D0859851

HARRAP'S
POCKET
ITALIAN
AND ENGLISH
DICTIONARY

GRANDE UNIVERSALE MURSIA

HARRAP'S
POCKET
ITALIAN
AND ENGLISH
DICTIONARY

English-Italian/Italian-English

HARRAP
London

Hanno collaborato alla redazione del presente dizionario
Annamaria Fattore Maiocchi e Ada de Bichiacchi

First published as
Harrap's Compact Italian & English Dictionary
in 1968

First published in this edition in Great Britain 1984
by HARRAP LIMITED
19–23 Ludgate Hill, London EC4M 7PD

© Copyright 1967 U. Mursia & C. – Milano – Via Tadino, 29

ISBN 0 245–54231–0

Printed and bound in Great Britain by
REDWOOD BURN LIMITED
Trowbridge, Wiltshire

NORME, REGOLE E INFORMAZIONI

NORME PER L'USO DEL DIZIONARIO

1. La parte iniziale del presente **Piccolo dizionario** comprende una serie di informazioni che valgono a completare l'opera, a facilitarne la consultazione o ad arricchire le conoscenze del lettore; tali si debbono considerare le **regole di pronuncia**, l'elenco dei **verbi irregolari inglesi**, la **tabella di raffronto fra le unità inglesi o americane e il sistema metrico**, le indicazioni relative al **sistema monetario inglese e americano**, l'elenco dei **numeri ordinali e cardinali** e, infine, l'**elenco delle abbreviazioni** usate nel dizionario stesso.

Inoltre comprende una serie di informazioni in inglese a facilitarne la consultazione per il lettore inglese.

2. La seconda parte comprende il **Compact English-Italian Dictionary** e reca in appendice un ampio elenco di **nomi propri, storici e geografici** (con la relativa traduzione in italiano), nonché l'elenco delle **sigle e abbreviazioni usate nei Paesi di lingua inglese** con l'indicazione dell'equivalente italiano.

3. La terza parte comprende il **Piccolo dizionario italiano-inglese** e reca in appendice un ampio elenco di **nomi propri, storici e geografici** (con la relativa traduzione in inglese), nonché l'elenco delle **sigle e abbreviazioni usate in Italia** con l'indicazione dell'equivalente inglese.

4. Nella parte **italiano-inglese**, i lemmi italiani non recano accento se si tratta di parole piane (es.: *violino, rosa, determinazione*); recano l'accento se si tratta di parole tronche (es.: *così, però, lassù*) o sdrucciole (es.: *richiùdere, rimpròvero, nàutico*) o bisdrucciole o terminanti in *ia, io* con l'accento sulla *i* (es.: *filosofìa, mormorìo*). Tali accenti sono tutti gravi, salvo nelle parole con accento su una *e*, nel qual caso ci si è attenuti a un criterio strettamente ortoepico (es.: *règola, desèrtico, maneggévole, pregévole*): si è, cioè, distinto fra accento grave (pronuncia aperta) e accento acuto (pronuncia chiusa).

5. Nel corpo delle singole voci sono stati ampiamente adottati, secondo la consuetudine generale dei grandi dizionari, i seguenti **segni grafici**:

a) la **doppia barra** (||) che sta a segnalare la peculiarità della fraseologia o una certa differenza di significato nell'ambito del lemma o il passaggio da un senso proprio a uno figurato o il passaggio dal significato corrente a uno più specialistico o, infine, l'inizio dell'elencazione di parole composte e di analoghe associazioni semantiche;

b) i **numeri arabi in neretto** (1., 2., 3. ecc.) che valgono ad attirare l'attenzione sui diversi significati in cui è stato possibile articolare una determinata voce del dizionario;

c) la **losanga nera** (♦) che sta a indicare il cambiamento di natura grammaticale che sopravviene internamente a due omonimi appartenenti a un medesimo gruppo etimologico (es.: passaggio da sostantivo maschile a sostantivo femminile; da sostantivo ad aggettivo; da aggettivo ad avverbio; da verbo transitivo a verbo riflessivo ecc.);

d) gli **esponenti in numeri arabi** (¹, ², ³ ecc.) che servono a distinguere parole omonime appartenenti però a gruppi etimologici diversi.

6. In entrambe le parti, nel caso di sostantivi che abbiano **numero diverso** nelle due lingue, si è data l'indicazione del numero stesso sùbito dopo il lemma. Es.: **fare** *sm.* manners (*pl.*) - **postage** *s.* spese postali (*pl.*) - **embers** *s. pl.* brace (*sing.*).

7. Per i **plurali irregolari inglesi** si sono usati i seguenti criteri:

a) nella parte **inglese-italiano** si è fatta seguire al lemma, fra parentesi, la forma plurale irregolare, per esteso - es.: **child** *s.* (*pl.* children) - nei casi generali o abbreviata - es.: **diagnosis** *s.* (*pl.* -ses) - nei casi di parole derivanti da altre lingue antiche o moderne. Nel primo caso i plurali sono stati elencati anche come voce a sé e con rimando: es.: **children** V. *child*;

b) nella parte **italiano-inglese** si è fatta seguire alla traduzione, fra parentesi, la forma plurale irregolare, per esteso - es.: **bambino** *sm.* child (*pl.* children) - nei casi generali o abbreviata - es.: **diàgnosi** *sf.* diagnosis (*pl.* -ses) - nei casi di parole derivanti da altre lingue antiche o moderne.

8. Per i **verbi irregolari inglesi** si sono usati i seguenti criteri:

a) nella parte **inglese-italiano** si è fatto seguire al lemma, fra parentesi, il paradigma: es.: **to bring (brought, brought).** Le due forme del passato remoto e del participio passato sono state elencate anche come voce a sé e con rimando: es.: **brought** V. *to bring*;

b) nella parte **italiano-inglese** si è fatta seguire alla traduzione, fra parentesi, l'indicazione dell'irregolarità - es.: **costare** *vi.* to cost (*v. irr.*) - a meno che lo stesso verbo inglese ricorra più volte nell'ambito della stessa voce ed escludendo inoltre i due verbi ausiliari *to be* e *to have* (per i quali ultimi si suppone una costante attenzione del lettore circa l'irregolarità).

9. Per i **comparativi** e i **superlativi irregolari inglesi** sono stati seguiti analoghi criteri.

REGOLE DI PRONUNCIA

Alfabeto

L'alfabeto inglese è composto di 26 lettere, 5 in più dell'alfabeto italiano e precisamente: *j, k, w, x, y.* L'elenco completo delle lettere è il seguente:

a	(pron. *ei*)	**n**	(pron. *en*)
b	(pron. *bi*, con la *i* allungata)	**o**	(pron. *ou*)
c	(pron. *si*, con la *i* allungata e la *s* aspra, come in *sordo*)	**p**	(pron. *pi*, con la *i* allungata)
		q	(pron. *chiù*)
d	(pron. *di*, con la *i* allungata)	**r**	(pron. *ar*, con la *a* allungata)
e	(pron. *i*, con la *i* allungata)	**s**	(pron. *es*, con la *s* aspra)
f	(pron. *ef*)	**t**	(pron. *ti*, con la *i* allungata)
g	(pron. *gi*, con la *i* allungata)	**u**	(pron. *iù*)
h	(pron. *eic*, con la *c* dolce)	**v**	(pron. *vi*, con la *i* allungata)
i	(pron. *ai*)	**w**	(pron. *dabliu*)
j	(pron. *gei*)	**x**	(pron. *ecs*)
k	(pron. *kei*)	**y**	(pron. *uai*)
l	(pron. *el*)	**z**	(pron. *sed*, con la *s* dolce, come in *rosa*).
m	(pron. *em*)		

La pronuncia inglese è particolarmente difficile da apprendere ed è altresì difficile dare norme precise per l'apprendimento della stessa. Diamo comunque, qui di seguito, un elenco delle vocali, dei gruppi vocalici, delle consonanti e di alcuni gruppi consonantici con indicazioni approssimative sulla pronuncia.

Vocali

La vocale A ha vari suoni:

1. **ei** in sillaba tonica aperta come nella parola *tale* (racconto); nei gruppi **ange** e **aste** come nelle parole *danger* (pericolo) e *haste* (fretta);

2. **e** aperta in sillaba tonica chiusa come nella parola *cat* (gatto);

3. ha un suono incerto tra **e** aperta e **a** in sillabe atone iniziali o mediane come nelle parole *about* (circa) e *final* (finale);

4. **a** allungata quando è seguita da **r** finale (**r** muta) come nelle parole *car* (automobile) e *far* (lontano);

5. **ea** se è seguita da **re** finale (**e** aperta e **a** appena accennata) come nelle parole *care* (cura) e *dare* (sfida);

6. **o** breve in molti vocaboli che cominciano con il gruppo **qua** come in *quality* (qualità) e in *quantity* (quantità);

7. **o** aperta e prolungata se seguita da **l** o **ll** come in *all* (tutto), *tall* (alto);

nel gruppo **alk** (l muta) come in *talk* (chiacchiera); preceduta da **w** (ma non seguita da **k** o **g**) come in *war* (guerra);

8. **a** allungata nei gruppi **ance, and, ant, ask, alf** (l muta), **ast, alm** (l muta), **aff, aft, asp** e **ath** quando la **a** è tonica;

9. **i** breve e velata nelle desinenze **age** e **ate** non accentate.

La vocale E ha vari suoni:

1. **i** allungata in sillaba tonica aperta come in *these* (questi) e nei monosillabi, come in *me* (me);

2. **e** aperta come nella parola italiana *bello*, in sillaba tonica chiusa, come in *let* (lasciare);

3. **i** come nella parola italiana *vita*, in sillaba atona, come in *repeat* (ripetere);

4. **i** brevissima quando è preceduta da **s, z, c, ch, sh, g** e seguita da **s** come in *roses* (rose) e quando è tra due dentali come in *rested* (riposato);

5. è muta in fine di parola in *love* (amore) e nelle desinenze **es, ed**, come in *loves* (amori) e *loved* (amato);

6. **eu** francese quando è seguita da **r** in sillaba tonica, come in *term* (termine);

7. **a** gutturale quando è nel gruppo **er** in fine di parola, come in *letter* (lettera);

8. **ia** con la **a** appena accennata quando è seguita da **re** in fine di parola come in *severe* (severo) e in *mere* (semplice).

La vocale I ha vari suoni:

1. **ai** in sillaba tonica aperta, come in *fine* (bello) e in sillaba chiusa quando è seguita dai gruppi **gh** (muto), come in *high* (alto); **ght** (gh muto) come in *night* (notte); **gn** (g muta), come in *sign* (segno); **ld**, come in *child* (bambino) e **nd**, come in *mind* (mente);

2. **i** breve in sillaba tonica chiusa, come in *tin* (stagno);

3. **eu** francese, se seguita da **r** come in *fir* (abete);

4. **aia**, se seguita da **re** come in *fire* (fuoco).

La vocale O ha vari suoni:

1. **ou** (con la **o** chiusa) in sillaba tonica aperta, come in *home* (casa) e se seguita da **ld** come in *cold* (freddo);

2. **o** aperta e breve in sillaba tonica chiusa come in *not* (non);

3. **ò** aperta e lunga se seguita da **r** come in *morning* (mattino);

4. **oa** se seguita da **re** in fine di parola come in *more* (più);

5. **eu** francese se preceduta da **w** e seguita da **r** come in *work* (lavoro);

6. **u** allungata nei seguenti vocaboli: *to do* (fare); *to move* (muovere); *to prove* (provare); *to lose* (perdere); *who* (chi); *two* (due); *tomb* (tomba); *womb* (grembo); *shoe* (scarpa); *wolf* (lupo); *woman* (donna);

7. **a** se preceduta da **w** e seguita da **n** come in *won* (vinto);
8. **ua** in *one* (uno).

La vocale **U** ha vari suoni:

1. **iù** in sillaba tonica aperta, come in *tune* (tono);
2. **a** in sillaba tonica chiusa, come in *but* (ma);
3. **u** allungata se preceduta da **l** o **r**, come in *Lucy* (Lucia) e *rule* (regola);
4. **u** breve, se preceduta da **b, f, p** e seguita da **l, ll, sh**, come in *bush* (cespuglio); *to push* (spingere); *bull* (toro); *full* (pieno); *to pull* (tirare);
5. **eu** francese se seguita da **r** in sillaba aperta, come in *fur* (pelliccia);
6. **iua** se seguita da **re** in fine di parola, come in *pure* (puro).

Gruppi vocalici

AI si pronuncia **ea** se seguito da **r**, come in *air* (aria).

AU, AW si pronunciano **o** allungata, come in *fraud* (frode) e *law* (legge).

EA si pronuncia **e** in circa 40 parole e loro composti; *bread* (pane); *dead* (morto); *death* (morte); *head* (testa); *heavy* (pesante) ecc.;
    i lunga in moltissime sillabe toniche: *beat* (calore); *meat* (carne); **ei** nelle seguenti parole: *great* (grande); *break* (rompere); *steak* (bistecca); **eu** francese se all'inizio di parola e seguito da **r** come in *earth* (terra); **ea** se in fine di parola seguito da **r**, come in *bear* (sopportare); in molte parole suona però **ia**, come in *tear* (lacrima), o **a** allungata, come in *heart* (cuore).

EE si pronuncia **i** allungata, come in *feeling* (sentimento).

EI si pronuncia **ei** in genere, come in *rein* (briglia);
    i se preceduto da sibilante, come in *ceiling* (soffitto).

EY si pronuncia **ei** in sillaba tonica, come in *prey* (preda);
    i in sillaba atona, come in *money* (denaro). L'eccezione più comune è *key* (chiave) che si pronuncia **ki**.

EU, EW si pronunciano **iù** come in *Europe* (Europa) e in *new* (nuovo).

IE si pronuncia **i** allungata come in *piece* (pezzo).

OI, OY si pronunciano **oi** come in *soil* (suolo) e *royal* (reale).

OA si pronuncia **ou** come in *boat* (barca).

OO si pronuncia **u** allungata, come in *moon* (luna);
    u breve se seguita da **k** come in *book* (libro).
    Vi sono alcune eccezioni come *door* (porta) e *floor* (pavimento) dove il gruppo **oo** viene pronunciato **oa** e *blood* (sangue) e *flood* (alluvione) dove il gruppo **oo** viene pronunciato **a**.

OU, OW si pronunciano **au** come in *mouth* (bocca) e *now* (ora).

Consonanti

B è in generale pronunciata come in italiano; è però muta nei gruppi **bt** e **mb** in fine di parola, come in *debt* (debito) e *comb* (pettine).

C suona **s** aspra come nell'italiano *sordo* davanti a **e, i, y**, come in *cellar* (cantina), *city* (città) e *cyder* (sidro); suona **k** in fine di parola, come in *logic* (logico);
cce, cci, suonano **kse** e **ksi**;
ch suona **c** palatale come nell'italiano *città*, se seguito da vocale o in fine di parola; suona **k** in parole di origine greca o orientale. Suona **sc** come in italiano *sciare*, in parole di origine francese, come *machine* (macchina);
ck suona **k**;
tch suona **c** dolce.

G in fine di parola suona **g** gutturale come nell'italiano *gomma*;
ge, gi hanno suono palatale come nell'italiano *gesto, gita* in parole di origine latina; hanno suono gutturale in parole di origine germanica;
gh seguito da **t** o in fine di parola è muto;
gn ha la **g** muta quando le due lettere fanno parte della stessa sillaba, come in *sign* (segno); si pronunciano separate e la **g** ha suono gutturale quando le due lettere appartengono a due sillabe diverse, come in *signal* (segnale);
dge suona **g** palatale.

H è sempre aspirata tranne in *heir* (erede); *honest* (onesto); *honour* (onore) e *hour* (ora) e loro derivati.

J suona **g** palatale.

K è muta davanti a **n** come in *knee* (ginocchio).

L come in italiano.

M come in italiano.

N è nasale nei gruppi **ng** come in *ring* (anello) (la **g** è muta).

P suona **f** nei gruppi **ph**; è muta nel gruppo iniziale **psy**.

Q come in italiano.

R in genere, se mediana, non si pronuncia, ma allunga il suono della vocale che precede, come in *farm* (fattoria). Se è finale non si pronuncia.

S è in genere aspra all'inizio di parola o sillaba; è dolce se è posta tra due vocali;
sc suona **s** aspra se è seguita da **e, i, y**;
sh suona **sc** come nell'italiano *sciare*.
La **s** è muta in *aisle* (navata); *isle* e *island* (isola); *viscount* (visconte).

T ha due pronunce caratteristiche nel gruppo **th**:
a) un suono duro pronunciato con la lingua tra i denti, come in *thin* (sottile);
b) un suono dolce pronunciato con la lingua tra i denti, come in *this* (questo).

V come in italiano.

W in principio di parola suona **u** come in *west*; seguita da **r** è muta, come in *wrong* (sbagliato).

X finale ha il suono sordo **ks**; mediana può avere il suono sordo **ks** o il suono dolce **gs**; in principio di parola suona come la **s** dolce di *rosa*.

Y è semivocale; all'inizio di parola ha il suono consonantico **i**, come in *yes* (sì); ha tale suono anche in fine di polisillabi, come in *dignity* (dignità), e nel corpo della parola, come in *graveyard* (cimitero); in fine di monosillabi, invece, si pronuncia **ai**, come in *fly* (mosca) e in *cry* (grido).

Z **s** dolce di *rosa*.

Osservazioni

1. I gruppi finali **ble, cle, kle, gle** hanno la **l** appena accennata e le due consonanti vengono pronunciate staccate.
2. Nei gruppi **gua, gue, gui, build** e **cuit** finale la **u** è muta, come in *building* (fabbricato).
3. **ough** seguito da **t** si pronuncia **o** allungato, come in *thought* (pensiero); **ough** suona **of** in: *cough* (tosse) e *trough* (trogolo); suona **af** in: *enough* (abbastanza), *rough* (ruvido) e *tough* (duro); suona **au** in: *plough* (arare) e *bough* (ramo); suona **ou** in *though* (sebbene) e *dough* (pasta); suona **u** allungato in *through* (attraverso).
4. I gruppi **ci, sci, si, ti, xi** seguiti da vocale suonano **sc** come in *scelto*.
5. I gruppi finali **sten** e **stle** suonano rispettivamente **sn** e **sl**.
6. Il gruppo finale **sure** suona **ja** (**j** francese).
7. Il gruppo finale **ture** suona **cia** con la **a** allungata.

I SEGNI D'INTERPUNZIONE (PUNCTUATION MARKS)

,	*comma*	virgola
;	*semicolon*	punto e virgola
:	*colon*	due punti
.	*full stop*	punto
?	*question mark*	punto di domanda
!	*exclamation mark*	punto esclamativo
'	*apostrophe*	apostrofo
—	*dash*	lineetta
-	*hyphen*	trattino d'unione
« »	*quotation marks*	virgolette basse o quadre
' '	*inverted commas*	virgolette alte o inglesi
( )	*brackets*	parentesi rotonde
[ ]	*square brackets*	parentesi quadre
*	*asterisk*	asterisco
...	*dots*	puntini
	new paragraph	a capo
	full stop and new paragraph	punto e a capo
	capital letter	lettera maiuscola
	small letter	lettera minuscola

VERBI IRREGOLARI INGLESI [1]

Infinito	Passato	Participio passato	
to abide	abode	abode	dimorare
to arise	arose	arisen	sorgere
to awake*	awoke	awoke, awaked	svegliare, svegliarsi
to be	was	been	essere
to bear	bore	born, borne	sopportare, generare
to beat	beat	beaten, beat	battere
to become	became	become	diventare
to befall	befell	befallen	accadere
to beget	begot	begot, begotten	generare
to begin	began	begun	cominciare
to behold	beheld	beheld	mirare
to bend	bent	bent	piegare
to bereave*	bereft	bereft	orbare
to bet	bet	bet	scommettere
to bid	bade, bid	bidden, bid	ordinare
to bind	bound	bound	(ri)legare
to bite	bit	bitten, bit	mordere
to bleed	bled	bled	sanguinare
to blow	blew	blown	soffiare
to break	broke	broken	rompere
to breed	bred	bred	allevare
to bring	brought	brought	portare
to build	built	built	costruire
to burn*	burnt	burnt	bruciare
to burst	burst	burst	scoppiare
to buy	bought	bought	comperare
to cast	cast	cast	gettare, fondere
to catch	caught	caught	prendere, acchiappare
to chide*	chid	chid	sgridare
to choose	chose	chosen	scegliere
to cleave	cleft	cleft	fendere
to cling	clung	clung	attaccarsi
to come	came	come	venire
to cost	cost	cost	costare
to creep	crept	crept	strisciare
to cut	cut	cut	tagliare
to deal	dealt	dealt	trattare, commerciare
to dig*	dug	dug	scavare
to do	did	done	fare
to draw	drew	drawn	tirare, disegnare
to dream*	dreamt	dreamt	sognare
to drink	drank	drunk	bere
to drive	drove	driven	guidare
to dwell*	dwelt	dwelt	dimorare

[1] L'elenco, compilato per comodità del lettore, comprende i verbi di uso più comune. L'asterisco apposto accanto a un verbo indica l'esistenza, per il verbo stesso, di forme anche regolari.

to eat	ate, eat	eaten	mangiare
to fall	fell	fallen	cadere
to feed	fed	fed	nutrire
to feel	felt	felt	sentire, tastare
to fight	fought	fought	combattere
to find	found	found	trovare
to flee	fled	fled	fuggire
to fling	flung	flung	scagliare
to fly	flew	flown	volare
to forbid	forbade	forbidden	proibire
to forecast	forecast	forecast	predire
to forget	forgot	forgotten	dimenticare
to forgive	forgave	forgiven	perdonare
to forsake	forsook	forsaken	abbandonare
to freeze	froze	frozen	gelare
to get	got	got, gotten	ottenere, diventare
to gird	girt	girt	cingere
to give	gave	given	dare
to go	went	gone	andare
to grind	ground	ground	macinare
to grow	grew	grown	crescere, coltivare
to hang	hung	hung, hanged	appendere
to have	had	had	avere
to hear	heard	heard	udire
to hew*	hewed	hewn	recidere
to hide	hid	hidden, hid	nascondere
to hit	hit	hit	colpire
to hold	held	held	tenere, trattenere
to hurt	hurt	hurt	far male, ferire
to keep	kept	kept	tenere, conservare
to kneel*	knelt	knelt	inginocchiarsi
to knit*	knit	knit	lavorare a maglia
to know	knew	known	conoscere, sapere
to lay	laid	laid	deporre, posare
to lead	led	led	condurre, guidare
to lean	leant	leant	appoggiarsi, inclinarsi
to leap	leapt	leapt	saltare
to learn*	learnt	learnt	imparare
to leave	left	left	lasciare, partire
to lend	lent	lent	prestare
to let	let	let	lasciare
to lie	lay	lain	giacere, trovarsi
to light*	lit	lit	accendere
to lose	lost	lost	perdere
to make	made	made	fare
to mean	meant	meant	intendere, significare
to meet	met	met	incontrare
to mislay	mislaid	mislaid	smarrire
to mislead	misled	misled	sviare
to mistake	mistook	mistaken	sbagliare
to mow*	mowed	mown	falciare
to pay	paid	paid	pagare
to put	put	put	mettere

to read	read	read	leggere
to rend	rent	rent	strappare
to ride	rode	ridden	cavalcare
to ring	rang	rung	suonare
to rise	rose	risen	alzarsi, sorgere
to run	ran	run	correre
to saw	sawed	sawn	segare
to say	said	said	dire
to see	saw	seen	vedere
to seek	sought	sought	cercare
to sell	sold	sold	vendere
to send	sent	sent	mandare
to set	set	set	porre
to sew	sewed	sewn	cucire
to shake	shook	shaken	scuotere, tremare
to shear*	sheared	shorn	tosare
to shed	shed	shed	spargere
to shine	shone	shone	brillare, splendere
to shoe	shod	shod	calzare
to shoot	shot	shot	sparare
to show	showed	shown	mostrare
to shred	shred	shred	tagliuzzare
to shrink	shrank, shrunk	shrunk, shrunken	restringersi
to shut	shut	shut	chiudere
to sing	sang	sung	cantare
to sink	sank, sunk	sunk	affondare
to sit	sat	sat	sedere
to slay	slew	slain	trucidare
to sleep	slept	slept	dormire
to slink	slunk	slunk	svignarsela
to smell*	smelt	smelt	fiutare, odorare
to sow*	sowed	sown	seminare
to speak	spoke	spoken	parlare
to spell	spelt	spelt	compitare
to spend	spent	spent	spendere
to spill*	spilt	spilt	spandere, versare
to spin	spun, span	spun	filare
to spit	spat, spit	spat, spit	sputare
to split	split	split	spaccare
to spoil	spoilt	spoilt	guastare, viziare
to spread	spread	spread	diffondere, stendere
to spring	sprang	sprung	saltare
to stand	stood	stood	stare (in piedi)
to steal	stole	stolen	rubare
to stick	stuck	stuck	appicciare
to sting	stung	stung	pungere
to stink	stank, stunk	stunk	puzzare
to strike	struck	struck	battere, colpire
to strive	strove	striven	sforzarsi
to swear	swore	sworn	giurare
to sweat*	sweat	sweat	sudare
to sweep	swept	swept	spazzare
to swell*	swelled	swollen	gonfiare
to swim	swam	swum	nuotare
to swing	swung	swung	dondolare
to take	took	taken	prendere

to **teach**	taught	taught	insegnare
to **tear**	tore	torn	lacerare
to **tell**	told	told	dire, raccontare
to **think**	thought	thought	pensare
to **thrive**	throve	thriven	prosperare
to **throw**	threw	thrown	gettare
to **thrust**	thrust	thrust	spingere, gettare
to **tread**	trode	trod, trodden	calpestare
to **understand**	understood	understood	capire
to **upset**	upset	upset	capovolgere
to **wake**	woke	woke, woken	svegliare, svegliarsi
to **wear**	wore	worn	indossare, logorare
to **weave**	wove	woven	intrecciare, tessere
to **weep**	wept	wept	piangere
to **win**	won	won	vincere
to **wind**	wound	wound	serpeggiare
to **withdraw**	withdrew	withdrawn	ritirare, ritirarsi
to **wring**	wrung	wrung	torcere
to **write**	wrote	written	scrivere

TABELLA DI RAFFRONTO
FRA LE UNITÀ INGLESI O AMERICANE
E IL SISTEMA METRICO

	denominazione delle unità inglesi o americane	valore	equivalenza col sistema metrico *	equivalenza del sistema metrico con le unità inglesi **
misure lineari	pollice (inch - in)	—	2,54 cm	0,3937 (cm)
	piede (foot - ft)	12 in	0,304 m	3,28 (m)
	yarda (yard - yd)	3 ft	0,914 m	1,09 (m)
	fathom	6 ft	1,828 m	0,546 (m)
	miglio terrestre (statute mile)	5280 ft	1,609 km	0,621 (km)
	miglio inglese	5000 ft	1,523 km	0,656 (km)
	nodo (nautical mile)	6080 ft	1,853 km	0,539 (km)
superfici	pollice quadr. (square inch - sq.in)	—	6,45 cm²	0,155 (cm²)
	piede quadr. (square foot - sq.ft)	144 sq.in	829 cm²	10,76 (m²)
	yarda quadr. (square yard - sq.yd)	1296 sq.in	0,836 m²	1,196 (m²)
	miglio quadr. (square mile)	—	2,59 km²	0,386 (km²)
volumi e capacità	pollice cubo (cubic inch - cu.in)	—	16,38 cm³	0,061 (cm³)
	piede cubo (cubic foot - cu.ft)	1728 cu.in	28,32 dm³	0,0353 (dm³)
	yarda cubica (cubic yard - cu.yd)	27 cu.ft	0,764 m³	1,308 (m³)
	register ton	100 cu.ft	2,832 m³	0,353 (m³)
	oncia fluida americana (U.S. fl.oz)	1,8 cu.in	29,57 cm³	0,0338 (cm³)
	oncia fluida inglese (imp. fl.oz)	1,73 cu.in	28,4 cm³	0,0353 (cm³)
	bushel	8 gals	28,3 l	0,035 (l)
	gallone americano (U.S. gal)	231 cu.in	3,78 l	0,26 (l)
	gallone inglese (imp. gal)	277 cu.in	4,54 l	0,22 (l)
	pinta (pint)	1/8 gal	0,47 l	2,11 (l)
pesi	oncia avoirdupois (ounce - oz)	—	28,35 g	0,0352 (g)
	oncia troy (ounce troy - oz)	—	31,1 g	0,0321 (g)
	libbra avoirdupois (pound - lb)	16 oz.a.d.p.	453 g	2,204 kg)
	libbra troy (pound - lb)	12 oz.t.	373 g	2,679 (kg)
	tonnellata americana (short ton - ton)	2000 lbs	907 kg	0,102 (t)
	tonnellata ingl. (long ton - ton)	2240 lbs	1016 kg	0,984 (t)

Con la graduale introduzione del sistema metrico, le unità di misura inglesi e americane diventeranno progressivamente meno diffuse.

* Coefficiente per il quale si deve moltiplicare il valore della grandezza per ottenere la misura nel sistema metrico.

** Coefficiente per il quale si deve moltiplicare il valore espresso nell'unità metrica segnato tra parentesi per ottenere la misura nel sistema inglese.

SISTEMA MONETARIO INGLESE
(Denaro circolante)
Unità base = **pound**, sterlina.

Monete *(coins)*

½p piece (half-penny), duecentesima parte della sterlina;
1p piece (one penny), centesima parte sterlina;
2p piece (two pence), cinquantesima parte della sterlina;
5p piece (five pence), ventesima parte della sterlina;
10p piece (ten pence), decima parte della sterlina;
50p piece (fifty pence), metà della sterlina.

Banconote *(banknotes)*

pound note (£1), sterlina carta;
five-pound note (£5), cinque sterline;
ten-pound note (£10), dieci sterline;
twenty-pound note (£20), venti sterline.

Monete nominali *(nominal coins* – usate nelle parcelle dei professionisti, prezzi par articoli di lusso, per libri, ecc.)

guinea (£1.05, 105p), ghinea, centocinque pence;
half (a) guinea (52½p), mezza ghinea, cinquantadue pence e mezzo.

SISTEMA MONETARIO AMERICANO
(Denaro circolante)
Unità base = **dollar**, dollaro.

Rame *(copper)*:
  cent o *penny (1 c.)*, un centesimo di dollaro.
Lega di rame e nichel *(copper and nickel alloy)*:
  nickel o *five cents (5 c.)*, cinque centesimi di dollaro.
Argento *(silver)*:
  dime (10 c.), dieci centesimi di dollaro;
  quarter (25 c.), un quarto di dollaro;
  half-dollar (50 c.), mezzo dollaro, cinquanta centesimi;
  dollar ($ 1), dollaro (generalmente in banconota).
Banconote *(bills)*:
  si hanno tagli da $ 1, 2, 5, 10, 20, 50, 100, 500.
  Esistono inoltre, sebbene non in circolazione normale, banconote da $ 1,000, 5,000 e 10,000.

I NUMERI

CARDINALI

1	one
2	two
3	three
4	four
5	five
6	six
7	seven
8	eight
9	nine
10	ten
11	eleven
12	twelve
13	thirteen
14	fourteen
15	fifteen
16	sixteen
17	seventeen
18	eighteen
19	nineteen
20	twenty
21	twenty-one
22	twenty-two
30	thirty
40	forty
50	fifty
60	sixty
70	seventy
80	eighty
90	ninety
100	one hundred
101	one hundred and one
200	two hundred
1.000	one thousand
1.001	one thousand and one
1.010	one thousand and ten
10.000	ten thousand
100.000	one hundred thousand
200.000	two hundred thousand
1.000.000	one million

ORDINALI

1°	1st	the first
2°	2nd	the second
3°	3rd	the third
4°	4th	the fourth
5°	5th	the fifth
6°	6th	the sixth
7°	7th	the seventh
8°	8th	the eighth
9°	9th	the ninth
10°	10th	the tenth
11°	11th	the eleventh
12°	12th	the twelfth
13°	13th	the thirteenth
14°	14th	the fourteenth
15°	15th	the fifteenth
16°	16th	the sixteenth
17°	17th	the seventeenth
18°	18th	the eighteenth
19°	19th	the nineteenth
20°	20th	the twentieth
21°	21st	the twenty-first
22°	22nd	the twenty-second
30°	30th	the thirtieth
40°	40th	the fortieth
50°	50th	the fiftieth
60°	60th	the sixtieth
70°	70th	the seventieth
80°	80th	the eightieth
90°	90th	the ninetieth
100°	100th	the (one) hundredth
101°	101st	the one hundred and first
200°	200th	the two hundredth
1.000°	$1,000^{th}$	the (one) thousandth
1.001°	$1,001^{st}$	the one thousand and first
1.010°	$1,010^{th}$	the one thousand and tenth
10.000°	10,000	the ten thousandth
100.000°	100,000	the one hundred thousandth
200.000°	200,000	the two hundred thousandth
1.000.000°	1,000,000	the one millionth

ELENCO DELLE ABBREVIAZIONI

abbr.	abbreviazione	*gen.*	genitivo
(*aer.*)	aeronautica	*general.*	generalmente
agg.	aggettivo	(*geogr.*)	geografia
(*agr.*)	agricoltura	(*geol.*)	geologia
(*amer.*)	americano, americanismo	(*geom.*)	geometria
		ger.	gerundio
amm.	amministrativo, amministrazione	(*gergo*)	gergo, gergale
		(*giorn.*)	giornalismo, giornalistico
(*anat.*)	anatomia		
(*ant.*)	anticamente, antiquato	(*giur.*)	giuridico
(*arch.*)	architettura	(*gramm.*)	grammatica
art.	articolo	*i.*	intransitivo
(*arte*)	arte, artistico	*id.*	idem
assol.	assoluto	*imp.*	impersonale
(*astr.*)	astronomia	*imperat.*	imperativo
attr.	attributo, attributivo	*ind.*	indicativo
aus.	ausiliare	*indef.*	indefinito
(*auto*)	automobilismo	*inf.*	infinito
avv.	avverbio	*int.*	interrogativo
(*bot.*)	botanica	*inter.*	interiezione, interiettivo
(*biol.*)	biologia	(*iron.*)	ironico
(*chim.*)	chimica	*irr.*	irregolare
(*chir.*)	chirurgia	(*itt.*)	ittiologia
(*cine*)	cinematografia	(*lat.*)	latino, latinismo
coll.	collettivo	*loc. avv.*	locuzione avverbiale
(*comm.*)	commercio, commerciale	*loc. cong.*	locuzione congiuntiva
comp.	comparativo	*loc. prep.*	locuzione prepositiva
compl.	complemento	(*lett.*)	letteratura, letterario
condiz.	condizionale	*m.*	maschile
cong.	congiunzione	(*mar.*)	marina, marittimo, marinaresco
(*costr.*)	costruzioni		
(*cuc.*)	cucina	(*mat.*)	matematica
(*dial.*)	dialettale	(*mecc.*)	meccanica
dif.	difettivo	(*med.*)	medicina
dim.	diminutivo	(*metal.*)	metallurgia
dimostr.	dimostrativo	(*mil.*)	militare
ecc., etc.	eccetera	(*min.*)	mineralogia, minerario
(*eccl.*)	ecclesiastico	(*mit.*)	mitologia
(*econ.*)	economia	(*mus.*)	musica
(*edil.*)	edilizia	*neg.*	negazione, negativo
(*elettr.*)	elettricità, elettrotecnica	(*neol.*)	neologismo
escl.	esclamativo, in esclamazione	*ogg.*	oggetto
		(*ott.*)	ottica
f.	femminile	*p.*	participio
(*fam.*)	familiare	*pass.*	passato
(*farm.*)	farmacia, farmaceutico	*pers.*	persona, personale
(*ferr.*)	ferrovia	(*pitt.*)	pittura
(*fig.*)	figurato	*pl.*	plurale
(*fil.*)	filosofia	(*poet.*)	poetico
(*fis.*)	fisica	(*pol.*)	politica
(*foto*)	fotografia	(*pop.*)	popolare
fut.	futuro	*poss.*	possessivo

pp.	participio passato	*sost.*	sostantivato
prep.	preposizione	*spec.*	specialmente
pred.	predicato, predicativo	*(sport)*	sport, sportivo
pres.	presente	*(spreg.)*	spregiativo
pron.	pronome, pronominale	*sthg.*	something
prov.	proverbio, proverbiale	*(stor.)*	storia
(psicol.)	psicologia	*superl.*	superlativo
qc.	qualcosa	*t.*	transitivo
qu.	qualcuno	*(teat.)*	teatro
r.	riflessivo	*(tec.)*	tecnica
(radio)	radiofonia	*(tel.)*	telefonia, telefono
rec.	reciproco	*(teol.)*	teologia
reg.	regolare	*(tip.)*	tipografia
rel.	relativo	*(tv.)*	televisione
(relig.)	religione	*(us.)*	uso, usato
s.	(dall'inglese) sostantivo	*v.*	verbo
s.	(dall'italiano) sostantivo	*V.*	vedi
	maschile e femminile	*(vezz.)*	vezzeggiativo
semidif.	semidifettivo	*v. dif.*	verbo difettivo
sf.	sostantivo femminile	*vi.*	verbo intransitivo
sm.	sostantivo maschile	*(v. irr.)*	verbo irregolare
(scherz.)	scherzoso	*(volg.)*	volgare
(scol.)	scolastico	*vr.*	verbo riflessivo
(scult.)	scultura	*v. semidif.*	verbo semidifettivo
sing.	singolare	*vt.*	verbo transitivo
so.	someone	*(zool.)*	zoologia
sogg.	soggetto		

INGLESE-ITALIANO

A

a *art.* **1.** un, uno, una **2.** un certo ‖ *once a week*, una volta alla settimana.

A *s.* (*mus.*) la.

aback *avv.* alla sprovvista.

abacus *s.* **1.** abaco **2.** pallottoliere.

abandon *s.* abbandono.

to **abandon** *vt.* abbandonare.

to **abase** *vt.* abbassare, umiliare.

abasement *s.* umiliazione.

to **abash** *vt.* confondere.

abashment *s.* confusione.

to **abate** *vt.* diminuire. ♦ to **abate** *vi.* placarsi (*di tempo atmosferico*).

abatement *s.* diminuzione.

abbess *s.* badessa.

abbey *s.* abbazia.

abbot *s.* abate.

abbreviation *s.* abbreviazione.

to **abdicate** *vt.* e *vi.* **1.** abdicare a **2.** dimettersi.

abdication *s.* abdicazione.

abdomen *s.* addome.

abdominal *agg.* addominale.

to **abduct** *vt.* rapire.

abduction *s.* rapimento.

abductor *s.* **1.** rapitore **2.** (*anat.*) abduttore.

aberration *s.* aberrazione.

abetter *s.* fautore.

abeyance *s.* sospensione.

to **abhor** *vt.* aborrire.

abhorrence *s.* aborrimento.

to **abide (abode, abode)** *vi.* abitare ‖ *to — by*, conformarsi a.

ability *s.* abilità, capacità.

abject *agg.* abietto.

abjection *s.* abiezione.

abjuration *s.* abiura.

to **abjure** *vt.* abiurare.

ablation *s.* ablazione.

ablative *agg.* e *s.* ablativo.

able *agg.* capace ‖ *to be — to*, essere in grado di, potere.

ablution *s.* abluzione.

abnegation *s.* **1.** abnegazione **2.** rinuncia.

abnormal *agg.* anormale.

aboard *avv.* e *prep.* a bordo.

abode V. *to abide.* ♦ **abode** *s.* dimora.

to **abolish** *vt.* abolire.

abolishment, abolition *s.* abolizione.

abolitionism *s.* abolizionismo.

abolitionist *agg.* e *s.* abolizionista.

abominable *agg.* abominevole.

to **abominate** *vt.* detestare.

abomination *s.* abominazione.

aboriginal *agg.* e *s.* aborigeno.

to **abort** *vi.* abortire.

abortion *s.* aborto.

abortive *agg.* abortivo.

to **abound** *vi.* abbondare.

about *avv.* **1.** circa **2.** intorno ‖ *to be —*, stare per. ♦ **about** *prep.* **1.** intorno a **2.** presso di **3.** riguardo a.

above *prep.* **1.** al di sopra di **2.** più di ‖ *— mentioned*, suddetto. ♦ **above** *avv.* in alto, sopra.

abrasion *s.* abrasione.

to **abridge** *vt.* **1.** abbreviare **2.** privare di.

abridg(e)ment *s.* **1.** abbreviazione, sommario **2.** privazione.

abroad *avv.* **1.** all'estero **2.** fuori.

to **abrogate** *vt.* abrogare.

abrogation *s.* abrogazione.

abrupt *agg.* **1.** scosceso **2.** brusco **3.** inaspettato.

abruptness *s.* **1.** ripidezza **2.** rudezza **3.** precipitazione.

abscess *s.* ascesso.

abscissa *s.* ascissa.

absence *s.* assenza.

absent *agg.* assente ‖ *— -minded*, distratto; *— -mindedness*, distrazione.

to **absent** *vt.* *to — oneself*, assentarsi.

absenteeism *s.* assenteismo.

absinth(e) *s.* assenzio.

absolute *agg.* e *s.* assoluto.

absolution *s.* assoluzione.

absolutism *s.* assolutismo.

absolutist *agg.* e *s.* assolutista.

to **absolve** *vt.* assolvere.

to **absorb** *vt.* assorbire.

absorbent *agg.* e *s.* assorbente.

absorption *s.* assorbimento.

to **abstain** *vi.* astenersi.

abstemious *agg.* sobrio.

abstention *s.* astensione.

abstentionist *s.* astensionista.

abstinence *s.* astinenza.

abstract *agg.* astratto. ♦ **abstract** *s.* **1.** astrazione **2.** estratto.

to **abstract** *vt.* **1.** astrarre **2.** estrarre **3.** sottrarre **4.** riassumere.

abstraction *s.* **1.** astrazione **2.** distrazione **3.** furto.

abstractly *avv.* astrattamente.

abstruse *agg.* astruso.

abstruseness *s.* astrusità.

absurd agg. assurdo.
absurdity s. assurdità.
absurdly avv. assurdamente.
abundance s. abbondanza.
abundant agg. abbondante.
abuse s. **1.** abuso **2.** ingiuria.
to **abuse** vt. **1.** abusare **2.** ingiuriare.
abusive agg. **1.** abusivo **2.** ingiurioso.
abysm, abyss s. abisso.
abysmal, abyssal agg. abissale.
academic agg. e s. accademico.
academician s. accademico.
academy s. accademia: — of music, conservatorio.
acanthus s. acanto.
acarus s. (pl. -ri) acaro.
to **accelerate** vt. accelerare.
acceleration s. accelerazione.
accelerative agg. accelerativo.
accelerator s. acceleratore.
accent s. accento.
to **accent** vt. **1.** accentare **2.** accentuare.
to **accentuate** V. to accent.
accentuation s. accentuazione.
to **accept** vt. accettare, approvare.
acceptable agg. accettabile.
acceptance s. **1.** accettazione **2.** consenso.
acceptation s. accezione, significato.
access s. accesso.
accessible agg. accessibile.
accession s. **1.** assunzione (al trono) **2.** adesione **3.** aggiunta.
accessory agg. e s. **1.** accessorio **2.** complice.
accident s. **1.** caso: by —, per caso **2.** incidente **3.** irregolarità.
accidental agg. accidentale.
to **acclaim** vt. acclamare.
acclamation s. acclamazione.
acclimation, acclimatization s. acclimazione, acclimatazione.
to **acclimate**, to **acclimatize** vt. acclimatare. ♦ to **acclimate**, to **acclimatize** vi. acclimatarsi.
to **accommodate** vt. **1.** adattare **2.** ospitare **3.** fornire.
accommodating agg. accomodante.
accommodation s. **1.** accomodamento **2.** comodità **3.** alloggio **4.** (comm.) facilitazione.
accompaniment s. accompagnamento.
accompanist s. (mus.) accompagnatore.
to **accompany** vt. accompagnare

(anche mus.).
accomplice s. complice.
to **accomplish** vt. compiere, realizzare.
accomplishment s. **1.** compimento **2.** compitezza **3.** dote.
accord s. accordo.
to **accord** vt. accordare. ♦ to **accord** vi. accordarsi.
accordance s. accordo.
accordant agg. concorde, conforme.
according agg. **1.** concordante, conforme **2.** armonioso. ♦ **according** avv. — as, secondo che; — to, secondo.
accordingly avv. **1.** in conseguenza **2.** conformemente.
accordion s. fisarmonica.
accordionist s. fisarmonicista.
account s. **1.** (comm.) conto **2.** (comm.) acconto **3.** valore **4.** resoconto || to take into —, prendere in considerazione; on — of, a causa di.
to **account** vt. considerare || to — for, essere responsabile di.
accountable agg. responsabile.
accountancy s. ragioneria.
accountant s. contabile || chartered —, ragioniere.
to **accredit** vt. accreditare.
to **accrue** vi. **1.** derivare **2.** accumularsi.
to **accumulate** vt. accumulare. ♦ to **accumulate** vi. accumularsi.
accumulation s. accumulazione.
accumulative agg. accumulativo.
accumulator s. accumulatore.
accuracy s. esattezza.
accurate agg. esatto.
accusation s. accusa.
accusative agg. e s. accusativo.
to **accuse** vt. accusare.
accused s. accusato.
accuser s. accusatore.
to **accustom** vt. abituare.
accustomed agg. **1.** abituale **2.** abituato.
ace s. asso.
acetone s. acetone.
acetylene s. acetilene.
ache s. dolore.
to **ache** vi. far male: my head aches, mi fa male la testa.
to **achieve** vt. **1.** compiere **2.** ottenere.
achievement s. **1.** compimento **2.** conseguimento **3.** gesta.
aching agg. **1.** doloroso **2.** afflitto.

◆ **aching** s. dolore.
acid agg. e s. acido.
acidity s. acidità.
aciduous agg. acidulo.
to **acknowledge** vt. riconoscere ‖ to — receipt of, accusare ricevuta di.
acknowledg(e)ment s. riconoscimento.
acolyte s. accolito.
acorn s. ghianda.
acoustic(al) agg. acustico.
acoustics s. acustica.
to **acquaint** vt. informare ‖ to become acquainted with, fare la conoscenza di.
acquaintance s. conoscenza.
acquiescence s. acquiescenza.
to **acquire** vt. acquisire, acquistare.
acquisition s. acquisto.
to **acquit** vt. **1.** pagare **2.** liberare **3.** assolvere.
acquittal s. (giur.) assoluzione.
acquittance s. **1.** saldo **2.** quietanza.
acrid agg. acre.
acridity s. asprezza.
acrimony s. acrimonia.
acrobat s. acrobata.
acrobatic(al) agg. acrobatico.
acrobatics s. pl. acrobazia (sing.).
acropolis s. acropoli.
across avv. per traverso. ◆ **across** prep. attraverso ‖ to come —. incontrare.
act s. atto, legge.
to **act** vt. e vi. **1.** agire, fare **2.** (teat.) recitare.
acting agg. facente funzione di. ◆ **acting** s. **1.** azione **2.** (teat.) rappresentazione.
action s. **1.** azione **2.** (giur.) processo **3.** (mecc.) funzionamento.
active agg. attivo.
activism s. attivismo.
activist s. attivista.
activity s. attività.
actor s. attore.
actress s. attrice.
actual agg. reale.
actuality s. realtà.
actually avv. realmente.
to **actuate** vt. mettere in moto.
acuminate agg. acuminato.
acute agg. acuto.
ad s. V. advertisement.
adamantine agg. adamantino.
to **adapt** vt. adattare.
adaptable agg. adattabile.
adaptation s. adattamento.

to **add** vt. aggiungere ‖ to — up, fare una somma.
addendum s. (pl. -da) aggiunta.
adder s. vipera.
addict s. tossicomane.
addition s. **1.** (mat.) addizione **2.** aggiunta.
additional agg. supplementare.
address s. **1.** indirizzo **2.** abilità. ◆ **addresses** s. pl. omaggi.
to **address** vt. e vi. indirizzare, arringare. ◆ to **address** vi. rivolgersi.
addressee s. destinatario.
addresser s. mittente.
to **adduce** vt. addurre.
adenoids s. pl. adenoidi.
adept agg. e s. perito, esperto.
adequate agg. adeguato.
to **adhere** vi. aderire.
adherence s. aderenza, adesione.
adherent agg. e s. aderente.
adhesion s. V. adherence.
adhesive agg. e s. adesivo.
adipose agg. adiposo.
adjacent agg. adiacente.
adjective agg. **1.** aggettivale **2.** addizionale. ◆ **adjective** s. aggettivo.
to **adjoin** vt. **1.** aggiungere **2.** essere contiguo.
adjoining agg. adiacente.
to **adjourn** vt. aggiornare.
adjournment s. aggiornamento.
adjunct s. **1.** aggiunta **2.** aggiunto **3.** (gramm.) complemento.
adjuration s. implorazione.
to **adjust** vt. **1.** aggiustare **2.** adattare **3.** regolare.
adjustment s. **1.** adattamento, compromesso **2.** (comm.) liquidazione.
adjutant s. aiutante.
to **administer** vt. **1.** amministrare **2.** fornire. ◆ to **administer** vi. contribuire.
administration s. **1.** amministrazione **2.** somministrazione.
administrative agg. amministrativo.
administrator s. amministratore.
admirable agg. ammirabile.
admiral s. ammiraglio.
admiralty s. ammiragliato.
admiration s. ammirazione.
to **admire** vt. ammirare.
admirer s. ammiratore.
admiringly avv. con ammirazione.
admissible agg. ammissibile.
admission s. **1.** ammissione **2.** con-

fessione.

to **admit** *vt.* **1.** ammettere **2.** contenere.

admittance *s.* ammissione, ingresso.

to **admonish** *vt.* ammonire.

admonition *s.* ammonimento.

ado *s.* **1.** fatica **2.** confusione.

adolescence *s.* adolescenza.

adolescent *agg.* e *s.* adolescente.

to **adopt** *vt.* adottare.

adoption *s.* adozione.

adoptive *agg.* adottivo.

adorable *agg.* adorabile.

adoration *s.* adorazione.

to **adore** *vt.* adorare.

to **adorn** *vt.* adornare.

adornment *s.* ornamento.

adrenalin *s.* adrenalina.

adrift *avv.* alla deriva.

to **adulate** *vt.* adulare.

adulation *s.* adulazione.

adulator *s.* adulatore.

adult *agg.* e *s.* adulto.

to **adulterate** *vt.* adulterare.

adulteration *s.* adulterazione.

adulterer *s.* adultero.

adulteress *s.* adultera.

adulterine *agg.* adulterino.

adultery *s.* adulterio.

advance *s.* **1.** avanzamento **2.** anticipo **3.** approccio.

to **advance** *vt.* **1.** portar avanti **2.** anticipare (*denaro*) **3.** (*comm.*) aumentare. ♦ to **advance** *vi.* avanzare.

advancement *s.* **1.** avanzamento **2.** (*comm.*) rialzo.

advantage *s.* vantaggio || *to take — of,* approfittare di.

to **advantage** *vt.* avvantaggiare.

advantageous *agg.* vantaggioso.

advent *s.* avvento.

adventure *s.* avventura.

to **adventure** *vt.* rischiare. ♦ to **adventure** *vi.* avventurarsi.

adventurer *s.* avventuriero.

adventurous *agg.* avventuroso.

adverb *s.* avverbio.

adverbial *agg.* avverbiale.

adversary *s.* avversario.

adverse *agg.* avverso.

adversity *s.* avversità.

to **advert** *vi.* alludere, riferirsi.

to **advertise** *vt.* e *vi.* fare pubblicità a, divulgare.

advertisement *s.* **1.** avviso **2.** cartellone pubblicitario **3.** inserzione.

advertiser *s.* inserzionista.

advertising *agg.* pubblicitario. ♦ **advertising** *s.* pubblicità.

advice *s.* **1.** consiglio **2.** notizia.

advisability *s.* opportunità.

advisable *agg.* consigliabile.

to **advise** *vt.* **1.** consigliare **2.** avvisare || *to — with so.,* consultarsi con qu.

advised *agg.* giudizioso.

adviser *s.* consigliere.

advocacy *s.* avvocatura.

advocate *s.* difensore.

aegis *s.* egida.

Aeolian *agg.* eolio.

to **aerate** *vt.* **1.** aerare **2.** gassare.

aeration *s.* **1.** aerazione **2.** (*chim.*) aggiunta di acido carbonico.

aerial *agg.* aereo. ♦ **aerial** *s.* (*radio*) antenna.

aerodrome *s.* aerodromo.

aerodynamics *s.* aerodinamica.

aeronaut *s.* aeronauta.

aeronautics *s.* aeronautica.

aeroplane *s.* aeroplano.

aerostat *s.* aerostato.

aerostatics *s.* aerostatica.

aesthete *s.* esteta.

aesthetic(al) *agg.* estetico.

aestheticism *s.* estetismo.

aesthetics *s.* estetica.

aestivation *s.* letargo estivo.

aether *s.* etere.

afar *avv.* lontano.

affability *s.* affabilità.

affable *agg.* affabile.

affair *s.* **1.** affare **2.** tresca.

to **affect**[1] *vt.* **1.** ostentare **2.** simulare.

to **affect**[2] *vt.* **1.** concernere **2.** commuovere **3.** (*med.*) intaccare.

affectation *s.* affettazione.

affected *agg.* **1.** affettato **2.** affetto **3.** commosso **4.** disposto.

affection *s.* **1.** affetto **2.** (*med.*) affezione.

affectionate *agg.* affezionato, affettuoso.

affective *agg.* affettivo.

to **affiliate** *vt.* affiliare. ♦ to **affiliate** *vi.* affiliarsi.

affiliation *s.* affiliazione.

affinity *s.* affinità, parentela.

to **affirm** *vt.* **1.** affermare **2.** ratificare.

affirmation *s.* **1.** affermazione **2.** ratificazione.

affirmative *agg.* affermativo || *in the —,* affermativamente.

to **affix** *vt.* aggiungere, apporre.

to **afflict** *vt.* affliggere.
affliction *s.* afflizione.
affluence *s.* **1.** affluenza **2.** abbondanza.
affluent *agg.* ricco. ♦ **affluent** *s.* (*geogr.*) affluente.
afflux *s.* afflusso.
to **afford** *vt.* offrire || *can* —, potersi permettere.
to **afforest** *vt.* imboschire.
afforestation *s.* imboschimento.
affront *s.* affronto || *to take* — *at*, offendersi per.
to **affront** *vt.* **1.** affrontare **2.** insultare.
afloat *avv.* a galla. ♦ **afloat** *agg.* **1.** galleggiante **2.** in circolazione.
afore *avv.* precedentemente. ♦ **afore** *prep.* prima di.
aforementioned, aforesaid *agg.* predetto.
afraid *agg.* spaventato || *to be* —, temere.
African *agg.* e *s.* africano.
after *agg.* seguente. ♦ **after** *prep.* **1.** dopo, dietro **2.** secondo **3.** alla maniera di. ♦ **after** *avv.* dopo. ♦ **after** *cong.* dopo che.
afternoon *s.* pomeriggio.
afterthought *s.* riflessione.
afterward(s) *avv.* poi.
again *avv.* ancora, di nuovo.
against *prep.* **1.** contro **2.** in previsione di.
agape *agg.* e *avv.* a bocca aperta.
age *s.* **1.** età **2.** secolo || *old* —, vecchiaia; *to be of* —, essere maggiorenne; *to be under* —, essere minorenne; *Middle Ages*, Medioevo.
to **age** *vt.* e *vi.* invecchiare.
aged *agg.* **1.** vecchio **2.** dell'età di.
agency *s.* **1.** causa, azione **2.** (*comm.*) agenzia, rappresentanza.
agent *s.* agente.
agglomerate *agg.* e *s.* agglomerato.
to **agglomerate** *vt.* agglomerare.
♦ to **agglomerate** *vi.* agglomerarsi.
agglomeration *s.* agglomerazione.
to **agglutinate** *vt.* agglutinare. ♦ to **agglutinate** *vi.* agglutinarsi.
to **aggravate** *vt.* **1.** aggravare **2.** irritare.
aggravation *s.* **1.** aggravamento **2.** esasperazione.
aggregate *agg.* e *s.* aggregato.
to **aggregate** *vt.* **1.** aggregare **2.** ammontare a. ♦ to **aggregate** *vi.* aggregarsi.

aggregation *s.* aggregazione.
aggression *s.* aggressione.
aggressive *agg.* aggressivo.
aggressiveness *s.* aggressività.
aggressor *s.* aggressore.
aghast *agg.* **1.** atterrito **2.** stupefatto.
agile *agg.* agile.
agility *s.* agilità.
to **agitate** *vt.* agitare.
agitation *s.* agitazione.
agitator *s.* agitatore.
agnostic *agg.* e *s.* agnostico.
ago *agg.* e *avv.* fa.
agonistic(al) *agg.* agonistico.
to **agonize** *vt.* tormentare. ♦ to **agonize** *vi.* **1.** tormentarsi **2.** agonizzare.
agony *s.* **1.** agonia **2.** dolore.
agrarian *agg.* e *s.* agrario.
to **agree** *vt.* e *vi.* **1.** accordarsi **2.** accettare **3.** essere adatto.
agreeable *agg.* **1.** gradevole **2.** conforme.
agreement *s.* **1.** accordo **2.** conformità **3.** consenso.
agricultural *agg.* agricolo.
agriculture *s.* agricoltura.
agronomist *s.* agronomo.
agronomy *s.* agronomia.
ague *s.* febbre malarica.
ahead *avv.* avanti.
aid *s.* aiuto.
to **aid** *vt.* aiutare, soccorrere.
to **ail** *vt.* affliggere. ♦ to **ail** *vi.* sentirsi male.
aileron *s.* alettone.
aim *s.* **1.** mira **2.** scopo.
to **aim** *vt.* e *vi.* **1.** mirare **2.** aspirare a.
aimless *agg.* senza scopo.
air *s.* aria || — *conditioning*, condizionamento d'aria; — *lift*, ponte aereo; —*line*, aviolinea; —*raid*, incursione aerea; — *-mail*, posta aerea.
to **air** *vt.* aerare.
aircraft *s.* aereo, aerei || — *-carrier*, portaerei.
airfield *s.* campo d'aviazione.
airiness *s.* leggerezza, disinvoltura.
airing *s.* **1.** ventilazione **2.** passeggiata.
to **air-mail** *vt.* trasportare per via aerea.
airman *s.* aviatore.
airport *s.* aeroporto.
airship *s.* aeronave.
airsickness *s.* mal d'aria.

airstrip s. pista (d'areoporto).
airtight agg. a tenuta d'aria.
airway s. via aerea.
airy agg. **1.** arioso **2.** aereo **3.** gaio.
aisle s. navata (laterale).
ajar avv. socchiuso.
akin agg. **1.** consanguineo **2.** simile.
alacrity s. alacrità.
alarm s. allarme || — -clock, sveglia; to take —, allarmarsi.
to alarm vt. allarmare.
alas inter. ahimè.
Albanian agg. e s. albanese.
albatross s. albatro.
albumen s. albume.
albumin s. albumina.
alchemist s. alchimista.
alchemy s. alchimia.
alcohol s. alcool: wood —, alcool metilico.
alcoholic agg. alcolico. ♦ **alcoholic** sm. alcolizzato.
alcoholism s. alcoolismo.
alcove s. alcova.
alder s. ontano.
alderman s. assessore.
ale s. birra || —house, birreria.
aleatory agg. aleatorio.
alembic s. alambicco.
alert agg. **1.** all'erta **2.** svelto. ♦ alert s. allarme.
algebraic(al) agg. algebrico.
alien agg. e s. **1.** estraneo **2.** straniero.
to alienate vt. alienare.
alienation s. alienazione.
alienist s. alienista.
alight agg. illuminato.
to alight vi. **1.** scendere **2.** posarsi, atterrare.
to align vt. allineare. ♦ to align vi. allinearsi.
alignment s. allineamento.
alike agg. simile. ♦ alike avv. similmente.
aliment s. alimento.
alimentary agg. alimentare.
alimentation s. alimentazione.
aliquot agg. e s. aliquota.
alive agg. **1.** vivo **2.** vivace **3.** sensibile.
alkaline agg. alcalino.
all agg. tutto, tutti, ogni || — the way, lungo tutto il cammino. ♦ **all** pron. tutto, tutti || not at —, niente affatto; — the better, tanto meglio || — of us, noi tutti; it is — up, tutto è finito. ♦ all avv. completamente, interamente || —

right, va bene; — but, quasi. ♦ all s. tutto, totalità.
to allege vt. addurre.
allegiance s. fedeltà.
allegoric(al) agg. allegorico.
allegory s. allegoria.
allergic agg. allergico.
allergy s. allergia.
to alleviate vt. alleviare.
alleviation s. alleviamento.
alley s. vialetto, vicolo.
alliance s. **1.** alleanza **2.** unione.
allied agg. alleato.
alligator s. alligatore.
alliteration s. allitterazione.
alliterative agg. allitterativo.
to allocate vt. assegnare, distribuire.
allocution s. allocuzione.
to allot vt. assegnare.
allotment s. **1.** distribuzione **2.** lotto (di terreno).
to allow vt. **1.** permettere **2.** riconoscere **3.** concedere.
allowance s. **1.** permesso **2.** assegno, indennità **3.** razione **4.** riconoscimento **5.** sconto.
alloy s. (metal.) lega.
to allude vi. alludere.
to allure vt. attrarre.
allurement s. allettamento.
allusion s. allusione.
allusive agg. allusivo.
alluvion s. alluvione.
ally s. alleato.
to ally vt. **1.** unire **2.** alleare. ♦ to ally vi. allearsi.
almanac s. almanacco.
almighty agg. onnipotente: the Almighty, l'Onnipotente.
almond s. mandorla || — -tree, mandorlo.
almost avv. quasi.
alms s. elemosina || — -house, ospizio per i poveri; — -man, accattone.
alone agg. e avv. solo.
along avv. e prep. **1.** lungo **2.** avanti.
alongside avv. (mar.) accanto, accosto. ♦ **alongside** prep. a fianco di, lungo.
aloof avv. a distanza. ♦ **aloof** agg. riservato, scontroso.
aloofness s. freddezza.
aloud avv. ad alta voce.
alp s. alpe.
alpha s. alfa.
alphabet s. alfabeto.
alphabetic(al) agg. alfabetico.

alpine *agg.* alpino.

already *avv.* già.

also *avv.* anche, inoltre.

altar *s.* altare || — *-boy*, chierichetto; — *-piece*, pala d'altare.

to **alter** *vt.* alterare. ♦ to **alter** *vi.* alterarsi, trasformarsi.

alteration *s.* alterazione.

altercation *s.* alterco.

alternacy *s.* alternanza.

alternate *agg.* alterno, alternato.

to **alternate** *vt.* alternare. ♦ to **alternate** *vi.* alternarsi.

alternation *s.* alternazione.

alternative *agg.* alternativo. ♦ **alternative** *s.* alternativa.

alternator *s.* (*elettr.*) alternatore.

although *cong.* benché.

altimeter *s.* altimetro.

altitude *s.* **1.** altitudine **2.** (*aer.*) quota.

altogether *avv.* interamente.

altruism *s.* altruismo.

altruist *s.* altruista.

altruistic *agg.* altruistico.

aluminium *s.* alluminio.

always *avv.* sempre.

amalgam *s.* amalgama.

to **amalgamate** *vt.* amalgamare. ♦ to **amalgamate** *vi.* amalgamarsi.

amalgamation *s.* amalgamazione.

amaranth *s.* amaranto.

to **amass** *vt.* ammucchiare.

amateur *agg.* e *s.* amatore, dilettante.

amateurism *s.* dilettantismo.

to **amaze** *vt.* stupire.

amazement *s.* sorpresa.

amazing *agg.* sorprendente.

Amazon *s.* amazzone.

ambages *s. pl.* ambagi.

ambassador *s.* ambasciatore.

amber *s.* ambra.

ambient *agg.* circostante. ♦ **ambient** *s.* ambiente.

ambiguity *s.* ambiguità.

ambiguous *agg.* ambiguo.

ambit *s.* ambito.

ambition *s.* ambizione.

ambitious *agg.* ambizioso.

ambivalence *s.* ambivalenza.

ambivalent *agg.* ambivalente.

amble *s.* ambio.

ambo *s.* ambone.

ambulance *s.* ambulanza.

ambush *s.* imboscata.

to **ambush** *vt.* e *vi.* tendere una imboscata (a).

to **ameliorate** *vt.* e *vi.* migliorare.

to **amend** *vt.* emendare. ♦ to **amend** *vi.* emendarsi.

amendment *s.* emendamento.

amends *s.* ammenda.

amenity *s.* amenità.

American *agg.* e *s.* americano.

Americanism *s.* americanismo.

amethyst *s.* ametista.

amiability *s.* amabilità.

amiable *agg.* amabile.

amiably *avv.* amabilmente.

amianthus *s.* amianto.

amicable *agg.* amichevole.

amid *prep.* in mezzo a, tra, fra.

amiss *avv.* a male; *to take sthg.* —, aversene a male. ♦ **amiss** *agg.* inopportuno, errato.

amity *s.* amicizia.

ammonia *s.* ammoniaca.

ammunition *s.* munizioni.

amnesty *s.* amnistia.

to **amnesty** *vt.* amnistiare.

amoeba *s.* ameba.

among(st) *prep.* tra, fra (*più di due*); in mezzo a.

amoral *agg.* amorale.

amorality *s.* amoralità.

amorous *agg.* amoroso.

amorphous *agg.* amorfo.

to **amortize** *vt.* (*comm.*) ammortizzare.

amount *s.* **1.** somma **2.** totale **3.** valore **4.** quantità.

to **amount** *vi.* **1.** ammontare **2.** equivalere.

amperometer *s.* amperometro.

amphibian *agg.* e *s.* anfibio.

amphibious *agg.* anfibio.

amphitheatre *s.* anfiteatro.

amphitryon *s.* anfitrione.

amphora *s.* anfora.

ample *agg.* ampio.

amplification *s.* amplificazione.

amplifier *s.* amplificatore.

to **amplify** *vt.* amplificare. ♦ to **amplify** *vi.* dilungarsi.

to **amputate** *vt.* amputare.

amputation *s.* amputazione.

amulet *s.* amuleto.

to **amuse** *vt.* divertire.

amusement *s.* divertimento.

an *art.* V. *a.*

anachronic *agg.* anacronistico.

anachronism *s.* anacronismo.

anachronistic(al) *agg.* anacronistico.

anaemia *s.* anemia.

anaemic *agg.* anemico.

anaesthesia *s.* anestesia.

anaesthetic *agg.* e *s.* anestetico.
anaesthetist *s.* anestesista.
to **anaesthetize** *vt.* anestetizzare.
anagram *s.* anagramma.
anal *agg.* anale.
analgesic *agg.* e *s.* analgesico.
analogic(al) *agg.* analogico.
analogous *agg.* analogo.
analogy *s.* analogia.
to **analyse** *vt.* analizzare.
analysis *s.* (*pl.* -ses) analisi.
analyst *s.* analista.
analytic(al) *agg.* analitico.
anarchic(al) *agg.* anarchico.
anarchism *s.* anarchia.
anarchist *s.* anarchico.
anarchy *s.* anarchia.
anathema *s.* anatema.
anatomic(al) *agg.* anatomico.
anatomist *s.* anatomista.
to **anatomize** *vt.* anatomizzare.
anatomy *s.* anatomia.
ancestor *s.* antenato.
ancestral *agg.* ancestrale.
ancestry *s.* stirpe.
anchor *s.* (*mar.*) ancora.
to **anchor** *vt.* ancorare. ♦ to **anchor** *vi.* ancorarsi.
anchorage *s.* ancoraggio.
anchoret *s.* anacoreta.
anchovy *s.* acciuga.
ancient *agg.* e *s.* antico.
and *cong.* e.
androgynous *agg.* androgino.
anecdote *s.* aneddoto.
anecdotic(al) *agg.* aneddotico.
anew *avv.* di nuovo.
anfractuosity *s.* anfrattuosità.
anfractuous *agg.* anfrattuoso.
angel *s.* angelo: *guardian* —, angelo custode.
angelic(al) *agg.* angelico.
anger *s.* collera.
to **anger** *vt.* irritare.
angle *s.* (*geom.*) angolo || *at right angles*, perpendicolarmente.
to **angle** *vi.* **1.** pescare (*con l'amo*) **2.** *to* — *for*, andare in cerca di.
angler *s.* pescatore (*con l'amo*).
Anglican *agg.* e *s.* anglicano.
Anglo-Saxon *agg.* e *s.* anglosassone.
angrily *avv.* irosamente.
angry *agg.* irato, arrabbiato || *to get* —, adirarsi.
anguish *s.* angoscia.
to **anguish** *vt.* angosciare. ♦ to **anguish** *vi.* angosciarsi.
angular *agg.* angolare.
anhydride *s.* anidride.

aniline *s.* anilina.
animadversion *s.* biasimo.
to **animadvert** *vi.* criticare: *to* — *on so., sthg.*, criticare qu., qc.
animal *agg.* e *s.* animale.
to **animate** *vt.* animare.
animatedly *avv.* animatamente.
animation *s.* animazione.
animator *s.* animatore.
animism *s.* animismo.
animosity *s.* animosità.
anise *s.* anice.
ankle *s.* caviglia.
ankylosis *s.* anchilosi.
annals *s. pl.* annali.
Annelida *s. pl.* anellidi.
to **annex** *vt.* annettere.
annexation *s.* annessione.
to **annihilate** *vt.* annichilire.
annihilation *s.* annichilimento.
anniversary *s.* anniversario.
to **annotate** *vt.* e *vi.* annotare.
annotation *s.* annotazione.
to **announce** *vt.* annunciare.
announcement *s.* annuncio.
announcer *s.* annunciatore.
to **annoy** *vt.* infastidire.
annoyance *s.* fastidio.
annoying *agg.* fastidioso.
annual *agg.* annuale. ♦ **annual** *s.* annuario.
annuity *s.* rendita annuale.
to **annul** *vt.* annullare.
annulment *s.* annullamento.
to **annunciate** *vt.* annunciare.
annunciation *s.* annuncio, annunciazione.
anode *s.* anodo.
anodyne *agg.* e *s.* anodino.
to **anoint** *vt.* ungere, consacrare.
anomalous *agg.* anomalo.
anomaly *s.* anomalia.
anonym *s.* anonimo.
anonymous *agg.* anonimo.
another *agg.* e *pron.* un altro || *one* —, l'un l'altro.
answer *s.* risposta.
to **answer** *vt.* e *vi.* rispondere.
ant *s.* formica || — -*bear*, formichiere.
antagonism *s.* antagonismo.
antagonist *s.* antagonista.
Antarctic *agg.* antartico.
antecedent *agg.* e *s.* antecedente. ♦ **antecedents** *s. pl.* antenati.
to **antedate** *vt.* **1.** antidatare **2.** anticipare.
antediluvian *agg.* e *s.* antidiluviano.

antelope s. antilope.
anteroom s. anticamera.
anthem s. inno.
anthological agg. antologico.
anthology s. antologia.
anthracite s. antracite.
anthropocentric agg. antropocentrico.
anthropologist s. antropologo.
anthropology s. antropologia.
anthropomorphic agg. antropomorfo.
anthropomorphism s. antropomorfismo.
anthropomorphous agg. antropomorfo.
anthropophagous agg. e s. (pl. -gi) antropofago.
anthropophagy s. antropofagia.
antiaesthetic agg. antiestetico.
anti-aircraft agg. antiaereo.
antibiotic agg. e s. antibiotico.
antibody s. anticorpo.
to **anticipate** vt. 1. anticipare 2. prevedere 3. pregustare.
anticipation s. 1. anticipo 2. previsione 3. pregustazione.
anticlerical agg. anticlericale.
anticlericalism s. anticlericalismo.
anticonceptive s. antifecondativo.
anticonstitutional agg. anticostituzionale.
anticyclone s. anticiclone.
anti-dazzle agg. antiabbagliante.
antidote s. antidoto.
anti-freeze s. anticongelante.
anti-gas agg. antigas.
antimilitarism s. antimilitarismo.
antimilitarist s. antimilitarista.
antimony s. antimonio.
antinomy s. antinomia.
antiparticle s. antiparticella.
antipathetic(al) agg. avverso.
antipathy s. antipatia.
antiphon(y) s. antifona.
antipodal agg. degli, agli antipodi.
antipode s. antipodo.
antiquarian agg. e s. antiquario.
antiquary s. antiquario.
antiquated agg. antiquato.
antique agg. antico. ♦ **antique** s. antichità || — dealer, antiquario.
antiquity s. antichità.
antirheumatic agg. antireumatico.
anti-rust agg. e s. antiruggine.
anti-Semite s. antisemita.
anti-Semitism s. antisemitismo.
antiseptic agg. e s. antisettico.
antisocial agg. antisociale.

antispasmodic agg. e s. antispasmodico.
anti-tank agg. anticarro.
antitetanic agg. antitetanico.
anti-theft agg. e s. antifurto.
antithesis s. (pl. -ses) antitesi.
antithetic(al) agg. antitetico.
antitoxic agg. antitossico.
anus s. ano.
anvil s. incudine.
anxiety s. ansietà.
anxious agg. ansioso.
any agg. 1. qualunque 2. (in frasi neg.; int.; dubitative) qualche, nessuno, del || at — rate, in ogni modo. ♦ **any** pron. 1. alcuno, nessuno 2. ne || have you — bread?, hai del pane?; I haven't —, non ne ho.
anybody pron. 1. chiunque 2. (in frasi neg.; int.; dubitative) qualcuno, nessuno.
anyhow avv. e cong. comunque.
anyone pron. V. anybody.
anything pron. 1. qualunque cosa 2. (in frasi neg.; int.; dubitative) qualche cosa, niente.
anyway avv. in ogni modo, comunque.
anywhere avv. dovunque.
apace avv. presto.
apanage s. appannaggio.
apart avv. 1. a parte 2. lontano.
apartheid s. discriminazione razziale.
apartment s. alloggio (in affitto).
apathy s. apatia.
ape s. scimmia.
to **ape** vt. scimmiottare.
aperitif s. aperitivo.
apex s. apice.
aphaeresis s. aferesi.
aphonia s. afonia.
aphorism s. aforisma.
aphrodisiac agg. e s. afrodisiaco.
aphtha s. afta.
apiece avv. a testa.
apish agg. scimmiesco.
apocalypse s. apocalisse.
apocalyptic(al) agg. apocalittico.
apocrypha s. pl. libri apocrifi.
apocryphal agg. apocrifo.
apogee s. apogeo.
apologetic(al) agg. apologetico.
apologist s. apologista.
to **apologize** vi. scusarsi.
apologue s. apologo.
apology s. scusa.
apoplexy s. apoplessia.

apostasy *s.* apostasia.
apostate *agg.* e *s.* apostata.
apostle *s.* apostolo.
apostolate *s.* apostolato.
apostolic(al) *agg.* apostolico.
apostrophe *s.* apostrofo.
to apostrophize *vt.* apostrofare.
apothecary *s.* farmacista.
apotheosis *s.* (*pl.* -ses) apoteosi.
to appal *vt.* spaventare.
appalling *agg.* spaventoso.
apparatus *s.* apparato.
apparent *agg.* 1. visibile, evidente 2. (*giur.*) legittimo.
apparition *s.* apparizione.
appeal *s.* 1. appello 2. attrattiva.
to appeal *vi.* 1. appellarsi 2. attrarre.
appealing *agg.* 1. supplichevole 2. attraente.
to appear *vi.* 1. apparire 2. sembrare.
appearance *s.* 1. apparenza, aspetto 2. apparizione.
to appease *vt.* placare.
appeasement *s.* pacificazione, tregua.
appellative *agg.* e *s.* appellativo.
appendicitis *s.* appendicite.
appendix *s.* appendice.
appetite *s.* appetito.
appetizer *s.* aperitivo.
appetizing *agg.* appetitoso.
to applaud *vt.* e *vi.* applaudire.
applauding *agg.* plaudente.
applause *s.* applauso.
apple *s.* mela || — -tree, melo.
appliance *s.* 1. applicazione 2. apparecchio.
applicant *s.* richiedente.
application *s.* 1. applicazione 2. domanda.
to apply *vt.* applicare. ♦ to apply *vi.* 1. applicarsi 2. rivolgersi.
to appoint *vt.* 1. fissare 2. nominare, assegnare.
appointee *s.* persona designata.
appointment *s.* 1. appuntamento 2. nomina 3. impiego.
apposition *s.* apposizione.
appraisal *s.* stima.
to appraise *vt.* stimare.
appreciable *agg.* apprezzabile.
to appreciate *vt.* 1. apprezzare 2. rendersi conto di. ♦ to appreciate *vi.* aumentare di valore.
appreciation *s.* 1. apprezzamento 2. aumento di valore.
to apprehend *vt.* assodare.

apprehension *s.* 1. apprensione 2. percezione 3. arresto.
apprehensive *agg.* 1. apprensivo 2. perspicace.
apprentice *s.* apprendista.
apprenticeship *s.* apprendistato.
approach *s.* 1. avvicinamento 2. approccio 3. impostazione (*di una pratica ecc.*).
to approach *vt.* avvicinare. ♦ to approach *vi.* avvicinarsi.
approachable *agg.* accessibile.
appropriate *agg.* appropriato.
to appropriate *vt.* 1. appropriarsi di 2. stanziare.
appropriation *s.* 1. appropriazione 2. stanziamento.
approval *s.* 1. approvazione 2. (*comm.*) prova: on —, in prova.
to approve *vt.* 1. approvare 2. mostrare.
approximate *agg.* approssimativo.
to approximate *vt.* approssimare. ♦ to approximate *vi.* approssimarsi.
approximation *s.* approssimazione.
approximative *agg.* approssimativo.
apricot *s.* albicocca || — -tree, albicocco.
April *s.* aprile.
apron *s.* 1. grembiale 2. riparo 3. (*teat.*) proscenio.
apse *s.* abside.
apt *agg.* 1. atto 2. intelligente 3. proclive.
aptitude, aptness *s.* 1. idoneità 2. intelligenza 3. proprietà (*di vocabolo*).
aqualung *s.* autorespiratore.
aquamarine *s.* acquamarina.
aquarium *s.* acquario.
aquatic(al) *agg.* acquatico.
aqueduct *s.* acquedotto.
aqueous *agg.* acqueo, acquoso.
Arab *agg.* e *s.* arabo.
arabesque *s.* arabesco.
Arabian *agg.* e *s.* arabo.
Arabic *agg.* arabico.
arable *agg.* arabile.
arbiter *s.* arbitro.
arbitrage *s.* arbitraggio.
arbitrary *agg.* arbitrario.
to arbitrate *vt.* e *vi.* arbitrare.
arbitrator *s.* (*giur.*) arbitro.
arboreal, arboreous *agg.* arboreo.
arboriculture *s.* arboricoltura.
arbour *s.* pergolato.
arc *s.* arco.
arcade *s.* galleria.

Arcadian *agg.* e *s.* arcadico.
arch *s.* arco.
to arch *vt.* **1.** fabbricare ad arco **2.** inarcare. ◆ **to arch** *vi.* inarcarsi.
archaeologic(al) *agg.* archeologico.
archaeologist *s.* archeologo.
archaeology *s.* archeologia
archaic(al) *agg.* arcaico.
archaism *s.* arcaismo.
archangel *s.* arcangelo.
archbishop *s.* arcivescovo
archduke *s.* arciduca.
archer *s.* arciere.
archetype *s.* archetipo.
archipelago *s.* arcipelago.
architect *s.* architetto.
architectonic, architectural *agg* architettonico.
architecture *s.* architettura.
archive *s.* archivio.
archivist *s.* archivista.
Arctic *agg.* e *s.* artico.
ardent *agg.* ardente.
ardour *s.* ardore.
arduous *agg.* arduo.
area *s.* area.
arena *s.* (*arch.*) arena.
Areopagus *s.* areopago.
argent *s.* argenteo.
Argentine *agg.* e *s.* argentino.
argil *s.* argilla.
to argue *vi.* **1.** discutere **2.** ragionare. ◆ **to argue** *vt.* dimostrare.
argument *s.* **1.** discussione **2.** argomentazione.
arid *agg.* arido.
aridity *s.* aridità.
to arise (arose, arisen) *vi.* **1.** alzarsi **2.** (*fig.*) nascere.
aristocracy *s.* aristocrazia.
aristocrat *s.* aristocratico.
aristocratic(al) *agg.* aristocratico.
Aristotelian *agg.* e *s.* aristotelico.
arithmetic *s.* aritmetica.
arithmetic(al) *agg.* aritmetico.
arm[1] *s.* braccio || — *-in-* —, a braccetto.
arm[2] *s.* arma || *coat of arms*, stemma.
to arm *vt.* armare. ◆ **to arm** *vi.* armarsi.
armament *s.* armamento.
armchair *s.* poltrona.
armful *s.* bracciata.
armistice *s.* armistizio.
armless *agg.* inerme.
armlet *s.* braccialetto.
armour *s.* corazza.
to armour *vt.* corazzare || *armour-*

ed-car, autoblinda.
armoury *s.* **1.** arsenale **2.** armeria.
armpit *s.* ascella.
army *s.* esercito.
aromatic(al) *agg.* aromatico.
arose V. *to arise.*
around *avv.* intorno. ◆ **around** *prep.* **1.** intorno a **2.** circa.
to arouse *vt.* **1.** destare **2.** eccitare.
to arrange *vt.* **1.** accomodare **2.** predisporre **3.** (*mus.*) arrangiare.
arrangement *s.* **1.** accomodamento **2.** (*mus.*) arrangiamento **3.** dispositivo. ◆ **arrangements** *s. pl.* preparativi.
arras *s.* arazzo.
array *s.* **1.** apparato **2.** (*mil.*) spiegamento.
to array *vt.* **1.** ornare **2.** (*mil.*) schierare.
arrest *s.* arresto.
to arrest *vt.* arrestare.
arrival *s.* arrivo.
to arrive *vi.* arrivare.
arrogance *s.* arroganza.
arrogant *agg.* arrogante.
to arrogate *vt.* arrogarsi.
arrow *s.* freccia.
arsenal *s.* arsenale.
arsenic *s.* arsenico.
art *s.* arte.
arteriosclerosis *s.* arteriosclerosi.
artery *s.* arteria.
artesian *agg.* artesiano.
artful *agg.* **1.** abile **2.** artificioso **3.** astuto.
arthritic(al) *agg.* artritico.
arthritis *s.* artrite.
artichoke *s.* carciofo.
article *s.* articolo.
articulate *agg.* **1.** articolato **2.** chiaro.
to articulate *vt.* articolare. ◆ **to articulate** *vi.* articolarsi.
articulation *s.* articolazione.
artifice *s.* **1.** artificio **2.** abilità.
artificial *agg.* artificiale.
artificiality *s.* artificiosità.
artillery *s.* artiglieria.
artilleryman *s.* artigliere.
artist *s.* artista.
artistic(al) *agg.* artistico.
artistry *s.* abilità artistica.
artless *agg.* ingenuo.
Aryan *agg.* e *s.* ariano.
as *avv.* come || — ... —, tanto ... quanto; *so* — (*con infinito*), in modo da; — *for,* quanto a; — *far* —, sin dove, fino a; — *much,* al-

trettanto; — *well*, come pure. ♦
as *cong.* **1.** poiché **2.** mentre.
asbestos *s.* asbesto.
to **ascend** *vi.* ascendere. ♦ to
ascend *vt.* risalire, scalare.
ascendancy *s.* ascendente.
ascendant *agg.* e *s.* ascendente.
ascension *s.* ascensione.
ascent *s.* ascesa.
to **ascertain** *vt.* accertarsi di.
ascertainment *s.* accertamento.
ascetic *s.* asceta.
ascetic(al) *agg.* ascetico.
asceticism *s.* ascetismo.
to **ascribe** *vt.* ascrivere.
asepsis *s.* asepsi.
aseptic *agg.* e *s.* asettico.
asexual *agg.* asessuale.
ash *s.* cenere || — *-tray*, portacenere.
ash(-tree) *s.* frassino.
ashamed *agg.* vergognoso || *to be*
—, aver vergogna.
ashore *avv.* a terra.
ashy *agg.* cinereo.
Asiatic *agg.* e *s.* asiatico.
aside *avv.* a parte, da parte.
asininity *s.* asinità.
to **ask** *vt.* e *vi.* **1.** chiedere **2.** invi-
tare || *to — so. for sthg.*, chiedere
a qu. qc.; *to — for trouble*, cer-
car fastidi.
askance *avv.* di traverso.
asker *s.* interrogante.
asleep *agg.* addormentato.
asocial *agg.* asociale.
asp *s.* aspide.
asparagus *s. coll.* asparago, aspa-
ragi.
aspect *s.* aspetto.
aspen *s.* pioppo tremulo.
aspergillum *s.* aspersorio.
asperity *s.* **1.** asperità **2.** (*fig.*)
asprezza.
aspersion *s.* **1.** aspersione **2.** calunnia.
asphalt *s.* asfalto.
asphyxia *s.* asfissia.
to **asphyxiate** *vt.* asfissiare.
aspirant *agg.* e *s.* aspirante.
to **aspirate** *vt.* aspirare.
aspiration *s.* aspirazione.
aspirator *s.* aspiratore.
to **aspire** *vi.* aspirare.
aspirin *s.* aspirina.
aspiring *agg.* ambizioso.
asquint *avv.* di traverso.
ass *s.* asino || *to make an — of one-
self*, rendersi ridicolo.
to **assail** *vt.* assalire.

assailant, assailer *s.* assalitore.
assassin *s.* assassino.
to **assassinate** *vt.* assassinare.
assassination *s.* assassinio.
assault *s.* assalto, aggressione.
to **assault** *vt.* assalire.
assaulter *s.* assalitore.
to **assay** *vt.* saggiare.
assayer *s.* (as)saggiatore.
to **assemble** *vt.* riunire. ♦ to **assemble** *vi.* riunirsi.
assembly *s.* **1.** assemblea **2.** (*mil.*)
adunata **3.** (*mecc.*) montaggio: —
line, catena di montaggio.
assent *s.* consenso.
to **assent** *vt.* approvare.
to **assert** *vt.* asserire || *to — one-
self*, farsi valere.
assertion *s.* asserzione.
assertor *s.* assertore.
to **assess** *vt.* **1.** tassare **2.** (*comm.*)
ripartire.
assessment *s.* **1.** valutazione **2.** tassazione.
assessor *s.* agente delle tasse.
asset *s.* **1.** bene, vantaggio. ♦ **assets** *s. pl.* patrimonio, attività
(*sing.*).
assiduity *s.* assiduità.
assiduous *agg.* assiduo.
to **assign** *vt.* **1.** assegnare **2.** trasferire **3.** designare.
assignation *s.* **1.** assegnazione **2.**
(*giur.*) cessione **3.** appuntamento.
assignment *s.* **1.** assegnazione **2.**
(*giur.*) cessione.
assimilable *agg.* assimilabile.
to **assimilate** *vt.* **1.** assimilare **2.**
confrontare. ♦ to **assimilate** *vi.*
assimilarsi.
assimilation *s.* **1.** assimilazione **2.**
confronto. ·
to **assist** *vt.* e *vi.* assistere.
assistance *s.* assistenza.
assistant *agg.* e *s.* assistente || *shop*
—, commesso.
assize *s.* **1.** (*giur.*) seduta. ♦ **Assizes** *s. pl.* Assise.
associate *agg.* e *s.* associato.
to **associate** *vt.* associare. ♦ to
associate *vi.* associarsi.
association *s.* associazione.
assonance *s.* assonanza.
to **assort** *vt.* **1.** assortire **2.** classificare. ♦ to **assort** *vi.* **1.** armonizzarsi **2.** frequentare: *to — with
so.*, frequentare qu.
to **assume** *vt.* **1.** assumere **2.** fingere **3.** presumere.

assuming *agg.* presuntuoso.

assumption *s.* **1.** assunzione **2.** finzione **3.** supposizione **4.** presunzione.

assurance *s.* **1.** assicurazione **2.** sicurezza **3.** fiducia.

to **assure** *vt.* **1.** assicurare **2.** rassicurare.

assurer *s.* assicuratore.

asterisk *s.* asterisco.

astern *avv.* a poppa.

asteroid *s.* asteroide.

asthenia *s.* astenia.

asthma *s.* asma.

asthmatic *agg.* e *s.* asmatico.

astigmatic *agg.* astigmatico.

astigmatism *s.* astigmatismo.

astir *agg.* e *avv.* in moto.

to **astonish** *vt.* stupire.

astonishing *agg.* sorprendente

astonishment *s.* sorpresa.

to **astound** *vt.* sbalordire.

astragal(us) *s.* astragalo.

astrakhan *s.* astracan.

astral *agg.* astrale.

astray *agg.* e *avv.* fuori strada.

astride *agg.* e *avv.* a cavalcioni. ♦ **astride** *prep.* a cavalcioni di.

astringent *agg.* e *s.* astringente

astrolabe *s.* astrolabio.

astrologer *s.* astrologo.

astrology *s.* astrologia.

astronaut *s.* astronauta.

astronautics *s.* astronautica.

astronomer *s.* astronomo.

astronomic(al) *agg.* astronomico.

astronomy *s.* astronomia.

astute *agg.* astuto.

asunder *avv.* **1.** separatamente **2.** in pezzi.

asylum *s.* **1.** asilo, ricovero **2.** manicomio.

asymmetric(al) *agg.* asimmetrico.

asymmetry *s.* asimmetria.

at *prep.* (*stato, tempo, modo*) a, da, in: *to arrive — a place,* arrivare in un luogo; *— that time,* in quel momento; *— will,* a volontà.

atavistic *agg.* atavico.

atavism *s.* atavismo.

ataxy *s.* atassia.

ate V. *to eat.*

atheism *s.* ateismo.

atheist *s.* ateo.

atheistic(al) *agg.* ateistico.

athlete *s.* atleta.

athletic *agg.* atletico.

athletics *s.* atletica.

atlas *s.* atlante.

atmosphere *s.* atmosfera.

atmospheric(al) *agg.* atmosferico.

atoll *s.* atollo.

atom *s.* atomo.

atomic(al) *agg.* atomico.

atomism *s.* atomismo.

to **atomize** *vt.* nebulizzare.

atomizer *s.* atomizzatore, nebulizzatore.

atomy *s.* atomo.

to **atone** *vt.* espiare.

atonement *s.* espiazione.

atonic *agg.* **1.** atono **2.** atonico.

atrocious *agg.* atroce.

atrocity *s.* atrocità.

atrophic *agg.* atrofico.

atrophy *s.* atrofia.

to **atrophy** *vt.* atrofizzare. ♦ to **atrophy** *vi.* atrofizzarsi.

atropin(e) *s.* atropina.

to **attach** *vt.* **1.** attaccare, unire **2.** attribuire **3.** attrarre. ♦ to **attach** *vi.* attaccarsi.

attaché *s.* addetto.

attachment *s.* **1.** attaccamento **2.** (*mecc.*) accessorio.

attack *s.* attacco.

to **attack** *vt.* attaccare.

attacker *s.* assalitore.

to **attain** *vt.* raggiungere. ♦ to **attain** *vi.* giungere.

attainable *agg.* raggiungibile.

attainment *s.* **1.** raggiungimento **2.** cultura.

attempt *s.* **1.** tentativo **2.** attentato.

to **attempt** *vt.* **1.** tentare **2.** attentare a.

to **attend** *vi.* **1.** badare a **2.** obbedire ‖ *to — on,* essere al servizio di. ♦ to **attend** *vt.* **1.** assistere **2.** accompagnare **3.** frequentare.

attendance *s.* **1.** servizio **2.** assistenza **3.** frequenza.

attendant *s.* **1.** servitore **2.** assistente **3.** assiduo frequentatore.

attention *s.* attenzione: *to pay —,* fare attenzione.

attentive *agg.* **1.** attento **2.** sollecito.

to **attenuate** *vt.* **1.** assottigliare **2.** attenuare. ♦ to **attenuate** *vi.* **1.** assottigliarsi **2.** attenuarsi.

attenuation *s.* **1.** assottigliamento **2.** attenuazione.

to **attest** *vt.* attestare.

attic *agg.* e *s.* attico.

to **attire** *vt.* vestire, agghindare. ♦ to **attire** *vi.* vestirsi.

attitude *s.* atteggiamento.

attorney s. **1.** procura **2.** procuratore || — (-at-law), procuratore legale.

to **attract** vt. attrarre.

attraction s. **1.** attrazione **2.** attrattiva.

attractive agg. attraente.

attribute s. attributo.

to **attribute** vt. attribuire.

attribution s. attribuzione.

attributive agg. attributivo. ♦ **attributive** s. attributo.

aubergine s. melanzana.

auction s. asta: — sale, vendita all'asta.

to **auction** vt. vendere all'asta.

auctioneer s. banditore.

audible agg. udibile.

audience s. **1.** udienza **2.** uditorio.

audiovisual agg. audiovisivo.

audit s. verifica, revisione.

audition s. audizione.

auditory agg. e s. uditorio.

auger s. trivella, succhiello.

to **augment** vt. aumentare. ♦ to **augment** vi. crescere.

augmentative agg. e s. accrescitivo.

to **augur** vt. e vi. predire.

august agg. augusto.

August s. agosto.

aunt s. zia || great- —, prozia.

auricle s. **1.** padiglione auricolare **2.** (med.) orecchietta.

auricular agg. auricolare.

auriferous agg. aurifero.

to **auscultate** vt. auscultare.

auscultation s. auscultazione.

auscultator s. stetoscopio.

auspice s. auspicio.

auspicious agg. propizio.

austere agg. austero.

austerity s. austerità.

austral agg. australe.

Australian agg. e s. australiano.

Austrian agg. e s. austriaco.

autarky s. autarchia.

authentic(al) agg. autentico.

to **authenticate** vt. autenticare.

authentication s. autenticazione.

authenticity s. autenticità.

author s. autore.

authoress s. autrice.

authoritative agg. **1.** autoritario **2.** autorevole.

authoritativeness s. autorevolezza.

authority s. autorità.

authorization s. autorizzazione.

to **authorize** vt. autorizzare.

authorless agg. anonimo.

authorship s. paternità (di un libro).

autobiographic(al) agg. autobiografico.

autobiography s. autobiografia.

autochthon s. autoctono.

autochthonous agg. autoctono.

autocracy s. autocrazia.

autocrat s. autocrate.

autocriticism s. autocritica.

autoeducation s. autoeducazione.

autofinancing s. autofinanziamento.

autograph s. autografo.

autography s. autografia.

autolesion s. autolesione.

automatic agg. automatico. ♦ **automatic** s. arma automatica.

automation s. automazione.

automatism s. automatismo.

automaton s. automa.

autonomist s. autonomista.

autonomous agg. autonomo.

autonomy s. autonomia.

autopsy s. autopsia.

auto-suggestion s. autosuggestione.

autumn s. autunno.

autumnal agg. autunnale.

auxiliary agg. e s. ausiliare.

avail s. utilità.

to **avail** vt. e vi. servire a || to — oneself of, approfittare di.

availability s. **1.** disponibilità **2.** validità.

available agg. **1.** disponibile **2.** valevole.

avalanche s. valanga.

avarice s. **1.** avarizia **2.** cupidigia.

avaricious agg. **1.** avaro **2.** cupido.

to **avenge** vt. vendicare.

avenger s. vendicatore.

avenue s. viale.

to **aver** vt. asserire, dichiarare.

average agg. medio. ♦ **average** s. **1.** media **2.** (comm.) avaria.

averse agg. avverso.

aversion s. avversione.

to **avert** vt. sviare.

aviary s. uccelliera.

aviation s. aviazione.

aviator s. aviatore.

avid agg. avido.

avidity s. avidità.

to **avoid** vt. **1.** evitare **2.** (giur.) annullare.

avoidable agg. **1.** evitabile **2.** (giur.) annullabile.

to **avow** vt. dichiarare, ammettere.

avowal s. dichiarazione, ammissione.

to **await** vt. attendere.
awake agg. **1.** sveglio **2.** conscio.
to **awake** (awoke, awoke) vt. svegliare. ♦ to **awake** (awoke, awoke) vi. svegliarsi.
to **awaken** vt. risvegliare, far aprire gli occhi. ♦ to **awaken** vi. risvegliarsi, aprire gli occhi.
awakening s. risveglio.
award s. **1.** sentenza **2.** ricompensa.
to **award** vt. aggiudicare.
aware agg. conscio.
away avv. via, lontano || right —, subito, seduta stante.
awe s. timore reverenziale.
awful agg. **1.** terribile **2.** imponente.
awkward agg. **1.** goffo, imbarazzato **2.** scomodo **3.** inopportuno **4.** delicato.
awkwardness s. **1.** goffaggine **2.** imbarazzo.
awl s. lesina.
awning s. tenda.
awoke V. to awake.
awry agg. **1.** storto **2.** bieco. ♦ **awry** avv. **1.** per traverso **2.** perversamente.
ax(e) s. scure.
axiom s. assioma.
axiomatic(al) agg. assiomatico.
axis s. (pl. axes) asse.
axle s. (mecc.) asse.
azimuth s. azimut.
azote s. azoto.
to **azotize** vt. azotare.
Aztec agg. e s. azteco.
azure agg. e s. azzurro.

B

b s. (mus.) si.
babble s. balbettio.
to **babble** vi. e vt. **1.** balbettare **2.** mormorare (di acque).
babe s. bambino.
babel s. babele.
baboon s. babbuino.
baby s. bimbo, neonato || — -sitter, chi accudisce i bambini.
babyhood s. infanzia.
babyish agg. infantile.
baccarat s. baccarà.
Bacchanal s. **1.** baccante **2.** baccanale (anche fig.).
Bacchante s. baccante.

bacchic(al) agg. bacchico.
bachelor s. scapolo || Bachelor of Arts, titolo universitario in lettere.
bachelorhood s. celibato.
bacillus s. (pl. -li) bacillo.
back[1] agg. posteriore. ♦ **back** avv. dietro, indietro || to be —, essere di ritorno; to go, to come —, ritornare.
back[2] s. **1.** dorso, schiena **2.** spalle **3.** rovescio **4.** schienale **5.** fondo.
to **back** vt. **1.** sostenere **2.** fare indietreggiare || to — a bill, avallare una cambiale. ♦ to **back** vi. indietreggiare || — down, abbandonare la contesa.
to **backbite** vt. denigrare.
backbiter s. calunniatore.
backbiting agg. maldicente. ♦ **backbiting** s. maldicenza.
backbone s. **1.** spina dorsale **2.** (fig.) fermezza.
backer s. **1.** scommettitore **2.** sostenitore.
backfire s. ritorno di fiamma.
background s. **1.** sfondo **2.** curriculum **3.** ambiente.
backing s. **1.** sostegno **2.** marcia indietro.
backlash s. rimbalzo.
backslider s. apostata.
backward agg. **1.** lento **2.** tardo.
backward(s) avv. indietro.
backwash s. risacca.
bacon s. lardo affumicato, pancetta.
bacterial agg. batterico.
bacteriology s. batteriologia.
bacterium s. (pl. -ia) batterio.
bad (worse, worst) agg. **1.** cattivo **2.** brutto. ♦ **bad** s. **1.** male **2.** rovina.
bade V. to bid.
badge s. insegna.
badger s. tasso.
badly avv. male, malamente.
badness s. **1.** cattiveria **2.** cattiva qualità.
baffle s. (-plate) deflettore, diaframma.
to **baffle** vt. **1.** eludere **2.** confondere.
bag s. **1.** sacco **2.** borsa || sleeping- —, sacco a pelo.
to **bag** vt. **1.** gonfiare **2.** rubare **3.** insaccare.
baggage s. bagaglio.
bagpipe s. cornamusa.
bail s. **1.** cauzione **2.** garante.
to **bail**[1] vt. **1.** dar garanzia per **2.**

affidare (*dietro cauzione*).

to **bail**[2] *vt.* e *vi.* (*mar.*) aggottare || *to — out*, lanciarsi col paracadute.

bailiff *s.* **1.** magistrato inquirente **2.** ufficiale fiscale.

bain-marie *s.* bagnomaria.

bait *s.* **1.** esca **2.** sosta (*per ristoro*).

to **bait** *vt.* **1.** adescare **2.** tormentare. ♦ to **bait** *vi.* fermarsi (*per prendere ristoro*).

to **bake** *vt.* e *vi.* cuocere al forno.

baker *s.* fornaio.

bakery *s.* forno.

baking *s.* cottura al forno.

balance *s.* **1.** bilancia **2.** bilanciere **3.** equilibrio **4.** bilancio.

to **balance** *vt.* **1.** pesare **2.** pareggiare. ♦ to **balance** *vi.* **1.** bilanciarsi **2.** oscillare.

balanced *agg.* equilibrato.

balancer *s.* acrobata.

balcony *s.* **1.** balcone **2.** (*teat.*).balconata.

bald *agg.* **1.** calvo, pelato **2.** povero, nudo.

baldness *s.* **1.** calvizie **2.** (*fig.*) nudità.

baldric *s.* bandoliera.

bale *s.* (*comm.*) balla.

Balkan *agg.* balcanico.

ball *s.* **1.** palla **2.** ballo || *— -bearing*, cuscinetto a sfere.

to **ball** *vt.* appallottolare. ♦ to **ball** *vi.* appallottolarsi.

ballad *s.* ballata.

ballast *s.* zavorra.

to **ballast** *vt.* zavorrare.

ballet *s.* balletto || *— -dancer*, ballerino classico.

ballistics *s.* balistica.

balloon *s.* **1.** pallone **2.** lambicco **3.** fumetto.

ballot *s.* **1.** pallina, scheda (*per votazione*) **2.** voto **3.** scrutinio || *— -box*, urna.

to **ballot** *vt.* mettere in ballottaggio.

balm *s.* balsamo.

balm-cricket *s.* (*zool.*) cicala.

balmy *agg.* balsamico.

Baltic *agg.* baltico.

balustrade *s.* balaustrata.

bamboo *s.* bambù.

ban *s.* bando.

to **ban** *vt.* proibire.

banal *agg.* banale.

banality *s.* banalità.

banana *s.* **1.** banana **2.** banano.

band *s.* **1.** legame **2.** benda **3.** nastro **4.** banda.

to **band** *vt.* **1.** legare **2.** bendare.

bandage *s.* bendaggio.

to **bandage** *vt.* bendare.

banderole *s.* banderuola.

bandit *s.* bandito.

bandmaster *s.* capobanda.

bandog *s.* cane da guardia.

bandsman *s.* bandista.

bane *s.* **1.** calamità **2.** veleno.

baneful *agg.* velenoso.

bang *s.* **1.** botta **2.** detonazione.

to **bang** *vt.* e *vi.* sbattere violentemente.

banging *s.* **1.** colpi violenti **2.** detonazioni.

to **banish** *vt.* bandire, esiliare.

banishment *s.* bando, esilio.

banister *s.* ringhiera (*di scala*).

bank *s.* **1.** banca **2.** banco **3.** argine **4.** terrapieno.

to **bank** *vt.* **1.** arginare **2.** depositare in banca || *to — upon*, contare su. ♦ to **bank** *vi.* gestire una banca.

bankbook *s.* libretto bancario.

banker *s.* banchiere.

banking *agg.* bancario. ♦ **banking** *s.* tecnica, professione bancaria.

bank note *s.* banconota.

bankrupt *agg.* e *s.* fallito || *to go —*, fallire.

bankruptcy *s.* fallimento.

banner *s.* vessillo.

banns *s. pl.* pubblicazioni matrimoniali.

banquet *s.* banchetto.

to **banquet** *vi.* banchettare.

banter *s.* scherzo, beffa.

to **banter** *vt.* canzonare.

baptism *s.* battesimo.

baptist(e)ry *s.* battistero.

to **baptize** *vt.* battezzare.

bar *s.* **1.** sbarra **2.** diga **3.** striscia **4.** ostacolo **5.** (*fig.*) tribunale **6.** bar **7.** (*mus.*) battuta.

to **bar** *vt.* **1.** sbarrare **2.** ostacolare **3.** proibire.

barbarian *agg.* e *s.* barbaro.

barbaric *agg.* barbarico.

barbarism *s.* **1.** barbarie **2.** (*gramm.*) barbarismo.

barbarous *agg.* barbaro.

barbarousness *s.* barbarie.

barbecue *s.* **1.** animale arrostito intero **2.** festa campestre.

to **barbecue** *vt.* arrostire un animale intero.

barbed *agg.* dentato.

barber *s.* barbiere.

barbiturate s. barbiturico.
bard s. bardo, trovatore.
bare agg. **1.** nudo **2.** logoro.
to **bare** vt. **1.** denudare **2.** snudare **3.** smascherare.
barefoot agg. scalzo.
barehanded agg. e avv. **1.** a mano nuda **2.** senz'armi.
bareheaded agg. a capo scoperto.
barely avv. **1.** apertamente **2.** appena.
bargain s. affare.
to **bargain** vt. e vi. contrattare.
bargaining s. contrattazione.
barge s. chiatta.
baritone s. baritono.
bark[1] s. corteccia.
bark[2] s. latrato.
to **bark**[1] vt. scortecciare.
to **bark**[2] vi. latrare, abbaiare.
barking[1] s. scortecciamento.
barking[2] s. abbaiamento.
barley s. orzo.
barmaid s. barista (donna).
barman s. barista.
barn s. granaio.
barometer s. barometro.
barometric(al) agg. barometrico.
baron s. barone.
baroness s. baronessa.
baroque agg. e s. barocco.
barracks s. pl. caserma (sing.).
barrage s. sbarramento.
barrel s. **1.** barile **2.** cilindro **3.** canna (di arma da fuoco) || — -organ, organetto.
to **barrel** vt. mettere in barili.
barrelled agg. double- — gun, fucile a due canne.
barren agg. sterile.
barrenness s. sterilità.
barricade s. barricata.
to **barricade** vt. barricare.
barrier s. barriera || transonic —, muro del suono.
barrister s. avvocato (che può discutere cause nelle corti superiori).
barrow s. **1.** barella **2.** carriola.
bartender s. barista.
barter s. baratto.
to **barter** vt. e vi. barattare.
basal agg. basilare.
basalt s. basalto.
base[1] agg. basso, vile.
base[2] s. base.
to **base** vt. basare.
baseless agg. senza base.
basement s. **1.** fondamento **2.** seminterrato.

baseness s. bassezza.
to **bash** vt. colpire.
bashful agg. timido.
bashfulness s. timidezza.
basic agg. **1.** fondamentale **2.** (chim.) basico.
basil s. basilico.
basilar agg. basilare.
basilisk s. basilisco.
basin s. **1.** bacino **2.** catino, lavabo || sugar —, zuccheriera.
basis s. (pl. -ses) base.
to **bask** vi. crogiolarsi (al sole, al fuoco).
basket s. cesto || —ball, pallacanestro; — -chair, poltroncina di vimini.
Basque agg. e s. basco.
bas-relief s. bassorilievo.
bass agg. e s. (mus.) basso.
bass s. pesce persico.
bassoon s. (mus.) fagotto.
bastard agg. e s. bastardo.
to **baste** vt. imbastire.
basting s. imbastitura.
bastion s. bastione.
bat[1] s. pipistrello.
bat[2] s. (sport) mazza.
batch s. **1.** infornata **2.** gruppo.
to **bate** vt. ridurre.
bath s. bagno || — -robe, accappatoio; — -tub, vasca da bagno.
to **bath** vt. bagnare. ♦ to **bath** vi. bagnarsi, fare il bagno.
bathe s. bagno (in mare, lago ecc.).
to **bathe** vt. bagnare. ♦ to **bathe** vi. bagnarsi, fare il bagno (in mare, lago ecc.).
bather s. bagnante.
bathing s. il bagnarsi || — -suit, costume da bagno.
bathroom s. stanza da bagno.
bathysphere s. batisfera.
batiste s. batista.
batman s. attendente.
baton s. **1.** bastone **2.** bacchetta (di direttore d'orchestra).
batrachian s. batrace.
batsman s. (sport) battitore.
battalion s. battaglione.
to **batten** vt. (mar.) chiudere (i boccaporti).
batter s. (cuc.) pastella.
to **batter** vt. battere || to — down, abbattere; to — in, sfondare.
battering s. cannoneggiamento.
battery s. batteria || storage —, accumulatore.
battle s. battaglia.

to **battle** vt. e vi. combattere.

battledore s. racchetta di legno || — and shuttlecock, volano.

battlement s. (arch.) merlo.

battleship s. nave da guerra.

bauxite s. bauxite.

bawdiness s. oscenità.

bawdy agg. osceno || — house, bordello.

bawl s. grido.

to **bawl** vt. e vi. gridare, vociare.

bay[1] s. 1. baia 2. insenatura, recesso (nelle montagne).

bay[2] s. alloro || — -tree, lauro.

bay[3] s. 1. rientranza 2. campata || — -window, bovindo.

bay[4] s. latrato || at —, senza scampo.

bay[5] agg. e s. baio.

to **bay**[1] vt. arginare.

to **bay**[2] vi. latrare.

bayonet s. baionetta.

baza(a)r s. 1. bazar 2. vendita di beneficienza.

to **be (was, been)** vi. 1. essere 2. stare 3. andare 4. costare: how much is it?, quanto costa? 5. dovere || to — in, essere in casa; to — about, stare per; so be it, così sia.

beach s. spiaggia.

beacon s. faro.

to **beacon** vt. guidare con segnalazioni luminose.

bead s. 1. goccia 2. perlina. ◆ **beads** s. pl. rosario (sing.).

to **bead** vt. imperlare. ◆ to **bead** vi. imperlarsi.

beak s. 1. becco, rostro 2. beccuccio.

to **beak** vt. beccare.

beaker s. boccale.

beam s. 1. trave 2. raggio 3. asta (di bilancia) 4. fiancata (di nave).

to **beam** vi. brillare. ◆ to **beam** vt. irradiare.

beaming agg. raggiante.

bean s. fagiolo || French —, fagiolino; coffee —, grano di caffè.

bear s. orso.

to **bear**[1] vt. e vi. speculare al ribasso (in Borsa).

to **bear**[2] (bore, born(e)) vt. 1. portare 2. sopportare 3. generare. ◆ to **bear** (bore, borne) vi. 1. resistere 2. appoggiarsi 3. pazientare || to — with, aver pazienza con.

bearable agg. sopportabile.

beard s. 1. barba 2. chioma (di cometa).

to **beard** vt. affrontare, sfidare.

bearded agg. barbuto.

beardless agg. senza barba.

bearer s. portatore.

bearing s. 1. sopportazione 2. portamento 3. condotta 4. relazione 5. sostegno 6. raccolto || to lose one's bearings, perdere l'orientamento; to take the bearings of a coast (mar.), rilevare una costa.

beast s. bestia.

beastliness s. bestialità.

beastly agg. bestiale. ◆ **beastly** avv. bestialmente.

beat s. 1. battito 2. (mus.) battuta.

to **beat (beat, beat(en))** vt. e vi. battere || to — down, abbattere; to — back, respingere.

beaten agg. abbattuto, vinto.

beater s. battitore.

beatification s. beatificazione.

beating s. 1. battito 2. bastonatura 3. sconfitta.

beatitude s. beatitudine.

beautiful agg. bello.

beautifully avv. magnificamente.

to **beautify** vt. abbellire. ◆ to **beautify** vi. abbellirsi.

beauty s. bellezza.

beaver s. castoro.

became V. to become.

because cong. perché || — of, a causa di.

beck[1] s. ruscello.

beck[2] s. cenno, gesto.

to **become (became, become)** vi. 1. divenire 2. avvenire. ◆ to **become (became, become)** vt. addirsi a.

becoming agg. adatto.

bed s. 1. letto 2. fondo 3. (geol.) strato || double —, letto matrimoniale || flower- —, aiuola; — -cover, copriletto.

bedclothes s. pl. lenzuola.

bedlam s. manicomio.

bedouin agg. e s. beduino.

bedroom s. camera da letto.

bedside s. capezzale.

bedstead s. telaio del letto.

bedtime s. ora di andare a letto.

bee s. ape.

beech s. faggio || — -marten, faina.

beef s. manzo.

beefsteak s. bistecca.

beehive s. alveare.

beeline s. linea diretta, linea d'aria.

been V. to be.

beer s. birra.

beet *s.* barbabietola.
beetle *s.* coleottero, scarafaggio.
beetroot *s.* V. *beet.*
to befall (befell, befallen) *vt.* e
vi. accadere.
before *avv.* prima, già || — *-men-
tioned*, già citato. ◆ before *prep.*
1. prima (di) 2. davanti a. ◆ before *cong.* 1. prima che 2. piuttosto che.
beforehand *avv.* anticipatamente.
to beg *vt.* e *vi.* 1. chiedere, pregare
2. elemosinare.
began V. *to begin.*
to beget (begot, begot(ten)) *vt.*
generare.
beggar *s.* mendicante.
beggarly *agg.* misero. ◆ beggarly
avv. miseramente.
beggary *s.* mendicità.
begging *agg.* mendicante. ◆ begging *s.* accattonaggio.
to begin (began, begun) *vt.* e *vi.*
cominciare || *to — with*, in primo
luogo, per cominciare.
beginner *s.* 1. iniziatore 2. principiante.
beginning *s.* inizio.
begot V. *to beget.*
begotten V. *to beget.*
to begrime *vt.* insudiciare.
begun V. *to begin.*
behalf *s.* profitto, favore: *on — of*,
da parte di, a nome di.
to behave *vi.* comportarsi: *to —
oneself*, comportarsi bene || *ill
-behaved*, maleducato.
behaviour *s.* comportamento, condotta.
to behead *vt.* decapitare.
beheld V. *to behold.*
behind *avv.* dietro, indietro. ◆
behind *prep.* dietro (a). ◆ behind *s.* parte posteriore.
to behold (beheld, beheld) *vt.*
guardare.
beholder *s.* spettatore.
to behove *vt. imp.* convenire, essere doveroso.
being *agg.* presente. ◆ being *s.* 1.
esistenza 2. essere vivente.
belch *s.* 1. rutto 2. eruzione.
to belch *vi.* ruttare. ◆ to belch
vt. eruttare.
belfry *s.* campanile.
Belgian *agg.* e *s.* belga.
to belie *vt.* 1. smentire 2. deludere.
belief *s.* credenza, fede.
to believe *vt.* e *vi.* credere, aver
fede.
believer *s.* credente.
to belittle *vt.* sminuire.
bell *s.* 1. campana 2. campanello ||
— *-boy*, fattorino d'albergo; —
-ringer, campanaro; — *-tower*,
campanile.
belligerency *s.* belligeranza.
belligerent *agg.* e *s.* belligerante.
bellow *s.* muggito.
to bellow *vi.* muggire.
bellows *s. pl.* mantice, soffietto
(*sing.*).
belly *s.* ventre.
to belong *vi.* 1. appartenere 2. concernere.
belongings *s. pl.* proprietà (*sing.*).
beloved *agg.* e *s.* amato.
below *avv.* giù, al di sotto. ◆ below *prep.* sotto: — *zero*, sotto
zero.
belt *s.* 1. cintura 2. zona.
to belt *vt.* 1. cingere 2. staffilare.
to bemire *vt.* infangare. ◆ to bemire *vi.* impantanarsi.
bench *s.* 1. panca 2. banco 3. seggio 4. corte giudiziaria.
bend *s.* 1. curva 2. curvatura 3.
(*mar.*) nodo.
to bend (bent, bent) *vt.* 1. piegare 2. tendere. ◆ to bend (bent,
bent) *vi.* piegarsi.
bending *s.* V. *bend.*
beneath *avv.* e *prep.* V. *below.*
benediction *s.* benedizione.
benefactor *s.* benefattore.
benefactress *s.* benefattrice.
benefice *s.* beneficio.
beneficence *s.* beneficenza.
beneficent *agg.* beneficente.
beneficiary *agg.* e *s.* beneficiario.
benefit *s.* 1. vantaggio 2. indennità
3. (*giur.*) beneficio.
to benefit *vt.* giovare, beneficare.
◆ to benefit *vi.* approfittare.
benevolence *s.* benevolenza.
benevolent *agg.* benevolo.
Bengal-light *s.* bengala.
benign *agg.* benigno.
benignity *s.* benignità.
bent V. *to bend.* ◆ bent *agg.* risoluto. ◆ bent *s.* inclinazione.
to benumb *vt.* intorpidire.
benumbing *s.* intorpidimento.
benzol *s.* benzolo.
to bequeath *vt.* lasciare per testamento.
bequest *s.* lascito.
Berber *agg.* e *s.* berbero.

to **bereave** (**bereaved, bereft**) *vt.* privare.

bergamot *s.* bergamotto.

berlin(e) *s.* berlina.

berry *s.* bacca.

berth *s.* 1. cuccetta 2. (*mar.*) ancoraggio 3. (*fig.*) posto.

to **berth** *vt.* ancorare.

beryllium *s.* berillio.

to **beseech** (**besought, besought**) *vt.* supplicare.

beseeching *s.* supplica.

to **beseem** *vt.* addirsi a.

beseeming *agg.* adatto.

beside *prep.* 1. vicino a 2. fuori di.

besides *avv.* inoltre. ♦ **besides** *prep.* oltre a.

to **besiege** *vt.* assediare.

besieger *s.* assediante.

besought V. *to beseech.*

to **besprinkle** *vt.* spruzzare.

best *agg.* (*superl. di* good) il migliore || — -*seller*, libro molto venduto. ♦ **best** *s.* il meglio. ♦ **best** *avv.* 1. nel modo migliore 2. maggiormente.

bestial *agg.* bestiale.

bestiality *s.* bestialità.

to **bestialize** *vt.* abbrutire.

to **bestir** *vt.* agitare.

to **bestow** *vt.* concedere.

bestowal *s.* conferimento.

to **bestrew** (**bestrewed, bestrewn**) *vt.* cospargere, disseminare.

bet *s.* scommessa.

to **bet** (**bet, bet**) *vt. e vi.* scommettere.

to **betake** (**betook, betaken**) *vr.* — *oneself:* dirigersi, recarsi.

to **betray** *vt.* tradire.

betrayal *s.* tradimento.

betrayer *s.* traditore.

betrothal *s.* fidanzamento.

betrothed *agg. e s.* fidanzato.

better[1] *s.* scommettitore.

better[2] *agg.* (*comp. di* good) migliore. ♦ **better** *avv.* meglio || *bad* —, sarebbe meglio che; *all the* —, *so much the* —, tanto meglio. ♦ **better** *s.* 1. il meglio 2. superiore.

to **better** *vt. e vi.* migliorare.

between *avv.* in mezzo. ♦ **between** *prep.* tra, fra (*due cose, due persone*).

beverage *s.* bevanda.

bevy *s.* stormo, frotta.

to **beware** *vi.* guardarsi, diffidare.

to **bewilder** *vt.* sconcertare.

bewildering *agg.* sbalorditivo.

bewilderment *s.* confusione.

to **bewitch** *vt.* incantare.

bewitcher *s.* incantatore.

bewitching *agg.* affascinante.

beyond *avv.* più in là. ♦ **beyond** *prep.* al di là di. ♦ **beyond** *s.* l'al di là.

bias *s.* 1. pregiudizio 2. predisposizione.

to **bias** *vt.* influenzare.

bib *s.* bavaglino.

Bible *s.* Bibbia.

biblical *agg.* biblico.

bibliographic(al) *agg.* bibliografico.

bibliography *s.* bibliografia.

bicameral *agg.* bicamerale.

bicarbonate *s.* bicarbonato.

bicentennial *agg. e s.* bicentenario.

bicephalous *agg.* bicipite.

biceps *s.* bicipite.

to **bicker** *vi.* litigare.

bicoloured *agg.* bicolore.

biconcave *agg.* biconcavo.

bicycle *s.* bicicletta.

bid *s.* 1. offerta (*a un'asta*) 2. appalto.

to **bid**[1] (**bid, bid**) *vt.* offrire (*a un'asta*). ♦ to **bid** (**bid, bid**) *vi.* fare offerta di appalto.

to **bid**[2] (**bade, bidden**) *vt. e vi.* 1. comandare 2. dire || *to* — *goodbye,* accomiatarsi.

biennial *agg.* biennale.

biennium *s.* (*pl.* -biennia) biennio.

bier *s.* bara.

big *agg.* 1. grosso 2. gravido 3. importante.

bigamous *agg.* bigamo.

bigamy *s.* bigamia.

bigness *s.* grossezza.

bigot *s.* bigotto.

bigoted *agg.* bigotto, fanatico.

bilateral *agg.* bilaterale.

bilberry *s.* mirtillo.

bile *s.* bile.

bilingual *agg.* bilingue.

bilious *agg.* 1. biliare 2. collerico.

bill[1] *s.* becco.

bill[2] *s.* 1. progetto di legge 2. certi- 5. lista 6. affisso || — *of lading,* polizza di carico; — *of rights,* dichiarazione dei diritti.

to **bill** *vt.* 1. fatturare 2. affiggere 3. (*teat.*) mettere in programma.

billhook *s.* falcetto.

billiard *agg.* di, da bigliardo: —

-cue, stecca da bigliardo.

billiards *s. pl.* bigliardo (*sing.*).

billion *s.* **1.** bilione **2.** (*amer.*) miliardo.

billow *s.* onda.

bimestrial *agg.* bimestrale.

bimonthly *agg.* e *s.* bimestrale. ♦ **bimonthly** *avv.* bimestralmente.

bin *s.* recipiente || *dust- —*, bidone della spazzatura.

bind *s.* **1.** legame **2.** fascia.

to **bind** (**bound, bound**) *vt.* **1.** legare **2.** fasciare **3.** rilegare **4.** obbligare.

binder *s.* **1.** rilegatore **2.** (*mecc.*) legatrice.

binding *agg.* impegnativo. ♦ **binding** *s.* **1.** legame **2.** fasciatura **3.** rilegatura.

binocular *s.* binocolo.

binomial *s.* binomio.

biochemistry *s.* biochimica.

biographer *s.* biografo.

biographic(al) *agg.* biografico.

biography *s.* biografia.

biological *agg.* biologico.

biologist *s.* biologo.

biology *s.* biologia.

biophysics *s.* biofisica.

biosphere *s.* biosfera.

bipartite *agg.* bipartito.

bipartition *s.* bipartizione.

biped *agg.* e *s.* bipede.

biplane *s.* biplano.

bipolar *agg.* bipolare.

birch *s.* **1.** betulla **2.** verga.

bird *s.* uccello.

birdcage *s.* gabbia (*per uccelli*).

birdseed *s.* miglio.

birth *s.* **1.** nascita **2.** stirpe.

birthday *s.* compleanno.

birthmark *s.* voglia, segno caratteristico (*di persona*).

birthplace *s.* luogo di nascita.

biscuit *s.* biscotto.

bisection *s.* bisezione.

bisector *s.* bisettrice.

bisexual *agg.* ermafrodito.

bishop *s.* vescovo.

bishopric *s.* vescovato.

bismuth *s.* bismuto.

bison *s.* bisonte.

bistoury *s.* bisturi.

bistre *s.* bistro.

bit *s.* **1.** pezzettino **2.** un poco **3.** (*mecc.*) parte tagliente di un utensile **4.** morso (*del cavallo*).

bit V. *to bite.*

bitch *s.* cagna.

bite *s.* **1.** morso **2.** presa.

to **bite** (**bit, bit(ten)**) *vt.* mordere. ♦ to **bite** (**bit, bit(ten)**) *vi.* abboccare || *to — in*, corrodere.

biting *agg.* **1.** mordente **2.** mordace.

bitten V. *to bite.*

bitter *agg.* **1.** amaro **2.** aspro **3.** (*di clima*) rigido || *— -sweet*, agrodolce. ♦ **bitter** *s.* amaro.

bitterish *agg.* amarognolo.

bitterness *s.* **1.** amarezza **2.** rancore **3.** rigidità (*di clima*).

bitumen *s.* bitume.

bivalent *agg.* bivalente.

bivouac *s.* bivacco.

bi-weekly *agg.* e *s.* bisettimanale. ♦ **bi-weekly** *avv.* due volte alla settimana.

to **blab** *vt.* e *vi.* **1.** chiacchierare **2.** spifferare.

black *agg.* **1.** nero **2.** negro **3.** (*fig.*) malvagio, minaccioso. ♦ **black** *s.* **1.** colore nero **2.** negro.

to **black** *vt.* annerire. ♦ to **black** *vi.* annerirsi.

to **blackball** *vt.* votare contro, bocciare.

blackberry *s.* mora selvatica.

blackbird *s.* merlo.

blackboard *s.* lavagna.

to **blacken** *vt.* **1.** annerire **2.** (*fig.*) diffamare. ♦ to **blacken** *vi.* diventare nero.

blackguard *s.* mascalzone.

blackish *agg.* nerastro.

blackleg *s.* **1.** truffatore **2.** crumiro.

blackmail *s.* ricatto.

to **blackmail** *vt.* ricattare.

blackmailer *s.* ricattatore.

blackness *s.* **1.** nerezza **2.** oscurità.

blackout *s.* oscuramento.

blacksmith *s.* fabbro ferraio.

bladder *s.* vescica.

blade *s.* **1.** stelo **2.** lama.

blamable *agg.* biasimevole.

blame *s.* **1.** biasimo **2.** colpa.

to **blame** *vt.* **1.** biasimare **2.** incolpare.

blameful *agg.* biasimevole.

blameless *agg.* irreprensibile.

bland *agg.* blando.

blandishment *s.* blandizie (*pl.*).

blandly *avv.* blandamente.

blank *agg.* **1.** vuoto **2.** in bianco || *— verse*, verso sciolto.. ♦ **blank** *s.* **1.** vuoto **2.** spazio in bianco **3.** mira || *point- —*, di punto in bianco.

blanket *s.* coperta.

blankly *avv.* **1.** senza espressione **2.** decisamente.

blare *s.* squillo (*di tromba*).

to **blaspheme** *vt.* e *vi.* bestemmiare.

blasphemous *agg.* blasfemo.

blasphemously *avv.* empiamente.

blasphemy *s.* bestemmia, empietà.

blast *s.* **1.** raffica **2.** squillo **3.** scoppio **4.** flagello || — *-furnace*, altoforno.

to **blast** *vt.* **1.** far esplodere **2.** rovinare.

blaze *s.* **1.** fiamma **2.** scoppio.

to **blaze** *vi.* ardere. ♦ to **blaze** *vt.* **1.** bruciare **2.** divulgare.

blazer *s.* giacca sportiva.

blazing *s.* **1.** fiamma **2.** splendore **3.** vanteria.

blazon *s.* **1.** blasone **2.** ostentazione.

bleach *s.* imbianchimento, candeggio.

to **bleach** *vt.* imbiancare, candeggiare. ♦ to **bleach** *vi.* imbiancarsi.

bleacher *s.* recipiente per candeggio.

bleaching *s.* V. *bleach*.

bleak *agg.* **1.** brullo **2.** desolato **3.** incolore.

bleakness *s.* **1.** freddezza **2.** squallore.

blear *agg.* **1.** cisposo **2.** ottuso.

bleat *s.* belato.

to **bleat** *vi.* belare.

to **bleed (bled, bled)** *vi.* sanguinare. ♦ to **bleed (bled, bled)** *vt.* salassare.

bleeding *s.* **1.** emorragia **2.** salasso **3.** fuga.

blemish *s.* difetto.

blend *s.* miscela.

to **blend** *vt.* mescolare. ♦ to **blend** *vi.* mescolarsi.

to **bless** *vt.* benedire.

blessed *agg.* beato, santo.

blessing *s.* benedizione.

blew V. *to blow*.

blind *agg.* cieco. ♦ **blind** *s.* **1.** tenda **2.** persiana **3.** paraocchi **4.** finzione.

to **blind** *vt.* **1.** accecare **2.** oscurare **3.** nascondere.

blindness *s.* cecità.

to **blink** *vi.* **1.** battere le palpebre **2.** lampeggiare **3.** (*fig.*) chiudere gli occhi.

blinker *s.* **1.** lampeggiatore **2.** paraocchi.

blinking *agg.* **1.** ammiccante **2.** scintillante. ♦ **blinking** *s.* ammicco.

bliss *s.* beatitudine.

blissful *agg.* **1.** beato **2.** delizioso.

blister *s.* bolla.

blithe *agg.* gaio.

blizzard *s.* tormenta (*di neve*).

block *s.* **1.** ceppo **2.** masso **3.** isolato (*di case*) **4.** ostacolo **5.** persona stupida || — *letters*, stampatello.

to **block** *vt.* bloccare.

blockade *s.* blocco.

blockhead *s.* stupido.

blonde *s.* donna bionda.

blood *s.* sangue.

bloodhound *s.* segugio.

bloodless *agg.* **1.** esangue **2.** incruento **3.** (*fig.*) insensibile.

bloodshed *s.* spargimento di sangue.

bloodshot *agg.* iniettato di sangue.

bloody *agg.* **1.** sanguinante **2.** sanguinoso **3.** sanguinario **4.** maledetto.

bloom *s.* **1.** fiore **2.** rossore.

to **bloom** *vi.* **1.** fiorire **2.** arrossire.

blossom *s.* fiore.

to **blossom** *vi.* **1.** fiorire **2.** diventare.

blot *s.* macchia.

to **blot** *vt.* **1.** macchiare **2.** assorbire.

blotch *s.* **1.** macchia **2.** pustola.

blotting *s.* **1.** il macchiare **2.** l'asciugare || — *-paper*, carta assorbente; — *-pad*, tampone di carta assorbente.

blouse *s.* camicetta.

blow *s.* **1.** soffio **2.** colpo **3.** fioritura || *to come to blows*, venire alle mani.

to **blow (blew, blown)** *vt.* **1.** soffiare **2.** suonare (*strumenti a fiato*) || *to — up*, (far) saltare in aria. ♦ to **blow (blew, blown)** *vi.* sbocciare.

blower *s.* **1.** soffiatore **2.** sfiatatoio.

blown V. *to blow*.

blowpipe *s.* **1.** cannello per soffiare **2.** cerbottana.

blue *agg.* **1.** azzurro, blu **2.** livido **3.** triste.

bluebell *s.* campanula.

bluebottle[1] *s.* fiordaliso.

bluebottle[2] *s.* tafano.

blueprint *s.* cianografia.

bluff *s.* ripida scogliera.

bluish *agg.* bluastro.

blunder *s.* errore.

blunt *agg.* **1.** smussato **2.** ottuso **3.** schietto.

blush *s.* rossore.

to **blush** vi. arrossire.

board s. 1. asse, tavola 2. vitto 3. pensione 4. consiglio, ministero 5. (mar.) bordo || on —, a bordo; full —, pensione completa. ♦ **boards** s. pl. palcoscenico (sing.).

to **board** vt. 1. fornire di assi 2. prendere a pensione 3. (mar.) abbordare. ♦ to **board** vi. 1. essere a pensione 2. imbarcarsi.

boarder s. pensionante.

boarding s. assito || — -house, pensione; — -school, collegio.

boast s. vanto.

to **boast** vt. vantare. ♦ to **boast** vi. vantarsi.

boaster s. spaccone.

boastful agg. vanaglorioso.

boastfulness s. millanteria.

boasting s. vanteria.

boat s. barca, battello || flying- —, idrovolante; sauce- —, salsiera; ferry- —, traghetto.

boating s. canottaggio.

boatman s. barcaiolo.

boatswain s. nostromo.

to **bob** vi. dondolarsi, oscillare || to — up, venire a galla.

bobbin s. bobina.

bobsled s. guidoslitta.

bodice s. busto.

bodkin s. punteruolo, stiletto.

body s. 1. corpo 2. corporazione, ente 3. massa || — belt, panciera.

bodymaker s. carrozziere.

Boeotian agg. e s. beota.

bog s.

boggy agg. paludoso.

bogy s. spauracchio.

boil s. bollitura.

to **boil** vt. e vi. bollire, ribollire || to — away, consumarsi; to — over, traboccare bollendo.

boiler s. bollitore, caldaia.

boiling agg. bollente. ♦ **boiling** s. ebollizione.

boisterous agg. 1. rumoroso 2. violento.

boisterousness s. fracasso.

bold agg. 1. audace 2. sfacciato 3. vigoroso || — -face, neretto.

boldness s. 1. audacia 2. sfacciataggine.

bolide s. bolide.

Bolshevism s. bolscevismo.

Bolshevist agg. e s. bolscevico.

bolster s. cuscino 2. supporto.

bolt s. 1. catenaccio 2. bullone 3. otturatore 4. freccia 5. fulmine.

to **bolt**[1] vt. 1. sprangare 2. imbullonare.

to **bolt**[2] vt. setacciare, vagliare.

bolter s. setaccio.

bomb s. bomba.

to **bomb** vt. bombardare.

to **bombard** vt. bombardare.

bombardier s. bombardiere.

bombardment s. bombardamento.

bombastic agg. ampolloso.

bomber s. bombardiere.

bond s. 1. vincolo 2. patto 3. (comm.) titolo 4. cauzione || — -holder, portatore di obbligazioni; goods in —, merci in attesa di sdoganamento.

bondage s. schiavitù.

bone s. 1. osso 2. lisca.

to **bone** vt. 1. disossare 2. spinare.

bonfire s. falò.

bonnet s. 1. cuffia 2. (auto) cofano.

bonus s. gratifica || cost of living —, carovita.

bony agg. 1. osseo 2. ossuto.

bonze s. bonzo.

booby s. sciocco.

book s. 1. libro 2. registro || note- —, taccuino; copy- —, quaderno.

to **book** vt. 1. registrare 2. prenotare.

bookbinding s. rilegatura.

bookcase s. libreria.

booking s. 1. registrazione 2. prenotazione || — -office, biglietteria.

bookish agg. 1. studioso 2. libresco.

bookkeeper s. contabile.

bookkeeping s. contabilità.

booklet s. libretto.

bookmaker s. allibratore.

bookseller s. libraio.

bookshelf s. (pl. -lves) scaffale.

bookshop s. libreria.

bookstall s. edicola, bancarella (di libri).

boom s. 1. rombo 2. periodo di prosperità.

to **boom** vi. 1. rimbombare 2. essere in periodo di prosperità.

boor s. persona zotica.

boorish agg. rustico.

boorishness s. rozzezza.

boot s. 1. stivale, scarpa 2. (auto) portabagagli.

bootblack s. lustrascarpe.

booth s. baracca || telephone —, cabina telefonica.

booty s. bottino.

border *s.* 1. orlo 2. frontiera.
to **border** *vt.* orlare || *to* — *on,* confinare con.
borderer *s.* abitante di confine.
bordering *s.* 1. il bordare 2. il confinare.
bore V. *to bear.*
bore[1] *s.* 1. buco 2. calibro (*di arma*).
bore[2] *s.* 1. seccatura 2. seccatore.
to **bore**[1] *vt.* forare.
to **bore**[2] *vt.* annoiare.
boreal *agg.* boreale.
boredom *s.* noia.
boric *agg.* borico.
boring[1] *agg.* noioso.
boring[2] *s.* perforazione || — *test,* sondaggio.
born V. *to bear.* ✦ **born** *agg.* nato, generato || *to be* —, nascere.
borne V. *to bear.*
borough *s.* 1. municipio 2. circoscrizione elettorale.
to **borrow** *vt.* prendere a prestito.
borrower *s.* chi prende a prestito.
bosom *s.* seno || — *friend,* amico intimo.
boss[1] *s.* 1. protuberanza 2. (*arch.*) bugna.
boss[2] *s.* capo, padrone.
bossy[1] *agg.* a bugnato.
bossy[2] *agg.* (*gergo*) prepotente.
botanist *s.* botanico.
botany *s.* botanica.
botch *s.* pasticcio.
to **botch** *vt.* 1. rattoppare 2. arruffare.
botcher *s.* pasticcione.
both *agg.* e *pron.* entrambi, tutti e due. ✦ **both** *avv.* nel medesimo tempo || — ... *and,* sia... sia, tanto... quanto.
bother *s.* seccatura.
to **bother** *vt.* infastidire. ✦ to **bother** *vi.* preoccuparsi.
bothersome *agg.* fastidioso.
bottle *s.* bottiglia || *feeding-* —, poppatoio; — *-feeding,* allattamento artificiale.
to **bottle** *vt.* imbottigliare.
bottling *s.* imbottigliamento.
bottom *agg.* 1. inferiore 2. basilare. ✦ **bottom** *s.* 1. fondo 2. fondamento 3. deretano 4. (*mar.*) chiglia.
to **bottom** *vt.* 1. mettere il fondo (a) 2. impagliare 3. capire. ✦ to **bottom** *vi.* posare, essere posato.
bottomless *agg.* 1. senza fondo 2.

senza fine.
bough *s.* ramo (*d'albero*).
bought V. *to buy.*
boulder *s.* macigno.
boulevard *s.* viale.
bounce *s.* 1. balzo 2. vanteria.
to **bounce** *vt.* far rimbalzare. ✦ to **bounce** *vi.* 1. rimbalzare 2. gloriarsi.
bouncer *s.* fanfarone.
bound[1] *s.* limite, confine.
bound[2] *s.* salto.
bound[3] V. *to bind.*
bound[4] *agg.* 1. destinato 2. diretto a 3. certo.
to **bound**[1] *vt.* confinare, limitare.
to **bound**[2] *vi.* balzare.
boundary *s.* limite, frontiera.
boundless *agg.* illimitato.
bounteous *agg.* generoso.
bounty *s.* generosità.
bourgeois *agg.* e *s.* borghese.
bourgeoisie *s.* borghesia.
bow[1] *s.* 1. arco 2. archetto 3. fiocco || — *-window,* bovindo.
bow[2] *s.* inchino.
bow[3] *s.* prua.
to **bow** *vt.* piegare. ✦ to **bow** *vi.* 1. piegarsi 2. inclinarsi.
bowels *s. pl.* viscere.
bower *s.* 1. pergolato 2. dimora.
bowl[1] *s.* ciotola.
bowl[2] *s.* boccia.
to **bowl** *vt.* far rotolare. ✦ to **bowl** *vi.* 1. rotolare 2. giocare a bocce.
bowler *s.* giocatore di bocce || — *hat,* bombetta.
bowling *s.* gioco delle bocce.
bowman *s.* arciere.
bowshot *s.* tiro d'arco.
box[1] *s.* 1. scatola 2. stanzetta 3. stalla 4. (*teat.*) palco 5. (*giur.*) banco || *letter-* —, buca per le lettere; *money-* —, salvadanaio; *strong-* —, cassaforte.
box[2] *s.* pugno, ceffone.
to **box**[1] *vt.* mettere in scatola.
to **box**[2] *vt.* schiaffeggiare. ✦ to **box** *vi.* fare del pugilato.
boxer *s.* pugile.
boxing *s.* pugilato.
boy *s.* ragazzo.
to **boycott** *vt.* boicottare.
boyhood *s.* fanciullezza.
boyish *agg.* fanciullesco.
bra *s.* reggipetto.
brace *s.* 1. sostegno 2. coppia, paio 3. (*mar.*) braccio. ✦ **braces** *s. pl.* bretelle.

to **brace** vt. **1.** legare **2.** fortificare.
bracelet s. braccialetto.
brachycardia s. brachicardia.
bracket s. **1.** mensola, sostegno **2.** parentesi.
brackish agg. salato, salso.
brag s. **1.** millanteria **2.** millantatore.
to **brag** vt. vantare. ♦ to **brag** vi. vantarsi.
braggart agg. e s. spaccone.
bragging s. millanteria.
braid s. **1.** treccia **2.** gallone.
to **braid** vt. **1.** intrecciare **2.** guarnire.
brain s. cervello.
brainless agg. scervellato.
brake[1] s. **1.** felce **2.** boschetto.
brake[2] s. freno.
to **brake** vt. frenare.
braksesman s. frenatore.
bramble s. rovo.
bran s. crusca.
branch s. **1.** ramo **2.** filiale.
to **branch** vt. ramificare. ♦ to **branch** vi. ramificarsi || to — out, estendersi (di attività commerciale, affari).
branching s. ramificazione.
brand s. **1.** tizzone **2.** marchio (a fuoco) **3.** marca || — -new, nuovo fiammante.
to **brand** vt. **1.** marchiare **2.** stigmatizzare.
to **brandish** vt. brandire.
brass agg. **1.** di ottone **2.** (fig.) sfacciato. ♦ **brass** s. **1.** ottone **2.** (mecc.) bronzina **3.** (fig.) sfacciataggine || — band, fanfara
brassy agg. V. brass.
bravado s. bravata.
brave agg. e s. prode, coraggioso.
bravely avv. coraggiosamente.
bravery s. **1.** coraggio **2.** splendore.
brawl s. rissa.
to **brawl** vi. rissare.
brawn s. muscolo, forza muscolare.
brawny agg. muscoloso.
bray s. raglio.
to **bray**[1] vi. **1.** ragliare **2.** (fig.) stonare.
to **bray**[2] vt. frantumare, sminuzzare.
brazen agg. V. brass.
brazier[1] s. calderaio.
brazier[2] s. braciere.
Brazilian agg. e s. brasiliano.
breach s. **1.** rottura **2.** breccia **3.** infrazione || — of promise, rottura di fidanzamento.

bread s. pane.
to **bread** vt. rimpanare.
breadth s. **1.** larghezza **2.** altezza (di stoffe).
breadthwise avv. in larghezza (di stoffe).
break s. **1.** rottura **2.** interruzione, intervallo **3.** infrazione || — -up, collasso, smembramento, fine.
to **break** (broke, broken) vt. **1.** rompere **2.** interrompere **3.** domare **4.** rovinare. ♦ to **break** (broke, broken) vi. **1.** rompersi **2.** irrompere || to — down, demolire, (auto) restare in panne, esaurirsi; to — off, mandare a monte; to — up, fare a pezzi.
breakdown s. **1.** collasso **2.** rottura **3.** dissesto || nervous —, esaurimento nervoso.
breaker s. **1.** rompitore **2.** violatore **3.** domatore **4.** (mecc.) macchina rompitrice **5.** (mar.) frangente **6.** (elett.) interruttore.
breakfast s. prima colazione.
to **breakfast** vi. fare la prima colazione.
breaking s. **1.** rottura **2.** (comm.) fallimento.
breakneck agg. a rotta di collo.
breakwater s. frangiflutti.
breast s. petto || — -bone, sterno.
breasted agg. dal petto || double-—, a doppio petto.
breath s. **1.** soffio **2.** respiro.
breathable agg. respirabile.
to **breathe** vi. **1.** respirare **2.** spirare. ♦ to **breathe** vt. **1.** infondere **2.** sussurrare.
breathing s. V. breath.
breathless agg. **1.** ansante **2.** esanime.
breathlessness s. affanno.
bred V. to breed. ♦ **bred** agg. ill-—, maleducato.
breech s. **1.** parte posteriore **2.** culatta (di arma).
breeches s. pl. calzoni.
breed s. razza.
to **breed** (bred, bred) vt. **1.** generare **2.** allevare. ♦ to **breed** (bred, bred) vi. nascere.
breeder s. **1.** chi genera **2.** allevatore.
breeding s. **1.** generazione **2.** allevamento **3.** educazione.
breeze s. brezza.
breezy agg. **1.** ventilato **2.** cordiale.
brethren s. pl. confratelli.

breviary s. breviario.

brevity s. brevità.

brew s. **1.** mistura **2.** fermentazione (*di birra*).

to **brew** vt. **1.** mescolare **2.** (*fig.*) macchinare. ♦ to **brew** vi. fare la birra.

brewer s. birraio.

brewery s. fabbrica di birra.

bribe s. dono (*a scopo di corruzione*), allettamento.

to **bribe** vt. corrompere.

briber s. corruttore.

bribery s. corruzione.

brick s. mattone.

bricklayer s. muratore.

brickwork s. muratura in mattoni.

brickyard s. mattonaia.

bride s. sposa.

bridegroom s. sposo.

bridge s. ponte ‖ *swing-* —, ponte girevole; *toll-* —, ponte a pedaggio; — *-head*, testa di ponte.

bridle s. briglia, freno.

to **bridle** vt. imbrigliare.

bridling s. imbrigliamento.

brief agg. breve. ♦ **brief** s. riassunto.

to **brief** vt. **1.** riassumere **2.** (*giur.*) nominare (il proprio avvocato) **3.** dare istruzioni.

briefness s. brevità, concisione.

brier s. **1.** rovo **2.** rosa selvatica.

brig s. brigantino.

brigade s. brigata.

bright agg. **1.** chiaro, splendente **2.** vivace.

to **brighten** vt. **1.** far brillare **2.** animare. ♦ to **brighten** vi. **1.** brillare **2.** animarsi.

brightness s. **1.** splendore **2.** gaiezza.

brill s. (*itt.*) rombo.

brilliance, brilliancy s. brillantezza.

brilliant agg. e s. brillante.

brilliantine s. brillantina.

brim s. **1.** orlo **2.** ala (*di cappello*).

brimful agg. colmo.

brindled agg. pezzato.

brine s. acqua salata.

to **bring** (**brought, brought**) vt. **1.** portare **2.** indurre ‖ *to — about*, causare; *to — back*, richiamare alla memoria; *to — forth*, dare alla luce; *to — up*, educare, allevare.

brink s. orlo.

brisk agg. **1.** vivace **2.** frizzante.

briskness s. vivacità.

bristle s. setola.

to **bristle** vi. essere irto di.

bristly agg. **1.** setoloso **2.** ruvido.

British agg. britannico.

Briton agg. e s. britanno.

broad agg. **1.** ampio **2.** chiaro **3.** marcato **4.** volgare ‖ — *daylight*, pieno giorno. ♦ **broad** s. larghezza. ♦ **broad** avv. ampiamente.

broadcast s. **1.** radiodiffusione **2.** radiocomunicazione.

to **broadcast** (**broadcast, broadcast**) (*anche reg.*) vt. e vi. radiotrasmettere.

broadcaster s. trasmettitore.

broadcasting s. radiodiffusione.

to **broaden** vt. allargare. ♦ to **broaden** vi. allargarsi, estendersi.

broadness s. **1.** larghezza **2.** grossolanità.

broadside s. (*mar.*) **1.** bordo, fiancata **2.** bordata.

brocade s. broccato.

bro(c)coli s. broccolo.

broil s. rissa.

to **broil** vt. cuocere alla griglia. ♦ to **broil** vi. abbrustolirsi (*al sole*).

broke V. *to break.*

broken V. *to break.* ♦ **broken** agg. **1.** variabile (*di tempo*) **2.** accidentato (*di terreno*) **3.** indebolito **4.** avvilito **5.** scorretto.

broker s. **1.** (*comm.*) agente **2.** mediatore.

bromide s. bromuro.

bromine s. bromo.

bronchial agg. bronchiale.

bronchia s. pl. bronchi.

bronchitis s. bronchite.

broncho-pneumonia s. bronchopolmonite.

bronze s. bronzo.

to **bronze** vt. abbronzare. ♦ to **bronze** vi. abbronzarsi.

brooch s. spilla.

brood s. covata.

to **brood** vt. **1.** covare **2.** (*fig.*) rimuginare, meditare.

brooding s. **1.** cova **2.** meditazione.

brook s. ruscello.

to **brook** vt. sopportare, tollerare.

brooklet s. ruscelletto.

broom s. **1.** ginestra **2.** scopa.

broth s. brodo.

brothel s. bordello.

brother s. **1.** fratello **2.** collega ‖ — *-in-law*, cognato; *half-* —, fratellastro.

brotherhood s. 1. fratellanza 2. confraternita.
brotherlike agg. fraterno.
brotherly agg. fraterno. ♦ **brotherly** avv. fraternamente.
brought V. to bring.
brow s. fronte. ♦ **brows** s. pl. sopracciglia.
brown agg. 1. bruno 2. marrone. ♦ **brown** s. marrone.
to **brown** vt. 1. rendere bruno 2. rosolare. ♦ to **brown** vi. 1. diventare bruno 2. abbronzarsi
to **browse** vt. e vi. brucare.
bruise s. contusione.
to **bruise** vt. ammaccare. ♦ to **bruise** vi. ammaccarsi.
bruiser s. 1. pugilatore 2. (fig.) gradasso.
brush s. 1. spazzola, spazzolino 2. spazzolata 3. pennello 4. rissa || — -up, ripasso.
to **brush** vt. 1. spazzolare 2. sfiorare || to — aside (fig.), ignorare; to — up, ripassare.
brushwood s. sottobosco.
brushy agg. 1. ispido 2. folto (di bosco).
brusque agg. brusco.
brutal agg. brutale.
brutality s. brutalità.
to **brutalize** vt. 1. abbrutire 2. maltrattare. ♦ to **brutalize** vi. abbrutirsi.
brute agg. brutale. ♦ **brute** s. bruto.
brutish agg. brutale, rozzo.
bubble s. 1. bolla 2. gorgoglio.
to **bubble** vi. gorgogliare || to — over, traboccare.
bubo s. bubbone.
bubonic agg. bubbonico.
buccaneer s. bucaniere.
buck s. 1. daino 2. maschio (di molti animali).
to **buck** vi. sgroppare.
bucket s. secchio.
buckle s. fibbia.
to **buckle** vt. 1. affibbiare 2. piegare. ♦ to **buckle** vi. piegarsi.
bucolic agg. bucolico.
bud s. 1. gemma 2. germe.
to **bud** vi. germogliare.
Buddhism s. buddismo.
Buddhist agg. e s. buddista.
budget s. 1. raccolta (di documenti) 2. bilancio.
buffalo s. bufalo.
buffer s. respingente.

buffet¹ s. schiaffo.
buffet² s. credenza.
to **buffet** vt. schiaffeggiare.
buffoon s. buffone.
bug s. 1. coleottero 2. cimice || big —, (gergo) pezzo grosso.
bugbear s. spauracchio.
bugger s. sodomita.
build s. costruzione, struttura.
to **build (built, built)** vt. costruire || to — up, murare.
builder s. costruttore.
building agg. edilizio. ♦ **building** s. edificio.
built V. to build.
bulb s. 1. bulbo 2. lampadina || — socket, portalampada.
Bulgarian agg. e s. bulgaro.
bulge s. gonfiore.
to **bulge** vi. gonfiarsi. ♦ to **bulge** vt. 1. sporgere 2. gonfiare.
bulgy agg. rigonfio.
bulk s. 1. massa 2. carico.
bulkhead s. paratia.
bulky agg. massiccio.
bull s. 1. toro 2. maschio (di alcuni mammiferi) || —'s eye, oblò.
bulldog s. mastino.
bullet s. pallottola.
bulletin s. bollettino || news —, giornale radio.
bullfight s. corrida.
bullfighter s. torero.
bullock s. torello.
bully agg. borioso.
to **bully** vt. e vi. fare il prepotente (verso).
bulwark s. 1. bastione 2. (mar.) parapetto.
bumble-bee s. calabrone.
bump s. 1. urto 2. bernoccolo.
to **bump** vt. e vi. urtare, andare a sbattere contro.
bumper s. 1. paraurti 2. respingente.
bun s. 1. focaccia 2. crocchia.
bunch s. 1. mazzo 2. grappolo.
bundle s. 1. fagotto 2. fascio.
to **bundle** vt. riunire in fascio, fare un involto.
bung s. tappo.
bungler agg. e s. confusionario.
bunny s. coniglietto.
buoy s. boa.
buoyancy s. 1. galleggiabilità 2. ottimismo.
buoyant agg. 1. galleggiante 2. ottimista.
burden s. 1. peso 2. tonnellaggio.

to **burden** vt. caricare.
burdensome agg. gravoso.
bureau s. (pl. bureaux) ufficio.
bureaucracy s. burocrazia.
bureaucrat s. burocrate.
bureaucratic agg. burocratico.
burglar s. scassinatore (notturno).
burglary s. furto (notturno) con scasso.
to **burgle** vt. e vi. svaligiare con scasso.
burgomaster s. borgomastro.
burial s. sepoltura || -ground, cimitero; — -service, ufficio funebre.
burin s. bulino.
burly agg. corpulento.
burn s. ustione.
to **burn** (burnt, burnt) (anche reg.) vt. e vi. bruciare, ardere.
burner s. bruciatore.
burning s. 1. incendio 2. (metal.) fusione.
to **burnish** vt. lustrare.
burnt V. to burn.
burrow s. tana, buca.
bursar s. economo.
bursary s. 1. ufficio dell'economato 2. borsa di studio.
burst s. 1. scoppio 2. squarcio.
to **burst** (burst, burst) vt. 1. far esplodere 2. sfondare. ◆ to **burst** (burst, burst) vi. 1. scoppiare 2. irrompere.
bursting s. scoppio.
to **bury** vt. seppellire.
bus s. autobus.
busby s. colbac.
bush s. cespuglio.
bushel s. staio.
bushy agg. folto.
busily avv. attivamente.
business s. 1. affare 2. mestiere 3. ditta 4. scopo || — -man, uomo d'affari; — -like, metodico, sistematico.
bust s. busto.
bustle s. trambusto.
to **bustle** vi. agitarsi.
busy agg. occupato.
to **busy** vt. occupare.
busybody s. ficcanaso.
but cong. ma. ◆ **but** avv. solo. ◆ **but** prep. tranne || — for, se non fosse per; — that, se non; cannot —, non poter far a meno di; all —, pressoché.
butane s. butano.
butcher s. macellaio.
butchery s. macello.

butler s. maggiordomo.
butt[1] s. 1. calcio (di arma) 2. impugnatura (di utensile) 3. mozzicone.
butt[2] s. urto.
to **butt** vt. e vi. cozzare.
butter s. burro.
to **butter** vt. imburrare.
buttercup s. ranuncolo.
butterfly s. farfalla.
buttery agg. burroso.
buttock s. natica.
button s. bottone.
to **button** vt. abbottonare.
button-hole s. occhiello.
to **button-hole** vt. 1. fare asole a 2. (fig.) attaccar bottone.
button-holer s. attaccabottoni.
buttress s. contrafforte.
buxom agg. formoso, avvenente (di donna).
to **buy** (bought, bought) vt. comprare || to — off, riscattare; to — up, accaparrare.
buyable agg. acquistabile.
buyer s. acquirente.
buzz s. ronzio.
buzzard s. poiana.
to **buzz** vi. e vt. ronzare, bisbigliare.
buzzer s. 1. insetto che ronza 2. cicala, segnale acustico.
by avv. 1. vicino 2. da parte, in disparte || — and —, fra poco; — and large, complessivamente. ◆ **by** prep. 1. (agente, causa, mezzo) per, da, con, di || a book (written) — Shakespeare, un libro di Shakespeare; to travel — train, viaggiare col treno 2. (tempo) entro, per, durante || day — day, di giorno in giorno; — night, di notte 3. (luogo) vicino a, a fianco di, attraverso || a house — the sea, una casa sul mare. ◆ **by** agg. secondario.
bye-bye inter. arrivederci.
bygone agg. e s. passato.
by-line s. (giorn.) firma.
byname s. soprannome.
by-pass s. 1. circonvallazione 2. deviazione.
by-product s. sottoprodotto.
byroad s. strada secondaria.
byssus s. bisso.
bystander s. spettatore.
bystreet s. viuzza.
byway s. via traversa.
byword s. proverbio, epiteto.
bywork s. lavoro supplementare (a tempo perso).
Byzantine agg. e s. bizantino.

C

C (*mus.*) do.
cab *s.* vettura di piazza.
cabal *s.* intrigo, cospirazione.
cabbage *s.* cavolo.
cab(b)ala *s.* cabala.
cab(b)alistic *agg.* cabalistico.
cabin *s.* **1.** capanna **2.** (*aer.*; *fer.*; *mar.*) cabina.
cabinet *s.* **1.** stanzino **2.** stipo, armadietto **3.** (*pol.*) gabinetto, consiglio dei ministri || — *-maker*, ebanista; — *-minister*, membro del gabinetto.
cable *s.* **1.** cavo **2.** cablogramma || — *-way*, teleferica.
to cable *vt.* e *vi.* **1.** fornire di cavo **2.** trasmettere un cablogramma.
cablegram *s.* cablogramma.
cabman *s.* tassista.
caboose (*mar.*) cambusa.
cabotage *s.* cabotaggio.
cacao *s.* cacao.
cacophony *s.* cacofonia.
cactus *s.* cactus.
cadaverous *agg.* **1.** cadaverico **2.** esangue.
cadence *s.* cadenza, ritmo.
cadet *s.* cadetto.
caducity *s.* caducità.
Caesarean *agg.* cesareo, imperiale || — *operation*, parto cesareo.
caesura *s.* cesura.
café *s.* caffè (*locale pubblico*).
caffeine *s.* caffeina.
cage *s.* **1.** gabbia **2.** impalcatura.
to cage *vt.* mettere in gabbia.
cake *s.* torta, focaccia.
calamary *s.* calamaro.
calamitous *agg.* calamitoso.
calamity *s.* calamità.
calcareous *agg.* calcareo.
calcification *s.* calcificazione.
to calcify *vt.* calcificare. ✦ to calcify *vi.* calcificarsi.
calcination *s.* calcinazione.
to calcine V. *to calcify.*
calcite *s.* calcite.
calcium *s.* calcio.
to calculate *vt.* **1.** calcolare **2.** contare. ✦ to calculate *vi.* fare affidamento.
calculated *agg.* **1.** calcolato **2.** premeditato **3.** (*fig.*) idoneo.
calculating *agg.* calcolatore || — *machine*, macchina calcolatrice.
calculation *s.* calcolo.

calculator *s.* calcolatore, calcolatrice.
calendar *s.* calendario, almanacco.
calf¹ *s.* (*pl.* calves) vitello.
calf² *s.* polpaccio.
to calibrate *vt.* **1.** calibrare **2.** (*mecc.*) tarare.
calibration *s.* calibratura, taratura.
calibre *s.* calibro.
calico *s.* calicò.
call *s.* **1.** richiamo, chiamata **2.** breve visita: *to pay* (*v. irr.*) *so. a* —, fare una breve visita a qu. **3.** (*giur.*) appello **4.** (*mil.*) adunata **5.** (*mar.*) scalo || — *bird*, uccello da richiamo; — *box*, cabina telefonica; — *up*, chiamata alle armi; *trunk* —, chiamata intercontinentale.
to call *vt.* e *vi.* **1.** chiamare, richiamare: *to* — *aside*, chiamare in disparte; *to* — *to arms*, chiamare alle armi; *to* — *to mind*, richiamare alla mente **2.** esortare, ordinare || *to* — *into being*, creare; *to* — *out*, chiamare ad alta voce, esclamare; *to* — *up*, telefonare; *to* — *at*, fare scalo a; *to* — *for*, passare a prendere; *to* — *on*, fare una breve visita a; *to* — *upon*, implorare, invocare.
caller *s.* visitatore, visitatrice.
calligrapher *s.* calligrafo.
calligraphic *agg.* calligrafico.
calling *s.* **1.** appello **2.** mestiere, professione **3.** vocazione.
callosity *s.* **1.** callosità **2.** (*fig.*) insensibilità.
callous *agg.* **1.** calloso **2.** (*fig.*) insensibile.
calm *agg.* calmo. ✦ calm *s.* calma.
to calm *vt.* calmare. ✦ to calm *vi.* to — *down*, calmarsi (*di tempesta ecc.*).
calming *agg.* calmante.
calmly *avv.* con calma.
calmness *s.* calma, tranquillità.
calorific *agg.* calorifico.
calorimeter *s.* calorimetro.
calory *s.* caloria.
to calumniate *vt.* calunniare.
Calvary *s.* Calvario.
calves V. *calf.*
Calvinism *s.* calvinismo.
Calvinist *agg.* e *s.* calvinista.
came V. *to come.*
camel *s.* cammello.
camellia *s.* camelia.
cameo *s.* cammeo.
camera *s.* **1.** (*foto*) macchina foto-

grafica **2.** (*giur.*) Camera di Consiglio.

camisole *s.* corpetto, farsetto.

camouflage *s.* **1.** mascheramento **2.** (*mil.*) mimetizzazione.

to camouflage *vt.* **1.** mascherare **2.** (*mil.*) mimetizzare.

camp *s.* **1.** (*mil.*) campo **2.** campeggio || — *bed*, brandina.

to camp *vt.* (*mil.*) accampare. ♦ **to camp** *vi.* **1.** accamparsi **2.** attendarsi.

campaign *s.* (*mil.*) campagna.

camper *s.* campeggiatore.

camphor *s.* canfora.

camping *s.* **1.** (*mil.*) accampamento **2.** campeggio.

can[1] *s.* recipiente di latta, bidone.

can[2] *v. dif.* (*ind. cong. pres.*) **could** (*ind. cong. pass. e condiz.*) potere, essere in grado di.

Canadian *agg. e s.* canadese.

canal *s.* canale.

canalization *s.* canalizzazione.

to canalize *vt.* canalizzare.

canary *agg.* giallo canarino. ♦ **canary** *s.* canarino.

to cancel *vt.* annullare, cancellare.

cancellation *s.* annullamento, cancellatura.

cancer *s.* cancro.

candid *agg.* sincero, candido.

candidate *s.* candidato.

candidature *s.* candidatura.

candidly *avv.* sinceramente, candidamente.

candied *agg.* candito.

candle *s.* candela || — *-end*, moccolo; — *-holder*, candelabro; *by* — *-light*, a lume di candela.

candlestick *s.* candeliere.

candour *s.* candore, ingenuità.

candy *s.* candito.

to candy *vt.* candire. ♦ **to candy** *vi.* cristallizzarsi (*di zucchero*).

cane *s.* **1.** giunco, canna **2.** bastone da passeggio.

to cane *vt.* bastonare (*con una canna*).

canine *s.* dente canino.

caning *s.* bastonatura.

canned *agg.* conservato in scatola.

cannibal *s.* cannibale.

cannibalism *s.* cannibalismo.

cannon *s.* **1.** cannone **2.** carambola (*al biliardo*).

to cannon *vi.* **1.** cannoneggiare **2.** far carambola.

canoe *s.* canoa.

canon *s.* **1.** canone **2.** (*eccl.*) canonico: — *law*, diritto canonico.

canonical *agg.* canonico.

to canonize *vt.* canonizzare.

canopy *s.* **1.** baldacchino **2.** volta (*del cielo*).

cant *s.* **1.** (*arch.*) angolo esterno **2.** inclinazione **3.** gergo.

canteen *s.* **1.** (*mil.*) dispensa **2.** mensa aziendale.

canvas *s.* **1.** canovaccio **2.** (*mar.*) velatura **3.** tela **4.** tendone.

canyon *s.* burrone.

cap *s.* **1.** berretto **2.** (*arch.*) capitello **3.** (*mecc.; elettr.*) cappuccio, capsula.

capability *s.* capacità, abilità.

capable *agg.* abile, capace.

capacitor *s.* condensatore.

capacity *s.* **1.** capacità **2.** (*elettr.*) potenza (*di motore*).

cape[1] *s.* capo, promontorio.

cape[2] *s.* cappa.

caper[1] *s.* cappero.

caper[2] *s.* piroetta, capriola.

to caper *vi.* far capriole.

capercaillie *s.* gallo cedrone.

capillarity *s.* capillarità.

capillary *agg.* capillare. ♦ **capillary** *s.* (*anat.*) vaso capillare.

capital[1] *agg. e s.* capitale.

capital[2] *s.* (*arch.*) capitello.

capitalism *s.* capitalismo.

capitalist *s.* capitalista.

capitalistic *agg.* capitalistico.

to capitalize *vt.* capitalizzare.

capitular *agg.* capitolare.

capitulary *s.* capitolare.

to capitulate *vi.* capitolare.

capitulation *s.* capitolazione.

capon *s.* cappone.

caprice *s.* capriccio.

to capsize *vt.* capovolgere. ♦ **to capsize** *vi.* capovolgersi.

capstan *s.* argano.

capsule *s.* capsula.

to capsule *vt.* incapsulare.

captain *s.* **1.** capitano **2.** (*comm.*) magnate.

captious *agg.* capzioso.

to captivate *vt.* cattivare, ammaliare.

captivating *agg.* cattivante, ammaliante.

captive *s.* prigioniero: *to take* —, far prigioniero.

captivity *s.* prigionia, cattività.

capture *s.* cattura.

to capture *vt.* far prigioniero, prendere (*di città ecc.*).

Capuchin *s.* **1.** (*eccl.*) Cappuccino **2.** scimmia cappuccina.

car *s.* **1.** carro **2.** automobile **3.** (*ferr.*) vagone || — *-licence*, permesso di circolazione; *dining-* —, vagone ristorante; *sleeping-* —, vagone letto.

carabin *s.* carabina.

carabineer *s.* carabiniere.

to **caracole** *vi.* caracollare.

carafe *s.* caraffa.

caramel *s.* caramello.

carat *s.* carato.

caravan *s.* **1.** carovana **2.** carro (*di zingari ecc.*).

caravel *s.* caravella.

carbon *s.* carbonio || — *paper*, carta carbone.

carbonate *s.* carbonato.

carboniferous *agg.* carbonifero.

to **carbonize** *vt.* carbonizzare.

carbuncle *s.* carbonchio.

carburation *s.* carburazione.

carburetter, carburettor *s.* carburatore.

carcase *s.* carcassa.

carcinogen *s.* sostanza cancerogena.

card *s.* **1.** cartoncino, biglietto **2.** carta da giuoco.

to **card** *vt.* schedare.

cardan *s.* cardano || — *joint*, giunto cardanico.

cardboard *s.* cartone.

cardiac *agg.* cardiaco.

cardigan *s.* giacca di lana.

cardinal *agg.* e *s.* cardinale.

cardiogram *s.* cardiogramma.

cardiologist *s.* cardiologo.

cardiopathy *s.* cardiopatia.

care *s.* **1.** cura, attenzione, protezione: *take* —!, attenzione!; *to take* — *of*, aver cura **2.** preoccupazione || — *-free*, senza pensieri; — *-worn*, pieno di pensieri.

to **care** *vi.* curarsi, interessarsi.

career *s.* **1.** carriera **2.** andatura veloce.

careful *agg.* **1.** accurato **2.** prudente.

carefully *avv.* **1.** accuratamente **2.** attentamente.

careless *agg.* noncurante.

carelessly *avv.* negligentemente.

carelessness *s.* trascuratezza.

caress *s.* carezza.

to **caress** *vt.* accarezzare.

caressing *agg.* carezzevole.

caretaker *s.* guardiano, custode.

caricature *s.* caricatura.

Carmelite *s.* carmelitano.

carmine *agg.* e *s.* carminio.

carnage *s.* carneficina, strage.

carnal *agg.* carnale, sensuale.

carnation *agg.* carnicino. ♦ **carnation** *s.* garofano.

carnival *s.* carnevale.

carnivore *s.* carnivoro.

carnivorous *agg.* carnivoro.

carol *s.* canto, inno.

carotid *s.* carotide.

carousel *s.* carosello.

carp *s.* carpa.

carpenter *s.* carpentiere, falegname.

carpet *s.* tappeto || *bedside* —, scendiletto.

carriage *s.* **1.** carrozza, vettura **2.** (*comm.*) trasporto.

carrier *s.* **1.** portatore, spedizioniere **2.** (*mecc.*) trasportatore **3.** supporto.

carrion *s.* carogna.

carrot *s.* carota.

carry *s.* portata (*di arma da fuoco ecc.*).

to **carry** *vt.* e *vi.* **1.** portare (*un peso*), trasportare **2.** trasmettere (*suoni*) || *to* — *about*, portare addosso; *to* — *on*, continuare; *to* — *out*, eseguire, realizzare, compiere; *to* — *through*, portare a buon fine.

carrying *s.* trasporto.

cart *s.* carro.

cartel *s.* (*econ.; pol.*) cartello.

cartilage *s.* cartilagine.

cartography *s.* cartografia.

cartomancy *s.* cartomanzia.

carton *s.* scatola di cartone.

cartoon *s.* **1.** vignetta **2.** (*cine*) disegno animato.

cartridge *s.* **1.** cartuccia **2.** (*foto*) rotolo.

to **carve** *vt.* e *vi.* scolpire, incidere, cesellare.

carver *s.* intagliatore, scultore (*in legno e avorio*).

carving *s.* scultura, intaglio (*in legno e avorio*).

caryatid *s.* cariatide.

cascade *s.* piccola cascata (*d'acqua*).

case[1] *s.* **1.** caso, avvenimento **2.** (*giur.*) causa.

case[2] *s.* **1.** astuccio **2.** cassa, cassetta.

to **case** *vt.* imballare.

casement *s.* telaio di finestra (*a due battenti*), finestra.

cash s. cassa, contanti || — *on delivery*, pagamento alla consegna; *by ready* —, in contanti.

to cash vt. incassare, riscuotere.

cashier s. cassiere.

to cashier vt. destituire.

casing s. involucro, copertura.

cask s. barile, botte.

casket s. scrigno.

cassation s. cassazione.

cassock s. tunica (*del clero anglicano*).

cast s. **1.** getto, lancio **2.** (*metal.*) gettata, stampo **3.** complesso (*di attori*) || — *-iron*, ghisa.

to cast (cast, cast) vt. e vi. **1.** gettare, lanciare **2.** (*metal.*) fondere (*in stampo*) || to — *aside*, gettare da parte; to — *down*, abbassare (*gli occhi*).

castanets s. pl. nacchere.

castaway agg. arenato, respinto. ♦ **castaway** s. naufrago, reprobo.

caste s. casta.

caster s. V. *castor*.

to castigate vt. castigare, punire.

casting s. **1.** il gettare **2.** (*metal.*) getto, colata **3.** distribuzione (*delle parti agli attori*).

castle s. castello.

castor s. **1.** pepaiuola, saliera **2.** rotella da mobili.

castor-oil s. olio di ricino.

to castrate vt. castrare.

casual agg. casuale, fortuito.

casually avv. per caso.

casualness s. irregolarità, noncuranza.

casualty s. **1.** infortunio **2.** infortunato.

casuistry s. casistica.

cat s. gatto.

cataclysm s. cataclisma.

catacomb s. catacomba.

catalepsy s. catalessi.

cataleptic agg. e s. catalettico.

catalogue s. catalogo.

to catalogue vt. e vi. catalogare.

catalyst s. catalizzatore.

cataplasm s. cataplasma.

catapult s. catapulta.

cataract s. cateratta.

catarrh s. catarro.

catastrophe s. catastrofe, calamità.

catastrophic(al) agg. catastrofico.

catch s. **1.** presa, cattura **2.** trappola || — *-as-* — *-can*, lotta libera.

to catch (caught, caught) vt. **1.** afferrare, acchiappare, prendere: to

— *the train*, prendere il treno **2.** pescare, sorprendere.

catching agg. **1.** attraente **2.** orecchiabile (*di melodia*) **3.** (*med.*) contagioso.

catchy agg. **1.** attraente **2.** orecchiabile (*di melodia*) **3.** insidioso.

catechism s. catechismo.

to catechize vt. catechizzare.

catechumen s. catecumeno.

categoric(al) agg. categorico.

category s. categoria.

to cater vi. **1.** provvedere cibo **2.** procurare svaghi.

caterpillar s. **1.** bruco **2.** (*mecc.*) cingolo **3.** trattore a cingoli.

catharsis s. catarsi.

cathartic agg. catartico.

cathedral s. cattedrale.

Catherine-wheel s. girandola.

cathode s. catodo.

cathodic agg. catodico.

catholic agg. e s. cattolico.

Catholicism s. cattolicesimo.

cation s. catione.

cattish agg. felino.

cattle s. bestiame, armenti || — *-dealer*, negoziante di bestiame; — *-lifter*, ladro di bestiame.

caught V. to *catch*.

cauldron s. caldaia.

cauliflower s. cavolfiore.

causal agg. causale.

causality s. causalità.

causative agg. causativo.

cause s. **1.** causa, ragione, motivo **2.** (*giur.*) processo, causa.

to cause vt. causare, cagionare.

causeway s. strada rialzata.

caustic agg. caustico (*anche fig.*).

caustically avv. causticamente (*anche fig.*).

causticity s. causticità (*anche fig.*).

cauterization s. cauterizzazione.

to cauterize vt. cauterizzare.

caution s. **1.** prudenza, cautela **2.** cauzione, garanzia || — *-money*, cauzione, pegno.

to caution vt. mettere in guardia.

cautious agg. cauto, prudente.

cautiously avv. cautamente.

cavalier s. cavaliere.

cavalry s. cavalleria.

cave s. caverna, spelonca.

to cave vt. e vi. scavare || to — *in*, sprofondare.

cavernous agg. cavernoso (*anche fig.*).

caviar(e) s. caviale.

cavil s. cavillo.
to cavil vi. cavillare.
cavity s. cavità.
cavy s. cavia.
cayman s. caimano.
to cease vt. e vi. cessare, finire.
cedar s. cedro.
cedilla s. cediglia.
ceiling s. soffitto.
to celebrate vt. e vi. celebrare, solennizzare.
celebrated agg. famoso.
celebration s. celebrazione.
celebrity s. celebrità, persona fa-
mosa.
celerity s. celerità.
celery s. sedano.
celestial agg. celestiale, paradisiaco.
celibacy s. celibato.
cell s. 1. cella 2. cellula.
cellar s. cantina.
cellarman s. cantiniere.
cellular agg. cellulare, alveolare.
cellulitis s. cellulite.
celluloid agg. e s. celluloide.
cellulose s. cellulosa.
Celt s. celta.
Celtic agg. celtico.
cement s. 1. cemento 2. stucco, mastice.
to cement vt. cementare (anche fig.).
cemetery s. cimitero.
to cense vt. incensare.
censer s. turibolo.
censor s. censore.
to censor vt. censurare.
censorial agg. censorio.
censorship s. censura, censorato.
censure s. censura.
to censure vt. censurare.
census s. censo.
cent s. centesimo (di dollaro).
centaur s. centauro.
centenarian agg. e s. centenario.
centenary agg. e s. centenario.
centennial agg. centennale.
centesimal agg. centesimale.
centigrade agg. centigrado.
centigramme s. centigrammo.
centilitre s. centilitro.
centimetre s. centimetro.
central agg. 1. centrale 2. fondamentale.
centralism s. accentramento.
centralization s. concentrazione (di
poteri).
to centralize vt. e vi. accentrare.
centre s. centro, parte centrale, interno.

centrifugal agg. centrifugo.
centripetal agg. centripeto.
centrism s. centrismo.
to centuplicate vt. centuplicare.
centurion s. centurione.
century s. 1. secolo 2. (stor.) centuria.
cephalalgia s. cefalea.
ceramics s. (arte della) ceramica.
cereal agg. e s. cereale.
cerebral agg. cerebrale.
cerebro-spinal agg. cerebro-spinale.
cerebrum s. cervello.
ceremonial agg. da cerimonia. ♦
ceremonial s. cerimoniale.
ceremonious agg. cerimonioso.
ceremony s. cerimonia || to stand
on —, far complimenti.
certain agg. 1. certo, sicuro 2. indeterminato, certo.
certainly avv. certamente.
certainty s. certezza.
certificate s. certificato.
to certify vt. certificare, attestare.
certitude s. certezza.
cervical agg. cervicale. ♦ **cervical**
s. vertebra cervicale. ♦ **cervicals**
s. pl. nervi cervicali.
cessation s. cessazione.
cession s. cessione.
cess-pit, cess-pool s. pozzo nero.
cetacean agg. di cetaceo. ♦ **cetacean** s. cetaceo.
to chafe vt. 1. riscaldare 2. irritare.
to chafe vi. 1. strofinarsi 2. irritarsi.
chaff s. 1. pula, paglia trinciata 2.
(fig.) oggetto di nessun valore.
chaffer s. contrattazione, baratto.
chain s. 1. catena 2. serie, concatenamento.
to chain vt. 1. incatenare 2. (fig.)
mettere in ceppi.
chain-stores s. pl. catene (di negozi o grandi magazzini).
chair s. 1. sedia: deck- —, sedia a
sdraio; easy- —, poltrona 2. cat-
tedra (universitaria).
chairman s. presidente (di consiglio, assemblea ecc.).
chalice s. calice.
chalk s. 1. gesso 2. (min.) calcare
|| — -drawing, disegno a pastello;
— -stone (pat.), calcolo.
chalky agg. gessoso.
challenge s. 1. sfida 2. (mil.) intimazione.
to challenge vt. 1. sfidare 2. (mil.)
intimare.

challenger s. sfidatore, sfidante.
chamber s. 1. sala, aula 2. (pol.; comm.) camera || — -music, musica da camera; —maid, cameriera (specialmente d'albergo).
chamberlain s. 1. ciambellano 2. tesoriere.
chameleon s. camaleonte.
chamois s. camoscio.
champion s. 1. campione 2. difensore.
championship s. campionato.
chance s. 1. avvenimento fortuito, caso 2. occasione.
to chance vi. accadere.
chancellery s. cancelleria.
chancellor s. cancelliere.
chancery s. cancelleria.
chandelier s. candeliere, lampadario.
change s. 1. cambio, mutamento || — for a —, tanto per cambiare 2. moneta spicciola.
to change vt. e vi. cambiare.
changeability s. mutabilità.
changeable agg. 1. mutabile 2. incostante (di tempo).
changing agg. cangiante, mutevole.
♦ changing s. cambio.
channel s. 1. canale, stretto. ♦ channels s. pl. vie di comunicazione.
chant s. canto, cantilena.
to channel vt. 1. fare canali 2. incanalare.
chaos s. caos.
chap[1] s. (fam.) individuo, ragazzo.
chap[2] s. screpolatura.
chapel s. cappella.
chaplain s. cappellano.
chaplet s. ghirlanda, corona (di fiori).
chapter s. capitolo.
to char vt. carbonizzare. ♦ to char vi. carbonizzarsi.
character s. 1. carattere, indole 2. scrittura 3. (lett.) personaggio.
characteristic agg. caratteristico.
♦ characteristic s. caratteristica.
characterization s. caratterizzazione.
to characterize vt. caratterizzare.
charade s. sciarada.
charcoal s. carbone di legna.
charge s. 1. prezzo richiesto, spesa 2. incarico, sorveglianza 3. (giur.) accusa.
to charge vt. 1. far pagare, addebitare 2. incaricare 3. accusare: to

— so. with a crime, accusare qu. di un delitto.
chargeable agg. 1. a carico di, da addebitarsi a 2. accusabile.
chariot s. cocchio.
charitable agg. caritatevole.
charitably avv. caritatevolmente.
charity s. 1. carità, benevolenza 2. istituzione benefica.
charlatan s. ciarlatano.
charm s. 1. fascino 2. incantesimo, malia.
to charm vt. 1. affascinare 2. sottoporre a magia.
charming agg. affascinante.
charmingly avv. in modo affascinante.
charnel(-house) s. ossario.
chart s. 1. grafico 2. carta marina.
charter s. 1. licenza, brevetto 2. carta costituzionale.
chartography s. cartografia.
charwoman s. domestica ad ore.
charwork s. lavoro di domestica ad ore.
chase s. 1. inseguimento, caccia 2. riserva di caccia, cacciagione.
to chase[1] vt. inseguire, cacciare.
to chase[2] vt. cesellare.
chaser[1] s. cacciatore, inseguitore.
chaser[2] s. cesellatore.
chasing s. 1. cesellatura 2. filettatura (di una vite).
chasm s. baratro, abisso.
chaste agg. casto, puro.
chastely avv. castamente, virtuosamente.
chastity s. castità.
chat s. chiacchiera.
to chat vi. chiacchierare.
chatter s. 1. chiacchiera, chiacchierio 2. il battere dei denti.
to chatter vi. 1. chiacchierare 2. battere i denti.
chatterbox s. chiacchierone, chiacchierona.
chattering s. 1. chiacchierio 2. il battere dei denti.
chauvinism s. sciovinismo.
chauvinist s. sciovinista.
cheap agg. e avv. a buon mercato.
cheaply avv. economicamente, in modo poco costoso.
cheat s. 1. frode 2. imbroglione.
to cheat vt. e vi. imbrogliare.
cheater s. truffatore, baro.
cheating s. inganno.
check[1] s. 1. scacco 2. controllo, verifica 3. scontrino, contromarca.

check² s. disegno a scacchi.
to **check** vi. dare scacco. ♦ to **check** vt. controllare, verificare.
checked agg. quadrettato.
checkmate s. scacco matto.
to **checkmate** vt. dare scacco matto.
cheek s. guancia.
cheekily avv. sfacciatamente.
cheeky agg. sfacciato.
to **cheer** vt. rallegrare, incoraggiare. ♦ to **cheer** vi. essere di buon umore, rallegrarsi.
cheerful agg. di buon umore.
cheerfully avv. allegramente.
cheerfulness s. buon umore.
cheering agg. incoraggiante. ♦ **cheering** s. acclamazioni (pl.).
cheese s. formaggio.
cheetah s. ghepardo.
chemical agg. chimico.
chemically avv. chimicamente.
chemicals s. pl. prodotti chimici.
chemisette s. camicetta.
chemist s. 1. chimico 2. farmacista.
chemistry s. chimica.
cheque s. assegno: to cash a —, cambiare un assegno; — -book, libretto d'assegni; blank —, assegno in bianco; crossed —, assegno sbarrato.
to **cherish** vt. 1. (fig.) nutrire 2. curare teneramente, coccolare.
cherry s. ciliegia.
cherub s. cherubino.
chess s. giuoco degli scacchi || — -board, scacchiera; — -men, pezzi degli scacchi.
chest s. 1. cassetta, cassone 2. torace.
chestnut agg. castano. ♦ **chestnut** s. 1. castagno 2. castagna.
to **chew** vt. e vi. masticare.
chicanery s. cavillo (legale).
chick s. 1. pulcino 2. (fig.) bambino.
chicken s. gallinella, pollo.
chicory s. cicoria.
to **chide** (chid, chid) (anche reg.) vt. e vi. redarguire, sgridare.
chief agg. principale. ♦ **chief** s. capo, comandante.
chiefly avv. principalmente.
chieftain s. capo (di tribù, clan ecc.).
chilblain s. gelone.
child s. (pl. children) 1. bambino, bambina 2. figlio, figlia.
childhood s. infanzia.
childish agg. infantile.

childishness s. fanciullaggine, puerilità.
childless agg. senza figli.
childlike agg. infantile.
children V. child.
Chilean agg. e s. cileno.
chill s. 1. colpo di freddo 2. (metal.) conchiglia.
to **chill** vt. 1. raffreddare, agghiacciare (anche fig.) 2. (metal.) fondere in conchiglia. ♦ to **chill** vi. raffreddarsi.
chilled agg. 1. congelato 2. (metal.) fuso in conchiglia.
chilliness s. 1. freddo 2. (fig.) freddezza.
chilly agg. 1. freddoloso (di persona) 2. fresco (di tempo).
chime s. scampanio.
to **chime** vt. e vi. scampanare, suonare a festa.
chiming s. lo scampanare.
chimney s. camino, comignolo || — -sweeper, spazzacamino.
chimpanzee s. scimpanzè.
chin s. mento || — -strap, sottogola.
china s. 1. porcellana fine 2. (fam.) stoviglie di porcellana.
chinchilla s. cincillà.
chine s. spina dorsale.
Chinese agg. e s. cinese.
chink s. fessura, crepa.
chip s. 1. scheggia 2. (cuc.) patatina fritta.
to **chip** vt. 1. scheggiare 2. rompere. ♦ to **chip** vi. scheggiarsi, frantumarsi.
chiromancer s. chiromante.
chiromancy s. chiromanzia.
chiropodist s. pedicure.
chirp s. 1. cinguettio, pigolio 2. stridio, il frinire (di cicale ecc.).
to **chirp** vi. 1. cinguettare, pigolare 2. frinire, stridere (di cicale ecc.).
chisel s. cesello.
to **chisel** vt. cesellare.
chiseller s. cesellatore.
chitterlings s. pl. trippa.
chivalrous agg. cavalleresco.
chivalry s. 1. cavalleria 2. condotta cavalleresca.
chloride s. cloruro.
chlorine s. cloro.
chlorite s. clorito.
chloroform s. cloroformio.
chlorophyl(l) s. clorofilla.
chock s. 1. cuneo, bietta 2. (mar.) passacavi.
chocolate agg. 1. di cioccolato 2.

color cioccolata. ♦ **chocolate** s. cioccolato: *cake of —*, tavoletta di cioccolato.

choice agg. di prima qualità, scelto. ♦ **choice** s. **1.** scelta **2.** la cosa scelta **3.** assortimento.

choir s. coro.

choke s. **1.** soffocamento **2.** strozzatura (*di tubo*).

to **choke** vt. **1.** soffocare (*anche fig.*) **2.** ingorgare. ♦ to **choke** vi. ostruirsi.

choker s. soffocatore.

cholera s. colera.

cholesterol s. colesterolo.

to **choose (chose, chosen)** vt. scegliere.

chooser s. chi sceglie.

chop s. **1.** (*cuc.*) braciola **2.** colpo (*di scure ecc.*).

to **chop** vt. e vi. **1.** fendere, tagliare **2.** (*cuc.*) tritare || *to — down*, abbattere (*alberi*); *to — off*, tagliar via.

chopper s. **1.** ascia **2.** chi taglia con l'ascia **3.** tagliatrice.

choppy agg. **1.** screpolato **2.** increspato (*del mare*).

choral agg. corale.

chord s. **1.** (*mus.; anat.; geom.*) corda **2.** (*mus.*) accordo.

choreographer s. coreografo.

choreographic agg. coreografico.

choreography s. coreografia.

chorus s. coro || *— -singer*, corista.

chose V. to choose.

chosen V. to choose.

chrism s. crisma.

to **christen** vt. battezzare.

Christendom s. cristianità.

christening s. battesimo.

Christian agg. e s. cristiano || *— name*, nome di battesimo.

Christianity s. cristianesimo.

to **christianize** vt. convertire al cristianesimo.

Christmas s. Natale.

chromatic agg. cromatico.

chromatically avv. cromaticamente.

chromatism s. cromatismo.

chromatography s. cromatografia.

chrome s. cromo.

to **chrome** vt. cromare.

chromium s. cromo || *— -plated*, cromato; *— -plating*, cromatura.

chromolithograph s. cromolitografia.

chromosome s. cromosoma.

chromosphere s. cromosfera.

chronic agg. cronico (*anche fig.*).

chronicle s. cronaca.

chronicler s. cronista.

chronologic(al) agg. cronologico.

chronologically avv. cronologicamente.

chronology s. cronologia.

chronometer s. cronometro.

chrysalid s. crisalide.

chrysanthemum s. crisantemo.

chubby agg. paffuto.

church s. **1.** chiesa **2.** comunità religiosa || *— -going*, assiduità ai servizi religiosi; *— -living*, beneficio ecclesiastico; *— -service*, funzione religiosa.

churchman s. **1.** ecclesiastico **2.** membro della chiesa anglicana.

churchy agg. bigotto.

churchyard s. cimitero.

chyle s. (*fisiol.*) chilo.

ciborium s. ciborio.

cicada s. cicala.

to **cicatrize** vt. cicatrizzare. ♦ to **cicatrize** vi. cicatrizzarsi.

cider s. sidro.

cigar s. sigaro || *— -case*, portasigari, *— -end*, mozzicone; *— -holder*, bocchino per sigari.

cigarette s. sigaretta || *— -case*, portasigarette, *— -end*, mozzicone, *— -holder*, bocchino; *— paper*, cartina per sigaretta.

cilice s. cilicio.

cinder s. **1.** brace **2.** scoria.

cine-camera s. macchina da presa.

cinema s. cinematografo.

cinematograph s. **1.** proiettore cinematografico **2.** macchina da presa.

cinematographer s. **1.** operatore cinematografico **2.** cineasta.

cinematographic agg. cinematografico.

cinematography s. cinematografia.

cine-projector s. proiettore cinematografico.

cinerary agg. cinerario.

cinnabar s. cinabro.

cinnamon s. cannella.

cipher s. **1.** cifrario **2.** monogramma **3.** (*mat.; anche fig.*) zero, nullità.

to **cipher** vt. e vi. cifrare.

circle s. **1.** cerchio, circolo (*anche fig.*) **2.** orbita (*dei pianeti*) **3.** galleria (*di teatro*).

circlet s. cerchietto.

circuit *s.* **1.** cinta, circonvallazione **2.** rivoluzione, rotazione (*di astri*) **3.** (*elettr.; sport*) circuito.

circular *agg.* circolare. ♦ **circular** *s.* lettera circolare.

to **circulate** *vt.* mettere in circolazione, diffondere. ♦ to **circulate** *vi.* circolare.

circulating *agg.* circolante.

circulation *s.* **1.** circolazione **2.** diffusione **3.** (*giorn.*) tiratura.

circulatory *agg.* circolatorio.

to **circumcise** *vt.* circoncidere.

circumcision *s.* circoncisione.

circumference *s.* circonferenza.

circumflex *agg.* circonflesso.

circumlocution *s.* circonlocuzione.

to **circumnavigate** *vt.* circumnavigare.

circumnavigation *s.* circumnavigazione.

circumnavigator *s.* circumnavigatore.

to **circumscribe** *vt.* circoscrivere.

circumscription *s.* circoscrizione.

circumspect *agg.* circospetto.

circumspection *s.* circospezione.

circumstance *s.* circostanza.

circumstantial *agg.* **1.** circostanziale **2.** circostanziato.

circumstantiality *s.* abbondanza di particolari.

circumstantially *avv.* circostanziatamente.

to **circumvent** *vt.* circuire.

circumvention *s.* raggiro.

circumvolution *s.* circonvoluzione.

circus *s.* **1.** circo, arena **2.** piazza rotonda.

cirrhosis *s.* cirrosi.

cisalpine *agg.* cisalpino.

cistern *s.* cisterna.

citadel *s.* cittadella.

to **cite** *vt.* citare.

citizen *s.* cittadino.

citizenhood *s.* cittadinanza.

citizenship *s.* diritto di cittadinanza.

citrate *s.* citrato.

citric *agg.* citrico.

citron *s.* cedro.

city *s.* **1.** città (*grande*) **2.** centro di grande traffico di una città.

civic *agg.* civico.

civil *agg.* civile, cortese.

civilian *agg.* e *s.* civile, borghese.

civility *s.* civiltà, cortesia.

civilization *s.* civilizzazione, civiltà.

to **civilize** *vt.* civilizzare.

civilly *avv.* civilmente.

civism *s.* civismo.

claim *s.* **1.** richiesta **2.** (*giur.*) rivendicazione **3.** (*comm.*) reclamo.

to **claim** *vt.* **1.** esigere, chiedere **2.** (*giur.*) rivendicare **3.** (*comm.*) reclamare.

claimant *s.* **1.** rivendicatore **2.** richiedente.

clairvoyance *s.* chiaroveggenza.

clairvoyant *agg.* e *s.* chiaroveggente.

to **clamber** *vi.* arrampicarsi.

clammy *agg.* vischioso.

clamour *s.* clamore, vocio.

to **clamour** *vt.* e *vi.* vociferare.

clan *s.* gruppo familiare, tribù.

clandestine *agg.* clandestino.

to **clang** *vi.* emettere un suono, un grido. ♦ to **clang** *vt.* far risonare.

clangour *s.* fragore.

to **clank** *vi.* tintinnare. ♦ to **clank** *vt.* far tintinnare.

clap *s.* **1.** applauso **2.** rumore improvviso **3.** piccolo colpo (*con la mano*).

to **clap** *vt.* e *vi.* **1.** applaudire **2.** dare un colpo (*con la mano*) **3.** battere (*le ali*).

clapper *s.* **1.** battente (*di porta*) **2.** (*teat.*) membro della « claque ».

claret *s.* **1.** color rosso-violetto **2.** vino chiaretto.

clarification *s.* chiarificazione.

to **clarify** *vt.* chiarificare. ♦ to **clarify** *vi.* chiarificarsi.

clarinet *s.* clarinetto.

clarity *s.* chiarità.

clash *s.* **1.** cozzo, urto **2.** scontro (*d'opinioni*).

to **clash** *vt.* e *vi.* **1.** cozzare, far strepito **2.** scontrarsi (*d'opinioni*).

clasp *s.* fermaglio, fibbia.

to **clasp** *vt.* afferrare.

class *s.* **1.** classe, categoria **2.** (*scol.*) classe **3.** (*fig.*) distinzione.

classic *agg.* e *s.* classico.

classical *agg.* classico.

classically *avv.* classicamente.

classicism *s.* classicismo.

classification *s.* classificazione.

to **classify** *vt.* classificare.

classmate *s.* compagno di classe.

classroom *s.* aula.

classy *agg.* (*fam.*) di classe.

clatter *s.* fracasso.

to **clatter** *vi.* far fracasso.

clause *s.* clausola.

claustrophobia *s.* claustrofobia.

claw *s.* **1.** artiglio, zampa con artigli **2.** uncino **3.** chela.

to claw *vt.* artigliare.

clawed *agg.* munito di artigli.

clay *s.* argilla: *fire-* —, argilla refrattaria || — *pigeon*, piattello.

clayey *agg.* argilloso.

clean *agg.* **1.** pulito **2.** netto, nitido **3.** (*fig.*) puro, schietto.

to clean *vt.* pulire.

cleaner *s.* pulitore, pulitrice || *dry-* —, smacchiatore a secco.

cleaning *s.* pulitura.

cleanliness *s.* pulizia.

cleanly *agg.* pulito. ♦ **cleanly** *avv.* in modo pulito.

cleanness *s.* **1.** pulizia (*anche fig.*) **2.** nitidezza.

to cleanse *vt.* **1.** pulire **2.** purificare.

cleanser *s.* **1.** pulitore **2.** detersivo.

cleansing *agg.* purificante. ♦ **cleansing** *s.* **1.** purificazione **2.** depurazione.

clear *agg.* **1.** chiaro, limpido **2.** distinto, evidente || — *-cut*, nettamente stagliato; — *-sighted*, dalla vista buona.

to clear *vt.* **1.** chiarire, schiarire **2.** discolpare (*comm.*) svincolare || *to* — *away*, sparecchiare, dissiparsi (*di nebbia*); *to* — *up*, rassettare (*una stanza*), chiarire (*un malinteso*). ♦ **to clear** *vi.* schiarirsi.

clearance *s.* **1.** chiarificazione **2.** sgombero **3.** (*comm.*) sdoganamento.

clearing *s.* **1.** chiarimento **2.** rimozione.

clearly *avv.* chiaramente.

clearness *s.* **1.** chiarezza **2.** (*fig.*) limpidezza.

cleavage *s.* **1.** spaccatura **2.** (*min.*) clivaggio.

to cleave (cleft, cleft) *vt.* e *vi.* fendere, spaccare.

cleft *s.* fenditura.

clemency *s.* clemenza.

clement *agg.* **1.** clemente **2.** dolce, gentile (*di carattere*) **3.** mite (*di tempo*).

to clench *vt.* **1.** stringere (*mani, denti ecc.*) **2.** ribadire.

clergy *s.* clero.

clergyman *s.* ecclesiastico.

clerical *agg.* **1.** clericale **2.** impiegatizio.

clericalism *s.* clericalismo.

clerk *s.* impiegato || *chief* —, ca-

poufficio.

to clerk *vi.* lavorare come impiegato.

clever *agg.* intelligente, abile, ingegnoso.

cleverly *avv.* intelligentemente.

cleverness *s.* intelligenza, abilità, ingegnosità.

clew *s.* gomitolo (*di filo*).

click *s.* scatto, rumore secco.

client *s.* cliente.

cliff *s.* scogliera.

climate *s.* clima.

climatic *agg.* climatico.

climax *s.* apice, culmine.

climb *s.* **1.** rampa **2.** ascesa.

to climb *vt.* e *vi.* **1.** arrampicarsi **2.** scalare (*anche fig.*).

climber *s.* **1.** scalatore **2.** (*fig.*) arrivista **3.** pianta rampicante.

climbing *s.* **1.** scalata **2.** (*fig.*) arrivismo. ♦ **climbing** *agg.* rampicante.

to cling (clung, clung) *vi.* attaccarsi, aggrapparsi (*anche fig.*): *to* — *to a hope*, aggrapparsi ad una speranza.

clinical *agg.* clinico.

clinician *s.* clinico.

clinking *s.* tintinnio.

clip *s.* **1.** fermaglio, molletta || *hair* —, forcina per capelli **2.** graffa (*per ferite*) **3.** tosatura (*di pecore*).

to clip *vt.* **1.** tenere insieme (*con un fermaglio*) **2.** tosare (*pecore ecc.*).

clipper *s.* **1.** tosatore **2.** (*mar.*) "clipper". ♦ **clippers** *s.* *pl.* **1.** forbici **2.** macchinetta per tosare (*sing.*).

cloak *s.* **1.** mantello **2.** (*fig.*) manto, velo.

clock *s.* orologio (*da muro, da tavolo*) || *alarm-* —, sveglia.

clockwise *agg.* in senso orario || *counter-* —, in senso antiorario.

clockwork *s.* meccanismo a orologeria.

clod *s.* zolla.

clog *s.* **1.** impedimento, intoppo **2.** zoccolo.

to clog *vt.* ostruire, impedire (*anche fig.*). ♦ **to clog** *vi.* incepparsi.

cloister *s.* chiostro.

close *agg.* **1.** chiuso **2.** serrato: — *combat*, combattimento corpo a corpo **3.** afoso, viziato (*di aria*) **4.** intimo: — *friend*, amico intimo **5.** accurato, attento || — *-fitting*, aderente (*di vestiti*); —

-mouthed, riservato; — *-shaven*, rasato con cura.

close *s.* **1.** spazio cintato **2.** fine, termine **3.** corpo a corpo.

close *avv.* vicino, presso.

to close *vt.* chiudere || *to — up*, turare, sbarrare (*di strada*). ♦ **to close** *vi.* chiudersi || *to — in*, avvicinarsi, accorciarsi (*di giorni*); *to — with*, venire a un accordo.

closed *agg.* chiuso.

closely *avv.* **1.** da vicino **2.** attentamente.

closeness *s.* **1.** afa, mancanza d'aria **2.** compattezza **3.** intimità **4.** vicinanza **5.** accuratezza.

closet *s.* **1.** studio, salotto privato **2.** armadio a muro **3.** gabinetto.

close-up *s.* (*cine*) primo piano.

closing *s.* chiusura (*di negozi, teatri ecc.*).

clot *s.* grumo.

to clot *vt.* raggrumare, coagulare. ♦ **to clot** *vi.* raggrumarsi, coagularsi.

cloth *s.* tessuto, stoffa, tela || (*table-*) —, tovaglia.

to clothe *vt.* vestire.

clothes *s. pl.* abiti, indumenti || *-book*, attaccapanni; *-line*, corda (*per stendere il bucato*); *-peg*, molletta (*fermabucato*).

clothing *s.* **1.** vestiario **2.** copertura.

cloud *s.* **1.** nuvola, nube **2.** nugolo (*di insetti*).

to cloud *vt.* e *vi.* annuvolare, oscurare || *to — (up, over)*, annuvolarsi.

clouded *agg.* **1.** coperto (*di nubi*) **2.** torbido (*di liquidi*).

cloudily *avv.* nebulosamente.

cloudy *agg.* **1.** nuvoloso **2.** torbido.

clover *s.* trifoglio.

clown *s.* pagliaccio.

clownish *agg.* pagliaccesco.

club *s.* **1.** mazza, randello **2.** circolo, associazione **3.** (*carte*) fiori.

clue *s.* **1.** indizio, traccia **2.** filo di un racconto.

clumsily *avv.* goffamente.

clumsiness *s.* goffaggine.

clumsy *agg.* goffo, senza grazia.

clung V. *to* **cling**.

cluster *s.* **1.** grappolo (*d'uva*), mazzo (*di fiori*), gruppo **2.** folla, capannello (*di gente*) **3.** sciame.

clutch *s.* **1.** stretta, grinfia **2.** (*auto*) frizione.

to clutch *vt.* e *vi.* afferrare, afferrarsi, agguantare.

coach *s.* **1.** carrozza, cocchio **2.** pullman **3.** carrozza ferroviaria **4.** (*sport*) allenatore, istruttore || *-house*, rimessa; *mourning-* —, carro funebre; *stage-* —, diligenza.

coachman *s.* cocchiere.

coachwork *s.* carrozzeria.

coadjutor *s.* coadiutore.

coagulant *s.* sostanza coagulante.

to coagulate *vt.* coagulare. ♦ **to coagulate** *vi.* coagularsi.

coagulation *s.* coagulazione.

coagulator *s.* coagulatore.

coal *s.* carbone: — *-bed*, bacino carbonifero; — *-black*, nero come il carbone; — *-fed*, alimentato a carbone; — *-mine*, miniera di carbone.

to coalesce *vi.* **1.** coalizzarsi, unirsi **2.** fondersi.

coalition *s.* coalizione.

coarse *agg.* **1.** grossolano, rozzo **2.** ruvido, grosso (*di materiale*).

coarsely *avv.* grossolanamente.

coarseness *s.* **1.** grossolanità **2.** ruvidezza (*di stoffe ecc.*).

coast *s.* costa || *-guard*, polizia costiera.

coastal *agg.* costiero.

coaster *s.* **1.** nave cabotiera **2.** sottobicchiere.

coat *s.* **1.** giacca, soprabito **2.** manto (*anche fig.*), pelliccia (*di animale*) **3.** rivestimento, intonaco || — *of arms*, stemma.

to coat *vt.* rivestire, coprire.

coating *s.* rivestimento, mano di vernice.

to coax *vt.* blandire, circuire. ♦ **to coax** *vi.* far moine.

coaxial *agg.* coassiale.

cobalt *s.* cobalto.

cobble *s.* ciottolo.

to cobble *vt.* **1.** pavimentare (*con ciottoli*) **2.** rappezzare (*scarpe*).

cobbler *s.* ciabattino.

cobra *s.* cobra.

cobweb *s.* ragnatela.

cocaine *s.* cocaina.

coccyx *s.* (*pl.* *-cyges*) coccige.

cock *s.* **1.** gallo **2.** cane di fucile.

cockade *s.* coccarda.

cockatoo *s.* cacatoa.

cockboat *s.* (*mar.*) lancia.

cockerel *s.* galletto.

cock-eyed *agg.* strabico.

cockish *agg.* sfrontato.

cockney *agg.* e *s.* dialetto londinese.

cockpit *s.* **1.** arena (*per combattimento di galli*) **2.** (*mar.*) castello di poppa.

cockroach *s.* scarafaggio.

cockscomb *s.* **1.** cresta (*di gallo*) **2.** (*fig.*) zerbinotto.

cocktail *s.* **1.** cavallo con coda mozzata **2.** cocktail.

cocoa *s.* cacao.

coconut *s.* noce di cocco.

cocoon *s.* bozzolo.

cod *s.* merluzzo.

code *s.* codice.

to **code** *vt.* **1.** codificare **2.** cifrare (*un dispaccio*).

codeine *s.* codeina.

codex *s.* codice, manoscritto antico.

codfish *s.* merluzzo.

codicil *s.* codicillo.

codification *s.* codificazione.

to **codify** *vt.* codificare.

co-director *s.* condirettore.

co-education *s.* istruzione nella scuola mista.

co-educational *agg.* (*scol.*) misto.

coefficient *agg.* e *s.* coefficiente.

coenobium *s.* cenobio.

coercible *agg.* coercibile.

coercion *s.* coercizione.

coercive *agg.* coercitivo.

coeval *agg.* e *s.* coevo.

to **coexist** *vi.* coesistere.

coexistence *s.* coesistenza.

coffee *s.* caffè: — -*bean*, chicco di caffè; — -*grounds*, fondi di caffè || — -*house*, caffè, bar; — -*mill*, macinino; — -*pot*, caffettiera.

coffer *s.* cassa, cofano.

coffin *s.* bara.

cog *s.* dente (*di ruota*).

cognate *agg.* e *s.* consanguineo, congiunto.

cognition *s.* cognizione.

cognitive *agg.* avente conoscenza.

cognizable *agg.* **1.** conoscibile **2.** (*giur.*) entro la giurisdizione di una corte.

to **cohabit** *vi.* coabitare.

cohabitation *s.* coabitazione.

coheir *s.* coerede.

coheiress *s.* (*donna*) coerede.

coherence *s.* **1.** coerenza **2.** aderenza.

coherent *agg.* **1.** coerente **2.** aderente.

coherently *avv.* coerentemente.

cohesion *s.* coesione.

cohesive *agg.* coesivo.

cohort *s.* coorte.

coil *s.* **1.** rotolo, spira **2.** (*elettr.; mecc.*) bobina.

coin *s.* moneta (*di metallo*).

to **coin** *vt.* coniare (*anche fig.*).

coinage *s.* conio.

to **coincide** *vi.* coincidere.

coincidence *s.* coincidenza.

coiner *s.* falsario.

colander *s.* colino.

cold *agg.* **1.** freddo: *to be* —, aver freddo **2.** freddo (*di carattere*), apatico: *in — blood*, a sangue freddo. ♦ **cold** *s.* **1.** freddo **2.** raffreddore: *to catch a* —, prendere il raffreddore.

coldness *s.* freddezza (*anche fig.*).

Coleoptera *s. pl.* coleotteri.

colic *s.* colica.

colitis *s.* colite.

to **collaborate** *vi.* collaborare.

collaboration *s.* collaborazione.

collaborationist *s.* collaborazionista.

collaborator *s.* collaboratore.

collapse *s.* **1.** crollo (*anche fig.*) **2.** collasso.

to **collapse** *vi.* crollare (*anche fig.*).

collar *s.* **1.** colletto **2.** collare.

to **collate** *vt.* **1.** collezionare, confrontare **2.** riordinare (*pagine di un'opera*).

collateral *agg.* collaterale.

colleague *s.* collega.

to **collect** *vt.* **1.** riunire **2.** incassare, riscuotere **3.** fare una raccolta. ♦ to **collect** *vi.* **1.** riunirsi **2.** riscuotere.

collecting *s.* il raccogliere: *stamp* —, il raccogliere francobolli.

collection *s.* **1.** raccolta, collezione **2.** riunione di persone **3.** questua, colletta.

collective *agg.* collettivo || — *title* (*tip.*), titolo generale.

collectivism *s.* collettivismo.

collectivity *s.* collettività.

collectivization *s.* collettivizzazione.

to **collectivize** *vt.* collettivizzare.

collector *s.* **1.** collezionista **2.** esattore.

college *s.* **1.** collegio **2.** scuola secondaria (*con internato*).

collegial *agg.* collegiale.

collier *s.* minatore.

colliery *s.* miniera di carbone.

collimator *s.* collimatore.

collision s. 1. collisione 2. urto, conflitto (d'interessi).

collocation s. collocazione.

colloidal agg. colloidale.

colloquial agg. d'uso corrente, familiare.

colloquialism s. espressione familiare.

colloquially avv. nella lingua parlata.

colloquy s. colloquio.

collusion s. collusione.

colon s. (gramm.) due punti.

colonel s. colonnello.

colonial agg. coloniale.

colonialism s. sistema coloniale.

colonialist s. colonialista.

colonist s. 1. colono 2. colonizzatore.

colonization s. colonizzazione.

to **colonize** vt. colonizzare. ◆ to **colonize** vi. stabilirsi in colonia.

colonizer s. colonizzatore.

colonnade s. colonnato.

colony s. colonia.

colossal agg. colossale.

colossus s. colosso.

colour s. 1. colore 2. colorito || — -bearer, portabandiera; — -blind, daltonico; — -print, stampa a colori. ◆ **colours** s. pl. bandiera (sing.) || with the —, sotto le armi.

to **colour** vt. colorare, tingere. ◆ to **colour** vi. colorirsi, prender colore.

colourable agg. verosimile.

colouration s. colorazione.

coloured agg. colorato, colorito (anche fig.).

colourful agg. colorito, pittoresco.

colouring s. 1. colorante 2. coloramento.

colourless agg. incolore.

colt s. 1. puledro 2. (fig.) novellino.

columbarium s. (pl. -ria) colombario.

column s. colonna (anche fig.).

columnist s. giornalista (che cura una rubrica).

coma s. coma.

comatose agg. comatoso.

comb s. 1. pettine 2. cresta (gallo, onde ecc.).

to **comb** vt. pettinare. ◆ to **comb** vi. frangersi (di onde) || to — one's hair, pettinarsi.

combat s. combattimento, lotta.

combination s. 1. combinazione 2. associazione.

to **combine** vt. 1. unire 2. (chim.) combinare 3. contribuire. ◆ to **combine** vi. 1. unirsi 2. combinarsi.

combing s. pettinata.

comb-out s. rastrellamento.

combustible agg. e s. combustibile.

combustion s. combustione.

to **come** (came, come) vi. venire, arrivare, giungere, provenire || to — about, accadere; to — across, incontrare per caso; to — along (fam.), capitare; to — back, ritornare; to — down, scendere; to — in, entrare, salire (di marea); to — on, avanzare, sopraggiungere (di malattie, stagioni ecc.), entrare in scena (di attori); to — through, superare; to — under, essere soggetti, essere catalogati; to — upon, trovare per caso.

comedian s. autore, attore di commedie.

comedy s. commedia.

comeliness s. avvenenza.

comely agg. avvenente.

comer s. chi viene.

comet s. cometa.

comfit s. confetto.

comfort s. 1. conforto 2. comodità.

to **comfort** vt. 1. confortare 2. ristorare.

comfortable agg. comodo, confortevole || to be —, sentirsi a proprio agio.

comfortably avv. comodamente.

comforting agg. confortante.

comic agg. comico, buffo. ◆ **comic** s. 1. attore comico 2. il ridicolo, il comico. ◆ **comics** s. pl. (fam.) fumetti.

comical agg. comico, buffo.

comicality s. comicità.

coming agg. prossimo, futuro. ◆ **coming** s. 1. venuta, arrivo || — away, partenza; — back, ritorno; — down, discesa, calo (dei prezzi).

comity s. cortesia, gentilezza.

comma s. virgola || inverted commas, virgolette.

command s. 1. comando, ordine 2. padronanza.

to **command** vt. e vi. 1. comandare 2. dominare (anche fig.).

commandant s. comandante.

commander s. comandante.

commandership s. funzioni di comandante.

commandment *s.* comandamento.
to **commemorate** *vt.* commemorare.
commemoration *s.* commemorazione.
commemorative *agg.* commemorativo.
to **commend** *vt.* lodare, encomiare.
commendable *agg.* lodevole.
commendably *avv.* lodevolmente.
commendation *s.* elogio, lode.
commendatory *agg.* laudativo.
commensal *s.* commensale.
commensurability *s.* commensurabilità.
commensurable *agg.* commensurabile.
commensurate *agg.* proporzionato.
comment *s.* 1. commento 2. critica.
to **comment** *vt.* e *vi.* commentare: *to — up (on) a test*, commentare un testo.
commentary *s.* commentario.
commentation *s.* annotazione, commento.
commentator *s.* 1. commentatore 2. radiocronista.
commerce *s.* commercio.
commercial *agg.* commerciale.
commercialism *s.* mercantilismo.
commercialist *s.* commercialista.
to **commercialize** *vt.* rendere commerciabile.
commercially *avv.* commercialmente.
commination *s.* comminazione.
to **commiserate** *vt.* e *vi.* commiserare.
commissary *s.* commissario, delegato.
commissaryship *s.* commissariato.
commission *s.* 1. commissione, comitato 2. commissione, incarico || *— agent (o merchant)*, commissionario.
to **commission** *vt.* 1. commissionare 2. delegare.
commissioned *agg.* munito di autorità || *non- — officer*, sottufficiale.
commissioner *s.* (*pol.*) delegato.
to **commit** *vt.* 1. affidare, rimettere: *to — one's soul to God*, rimettere la propria anima a Dio 2. commettere.
commitment, committal *s.* 1. consegna 2. incarico.
committed *agg.* (*neol.*) impegnato.
committee *s.* comitato.

commodity *s.* merce, oggetto di prima necessità || *free commodities*, merci esenti da dogana.
common *agg.* 1. comune 2. solito, abituale || *— law*, legge consacrata dalla consuetudine.
commoner *s.* 1. cittadino (*non nobile*) 2. membro della Camera dei Comuni.
commonness *s.* 1. banalità 2. frequenza (*di un avvenimento*).
commonplace *s.* luogo comune.
commons *s. pl.* il popolo (*sing.*) || *the House of —*, la Camera dei Comuni.
commonwealth *s.* 1. confederazione 2. repubblica (*anche fig.*).
commotion *s.* 1. agitazione, confusione 2. insurrezione, tumulto.
communal *agg.* della comunità.
commune *s.* comune.
communicability *s.* comunicabilità.
communicable *agg.* comunicabile.
to **communicate** *vt.* comunicare, trasmettere (*malattie, calore ecc.*).
♦ to **communicate** *vi.* mettersi in comunicazione.
communication *s.* 1. comunicazione, informazione 2. relazione, rapporto.
communicative *agg.* comunicativo.
communicativeness *s.* comunicativa.
communion *s.* comunione, comunanza || *Holy Communion*, Eucarestia.
communism *s.* comunismo.
communist *s.* comunista.
communistic *agg.* comunista.
community *s.* 1. comunanza (*di beni ecc.*) 2. collettività, società 3. (*eccl.*) comunità.
commutability *s.* permutabilità, commutabilità.
commutable *agg.* permutabile, commutabile.
commutative *agg.* commutativo.
commutator *s.* commutatore.
to **commute** *vt.* commutare.
compact[1] *s.* patto, contratto.
compact[2] *agg.* 1. compatto 2. ridotto.
compactness *s.* 1. compattezza 2. concisione (*di stile*).
companion[1] *s.* compagno.
companion[2] *s.* (*mar.*) boccaporto: *— -way*, scaletta (*di boccaporto*), scalandrone.
companionable *agg.* socievole.

companionship s. amicizia, cameratismo.

company s. **1.** compagnia **2.** comitiva **3.** (*comm.*) società.

comparable agg. paragonabile.

comparative agg. **1.** comparativo **2.** comparato. ♦ **comparative** s. (*gramm.*) comparativo.

comparatively avv. **1.** comparativamente **2.** relativamente.

to **compare** vt. paragonare, verificare. ♦ to **compare** vi. competere, rivaleggiare, reggere al confronto.

comparison s. **1.** paragone, confronto **2.** (*gramm.*) comparazione.

compartment s. compartimento, scompartimento.

compass s. **1.** circonferenza, spazio, estensione **2.** bussola. ♦ **compasses** s. pl. (*a pair of* —) compasso (*sing.*).

to **compass** vt. circondare.

compassion s. compassione: *out of* —, per compassione.

compassionate agg. compassionevole.

to **compassionate** vt. compassionare.

compassionately avv. con compassione.

compatibility s. compatibilità.

compatible agg. compatibile.

compatibly avv. compatibilmente.

to **compel** vt. costringere, obbligare.

compelling agg. irresistibile.

compendious agg. compendioso.

to **compensate** vt. ricompensare, risarcire. ♦ to **compensate** vi. supplire.

compensation s. **1.** compenso **2.** (*mecc.*) compensazione **3.** indennità, risarcimento.

compensator s. compensatore.

compensatory agg. compensativo.

to **compete** vi. competere, gareggiare.

competence s. **1.** competenza **2.** mezzi sufficienti per vivere (*pl.*).

competent agg. competente, abile.

competently avv. con competenza.

competition s. **1.** competizione, gara **2.** rivalità.

competitive agg. **1.** di competizione **2.** (*comm.*) di concorrenza.

competitively avv. per mezzo di concorso.

competitor s. concorrente, rivale.

compilation s. compilazione.

to **compile** vt. compilare.

compiler s. compilatore.

complacency s. **1.** soddisfazione **2.** compiacenza di sé.

complacent agg. **1.** compiacente **2.** soddisfatto di sé.

to **complain** vi. lagnarsi, dolersi.

complaint s. **1.** lamento **2.** reclamo.

complaisant agg. compiacente.

complement s. complemento.

complemental agg. complementare.

complementary agg. complementare.

complete agg. completo.

to **complete** vt. **1.** completare **2.** riempire (*moduli ecc.*).

completely avv. completamente.

completeness s. completezza.

completion s. compimento.

complex agg. **1.** complicato **2.** (*gramm.*) composto. ♦ **complex** s. complesso.

complexion s. carnagione, colorito.

complexity s. complessità.

compliance s. **1.** condiscendenza **2.** servilismo.

compliant agg. **1.** compiacente **2.** servile.

to **complicate** vt. complicare.

complicated agg. complicato.

complication s. complicazione.

complicity s. complicità.

compliment s. complimento: *to pay so. a* —, far un complimento a qu.

to **compliment** vt. complimentare, congratularsi con.

complimentary agg. **1.** complimentoso **2.** di favore: — *tickets*, biglietti di favore.

to **comply** vi. accondiscendere, conformarsi.

component agg. e s. componente.

to **comport** vi. comportarsi.

to **compose** vt. **1.** comporre, costituire **2.** (*mus.*) comporre || *to* — *a quarrel*, comporre una vertenza.

composed agg. **1.** composto **2.** calmo.

composer s. compositore.

composing agg. calmante. ♦ **composing** s. **1.** il comporre **2.** (*tip.*) composizione.

composite agg. composto.

composition s. **1.** composizione **2.** compromesso **3.** concordato, intesa.

compositor s. (*tip.*) compositore.

composure s. posatezza, sangue freddo.

compote *s.* conserva di frutta.
compound **1.** miscela **2.** (*chim.*) composto **3.** (*gramm.*) parola composta.
to **compound** *vt.* e *vi.* **1.** comporre, mescolare **2.** combinare (*ingredienti, elementi ecc.*).
to **comprehend** *vt.* **1.** contenere **2.** capire.
comprehensibility *s.* comprensibilità.
comprehensible *agg.* **1.** comprensibile **2.** delimitato.
comprehension *s.* **1.** comprensione **2.** portata.
comprehensive *agg.* **1.** di vasta portata **2.** comprensivo.
comprehensively *avv.* comprensivamente.
compress *s.* compressa (*di garza*).
to **compress** *vt.* **1.** comprimere **2.** (*fig.*) condensare (*idee ecc.*).
compressibility *s.* compressibilità.
compression *s.* **1.** compressione **2.** (*fig.*) concentrazione.
to **comprise** *vt.* contenere, includere.
compromise *s.* compromesso.
to **compromise** *vt.* compromettere. ♦ to **compromise** *vi.* venire a un compromesso.
compromising *agg.* compromettente.
compulsion *s.* costrizione: *under* —, per costrizione.
compulsive *agg.* coercitivo.
compulsory *agg.* obbligatorio.
compunction *s.* compunzione.
computable *agg.* calcolabile.
computation *s.* calcolo.
to **compute** *vt.* computare, calcolare.
computer *s.* calcolatore.
comrade *s.* camerata, compagno.
comradeship *s.* cameratismo.
to **concatenate** *vt.* concatenare.
concatenation *s.* concatenazione.
concave *agg.* concavo.
to **conceal** *vt.* nascondere.
concealment *s.* **1.** occultamento **2.** nascondiglio.
conceit *s.* vanità, presunzione.
conceited *agg.* presuntuoso, vanitoso.
conceivability *s.* concepibilità.
conceivable *agg.* concepibile.
to **conceive** *vt.* **1.** concepire, generare **2.** immaginare, ideare.
to **concentrate** *vt.* **1.** concentrare

2. convergere. ♦ to **concentrate** *vi.* concentrarsi.
concentration *s.* **1.** concentrazione **2.** concentramento.
concentric *agg.* concentrico.
concept *s.* concetto.
conception *s.* **1.** concezione, concepimento **2.** concetto.
conceptional *agg.* concezionale.
conceptual *agg.* concettuale.
conceptualism *s.* concettualismo.
concern *s.* **1.** interesse, rapporto **2.** affare **3.** sollecitudine **4.** (*comm.*) ditta, azienda.
to **concern** *vt.* concernere, riguardare.
concerned *agg.* **1.** interessato **2.** ansioso, preoccupato || *as far as I am* —, per quanto mi riguarda.
concerning *prep.* riguardo a, circa.
concert *s.* **1.** concerto **2.** accordo.
concerted *agg.* **1.** (*mus.*) concertato **2.** convenuto.
concession *s.* concessione.
concessionary *agg.* e *s.* concessionario.
concettism *s.* concettismo.
conch *s.* conchiglia, mollusco.
conchoid *s.* concoide.
conchoidal *agg.* concoidale.
conciliar *agg.* conciliare.
to **conciliate** *vt.* conciliare.
conciliation *s.* conciliazione.
conciliator *s.* conciliatore, conciliatrice.
conciliatory *agg.* conciliante.
concise *agg.* conciso, succinto.
concision *s.* concisione.
conclave *s.* conclave.
to **conclude** *vt.* terminare, concludere. ♦ to **conclude** *vi.* terminare, concludersi.
conclusion *s.* conclusione.
conclusive *agg.* conclusivo.
to **concoct** *vt.* **1.** mescolare (*di ingredienti*) **2.** preparare, tramare.
concomitance *s.* concomitanza.
concomitant *agg.* concomitante.
concomitantly *avv.* simultaneamente.
concord *s.* **1.** concordia **2.** (*mus.*) accordo **3.** (*gramm.*) concordanza.
concordant *agg.* **1.** concorde **2.** (*mus.*) armonioso.
concordat *s.* concordato.
concourse *s.* concorso, affluenza (*di persone ecc.*).
concrete *agg.* concreto. ♦ **concrete** *s.* calcestruzzo.

concreteness s. concretezza.
concretion s. concrezione.
concubinage s. concubinato.
concubine s. concubina.
concupiscence s. concupiscenza.
to **concur** vi. concorrere, contribuire (di cause, avvenimenti).
concurrence s. **1.** concorso (di circostanze) **2.** cooperazione (di persone) **3.** (geom.) convergenza.
concurrent agg. concorrente, simultaneo.
to **concuss** vt. **1.** urtare **2.** (med.) provocare un trauma **3.** intimidire.
concussion s. **1.** urto **2.** (med.) commozione cerebrale, trauma.
to **condemn** vt. **1.** condannare **2.** biasimare, censurare.
condemnable agg. **1.** condannabile **2.** censurabile.
condemnation s. **1.** condanna **2.** biasimo, censura.
condensability s. condensabilità.
condensable agg. condensabile.
condensate s. (fis.; chim.) condensamento.
condensation s. condensazione.
to **condense** vt. condensare, abbreviare. ♦ to **condense** vi. condensarsi, concentrarsi.
condenser s. condensatore.
to **condescend** vi. accondiscendere.
condescending agg. condiscendente.
condescendingly avv. con condiscendenza.
condescension s. **1.** condiscendenza **2.** affabilità.
condition s. condizione, clausola: on — that, a condizione che.
to **condition** vt. condizionare.
conditional agg. e s. condizionale.
conditionally avv. condizionatamente.
conditioned agg. condizionato: — air, aria condizionata.
conditioning s. **1.** condizionatura (di tessili) **2.** condizionamento.
condolence s. condoglianza.
conduct s. **1.** condotta, comportamento **2.** metodo.
to **conduct** vt. **1.** condurre, guidare, dirigere **2.** (fis.) condurre, trasmettere. ♦ to **conduct** vi. **1.** comportarsi **2.** indicare la via.
conductibility s. conducibilità.
conductivity s. conducibilità.
conductor s. **1.** guida (di persone) **2.** (mus.) direttore **3.** bigliettario.

conduit s. **1.** conduttura **2.** passaggio segreto.
cone s. **1.** cono **2.** pigna.
to **confabulate** vi. confabulare.
confectionary agg. di pasticceria.
confectioner s. pasticciere.
confectionery s. pasticceria.
confederate agg. confederato. ♦ **confederate** s. **1.** confederato **2.** complice.
to **confederate** vt. confederare. ♦ to **confederate** vi. confederarsi.
confederation s. confederazione.
to **confer** vt. conferire, dare. ♦ to **confer** vi. conferire, consultarsi.
conference s. **1.** conferenza **2.** congresso.
to **confess** vt. e vi. confessare, professare.
confessedly avv. apertamente, dichiaratamente.
confession s. confessione, professione: — of faith, professione di fede.
confessional agg. e s. confessionale.
confessionary agg. confessionale.
confessor s. **1.** confessore **2.** chi si confessa.
confetti s. pl. coriandoli.
confidant s. confidente.
to **confide** vt. confidare. ♦ to **confide** vi. confidarsi: to — in so., confidarsi con qu.
confidence s. **1.** fiducia **2.** confidenza **3.** sicurezza in se stessi.
confident agg. fiducioso.
confidential agg. confidenziale, riservato.
confidently avv. con sicurezza, con fiducia.
confiding agg. senza sospetti.
configuration s. configurazione.
to **configure** vt. configurare.
to **confine** vt. relegare, limitare. ♦ to **confine** vi. confinare, essere contiguo.
confinement s. **1.** reclusione **2.** limitazione **3.** puerperio.
to **confirm** vt. **1.** confermare **2.** cresimare.
confirmation s. **1.** conferma **2.** cresima **3.** (pol.; giur.) ratifica.
confirmatory agg. confermativo.
confiscable agg. confiscabile.
to **confiscate** vt. confiscare.
confiscation s. confisca.
conflagration s. conflagrazione.
conflict s. conflitto, contrasto.

confluence s. **1.** confluenza **2.** incrocio (di strade ecc.).

confluent agg. confluente.

to **conform** vt. conformare. ♦ to **conform** vi. conformarsi, ottemperare.

conformation s. **1.** conformazione **2.** adattamento.

conformist s. conformista.

conformity s. **1.** conformità **2.** conformismo.

to **confound** vt. **1.** confondere, disorientare **2.** sconvolgere.

confounded agg. attonito, confuso.

confraternity s. confraternita.

to **confront** vt. **1.** affrontare **2.** trovarsi di fronte a.

confrontation s. confronto.

Confucianism s. confucianesimo.

to **confuse** vt. **1.** disorientare, sconcertare **2.** confondere.

confusedly avv. confusamente.

confusion s. **1.** disordine, confusione **2.** turbamento.

confutation s. confutazione.

to **confute** vt. confutare.

to **congeal** vt. ghiacciare. ♦ to **congeal** vi. gelarsi.

congenial agg. **1.** congeniale, affine **2.** amabile, simpatico.

congeniality s. **1.** affinità **2.** carattere simpatico.

congenially avv. amabilmente.

congenital agg. congenito.

conger s. anguilla marina.

congeries s. congerie.

to **congest** vt. congestionare. ♦ to **congest** vi. congestionarsi.

congested agg. congestionato.

congestion s. congestione.

to **conglobate** vt. conglobare. ♦ to **conglobate** vi. conglobarsi.

conglobation s. conglobazione.

conglomerate agg. e s. conglomerato.

to **conglomerate** vt. conglomerare. ♦ to **conglomerate** vi. conglomerarsi.

conglomeration s. conglomerazione.

to **congratulate** vt. congratulare, congratularsi con.

congratulation s. congratulazione.

congratulatory agg. congratulatorio.

to **congregate** vt. adunare. ♦ to **congregate** vi. adunarsi.

congregation s. **1.** unione, adunata, assemblea **2.** (relig.) congregazione.

congregational agg. della congregazione.

congress s. congresso, riunione.

congressional agg. di congresso.

congruence s. congruenza.

congruent agg. congruente, conforme.

congruity s. conformità.

congruous agg. congruente, conforme.

conic(al) agg. conico.

conifer s. conifera.

coniferous agg. conifero.

conjecture s. congettura.

to **conjecture** vt. e vi. congetturare, ipotizzare.

conjointly avv. congiuntamente.

conjugal agg. coniugale.

conjugate agg. congiunto. ♦ **conjugate** s. **1.** (mat.) coniugato **2.** (biol.) fusione.

to **conjugate** vt. coniugare. ♦ to **conjugate** vi. coniugarsi.

conjugation s. coniugazione.

conjunction s. congiunzione.

conjunctiva s. (anat.) congiuntiva.

conjunctive agg. **1.** (biol.) connettivo **2.** (gramm.) congiuntivo. ♦ **conjunctive** s. congiuntivo.

conjunctivitis s. congiuntivite.

conjuncture s. congiuntura, circostanza.

conjuration s. **1.** incantesimo **2.** evocazione solenne.

to **conjure** vt. **1.** scongiurare **2.** evocare. ♦ to **conjure** vi. fare giochi di prestigio.

conjurer s. prestigiatore.

conjuring s. prestidigitazione.

connatural agg. connaturale.

to **connect** vt. **1.** connettere, collegare, unire **2.** associare (mentalmente). ♦ to **connect** vi. **1.** avere relazioni, collegarsi **2.** (ferr.) far coincidenza.

connecting agg. che connette. ♦ **connecting** s. (elettr.) collegamento.

connection s. **1.** collegamento, connessione **2.** relazione, parentela **3.** coincidenza **4.** (comm.) clientela.

connective agg. connettivo.

conning-tower s. (mar.) torretta di comando.

connivance s. connivenza.

to **connive** vi. essere connivente.

connotation s. significato implicito.

to **connote** vt. implicare, significare.

to **conquer** *vt.* conquistare.
conqueror *s.* conquistatore.
conquest *s.* conquista.
consanguine *agg.* consanguineo.
consanguinity *s.* consanguineità.
conscience *s.* coscienza: *for —' sake*, per scrupolo di coscienza; *to be — -stricken*, sentirsi rimordere la coscienza.
conscienceless *agg.* senza scrupoli.
conscientious *agg.* scrupoloso || — *objector*, obiettore di coscienza.
conscientiously *avv.* coscienziosamente.
conscious *agg.* consapevole, conscio.
consciousness *s.* coscienza, consapevolezza.
conscript *agg.* e *s.* coscritto.
conscription *s.* coscrizione.
to **consecrate** *vt.* consacrare, dedicare.
consecration *s.* consacrazione, dedizione.
consecutive *agg.* consecutivo.
consecutively *avv.* consecutivamente.
consensual *agg.* consensuale.
consensus *s.* consenso, accordo || — *of opinion*, unanimità.
consent *s.* consenso, accordo || *by mutual —*, amichevolmente.
to **consent** *vi.* acconsentire.
consequence *s.* 1. conseguenza, effetto 2. importanza.
consequent *agg.* conseguente, risultante.
consequential *agg.* consequenziale.
consequently *avv.* di conseguenza.
conservatism *s.* conservatorismo.
conservative *agg.* conservativo. ♦ **Conservative** *s.* conservatore.
conservator *s.* 1. conservatore 2. sovrintendente (*di museo ecc.*).
conserve *s.* conserva di frutta.
to **consider** *vt.* considerare, riflettere, stimare.
considerable *agg.* considerevole, importante.
considerate *agg.* rispettoso, pieno di riguardi.
consideration *s.* 1. considerazione 2. rimunerazione 3. (*comm.*) provvigione.
considering *prep.* tenuto conto di, considerando.
to **consign** *vt.* 1. (*comm.*) inviare, consegnare 2. depositare (*soldi in banca*).

consignation *s.* 1. (*comm.*) pagamento 2. consegna (*di merce*).
consignee *s.* consegnatario.
consigner *s.* mittente.
consignment *s.* 1. invio, spedizione 2. consegna, deposito.
to **consist** *vi.* consistere, essere composto.
consistence, consistency *s.* 1. consistenza, compattezza 2. costanza.
consistent *agg.* coerente, logico.
consistently *avv.* coerentemente.
consistory *s.* concistoro.
consolation *s.* consolazione.
consolatory *agg.* consolante.
to **console** *vt.* consolare.
to **consolidate** *vt.* consolidare. ♦ to **consolidate** *vi.* consolidarsi.
consolidation *s.* consolidazione.
consoling *agg.* consolante.
consonance *s.* consonanza, accordo.
consonant *agg.* consono. ♦ **consonant** *s.* consonante.
consort *s.* 1. consorte 2. compagno, collega.
to **consort** *vi.* associarsi, unirsi. ♦ to **consort** *vt.* associare, unire.
conspicuous *agg.* cospicuo, notevole.
conspicuousness *s.* cospicuità.
conspiracy *s.* congiura.
conspirator *s.* cospiratore.
to **conspire** *vt.* e *vi.* cospirare.
constable *s.* 1. agente di polizia 2. conestabile.
constabulary *s.* corpo della polizia.
constancy *s.* costanza.
constant *agg.* costante, fedele. ♦ **constant** *s.* (*mat.*) costante.
constantly *agg.* costantemente.
constellation *s.* costellazione.
consternation *s.* costernazione.
constipation *s.* stitichezza.
constituency *s.* 1. gli elettori (*pl.*) 2. circoscrizione elettorale.
constituent *agg.* costituente. ♦ **constituent** *s.* 1. elemento costitutivo 2. (*pol.*) elettore.
to **constitute** *vt.* 1. costituire 2. eleggere.
constitution *s.* 1. costituzione, statuto 2. costituzione, composizione (*del corpo, dell'aria ecc.*).
constitutional *agg.* costituzionale.
constitutionalism *s.* costituzionalismo.
constitutionality *s.* costituzionalità.

constitutive *agg.* costitutivo.
to constrain *vt.* costringere.
constrained *agg.* costretto, forzato.
constraint *s.* **1.** costrizione **2.** imbarazzo.
to constrict *vt.* costringere.
constriction *s.* costrizione.
to construct *vt.* costruire (*anche fig.*).
construction *s.* **1.** costruzione **2.** (*giur.*) interpretazione.
constructive *agg.* costruttivo.
to construe *vt.* **1.** costruire grammaticalmente **2.** interpretare. ♦ **to construe** *vi.* fare l'analisi grammaticale.
consuetudinary *agg.* consuetudinario: — *law*, diritto consuetudinario.
consul *s.* console.
consular *agg.* consolare.
consulate *s.* consolato.
to consult *vt.* consultare. ♦ **to consult** *vi.* consultarsi.
consultation *s.* **1.** consultazione **2.** consulto.
consultative *agg.* consultativo.
consulting *agg.* consulente || — -*room*, ambulatorio.
to consume *vt.* consumare. ♦ **to consume** *vi.* consumarsi.
consumer *s.* consumatore, utente.
consummate *agg.* consumato, perfetto.
consumption *s.* **1.** consumo **2.** sciupio **3.** distruzione **4.** tubercolosi.
consumptive *s.* tisico, tubercolotico.
contact *s.* contatto, relazione.
to contact *vt.* e *vi.* mettere, mettersi in contatto con, prender contatto.
contagion *s.* contagio.
contagious *agg.* contagioso.
to contain *vt.* **1.** contenere, comprendere **2.** reprimere, frenare (*i sentimenti*).
contained *agg.* frenato, contenuto (*di comportamento*).
container *s.* recipiente.
contamination *s.* contaminazione.
to contemplate *vt.* e *vi.* contemplare, meditare.
contemplation *s.* contemplazione.
contemplative *agg.* contemplativo.
contemplator *s.* contemplatore.
contemporaneousness *s.* contemporaneità.
contemporary *agg.* e *s.* contemporaneo.

contempt *s.* disprezzo || — *of Court* (*giur.*), vilipendio della Corte.
contemptibility *s.* spregevolezza.
contemptible *agg.* spregevole.
contemptuous *agg.* sprezzante.
contemptuously *avv.* sprezzantemente.
to contend *vi.* **1.** contendere. ♦ **to contend** *vt.* sostenere, affermare.
contending *agg.* contendente, rivale.
content *s.* **1.** volume, capacità **2.** contenuto. ♦ **contents** *s. pl.* indice (*di libro*) (*sing.*). ♦ **content** *agg.* contento, soddisfatto.
to content *vt.* contentare, soddisfare.
contented *agg.* contento, pago.
contention *s.* **1.** contesa **2.** emulazione **3.** controversia.
contentious *agg.* litigioso.
contest *s.* contestazione, contesa.
to contest *vt.* contestare, contendere. ♦ **to contest** *vi.* competere, rivaleggiare.
context *s.* contesto.
contiguity *s.* contiguità.
continence *s.* continenza.
continent *agg.* continente. ♦ **continent** *s.* (*geogr.*) continente.
continental *agg.* e *s.* continentale.
contingency *s.* contingenza, caso.
contingent *agg.* eventuale, imprevisto.
continual *agg.* continuo.
continuation *s.* continuazione, seguito.
to continue *vt.* e *vi.* continuare, far continuare.
continuity *s.* **1.** continuità **2.** (*cine*) sceneggiatura.
continuous *agg.* continuo.
to contort *vt.* contorcere.
contortion *s.* contorsione.
contortionist *s.* contorsionista.
contour *s.* contorno, profilo.
contraband *s.* contrabbando.
contraceptive *s.* anticoncezionale.
contract *s.* contratto, patto.
to contract *vt.* **1.** contrarre (*matrimonio, amicizia ecc.*) **2.** (*comm.*) contrattare **3.** contrarre, restringere. ♦ **to contract** *vi.* contrarsi, restringersi.
contractile *agg.* contrattile.
contraction *s.* accorciamento.
contractor *s.* **1.** contraente **2.** appaltatore **3.** imprenditore.

contractual *agg.* contrattuale.
to contradict *vt.* contraddire.
contradiction *s.* contraddizione.
contradictory *agg.* contraddittorio.
to contraindicate *vt.* controindicare.
contraindication *s.* controindicazione.
contraposition *s.* opposizione, antitesi.
contrarily *avv.* contrariamente.
contrary *agg.* contrario, opposto.
◆ **contrary** *s.* il contrario: *on the —*, al contrario. ◆ **contrary** *avv.* contrariamente, all'opposto.
contrast *s.* contrasto, opposizione.
to contrast *vt.* e *vi.* far contrasto, mettere in contrasto.
to contravene *vt.* contravvenire.
to contribute *vt.* contribuire. ◆ **to contribute** *vi.* collaborare (*a un giornale*).
contribution *s.* **1.** contributo **2.** (*comm.*) apporto di capitale **3.** collaborazione (*a un giornale*).
contributor *s.* **1.** contributore **2.** collaboratore (*di giornale ecc.*).
contrite *agg.* contrito.
contrition *s.* contrizione.
contrivance *s.* **1.** espediente **2.** apparato, congegno **3.** invenzione.
to contrive *vt.* escogitare. ◆ **to contrive** *vi.* adoperarsi, riuscire.
control *s.* autorità, influenza, dominio, controllo || — *device* (*mecc.*), dispositivo di controllo; — *room*, camera di manovra; *birth-* —, limitazione delle nascite; *self-* —, autocontrollo. ◆ **controls** *s. pl.* (*mecc.*) comandi.
to control *vt.* controllare, dirigere.
controller *s.* controllore, sovrintendente.
controversial *agg.* controverso.
controversy *s.* controversia, polemica.
controvertible *agg.* controvertibile.
contumacious *agg.* **1.** insubordinato **2.** contumace.
contumacy *s.* **1.** ribellione **2.** contumacia.
contumely *s.* onta, contumelia.
contusion *s.* contusione.
contusive *agg.* contundente.
convalescence *s.* convalescenza.
convalescent *agg.* e *s.* convalescente.
to convene *vt.* **1.** convocare, riunire **2.** (*giur.*) citare. ◆ *to* **convene**

vi. riunirsi, incontrarsi.
convenience *s.* **1.** comodo, vantaggio. ◆ **conveniences** *s. pl.* comodità.
convenient *agg.* conveniente, comodo, adatto.
convent *s.* convento.
conventicle *s.* conventicola.
convention *s.* **1.** patto, convenzione **2.** assemblea **3.** regola (*di gioco*). ◆ **conventions** *s. pl.* convenzioni (*sociali*).
conventional *agg.* convenzionale, comune.
conventionality *s.* convenzionalità.
conventual *agg.* e *s.* conventuale.
to converge *vi.* convergere. ◆ **to converge** *vt.* far convergere.
convergence *s.* convergenza.
convergent *agg.* convergente.
conversation *s.* conversazione.
converse *agg.* e *s.* inverso, contrario.
conversely *avv.* viceversa.
conversion *s.* conversione, trasformazione.
convert *s.* convertito.
to convert *vt.* **1.** convertire **2.** trasformare.
converter *s.* **1.** convertitore **2.** (*elettr.; mecc.*) convertitore, trasformatore.
convertible *agg.* convertibile || — *car*, automobile decappottabile.
convex *agg.* convesso.
convexity *s.* convessità.
to convey *vt.* **1.** trasportare, convogliare **2.** trasmettere (*suoni, odori ecc.*) **3.** dare l'idea, suggerire.
conveyable *agg.* trasportabile, trasmissibile.
conveyance *s.* **1.** trasporto **2.** trasmissione **3.** convogliamento.
conveyancer *s.* notaio.
conveyer *s.* **1.** trasportatore **2.** trasmettitore **3.** convogliatore.
convict *s.* condannato, forzato.
to convict *vt.* condannare, dichiarare colpevole.
conviction *s.* **1.** (*giur.*) verdetto di colpevolezza, condanna **2.** convinzione.
to convince *vt.* convincere.
convincing *agg.* convincente.
convincingly *avv.* in modo convincente.
convivial *agg.* allegro, conviviale, gioviale.
conviviality *s.* giovialità.

convivially *avv.* convivialmente.

to **convocate** *vt.* convocare.

convocation *s.* convocazione.

convolution *s.* circonvoluzione.

convoy *s.* **1.** (*mar.; mil.*) convoglio **2.** scorta.

to **convoy** *vt.* **1.** (*mar.; mil.*) convogliare **2.** scortare.

convulsion *s.* **1.** convulsione **2.** rivolgimento.

convulsive *agg.* convulso.

to **coo** *vi.* tubare.

cook *s.* cuoco, cuoca: *head* —, capocuoco.

to **cook** *vt.* e *vi.* cucinare, cuocere.

cookery *s.* arte culinaria, cucina.

cooking *s.* **1.** cottura **2.** arte culinaria, cucina.

cool *agg.* **1.** fresco **2.** leggero (*di abito*) **3.** calmo **4.** freddo, senza entusiasmo **5.** sfacciato.

to **cool** *vt.* **1.** rinfrescare **2.** calmare. ♦ to **cool** *vi.* **1.** rinfrescarsi **2.** calmarsi.

cooling *agg.* rinfrescante. ♦ **cooling** *s.* abbassamento di temperatura.

coolness *s.* **1.** frescura **2.** freddezza, calma, sangue freddo.

coop *s.* stia.

to **coop** *vt.* mettere nella stia.

cooper *s.* bottaio.

to **co-operate** *vi.* cooperare.

co-operation *s.* cooperazione.

co-operative *agg.* cooperativo.

co-operator *s.* cooperatore.

to **co-opt** *vt.* eleggere membro (*di comitato*).

co-ordinate *agg.* **1.** dello stesso rango **2.** coordinato. ♦ **co-ordinate** *s.* (*mat.*) coordinata.

to **co-ordinate** *vt.* coordinare.

co-ordination *s.* coordinazione.

co-ordinative *agg.* coordinativo.

co-owner *s.* comproprietario.

co-ownership *s.* comproprietà.

cop[1] *s.* cima (*di collina ecc.*).

cop[2] *s.* (*gergo*) poliziotto.

copartnership *s.* società, associazione.

to **cope** *vi.* fronteggiare, tener testa.

co-pilot *s.* (*aer.*) secondo pilota.

copper *s.* **1.** rame **2.** moneta di rame.

to **copper** *vt.* rivestire di rame.

copperplate *s.* **1.** lastra di rame (*per incisione*) **2.** incisione in rame.

Coptic *agg.* copto.

copulation *s.* copulazione.

copulative *agg.* copulativo.

copy *s.* **1.** copia, trascrizione **2.** riproduzione **3.** esemplare || —-*book*, quaderno; — -*reader*, revisore di stampa; *fair* —, bella copia; *rough* —, brutta copia.

to **copy** *vt.* **1.** copiare **2.** imitare.

copyist *s.* copista.

copyright *s.* diritto d'autore, proprietà letteraria.

coquetry *s.* civetteria.

coral *s.* corallo.

cord *s.* corda, spago || *spinal* —, midollo spinale.

cordage *s.* cordame.

cordial *agg.* cordiale. ♦ **cordial** *s.* (*bevanda*) cordiale.

cordiality *s.* cordialità.

cordially *avv.* cordialmente.

cordon *s.* cordone.

core *s.* **1.** torsolo **2.** centro, cuore.

co-respondent *s.* (*giur.*) correo (*in adulterio*).

coriaceous *agg.* coriaceo.

cork *s.* **1.** sughero **2.** tappo, turacciolo || — *jacket*, cintura di salvataggio.

corkscrew *s.* cavaturaccioli.

cormorant *s.* cormorano.

corn[1] *s.* **1.** grano **2.** cereale || *ear of* —, spiga di grano; — -*cob*, pannocchia.

corn[2] *s.* callo, durone.

cornea *s.* cornea.

corner *s.* **1.** angolo **2.** (*comm.*) accaparramento (*di merci*).

to **corner** *vt.* **1.** mettere, spingere in un angolo **2.** (*fig.*) mettere con le spalle al muro. ♦ to **corner** *vi.* formare un angolo.

cornet *s.* cornetta.

cornice *s.* cornicione.

corolla *s.* corolla.

corollary *s.* corollario.

coronary *agg.* coronario.

coronation *s.* incoronazione.

coroner *s.* magistrato inquirente.

corporal[1] *agg.* corporale.

corporal[2] *s.* caporale.

corporation *s.* **1.** corporazione **2.** azienda municipale.

corporative *agg.* corporativo: — *system*, sistema corporativo.

corporeal *agg.* corporeo.

corpse *s.* cadavere.

corpulent *agg.* corpulento.

corpuscle *s.* corpuscolo.

corral *s.* recinto (*per bestiame*).

correct *agg.* corretto.
to correct *vt.* correggere.
correction *s.* correzione, rettifica.
corrective *agg.* e *s.* correttivo.
correctness *s.* correttezza.
corrector *s.* correttore: — *of the press (tip.)*, correttore di bozze.
to correlate *vt.* essere, mettere in correlazione. ♦ **to correlate** *vi.* essere in correlazione.
correlation *s.* correlazione.
correlative *agg.* correlativo.
to correspond *vi.* 1. corrispondere, essere in rapporti epistolari 2. rispondere a *(esigenze ecc.)* 3. equivalere.
correspondence 1. corrispondenza 2. accordo, rispondenza.
correspondent *s.* corrispondente.
corridor *s.* corridoio.
corroborant *agg.* corroborante.
corroboration *s.* conferma, convalida.
to corrode *vt.* corrodere. ♦ **to corrode** *vi.* corrodersi.
corrosion *s.* corrosione.
corrosive *agg.* e *s.* corrosivo.
to corrugate *vt.* corrugare.
corrugation *s.* corrugamento.
corrupt *agg.* corrotto, guasto, depravato.
to corrupt *vt.* corrompere, alterare. ♦ **to corrupt** *vi.* corrompersi, alterarsi.
corruption *s.* corruzione.
corsair *s.* corsaro.
corset *s.* corsetto.
cortisone *s.* cortisone.
corvette *s.* corvetta.
corvine *agg.* corvino.
coryphaeus *s. (pl.* -aei) corifeo.
cosecant *s.* cosecante.
cosily *avv.* comodamente.
cosine *s.* coseno.
cosmetic *agg.* e *s.* cosmetico.
cosmic(al) *agg.* cosmico.
cosmogony *s.* cosmogonia.
cosmographer *s.* cosmografo.
cosmography *s.* cosmografia.
cosmology *s.* cosmologia.
cosmopolitan *agg.* e *s.* cosmopolita.
cosmopolitanism *s.* cosmopolitismo.
cosmopolite *agg.* e *s.* cosmopolita.
cosmopolitism *s.* cosmopolitismo.
cosmos *s.* cosmo.
Cossack *s.* cosacco.
cost *s.* costo, prezzo || — *of living*, carovita; *at all costs*, ad ogni costo;

extra —, spesa supplementare.
to cost (cost, cost) *vt.* e *vi.* costare.
costal *agg.* costale.
coster, costermonger *s.* venditore ambulante *(di frutta, verdura ecc.)*.
costly *agg.* costoso.
costume *s.* 1. costume 2. abito.
cosy *agg.* comodo, intimo.
cot[1] *s.* capanna.
cot[2] 1. *(mar.)* cuccetta 2. culla.
cotangent *s.* cotangente.
cotenant *s.* ;coaffittuario.
cothurnus *s. (pl.*-ni) coturno.
cottage *s.* villino.
cotton *s.* cotone || — *-mill*, cotonificio; — *-spinner*, operaio di filatura; — *-wool*, ovatta; — *-waste*, cascame‚
couch *s.* divano.
cough *s.* tosse.
to cough *vt.* e *vi.* tossire.
could v. *can.*
council *s.* 1. consiglio *(adunanza di persone)* 2. *(eccl.)* concilio.
councillor *s.* consigliere.
counsel *s.* 1. consultazione 2. consiglio 3. legale.
to counsel *vt.* e *vi.* consigliare.
counsellor *s.* 1. consigliere 2. legale.
count[1] *s.* 1. conto, calcolo 2. *(pol.)* scrutinio 3. *(giur.)* capo d'accusa.
count[2] *s.* conte.
to count *vt.* e *vi.* 1. contare, calcolare 2. considerare, avere importanza.
countable *agg.* numerabile.
countenance *s.* espressione del volto, aria.
counter[1] *s.* calcolatore, contatore || *revolution* —, contagiri.
counter[2] *s.* volta di poppa.
counter[3] *s.* 1. banco, cassa *(di negozio)* 2. sportello 3. gettone *(da gioco)*.
counter[4] *agg.* contrario, opposto || — *clockwise*, in senso antiorario; — *poison*, antidoto. ♦ **counter** *avv.* in senso ontrario.
to counteract *vt.* agir contro, contrapporsi a.
counter-attack *s.* contrattacco.
to counter-attack *vt.* e *vi.* contrattaccare.
counterbalance *s.* contrappeso.
to counterbalance *vt.* controbilanciare.
counterblow *s.* contraccolpo.

countercharge s. controaccusa.

counterfeit agg. contraffatto, simulato. ♦ **counterfeit** s. contraffazione, simulazione.

counterfeiter s. **1.** falsario **2.** simulatore.

counterfoil s. matrice.

countermand s. revoca, contrordine.

counterpane s. copriletto.

counterpart s. **1.** sostituto **2.** duplicato, sosia **3.** complemento.

counterpoint s. contrappunto.

countershaft s. contralbero.

countersign s. contrassegno.

counterweight s. contrappeso.

countess s. contessa.

countless agg. innumerevole.

countrified agg. campagnolo, rurale.

country s. **1.** paese, regione **2.** campagna **3.** patria **4.** nazione.

countryman s. **1.** compaesano, compatriota **2.** contadino.

countryside s. campagna.

countrywoman s. **1.** compaesana, compatriota **2.** contadina.

county s. contea, provincia.

coup s. **1.** colpo **2.** (fig.) impressione.

couple s. coppia, paio.

to **couple** vt. accoppiare. ♦ to **couple** vi. accoppiarsi.

coupling s. accoppiamento.

coupon s. cedola, tagliando.

courage s. coraggio, ardire.

courageous agg. coraggioso.

course s. **1.** corso (del tempo), corso (di lezioni, conferenze) **2.** serie **3.** portata (dei pasti) **4.** (sport) circuito || of —, naturalmente; in due — a tempo debito.

court s. **1.** corte, cortile **2.** (giur.) corte || — of justice, tribunale.

to **court** vt. corteggiare.

courtier s. cortigiano.

courting s. corteggiamento.

courtyard s. cortile.

courtship s. corteggiamento.

cousin s. cugino, cugina.

cove s. **1.** insenatura **2.** grotta.

covenant s. convenzione, patto.

cover s. **1.** coperta, copertura **2.** calotta **3.** copertina (di libro) **4.** riparo, ricovero **5.** coperto (a tavola).

to **cover** vt. **1.** coprire, ricoprire **2.** proteggere **3.** percorrere **4.** nascondere **5.** comprendere, includere.

covering s. copertura, rivestimento.

coverlet s. copriletto.

covert s. ricovero, rifugio.

covertly avv. nascostamente.

to **covet** vt. agognare.

covetousness s. cupidigia.

cow s. mucca, vacca || — bell, campanaccio; — -grass, trifoglio di campo; — -shed, stalla.

coward s. codardo, vile.

cowardice s. codardia, viltà.

cowardly agg. codardo. ♦ **cowardly** avv. vilmente.

cowboy s. bovaro.

cowherd s. vaccaro.

cowl s. **1.** cappuccio, tonaca (di frate) **2.** (auto; aer.) cofano del motore.

coxswain s. timoniere.

coy agg. timido, riservato.

crab s. granchio.

crabbed agg. sgarbato, bisbetico.

crack s. **1.** schianto, detonazione, schiocco **2.** incrinatura, rottura.

to **crack 1.** vt. schiantare, rompere, incrinare **2.** schioccare. ♦ to **crack** vi. **1.** screpolarsi, spezzarsi **2.** scricchiolare.

cracked agg. **1.** incrinato **2.** fesso (di voce).

cracker s. petardo || nut-crackers, schiaccianoci; — of jokes, burlone.

crackle s. **1.** crepitio **2.** screpolatura, incrinatura.

to **crackle** vi. scoppiettare, scricchiolare. ♦ to **crackle** vt. screpolare.

crackling s. scoppiettio.

cradle s. culla (anche fig.).

craft s. **1.** abilità, mestiere, professione **2.** astuzia, inganno.

craftsman s. artigiano.

craftsmanship s. artigianato.

crafty agg. astuto, abile.

crag s. rupe, cresta.

to **cram** vt. riempire, stipare, rimpinzare. ♦ to **cram** vi. rimpinzarsi.

cramp s. crampo.

to **cramp** vt. (fig.) bloccare, paralizzare.

crane s. gru (anche mecc.).

to **crane** vt. e vi. **1.** sollevare o abbassare (mediante una gru) **2.** allungare (il collo).

cranium s. cranio.

crank[1] s. manovella, manubrio.

crank[2] agg. **1.** piegato **2.** disinnestato.

to **crank** vt. e vi. **1.** piegare a gomito **2.** mettere in moto (con manovella).

cranking s. avviamento (di motore).

crash s. **1.** strepito, fracasso **2.** caduta **3.** scontro, collisione **4.** rovina (anche morale).

to **crash** vt. e vi. **1.** abbattere, precipitare, crollare con grande rumore **2.** scontrare, scontrarsi.

crate s. cassa da imballaggio.

crater s. cratere.

to **crawl** vi. **1.** strisciare, andar carponi **2.** brulicare **3.** avere la pelle d'oca.

crawl s. **1.** strisciamento **2.** (nuoto) « crawl ».

crayfish s. gambero (d'acqua dolce).

craze s. mania, smania.

craziness s. pazzia, follia.

crazy agg. **1.** folle **2.** maniaco, entusiasta.

to **creak** vi. cigolare, stridere.

cream s. **1.** panna, crema **2.** ogni sostanza densa e untuosa.

creamery s. caseificio.

creamy agg. cremoso.

crease s. piega, grinza.

to **crease** vt. fare pieghe, sgualcire. ♦ to **crease** vi. sgualcirsi.

to **create** vt. **1.** creare, produrre, suscitare **2.** nominare.

creation s. **1.** creazione **2.** universo, natura, il creato.

creative agg. creativo.

creator s. creatore.

creature s. **1.** essere vivente **2.** creatura (anche fig.), favorito.

credence s. credenza, fede.

credentials s. pl. credenziali.

credibility s. credibilità.

credible agg. credibile.

credit s. **1.** fiducia **2.** credito, reputazione, autorità **3.** (comm.) fido, credito.

to **credit** vt. **1.** prestar fede **2.** attribuire **3.** (comm.) accreditare

creditor s. creditore.

credulity s. credulità.

credulous agg. credulo.

creed s. credo, credenza religiosa.

creek s. **1.** insenatura **2.** (amer.) torrente.

to **creep (crept, crept)** vi. **1.** strisciare, avanzare lentamente **2.** arrampicarsi (di piante) || to — along, avanzare strisciando; to — away, allontanarsi strisciando.

creeper s. **1.** rettile, verme **2.** persona strisciante **3.** pianta rampicante.

creepy agg. **1.** strisciante **2.** che dà i brividi.

to **cremate** vt. cremare.

cremation s. cremazione.

crematory s. crematoio.

creole agg. e s. creolo.

crept V. to creep.

crepuscular agg. crepuscolare.

crescent agg. **1.** crescente **2.** a mezzaluna. ♦ **crescent** s. **1.** luna crescente **2.** mezzaluna (emblema turco) **3.** strada a semicerchio.

cress s. crescione.

crest s. **1.** cresta **2.** ciuffo, pennacchio **3.** criniera.

to **crest** vt. ornare di pennacchio. ♦ to **crest** vi. incresparsi (di onde).

crevasse s. crepaccio.

crevice s. fessura.

crew[1] s. equipaggio, ciurma.

crew[2] V. to crow.

crib s. **1.** greppia **2.** presepio **3.** stalla, capanna.

crick s. crampo || a — in the neck, torcicollo.

cricket s. grillo.

crime s. delitto, crimine.

criminal agg. e s. criminale.

criminalist s. penalista.

criminality s. criminalità.

criminology s. criminologia.

crimson s. cremisi.

to **cringe** vi. (fig.) farsi piccolo, umiliarsi.

cripple agg. e s. storpio, zoppo.

to **cripple** vt. storpiare. ♦ to **cripple** vi. essere zoppo.

crisis s. crisi.

crisp agg. **1.** croccante **2.** crespo **3.** tonificante. ♦ **crisp** s. patatina fritta, croccante.

criss-cross agg. incrociato.

critic s. critico.

critical agg. critico.

criticism s. critica.

to **criticize** vt. criticare.

critique s. critica, recensione.

croak s. gracidamento.

to **croak** vt. e vi. **1.** gracidare **2.** (fig.) brontolare.

Croatian agg. e s. croato.

crochet s. lavoro all'uncinetto || — -book (o — -pin), uncinetto.

crock[1] s. coccio, vaso di terracotta.

crock[2] s. **1.** ronzino **2.** persona vecchia e malandata.

crock[3] s. fuliggine, sudiciume.

crockery s. terraglia.

crocodile s. coccodrillo.

croft s. piccolo podere, campicello.

crook s. **1.** gancio, uncino **2.** curva, flessione **3.** (gergo) truffatore.

crookback s. gobba.

crooked agg. **1.** curvo, storto, deforme **2.** (fig.) perverso.

crookedly avv. **1.** tortuosamente **2.** indirettamente **3.** perversamente.

crop s. **1.** raccolto, messe **2.** gozzo (di uccello) **3.** (fig.) gruppo **4.** rapata (di capelli).

to **crop** vt. **1.** mietere **2.** tosare.

cropper[1] s. mietitore.

cropper[2] s. (fam.) capitombolo.

cross agg. **1.** obliquo, trasversale **2.** adirato || — -bar, traversa; — -road, incrocio. ♦ **cross** s. **1.** croce **2.** tribolazione, pena.

to **cross** vt. e vi. **1.** fare il segno della croce **2.** attraversare **3.** incrociare **4.** cancellare || to — one's legs, accavallare le gambe.

crossbeam s. trave maestra.

crossbelt s. cartucciera a tracolla.

crossbow s. balestra.

crossbreed s. ibrido, incrocio.

cross-country agg. campestre.

cross-examination s. controinterrogatorio.

to **cross-examine** vt. controinterrogare.

cross-hatch s. tratteggio.

crossing s. **1.** passaggio, traversata **2.** incrocio || level —, passaggio a livello.

crossly avv. di malumore.

crosswise avv. **1.** di traverso **2.** a forma di croce.

crossword s. parole incrociate (pl.) || — puzzle, cruciverba.

crouch s. l'accovacciarsi.

to **crouch** vi. accovacciarsi, rannicchiarsi.

crow[1] s. corvo, cornacchia || a white —, una mosca bianca; to eat (v. irr.) a —, inghiottire un rospo.

crow[2] s. canto del gallo.

to **crow** (**crew, crowed**) vi. cantare (del gallo).

crowd s. folla, massa, moltitudine.

to **crowd** vt. affollare. ♦ to **crowd** vi. affollarsi, accalcarsi || to — together, stringere insieme.

crown[1] s. **1.** corona **2.** cocuzzolo **3.** coronamento, successo **4.** (moneta) corona: half a —, mezza corona.

to **crown** vt. **1.** incoronare **2.** coronare, ricompensare.

crowning s. **1.** incoronazione **2.** coronamento.

crucial agg. cruciale.

crucible s. **1.** crogiuolo **2.** (fig.) dura prova.

crucifix s. crocifisso.

crucifixion s. crocifissione.

to **crucify** vt. crocifiggere.

crude agg. grezzo, rozzo, primitivo.

crudity s. asprezza.

cruel agg. crudele.

cruelty s. crudeltà.

cruet s. ampolla.

cruise s. crociera: to go on a —, fare una crociera.

cruiser s. incrociatore.

cruising s. crociera.

crumb s. **1.** briciola **2.** mollica.

to **crumb** vt. **1.** sbriciolare **2.** impanare.

to **crumble** vt. sbriciolare. ♦ to **crumble** vi. sbriciolarsi.

crumbly agg. friabile.

to **crumple** vt. spiegazzare. ♦ to **crumple** vi. spiegazzarsi.

to **crunch** vt. e vi. sgranocchiare rumorosamente.

crusade s. crociata.

crusader s. crociato.

crush s. **1.** folla, calca **2.** frantumazione **3.** (gergo) cotta.

to **crush** vt. **1.** frantumare, torchiare **2.** (fig.) annientare, sconfiggere. ♦ to **crush** vi. accalcarsi, affollarsi.

crushing agg. schiacciante (anche fig.).

crust s. **1.** crosta **2.** incrostazione.

Crustacea s. pl. crostacei.

crutch s. **1.** gruccia, stampella **2.** forcella (di ramo).

cry s. grido, lamento, pianto || within —, a portata di voce.

to **cry** vt. e vi. **1.** gridare **2.** piangere || to — out, alzare la voce, protestare.

crypt s. cripta.

cryptogam s. crittogama.

cryptogram s. crittogramma.

cryptography s. crittografia.

crystal agg. cristallino. ♦ **crystal** s. cristallo || — work, cristalleria.

crystalline agg. cristallino (anche fig.).

crystallization s. cristallizzazione.

to **crystallize** vt. cristallizzare. ♦ to **crystallize** vi. cristallizzarsi.

crystallography *s.* cristallografia.
cub *s.* **1.** volpacchiotto **2.** (*fam.*) ragazzaccio.
cubage *s.* cubatura.
Cuban *agg.* e *s.* cubano.
cubature *s.* cubatura.
cube *s.* cubo || — *root*, radice cubica.
cubic *agg.* cubico.
cubism *s.* cubismo.
cubit *s.* cubito.
cuckold *s.* becco, cornuto.
to cuckold *vt.* tradire (*il marito*).
cuckoo *s.* cuculo.
cucumber *s.* cetriolo.
cudgel *s.* randello.
to cudgel *vt.* randellare.
cuff *s.* polsino (*di camicia*).
cuirass *s.* corazza.
cuirassier *s.* corazziere.
culinary *agg.* culinario.
to cull *vt.* scegliere.
culminant *agg.* culminante.
to culminate *vi.* culminare, giungere al culmine.
culottes *s. pl.* gonna pantaloni.
culprit *s.* **1.** colpevole **2.** imputato.
cult *s.* culto.
cultivable *agg.* coltivabile.
to cultivate *vt.* coltivare (*anche fig.*).
cultivation *s.* coltivazione.
cultural *agg.* culturale.
culture *s.* **1.** coltura, coltivazione **2.** cultura.
cultured *agg.* colto, educato.
cumbersome *agg.* ingombrante.
cumulative *agg.* cumulativo.
cumulus *s.* (*pl.* -li) cumulo.
cuneiform *agg.* cuneiforme.
cunette *s.* cunetta (*di trincea*).
cunning *agg.* astuto, furbo. ♦ **cunning** *s.* astuzia.
cup *s.* **1.** tazza **2.** (*sport*) coppa, trofeo || — *-bearer*, coppiere; *tea- —*, tazza da tè.
cupboard *s.* credenza, armadio.
cupel *s.* coppella.
cupidity *s.* cupidigia.
cupreous *agg.* cupreo.
cupric *agg.* ramico.
cur *s.* **1.** cane bastardo **2.** mascalzone.
curable *agg.* curabile.
curacy *s.* vicariato, cura.
curare *s.* curaro.
curate *s.* curato, vicario.
curative *agg.* curativo.
curator *s.* direttore (*di museo, istituto ecc.*).

curb *s.* **1.** cordone del marciapiede **2.** freno (*fig.*) || — *-bit*, morso della briglia.
curd *s.* giuncata.
to curdle *vt.* cagliare, coagulare. ♦ **to curdle** *vi.* cagliarsi, coagularsi.
curdy *agg.* cagliato, coagulato.
cure *s.* **1.** cura, rimedio: *to take a —*, fare una cura **2.** (*eccl.*) cura **3.** vulcanizzazione (*di gomma*).
to cure *vt.* **1.** curare, rimediare **2.** salare, affumicare (*di cibi*) **3.** vulcanizzare (*una gomma*). ♦ **to cure** *vi.* curarsi.
cureless *agg.* incurabile.
curette *s.* (*chir.*) raschiatoio.
curfew *s.* coprifuoco.
curio *s.* oggetto raro.
curiosity *s.* curiosità: *out of —*, per curiosità.
curious *agg.* **1.** curioso **2.** strano, singolare.
curl *s.* **1.** ricciolo **2.** curva, spirale.
to curl *vt.* **1.** arricciare **2.** torcere. ♦ **to curl** *vi.* **1.** arricciarsi **2.** torcersi **3.** sollevarsi in spire.
curler *s.* ferro per arricciare i capelli, bigodino.
curly *agg.* **1.** ricciuto **2.** a spirale.
currency *s.* **1.** (*comm.*) circolazione monetaria **2.** corso, credito, voga.
current *agg.* corrente. ♦ **current** *s.* corrente (*anche fig.*) || *alternating —*, corrente alternata; *direct —*, corrente continua.
currently *avv.* comunemente.
curriculum *s.* curriculum.
to curry *vt.* **1.** strigliare **2.** conciare (*di cuoio*).
curry-comb *s.* striglia.
curse *s.* maledizione, anatema: *a — upon him!*, sia maledetto!
to curse *vt.* **1.** maledire **2.** scomunicare. ♦ **to curse** *vi.* imprecare, pronunciare bestemmie.
cursed *agg.* maledetto.
cursive *agg.* e *s.* corsivo.
to curtail *vt.* accorciare, abbreviare.
curtain *s.* **1.** tenda, tendina **2.** cortina **3.** sipario || — *-call*, chiamata alla ribalta.
curtain-raiser *s.* avanspettacolo.
curtly *avv.* brevemente, bruscamente.
curtsey *s.* riverenza, inchino (*di donna*).
curve *s.* curva, svolta.
to curve *vt.* curvare. ♦ **to curve** *vi.*

curvarsi.
curvet s. falcata.
curvilinear agg. curvilineo.
cushion s. cuscino.
cusp s. **1.** cuspide **2.** (geom.) vertice.
custard s. crema (di uova e latte).
custody s. **1.** custodia, vigilanza **2.** arresto, detenzione.
custom s. costume, consuetudine. ♦ **customs** s. pl. dogana (sing.) || — -house officer, doganiere.
customary agg. **1.** abituale, d'uso comune **2.** (giur.) consuetudinario.
customer s. cliente, avventore.
cut s. **1.** taglio **2.** decurtazione **3.** (sport) colpo secco.
to **cut** (cut, cut) vt. e vi. **1.** tagliare, tagliarsi || to — a poor figure, fare una brutta figura **2.** (comm.) ridurre **3.** praticare un'apertura || to — down, abbattere; to — out, ritagliare; to — up, trinciare (il pollo), sradicare (alberi).
cutlet s. costoletta.
cut-off s. **1.** scorciatoia **2.** ritaglio di giornale.
cutter[1] s. **1.** tagliatore **2.** (mecc.) fresa.
cutter[2] s. (mar.) "cutter".
cut-throat agg. spietato. ♦ **cut-throat** s. tagliagole.
cutting agg. tagliente, sferzante. ♦ **cutting** s. **1.** taglio, incisione **2.** ritaglio, truciolo **3.** (comm.) riduzione.
cuttlefish s. seppia.
cyanide s. cianuro.
cybernetics s. cibernetica.
cycle s. ciclo.
cycling s. ciclismo.
cyclostyle s. ciclostile.
cyclotron s. ciclotrone.
cyclist s. ciclista.
cyclometer s. contachilometri.
cylinder s. **1.** cilindro **2.** rullo.
cylindrical agg. cilindrico.
cynic agg. e s. cinico.
cynicism s. cinismo.
cypress s. cipresso.
Cyprian agg. e s. cipriota.
Cyrillic agg. cirillico.
cyst s. cisti.
cystitis s. cistite.
cytology s. citologia.
Czar s. zar.
Czech agg. e s. ceco.
Czecho-Slovak agg. e s. cecoslovacco.

D

D s. (mus.) re.
dab s. **1.** colpo **2.** macchia.
to **dab** vt. **1.** sfiorare **2.** applicare.
to **dabble** vt. inumidire. ♦ to **dabble** vi. **1.** inumidirsi **2.** sguazzare || to — in (at), dilettarsi di.
dachshund s. cane bassotto.
dad(dy) s. (fam.) papà, babbo.
daffodil s. narciso selvatico.
daft agg. sciocco, pazzoide.
dagger s. **1.** pugnale **2.** (tip.) croce || at daggers drawn, ai ferri corti.
daguerreotype s. dagherrotipo.
daguerreotypy s. dagherrotipia.
dahlia s. dalia.
daily agg. quotidiano, giornaliero. ♦ **daily** s. (giornale) quotidiano. ♦ **daily** avv. ogni giorno.
daintily avv. delicatamente.
daintiness s. squisitezza.
dainty agg. **1.** squisito **2.** esigente **3.** raffinato (di gusti). ♦ **dainty** s. leccornia.
dairy s. latteria.
dairymaid s. lattaia.
dairyman s. lattaio.
dais s. piattaforma.
daisy s. margherita.
dalliance s. amoreggiamento.
to **dally** vi. gingillarsi, oziare.
Dalmatian agg. e s. dalmata.
daltonism s. daltonismo.
dam[1] s. diga, sbarramento.
dam[2] s. madre (di animali).
to **dam** vt. arginare.
damage s. danno. ♦ **damages** s. pl. (giur.) indennizzo, risarcimento (sing.).
to **damage** vt. danneggiare.
damaging agg. dannoso.
damask s. damasco.
to **damask** vt. damascare.
dame s. dama, gentildonna.
damn s. maledizione.
to **damn** vt. **1.** dannare **2.** (spesso scritto d-) maledire, mandare all'inferno.
damnation s. dannazione.
damnatory agg. compromettente (di prove).
damp agg. umido. ♦ **damp** s. **1.** umidità **2.** (fig.) depressione || fire-—, grisù.
to **damp** vt. **1.** inumidire **2.** (fig.) deprimere, smorzare.

damper s. **1.** regolatore (*di stufa, fornace ecc.*) **2.** (*mus.*) sordina.
dampness s. umidità.
dance s. danza.
to dance *vt.* e *vi.* danzare || *to — attendance on,* essere a disposizione di.
dancer s. ballerino.
dancing s. danza.
dandelion s. (*bot.*) soffione.
dandruff s. forfora.
dandy *agg.* elegante, raffinato. ♦
dandy s. zerbinotto.
Dane s. danese.
danger s. pericolo.
dangerous *agg.* pericoloso.
to dangle *vi.* ciondolare, penzolare ♦ **to dangle** *vt.* far penzolare.
dangling *agg.* penzolante.
Danish *agg.* danese.
dank *agg.* umido.
Dantean, Dantesque *agg.* dantesco.
dapple s. macchia || *— -grey,* leardo pomellato.
to dapple *vt.* chiazzare.
dare (dared, durst) *v. dif.* osare.
to dare *vt.* **1.** affrontare **2.** sfidare.
daredevil s. scavezzacollo.
daring *agg.* audace. ♦ **daring** s. audacia.
dark *agg.* **1.** scuro **2.** triste **3.** segreto. ♦ **dark** s. **1.** oscurità **2.** (*fig.*) ignoranza.
to darken *vt.* oscurare. ♦ **to darken** *vi.* oscurarsi.
darkling *agg.* oscuro. ♦ **darkling** *avv.* nell'oscurità.
darkness s. oscurità.
darling *agg.* e s. caro.
darn s. rammendo.
to darn *vt.* rammendare.
darnel s. loglio.
darner s. rammendatrice.
darning s. rammendo.
dart s. **1.** dardo **2.** slancio.
to dart *vt.* lanciare. ♦ **to dart** *vi.* lanciarsi (*in avanti*).
darting *agg.* dardeggiante.
Darwinism s. darwinismo.
dash s. **1.** slancio **2.** attacco **3.** tonfo **4.** spruzzo **5.** lineetta || *— -board,* cruscotto (*di automobili*).
to dash *vt.* **1.** frantumare **2.** macchiare. ♦ **to dash** *vi.* **1.** precipitarsi **2.** infrangersi.
dashing *agg.* impetuoso.
dastard s. vigliacco, furfante.
date[1] s. **1.** data **2.** appuntamento || *up to —,* aggiornato; *out of —,*

antiquato.
date[2] s. dattero.
to date *vt.* e *vi.* datare || *to — a girl,* dare un appuntamento a una ragazza.
dating s. datazione.
dative *agg.* e s. dativo.
datum s. (*pl.* data) dato, elemento.
to daub *vt.* **1.** intonacare **2.** impiastrare.
dauber s. imbrattatore.
daughter s. figlia || *— -in-law,* nuora; *grand- —* (*di nonni*), nipotina.
to daunt *vt.* spaventare, intimidire.
dauntless *agg.* intrepido.
to dawdle *vi.* oziare, bighellonare.
dawn s. alba.
to dawn *vi.* **1.** albeggiare **2.** apparire, balenare (*nella mente*).
day s. giorno || *— labourer,* lavoratore a giornata; *the — after tomorrow,* dopodomani; *the — before yesterday,* l'altro ieri; *this — week,* oggi a otto; *— off,* giorno di riposo; *— out,* giorno di libera uscita.
daybook s. (*comm.*) brogliaccio.
daybreak s. alba.
daydream s. fantasticheria.
to daydream *vi.* fantasticare.
daydreamer s. sognatore.
daylight s. luce del giorno.
daylong *agg.* che dura tutto il giorno. ♦ **daylong** *avv.* per tutto il giorno.
daytime s. giornata.
daze s. sbalordimento.
to daze *vt.* sbalordire.
dazzle s. abbagliamento || *— lamps* (*auto*), fari abbaglianti.
to dazzle *vt.* abbagliare.
deacon s. diacono.
dead *agg.* **1.** morto **2.** assoluto || *— drunk,* ubriaco fradicio. ♦
dead *avv.* assolutamente || *— sure,* arcisicuro.
to deaden *vt.* **1.** attutire **2.** isolare (*acusticamente*). ♦ **to deaden** *vi.* attutirsi.
deadening s. isolamento acustico.
deadline s. **1.** linea non superabile **2.** scadenza, termine massimo.
deadly *agg.* mortale. ♦ **deadly** *avv.* mortalmente.
deadness s. torpore.
deaf *agg.* sordo.
to deafen *vt.* assordare.
deaf-mute s. sordomuto.

deafness s. sordità.
deal s. **1.** quantità **2.** accordo **3.** affare **4.** mano (*del gioco delle carte*) || *a great —*, moltissimo.
to deal (dealt, dealt) *vt.* distribuire, dare. ♦ **to deal (dealt, dealt)** *vi.* trattare, comportarsi || *to — in*, commerciare in.
dealer s. **1.** commerciante **2.** mazziere (*delle carte*).
dealing s. **1.** commercio **2.** distribuzione **3.** relazione || *double- —*, slealtà.
dealt V. *to deal*.
deambulatory *agg.* deambulatorio.
dean s. **1.** decano **2.** preside (*di facoltà universitaria*).
dear *agg.* caro || *— me!*, povero me!
dearly *avv.* **1.** caramente **2.** a caro prezzo.
dearness s. amorevolezza.
dearth s. penuria.
death s. morte || *— -rattles*, rantoli dell'agonia; *— -warrant*, ordine di esecuzione capitale.
deathly *agg.* e *avv.* V. *deadly*.
to debase *vt.* **1.** avvilire **2.** svalutare.
to debar *vt.* escludere, privare.
to debark *vt.* e *vi.* sbarcare.
debate s. dibattito.
to debate *vt.* e *vi.* **1.** discutere **2.** ponderare.
debauch s. intemperanza, corruzione.
debauched *agg.* corrotto.
debauchery s. **1.** corruzione **2.** dissolutezza.
debenture s. (*comm.*) obbligazione.
debit s. debito.
to debit *vt.* addebitare.
to debouch *vi.* sfociare.
debris s. detriti (*pl.*).
debt s. debito.
debtor s. debitore.
début s. debutto.
decadence s. decadenza.
decadent *agg.* e *s.* decadente.
decagram(m)e s. decagrammo.
decahedron s. decaedro.
to decalcify *vt.* decalcificare.
decalitre s. decalitro.
decalogue s. decalogo.
decametre s. decametro.
to decamp *vi.* levare le tende.
to decant *vt.* travasare.
decantation s. decantazione.
decanter s. caraffa.
to decapitate *vt.* decapitare.

decasyllabic *agg.* decasillabico.
decay s. **1.** decadimento **2.** rovina **3.** carie (*dei denti*).
to decay *vt.* **1.** far decadere **2.** mandare in rovina. ♦ **to decay** *vi.* **1.** decadere **2.** andare in rovina **3.** cariarsi.
decayable *agg.* deperibile.
decease s. decesso.
to decease *vi.* morire.
deceit s. **1.** inganno **2.** falsità.
deceitful *agg.* **1.** ingannevole **2.** falso.
to deceive *vt.* ingannare.
deceiving *agg.* ingannatore.
to decelerate *vt.* e *vi.* rallentare.
deceleration s. rallentamento.
decelerator s. rallentatore.
December s. dicembre.
decency s. decenza. ♦ **decencies** *s. pl.* convenienze.
decennary *agg.* decennale. ♦ **decennary** s. decennio.
decennial *agg.* e *s.* decennale.
decent *agg.* decente || *a — fellow*, un buon diavolo.
decentralization s. decentramento.
to decentralize *vt.* decentrare.
deception s. inganno.
deceptive *agg.* ingannevole.
to decide *vt.* decidere. ♦ **to decide** *vi.* decidersi, pronunciarsi.
decigram(me) s. decigrammo.
decimal *agg.* e *s.* decimale.
to decimate *vt.* decimare.
decimation s. decimazione.
decimetre s. decimetro.
to decipher *vt.* decifrare.
deciphering s. decifrazione.
decision s. decisione.
decisive *agg.* **1.** decisivo **2.** deciso.
deck s. (*mar.*) ponte, coperta || *— -chair*, sedia a sdraio; *quarter- —*, cassero.
to deck *vt.* ornare.
decker s. *double- —*, autobus a due piani.
to declaim *vt.* e *vi.* declamare.
declaimer s. declamatore.
declamation s. declamazione.
declamatory *agg.* declamatorio.
declaration s. dichiarazione.
to declare *vt.* e *vi.* dichiarare.
declension s. **1.** declino **2.** (*gramm.*) declinazione.
declinable *agg.* declinabile.
declination s. **1.** inclinazione **2.** declino.
decline s. declino, deperimento.

to **decline** *vt.* e *vi.* declinare.

declining *s.* 1. declinazione 2. deperimento 3. rifiuto.

declivity *s.* declivio.

to **decode** *vt.* decifrare, tradurre (*testi in codice*).

decolorization *s.* decolorazione.

decoloration *s.* decolorazione.

to **decolour(ize)** *vt.* decolorare.

decomposable *agg.* scomponibile.

to **decompose** *vt.* 1. decomporre 2. scomporre. ♦ to **decompose** *vi.* 1. decomporsi 2. scomporsi.

decomposition *s.* decomposizione.

to **deconsecrate** *vt.* sconsacrare.

to **decorate** *vt.* decorare.

decoration *s.* decorazione.

decorative *agg.* decorativo.

decorator *s.* decoratore.

decorous *agg.* decoroso.

decoy *s.* esca, richiamo.

decrease *s.* diminuzione.

to **decrease** *vt.* e *vi.* diminuire.

decree *s.* decreto.

to **decree** *vt.* decretare.

decrepit *agg.* decrepito.

decrepitude *s.* decrepitezza.

to **decry** *vt.* stigmatizzare, denigrare.

to **decuple** *vt.* decuplicare.

to **dedicate** *vt.* dedicare.

dedicatee *s.* persona a cui è dedicato qc.

dedication *s.* 1. dedica 2. consacrazione.

dedicative, dedicatory *agg.* dedicatorio.

to **deduce** *vt.* 1. dedurre 2. derivare.

to **deduct** *vt.* detrarre.

deduction *s.* 1. deduzione 2. detrazione.

deductive *agg.* deduttivo.

deed *s.* atto, azione.

to **deem** *vt.* giudicare.

deep *agg.* 1. profondo 2. cupo || — -*freeze*, surgelamento; — *mourning*, lutto stretto. ♦ **deep** *s.* abisso, profondità. ♦ **deep** *avv.* profondamente || — *into the night*, fino a notte tarda.

to **deepen** *vt.* 1. approfondire 2. incupire. ♦ to **deepen** *vi.* 1. approfondirsi 2. incupirsi.

deeply *avv.* profondamente.

deepness *s.* profondità.

deep-rooted *agg.* radicato.

deer *s.* cervo || (*fallow*) —, daino.

to **deface** *vt.* sfregiare.

defacement *s.* sfregio.

defamation *s.* diffamazione.

defamatory *agg.* diffamatorio.

to **defame** *vt.* diffamare.

defamer *s.* diffamatore.

default *s.* 1. mancanza 2. inadempienza 3. (*giur.*) contumacia: *judgement by* —, giudizio in contumacia.

defaulting *agg.* (*comm.*) insolvente.

defeat *s.* 1. sconfitta 2. fallimento.

to **defeat** *vt.* 1. sconfiggere 2. frustrare.

defeatism *s.* disfattismo.

defeatist *agg.* e *s.* disfattista.

to **defecate** *vt.* purificare. ♦ to **defecate** *vi.* defecare.

defect *s.* difetto.

defection *s.* defezione.

defective *agg.* 1. difettoso 2. (*gramm.*) difettivo. ♦ **defective** *s.* anormale.

defence *s.* difesa.

defenceless *agg.* indifeso.

to **defend** *vt.* difendere.

defendant *s.* imputato.

defender *s.* difensore.

defenestration *s.* defenestrazione.

defensible *agg.* difensibile.

defensive *agg.* difensivo. ♦ **defensive** *s.* difensiva.

to **defer**[1] *vt.* e *vi.* differire || *deferred payment*, pagamento a rate.

to **defer**[2] *vt.* rimettere. ♦ to **defer** *vi.* rimettersi.

deference *s.* deferenza.

deferential *agg.* deferente.

deferment *s.* differimento.

defiance *s.* sfida.

defiant *agg.* ardito.

deficiency *s.* 1. deficienza 2. disavanzo.

deficient *agg.* e *s.* deficiente.

deficit *s.* (*comm.*) disavanzo.

to **defile** *vi.* marciare in fila. ♦ to **defile** *vt.* 1. insozzare 2. profanare.

defilement *s.* 1. contaminazione 2. profanazione.

definable *agg.* definibile.

to **define** *vt.* definire.

definite *agg.* definito.

definitely *avv.* in modo preciso.

definiteness *s.* precisione.

definition *s.* 1. definizione 2. nitidezza.

definitive *agg.* definitivo.

to **deflagrate** *vt.* far deflagrare. ♦ to **deflagrate** *vi.* deflagrare.

deflagration s. deflagrazione.
to deflate vt. sgonfiare. ♦ to deflate vi. sgonfiarsi.
deflation s. 1. sgonfiamento 2. deflazione.
to deflect vt. e vi. deviare.
deflection s. deviazione.
defloration s. deflorazione.
to deflower vt. 1. deflorare 2. devastare 3. spogliare (dei fiori).
to deforest vt. diboscare.
deforestation s. diboscamento.
to deform vt. deformare. ♦ to deform vi. deformarsi.
deformation s. deformazione.
deformed agg. deforme.
deformity s. deformità.
to defraud vt. defraudare.
defrauder s. frodatore.
to defray vt. pagare, risarcire.
defrayal s. pagamento, risarcimento.
to defrost vt. sgelare.
defroster s. riscaldatore.
deft agg. abile, destro.
to defy vt. sfidare.
degenerate agg. e s. degenerato.
to degenerate vt. e vi. degenerare.
degeneration s. degenerazione.
degradation s. degradazione.
to degrade vt. degradare.
degree s. 1. grado 2. rango 3. laurea, diploma || by degrees, gradatamente.
to dehydrate vt. disidratare.
dehydration s. disidratazione.
to deify vt. deificare.
deism s. deismo.
deity s. divinità.
to deject vt. abbattere, scoraggiare.
dejected agg. triste, abbattuto.
dejectedly avv. con aria abbattuta.
dejection s. abbattimento.
delation s. delazione.
delator s. delatore.
delay s. 1. ritardo 2. proroga.
to delay vt. e vi. ritardare.
delegacy s. delegazione.
delegate s. delegato.
to delegate vt. delegare.
delegation s. delegazione.
to delete vt. cancellare (anche fig.).
deliberate agg. 1. deliberato 2. cauto.
to deliberate vt. e vi. deliberare.
deliberately avv. deliberatamente.
deliberation s. 1. deliberazione 2. ponderatezza.
delicacy s. 1. delicatezza 2. ghiottoneria.

delicate agg. 1. delicato 2. esigente.
delicatessen s. pl. 1. ghiottonerie 2. salumeria (sing.).
delicious agg. delizioso.
delict s. (giur.) delitto.
delight s. delizia, gioia.
to delight vt. deliziare. ♦ to delight vi. dilettarsi.
delighted agg. lietissimo, entusiasta.
delightful agg. delizioso.
to delimit(ate) vt. delimitare.
delimitation s. delimitazione.
to delineate vt. delineare.
delineation s. delineazione.
delinquency s. 1. delinquenza 2. colpevolezza.
delinquent agg. colpevole. ♦ delinquent s. delinquente.
delirious agg. delirante.
deliriously avv. in modo delirante.
delirium s. delirio, frenesia.
to deliver vt. 1. liberare 2. consegnare 3. partorire 4. pronunciare (un discorso).
deliverance s. liberazione.
delivery s. 1. liberazione 2. consegna 3. parto 4. resa 5. dizione, pronuncia || — -man, fattorino.
deltoid agg. triangolare.
to delude vt. ingannare.
deluge s. diluvio.
delusion s. illusione.
delusive agg. illusorio.
to delve vt. scavare, esumare. ♦ to delve vi. compiere ricerche, frugare.
demagnetization s. demagnetizzazione.
to demagnetize vt. demagnetizzare.
demagogic(al) agg. demagogico.
demagogue s. demagogo.
demagogy s. demagogia.
demand s. 1. domanda 2. esigenza || on —, a richiesta.
to demand vt. 1. domandare 2. esigere.
demarcation s. demarcazione.
demeanour s. contegno.
demerit s. demerito.
demesne s. dominio, proprietà terriera.
demigod s. semidio.
demijohn s. damigiana.
demilitarization s. smilitarizzazione.
to demilitarize vt. smilitarizzare.
demise s. 1. trapasso (di proprietà)

2. decesso.
demiurge s. demiurgo.
demobilization s. smobilitazione.
to **demobilize** vt. smobilitare.
democracy s. democrazia.
democrat s. democratico.
democratic(al) agg. democratico.
democratization s. democratizza-
zione.
to **democratize** vt. democratizzare.
demographic(al) agg. demografico.
demography s. demografia.
to **demolish** vt. demolire.
demolisher s. demolitore.
demolition s. demolizione.
demon s. demonio.
demoniac(al) agg. demoniaco.
demonology s. demonologia.
demonstrability s. dimostrabilità.
demonstrable agg. dimostrabile.
demonstrant s. dimostrante.
to **demonstrate** vt. e vi. dimostrare.
demonstration s. dimostrazione.
demonstrative agg. **1.** dimostrativo
2. espansivo.
demonstrativeness s. **1.** dimostrazione **2.** espansività.
demonstrator s. **1.** dimostratore **2.**
dimostrante.
demoralization s. **1.** depravazione
2. demoralizzazione.
to **demoralize** vt. **1.** depravare **2.**
demoralizzare.
to **demur** vi. titubare, esitare.
demure agg. riservato, pudico.
demureness s. riservatezza, pudore.
den s. tana.
to **denationalize** vt. snazionalizzare.
to **denature** vt. denaturare.
deniable agg. negabile.
denial s. rifiuto || self- —, abnega-
zione.
to **denigrate** vt. denigrare.
denigration s. denigrazione.
denigrator s. denigratore.
to **denominate** vt. denominare.
denomination s. **1.** denominazione
2. setta **3.** valore (di monete).
denominational agg. confessionale.
denominative agg. denominativo.
denominator s. denominatore.
denotation s. **1.** indicazione **2.** significato.
to **denote** vt. denotare, indicare.
to **denounce** vt. denunciare.
dense agg. **1.** denso **2.** opaco **3.** stupido.
density s. **1.** densità **2.** opacità **3.**

stupidità.
dent s. incavo, tacca.
dental agg. e s. dentale.
dentary agg. dentario.
dentine s. dentina.
dentist s. dentista.
dentistry s. odontoiatria.
dentition s. dentizione.
denture s. dentiera.
denudation s. denudazione.
to **denude** vt. denudare.
denunciation s. denunzia.
to **deny** vt. negare, rifiutare.
deodorant agg. e s. deodorante.
to **deodorize** vt. deodorare.
deontology s. deontologia.
deoxidization s. disossidazione.
to **deoxidize** vt. disossidare.
to **depart** vi. partire, allontanarsi.
department s. **1.** reparto **2.** (amer.)
ministero || — store, grande ma-
gazzino.
departure s. **1.** partenza **2.** allontanamento.
to **depend** vi. **1.** dipendere: it all
depends on circumstances, tutto dipende dalle circostanze **2.** contare:
— on so., contare su qu.
dependable agg. fidato.
dependant agg. e s. dipendente.
dependence s. **1.** dipendenza **2.** fiducia.
dependency s. territorio dipendente.
dependent agg. dipendente.
to **depict** vt. dipingere.
to **depilate** vt. depilare.
depilatory agg. e s. depilatorio.
to **deplete** vt. **1.** vuotare **2.** esaurire.
depletion s. esaurimento.
deplorable agg. deplorevole.
to **deplore** vt. deplorare.
to **deploy** vt. schierare, spiegare. ◆
to **deploy** vi. schierarsi (di truppe ecc.).
to **depone** vt. deporre (in un processo).
deponent s. testimone.
to **depopulate** vt. spopolare.
to **deport** vt. deportare || to — one-
self, comportarsi.
deportation s. deportazione.
deportment s. atteggiamento.
deposal s. deposizione.
to **depose** vt. e vi. deporre.
deposit s. deposito.
to **deposit** vt. depositare.
deposition s. **1.** deposizione **2.** de-

posito.
depositor s. depositante.
depot s. deposito.
to **deprave** vt. depravare.
depravity s. depravazione.
deprecable agg. deprecabile.
to **deprecate** vt. disapprovare.
deprecation s. disapprovazione.
deprecative, deprecatory agg. disapprovante.
to **depreciate** vt. svalutare. ♦ to **depreciate** vi. svalutarsi.
depreciation s. 1. svalutazione 2. ammortamento: — charge, quota d'ammortamento.
depreciative, depreciatory agg. spregiativo.
depredation s. saccheggio.
depredatory agg. predatorio.
to **depress** vt. 1. deprimere 2. abbassare.
depression s. 1. depressione 2. (econ.) crisi.
depressor s. depressore.
deprivation s. privazione.
to **deprive** vt. privare.
depth s. 1. profondità 2. (mar.) fondale.
to **depurate** vt. depurare. ♦ to **depurate** vi. depurarsi.
depuration s. depurazione.
depurative agg. e s. depurativo.
depurator s. depuratore.
deputation s. delega.
to **depute** vt. deputare.
deputy s. 1. deputato 2. sostituto.
derailment s. deragliamento.
to **derange** vt. sconvolgere.
derangement s. sconvolgimento.
deratization s. derattizzazione.
to **deride** vt. deridere.
derision s. 1. derisione 2. zimbello.
derisive, derisory agg. derisorio.
derivable agg. derivabile.
derivation s. derivazione.
derivative agg. e s. derivato.
derivatively avv. per derivazione.
to **derive** vt. e vi. derivare.
derm s. derma.
dermatologist s. dermatologo.
dermatology s. dermatologia.
to **derogate** vi. derogare.
derogation s. deroga.
derogatory agg. derogatorio.
derrick s. 1. argano 2. torre di trivellazione.
descant s. 1. melodia 2. dissertazione.
to **descend** vt. e vi. (di)scendere ||

to — upon so., aggredire qu.
descendance s. discendenza.
descendant s. discendente.
descent s. 1. discesa 2. incursione 3. lignaggio 4. caduta.
describable agg. descrivibile.
to **describe** vt. descrivere.
description s. descrizione.
descriptive agg. descrittivo.
to **descry** vt. scoprire.
to **desecrate** vt. profanare.
desert[1] agg. deserto. ♦ **desert** s. deserto.
desert[2] s. 1. merito 2. compenso.
to **desert** vt. abbandonare. ♦ to **desert** vi. disertare.
deserted agg. deserto.
deserter s. disertore.
desertion s. 1. abbandono 2. diserzione.
to **deserve** vt. meritare.
deservedly avv. meritatamente.
deserving agg. meritevole.
design s. disegno.
to **design** vt. 1. destinare 2. progettare 3. disegnare.
designate agg. designato.
to **designate** vt. 1. designare 2. indicare.
designation s. designazione.
designer s. disegnatore.
designing agg. astuto. ♦ **designing** s. 1. disegno 2. complotto.
desirable agg. desiderabile.
desire s. desiderio.
to **desire** vt. 1. desiderare 2. domandare.
desirous agg. desideroso.
to **desist** vi. desistere.
desk s. 1. scrivania 2. cassa || school- master's —, cattedra (di insegnante).
desolate agg. desolato.
to **desolate** vt. 1. affliggere 2. devastare.
desolation s. desolazione.
despair s. disperazione.
to **despair** vi. disperare.
despairing agg. disperato.
desperate agg. disperato.
despicable agg. spregevole.
despicableness s. spregevolezza.
despisable agg. spregevole.
to **despise** vt. disprezzare.
despite prep. malgrado.
despiteful agg. maligno, dispettoso.
despondency s. scoraggiamento.
despondent agg. scoraggiato.
despot s. despota.

despotic(al) *agg.* dispotico.
despotism *s.* dispotismo.
destination *s.* destinazione.
to **destine** *vt.* destinare.
destiny *s.* destino.
destitute *agg.* 1. povero 2. privo.
destitution *s.* 1. povertà 2. privazione.
to **destroy** *vt.* distruggere.
destroyable *agg.* distruggibile.
destroyer *s.* 1. distruttore 2. cacciatorpediniere.
destroying *agg.* distruttore.
destruction *s.* distruzione, rovina.
destructive *agg.* distruttivo.
destructor *s.* distruttore.
desuetude *s.* disuso.
desultory *agg.* saltuario.
to **detach** *vt.* distaccare.
detachable *agg.* staccabile.
detached *agg.* 1. distaccato 2. isolato.
detachment *s.* 1. distacco 2. (*mil.*) distaccamento.
detail *s.* 1. dettaglio, particolare 2. pattuglia.
to **detail** *vt.* 1. dettagliare 2. (*mil.*) distaccare (*una pattuglia*).
to **detain** *vt.* 1. detenere 2. trattenere.
to **detect** *vt.* scoprire.
detectable *agg.* scopribile.
detection *s.* scoperta.
detective *s.* investigatore || — *novel*, romanzo poliziesco.
detector *s.* (*radio*) rivelatore.
detent *s.* (*mecc.*) arpione.
detention *s.* 1. detenzione 2. ritardo forzato.
to **deter** *vt.* trattenere.
to **deterge** *vt.* detergere.
detergent *agg.* e *s.* detergente, detersivo.
to **deteriorate** *vt.* deteriorare. ♦ to **deteriorate** *vi.* deteriorarsi.
deterioration *s.* deterioramento.
determinable *agg.* determinabile.
determinant *s.* causa determinante.
determinate *agg.* determinato.
determination *s.* determinazione.
determinative *agg.* determinativo.
to **determine** *vt.* determinare, decidere. ♦ to **determine** *vi.* risolversi || *to — on*, fissarsi su.
determined *agg.* deciso.
determinism *s.* determinismo.
determinist *agg.* e *s.* determinista.
deterrent *agg.* e *s.* (*neol.*) deterrente.

detersive *agg.* e *s.* detersivo.
to **detest** *vt.* detestare.
detestable *agg.* detestabile.
detestation *s.* 1. odio 2. esecrazione.
dethronement *s.* deposizione (*dal trono*).
to **detonate** *vt.* e *vi.* esplodere.
detonator *s.* detonatore.
detour *s.* deviazione, giravolta.
to **detract** *vt.* e *vi.* diminuire.
detraction *s.* detrazione.
detractor *s.* detrattore.
detriment *s.* detrimento.
detrimental *agg.* dannoso.
to **devaluate** *vt.* svalutare.
devaluation *s.* svalutazione.
to **devastate** *vt.* devastare.
devastation *s.* devastazione.
to **develop** *vt.* sviluppare. ♦ to **develop** *vi.* svilupparsi.
developer *s.* sviluppatore.
development *s.* sviluppo.
to **deviate** *vt.* e *vi.* deviare.
deviation *s.* deviazione.
deviationism *s.* deviazionismo.
device *s.* 1. trovata 2. dispositivo. ♦ **devices** *s. pl.* capriccio, inclinazione (*sing.*).
devil *s.* diavolo.
devilish *agg.* diabolico.
devious *agg.* 1. remoto 2. errante.
to **devise** *vt.* 1. escogitare 2. lasciare in eredità.
deviser *s.* inventore.
devising *s.* invenzione.
devoid *agg.* privo.
devolution *s.* 1. trasmissione (*di beni*) 2. degenerazione.
to **devolve** *vt.* trasmettere. ♦ to **devolve** *vi.* trasferirsi.
to **devote** *vt.* dedicare.
devoted *agg.* 1. devoto 2. votato.
devotion *s.* devozione.
devotional *agg.* devoto.
to **devour** *vt.* divorare.
devourer *s.* divoratore.
devout *agg.* devoto, pio, religioso.
dew *s.* rugiada.
dewy *agg.* rugiadoso.
dexterity *s.* destrezza.
dexterous *agg.* destro.
dextrin(e) *s.* destrina.
diabetes *s.* diabete.
diabetic *agg.* e *s.* diabetico.
diabolic(al) *agg.* diabolico.
diadem *s.* diadema.
to **diagnose** *vt.* diagnosticare.
diagnosis *s.* (*pl.* -ses) diagnosi.

diagnostic *agg.* diagnostico.
diagonal *agg.* e *s.* diagonale.
diagram *s.* diagramma.
dial *s.* quadrante.
to **dial** *vt.* comporre (*un numero telefonico*) || *to — so.*, telefonare a qu.
dialect *s.* dialetto.
dialectal *agg.* dialettale.
dialectic(al) *agg.* dialettico.
dialectics *s.* dialettica.
dialogue *s.* dialogo.
to **dialogue** *vt.* e *vi.* dialogare.
diameter *s.* diametro.
diametrically *avv.* diametralmente.
diamond *s.* **1.** diamante **2.** losanga.
diaper *s.* **1.** arabesco **2.** pannolino.
diaphanous *agg.* diafano.
diaphragm *s.* diaframma.
diapositive *s.* diapositiva.
diarchy *s.* diarchia.
diarist *s.* diarista.
diarrhoea *s.* diarrea.
diary *s.* diario.
diatribe *s.* diatriba.
dice V. *die.*
to **dice** *vt.* **1.** giocare ai dadi **2.** tagliare a dadi **3.** quadrettare.
dictaphone *s.* dittafono.
dictate *s.* dettame.
to **dictate** *vt.* e *vi.* dettare.
dictation *s.* **1.** dettato **2.** dettame.
dictator *s.* dittatore.
dictatorial *agg.* dittatoriale.
dictatorship *s.* dittatura.
diction *s.* **1.** stile **2.** dizione.
dictionary *s.* dizionario.
dictograph *s.* dittografo.
did V. *to do.*
didactic *agg.* didattico.
didactics *s.* didattica.
die *s.* (*pl.* dice) dado.
to **die** *vi.* morire || *to — away*, svanire; *to — out*, estinguersi.
dielectric *agg.* e *s.* dielettrico.
diet *s.* dieta.
to **diet** *vt.* mettere a dieta. ♦ to **diet** *vi.* essere a dieta.
dietarian *s.* chi sta a dieta.
dietary *agg.* dietetico. ♦ **dietary** *s.* dieta.
dietetic(al) *agg.* dietetico.
to **differ** *vi.* differire.
difference *s.* **1.** differenza **2.** divergenza.
different *agg.* differente.
differential *agg.* e *s.* differenziale.
to **differentiate** *vt.* differenziare. ♦ to **differentiate** *vi.* differenziarsi.
differentiation *s.* differenziazione.
differently *avv.* differentemente.
differing *agg.* **1.** differente, discordante.
difficult *agg.* difficile.
difficulty *s.* difficoltà.
diffidence *s.* timidezza.
diffident *agg.* esitante.
diffraction *s.* diffrazione.
diffuse *agg.* diffuso.
to **diffuse** *vt.* diffondere. ♦ to **diffuse** *vi.* diffondersi.
diffusedly, diffusely *avv.* **1.** diffusamente **2.** ovunque.
diffuser *s.* (*foto*) diffusore.
diffusion *s.* **1.** diffusione **2.** prolissità.
diffusive *agg.* **1.** diffusivo **2.** prolisso.
diffusor *s.* diffusore.
to **dig (dug, dug)** *vt.* vangare, scavare || *to — in*, affondare; *to — out*, estrarre.
digest *s.* **1.** sommario **2.** condensato.
to **digest** *vt.* classificare, condensare, redigere. ♦ to **digest** *vt.* e *vi.* digerire.
digestibility *s.* digeribilità.
digestible *agg.* digeribile.
digestion *s.* digestione.
digestive *agg.* e *s.* digestivo.
digger *s.* **1.** zappatore **2.** scavatrice.
digging *s.* **1.** scavo **2.** miniera. ♦ **diggings** *s. pl.* (*gergo*) alloggio (*sing.*).
digital *agg.* digitale.
dignified *agg.* dignitoso.
to **dignify** *vt.* elevare, nobilitare.
dignitary *s.* dignitario.
dignity *s.* **1.** dignità **2.** dignitario.
digression *s.* digressione.
digressive *agg.* digressivo.
dike *s.* diga.
to **dike** *vt.* arginare.
to **dilapidate** *vt.* dilapidare. ♦ to **dilapidate** *vi.* andare in rovina.
dilatability *s.* dilatabilità.
dilatable *agg.* dilatabile.
dilatation *s.* dilatazione.
to **dilate** *vt.* dilatare. ♦ to **dilate** *vi.* dilatarsi.
dilatory *agg.* **1.** dilatorio **2.** lento.
diligence *s.* diligenza.
diligent *agg.* diligente.
diluent *agg.* e *s.* diluente.
to **dilute** *vt.* diluire.
dilution *s.* **1.** diluzione **2.** sostanza

diluita.
diluvial *agg.* diluviale.
dim *agg.* **1.** debole **2.** appannato **3.** oscuro.
to **dim** *vt.* **1.** indebolire **2.** oscurare. ♦ to **dim** *vi.* **1.** indebolirsi **2.** oscurarsi.
dime *s.* quarto di dollaro.
dimension *s.* dimensione.
dimeter *s.* dimetro.
to **diminish** *vt.* e *vi.* diminuire.
diminishable *agg.* diminuibile.
diminution *s.* diminuzione.
diminutive *agg.* minuscolo. ♦ **diminutive** *s.* diminutivo.
dimissory *agg.* dimissorio.
dimly *avv.* **1.** debolmente **2.** oscuramente.
dimness *s.* **1.** debolezza **2.** offuscamento (*di vista*).
dimple *s.* fossetta.
din *s.* baccano.
to **din** *vt.* e *vi.* rintronare.
to **dine** *vi.* pranzare.
diner *s.* commensale.
to **ding** *vt.* e *vi.* suonare, scampanellare.
dingy *agg.* scuro, sporco.
dining *s.* il pranzare || — *-room*, sala da pranzo.
dinner *s.* pranzo || — *-wagon*, carrello (*per i pasti*); — *-car*, vagone ristorante.
dinosaur *s.* dinosauro.
dint *s.* tacca || *by* — *of*, a forza di.
diocesan *agg.* e *s.* diocesano.
diocese *s.* diocesi.
diode *s.* diodo.
Dionysiac, Dionysian *agg.* dionisiaco.
diopter *s.* diottria.
dioptric *agg.* diottrico.
dioxid(e) *s.* biossido.
dip *s.* **1.** bagno **2.** inclinazione **3.** (*aer.*) picchiata **4.** tuffo.
to **dip** *vt.* **1.** immergere **2.** abbassare. ♦ to **dip** *vi.* **1.** immergersi **2.** abbassarsi **3.** tuffarsi.
diphtheria *s.* difterite.
diphtheric *agg.* difterico.
diphthong *s.* dittongo.
diplomacy *s.* diplomazia.
diplomat *s.* diplomatico.
diplomatic *agg.* diplomatico.
diplomatically *avv.* diplomaticamente.
diplomatics *s.* diplomazia.
diplomatist *s.* diplomatico.
dipody *s.* dipodia.

dipper *s.* **1.** tuffatore **2.** mestolo || *the Big* —, l'Orsa Maggiore.
dipsomaniac *s.* dipsomane.
dipteral *agg.* dittero.
diptych *s.* dittico.
dire *agg.* terribile, orrendo.
direct *agg.* diretto.
to **direct** *vt.* **1.** dirigere **2.** ordinare.
direction *s.* **1.** direzione **2.** indicazione.
directional *agg.* direzionale.
directive *agg.* direttivo. ♦ **directive** *s.* direttiva.
directly *avv.* **1.** direttamente **2.** subito.
director *s.* **1.** direttore **2.** regista.
directorial *agg.* direttivo.
directory *agg.* direttivo. ♦ **directory** *s.* **1.** (*tel.*) guida **2.** (*amer.*) consiglio di amministrazione.
direful *agg.* orrendo.
dirge *s.* canto funebre.
diriment *agg.* dirimento.
dirt *s.* sporcizia.
dirtiness *s.* sozzura.
dirty *agg.* **1.** sporco **2.** brutto **3.** sboccato.
to **dirty** *vt.* sporcare. ♦ to **dirty** *vi.* sporcarsi.
disability *s.* **1.** incapacità **2.** invalidità.
to **disable** *vt.* rendere incapace, inabile.
to **disabuse** *vt.* disingannare.
to **disaccustom** *vt.* disabituare.
disadvantage *s.* svantaggio.
disadvantageous *agg.* svantaggioso.
to **disagree** *vi.* dissentire.
disagreeable *agg.* sgradevole.
disagreeableness *s.* sgradevolezza.
disagreement *s.* dissenso.
to **disappear** *vi.* scomparire.
disappearance *s.* sparizione.
to **disappoint** *vt.* deludere.
disappointingly *avv.* in modo deludente.
disappointment *s.* delusione.
disapprobation, disapproval *s.* disapprovazione.
to **disapprove** *vt.* e *vi.* disapprovare.
disapprovingly *avv.* con disapprovazione.
to **disarm** *vt.* e *vi.* disarmare.
disarmament *s.* disarmo.
to **disarrange** *vt.* scompigliare.
disarrangement *s.* scompiglio.
disarray *s.* scompiglio, confusione.

to **disassemble** *vt*. smontare.
disassembling *s*. smontaggio.
disaster *s*. disastro.
disastrous *agg*. disastroso.
to **disavow** *vt*. ripudiare.
to **disband** *vt*. sciogliere. ♦ to **disband** *vi*. sbandarsi.
disbelief *s*. incredulità.
to **disbelieve** *vt*. e *vi*. non credere.
disbeliever *s*. incredulo.
disbursement *s*. pagamento.
to **discard** *vt*. scartare.
to **discern** *vt*. discernere.
discernible *agg*. visibile.
discernment *s*. discernimento.
discharge *s*. **1.** scarico **2.** scarica **3.** congedo **4.** assoluzione **5.** liberazione **6.** pagamento.
to **discharge** *vt*. **1.** scaricare **2.** congedare **3.** assolvere **4.** liberare. ♦ to **discharge** *vi*. scaricarsi.
disciple *s*. discepolo.
disciplinable *agg*. disciplinabile.
disciplinary *agg*. disciplinare.
discipline *s*. disciplina.
to **disclaim** *vt*. rifiutare, declinare (*responsabilità*).
disclaimer *s*. rinuncia, rifiuto.
to **disclose** *vt*. svelare.
disclosure *s*. rivelazione.
discoid *agg*. e *s*. discoide.
to **discolour** *vt*. scolorire. ♦ to **discolour** *vi*. scolorirsi.
discolouration *s*. scoloramento.
to **discomfit** *vt*. **1.** sconfiggere **2.** disorientare.
to **discomfort** *vt*. mettere a disagio.
to **discompose** *vt*. agitare.
to **disconcert** *vt*. turbare.
to **disconnect** *vt*. separare, disunire.
disconnected *agg*. **1.** sconnesso **2.** disinnestato.
disconnectedness *s*. sconnessione.
disconsolate *agg*. sconsolato.
discontent *s*. scontento.
to **discontinue** *vt*. e *vi*. cessare.
discontinuity *s*. discontinuità.
discontinuous *agg*. discontinuo.
discord *s*. **1.** discordia, dissenso **2.** (*mus.*) dissonanza.
discordance *s*. **1.** disaccordo **2.** discordanza (*di suoni*).
discordant *agg*. discorde.
discordantly *avv*. in disaccordo.
discount *s*. sconto || *at a* —, sottocosto.
to **discount** *vt*. **1.** scontare **2.** tenere in poco conto.

discountable *agg*. **1.** scontabile **2.** poco attendibile.
to **discourage** *vt*. scoraggiare.
discouragement *s*. scoraggiamento.
to **discover** *vt*. scoprire.
discoverer *s*. scopritore.
discovery *s*. scoperta.
discredit *s*. **1.** discredito **2.** dubbio.
to **discredit** *vt*. **1.** screditare **2.** mettere in dubbio.
discreditable *agg*. vergognoso, infamante.
discreet *agg*. prudente, discreto.
discrepancy *s*. disaccordo.
discrete *agg*. separato, distinto.
discretion *s*. **1.** discrezione **2.** saggezza.
discretionary *agg*. discrezionale.
discriminate *agg*. discriminato.
to **discriminate** *vt*. e *vi*. discriminare.
discriminating *agg*. **1.** sagace **2.** discriminante.
discrimination *s*. **1.** discriminazione **2.** discernimento.
discursive *agg*. divagante.
discus *s*. disco || — *-thrower*, discobolo.
to **discuss** *vt*. discutere.
discussion *s*. discussione.
disdain *s*. sdegno.
to **disdain** *vt*. disdegnare.
disdainful *agg*. sdegnoso.
disease *s*. malattia.
to **disembark** *vt*. e *vi*. sbarcare.
to **disembarrass** *vt*. sbarazzare.
to **disembody** *vt*. **1.** disincarnare **2.** congedare.
to **disembowel** *vt*. sventrare.
disembowelment *s*. sventramento.
to **disenchant** *vt*. disincantare.
disenchantment *s*. disincanto.
to **disengage** *vt*. **1.** disimpegnare **2.** disinnestare. ♦ to **disengage** *vi*. liberarsi.
disengagement *s*. **1.** liberazione **2.** disinnesto.
to **disentangle** *vt*. districare. ♦ to **disentangle** *vi*. districarsi.
disentanglement *s*. districamento.
disesteem *s*. disistima.
to **disesteem** *vt*. disprezzare.
disfavour *s*. **1.** disgrazia **2.** disapprovazione.
to **disfigure** *vt*. sfigurare.
disfigurement *s*. deturpamento.
to **disfranchise** *vt*. privare dei diritti (*civili o di voto*).
to **disgorge** *vt*. **1.** emettere **2.** vomi-

tare (*anche fig.*).
disgrace *s.* **1.** vergogna **2.** disgrazia.
to **disgrace** *vt.* disonorare.
disgraceful *agg.* vergognoso.
disgregation *s.* disgregazione.
disguise *s.* travestimento || *in* —, travestito, camuffato.
to **disguise** *vt.* mascherare.
disgust *s.* disgusto.
tò **disgust** *vt.* disgustare.
disgustedly *avv.* con disgusto.
disgustful, disgusting *agg.* disgustoso.
dish *s.* **1.** piatto **2.** vivanda || —-*washer*, lavapiatti.
to **dish** *vt.* servire || *to* — *up*, servire in tavola.
to **disharmonize** *vt.* disarmonizzare.
to **dishearten** *vt.* scoraggiare.
disheartenment *s.* scoraggiamento.
to **dishevel** *vt.* arruffare.
dishonest *agg.* disonesto.
dishonesty *s.* disonestà.
dishonour *s.* **1.** disonore **2.** mancato pagamento.
to **dishonour** *·vt.* **1.** disonorare **2.** rifiutare di pagare.
dishonourable *agg.* disonorevole.
dishonourableness *s.* disonorabilità.
disillusion(ment) *s.* disillusione.
to **disinfect** *vt.* disinfettare.
disinfectant *s.* disinfettante.
disinfection *s.* disinfezione.
to **disinfest** *vt.* disinfestare.
disinfestation *s.* disinfestazione.
to **disinherit** *vt.* diseredare.
to **disintegrate** *vt.* disintegrare. ♦ to **disintegrate** *vi.* disintegrarsi.
disintegration *s.* disintegrazione.
disintegrator *s.* disintegratore.
to **disinter** *vt.* dissotterrare.
disinterested *agg.* disinteressato.
disinterment *s.* dissotterramento.
to **disjoin** *vt.* disgiungere. ♦ to **disjoin** *vi.* disgiungersi.
to **disjoint** *vt.* **1.** disgregare **2.** disarticolare. ♦ to **disjoint** *vi.* disgregarsi.
disjunction *s.* separazione.
disjunctive *agg.* disgiuntivo.
disjunctively *avv.* disgiuntamente.
disk *s.* disco.
dislike *s.* avversione.
to **dislike** *vt.* detestare, provar avversione per.
to **dislocate** *vt.* **1.** spostare **2.** slogare **3.** disorganizzare.

dislocation *s.* **1.** dislocazione **2.** slogatura **3.** disorganizzazione.
to **dislodge** *vt.* sloggiare.
disloyal *agg.* sleale.
disloyalty *s.* slealtà.
dismal *agg.* tetro.
to **dismantle** *vt.* smantellare.
dismantlement *s.* smantellamento.
to **dismast** *vt.* (*mar.*) disalberare.
dismay *s.* costernazione.
to **dismay** *vt.* costernare.
to **dismember** *vt.* smembrare.
dismemberment *s.* smembramento.
to **dismiss** *vt.* **1.** congedare **2.** licenziare **3.** bandire.
dismissal *s.* **1.** congedo **2.** licenziamento **3.** destituzione **4.** rigetto.
to **dismount** *vt.* e *vi.* smontare.
disobedience *s.* disubbidienza.
disobedient *agg.* disubbidiente.
to **disobey** *vt.* disubbidire.
to **disoblige** *vt.* essere scortese con.
disobliging *agg.* scortese.
disorder *s.* **1.** disordine **2.** disturbo.
to **disorder** *vt.* **1.** scompigliare **2.** disturbare.
disorderly *agg.* **1.** disordinato **2.** turbolento.
disorganization *s.* disorganizzazione.
to **disorganize** *vt.* disorganizzare.
to **disorient(ate)** *vt.* disorientare.
disorientation *s.* disorientamento.
to **disown** *vt.* rinnegare.
disowning *s.* rinnegamento.
to **disparage** *vt.* **1.** deprezzare **2.** screditare.
disparagement *s.* **1.** deprezzamento **2.** denigrazione.
disparaging *agg.* **1.** sprezzante **2.** denigratorio.
disparate *agg.* disparato.
disparity *s.* disparità.
dispassionate *agg.* spassionato.
dispatch *s.* **1.** spedizione **2.** dispaccio **3.** disbrigo **4.** celerità.
to **dispatch** *vt.* **1.** spedire **2.** sbrigare.
to **dispel** *vt.* dissipare.
dispensary *s.* dispensario.
dispensation *s.* **1.** (*eccl.*) dispensa **2.** distribuzione **3.** beneficio.
to **dispense** *vt.* dispensare. ♦ to **dispense** *vi.* fare a meno di: *to* — *with so.*, fare a meno di qu.
dispersal *s.* dispersione.
to **disperse** *vt.* disperdere. ♦ to **disperse** *vi.* disperdersi.
dispersion *s.* dispersione.

dispersive *agg.* dispersivo.
dispirited *agg.* depresso.
to **displace** *vt.* 1. spostare 2. destituire.
displacement *s.* 1. spostamento 2. sostituzione 3. (*mar.*) dislocamento.
display *s.* mostra, esibizione.
to **display** *vt.* mostrare, esporre.
to **displease** *vt.* dispiacere.
displeasing *agg.* spiacevole.
displeasure *s.* dispiacere.
disposal *s.* 1. disposizione 2. cessione.
to **dispose** *vt.* e *vi.* disporre || to — of, disfarsi di, smerciare.
disposition *s.* 1. disposizione 2. indole.
to **dispossess** *vt.* spogliare.
dispossession *s.* 1. spoliazione 2. (*giur.*) esproprio.
disproportion *s.* sproporzione.
disproportionate, disproportioned *agg.* sproporzionato.
to **disprove** *vt.* 1. confutare 2. dimostrare la falsità di.
disputable *agg.* discutibile.
dispute *s.* controversia, disputa.
to **dispute** *vt.* 1. disputare 2. contestare.
disqualification *s.* 1. incapacità 2. (*giur.*) interdizione 3. squalifica.
to **disqualify** *vt.* 1. rendere incapace 2. (*giur.*) interdire 3. squalificare.
disquieting *agg.* inquietante.
disquisition *s.* 1. disquisizione 2. inchiesta.
disregard *s.* noncuranza.
to **disregard** *vt.* ignorare.
disreputable *agg.* 1. sconveniente 2. screditato.
disreputably *avv.* disonorevolmente.
disrepute *s.* discredito.
disrespectful *agg.* irrispettoso.
to **disrobe** *vt.* svestire. ♦ to **disrobe** *vi.* svestirsi.
disruption *s.* rottura.
disruptive *agg.* 1. che smembra 2. dirompente.
dissatisfaction *s.* insoddisfazione.
dissatisfactory *agg.* insoddisfacente.
dissatisfied *agg.* scontento.
to **dissatisfy** *vt.* scontentare.
to **dissect** *vt.* sezionare.
dissection *s.* 1. sezionamento 2. parte sezionata.
to **dissemble** *vt.* e *vi.* dissimulare,

ignorare.
dissembling *s.* dissimulazione. ♦ **dissembling** *agg.* ipocrita.
dissemblingly *avv.* ingannevolmente.
to **disseminate** *vt.* (dis)seminare.
dissemination *s.* disseminazione.
disseminator *s.* propagatore.
dissension *s.* divergenza.
dissent *s.* 1. dissenso 2. (*relig.*) separazione, scisma.
to **dissent** *vi.* dissentire.
dissenter *s.* dissidente.
dissenting *agg.* dissenziente.
to **dissertate** *vi.* dissertare.
dissertation *s.* dissertazione.
dissertator *s.* dissertatore.
disservice *s.* cattivo servizio.
to **dissever** *vt.* scindere. ♦ to **dissever** *vi.* scindersi.
dissidence *s.* dissidio.
dissident *agg.* e *s.* dissidente.
dissimilar *agg.* dissimile.
dissimilarity *s.* dissomiglianza.
dissimilation *s.* dissimilazione.
to **dissimulate** *vt.* e *vi.* dissimulare.
dissimulation *s.* dissimulazione.
dissimulator *s.* dissimulatore.
to **dissipate** *vt.* dissipare. ♦ to **dissipate** *vi.* dissiparsi.
dissipation *s.* dissipazione.
dissociable *agg.* 1. dissociabile 2. riservato.
to **dissociate** *vt.* dissociare. ♦ to **dissociate** *vi.* dissociarsi.
dissociation *s.* 1. dissociazione 2. sdoppiamento (*della personalità*).
dissolubility *s.* dissolubilità.
dissoluble *agg.* dissolubile.
dissolute *agg.* dissoluto.
dissoluteness *s.* dissolutezza.
dissolution *s.* dissoluzione.
to **dissolve** *vt.* dissolvere. ♦ to **dissolve** *vi.* dissolversi.
dissolvent *agg.* e *s.* dissolvente.
dissonance *s.* dissonanza.
dissonant *agg.* dissonante.
to **dissuade** *vt.* dissuadere.
dissuasion *s.* dissuasione.
dissyllabic *agg.* bisillabico.
dissyllable *s.* bisillabo.
dissymmetry *s.* asimmetria.
distaff *s.* conocchia.
distance *s.* distanza || long- — call, telefonata interurbana; at a —, da lontano.
distant *agg.* 1. lontano 2. riservato.
distantly *avv.* (da) lontano.
distaste *s.* ripugnanza.

distasteful *agg.* repellente.

distemper[1] *s.* **1.** turbamento fisico **2.** cimurro **3.** tumulto.

distemper[2] *s.* tempera.

to distend *vt.* distendere. ♦ **to distend** *vi.* distendersi.

to distil(l) *vt.* e *vi.* (di)stillare.

distillate *s.* distillato.

distillation *s.* distillazione.

distiller *s.* distillatore.

distillery *s.* distilleria.

distinct *agg.* distinto.

distinction *s.* distinzione.

distinctive *agg.* distintivo.

to distinguish *vt.* e *vi.* distinguere.

distinguished *agg.* **1.** distinto **2.** illustre.

to distort *vt.* distorcere.

distortion *s.* distorsione.

to distract *vt.* **1.** distrarre **2.** turbare, far impazzire.

distraction *s.* **1.** distrazione **2.** follia: *to love to* —, amare alla follia.

to distrain *vi.* sequestrare.

distrait *agg.* distratto, smarrito.

distraught *agg.* **1.** folle **2.** sconvolto.

distress *s.* **1.** angoscia **2.** pericolo **3.** sequestro.

to distress *vt.* **1.** affliggere **2.** sequestrare.

distressful *agg.* penoso.

distributable *agg.* distribuibile.

to distribute *vt.* distribuire.

distribution *s.* distribuzione.

distributive *agg.* distributivo.

distributor *s.* distributore.

district *s.* distretto.

distrust *s.* diffidenza.

to distrust *vt.* diffidare di.

distrustful *agg.* diffidente.

to disturb *vt.* **1.** disturbare **2.** turbare.

disturbance *s.* agitazione.

disturber *s.* disturbatore.

disunion *s.* separazione.

to disunite *vt.* disunire. ♦ **to disunite** *vi.* separarsi.

disunited *agg.* disunito.

disuse *s.* disuso.

disused *agg.* disusato.

ditch *s.* fosso || *to die in the last* —, resistere ad oltranza.

to ditch *vi.* scavare fossi.

dithyramb *s.* ditirambo.

dithyrambic *agg.* ditirambico.

ditty *s.* **1.** canzone **2.** poemetto.

diuretic *agg.* e *s.* diuretico.

diurnal *agg.* **1.** diurno **2.** quotidiano.

diuturnal *agg.* diuturno.

diuturnity *s.* diuturnità.

divan *s.* divano.

dive *s.* **1.** tuffo **2.** (*aer.*) picchiata.

to dive *vi.* **1.** tuffarsi **2.** (*aer.*) lanciarsi in picchiata.

diver *s.* **1.** tuffatore **2.** palombaro.

to diverge *vi.* divergere.

divergence *s.* divergenza.

divergent *agg.* divergente.

diverse *agg.* **1.** diverso **2.** mutevole.

to diversify *vt.* rendere diverso.

diversion *s.* **1.** diversione **2.** passatempo.

diversity *s.* diversità.

to divert *vt.* **1.** deviare **2.** divertire.

to divest *vt.* spogliare.

to divide *vt.* dividere. ♦ **to divide** *vi.* dividersi.

dividend *s.* dividendo.

dividing *s.* divisione.

divination *s.* divinazione.

divinatory *agg.* divinatorio.

divine *agg.* divino. ♦ **divine** *s.* (*eccl.*) teologo.

to divine *vt.* e *vi.* predire.

diviner *s.* indovino || *water* —, rabdomante.

diving *s.* tuffo || — *-bell*, campana subacquea; — *-board*, trampolino.

divining *s.* divinazione.

divinity *s.* **1.** divinità **2.** teologia.

divisibility *s.* divisibilità.

divisible *agg.* divisibile.

division *s.* divisione.

divisional *agg.* di divisione.

divisor *s.* divisore.

divorce *s.* divorzio.

to divorce *vt.* divorziare.

divulgation *s.* divulgazione.

to divulge *vt.* divulgare.

divulger *s.* divulgatore.

dizzily *avv.* vertiginosamente.

dizziness *s.* vertigine.

dizzy *agg.* **1.** vertiginoso **2.** preso da vertigine **3.** stordito.

to do (**did, done**) *vt.* e *vi.* **1.** (*v. aus. in frasi int., neg., int.-neg.*) — *you understand English?*, capisci l'inglese?; *I do not* (*I don't*), non capisco; *he does not* (*he doesn't*) *speak English*, non parla l'inglese **2.** (*uso enfatico*) *I do study!*, studio veramente! **3.** (*sostitutivo*) *he said he would come and he did*, disse che sarebbe venuto e venne **4.** fare (*in senso generale, astratto*) *what are you doing?*, che cosa stai facendo?; *to*

— one's duty, fare il proprio dovere **5.** bastare: *that will do*, ciò basta **6.** addirsi, convenire: *this house will do me*, questa casa mi va bene || *to — without*, fare a meno.

docile agg. docile.

docility s. docilità.

dock[1] s. bacino: *dry- —*, bacino di carenaggio || *— -master*, capitano di porto; *wet- —*, darsena.

dock[2] s. banco degli imputati (*in tribunale*).

docker s. scaricatore.

docket s. **1.** (*giur.*) estratto verbale **2.** etichetta.

dockyard s. cantiere.

doctor s. dottore.

doctoral agg. dottorale.

doctorate s. dottorato.

doctrinaire agg. e s. dottrinario.

doctrinal agg. dottrinale.

doctrine s. dottrina.

document s. documento.

to **document** vt. documentare.

documentary agg. e s. documentario.

documentation s. documentazione.

to **dodder** vi. tremare, vacillare.

dodecagon s. dodecagono.

dodecahedron s. dodecaedro.

dodge s. **1.** schivata **2.** balzo.

to **dodge** vt. schivare. ♦ to **dodge** vi. scansarsi.

doe s. femmina (*di daino, cervo ecc.*).

doer s. chi agisce, chi fa.

dog s. **1.** cane **2.** (*mecc.*) gancio || *— -cart*, calesse; *— catcher*, accalappiacani; *— -days*, giorni di canicola; *— -ear*, orecchia (*a una pagina*); *— -tired*, stanco morto.

to **dog** vt. inseguire.

dogged agg. ostinato.

doggerel s. filastrocca.

dogmatic(al) agg. dogmatico.

dogmatism s. dogmatismo.

doily s. tovagliolino.

doings s. pl. azioni, imprese.

dole s. **1.** ripartizione **2.** sussidio.

doleful agg. triste.

dolichocephalic agg. dolicocefalo.

doll s. bambola.

dollar s. dollaro.

dolly s. **1.** bambola **2.** (*cine*) carrello.

dolomitic agg. dolomitico.

dolphin s. **1.** delfino **2.** boa.

dolt s. stupido.

domain s. dominio.

dome s. cupola.

domestic agg. **1.** domestico **2.** nazionale. ♦ **domestic** s. domestico.

domicile s. domicilio.

domiciliary agg. domiciliare.

dominant agg. dominante.

to **dominate** vt. e vi. dominare.

domination s. dominazione.

domineering agg. dispotico.

Dominican agg. e s. domenicano.

dominion s. dominio, possedimento (*di territori*).

donation s. donazione.

donative s. dono.

done V. *to do* || *over- —*, troppo cotto; *under- —*, poco cotto.

donjon s. torrione.

donkey s. asino.

donor s. donatore.

doodle s. ghirigoro.

doom s. **1.** destino **2.** giudizio.

to **doom** vt. condannare.

doomsday s. giudizio universale.

door s. porta, portiera || *— -keeper*, portinaio; *— -post*, stipite; *— -way*, soglia.

dope s. **1.** vernice **2.** stupefacente.

to **dope** vt. **1.** verniciare **2.** drogare.

doping s. drogaggio.

Doric agg. dorico.

dormer (window) s. abbaino.

dormitory s. dormitorio.

dormouse s. (*pl.* dormice) ghiro.

dorsal agg. dorsale.

dosage s. dosaggio.

to **dose** vt. **1.** dosare **2.** adulterare.

dosimeter s. dosatore.

dossal s. dossale.

dossier s. incartamento.

dot s. punto, puntino.

to **dot** vt. punteggiare.

dotage s. **1.** rimbambimento **2.** infatuazione.

dotal agg. dotale.

doting agg. **1.** senile **2.** infatuato. ♦ **doting** s. senilità.

double agg. doppio. ♦ **double** s. **1.** doppio **2.** (*cine*) controfigura. ♦ **double** avv. **1.** doppiamente **2.** in due.

to **double** vt. **1.** raddoppiare **2.** doppiare **3.** piegare. ♦ to **double** vi. **1.** raddoppiarsi **2.** piegarsi.

double-dealing s. imbroglio.

doubleness s. doppiezza.

doubling s. raddoppiamento.

doubly avv. doppiamente.

doubt s. dubbio || *no —*, indubbiamente.

to **doubt** vt. e vi. dubitare.

doubtful *agg.* incerto, dubbio.
doubtfulness *s.* dubbiosità.
doubtless *agg.* indubbio. ♦ **doubtless** *avv.* indubbiamente.
dough *s.* pasta.
dove *s.* colomba || — -*cot(e)*, colombaia.
dowdy *agg.* sciatto.
dower *s.* dote.
down[1] *s.* **1.** duna **2.** collina.
down[2] *s.* **1.** piumino **2.** lanugine.
down[3] *agg.* **1.** diretto verso il basso **2.** depresso.
down[4] *avv.* (in) giù || — *with!*, abbasso: — *with the tyrant!*, abbasso il tiranno! ♦ **down** *prep.* giù per.
to **down** *vt.* abbattere, rovesciare.
downcast *agg.* abbattuto.
downfall *s.* rovescio.
downhearted *agg.* scoraggiato.
downhill *agg.* discendente, inclinato. ♦ **downhill** *avv.* in discesa.
downpour *s.* acquazzone.
downright *agg.* vero, sincero. ♦ **downright** *avv.* completamente.
downstairs *avv.* giù. ♦ **downstairs** *agg.* dabbasso. ♦ **downstairs** *s.* pianterreno.
downtrodden *agg.* calpestato, oppresso.
downward *agg.* in giù, discendente.
downward(s) *avv.* in giù.
downy[1] *agg.* ondulato.
downy[2] *agg.* **1.** lanuginoso **2.** morbido.
dowry *s.* dote.
dowser *s.* rabdomante.
doze *s.* sonnellino.
to **doze** *vi.* sonnecchiare.
dozen *s.* dozzina.
drab *s.* **1.** sciattona **2.** sgualdrina.
draff *s.* feccia.
draft *s.* **1.** tiro **2.** sorso **3.** abbozzo **4.** corrente d'aria **5.** (*comm.*) tratta **6.** (*mar.*) pescaggio.
to **draft** *vt.* **1.** tirare **2.** abbozzare.
drag *s.* **1.** erpice **2.** (*mar.*) draga **3.** ostacolo.
to **drag** *vt.* **1.** trascinare **2.** dragare. ♦ to **drag** *vi.* trascinarsi || *to — on*, tirare in lungo.
to **draggle** *vt.* inzaccherare. ♦ to **draggle** *vi.* inzaccherarsi.
dragon *s.* drago || — -*fly*, libellula.
drain *s.* **1.** canale, fogna **2.** fuga.
to **drain** *vt.* prosciugare. ♦ to **drain** *vi.* **1.** prosciugarsi **2.** defluire.
drainage *s.* **1.** fognatura **2.** drenaggio.

draining *s.* **1.** scolatura **2.** drenaggio.
dram *s.* dramma (*unità di peso*).
drama *s.* dramma.
dramatic(al) *agg.* drammatico.
dramatics *s. pl.* produzioni drammatiche (*di dilettanti*).
dramatist *s.* drammaturgo.
to **dramatize** *vt. e vi.* drammatizzare.
dramaturgy *s.* drammaturgia.
drank V. *to drink.*
to **drape** *vt.* drappeggiare.
draper *s.* negoziante di tessuti.
drapery *s.* **1.** tessuti **2.** drappeggi.
drastic *agg.* drastico.
draught *s.* V. *draft.* ♦ **draughts** *s. pl.* gioco della dama (*sing.*).
draught-board *s.* scacchiera.
draw *s.* **1.** tiro **2.** estrazione **3.** attrazione.
to **draw** (**drew, drawn**) *vt.* **1.** tirare **2.** attirare **3.** disegnare **4.** estrarre **5.** (*comm.*) emettere || *to — up*, compilare. ♦ to **draw** (**drew, drawn**) *vi.* tirarsi || *to — on*, avvicinarsi; *to — in*, ritirarsi; *to — up*, fermarsi.
drawback *s.* ostacolo.
drawbridge *s.* ponte levatoio.
drawer *s.* **1.** estrattore **2.** disegnatore **3.** cassetto.
drawers *s. pl.* mutande.
drawing *s.* **1.** disegno **2.** estrazione **3.** attrazione || — -*pen*, tiralinee; — -*pin*, puntina da disegno.
drawing-room *s.* salotto.
to **drawl** *vt.* strascicare la voce.
drawn V. *to draw* ||
dread *s.* spavento.
dreadful *agg.* terribile.
dreadnought *s.* **1.** impavido **2.** (*mar.*) corazzata.
dream *s.* sogno.
to **dream** (**dreamt, dreamt**) (*anche reg.*) *vt. e vi.* sognare.
dreamer *s.* sognatore.
dreamt V. *to dream.*
dreamless *agg.* senza sogni.
dreamy *agg.* **1.** sognante **2.** vago.
dreariness *s.* tristezza.
dreary *agg.* tetro, squallido.
dredge *s.* draga.
to **dredge**[1] *vt. e vi.* dragare.
to **dredge**[2] *vt.* cospargere, spolverizzare.
dredger[1] *s.* draga.
dredger[2] *s.* spolverizzatore.
dredging *s.* dragaggio.

dregs s. pl. **1.** feccia (sing.) **2.** sedimento (sing.).

to drench vt. inzuppare || to get drenched, inzupparsi.

dress s. abito, abbigliamento.

to dress vt. **1.** vestire **2.** bendare **3.** condire, rifinire. ♦ to **dress** vi. vestirsi.

dressing s. **1.** abbigliamento **2.** medicazione **3.** condimento || — -gown, vestaglia; — -table, toletta.

dressmaker s. sarta.

dressmaking s. sartoria.

drew V. to draw.

dribble s. **1.** gocciolamento **2.** (sport) palleggio.

to dribble vt. e vi. **1.** stillare **2.** (sport) palleggiare.

dribbling s. V. dribble.

drier s. essiccatore.

drift s. **1.** spinta **2.** deriva **3.** raffica **4.** (fig.) significato.

to drift vt. sospingere. ♦ to **drift** vi. andare alla deriva, essere trascinato.

drill s. **1.** trapano, trivella **2.** esercitazione.

to drill vt. **1.** trapanare, trivellare **2.** esercitare.

drilling s. **1.** trapanazione, trivellazione **2.** esercitazione || — machine, trapano.

drink s. **1.** il bere **2.** bevanda.

to drink (drank, drunk) vt. e vi. bere.

drinkable agg. bevibile.

drinker s. bevitore.

drinking s. il bere.

drip s. gocciolamento.

to drip vt. e vi. gocciolare.

dripping s. gocciolio.

drive s. **1.** gita (in auto) **2.** viale (carrozzabile) **3.** spinta.

to drive (drove, driven) vt. **1.** condurre **2.** guidare **3.** azionare || to — away, scacciare; to — in, conficcare. ♦ to **drive (drove, driven)** vi. andare (in veicolo) || to — off, partire (in veicolo); to — up, arrivare (in veicolo).

drive-in s. cinema, banca ecc. in cui si entra in auto.

driver s. conducente.

driving s **1.** guida **2.** comando.

drizzle s. pioggerella.

to drizzle vi. piovigginare.

drizzly agg. piovigginoso.

droll agg. buffo.

drollery s. **1.** buffoneria **2.** scherzo.

dromedary s. dromedario.

drone s. **1.** fuco **2.** ronzio.

to drone vt. e vi. ronzare.

to droop vt. abbassare. ♦ to **droop** vi. afflosciarsi, languire.

drooping agg. **1.** pendente, abbassato **2.** abbattuto.

drop s. **1.** goccia **2.** caduta **3.** ribasso.

to drop vt. lasciar cadere. ♦ to **drop** vi. cadere || to — in, fare una visitina; to — away, scomparire.

dropper s. contagocce.

dropsical agg. idropico.

dropsy s. idropisia.

dross s. scoria.

drought s. siccità.

drove V. to drive.

to drown vt. **1.** annegare **2.** smorzare. ♦ to **drown** vi. annegare.

drowning s. annegamento.

to drowse vi. sonnecchiare, assopirsi.

drowsily avv. in modo sonnolento.

drowsiness s. sonnolenza.

drowsy agg. sonnolento.

to drub vt. percuotere, bastonare.

drudge s. sgobbone.

to drudge vi. sfacchinare.

drudgery s. lavoro faticoso.

drug s. **1.** medicina **2.** droga || — -store, farmacia (in cui si vendono articoli vari).

to drug vt. drogare.

druggist s. farmacista.

Druid s. druido.

drum s. **1.** tamburo **2.** timpano.

to drum vi. suonare il tamburo. ♦ to **drum** vt. (fig.) inculcare.

drummer s. tamburino.

drumming s. tambureggiamento.

drunk V. to drink. ♦ **drunk** agg. ubriaco.

drunkard s. ubriacone.

drunken agg. ubriaco.

drunkenness s. ubriachezza.

dry agg. asciutto, arido, secco || — cleaning, lavaggio a secco.

to dry vt. **1.** seccare **2.** asciugare. ♦ to **dry** vi. **1.** seccarsi **2.** asciugatsi || to — up, ammutolire.

dryad s. driade.

drying agg. essiccante. ♦ **drying** s. essiccamento.

dual agg. duplice.

dualism s. dualismo.

dualist s. dualista.

dualistic agg. dualistico.

duality *s.* dualità.
to dub[1] *vt.* creare cavaliere.
to dub[2] *vt.* (*cine*) doppiare.
dubbing *s.* doppiaggio.
dubious *agg.* 1. dubbio 2. dubbioso.
dubiousness *s.* dubbiosità.
dubitative *agg.* dubitativo.
ducal *agg.* ducale.
duchess *s.* duchessa.
duchy *s.* ducato.
duck[1] *s.* anitra.
duck[2] *s.* tela.
duck[3] *s.* tuffo.
to duck *vt.* 1. tuffare 2. piegare. ♦
to duck *vi.* 1. tuffarsi 2. piegarsi.
duckling *s.* anatroccolo.
duct *s.* condotto.
ductile *agg.* duttile.
ductility *s.* duttilità.
due *agg.* e *s.* dovuto || *to be* —, do-
ver arrivare; *to fall* —, scadere.
duel *s.* duello.
to duel *vi.* duella.e.
duet *s.* duetto.
dug *V. to dig.*
duke *s.* duca.
dukedom *s.* ducato.
dull *agg.* 1. tardo, sciocco 2. sordo
3. triste 4. noioso 5. opaco.
to dull *vt.* 1. istupidire 2. intorpidire 3. smorzare. ♦ to dull *vi.*
1. istupidirsi 2. intorpidirsi 3.
smorzarsi.
dullard *s.* imbecille.
dul(l)ness *s.* 1. lentezza 2. noia
3. opacità 4. ottusità.
dully *avv.* 1. ottusamente 2. lentamente 3. in modo noioso 4. debolmente.
duly *avv.* debitamente.
dumb *agg.* muto || — *-show*, pan-
tomima.
to dumbfound *vt.* confondere.
dumbness *s.* mutismo.
dumb-waiter *s.* montavivande.
dummy *agg.* 1. muto 2. falso. ♦
dummy *s.* fantoccio.
dump *s.* 1. colpo sordo 2. ammasso.
dumping *s.* «dumping» (*tipo di
vendita concorrenziale sui mercati
esteri*).
dunce *s.* ignorante.
dune *s.* duna.
dung *s.* 1. sterco 2. letame.
dungarees *s. pl.* tuta (*da lavoro*)
(*sing.*).
dungeon *s.* 1. torrione 2. prigione
sotterranea.
dunghill *s.* letamaio.

to dunk *vt.* e *vi.* inzuppare.
duodenal *agg.* duodenale.
duodenum *s.* (*pl.* -na) duodeno.
dupe *s.* gonzo.
duplex *agg.* duplice.
duplicate *agg.* doppio. ♦ duplicate *s.* duplicato.
to duplicate *vt.* duplicare.
duplication *s.* 1. raddoppiamento
2. riproduzione.
duplicator *s.* copialettere.
duplicity *s.* doppiezza.
durability *s.* durata.
durable *agg.* durevole.
durallumin *s.* duralluminio.
duration *s.* durata.
duress *s.* 1. prigionia 2. coercizione.
during *prep.* durante.
durst *V.* dare.
dusk *s.* 1. oscurità 2. crepuscolo.
dusky *agg.* oscuro.
dust *s.* polvere || — *-bin*, pattu-
miera.
to dust *vt.* 1. impolverare 2. spolverare. ♦ to dust *vi.* impolverarsi.
duster *s.* 1. strofinaccio (*per la polvere*) 2. polverizzatore.
dustman *s.* spazzino.
dusty *agg.* polveroso.
Dutch *agg.* olandese.
Dutchman *s.* olandese.
dutiful *agg.* rispettoso.
duty *s.* 1. ubbidienza 2. dovere 3.
tassa.
duumvirate *s.* duumvirato.
dwarf *s.* nano.
dwarfish *agg.* nano.
to dwell (dwelt, dwelt) *vi.* 1.
abitare 2. fermarsi.
dweller *s.* abitatore.
dwelling *s.* abitazione.
dwelt *V. to dwell.*
dye *s.* tintura.
to dye *vt.* tingere. ♦ to dye *vi.* tin-
gersi.
dyer *s.* tintore.
dyerworks *s. pl.* tintoria (*sing.*).
dying *agg.* morente.
dynamic(al) *agg.* dinamico.
dynamics *s.* dinamica.
dynamism *s.* dinamismo.
dynamite *s.* dinamite.
dynamiter *s.* dinamitardo.
dynamo *s.* dinamo.
dynamometer *s.* dinamometro.
dynast *s.* dinasta.
dynastic(al) *agg.* dinastico.
dynasty *s.* dinastia.
dyne *s.* dina.

dysenteric *agg.* dissenterico.
dysentery *s.* dissenteria.
dyspepsia *s.* dispepsia.
dyspeptic(al) *agg.* dispeptico.

E

E (*mus.*) mi.
each *agg.* ogni, ciascuno. ♦ **each**
pron. ognuno, ciascuno || — *other*,
l'un l'altro.
eager *agg.* **1.** ardente, appassionato
2. avido, desideroso.
eagerly *avv.* **1.** ardentemente **2.** avidamente.
eagerness *s.* **1.** ardore **2.** impazienza, premura.
eagle *s.* aquila.
ear[1] orecchio || — -*ache* mal d'o-
recchi — -*drum;* timpano; —
-*ring*, orecchino; — -*vax*, ceru-
me; *within* — -*shot*, a portata di
voce.
ear[2] *s.* spiga (*di grano*).
earl *s.* conte.
earldom *s.* **1.** titolo di conte **2.**
contea.
early *agg.* **1.** primo, il principio, la
prima parte (*di qualsiasi tempo*)
2. mattiniero **3.** prematuro **4.** re-
moto || — *train*, treno del primo
mattino.
early *avv.* **1.** presto, di buon'ora,
per tempo **2.** al principio.
earmark *s.* **1.** marchio, caratteristica **2.** (*comm.*) contrassegno.
to **earn** *vt.* guadagnare, meritare.
earnest *agg.* **1.** serio, zelante **2.** ardente. ♦ **earnest** *s.* caparra, pe-
gno.
earnestly *avv.* **1.** seriamente **2.** con
ardore.
earnestness *s.* **1.** serietà **2.** ardore.
earnings *s. pl.* **1.** guadagni **2.**
(*comm.*) utili.
earth *s.* **1.** terra, mondo **2.** terreno.
earth-bound *agg.* radicato, attacca-
to ai beni terreni.
earthen *agg.* di terra, di terracotta.
earthenware *s.* terraglia.
earthly *agg.* terrestre.
earthquake *s.* terremoto.
earthworm *s.* lombrico.
earthy *agg.* terroso, di terra.
ease *s.* **1.** tranquillità (*di spirito*),

benessere **2.** facilità, agevolezza **3.**
sollievo.
to **ease** *vt.* e *vi.* **1.** alleviare, calmare
2. liberare, alleggerire.
easeful *agg.* tranquillo.
easel *s.* cavalletto, telaio.
easily *avv.* **1.** facilmente **2.** comodamente.
easiness *s.* **1.** comodità, benessere
2. facilità.
east *s.* est, oriente: *the Far East*,
l'Estremo Oriente. ♦ **east** *avv.*
ad est, verso est.
Easter *s.* Pasqua.
easterly *agg.* dell'est, dall'est, orientale.
eastern *agg.* dell'est, orientale.
eastward *agg.* verso est.
easy *agg.* **1.** facile **2.** agiato,
modo **3.** piacevole.
easy *avv.* facilmente, comodamente.
easygoing *agg.* facilone, indolente.
to **eat (ate, eaten)** *vt.* e *vi.* **1.**
mangiare **2.** rodere, corrodere.
eatable *agg.* mangiabile, commesti-
bile.
eatables *s. pl.* vivande, viveri.
eaten V. *to eat.*
eater *s.* mangiatore.
eating *s.* il mangiare.
eaves *s. pl.* gronda, cornicione
(*sing.*).
to **eavesdrop** *vi.* origliare.
ebb *s.* **1.** riflusso, l'abbassarsi della
marea **2.** (*fig.*) decadenza || — *-tide*,
bassa marea.
ebbing *agg.* **1.** defluente **2.** in declino.
ebonist *s.* ebanista.
ebonite *s.* ebanite.
ebony *s.* ebano.
ebullition *s.* ebollizione.
eccentric *agg.* e *s.* eccentrico (*anche fig.*).
eccentricity *s.* eccentricità.
ecclesiastic *agg.* e *s.* ecclesiastico.
ecclesiastical *agg.* ecclesiastico.
echelon *s.* scaglione.
echinoderm *s.* echinoderma.
echo *s.* eco.
to **echo** *vt.* e *vi.* **1.** far eco (a) **2.** e-
cheggiare.
eclectic *agg.* e *s.* eclettico.
eclecticism *s.* eclettismo.
eclipse *s.* eclissi.
to **eclipse** *vt.* eclissare.
ecliptic *agg.* eclittico.
eclogue *s.* egloga.
ecology *s.* ecologia.

economic *agg.* economico.
economical *agg.* economico.
economics *s.* scienze economiche.
economist *s.* economista.
to **economize** *vt.* e *vi.* economizzare.
economy *s.* economia.
ecstasy *s.* estasi.
ecstatic *agg.* estatico.
ecstatically *avv.* estaticamente.
ecumenic(al) *agg.* ecumenico.
eczema *s.* eczema.
eddy *s.* **1.** turbine d'aria, vortice **2.** gorgo, risucchio.
edge *s.* **1.** orlo, margine **2.** ciglio, sponda **3.** taglio (*di lama*) **4.** spigolo.
to **edge** *vt.* e *vi.* **1.** bordare, fare un bordo **2.** affilare, arrotare, aguzzare (*anche fig.*).
edged *agg.* affilato, tagliente || *double- —*, a doppio taglio (*anche fig.*).
edgeless *agg.* **1.** senza bordo **2.** smussato, che non taglia.
edging *s.* orlatura, fettuccia.
edible *agg.* mangereccio.
edibles *s.* *pl.* commestibili.
edict *s.* editto.
edifice *s.* edificio (*anche fig.*).
edifying *agg.* edificante.
to **edit** *vt.* **1.** pubblicare, curare (*un libro*) **2.** redigere **3.** (*cine*) montare.
editing *s.* **1.** redazione, commento (*di un testo*) **2.** direzione (*di un giornale, ecc.*).
edition *s.* edizione.
editor *s.* **1.** commentatore, curatore (*di un testo*) **2.** direttore, redattore (*di un giornale*).
editorial *s.* editoriale, articolo di fondo. ◆ **editorial** *agg.* editoriale.
editorship *s.* direzione, redazione (*di giornali*).
to **educate** *vt.* **1.** istruire, educare **2.** affinare, esercitare.
educated *agg.* **1.** istruito, colto **2.** addestrato (*di animali*).
education *s.* **1.** cultura, educazione **2.** istruzione, insegnamento.
educational *agg.* educativo.
educative *agg.* istruttivo.
educator *s.* educatore.
to **educe** *vt.* estrarre, sviluppare.
educible *agg.* che si può estrarre.
to **edulcorate** *vt.* dolcificare.
eel *s.* anguilla.
eerie, eery *agg.* irreale, sovrannaturale.

to **efface** *vt.* cancellare, distruggere.
effect *s.* **1.** effetto, risultato **2.** impressione. ◆ **effects** *s.* *pl.* effetti personali.
to **effect** *vt.* effettuare, eseguire.
effective *agg.* **1.** efficace **2.** effettivo.
effectiveness *s.* efficacia.
effectual *agg.* efficace.
effectuality *s.* efficacia, validità.
effectuation *s.* effettuazione.
effeminacy *s.* effeminatezza.
effeminate *agg.* effeminato.
effervescence *s.* **1.** effervescenza **2.** (*fig.*) eccitamento.
effete *agg.* logoro, esaurito.
efficacious *agg.* efficace.
efficaciousness *s.* **1.** efficacia **2.** rendimento (*di una macchina*).
efficiency *s.* efficienza, rendimento.
efficient *agg.* **1.** efficiente, di alto rendimento **2.** abile, capace.
effigy *s.* effigie.
to **effloresce** *vi.* fiorire, germogliare.
effluent *agg.* defluente.
effort *s.* sforzo, fatica.
effortless *agg.* senza sforzo, facile.
effrontery *s.* sfrontatezza.
effulgence *s.* splendore.
effusion *s.* effusione, esuberanza.
effusive *agg.* espansivo, esuberante.
egg *s.* uovo || *boiled —*, uovo alla coque; *hard-boiled —*, uovo sodo.
to **egg** *vt.* to *— on so.*, istigare, incitare qu.
egocentric *agg.* egocentrico.
egocentrism *s.* egocentrismo.
egoism *s.* egoismo.
egoist *s.* egoista.
egoistic(al) *agg.* egoistico.
egotism *s.* egotismo.
egotist *s.* egotista.
egregious *agg.* insigne, eminente.
egress *s.* uscita.
Egyptian *agg.* e *s.* egiziano.
eider-down *s.* piumino (*da letto*).
eight *agg.* otto.
eighteen *agg.* diciotto.
eighteenth *agg.* diciottesimo.
eighth *agg.* ottavo.
eightieth *agg.* ottantesimo.
eighty *agg.* ottanta.
either *agg.* **1.** l'uno o l'altro **2.** ciascuno dei due, tutti e due. ◆ **either** *avv.* anche, pure. ◆ **either** *avv.* (*in frasi neg.*) neanche, neppure. ◆ **either** *cong.* (*seguito da* or) o, oppure.
to **ejaculate** *vt.* **1.** eiaculare **2.** e-

sclamare.

ejaculation s. 1. eiaculazione 2. esclamazione.

to **eject** vt. gettar fuori.

ejection s. 1. espulsione 2. (fig.) destituzione.

ejector s. espulsore.

elaborate agg. elaborato, accurato.

to **elaborate** vt. e vi. elaborare.

elaboration s. elaborazione.

to **elapse** vi. trascorrere, passare (del tempo).

elastic agg. elastico (anche fig.).

elasticity s. elasticità.

to **elate** vt. inebriare, esaltare.

elbow s. gomito.

to **elbow** vt. e vi. spingere con il gomito, andare avanti a gomitate.

elder agg. (comp. di old) maggiore, più vecchio (tra due persone). ♦ **elder** s. maggiore, più vecchio (fra due).

elderly agg. attempato.

eldest agg. (superl. di old) maggiore (tra fratelli), primogenito.

elect agg. eletto, scelto.

to **elect** vt. eleggere.

election s. 1. elezione 2. scelta.

elective agg. 1. elettivo 2. elettorale.

elector s. elettore.

electoral agg. elettorale.

electorate s. elettorato.

electric(al) agg. elettrico.

electrician s. elettricista.

electricity s. elettricità.

to **electrify** vt. 1. elettrificare 2. elettrizzare.

electrization s. elettrizzazione.

electrocardiogram s. elettrocardiogramma.

to **electrocute** vt. fulminare mediante elettricità.

electrocution s. elettroesecuzione.

electrode s. elettrodo.

electrodynamics s. elettrodinamica.

electrolysis s. elettrolisi.

electro-magnet s. elettromagnete.

electromagnetic agg. elettromagnetico.

electron s. elettrone.

electronic agg. elettronico.

electronics s. elettronica.

electrostatics s. elettrostatica.

elegance s. eleganza.

elegant agg. elegante, raffinato.

elegiac agg. elegiaco.

elegy s. elegia.

element s. 1. elemento 2. principio costitutivo.

elemental agg. 1. dei quattro elementi 2. elementare 3. fondamentale.

elementary agg. elementare.

elephant s. elefante.

elephantiasis s. elefantiasi.

elephantine agg. elefantesco.

to **elevate** vt. innalzare, elevare (anche fig.).

elevated agg. 1. elevato 2. sopraelevato.

elevation s. 1. elevazione 2. collina, luogo alto.

elevator s. ascensore, montacarichi.

eleven agg. undici.

elevenses s. (fam.) spuntino a metà mattina.

eleventh agg. undicesimo.

elf s. (pl. elves) elfo, folletto.

elfish agg. 1. incantato 2. vivace.

to **elicit** vt. estrarre, strappare.

eligibility s. eleggibilità.

eligible agg. eleggibile.

to **eliminate** vt. eliminare.

elimination s. eliminazione.

elision s. elisione.

elixir s. elisir.

elk s. alce.

ellipse s. ellisse.

ellipsis s. ellissi.

elliptic(al) agg. ellittico.

elm s. olmo.

elocution s. 1. elocuzione 2. dizione.

to **elope** vi. fuggire (con un amante).

elopement s. fuga (con un amante).

eloquence s. eloquenza.

eloquent agg. eloquente (anche fig.).

else avv. (dopo avv. e pron. int., indef.) altro.

elsewhere avv. altrove.

to **elude** vt. eludere, schivare.

elusive agg. 1. elusivo, ambiguo 2. sfuggevole.

elytron s. (pl. elytra) elitra.

Elzevir agg. e s. elzeviro.

to **emaciate** vt. far deperire, far dimagrire.

emaciated agg. emaciato.

to **emanate** vi. emanare.

emanation s. emanazione.

to **emancipate** vt. emancipare.

emancipation s. emancipazione.

to **embalm** vt. 1. imbalsamare 2. profumare.

embalmer s. imbalsamatore.

embankment s. 1. argine, diga 2. alzaia.

embarcation s. imbarco.

embargo s. embargo, fermo.

to **embark** vt. imbarcare (*truppe, merci*). ♦ to **embark** vi. imbarcarsi.

embarkation s. imbarco.

to **embarrass** vt. mettere in imbarazzo.

embarrassing agg. imbarazzante.

embarrassment s. 1. imbarazzo 2. difficoltà.

embassy s. ambasciata.

to **embattle** vt. disporre in ordine di battaglia, fortificare.

to **embed** vt. incassare, conficcare.

to **embellish** vt. abbellire, ornare.

embellishment s. abbellimento, ornamento.

ember s. tizzone. ♦ **embers** s. pl. brace (*sing.*).

embezzler s. malversatore.

to **embitter** vt. 1. rendere amaro 2. (*fig.*) amareggiare.

embitterment s. amarezza, inasprimento.

to **emblazon** vt. 1. decorare 2. celebrare.

emblem s. emblema, simbolo (*fig.*).

emblematic(al) agg. emblematico.

embodiment s. 1. incarnazione 2. incorporamento.

to **embody** vt. 1. incarnare 2. personificare 3. incorporare.

to **embolden** vt. incoraggiare.

embolism s. embolia.

embolus s. (*pl.* -li) embolo.

to **emboss** vt. 1. scolpire 2. stampare in rilievo.

embossed agg. 1. sbalzato 2. fatto in rilievo.

embrace s. abbraccio, amplesso.

to **embrace** vt. abbracciare (*anche fig.*). ♦ to **embrace** vi. abbracciarsi.

embrasure s. 1. vano (*di porta, finestra*) 2. feritoia.

to **embroider** vt. ricamare.

embroiderer s. ricamatore.

embroidery s. ricamo.

to **embroil** vt. coinvolgere in una disputa.

embryo s. embrione.

embryonic agg. embrionale (*anche fig.*).

to **emend** vt. emendare.

emendation s. emendamento.

emerald s. smeraldo.

to **emerge** vi. 1. emergere, affiorare 2. (*fig.*) risultare.

emergency s. emergenza, caso imprevisto || — -*door,* uscita di sicurezza; — *means,* mezzi di fortuna.

emersion s. emersione.

emery s. smeriglio || — -*paper,* carta smerigliata.

emetic agg. e s. emetico.

emigrant agg. e s. emigrante.

to **emigrate** vi. emigrare.

emigration s. emigrazione.

eminence s. 1. luogo, parte eminente 2. (*anat.*) protuberanza 3. (*fig.*) eminenza, eccellenza.

eminent agg. eminente (*anche fig.*).

eminently avv. eminentemente.

emir s. emiro.

emissary s. emissario, agente segreto.

emission s. emissione.

to **emit** vt. 1. emettere 2. esalare.

emollient agg. e s. emolliente.

emolument s. remunerazione, salario.

emotion s. emozione, turbamento.

emotional agg. 1. emotivo, impressionabile 2. commovente.

emotionalism s. emotività.

emotionally avv. con emozione.

emotive agg. 1. commovente 2. emotivo.

emperor s. imperatore.

emphasis s. 1. accentuazione, rilievo 2. enfasi.

to **emphasize** vt. accentuare.

emphatic agg. 1. accentuato 2. enfatico.

emphysema s. enfisema.

emphyteusis s. enfiteusi.

empire s. impero.

empiric s. empirico.

empirical agg. empirico.

empiricism s. empirismo.

emplacement s. 1. collocazione 2. (*mil.*) piazzuola.

employ s. impiego: out of —, senza impiego.

to **employ** vt. 1. impiegare, adoperare 2. assumere.

employee s. impiegato.

employer s. datore di lavoro.

employment s. impiego, occupazione.

to **empoison** vt. avvelenare.

emporium s. 1. centro commerciale 2. emporio.

to **empower** vt. dare pieni poteri a.

emptiness s. **1.** vuoto **2.** vanità.

empty agg. **1.** vuoto **2.** vano **3.** vacante ‖ — -handed, a mani vuote.

to empty vt. vuotare. ♦ **to empty**
vi. vuotarsi.

to emulate vt. emulare.

emulation s. emulazione.

emulator s. emulatore.

emulous agg. emulo.

to emulsify vt. emulsionare.

emulsion s. emulsione.

emulsive agg. emulsivo.

to enable vt. mettere in grado.

to enact vt. decretare, emanare (una
legge).

enactment s. **1.** promulgazione **2.**
legge.

enamel s. smalto.

to enamel vt. smaltare.

to encamp vi. accamparsi.

encaustic agg. encaustico.

encephalic agg. encefalico.

encephalitis s. encefalite.

to enchant vt. incantare, affascinare.

enchanter s. incantatore, mago.

enchanting agg. incantevole.

enchantment s. incanto, incantesimo.

enchantress s. incantatrice.

to encircle vt. circondare, cingere.

enclitic agg. enclitico.

to enclose vt. **1.** racchiudere, cingere
2. accludere.

enclosed agg. **1.** racchiuso, circon-
dato **2.** accluso.

enclosure s. recinto, staccionata
2. allegato.

encomiast s. encomiasta.

to encompass vt. circondare (anche
fig.).

encore avv. (teat.) bis.

to encore vt. chiedere il bis.

encounter s. scontro.

to encourage vt. incoraggiare, animare.

encouragement s. incoraggiamento.

encouraging agg. incoraggiante.

to encroach vt. **1.** usurpare, invadere **2.** (giur.) ledere.

to encrust vt. incrostare.

to encumber vt. **1.** ingombrare, imbarazzare **2.** ostruire.

encumbrance s. ingombro, impedimento.

encyclic(al) agg. enciclico. ♦ **en-
cyclic(al)** s. enciclica.

encyclop(a)edia s. enciclopedia.

encyclop(a)edic(al) agg. enciclo-

pedico.

end s. **1.** estremità, fine, termine **2.**
scopo, mira **3.** morte.

to end vt. e vi. finire, concludere.

to endanger vt. mettere in pericolo,
compromettere.

to endear vt. affezionare, rendere
caro.

endearing agg. affettuoso, tenero.

endearment s. tenerezza. ♦ **en-
dearments** s. pl. blandizie.

to endeavo(u)r vi. sforzarsi. ♦
to endeavo(u)r vt. tentare.

endemic agg. endemico.

ending agg. finale, ultimo. ♦ **ending** s. fine, conclusione.

endless agg. senza fine, eterno, continuo.

endocarditis s. endocardite.

endocardium s. endocardio.

endocarp s. endocarpo.

endocrine agg. endocrino.

endocrinology s. endocrinologia.

endogeny s. endogenesi.

to endorse vt. (comm.) girare, vistare.

endorsee s. (comm.) giratario.

endorsement s. (comm.) girata.

endorser s. (comm.) girante.

to endow vt. **1.** dotare **2.** fare una
donazione.

endowment s. **1.** costituzione di
dote, donazione **2.** (fig.) talento.

endurance s. **1.** resistenza, sopportazione **2.** durata.

to endure vt. tollerare, sopportare.
♦ **to endure** vi. resistere, durare.

enduring agg. **1.** tollerante, paziente **2.** durevole.

enema s. clistere.

enemy agg. e s. nemico.

energetic(al) agg. **1.** energico **2.**
energetico.

to energize vt. infondere energia.

energumen s. energumeno.

energy s. energia, forza.

to enervate vt. snervare, indebolire.

enervation s. indebolimento.

to enfeeble vt. indebolire.

to enfold vt. **1.** avvolgere **2.** cingere.

to enforce vt. **1.** imporre, far rispettare **2.** mettere in vigore (una
legge).

to enframe vt. incorniciare.

to enfranchise vt. affrancare, liberare.

enfranchisement s. affrancamento,

liberazione.

to **engage** vt. 1. impegnare 2. ingaggiare 3. attrarre (l'attenzione). ◆ to **engage** vi. impegnarsi || to — in conversation, prendere parte alla conversazione.

engaged agg. 1. impegnato 2. fidanzato 3. occupato, riservato.

engagement s. 1. impegno 2. fidanzamento 3. assunzione, impiego.

engaging agg. attraente, avvincente.

engagingly avv. in modo attraente.

to **engender** vt. produrre, causare.

engine s. 1. macchina, motore 2. (ferr.) locomotrice || fire- —, autopompa.

engineer s. 1. ingegnere 2. tecnico.

engineering s. 1. ingegneria 2. costruzione meccanica.

English agg. inglese. ◆ **English** s. lingua inglese.

Englishman s. (uomo) inglese.

Englishwoman s. (donna) inglese.

to **engrave** vt. 1. intagliare, incidere 2. (fig.) imprimere.

engraver s. incisore.

engraving s. arte dell'incisione || wood- —, xilografia.

to **engross** vt. 1. copiare (un atto legale), redigere (un documento) 2. assorbire (l'attenzione).

engrossment s. copiatura (di documento).

to **enhance** vt. accrescere.

enigma s. enigma.

enigmatic(al) agg. enigmatico.

to **enjoy** vt. 1. godere, gioire 2. gustare, provar piacere di || to — oneself, divertirsi.

enjoyable agg. piacevole, gradevole.

enjoyably avv. piacevolmente.

enjoyment s. godimento, piacere.

to **enkindle** vt. infiammare, eccitare. ◆ to **enkindle** vi. infiammarsi, eccitarsi.

to **enlarge** vt. 1. allargare, ampliare 2. (foto) ingrandire. ◆ to **enlarge** vi. allargarsi, ampliarsi.

enlargement s. 1. allargamento 2. (foto) ingrandimento.

enlarger s. (foto) ingranditore.

to **enlighten** vt. rischiarare, illuminare (anche fig.).

enlightenment s. 1. spiegazione, schiarimento 2. (lett.) l'illuminismo.

to **enlist** vt. arruolare. ◆ to **enlist** vi. arruolarsi.

enlistment s. arruolamento, in-

gaggio.

to **enliven** vt. rianimare, ravvivare.

to **enmesh** vt. impegolare, irretire.

enmity s. ostilità, inimicizia.

to **ennoble** vt. nobilitare.

enormity s. mostruosità.

enormous agg. enorme, immenso.

enough avv. abbastanza, sufficientemente. ◆ **enough** agg. sufficiente. ◆ **enough** s. il necessario, quanto basta.

to **enrage** vt. far arrabbiare, esasperare.

to **enrapture** vt. rapire, estasiare.

to **enrich** vt. 1. arricchire (anche fig.) 2. abbellire.

enrichment s. 1. arricchimento 2. abbellimento.

to **enrol** vt. 1. arruolare, ingaggiare 2. iscrivere.

enrolment s. 1. arruolamento, iscrizione 2. (giur.) registrazione.

ensign s. 1. bandiera, stendardo 2. portabandiera.

to **enslave** vt. assoggettare, far schiavo (anche fig.).

enslavement s. asservimento, schiavitù (anche fig.).

to **ensnare** vt. adescare, intrappolare (anche fig.).

to **ensue** vt. e vi. seguire.

to **ensure** vt. assicurare, garantire.

entail s. eredità, ordine di successione (vincolato).

to **entangle** vt. impigliare, intralciare (anche fig.).

entanglement s. groviglio, impiccio.

to **enter** vt. e vi. 1. entrare, penetrare 2. iscrivere 3. (comm.) registrare || to — upon, intraprendere (una carriera).

enteric agg. enterico.

enteritis s. enterite.

enterocolitis s. enterocolite.

enterogastritis s. gastroenterite.

enterprise s. 1. impresa 2. iniziativa, intraprendenza.

enterprising agg. intraprendente.

to **entertain** vt. 1. ricevere, ospitare 2. intrattenere, divertire 3. carezzare (un'idea), nutrire (dubbi, speranze).

entertainer s. 1. anfitrione, ospite 2. comico.

entertaining agg. divertente.

entertainment s. 1. trattenimento, spettacolo 2. ricevimento, festa 3. divertimento.

to **enthral** *vt.* (*fig.*) affascinare, incantare.

enthralment *s.* incanto, malia.

to **enthrone** *vt.* mettere sul trono.

enthronement *s.* investitura, intronizzazione.

enthusiasm *s.* entusiasmo.

enthusiast *s.* entusiasta.

enthusiastic(al) *agg.* entusiastico.

enthusiastically *avv.* entusiasticamente.

to **entice** *vt.* sedurre, allettare.

enticement *s.* **1.** attrattiva **2.** adescamento, istigazione.

enticing *agg.* seducente, attraente.

entire *agg.* intero, completo.

entirely *avv.* interamente, completamente.

to **entitle** *vt.* **1.** intitolare (*un libro*) **2.** dare un titolo.

entity *s.* entità, esistenza.

entomological *agg.* entomologico.

entomologist *s.* entomologo.

entomology *s.* entomologia.

entrails *s. pl.* intestino (*sing.*), visceri.

entrance *s.* **1.** ingresso, entrata **2.** ammissione || — *hall*, vestibolo.

to **entrap** *vt.* prendere in trappola, truffare.

to **entreat** *vt.* pregare, supplicare.

entreaty *s.* supplica, istanza.

to **entrench** *vt.* e *vi.* trincerare, fortificare (*anche fig.*) || *to* — *upon*, usurpare.

entrepreneur *s.* **1.** (*teat.*) impresario **2.** imprenditore.

to **entrust** *vt.* affidare, commettere.

entry *s.* **1.** entrata **2.** ingresso, passaggio **3.** (*comm.*) registrazione.

to **entwine** *vt.* attorcigliare, intrecciare. ◆ to **entwine** *vi.* arrotolarsi.

to **enucleate** *vt.* spiegare, chiarire.

enucleation *s.* spiegazione, chiarimento.

to **enumerate** *vt.* enumerare.

enumeration *s.* enumerazione.

enumerator *s.* numeratore.

to **enunciate** *vt.* enunciare, proclamare.

enunciation *s.* enunciazione.

to **envelop** *vt.* avvolgere, avviluppare.

envelope *s.* busta, involucro.

envelopment *s.* avvolgimento.

enviable *agg.* invidiabile.

envious *agg.* invidioso.

to **environ** *vt.* circondare, accerchiare.

environment *s.* ambiente.

environs *s. pl.* dintorni.

envy *s.* invidia.

to **envy** *vt.* invidiare.

enzyme *s.* enzima.

epaulet(te) *s.* (*mil.*) spallina.

ephebe *s.* efebo.

ephemeral *agg.* effimero.

ephemeris *s.* (*pl.* -ides) effemeride.

epic *agg.* epico. ◆ **epic** *s.* poema epico.

epically *avv.* epicamente.

epicentre *s.* epicentro.

epicurean *agg.* e *s.* epicureo.

epidemic(al) *agg.* epidemico.

epidemically *avv.* epidemicamente.

epidermal *agg.* epidermico.

epidermis *s.* epidermide.

epigastric *agg.* epigastrico.

epigram *s.* epigramma.

epigrammatic *agg.* epigrammatico.

epigrammatist *s.* epigrammista.

epigraph *s.* epigrafe.

epigraphy *s.* epigrafia.

epilepsy *s.* epilessia.

epileptic *agg.* epilettico.

epilogue *s.* epilogo.

Epiphany *s.* Epifania.

episcopacy *s.* episcopato.

episcopal *agg.* episcopale.

episcopate *s.* episcopato.

episode *s.* episodio.

episodic(al) *agg.* episodico.

epistle *s.* epistola.

epistolary *agg.* epistolare.

epitaph *s.* epitaffio.

epithalamium *s.* epitalamio.

epithet *s.* epiteto.

epitome *s.* epitome, riassunto.

epoch *s.* epoca, età.

epopee *s.* epopea.

equability *s.* uguaglianza, uniformità.

equal *agg.* uguale, simile, stesso. ◆ **equal** *s.* pari (*di rango*).

equality *s.* uguaglianza, parità.

equalization *s.* eguagliamento.

to **equalize** *vt.* e *vi.* uguagliare.

equally *avv.* ugualmente, imparzialmente.

equanimity *s.* equanimità.

equanimous *agg.* equanime.

equation *s.* **1.** equazione **2.** pareggio.

equator *s.* equatore.

equatorial *agg.* equatoriale.

equestrian *agg.* equestre.

equidistant *agg.* equidistante.

equilateral *agg.* equilatero.

equine agg. equino.
equinoctial agg. equinoziale.
equinox s. equinozio.
to **equip** vt. 1. equipaggiare 2. fornire, arredare.
equipment s. 1. equipaggiamento 2. attrezzatura.
equipoise s. equilibrio.
equipollent agg. equipollente.
equitation s. equitazione.
equity s. giustizia, equità.
equivalence s. equivalenza.
equivalent agg. e s. equivalente.
equivocal agg. 1. ambiguo, equivoco 2. sospetto, losco.
equivocally avv. 1. ambiguamente 2. in modo losco.
to **equivocate** vi. equivocare, giocare sull'equivoco.
equivocation s. 1. l'equivocare 2. equivoco.
equivoke s. 1. gioco di parole 2. ambiguità (d'espressione).
era s. era, epoca.
eradicable agg. estirpabile.
to **eradicate** vt. sradicare, estirpare.
to **erase** vt. raschiare, cancellare.
eraser s. 1. raschietto 2. gomma per cancellare.
erasure s. raschiatura, cancellatura.
erect agg. diritto, ritto.
to **erect** vt. 1. raddrizzare 2. costruire.
erection s. 1. raddrizzamento 2. erezione.
eremite s. eremita.
ermine s. ermellino.
to **erode** vt. corrodere, logorare.
erosion s. erosione.
erosive agg. corrosivo.
erotic agg. erotico.
eroticism s. erotismo.
to **err** vi. 1. sbagliare 2. errare, vagabondare.
errand s. commissione || — -boy, fattorino.
errant agg. 1. errante 2. che sbaglia.
erratic agg. 1. erratico 2. irregolare.
erratically avv. 1. irregolarmente 2. eccentricamente.
erring agg. 1. errante 2. che sbaglia.
erroneous agg. erroneo.
error s. 1. errore 2. torto.
erudite agg. erudito.
erudition s. erudizione.
to **erupt** vi. eruttare.
eruption s. eruzione.
eruptive agg. eruttivo.
escalade s. scalata.

escalator s. scala mobile.
escape s. 1. fuga, evasione 2. scampo, salvezza.
to **escape** vt. e vi. 1. fuggire, evadere 2. scampare.
escapism s. evasione dalla realtà.
escapist s. chi cerca di evadere dalla realtà.
eschatology s. escatologia.
to **eschew** vt. evitare, astenersi da.
escort s. scorta.
to **escort** vt. scortare, accompagnare.
Eskimo s. esquimese.
esoteric agg. esoterico.
especial agg. speciale.
especially avv. specialmente.
espionage s. spionaggio.
esplanade s. spianata.
to **espy** vt. scorgere, avvistare.
esquire s. (titolo di cortesia) John Smith Esq., egregio sig. John Smith.
essay s. 1. esperimento, prova 2. (lett.) saggio.
to **essay** vt. provare, mettere alla prova.
essayist s. saggista.
essence s. essenza.
essential agg. essenziale.
to **establish** vt. 1. affermare (un diritto ecc.) 2. instaurare 3. (comm.) fondare, costituire.
established agg. 1. stabilito, affermato 2. fondato.
establishment s. 1. affermazione, conferma 2. instaurazione 3. stabilimento, azienda.
estate s. 1. terra, proprietà (terriera) 2. stato, gruppo politico 3. condizione, classe sociale || — agent, mediatore.
esteem s. stima, considerazione.
to **esteem** vt. 1. stimare, tenere in gran conto 2. considerare.
estimable agg. degno di stima.
estimate s. 1. stima, giudizio 2. (comm.) preventivo.
to **estimate** vt. 1. stimare, valutare 2. preventivare.
estimator s. perito, stimatore.
to **estrange** vt. alienare, alienarsi, allontanare.
estrangement s. alienazione, allontanamento.
estuary s. estuario.
etching s. acquaforte.
eternal agg. eterno.
eternity s. eternità.

ether *s.* etere.
ethereal *agg.* etereo.
ethic(al) *agg.* etico.
ethics *s.* etica.
Ethiopian *agg.* etiopico. ♦ **Ethiopian** *s.* etiope.
Ethiopic *agg.* etiopico.
ethnic(al) *agg.* etnico.
ethnography *s.* etnografia.
ethnologist *s.* etnologo.
ethnology *s.* etnologia.
ethylene *s.* etilene.
ethylic *agg.* etilico.
etiquette *s.* **1.** etichetta **2.** cerimoniale.
Etrurian, Etruscan *agg.* e *s.* etrusco.
etymologic(al) *agg.* etimologico.
etymology *s.* etimologia.
eucalyptus *s.* eucalipto.
Eucharist *s.* Eucaristia.
eucharistic(al) *agg.* eucaristico.
eugenics *s.* eugenetica.
eulogist *s.* elogiatore.
to **eulogize** *vt.* elogiare.
eulogy *s.* elogio, panegirico.
eunuch *s.* eunuco.
euphemism *s.* eufemismo.
euphonic *agg.* eufonico.
euphony *s.* eufonia.
euphoria *s.* euforia.
euphuism *s.* eufuismo.
euphuist *s.* affettato.
euphuistic *agg.* affettato, ricercato (*di stile*).
European *agg.* e *s.* europeo.
Eurovision *s.* eurovisione.
euthanasia *s.* eutanasia.
to **evacuate** *vt.* e *vi.* evacuare, sfollare.
evacuation *s.* evacuazione, sfollamento.
to **evade** *vt.* evitare, schivare, eludere.
to **evaluate** *vt.* valutare.
evaluation *s.* valutazione.
evanescent *agg.* evanescente.
evangelic(al) *agg.* evangelico.
evangelist *s.* evangelista.
evangelistic *agg.* di un evangelista, missionario.
evangelization *s.* evangelizzazione.
to **evangelize** *vt.* evangelizzare.
to **evaporate** *vi.* evaporare. ♦ to **evaporate** *vt.* far evaporare.
evaporation *s.* evaporazione.
evasion *s.* **1.** evasione, scappatoia **2.** scusa, pretesto.
evasive *agg.* evasivo.

evasively *avv.* evasivamente.
evasiveness *s.* ambiguità.
eve *s.* vigilia.
even *agg.* **1.** uguale, uniforme, costante, regolare **2.** pari, equo. ♦ **even** *avv.* **1.** ancora (*con comp.*) **2.** persino, anche || — *as*, nel momento in cui.
evening *s.* **1.** sera, serata **2.** (*fig.*) declino, fine.
evenly *avv.* in modo uguale, uniformemente.
evensong *s.* vespro.
event *s.* **1.** caso, eventualità **2.** avvenimento **3.** (*sport*) prova.
eventful *agg.* ricco di avvenimenti, movimentato.
eventual *agg.* finale, definitivo.
eventuality *s.* eventualità.
eventually *avv.* alla fine.
ever *avv.* **1.** mai **2.** sempre.
evergreen *s.* sempreverde.
everlasting *agg.* eterno.
everliving *agg.* immortale.
evermore *avv.* perpetuamente.
every *agg.* ogni, ciascuno, tutti.
everybody *pron. indef.* ognuno, tutti.
everyday *agg.* di tutti i giorni, quotidiano.
everyone *pron. indef.* V. *everybody*.
everything *pron. indef.* ogni cosa, tutto.
everywhere *avv.* ovunque.
to **evict** *vt.* sfrattare, espellere.
eviction *s.* sfratto.
evidence *s.* **1.** evidenza **2.** prova.
to **evidence** *vt.* provare, dimostrare.
evident *agg.* evidente, chiaro.
evil *agg.* cattivo, malvagio || — *-eye*, malocchio. ♦ **evil** *s.* male, peccato.
to **evirate** *vt.* evirare.
to **evocate** *vt.* evocare.
evocation *s.* evocazione.
evocative *agg.* evocatore.
to **evoke** *vt.* evocare.
evolution *s.* evoluzione.
evolutional *agg.* evolutivo.
evolutionism *s.* evoluzionismo.
to **evolve** *vt.* evolvere. ♦ to **evolve** *vi.* evolversi.
evolvement *s.* evoluzione, sviluppo.
ewe *s.* pecora (*femmina*).
to **exacerbate** *vt.* esacerbare, inasprire.
exacerbation *s.* esacerbazione, inasprimento.
exact *agg.* **1.** esatto, giusto **2.** puntuale, rigoroso.

to **exact** vt. **1.** esigere **2.** rendere necessario.

exacting agg. **1.** esigente **2.** impegnativo.

exaction s. esazione, estorsione.

exactitude s. esattezza, precisione.

exactly avv. esattamente.

exactness s. esattezza, precisione.

to **exaggerate** vt. esagerare, ingrandire.

exaggeration s. esagerazione.

to **exalt** vt. **1.** innalzare, elevare **2.** esaltare, lodare.

exaltation s. **1.** innalzamento **2.** esaltazione.

exalted agg. **1.** elevato (di grado ecc.) **2.** esaltato, eccitato.

examination s. **1.** esame, ispezione **2.** esame scolastico **3.** (giur.) interrogatorio.

to **examine** vt. **1.** verificare, ispezionare **2.** esaminare **3.** (giur.) istruire un processo.

examiner s. esaminatore.

example s. esempio.

to **exasperate** vt. **1.** peggiorare, aggravare **2.** esasperare.

exasperatingly avv. in modo esasperante.

exasperation s. esasperazione.

to **excavate** vt. scavare, fare scavi (archeologici).

excavation s. **1.** scavo **2.** fossa, buca.

excavator s. **1.** operaio scavatore **2.** (mecc.) escavatore.

to **exceed** vt. e vi. **1.** eccedere, superare (i limiti) **2.** essere superiore.

exceeding agg. esagerato.

exceedingly avv. eccessivamente, troppo.

to **excel** vt. superare. ♦ to **excel** vi. primeggiare.

excellence s. **1.** eccellenza **2.** pregio, superiorità.

Excellency s. (titolo) Eccellenza.

excellent agg. eccellente.

except prep. eccetto, tranne.

to.**except** vt. eccettuare, escludere. ♦ to **except** vi. obiettare, sollevare eccezioni.

excepting prep. eccetto, tranne.

exception s. eccezione.

exceptional agg. eccezionale, straordinario.

excerpt s. brano scelto.

excess s. **1.** eccesso, intemperanza **2.** supplemento.

exchange s. **1.** scambio **2.** (finanza) cambio **3.** borsa, mercato || bill of —, cambiale; — -broker, agente di cambio.

excessive agg. eccessivo, smoderato.

to **exchange** vt. cambiare, scambiare. ♦ to **exchange** vi. fare un cambio.

exchangeable agg. scambiabile.

exchanger s. cambiavalute.

exchequer s. Tesoro, Scacchiere, fisco.

excise s. imposta indiretta || — duty, dazio.

to **excise**[1] vt. tassare.

to **excise**[2] vt. estirpare, mutilare (un testo).

exciseman s. daziere, funzionario degli uffici delle imposte.

excision s. taglio, recisione.

excitability s. eccitabilità.

excitable agg. eccitabile.

excitant agg. e s. eccitante.

excitation s. eccitazione.

to **excite** vt. **1.** provocare, far nascere (una rivolta, un sentimento ecc.) **2.** eccitare, animare.

excited agg. eccitato.

excitement s. eccitazione.

to **exclaim** vt. e vi. esclamare.

exclamation s. esclamazione.

exclamatory agg. esclamativo.

to **exclude** vt. escludere.

exclusion s. esclusione.

exclusive agg. **1.** altezzoso **2.** chiuso, scelto (di ambiente) **3.** esclusivo.

exclusiveness s. esclusività.

to **excogitate** vt. escogitare.

excommunicable agg. scomunicabile.

excommunicate agg. e s. scomunicato.

to **excommunicate** vt. scomunicare.

excommunication s. scomunica.

excrement s. escremento.

excrescence s. escrescenza, protuberanza.

excruciating agg. tormentoso, straziante.

to **exculpate** vt. giustificare, scolpare.

excursion s. **1.** escursione, gita **2.** (mil.) sortita.

excursionist s. escursionista, gitante.

excusable agg. scusabile.

excuse s. **1.** scusa, giustificazione **2.**

pretesto.

to excuse *vt.* scusare, giustificare.

execrable *agg.* esecrabile.

to execrate *vt.* e *vi.* **1.** esecrare, detestare **2.** maledire.

execration *s.* **1.** esecrazione **2.** maledizione.

executant *s.* esecutore.

to execute *vt.* **1.** eseguire, mettere in esecuzione **2.** (*giur.*) convalidare **3.** giustiziare.

execution *s.* **1.** compimento, attuazione **2.** esecuzione.

executioner *s.* esecutore, boia.

executive *agg.* esecutivo.

executor *s.* esecutore.

exedra *s.* esedra.

exegesis *s.* (*pl.* -ses)· esegesi.

exegete *s.* esegeta.

exemplary *agg.* esemplare.

exemplification *s.* esemplificazione.

to exemplify *vt.* esemplificare.

exempt *agg.* esente, esonerato.

to exempt *vt.* esentare, esonerare.

exemption *s.* esenzione, esonero.

exequies *s. pl.* esequie.

exercise *s.* esercizio, esercitazione || — *-book*, quaderno.

to exercise *vt.* esercitare, usare. ♦ **to exercise** *vi.* esercitarsi, allenarsi.

exercitation *s.* esercizio, uso (*di una facoltà*).

to exert *vt.* esercitare.

exertion *s.* **1.** esercizio (*di autorità*) **2.** sforzo.

exhalation *s.* esalazione.

to exhale *vt.* e *vi.* esalare, emettere.

exhaust *s.* **1.** (*mecc.*) scarico, scappamento **2.** apparato aspiratore.

to exhaust *vt.* e *vi.* **1.** aspirare (*aria, gas ecc.*) **2.** esaurire (*anche fig.*).

exhausted *agg.* **1.** aspirato **2.** esausto, spossato.

exhausting *agg.* che esaurisce.

exhaustion *s.* **1.** aspirazione **2.** esaurimento.

exhaustive *agg.* **1.** esauriente **2.** spossante.

exhibit *s.* **1.** insieme di oggetti in mostra **2.** (*giur.*) documento.

to exhibit *vt.* **1.** esibire, mostrare **2.** (*giur.*) produrre (*documenti ecc.*).

exhibition *s.* **1.** presentazione (*di documenti*) **2.** esposizione, mostra.

exhibitionism *s.* esibizionismo.

exhibitionist *s.* esibizionista.

exhibitor *s.* espositore.

to exhilarate *vt.* rallegrare, esilarare.

exhilarating *agg.* esilarante.

to exhort *vt.* esortare, ammonire.

exhortation *s.* esortazione.

exhortative *agg.* esortativo.

exhumation *s.* esumazione.

to exhume *vt.* esumare.

exigence *s.* **1.** esigenza, necessità **2.** situazione critica.

exigent *agg.* **1.** pressante, urgente **2.** esigente.

exigible *agg.* esigibile.

exiguity *s.* esiguità.

exiguous *agg.* esiguo.

exile *s.* **1.** esilio, bando **2.** esule.

to exile *vt.* esiliare.

to exist *vi.* esistere.

existence *s.* esistenza.

existent *agg.* esistente.

existential *agg.* esistenziale.

existentialism *s.* esistenzialismo.

existentialist *agg.* e *s.* esistenzialista.

existing *agg.* esistente, attuale.

exit *s.* uscita.

exode, exodus *s.* esodo.

exogenous *agg.* esogeno.

to exonerate *vt.* **1.** esonerare, dispensare **2.** giustificare.

exoneration *s.* **1.** dispensa, esonero **2.** giustificazione.

exorbitant *agg.* esorbitante.

to exorcise *vt.* esorcizzare.

exorciser *s.* esorcista.

exorcism *s.* esorcismo.

exorcist *s.* esorcista.

exothermic *agg.* esotermico.

exotic *agg.* esotico.

exoticism *s.* esotismo.

to expand *vt.* espandere, dilatare, allargare. ♦ **to expand** *vi.* espandersi, dilagare, dilatarsi, allargarsi, svilupparsi.

expanse *s.* distesa, estensione, spazio.

expansion *s.* espansione, dilatazione, allargamento.

expansionism *s.* espansionismo.

expansive *agg.* **1.** espansivo **2.** dilatabile.

to expatiate *vi.* **1.** errare, vagabondare **2.** parlare e scrivere diffusamente.

expatiation *s.* **1.** dissertazione **2.** prolissità.

expatriate *agg.* e *s.* espatriato.

to expatriate *vt.* esiliare. ♦ to

expatriate vi. espatriare.
expatriation s. espatrio.
to expect vt. **1.** aspettare, aspettarsi **2.** esigere, insistere **3.** pensare, credere || to — somebody to come, prevedere la venuta di qu.
expectance s. aspettativa, attesa.
expectant s. **1.** chi attende **2.** candidato.
expectation s. attesa, aspettativa. ♦ **expectations** s. pl. speranze.
expectorant agg. e s. espettorante.
expectoration s. espettorazione.
expediency s. **1.** convenienza **2.** opportunismo.
expedient s. espediente, ripiego.
to expedite vt. affrettare.
expedition s. **1.** spedizione **2.** prontezza, celerità.
expeditious s. svelto, sbrigativo.
to expel vt. espellere, cacciare.
expense s. **1.** spesa, sborso **2.** (fig.) sacrificio, prezzo.
expensive agg. costoso, caro.
experience s. esperienza.
to experience vt. sperimentare, provare.
experienced agg. pratico, esperto.
experiment s. esperimento, prova.
experimental agg. sperimentale.
experimentation s. sperimentasmo.
experimentalist s. sperimentalista.
experimentation s. sperimentazione.
expert agg. esperto. ♦ **expert** s. esperto, perito, competente.
expertly avv. abilmente.
to expiate vt. espiare.
expiation s. espiazione.
expiatory agg. espiatorio.
expiration s. **1.** fine, scadenza **2.** espirazione.
expiratory agg. espiratorio.
to expire vt. e vi. **1.** finire, scadere **2.** spirare, morire.
expiring agg. **1.** che scade **2.** spirante, morente.
expiry s. fine, cessazione.
to explain vt. e vi. spiegare, chiarire.
explanation s. spiegazione, delucidazione.
expletive agg. espletivo, pleonastico. ♦ **expletive** s. **1.** imprecazione **2.** pleonasmo.
explicable agg. spiegabile.
to explicate vt. sviluppare (un prin-

cipio, un'idea ecc.).
explication s. spiegazione, sviluppo.
explicit agg. esplicito, chiaro.
to explode vt. esplodere, far esplodere. ♦ **to explode** vi. scoppiare, esplodere.
to exploit vt. **1.** utilizzare, sfruttare **2.** approfittare di.
exploitation s. sfruttamento, utilizzazione.
exploiter s. **1.** chi valorizza (idea, invenzione ecc.) **2.** sfruttatore.
exploration s. esplorazione.
to explore vt. esplorare.
explorer s. esploratore, esploratrice.
explosion s. esplosione, scoppio.
explosive agg. e s. esplosivo.
exponent s. **1.** divulgatore **2.** esponente.
exponential agg. esponenziale.
export s. esportazione.
to export vt. esportare.
exportation s. esportazione.
exporter s. esportatore.
to expose vt. **1.** esporre **2.** (foto) impressionare.
exposé s. esposto, resoconto.
exposition s. **1.** spiegazione, commento **2.** mostra, esposizione.
expositive agg. espositivo.
expositor s. commentatore.
expository agg. esplicativo.
exposure s. **1.** esposizione (al freddo, al caldo ecc.) **2.** mostra **3.** (foto) (tempo di) esposizione.
to expound vt. spiegare (una teoria).
express agg. **1.** chiaro, preciso **2.** espresso, diretto. ♦ **express** s. espresso, corriere || — train, direttissimo.
to express vt. esprimere, manifestare.
expression s. espressione.
expressionism s. espressionismo.
expressionist s. espressionista.
expressive agg. espressivo, significativo.
expressly avv. espressamente.
to expropriate vt. espropriare.
expropriation s. espropriazione.
expulsion s. espulsione.
expulsive agg. espulsivo.
expunction s. cancellatura.
to expurgate vt. espurgare (uno scritto).
expurgation s. espurgazione (di uno scritto).

exquisite *agg.* 1. squisito 2. fine, sensibile. ♦ **exquisite** *s.* raffinato.
exquisiteness *s.* squisitezza, finezza.
extant *agg.* ancora esistente.
extemporaneous, extemporary *agg.* estemporaneo.
extempore *agg.* improvvisato.
extemporization *s.* improvvisazione.
to **extemporize** *vt.* e *vi.* improvvisare.
to **extend** *vt.* 1. estendere, allungare, prolungare. ♦ to **extend** *vi.* estendersi, allungarsi, prolungarsi.
extendible *agg.* estendibile.
extensible *agg.* estensibile.
extension *s.* 1. estensione, allungamento 2. (*comm.*) proroga.
extensive *agg.* 1. esteso, ampio 2. estensivo.
extent *s.* 1. estensione 2. volume 3. limite, grado.
to **extenuate** *vt.* attenuare.
extenuation *s.* attenuazione.
exterior *agg.* esterno, esteriore. ♦ **exterior** *s.* 1. l'esterno 2. esteriorità.
exteriority *s.* esteriorità.
exteriorization *s.* esteriorizzazione.
to **exteriorize** *vt.* esternare.
to **exterminate** *vt.* sterminare.
extermination *s.* sterminio.
external *agg.* esteriore, esterno.
externality *s.* superficialità.
to **externalize** *vt.* esternare.
externally *avv.* esternamente, esteriormente.
exterritorial *agg.* estraterritoriale.
extinct *agg.* 1. estinto 2. spento.
extinction *s.* estinzione.
to **extinguish** *vt.* 1. estinguere, spegnere 2. pagare, ammortizzare.
extinguisher *s.* spegnitore, estintore.
to **extirpate** *vt.* estirpare, sradicare.
extirpation *s.* estirpazione, sradicamento.
to **extol** *vt.* lodare, magnificare
to **extort** *vt.* estorcere, strappare.
extorter *s.* chi estorce.
extortion *s.* estorsione.
extortioner *s.* ricattatore.
extra *agg.* 1. straordinario 2. in più, extra. ♦ **extra** *s.* 1. supplemento 2. (*giorn.*) edizione straordinaria 3. (*cine*) comparsa. ♦ **extra** *avv.* extra, di più, in più, insolitamente.
extract *s.* 1. estratto 2. citazione.

to **extract** *vt.* estrarre, togliere.
extractable *agg.* estraibile.
extraction *s.* 1. estrazione 2. origine, stirpe.
extractive *agg.* estrattivo.
extractor *s.* estrattore.
to **extradite** *vt.* estradare.
extradition *s.* estradizione.
extraneous *agg.* estraneo.
extraordinary *agg.* straordinario, eccezionale.
extraterritorial *agg.* estraterritoriale.
extraterritoriality *s.* estraterritorialità.
extravagance *s.* 1. prodigalità, sperpero 2. stravaganza.
extravagant *agg.* 1. prodigo 2. stravagante.
extreme *agg.* 1. estremo, ultimo 2. grave. ♦ **extreme** *s.* estremo, estremità.
extremely *avv.* estremamente.
extremism *s.* estremismo.
extremist *s.* estremista.
extremity *s.* estremità.
extrinsic(al) *agg.* estrinseco.
extrovert *s.* estroverso.
to **extrude** *vt.* estromettere.
exuberance *s.* esuberanza.
exuberant *agg.* 1. copioso, abbondante 2. esuberante, pieno di vita.
exudation *s.* essudazione.
to **exude** *vt.* e *vi.* trasudare.
to **exult** *vi.* gioire, esultare.
exultant *agg.* esultante.
exultation *s.* esultanza.
eye *s.* occhio.
eyeball *s.* bulbo oculare.
eyebrow *s.* sopracciglio.
eyeglass *s.* lente, monocolo.
eyehole *s.* orbita, occhiaia.
eyelash *s.* ciglio.
eyelet *s.* occhiello, asola.
eyelid *s.* palpebra.
eyesight *s.* vista.
eyesore *s.* cosa brutta e spiacevole.
eyewitness *s.* testimone oculare.

F

F *s.* (*mus.*) fa.
fable *s.* favola.
fabled *agg.* 1. mitico 2. inventato.
fabric *s.* 1. tessuto 2. manufatto 3.

struttura **4.** fabbricazione.

to **fabricate** vt. **1.** fabbricare **2.** inventare.

fabrication s. **1.** fabbricazione **2.** invenzione.

fabulist s. **1.** favolista **2.** bugiardo.

fabulosity s. favolosità.

fabulous agg. favoloso.

façade s. facciata.

face s. **1.** faccia **2.** aspetto **3.** sfrontatezza **4.** facciata **5.** quadrante (*di orologio*) || *to pull faces*, fare boccacce || *— -powder*, cipria; *— value*, (*comm.*) valore nominale.

to **face** vt. **1.** fronteggiare **2.** affrontare **3.** ricoprire || *to — about*, fare dietro-front.

facet s. sfaccettatura.

facetious agg. faceto.

facetiousness s. lepidezza.

facial agg. facciale.

facile agg. **1.** facile **2.** pronto **3.** accomodante.

to **facilitate** vt. facilitare.

facilitation s. facilitazione.

facility s. facilità. ♦ **facilities** s. pl. facilitazioni.

facing agg. che sta di fronte. ♦ **facing** s. rivestimento. ♦ **facings** s. pl. mostrine.

fact s. **1.** fatto **2.** realtà || *in —*, infatti, di fatto; *as a matter of —*, effettivamente.

faction s. **1.** fazione **2.** faziosità.

factious agg. fazioso.

factiousness s. faziosità.

factitious agg. fittizio.

factitiousness s. artificiosità.

factor s. **1.** fattore **2.** agente.

factory s. fabbrica.

factual agg. effettivo.

facultative agg. **1.** facoltativo **2.** casuale.

faculty s. facoltà.

fad s. **1.** mania **2.** capriccio.

faddist s. maniaco.

faddy agg. capriccioso.

fade s. (*radio*) variazione graduale.

to **fade** vi. **1.** appassire **2.** sbiadire **3.** svanire || *to — in* (*cine*) aprire in dissolvenza; *to — out*, (*cine*) chiudere in dissolvenza. ♦ to **fade** vt. **1.** far sbiadire **2.** far svanire.

fading s. **1.** appassimento **2.** scolorimento **3.** affievolimento **4.** dissolvenza.

to **fag** vt. affaticare. ♦ to **fag** vi. **1.** affaticarsi **2.** sfacchinare.

fag(g)ot s. fascina.

faience s. terracotta.

fail s. fallo.

to **fail** vi. **1.** fallire **2.** mancare, venir meno **3.** indebolirsi **4.** esser bocciato. ♦ to **fail** vt. **1.** mancare di **2.** bocciare **3.** abbandonare.

failing[1] agg. debole. ♦ **failing** s. **1.** debolezza **2.** mancanza **3.** fallimento.

failing[2] prep. in mancanza di.

failure s. **1.** fallimento **2.** incapacità **3.** mancanza **4.** indebolimento **5.** guasto || *to be a —*, essere un fallito.

fain agg. contento, disposto. ♦ **fain** avv. volentieri || *I would — stay*, preferirei restare.

faint agg. **1.** debole **2.** timido **3.** vago.

faint s. svenimento || *— -hearted*, codardo.

to **faint** vi. svenire.

faintness s. **1.** debolezza **2.** timidezza.

fair[1] agg. **1.** onesto **2.** biondo **3.** gentile **4.** bello **5.** sereno (*di tempo*) **6.** (*comm.*) libero || *— -play*, comportamento leale. ♦ **fair** avv. **1.** con onestà **2.** con precisione.

fair[2] s. fiera || *fun —*, Luna Park.

fairly avv. **1.** onestamente **2.** abbastanza.

fairness s. **1.** bellezza **2.** onestà **3.** color biondo **4.** bianchezza (*di carnagione*).

fairway s. canale navigabile.

fairy agg. **1.** fatato **2.** immaginario. ♦ **fairy** s. fata || *— -tale*, fiaba.

fairyland s. paese delle fate.

fairylike agg. simile a fata.

faith s. **1.** fede **2.** promessa || *— -healer*, guaritore.

faithful agg. **1.** fedele **2.** degno di fiducia.

faithfulness s. fedeltà.

faithless agg. **1.** senza fede **2.** sleale.

to **fake** vt. (*gergo*) falsificare.

fakir s. fachiro.

falcon s. falcone.

falconry s. falconeria.

fall s. **1.** caduta, cascata **2.** (*amer.*) autunno.

to **fall (fell, fallen)** vi. **1.** cadere **2.** abbassarsi **3.** capitare in sorte **4.** dividersi || *to — back*, ritirarsi; *to — behind*, restare indietro; *to — in with*, imbattersi; *to — short*, essere insufficiente; *to — away*, deperire; *to — down*, far fiasco; *to — due*, scadere.

fallacious *agg.* fallace.

fallaciousness *s.* fallacia.

fallacy *s.* **1.** fallacia **2.** errore **3.** sofisma.

fallen V. *to fall*.

fallibility *s.* fallibilità.

fallible *agg.* fallibile.

falling *agg.* cadente. ♦ **falling** *s.* caduta || *— back*, ripiegamento; *— off*, diminuzione; *— short*, insufficienza.

fall-out *s.* pioggia radioattiva.

fallow *agg.* incolto.

false *agg.* **1.** falso **2.** stonato **3.** ingannevole || *— bottom*, doppio fondo.

falsehood *s.* falsità.

falsely *avv.* falsamente.

falseness *s.* falsità.

falsifiable *agg.* falsificabile.

falsification *s.* falsificazione.

falsifier *s.* falsificatore.

to falsify *vt.* **1.** falsificare **2.** smentire.

falsity *s.* falsità.

to falter *vi.* vacillare. ♦ **to falter** *vt.* balbettare.

fame *s.* fama.

famed *agg.* celebre.

familiar *agg.* familiare. ♦ **familiar** *s.* amico intimo || *to be — with*, esser pratico di.

familiarity *s.* familiarità.

familiarization *s.* familiarità.

to familiarize *vt.* familiarizzare.

family *s.* famiglia.

famine *s.* carestia.

to famish *vt.* far morire di fame. ♦ **to famish** *vi.* morire di fame.

famous *agg.* famoso.

fan[1] *s.* **1.** ventaglio **2.** ventilatore **3.** pala (*d'elica*).

fan[2] *s.* (*gergo*) tifoso, ammiratore.

to fan *vt.* **1.** sventolare **2.** (*agr.*) vagliare.

fanatic *agg. e s.* fanatico.

fanatical *agg.* fanatico.

fanaticism *s.* fanatismo.

to fanaticize *vt.* rendere fanatico. ♦ **to fanaticize** *vi.* agire da fanatico.

fanciful *agg.* **1.** fantasioso **2.** fantastico.

fancifulness *s.* **1.** fantasia **2.** capriccio.

fancy *agg.* **1.** immaginario **2.** stravagante **3.** decorato. ♦ **fancy** *s.* **1.** fantasia **2.** capriccio **3.** inclinazione || *— ball*, ballo in costume; *— -dress*, costume.

to fancy *vt.* **1.** immaginare **2.** ritenere.

fang *s.* **1.** zanna **2.** dente (*velenoso*).

fanning *s.* ventilazione.

fantastic(al) *agg.* **1.** immaginario **2.** bizzarro.

to fantasticate *vt. e vi.* fantasticare.

fantasy *s.* **1.** fantasia **2.** capriccio.

far *agg.* (**farther, farthest**) (**further, furthest**) lontano. ♦ **far** *avv.* **1.** lontano **2.** di gran lunga || *— away*, *— off*, lontano; *as — as*, fino a, per quanto; *so —*, finora; *— -gone*, a uno stadio avanzato (*di malattie*).

farce *s.* farsa.

farcical *agg.* farsesco.

farcicality *s.* qualità farsesca.

fare *s.* **1.** tariffa **2.** vitto **3.** passegero || *bill of —*, lista delle vivande.

to fare *vi.* **1.** andare **2.** riuscire **3.** nutrirsi || *to — badly*, andar male.

farewell *s.* congedo. ♦ **farewell** *inter.* addio.

farfetched *agg.* remoto.

farinaceous *agg.* farinaceo.

farinose *agg.* farinoso.

farm *s.* fattoria || *— -yard*, aia.

to farm *vt.* coltivare. ♦ **to farm** *vi.* fare l'agricoltore.

farmer *s.* agricoltore.

farmhouse *s.* casa colonica.

farming *s.* agricoltura.

farmstead *s.* cascina.

farraginous *agg.* farraginoso.

farrier *s.* maniscalco.

farsighted *agg. e s.* presbite.

farther *agg.* (*comp. di* far) più lontano, ulteriore. ♦ **farther** *avv.* **1.** (*di*) più **2.** più lontano **3.** inoltre.

farthermost *agg.* il più lontano.

farthest *agg.* (*superl. di* far) il più lontano, estremo. ♦ **farthest** *avv.* (il) più lontano.

farthing *s.* "farthing" (*moneta inglese: un quarto di penny*).

fascicle *s.* fascicolo.

to fascinate *vt.* affascinare.

fascinating *agg.* affascinante.

fascination *s.* fascino.

fascinator *s.* affascinatore.

fascism *s.* fascismo.

fascist *agg. e s.* fascista.

fashion s. 1. modo 2. abitudine 3. moda || — -plate, figurino; a man of —, un uomo di mondo.

to **fashion** vt. foggiare.

fashionable agg. 1. alla moda 2. elegante.

fast agg. 1. fermo 2. fedele 3. inalterabile 4. rapido 5. (fig.) dissoluto 6. in anticipo (di orologio). ♦ **fast** avv. 1. fermamente 2. fortemente 3. velocemente 4. in modo dissoluto.

fast s. digiuno.

to **fast** vi. digiunare.

to **fasten** vt. 1. attaccare 2. allacciare 3. chiudere 4. fissare. ♦ to **fasten** vi. 1. allacciarsi 2. chiudersi 3. fissarsi.

fastener s. 1. fermaglio 2. legaccio, chiusura || snap —, automatico.

fastening s. 1. legatura 2. gancio, chiavistello.

faster s. digiunatore.

fastidious agg. schizzinoso.

fastidiousness s. schizzinosità.

fastness s. 1. velocità 2. fermezza 3. solidità 4. dissolutezza.

fat agg. 1. grasso 2. (fig.) proficuo. ♦ **fat** s. grasso || — -head, zuccone.

to **fat** V. to fatten.

fatal agg. fatale.

fatalism s. fatalismo.

fatalist s. fatalista.

fatalistic agg. fatalistico.

fatality s. 1. fatalità 2. fatalismo.

fatally avv. 1. in modo fatale 2. fatalmente.

fate s. fato.

father s. padre || — -in-law, suocero.

fatherhood s. paternità.

fatherland s. madrepatria.

fatherless agg. senza padre.

fatherlike agg. paterno. ♦ **fatherlike** avv. paternamente.

fatherly agg. e avv. V. fatherlike.

fathom s. (mar.) braccio (misura di profondità).

to **fathom** vt. scandagliare.

fathomless agg. 1. incommensurabile 2. incomprensibile.

fatidic(al) agg. fatidico.

fatigue s. fatica.

to **fatigue** vt. affaticare. ♦ to **fatigue** vi. affaticarsi.

fatness s. grassezza.

to **fatten** vt. ingrassare. ♦ to **fatten** vi. ingrassarsi.

fattener s. ingrassatore.

fattening s. ingrassamento.

fattiness s. grassezza.

fatty agg. grasso.

fatuity s. fatuità.

fatuous agg. fatuo.

fault s. 1. fallo 2. colpa 3. difetto || — -finder, criticone.

faultiness s. imperfezione.

faultless agg. 1. perfetto 2. irreprensibile.

faulty agg. difettoso.

faun s. fauno.

favour s. favore.

to **favour** vt. 1. favorire 2. sostenere 3. (fam.) assomigliare a.

favourable agg. favorevole.

favourite agg. e s. favorito.

favouritism s. favoritismo.

fawn s. cerbiatto.

to **fawn** vt. fare le feste || to — on, adulare.

fawner s. adulatore.

fawning s. servilismo.

fear s. paura, timore.

to **fear** vt. e vi. temere, aver paura.

fearful agg. 1. terribile 2. timoroso.

fearfulness s. 1. aspetto terribile 2. timore.

fearless agg. intrepido.

feasibility s. fattibilità.

feasible agg. fattibile.

feast s. 1. festa 2. banchetto.

to **feast** vt. 1. rallegrare 2. festeggiare. ♦ to **feast** vi. banchettare.

feaster s. convitato.

feat s. impresa, prodezza.

feather s. penna, piuma.

to **feather** vt. 1. coprire di penne, piume 2. (mar.) spalare.

feathered agg. 1. pennuto 2. (fig.) alato.

feathering s. piumaggio.

featherless agg. implume.

feature s. 1. lineamento 2. (cine) attrazione 3. caratteristica || — film, parte principale di un film.

to **feature** vt. 1. caratterizzare 2. (teat.) dare una parte importante a.

featureless agg. senza caratteristiche.

febrifuge s. febbrifugo.

febrile agg. febbrile.

February s. febbraio.

fecal agg. fecale.

fecund agg. fecondo.

to **fecundate** vt. fecondare.

fecundation s. fecondazione.

fecundity s. fecondità.
fed V. to feed.
federacy s. federazione.
federal agg. federale.
federalism s. federalismo.
federate agg. confederato.
to **federate** vt. confederare. ♦ to
federate vi. confederarsi.
federation s. (con)federazione.
federative agg. federativo.
fee s. 1. onorario 2. tassa 3. (giur.)
proprietà ereditaria.
feeble agg. debole.
feebleness s. debolezza.
feed s. 1. alimentazione 2. pascolo.
to **feed (fed, fed)** vt. 1. nutrire
2. pascere 3. rifornire || to be fed
up, essere stufo. ♦ to **feed (fed,
fed)** vi. nutrirsi || to — up, in-
grassare.
feeder s. 1. ciò che, chi nutre 2.
cavo di alimentazione 3. affluente
4. serbatoio.
feeding s. alimentazione.
feel s. tatto.
to **feel (felt, felt)** vt. 1. sentire
(col tatto o col sentimento) 2. tastare, sondare. ♦ to **feel (felt,
felt)** vi. 1. sentirsi 2. andare a tastoni.
feeling agg. sensibile. ♦ **feeling** s.
1. sentimento 2. sensibilità 3. sensazione.
feet V. foot.
to **feign** vt. 1. inventare 2. falsificare. ♦ to **feign** vi. fingersi.
feignedly avv. simulatamente.
feigner s. simulatore.
feint s. 1. finta 2. simulazione.
to **feint** vi. fare una finta.
feldspar s. feldspato.
to **felicitate** vt. felicitarsi con || to
— so. on sthg., felicitarsi con qu.
di qc.
felicitation s. felicitazione.
felicitous agg. appropriato.
feline agg. e s. felino.
fell[1] V. to fall.
fell[2] agg. 1. crudele 2. funesto.
to **fell** vt. abbattere.
felling s. taglio (di un bosco).
fellow s. 1. individuo 2. compagno,
collega || — -citizen, concittadi-
no; — -creature, simile; a good
—, un buon diavolo.
fellowship s. 1. amicizia 2. associazione.
felon agg. e s. criminale.
felony s. crimine, delitto.

felt[1] V. to feel.
felt[2] s. feltro.
to **felt** vt. feltrare.
felucca s. feluca.
female agg. 1. femminile 2. (mecc.)
femmina. ♦ **female** s. femmina.
feminine agg. e s. femminile.
femininity s. femminilità.
feminism s. femminismo.
femur s. femore.
fen s. palude || — -berry, mirtillo;
— -fire, fuoco fatuo.
fence s. 1. recinto 2. scherma 3.
(fam.) ricettatore.
to **fence** vt. cintare. ♦ to **fence** vi.
tirar di scherma.
fencer s. schermidore.
fencing s. 1. cinta 2. scherma.
fender s. 1. riparo 2. paraurti 3.
(mar.) parabordo.
fennel s. finocchio.
feracity s. feracità.
feral[1] agg. ferale, funesto.
feral[2] agg. ferino.
ferial agg. feriale.
ferine agg. ferino.
ferment s. fermento.
to **ferment** vi. 1. fermentare 2. agitarsi. ♦ to **ferment** vt. 1. far fermentare 2. eccitare.
fermentation s. 1. fermentazione 2.
fermento.
fermentative agg. fermentativo.
fern s. felce.
ferocious agg. feroce.
ferocity s. ferocia.
ferreous agg. 1. ferroso 2. ferreo.
ferret[1] s. furetto.
ferret[2] s. nastro, fettuccia.
ferro-concrete s. cemento armato.
ferrous agg. ferroso.
ferruginous agg. ferruginoso.
ferry s. traghetto.
to **ferry** vt. e vi. traghettare.
ferryman s. traghettatore.
fertile agg. fertile.
fertility s. fertilità.
fertilization s. fertilizzazione.
to **fertilize** vt. 1. fertilizzare 2. fecondare.
fertilizer s. fertilizzante.
fervency s. fervore.
fervent, fervid agg. ardente.
fervour s. ardore.
festal agg. festivo.
fester s. suppurazione, piaga.
to **fester** vi. suppurare (di ferita).
festival s. 1. festa 2. festival.
festive agg. 1. festivo 2. festoso.

festivity s. festività. ♦ **festivities** s. pl. festeggiamenti.

festoon s. festone.

to **fetch** vt. 1. andare a prendere 2. tirare 3. fruttare, rendere || to — back, riportare.

fetid agg. fetido.

fetish s. feticcio.

fetishism s. feticismo.

fetishist s. feticista.

fetter s. ceppo, catena.

to **fetter** vt. incatenare.

fettle s. condizione || in fine —, in forma.

feud[1] s. ostilità.

feud[2] s. feudo.

feudal agg. feudale.

feudalism s. feudalesimo.

feudality s. 1. feudalesimo 2. feudo.

feudatory agg. e s. feudatario.

fever s. febbre || to be in a —, avere la febbre.

feverish agg. 1. febbricitante 2. febbrile.

few agg. e pron. pochi || a —, alcuni; quite a —, un numero considerevole; a good —, parecchi.

fewness s. scarsità, esiguità.

fiancé s. fidanzato.

fib s. fandonia.

to **fib** vi. dire fandonie.

fibre s. fibra.

fibroid, fibrous agg. fibroso.

fickle agg. incostante.

fickleness s. incostanza.

fictile agg. fittile.

fiction s. 1. narrativa 2. finzione.

fictional agg. immaginario.

fictitious agg. fittizio.

fiddle s. violino || fit as a —, in ottima salute.

to **fiddle** vi. 1. suonare il violino 2. gingillarsi.

fiddler s. violinista.

fiddlestick s. archetto. ♦ **fiddlesticks** s. pl. sciocchezze.

fidelity s. fedeltà.

to **fidget** vt. agitare. ♦ to **fidget** vi. agitarsi.

fidgety agg. irrequieto.

fiduciary agg. e s. fiduciario.

field s. campo || — -glass, binocolo; — -day, giorno di esercitazioni; — -officer, ufficiale superiore.

fiend s. demonio.

fiendish agg. diabolico.

fierce agg. 1. fiero 2. selvaggio 3. ardente.

fierceness s. 1. ferocia 2. ardore.

fiery agg. 1. di fuoco 2. focoso 3. infiammabile.

fife s. piffero.

fifteen agg. e s. quindici.

fifteenth agg. e s. quindicesimo.

fifth agg. e s. quinto.

fiftieth agg. e s. cinquantesimo.

fifty agg. e s. cinquanta || — - —, a metà.

fig[1] s. fico.

fig[2] s. tenuta, vestiario.

fight s. 1. lotta 2. spirito combattivo.

to **fight** (**fought, fought**) vt. e vi. combattere || to — down, vincere; to — off, respingere; to — shy of, tenersi alla larga da.

fighter s. 1. combattente 2. (aer.) caccia.

fighting s. combattimento, rissa.

figuration s. figurazione.

figurative agg. 1. figurativo 2. figurato.

figure s. 1. figura, forma 2. cifra 3. diagramma.

to **figure** vt. raffigurare. ♦ to **figure** vi. 1. immaginarsi 2. passare per.

figurehead s. 1. prestanome 2. (mar.) polena.

filament s. filamento.

filamentary, filamentous agg. filamentoso.

filcher s. ladruncolo.

file[1] s. lima.

file[2] s. 1. schedario, archivio 2. fila 3. raccolta.

to **file**[1] vt. limare.

to **file**[2] vt. 1. archiviare 2. ordinare. ♦ to **file** vi. marciare in fila.

filial agg. filiale.

filiation s. filiazione.

filibuster s. filibustiere.

filigree s. filigrana.

filing[1] s. limatura.

filing[2] s. 1. archiviazione 2. sfilata.

fill s. sazietà.

to **fill** vt. 1. riempire 2. occupare 3. otturare (di denti) || to — in, to — up, riempire, compilare. ♦ to **fill** vi. riempirsi.

fillet s. 1. nastro 2. (cuc.) filetto.

filling s. 1. riempitura 2. otturazione 3. (cuc.) ripieno || — station, stazione di rifornimento.

fillip s. 1. schiocco (delle dita) 2. stimolo.

film s. 1. pellicola 2. velo 3. membrana.

to **film** vt. 1. coprire con una pellicola 2. filmare. ♦ to **film** vi. 1. coprirsi con una pellicola 2. girare un film.

filmy agg. velato.

filter s. filtro.

to **filter** vt. e vi. filtrare.

filth s. sozzura.

filthily avv. in modo sudicio.

filthiness s. 1. sozzura 2. corruzione morale.

filthy agg. 1. sozzo 2. corrotto.

filtration s. filtrazione.

fin s. 1. pinna 2. (mecc.) aletta.

final agg. e s. finale.

finalist s. finalista.

finality s. 1. finalità 2. carattere definitivo.

finally avv. alla fine.

finance s. finanza.

to **finance** vt. finanziare.

financial agg. finanziario.

financier s. 1. finanziere 2. finanziatore.

financing s. finanziamento.

finch s. fringuello.

find s. scoperta, ritrovamento.

to **find (found, found)** vt. 1. trovare 2. provvedere 3. ritenere || to — out, scoprire.

finding s. 1. scoperta 2. sentenza.

fine¹ agg. 1. bello 2. fine. ♦ **fine** avv.

fine² s. multa.

to **fine¹** vt. raffinare. ♦ to **fine** vi. raffinarsi.

to **fine²** vt. multare.

finely avv. 1. bene 2. finemente.

finger s. dito || — -print, impronta digitale; — -tip, punta delle dita; — -post, cartello segnavia.

to **finger** vt. 1. toccare con le dita 2. rubare || to be light-fingered (fig.), avere le mani lunghe.

finish s. 1. fine 2. finezza 3. finitura.

to **finish** vt. e vi. finire.

finished agg. (fig.) perfetto.

finishing agg. ultimo, conclusivo. ♦ **finishing** s. (ri)finitura.

finite agg. limitato.

Finn s. finlandese.

Finnic, Finnish agg. finlandese.

fir (-tree) s. abete || — -wood, abetaia.

fire s. 1. fuoco 2. incendio || on —, in fiamme; — -guard, parafuoco; — -plug, bocca da incendio; — station, caserma dei pompieri; — -works, fuochi d'artificio.

to **fire** vt. 1. dar fuoco 2. far fuoco

3. (fig.) infiammare. ♦ to **fire** vi. 1. prender fuoco 2. (fig.) infiammarsi.

firedamp s. grisù.

fire escape s. 1. scala di sicurezza 2. scala dei pompieri.

firefly s. lucciola.

fireman s. pompiere.

fireplace s. caminetto.

fireproof agg. incombustibile.

fireside s. angolo del focolare.

firewood s. legna da ardere.

firing s. 1. accensione 2. sparo 3. alimentazione (di un fuoco) || — squad, plotone d'esecuzione.

firm¹ agg. 1. fisso 2. solido 3. deciso.

firm² s. azienda, ditta.

firmament s. firmamento.

firmly avv. 1. fermamente 2. solidamente.

firmness s. 1. fermezza 2. stabilità.

first agg. primo || — -aid, pronto soccorso; — -born, primogenito; — -class, di prima qualità; — -name, nome di battesimo. ♦ **first** avv. 1. prima di tutto 2. per la prima volta || at —, sulle prime. ♦ **first** s. 1. primo 2. principio.

firth s. fiordo.

fiscal agg. fiscale.

fish s. pesce || — -hook, amo.

to **fish** vi. 1. pescare 2. cercare. ♦ to **fish** vt. pescare.

fisher s. pescatore.

fisherman s. pescatore.

fishery s. pesca.

fishing s. pesca || — -boat, peschereccio; — -line, lenza.

fishmonger s. pescivendolo.

fishy agg. 1. di pesce 2. pescoso 3. (fig.) equivoco.

fission s. fissione.

fist s. pugno.

fit¹ agg. 1. adatto 2. pronto.

fit² s. 1. giusta misura 2. attacco, accesso (di febbre, ira ecc.).

to **fit** vt. 1. adattare 2. andar bene a 3. provare || to — out, equipaggiare.

fitful agg. 1. irregolare 2. spasmodico.

fitfulness s. irregolarità.

fitness s. convenienza.

fitter s. 1. aggiustatore 2. montatore.

fitting agg. adatto, conveniente. ♦ **fitting** s. 1. adattamento, prova 2. equipaggiamento. ♦ **fittings**

s. *pl.* **1.** accessori **2.** arredamento (*sing.*).

five *agg.* e *s.* cinque.

fix *s.* **1.** difficoltà **2.** (*mar.*) punto.

to fix *vt.* fissare || *to — up*, sistemare, riparare. ♦ **to fix** *vi.* stabilirsi.

fixation *s.* fissazione.

fixed *agg.* **1.** fisso **2.** stabilito.

fixer *s.* **1.** montatore **2.** fissatore.

fixing *s.* **1.** collocamento **2.** messa in opera **3.** fissaggio.

fixity *s.* **1.** stabilità **2.** fissità.

fizz *s.* **1.** effervescenza **2.** bevanda effervescente.

to fizz *vi.* frizzare.

fjord *s.* fiordo.

flabbiness *s.* **1.** mollezza **2.** fiacchezza (*di carattere ecc.*).

flabby *agg.* **1.** floscio **2.** fiacco.

flaccid *agg.* flaccido.

flaccidness *s.* flaccidezza.

flag¹ *s.* bandiera || *— -ship*, nave ammiraglia.

flag² *s.* lastra di pietra (*per pavimentazione*).

to flag¹ *vt.* **1.** imbandierare **2.** pavesare. ♦ **to flag** *vi.* **1.** pendere **2.** avvizzire.

to flag² *vt.* lastricare.

to flagellate *vt.* flagellare.

flagellation *s.* flagellazione.

flagellator *s.* flagellatore.

flagrancy *s.* flagranza.

flagrant *agg.* flagrante.

flagstaff *s.* asta di bandiera.

flair *s.* fiuto, intuizione.

flake *s.* **1.** fiocco (*di neve, lana ecc.*) **2.** favilla **3.** lamina **4.** scaglia.

to flake *vt.* **1.** sfaldare **2.** squamare **3.** coprire di fiocchi. ♦ **to flake** *vi.* **1.** sfaldarsi **2.** squamarsi **3.** cadere in fiocchi.

flaky *agg.* **1.** a falde **2.** a lamine, a scaglie.

flame *s.* fiamma || *— -thrower*, lanciafiamme.

to flame *vi.* fiammeggiare.

flaming *agg.* ardente.

flange *s.* orlo, frangia.

flank *s.* fianco.

to flank *vt.* **1.** fiancheggiare **2.** (*mil.*) attaccare il fianco di.

flannel *s.* flanella. ♦ **flannels** *s. pl.* calzoni di flanella.

flap *s.* **1.** lembo, falda **2.** colpo, agitazione **3.** linguetta **4.** (*aer.*) alettone.

flare *s.* **1.** fiammata improvvisa **2.** chiarore.

to flare *vi.* **1.** brillare (*di luce incerta*) **2.** agitarsi **3.** divampare.

flash *s.* **1.** lampo **2.** chiusa || *— -back*, scena retrospettiva; *— -light*, lampo al magnesio.

to flash *vt.* **1.** proiettare **2.** diffondere. ♦ **to flash** *vi.* **1.** lampeggiare **2.** muoversi rapidamente.

flashing *agg.* risplendente. ♦ **flashing** *s.* splendore, scintillio.

flask *s.* fiasca.

flat¹ *agg.* **1.** piatto, piano **2.** disteso **3.** deciso **4.** sgonfio (*di pneumatico*).

flat² *s.* **1.** superficie piana **2.** pianura **3.** bassofondo **4.** chiatta **5.** appartamento **6.** (*mus.*) bemolle || *— -iron*, ferro da stiro.

flatly *avv.* **1.** pianamente **2.** scialbamente **3.** recisamente.

flatness *s.* **1.** piattezza **2.** decisione.

to flatten *vt.* **1.** appiattire **2.** smorzare. ♦ **to flatten** *vi.* **1.** appiattirsi **2.** indebolirsi.

to flatter *vt.* **1.** adulare **2.** illudere.

flatterer *s.* adulatore.

flattery *s.* adulazione.

flatulence, flatulency *s.* **1.** flatulenza **2.** vanità.

flatus *s.* flatulenza.

to flaunt *vt.* **1.** sventolare **2.** ostentare.

flavour *s.* gusto, aroma.

to flavour *vt.* aromatizzare, dare gusto a.

flavoured *agg.* **1.** profumato **2.** saporito.

flavouring *s.* **1.** aroma **2.** condimento.

flavourless *agg.* insipido.

flaw *s.* **1.** screpolatura **2.** falla, pecca.

flawless *agg.* perfetto.

flax *s.* lino.

flaxen *agg.* **1.** di lino **2.** biondo.

to flay *vt.* **1.** scorticare **2.** criticare aspramente.

flea *s.* pulce || *— -bite* (*fig.*), inezia.

fleck *s.* **1.** macchia **2.** scaglia.

to flee (fled, fled) *vt.* **1.** abbandonare **2.** evitare, schivare. ♦ **to flee (fled, fled)** *vi.* **1.** fuggire **2.** svanire.

fleece *s.* vello.

fleecy *agg.* lanoso.

to fleer *vt.* e *vi.* far beffe (a).

fleet *s.* flotta.

fleeting *agg.* fugace.

Flemish *agg.* fiammingo.

flesh *s.* carne || *to lose* —, dimagrire; *to put on* —, ingrassare.

fleshiness *s.* **1.** carnosità **2.** corpulenza.

fleshless *agg.* scarno.

fleshly *agg.* carnale, sensuale.

flew V. *to fly.*

to flex *vt.* flettere, piegare. ♦ to **flex** *vi.* flettersi.

flexibility *s.* **1.** flessibilità **2.** docilità.

flexible *agg.* **1.** flessibile **2.** docile.

flexion *s.* **1.** flessione **2.** curva.

flexuosity *s.* flessuosità.

flexuous *agg.* flessuoso.

flicker *s.* tremolio, bagliore.

to flicker *vi.* **1.** tremolare **2.** guizzare. ♦ to **flicker** *vt.* far tremolare.

flight[1] *s.* **1.** volo **2.** stormo **3.** rampa (*di scale*).

flight[2] *s.* fuga.

flimsiness *s.* leggerezza, frivolezza.

flimsy *agg.* leggero, sottile.

to flinch *vi.* indietreggiare, ritirarsi.

fling *s.* **1.** getto **2.** beffa **3.** tentativo.

to fling (flung, flung) *vt.* gettare. || *to* — *open*, spalancare. ♦ to **fling (flung, flung)** *vi.* gettarsi.

flint *s.* selce, pietra focaia.

to flip *vt.* **1.** far schioccare **2.** sbattere.

flippancy *s.* leggerezza.

flippant *agg.* leggero.

flipper *s.* pinna.

flirt *s.* **1.** movimento rapido **2.** amoreggiamento.

to flirt *vt.* muovere rapidamente. ♦ to **flirt** *vi.* amoreggiare.

flirtation *s.* amoreggiamento.

to flit *vi.* **1.** volare **2.** scorrere.

float *s.* galleggiante.

to float *vt.* **1.** trasportare **2.** inondare **3.** (*comm.*) varare (*un progetto ecc.*). ♦ to **float** *vi.* **1.** galleggiare **2.** spandersi.

floatage *s.* **1.** galleggiamento **2.** relitto.

floatation *s.* (*comm.*) varo.

floater *s.* galleggiante.

floating *agg.* **1.** galleggiante **2.** oscillante, fluttuante.

flock *s.* **1.** bioccolo **2.** gregge **3.** cascame.

to flock *vi.* affollarsi.

floe *s.* banchisa.

to flog *vt.* fustigare || *to* — *a dead horse*, fare una fatica inutile.

flogger *s.* fustigatore.

flood *s.* inondazione, diluvio.

to flood *vt.* inondare. ♦ to **flood** *vi.* straripare.

flooding *s.* **1.** inondazione **2.** emorragia.

floodlight *s.* illuminazione con riflettore.

flood tide *s.* flusso della marea.

floor *s.* **1.** pavimento **2.** piano || — -*lamp*, lampada a stelo.

to floor *vt.* pavimentare.

flooring *s.* impiantito.

flop *s.* **1.** tonfo **2.** insuccesso.

floral *agg.* floreale.

floriculture *s.* floricultura.

floriculturist *s.* floricoltore.

florid *agg.* **1.** florido **2.** fiorito (*di stile*).

floridity *s.* floridezza.

florin *s.* fiorino.

florist *s.* fiorista.

flotilla *s.* flottiglia.

to flounce *vi.* agitarsi || *to* — *out*, andarsene furibondo.

flour *s.* farina || *potato-* —, fecola.

to flour *vt.* **1.** infarinare **2.** macinare.

flourish *s.* **1.** ornamento **2.** squillo di tromba.

to flourish *vi.* **1.** prosperare **2.** essere attivo.

flourishing *agg.* **1.** fiorente **2.** pomposo.

floury *agg.* **1.** farinoso **2.** infarinato.

flow *s.* corrente, flusso.

to flow *vi.* **1.** scorrere **2.** derivare da. ♦ to **flow** *vt.* inondare.

flower *s.* fiore || — -*bed*, aiuola; — -*bud*, bocciuolo.

to flower *vi.* fiorire. ♦ to **flower** *vt.* infiorare.

flowering *agg.* in fiore. ♦ **flowering** *s.* fioritura.

flowerless *agg.* senza fiori.

flowery *agg.* fiorito.

flowing *agg.* **1.** fluente **2.** fluido.

flown V. *to fly.*

flu *s.* influenza.

to fluctuate *vi.* **1.** fluttuare **2.** ondeggiare.

fluctuation *s.* oscillazione.

flue *s.* condotto per l'aria.

fluency *s.* **1.** fluidità **2.** scioltezza.

fluent *agg.* **1.** fluente **2.** dalla parola facile.

fluently *avv.* **1.** fluentemente **2.** speditamente.

fluff *s.* peluria.

fluffy agg. **1.** soffice, vaporoso **2.** coperto di peluria.
fluid agg. e s. fluido.
fluidity s. fluidità.
flung V. to fling.
fluorescence s. fluorescenza.
fluorescent agg. fluorescente.
fluoride s. fluoruro.
fluorine s. fluoro.
flurry s. **1.** ventata **2.** agitazione.
to **flurry** vt. agitare.
flush agg. **1.** abbondante **2.** pieno di vita **3.** a pari livello **4.** ben fornito. ♦ **flush** s. **1.** flusso **2.** vampata **3.** vigore.
to **flush** vt. **1.** lavare **2.** far scorrere **3.** rianimare. ♦ to **flush** vi. **1.** scorrere **2.** arrossire.
flute s. **1.** flauto **2.** increspatura.
fluted agg. **1.** flautato **2.** increspato.
flutter s. **1.** battito, movimento rapido **2.** eccitazione.
to **flutter** vt. agitare. ♦ to **flutter** vi. **1.** agitarsi **2.** battere le ali.
fluttering agg. **1.** svolazzante **2.** palpitante. ♦ **fluttering** s. **1.** svolazzamento **2.** palpitazione.
fluxion s. flusso.
fly[1] s. **1.** volo **2.** calesse **3.** (mecc.) volano.
fly[2] s. mosca.
to **fly** (**flew, flown**) vi. volare. ♦ to **fly** (**flew, flown**) vt. **1.** far volare **2.** sventolare || to — about, svolazzare; to — away, fuggire; to off (aer.), decollare.
flying agg. **1.** rapido **2.** sventolante || —boat, idrovolante.
flypaper s. carta moschicida.
foam s. schiuma || — rubber gommapiuma.
to **foam** vi. spumeggiare.
foamy agg. spumeggiante.
focal agg. focale.
focus s. **1.** fuoco **2.** focolaio.
to **focus** vt. mettere a fuoco.
fodder s. foraggio.
to **fodder** vt. foraggiare.
foe s. nemico.
foetus s. feto.
fog s. nebbia.
foggy agg. nebbioso (anche fig.).
foible s. debolezza.
foil[1] s. **1.** fioretto **2.** traccia.
foil[2] s. lamina.
fold[1] s. ovile.
fold[2] s. **1.** piega **2.** spira.
to **fold**[1] vt. **1.** piegare **2.** avvolgere **3.** abbracciare. ♦ to **fold** vi. pie-

garsi.
to **fold**[2] vt. chiudere nell'ovile.
folder s. **1.** volantino **2.** cartelletta.
folding agg. pieghevole. ♦ **folding** s. **1.** piega, piegatura **2.** avvolgimento **3.** abbraccio.
foliage s. fogliame.
folio s. (tip.) fo(g)lio.
folk s. gente, popolo.
folklore s. folclore.
folkloristic agg. folcloristico.
to **follow** vt. e vi. seguire.
follower s. seguace.
following agg. seguente. ♦ **following** s. seguito.
folly s. follia.
to **foment** vt. fomentare.
fomentation s. fomentazione.
fomenter s. fomentatore.
fond agg. **1.** amante **2.** affettuoso.
to **fondle** vt. vezzeggiare.
fondly avv. **1.** amorevolmente **2.** ingenuamente.
fondness s. tenerezza, amore.
font s. **1.** fonte battesimale **2.** acquasantiera.
food s. cibo.
foodstuff s. alimenti (pl.).
fool s. **1.** sciocco **2.** buffone || to make a — of, beffarsi di.
to **fool** vt. ingannare. ♦ to **fool** vi. fare lo sciocco || to — away, sperperare.
foolery s. follia.
foolhardiness s. folle temerarietà.
foolhardy agg. temerario.
foolish agg. sciocco.
foolishness s. sciocchezza.
foot s. (pl. feet) **1.** piede **2.** zampa || on —, a piedi.
football s. pallone.
footballer s. calciatore.
foot-bath s. pediluvio.
footboard s. predellino.
footbridge s. cavalcavia.
footfall s. passo.
footing s. punto d'appoggio.
footlights s. pl. luci della ribalta.
footman s. domestico.
footmark s. orma.
footnote s. poscritto.
footpath s. sentiero.
footprint, footstep s. orma.
footstool s. sgabello.
footway s. passaggio pedonale.
fop s. damerino.
foppery s. fatuità.
foppish agg. fatuo.
for[1] prep. per || — all that, ciò no-

nostante; *as* —, in quanto a.
for[2] *cong.* poiché.
forage *s.* foraggio.
foray *s.* incursione, saccheggio.
forbade V. *to forbid.*
to forbear (forbore, forborne)
vi. **1.** astenersi **2.** essere paziente.
forbearance *s.* **1.** astensione **2.**
pazienza.
forbearing *agg.* paziente.
to forbid (forbade, forbidden)
vt. proibire, impedire.
forbidding *agg.* **1.** severo **2.** ripugnante.
forbore V. *to forbear.*
forborne V. *to forbear.*
force *s.* forza. ♦ **forces** *s. pl.* truppe ‖ *the Armed Forces*, le Forze
Armate.
to force *vt.* **1.** forzare **2.** costringere ‖ *to — back*, respingere; *to
— in*, sfondare; *to — on*, far avanzare.
forceful *agg.* forte.
forceps *s.* **1.** forcipe **2.** pinza.
forcible *agg.* **1.** violento **2.** potente.
ford *s.* guado.
to ford *vt.* guadare.
fordable *agg.* guadabile.
fore *agg.* anteriore. ♦ **fore** *s.* prua.
forearm *s.* avambraccio.
to forearm *vt.* premunire.
to forebode *vt.* presagire (*un male*).
foreboding *s.* presagio.
forecast *s.* previsione.
to forecast (forecast, forecast)
vt. prevedere.
forecastle *s.* castello di prua.
forefather *s.* antenato.
forefinger *s.* indice.
foreground *s.* primo piano.
forehead *s.* fronte.
foreign *agg.* **1.** straniero **2.** estraneo ‖ *— Office*, Ministero degli
Esteri.
foreigner *s.* straniero.
forelock *s.* ciuffo.
foreman *s.* caposquadra, caporeparto.
foremast *s.* albero di trinchetto.
forename *s.* nome di battesimo.
forensic(al) *agg.* forense.
to forerun (foreran, forerun) *vt.*
precorrere.
forerunner *s.* **1.** precursore **2.** messaggero.
foresail *s.* vela di trinchetto.
to foresee (foresaw, foreseen)
vt. prevedere.

foreseeable *agg.* prevedibile.
foreseeing *s.* previsione.
foreseen V. *to foresee.*
to foreshadow *vt.* adombrare.
foreshortening *s.* scorcio.
foresight *s.* **1.** previsione **2.** previdenza.
forest *s.* foresta.
forestal *agg.* forestale.
to forestall *vt.* **1.** prevenire **2.** accaparrare.
forestalling *s.* **1.** anticipazione **2.**
accaparramento.
forester *s.* **1.** guardia forestale **2.**
abitante di foreste.
forestry *s.* **1.** foresta **2.** silvicultura.
foretaste *s.* pregustazione.
to foretaste *vt.* pregustare.
to foretell (foretold, foretold)
vt. predire.
forethought *agg.* premeditato. ♦
forethought *s.* **1.** premeditazione
2. previdenza.
foretold V. *to foretell.*
forever *avv.* per sempre.
to forewarn *vt.* avvertire.
foreword *s.* prefazione.
forfeit *s.* **1.** perdita **2.** ammenda **3.**
penitenza.
forfeiture *s.* **1.** multa **2.** confisca.
to forgather *vi.* riunirsi, associarsi.
forgave V. *to forgive.*
forge *s.* fucina.
to forge *vt.* **1.** foggiare, fabbricare
2. contraffare.
forger *s.* **1.** fabbro **2.** falsario.
forgery *s.* contraffazione.
to forget (forgot, forgotten) *vt.*
e *vi.* dimenticare, dimenticarsi.
forgetful *agg.* **1.** immemore **2.** negligente.
forgetfulness *s.* **1.** oblio **2.** negligenza.
forget-me-not *s.* non-ti-scordar-di--me.
to forgive (forgave, forgiven)
vt. perdonare.
forgiveness *s.* perdono.
forgot V. *to forget.*
forgotten V. *to forget.*
fork *s.* **1.** forchetta **2.** forca **3.** forcella **4.** biforcazione.
to fork *vi.* biforcarsi ‖ *to — out*,
(*gergo*) pagare. ♦ **to fork** *vt.*
biforcare.
forked *agg.* biforcuto.
forlorn *agg.* abbandonato.
form *s.* **1.** forma **2.** modulo **3.**
banco.

to **form** vt. formare. ♦ to **form** vi. formarsi.

formal agg. formale || — dress, abito da cerimonia.

formalism s. formalismo.

formalist s. formalista.

formality s. formalità.

to **formalize** vt. 1. formare 2. formalizzare.

format s. formato.

formation s. formazione.

formative agg. formativo.

forme s. (tip.) forma di stampa.

former¹ agg. e pron. precedente, il primo (fra due).

former² s. 1. artefice 2. stampo.

formerly avv. precedentemente.

formic agg. formico.

formidable agg. 1. formidabile 2. spaventoso.

formless agg. informe.

formulary s. formulario.

to **formulate** vt. formulare.

formulation s. formulazione.

to **forsake** (**forsook, forsaken**) vt. abbandonare.

forsaking s. abbandono.

forsook V. to forsake.

to **forswear** (**forswore, forsworn**) vt. 1. abiurare 2. spergiurare.

fort s. (mil.) fortezza.

forth avv. 1. avanti 2. fuori || and so —, e così via.

forthcoming agg. prossimo.

fortieth agg. e s. quarantesimo.

fortification s. fortificazione.

to **fortify** vt. fortificare.

fortitude s. forza d'animo.

fortnight s. due settimane.

fortnightly agg. quindicinale. ♦ **fortnightly** avv. ogni due settimane.

fortress s. (mil.) fortezza.

fortuitous agg. fortuito.

fortunate agg. 1. fortunato 2. propizio.

fortune s. 1. sorte: to tell fortunes, predire la sorte 2. fortuna.

fortune-teller s. indovino.

forty agg. e s. quaranta.

forward agg. 1. avanzato 2. precoce 3. pronto.

to **forward** vt. 1. promuovere 2. spedire.

forwarder s. spedizioniere.

forwarding s. spedizione.

forward(s) avv. avanti, in avanti.

fossil agg. e s. fossile.

fossilization s. fossilizzazione.

to **fossilize** vt. fossilizzare. ♦ to **fossilize** vi. fossilizzarsi.

to **foster** vt. 1. favorire 2. allevare, nutrire.

fought V. to fight.

foul agg. 1. sporco 2. tempestoso.

foulmouthed agg. sboccato.

to **foul** vt. 1. sporcare 2. urtare. ♦ to **foul** vi. 1. sporcarsi 2. urtarsi.

found V. to find.

to **found**¹ vt. fondare.

to **found**² vt. fondere.

foundation s. 1. fondazione 2. fondamenta 3. fondamento.

founder¹ s. fondatore.

founder² s. fonditore.

to **founder** vi. crollare. ♦ to **founder** vi. affondare.

foundling s. trovatello || — -hospital, brefotrofio.

foundry s. fonderia.

fountain s. 1. fontana 2. sorgente || — -pen, penna stilografica.

four agg. e s. quattro || — -handed, quadrumane; — -footed, quadrupede.

fourscore agg. ottanta.

fourteen agg. e s. quattordici.

fourteenth agg. e s. quattordicesimo.

fourth agg. e s. quarto.

fowl s. pollo, pollame.

fox s. volpe: — -hunt, caccia alla volpe.

foxglove s. digitale.

foxy agg. 1. volpino 2. rossiccio 3. scolorito 4. aspro.

foyer s. ridotto.

fraction s. frazione.

fractional agg. frazionario.

to **fractionize** vt. frazionare.

fracture s. frattura.

to **fracture** vt. fratturare. ♦ to **fracture** vi. fratturarsi.

fragile agg. fragile.

fragility s. fragilità.

fragment s. frammento.

fragmentary agg. frammentario.

fragrance s. fragranza.

fragrant agg. fragrante.

frail agg. 1. debole 2. caduco.

frailness, frailty s. debolezza.

frame s. 1. cornice 2. struttura, intelaiatura.

to **frame** vt. 1. incorniciare 2. formare.

framework s. struttura.

framing s. incorniciatura.

franc s. franco.
franchise s. franchigia.
Franciscan agg. e s. francescano.
frank agg. franco.
frankness s. franchezza.
frantic agg. frenetico.
fraternal agg. fraterno.
fraternity s. 1. fraternità 2. confraternita.
fraternization s. affratellamento.
to **fraternize** vi. fraternizzare.
fratricidal agg. fratricida.
fratricide s. 1. fratricida 2. fratricidio.
fraud s. 1. frode 2. impostura 3. (fam.) impostore.
fraudulence s. frode.
fraudulent agg. fraudolento.
fray s. zuffa.
to **fray** vt. consumare. ♦ to **fray** vi. consumarsi.
freak s. 1. capriccio 2. macchiolina.
freakish, freaky agg. capriccioso.
freckle s. lentiggine.
freckled, freckly agg. lentigginoso.
free agg. 1. libero 2. (comm.) franco 3. abbondante 4. gratuito || — on board, franco porto. ♦ **free** avv. gratuitamente.
to **free** vt. liberare.
freedom s. libertà.
freely avv. 1. liberamente 2. gratuitamente.
freemason s. massone.
freemasonry s. massoneria.
freethinker s. libero pensatore.
freethinking s. libertà di pensiero.
freetrade s. libero scambio.
freetrader s. libero scambista.
freeze s. gelo, congelamento.
to **freeze (froze, frozen)** vt. e vi. 1. gelare 2. (imp.) far freddo.
freezer s. cella frigorifera.
freezing agg. glaciale, congelante. ♦ **freezing** s. congelamento.
freight s. 1. trasporto 2. nolo.
to **freight** vt. 1. trasportare 2. noleggiare 3. caricare.
French agg. francese. ♦ **French** s. lingua francese.
to **frenchify** vt. francesizzare. ♦ to **frenchify** vi. francesizzarsi.
Frenchman s. francese (uomo).
Frenchwoman s. francese (donna).
frenzied agg. frenetico.
frenzy s. frenesia, delirio.
frequency s. frequenza.
frequent agg. frequente.
to **frequent** vt. frequentare.

fresco s. affresco.
fresh agg. fresco, nuovo, puro || — water, acqua dolce. ♦ **fresh** s. sorgente.
fresh-water agg. d'acqua dolce.
to **freshen** vt. 1. rinfrescare 2. desalinizzare. ♦ to **freshen** vi. rinfrescarsi.
freshly avv. 1. in modo fresco 2. recentemente.
freshman s. matricola.
freshness s. 1. freschezza 2. inesperienza.
fret[1] s. agitazione.
fret[2] s. 1. fregio 2. traforo.
to **fret**[1] vt. rodere. ♦ to **fret** vi. 1. affliggersi 2. agitarsi.
to **fret**[2] vt. 1. ornare 2. traforare.
fretful agg. irritabile.
fretfully avv. con irritazione.
fretfulness s. irritabilità.
fretwork s. intaglio ornamentale.
friability s. friabilità.
friable agg. friabile.
friar s. frate || Black- —, domenicano; Grey- —, francescano; White- —, carmelitano.
friction s. frizione, attrito.
Friday s. venerdì: Good —, Venerdì Santo.
fried agg. fritto.
friend s. amico || to make friends, fare amicizia; the Society of Friends, i quaccheri.
friendless agg. senza amici.
friendliness s. cordialità.
friendly agg. amichevole. ♦ **friendly** avv. amichevolmente.
friendship s. amicizia.
frigate s. fregata.
fright s. spavento.
to **frighten** vt. spaventare.
frightful agg. spaventevole.
frightfulness s. spavento.
frigid agg. 1. glaciale 2. frigido.
frigidity s. 1. freddezza 2. frigidità.
frill s. 1. fronzolo 2. gala increspata.
to **frill** vt. ornare di gale.
fringe s. 1. frangia 2. bordo.
to **fringe** vt. orlare.
frippery s. cianfrusaglie (pl.).
to **frisk** vi. fare capriole.
frisky agg. gaio.
frivolity s. frivolezza.
frivolous agg. frivolo.
frizzly, frizzy agg. crespo.
frock s. 1. abito 2. tonaca.
frog[1] s. rana.

frog² *s.* alamaro.

frogman *s.* sommozzatore.

frolic *s.* scherzo.

frolicsome *agg.* scherzoso.

from *prep.* da, di.

front *agg.* anteriore. ♦ **front** *s.* **1.** fronte **2.** sfrontatezza.

to front *vt.* fronteggiare.

frontal *agg.* frontale.

frontier *s.* frontiera.

frontispiece *s.* frontespizio.

frost *s.* **1.** gelo **2.** brina || *—bite,* congelamento; *hoar- —,* brinata.

to frost *vt.* **1.** gelare **2.** (*cuc.*) glassare **3.** smerigliare.

frosty *agg.* **1.** gelato **2.** gelido **3.** canuto.

froth *s.* **1.** schiuma **2.** frivolezza.

to froth *vi.* far schiuma.

frothy *agg.* **1.** schiumoso **2.** leggero.

frown *s.* **1.** l'aggrottare le ciglia **2.** cipiglio.

to frown *vi.* **1.** aggrottare le ciglia **2.** accigliarsi.

frowning *agg.* accigliato.

froze V. *to freeze.*

frozen V. *to freeze.*

fructiferous *agg.* fruttifero.

to fructify *vi.* fruttificare. ♦ **to fructify** *vt.* fertilizzare.

frugal *agg.* frugale.

frugalist *s.* persona frugale.

frugality *s.* frugalità.

fruit *s.* **1.** frutta **2.** frutto.

fruiterer *s.* fruttivendolo.

fruitful *agg.* **1.** fruttifero **2.** fertile **3.** redditizio.

fruitfulness *s.* **1.** fertilità **2.** vantaggio.

fruition *s.* **1.** godimento **2.** realizzazione.

fruitless *agg.* infruttuoso.

to frustrate *vt.* frustrare.

frustration *s.* frustrazione.

frustum *s.* (*pl.* -ta) (*geom.*) tronco.

fry *s.* fritto, frittura.

to fry *vt.* e *vi.* friggere.

fudge *s.* fandonia, sciocchezza.

to fudge *vt.* rattoppare.

fuel *s.* combustibile || *— oil,* nafta.

to fuel *vt.* alimentare di combustibile.

fugacity *s.* fugacità.

fugitive *agg.* **1.** fuggitivo **2.** effimero. ♦ **fugitive** *s.* **1.** fuggitivo **2.** rifugiato.

fugitiveness *s.* fuggevolezza.

fugue *s.* (*mus.*) fuga.

fulcrum *s.* (*pl.* fulcra) fulcro.

to fulfil *vt.* **1.** compiere **2.** adempiere, esaurire.

fulfilment *s.* **1.** compimento **2.** adempimento, esaudimento.

fulgency *s.* fulgidezza.

fulgent *agg.* fulgente.

fulgid *agg.* fulgido.

fulguration *s.* folgorazione.

full *agg.* pieno || *— up,* completo; *— -stop,* punto. ♦ **full** *avv.* interamente. ♦ **full** *s.* **1.** intero **2.** massimo.

fullness *s.* pienezza.

fully *avv.* completamente.

fulminant *agg.* fulminante.

fulmination *s.* **1.** fulminazione **2.** imprecazione.

fumarole *s.* fumarola.

to fumble *vi.* annaspare. ♦ **to fumble** *vt.* maneggiare goffamente.

fume *s.* **1.** fumo **2.** eccitazione.

to fume *vi.* **1.** fumare **2.** irritarsi.

fun *s.* **1.** divertimento **2.** facezia || *to make — of so.,* canzonare qu.; *to have good —,* divertirsi molto.

funambulism *s.* funambolismo.

funambulist *s.* funambolo.

function *s.* funzione.

to function *vi.* **1.** funzionare **2.** fungere da.

functional *agg.* funzionale.

functionary *s.* funzionario.

fund *s.* fondo, riserva.

to fund *vt.* **1.** accumulare **2.** investire in obbligazioni.

fundament *s.* base.

fundamental *agg.* fondamentale. ♦ **fundamental** *s.* fondamento.

funeral *agg.* funebre. ♦ **funeral** *s.* funerale.

funerary, funereal *agg.* funereo.

funicular *agg.* e *s.* funicolare.

funnel *s.* **1.** imbuto **2.** camino, ciminiera.

funny *agg.* **1.** comico **2.** strano.

fur *s.* **1.** pelliccia **2.** patina, rivestimento.

to fur *vt.* coprire con pelliccia.

furbelow *s.* falpalà.

furious *agg.* furioso.

to furl *vt.* **1.** piegare, chiudere **2.** ammainare (*vele ecc.*). ♦ **to furl** *vi.* piegarsi, chiudersi.

furnace *s.* fornace.

to furnish *vt.* **1.** fornire **2.** ammobiliare.

furnisher *s.* fornitore.

furnishings *s. pl.* arredamento (*sing.*).

furniture s. **1.** mobilio **2.** contenuto.
furrier s. pellicciaio.
furriery s. pellicceria.
furrow s. **1.** solco **2.** scia.
to **furrow** vt. **1.** solcare **2.** arare.
further agg. (comp. di far) **1.** più lontano **2.** ulteriore. ♦ **further** avv. **1.** più in là **2.** ancora.
to **further** vt. favorire.
furthermore avv. inoltre.
furthermost agg. il più lontano.
furthest agg. (superl. di far) estremo. ♦ **furthest** avv. all'estremo limite.
furtive agg. furtivo.
furunculosis s. furuncolosi.
fury s. furia.
fuse s. **1.** valvola, fusibile **2.** spoletta **3.** miccia.
to **fuse** vt. **1.** fondere **2.** liquefare. ♦ to **fuse** vi. **1.** fondersi **2.** saltare (di valvola).
fuselage s. fusoliera.
fusible agg. fusibile.
fusion s. fusione.
fuss s. **1.** trambusto **2.** smancerie.
to **fuss** vi. far confusione. ♦ to **fuss** vt. irritare.
fussily avv. **1.** con inutile scalpore **2.** con esagerata importanza.
fussy agg. **1.** che fa confusione **2.** meticoloso.
fusty agg. stantio.
futility s. futilità.
future agg. e s. futuro.
futurism s. futurismo.
fuzz s. lanuggine.
fuzzily avv. confusamente.
fuzziness s. **1.** increspatura (di capelli) **2.** (foto) sfocatura.
fuzzy agg. **1.** lanuginoso **2.** confuso **3.** (foto) sfocato.

G

G s. (mus.) sol.
to **gabble** vt. e vi. parlare in modo confuso.
gabbler s. chiacchierone.
gable s. frontone.
gadfly s. **1.** tafano **2.** (fig.) persona irritante.
gadget s. aggeggio.
Gael s. gaelico.
Gaelic agg. e s. gaelico.

gaff s. uncino, rampone.
gag s. **1.** bavaglio **2.** improvvisazione **3.** trovata geniale.
to **gag** vt. imbavagliare. ♦ to **gag** vi. improvvisare (motti di spirito).
gage s. garanzia.
to **gage** vt. dare in pegno.
gaiety s. gaiezza. ♦ **gaieties** s. pl. divertimenti.
gaily avv. gaiamente.
gain s. **1.** guadagno **2.** aumento, miglioramento.
to **gain** vt. e vi. **1.** guadagnare **2.** aumentare || to — on, guadagnar terreno su.
gainer s. chi guadagna.
gainful agg. lucroso.
gainings s. pl. guadagni.
to **gainsay** vt. contraddire.
gainsaying s. contraddizione.
gait s. andatura.
gaiter s. ghetta.
galalith s. galalite.
galantine s. galantina.
galaxy s. galassia.
gale s. tempesta.
galenic agg. galenico.
Galilean agg. e s. galileo.
gall[1] s. bile, fiele || — -bladder, cistifellea.
gall[2] s. **1.** scorticatura **2.** irritazione.
to **gall** vt. irritare. ♦ to **gall** vi. irritarsi.
gallant agg. **1.** prode **2.** galante. ♦ **gallant** s. uomo di mondo.
gallantry s. **1.** galanteria **2.** coraggio **3.** atto, discorso amoroso.
galleon s. galeone.
gallery s. galleria || picture- —, pinacoteca.
galley s. **1.** (mar.) galea **2.** (mar.) cambusa **3.** (tip.) vantaggio || — proof (tip.), bozza in colonna; — slave, galeotto.
Gallic agg. e s. gallico.
gallicism s. francesismo.
gallinacean agg. e s. gallinaceo.
gallium s. gallio.
gallon s. gallone (misura).
galloon s. gallone (ornamento).
gallooned agg. gallonato.
gallop s. **1.** galoppo: at a —, al galoppo **2.** galoppata.
to **gallop** vt. far galoppare. ♦ to **gallop** vi. galoppare.
gallows s. pl. patibolo (sing.).
galore s. abbondanza. ♦ **galore** avv. in abbondanza.
galosh(e) s. galoscia.

galvanic(al) *agg.* **1.** galvanico **2.** (*fig.*) galvanizzante.
galvanization *s.* galvanizzazione.
to **galvanize** *vt.* galvanizzare.
galvanometer *s.* galvanometro.
galvanoplastic *agg.* galvanoplastico.
gamble *s.* gioco d'azzardo.
to **gamble** *vt.* e *vi.* giocare (*d'azzardo*).
gambler *s.* giocatore d'azzardo.
gambling *s.* V. *gamble* || — *-house*, casa da gioco.
gambol *s.* piroetta. ♦ **game** *s.* **1.** gioco (*con regole*), mano (*in una partita*) **2.** (*fig.*) progetto **3.** selvaggina (*coll.*).
to **game** V. *to gamble*.
gamekeeper *s.* guardacaccia.
gamely *avv.* coraggiosamente.
gamesome *agg.* scherzoso.
gamester *s.* giocatore.
gammon *s.* (*mar.*) trinca di bompresso.
gang *s.* **1.** squadra **2.** banda.
to **gang** *vt.* e *vi.* formare una banda.
ganglion *s.* (*pl.* ganglia) ganglio.
gangrene *s.* cancrena.
to **gangrene** *vi.* andare in cancrena.
gangster *s.* bandito.
gangsterism *s.* banditismo.
gangway *s.* **1.** passaggio (*tra file di sedie ecc.*) **2.** (*mar.*) passerella.
gaol *s.* prigione.
to **gaol** *vt.* imprigionare.
gaoler *s.* carceriere.
gap *s.* **1.** apertura, breccia **2.** intervallo **3.** divergenza **4.** lacuna.
gape *s.* **1.** sbadiglio **2.** apertura **3.** stupore.
to **gape** *vi.* **1.** spalancare la bocca **2.** sbadigliare **3.** restare a bocca aperta.
gaping *agg.* **1.** aperto **2.** stupito.
garage *s.* autorimessa || — *keeper*, garagista.
garb *s.* costume.
garbage *s.* rifiuto.
garden *s.* giardino.
to **garden** *vi.* fare del giardinaggio.
gardener *s.* giardiniere.
gardening *s.* giardinaggio.
gargarism *s.* gargarismo.
gargle *s.* liquido per gargarismi.
to **gargle** *vt.* e *vi.* gargarizzare.
gargoyle *s.* doccione.
garish *agg.* **1.** abbagliante **2.** appariscente.

garland *s.* ghirlanda.
garlic *s.* aglio.
garment *s.* abito, indumento.
garnet[1] *s.* granato.
garnet[2] *s.* (*mar.*) paranco.
to **garnish** *vt.* guarnire.
garnish(ment) *s.* ornamento.
garret *s.* soffitta.
garrison *s.* guarnigione.
to **garrison** *vt.* presidiare.
garrulity *s.* garrulità.
garrulous *agg.* garrulo.
garter *s.* giarrettiera || *knight o, the Garter*, Cavaliere dell'Ordine della Giarrettiera.
gas *s.* gas || — *-fitter*, gassista; — *-mask*, maschera antigas; — *-meter*, contatore del gas.
to **gas** *vt.* **1.** fornire di gas **2.** asfissiare col gas.
Gascon *agg.* e *s.* guascone.
gasconade *s.* guasconata.
gaseous *agg.* gassoso.
gash *s.* sfregio.
to **gash** *vt.* sfregiare.
gas oil *s.* gasolio.
gasoline *s.* (*amer.*) benzina.
gasp *s.* respiro affannoso.
to **gasp** *vi.* **1.** ansare **2.** restare senza fiato **3.** parlare affannosamente.
gassy *agg.* gassoso.
gastric *agg.* gastrico.
gastritis *s.* gastrite.
gastroenteritis *s.* gastroenterite.
gastronome *s.* gastronomo.
gastronomic(al) *agg.* gastronomico.
gastronomy *s.* gastronomia.
gate *s.* **1.** cancello **2.** porta.
gatekeeper *s.* portiere, custode.
gateway *s.* portone, ingresso.
to **gather** *vt.* **1.** raccogliere **2.** acquistare **3.** dedurre. ♦ to **gather** *vi.* raccogliersi.
gathering *s.* **1.** raccolta **2.** (*med.*) ascesso.
gaud *s.* fronzolo.
gaudiness *s.* sfarzo.
gaudy *agg.* sfarzoso. ♦ **gaudy** *s.* festa (*universitaria*).
gauge *s.* **1.** misura **2.** calibro **3.** (*ferr.*) scartamento **4.** pescaggio || *narrow* —, scartamento ridotto.
to **gauge** *vt.* misurare.
gaunt *agg.* scarno.
gauze *s.* garza, velo, mussolina.
gauzy *agg.* trasparente.
gave V. *to give*.
gay *agg.* **1.** gaio **2.** licenzioso.
gayety *s.* gaiezza.

gaze s. sguardo fisso.

to gaze vi. fissare.

gazelle s. gazzella.

gazette s. gazzetta.

gazetteer s. **1.** giornalista **2.** dizionario geografico.

gear s. **1.** meccanismo **2.** (auto) marcia, cambio **3.** (mecc.) ingranaggio.

to gear vt. ingranare || to — up, down, aumentare, diminuire la velocità.

gearing s. ingranaggio, innesto.

geese V. goose.

gelatin(e) s. gelatina.

gelatinous agg. gelatinoso.

to geld vt. castrare.

gelid agg. gelido.

gem s. gemma.

gemmy agg. pieno di gemme.

gender s. genere.

genderless agg. di genere comune.

genealogical agg. genealogico.

genealogy s. genealogia.

generable agg. generabile.

general agg. e s. generale.

generality s. **1.** generalità **2.** maggioranza.

generalization s. generalizzazione.

to generalize vt. e vi. generalizzare.

generally avv. generalmente.

to generate vt. generare.

generation s. generazione.

generative agg. generativo.

generator s. generatore.

generic(al) agg. generico.

generosity s. generosità.

generous agg. **1.** generoso **2.** abbondante.

genesis s. (pl. -ses) genesi.

genetic(al) agg. genetico.

genetics s. genetica.

genial agg. **1.** gioviale **2.** geniale **3.** mite (di clima).

geniality s. **1.** giovialità **2.** mitezza (di clima).

genital agg. e s. genitale.

genitive agg. e s. genitivo.

genius s. genio.

genocide s. genocidio.

genre s. genere.

genteel agg. raffinato.

gentian s. genziana.

gentile agg. e s. pagano.

gentility s. signorilità.

gentle agg. **1.** nobile **2.** garbato **3.** moderato **4.** facile.

gentleman s. **1.** signore **2.** gentiluomo.

gentlemanlike, gentlemanly agg.
da gentiluomo.

gentleness s. gentilezza.

gentlewoman s. gentildonna.

gently avv. **1.** gentilmente, con delicatezza **2.** gradualmente.

gentry s. classe gentilizia.

to genuflect vi. genuflettersi.

genuflection s. genuflessione.

genuine agg. **1.** autentico **2.** sincero **3.** puro.

genuineness s. **1.** autenticità **2.** sincerità.

genus s. (pl. -nera) genere.

geodesy s. geodesia.

geographer s. geografo.

geographic(al) agg. geografico.

geography s. geografia.

geologic(al) agg. geologico.

geologist s. geologo.

geology s. geologia.

geometer s. geometra.

geometric(al) agg. geometrico.

geometrician s. geometra.

geometry s. geometria.

geophysics s. geofisica.

geopolitics s. geopolitica.

georgic agg. georgico.

geranium s. geranio.

gerent s. gerente.

germ s. germe.

german agg. germano.

German agg. e s. tedesco.

Germanic agg. germanico.

Germanism s. germanesimo.

Germanist s. germanista.

germanium s. germanio.

germinal agg. germinale.

to germinate vt. far germinare. ♦ **to germinate** vi. germinare.

germination s. germinazione.

gerontology s. gerontologia.

gerund s. gerundio.

gerundial agg. gerundivo.

gerundive agg. e s. gerundivo.

gestation s. gestazione.

to gesticulate vi. gesticolare.

gesticulation s. gesticolazione.

gesture s. **1.** gesto **2.** il gestire.

to gesture vi. far gesti.

to get (got, got) vt. **1.** ottenere, procurare **2.** prendere **3.** portare **4.** fare. ♦ **to get (got, got)** vi. **1.** andare **2.** divenire || to — off, scendere; to — over, scavalcare; to — out, (far) uscire; to — up, alzarsi; to — married, sposarsi; to — hold of, impossessarsi di.

getaway s. **1.** fuga **2.** (sport) partenza.

gettable *agg.* ottenibile.

get-up *s.* **1.** equipaggiamento **2.** presentazione (*di libro, giornale ecc.*).

geyser *s.* **1.** geyser **2.** scaldabagno.

ghastliness *s.* **1.** aspetto spaventoso **2.** pallore spettrale.

ghastly *agg.* **1.** spaventoso **2.** spettrale.

gherkin *s.* cetriolo.

Ghibelline *agg.* e *s.* ghibellino.

ghost *s.* **1.** spirito **2.** spettro || *to give up the* —, spirare.

ghostliness *s.* **1.** l'essere spettrale **2.** spiritualità.

ghostly *agg.* **1.** spettrale **2.** spirituale.

giant *s.* gigante.

giantism *s.* gigantismo.

gibbet *s.* patibolo.

to gibbet *vt.* **1.** impiccare **2.** (*fig.*) mettere alla berlina.

gibbosity *s.* gibbosità.

gibbous *agg.* gibboso.

gibe *s.* scherno.

to gibe *vt.* e *vi.* schernire.

giblets *s. pl.* regaglie.

giddily *avv.* vertiginosamente.

giddiness *s.* **1.** capogiro **2.** (*fig.*) frivolezza.

giddy *agg.* **1.** stordito **2.** vertiginoso **3.** frivolo.

to giddy *vt.* stordire. ♦ **to giddy** *vi.* aver le vertigini.

gift *s.* **1.** dono **2.** dote.

to gift *vt.* dotare.

gig[1] *s.* **1.** calessino **2.** (*mar.*) iole.

gig[2] *s.* rampone, fiocina.

gigantean, gigantic *agg.* gigantesco.

giggle *s.* risatina.

to giggle *vi.* fare risatine.

to gild (gilt, gilt) (*anche reg.*) *vt.* (in)dorare.

gilder *s.* doratore.

gilding *s.* doratura.

gill *s.* **1.** branchia **2.** pappagorgia.

gilt V. *to gild.*

gilt *s.* doratura.

gimlet *s.* succhiello.

gin[1] *s.* "gin" (*liquore*).

gin[2] *s.* **1.** elevatore **2.** trappola (*per animali*).

ginger *s.* zenzero.

gingerly *agg.* cauto. ♦ **gingerly** *avv.* cautamente.

gipsy *s.* zingaro.

gipsydom *s.* gli zingari (*pl.*).

gipsyish *agg.* zingaresco.

giraffe *s.* giraffa.

to gird (girt, girt) (*anche reg.*) *vt.* cingere.

girder *s.* **1.** trave maestra **2.** sbarra

girdle *s.* **1.** cintura **2.** reggicalze.

to girdle *vt.* cingere.

girl *s.* ragazza || *flower* —, fioraia.

girlhood *s.* adolescenza (*di ragazza*).

Girondist *agg.* e *s.* girondino.

girt V. *to gird.*

girth *s.* **1.** circonferenza **2.** cinghia.

to give (gave, given) *vt.* dare || *to* — *in*, cedere; *to* — *out*, annunciare, venir meno; *to* — *up*, smettere, abbandonare; *to* — *birth to*, generare; *to* — *oneself up*, costituirsi (*alla polizia*); *to* — *oneself up to*, dedicarsi (a); *to* — *off*, emettere (*luce ecc.*).

giver *s.* datore.

glacial *agg.* glaciale.

glaciation *s.* glaciazione.

glacier *s.* ghiacciaio.

glacis *s.* spalto.

glad *agg.* lieto.

to gladden *vt.* rallegrare. ♦ **to gladden** *vi.* rallegrarsi.

glade *s.* radura.

gladiator *s.* gladiatore.

gladiolus *s.* (*pl.* -li) gladiolo.

gladly *avv.* con piacere.

gladness *s.* contentezza.

glair *s.* albume.

gladsome *agg.* gioioso.

glair *s.* albume.

glamorous *agg.* affascinante.

glamour *s.* **1.** fascino **2.** incantesimo

glance *s.* **1.** occhiata **2.** colpo obliquo.

to glance *vt.* e *vi.* **1.** gettare uno sguardo **2.** sfiorare **3.** balenare || *to* — *off*, sorvolare su.

gland *s.* **1.** ghiandola **2.** ghianda.

glandiferous *agg.* ghiandifero.

glandular *agg.* glandolare.

glare *s.* **1.** luce abbagliante **2.** sguardo truce **3.** abbagliamento.

to glare *vi.* **1.** splendere **2.** guardare tormentosamente.

glaring *agg.* **1.** abbagliante **2.** evidente.

glass *s.* **1.** vetro **2.** bicchiere **3.** specchio || — *-ware*, articoli in vetro; — *-work*, fabbrica di vetro; — *-paper*, carta vetrata. ♦ **glasses** *s. pl.* occhiali, cannocchiale (*sing.*).

to glass *vt.* **1.** specchiare **2.** imbottigliare.

glassy *agg.* **1.** vitreo **2.** cristallino.

glaucous *agg.* glauco.
glaze *s.* superficie vetrosa.
to glaze *vt.* **1.** smaltare **2.** mettere vetri a. ♦ **to glaze** *vi.* diventare vitreo.
glazier *s.* vetraio.
glazy *agg.* vitreo.
gleam *s.* barlume.
to gleam *vi.* scintillare.
gleamy *agg.* scintillante.
to glean *vt.* e *vi.* spigolare.
gleaner *s.* spigolatore.
gleaning *s.* spigolatura.
glee *s.* allegria.
gleeful *agg.* allegro.
glib *agg.* **1.** liscio **2.** facondo **3.** sciolto.
glibness *s.* **1.** disinvoltura **2.** facondia.
glide *s.* scivolata.
to glide *vt.* **1.** far scorrere **2.** trascorrere. ♦ **to glide** *vi.* **1.** scivolare **2.** passare.
glider *s.* aliante.
gliding *agg.* scorrevole. ♦ **gliding** *s.* volo a vela.
glimmer *s.* barlume.
to glimmer *vi.* brillare.
glimpse *s.* **1.** visione **2.** occhiata **3.** vaga idea.
to glimpse *vt.* e *vi.* intravedere.
glitter *s.* scintillio.
to glitter *vi.* scintillare.
gloaming *s.* crepuscolo.
to gloat *vi.* fissare avidamente.
global *agg.* globale.
globe *s.* **1.** globo **2.** pianeta.
globous, globular *agg.* sferico.
globule *s.* globulo.
gloom *s.* **1.** oscurità **2.** tristezza.
to gloom *vt.* **1.** oscurare **2.** rattristare. ♦ **to gloom** *vi.* **1.** oscurarsi **2.** rattristarsi.
gloomy *agg.* cupo.
glorification *s.* glorificazione.
to glorify *vt.* glorificare.
glorious *agg.* **1.** glorioso **2.** splendido.
gloriousness *s.* V. *glory.*
glory *s.* **1.** gloria **2.** splendore.
to glory *vi.* vantarsi.
gloss *s.* **1.** glossa **2.** lucentezza **3.** apparenza.
glossarist *s.* glossatore.
glossary *s.* glossario.
glossy *agg.* lucido.
glottis *s.* glottide.
glottologist *s.* glottologo.
glottology *s.* glottologia.

glove *s.* guanto || *to be hand in — with,* essere molto intimo con.
gloved *agg.* inguantato.
glover *s.* guantaio.
glow *s.* **1.** calore **2.** splendore **3.** colorito || *—worm,* lucciola.
to glow *vi.* ardere.
glucose *s.* glucosio.
glue *s.* colla.
to glue *vt.* incollare.
glut *s.* **1.** scorpacciata **2.** saturazione.
to glut *vt.* **1.** saziare **2.** saturare. ♦ **to glut** *vi.* fare una scorpacciata.
gluten *s.* glutine.
gluteus *s.* (*pl.* glutei) gluteo.
glutton *s.* ghiottone.
gluttonous *agg.* ghiottone.
gluttony *s.* ghiottoneria.
glycerin(e) *s.* glicerina.
glycogen *s.* glicogeno.
gnarled *agg.* nodoso. *
to gnash *vt.* e *vi.* digrignare.
gnat *s.* zanzara.
to gnaw *vt.* rodere.
gnawing *agg.* **1.** rosicante **2.** corrodente.
gnome[1] *s.* gnomo.
gnome[2] *s.* massima.
gnomic *agg.* gnomico.
gnosis *s.* gnosi.
gnostic *agg.* e *s.* gnostico.
gnosticism *s.* gnosticismo.
go *s.* **1.** movimento **2.** energia **3.** colpo || *— -between,* intermediario; *— -by,* evasione; *— -cart,* girello.
to go (went, gone) *vi.* **1.** andare **2.** divenire || *to — by,* passare; *to — for,* andare a cercare; *to — on,* continuare.
goad *s.* pungolo.
to goad *vt.* stimolare.
goal *s.* **1.** traguardo **2.** (*sport*) rete || *— -keeper,* portiere.
goat *s.* capra.
goatish *agg.* **1.** caprino **2.** lascivo.
to gobble *vt.* tranguggiare, inghiottire.
goblin *s.* folletto.
god *s.* **1.** dio, divinità **2.** Dio.
godchild *s.* (*pl.* -children) figlioccio.
goddaughter *s.* figlioccia.
goddess *s.* dea.
godfather *s.* padrino.
godless *agg.* **1.** ateo **2.** empio.
godlike *agg.* divino.
godliness *s.* devozione.
godly *agg.* religioso.
godmother *s.* madrina.

godown s. deposito.
godsend s. dono del cielo.
godship s. divinità.
godson s. figlioccio.
goggle agg. **1.** stralunato **2.** sporgente (di occhi).
to goggle vt. stralunare. ♦ **to goggle** vi. essere sporgenti (di occhi).
goggles s. pl. occhiali di protezione.
going s. **1.** l'andare **2.** partenza.
goitre s. gozzo.
goitrous agg. gozzuto.
gold agg. d'oro. ♦ **gold** s. oro || — -field, zona aurifera; — -dig *", cercatore d'oro.
golden agg. dorato, d'oro.
goldfinch s. cardellino.
goldsmith s. orefice.
gone V. to go.
gonfalon s. gonfalone.
goniometer s. goniometro.
goniometry s. goniometria.
good (better, best) agg. **1.** buono **2.** bravo **3.** bello. ♦ **good** inter. bene!
good s. **1.** bene **2.** utilità || for —, per sempre.
good-bye inter. e s. addio, arrivederci.
good-for-nothing s. buono a nulla.
goodly agg. bello.
goodness s. **1.** bontà **2.** il meglio || my —!, Dio mio!
goods s. pl. merce (sing.).
goodwill s. **1.** buona volontà **2.** benevolenza.
goody agg. troppo buono. ♦ **goody** inter. bene!
goose s. (pl. geese) oca.
gooseberry s. uva spina.
goose-step s. passo dell'oca.
gore s. sangue rappreso.
gorge s. gola.
to gorge V. to glut.
gorgeous agg. magnifico.
gorgeousness s. magnificenza.
gospel s. vangelo.
gossamer s. ragnatela.
gossip s. **1.** pettegolezzo **2.** pettegolo.
to gossip vi. far pettegolezzi.
gossiper s. pettegolo.
gossipy agg. pettegolo.
got V. to get.
Gothic agg. e s. gotico.
gothicism s. **1.** stile gotico **2.** rozzezza.
gouache s. guazzo.
gouge s. sgorbia.

gourd s. zucca.
gourmand s. goloso.
gourmet s. buongustaio.
gout s. **1.** gotta **2.** goccia.
gouty agg. gottoso.
to govern vt. **1.** governare **2.** controllare **3.** (gramm.) reggere.
governable agg. docile.
governess s. istitutrice.
government s. governo.
governmental agg. governativo.
governor s. **1.** governatore **2.** regolatore.
gown s. **1.** veste **2.** toga || dressing—, veste da camera; night- —, camicia da notte.
grab s. presa.
to grab vt. **1.** afferrare **2.** (mecc.) bloccare.
grace s. grazia.
to grace vt. adornare.
graceful agg. grazioso.
gracefulness s. grazia.
graceless agg. **1.** sgraziato **2.** depravato.
gracile agg. gracile.
gracility s. gracilità.
gracious agg. benigno || good —!, mio Dio!
gradation s. gradazione.
grade s. **1.** grado **2.** pendio.
to grade vt. **1.** graduare **2.** livellare.
gradient agg. che sale, scende gradatamente. ♦ **gradient** s. pendenza.
gradual agg. graduale.
graduality s. gradualità.
graduate s. laureato.
to graduate vt. **1.** graduare **2.** laureare. ♦ **to graduate** vi. laurearsi.
graduation s. **1.** graduazione **2.** laurea.
graft s. innesto.
to graft vt. innestare.
grain s. **1.** granaglie (pl.) **2.** chicco **3.** grano.
grainy agg. **1.** granuloso **2.** granoso.
gram s. grammo.
Gramineae s. pl. graminacee.
grammar s. grammatica.
grammarian s. grammatico.
grammatic(al) agg. grammaticale.
gramophone s. grammofono.
granary s. granaio.
grand agg. **1.** grande **2.** nobile || — -aunt, prozia; — -uncle, prozio; — -nephew, pronipote (maschio); — -niece, pronipote (femmina).

grandchild s. (*pl.* -children) nipote (*di nonni*).

granddaughter s. nipote (*femmina*) (*di nonni*).

grandeur s. grandiosità.

grandfather s. nonno.

grandiloquence s. magniloquenza.

grandiloquent agg. magniloquente.

grandiose agg. grandioso.

grandiosity s. grandiosità.

grandmother s. nonna.

grandmotherly agg. protettivo.

grandparents s. pl. nonni.

grandson s. nipote (*maschio*) (*di nonni*).

grange s. fattoria, casa colonica.

granite s. granito.

granitic agg. granitico.

granivorous agg. granivoro.

grant s. concessione.

to grant vt. concedere ‖ *to take for granted*, dare per scontato.

granular agg. granulare.

granularity s. granulosità.

to granulate vt. granulare. ♦ **to granulate** vi. granularsi.

granulation s. granulazione.

granulous agg. granuloso.

grape s. **1.** acino ‖ — *-shot*, mitraglia. ♦ **grapes** s. pl. uva.

grapefruit s. pompelmo.

grapevine s. **1.** vigna **2.** (*fam.*) notizia ufficiosa.

graph s. grafico.

graphic(al) agg. **1.** grafico **2.** pittoresco.

graphite s. grafite.

graphologist s. grafologo.

graphology s. grafologia.

graphomania s. grafomania.

graphomaniac s. grafomane.

grapnel s. (*mar.*) grappino.

to grapple vt. afferrare. ♦ **to grapple** vi. lottare.

grappling s. (*mar.*) aggancio ‖ — *irons*, grappini d'abbordaggio.

grasp s. **1.** stretta **2.** manico **3.** potere.

to grasp vt. e vi. afferrare.

grasping agg. avido.

grass s. erba.

grasshopper s. cavalletta.

grass-widow s. donna separata dal marito.

grassy agg. erboso.

grate s. **1.** grata **2.** graticola.

to grate vt. **1.** fornire di grata **2.** grattugiare. ♦ **to grate** vi. stridere.

grateful agg. grato.

gratefulness s. gratitudine.

grater s. grattugia.

to gratify vt. **1.** ricompensare **2.** appagare.

gratifying agg. soddisfacente.

grating[1] agg. **1.** irritante **2.** stridente. ♦ **grating** s. stridore.

grating[2] s. **1.** grata **2.** (*ott.*) reticolo.

gratitude s. gratitudine.

gratuitous agg. gratuito.

gratuity s. mancia.

grave[1] agg. grave.

grave[2] s. tomba.

gravel s. ghiaia.

to gravel vt. inghiaiare.

gravelly agg. ghiaioso.

graven agg. intagliato.

graver s. **1.** incisore **2.** bulino.

gravestone s. pietra tombale.

graveyard s. cimitero.

gravid agg. gravido.

to gravitate vi. gravitare.

gravitation s. gravitazione.

gravitational agg. gravitazionale.

gravity s. gravità.

gravy s. sugo.

gray agg. e s. grigio.

graze s. **1.** colpo di striscio **2.** escoriazione.

to graze[1] vt. e vi. **1.** graffiare **2.** sfiorare.

to graze[2] vt. e vi. pascolare, condurre al pascolo.

grazier s. allevatore (*di bestiame*).

grazing[1] s. abrasione.

grazing[2] s. pascolo.

grease s. grasso.

to grease vt. ungere, lubrificare.

greaser s. ingrassatore.

greasiness s. untuosità.

greasy agg. **1.** grasso **2.** unto, untuoso **3.** scivoloso.

great agg. grande ‖ — *-grandchild*, pronipote (*di nonni*); — *-grandfather*, bisnonno; — *-grandmother*, bisnonna.

greatness s. grandezza.

Grecian agg. e s. greco.

greed(iness) s. avidità.

greedy agg. avido.

Greek agg. e s. greco.

green agg. **1.** verde **2.** inesperto **3.** vigoroso **4.** recente. ♦ **green** s. prato. ♦ **greens** s. pl. frasche, verdura (*sing.*).

greenery s. **1.** vegetazione **2.** serra.

greengrocer s. erbivendolo.

greenhouse s. serra.

greenish agg. verdastro.
greenness s. **1.** color verde **2.** acerbezza **3.** ingenuità **4.** vigore.
greenroom s. (teat.) camerino.
to **greet** vt. e vi. salutare.
greeting s. saluto.
Gregorian agg. gregoriano.
grenadier s. granatiere.
grenadine s. granatina.
grew V. to grow.
grey agg. e s. grigio.
greyhound s. levriere.
greyness s. grigiore.
grid s. griglia.
gridiron s. graticola.
grief s. **1.** dolore **2.** fallimento || to come to —, fare fiasco.
grievance s. **1.** lagnanza **2.** torto.
to **grieve** vt. affliggere. ♦ to **grieve** vi. affliggersi.
grievous agg. **1.** doloroso **2.** grave.
griffon s. grifone.
grill s. **1.** graticola **2.** cibo ai ferri || -room, rosticceria.
to **grill** vt. e vi. arrostire (alla graticola).
grille s. inferriata.
grim agg. cupo.
grimace s. smorfia.
grime s. sudiciume.
to **grime** vt. insudiciare.
grimly avv. cupamente.
grimy agg. sudicio.
grin s. **1.** largo sorriso **2.** sogghigno.
to **grin** vi. **1.** fare un largo sorriso **2.** sogghignare.
to **grind** (ground, ground) vt. **1.** macinare **2.** molare **3.** digrignare **4.** (fig.) opprimere.
grinder s. **1.** mola **2.** molare **3.** arrotino || organ- —, suonatore di organetto.
grinding agg. irritante. ♦ **grinding** s. **1.** macinatura **2.** stridore **3.** affilatura **4.** (fig.) oppressione.
grindstone s. mola.
grip s. **1.** stretta **2.** manico **3.** (fig.) padronanza || to lose one's grips, perdere le staffe.
to **grip** vt. e vi. afferrare.
gripe s. **1.** presa **2.** freno. ♦ **gripes** s. pl. colica (sing.).
gripper s. pinza.
grist s. grano da macinare || to bring — to one's mill, tirar l'acqua al proprio mulino.
grit s. sabbia, arenaria.
grizzly agg. grigio. ♦ **grizzly** s. orso grigio.

groan s. gemito.
to **groan** vi. gemere.
groaning s. gemito.
grocer s. droghiere.
grocery s. drogheria. ♦ **groceries** s. pl. droghe e coloniali.
groggy agg. vacillante.
groin s. inguine.
groom s. stalliere.
to **groom** vt. strigliare.
groove s. solco.
to **grope** vi. brancolare.
gropingly avv. a tastoni.
gross agg. **1.** grossolano **2.** pesante **3.** lussureggiante **4.** (comm.) lordo.
grotesque agg. grottesco.
grotto s. grotta.
ground[1] V. to grind.
ground[2] s. **1.** suolo, terreno **2.** distanza, territorio **3.** motivi, ragioni (general. pl.) || — -floor, pianterreno.
to **ground** vt. fondare. ♦ to **ground** vi. **1.** fondarsi **2.** arenarsi.
grounded agg. interrato.
groundless agg. infondato.
groundlessness s. infondatezza.
grounds s. pl. **1.** fondi, sedimenti **2.** parco (sing.).
group s. gruppo.
to **group** vt. raggruppare. ♦ to **group** vi. raggrupparsi.
grouping s. raggruppamento.
grove s. boschetto || olive —, oliveto.
to **grovel** vi. **1.** strisciare a terra **2.** (fig.) umiliarsi.
grovelling s. strisciamento. ♦ **grovelling** agg. **1.** strisciante **2.** (fig.) abbietto.
to **grow** (grew, grown) vi. **1.** crescere **2.** diventare || to — better, migliorare; to — old, invecchiare; to — up, crescere, diventare maturo (di persone). ♦ to **grow** (grew, grown) vt. coltivare.
grower s. coltivatore.
growing s. coltivazione.
growl s. brontolio.
to **growl** vt. e vi. brontolare.
growler s. brontolone.
grown V. to grow.
grown-up agg. e s. adulto.
growth s. **1.** crescita **2.** produzione.
grub s. **1.** verme **2.** larva.
to **grub** vt. e vi. scavare.
grubby agg. **1.** bacato **2.** sporco.
grudge s. malanimo || to bear a — against so., nutrire rancore verso

qu.

to **grudge** vt. **1.** dare a malincuore **2.** invidiare.

grudging agg. **1.** riluttante **2.** invidioso.

gruesome agg. raccapricciante.

gruff agg. burbero.

grumble s. brontolio.

to **grumble** vt. e vi. brontolare.

grumbler s. brontolone.

grumbling s. brontolio.

grumpy agg. burbero, tetro.

grunt s. grugnito.

to **grunt** vt. e vi. grugnire.

gruyère s. gruviera.

guarantee s. **1.** garanzia **2.** garante.

to **guarantee** vt. garantire.

guard s. **1.** guardia **2.** capotreno **3.** parapetto.

to **guard** vt. custodire.

guardian s. **1.** guardiano **2.** tutore.

guardianship s. **1.** protezione **2.** tutela.

guardless agg. indifeso.

guardrail s. **1.** spartitraffico **2.** corrimano (di scala).

Guelph s. guelfo.

guerrilla s. **1.** guerriglia **2.** guerrigliere.

guess s. supposizione.

to **guess** vt. e vi. **1.** supporre **2.** indovinare.

guess-work s. congettura.

guest s. ospite || — -house, pensione.

guffaw s. riso sguaiato.

guide s. guida.

to **guide** vt. guidare.

guild s. corporazione.

guile s. insidia.

guileful agg. insidioso.

guileless agg. sincero.

guillotine s. ghigliottina.

guilt s. colpa.

guiltiness s. colpevolezza.

guiltless agg. innocente.

guilty agg. colpevole.

guinea s. ghinea.

Guinea-pig s. cavia.

guise s. **1.** aspetto, apparenza **2.** falso aspetto.

guitar s. chitarra.

guitarist s. chitarrista.

gulf s. golfo.

gull[1] s. gabbiano.

gull[2] s. sciocco.

to **gull** vt. truffare.

gully s. condotto (di scolo) || —

-hole, tombino.

gulp s. **1.** boccone **2.** sorso.

to **gulp** vt. inghiottire.

gum[1] s. gengiva.

gum[2] s. gomma.

to **gum** vt. ingommare.

gummy agg. gommoso.

gun s. **1.** cannone **2.** fucile **3.** rivoltella, pistola || — -barrel, canna da fucile; — -carriage, affusto di cannone.

gunfire s. sparatoria.

gunner s. artigliere.

gunpowder s. polvere da sparo.

gun-room s. armeria.

gunshot s. colpo di arma da fuoco.

gunsmith s. armaiolo.

gurgle s. gorgoglic.

to **gurgle** vi. gorgogliare.

gush s. **1.** getto **2.** effusione.

to **gush** vi. **1.** sgorgare **2.** essere espansivo.

gusher s. pozzo petrolifero.

gushing agg. **1.** sgorgante **2.** esuberante.

gust s. **1.** raffica **2.** (fig.) impeto.

gustative, gustatory agg. gustativo.

gusty agg. ventoso.

gut s. budello.

to **gut** vt. sventrare.

gutter s. **1.** grondaia **2.** rigagnolo.

to **gutter** vt. scanalare. ♦ to **gutter** vi. colare.

guttural agg. e s. gutturale.

to **guzzle** vt. tracannare.

gymkhana s. gincana.

gymnasium s. palestra.

gymnast s. ginnasta.

gymnastic(al) agg. ginnastico.

gymnastics s. ginnastica.

gynaeceum s. (pl. -cea) gineceo.

gynaecologic agg. ginecologico.

gynaecologist s. ginecologo.

gynaecology s. ginecologia.

gypsy s. V. gipsy.

to **gyrate** vi. girare.

gyroscope s. giroscopio.

gyves s. pl. ceppi, catene.

H

haberdasher s. merciaio.

haberdashery s. merceria.

habit s. **1.** abitudine **2.** temperamen-

to **3.** costume.
habitable *agg.* abitabile.
habitation *s.* abitazione.
habitual *agg.* abituale, consueto.
habitude *s.* abitudine.
hack[1] *s.* **1.** tacca, incisione **2.** piccone, mazza **3.** tosse secca.
hack[2] *s.* **1.** ronzino **2.** (*fig.*) scribacchino.
to **hack**[1] *vt.* sminuzzare. ♦ to **hack** *vi.* tossire a colpi secchi.
to **hack**[2] *vt.* e *vi.* **1.** adoperare cavalli da nolo **2.** adibire a un lavoro da scribacchino.
hackney *s.* **1.** cavallo da nolo **2.** vettura da nolo.
hacksaw *s.* seghetto.
had V. *to have.*
haematoma *s.* ematoma.
haemoglobin *s.* emoglobina.
haemophilia *s.* emofilia.
haemoptysis *s.* emottisi.
haemorrhage *s.* emorragia.
haemorrhoids *s. pl.* emorroidi.
haemostasia *s.* emostasi.
haemostatic *agg.* e *s.* emostatico.
haft *s.* manico, impugnatura.
hag *s.* **1.** strega, megera **2.** (*zool.*) lampreda.
haggard *agg.* sparuto, emaciato.
to **haggle** *vi.* mercanteggiare.
hagiographer *s.* agiografo.
hagiography *s.* agiografia.
hail[1] *s.* grandine ‖ — *-stone*, chicco di grandine; — *-storm*, grandinata.
hail[2] *inter.* salve!, salute!
to **hail**[1] *vi.* grandinare.
to **hail**[2] *vt.* e *vi.* salutare, chiamare.
hair *s.* **1.** capelli, capigliatura **2.** pelo, crine, setola ‖ — *-breadth*, spessore di un capello; — *-cut*, taglio dei capelli; — *-do*, acconciatura.
hairdresser *s.* parrucchiere.
hairiness *s.* pelosità.
hairless *agg.* senza capelli.
hairpin *s.* forcella (*per capelli*).
hairy *agg.* **1.** capelluto **2.** peloso.
halation *s.* alone.
halberd *s.* alabarda.
hale *agg.* robusto, gagliardo.
half *agg.* mezzo.
half *s.* (*pl.* halves) metà, mezzo. ♦ **half** *avv.* a mezzo, a metà ‖ — *-brother*, fratellastro; — *-length*, di media lunghezza; — *-mast*, a mezz'asta; — *-pay*, stipendio ridotto; — *-processed*, semilavorato; — *-sister*, sorellastra; — *-year*, se-

mestre.
halfpenny *s.* mezzo penny.
halfway *agg.* e *avv.* a mezza strada.
hall *s.* **1.** sala, salone **2.** refettorio, sala di ritrovo.
hallo! *int.* pronto (*al telefono*).
to **hallow** *vt.* santificare.
to **hallucinate** *vt.* allucinare.
hallucination *s.* allucinazione.
halo *s.* alone, aureola.
to **halt**[1] *vt.* fermare. ♦ to **halt** *vi.* fermarsi.
to **halt**[2] *vi.* zoppicare.
halter *s.* **1.** capestro **2.** cavezza.
to **halve** *vt.* dividere a metà.
halyard *s.* (*mar.*) drizza.
ham *s.* **1.** prosciutto. ♦ **hams** *s. pl.* natiche.
hamlet *s.* piccolo villaggio.
hammer *s.* martello, martelletto: — *-blow*, colpo di martello, di maglio ‖ *to bring under the* —, mettere all'asta.
to **hammer** *vt.* e *vi.* martellare.
hammering *s.* martellamento.
hammock *s.* amaca.
hamper[1] *s.* cesta.
hamper[2] *s.* impedimento.
to **hamper** *vt.* imbarazzare, ostacolare.
to **hamstring** *vt.* azzoppare.
hand *s.* **1.** mano: *hands off!*, via le mani!; *hands up!*, mani in alto! **2.** operaio, lavoratore **3.** calligrafia ‖ *at* —, a portata di mano; *first-*—, di prima mano.
to **hand** *vt.* porgere, dare ‖ *to* — *in*, consegnare; *to* — *out*, distribuire; *to* — *over*, rimettere.
handbag *s.* borsetta.
handbill *s.* volantino.
handbook *s.* manuale.
handcuffs *s. pl.* manette.
to **handcuff** *vt.* mettere le manette.
handful *s.* **1.** manciata **2.** piccolo numero (*di persone*)
handgrip *s.* stretta di mano, morsa della mano.
handicap *s.* svantaggio.
to **handicap** *vt.* svantaggiare, ostacolare.
handicraft *s.* **1.** lavoro manuale **2.** abilità manuale.
handicraftsman *s.* artigiano.
handily *avv.* **1.** abilmente **2.** a portata di mano.
handiwork *s.* lavoro fatto a mano.
handkerchief *s.* fazzoletto.
handle *s.* **1.** manico, impugnatura

2. (*fig.*) pretesto || — *-bar*, manubrio (*di bicicletta*).

to **handle** *vt.* **1.** maneggiare **2.** comportarsi verso.

handler *s.* manipolatore.

handling *s.* **1.** maneggiamento **2.** maniera di trattare.

handmade *agg.* fatto a mano.

handrail *s.* corrimano.

handshake *s.* stretta di mano.

handsome *agg.* bello, di bell'aspetto.

handwriting *s.* calligrafia.

handy *agg.* **1.** abile, destro **2.** a portata di mano || — *-man*, factotum.

hang *s.* inclinazione, pendio.

to **hang (hung, hung)** *vt.* appendere, attaccare.

to **hang (hung, hung)** *vi.* **1.** pendere **2.** appoggiarsi. ♦ to **hang** (*reg.*) *vt.* impiccare.

hanger *s.* gancio, uncino || — *on*, seguace, parassita; *dress-* —, attaccapanni; *paper-* —, tappezziere. ♦

hanging *agg.* pendente, sospeso. ♦

hanging *s.* impiccagione.

hangman *s.* boia, carnefice.

hank *s.* matassa.

hapless *agg.* sfortunato.

to **happen** *vi.* avvenire, accadere.

happening *s.* avvenimento.

happily *avv.* felicemente.

happiness *s.* felicità.

happy *agg.* felice, contento.

harangue *s.* arringa.

to **harangue** *vt.* e *vi.* arringare, pronunciare un discorso solenne.

to **harass** *vt.* tormentare, molestare.

harbinger *s.* precursore.

harbour *s.* **1.** porto **2.** (*fig.*) rifugio.

to **harbour** *vt.* **1.** accogliere, dare asilo a **2.** nutrire (*pensieri ecc.*). ♦ to **harbour** *vi.* entrare in porto.

hard *agg.* **1.** duro **2.** severo, spietato **3.** difficile **4.** rigido (*di tempo*). ♦ **hard** *avv.* **1.** energicamente **2.** con difficoltà, duramente **3.** vicino, accanto || — *-boiled*, bollito fino a diventar duro; — *-headed*, ostinato; — *-set*, in bisogno.

to **harden** *vt.* indurire. ♦ to **harden** *vi.* indurirsi.

hardening *agg.* temprante. ♦ **hardening** *s.* tempra.

hardihood *s.* ardire, coraggio.

hardily *avv.* arditamente.

hardiness *s.* **1.** ardire **2.** robustezza.

hardly *avv.* **1.** a stento, a malapena **2.** quasi **3.** duramente, severamente.

hardness *s.* durezza (*anche fig.*).

hardship *s.* **1.** avversità **2.** stento.

hardware *s.* ferramenta.

hardy *agg.* ardito.

hare *s.* lepre || — *-brained*, scervellato; — *-lip*, labbro leporino.

to **hark** *vt.* e *vi.* ascoltare || to — *back*, risalire a (*col pensiero*).

harlequin *s.* arlecchino.

harlequinade *s.* arlecchinata.

harlot *s.* prostituta.

harm *s.* danno (*morale e fisico*) || out of — *'s way*, in salvo.

to **harm** *vt.* far male, far torto.

harmful *agg.* nocivo, dannoso.

harmfulness *s.* l'essere nocivo.

harmless *agg.* innocuo.

harmonic *agg.* **1.** armonico, armonioso **2.** (*mat.*) in progressione.

harmonious *agg.* armonioso.

harmonium *s.* armonium.

to **harmonize** *vt.* armonizzare. ♦ to **harmonize** *vi.* armonizzarsi.

harmony *s.* armonia, accordo.

harness *s.* finimenti (*pl.*).

to **harness** *vt.* bardare, mettere i finimenti a.

harp *s.* arpa.

harpist *s.* arpista.

harpoon *s.* rampone, fiocina.

harpsichord *s.* clavicembalo.

harrow *s.* erpice.

harsh *agg.* **1.** duro, ruvido **2.** aspro **3.** discordante (*di suono*).

harshness *s.* asprezza, durezza.

harvest *s.* raccolto, messe.

harvester *s.* **1.** mietitore **2.** mietitrice meccanica.

haste *s.* fretta, rapidità || to make —, far presto.

to **haste,** to **hasten** *vt.* affrettare. ♦ to **haste,** to **hasten** *vi.* affrettarsi.

hastily *avv.* **1.** frettolosamente **2.** precipitosamente.

hasty *agg.* **1.** frettoloso, affrettato **2.** avventato, impetuoso.

hat *s.* cappello.

hatch *s.* **1.** portello, mezza porta **2.** (*mar.*) boccaporto.

hatchet *s.* accetta.

hate *s.* odio.

to **hate** *vt.* odiare, avere in odio.

hateful *agg.* **1.** odioso **2.** pieno di odio.

hatred *s.* odio.

hatstand *s.* attaccapanni.

hatter *s.* cappellaio.

haughtily *avv.* altezzosamente.

haughtiness s. alterigia, boria.

haughty agg. altezzoso, arrogante.

haul s. 1. trazione, tiro 2. raccolta, retata.

to **haul** vt. tirare, trainare. ♦ to **haul** vi. cambiare (di vento).

haulage s. 1. trasporto 2. costo del trasporto.

haunt s. 1. ricovero, ritiro 2. covo, tana.

to **haunt** vt. 1. frequentare assiduamente 2. perseguitare (di ricordi, pensieri ecc.).

haunted agg. 1. frequentato 2. perseguitato.

haunting agg. che perseguita.

to **have (had, had)** vt. 1. (ausiliare) avere: I — gone, sono andato; I — not (I haven't) read the book, non ho letto il libro 2. avere, possedere || to — breakfast, far colazione 3. dovere: I — to go there, devo andarci 4. ricevere, ottenere || had better, sarebbe meglio che; I had rather, preferirei.

haven s. (fig.) porto, rifugio.

havoc s. strage, rovina.

hawk s. 1. falco, sparviero 2. (fig.) avvoltoio.

hawker[1] s. falconiere.

hawker[2] venditore ambulante.

hawser s. gomena.

hawthorn s. biancospino.

hay s. fieno, paglia || — -loft, fienile; — -making, falciatura.

haycock s. mucchio di fieno.

hayseed s. seme di erba.

haystack s. mucchio di fieno.

hazard s. 1. azzardo, rischio 2. giuoco di dadi.

to **hazard** vt. azzardare, arrischiare.

haze s. foschia, nebbia.

hazel s. nocciuolo || — -nut, nocciuola.

hazily avv. indistintamente.

haziness s. 1. foschia 2. (fig.) confusione.

hazy agg. 1. nebbioso 2. indistinto (anche fig.).

he pron. sogg. m. egli, lui, colui.

head s. 1. testa 2. capo, direttore 3. individuo 4. parte alta di una cosa 5. capo, unità di bestiame || — -first, a capofitto; — -master, direttore di una scuola; — -money, taglia; — -work, lavoro mentale.

to **head** vt. 1. colpire con la testa 2. dirigere, comandare 3. intestare. ♦ to **head** vi. dirigersi.

headache s. mal di testa.

headed agg. munito di testa || hot- —, esaltato; pig- —, ostinato; swollen- —, tronfio; wrong- —, caparbio.

heading s. 1. intestazione, titolo (di un capitolo) 2. (aer.) rotta.

headland s. promontorio.

headless agg. senza testa (anche fig.).

headlight s. faro anteriore.

headline s. intestazione di capitolo, articolo.

headlong avv. a capofitto, precipitosamente.

headquarters s. pl. quartier generale (sing.).

headstone s. pietra tombale.

to **heal** vt. 1. guarire, curare 2. (fig.) sanare. ♦ to **heal** vi. 1. guarire 2. sanarsi.

healer s. guaritore.

healing agg. salutare.

health s. 1. salute 2. salvezza divina.

healthful agg. salubre.

healthily avv. salubremente.

healthiness s. 1. salute 2. salubrità.

healthy agg. 1. sano, robusto 2. salutare.

heap s. mucchio, cumulo.

to **heap** vt. ammucchiare, accumulare.

to **hear (heard, heard)** vt. e vi. 1. sentire, udire 2. sentir dire, venire a sapere.

hearing s. 1. udito 2. udienza.

hearsay s. diceria, voce.

hearse s. carro funebre.

heart s. 1. cuore (anche fig.) 2. affetto, coraggio 3. centro, parte principale || — -beat, pulsazione; — -break, crepacuore; — -breaking, straziante; — -failure, collasso cardiaco; — -felt, sincero, di cuore.

heartache s. angoscia, angustia.

heartburn s. bruciore di stomaco.

hearted agg. dal cuore, di cuore || broken- —, desolato; chicken- —, pauroso; down- —, depresso; lion- —, dal cuore di leone; whole- —, generoso.

to **hearten** vt. incoraggiare. ♦ to **hearten** vi. prendere coraggio.

hearth s. 1. focolare (anche fig.) 2. (metal.) crogiuolo, letto di fusione.

heartily avv. cordialmente.

heartiness s. 1. cordialità.

heartless agg. senza cuore.
hearty agg. 1. sincero, cordiale 2. sano, robusto.
heat s. 1. calore, caldo 2. animosità || — -stroke, colpo di calore; — -wave, ondata di calore.
to heat vt. 1. scaldare 2. animare. ♦ **to heat** vi. 1. scaldarsi 2. animarsi.
heater s. bollitore, riscaldatore.
heath s. brughiera.
heathen agg. e s. pagano.
heather s. erica.
heating s. riscaldamento.
heave s. 1. sforzo 2. rigonfiamento (di onde) 3. sollevamento.
heaven s. 1. cielo, paradiso (anche fig.) 2. stato di gioia.
heavenly agg. divino, celeste.
heavenward agg. rivolto al cielo.
heavily avv. pesantemente, gravemente.
heaviness s. pesantezza.
heavy agg. 1. pesante 2. violento, forte 3. fangoso, pesante (di terreno).
Hebrew agg. e s. ebreo.
hecatomb s. ecatombe.
hectare s. ettaro.
hectic agg. 1. tisico, etico 2. febbricitante.
hectogram(me) s. ettogrammo.
hectolitre s. ettolitro.
hectometre s. ettometro.
hedge s. 1. siepe 2. barriera.
to hedge vt. circondare con una siepe. ♦ **to hedge** vi. essere evasivo.
hedgehog s. riccio, porcospino.
hedonism s. edonismo.
hedonist s. edonista.
heed s. attenzione, cura.
heedful agg. attento, vigile.
heedless agg. sventato.
heedlessness s. sventatezza, trascuratezza.
heel s. 1. calcagno, tallone 2. sperone (di uccelli).
Hegelian agg. hegeliano.
hegemony s. egemonia.
heifer s. giovenca.
heigh inter. ehi!
height s. 1. altezza 2. altitudine 3. altura, collina 4. sommità, il più alto grado.
to heighten vt. 1. innalzare 2. accrescere, intensificare. ♦ **to heighten** vi. innalzarsi.
heinous agg. atroce.

heir s. erede.
heiress s. ereditiera.
held V. to hold.
helicoid agg. elicoidale.
helicopter s. elicottero.
heliocentric(al) agg. eliocentrico.
heliotherapy s. elioterapia.
heliport s. eliporto.
helium s. elio.
hell s. inferno (anche fig.).
Hellenic agg. ellenico.
Hellenism s. ellenismo.
Hellenist s. ellenista.
hellish agg. infernale.
hello inter. salve!
helm¹ s. elmo, casco.
helm² s. timone (anche fig.).
helmet s. elmetto, casco.
helmsman s. timoniere.
help s. aiuto, soccorso.
to help vt. 1. aiutare, soccorrere 2. servire (cibo) || cannot —, non poter fare a meno di; to — oneself to, servirsi di (cibo).
helper s. aiutante.
helpful agg. utile, servizievole.
helpless agg. senza aiuto, indifeso.
helpmate s. collaboratore.
Helvetic agg. elvetico.
hem¹ s. orlo, bordo.
hem² inter. ehm!.
to hem¹ vt. orlare || to — in, circondare, accerchiare.
to hem² vi. schiarirsi la gola.
hemicycle s. emiciclo.
hemiplegia s. emiplegia.
hemisphere s. emisfero.
hemispheric(al) agg. emisferico.
hemlock s. cicuta.
hemp s. canapa.
hen s. 1. gallina 2. femmina (di uccelli) || — -house, pollaio.
hence avv. 1. di qui, da questo momento 2. donde.
henceforth avv. d'ora innanzi.
hendecasyllabic agg. endecasillabico.
hendecasyllable s. endecasillabo.
henna s. alcanna.
hepatic agg. epatico.
hepatitis s. epatite.
heptagon s. ettagono.
heptagonal agg. ettagonale.
her agg. poss. f. suo, sua, suoi, sue. ♦ **her** pron. compl. f. la, lei, le, colei.
herald s. 1. araldo 2. nunzio 3. (fig.) precursore.

heraldic *agg.* araldico.
herb *s.* **1.** erba **2.** pianta medicinale.
herbaceous *agg.* erbaceo.
herbal *agg.* di erba.
herbarium *s.* erbario.
herbivorous *agg.* erbivoro.
herborist *s.* erborista.
Herculean *agg.* erculeo.
herd *s.* gregge, mandria.
herdsman *s.* mandriano.
here *avv.* qui, qua || — *I am*, eccomi.
hereabouts *avv.* qui intorno.
hereafter *avv.* d'ora innanzi.
hereby *avv.* **1.** con questo mezzo **2.** qui vicino.
hereditary *agg.* ereditario.
heredity *s.* (*biol.*) ereditarietà.
herein *avv.* **1.** in questo **2.** (*comm.*) nella presente.
heresiarch *s.* eresiarca.
heresy *s.* eresia.
heretic(al) *agg.* e *s.* eretico.
herewith *avv.* qui accluso.
heritable *agg.* ereditabile.
heritage *s.* eredità.
hermaphrodite *agg.* e *s.* ermafrodito.
hermeneutics *s.* ermeneutica.
hermetic(al) *agg.* ermetico.
hermetically *avv.* ermeticamente.
hermit *s.* eremita.
hermitage *s.* eremo, eremitaggio.
hernia *s.* ernia.
hernial *agg.* erniario.
hero *s.* eroe.
heroic(al) *agg.* eroico.
heroin *s.* (*chim.*) eroina.
heroine *s.* eroina.
heroism *s.* eroismo.
heron *s.* airone.
herpes *s.* erpete.
herring *s.* aringa || — *-bone*, spina di pesce (*nei tessuti ecc.*).
hers *pron. poss. f.* il suo, la sua, i suoi, le sue.
herself *pron. r. f.* **1.** se stessa, sé, si **2.** ella stessa.
hesitant *agg.* esitante.
to hesitate *vi.* esitare.
hesitatingly *avv.* con esitazione.
hesitation *s.* esitazione.
heteroclite *agg.* eteroclito.
heterodox *agg.* eterodosso.
heterodoxy *s.* eterodossia.
heterogeneity *s.* eterogeneità.
heterogeneous *agg.* eterogeneo.
to hew (hewed, hewn) *vt.* fendere, recidere || *to* — *down*, abbat-

tere.
hexagon *s.* esagono.
hexagonal *agg.* esagonale.
hexahedron *s.* esaedro.
hexameter *s.*, esametro.
hiatus *s.* iato.
to hibernate *vi.* (*zool.*) cadere in letargo invernale.
hibernation *s.* **1.** svernamento **2.** ibernazione.
hiccough, hiccup *s.* singhiozzo, singulto.
hid V. *to hide.*
hidden V. *to hide.*
hide[1] *s.* pelle, cuoio.
hide[2] *s.* nascondiglio || — *-and-seek*, rimpiattino.
to hide[1] **(hid, hidden)** *vt.* nascondere, celare. ♦ **to hide (hid, hidden)** *vi.* nascondersi, celarsi.
to hide[2] *vt.* **1.** spellare, scorticare **2.** frustare.
hideous *agg.* orrendo, odioso.
hideousness *s.* odiosità, aspetto orribile.
hiding *s.* il nascondere.
hierarchy *s.* gerarchia.
hieratic *agg.* ieratico.
hieroglyph *s.* geroglifico.
hieroglyphic(al) *agg.* geroglifico.
high *agg.* **1.** alto, elevato (*anche fig.*) **2.** altezzoso **3.** forte, intenso (*di luce, colori*) || — *-born*, di alto lignaggio; — *-class*, di prim'ordine; — *-coloured*, dal colore acceso; — *-hearted*, pieno di coraggio; — *-life*, vita di alta società; — *school*, scuola media; — *sea*, mare aperto; — *-speed*, ad alta velocità. ♦ **high** *avv.* **1.** alto, in alto **2.** fortemente.
highbrow *agg.* e *s.* intellettuale.
highland *s.* regione montuosa.
highlander *s.* montanaro.
highly *avv.* **1.** molto, assai **2.** altamente, nobilmente.
highness *s.* **1.** altezza, elevatezza **2.** eccellenza, valore.
highway *s.* strada maestra.
highwayman *s.* bandito, rapinatore.
hilarious *agg.* ilare.
hill *s.* collina, altura.
hillock *s.* collinetta.
hillside *s.* pendio.
hilltop *s.* sommità della collina.
hilly *agg.* collinoso.
hilt *s.* elsa.
him *pron. pers. m.* lo, lui, gli, colui, sé.
himself *pron. r. m.* **1.** si, sé, se

stesso **2.** egli stesso.

hind[1] *s.* cerva, daina.

hind[2] *s.* colono, fattore.

hind(er) *agg.* posteriore.

to hinder *vt.* e *vi.* **1.** impedire, ostruire **2.** imbarazzare.

hindrance *s.* ostacolo, impaccio.

Hindu *agg.* e *s.* indù.

hinge *s.* **1.** cardine **2.** (*fig.*) perno.

to hinge *vt.* munire di cardini. ♦ to hinge *vi.* **1.** girare sui cardini **2.** essere imperniato.

hint *s.* **1.** cenno, allusione **2.** consiglio.

to hint *vt.* e *vi.* alludere, accennare, suggerire.

hinterland *s.* retroterra.

hip *s.* anca, fianco.

hippocampus *s.* (*pl.* -pi.) ippocampo.

hippopotamus *s.* ippopotamo.

hire *s.* affitto, nolo.

to hire *vt.* prendere a servizio, noleggiare.

hireling *s.* mercenario.

his *agg. poss. m.* suo, sua, suoi, sue. ♦ his *pron. poss. m.* il suo, la sua, i suoi, le sue.

Hispanic *agg.* ispanico.

Hispanicism *s.* ispanismo.

Hispanist *s.* ispanista.

hispid *agg.* ispido.

hiss *s.* sibilo, fischio.

to hiss *vt.* e *vi.* **1.** sibilare **2.** fischiare.

histology *s.* istologia.

historian *s.* storico.

historic(al) *agg.* storico.

historicity *s.* storicità.

historiographer *s.* storiografo.

historiography *s.* storiografia.

history *s.* storia.

histrion *s.* istrione.

histrionic(al) *agg.* istrionico.

histrionism *s.* istrionismo.

hit *s.* **1.** colpo, botta **2.** osservazione sarcastica **3.** caso fortunato **4.** (*teat.*) successo.

to hit (hit, hit) *vt.* e *vi.* **1.** battere, picchiare **2.** urtare, venire a contatto **3.** (*fig.*) toccare, colpire || to — the mark, colpire nel segno.

hitch *s.* **1.** colpo, strattone, balzo repentino **2.** nodo.

to hitch *vt.* **1.** muovere a sbalzi **2.** legare, attaccare. ♦ to hitch *vi.* muoversi a sbalzi.

to hitchhike *vi.* fare l'autostop.

hitchhiker *s.* autostoppista.

hitchhiking *s.* autostop.

hive *s.* **1.** alveare, arnia **2.** sciame (*anche fig.*).

hives *s. pl.* orticaria, eruzione cutanea.

hoar *s.* candore, vecchiaia || — -frost, brina.

hoard *s.* gruzzolo.

to hoard *vt.* ammassare, ammucchiare. ♦ to hoard *vi.* ammucchiarsi.

hoarder *s.* incettatore.

hoarding *s.* recinto provvisorio.

hoarse *agg.* rauco, fioco.

hoarseness *s.* raucedine.

hoary *agg.* **1.** bianco, canuto **2.** venerando.

hobble *s.* **1.** zoppicamento **2.** imbarazzo.

to hobble *vi.* zoppicare. ♦ to hobble *vt.* azzoppare.

hobby *s.* svago preferito, passatempo.

hobnail *s.* chiodo (*per scarponi*).

hobnailed *agg.* chiodato.

hodman *s.* manovale.

hoe *s.* zappa.

to hoe *vt.* zappare, estirpare le erbacce.

hog *s.* maiale.

hogshead *s.* barilotto (*per tabacco, zucchero*).

hoist *s.* montacarichi.

to hoist *vt.* alzare, sollevare.

hold[1] *s.* **1.** presa **2.** (*fig.*) ascendente.

hold[2] *s.* (*mar.*) stiva.

to hold (held, held) *vt.* e *vi.* **1.** tenere, sostenere **2.** contenere **3.** ritenere, credere, pensare **4.** occupare una carica, possedere **5.** resistere, aggrapparsi || to — up, sollevare; to — back, esitare.

holder *s.* **1.** possessore, detentore, proprietario **2.** sostegno, supporto **3.** dente canino.

holdings *s. pl.* beni, titoli.

hold-up *s.* intoppo nel traffico, panna di automobile.

hole *s.* **1.** foro, apertura, buco **2.** antro, tana.

holiday *s.* **1.** festa, giorno festivo **2.** vacanza.

holiness *s.* santità.

hollow *agg.* **1.** concavo, infossato **2.** cupo, cavernoso **3.** (*fig.*) falso, irreale, vuoto.

to hollow *vt.* scavare, incavare.

hollow *avv.* (*fam.*) completamente.

hollowness *s.* **1.** cavità **2.** timbro

cavernoso (*di voce*).

holly *s.* agrifoglio.

holocaust *s.* olocausto.

holograph *agg. e s.* documento olografo.

holy *agg.* santo, sacro.

homage *s.* omaggio.

home[1] *s.* **1.** casa, focolare domestico **2.** patria **3.** rifugio, asilo, ospizio.

home[2] *agg.* domestico, casalingo.

home[3] *avv.* **1.** a casa, in patria **2.** direttamente, al segno || — *-born*, indigeno, locale; — *-bred*, allevato in casa; — *-made*, fatto in casa; — *-market*, mercato nazionale; — *-town*, città natia; — *-trade*, commercio interno

homeland *s.* patria.

homeless *agg.* senza casa.

homelike *agg.* domestico, familiare.

homely *agg.* **1.** semplice, modesto **2.** domestico.

homeopathic *agg.* omeopatico

homeopathy *s.* omeopatia.

Homeric *agg.* omerico.

homesick *agg.* nostalgico.

homesickness *s.* nostalgia.

homeward *agg. e avv.* verso casa, verso la patria.

homework *s. coll.* compiti per casa.

homicidal *agg.* omicida.

homicide *s.* omicidio.

homily *s.* omelia.

homogeneity *s.* omogeneità.

homogeneous *agg.* omogeneo.

to **homogenize** *vt.* omogeneizzare.

to **homologate** *vt.* omologare.

homologation *s.* omologazione.

homologous *agg.* omologo.

homology *s.* omologia.

homonymous *agg.* omonimo.

homonymy *s.* omonimia.

homosexual *agg. e s.* omosessuale.

homosexuality *s.* omosessualità.

homy *agg.* casalingo.

honest *agg.* **1.** onesto, integro **2.** leale.

honesty *s.* **1.** onestà, probità **2.** lealtà.

honey *s.* miele.

honeycomb *s.* favo.

honeyed *agg.* **1.** coperto di miele **2.** (*fig.*) sdolcinato, adulatorio.

honeymoon *s.* luna di miele.

honeysuckle *s.* caprifoglio.

honorary *agg.* onorario, onorifico.

honorific *agg.* onorifico.

honour *s.* **1.** onore, reputazione **2.** stima, reverenza **3.** Eccellenza.

to **honour** *vt.* onorare, fare onore a.

honourable *agg.* stimato, onorevole.

honourableness *s.* onorabilità.

hood *s.* cappuccio.

to **hood** *vt.* incappucciare, fornire di cappuccio.

hoof *s.* zoccolo (*di animale*).

hook *s.* **1.** uncino, gancio **2.** amo **3.** tagliola **4.** falce per grano || *by* — *or by crook*, di riffa o di raffa.

to **hook** *vt.* agganciare. ♦ to **hook** *vi.* agganciarsi.

hooked *agg.* **1.** fornito di uncini **2.** adunco, uncinato.

hoop *s.* collare, cerchio (*di botte, ruota ecc.*).

to **hoop** *vt.* cerchiare (*una botte*).

to **hoot** *vt. e vi.* **1.** urlare, gridare **2.** suonare il clacson.

hop[1] *s.* salto (*su una gamba sola*).

hop[2] *s.* luppolo.

to **hop** *vt. e vi.* saltare su una gamba sola.

hope *s.* speranza.

to **hope** *vt. e vi.* sperare, essere fiducioso.

hopeful *agg.* pieno di speranza, fiducioso.

hopefulness *s.* fiducia, buona speranza.

hopeless *agg.* senza speranza, irrimediabile.

hopelessness *s.* disperazione.

hopper *s.* persona od insetto che saltella.

horde *s.* orda.

horizon *s.* orizzonte.

horizontal *agg.* orizzontale.

horizontally *avv.* orizzontalmente.

hormone *s.* ormone.

horn *s.* **1.** corno, tentacolo, antenna **2.** (*mus.*) corno, tromba.

to **horn** *vt.* **1.** fornire di corna **2.** ferire con le corna.

hornet *s.* vespa, calabrone.

hornpipe *s.* cornamusa.

horology *s.* orologeria.

horoscope *s.* oroscopo: *to cast a* —, fare un oroscopo.

horrible *agg.* **1.** orribile, orrendo **2.** (*fam.*) eccessivo.

horribly *avv.* orribilmente.

horrid *agg.* orrido, orrendo.

horrific *agg.* orribile, orripilante.

to **horrify** *vt.* **1.** atterrire, incutere timore **2.** scandalizzare.

horror *s.* **1.** orrore, spavento **2.** cosa orribile || — *-stricken*, atterrito.

hors-d'oeuvre s. antipasto.

horse s. cavallo || — -bean, fava; — -boy, mozzo di stalla; — -chestnut, ippocastano; — -doctor, veterinario; — -race, corsa ippica; — -shoe, ferro di cavallo.

horseback s. dorso di cavallo || on —, a cavallo.

horseman s. cavaliere.

horticultural agg. attinente all'orticultura.

horticulture s. orticultura.

hosanna inter. osanna.

hose s. **1.** idrante **2.** calze (pl.).

hosier s. commerciante in calze.

hosiery s. maglieria.

hospice s. alloggio, ospizio.

hospitable agg. ospitale.

hospital s. ospedale.

hospitality s. ospitalità.

host[1] s. folla, moltitudine.

host[2] s. ospite, anfitrione.

hostage s. ostaggio.

hostel s. pensionato (per giovani, studenti, militari ecc.).

hostess s. **1.** ospite, padrona di casa **2.** assistente di volo.

hostile agg. ostile, nemico.

hostility s. inimicizia, ostilità.

hot agg. **1.** caldo, ardente **2.** forte, piccante **3.** violento, impetuoso || — -headed, scalmanato.

hotel s. albergo || — -keeper, albergatore.

hothead s. testa calda.

hothouse s. serra.

hotly avv. caldamente.

hotspur s. persona impulsiva.

hound s. bracco, segugio.

to **hound** vt. cacciare (con bracchi).

hour s. **1.** ora **2.** periodo. ♦ **hours** s. pl. orario (sing.).

hourly agg. **1.** continuo **2.** all'ora **3.** ad ogni ora. ♦ **hourly** avv. **1.** continuamente **2.** ad ogni ora **3.** d'ora in ora.

house s. **1.** casa, abitazione **2.** albergo, pensione **3.** clinica **4.** convento **5.** casato, dinastia **6.** teatro **7.** (comm.) ditta **8.** (mar.) tuga.

to **house** vt. **1.** alloggiare, ricevere in casa **2.** (fig.) offrire un rifugio. ♦ to **house** vi. **1.** prendere alloggio **2.** rifugiarsi.

housebreaker s. scassinatore.

housebreaking s. demolizione edilizia.

household s. famiglia: Royal Household, la famiglia reale.

householder s. capofamiglia.

housekeeper s. governante, domestica.

housekeeping s. il governo della casa.

houseless agg. senza casa.

housemaid s. domestica, cameriera.

housewife s. (pl. -wives) massaia, casalinga.

housework s. lavoro domestico.

housing s. **1.** il ricevere, l'accogliere **2.** alloggio, rifugio, riparo.

hovel s. **1.** tana **2.** baracca.

to **hover** vi. **1.** librarsi, svolazzare **2.** gironzolare.

how avv. come, in che modo.

however avv. **1.** comunque **2.** però, tuttavia.

howitzer s. obice.

howl s. urlo, grido.

to **howl** vt. e vi. urlare, ululare.

howling agg. urlante, ululante.

hub s. mozzo di ruota.

hubbub s. tumulto, fracasso.

huddle s. calca, folla.

to **huddle** vt. ammucchiare. ♦ to **huddle** vi. affollarsi, accalcarsi.

hue s. tinta, colore.

hug s. abbraccio.

to **hug** vt. abbracciare (anche fig.) || to — oneself, compiacersi.

huge agg. enorme, vasto.

hugeness s. grandezza, enormità.

huil s. scafo.

hullabaloo s. tumulto, fracasso.

hullo inter. **1.** (fam.) salve **2.** (tel.) pronto.

hum s. ronzio, mormorio.

to **hum** vt. e vi. **1.** ronzare, mormorare **2.** cantare a bocca chiusa.

human agg. **1.** umano **2.** sensibile.

humane agg. umano, compassionevole.

humaneness s. benevolenza, umanità.

humanism s. umanesimo.

humanist s. umanista.

humanistic agg. umanistico.

humanitarian agg. filantropico, umanitario.

humanity s. **1.** umanità, il genere umano **2.** bontà, benevolenza.

to **humanize** vt. **1.** rendere umano **2.** adattare alla natura umana. ♦ to **humanize** vi. acquisire sentimenti migliori.

humankind s. il genere umano.

humble agg. umile, modesto.

to **humble** vt. umiliare.

humbleness s. umiltà.

humbly avv. umilmente.

humbug s. frode, impostura.

humdrum s. monotonia, tedio. ♦ **humdrum** agg. monotono.

humeral agg. omerale.

humerus s. (pl. -ri) omero.

humid agg. umido.

humidity s. umidità.

to **humiliate** vt. umiliare, mortificare.

humiliation s. umiliazione.

humility s. umiltà.

humming agg. ronzante. ♦ **humming** s. ronzio.

humorist s. umorista.

humorous agg. arguto, dotato di senso dell'umorismo.

humour s. 1. umorismo 2. umore.

hump s. 1. gobba, gibbosità 2. collinetta, cresta.

humpback s. 1. gobba 2. gobbo.

hunch s. gobba, gibbosità.

hunchback s. persona gobba.

hundred agg. cento. ♦ **hundred** s. centinaio.

hundredth agg. centesimo.

hung V. to *hang*.

Hungarian agg. e s. ungherese.

hunger s. 1. fame, appetito 2. (fig.) ingordigia.

hungrily avv. 1. con grande appetito 2. avidamente.

hungry agg. 1. affamato || to be —, aver fame 2. (fig.) avido, bramoso.

hunt s. 1. caccia 2. ricerca, inseguimento.

to **hunt** vt. e vi. 1. cacciare, andare a caccia 2. cercare affannosamente.

hunter s. cacciatore (anche fig.).

hunting s. 1. caccia 2. ricerca.

huntsman s. cacciatore.

hurdle s. ostacolo (anche fig.).

hurl s. lancio violento.

to **hurl** vt. lanciare, scagliare (anche fig.).

hurrah inter. urrah!

hurricane s. uragano, ciclone (anche fig.).

hurried agg. affrettato, precipitoso.

hurry s. fretta, precipitazione: to be in a —, aver fretta.

to **hurry** vt. affrettare. ♦ to **hurry** vi. affrettarsi || — up!, fa presto!

hurt s. lesione, ferita (anche fig.).

to **hurt** (hurt, hurt) vt. e vi. 1. dolere 2. recar dolore, offendere.

hurtful agg. 1. dannoso 2. offensivo.

husband s. marito.

husbandry s. 1. agricoltura 2. amministrazione domestica.

hush inter. silenzio.

to **hush** vt. 1. zittire, tacere 2. (fig.) calmare.

husk s. 1. guscio, baccello 2. involucro 3. (pl.) rifiuti.

to **husk** vt. sgusciare, sbucciare.

husky agg. rugoso, secco.

hussar s. ussaro.

hut s. 1. capanna, casupola 2. rifugio alpino.

hyacinth s. giacinto.

hybrid agg. e s. ibrido.

hybridism s. ibridismo.

hybridization s. ibridazione.

hydra s. idra.

hydrangea s. ortensia.

hydrant s. idrante.

hydrate s. idrato.

to **hydrate** vt. idratare.

hydraulic agg. idraulico.

hydraulics s. idraulica.

hydric agg. contenente idrogeno.

hydrocarbon s. idrocarburo.

hydrocephalus s. idrocefalo.

hydroelectric agg. idroelettrico.

hydrofluoric agg. fluoridrico.

hydrofoil boat s. aliscafo.

hydrogen s. idrogeno.

hydrology s. idrologia.

hydrolysis s. (pl. -ses) idrolisi.

hydrostatic(al) agg. idrostatico.

hyena s. iena.

hygiene s. igiene.

hygienics s. la scienza dell'igiene.

hygienist s. igienista.

hygrometry s. igrometria.

hymn s. inno.

hyperbole s. iperbole.

hyperbolic(al) agg. iperbolico.

hyperborean agg. e s. iperboreo.

hypercritical agg. ipercritico.

hypermetropy s. ipermetropia.

hypernutrition s. supernutrizione.

hypersensitive agg. ipersensibile.

hypersensitivity s. ipersensibilità.

hypertension s. ipertensione.

hypertrophy s. ipertrofia.

hyphen s. lineetta d'unione.

hypnosis s. (pl. -ses) ipnosi.

hypnotic agg. e s. ipnotico.

hypnotism s. ipnotismo.

to **hypnotize** vt. ipnotizzare.

hypochondria s. ipocondria.

hypochondriac agg. e s. ipocondriaco.

hypocrisy s. ipocrisia.

hypocrite *s.* ipocrita.
hypocritic(al) *agg.* ipocrita.
hypodermic *agg.* ipodermico.
hypodermoclysis *s.* ipodermoclisi.
hyposulphite *s.* iposolfito.
hypotenuse *s.* ipotenusa.
hypothecary *agg.* ipotecario.
to **hypothecate** *vt.* ipotecare.
hypothesis *s.* (*pl.* -ses) ipotesi.
to **hypothesize** *vi.* fare ipotesi.
hypothetic(al) *agg.* ipotetico.
hypothetically *avv.* ipoteticamente.
hysteria *s.* isterismo.
hysteric(al) *agg.* isterico.
hysterics *s.* attacco isterico.

I

I *pron. pers.* io.
iamb *s.* giambo.
iambic *agg.* giambico.
Iberian *agg.* e *s.* iberico.
ice *s.* ghiaccio || — -box, ghiacciaia;
— -breaker, rompighiaccio; —
-cream, gelato.
to **ice** *vt.* **1.** ghiacciare **2.** (*cuc.*) glassare.
iceboat *s.* nave rompighiaccio.
Icelander *s.* islandese.
Icelandic *agg.* islandese.
ichtyologist *s.* ittiologo.
ichthyology *s.* ittiologia.
icicle *s.* ghiacciuolo.
iciness *s.* gelo.
icing *s.* glassatura.
icon *s.* icona.
iconoclast *s.* iconoclasta.
iconoclastic *agg.* iconoclastico.
iconography *s.* iconografia.
icy *agg.* gelido, gelato.
idea *s.* idea.
ideal *agg.* e *s.* ideale.
idealism *s.* idealismo.
idealist *s.* idealista.
idealistic(al) *agg.* idealistico.
idealization *s.* idealizzazione.
to **idealize** *vt.* idealizzare.
ideally *avv.* idealmente.
to **ideate** *vt.* ideare.
ideation *s.* ideazione.
identic(al) *agg.* identico.
identifiable *agg.* identificabile.
identification *s.* identificazione.
to **identify** *vt.* identificare || *to* —
oneself with, immedesimarsi con.

identity *s.* identità.
ideogram *s.* ideogramma.
ideography *s.* ideografia.
ideologic(al) *agg.* ideologico.
ideologist *s.* ideologo.
ideology *s.* ideologia.
idiocy *s.* idiozia.
idiom *s.* **1.** idioma **2.** idiotismo.
idiomatic(al) *agg.* idiomatico.
idiosyncrasy *s.* idiosincrasia.
idiot *s.* idiota.
idiotic(al) *agg.* idiota.
idle *agg.* **1.** ozioso **2.** vano.
to **idle** *vi.* oziare.
idleness *s.* **1.** ozio **2.** futilità.
idler *s.* ozioso.
idly *avv.* oziosamente.
idol *s.* idolo.
idolater *s.* idolatra.
to **idolatrize** *vt.* idolatrare.
idolatrous *agg.* idolatrico.
idolatry, idolism *s.* idolatria.
idyl(l) *s.* idillio.
idyllic *agg.* idillico.
if *cong.* se || *as* —, come se.
igneous *agg.* igneo.
to **ignite** *vt.* accendere. ♦ to **ignite**
vi. accendersi.
ignition *s.* accensione || *battery
coil* —, spinterogeno.
ignobility *s.* ignobilità.
ignoble *agg.* ignobile.
ignominious *agg.* ignominioso.
ignominy, ignomy *s.* ignominia.
ignorance *s.* ignoranza.
ignorant *agg.* ignorante.
to **ignore** *vt.* ignorare.
ilex *s.* leccio.
iliac *agg.* iliaco.
ill (**worse, worst**) *agg.* **1.** ammala-
to **2.** cattivo. ♦ **ill** *avv.* male ||
— -advised, sconsiderato; — -dis-
posed, malevolo; — -fated, sfortunato; — -mannered, maleducato.
♦ **ill** *s.* male.
illation *s.* illazione.
illegal *agg.* **1.** illegale **2.** illecito.
illegality *s.* illegalità.
illegible *agg.* illeggibile.
illegitimacy *s.* illegittimità.
illegitimate *agg.* illegittimo.
illiberal *agg.* **1.** illiberale **2.** meschino.
illiberality *s.* **1.** illiberalità **2.** meschinità.
illicit *agg.* illecito.
illimitable *agg.* illimitato.
illiteracy *s.* **1.** analfabetismo **2.** i-
gnoranza.

illiterate *agg.* e *s.* **1.** analfabeta **2.** ignorante.
illness *s.* malattia.
illogical *agg.* illogico.
illogicality *s.* illogicità.
to **ill-treat** *vt.* maltrattare.
to **illuminate** *vt.* illuminare.
illumination *s.* illuminazione.
to **illumine** *vt.* illuminare.
illuminism *s.* illuminismo.
ill-usage *s.* maltrattamento.
to **ill-use** *vt.* maltrattare.
illusion *s.* illusione.
illusionism *s.* illusionismo.
illusionist *s.* illusionista.
illusive *agg.* illusorio.
illusiveness *s.* illusorietà.
illusory *agg.* illusorio.
to **illustrate** *vt.* illustrare.
illustration *s.* illustrazione.
illustrative *agg.* illustrativo.
illustrator *s.* illustratore.
illustrious *agg.* illustre.
ill-will *s.* malevolenza.
ill-wisher *s.* malevolo.
image *s.* immagine.
to **image** *vt.* **1.** immaginare **2.** descrivere **3.** riflettere.
imagery *s.* raffigurazione.
imaginable *agg.* immaginabile.
imaginary *agg.* immaginario.
imagination *s.* immaginazione.
imaginative *agg.* immaginativo.
to **imagine** *vt.* e *vi.* immaginare.
imagining *s.* immaginazione.
imbecile *agg.* e *s.* **1.** debole **2.** imbecille.
imbecility *s.* **1.** debolezza **2.** imbecillità.
to **imbibe** *vt.* assorbire. ♦ to **imbibe** *vi.* imbeversi.
to **imbue** *vt.* impregnare.
imitable *agg.* imitabile.
to **imitate** *vt.* imitare.
imitation *s.* imitazione.
imitative *agg.* imitativo.
imitator *s.* imitatore.
immaculate *agg.* immacolato.
immanence *s.* immanenza.
immanent *agg.* immanente.
immanentism *s.* immanentismo.
immaterial *agg.* **1.** immateriale **2.** irrilevante.
immaterialism *s.* immaterialismo.
immaterialist *s.* immaterialista.
immateriality *s.* immaterialità.
immature *agg.* immaturo.
immaturity *s.* immaturità.
immeasurability *s.* incommensurabilità.

immeasurable *agg.* incommensurabile.
immediacy *s.* **1.** immediatezza **2.** rapporto diretto.
immediate *agg.* **1.** immediato **2.** diretto.
immediateness *s.* V. *immediacy.*
immemorial *agg.* immemorabile.
immense *agg.* immenso.
immenseness, immensity *s.* immensità.
immensurability *s.* immensurabilità.
immensurable *agg.* immensurabile.
to **immerge,** to **immerse** *vt.* immergere. ♦ to **immerge** *vi.* immergersi.
immersion *s.* **1.** immersione **2.** eclisse.
immigrant *agg.* e *s.* immigrante.
to **immigrate** *vi.* immigrare.
immigration *s.* immigrazione.
imminence *s.* **1.** imminenza **2.** pericolo.
imminent *agg.* **1.** imminente **2.** sovrastante.
immobile *agg.* immobile.
immobility *s.* immobilità.
immobilization *s.* immobilizzazione.
to **immobilize** *vt.* immobilizzare.
immoderate *agg.* smodato.
immoderateness *s.* smoderatezza.
immodest *agg.* **1.** immodesto **2.** indecente.
immodesty *s.* **1.** immodestia **2.** indecenza.
to **immolate** *vt.* immolare.
immolation *s.* immolazione.
immolator *s.* immolatore.
immoral *agg.* immorale.
immorality *s.* immoralità.
immortal *agg.* e *s.* immortale.
immortality *s.* immortalità.
immortalization *s.* l'immortalare.
to **immortalize** *vt.* immortalare.
immovability *s.* **1.** immobilità **2.** inamovibilità.
immovable *agg.* **1.** immobile **2.** inamovibile.
immovables *s. pl.* beni immobili.
immune *agg.* **1.** immune **2.** esente.
immunity *s.* **1.** immunità **2.** esenzione.
immunization *s.* immunizzazione.
to **immunize** *vt.* immunizzare.
to **immure** *vt.* **1.** murare **2.** impri-

gionare **3.** chiudere fra mura.
immutability *s.* immutabilità.
immutable *agg.* immutabile.
imp *s.* diavoletto.
impact *s.* urto, collisione.
to **impact** *vt.* conficcare.
to **impair** *vt.* menomare.
impairment *s.* menomazione.
to **impale** *vt.* impalare.
impalpability *s.* impalpabilità.
impalpable *agg.* impalpabile.
imparity *s.* imparità.
to **impart** *vt.* **1.** impartire **2.** rivelare.
impartial *agg.* imparziale.
impartiality *s.* imparzialità.
impassable *agg.* invalicabile, impraticabile.
impassibility *s.* impassibilità.
impassible *agg.* impassibile.
to **impassion** *vt.* appassionare.
impassionate, impassioned *agg.* eccitato, ardente.
impassive *agg.* impassibile.
impatience *s.* **1.** impazienza **2.** avversione.
impatient *agg.* **1.** impaziente **2.** intollerante.
impavid *agg.* impavido.
to **impeach** *vt.* **1.** imputare **2.** biasimare || *to — so. for high treason,* accusare qu. di alto tradimento.
impeachable *agg.* accusabile.
impeacher *s.* accusatore.
impeachment *s.* accusa.
impeccability *s.* impeccabilità.
impeccable *agg.* impeccabile.
impecunious *agg.* povero.
to **impede** *vt.* **1.** impedire **2.** ostacolare.
impediment *s.* impedimento.
to **impel** *vt.* spingere, incitare.
impellent *agg.* impellente. ◆ **impellent** *s.* incentivo.
to **impend** *vi.* incombere.
impendence *s.* imminenza.
impendent *agg.* incombente.
impenetrability *s.* impenetrabilità.
impenetrable *agg.* impenetrabile.
impenitence *s.* impenitenza.
impenitent *agg.* impenitente.
imperative *agg.* e *s.* imperativo.
imperator *s.* imperatore.
imperceptibility *s.* impercettibilità.
imperceptible *agg.* impercettibile.
imperfect *agg.* **1.** imperfetto **2.** incompiuto.
imperfection *s.* **1.** imperfezione **2.**

incompiutezza.
imperial *agg.* imperiale.
imperialism *s.* imperialismo.
imperialist *s.* imperialista.
imperialistic *agg.* imperialistico.
to **imperil** *vt.* mettere in pericolo.
imperious *agg.* **1.** imperioso **2.** impellente.
imperiousness *s.* **1.** imperiosità **2.** urgenza.
imperishability *s.* indistruttibilità.
imperishable *agg.* indistruttibile, imperituro.
impermeability *s.* impermeabilità.
impermeable *agg.* impermeabile.
impersonal *agg.* impersonale.
impersonality *s.* l'essere impersonale.
to **impersonate** *vt.* impersonare.
impersonation *s.* personificazione.
impertinence *s.* **1.** impertinenza **2.** non pertinenza.
impertinent *agg.* **1.** impertinente **2.** non pertinente.
imperturbability *s.* imperturbabilità.
imperturbable *agg.* imperturbabile.
impervious *agg.* **1.** impervio **2.** impermeabile.
to **impetrate** *vt.* impetrare.
impetration *s.* impetrazione.
impetuosity *s.* impetuosità.
impetuous *agg.* impetuoso.
impetus *s.* impeto.
impiety *s.* empietà.
impious *agg.* empio.
impish *agg.* birichino.
implacability *s.* implacabilità.
implacable *agg.* implacabile.
to **implant** *vt.* **1.** impiantare **2.** inculcare.
implement *s.* utensile.
to **implement** *vt.* **1.** compiere **2.** attrezzare.
to **implicate** *vt.* implicare.
implication *s.* implicazione.
implicit, implied *agg.* implicito.
to **implore** *vt.* implorare.
imploring *agg.* supplichevole.
to **imply** *vt.* implicare.
impolite *agg.* scortese.
impoliteness *s.* scortesia.
impolitic *agg.* impolitico.
imponderability *s.* imponderabilità.
imponderable *agg.* imponderabile.
import *s.* **1.** importanza **2.** significato **3.** (*comm.*) importazione.
to **import** *vt.* **1.** importare **2.** si-

gnificare 3. (*comm.*) importare.
importance *s.* importanza.
important *agg.* importante.
importer *s.* importatore.
importunate, importune *agg.* urgente.
to **importune** *vt.* importunare.
importunity *s.* 1. insistenza 2. urgenza.
to **impose** *vt.* 1. imporre 2. (*tip.*) impaginare. ◆ to **impose** *vi.* imporsi || *to — on*, ingannare.
imposing *agg.* imponente.
imposition *s.* 1. imposizione 2. imposta 3. inganno 4. (*tip.*) messa in macchina.
impossibility *s.* impossibilità.
impossible *agg.* impossibile.
impostor *s.* impostore.
imposture *s.* impostura.
impotence *s.* impotenza.
impotent *agg.* impotente.
to **impoverish** *vt.* impoverire.
impoverishment *s.* impoverimento.
impracticability *s.* 1. inattuabilità 2. impraticabilità 3. intrattabilità.
impracticable *agg.* 1. inattuabile 2. impraticabile 3. intrattabile.
imprecation *s.* imprecazione.
imprecatory *agg.* imprecatorio.
impregnable *agg.* inespugnabile.
to **impregnate** *vt.* 1. impregnare 2. fecondare.
impregnation *s.* fecondazione.
to **impress** *vt.* 1. imprimere, stampare 2. impressionare.
impression *s.* 1. impressione 2. ristampa.
impressionability *s.* impressionabilità.
impressionable *agg.* impressionabile.
impressionism *s.* impressionismo.'
impressionist *agg. e s.* impressionista.
impressive *agg.* impressionante.
imprint *s.* 1. impronta 2. stampa.
to **imprint** *vt.* 1. imprimere 2. stampare.
to **imprison** *vt.* imprigionare.
imprisonment *s.* prigionia.
improbability *s.* improbabilità.
improbable *agg.* improbabile.
improbably *avv.* improbabilmente.
impromptu *agg.* improvvisato. ◆ **impromptu** *s.* improvvisazione.
improper *agg.* 1. erroneo 2. inadatto 3. sconveniente, irregolare.

impropriety *s.* 1. scorrettezza 2. sconvenienza.
to **improve** *vt.* 1. migliorare 2. valorizzare. ◆ to **improve** *vi.* migliorare, perfezionarsi.
improvement *s.* miglioramento.
improvidence *s.* imprevidenza.
improvident *agg.* imprevidente.
improvisation *s.* improvvisazione.
improvisator *s.* improvvisatore.
to **improvise** *vt. e vi.* improvvisare.
imprudence *s.* imprudenza.
imprudent *agg.* imprudente.
impudence *s.* impudenza.
impudent *agg.* impudente.
to **impugn** *vt.* (*giur.*) impugnare.
impugnable *agg.* (*giur.*) impugnabile.
impugner *s.* oppositore.
impulse, impulsion *s.* impulso.
impulsive *agg.* impulsivo.
impulsiveness, impulsivity *s.* impulsività.
impunity *s.* impunità.
impure *agg.* impuro.
impurity *s.* impurità.
imputable *agg.* imputabile.
imputation *s.* imputazione.
to **impute** *vt.* imputare.
in *avv. e prep.* a, in, dentro, entro, durante || *to be — Paris*, essere a Parigi; *the best — the world*, il migliore del mondo; *— my opinion*, secondo me; *— all*, in tutto; *— that*, in quanto che.
inability *s.* incapacità.
inaccessibility *s.* inaccessibilità.
inaccessible *agg.* inaccessibile.
inaccuracy *s.* inesattezza.
inaccurate *agg.* inesatto.
inaction *s.* inattività.
inactive *agg.* inattivo.
inactivity *s.* inattività.
inadaptability *s.* inadattabilità.
inadequacy *s.* inadeguatezza.
inadequate *agg.* inadeguato.
inadmissibility *s.* inammissibilità.
inadmissible *agg.* inammissibile.
inadvertence *s.* inavvertenza.
inadvertent *agg.* 1. disattento 2. involontario.
inalienability *s.* inalienabilità.
inalienable *agg.* inalienabile.
inalterability *s.* inalterabilità.
inalterable *agg.* inalterabile.
inane *agg. e s.* vuoto.
inanimate *agg.* 1. inanimato 2. fiacco.
inanity *s.* inanità.

inappeasable *agg.* implacabile.
inappellable *agg.* inappellabile.
inappetence *s.* inappetenza.
inapplicable *agg.* inapplicabile.
inappropriate *agg.* inadeguato.
inapt *agg.* 1. inadatto 2. inetto.
inarticulate *agg.* inarticolato.
inattention *s.* 1. disattenzione 2. negligenza.
inattentive *agg.* 1. disattento 2. negligente.
inaudible *agg.* impercettibile.
inaugural *agg.* inaugurale.
to inaugurate *vt.* inaugurare.
inauguration *s.* inaugurazione.
inboard *agg.* interno. ♦ inboard *avv.* internamente.
inborn, inbred *agg.* innato.
incalculable *agg.* 1. incalcolabile 2. incerto.
incandescence *s.* incandescenza.
incandescent *agg.* incandescente.
incantation *s.* incantesimo.
incapability *s.* incapacità.
incapable *agg.* incapace.
incapacity *s.* incapacità.
to incarnate *vt.* 1. incarnare 2. realizzare.
incarnation *s.* incarnazione.
incatenation *s.* incatenamento.
incautious *agg.* incauto.
incendiary *agg. e s.* 1. incendiario 2. sovversivo.
incensation *s.* incensamento.
incense *s.* incenso.
to incense[1] *vt.* incensare.
to incense[2] *vt.* provocare.
incensurable *agg.* incensurabile.
incentive *agg.* stimolante. ♦ incentive *s.* incentivo.
incertitude *s.* incertezza.
incessant *agg.* incessante.
incest *s.* incesto.
incestuous *agg.* incestuoso.
inch *s.* pollice (*misura*).
incidence *s.* incidenza.
incident *agg.* probabile. ♦ incident *s.* avvenimento.
incidental *agg.* fortuito. ♦ incidental *s.* caso.
incipient *agg.* incipiente.
to incise *vt.* incidere.
incisive *agg.* incisivo.
incisiveness *s.* incisività.
incisor *s.* incisivo.
incitation *s.* incitamento.
to incite *vt.* incitare.
incivility *s.* villania.
inclemency *s.* inclemenza.

inclement *agg.* inclemente.
inclinable *agg.* incline.
inclination *s.* inclinazione.
to incline *vt.* inclinare. ♦ to incline *vi.* propendere.
inclined *agg.* 1. inclinato 2. incline.
to include *vt.* includere.
included *agg.* incluso, compreso.
inclusion *s.* inclusione.
inclusive *agg.* compreso.
incoherence *s.* incoerenza.
incoherent *agg.* incoerente.
incombustible *agg.* incombustibile.
income *s.* rendita, reddito || — -tax, imposta sul reddito.
incoming *s.* entrata. ♦ incoming *agg.* entrante.
incommensurability *s.* incommensurabilità.
incommensurable *agg.* incommensurabile.
incommensurate *agg.* 1. inadeguato 2. smisurato.
incommunicability *s.* incomunicabilità.
incommunicable *agg.* incomunicabile.
incommutable *agg.* incommutabile.
incomparable *agg.* incomparabile.
incompatibility *s.* incompatibilità.
incompatible *agg.* incompatibile.
incompetence *s.* incompetenza.
incompetent *agg. e s.* incompetente.
incomplete *agg.* incompleto.
incompleteness, incompletion *s.* incompletezza.
incomprehensibility *s.* incomprensibilità.
incomprehensible *agg.* incomprensibile.
incomprehension *s.* incomprensione.
inconceivability *s.* inconcepibilità.
inconceivable *agg.* inconcepibile.
inconclusive *agg.* inconcludente.
inconclusiveness *s.* inconcludenza.
incongruity *s.* incongruenza.
incongruous *agg.* incongruo.
inconsequence *s.* incongruenza.
inconsequent *agg.* incongruente.
inconsequential *agg.* 1. incoerente 2. irrilevante.
inconsiderate *agg.* sconsiderato.
inconsistence *s.* incoerenza.
inconsistent *agg.* incoerente.
inconsolable *agg.* inconsolabile.
inconstancy *s.* incostanza.
inconstant *agg.* incostante.

incontestability s. incontestabilità.

incontestable agg. incontestabile.

incontinence s. incontinenza.

incontinent agg. incontinente.

incontinently avv. smoderatamente.

incontrollable agg. incontrollabile.

incontrovertible agg. incontrovertibile.

inconvenience s. 1. disturbo 2. scomodità.

to **inconvenience** vt. scomodare.

inconvenient agg. incomodo.

inconvertible agg. inconvertibile.

to **incorporate** vt. 1. incorporare 2. (comm.) costituire. ♦ to **incorporate** vi. incorporarsi.

incorporated agg. 1. (comm.) anonimo 2. incorporato.

incorporation s. 1. incorporazione 2. (comm.) costituzione.

incorporeal agg. incorporeo.

incorrect agg. scorretto.

incorrectness s. scorrettezza.

incorrigible agg. incorreggibile.

incorrupt agg. incorrotto.

incorruptibility s. incorruttibilità.

incorruptible agg. incorruttibile.

increase s. aumento.

to **increase** vt. e vi. aumentare.

increasing agg. crescente.

increasingly avv. sempre più.

incredibility s. incredibilità.

incredible agg. incredibile.

incredulity s. incredulità.

incredulous agg. incredulo.

increment s. incremento.

to **incriminate** vt. incriminare.

incrimination s. incriminazione.

incriminatory agg. incriminante.

incrustation s. incrostazione.

incubation s. incubazione.

incubator s. incubatrice.

to **inculcate** vt. inculcare.

inculcation s. inculcazione.

inculpable agg. innocente.

inculpation s. accusa.

incumbent agg. incombente.

to **incur** vt. incorrere in.

incurability s. incurabilità.

incurable agg. incurabile.

incursion s. incursione.

indebted agg. 1. indebitato 2. obbligato.

indecency s. indecenza.

indecent agg. indecente.

indecipherable agg. indecifrabile.

indecision s. indecisione.

indecisive agg 1. indeciso 2. non decisivo.

indeclinable agg. indeclinabile.

indecomposable agg. indecomponibile.

indecorous agg. indecoroso.

indeed avv. in verità, davvero.

indefatigable agg. infaticabile.

indefeasible agg. irrevocabile.

indefinable agg. indefinibile.

indefinite agg. indefinito.

indefiniteness s. indeterminatezza.

indelible agg. indelebile.

indelicacy s. 1. rozzezza 2. sconvenienza.

indelicate agg. 1. sgarbato 2. sconveniente.

to **indemnify** vt. 1. indennizzare 2. assicurare.

indemnity s. 1. indennità 2. assicurazione.

indemonstrable agg. indimostrabile.

indent s. 1. dentellatura 2. incavo 3. (comm.) ordinazione 4. (tip.) capoverso.

to **indent** vt. 1. dentellare, frastagliare 2. intagliare 3. (comm.) ordinare (merci).

indentation, indention s. 1. dentellatura 2. incisione.

indenture s. 1. dentellatura 2. contratto.

independence s. indipendenza.

independent agg. e s. indipendente.

indescribable agg. indescrivibile.

indestructibility s. indistruttibilità.

indestructible agg. indistruttibile.

indeterminable agg. indeterminabile.

indeterminate agg. indeterminato.

indetermination s. indeterminazione.

index s. indice.

Indian agg. e s. indiano.

to **indicate** vt. indicare.

indicating agg. indicatore.

indication s. 1. indicazione 2. segno.

indicative agg. e s. indicativo.

indicator s. indicatore.

to **indict** vt. accusare.

indictment s. (giur.) accusa.

indifference s. 1. indifferenza 2. imparzialità 3. mancanza di valore.

indifferent agg. 1. indifferente 2.

imparziale **3.** mediocre.

indifferentism s. indifferentismo.

indifferentist s. indifferentista.

indigence s. indigenza.

indigenous agg. indigeno.

indigent agg. indigente.

indigestible agg. indigesto.

indigestion s. dispepsia.

indignant agg. indignato.

indignation s. indignazione.

indignity s. **1.** indegnità **2.** offesa.

indigo s. indaco.

indirect agg. **1.** indiretto **2.** tortuoso.

indiscernible agg. indistinguibile.

indiscipline s. indisciplina.

indiscreet agg. **1.** sconsiderato **2.** indiscreto.

indiscrete agg. compatto.

indiscretion s. **1.** sconsideratezza **2.** indiscrezione.

indiscriminate agg. indiscriminato.

indispensable agg. indispensabile.

indisposed agg. indisposto.

indisposition s. **1.** avversione **2.** indisposizione.

indisputability s. indiscutibilità.

indisputable agg. indiscutibile.

indisputed agg. indiscusso.

indissolubility s. indissolubilità.

indissoluble agg. indissolubile.

indistinct agg. indistinto.

indistinguishable agg. indistinguibile.

individual agg. individuale. ♦ **individual** s. individuo.

individualism s. individualismo.

individualist agg. e s. individualista.

individualistic agg. individualistico.

individuality s. individualità.

individualization s. individualizzazione.

to **individualize** vt. individualizzare.

indivisibility s. indivisibilità.

indivisible agg. indivisibile.

indocility s. indocilità.

Indo-European agg. e s. indo-europeo.

indolence s. indolenza.

indolent agg. indolente.

indomitable agg. indomabile.

indoor agg. in casa.

indoors avv. in casa.

indraft, indraught s. risucchio, vortice.

indubitable agg. indubitabile.

to **induce** vt. indurre.

inducement s. **1.** allettamento **2.** movente.

induction s. **1.** induzione **2.** insediamento.

inductive agg. induttivo.

inductor s. induttore.

to **indulge** vt. essere indulgente verso. ♦ to **indulge** vi. indulgere.

indulgence s. **1.** indulgenza **2.** proroga.

indulgent agg. indulgente.

indult s. indulto.

industrial agg. industriale. ♦ **industrial** s. lavoratore dell'industria.

industrialism s. industrialismo.

industrialist s. industriale.

industrialization s. industrializzazione.

to **industrialize** vt. industrializzare.

industrious agg. industrioso.

industry s. **1.** industria **2.** operosità, diligenza.

inebriate agg. e s. ubriaco.

to **inebriate** vt. inebriare.

inedited agg. inedito.

ineffable agg. ineffabile.

ineffective agg. **1.** inefficace **2.** inefficiente.

ineffectiveness s. **1.** inefficacia **2.** inefficienza.

ineffectual agg. inutile.

inefficacy s. inefficacia.

inefficient agg. V. ineffective.

inelegance s. ineleganza.

inelegant agg. inelegante.

ineligibility s. ineleggibilità.

ineligible agg. ineleggibile.

ineluctable agg. ineluttabile.

inept agg. inadatto.

ineptitude, ineptness s. inettitudine.

inequality s. diseguaglianza.

inequity s. ingiustizia.

ineradicable agg. inestirpabile.

inerrability s. infallibilità.

inerrable agg. infallibile.

inert agg. inerte.

inertness s. inerzia.

inescapable agg. inevitabile.

inestimable agg. inestimabile.

inevitability s. inevitabilità.

inevitable agg. inevitabile.

inevitableness s. inevitabilità.

inexact agg. inesatto.

inexactitude s. inesattezza.

inexcusability s. inescusabilità.

inexcusable agg. imperdonabile.

inexecutable *agg.* ineseguibile.
inexhaustibility *s.* inesauribilità.
inexhaustible *agg.* inesauribile.
inexistence *s.* inesistenza.
inexistent *agg.* inesistente.
inexorability *s.* inesorabilità.
inexorable *agg.* inesorabile.
inexpedient *agg.* inopportuno.
inexpensive *agg.* poco costoso.
inexperience *s.* inesperienza.
inexperienced, inexpert *agg.* inesperto.
inexpiable *agg.* inespiabile.
inexplicable *agg.* inesplicabile.
inexplorable *agg.* inesplorabile.
inexpressible *agg.* inesprimibile.
inexpressive *agg.* inespressivo.
inexpressiveness *s.* inespressività.
inexpugnability *s.* inespugnabilità.
inexpugnable *agg.* inespugnabile.
inextinguishable *agg.* inestinguibile.
inextricable *agg.* inestricabile.
infallibility *s.* infallibilità.
infallible *agg.* infallibile.
infamous *agg.* infame.
infamy *s.* infamia.
infancy *s.* infanzia.
infant *agg.* infantile. ♦ infant *s.* 1. neonato 2. *(giur.)* minore.
infanticide *s.* 1. infanticida 2. infanticidio.
infantile *agg.* infantile.
infantilism *s.* infantilismo.
infantry *s.* fanteria || — -man, fante.
infarct *s.* infarto.
to infatuate *vt.* infatuare.
infatuation *s.* infatuazione.
to infect *vt.* contagiare.
infection *s.* contagio.
infectious *agg.* contagioso.
infective *agg.* infettivo.
infecund *agg.* infecondo.
infelicitous *agg.* infelice.
infelicity *s.* infelicità.
to infer *vt.* dedurre.
inferable *agg.* deducibile.
inference *s.* deduzione.
inferior *agg.* e *s.* inferiore.
inferiority *s.* inferiorità.
infernal *agg.* infernale.
to infest *vt.* infestare.
infestation *s.* infestamento.
infidel *agg.* e *s.* infedele.
infidelity *s.* 1. miscredenza 2. infedeltà.
to infiltrate *vt.* infiltrare. ♦ to infiltrate *vi.* infiltrarsi.
infiltration *s.* infiltrazione.

infinite *agg.* e *s.* infinito.
infinitesimal *agg.* infinitesimale.
infinitive *agg.* e *s.* infinito.
infinitude *s.* infinità.
infinity *s.* infinità, infinito.
infirm *agg.* 1. infermo 2. irresoluto.
infirmary *s.* infermeria.
infirmity *s.* 1. infermità 2. irresolutezza.
to inflame *vt.* infiammare. ♦ to inflame *vi.* infiammarsi.
inflammability *s.* infiammabilità.
inflammable *agg.* infiammabile.
inflammation *s.* 1. l'infiammare, l'infiammarsi 2. infiammazione.
inflammatory *agg.* infiammatorio.
to inflate *vt.* gonfiare.
inflation *s.* 1. gonfiore, gonfiatura 2. *(comm.)* inflazione.
inflationary *agg.* inflazionistico.
to inflect *vt.* 1. flettere 2. modulare.
inflection *s.* 1. flessione 2. inflessione.
inflexibility *s.* inflessibilità.
inflexible *agg.* inflessibile.
to inflict *vt.* infliggere.
infliction *s.* 1. inflizione 2. pena.
inflorescence *s.* infiorescenza.
influence *s.* 1. influenza 2. *(elettr.)* induzione.
to influence *vt.* influenzare.
influential *agg.* influente.
influenza *s.* *(med.)* influenza.
influx *s.* 1. affluenza 2. sbocco *(di fiume)*.
inform *agg.* informe.
to inform *vt.* 1. informare 2. dar forma a.
informal *agg.* non ufficiale.
informality *s.* assenza di formalità.
information *s.* *(solo sing.)* 1. informazione 2. sapere 3. accusa.
informative, informatory *agg.* informativo.
informed *agg.* istruito.
informer *s.* 1. informatore 2. accusatore.
infraction *s.* 1. infrazione 2. violazione.
infrangibility *s.* infrangibilità.
infrangible *agg.* 1. infrangibile 2. inviolabile.
infrared *agg.* infrarosso.
infrequent *agg.* raro.
to infringe *vt.* violare.
infringement *s.* violazione.
infringer *s.* trasgressore.
infructuous *agg.* infruttuoso.

to **infuse** *vt.* **1.** versare **2.** infondere **3.** mettere in infusione.
infusible *agg.* infusibile.
infusion *s.* **1.** infusione **2.** infuso.
ingenious *agg.* ingegnoso.
ingenuity *s.* ingegnosità.
ingenuous *agg.* **1.** ingenuo **2.** franco.
ingenuousness *s.* ingenuità.
to **ingest** *vt.* ingerire.
ingestion *s.* ingestione.
inglorious *agg.* inglorioso.
ingot *s.* lingotto.
ingratitude *s.* ingratitudine.
ingredient *s.* ingrediente.
inguen *s.* inguine.
inguinal *agg.* inguinale.
to **inhabit** *vt.* abitare.
inhabitable *agg.* abitabile.
inhabitancy *s.* domicilio.
inhabitant *s.* abitante.
inhalant *s.* **1.** inalatore **2.** sostanza da inalare.
inhalation *s.* inalazione.
to **inhale** *vt.* e *vi.* **1.** aspirare **2.** inalare.
inhaler *s.* inalatore.
inherent *agg.* inerente.
to **inherit** *vt.* e *vi.* ereditare.
inheritance *s.* eredità.
to **inhibit** *vt.* **1.** inibire **2.** interdire.
inhibition *s.* **1.** inibizione **2.** interdizione.
inhibitory *agg.* inibitorio.
inhospitable *agg.* inospitale.
inhospitality *s.* inospitalità.
inhuman *agg.* inumano.
inhumanity *s.* inumanità.
inhumation *s.* inumazione.
inimical *agg.* nemico.
inimitable *agg.* inimitabile.
iniquitous *agg.* iniquo.
iniquity *s.* iniquità.
initial *agg.* e *s.* iniziale.
to **initial** *vt.* siglare.
initiate *agg.* e *s.* iniziato.
to **initiate** *vt.* iniziare.
initiation *s.* **1.** inizio **2.** iniziazione.
initiative *agg.* introduttivo. ♦ **initiative** *s.* iniziativa.
initiator *s.* iniziatore.
to **inject** *vt.* iniettare.
injection *s.* iniezione.
injector *s.* iniettore.
injunction *s.* ingiunzione.
to **injure** *vt.* ledere, ferire.
injurer *s.* **1.** danneggiatore **2.** feritore.
injury *s.* **1.** torto, danno **2.** ferita.

injustice *s.* ingiustizia.
ink *s.* inchiostro || — *-pot,* calamaio.
inkholder *s.* calamaio.
inkling *s.* indizio.
inky *agg.* **1.** di, simile a inchiostro **2.** macchiato d'inchiostro.
inlaid V. *to inlay.*
inland *agg.* e *s.* interno. ♦ **inland** *avv.* all'interno.
inlay *s.* intarsio.
to **inlay (inlaid, inlaid)** *vt.* intarsiare.
inlet *s.* **1.** piccola insenatura **2.** apertura.
inmate *s.* **1.** inquilino **2.** ricoverato.
inmost *agg.* più interno.
inn *s.* locanda || — *-keeper,* locandiere; — *of court,* scuola di legge.
innate *agg.* innato.
innavigable *agg.* non navigabile.
inner *agg.* interno, intimo.
innermost *agg.* V. *inmost.*
innervation *s.* innervazione.
innocence *s.* innocenza.
innocent *agg.* e *s.* innocente.
innocuity *s.* innocuità.
innocuous *agg.* innocuo.
innominate *agg.* innominato.
to **innovate** *vt.* e *vi.* innovare.
innovation *s.* innovazione.
innovator *s.* innovatore.
innumerability *s.* innumerabilità.
innumerable *agg.* innumerevole.
inobservance *s.* **1.** inosservanza **2.** disattenzione.
inobservant *agg.* **1.** inosservante **2.** disattento.
to **inoculate** *vt.* **1.** inoculare **2.** inculcare.
inoculation *s.* inoculazione.
inodorous *agg.* inodoro.
inoffensive *agg.* inoffensivo.
inopportune *agg.* inopportuno.
inopportuneness *s.* inopportunità.
inordinate *agg.* smoderato.
inorganic *agg.* inorganico.
inoxidizable *agg.* inossidabile.
inpouring *agg.* affluente. ♦ **inpouring** *s.* afflusso.
input *s.* (*mecc.; elettr.*) alimentazione, entrata.
inquest *s.* **1.** inchiesta **2.** giuria.
inquietude *s.* inquietudine.
to **inquire** *vt.* e *vi.* chiedere || *to* — *after,* chiedere informazioni su; *to* — *into,* indagare su.
inquirer *s.* investigatore.
inquiring *agg.* **1.** indagatore **2.** cu-

rioso.

inquiry s. **1.** ricerca **2.** domanda **3.** inchiesta.

inquisition s. **1.** ricerca **2.** inchiesta.

inquisitive agg. V. *inquiring.*

inquisitiveness s. curiosità

inrush s. irruzione.

insalubrity s. insalubrità.

insane agg. insano.

insanitary agg. malsano.

insanity s. insania.

insatiability s. insaziabilità.

insatiable, insatiate agg. insaziabile.

to **inscribe** vt. **1.** iscrivere **2.** scolpire **3.** dedicare.

inscription s. **1.** iscrizione **2.** dedica.

inscrutability s. inscrutabilità.

inscrutable agg. inscrutabile.

inscrutableness s. inscrutabilità.

insect s. insetto.

insecticide s. insetticida.

insectivorous agg. insettivoro.

insecure agg. insicuro.

insecurity s. insicurezza.

insensate agg. **1.** insensibile **2.** insensato.

insensibility s. insensibilità.

insensible agg. **1.** insensibile **2.** inconscio.

insensitive agg. insensibile.

inseparable agg. inseparabile.

insert s. inserzione.

to **insert** vt. inserire.

insertion s. inserzione.

to **inset (inset, inset)** vt. inserire.

inside agg. e s. interno. ♦ **inside** avv. e prep. dentro.

insidious agg. insidioso.

insight s. **1.** intuito **2.** penetrazione.

insignificant agg. insignificante.

insincere agg. insincero.

insincerity s. falsità.

to **insinuate** vt. insinuare.

insinuation s. insinuazione.

insinuative agg. insinuante.

insipid agg. insipido.

insipidity, insipidness s. insipidezza.

insipience s. insipienza.

insipient agg. insipiente.

to **insist** vi. insistere.

insistence s. insistenza.

insistent agg. insistente.

insolation s. insolazione.

insolence s. insolenza.

insolent agg. e s. insolente.

insolubility s. insolubilità.

insoluble agg. insolubile.

insolvable agg. insolubile.

insolvency s. insolvenza.

insolvent agg. insolvente. ♦ **insolvent** s. debitore insolvente.

insomnia s. insonnia.

to **inspect** vt. ispezionare.

inspection s. ispezione.

inspector s. ispettore.

inspectoral agg. di ispettore, di ispezione.

inspectorate s. ispettorato.

inspiration s. **1.** inspirazione **2.** ispirazione.

to **inspire** vt. **1.** inspirare **2.** ispirare.

inspirer s. ispiratore.

inspiring agg. ispiratore.

instability s. instabilità.

to **install** vt. installare.

installation s. installazione.

instalment s. **1.** rata **2.** puntata.

instance s. **1.** esempio **2.** caso **3.** istanza.

instancy s. **1.** urgenza **2.** insistenza.

instant agg. **1.** urgente **2.** corrente. ♦ **instant** s. istante.

instantaneous agg. istantaneo.

instantly avv. all'istante. ♦ **instantly** cong. non appena che.

instead avv. invece.

instep s. **1.** collo del piede **2.** collo di scarpa.

to **instigate** vt. istigare.

instigation s. istigazione.

instigator s. istigatore.

to **instil(l)** vt. instillare.

instinct agg. imbevuto. ♦ **instinct** s. istinto.

instinctive agg. istintivo.

institute s. istituto. ♦ **institutes** s. pl. istituzioni.

to **institute** vt. istituire.

institution s. istituto.

institutional agg. istituzionale.

institutor s. istitutore.

to **instruct** vt. **1.** istruire **2.** informare **3.** ordinare.

instruction s. istruzione.

instructive agg. istruttivo.

instructor s. istruttore.

instrument s. **1.** strumento **2.** atto giuridico.

to **instrument** vt. **1.** strumentare **2.** redigere.

instrumental agg. **1.** strumentale **2.** utile.

instrumentation s. **1.** orchestrazio-

ne **2.** uso di strumenti.
insubordinate *agg.* insubordinato.
insubordination *s.* insubordinazione.
insubstantial *agg.* incorporeo.
insufferable *agg.* insopportabile.
insufficiency *s.* insufficienza.
insufficient *agg.* insufficiente.
insular *agg.* **1.** insulare **2.** (*fig.*) di mentalità ristretta.
to **insulate** *vt.* isolare.
insulation *s.* isolamento.
insulator *s.* isolatore.
insulin *s.* insulina.
insult *s.* insulto.
to **insult** *vt.* insultare.
insuperable *agg.* insuperabile.
insuppressible *agg.* insopprimibile.
insurance *s.* assicurazione.
insurant *s.* assicurato.
to **insure** *vt.* assicurare.
insurer *s.* assicuratore.
insurgency *s.* insurrezione.
insurgent *agg.* e *s.* insorto.
insurmountable *agg.* insormontabile.
insurrection *s.* insurrezione.
insurrectional, insurrectionary *agg.* insurrezionale.
insurrectionist *s.* insorto.
intact *agg.* intatto.
intake *s.* **1.** presa **2.** energia assorbita.
intangible *agg.* intangibile.
integrable *agg.* integrabile.
integral *agg.* integrale.
integrant *agg.* integrante.
to **integrate** *vt.* integrare.
integration *s.* integrazione.
integrity *s.* integrità.
intellect *s.* intelletto.
intellective *agg.* intellettivo.
intellectual *agg.* e *s.* intellettuale.
intellectualism *s.* intellettualismo.
intelligence *s.* **1.** intelligenza **2.** informazioni (*pl.*).
intelligent *agg.* intelligente.
intelligibility *s.* intelligibilità.
intelligible *agg.* intelligibile.
intemperance *s.* intemperanza.
intemperate *agg.* **1.** smoderato **2.** rigido (*di clima*).
to **intend** *vt.* **1.** intendere **2.** destinare.
intendant *s.* intendente.
intended *agg.* progettato.
intense *agg.* intenso.
intensification *s.* intensificazione.
to **intensify** *vt.* intensificare. ♦ to

intensify *vi.* intensificarsi.
intensity *s.* **1.** intensità **2.** vigore.
intensive *agg.* intensivo, intenso.
intent *agg.* intento, dedito. ♦ **intent** *s.* intenzione, scopo.
intention *s.* intenzione.
intentional *agg.* intenzionale.
intently *avv.* intensamente.
to **inter** *vt.* seppellire.
to **intercalate** *vt.* intercalare.
to **intercede** *vi.* intercedere.
to **intercept** *vt.* intercettare.
interception *s.* intercettamento.
interceptor *s.* intercettatore.
intercession *s.* intercessione.
intercessor *s.* intercessore.
interchange *s.* scambio.
to **interchange** *vt.* scambiare. ♦ to **interchange** *vi.* scambiarsi.
interchangeable *agg.* scambievole.
intercom *s.* citofono.
intercommunication *s.* intercomunicazione.
intercontinental *agg.* intercontinentale.
intercostal *agg.* intercostale.
intercourse *s.* rapporto, relazione || *trade* —, scambi commerciali.
interdependence *s.* interdipendenza.
interdependent *agg.* interdipendente.
interdict *s.* **1.** interdizione **2.** interdetto **3.** proibizione.
to **interdict** *vt.* **1.** interdire **2.** proibire.
interdiction *s.* V. *interdict*.
interest *s.* interesse.
to **interest** *vt.* interessare.
interested *agg.* interessato || *those* —, gli interessati.
interesting *agg.* interessante.
to **interfere** *vi.* **1.** interferire **2.** scontrarsi.
interference *s.* **1.** interferenza **2.** collisione.
interior *agg.* e *s.* interno.
to **interject** *vt.* intromettere.
interjection *s.* intromissione.
to **interlace** *vt.* intrecciare. ♦ to **interlace** *vi.* intrecciarsi.
interlacing *s.* intreccio.
to **interline** *vt.* interlineare.
interlinear *agg.* interlineare.
interlineation *s.* interlineazione.
to **interlink** *vt.* concatenare.
to **interlock** *vt.* sincronizzare.
interlocution *s.* interlocuzione.
interlocutor *s.* interlocutore.

to **interlope** vi. immischiarsi.
interlude s. **1.** intervallo **2.** intermezzo.
intermarriage s. matrimonio tra membri di famiglie, razze diverse.
to **intermarry** vt. e vi. imparentarsi per mezzo di matrimonio.
to **intermeddle** vi. intromettersi.
intermeddler s. intrigante.
intermediary agg. intermedio, frapposto. ♦ **intermediary** s. **1.** intermediario, mediatore **2.** cosa intermedia.
intermediate agg. V. *intermediary.*
intermediation s. mediazione.
interment s. sepoltura.
interminable agg. interminabile.
to **intermingle** vt. mescolare. ♦ to **intermingle** vi. mescolarsi.
intermission s. sosta, pausa.
to **intermit** vt. interrompere. ♦ to **intermit** vi. interrompersi, essere intermittente.
intermittence s. intermittenza.
intermittent agg. intermittente.
to **intern** vt. internare.
internal agg. interno.
international agg. internazionale.
internationalism s. internazionalismo.
internationalist s. internazionalista.
to **internationalize** vt. internazionalizzare.
internment s. internamento.
to **interpellate** vt. interpellare.
interpellation s. interpellanza.
interphone s. citofono.
interplanetary agg. interplanetario.
interplay s. azione reciproca.
to **interpolate** vt. interpolare.
interpolation s. interpolazione.
to **interpose** vt. interporre. ♦ to **interpose** vi. interporsi.
interposition s. interposizione.
to **interpret** vt. interpretare. ♦ to **interpret** vi. fare l'interprete.
interpretation s. interpretazione.
interpretative agg. interpretativo.
interpreter s. interprete.
interpunction s. interpunzione.
interregnum s. **1.** interregno **2.** intervallo.
interrelation s. relazione.
interrelationship s. interdipendenza.
to **interrogate** vt. interrogare.
interrogation s. interrogazione || — -*mark,* punto interrogativo.

interrogative agg. e s. interrogativo.
interrogatory agg. interrogativo. ♦ **interrogatory** s. **1.** interrogazione **2.** interrogatorio.
to **interrupt** vt. e vi. interrompere.
interrupter s. interruttore.
interruption s. interruzione.
to **intersect** vt. intersecare. ♦ to **intersect** vi. intersecarsi.
intersection s. intersezione.
interspace s. intervallo, spazio.
to **intersperse** vt. cospargere.
interstice s. interstizio.
to **intertwine** vt. attorcigliare. ♦ to **intertwine** vi. attorcigliarsi.
interurban agg. interurbano.
interval s. intervallo.
to **intervene** vi. intervenire.
intervener s. chi interviene.
intervention s. intervento.
interventionist s. interventista.
interview s. intervista.
to **interview** vt. intervistare.
interviewer s. intervistatore.
to **interweave (interwove, interwoven)** vt. intessere, intrecciare.
intestinal agg. intestinale.
intestine agg. e s. intestino.
intimacy s. intimità.
intimate agg. intimo. ♦ **intimate** s. amico intimo.
to **intimate** vt. **1.** intimare **2.** accennare.
intimation s. **1.** intimazione **2.** preannunzio.
intimidation s. intimidazione.
intimidatory agg. intimidatorio.
into prep. in, dentro || *to go — the, park,* entrare nel parco; *far — the night,* fino a tarda notte.
intolerable agg. intollerabile.
intolerance s. intolleranza.
intolerant agg. e s. intollerante.
to **intonate** vt. intonare.
intonation s. intonazione.
to **intone** vt. intonare.
to **intoxicate** vt. inebriare.
intoxication s. ebbrezza.
intractable agg. intrattabile.
intramuscular agg. intramuscolare.
intransgressible agg. che non può essere trasgredito.
intransigence s. intransigenza.
intransigent agg. e s. intransigente.
intransitive agg. intransitivo.
intravenous agg. endovenoso.
intrepid agg. intrepido.

intrepidity s. intrepidezza.
intricacy s. complicazione.
intricate agg. intricato.
intrigant s. intrigante.
intrigue s. intrigo.
to **intrigue** vt. **1.** ingannare **2.** rendere perplesso **3.** affascinare. ♦ to **intrigue** vi. avere una tresca.
intriguer s. intrigante.
intrinsic agg. intrinseco.
to **introduce** vt. **1.** introdurre **2.** presentare.
introduction s. **1.** introduzione **2.** presentazione.
introductive, introductory agg. introduttivo.
intromission s. interferenza.
to **intromit** vt. introdurre.
to **introspect** vi. autoesaminarsi.
introspection s. introspezione.
introspective agg. introspettivo.
introversion s. introversione.
introvert agg. e s. introverso.
to **intrude** vt. imporre. ♦ to **intrude** vi. intromettersi.
intruder s. **1.** intruso **2.** importuno.
intrusion s. intrusione.
intrusive agg. **1.** intruso **2.** importuno.
intrusiveness s. indiscrezione.
intuition s. intuizione.
intuitional agg. intuitivo.
intuitionism s. intuizionismo.
intuitive agg. intuitivo.
to **inundate** vt. inondare.
inundation s. inondazione.
inurbane agg. inurbano.
inurbanity s. inurbanità.
to **inure** vt. abituare. ♦ to **inure** vi. venire in uso.
inurement s. abitudine.
inutility s. inutilità.
to **invade** vt. **1.** invadere **2.** violare.
invader s. invasore.
invalid agg. **1.** invalido **2.** nullo. ♦ **invalid** s. invalido.
to **invalid** vt. **1.** rendere invalido **2.** riformare.
to **invalidate** vt. invalidare.
invalidation s. invalidazione.
invalidity s. invalidità.
invaluable agg. inestimabile.
invariability s. invariabilità.
invariable agg. invariabile.
invasion s. invasione.
invective s. invettiva.
to **inveigh** vi. inveire.

to **invent** vt. inventare.
invention s. **1.** invenzione **2.** inventiva.
inventive agg. inventivo.
inventor s. inventore.
inventory s. inventario.
to **inventory** vt. fare l'inventario di.
inverse agg. e s. inverso.
inversion s. inversione.
invert agg. e s. invertito.
to **invert** vt. invertire.
invertebrate agg. e s. invertebrato.
invertible agg. invertibile.
to **invest** vt. **1.** investire **2.** rivestire.
to **investigate** vt. e vi. investigare.
investigation s. investigazione.
investigative agg. investigativo.
investigator s. investigatore.
investiture s. investitura.
investment s. investimento.
investor s. investitore.
inveterate agg. inveterato.
invidious agg. odioso.
invidiousness s. odiosità.
to **invigorate** vt. rinvigorire.
invigorative agg. rinforzante.
invincibility s. invincibilità.
invincible agg. invincibile.
inviolability s. inviolabilità.
inviolable agg. inviolabile.
inviolate agg. inviolato.
invisibility s. invisibilità.
invisible agg. invisibile.
invitation s. invito.
to **invite** vt. **1.** invitare **2.** provocare.
invocation s. invocazione.
invoice s. fattura.
to **invoice** vt. fatturare.
to **invoke** vt. **1.** invocare **2.** evocare.
involuntary s. involontario.
involute agg. **1.** involuto **2.** a spirale.
involution s. **1.** involuzione **2.** intrico **3.** (mat.) elevazione a potenza.
to **involve** vt. **1.** avvolgere **2.** implicare **3.** complicare.
invulnerability s. invulnerabilità.
invulnerable agg. invulnerabile.
inward agg. interiore.
inwardness s. interiorità.
inwards avv. internamente.
iodine s. iodio.
to **iodize** vt. iodare.
ion s. ione.
Ionic agg. ionico.

Ionization s. ionizzazione.
Ionosphere s. ionosfera.
Iranian agg. e s. iraniano.
Iraqi agg. e s. iracheno.
Irascibility s. irascibilità.
Irascible agg. irascibile.
Irate agg. adirato.
Ireful agg. irato.
Iridescence s. iridescenza.
Iridescent agg. iridescente.
Iris s. iride.
Irish agg. irlandese.
Irishman s. irlandese.
Irksome agg. noioso.
Iron agg. di ferro. ◆ **iron** s. ferro ‖ — -*foundry*, ferriera. ◆ **irons** s. pl. catene.
to Iron vt. **1.** rivestire di ferro **2.** stirare.
Ironclad agg. corazzato. ◆ **ironclad** s. corazzata.
Ironic(al) agg. ironico.
Ironing s. stiratura.
Ironmonger s. negoziante in ferramenta.
Ironsmith s. fabbro ferraio.
Ironware s. ferramenta.
Ironwork s. lavoro in ferro. ◆ **ironworks** s. pl. ferriera (*sing.*).
Irony s. ironia.
to Irradiate vt. irradiare. ◆ **to irradiate** vi. risplendere.
Irradiation s. **1.** illuminazione **2.** irradiazione.
Irrational agg. irrazionale.
Irrationalism, irrationality s. irrazionalità.
Irrealizable agg. irrealizzabile.
Irreconcilability s. inconciliabilità.
Irreconcilable agg. irreconciliabile.
Irrecoverable agg. **1.** irrecuperabile **2.** irrimediabile.
Irredentism s. irredentismo.
Irredentist s. irredentista.
Irreducible agg. irriducibile.
Irreflection s. irriflessione.
Irreflective agg. irriflessivo.
Irrefutable agg. irrefutabile.
Irregular agg. e s. irregolare.
Irregularity s. irregolarità.
Irrelevant agg. **1.** non pertinente **2.** insignificante.
Irreligious agg. irreligioso.
Irremediable agg. irrimediabile.
Irremissible agg. irremissibile.
Irremovability s. irremovibilità.
Irremovable agg. irremovibile.
Irreparable agg. irreparabile.
Irreplaceable agg. insostituibile.

Irreprehensible agg. irreprensibile.
Irrepressible agg. irrefrenabile.
Irrepressibleness s. irrefrenabilità.
Irreproachable agg. irreprensibile.
Irreprovable agg. irreprensibile.
Irresistible agg. irresistibile.
Irresolute agg. irresoluto.
Irresoluteness, irresolution s. irresolutezza.
Irresolvable agg. insolubile.
Irrespective agg. noncurante.
Irresponsibility s. irresponsabilità.
Irresponsible agg. **1.** irresponsabile **2.** insolvibile.
Irresponsive agg. che non risponde.
Irretrievable agg. irrecuperabile.
Irreverence s. irriverenza.
Irreverent agg. irriverente.
Irreversibility s. irreversibilità.
Irreversible agg. irreversibile.
Irrevocable agg. irrevocabile.
Irrigable agg. irrigabile.
to Irrigate vt. irrigare.
Irrigation s. irrigazione.
Irritability s. irritabilità.
Irritable agg. irritabile.
Irritant agg. e s. irritante.
to Irritate vt. irritare.
Irritation s. irritazione.
Irritative agg. irritante.
Irruption s. irruzione.
Islamic agg. islamico.
Islamism s. islamismo.
Island s. **1.** isola **2.** salvagente stradale.
Islander s. isolano.
Isle s. piccola isola ‖ *the British Isles*, le isole britanniche.
Islet s. isolotto.
Isochronism s. isocronismo.
to Isolate vt. isolare.
Isolation s. isolamento.
Isolationism s. isolazionismo.
Isolationist s. isolazionista.
Isolator s. isolatore.
Isomorphism s. isomorfismo.
Isomorphous agg. isomorfo.
Isosceles agg. isoscele.
Isotherm s. isoterma.
Isothermal agg. isotermico.
Isotope s. isotopo.
Isotrope s. isotropo.
Israeli agg. e s. israeliano.
Israelite s. israelita.
Issue s. **1.** uscita, sbocco, foce **2.** conclusione **3.** prole, stirpe **4.** problema **5.** emissione, pubblicazione.
to Issue vt. **1.** emettere, pubblicare **2.** rilasciare. ◆ **to issue** vi. **1.**

uscire 2. risultare 3. discendere.
issueless *agg.* **1.** senza sbocco **2.** senza prole.
isthmus *s.* istmo.
it *pron. neutro* esso, essa, ciò, lo, gli, le, ne, sé || *I don't believe —,* non ci credo; *— is raining,* piove; *— is Sunday,* è domenica.
Italian *agg.* e *s.* italiano.
to **italicize** *vt.* e *vi.* **1.** stampare in corsivo **2.** sottolineare.
itch *s.* **1.** prurito **2.** scabbia.
to **itch** *vi.* **1.** prudere **2.** aver voglia di.
itching *s.* prurito.
item *s. (comm.)* voce.
to **itemize** *vt.* specificare, elencare.
to **iterate** *vt.* ripetere.
itinerant *agg.* ambulante.
itinerary *s.* itinerario.
its *agg.* e *pron. poss. neutro* suo, sua, suoi, sue.
itself *pron. r. neutro* esso stesso, essa stessa, sé, si || *by —,* da solo.
ivory *s.* avorio.
ivy *s.* edera.

J

jab *s.* **1.** stoccata **2.** colpo improvviso.
jack *s.* **1.** *(fam.)* marinaio **2.** fante *(gioco delle carte)* **3.** bandiera *(di nave)* **4.** maschio *(di certi animali)* **5.** uomo di fatica **6.** *(mecc.)* cricco.
jackal *s.* sciacallo.
jackass *s.* somaro.
jackdaw *s.* cornacchia.
jacket *s.* **1.** giacchetta **2.** rivestimento protettivo, isolante.
Jacobin *s.* giacobino.
jade¹ *s.* giada.
jade² *s.* **1.** cavallo, ronzino **2.** megera.
to **jag** *vt.* frastagliare, dentellare.
jaguar *s.* giaguaro.
jail *s.* carcere.
to **jail** *vt.* incarcerare.
jailer *s.* carceriere.
to **jam** *vt.* premere, serrare, pigiare. ♦ to **jam** *vi.* bloccarsi, incepparsi.
jam¹ *s.* marmellata.
jam² *s.* **1.** ammasso **2.** compressione **3.** ingorgo.
jamb *s.* stipite.

Jansenism *s.* giansenismo.
Jansenist *s.* giansenista.
January *s.* gennaio.
Japanese *agg.* e *s.* giapponese.
jar *s.* rumore aspro, stridio.
to **jar** *vi.* **1.** discordare **2.** stridere. ♦ to **jar** *vt.* **1.** far discordare **2.** far stridere.
jargon *s.* **1.** gergo **2.** linguaggio professionale.
jarring *agg.* discorde, stridente.
jasmin(e) *s.* gelsomino.
jasper *s.* diaspro.
jaundice *s.* itterizia.
javelin *s.* giavellotto.
jaw *s.* **1.** mascella, mandibola **2.** morsa, ganascia. ♦ **jaws** *s. pl.* stretta, gola.
jealous *agg.* geloso.
jealously *avv.* gelosamente.
jealousness, jealousy *s.* gelosia.
jeer *s.* beffa, scherno.
jelly *s.* gelatina *(anche di frutta)*.
to **jeopardize** *vt.* mettere a repentaglio.
jeopardy *s.* rischio, pericolo.
jerk *s.* **1.** scatto, strattone **2.** spinta **3.** sussulto, tic nervoso.
to **jerk** *vt.* dare uno strattone. ♦ to **jerk** *vi.* sobbalzare || *to — along,* avanzare a scatti.
jerky *agg.* **1.** sussultante **2.** convulso.
jersey *s.* camicetta a maglia con maniche.
jest *s.* facezia, scherzo.
to **jest** *vi.* scherzare, dire delle facezie.
jester *s.* burlone.
jestful *agg.* incline allo scherzo.
Jesuit *s.* gesuita.
Jesuitical *agg.* gesuitico.
jet¹ *agg.* nero lucido.
jet² *s.* **1.** getto, spruzzo **2.** spruzzatore || *— engine,* motore a reazione; *— plane,* aeroplano a reazione.
to **jet** *vt.* schizzare, sprizzare. ♦ to **jet** *vi.* slanciarsi.
jetty *s.* molo || *landing —,* imbarcadero.
Jew *s.* ebreo.
jewel *s.* gioiello.
jewelcase *s.* scrigno.
jeweller *s.* gioielliere.
jewellery *s.* **1.** gioielli **2.** commercio delle gemme.
Jewish *agg.* ebraico, ebreo.
to **jib** *vi.* recalcitrare, impuntarsi.
jig *s.* **1.** giga **2.** *(mecc.)* maschera.

jigsaw s. sega da traforo.
to **jingle** vt. far tintinnare. ♦ to
jingle vi. tintinnare.
job s. 1. lavoro, impiego 2. (fam.)
faccenda, situazione.
jobber s. 1. noleggiatore 2. lavoratore a cottimo 3. trafficante disonesto.
jockey s. fantino.
jocose agg. giocoso, allegro.
jocosity s. giocondità.
jocund agg. giocondo, gaio.
jocundity s. allegria, giocondità.
join s. giuntura.
to **join** vt. 1. unire 2. raggiungere.
♦ to **join** vi. 1. unirsi 2. essere
contiguo.
joiner s. falegname.
joinery s. falegnameria.
joining s. congiunzione.
joint agg. unito, associato || — ac-
count, conto di partecipazione; —
-heir, coerede; — -stock, capitale
sociale; — -tenant, comproprietario.
joint s. 1. giuntura, congiunzione
2. trancio di carne 3. articolazione.
jointer s. pialla.
jointly avv. unitamente.
joke s. scherzo, burla, facezia.
to **joke** vt. burlarsi di, canzonare.
♦ to **joke** vi. celiare.
joker s. tipo ameno, burlone.
jolly agg. gaio, vivace.
to **jolt** vt. far sobbalzare, scuotere.
♦ to **jolt** vi. traballare.
to **jostle** vt. spingere. ♦ to **jostle**
vi. spingersi.
journal s. 1. giornale 2. diario.
journalism s. giornalismo.
journalist s. giornalista.
journalistic agg. giornalistico.
journey s. viaggio (general. per
terra).
to **journey** vi. fare un viaggio.
journey-man s. operaio specializzato.
jovial agg. gioviale, allegro.
joviality s. giovialità.
jowl¹ s. 1. mascella 2. guancia.
jowl² s. gozzo.
joy s. gioia, contentezza.
joyful agg. giulivo, allegro.
joyfully avv. gaiamente, allegramente.
joyless agg. mesto, senza gioia.
joyous agg. gioioso, gaio.
joyously avv. gioiosamente.
jubilant agg. giubilante, trionfante.

to **jubilate** vi. esultare.
jubilation s. giubilo.
jubilee s. giubileo.
Judaic agg. giudaico.
Judaism s. giudaismo.
judge s. 1. giudice 2. intenditore.
to **judge** vt. e vi. 1. fare da giudice,
giudicare 2. supporre, stimare.
judgement s. 1. giudizio 2. verdetto, sentenza 3. parere.
judicial agg. giudiziale, giudiziario.
judiciary agg. giudiziario. ♦ judiciary s. magistratura.
judicious agg. giudizioso.
jug s. 1. boccale 2. caraffa, bricco.
juggler s. 1. giocoliere 2. impostore.
jugular agg. e s. giugulare.
juice s. succo (di frutta ecc.).
juiciness s. succosità.
juicy agg. succoso.
jujube s. giuggiola.
Julian agg. giuliano.
July s. luglio.
jumble s. guazzabuglio.
jump s. salto, balzo: high — (sport),
salto in alto.
to **jump** vt. 1. saltare, superare con
un salto 2. mangiare (giuoco della
dama). ♦ to **jump** vi. 1. saltare
2. trasalire.
jumper¹ s. saltatore.
jumper² s. maglione.
jumping agg. saltatore.
junction s. 1. congiunzione 2. nodo ferroviario.
juncture s. 1. articolazione 2. (fig.)
congiuntura, momento critico.
June s. giugno.
jungle s. giungla.
junior agg. 1. minore, di secondaria
importanza 2. il più giovane. ♦
junior s. 1. cadetto 2. minore.
juniper s. ginepro.
junk¹ s. 1. avanzo, rifiuto 2. gomena vecchia 3. carne salata.
junk² s. (mar.) giunca.
juridic(al) agg. giuridico.
jurisdiction s. giurisdizione.
jurisdictional agg. giurisdizionale.
jurisprudence s. giurisprudenza.
jurisprudent s. giurisprudente.
jurisprudential agg. legale.
jurist s. giurista.
jury s. giuria, giurì.
juryman s. giurato.
just agg. giusto, retto. ♦ **just** avv.
appena, appunto, esattamente ||
— now, proprio ora; — so., proprio così; — then, proprio allora.

justice s. giustizia, imparzialità.
justiciable agg. processabile.
justiciary agg. giudiziario.
justifiability s. legittimità di difesa.
justifiable agg. giustificabile, legittimo || — homicide, omicidio per legittima difesa.
justification s. giustificazione.
justificative agg. giustificativo.
to justify vt. 1. giustificare 2. difendere 3. perdonare.
justly avv. giustamente, esattamente.
jut s. sporgenza.
to jut vt. e vi. sporgere.
jute s. iuta.
juvenile agg. giovanile.
juxtaposition s. accostamento.

K

kaleidoscope s. caleidoscopio.
kalends s. pl. calende.
kangaroo s. canguro.
kaolin(e) s. caolino.
karting s. andare in « go-kart ».
kathode s. catodo.
keel s. 1. chiglia 2. chiatta (da carbone).
to keel vt. 1. rovesciare 2. (mar.) carenare.
keen agg. 1. aguzzo, affilato 2. pungente 3. forte 4. appassionato 5. acuto.
keenly avv. 1. in modo penetrante 2. dolorosamente 3. avidamente 4. (comm.) al minimo.
keenness s. 1. sottigliezza 2. intensità 3. ardore 4. acume.
keep s. 1. sostentamento 2. torrione.
to keep (kept, kept) vi. 1. restare 2. conservarsi || to — on, continuare; to — off, tenersi in disparte. ◆ **to keep (kept, kept)** vt. 1. tenere 2. mantenere 3. custodire 4. rispettare || to — back, dissimulare; to — up, tener alto, sostenere.
keeper s. guardiano.
keeping s. 1. sorveglianza 2. mantenimento 3. armonia.
keepsake s. oggetto ricordo.
keg s. barilotto.
kennel s. 1. canile 2. muta di cani 3. rigagnolo.

to kennel vt. tenere in un canile.
◆ **to kennel** vi. rintanarsi.
kepi s. chepì.
kept V. to keep.
kerbstone s. cordonatura (del marciapiede).
kerchief s. fazzoletto.
kernel s. 1. gheriglio 2. seme 3. (fig.) essenza.
kettle s. bollitore, bricco.
key s. 1. chiave 2. tasto || — -money, buonuscita.
to key vt. 1. (mecc.) inchiavettare 2. (mus.) accordare 3. chiudere a chiave || to — up (fig.), eccitare.
keyboard s. tastiera.
keyed agg. 1. munito di chiavi 2. (mus.) a tasti.
keyhole s. buco della serratura.
keyless agg. senza chiave.
keystone s. chiave di volta.
kick s. 1. calcio 2. rinculo || — -off (sport), calcio d'inizio.
to kick vt. prendere a calci. ◆ **to kick** vi. 1. tirar calci 2. rinculare (di armi) 3. recalcitrare.
kicker s. chi scalcia.
kid[1] s. 1. capretto 2. bimbo.
kid[2] s. tinozza.
to kidnap vt. rapire.
kidnapper s. rapitore.
kidnapping s. ratto.
kidney s. 1. rene 2. temperamento || stones in the kidneys, calcoli renali.
kier s. caldaia.
to kill vt. 1. uccidere 2. respingere 3. smorzare 4. fermare.
killer s. uccisore || lady- —, dongiovanni.
killing agg. mortale. ◆ **killing** s. uccisione.
killjoy s. guastafeste.
kiln s. fornace.
kilo, kilogram(me) s. chilo(grammo).
kilometer s. chilometro.
kilt s. gonnellino degli scozzesi.
kin agg. consanguineo, affine. ◆ **kin** s. parentela.
kind[1] agg. gentile || very — of you, molto gentile da parte tua.
kind[2] s. specie, tipo.
to kindle vt. accendere. ◆ **to kindle** vi. accendersi.
kindliness s. gentilezza.
kindling s. 1. accensione 2. legna facilmente infiammabile.
kindly agg. gentile. ◆ **kindly** avv.

gentilmente.

kindness s. gentilezza.

kindred agg. **1.** imparentato **2.** affine. ♦ **kindred** s. parentela.

kinematics s. cinematica.

kinetic agg. cinetico.

kinetics s. cinetica.

king s. re || *king's English*, la lingua inglese ufficiale.

kingdom s. regno.

kinghood s. regalità.

kingly agg. regale, regio.

kingship s. regalità.

kinless agg. senza parenti.

kinsfolk s. pl. parenti.

kinship s. parentela.

kinsman s. parente.

kinswoman s. parente (*donna*).

kiosk s. chiosco || *newspaper —*, edicola.

kipper s. aringa, salmone affumicato.

to **kipper** vt. affumicare (*pesce*).

kiss s. bacio.

to **kiss** vt. baciare || *to — the dust*, mordere la polvere.

kit s. **1.** cassetta **2.** equipaggiamento.

kitchen s. cucina || *— garden*, orto.

kitchener s. cuciniere.

kitchenette s. cucinino.

kitchenware s. batteria da cucina.

kite s. **1.** nibbio **2.** aquilone **3.** aliante.

kitten s. gattino.

kleptomania s. cleptomania.

kleptomaniac agg. e s. cleptomane.

knack s. **1.** abilità **2.** dispositivo ingegnoso.

knapsack s. zaino (*per soldati*).

knave s. furfante.

knavery s. disonestà.

knavish agg. disonesto.

to **knead** vt. impastare.

kneader s. **1.** chi impasta **2.** impastatrice.

kneading s. impasto || *— trough*, madia.

knee s. **1.** ginocchio **2.** tubo a gomito || *— -cap*, rotula, ginocchiera.

to **kneel (knelt, knelt)** vi. inginocchiarsi.

kneeler s. **1.** chi s'inginocchia **2.** inginocchiatoio.

knell s. rintocco funebre.

to **knell** vt. chiamare a raccolta. ♦ to **knell** vi. sonare a morto.

knelt V. *to kneel*.

knew V. *to know*.

knickerbockers s. pl. calzoni alla zuava.

knick-knack s. ninnolo.

knick-knackery s. cianfrusaglie.

knife s. (*pl.* knives) **1.** coltello **2.** bisturi || *pen- —*, temperino; *pruning- —*, falcetto || *— -grinder*, arrotino.

to **knife** vt. **1.** tagliare **2.** accoltellare.

knight s. cavaliere.

knighthood s. **1.** rango di cavaliere **2.** cavalleria.

knightliness s. cavalleria.

knightly agg. cavalleresco. ♦ **knightly** avv. cavallerescamente.

to **knit (knit, knit)** (*anche reg.*) vt. **1.** lavorare a maglia **2.** corrugare **3.** unire. ♦ to **knit (knit, knit)** (*anche reg.*) vi. unirsi, saldarsi.

knitter s. **1.** magliaia **2.** telaio per maglieria.

knitting s. lavoro a maglia.

knitwear s. maglieria.

knob s. **1.** protuberanza **2.** pomo, manopola.

knobby agg. nodoso.

knock s. **1.** colpo **2.** (*mecc.*) battito in testa.

to **knock** vt. urtare. ♦ to **knock** vi. **1.** bussare **2.** detonare || *to — down*, abbattere; *to — out*, sopraffare.

knocker s. battente.

knot s. **1.** nodo **2.** coccarda **3.** gruppo **4.** difficoltà.

to **knot** vt. annodare. ♦ to **knot** vi. annodarsi.

knottiness s. **1.** nodosità **2.** (*fig.*) difficoltà.

knotty agg. **1.** nodoso **2.** (*fig.*) difficile.

to **know (knew, known)** vt. **1.** conoscere **2.** sapere **3.** riconoscere || *to — of*, aver sentito parlare di; *to — about*, essere al corrente di.

knowable agg. **1.** comprensibile **2.** riconoscibile.

knowing agg. **1.** intelligente **2.** istruito.

knowledge s. conoscenza.

known V. *to know*.

knuckle s. articolazione, nocca || *— -duster*, pugno di ferro.

to **knuckle** vi. **1.** (*fig.*) cedere **2.** applicarsi || *to — under*, sottomettersi.

knurl s. zigrinatura.
to **knurl** vt. zigrinare.
Korean agg. e s. coreano.

L

la s. (mus.) la.
label s. etichetta.
to **label** vt. **1.** mettere l'etichetta a **2.** classificare.
labial agg. e s. labiale.
laboratory s. laboratorio.
laborious agg. laborioso.
laboriousness s. laboriosità.
labour s. **1.** lavoro, fatica **2.** mano d'opera **3.** doglie (pl.) || hard —, lavori forzati; — party, partito laborista.
to **labour** vi. **1.** lavorare, faticare **2.** avere le doglie. ♦ to **labour** vt. elaborare, sviluppare.
laboured agg. **1.** elaborato **2.** penoso.
labourer s. lavoratore.
labouring agg. laborioso.
labourism s. laburismo.
labourist s. laburista.
labyrinth s. labirinto.
lace s. **1.** laccio **2.** pizzo **3.** passamaneria.
to **lace** vt. **1.** allacciare **2.** guarnire con merletti, galloni.
to **lacerate** vt. lacerare.
lachrymal agg. lacrimale.
lachrymator s. gas lacrimogeno.
lack s. mancanza.
to **lack** vt. mancare di. ♦ to **lack** vi. mancare, scarseggiare.
lacker s. **1.** lacca **2.** oggetto laccato.
to **lacker** vt. laccare.
laconic(al) agg. laconico.
to **lacquer** V. to lacker.
lactation s. **1.** lattazione **2.** allattamento.
lacteal, lacteous agg. latteo.
lactose s. lattosio.
lacunar agg. lacunoso. ♦ **lacunar** s. soffitto a cassettoni.
lacustrine agg. lacustre.
lacy agg. simile a pizzo.
lad s. ragazzo.
ladder s. **1.** scala a pioli **2.** smagliatura.
to **ladder** vt. munire di scala. ♦ to

ladder vi. smagliarsi.
to **lade** (laded, laden) vt. caricare.
laden agg. (fig.) oppresso.
lading s. carico: bill of —, polizza di carico.
ladle s. mestolo.
to **ladle** vt. versare con un mestolo.
lady s. signora || Our Lady, la Madonna; — doctor, dottoressa.
ladybird s. coccinella.
ladykiller s. (fam.) dongiovanni.
ladylike agg. signorile, raffinato.
ladyship s. **1.** rango di nobildonna **2.** Signoria.
lag s. ritardo, rallentamento.
to **lag** vi. ritardare, restare indietro.
laggard agg. e s. pigro.
lagoon s. laguna.
to **laicize** vt. laicizzare.
laid V. to lay.
lain V. to lie.
lair s. tana.
laity s. **1.** i laici **2.** i profani.
lake s. lago.
laky agg. lacustre.
lamb s. agnello.
lambent agg. **1.** lambente **2.** scintillante.
lame agg. **1.** zoppo **2.** (fig.) debole (di argomenti).
to **lame** vt. storpiare.
lamellar agg. lamellare.
lameness s. **1.** zoppaggine **2.** imperfezione.
lament s. lamento.
to **lament** vt. lamentare. ♦ to **lament** vi. lamentarsi.
lamentable agg. lamentevole.
lamentation s. lamento.
lamented agg. **1.** deplorato **2.** compianto.
to **laminate** vt. laminare.
lamination s. **1.** laminazione **2.** lamina.
lamp s. lampada || — -black, nerofumo; — -shade, paralume.
lamplight s. luce artificiale.
lampoon s. libello.
lamprey s. lampreda.
lance s. **1.** lancia **2.** fiocina.
to **lance** vt. (med.) incidere.
lancer s. lanciere.
lancet s. bisturi.
land s. **1.** terra **2.** paese, contrada **3.** campagna, terreno || — -surveying, agrimensura; — surveyor, agrimensore.
to **land** vi. **1.** sbarcare **2.** atterrare. ♦ to **land** vt. **1.** sbarcare **2.** de-

porre **3.** prendere possesso di.
landed *agg.* fondiario.
landing *s.* **1.** sbarco **2.** atterraggio
3. pianerottolo || — *-stage*, pontile di sbarco; — *-strip*, pista d'atterraggio.
landlady *s.* **1.** padrona di casa **2.** albergatrice.
landless *agg.* senza terreni.
landlord *s.* **1.** padrone di casa, di terra **2.** albergatore.
landmark *s.* **1.** punto di riferimento **2.** pietra miliare.
landowner *s.* proprietario terriero.
landscape *s.* paesaggio || — *-painter*, paesaggista.
landslide, landslip *s.* frana.
lane *s.* **1.** viottolo, vicolo **2.** (*mar.*) rotta **3.** corsia (*di strada*).
language *s.* linguaggio.
languid *agg.* languido.
languish *s.* languore.
to **languish** *vi.* languire.
languor *s.* languore.
languorous *agg.* languido.
lank *agg.* **1.** allampanato **2.** liscio (*di capelli*).
lanolin(e) *s.* lanolina.
lantern *s.* lanterna.
lap[1] *s.* **1.** grembo **2.** valletta **3.** lembo.
lap[2] *s.* **1.** sovrapposizione **2.** (*sport*) giro di pista.
to **lap** *vt.* **1.** piegare **2.** avvolgere **3.** lambire **4.** bere avidamente. ♦ to **lap** *vi.* ripiegarsi.
laparotomy *s.* laparotomia.
lapel *s.* risvolto (*di giacca, soprabito*).
lapidary *agg.* lapidario. ♦ **lapidary** *s.* tagliatore di pietre.
lapidation *s.* lapidazione.
Lapp *agg.* e *s.* lappone.
lappet *s.* **1.** falda **2.** lobo dell'orecchio.
lapse *s.* **1.** errore **2.** intervallo.
to **lapse** *vi.* **1.** errare **2.** scivolare.
larboard *s.* fiancata sinistra (*di nave*).
larceny *s.* furto.
larch *s.* larice.
lard *s.* lardo.
to **lard** *vt.* **1.** ungere con lardo **2.** lardellare.
larder *s.* dispensa.
large *agg.* **1.** largo **2.** grande, ampio **3.** generoso || *at* —, in genere; *to be at* —, essere in libertà.
largeness *s.* **1.** ampiezza, grandezza **2.** generosità.

lark *s.* allodola.
laryngitis *s.* laringite.
larynx *s.* laringe.
lascivious *agg.* lascivo.
lasciviousness *s.* lascivia.
lash *s.* **1.** frusta **2.** frustata **3.** (*eye*)-—, ciglio.
to **lash** *vt.* frustare || *to* — *at*, sferzare.
lashing *s.* **1.** frustata **2.** legatura.
lass, lassie *s.* ragazzina.
last *agg.* (*superl. di late*) **1.** ultimo **2.** scorso **3.** massimo || *the* — *but one*, il penultimo. ♦ **last** *s.* **1.** fine **2.** ultimo. ♦ **last** *avv.* **1.** ultimo **2.** l'ultima volta || *at* —, alla fine.
to **last** *vi.* durare.
lasting *agg.* durevole. ♦ **lasting** *s.* durata.
latch *s.* chiavistello.
late (**later, latter; latest, last**) *agg.* **1.** tardi **2.** in ritardo **3.** tardo **4.** precedente **5.** defunto. ♦ **late** *avv.* **1.** tardi **2.** in ritardo.
lately *avv.* recentemente.
latent *agg.* latente.
later *agg.* (*comp. di late*) posteriore. ♦ **later** *avv.* più tardi.
lateral *agg.* laterale.
latest *agg.* (*superl. di late*) ultimo, recentissimo || *at the* —, al più tardi.
latex *s.* lattice.
lathe *s.* tornio.
lather *s.* schiuma.
to **lather** *vt.* insaponare. ♦ to **lather** *vi.* schiumare.
Latin *agg.* e *s.* latino.
Latinism *s.* latinismo.
Latinist *s.* latinista.
Latinity *s.* latinità.
latitude *s.* **1.** latitudine **2.** ampiezza.
latter *agg.* (*comp. di late*) **1.** posteriore **2.** ultimo **3.** secondo.
latterly *avv.* recentemente.
lattice *s.* grata, traliccio.
latticed *agg.* munito di grata.
laudable *agg.* lodevole.
laudanum *s.* laudano.
laudatory *agg.* laudatorio.
laugh *s.* risata.
to **laugh** *vi.* ridere || *to* — *at*, deridere.
laughable *agg.* comico.
laughing *s.* risata || — *-stock*, zimbello.
laughter *s.* riso || *to burst into* —, scoppiare a ridere.

launch[1] *s.* varo.
launch[2] *s.* (*mar.*) lancia.
to launch *vt.* 1. lanciare 2. varare.
to launder *vt.* e *vi.* 1. fare il bucato 2. lavare e stirare.
launderette *s.* lavanderia con macchine automatiche.
laundress *s.* lavandaia.
laundry *s.* 1. lavanderia 2. bucato.
laureate *agg.* coronato d'alloro.
laurel *s.* lauro, alloro.
to laurel *vt.* coronare d'alloro.
lavatory *s.* gabinetto.
lavender *s.* lavanda.
lavish *agg.* prodigo.
to lavish *vt.* prodigare.
lavishness *s.* prodigalità.
law *s.* 1. legge 2. professione legale 3. processo, causa || — -court, tribunale; *to go to* —, ricorrere in giudizio.
lawful *agg.* 1. legale 2. legittimo.
lawfulness *s.* 1. legalità 2. legittimità.
lawgiver *s.* legislatore.
lawless *agg.* 1. illegale 2. sregolato.
lawn *s.* prato (*rasato*).
lawsuit *s.* (*giur.*) processo.
lawyer *s.* avvocato.
lax *agg.* allentato.
laxative *agg.* e *s.* lassativo.
laxity *s.* 1. negligenza 2. rilassatezza.
lay V. *to lie.*
lay *agg.* 1. laico 2. profano || -brother, converso; — -sister, conversa. ♦ **lay** *s.* configurazione.
to lay (laid, laid) *vt.* 1. porre 2. deporre 3. preparare 4. calmare || *to* — *aside*, mettere da parte; *to* — *out*, stendere, spendere.
lay-by *s.* piazzola di sosta.
layer *s.* 1. strato 2. gallina che fa uova 3. (*mil.*) puntatore.
laying *s.* 1. posa 2. covata.
layoff *s.* stagione morta (*di lavoro*).
layout *s.* 1. esposizione 2. schema.
lazaret *s.* lazzaretto.
laziness *s.* pigrizia.
lazy *agg.* pigro.
lead[1] *s.* 1. piombo 2. grafite || red- —, minio; white- —, biacca.
lead[2] *s.* 1. comando 2. guinzaglio 3. mano (*di carte*).
to lead[1] *vt.* impiombare.
to lead[2] **(led, led)** *vt.* 1. condurre, capeggiare 2. indurre.
leaden *agg.* di piombo, plumbeo.

leader *s.* 1. capo 2. articolo di fondo.
leadership *s.* direzione.
leading[1] *agg.* 1. dominante 2. primo. ♦ **leading** *s.* guida.
leading[2] *s.* impiombatura.
leaf *s.* (*pl.* leaves) 1. foglia 2. foglio.
to leaf *vt.* sfogliare. ♦ **to leaf** *vi.* mettere le foglie.
leafless *agg.* senza foglie.
leaflet *s.* 1. fogliolina 2. volantino.
league *s.* lega.
to league *vi.* allearsi.
leak *s.* 1. fessura 2. (*mar.*) falla 3. perdita.
to leak *vi.* perdere || *to* — *out*, trapelare.
leakage *s.* 1. colatura 2. dispersione.
leaky *agg.* che cola, perde.
lean[1] *agg.* magro, esile.
lean[2] *s.* inclinazione.
to lean (leant, leant) (*anche reg.*) *vt.* e *vi.* 1. pendere 2. appoggiarsi 3. sporgersi 4. inclinare.
leaning *s.* 1. inclinazione 2. l'appoggiarsi.
leanness *s.* magrezza.
leant V. *to lean.*
leap *s.* salto || — *-year*, anno bisestile.
to leap (leapt, leapt) (*anche reg.*) *vt.* e *vi.* saltare.
to learn (learnt, learnt) (*anche reg.*) *vt.* e *vi.* imparare, apprendere.
learned *agg.* colto.
learner *s.* allievo.
learning *s.* cultura.
learnt V. *to learn.*
lease *s.* 1. contratto d'affitto 2. durata (*di contratto*) || *on* —, in affitto.
to lease *vt.* affittare.
leash *s.* guinzaglio.
to leash *vt.* tenere al guinzaglio.
least *agg.* (*superl. di* little) il minimo. ♦ **least** *s.* (il) meno. ♦ **least** *avv.* (il) meno.
leather *s.* 1. cuoio 2. oggetto in cuoio || *patent* —, vernice.
leathern *agg.* di cuoio.
leave *s.* 1. permesso 2. congedo.
to leave (left, left) *vt.* lasciare. ♦ **to leave (left, left)** *vi.* partire || *to* — *off*, smettere.
leaven *s.* 1. lievito 2. (*fig.*) fermento.
to leaven *vt.* far lievitare.

leaves V. *leaf.*

leaving *s.* partenza.

lecherous *agg.* lascivo.

lechery *s.* lascivia.

lecture *s.* **1.** conferenza **2.** lezione **3.** rimprovero.

to lecture *vt.* rimproverare. ♦ **to lecture** *vi.* fare una conferenza.

lecturer *s.* **1.** conferenziere **2.** lettore universitario.

led V. *to lead.*

ledger *s.* (*comm.*) libro mastro.

lee *s.* feccia.

leech *s.* sanguisuga (*anche fig.*).

to leer *vt.* e *vi.* guardare di sbieco.

leeward *agg.* e *avv.* sottovento.

leeway *s.* deriva.

left *agg.* sinistro. ♦ **left** *s.* sinistra || — *-handed*, mancino.

left V. *to leave.*

leftist *s.* (*pol.*) uomo di sinistra.

leg *s.* **1.** gamba **2.** (*cuc.*) cosciotto || *to pull so.'s* —, canzonare qu.

legacy *s.* legato.

legal *agg.* legale.

legality *s.* legalità.

legalization *s.* legalizzazione.

to legalize *vt.* legalizzare.

legatee *s.* legatario.

legation *s.* legazione.

legend *s.* leggenda.

legendary *agg.* leggendario.

leggins *s. pl.* gambali.

legible *agg.* leggibile.

legion *s.* legione.

legionary *agg.* e *s.* legionario.

to legislate *vi.* fare leggi. ♦ **to legislate** *vt.* trasformare per mezzo di leggi.

legislation *s.* legislazione.

legislative *agg.* legislativo.

legislator *s.* legislatore.

legislature *s.* **1.** legislatura **2.** corpo legislativo.

legitimacy *s.* legittimità.

legitimate *agg.* legittimo.

to legitimate *vt.* legittimare.

legitimation *s.* legittimazione.

legume *s.* legume.

leguminous *agg.* leguminoso.

leisure *s.* **1.** agio **2.** tempo libero.

leisurely *agg.* e *avv.* con comodo.

lemon *s.* limone.

lemonade *s.* limonata.

to lend (lent, lent) *vt.* prestare.

lender *s.* prestatore.

length *s.* **1.** lunghezza **2.** durata, spazio di tempo || *at* —, alla fine.

to lengthen *vt.* allungare. ♦ **to lengthen** *vi.* allungarsi.

lengthy *agg.* lungo, prolisso.

lenient *agg.* **1.** emolliente **2.** mite.

lenitive *agg.* e *s.* calmante.

lens *s.* **1.** (*ott.*) lente **2.** (*foto*) obiettivo.

lent V. *to lend.*

Lent *s.* quaresima.

lentil *s.* lenticchia.

leonine *agg.* leonino.

leopard *s.* **1.** leopardo **2.** gattopardo.

leper *s.* lebbroso || — *hospital*, lebbrosario.

leporine *agg.* leporino.

leprosy *s.* lebbra.

leprous *agg.* lebbroso.

lesbian *agg.* e *s.* lesbica.

lesion *s.* lesione.

less *agg.* (*comp. di* little) minore, meno. ♦ **less** *s.* meno. ♦ **less** *avv.* meno. ♦ **less** *prep.* meno.

lessee *s.* affittuario.

to lessen *vt.* e *vi.* diminuire.

lesser *agg.* minore.

lesson *s.* lezione.

lest *cong.* per paura che.

to let (let, let) *vt.* **1.** lasciare, permettere **2.** affittare || *to* — *in*, far entrare; *to* — *off*, lasciar andare; *to* — *out*, lasciar uscire.

lethal *agg.* letale.

lethargy *s.* letargo.

letter *s.* lettera.

lettered *agg.* **1.** letterato **2.** intestato.

lettuce *s.* lattuga.

leucocyte *s.* leucocito.

leucocythaemia, leukemia *s.* leucemia.

levant *s.* levante.

level *agg.* **1.** livellato **2.** a livello **3.** regolato. ♦ **level** *s.* **1.** livello **2.** superficie piana **3.** livella || *on a* — *with*, sullo stesso piano di.

to level *vt.* **1.** livellare **2.** puntare (*un'arma*).

levelling *s.* **1.** livellamento **2.** puntamento (*di arma*).

lever *s.* **1.** manubrio **2.** leva.

to lever *vi.* far leva.

to levigate *vt.* **1.** levigare **2.** polverizzare.

levigation *s.* **1.** levigazione **2.** polverizzazione.

levity *s.* leggerezza.

levy *s.* **1.** leva **2.** imposta.

to levy *vt.* **1.** arruolare **2.** imporre (*di tasse*).

lewd *agg.* impudico.
lewdness *s.* impudicizia.
lexical *agg.* lessicale.
lexicographer *s.* lessicografo.
lexicography *s.* lessicografia.
lexicology *s.* lessicologia.
lexicon *s.* lessico.
liability *s.* 1. obbligo 2. tendenza 3. (*giur.*) responsabilità. ♦ **liabilities** *s. pl.* passività (*sing.*).
liable *agg.* 1. soggetto a 2. (*giur.*) responsabile.
liar *s.* bugiardo.
libation *s.* libagione.
libel *s.* 1. libello 2. (*giur.*) diffamazione.
to libel *vt.* 1. scrivere un libello contro 2. (*giur.*) sporgere querela.
liberal *agg.* 1. liberale 2. umanistico. ♦ **liberal** *s.* liberale.
liberalism *s.* liberalismo.
liberalist *s.* liberalista.
liberality *s.* liberalità.
to liberalize *vt.* rendere liberale.
to liberate *vt.* liberare.
liberation *s.* liberazione.
liberator *s.* liberatore.
liberticide *s.* 1. liberticida 2. liberticidio.
libertinage *s.* libertinaggio.
libertine *agg. e s.* libertino.
libertinism *s.* libertinaggio.
liberty *s.* libertà.
libidinous *agg.* libidinoso.
libido *s.* libidine.
librarian *s.* bibliotecario.
library *s.* biblioteca || *film* —, cineteca; *record* —, discoteca.
lice V. *louse.*
licence *s.* licenza || *driving* —, patente automobilistica.
to license *vt.* dare una licenza a.
licensed *agg.* autorizzato.
licentious *agg.* licenzioso.
licentiousness *s.* dissolutezza.
lichen *s.* lichene.
lick *s.* leccata.
to lick *vt.* 1. leccare 2. lambire.
lid *s.* coperchio.
lie[1] *s.* menzogna || *the* —, smentita.
lie[2] *s.* posizione.
to lie[1] *vi.* mentire.
to lie[2] (lay, lain) *vi.* giacere, trovarsi || *to* — *down,* coricarsi; *to* — *in,* partorire.
lieutenant *s.* tenente.
life *s.* (*pl.* lives) vita || — *-belt,* cintura di salvataggio; — *preserver,* salvagente.

lifeboat *s.* lancia di salvataggio.
lifeless *agg.* senza vita.
lifelike *agg.* vivido.
lift *s.* 1. ascensore 2. passaggio (*su un veicolo*) 3. sollevamento.
to lift *vt.* 1. alzare 2. rubare. ♦ to lift *vi.* alzarsi.
light[1] *agg.* 1. chiaro 2. biondo 3. leggero 4. agile 5. insignificante.
light[2] *s.* 1. luce 2. fuoco 3. lampada || *traffic lights,* semaforo.
to light (lit, lit) (*anche reg.*) *vt.* 1. accendere 2. illuminare. ♦ to light (lit, lit) (*anche reg.*) *vi.* 1. accendersi 2. illuminarsi 3. posarsi.
to lighten *vt.* 1. alleggerire, alleviare 2. illuminare. ♦ to lighten *vi.* 1. alleggerirsi 2. illuminarsi 3. (*imp.*) lampeggiare.
lighter *s.* 1. accenditore 2. (*mar.*) chiatta.
lighthouse *s.* faro.
lighting *s.* 1. accensione 2. luce (*di quadro*).
lightless *agg.* oscuro.
lightness *s.* 1. leggerezza 2. gaiezza 3. illuminazione.
lightning *s.* fulmine || — *-rod,* parafulmine.
Ligurian *agg. e s.* ligure.
like *agg.* 1. simile 2. caratteristico di. ♦ like *prep.* come || — *this,* — *that,* così; *to feel* —, aver voglia di; *to look* —, avere l'aria di.
like *s.* simile. ♦ likes *s. pl.* gusti.
to like *vt.* piacere. ♦ to like *vi.* volere.
likelihood *s.* probabilità.
likely *agg.* 1. probabile 2. adatto. ♦ likely *avv.* probabilmente.
likeness *s.* 1. somiglianza 2. immagine.
likewise *avv.* 1. allo stesso modo 2. anche.
liking *s.* 1. gusto 2. preferenza.
lilac *agg. e s.* lilla.
lily *agg.* bianco. ♦ lily *s.* giglio || *water-* —, ninfea.
limb *s.* 1. membro 2. ramo.
lime[1] *s.* 1. calce 2. pania.
lime[2] *s.* cedro.
lime[3] *s.* tiglio.
to lime *vt.* 1. cementare 2. invischiare.
limelight *s.* luce della ribalta.
limestone *s.* calcare.
limit *s.* limite.
to limit *vt.* limitare.

limitary *agg.* **1.** limitato **2.** limitativo **3.** situato alla frontiera.

limitation *s.* limitazione.

limitative *agg.* limitativo.

limited *agg.* limitato || — *company*, società a responsabilità limitata; — *monarchy*, monarchia costituzionale.

limp *agg.* molle.

to limp *vi.* zoppicare.

limpid *agg.* limpido.

limpidity *s.* limpidezza.

limping *s.* zoppicamento.

line *s.* **1.** linea, riga **2.** ruga **3.** discendenza **4.** attività **5.** verso **6.** (*comm.*) articolo.

to line *vt.* **1.** rigare **2.** fiancheggiare **3.** foderare || *to* — *up*, allineare, allinearsi.

lineage *s.* lignaggio.

lineal *agg.* in linea diretta.

lineament *s.* lineamento.

linear *agg.* lineare.

linen *agg.* di lino. ♦ **linen** *s.* **1.** tela di lino **2.** biancheria.

liner *s.* **1.** transatlantico **2.** aereo di linea.

to linger *vt.* e *vi.* indugiare.

linguist *s.* linguista.

linguistic(al) *agg.* linguistico.

linguistics *s.* linguistica.

liniment *s.* linimento.

lining *s.* **1.** rigatura **2.** allineamento **3.** fodera **4.** rivestimento.

link *s.* **1.** anello **2.** (*fig.*) legame || *cuff-links*, gemelli da polso.

to link *vt.* collegare. ♦ **to link** *vi.* collegarsi.

linotyping *s.* linotipia.

linotypist *s.* linotipista.

lint *s.* garza.

lintel *s.* architrave.

lion *s.* leone.

lioness *s.* leonessa.

lip *s.* **1.** labbro **2.** margine || —*-stick*, rossetto per labbra.

to lip *vt.* **1.** toccare (*con le labbra*) **2.** sussurrare.

liquefaction *s.* liquefazione.

to liquefy *vt.* liquefare. ♦ **to liquefy** *vi.* liquefarsi.

liqueur *s.* rosolio.

liquid *agg.* **1.** liquido **2.** chiaro **3.** armonioso **4.** instabile. ♦ **liquid** *s.* liquido.

to liquidate *vt.* liquidare.

liquidation *s.* liquidazione.

liquidator *s.* liquidatore.

liquor *s.* **1.** liquido **2.** bevanda alcolica.

liquorice *s.* liquirizia.

to lisp *vi.* parlare bleso.

lisping *agg.* bleso. ♦ **lisping** *s.* pronuncia blesa.

list¹ *s.* **1.** lista **2.** striscia **3.** cimosa. ♦ **lists** *s. pl.* lizza (*sing.*).

list² *s.* (*mar.*) sbandamento.

to list¹ *vt.* elencare, catalogare.

to list² *vi.* (*mar.*) sbandare.

to listen *vi.* ascoltare: *to* — *to so.*, ascoltare qu.; *to* — *in*, ascoltare la radio.

listener *s.* ascoltatore.

listening *s.* ascolto.

listless *agg.* disattento.

lit V. *to light.*

litany *s.* litania.

literal *agg.* **1.** letterale **2.** prosaico **3.** di lettera alfabetica.

literalism *s.* interpretazione letterale.

literary *agg.* letterario.

literate *agg.* e *s.* letterato.

literature *s.* letteratura.

lithe *agg.* agile.

lithograph *s.* litografia.

to lithograph *vt.* litografare.

lithographic(al) *agg.* litografico.

lithography *s.* (*arte della*) litografia.

litigant *s.* (*giur.*) contendente.

litmus *s.* tornasole.

litre *s.* litro.

litter *s.* **1.** lettiga, barella **2.** strame **3.** rifiuti **4.** figliata.

little (less, least) *agg.* **1.** piccolo **2.** breve **3.** poco || *a* —, un po' di. ♦ **little** *s.* poco. ♦ **little** *avv.* poco || *a* —, piuttosto.

liturgic(al) *agg.* liturgico.

liturgy *s.* liturgia.

live *agg.* **1.** vivo **2.** ardente **3.** carico (*di armi*).

to live *vi.* e *vt.* vivere, abitare.

livelihood *s.* mezzi di sussistenza.

liveliness *s.* vivacità.

lively *agg.* vivace.

liver *s.* fegato.

livery¹ *agg.* bilioso.

livery² *s.* **1.** livrea **2.** (*giur.*) passaggio di proprietà.

lives V. *life.*

livestock *s.* bestiame.

livid *agg.* livido.

living *agg.* **1.** vivo **2.** perfetto (*di somiglianza*). ♦ **living** *s.* **1.** mezzo di mantenimento **2.** vita || —*-room*, soggiorno.

lizard s. lucertola.
llama s. (zool.) lama.
load s. **1.** carico, peso **2.** (elettr.) carica, tensione.
to load vt. **1.** caricare **2.** adulterare.
loader s. caricatore.
loading s. caricamento.
loadstar s. stella polare.
loaf s. (pl. loaves) pagnotta || sugar- —, pan di zucchero.
to loaf vi. oziare.
loafer s. fannullone.
loan s. prestito: on —, a prestito.
to loan vt. prestare.
loath agg. riluttante.
to loathe vt. detestare.
loathing s. disgusto.
loathsome agg. **1.** odioso **2.** disgustoso.
loaves V. loaf.
lobby s. anticamera.
lobe s. lobo.
lobster s. aragosta.
local agg. e s. locale.
locality s. località.
to localize vt. localizzare.
to locate vt. **1.** situare **2.** individuare **3.** indicare.
location s. **1.** posizione **2.** locazione.
lock[1] s. **1.** ricciolo **2.** fiocco.
lock[2] s. **1.** serratura **2.** diga **3.** otturatore (di arma).
to lock vt. serrare. ♦ **to lock** vi. (mecc.) incepparsi.
locker s. armadio, bauletto a chiave.
locket s. medaglione.
lockout s. (econ.) serrata.
locomotion s. locomozione.
locomotive agg. locomotorio. ♦ **locomotive** s. locomotiva.
locust s. locusta || — -tree, carrubo, robinia.
locution s. locuzione.
lodge s. **1.** loggia **2.** padiglione.
to lodge vt. **1.** alloggiare **2.** collocare. ♦ **to lodge** vi. **1.** alloggiare **2.** entrare.
lodging s. alloggio, dimora.
loftiness s. **1.** altezza **2.** nobiltà.
lofty agg. **1.** alto, elevato **2.** orgoglioso, altero.
log s. ceppo || — -book, giornale di bordo.
logarithm s. logaritmo.
logic s. logica.
logical agg. logico.
logistic(al) agg. logistico.

logistics s. pl. (mil.) logistica (sing.).
logomachy s. logomachia.
loin s. lombo. ♦ **loins** s. pl. reni.
to loiter vt. sprecare (tempo ecc.). ♦ **to loiter** vi. bighellonare, oziare.
loitering s. il bighellonare, l'andare a zonzo.
Lombard agg. e s. lombardo.
Londoner s. londinese.
Londonese agg. londinese.
loneliness s. solitudine.
lonely, lonesome agg. solo, solitario.
long agg. lungo || — -distance call, telefonata interurbana. ♦ **long** s. molto tempo. ♦ **long** avv. a lungo || how —?, quanto tempo?; all day —, tutto il giorno; as — as, fino a, purché; so —!, arrivederci!; before —, tra poco.
to long vi. desiderare ardentemente: to — for sthg., desiderare ardentemente qc.
longanimity s. longanimità.
longboat s. lancia.
longevity s. longevità.
longevous agg. longevo.
longing agg. bramoso. ♦ **longing** s. brama.
longitude s. longitudine.
longitudinal agg. longitudinale.
long-sighted agg. **1.** presbite **2.** preveggente.
look s. sguardo. ♦ **looks** s. pl. aspetto (sing.).
to look vi. **1.** sembrare **2.** guardare || to — after, badare a; to — at, guardare; to — for, cercare; to — forward to, non veder l'ora di; to — like, somigliare; to — up, consultare (orario, dizionario ecc.); to — through, esaminare attentamente; to — up to, rispettare; to — down on, disprezzare.
looker-on s. spettatore.
looking-glass s. specchio.
lookout s. **1.** guardia **2.** vista panoramica **3.** prospettiva.
loom s. telaio.
to loom vt. tessere. ♦ **to loom** vi. apparire indistintamente.
loop s. **1.** cappio **2.** gancio.
loophole s. feritoia.
loose agg. **1.** sciolto **2.** ampio **3.** vago **4.** licenzioso **5.** allentato.
to loose vt. **1.** sciogliere **2.** liberare **3.** lanciare.

to **loosen** *vt.* **1.** sciogliere **2.** allentare.

looseness *s.* **1.** scioltezza **2.** ampiezza **3.** libertinaggio **4.** imprecisione.

to **lop** *vt.* potare, mozzare.

loquacious *agg.* loquace.

loquacity *s.* loquacità.

lord *s.* **1.** signore **2.** Pari || — *Mayor*, sindaco.

to **lord** *vt.* dominare.

lordly *agg.* **1.** fastoso, imponente **2.** altero.

lordship *s.* signoria, autorità.

lorry *s.* autocarro.

to **lose (lost, lost)** *vt.* e *vi.* perdere.

loser *s.* perdente.

losing, loss *s.* perdita.

lost V. *to lose.*

lot *s.* **1.** sorte **2.** parte **3.** lotto (*di terreno ecc.*) || *a — of*, una quantità di.

to **lot** *vt.* lottizzare.

lotion *s.* lozione.

lottery *s.* lotteria.

loud *agg.* forte, fragoroso, rumoroso || — *-speaker*, altoparlante. ♦ **loud(ly)** *avv.* ad alta voce.

lounge *s.* **1.** atrio (*di albergo, teat. ecc.*) **2.** lo stare in ozio.

to **lounge** *vi.* bighellonare.

lounger *s.* fannullone.

louse *s.* (*pl.* lice) pidocchio.

lousy *agg.* pidocchioso.

lovable *agg.* amabile.

love *s.* amore.

to **love** *vt.* amare.

loveless *agg.* senza amore.

loveliness *s.* bellezza.

lovely *agg.* bello.

lover *s.* amante, innamorato.

loving *agg.* amoroso.

lovingness *s.* affettuosità.

low[1] *agg.* **1.** basso **2.** debole || — *-spirited*, depresso. ♦ **low** *avv.* **1.** in basso **2.** a voce bassa **3.** a basso prezzo.

low[2] *s.* muggito.

to **low** *vi.* muggire.

to **lower** *vt.* **1.** abbassare **2.** abbattere. ♦ to **lower** *vi.* abbattersi.

lowering *s.* abbassamento.

lowland *s.* pianura.

lowly *agg.* **1.** basso **2.** umile. ♦ **lowly** *avv.* umilmente.

loyal *agg.* leale.

loyalty *s.* lealtà.

lozenge *s.* **1.** (*geom.*) rombo **2.** pastiglia.

lubber *s.* zoticone.

lubricant *agg.* e *s.* lubrificante.

to **lubricate** *vt.* lubrificare.

lubricating, lubrication *s.* lubrificazione.

lubricator *s.* lubrificatore.

lubricity *s.* **1.** viscosità **2.** (*fig.*) lascivia.

lubricous *agg.* lubrico.

lucent *agg.* lucente.

lucid *agg.* lucido, chiaro.

lucidity *s.* lucidità, chiarezza.

luck *s.* **1.** sorte **2.** fortuna || *to be in* —, *out of* —, essere fortunato, sfortunato.

luckily *avv.* fortunatamente.

luckless *agg.* sfortunato.

lucky *agg.* fortunato.

lucrative *agg.* lucrativo.

to **lucubrate** *vi.* fare delle elucubrazioni.

lucubration *s.* elucubrazione.

ludicrous *agg.* ridicolo.

ludicrousness *s.* comicità.

luggage *s.* bagaglio.

lugubrious *agg.* lugubre.

lukewarm *agg.* tiepido, apatico.

to **lull** *vt.* **1.** cullare **2.** calmare.

lullaby *s.* ninna-nanna.

lumbago *s.* lombaggine.

lumbar *agg.* lombare.

lumber *s.* **1.** cianfrusaglie (*pl.*) **2.** legname || — *-room*, ripostiglio.

to **lumber** *vt.* **1.** ammucchiare **2.** ingombrare. ♦ to **lumber** *vi.* **1.** tagliare legname **2.** muoversi pesantemente e rumorosamente.

lumbering *s.* commercio di legname.

luminary *s.* **1.** corpo luminoso **2.** luminare.

luminous *agg.* luminoso.

luminousness *s.* luminosità.

lump *s.* **1.** mucchio **2.** gonfiore **3.** zolletta **4.** (*comm.*) blocco **5.** persona goffa.

to **lump** *vt.* ammassare. ♦ to **lump** *vi.* raggrumarsi.

lumpy *agg.* **1.** granuloso **2.** increspato (*di mare*) **3.** pesante.

lunacy *s.* pazzia.

lunar *agg.* lunare.

lunatic *agg.* e *s.* pazzo.

lunation *s.* lunazione.

lunch *s.* seconda colazione, pasto del mezzogiorno.

to **lunch** *vi.* fare la seconda colazione. ♦ to **lunch** *vt.* offrire la colazione a.

luncheon s. spuntino.
lunette s. (*arch.*) lunetta.
lung s. polmone: *iron —*, polmone d'acciaio.
lupine s. lupino.
lure s. esca.
to **lure** vt. adescare.
lurid agg. **1.** spettrale **2.** orribile.
lurk s. nascondiglio.
to **lurk** vi. nascondersi.
luscious agg. **1.** dolce **2.** sensuale.
lust s. **1.** lussuria **2.** brama.
to **lust** vi. bramare: *to — for so.*, *sthg.*, bramare qu., qc.
lustful agg. **1.** sensuale **2.** bramoso.
lustfulness s. **1.** sensualità **2.** brama.
lustral agg. lustrale.
lustre[1] s. lustro, splendore.
lustre[2] s. lustro, quinquennio.
lusty agg. vigoroso, gagliardo.
lute s. liuto.
Lutheran agg. e s. luterano.
Lutheranism s. luteranesimo.
to **luxate** vt. (*med.*) lussare.
luxation s. lussazione.
luxuriant agg. lussureggiante.
to **luxuriate** vi. lussureggiare || *to — in*, deliziarsi di.
luxurious agg. lussuoso, sontuoso.
luxury s. **1.** lusso **2.** oggetto di lusso.
lye s. lisciva.
lying[1] agg. bugiardo.
lying[2] agg. giacente, situato.
lymph s. linfa.
lymphatic agg. linfatico. ♦ **lymphatic** s. vaso linfatico.
to **lynch** vt. linciare.
lynch law s. linciaggio.
lynx s. lince.
lyre s. lira.
lyric(al) agg. lirico. ♦ **lyric** s. lirica.
lyricism, lyrism s. lirismo.
lyrist s. poeta lirico.

M

macabre agg. macabro.
macaroni s. maccheroni.
macaroon s. amaretto.
mace s. mazza || *— -bearer*, mazziere.
to **macerate** vt. macerare. ♦ to

macerate vi. macerarsi.
maceration s. macerazione.
Machiavellian agg. machiavellico.
Machiavellism s. machiavellismo.
to **machinate** vt. macchinare.
machination s. macchinazione.
machine s. macchina || *sewing- —*, macchina da cucire.
to **machine** vt. e vi. lavorare a macchina.
machine-gun s. mitragliatrice.
to **machine-gun** vt. mitragliare.
machine-gunner s. mitragliere.
machinery s. **1.** macchinario **2.** meccanismo.
machining s. lavorazione (*a macchina*).
machinist s. macchinista.
mackerel s. sgombro || *— sky*, cielo a pecorelle.
mackintosh s. impermeabile.
macrocephalic agg. macrocefalo.
macrocosm s. macrocosmo.
macrocosmic agg. macrocosmico.
macromulecule s. macromolecola.
macroscopic agg. macroscopico.
to **maculate** vt. maculare.
maculation s. maculamento.
mad agg. **1.** pazzo **2.** idrofobo || *to go —*, impazzire.
madam s. signora.
madcap s. scervellato.
to **madden** vt. far impazzire. ♦ to **madden** vi. diventare matto.
madding agg. folle.
made V. *to make*.
madhouse s. manicomio.
madly avv. pazzamente.
madman s. pazzo.
madness s. **1.** pazzia **2.** idrofobia.
madrepore s. madrepora.
madrigal s. madrigale.
Maecenas s. mecenate.
magazine s. **1.** magazzino **2.** rivista **3.** arsenale.
maggot s. **1.** bruco **2.** (*fig.*) capriccio.
maggoty agg. **1.** bacato **2.** (*fig.*) capriccioso.
magic s. magia.
magic(al) agg. magico.
magician s. mago.
magisterial agg. **1.** di magistrato **2.** autoritario.
magistracy s. magistratura.
magistrate s. magistrato.
magistrature s. magistratura.
magnanimity s. magnanimità.
magnanimous agg. magnanimo.

magnesium *s.* magnesio.
magnet *s.* magnete, calamita.
magnetic(al) *agg.* magnetico.
magnetism *s.* magnetismo.
magnetization *s.* 1. magnetizzazione 2. forza d'attrazione.
to magnetize *vt.* magnetizzare.
magnetizer *s.* magnetizzatore.
magneto *s.* magnete.
magnetometer *s.* magnetometro.
magnification *s.* 1. esaltazione 2. ingrandimento.
magnificence *s.* magnificenza.
magnificent *agg.* magnifico.
magnifier *s.* 1. esaltatore 2. lente d'ingrandimento.
to magnify *vt.* 1. esaltare 2. ingrandire.
magniloquence *s.* magniloquenza.
magniloquent *agg.* magniloquente.
magnitude *s.* grandezza.
magpie *s.* gazza.
Magyar *agg.* e *s.* magiaro.
mahogany *s.* mogano.
maid *s.* 1. fanciulla 2. cameriera || *old* —, zitella.
maiden[1] *agg.* 1. vergine, puro 2. esordiente.
maiden[2] *s.* fanciulla || — *name*, nome da ragazza.
maidenhead, maidenhood *s.* verginità.
maidenliness *s.* modestia, verecondia.
maidenly *agg.* verginale.
maidservant *s.* cameriera.
maieutics *s.* maieutica.
maigre *agg.* magro.
mail *s.* posta || — *train*, treno postale.
to mail *vt.* mandare per posta.
to maim *vt.* storpiare.
main[1] *agg.* 1. principale 2. vigoroso || — *road*, strada maestra.
main[2] *s.* 1. alto mare 2. l'essenziale 3. condotto principale.
mainland *s.* terraferma.
mainly *avv.* principalmente.
mainmast *s.* (*mar.*) albero maestro.
mainsail *s.* vela maestra.
mainspring *s.* molla principale.
to maintain *vt.* 1. mantenere 2. asserire.
maintenance *s.* 1. mantenimento 2. manutenzione 3. difesa.
maize *s.* granoturco.
majestic(al) *agg.* maestoso.
majesty *s.* maestà.
major *agg.* maggiore, principale. ♦

major *s.* 1. maggiorenne 2. (*mil.*) maggiore.
majority *s.* 1. maggioranza 2. maggiore età.
make *s.* 1. fattura 2. costituzione 3. marca.
to make (made, made) *vt.* e *vi.* 1. fare 2. rendere 3. fabbricare || *to* — *for*, dirigersi; *to* — *up*, preparare, truccare; *to* — *up for*, compensare per || *to* — *oneself understood*, farsi capire; *to* — *so. confess*, obbligare qu. a confessare; *to* — *so. do what one likes*, far fare a qu. ciò che si vuole.
make-believe *s.* finzione.
maker *s.* 1. creatore 2. costruttore || — *-up*, truccatore.
makeshift *s.* espediente.
make-up *s.* 1. composizione 2. trucco 3. (*tip.*) impaginazione.
making *s.* 1. fattura 2. formazione. ♦ makings *s. pl.* il necessario (*sing.*).
maladjusted *agg.* 1. disadatto 2. disadattato.
maladjustment *s.* inadattabilità.
maladministration *s.* cattiva amministrazione.
maladroit *agg.* maldestro.
malady *s.* malattia.
malaise *s.* malessere.
Malayan *agg.* e *s.* malese.
malcontent *agg.* e *s.* malcontento.
male *agg.* maschio, maschile. ♦ male *s.* maschio.
malediction *s.* maledizione.
malefactor *s.* malfattore.
malefic *agg.* malefico.
maleficence *s.* malvagità.
maleficent *agg.* malefico.
malevolence *s.* malevolenza.
malevolent *agg.* malevolo.
malformation *s.* malformazione.
malformed *agg.* malformato.
malice *s.* 1. malignità 2. astio: *to bear* — *to so.*, nutrire rancore verso qu.
malicious *agg.* 1. maligno 2. premeditato.
malign *agg.* maligno.
malignancy *s.* malignità.
malignant *agg.* maligno.
malignity *s.* V. *malignancy*.
malleability *s.* malleabilità.
malleable *agg.* malleabile.
mallet *s.* mazzuolo.
mallow *s.* malva.
malnutrition *s.* malnutrizione.

malpractice *s.* pratica illecita.
malt *s.* malto.
Malthusian *agg.* e *s.* maltusiano.
Malthusianism *s.* maltusianesimo.
maltose *s.* maltosio.
to **maltreat** *vt.* maltrattare.
maltreatment *s.* maltrattamento.
malversation *s.* malversazione.
mama *s.* mamma.
mamma[1] *s.* mamma.
mamma[2] *s.* mammella.
mammal *s.* mammifero.
mammalian *agg.* e *s.* mammifero.
mammiferous *agg.* mammifero.
mammoth *agg.* enorme. ♦ **mammoth** *s.* mammut.
mammy *s.* mammina.
man *s.* (*pl.* men) **1.** uomo **2.** marito || — *-hour,* ora lavorativa; — *-of--war,* nave da guerra.
to **man** *vt.* munire, equipaggiare (*di uomini*).
manacle *s.* manetta.
to **manacle** *vt.* ammanettare.
to **manage** *vt.* **1.** dirigere **2.** maneggiare **3.** riuscire. ♦ to **manage** *vi.* destreggiarsi, cavarsela.
manageable *agg.* **1.** maneggevole **2.** fattibile.
management *s.* **1.** direzione, amministrazione **2.** abilità.
manager *s.* **1.** direttore **2.** amministratore **3.** impresario **4.** organizzatore.
manageress *s.* **1.** direttrice **2.** amministratrice.
managerial *agg.* direttivo.
managership *s.* **1.** direzione **2.** amministrazione.
managing *agg.* dirigente || — *director,* consigliere delegato.
mandarin *s.* mandarino.
mandatary *s.* mandatario.
mandate *s.* mandato.
mandator *s.* mandante.
mandatory *agg.* e *s.* mandatario.
mandible *s.* mandibola.
mandolin *s.* mandolino.
mandrake *s.* mandragora.
mandrel *s.* anima metallica.
mandrill *s.* mandrillo.
mane *s.* criniera.
manful *agg.* valoroso.
manganate *s.* manganato.
mange *s.* rogna.
manger *s.* mangiatoia.
to **mangle** *vt.* **1.** lacerare **2.** storpiare.
mangy *agg.* **1.** lacero **2.** rognoso **3.**

spregevole.
to **manhandle** *vt.* manovrare (*a mano*).
manhole *s.* botola.
manhood *s.* **1.** virilità **2.** vigore **3.** genere umano.
maniac *agg.* e *s.* maniaco, pazzo.
Manich(a)eism *s.* manicheismo.
manicurist *s.* manicure.
manifest *agg.* manifesto.
to **manifest** *vt.* manifestare.
manifestant *s.* manifestante.
manifestation *s.* manifestazione.
manifold *agg.* molteplice.
manifoldness *s.* molteplicità.
manikin *s.* **1.** omiciattolo **2.** manichino.
maniple *s.* manipolo.
to **manipulate** *vt.* manipolare.
manipulation *s.* manipolazione.
manipulator *s.* manipolatore.
mankind *s.* umanità.
manlike *agg.* **1.** civile **2.** antropomorfo.
manliness *s.* virilità.
manly *agg.* maschio, virile.
manner *s.* **1.** maniera **2.** contegno. ♦ **manners** *s. pl.* **1.** modi **2.** usanze.
mannered *agg.* manierato || *ill-* —, maleducato.
mannerism *s.* manierismo.
mannerly *agg.* cortese.
manoeuvrable *agg.* manovrabile.
manoeuvre *s.* manovra.
to **manoeuvre** *vt.* manovrare. ♦ to **manoeuvre** *vi.* fare le manovre.
manoeuvrer *s.* stratega.
manometer *s.* manometro.
manor *s.* feudo || — *-house,* castello.
manorial *agg.* feudale.
mansard *s.* mansarda.
manservant *s.* domestico.
mansion *s.* palazzo.
manslaughter *s.* omicidio preter-intenzionale.
mantelpiece, mantelshelf *s.* mensola di caminetto.
mantle *s.* manto, mantello.
to **mantle** *vt.* ammantare. ♦ to **mantle** *vi.* coprirsi.
manual *agg.* e *s.* manuale.
manufactory *s.* fabbrica.
manufacturable *agg.* fabbricabile.
manufacture *s.* **1.** manifattura **2.** manufatto.
to **manufacture** *vt.* fabbricare.
manufacturer *s.* fabbricante.

manufacturing *agg.* manifatturiero. ♦ **manufacturing** *s.* fabbricazione.

manure *s.* concime.

manuscript *agg.* e *s.* manoscritto.

many (more, most) *agg.* e *pron.* molti || — *a*, più di uno; — -*sided*, molteplice; *so* —, tanti; *too* —, troppi; *as* — *as*, tanti... quanti; *how* —?, quanti?

map *s.* carta geografica.

maple *s.* acero.

to mar *vt.* guastare.

marathon *s.* maratona.

to maraud *vt.* e *vi.* saccheggiare.

marauder *s.* predatore.

marble *s.* 1. marmo 2. biglia.

to marble *vt.* marmorizzare.

marble-cutter *s.* marmista.

March *s.* marzo.

march[1] *s.* confine.

march[2] *s.* marcia.

to march *vi.* 1. camminare 2. marciare || *to* — *in*, entrare marciando.

marching *agg.* in, di marcia.

marchioness *s.* marchesa.

mare *s.* cavalla.

margarine *s.* margarina.

margin *s.* margine.

marginal *agg.* marginale.

marine *agg.* marino, marittimo. ♦ **marine** *s.* 1. marina 2. fante di marina.

marital *agg.* maritale.

maritime *agg.* marittimo.

mark *s.* 1. segno 2. bersaglio 3. voto 4. marchio 5. importanza 6. marco || *question* —, punto interrogativo.

to mark *vt.* 1. segnare 2. dare i voti a 3. scegliere 4. osservare.

marked *agg.* notevole.

marker *s.* 1. chi segna 2. segnalibro.

market *s.* mercato.

to market *vt.* 1. vendere al mercato 2. introdurre sul mercato. ♦ to **market** *vi.* comprare, vendere sul mercato.

marketing *s.* 1. compra-vendita 2. « marketing » (*ricerche di mercato*).

marking *s.* segno.

marksman *s.* tiratore scelto.

marl *s.* marna.

marmalade *s.* marmellata (*d'arance*).

marmoreal *agg.* marmoreo.

marmot *s.* marmotta.

to maroon *vt.* abbandonare un luogo deserto.

marquee *s.* tendone.

marquess, marquis *s.* marchese.

marquise *s.* marchesa.

marriage *s.* matrimonio, unione.

married *agg.* 1. sposato 2. coniugale.

marrow *s.* midollo || (*vegetable*) —, zucca.

to marry *vt.* sposare. ♦ to **marry** *vi.* sposarsi.

marsh *s.* palude || — -*fever*, malaria; — *gas*, metano.

marshal *s.* maresciallo.

to marshal *vt.* 1. schierare 2. introdurre.

marshy *agg.* paludoso.

marsupial *agg.* e *s.* marsupiale.

marten *s.* martora.

martial *agg.* 1. marziale 2. di Marte.

Martian *agg.* e *s.* marziano.

martyr *s.* martire.

martyrdom *s.* martirio.

to martyrize *vt.* martirizzare.

martyrology *s.* martirologio.

marvel *s.* meraviglia.

to marvel *vi.* meravigliarsi.

marvellous *agg.* meraviglioso.

Marxism *s.* marxismo.

Marxist *agg.* e *s.* marxista.

marzipan *s.* marzapane.

mascot(te) *s.* mascotte.

masculine *agg.* e *s.* maschile.

masculinity *s.* mascolinità.

mash *s.* 1. mistura 2. puré.

to mash *vt.* 1. mescolare 2. schiacciare.

mask *s.* maschera.

to mask *vt.* mascherare.

masking *s.* il mascherarsi.

masochism *s.* masochismo.

mason *s.* muratore || *Free Mason*, massone.

masonry *s.* 1. arte del muratore 2. costruzione in muratura 3. massoneria.

masquerade *s.* mascherata.

to masquerade *vi.* 1. mascherarsi 2. fingersi.

mass[1] *s.* messa.

mass[2] *s.* massa, ammasso.

to mass *vt.* ammassare. ♦ to **mass** *vi.* ammassarsi.

massacre *s.* massacro.

to massacre *vt.* massacrare.

massage *s.* massaggio.

to massage *vt.* massaggiare.

masseur s. massaggiatore.
masseuse s. massaggiatrice.
massif s. massiccio.
massive agg. **1.** massiccio **2.** potente.
massiveness s. compattezza.
to **mass-produce** vt. produrre in serie.
mass-producer s. produttore in serie.
mass-production s. produzione in serie.
massy agg. massiccio.
mast s. (mar.) albero.
to **mast** vt. (mar.) alberare.
master s. **1.** padrone **2.** maestro ‖ — builder, capomastro; Master of Arts, laureato in lettere.
to **master** vt. **1.** conoscere a fondo **2.** dominare.
masterful agg. **1.** autoritario **2.** abile.
masterhood s. padronanza.
masterly agg. magistrale.
masterpiece s. capolavoro.
mastership s. **1.** autorità **2.** abilità.
masterstroke s. colpo magistrale.
mastery s. **1.** maestria **2.** signoria.
mastication s. masticazione.
mastiff s. mastino.
mastitis s. mastite.
mastodon s. mastodonte.
mastoid s. mastoide.
mastoiditis s. mastoidite.
masturbation s. masturbazione.
mat s. stuoia ‖ door- —, zerbino.
to **mat** vt. **1.** intrecciare **2.** coprire con stuoie **3.** smerigliare.
match[1] s. **1.** gara, incontro **2.** avversario **3.** l'uguale **4.** matrimonio.
match[2] s. fiammifero.
to **match** vt. **1.** accoppiare, maritare **2.** uguagliare. ♦ to **match** vi. **1.** accoppiarsi **2.** accordarsi **3.** rivaleggiare.
matchless agg. impareggiabile.
mate s. **1.** compagno **2.** aiuto **3.** (mar.) ufficiale in seconda.
to **mate** vt. accoppiare. ♦ to **mate** vi. accoppiarsi.
material agg. **1.** materiale **2.** essenziale. ♦ **material** s. **1.** materia, materiale **2.** stoffa. ♦ **materials** s. pl. articoli ‖ raw —, materie prime.
materialism s. materialismo.
materialist agg. e s. materialista.
materialistic agg. materialistico.

materialization s. materializzazione.
to **materialize** vt. materializzare.
♦ to **materialize** vi. **1.** materializzarsi **2.** avverarsi.
maternal agg. materno.
maternity s. maternità.
mathematic(al) agg. matematico.
mathematician s. matematico.
mathematics s. matematica.
matriarchy s. matriarcato.
matricidal agg. matricida.
matricide s. **1.** matricida **2.** matricidio.
to **matriculate** vt. immatricolare.
♦ to **matriculate** vi. immatricolarsi.
matriculation s. immatricolazione.
matrimonial agg. matrimoniale.
matrimony s. matrimonio.
matrix s. **1.** matrice **2.** (anat.) utero.
matron s. **1.** matrona **2.** direttrice **3.** governante.
matronal, matronly agg. matronale.
matter s. **1.** materia **2.** faccenda ‖ what is the — with you?, che cosa vi succede?; what is the —?, che succede?
to **matter** vi. **1.** importare: it matters little, poco importa **2.** (med.) suppurare.
matter-of-fact agg. pratico.
matting s. stuoia.
mattock s. piccone.
mattress s. materasso.
to **maturate** vi. **1.** maturare **2.** suppurare.
maturation s. **1.** maturazione **2.** suppurazione.
mature agg. maturo.
to **mature** vt. e vi. maturare.
maturity s. **1.** maturità **2.** (comm.) scadenza.
matutine agg. mattutino.
maudlin agg. **1.** sdolcinato **2.** querulo.
to **maunder** vi. **1.** parlare a vanvera **2.** girovagare.
mausoleum s. mausoleo.
mawkish agg. **1.** nauseante **2.** sdolcinato.
mawkishness s. **1.** sapore nauseante **2.** sdolcinatezza.
maxim s. massima.
maximalist s. massimalista.
maximum agg. e s. massimo.
May s. maggio ‖ — Day, primo maggio.

may (might) v. dif. potere (pres. ind. e congiuntivo) || — I go out?, posso uscire?; he — arrive to day, può darsi che arrivi oggi; — he live to repent it, possa egli vivere tanto da pentirsene

maybe avv. forse.

maybug s. maggiolino.

mayflower s. biancospino.

mayonnaise s. maionese.

mayor s. sindaco.

maze s. labirinto.

to maze vt. disorientare, confondere.

mazily avv. confusamente.

mazy agg. intricato.

me pron. pers. me, mi.

meadow s. prato.

meagre agg. **1.** magro **2.** scarso.

meal[1] s. farina.

meal[2] s. pasto.

mealy agg. **1.** farinoso **2.** infarinato **3.** pallido **4.** chiazzato.

mean[1] agg. **1.** meschino **2.** mediocre.

mean[2] s. punto medio, mezzo. ♦ **means** s. pl. mezzi || by no means, ben lungi da.

to mean (meant, meant) vt. e vi. **1.** intendere, significare **2.** destinare.

meander s. meandro.

to meander vi. serpeggiare.

meaning agg. **1.** disposto **2.** significativo. ♦ **meaning** s. **1.** significato **2.** idea.

meaningful agg. significativo.

meaningless agg. senza senso.

meanly avv. **1.** meschinamente **2.** umilmente.

meanness s. meschinità.

meant V. to mean.

meantime s. frattempo. ♦ **meantime** avv. frattanto.

meanwhile avv. frattanto.

measles s. morbillo || German —, rosolia.

measurable agg. misurabile.

measure s. **1.** misura **2.** ritmo.

to measure vt. e vi. misurare.

measureless agg. smisurato.

measurement s. misurazione.

measurer s. misuratore.

meat s. carne.

meaty agg. **1.** polposo **2.** sostanzioso.

mechanic s. meccanico.

mechanical agg. meccanico.

mechanics s. meccanica.

mechanism s. **1.** meccanismo **2.** tecnica.

mechanization s. meccanizzazione.

to mechanize vt. meccanizzare.

medal s. medaglia.

to meddle vi. immischiarsi.

meddler s. intrigante.

meddlesome agg. importuno.

medi(a)eval agg. medievale.

medi(a)evalism s. medievalismo.

medi(a)evalist s. medievalista.

medial agg. medio.

median agg. mediano.

mediate agg. mediato.

to mediate vt. conseguire con mediazione. ♦ **to mediate** vi. fare da intermediario.

mediation s. mediazione.

mediator s. mediatore.

medical agg. medico.

medicament s. medicamento.

medication s. medicazione.

medicative agg. curativo.

medicinal agg. medicinale.

medicine s. medicina || — -man, stregone.

mediocrity s. mediocrità.

to meditate vt. e vi. meditare.

meditation s. meditazione.

meditative agg. meditativo.

Mediterranean agg. mediterraneo.

medium agg. medio. ♦ **medium** s. mezzo.

mediumistic agg. medianico.

medlar s. nespola || — -tree, nespolo.

medley agg. misto. ♦ **medley** s. miscuglio.

medulla s. midollo.

medullar(y) agg. midollare.

meek agg. mite.

meekness s. mansuetudine.

to meet (met, met) vt. **1.** incontrare **2.** far fronte a. ♦ **to meet (met, met)** vi. incontrarsi || to — with, imbattersi in.

meeting s. **1.** incontro **2.** riunione || political —, comizio.

megalomaniac s. megalomane.

megaphone s. megafono.

melancholic agg. malinconico.

melancholy agg. malinconico. ♦ **melancholy** s. malinconia.

mellifluous agg. mellifluo.

mellow agg. **1.** maturo **2.** pastoso **3.** ubertoso.

to mellow vt. e vi. maturare.

mellowness s. **1.** maturità **2.** pastosità **3.** ubertosità.

melodic agg. melodico.

melodious *agg.* melodioso.
melodiousness *s.* melodiosità.
melodrama *s.* melodramma.
melodramatic *agg.* melodrammatico.
melody *s.* melodia.
melomaniac *s.* melomane.
melon *s.* melone || *water-* —, anguria.
melt *s.* fusione.
to **melt** *vt.* **1.** sciogliere **2.** intenerire. ♦ to **melt** *vi.* **1.** sciogliersi **2.** intenerirsi || *to* — *away*, svanire.
melter *s.* fonditore.
melting *s.* fusione || — *-pot*, crogiuolo.
meltingly *avv.* teneramente.
member *s.* membro.
membership *s.* **1.** qualifica di membro **2.** i membri.
membrane *s.* membrana.
memoirs *s. pl.* memorie.
memorable *agg.* memorabile.
memorandum *s.* (*pl.* -da) promemoria.
memorial *agg.* commemorativo. ♦ **memorial** *s.* **1.** monumento **2.** memoriale.
memorialist *s.* memorialista.
to **memorize** *vt.* imparare a memoria.
memory *s.* memoria.
men V. *man.*
menace *s.* minaccia.
to **menace** *vt.* e *vi.* minacciare.
menacing *agg.* minaccioso.
menagerie *s.* serraglio.
mend *s.* rattoppo.
to **mend** *vt.* **1.** riparare **2.** correggere. ♦ to **mend** *vi.* **1.** correggersi **2.** migliorare.
mendacious *agg.* mendace.
mendacity *s.* **1.** abitudine di mentire **2.** bugia.
mender *s.* **1.** riparatore **2.** rammendatrice.
mendicant *agg.* e *s.* mendicante.
mendicity *s.* mendicità.
mending *s.* **1.** riparazione **2.** rammendo.
menial *agg.* servile. ♦ **menial** *s.* servo.
meninx *s.* (*pl.* meninges) meninge.
meniscus *s.* menisco.
menopause *s.* menopausa.
menses *s. pl.* mestruazioni.
menstruation *s.* mestruazione.
mental *agg.* mentale || — *-hospital*, manicomio.
mentality *s.* **1.** mentalità **2.** intelligenza.
menthol *s.* mentolo.
mention *s.* menzione || *don't* — *it*, non c'è di che (*risposta a* « *grazie* »).
to **mention** *vt.* nominare.
mentionable *agg.* menzionabile.
mentor *s.* mentore.
mephitic *agg.* mefitico.
mercantile *agg.* mercantile.
mercantilism *s.* mercantilismo.
mercenary *agg.* e *s.* mercenario.
merchandise *s.* merce.
to **merchandise** *vt.* e *vi.* commerciare.
merchant *s.* mercante || — *ship*, nave mercantile.
merciful *agg.* pietoso.
merciless *agg.* spietato.
mercury *s.* mercurio.
mercy *s.* pietà, misericordia.
mere[1] *agg.* **1.** mero **2.** solo.
mere[2] *s.* confine.
mere[3] *s.* laghetto, stagno.
to **merge** *vt.* assorbire. ♦ to **merge** *vi.* **1.** essere assortito **2.** immergersi.
merger *s.* (*comm.*) fusione (*di società*).
meridian *agg.* **1.** meridiano **2.** culminante. ♦ **meridian** *s.* **1.** meridiano **2.** culmine.
meridional *agg.* e *s.* meridionale.
merit *s.* merito.
to **merit** *vt.* meritare.
meritorious *agg.* meritorio.
mermaid *s.* sirena.
merman *s.* tritone.
merrily *avv.* allegramente.
merry *agg.* gaio.
merry-go-round *s.* giostra.
merrymaking *s.* festa.
mesh *s.* maglia. ♦ **meshes** *s. pl.* reti.
mesocarp *s.* mesocarpo.
mesozoic *agg.* e *s.* mesozoico.
mess *s.* **1.** mensa **2.** confusione **3.** pasticcio.
to **mess** *vt.* mettere in disordine || *to* — *up*, mettere a soqquadro.
message *s.* **1.** messaggio **2.** commissione.
messenger *s.* messaggero || — *-boy*, fattorino.
Messiah *s.* Messia.
Messianic *agg.* messianico.
mestizo *s.* meticcio.

met V. *to meet.*
metabolism *s.* metabolismo.
metal *s.* **1.** metallo **2.** pietrisco.
metallic *agg.* metallico.
metallization *s.* metallizzazione.
to **metallize** *vt.* metallizzare.
metalloid *s.* metalloide.
metallurgic(al) *agg.* metallurgico.
metallurgist *s.* metallurgico.
metallurgy *s.* metallurgia.
metamorphic *agg.* metamorfico.
metamorphism *s.* metamorfismo.
metamorphosis *s.* (*pl.* -ses) metamorfosi.
metaphor *s.* metafora.
metaphoric(al) *agg.* metaforico.
metaphysic(al) *agg.* metafisico.
metaphysics *s.* metafisica.
metapsychic(al) *agg.* metapsichico.
metapsychics *s.* metapsichica.
metastasis *s.* (*pl.* -ses) metastasi.
metayage *s.* mezzadria.
metayer *s.* mezzadro.
mete *s.* segno di confine || *metes and bounds* (*giur.*), limiti e confini.
metempsychosis *s.* metempsicosi.
meteor *s.* meteora.
meteoric *agg.* **1.** meteorico **2.** transitorio.
meteoroid *s.* meteorite.
meteorologic(al) *agg.* meteorologico.
meteorologist *s.* meteorologo.
meteorology *s.* meteorologia.
meter *s.* **1.** contatore **2.** tassametro.
methane *s.* metano.
method *s.* metodo.
methodic(al) *agg.* metodico.
methodist *s.* metodista.
methodological *agg.* metodologico.
methodology *s.* metodologia.
meticulosity *s.* meticolosità.
meticulous *agg.* meticoloso.
metre *s.* **1.** metro **2.** (*mus.*) tempo.
metrical *agg.* metrico.
metrics *s.* metrica.
metronome *s.* metronomo.
metropolis *s.* metropoli.
metropolitan *agg.* metropolitano.
♦ **metropolitan** *s.* abitante di una metropoli.
mettle *s.* tempra.
mettled, mettlesome *agg.* focoso.
mew¹ *s.* gabbiano.
mew² *s.* miagolio.
to **mew**¹ *vt.* rinchiudere in gabbia.
to **mew**² *vi.* miagolare.
to **mewl** *vi.* vagire.

Mexican *agg.* e *s.* messicano.
mezzanine *s.* mezzanino.
miaul *s.* miagolio.
mice V. *mouse.*
microbe *s.* microbo.
microbial *agg.* microbico.
microbiology *s.* microbiologia.
microcosm *s.* microcosmo.
micrometer *s.* micrometro.
micrometry *s.* micrometria.
micro-organism *s.* microorganismo.
microphone *s.* microfono.
microphotography *s.* microfotografia.
microscope *s.* microscopio.
microscopic(al) *agg.* microscopico.
microscopy *s.* microscopia.
mid *agg.* medio, mezzo.
midday *s.* mezzogiorno.
middle *agg.* medio || *Middle Ages*, medioevo; — *-aged*, di mezza età.
♦ **middle** *s.* **1.** mezzo **2.** cintola.
middle class *s.* borghesia.
middleman *s.* intermediario.
middling *agg.* medio.
midge *s.* moscerino.
midget *s.* nano.
midland *agg.* centrale. ♦ **midlands** *s. pl.* regione centrale (*sing.*).
midnight *s.* mezzanotte.
midriff *s.* **1.** diaframma **2.** costume da bagno a due pezzi.
midshipman *s.* guardiamarina.
midst *s.* mezzo.
midsummer *s.* solstizio d'estate.
midway *agg.* e *avv.* a mezza strada.
mid-week *agg.* di metà settimana.
midwife *s.* (*pl.* -wives) levatrice.
midwinter *s.* solstizio d'inverno.
mien *s.* portamento.
might *s.* potenza.
might V. *may.*
mighty *agg.* potente.
migrant *agg.* e *s.* migratore.
to **migrate** *vi.* (e)migrare.
migration *s.* (e)migrazione.
migratory *agg.* migratore.
milady *s.* nobildonna.
mild *agg.* dolce.
mildew *s.* muffa.
mildness *s.* dolcezza.
mile *s.* miglio.
milestone *s.* pietra miliare.
milfoil *s.* millefoglio.
miliary *agg.* migliare.
militant *agg.* militante. ♦ **militant** *s.* attivista.

militarily *avv.* militarmente.
militarism *s.* militarismo.
militarist *s.* militarista.
militarization *s.* militarizzazione.
to **militarize** *vt.* militarizzare.
military *agg.* e *s.* militare.
militiaman *s.* milite.
milk *s.* latte || — -*jug*, lattiera.
to **milk** *vt.* mungere. ♦ to **milk** *vi.*
1. produrre latte 2. mungere.
milker *s.* 1. mungitore 2. mucca da
latte.
milking *s.* mungitura.
milkmaid *s.* mungitrice.
milkman *s.* lattaio.
milky *agg.* 1. latteo 2. (*fig.*) genti-
le || *the Milky Way*, la Via Lat-
tea.
mill *s.* 1. mulino 2. macinino 3. fab-
brica || *saw-* —, segheria.
to **mill** *vt.* 1. macinare 2. segare 3.
frullare.
millenary *agg.* millenario. ♦ **millenary** *s.* 1. millennio 2. millenario.
millennium *s.* millennio.
millepede *s.* millepiedi.
miller *s.* 1. mugnaio 2. fresatore 3.
fresa.
millet *s.* (*bot.*) miglio.
milliard *s.* 1. miliardo 2. (*amer.*)
bilione.
milligram(me) *s.* milligrammo.
millimetre *s.* millimetro.
milliner *s.* modista.
millinery *s.* modisteria.
milling *s.* 1. macinatura 2. fresa-
tura.
million *s.* milione.
millionaire *s.* milionario.
millstone *s.* macina.
mime *s.* mimo.
to **mime** *vi.* e *vt.* mimare.
to **mimeograph** *vt.* ciclostilare.
mimetic *agg.* mimetico.
mimic *agg.* imitativo || — *art*, mi-
mica. ♦ **mimic** *s.* imitatore.
to **mimic (mimicked, mimicked)**
vt. imitare.
mimicry *s.* 1. imitazione 2. mimetismo.
minaret *s.* minareto.
minatory *agg.* minatorio.
mince *s.* carne tritata.
to **mince** *vt.* 1. tritare 2. tagliuzzare
3. mitigare. ♦ to **mince** *vi.* camminare, parlare in modo affettato.
mincer *s.* tritacarne.
mincing *agg.* affettato.

mind *s.* 1. mente 2. opinione.
to **mind** *vt.* 1. badare a 2. spiacere
|| *never* —!, non importa!; *I do
not* —, non mi preoccupo di.
minded *agg.* incline || *broad-* —, di
larghe vedute; *narrow-* —, di idee
ristrette || *if you are so* —, se la
pensate così.
mindful *agg.* memore.
mindless *agg.* 1. disattento 2. stupido.
mine[1] *pron. poss.* il mio, la mia, i
miei, le mie || *a friend of* —, un
mio amico.
mine[2] *s.* 1. miniera 2. mina || —
-*sweeper*, dragamine.
to **mine** *vt.* 1. scavare 2. estrarre 3.
minare.
miner *s.* minatore.
mineral *agg.* e *s.* minerale.
to **mineralize** *vt.* mineralizzare.
mineralogy *s.* mineralogia.
to **mingle** *vt.* mescolare. ♦ to **mingle** *vi.* mescolarsi.
miniature *agg.* in miniatura. ♦
miniature *s.* miniatura.
to **miniature** *vt.* e *vi.* fare miniature.
miniaturist *s.* miniaturista.
minim *s.* 1. (*mus.*) minima 2. quantità minima 3. inezia.
minimal *agg.* minimo.
to **minimize** *vt.* minimizzare.
minimum *s.* (*pl.* -ma) minimo.
mining *agg.* minerario. ♦ **mining**
s. 1. scavo 2. estrazione 3. posa
di mine.
minion *s.* favorito.
miniskirt *s.* minigonna.
minister *s.* ministro.
to **minister** *vi.* assistere.
ministerial *agg.* ministeriale.
ministry *s.* ministero.
mink *s.* visone.
minor *agg.* minore. ♦ **minor** *s.*
minorenne.
minority *s.* 1. minoranza 2. età minore.
minstrel *s.* menestrello.
mint[1] *s.* zecca.
mint[2] *s.* menta.
to **mint** *vt.* coniare.
mintage *s.* conio.
minuend *s.* minuendo.
minuet *s.* minuetto.
minus *s.* e *prep.* meno.
minute *agg.* minuto, minuscolo.
minute *s.* 1. minuto 2. nota || —
-*hand*, lancetta dei minuti.

minutely[1] *avv.* minutamente.
minutely[2] *avv.* di minuto in minuto.
minuteness *s.* **1.** minutezza **2.** minuziosità.
miracle *s.* miracolo.
miraculous *agg.* miracoloso.
mirage *s.* miraggio.
mire *s.* fango.
to **mire** *vt.* infangare. ♦ to **mire** *vi.* infangarsi.
mirror *s.* specchio || *driving- —*, specchietto retrovisore.
to **mirror** *vt.* rispecchiare.
mirth *s.* allegria.
mirthful *agg.* allegro.
mirthless *agg.* triste.
miry *agg.* fangoso.
misadventure *s.* disavventura.
misanthrope *s.* misantropo.
misanthropy *s.* misantropia.
misapplication *s.* applicazione erronea.
to **misapply** *vt.* applicare erroneamente.
misapprehension *s.* malinteso.
misbehaviour *s.* cattivo contegno.
misbelief *s.* falsa credenza.
to **misbelieve** *vi.* avere una falsa credenza.
misbeliever *s.* miscredente.
misbelieving *agg.* eretico.
to **miscalculate** *vt.* e *vi.* calcolare male.
miscarriage *s.* **1.** disguido **2.** fallimento **3.** aborto.
to **miscarry** *vi.* **1.** smarrirsi **2.** fallire **3.** abortire.
miscellaneous *agg.* miscellaneo.
miscellany *s.* miscellanea.
mischance *s.* sfortuna.
mischief *s.* **1.** danno, male **2.** malizia **3.** birichinata.
mischievous *agg.* **1.** nocivo **2.** malizioso.
misconduct *s.* cattiva condotta.
miscount *s.* conteggio errato.
misdeed *s.* misfatto.
misdemeanour *s.* misfatto.
to **misdirect** *vt.* mandare in direzione sbagliata.
misdirection *s.* indicazione sbagliata.
misdoing *s.* misfatto.
miser *s.* avaro.
miserable *agg.* **1.** triste **2.** miserabile.
miserliness *s.* avarizia.
miserly *agg.* avaro.

misery *s.* **1.** miseria **2.** sofferenza.
misfire *s.* cilecca.
misfit *s.* **1.** cosa che si adatta male **2.** (*fig.*) pesce fuor d'acqua.
misfortune *s.* sventura.
to **misgive (misgave, misgiven)** *vt.* preoccupare. ♦ to **misgive (misgave, misgiven)** *vi.* preoccuparsi.
misgiving *s.* **1.** presentimento **2.** timore.
to **misgovern** *vt.* governare male.
misgovernment *s.* malgoverno.
to **misguide** *vt.* **1.** guidare male **2.** traviare.
to **mishandle** *vt.* maltrattare.
mishap *s.* infortunio.
to **misinform** *vt.* informare male.
misinformation *s.* informazione sbagliata.
to **misinterpret** *vt.* interpretare male.
misinterpretation *s.* interpretazione errata.
to **misjudge** *vt.* giudicare male.
misjudgement *s.* giudizio erroneo.
to **mislay (mislaid, mislaid)** *vt.* smarrire.
to **mislead (misled, misled)** *vt.* **1.** traviare **2.** ingannare.
misogamy *s.* misogamia.
misogynist *s.* misogino.
misogyny *s.* misoginia.
misoneism *s.* misoneismo.
to **misplace** *vt.* collocare male, fuori posto.
misplacement *s.* spostamento.
misprint *s.* errore di stampa, refuso.
to **misprint** *vt.* stampare con errori.
to **mispronounce** *vt.* pronunciare male.
mispronunciation *s.* pronuncia scorretta.
misquotation *s.* citazione erronea.
to **misquote** *vt.* citare erroneamente.
to **misread (misread, misread)** *vt.* leggere erroneamente.
mesreading *s.* falsa interpretazione.
to **misrepresent** *vt.* travisare.
misrepresentation *s.* travisamento.
miss[1] *s.* **1.** colpo mancato **2.** difetto.
miss[2] *s.* signorina: *Miss Jane Smith*, la signorina Jane Smith.
to **miss** *vt.* **1.** mancare (*il colpo*) **2.** perdere **3.** notare, sentire la man-

canza di **4.** evitare.

missal s. messale.

missile s. missile.

missing agg. mancante || the —, i dispersi.

mission s. missione.

missionary agg. e s. missionario.

missioner s. missionario.

to **misspell** vt. sbagliare l'ortografia.

mist s. **1.** bruma **2.** pioggerella **3.** appannamento.

to **mist** vt. appannare. ♦ to **mist** vi. appannarsi.

mistakable agg. suscettibile d'errore.

mistake s. errore.

to **mistake (mistook, mistaken)** vt. **1.** sbagliare **2.** scambiare **3.** non capire.

mistaken agg. **1.** in errore **2.** erroneo.

mister s. signore: Mr. Brown, il signor Brown.

mistletoe s. vischio.

mistook V. to mistake.

mistral s. maestrale.

mistranslation s. traduzione errata.

mistress s. **1.** signora: Mrs. Brown, la signora Brown **2.** insegnante **3.** amante.

mistrust s. diffidenza.

to **mistrust** vt. e vi. diffidare di, sospettare.

mistrustful agg. diffidente.

misty agg. **1.** nebbioso **2.** confuso.

to **misunderstand (misunderstood, misunderstood)** vt. e vi. fraintendere.

misunderstanding s. **1.** malinteso **2.** disaccordo.

misunderstood V. to misunderstand.

misusage, misuse s. **1.** cattivo uso **2.** maltrattamento.

to **misuse** vt. **1.** usar male **2.** maltrattare.

to **miswrite (miswrote, miswritten)** vt. scrivere scorrettamente.

mithridatic agg. immunizzante (contro veleni).

mithridatism s. immunizzazione (contro un veleno).

to **mitigate** vt. mitigare.

mitigation s. mitigazione.

mitral agg. mitrale.

mitre s. **1.** (eccl.) mitra **2.** giunto ad angolo.

mitt(en) s. manopola, guantone.

to **mix** vt. mescolare || to — up, confondere. ♦ to **mix** vi. mescolarsi.

mixed agg. misto, eterogeneo.

mixer s. (mecc.) mescolatore.

mixing s. mescolanza.

mixture s. **1.** mescolanza **2.** miscela.

mizzen s. (mar.) mezzana.

mnemonic agg. mnemonico.

mnemonics s. mnemonica.

moan s. gemito.

to **moan** vt. e vi. gemere.

moanful agg. lamentoso.

moaning s. lamento.

moat s. fossato.

mob s. **1.** folla **2.** plebaglia.

to **mob** vt. **1.** assalire **2.** affollare.

mobile agg. **1.** mobile **2.** mutevole.

mobility s. **1.** mobilità **2.** mutevolezza.

mobilization s. mobilitazione.

to **mobilize** vt. mobilitare.

moccasin s. mocassino.

mock agg. **1.** ironico **2.** finto || —-heroic, eroicomico. ♦ **mock** s. **1.** derisione **2.** imitazione.

to **mock** vt. e vi. beffare, prendersi gioco di.

mocker s. burlone.

mockery s. **1.** derisione **2.** contraffazione.

mocking agg. beffardo.

modal agg. modale.

modality s. modalità.

model agg. modello. ♦ **model** s. **1.** modello **2.** copia.

to **model** vt. modellare.

modeller s. **1.** modellatore **2.** modellista.

modelling s. **1.** modellatura **2.** creazione di modelli.

moderate agg. e s. moderato.

to **moderate** vt. moderare. ♦ to **moderate** vi. moderarsi.

moderateness s. moderatezza.

moderation s. moderazione.

moderator s. moderatore.

modern agg. e s. moderno.

modernism s. modernismo.

modernist s. modernista.

modernity s. modernità.

modernization s. **1.** rimodernamento **2.** aggiornamento.

to **modernize** vt. modernizzare. ♦ to **modernize** vi. modernizzarsi.

modest agg. **1.** modesto **2.** pudico.

modesty s. 1. modestia 2. pudore.
modifiable agg. modificabile.
modification s. modificazione.
modifier s. modificatore.
to **modify** vt. modificare.
to **modulate** vt. e vi. modulare.
modulation s. modulazione.
modulator s. modulatore.
mofette s. mofeta.
Mohammedan agg. e s. maomettano.
moist agg. umido.
to **moisten** vt. inumidire. ◆ to **moisten** vi. inumidirsi.
moistness s. umidità.
moisture s. vapore umido.
molar agg. e s. molare.
molasses s. melassa.
mole[1] s. neo.
mole[2] s. talpa.
mole[3] s. molo.
molecular agg. molecolare.
molecule s. molecola.
moleskin s. 1. pelle di talpa 2. fustagno. ◆ **moleskins** s. pl. calzoni di fustagno.
to **molest** vt. molestare.
molestation s. molestia.
molester s. molestatore.
to **mollify** vt. addolcire.
mollusc s. mollusco.
molybdenum s. molibdeno.
moment s. 1. momento 2. importanza.
momentary agg. momentaneo.
momentous agg. importante.
monachal agg. monacale.
monad s. monade.
monarch s. monarca.
monarchic(al) agg. monarchico.
monarchist s. monarchico.
monarchy s. monarchia.
monastery s. monastero.
monastic(al) agg. monastico.
Monday s. lunedì.
monetary agg. monetario.
monetization s. monetazione.
to **monetize** vt. monetizzare.
money s. denaro || — -bag, portamonete; — -order, vaglia; earnest —, caparra; paper —, valuta cartacea; ready —, contanti.
moneyed agg. 1. di, in denaro 2. ricco.
moneyless agg. squattrinato.
monger s. mercante || fish —, pescivendolo.
Mongolian agg. e s. mongolo.
mongolism s. mongolismo.

mongoloid agg. e s. mongoloide.
mongrel agg. misto. ◆ **mongrel** s. 1. bastardo 2. incrocio.
monism s. monismo.
monition s. 1. ammonizione 2. (giur.) citazione.
monitor s. 1. consigliere 2. capoclasse 3. dispositivo di controllo.
monitory agg. ammonitore.
monk s. monaco.
monkey s. scimmia.
monkeyish agg. scimmiesco.
monkhood s. monacato.
monkish agg. monastico, manacale.
monochromatic agg. monocromatico.
monochrome s. monocromia.
monocle s. monocolo.
monody s. monodia.
monogamist s. monogamo.
monogamy s. monogamia.
monogram s. monogramma.
monograph s. monografia.
monographic(al) agg. monografico.
monolith s. monolito.
monolithic agg. monolitico.
monologue s. monologo.
monometallic agg. monometallico.
monomial s. monomio.
monomolecular agg. monomolecolare.
monoplane s. monoplano.
monopolist s. monopolista.
to **monopolize** vt. monopolizzare.
monopoly s. monopolio.
monorail s. monorotaia.
monosyllabic agg. monosillabico.
monosyllable s. monosillabo.
monotheism s. monoteismo.
monotheist s. monoteista.
monotheistic(al) agg. monoteistico.
monotone s. tono uniforme.
monotonous agg. monotono.
monotony s. 1. tono uniforme 2. monotonia.
monotype s. monotipo.
monsoon s. monsone.
monster agg. colossale. ◆ **monster** s. mostro.
monstrance s. ostensorio.
monstrosity s. mostruosità.
monstrous agg. mostruoso.
montage s. montaggio.
month s. mese.
monthly agg. e s. mensile. ◆ **monthly** avv. mensilmente.
monument s. monumento.
monumental agg. monumentale.

mood s. **1.** umore **2.** (*gramm.*) modo. ♦ **moods** s. *pl.* capricci.
moodily *avv.* di malumore.
moodiness s. malumore.
moody *agg.* di malumore.
moon s. luna.
to **moon** *vi.* **1.** gingillarsi **2.** allunare || *to — about*, bighellonare.
mooncalf s. (*pl.* -lves) idiota.
mooning s. vagabondaggio.
moonlight s. chiaro di luna.
moonlit *agg.* illuminato dalla luna.
moonshine s. V. *moonlight*.
moonshiny *agg.* V. *moonlit*.
moony *agg.* **1.** lunare **2.** distratto.
Moor s. moro.
moor s. brughiera.
to **moor** *vt.* e *vi.* ormeggiare.
moorage s. ormeggio. ♦ **moorings** s. *pl.* **1.** gomena (*sing.*) **2.** ormeggi.
mop[1] s. **1.** scopa **2.** zazzera.
mop[2] s. smorfia.
to **mop**[1] *vt.* **1.** pulire **2.** asciugare || *to — up* (*mil.*), rastrellare.
to **mop**[2] *vi.* fare smorfie.
mope s. **1.** persona avvilita **2.** tristezza.
to **mope** *vt.* avvilire. ♦ to **mope** *vi.* avvilirsi.
mopish *agg.* avvilito.
moraine s. morena.
moral *agg.* morale. ♦ **moral** s. **1.** morale **2.** principio morale. ♦ **morals** s. *pl.* costumi.
morale s. il morale.
moralism s. moralismo.
moralist s. moralista.
moralistic *agg.* moralistico.
morality s. moralità.
moralization s. moralizzazione.
to **moralize** *vt.* moralizzare. ♦ to **moralize** *vi.* trarre la morale.
morass s. palude.
moratory *agg.* moratorio.
moratorium s. (*pl.* -ria) moratoria.
moray s. murena.
morbid *agg.* **1.** morboso **2.** patologico.
morbidity s. **1.** morbosità **2.** stato patologico.
mordacity, mordancy s. mordacità.
mordant *agg.* e s. mordente.
more (*comp. di* much, many) *agg.*, *pron.* e *avv.* più, di più, maggiormente || *— and —*, sempre più; *once —*, ancora una volta.
moreover *avv.* inoltre.

morganatic *agg.* morganatico.
morgue s. obitorio.
Mormon *agg.* e s. mormone.
morning s. mattino.
Moroccan *agg.* e s. marocchino.
moron s. deficiente.
morose *agg.* tetro.
morphia, morphine s. morfina.
morphinomaniac *agg.* e s. morfinomane.
morphologic(al) *agg.* morfologico.
morphology s. morfologia.
morsel s. boccone.
mortal *agg.* e s. mortale.
mortality s. mortalità.
mortally *avv.* mortalmente.
mortar[1] s. mortaio.
mortar[2] s. calcina.
mortgage s. ipoteca.
to **mortgage** *vt.* ipotecare.
mortagagee s. creditore ipotecario.
mortgager s. debitore ipotecario.
mortification s. mortificazione.
to **mortify** *vt.* **1.** mortificare **2.** incancrenire. ♦ to **mortify** *vi.* **1.** mortificarsi **2.** incancrenirsi.
mortuary *agg.* mortuario. ♦ **mortuary** s. camera mortuaria.
mosaic *agg.* musivo. ♦ **mosaic** s. mosaico.
Moslem *agg.* e s. mussulmano.
mosque s. moschea.
mosquito s. zanzara || *— -net*, zanzariera.
moss s. **1.** acquitrino **2.** muschio.
mossy *agg.* muscoso.
most *agg.* e *pron.* (*superl. di* much, many) il più, la maggior parte di, il massimo. ♦ **most** *avv.* **1.** il più **2.** molto **3.** maggiormente.
mostly *avv.* per lo più.
mote s. particella.
moth s. **1.** falena **2.** tignola.
mother s. madre || *— -country*, madrepatria; *— -in-law*, suocera.
motherhood s. maternità.
motherless *agg.* senza madre.
motherly *agg.* materno.
mothproof *agg.* inattaccabile dalle tarme.
motif s. motivo.
motion s. **1.** moto, movimento **2.** mozione || *— -picture*, film.
motionless *agg.* immobile.
to **motivate** *vt.* **1.** motivare **2.** stimolare.
motivation s. **1.** motivazione **2.** stimolo.
motive *agg.* motore. ♦ **motive** s.

motivo, movente.

motley *agg.* **1.** screziato **2.** eterogeneo. ♦ **motley** *s.* miscuglio.

motor *agg.* e *s.* motore || — *-cycle*, motocicletta; — *-car*, automobile, — *-boat*, motobarca; — *ship*, motonave.

to **motor** *vi.* andare in automobile.

motoring *s.* automobilismo.

motorist *s.* automobilista.

motorization *s.* motorizzazione.

to **motorize** *vt.* motorizzare.

mottle *s.* chiazza.

to **mottle** *vt.* chiazzare.

moufflon *s.* muflone.

mould[1] *s.* stampo.

mould[2] *s.* muffa.

mould[3] *s.* terriccio.

to **mould**[1] *vt.* modellare.

to **mould**[2] *vi.* ammuffire.

moulding *s.* **1.** il modellare **2.** cornice **3.** fusione.

mouldy *agg.* ammuffito.

mound *s.* monticello.

mount[1] *s.* monte, montagna.

mount[2] **1.** cavalcatura **2.** intelaiatura **3.** affusto di cannone **4.** montatura.

to **mount** *vt.* salire. ♦ to **mount** *vi.* **1.** montare **2.** ammontare.

mountain *s.* montagna.

mountaineer *s.* **1.** montanaro **2.** alpinista.

mountaineering *s.* alpinismo.

mountainous *agg.* montuoso.

mountebank *s.* ciarlatano.

mounter *s.* montatore.

to **mourn** *vt.* e *vi.* piangere.

mourner *s.* chi è in lutto.

mournful *agg.* lugubre.

mourning *s.* **1.** dolore **2.** lutto: *to go into* —, mettere il lutto.

mouse *s.* (*pl.* mice) topo.

moustache *s.* baffi (*pl.*).

mouth *s.* bocca.

to **mouth** *vt.* declamare. ♦ to **mouth** *vi.* fare smorfie.

mouthful *s.* boccone.

mouthpiece *s.* **1.** bocchino **2.** portavoce.

movable *agg.* mobile.

movables *s. pl.* beni mobili.

move *s.* **1.** movimento **2.** mossa **3.** trasloco.

to **move** *vt.* **1.** muovere **2.** commuovere. ♦ to **move** *vi.* **1.** muoversi

movement *s.* **1.** movimento, moto. **2.** traslocare **3.** commuoversi.

mover *s.* promotore.

movie *s.* film. ♦ **movies** *s. pl.* cinema (*sing.*).

moving *s.* **1.** spostamento **2.** trasloco.

mow *s.* covone.

to **mow (mowed, mown)** *vt.* falciare.

mower *s.* falciatore.

mowing *s.* falciatura.

mown V. *to mow.*

much (more, most) *agg.*, *s.* e *avv.* molto || *so* —, tanto; *too* —, troppo; *as* — *as*, tanto quanto; *how* —*?*, quanto?

muck *s.* letame.

mucous *agg.* mucoso.

mucus *s.* muco.

mud *s.* fango || — *-guard*, parafango.

to **mud** *vt.* infangare.

muddle *s.* confusione, pasticcio.

to **muddle** *vt.* confondere.

muddleheaded *agg.* confusionario.

muddler *s.* confusionario.

muddy *agg.* **1.** fangoso **2.** torbido **3.** infangato.

to **muddy** *vt.* infangare.

muff[1] *s.* manicotto.

muff[2] *s.* **1.** colpo mancato **2.** babbeo.

to **muffle** *vt.* **1.** avvolgere **2.** smorzare.

muffler *s.* **1.** sciarpa **2.** guantone **3.** silenziatore.

mug *s.* (*fam.*) faccia || — *shot* (*tv*), primo piano.

mulberry *s.* mora || — (*-tree*) gelso.

mule *s.* mulo.

mulish *agg.* (*fig.*) testardo.

muller *s.* pestello.

multiform *agg.* multiforme.

multimillionaire *s.* multimilionario.

multiple *agg.* e *s.* multiplo.

multiplicable *agg.* moltiplicabile.

multiplicand *s.* moltiplicando.

multiplication *s.* moltiplicazione.

multiplicity *s.* molteplicità.

multiplier *s.* moltiplicatore.

to **multiply** *vt.* moltiplicare. ♦ to **multiply** *vi.* moltiplicarsi.

multitude *s.* moltitudine.

multitudinous *agg.* **1.** innumerevole **2.** vasto.

mumble *s.* borbottio.

to **mumble** *vt.* e *vi.* borbottare.

mumbling *s.* V. *mumble.*

mummer *s.* guitto.

mummification s. mummificazione.
to **mummify** vt. mummificare.
mummy[1] s. mummia.
mummy[2] s. mammina.
mumps s. pl. orecchioni.
to **munch** vt. e vi. biascicare.
municipal agg. municipale.
municipality s. municipalità.
municipalization s. municipalizzazione.
to **municipalize** vt. municipalizzare.
munificence s. munificenza.
munificent agg. munifico.
munitions s. pl. munizioni.
mural agg. murale. ♦ **mural** s. affresco.
murder s. assassinio.
to **murder** vt. assassinare.
murderer s. assassino.
murderous agg. omicida.
muriatic agg. muriatico.
murky agg. tenebroso.
murmur s. 1. mormorio 2. brontolio.
to **murmur** vt. mormorare. ♦ to **murmur** vi. brontolare.
murmuring s. V. *murmur*.
muscat(el) s. moscato.
muscle s. muscolo.
muscled agg. muscoloso.
muscular agg. 1. muscolare 2. muscoloso.
musculature s. muscolatura.
Muse s. musa.
to **muse** vi. meditare.
museum s. museo.
mushroom s. fungo.
mushy agg. infrollito.
music s. musica.
musical agg. 1. musicale 2. appassionato di musica.
musicality s. musicalità.
musician s. musicista || *street —,* suonatore ambulante.
musicologist s. musicologo.
musicology s. musicologia.
musing agg. meditabondo. ♦ **musing** s. meditazione.
musk s. muschio.
musket s. moschetto.
musketeer s. moschettiere.
musky agg. muschiato.
Muslim agg. e s. mussulmano.
muslin s. mussola.
muss s. stato di confusione.
mussel s. mitilo.
must[1] s. mosto.
must[2] s. muffa.

must v. dif. (*pres. ind.*) dovere || *he — return here,* deve ritornare qui, *it — be true,* deve essere vero; *you — know him!,* non puoi non conoscerlo!
mustard s. senape.
muster s. adunata.
to **muster** vt. adunare. ♦ to **muster** vi. adunarsi.
mutability s. mutabilità.
mutable agg. mutevole.
mutation s. cambiamento.
mute agg. muto. ♦ **mute** s. 1. muto 2. sordina.
to **mutilate** vt. mutilare.
mutilation s. mutilazione.
mutineer s. ammutinato.
mutinous agg. ammutinato, ribelle.
mutiny s. ammutinamento.
to **mutiny** vi. ammutinarsi.
mutism s. mutismo.
to **mutter** V. *to murmur*.
mutton s. montone.
mutual agg. 1. reciproco 2. comune.
muzzle s. 1. muso 2. museruola 3. bocca (*di arma*).
to **muzzle** vt. mettere la museruola a.
my agg. poss. mio, mia, miei, mie,
mycosis s. (*pl.* -ses) micosi.
myocardial agg. miocardico.
myocarditis s. miocardite.
myocardium s. miocardio.
myopia s. miopia.
myopic agg. miope.
myosote s. miosotide.
myriad s. miriade.
myriagram s. miriagrammo.
myriametre s. miriametro.
Myriapoda s. pl. miriapodi.
myrrh s. mirra.
myrtle s. mirto.
myself pron. r. io stesso, me stesso, mi.
mysterious agg. misterioso.
mystery s. mistero.
mystic agg. e s. mistico.
mystical agg. mistico.
mysticism s. misticismo.
mystification s. mistificazione.
mystifier s. mistificatore.
to **mystify** vt. 1. disorientare 2. avvolgere nel mistero.
myth s. mito.
mythic(al) agg. mitico.
to **mythicize** vt. volgere in mito.
mythologic(al) agg. mitologico.
to **mythologize** vi. studiare i miti.
mythology s. mitologia.

mythomania s. mitomania.
mythomaniac agg. e s. mitomane.

N

nabob s. nababbo.
nacre s. madreperla.
to **nag** vt. e vi. brontolare.
naiad s. naiade.
nail s. **1.** unghia, artiglio **2.** chiodo.
to **nail** vt. **1.** inchiodare **2.** munire di chiodi.
nailer s. fabbricante di chiodi.
naïve agg. ingenuo, semplice.
naiveté s. ingenuità.
naked agg. **1.** nudo, spogliato **2.** spoglio, indifeso.
nakedness s. nudità.
name s. **1.** nome **2.** fama, reputazione || — -day, onomastico; full —, generalità.
to **name** vt. **1.** nominare, dare un nome **2.** designare.
nameless agg. **1.** senza nome **2.** innominabile.
namely avv. cioè.
nanny s. bambinaia, balia.
nap[1] s. siesta, sonnellino.
nap[2] s. pelo (di stoffe).
to **nap** vi. schiacciare un sonnellino, sonnecchiare.
nape s. nuca.
naphtha s. nafta.
napkin s. **1.** tovagliolo: — -ring, anello per tovagliolo **2.** pannolino.
narcissism s. narcisismo.
narcosis, narcotism s. narcosi.
narcotic agg. s. narcotico.
narcotization s. narcotizzazione.
to **narcotize** vt. narcotizzare.
to **narrate** vt. narrare.
narration s. narrazione, racconto.
narrative agg. narrativo. ♦ **narrative** s. resoconto, narrazione.
narrator s. narratore.
narrow agg. **1.** stretto, angusto, ristretto (anche fig.) **2.** esatto, minuzioso || — -minded, di idee ristrette. ♦ **narrow** s. stretto, strettoia.
to **narrow** vt. stringere, ridurre. ♦ to **narrow** vi. stringersi, contrarsi.
narrowness s. strettezza, limitatezza.
narwhal s. narvalo.
nasal agg. nasale. ♦ **nasal** s. **1.**

suono nasale **2.** osso nasale.
nascent agg. nascente.
nastily avv. **1.** sgradevolmente **2.** con cattiveria.
nastiness s. **1.** cattivo gusto **2.** cattiveria.
nasty agg. **1.** sporco, sgradevole **2.** cattivo, tempestoso (di tempo).
natal agg. natale.
natality s. natalità.
natant agg. natante.
natation s. nuoto.
natatorial agg. natatorio.
nation s. nazione.
national agg. nazionale.
nationalism s. nazionalismo.
nationalist s. nazionalista.
nationality s. **1.** nazionalità **2.** patriottismo.
nationalization s. **1.** nazionalizzazione **2.** naturalizzazione.
to **nationalize** vt. **1.** nazionalizzare **2.** naturalizzare.
native agg. **1.** innato **2.** natio, indigeno. ♦ **native** s. indigeno, nativo.
nativity s. nascita, natività.
natural agg. **1.** naturale, fisico **2.** spontaneo **3.** istintivo, innato.
naturalism s. naturalismo.
naturalist s. naturalista.
naturalistic agg. naturalistico.
naturalization s. **1.** naturalizzazione **2.** acclimatamento.
to **naturalize** vi. **1.** naturalizzare **2.** acclimatare.
nature s. **1.** natura **2.** carattere, temperamento || good —, bontà.
natured agg. di natura, per natura || good —, buono, di buon carattere.
naturism s. naturismo, nudismo.
naturist s. naturista.
naughtily avv. con cattiveria.
naughtiness s. cattiveria.
naughty agg. cattivo, impertinente.
to **nauseate** vt. nauseare, disgustare. ♦ to **nauseate** vi. avere la nausea, disgustarsi.
nauseating agg. nauseabondo.
nautical agg. nautico.
naval agg. navale.
nave[1] s. mozzo di ruota.
nave[2] s. navata centrale (di chiesa).
navel s. **1.** ombelico **2.** (fig.) centro.
navigability s. navigabilità.
navigable agg. navigabile.
to **navigate** vt. e vi. **1.** navigare **2.** regolare la rotta.

navigation *s.* **1.** navigazione **2.** rotta.

navigator *s.* navigatore, ufficiale di rotta.

navvy *s.* sterratore.

navy *s.* marina da guerra, flotta.

nay *avv.* anzi, non solo.

Nazi *agg.* e *s.* nazista.

Neapolitan *agg.* e *s.* napoletano.

near *agg.* **1.** vicino, prossimo **2.** affine, intimo **3.** fedele, esatto. ♦ **near** *prep.* vicino a, presso a. ♦ **near** *avv.* vicino, presso, accanto.

to **near** *vt.* e *vi.* avvicinarsi (a).

nearby *agg. avv. prep.* assai vicino.

nearly *avv.* quasi.

neat *agg.* **1.** pulito, lindo **2.** grazioso, di buon gusto **3.** chiaro, conciso.

neatly *avv.* **1.** lindamente, ordinatamente **2.** con semplicità, con buon gusto **3.** concisamente.

neatness *s.* **1.** pulizia, ordine **2.** grazia, armonia **3.** semplicità **4.** concisione.

nebula *s.* nebulosa.

nebular *agg.* nebulare.

nebulosity *s.* nebulosità.

nebulous *agg.* nebuloso, vago.

necessary *agg.* necessario.

to **necessitate** *vt.* **1.** rendere necessario **2.** obbligare.

necessity *s.* necessità.

neck *s.* collo || *stiff* —, torcicollo.

neckerchief *s.* fazzoletto da collo.

necklace *s.* collana, vezzo.

neckline *s.* scollatura.

necktie *s.* cravatta.

necrology *s.* necrologia.

necromancer *s.* negromante.

necromancy *s.* negromanzia.

necropolis *s.* necropoli.

necrosis *s.* (*pl.* -ses) necrosi.

nectar *s.* nettare.

need *s.* necessità, bisogno.

to **need** *vt.* e *vi.* essere necessario, occorrere, abbisognare, mancare di.

needful *agg.* necessario, indispensabile.

neediness *s.* bisogno, povertà.

needle *s.* **1.** ago **2.** puntina di grammofono.

to **needle** *vt.* **1.** cucire, pungere (*con un ago*) **2.** irritare.

needleful *s.* gugliata.

needless *agg.* inutile, superfluo.

needlewoman *s.* cucitrice.

needlework *s.* lavoro ad ago.

needs *avv.* necessariamente.

needy *agg.* povero, indigente.

ne'er *avv.* (*contrazione di* never) mai.

negation *s.* diniego.

negative *agg.* negativo. ♦ **negative** *s.* **1.** negazione **2.** qualità negativa.

neglect *s.* negligenza, trascuratezza.

to **neglect** *vt.* trascurare.

neglectful *agg.* negligente, noncurante.

negligence *s.* negligenza, trascuratezza.

negligent *agg.* negligente, trascurato.

negligible *agg.* trascurabile.

negotiable *agg.* negoziabile.

to **negotiate** *vt.* e *vi.* negoziare, trattare.

negotiation *s.* trattativa.

negress *s.* negra.

negro *agg.* e *s.* negro.

negroid *agg.* negroide.

neigh *s.* nitrito.

to **neigh** *vi.* nitrire.

neighbour *s.* vicino.

to **neighbour** *vi.* essere vicini di casa.

neighbourhood *s.* **1.** i vicini, vicinato **2.** paraggi, dintorni (*pl.*).

neighbouring *agg.* vicino, contiguo.

neither[1] *agg.* né l'uno né l'altro.

neither[2] *avv.* né, neppure, nemmeno: — ... *nor*, né ... né.

nemesis *s.* (*pl.* -ses) nemesi.

neo-classic(al) *agg.* neoclassico.

neo-classicism *s.* neoclassicismo.

neo-criticism *s.* neocriticismo.

neolithic *agg.* neolitico.

neologism *s.* neologismo.

neology *s.* neologia.

neon *s.* neon.

neophyte *s.* neofito.

neoplatonic *agg.* neoplatonico.

Neoplatonism *s.* neoplatonismo.

neopositivism *s.* neopositivismo.

neorealism *s.* neorealismo.

neorealist *s.* neorealista.

nephew *s.* nipote (*di zio*).

nephritic *agg.* nefritico.

nephritis *s.* nefrite.

nepotism *s.* nepotismo.

nerve *s.* **1.** nervo **2.** nervatura **3.** forza, energia, sangue freddo.

to **nerve** *vt.* tonificare, rinvigorire.

nerveless *agg.* snervato, inerte.

nervous *agg.* **1.** nervoso **2.** forte, vigoroso **3.** timido, apprensivo.

nervously *avv.* **1.** nervosamente **2.**

timidamente.

nervousness s. **1.** nervosismo, irritazione **2.** timidezza.

nervy agg. **1.** muscoloso, forte **2.** nervoso.

nescient agg. ignorante.

nest s. **1.** nido **2.** (fig.) covo, tana **3.** colonia (di vccelli, insetti ecc.).

to nest vi. fare il nido, nidificare.

to nestle vt. ospitare. ◆ **to nestle** vi. annidarsi, rifugiarsi.

nestling s. uccellino di nido.

net¹ agg. e s. netto.

net² s. **1.** rete **2.** (fig.) trappola.

to net vt. **1.** coprire con reti **2.** pescare con reti.

netful s. retata.

netting s. rete, reticolato.

nettle s. ortica || — rash, orticaria.

to nettle vt. pungere (di ortica).

network s. rete, reticolato.

neuralgia s. nevralgia.

neuralgic agg. nevralgico.

neurasthenia s. nevrastenia.

neurasthenic agg. nevrastenico.

neuritis s. nevrite.

neurologist s. neurologo.

neurology s. neurologia.

neuropathic agg. neuropatico.

neuropathology s. neuropatologia.

neurosis s. (pl. -ses) nevrosi.

neurotic s. neuropatico.

neuter s. parola neutra, neutro.

neutral agg. neutrale.

neutralism s. neutralismo.

neutralist s. neutralista.

neutrality s. neutralità.

neutralization s. neutralizzazione.

to neutralize vt. neutralizzare.

neutron s. neutrone.

never avv. mai, giammai || — again, mai più; — mind, non importa; now or —, ora o mai più; — -ending, eterno.

nevermore avv. mai più.

nevertheless avv. nonostante, ciò nondimeno.

new agg. nuovo, recente || — -born, neonato; — -comer, nuovo venuto; — -made, appena fatto.

newish agg. piuttosto nuovo.

newly avv. recentemente.

news s. notizia, notizie || — -man, strillone (di giornali); — -reel, cinegiornale.

newsmonger s. persona pettegola e curiosa.

newspaper s. giornale, quotidiano.

New Zealander s. neozelandese.

next agg. **1.** prossimo, vicino, il più vicino **2.** futuro, venturo **3.** primo, contiguo. ◆ **next** avv. dopo, in seguito, poi. ◆ **next** prep. presso, accanto.

nib s. pennino.

nibble s. morso.

to nibble vt. **1.** mordicchiare, sgranocchiare **2.** abboccare.

nibbler s. roditore.

nice agg. **1.** piacevole, bello, simpatico **2.** buono, gustoso **3.** accurato, minuzioso.

nicely avv. **1.** amabilmente, piacevolmente **2.** esattamente.

nicety s. **1.** finezza, precisione. ◆ **niceties** s. pl. minuzie.

niche s. nicchia.

nick s. tacca, intaccatura || in the — of time, al momento giusto.

to nick vt. **1.** intaccare **2.** colpire, afferrare al momento opportuno.

nickel s. nichel.

to nickel vt. nichelare.

nickname s. soprannome, nomignolo.

to nickname vt. soprannominare.

nicotine s. nicotina.

niece s. nipote (femmina) (di zio).

niggard agg. spilorcio.

niggardliness s. spilorceria.

niggardly agg. avaro, spilorcio.

nigger s. (spreg.) negro.

night s. **1.** notte, sera **2.** buio, oscurità || by —, di notte, good —, buona notte; — -bird, uccello notturno, nottambulo; — -dress, camicia da notte; — -shift, turno di notte.

nightcap s. berretto da notte.

nightfall s. tramonto.

nightingale s. usignolo.

nightly agg. notturno. ◆ **nightly** avv. di notte.

nightmare s. incubo.

nightpiece s. « notturno » (dipinto che rappresenta una scena notturna).

nihilism s. nichilismo.

nihilist s. nichilista.

nimble agg. **1.** agile, leggero **2.** acuto, sveglio.

nimbleness s. **1.** agilità **2.** prontezza, acutezza.

nimbly avv. **1.** agilmente, leggermente **2.** prontamente.

nine agg. nove.

ninepins s. pl. birilli.

nineteen agg. diciannove.

nineteenth *agg.* e *s.* diciannovesimo.
ninetieth *agg.* novantesimo.
ninety *agg.* novanta.
ninth *agg.* nono.
nip *s.* **1.** pizzicotto, morso **2.** stretta, presa **3.** morso (*di freddo, gelo ecc.*).
to nip *vt.* **1.** pizzicare, mordere (*anche di freddo ecc.*) **2.** stroncare.
nipple *s.* capezzolo.
nitrate *s.* nitrato.
nitric *agg.* nitrico.
nitrite *s.* (*chim.*) nitrito.
nitroglycerin(e) *s.* nitroglicerina.
no *agg.* nessuno. ◆ **no** *avv.* **1.** no **2.** in nessun modo.
nobiliary *agg.* nobiliare.
nobility *s.* nobiltà (*anche fig.*).
noble *agg.* **1.** nobile (*anche fig.*) **2.** superbo, grandioso. ◆ **noble** *s.* nobile.
nobleman *s.* nobiluomo.
nobleness *s.* nobiltà (*anche fig.*).
noblewoman *s.* nobildonna.
nobly *avv.* nobilmente.
nobody *pron. indef.* nessuno.
nocturnal *agg.* notturno.
nocturne *s.* (*pitt.; mus.*) notturno.
nod *s.* **1.** cenno del capo **2.** ordine, comando.
to nod *vt.* e *vi.* **1.** annuire col capo **2.** assopirsi, chinare il capo dal sonno **3.** inclinarsi (*di edifici ecc.*).
nodding *agg.* chinato, inclinato. ◆ **nodding** *s.* cenno del capo.
nodose *agg.* nodoso.
nodosity *s.* nodosità.
nodular *agg.* a forma di nodo.
nodule *s.* nodulo.
noise *s.* rumore, fragore, chiasso.
noiseless *agg.* senza rumore, silenzioso.
noisily *avv.* rumorosamente.
noisy *agg.* **1.** rumoroso, turbolento **2.** (*fig.*) vistoso, chiassoso.
nomad *agg.* e *s.* nomade.
nomadism *s.* nomadismo.
nomenclature *s.* nomenclatura.
nominal *agg.* nominale.
nominalism *s.* nominalismo.
nominalist *s.* nominalista.
nominalistic *agg.* nominalistico.
nominative *agg.* e *s.* nominativo.
nominator *s.* nominatore.
nonagenarian *agg.* e *s.* nonagenario.
non-aligned *agg.* non allineato.
non-alignment *s.* non allineamento.

non-appearance *s.* contumacia.
non-attendance *s.* assenza.
non-commital *agg.* evasivo.
non-conducting *agg.* isolante, non conduttore.
non-conductor *s.* isolante.
nonconformist *agg.* e *s.* anticonformista.
nonconformity *s.* anticonformismo.
non-delivery *s.* mancata consegna.
none *pron. sing.* e *pl.* nessuno, non uno. ◆ **none** *avv.* affatto, niente affatto.
nonentity *s.* **1.** cosa o persona insignificante **2.** inesistenza.
non-existence *s.* inesistenza.
non-resistance *s.* resistenza passiva.
nonsense *s.* assurdità, sciocchezza.
nonsensical *agg.* assurdo, sciocco.
non-stop *agg.* continuo, senza fermate. ◆ **non-stop** *avv.* di continuo, senza fermate.
non-transferable *agg.* non trasferibile.
noodle *agg.* sciocco, gonzo.
nook *s.* **1.** cantuccio, angolo **2.** ripostiglio.
noon *s.* mezzogiorno.
noose *s.* **1.** nodo scorsoio **2.** tranello.
nor *cong.* né, neppure || *neither I — he,* né io né lui.
normal *agg.* **1.** normale, regolare **2.** perpendicolare.
normality *s.* normalità.
normalization *s.* normalizzazione.
to normalize *vt.* normalizzare.
Norman *agg.* e *s.* normanno.
normative *agg.* normativo.
north *s.* nord, settentrione || *— wind,* vento di tramontana.
north-east *s.* nord-est.
northerly *agg.* del nord, settentrionale. ◆ **northerly** *avv.* verso il nord.
northern *agg.* nordico, settentrionale.
northerner *s.* abitante del nord.
northward(s) *agg.* e *avv.* verso nord.
Norwegian *agg.* e *s.* norvegese.
nose *s.* **1.** naso **2.** muso (*di animali*) **3.** prua (*mar.*).
to nose *vt.* e *vi.* **1.** fiutare **2.** indagare **3.** ficcare il naso.
nostril *s.* narice.
not *avv.* non || *— at all,* niente affatto.

notability *s.* notabilità.

notable *agg.* degno di nota, notevole.

notarial *agg.* notarile.

notary *s.* notaio.

notation *s.* 1. (*mus.*) notazione 2. (*mat.*) numerazione.

notch *s.* tacca, dentellatura.

to notch *vt.* 1. intaccare 2. intagliare.

note *s.* 1. (*mus.*) nota, tono 2. marchio, segno 3. nota, appunto, commento 4. (*comm.*) cedola, acconto 5. banconota.

to note *vt.* notare.

notebook *s.* taccuino.

notehead *s.* intestazione.

noteless *agg.* privo di interesse.

noteworthiness *s.* importanza.

noteworthy *agg.* notevole.

nothing *pron. indef.* nulla, niente, nessuna cosa.

nothingness *s.* 1. il nulla 2. nullità.

notice *s.* 1. avviso, avvertimento 2. (*giur.*) intimazione 3. licenziamento 4. attenzione, cura 5. recensione || — *-board*, cartello pubblicitario, tabella.

to notice *vt.* 1. osservare, fare attenzione a 2. recensire.

noticeable *agg.* notevole.

notifiable *agg.* da denunciarsi.

notification *s.* notifica.

to notify *vt.* notificare; far sapere.

notion *s.* 1. nozione 2. idea, teoria.

notional *agg.* 1. immaginario 2. speculativo.

notoriety *s.* notorietà.

notorious *agg.* 1. noto, conosciuto 2. famigerato.

notoriously *avv.* notoriamente.

notwithstanding *prep.* nonostante, malgrado.

nougat *s.* torrone.

nought *s.* 1. nulla 2. (*mat.*) zero.

noumenon *s.* (*pl.* -ena) noumeno.

noun *s.* (*gramm.*) nome, sostantivo.

to nourish *vt.* nutrire (*anche fig.*).

nourishing *agg.* nutriente.

nourishment *s.* nutrimento.

novel *s.* romanzo.

novelist *s.* romanziere.

to novelize *vt.* romanzare.

novelty *s.* novità.

November *s.* novembre.

novice *s.* 1. (*eccl.*) novizio 2. apprendista.

novitiate *s.* noviziato.

now *avv.* 1. ora, adesso, subito, al presente 2. allora 3. a dire il vero. ♦ **now** *cong.* ora che. ♦ **now** *s.* ora, il presente.

nowadays *avv.* al giorno d'oggi.

nowhere *avv.* in nessun luogo.

noxious *agg.* nocivo, dannoso.

nozzle *s.* becco, beccuccio (*di teiera, pompa ecc.*).

nuclear *agg.* nucleare.

nuclein *s.* nucleina.

nucleonics *s. pl.* fisica nucleare.

nucleus *s.* (*pl.* -ei) 1. nucleo 2. nocciolo, centro.

nude *agg.* 1. nudo 2. (*fig.*) semplice. ♦ **nude** *s.* (*pitt.; scult.*) nudo.

nudism *s.* nudismo.

nudist *agg.* e *s.* nudista.

nugget *s.* pepita.

nuisance *s.* 1. noia, seccatura 2. danno.

null *agg.* nullo.

nullification *s.* annullamento.

to nullify *vt.* annullare.

nullity *s.* 1. nullità 2. il non essere valido.

numb *agg.* 1. intorpidito, intirizzito 2. tramortito, intontito.

to numb *vt.* 1. intorpidire, intirizzire 2. (*fig.*) istupidire.

number *s.* 1. numero, cifra 2. numero, quantità 3. numero di giornale.

to number *vt.* 1. contare, numerare 2. annoverare 3. ammontare.

numberless *agg.* innumerevole.

numbness *s.* torpore (*anche fig.*).

numerable *agg.* numerabile, calcolabile.

numeral *agg.* e *s.* numerale.

numerator *s.* numeratore.

numerical *agg.* numerico.

numerically *avv.* numericamente.

numerous *agg.* numeroso.

numismatic *agg.* numismatico.

numismatics *s.* numismatica.

numismatist *s.* numismatico.

numismatology *s.* numismatica.

nun *s.* 1. monaca, suora 2. piccione dal cappuccio.

nuncio *s.* (*eccl.*) nunzio.

nunnery *s.* convento (*di suore*).

nuptial *agg.* nuziale.

nuptials *s. pl.* nozze, sponsali.

nurse *s.* 1. nutrice, balia 2. infermiera.

to nurse *vt.* 1. allattare, nutrire 2. allevare 3. curare (*ammalati*).

nursling *s.* lattante.

nursery s. **1.** camera dei bambini **2.** scuola materna **3.** vivaio || — *rhyme,* filastrocca per bambini.
nursing agg. **1.** che allatta, nutre **2.** che cura || — *home,* casa di cura. ♦ **nursing** s. **1.** allattamento **2.** il curare **3.** professione di infermiera.
nurture s. vitto, nutrimento.
to **nurture** vt. nutrire, allevare.
nut s. **1.** noce **2.** (*mecc.*) dado.
nutcracker s. schiaccianoci.
nutmeg s. noce moscata.
nutrition s. nutrizione.
nutritive agg. nutritivo.
nutshell s. guscio di noce.
nylon s. nailon.
nymph s. ninfa.

O

oak s. quercia.
oakum s. stoppa.
oar s. remo || — *-blade,* pala di remo.
to **oar** vi. remare.
oarsman s. rematore.
oasis s. (*pl.* -ses) oasi.
oats s. *pl.* avena (*sing.*).
oath s. **1.** giuramento **2.** bestemmia.
obduracy s. **1.** inesorabilità **2.** ostinazione.
obdurate agg. **1.** inesorabile **2.** ostinato.
obedience s. ubbidienza.
obedient agg. ubbidiente.
obeisance s. riverenza.
obelisk s. obelisco.
obese agg. obeso.
obesity s. obesità.
to **obey** vt. e vi. ubbidire.
to **obfuscate** vt. **1.** offuscare **2.** confondere.
obituary s. necrologio.
object s. oggetto.
to **object** vt. e vi. obiettare.
objectification s. oggettivazione.
to **objectify** vt. oggettivare.
objection s. **1.** obiezione **2.** avversione.
objectionable agg. **1.** biasimevole **2.** sgradevole.
objective agg. oggettivo. ♦ **objective** s. obiettivo.
objectiveness s. oggettività.

objectivism s. oggettivismo.
objectivity s. oggettività.
objector s. oppositore || *conscientious* —, obiettore di coscienza.
obligation s. obbligo.
obligatoriness s. obbligatorietà.
obligatory agg. obbligatorio.
to **oblige** vt. **1.** obbligare **2.** fare un favore a.
obliging agg. cortese.
oblique agg. obliquo.
obliqueness, obliquity s. obliquità.
to **obliterate** vt. cancellare.
obliteration s. cancellatura.
oblivion s. oblio || *Act of* —, amnistia.
oblivious agg. dimentico.
oblong agg. **1.** oblungo **2.** rettangolare. ♦ **oblong** s. (*geom.*) rettangolo.
obnoxious agg. odioso.
obscene agg. osceno.
obscenity s. oscenità.
obscurantism s. oscurantismo.
obscurantist agg. e s. oscurantista.
obscuration s. oscuramento.
obscure agg. oscuro. ♦ **obscure** s. oscurità.
to **obscure** vt. oscurare.
obscurity s. oscurità.
obsecration s. supplica.
obsequies s. *pl.* esequie.
obsequious agg. ossequioso.
observable agg. **1.** visibile **2.** notevole.
observance s. **1.** osservanza **2.** (*relig.*) regola.
observant agg. osservante.
observation s. osservazione.
observatory s. osservatorio.
to **observe** vt. e vi. osservare.
observer s. osservatore.
observing agg. attento.
to **obsess** vt. ossessionare.
obsession s. ossessione.
obsessive agg. ossessivo.
obsolescence s. disuso.
obsolescent agg. che sta cadendo in disuso.
obsolete agg. **1.** antiquato **2.** scaduto (*di prezzi*).
obstacle s. ostacolo.
obstetric(al) agg. ostetrico.
obstetrician s. ostetrico.
obstetrics s. ostetricia.
obstinacy s. ostinazione.
obstinate agg. ostinato.
to **obstruct** vt. **1.** ostruire **2.** ri-

tardare **3.** intasare.
obstruction s. ostruzione, ostacolo.
obstructionism s. ostruzionismo.
obstructionist s. ostruzionista.
to **obtain** vt. ottenere. ♦ to **obtain** vi. prevalere.
obtainable agg. ottenibile.
to **obtrude** vt. imporre. ♦ to **obtrude** vi. **1.** imporsi **2.** intromettersi.
obtruder s. **1.** intruso **2.** importuno.
obtrusion s. intrusione.
obtrusive agg. **1.** intruso **2.** importuno.
obtrusiveness s. **1.** intrusione **2.** invadenza.
to **obtund** vt. ottundere.
obtundent agg. ottundente.
to **obturate** vt. otturare.
obturation s. otturazione.
obturator s. otturatore.
obtuse agg. **1.** ottuso **2.** sordo.
obtuseness s. ottusità.
to **obviate** vt. ovviare.
obvious agg. ovvio.
obviousness s. chiarezza.
occasion s. **1.** occasione **2.** motivo.
occasional agg. occasionale.
occident s. occidente.
occidental agg. occidentale.
occidentalism s. occidentalismo.
to **occidentalize** vt. occidentalizzare.
occidentally avv. all'occidentale.
occipital agg. occipitale.
occiput s. (pl. -pita) occipite.
to **occlude** vt. occludere.
occlusion s. occlusione.
occlusive agg. occlusivo.
occult agg. occulto.
to **occult** vt. occultare. ♦ to **occult** vi. occultarsi.
occultation s. occultamento.
occultism s. occultismo.
occultist s. occultista.
occupant s. occupante.
occupation s. occupazione.
occupational agg. professionale.
occupier s. occupante.
to **occupy** vt. occupare: to — oneself with, occuparsi di.
to **occur** vi. **1.** accadere **2.** venire in mente **3.** ricorrere.
occurrence s. avvenimento.
ocean s. oceano.
oceanic agg. oceanico.
oceanography s. oceanografia.
ocellus s. (pl. -li) ocello.

ochre s. ocra.
octagon s. ottagono.
octagonal agg. ottagonale.
octahedron s. ottaedro.
octane s. ottano.
octave s. ottava.
October s. ottobre.
octogenarian agg. e s. ottuagenario.
octonarian agg. e s. ottonario.
octonary agg. di otto in otto. ♦ **octonary** s. strofa di otto versi.
octopus s. (pl. -pi) polipo, piovra.
octosyllabic agg. ottosillabico.
octosyllable s. verso, parola di otto sillabe.
ocular agg. e s. oculare.
oculate(d) agg. maculato.
oculist s. oculista.
oculistic agg. oculistico.
odalisque s. odalisca.
odd agg. **1.** dispari **2.** scompagnato **3.** in più **4.** occasionale **5.** bizzarro. ♦ **odd** s. cosa extra.
oddity, oddness s. stranezza.
odds s. pl. **1.** differenza **2.** disaccordo **3.** pronostico || — and ends, rimanenze.
ode s. ode.
odious agg. odioso.
odontological agg. odontoiatrico.
odontologist s. odontoiatra.
odontology s. odontoiatria.
odoriferous agg. odorifero.
odorous agg. odoroso.
odour s. odore.
odourless agg. inodoro.
oedema s. edema.
oenologist s. enologo.
oenology s. enologia.
oesophagus s. (pl. -gi) esofago.
of prep. **1.** di **2.** (tempo) a, in **3.** da parte di: very kind — you, molto gentile da parte vostra || — late, ultimamente.
off avv. **1.** lontano, via **2.** completamente || to be —, essere finito, fermo, in libertà. ♦ **off** prep. **1.** lontano, via da **2.** giù da. ♦ **off** agg. **1.** destro **2.** esterno **3.** lontano **4.** secondario **5.** libero || — day, giorno di libertà.
offence s. **1.** offesa **2.** colpa, delitto **3.** scandalo.
offenceless agg. **1.** inoffensivo **2.** innocente.
to **offend** vt. offendere. ♦ to **offend** vi. **1.** peccare **2.** violare la legge.
offender s. **1.** peccatore **2.** colpevole.

offensive *agg.* **1.** offensivo **2.** sgradevole. ♦ **offensive** *s.* offensiva.

offensiveness *s.* aggressività.

offer *s.* offerta.

to offer *vt.* offrire. ♦ **to offer** *vi.* offrirsi.

offerer *s.* offerente.

offering *s.* offerta.

offertory *s.* offertorio.

offhand *agg.* **1.** improvvisato **2.** spontaneo. ♦ **offhand** *avv.* lì per lì.

office *s.* ufficio, carica || *box-* —, botteghino.

officer *s.* ufficiale, funzionario || *non-commissioned* —, sottufficiale.

official *agg.* ufficiale. ♦ **official** *s.* funzionario.

officiant *s.* ufficiante.

to officiate *vi.* **1.** esercitare le funzioni di **2.** (*relig.*) ufficiare.

officious *agg.* **1.** ufficioso **2.** intrigante.

offing *s.* (*mar.*) largo.

offscourings *s. pl.* rifiuti, scarti.

offset *s.* **1.** compenso **2.** sperone (*di monte*) **3.** germoglio, progenie **4.** (*tip.*) fotolito.

offshoot *s.* **1.** germoglio **2.** ramo.

offshore *agg.* **1.** di terra **2.** lontano dalla costa. ♦ **offshore** *avv.* al largo.

offside *s.* (*sport*) fuori gioco.

offspring *s.* **1.** prole **2.** frutto.

often *avv.* spesso || *how* —?, quante volte?

ogive *s.* ogiva.

oil *s.* **1.** olio **2.** petrolio || — *cloth,* tela cerata; — *field,* giacimento petrolifero; — *-mill,* frantoio; — *paper,* carta oleata; — *pipeline,* oleodotto.

to oil *vt.* ungere, oliare.

oiler *s.* oliatore.

oily *agg.* oleoso, untuoso.

ointment *s.* unguento.

O.K. *avv.* bene: *to be* —, andar bene.

old (**elder, older; eldest, oldest**) *agg.* vecchio || *how* — *are you?,* quanti anni hai?; — *-fashioned,* antiquato. ♦ **old** *s.* passato.

oldish *agg.* attempato.

oleander *s.* oleandro.

oleograph *s.* oleografia.

oleographic *agg.* oleografico.

olfactory *agg.* olfattivo.

oligarch *s.* oligarchia.

oligarchic(al) *agg.* oligarchico.

oligarchy *s.* oligarchia.

olive *agg.* **1.** d'oliva **2.** olivastro. ♦ **olive** *s.* **1.** oliva **2.** (*-tree*) olivo.

Olympiad *s.* olimpiade.

Olympian *agg.* olimpico, olimpionico. ♦ **Olympian** *s.* olimpionico.

Olympic *agg.* V. *Olympian.*

omelet(te) *s.* frittata.

omen *s.* auspicio.

ominous *agg.* di cattivo augurio.

omission *s.* omissione.

to omit *vt.* omettere.

omnipotence *s.* onnipotenza.

omnipotent *agg. e s.* onnipotente.

omnipresent *agg.* onnipresente.

omniscience *s.* onniscienza.

omniscient *agg. e s.* onnisciente.

omnivorous *agg.* onnivoro.

on *prep.* **1.** su **2.** a, in, di, per || *on purpose,* apposta. ♦ **on** *avv.* **1.** su, indosso **2.** (in) avanti || *to be* —, essere in funzione, essere rappresentato; *and so* —, eccetera.

once *avv.* una volta || *at* —, subito; *all at* —, improvvisamente. ♦ **once** *cong.* una volta che.

on-coming *agg.* prossimo.

one *agg.* **1.** uno **2.** uno solo. ♦ **one** *pron.* **1.** (*dimostr.*) questo, quello **2.** (*indef.*) (l') uno || — *by* —, uno a uno. ♦ **one** *s.* uno || — *John Brown,* un certo John Brown.

one-eyed *agg.* guercio.

oneness *s.* unità, unicità.

onerous *agg.* oneroso.

oneself *pron. r.* se stesso.

one-sided *agg.* unilaterale.

one-sidely *avv.* unilateralmente.

oneway *agg.* a senso unico.

ongoings *s. pl.* avvenimenti.

onion *s.* cipolla || *spring-* —, cipollina.

onlooker *s.* spettatore.

only *agg. e avv.* solo.

onomastic *agg.* onomastico.

onomatopoeia *s.* onomatopeia.

onomatopoeic *agg.* onomatopeico.

onset *s.* **1.** attacco **2.** inizio.

onto *prep.* su, in cima a.

ontological *agg.* ontologico.

ontology *s.* ontologia.

onus *s.* onere.

onward *agg.* avanzato.

onward(s) *avv.* avanti.

onyx *s.* onice.

to ooze *vt. e vi.* stillare || *to* — *out,* trapelare.

oozy *agg.* melmoso.

opacity *s.* opacità.

opal s. opale.
opalescent agg. opalescente.
opaque agg. opaco.
open agg. aperto || wide —, spalancato; in the — air, all'aperto.
to open vt. aprire. ♦ to open vi. aprirsi.
open-handed agg. generoso.
opening s. 1. apertura 2. radura.
openly avv. apertamente.
open-minded agg. di larghe vedute.
open-mindedness s. larghezza di vedute.
openness s. 1. apertura 2. franchezza.
opera s. opera lirica || — -house, tèatro dell'opera; — glass, binocolo.
to operate vt. 1. operare 2. far funzionare 3. gestire. ♦ to operate vi. 1. operare 2. funzionare.
operatic agg. di opera.
operation s. 1. operazione 2. funzionamento 3. azione.
operative agg. 1. attivo 2. operatono, operaio (meccanico). sentenza. ♦ operative s. artigianista, telegrafista.
operator s. 1. operatore 2. teleforio || — part, dispositivo di una
ophthalmia s. oftalmia.
ophthalmic agg. oftalmico.
ophthalmology s. oftalmologia, oculistica.
ophthalmoscopy s. oftalmoscopia.
opiate agg. 1. oppiato 2. soporifero. ♦ opiate s. narcotico.
opinion s. opinione.
opinionated, opinionative agg. ostinato.
opium s. oppio.
opponent s. avversario.
opportune agg. opportuno.
opportunism s. opportunismo.
opportunist s. opportunista.
opportunist(ic) agg. opportunistico.
opportunity s. occasione.
opposable agg. opponibile.
to oppose vt. opporre. ♦ to oppose vi. opporsi.
opposed agg. 1. opposto 2. ostile.
opposer s. oppositore.
opposite agg. e s. opposto. ♦ opposite avv. di fronte. ♦ opposite prep. di fronte a, dirimpetto a.
opposition s. opposizione.

to oppress vt. opprimere.
oppression s. oppressione.
oppressive agg. opprimente.
oppressor s. oppressore.
opprobrious agg. obbrobrioso.
to opt vi. optare.
optic(al) agg. ottico.
optician s. ottico.
optics s. ottica.
optimism s. ottimismo.
optimist agg. e s. ottimista.
optimistic(al) agg. ottimistico.
option s. opzione.
optional agg. facoltativo.
opulence s. opulenza.
opulent agg. opulento.
or cong. o, oppure || either... —, sia... sia.
oracle s. oracolo.
oracular agg. profetico.
oral agg. e s. orale.
orange s. 1. arancia 2. arancio.
orangeade s. aranciata.
orangery s. aranceto.
oration s. discorso.
orator s. oratore.
oratorical agg. oratorio.
oratory[1] s. oratorio.
oratory[2] s. oratoria.
orb s. 1. cerchio 2. sfera.
orbit s. orbita.
orbital agg. orbitale.
orchard s. frutteto.
orchestra s. orchestra.
orchestral agg. orchestrale.
to orchestrate vt. orchestrare.
orchestration s. orchestrazione.
orchid, orchis s. orchidea.
to ordain vt. ordinare (anche eccl.).
ordeal s. 1. ordalia 2. dura prova.
order s. 1. ordine 2. classe || in — that, affinché; in — to, allo scopo di; postal —, vaglia postale; made to —, eseguito su ordinazione. ♦ orders s. pl. (relig.) ordini: to take —, farsi prete.
to order vt. 1. ordinare 2. riordinare.
ordering s. ordinamento.
orderly agg. ordinato. ♦ orderly s. 1. (mil.) ordinanza 2. (mil.) attendente.
ordinal agg. e s. ordinale.
ordinance s. 1. ordinanza 2. (relig.) rito.
ordinary agg. ordinario. ♦ ordinary s. 1. condizione ordinaria 2. pranzo a prezzo fisso.
ordinate s. ordinata.

ordination s. **1.** ordine **2.** (*relig.*) ordinazione.

ore s. minerale.

organ s. organo ‖ *barrel-* —, organetto; *mouth-* —, armonica.

organic *agg.* organico.

organism s. organismo.

organist s. organista.

organizable *agg.* organizzabile.

organization s. organizzazione.

to organize *vt.* organizzare. ♦ **to organize** *vi.* organizzarsi.

organizer s. organizzatore.

organzine s. organzino.

orgasm s. orgasmo.

orgeat s. orzata.

orgiastic *agg.* orgiastico.

orgy s. orgia.

orient s. oriente.

to orient *vt.* **1.** orientare **2.** volgere verso oriente.

oriental *agg.* e s. orientale.

orientalist s. orientalista.

orientation s. orientamento.

orifice s. orifizio.

origan s. origano.

origin s. origine.

original *agg.* e s. originale.

originality s. originalità.

originally *avv.* **1.** originalmente **2.** originariamente.

to originate *vt.* dare origine. ♦ **to originate** *vi.* aver origine.

originator s. iniziatore.

ornament s. ornamento.

ornamental *agg.* ornamentale.

ornamentation s. decorazione.

ornate *agg.* ornato.

ornithological *agg.* ornitologico.

ornithologist s. ornitologo.

ornithology s. ornitologia.

orographic(al) *agg.* orografico.

orography s. orografia.

orphan *agg.* e s. orfano.

orphanage s. **1.** la condizione di orfano **2.** orfanotrofio.

orthodox *agg.* ortodosso.

orthodoxy s. ortodossia.

orthogonal *agg.* ortogonale.

orthographic(al) *agg.* **1.** ortografico **2.** ortogonale.

orthography s. **1.** ortografia **2.** (*geom.*) proiezione ortogonale.

orthop(a)edic(al) *agg.* ortopedico.

orthop(a)edics s. ortopedia.

orthop(a)edist s. ortopedico.

to oscillate *vi.* oscillare.

oscillation s. oscillazione.

oscillator s. oscillatore.

oscillatory *agg.* oscillatorio.

oscillograph s. oscillografo.

osier s. vimine.

osmose, osmosis s. osmosi.

osseous *agg.* osseo.

ossification s. ossificazione.

to ossify *vt.* ossificare. ♦ **to ossify** *vi.* ossificarsi.

ostensible *agg.* apparente.

ostensory s. ostensorio.

ostentation s. ostentazione.

ostentatious *agg.* ostentato.

osteological *agg.* osteologico.

osteology s. osteologia.

ostracism s. ostracismo.

to ostracize *vt.* dare l'ostracismo a.

ostrich s. struzzo.

other *agg.* e *pron.* altro ‖ *each* —, l'un l'altro; *every* — *day,* un giorno sì e un giorno no. ♦ **others** *pron. pl.* altri ‖ *some...* —*...,* gli uni... gli altri.

otherwise *agg.* diverso. ♦ **otherwise** *avv.* altrimenti.

otherworld s. mondo ultraterreno.

otitis s. otite.

otorhinolaryngologist s. otorinolaringoiatra.

otter s. lontra.

Ottoman *agg.* e s. ottomano.

ought s. zero.

ought *v. dif.* (*condiz.*) dovere: *you* — *to wait,* dovresti aspettare.

ounce s. oncia.

our *agg. poss.* nostro, nostra, nostri, nostre.

ours *pron. poss.* il nostro, la nostra, i nostri, le nostre.

ourselves *pron. r. pl.* noi stessi.

out *agg.* esterno. ♦ **out** *avv.* fuori. ♦ **out** (*of*) *prep.* **1.** fuori (*di*) **2.** senza **3.** per ‖ — *-of-date,* fuori moda; — *-of-work,* disoccupato; — *-of-the-way,* remoto.

to outbid (**outbade, outbidden**) *vt.* offrire di più.

outboard *agg.* e *avv.* fuoribordo.

outbreak s. **1.** scoppio **2.** sommossa.

outburst s. scoppio.

outcast s. proscritto.

to outclass *vt.* surclassare.

outcome s. risultato.

outcry s. grido, scalpore.

outdid V. *to outdo.*

to outdistance *vt.* distanziare.

to outdo (**outdid, outdone**) *vt.* superare.

outdoor *agg.* all'aperto.

outdoors *avv.* all'aperto.

outer *agg.* esteriore.

outfit(ting) *s.* equipaggiamento.

to **outfit** *vt.* rifornire di equipaggiamento. ♦ to **outfit** *vi.* rifornirsi di equipaggiamento.

outfitter *s.* fornitore.

to **outfly** (**outflew, outflown**) *vt.* sorpassare nel volo.

outgone V. *to outgo.*

outgo *s.* uscita.

to **outgo** (**outwent, outgone**) *vt.* sorpassare.

outgoing *agg.* uscente, in partenza.

to **outgrow** (**outgrew, outgrown**) *vt.* **1.** diventare troppo grande per **2.** sorpassare (*in statura*).

outgrowth *s.* **1.** escrescenza **2.** risultato.

outhouse *s.* **1.** tettoia **2.** dipendenza.

outing *s.* escursione || — *clothes,* abiti sportivi.

outlandish *agg.* **1.** strano **2.** remoto.

outlaw *s.* fuorilegge.

outlawry *s.* (*giur.*) proscrizione.

outlay *s.* spesa.

outlet *s.* **1.** sbocco **2.** cortile.

outline *s.* **1.** contorno **2.** schema **3.** lineamento.

to **outline** *vt.* **1.** delineare **2.** abbozzare.

outliner *s.* bozzettista.

to **outlive** *vt.* sopravvivere a.

outlook *s.* **1.** veduta **2.** prospettiva **3.** vigilanza.

to **outnumber** *vt.* superare numericamente.

outpost *s.* avamposto.

outpour *s.* **1.** scroscio di pioggia **2.** (*fig.*) sfogo.

output *s.* produzione, rendimento.

outrage *s.* oltraggio.

to **outrage** *vt.* oltraggiare.

outrageous *agg.* **1.** oltraggioso **2.** violento.

outrageousness *s.* **1.** oltraggio **2.** violenza.

outran V. *to outrun.*

to **outrange** *vt.* avere una portata maggiore di.

to **outreach** *vt.* sorpassare.

outrider *s.* battistrada.

outright *agg.* **1.** franco **2.** completo. ♦ **outright** *avv.* **1.** francamente **2.** completamente.

outrightness *s.* **1.** immediatezza **2.** franchezza.

outroar *s.* fracasso.

to **outrun** (**outran, outrun**) *vt.* oltrepassare.

outrush *s.* fuga.

to **outsell** (**outsold, outsold**) *vt.* **1.** vendere in quantità superiore **2.** vendere a prezzo superiore.

outset *s.* esordio.

to **outshine** (**outshone, outshone**) *vt.* eclissare (*anche fig.*).

outside *agg.* e *s.* **1.** esterno **2.** massimo. ♦ **outside** *avv.* **1.** all'esterno **2.** all'aperto. ♦ **outside** *prep.* fuori di.

outsider *s.* **1.** profano **2.** estraneo **3.** (*sport*) non favorito.

outsize *agg.* fuori misura. ♦ **outsize** *s.* taglia fuori misura.

outskirt *s.* orlo. ♦ **outskirts** *s. pl.* periferia (*sing.*).

outsold V. *to outsell.*

outspoken *agg.* franco.

to **outspread** (**outspread, outspread**) *vt.* spiegare. ♦ to **outspread** (**outspread, outspread**) *vi.* spiegarsi.

outstanding *agg.* **1.** prominente **2.** resistente **3.** in sospeso.

to **outstretch** *vt.* distendere.

to **outstrip** *vt.* superare (*in velocità*).

outward *agg.* e *s.* esterno. ♦ **outward(s)** *avv.* esternamente.

outwent V. *to outgo.*

oval *agg.* e *s.* ovale.

ovary *s.* ovaia.

ovation *s.* ovazione.

oven *s.* forno.

over *avv.* **1.** di sopra **2.** eccessivamente || *to be* —, essere finito; — *and* — *again,* più e più volte. ♦ **over** *prep.* **1.** su **2.** più di **3.** durante || — *there,* dall'altra parte; — *and above,* oltre a.

overalls *s. pl.* tuta da lavoro (*sing.*).

overate V. *to overeat.*

to **overbear** (**overbore, overborne**) *vt.* dominare, sopraffare.

overbearing *agg.* imperioso.

overbearingness *s.* imperiosità.

overboard *avv.* in mare.

overbore V. *to overbear.*

overborne V. *to overbear.*

to **overburden** *vt.* sovraccaricare.

overcame V. *to overcome.*

overcast *agg.* scuro, nuvoloso.

to **overcast** (**overcast, overcast**) *vt.* oscurare. ♦ to **overcast** (**overcast, overcast**) *vi.* oscurarsi.

overcharge s. 1. sovraccarico 2. sovrapprezzo.

to **overcharge** vt. 1. sovraccaricare 2. far pagare troppo caro.

to **overcloud** vi. rannuvolarsi.

overcoat s. soprabito.

to **overcome** (overcame, overcome) vt. superare, vincere.

overcoming s. superamento, vittoria.

overconfident agg. troppo sicuro di sé.

overcredulity s. credulità eccessiva.

overcrowded agg. sovraffollato.

overcrowding s. sovraffollamento.

to **overdo** (overdid, overdone) vt. 1. esagerare 2. stancare.

overdone agg. troppo cotto.

overdose s. dose eccessiva.

overdrank V. to overdrink.

to **overdraw** (overdrew, overdrawn) vt. 1. esagerare 2. scoprire il conto in banca.

to **overdrink** (overdrank, overdrunk) vi. bere troppo.

overdue agg. scaduto.

to **overeat** (overate, overeaten) vi. mangiare troppo.

to **overestimate** vt. sopravvalutare.

overexcitability s. sovreccitabilità.

overexcitable agg. sovreccitabile.

to **overexcite** vt. sovreccitare.

overexcitement s. sovreccitazione.

to **overexert** vt. stancare.

to **overexpose** vt. sovresporre.

overfeeding s. superalimentazione.

overflew V. to overfly.

to **overflow** vt. inondare. ♦ to **overflow** vi. traboccare.

overflowing s. inondazione.

to **overfly** (overflew, overflown) vt. 1. sorvolare 2. superare in volo.

overfond agg. troppo appassionato.

to **overgrow** (overgrew, overgrown) vt. 1. coprire 2. superare. ♦ to **overgrow** (overgrew, overgrown) vi. 1. coprirsi 2. crescere troppo.

overgrowth s. 1. crescita eccessiva 2. vegetazione sovrabbondante.

overhang s. sporgenza, aggetto.

to **overhang** (overhung, overhung) vt. 1. sovrastare 2. ornare con tendaggi ecc.

to **overhaul** vt. 1. revisionare 2. sorpassare.

overhaul(ing) s. revisione.

overhead agg. 1. alto 2. (comm.) generale. ♦ **overhead** avv. in alto.

to **overhear** (overheard, overheard) vt. 1. udire per caso 2. origliare.

to **overheat** vt. surriscaldare. ♦ to **overheat** vi. surriscaldarsi.

overheating s. surriscaldamento.

overhung V. to overhang.

overindulgence s. eccessiva indulgenza.

overladen agg. sovraccarico.

overland avv. via terra.

overlap s. sovrapposizione.

overlay s. copertura.

to **overleap** vt. saltare di là da.

overload s. sovraccarico.

to **overload** vt. sovraccaricare.

to **overlook** vt. 1. guardare dall'alto 2. trascurare 3. ispezionare.

overlooker s. ispettore.

overnight agg. 1. compiuto durante la notte 2. per una notte. ♦ **overnight** avv. durante la notte.

overpaid V. to overpay.

to **overpass** vt. 1. attraversare 2. sorpassare 3. trasgredire.

overpast agg. passato.

to **overpay** (overpaid, overpaid) vt. pagare più del dovuto.

overpayment s. pagamento eccessivo.

overpeopled agg. sovrappopolato.

overplus s. soprappiù.

overpopulated agg. sovrappopolato.

overpopulation s. sovrappopolazione.

to **overpower** V. to overbear.

overpowering agg. 1. schiacciante 2. prepotente.

overpressure s. sovrapressione.

to **overprint** vt. sovrastampare.

to **overprize** vt. sopravvalutare.

to **overproduce** vt. produrre in eccesso.

overproduction s. sovraproduzione.

overproud agg. troppo orgoglioso.

overran V. to overrun.

to **overrate** vt. sopravvalutare.

to **overreach** vt. 1. oltrepassare 2. imbrogliare.

to **overrule** vt. 1. dirigere 2. annullare 3. dominare.

to **overrun** (overran, overrun) vt. 1. invadere 2. devastare 3. oltrepassare.

oversaw V. to oversee.

oversea(s) agg. e avv. d'oltremare.

to oversee (oversaw, overseen) vt. ispezionare.

overseer s. 1. ispettore 2. capo squadra.

to overset (overset, overset) vt. rovesciare. ♦ to overset (overset, overset) vi. rovesciarsi.

to overshadow vt. 1. ombreggiare 2. adombrare 3. proteggere.

overshoe s. soprascarpa.

to overshoot (overshot, overshot) vt. lanciare di là da || to — the mark, passare i limiti.

overside avv. lungo il fianco.

oversight s. 1. svista 2. sorveglianza.

to oversleep (overslept, overslept) vi. dormire oltre l'ora fissata.

to overspread (overspread, overre. ♦ to overspread (overspread, overspread) vi. spargersi.

to overstate vt. esagerare.

to overtake (overtook, overtaken) vt. 1. cogliere 2. superare.

overtaking s. sorpasso: no —, divieto di sorpasso.

overthrew V. to overthrow.

overthrow s. 1. rovesciamento 2. disfatta.

to overthrow (overthrew, overthrown) vt. 1. rovesciare 2. sconfiggere.

overtime s. straordinario (orario di lavoro).

overtook V. to overtake.

to overturn V. to overthrow.

overturnable agg. rovesciabile.

overturn(ing) s. rovesciamento.

overweary agg. stremato.

overweight agg. che supera il peso. ♦ overweight s. sovraccarico.

to overwhelm vt. 1. sommergere 2. sopraffare.

overwhelming agg. schiacciante.

overwork s. 1. lavoro eccessivo 2. straordinario.

to overwork vt. 1. far lavorare troppo 2. far eccessivo uso di. ♦ to overwork vi. lavorare troppo.

to overwrite (overwrote, overwritten) vi. scrivere troppo.

overwrought agg. 1. esausto 2. ricercato (di stile).

ovine agg. ovino.

oviparous agg. oviparo.

ovulation s. ovulazione.

ovule s. ovulo.

to owe vt. dovere, essere debitore di || you must pay what is owing, dovete pagare il vostro debito.

owing agg. dovuto.

owing to prep. a causa di.

owl s. gufo.

own agg. e pron. proprio.

to own vt. 1. possedere 2. ammettere || to — to, confessare.

owner s. proprietario || shipowner, armatore.

ownership s. proprietà.

ox (pl. oxen) s. bue.

oxidation s. ossidazione.

oxide s. ossido.

oxidizable agg. ossidabile.

to oxidize vt. ossidare. ♦ to oxidize vi. ossidarsi.

oxygen s. ossigeno || — tent, tenda ad ossigeno.

to oxygenate vt. ossigenare.

oxygenation s. ossigenazione.

to oxygenize vt. ossigenare.

oxyhydrogen agg. ossidrico: — blowpipe, cannello ossidrico.

oyster s. 1. ostrica 2. persona silenziosa, riservata.

ozone s. ozono.

to ozonize vt. ozonizzare.

P

pace s. passo.

to pace vi. andare al passo. ♦ to pace vt. percorrere. ♦ to pace vi. andare al passo, marciare.

paced agg. misurato (a passi) || slow- —, a passi lenti.

pachyderm s. pachiderma.

pacific agg. pacifico.

to pacificate vt. pacificare.

pacification s. pacificazione.

pacificator, pacifier s. pacificatore.

pacificatory agg. conciliante.

pacifism s. pacifismo.

pacifist agg. e s. pacifista.

to pacify vt. pacificare.

pack s. 1. pacco, balla, fagotto 2. carico 3. imballaggio 4. muta (di cani) 5. (med.) impacco || — -ice, banchisa; — -saddle, basto.

to pack vt. 1. impacchettare 2. im-

ballare **3.** raggruppare. ♦ **to pack**
vi. raggrupparsi ‖ *to — up,* fare
i bagagli.
package *s.* **1.** imballaggio **2.** pacco.
to package *vt.* **1.** imballare **2.** impacchettare.
packer *s.* **1.** imballatore **2.** impac-
chettatrice (*macchina*).
packet *s.* **1.** pacchetto **2.** (*mar.*) —
(*-boat*), postale.
packing *s.* **1.** imballaggio **2.** (*mecc.*)
guarnizione **3.** (*mar.*) baderna ‖
— -free, franco d'imballaggio.
pact *s.* patto.
pad[1] *s.* **1.** imbottitura **2.** zampa (*di
cane, lupo, volpe*) **3.** (*med.*) tampone.
pad[2] *s.* rumore sordo.
to pad *vt.* imbottire.
paddle *s.* **1.** pala **2.** pagaia.
to paddle *vi.* remare con pagaie.
paddy *s.* risaia.
padlock *s.* lucchetto.
to padlock *vt.* chiudere con lucchetto.
paediatric *agg.* pediatrico.
paediatrician *s.* pediatra.
paediatrics *s.* pediatria.
paediatrist *s.* pediatra.
pagan *agg.* e *s.* pagano.
paganism *s.* paganesimo.
page[1] *s.* paggio.
page[2] *s.* pagina.
to page *vt.* **1.** (*tip.*) impaginare **2.**
numerare le pagine.
pageant *s.* **1.** (*teat.*) scena (*di sacra rappresentazione*) **2.** parata,
corteo.
pageantry *s.* **1.** pompa, fasto **2.**
ostentazione.
to paginate *vt.* V. *to page.*
pagination *s.* **1.** paginatura **2.** impaginazione.
paid V. *to pay.*
pail *s.* secchio.
paillasse *s.* pagliericcio.
pain *s.* **1.** pena **2.** dolore, sofferenza.
♦ **pains** *s. pl.* doglie.
to pain *vt.* far male, far soffrire.
painful *agg.* penoso.
painless *agg.* indolore.
painstaking *agg.* diligente. ♦
painstaking *s.* cura.
paint *s.* **1.** pittura **2.** belletto.
to paint *vt.* dipingere. ♦ **to paint**
vi. imbellettarsi.
painter *s.* **1.** pittore **2.** imbianchino.
painting *s.* **1.** pittura **2.** dipinto,
quadro.

paintress *s.* pittrice.
pair *s.* paio, coppia.
to pair *vt.* accoppiare. ♦ **to pair**
vi. accoppiarsi.
palace *s.* palazzo.
paladin *s.* paladino.
palatable *agg.* **1.** gustoso **2.** (*fig.*)
gradevole.
palatal *agg.* e *s.* palatale.
palatalization *s.* palatalizzazione.
palate *s.* palato.
pale[1] *agg.* pallido.
pale[2] *s.* **1.** palo **2.** palizzata.
to pale *vt.* far impallidire. ♦ **to
pale** *vi.* impallidire.
paleness *s.* pallore.
paleochristian *agg.* paleocristiano.
paleographer *s.* paleografo.
paleography *s.* paleografia.
paleolithic *agg.* paleolitico.
paleologist *s.* paleologo.
paleology *s.* paleologia.
paleontologic(al) *agg.* paleontolo-
gico.
paleontologist *s.* paleontologo.
paleontology *s.* paleontologia.
paleozoic *agg.* paleozoico.
palette *s.* tavolozza.
palfrey *s.* palafreno.
palinode *s.* palinodia.
palisade *s.* palizzata.
pall *s.* **1.** drappo funebre **2.** (*eccl.*)
pallio.
to pall[1] *vt.* coprire con un drappo.
to pall[2] *vt.* saziare. ♦ **to pall** *vi.*
saziarsi.
pallet[1] *s.* pagliericcio.
pallet[2] *s.* **1.** paletta **2.** tavolozza.
to palliate *vt.* **1.** attenuare **2.** scusare.
palliation *s.* **1.** attenuazione **2.** scu-
sante.
palliative *agg.* e *s.* palliativo.
pallid *agg.* pallido.
pallor *s.* pallore.
palm[1] *s.* palma (*anche fig.*).
palm[2] *s.* (*anat.*) palmo.
to palm *vt.* toccare con la mano.
palmaceous *agg.* (*bot.*) di palma.
palmar *agg.* palmare.
palmate, palmated, *agg.* palmato.
palmiped *agg.* e *s.* palmipede.
palmistry *s.* chiromanzia.
palmy *agg.* **1.** coperto di palme **2.**
prosperoso, vittorioso.
palpability *s.* palpabilità.
palpable *agg.* palpabile.
to palpate *vt.* palpare.
to palpitate *vi.* palpitare.

palpitation s. palpitazione.
palsy s. paralisi.
to **palsy** vt. paralizzare.
to **palter** vi. tergiversare.
paltriness s. meschinità.
paltry agg. meschino.
to **pamper** vt. viziare.
pamphlet s. opuscolo.
pamphleteer s. autore di opuscoli.
pan s. **1.** padella **2.** vaschetta **3.** bacino **4.** piatto di bilancia || baking —, teglia.
pancake s. frittella.
panchromatic agg. pancromatico.
pancreatic agg. pancreatico.
pandemonium s. pandemonio.
pander s. mezzano, ruffiano.
to **pander** vi. fare il mezzano.
pane s. **1.** lastra di vetro **2.** (edil.) pannello **3.** faccia (di brillante).
panegyric s. panegirico.
panegyric(al) agg. laudativo.
panel s. **1.** pannello **2.** (neol.) commissione, comitato **3.** (giur.) lista di giurati.
pang s. **1.** fitta **2.** (fig.) stretta al cuore.
panic agg. e s. panico.
panicky agg. allarmato.
panicle s. pannocchia.
panification s. panificazione.
pannier s. paniere.
panoramic agg. panoramico.
pansy s. viola del pensiero.
pant s. **1.** palpito **2.** ansito.
to **pant** vi. **1.** palpitare **2.** ansimare.
pantagruelian agg. pantagruelico.
pantheism s. panteismo.
pantheist s. panteista.
pantheistic(al) agg. panteistico.
panther s. pantera.
panties s. pl. (fam.) mutandine.
panting s. **1.** palpitazione **2.** ansito **3.** ansia.
pantograph s. pantografo.
pantomime s. pantomima.
pantry s. dispensa.
pants s. pl. (fam.) mutande.
pap s. pappa.
papacy s. papato.
papal agg. papale.
paper s. **1.** carta **2.** prova d'esame
paper s. **1.** carta **2.** certificato, documento **3.** prova d'esame **4.** giornale || — back, libro in brossura; — board, cartone; — hanger, tappezziere; — hanging, tappezzeria.
to **paper** vt. **1.** incartare **2.** tappezzare.

papery agg. cartaceo.
papillary agg. papillare.
papism s. papismo.
papist s. papista.
papyrology s. papirologia.
papyrus s. (pl. -ri) papiro.
parable s. parabola.
parabolic(al) agg. **1.** parabolico **2.** di parabola.
paraboloid s. paraboloide.
parachute s. paracadute.
to **parachute** vt. paracadutare. ♦
to **parachute** vi. paracadutarsi.
parachutism s. paracadutismo.
parachutist s. paracadutista.
parade s. **1.** (mil.) parata **2.** mostra, sfoggio **3.** viale, passeggiata.
to **parade** vt. disporre in parata. ♦
to **parade** vi. marciare in parata.
paradigm s. paradigma.
paradisaic(al) agg. paradisiaco.
paradise s. paradiso.
paradisiac(al) agg. paradisiaco.
paradox s. paradosso.
paradoxical agg. paradossale.
paraffin s. paraffina.
paragon s. modello (di perfezione ecc.).
paragraph s. paragrafo.
to **paragraph** vt. dividere in paragrafi.
parallel agg. parallelo. ♦ **parallel** s. **1.** parallelo **2.** parallela.
to **parallel** vt. **1.** mettere in posizione parallela **2.** paragonare.
parallelepiped s. parallelepipedo.
parallelism s. parallelismo.
parallelogram s. parallelogramma.
paralogism s. paralogismo.
to **paralyse** vt. paralizzare.
paralysis s. (pl. -ses) paralisi.
paralytic agg. e s. paralitico.
parameter s. parametro.
paramount agg. supremo. ♦ **paramount** s. capo supremo.
paramour s. amante.
paranoia s. paranoia.
paranoiac agg. e s. paranoico.
paranymph s. paraninfo.
parapet s. parapetto.
paraphrase s. parafrasi.
to **paraphrase** vt. e vi. parafrasare.
parasite s. parassita.
parasitic(al) agg. parassitico.
parasitism s. parassitismo.
parasol s. parasole.
paratrooper s. paracadutista.
paratyphoid s. paratifo.

parcel s. **1.** pacco **2.** lotto, appezzamento di terreno **3.** gruppo.

to parcel vt. spartire.

parcelling s. spartizione.

parcener s. coerede.

to parch vt. **1.** arrostire **2.** disseccare. ♦ **to parch** vi. **1.** bruciarsi **2.** disseccarsi.

parchment s. pergamena.

pardon s. perdono.

to pardon vt. perdonare.

pardonable agg. perdonabile.

to pare vt. **1.** tagliare **2.** sbucciare.

parenchyma s. parenchima.

parent s. **1.** genitore **2.** causa, origine.

parentage s. **1.** discendenza **2.** nascita.

parental agg. paterno, materno.

parenthesis s. (pl. -ses) parentesi.

parenthetic(al) agg. parentetico.

parenthood s. paternità, maternità.

parentless agg. orfano.

paresis s. paresi.

pariah s. paria.

parietal agg. parietale.

parish s. parrocchia || — priest, parroco.

parishioner s. parrocchiano.

Parisian agg. e s. parigino.

parisyllabic agg. e s. parisillabo.

parity s. parità.

park s. **1.** parco **2.** posteggio.

to park vt. **1.** adibire a parco **2.** parcheggiare.

parking s. parcheggio || no —, divieto di sosta.

parkway s. (amer.) viale.

parley s. colloquio.

to parley vi. parlamentare.

parliament s. parlamento.

parliamentarian s. parlamentare.

parliamentarianism s. parlamentarismo.

parliamentary agg. parlamentare.

parlour s. **1.** salotto **2.** parlatorio || beauty —, istituto di bellezza.

Parmesan agg. parmigiano.

parochial agg. **1.** parrocchiale **2.** (fig.) ristretto.

parochialism s. ristrettezza di vedute.

parodist s. parodista.

parody s. parodia.

to parody vt. parodiare.

parole s. **1.** parola d'onore **2.** parola d'ordine.

paroxysm s. parossismo.

parricidal agg. parricida.

parricide s. **1.** parricidio **2.** parricida.

parrot s. pappagallo.

to parrot vt. ripetere pappagallescamente.

to parry vt. parare, schivare.

parsley s. prezzemolo.

parson s. parroco (anglicano).

parsonage s. (eccl.) canonica, parrocchia.

part s. parte.

to part vt. dividere. ♦ **to part** vi. dividersi.

to partake (partook, partaken) vi. partecipare, prendere parte.

parthenogenesis s. partenogenesi.

partial agg. parziale.

partiality s. parzialità.

partially avv. parzialmente.

participant agg. e s. partecipante.

to participate vi. **1.** partecipare **2.** condividere.

participation s. partecipazione.

participial agg. participiale.

participle s. participio.

particle s. . particella (anche gramm.).

particular agg. **1.** particolare **2.** particolareggiato **3.** esigente. ♦ **particular** s. particolare.

particularism s. particolarismo.

particularist s. particolarista.

particularity s. **1.** particolarità **2.** meticolosità.

to particularize vt. e vi. dettagliare.

parting s. separazione.

partisan agg. e s. partigiano.

partition s. **1.** divisione **2.** tramezzo.

to partition vt. dividere.

partitive agg. e s. partitivo.

partly avv. in parte.

partner s. **1.** socio **2.** coniuge.

partnership s. **1.** associazione **2.** (comm.) società.

partook V. to partake.

partridge s. pernice.

parturient agg. partoriente.

parturition s. parto.

party s. **1.** parte **2.** partito **3.** brigata **4.** trattenimento **5.** pattuglia.

pasha s. pascià.

pass[1] s. passo, gola.

pass[2] s. **1.** passaggio **2.** trapasso **3.** promozione **4.** lasciapassare.

to pass vt. e vi. passare || to — away, sparire; to — by, passar oltre.

passable *agg.* passabile.
passage *s.* **1.** passaggio **2.** corridoio **3.** brano.
passementerie *s.* passamaneria.
passenger *s.* passeggero.
passer *s.* — *-by,* passante.
passible *agg.* passibile.
passing *agg.* **1.** passeggero **2.** casuale. ♦ **passing** *s.* passaggio.
passion *s.* passione || — *-flower,* passiflora.
passional *agg.* passionale.
passionate *agg.* appassionato, passionale.
passionless *agg.* impassibile.
passive *agg.* e *s.* passivo.
passivism, passivity *s.* passività.
passport *s.* passaporto.
password *s.* parola d'ordine.
past *agg.* passato. ♦ **past** *s.* passato. ♦ **past** *avv.* vicino. ♦ **past** *prep.* al di là di.
paste *s.* pasta || *tooth* —, dentifricio.
to **paste** *vt.* **1.** incollare, appiccicare **2.** (*gergo*) attaccare.
pasteboard *agg.* di cartone. ♦ **pasteboard** *s.* cartone.
pastel *s.* pastello.
pasteurization *s.* pastorizzazione.
to **pasteurize** *vt.* pastorizzare.
pastime *s.* passatempo.
pastoral *agg.* e *s.* pastorale.
pastry *s.* dolci (*pl.*).
pasture *s.* pascolo.
to **pasture** *vt.* e *vi.* pascolare.
pasty *agg.* pastoso. ♦ **pasty** *s.* (*cuc.*) pasticcio.
pat *agg.* adatto. ♦ **pat** *avv.* esattamente. ♦ **pat** *s.* **1.** colpetto **2.** panetto di burro.
to **pat** *vt.* battere leggermente.
patch *s.* **1.** pezza, toppa **2.** macchia.
to **patch** *vt.* aggiustare, rattoppare, raffazzonare.
patching *s.* rattoppo.
patchy *agg.* **1.** rappezzato **2.** a macchie.
patent *agg.* **1.** chiaro, manifesto, evidente **2.** brevettato. ♦ **patent** *s.* brevetto.
to **patent** *vt.* brevettare.
patentee *s.* detentore di brevetto.
paternal *agg.* paterno.
paternalism *s.* paternalismo.
paternalistic *agg.* paternalistico.
paternity *s.* paternità.
path *s.* **1.** sentiero **2.** pista **3.** percorso, traiettoria.

pathetic *agg.* patetico.
pathfinder *s.* esploratore.
pathless *agg.* **1.** senza sentieri **2.** inesplorato.
pathogenic *agg.* patogeno.
pathologic(al) *agg.* patologico.
pathologist *s.* patologo.
pathology *s.* patologia.
pathway *s.* sentiero.
patience *s.* pazienza.
patient *agg.* **1.** paziente **2.** suscettibile. ♦ **patient** *s.* paziente.
patriarch *s.* patriarca.
patriarchal *agg.* patriarcale.
patriarchate *s.* patriarcato.
patrician *agg.* e *s.* patrizio.
patricide *s.* V. *parricide.*
patrimonial *agg.* patrimoniale.
patrimony *s.* patrimonio.
patriot *s.* patriota.
patriotic *agg.* patriottico.
patriotism *s.* patriottismo.
patrol *s.* pattuglia, ronda.
to **patrol** *vt.* e *vi.* pattugliare, fare la ronda.
patron *s.* patrono.
patronage *s.* patronato.
patronal *agg.* patronale.
patroness *s.* patronessa.
to **patronize** *vt.* **1.** patrocinare **2.** trattare con condiscendenza.
patronizing *agg.* **1.** protettivo **2.** condiscendente.
patter[1] *s.* gergo.
patter[2] *s.* picchiettio.
to **patter** *vi.* picchiettare.
pattern *s.* **1.** modello, campione **2.** disegno (*di stoffa ecc.*).
to **pattern** *vt.* modellare (su).
paunch *s.* pancia.
pauper *s.* povero.
pauperism *s.* povertà.
pause *s.* pausa.
to **pause** *vi.* **1.** fare una pausa **2.** esitare, indugiare.
pauseless *agg.* incessante.
to **pave** *vt.* **1.** pavimentare **2.** (*fig.*) appianare.
pavement *s.* **1.** pavimentazione **2.** marciapiede.
paver *s.* lastricatore.
pavilion *s.* padiglione.
paving *s.* pavimentazione.
paw *s.* zampa.
to **paw** *vt.* dare zampate. ♦ to **paw** *vi.* scalpitare (*di cavalli*).
pawn *s.* **1.** pegno **2.** pedina (*di scacchi*).

to **pawn** vt. impegnare (dare in pegno).

pawnbroker s. prestatore su pegno.

pawnbroking s. il prestare su pegno.

pawner s. chi dà qualcosa in pegno.

pawnshop s. agenzia di prestiti su pegno.

pay s. paga.

to **pay (paid, paid)** vt. e vi. 1. pagare 2. rendere, fruttare || to — off, liquidare.

payable agg. 1. pagabile 2. redditizio.

payee s. creditore.

payer s. pagatore.

paying out s. esborso.

payment s. pagamento.

payoff s. 1. giorno di paga 2. liquidazione.

payroll s. libro paga.

pea s. pisello || chick —, cece.

peace s. pace.

peaceable agg. pacifico.

peaceful s. pacifico, tranquillo.

peacefulness s. pace, calma.

peaceless agg. agitato.

peacemaker s. pacificatore.

peach s. (bot.) pesca.

peach-tree s. pesco.

peachy agg. simile a pesca.

peacock s. pavone.

to **peacock** vi. pavoneggiarsi.

peak s. 1. picco 2. punta 3. visiera.

peaky agg. appuntito.

peal s. 1. scampanio 2. scoppio, fragore, scroscio (di risa, applausi).

to **peal** vi. scampanare. ♦ to **peal** vt. far rimbombare.

peanut s. arachide.

pear s. pera.

pear-tree s. pero.

pearl s. perla.

to **pearl** vt. imperlare, ornare di perle. ♦ to **pearl** vi. imperlarsi.

pearly agg. 1. perlaceo 2. ricco di perle.

peasant s. contadino.

peasantry s. 1. condizione di contadino 2. i contadini (pl.).

peat s. torba || — -bog, torbiera.

pebble s. 1. ciottolo 2. cristallo di rocca.

to **pebble** vt. coprire con ciottoli.

peccary s. pecari.

peck s. beccata.

to **peck** vt. e vi. beccare.

pectoral agg. e s. pettorale.

peculation s. peculato.

peculiar agg. 1. particolare 2. strano.

peculiarity s. 1. particolarità 2. bizzarria, eccentricità.

pecuniary agg. pecuniario.

pedagogic(al) agg. pedagogico.

pedagogics s. pedagogia.

pedagogist s. pedagogista.

pedagogue s. pedagogo.

pedagogy s. pedagogia.

pedal s. pedale.

to **pedal** vt. e vi. pedalare.

pedant s. pedante.

pedantic agg. pedante.

pedantry s. pedanteria.

pedestal s. piedistallo.

pedestrian agg. pedestre. ♦ **pedestrian** s. pedone.

pediatrics ecc. V. paediatrics ecc.

pediment s. (arch.) frontone.

pedlar s. venditore ambulante.

peel s. buccia.

to **peel** vt. sbucciare. ♦ to **peel** vi. sbucciarsi.

peeling s. buccia.

peep[1] s. 1. sguardo furtivo 2. fessura.

peep[2] s. pigolio.

to **peep**[1] vi. 1. guardare furtivamente 2. far capolino.

to **peep**[2] vi. pigolare.

peeper[1] s. ficcanaso, persona curiosa.

peeper[2] s. piccioncino.

peer s. 1. pari 2. Pari, membro della Camera dei Lord.

to **peer** vt. uguagliare. ♦ to **peer** vi. 1. scrutare 2. far capolino.

peerage s. 1. i Pari 2. nobiltà.

peerless agg. senza pari.

peevish agg. irritabile.

peg s. piuolo.

to **peg** vt. fissare.

pejorative agg. e s. peggiorativo.

pelagic agg. oceanico.

pelican s. pellicano.

pellet s. 1. pallottolina (di carta ecc.) 2. pallottola 3. pillola.

pellucid agg. trasparente.

pelt[1] s. colpo (di proiettile ecc.).

pelt[2] s. pelle (di animale).

to **pelt** vt. colpire.

pelvic agg. pelvico.

pelvis s. bacino.

pen[1] s. penna || -nib, pennino; fountain- —, penna stilografica.

pen[2] s. recinto (per animali).

to **pen**[1] vt. scrivere.

to **pen**[2] vt. rinchiudere animali in un recinto.

penal *agg.* penale.
to penalize *vt.* (*sport.*) penalizzare.
penalty *s.* penalità, punizione.
penance *s.* penitenza.
pence *s.* V. *penny.*
pencil *s.* matita.
pendant, pendent *agg.* e *s.* pendente.
pending *prep.* **1.** durante **2.** fino a.
pendular *agg.* pendolare.
pendulous *agg.* pendulo.
pendulum *s.* pendolo || — -*clock,* pendola.
penetrable *agg.* penetrabile.
to penetrate *vt.* e *vi.* penetrare.
penetration *s.* penetrazione.
penetrative *agg.* penetrante.
penguin *s.* pinguino.
penicillin *s.* penicillina.
peninsula *s.* penisola.
peninsular *agg.* peninsulare.
penis *s.* pene.
penitence *s.* penitenza.
penitent *agg.* e *s.* penitente.
penitential *agg.* penitenziale.
penitentiary *agg.* penitenziale. ♦ **penitentiary** *s.* (*eccl.*) penitenziere **2.** riformatorio **3.** (*amer.*) penitenziario.
penknife *s.* (*pl.* -knives) temperino.
pennant *s.* (*mar.*) pennone.
penniless *agg.* senza un soldo.
pennon *s.* pennone.
penny *s.* (*numero delle monete*), **pence** (*loro valore*) *s.* "penny".
pension *s.* pensione.
to pension *vt.* pensionare.
pensionable *agg.* pensionabile.
pensioner *s.* pensionato.
pensive *agg.* pensoso.
pent *agg.* chiuso.
pentagon *s.* pentagono.
pentagonal *agg.* pentagonale.
pentagram *s.* pentagono.
pentahedron *s.* pentaedro.
pentameter *s.* pentametro.
pentane *s.* pentano.
pentathlon *s.* pentatlon.
Pentecost *s.* Pentecoste.
Pentecostal *agg.* pentecostale.
penthouse *s.* tettoia.
pentode *s.* (*elettr.*) pentodo.
pentose *s.* pentosio.
penult(imate) *agg.* e *s.* penultimo.
penury *s.* povertà.
peony *s.* peonia.
people *s.* (*costruzione al pl.*) **1.** popolo **2.** gente **3.** folla.
to people *vt.* popolare.

pepper *s.* pepe || — -*mill,* macinapepe.
to pepper *vt.* condire con pepe.
peppercorn *s.* grano di pepe.
peppermint *s.* menta peperita.
peppery *agg.* **1.** pepato **2.** collerico.
pepsin(e) *s.* pepsina.
per *prep.* per: — *cent,* per cento.
peracid *s.* peracido.
to perambulate *vt.* **1.** attraversare **2.** ispezionare. ♦ **to perambulate** *vi.* passeggiare.
perambulation *s.* **1.** ispezione **2.** passeggiata.
perambulator *s.* carrozzella per bambini.
percale *s.* percalle.
perceivable *agg.* percettibile.
to perceive *vt.* percepire, scorgere. ♦ **to perceive** *vi.* accorgersi.
percentage *s.* percentuale.
perceptible *agg.* percettibile.
perception *s.* percezione.
perceptive *agg.* percettivo.
perch[1] *s.* gruccia.
perch[2] *s.* pesce persico.
to perch *vi.* appollaiarsi.
perchlorate *s.* perclorato.
percipience *s.* percezione.
to percolate *vt.* e *vi.* filtrare, colare.
percolator *s.* filtro.
percussion *s.* percussione || — -*pin,* percussore.
perdition *s.* perdizione.
perdurable *agg.* durevole.
to peregrinate *vi.* peregrinare.
peregrination *s.* peregrinazione.
peremptory *agg.* perentorio.
perennial *agg.* perenne.
perfect *agg.* perfetto.
to perfect *vt.* perfezionare.
perfectibility *s.* perfettibilità.
perfectible *agg.* perfettibile.
perfecting *s.* **1.** perfezionamento **2.** completamento.
perfection *s.* **1.** perfezione **2.** perfezionamento.
perfectionism *s.* perfezionismo.
perfectionist *s.* perfezionista.
perfectly *avv.* perfettamente.
perfidious *agg.* perfido, sleale.
perfidy *s.* perfidia, slealtà.
to perforate *vt.* perforare.
perforation *s.* perforazione.
to perform *vt.* **1.** eseguire **2.** (*teat.*) rappresentare.
performable *agg.* **1.** eseguibile **2.** rappresentabile.

performance s. 1. esecuzione 2. atto 3. (teat.) rappresentazione.
performer s. 1 esecutore 2. attore.
performing agg. ammaestrato.
perfume s. profumo.
to **perfume** vt. profumare.
perfumer s. profumiere.
perfumery s. 1. profumeria 2. profumi.
perfunctory agg. superficiale.
to **perfuse** vt. aspergere.
perfusion s. aspersione.
perhaps avv. forse.
pericardium s. pericardio.
perigee s. perigeo.
peril s. pericolo.
perilous agg. pericoloso.
perimeter s. perimetro.
period s. 1. periodo 2. ora di lezione 3. stadio, fase (di una malattia) 4. (gramm.) punto.
periodic agg. periodico.
periodical agg. e s. periodico.
periodicity s. periodicità.
peripheral agg. periferico.
periphery s. 1. perimetro 2. superficie.
periphrase, periphrasis s. (pl. -ses) perifrasi.
periphrastic agg. perifrastico.
periscope s. periscopio.
to **perish** vi. perire.
perishable agg. 1. deperibile 2. mortale.
perishables s. pl. merci deteriorabili.
peristyle s. peristilio.
peritonitis s. peritonite.
periwig s. parrucca.
periwigged agg. imparruccato.
periwinkle s. pervinca.
to **perjure** vt. giurare falsamente.
perjurer, perjury s. spergiuro.
permanence s. permanenza.
permanent agg. permanente.
permanganate s. permanganato.
permeability s. permeabilità.
permeable agg. permeabile.
to **permeate** vt. permeare. ♦ to **permeate** vi. permearsi.
permission, permit s. permesso.
to **permit** vt. e vi. permettere.
to **permute** vt. permutare.
pernicious agg. pernicioso.
to **perorate** vi. perorare.
peroration s. perorazione.
peroxid(e) s. perossido || hydrogen —, acqua ossigenata.
to **peroxide** vt. ossigenare.

perpendicular agg. perpendicolare. ♦ **perpendicular** s. 1. perpendicolare 2. filo a piombo.
perpendicularity s. perpendicolarità.
to **perpetrate** vt. perpetrare.
perpetration s. perpetrazione.
perpetual agg. perpetuo.
to **perpetuate** vt. perpetuare.
perpetuity s. 1. perpetuità 2. rendita vitalizia.
to **perplex** vt. 1. rendere perplesso 2. complicare.
perplexed agg. perplesso.
perplexity s. 1. perplessità 2. complicazione.
to **persecute** vt. perseguitare.
persecution s. persecuzione.
persecutor s. persecutore.
perseverance s. perseveranza.
to **persevere** vi. perseverare.
Persian agg. e s. persiano.
persimmon s. (bot.) cachi.
to **persist** vi. persistere.
persistence s. persistenza.
persistent agg. persistente.
person s. persona.
personable agg. ben fatto.
personage s. personaggio.
personal agg. personale.
personality s. personalità.
personalization s. personificazione.
to **personalize** vt. personificare.
personally avv. personalmente.
personification s. personificazione.
to **personify** vt. personificare.
personnel s. personale.
perspective agg. prospettico. ♦ **perspective** s. prospettiva.
perspicacious agg. perspicace.
perspicacity s. perspicacia.
perspicuity s. perspicuità.
perspicuous agg. perspicuo.
perspiration s. traspirazione.
to **perspire** vt. e vi. sudare, trasudare.
to **persuade** vt. persuadere.
persuasion s. 1. persuasione 2. credenza.
persuasive agg. persuasivo.
pert agg. impertinente.
to **pertain** vi. appartenere.
pertinacious agg. pertinace.
pertinacy, pertinacity s. pertinacia.
pertinence s. pertinenza.
pertinent agg. pertinente.
pertly avv. insolentemente.
pertness s. insolenza.

to **perturb** *vt.* perturbare.
perturbation *s.* perturbazione.
perusal *s.* lettura attenta.
to **peruse** *vt.* leggere attentamente.
to **pervade** *vt.* pervadere.
pervasion *s.* penetrazione.
pervasive *agg.* penetrante.
perverse *agg.* 1. perverso 2. errato 3. ostinato.
perversion *s.* perversione.
perversity *s.* perversità.
pervert *s.* 1. pervertito 2. apostata.
to **pervert** *vt.* pervertire.
pessimism *s.* pessimismo.
pessimist *s.* pessimista.
pessimistic *agg.* pessimistico.
pessimistically *avv.* in modo pessimistico.
pest *s.* peste (*anche fig.*).
to **pester** *vt.* importunare.
pestiferous *agg.* pestifero.
pestilence *s.* pestilenza.
pestilent *agg.* 1. nocivo 2. molesto.
pestilential *agg.* pestilenziale.
pestle *s.* pestello.
pet *agg.* e *s.* favorito ‖ — *name,* vezzeggiativo.
to **pet** *vt.* vezzeggiare.
petal *s.* petalo.
petard *s.* petardo.
petition *s.* petizione, istanza.
to **petition** *vt.* e *vi.* fare una petizione (a).
petitioner *s.* postulante.
to **petrify** *vt.* pietrificare. ♦ to **petrify** *vi.* pietrificarsi.
petrography *s.* petrografia.
petrol *s.* benzina.
petticoat *s.* sottoveste.
pettifogger *s.* azzeccagarbugli.
petty *agg.* 1. meschino 2. subalterno.
petulant *agg.* petulante.
pew *s.* banco (*di chiesa*).
pewter *s.* peltro.
phagocyte *s.* fagocita.
phalanstery *s.* falansterio.
phalanx *s.* (*pl.* -ges) falange.
phallic *agg.* fallico.
phantasm *s.* fantasma.
phantasmagoria *s.* fantasmagoria.
phantasmagorial, phantasmagoric(al) *agg.* fantasmagorico.
phantom *s.* 1. fantasma 2. apparizione.
Pharaoh *s.* faraone.
Pharisee *s.* fariseo.
pharmaceutic(al) *agg.* farmaceutico.

pharmaceutics *s.* farmaceutica.
pharmacology *s.* farmacologia.
pharmacopoeia *s.* farmacopea.
pharmacy *s.* farmacia.
pharyngitis *s.* faringite.
pharynx *s.* (*pl.* -ges) faringe.
phase *s.* fase.
pheasant *s.* fagiano.
phenic *agg.* fenico.
phenol *s.* fenolo.
phenomenal *agg.* 1. fenomenico 2. fenomenale.
phenomenalism *s.* fenomenismo.
phenomenology *s.* fenomenologia.
phenomenon *s.* (*pl.* -na) fenomeno.
phial *s.* fiala.
to **philander** *vi.* fare il cascamorto.
philanderer *s.* cascamorto.
philanthrope *s.* filantropo.
philanthropic(al) *agg.* filantropico.
philanthropism *s.* filantropia.
philanthropist *s.* filantropo.
philanthropy *s.* filantropia.
philatelic(al) *agg.* filatelico.
philatelist *s.* filatelico.
philately *s.* filatelia.
philharmonic *agg.* filarmonico.
philippic *s.* filippica.
Philippine *agg.* filippino.
philologian, philologist *s.* filologo.
philology *s.* filologia.
philosopher *s.* filosofo.
philosophic(al) *agg.* filosofico.
philosophist *s.* pseudofilosofo.
to **philosophize** *vi.* filosofare.
philosophy *s.* filosofia.
phlebitis *s.* flebite.
phleboclysis *s.* fleboclisi.
phlegm *s.* flemma.
phlegmatic(al) *agg.* flemmatico.
phlegmon *s.* flemmone.
phlogistic *agg.* flogistico.
phobia *s.* fobia.
phoenix *s.* fenice.
phone *s.* V. *telephone.*
phones *s. pl.* cuffie.
phoneme *s.* fonema.
phonetics *s.* fonetica.
phonogram *s.* fonogramma.
phonograph *s.* fonografo.
phonology *s.* fonologia.
phosphate *s.* fosfato.
phosphor *s.* fosforo.
phosphorescence *s.* fosforescenza.
phosphorescent *agg.* fosforescente.
phosphoric *agg.* fosforico.
phosphorous *agg.* fosforoso.

PHOTO 204 **PILING**

photo s. foto.
photocell s. cellula fotoelettrica.
photocopy s. fotocopia.
photoelectric(al) agg. fotoelettrico.
photogenic agg. fotogenico.
photograph s. fotografia.
to photograph vt. fotografare.
photographer s. fotografo.
photography s. fotografia (come arte).
photometry s. fotometria.
photomontage s. fotomontaggio.
phrase s. 1. locuzione, frase 2. stile.
to phrase vt. esprimere.
phraseology s. fraseologia.
phrenetic(al) agg. frenetico.
phrenologist s. frenologo.
phrenology s. frenologia.
phthisiology s. tisiologia.
phthisis s. tisi.
phylloxera s. fillossera.
physic s. medicina.
physical agg. fisico.
physician s. medico.
physicist s. fisico.
physics s. fisica.
physiognomist s. fisionomista.
physiognomy s. fisionomia.
physiologic(al) agg. fisiologico.
physiologist s. fisiologo.
physiology s. fisiologia.
physiotherapy s. fisioterapia.
physique s. fisico.
pianist s. pianista.
picaresque agg. picaresco.
pick[1] s. 1. piccone 2. colpo di piccone || tooth —, stuzzicadenti.
pick[2] s. scelta, il meglio (di qc.).
to pick vt. 1. scavare 2. pulire 3. raccogliere 4. rubare.
pickax(e) s. piccone.
picker s. 1. piccone 2. zappatore 3. raccoglitore.
picket s. 1. piolo, palo 2. (mil.) picchetto.
pickle s. 1. salamoia 2. sottaceti (pl.).
to pickle vt. mettere in salamoia, sotto aceto.
picklock s. 1. scassinatore 2. grimaldello.
pickpocket s. borsaiolo.
pickup s. 1. raccolta 2. (mecc.) accelerazione 3. fonorivelatore.
pictorial agg. 1. illustrato 2. pittorico. ♦ **pictorial** s. giornale illustrato.
picture s. 1. quadro, dipinto, ritrat-

to 2. illustrazione. ♦ **pictures** s. pl. cinema (sing.) || — fook, libro illustrato.
to picture vt. dipingere || to — to oneself, immaginarsi, figurarsi.
picturesque agg. pittoresco.
pidgin agg. — English, inglese scorretto (usato tra cinesi ed europei).
pie[1] s. pica, gazza.
pie[2] s. torta, pasticcio.
pie[3] s. (tip.) refuso.
piece s. 1. pezzo 2. pezza (di tessuto) || by the —, a cottimo.
to piece vt. rappezzare, raggiustare.
piecemeal avv. pezzo per pezzo. ♦ **piecemeal** agg. frammentario.
piecework s. (lavoro a) cottimo.
pieceworker s. cottimista.
pied agg. screziato.
pier s. 1. molo 2. pilone || — -glass, specchiera.
to pierce vt. 1. forare 2. trafiggere.
piercer s. 1. punzone 2. punzonatore.
piercing agg. penetrante. ♦ **piercing** s. perforatoria.
pietism s. pietismo.
piety s. pietà, reverenza.
pig s. 1. maiale 2. (metal.) lingotto.
pigeon s. piccione || — -house, piccionaia; carrier —, piccione viaggiatore.
pigeonhole s. 1. colombaia 2. casella 3. (giur.) casellario.
to pigeonhole vt. incasellare.
piggish agg. porcino.
pigheaded agg. testardo.
pigment s. pigmento.
pigmentation s. pigmentazione.
pigmy agg. e s. pigmeo.
pigsty s. porcile.
pike[1] s. picca.
pike[2] s. (amer.) pedaggio.
pilaster s. pilastro.
pile s. 1. mucchio 2. fabbricato 3. rogo 4. (elettr.) pila 5. (fig.) gruzzolo.
to pile[1] vt. ammucchiare. ♦ **to pile** vi. ammucchiarsi.
to pile[2] vt. conficcare pali in, fare palizzate.
piles s. pl. emorroidi.
to pilfer vt. e vi. rubacchiare.
pilferer s. ladruncolo.
pilgrim s. pellegrino.
pilgrimage s. pellegrinaggio.
piling[1] s. ammucchiamento.
piling[2] s. palificazione di sostegno.

pill *s.* pillola: *contraceptive (pill),* pillola anticoncezionale.

pillage *s.* **1.** saccheggio **2.** bottino.

to **pillage** *vt.* saccheggiare.

pillar *s.* colonna, guanciale || — -*box,* cassetta delle lettere.

pillory *s.* berlina.

to **pillory** *vt.* mettere alla berlina.

pillow *s.* cuscino, guanciale || — -*case,* federa.

pilot *s.* pilota.

to **pilot** *vt.* pilotare.

pilotage *s.* pilotaggio.

pimple *s.* foruncolo.

pin *s.* **1.** spillo **2.** perno || *pins and needles,* formicolio.

to **pin** *vt.* **1.** puntare **2.** (*fig.*) inchiodare.

pinafore *s.* grembiulino.

pinaster *s.* pinastro.

to **pincer** *vt.* attanagliare.

pincers *s. pl.* tenaglie.

pinch *s.* **1.** pizzico, pizzicotto **2.** (*fig.*) angustia.

to **pinch** *vt.* **1.** pizzicare **2.** stringere **3.** causare dolore. ♦ to **pinch** *vi.* essere avaro.

pinchbeck *s.* princisbecco.

pincushion *s.* puntaspilli.

Pindaric *agg.* pindarico.

pine *s.* pino || — -*apple,* ananasso; — -*cone,* pigna; — -*wood,* pineta.

to **pine** *vi.* struggersi.

pinion¹ *s.* penna remigante.

pinion² *s.* (*mecc.*) pignone.

to **pinion** *vt.* tarpare le ali a.

pink *agg.* rosa. ♦ **pink** *s.* **1.** colore rosa **2.** garofano **3.** (*fig.*) quintessenza.

to **pink** *vt.* **1.** traforare **2.** trafiggere.

pinky *agg.* roseo.

pinnacle *s.* **1.** pinnacolo **2.** sommità.

pinpoint *s.* capocchia di spillo.

pint *s.* pinta.

pioneer *s.* pioniere.

pious *agg.* **1.** pio **2.** pietoso.

piousness *s.* pietà.

pip *s.* seme di frutto.

to **pip** *vi.* pigolare.

pipage *s.* **1.** tubatura **2.** trasporto per tubatura.

pipe *s.* **1.** tubo **2.** pipa **3.** strumento a fiato **4.** condotta.

to **pipe** *vi.* **1.** suonare (*piffero ecc.*) **2.** stridere. ♦ to **pipe** *vt.* **1.** suonare **2.** trasportare con tubature **3.** fornire di tubature.

pipeline *s.* oleodotto.

piper *s.* pifferaio.

pipet(te) *s.* (*chim.*) pipetta.

piping *agg.* **1.** flautato **2.** acuto. ♦ **piping** *s.* **1.** suono (*di piffero ecc.*) **2.** suono acuto **3.** tubatura.

piquancy *s.* gusto piccante.

piquant *agg.* piccante.

pique *s.* ripicco, risentimento.

piracy *s.* **1.** pirateria **2.** plagio.

pirate *s.* **1.** pirata **2.** plagiario.

pirogue *s.* piroga.

pirouette *s.* piroetta.

to **pirouette** *vi.* piroettare.

pistil *s.* pistillo.

pistol *s.* pistola.

piston *s.* pistone.

pit *s.* **1.** fossa **2.** cavità **3.** platea.

to **pit** *vt.* **1.** bucare **2.** mettere in una fossa.

pitch¹ *s.* **1.** lancio **2.** beccheggio **3.** (*mecc.*) passo **4.** (*mus.*) intonazione **5.** inclinazione.

pitch² *s.* pece, bitume || — -*dark,* nero come la pece.

to **pitch**¹ *vt.* **1.** sistemare **2.** gettare **3.** intonare. ♦ to **pitch** *vi.* **1.** beccheggiare **2.** (*aer.*) picchiare.

to **pitch**² *vt.* impeciare.

pitcher *s.* brocca.

pitchfork *s.* forcone.

to **pitchfork** *vt.* **1.** rimuovere **2.** spingere (*col forcone*).

pitching *s.* beccheggio.

pitchy *agg.* **1.** impeciato **2.** simile a pece.

piteous *agg.* pietoso.

pitfall *s.* trappola.

pith *s.* **1.** midollo **2.** (*fig.*) essenza.

pithy *agg.* (*fig.*) vigoroso.

pitiable, pitiful *agg.* pietoso.

pitiless *agg.* spietato.

pittance *s.* poco denaro.

pitted *agg.* butterato.

pity *s.* pietà || *what a* —!, che peccato!

to **pity** *vt.* aver pietà di, compatire.

pitying *agg.* pietoso.

pivot *s.* cardine.

to **pivot** *vt.* montare su cardini. ♦ to **pivot** *vi.* girare su cardini.

placable *agg.* placabile.

placard *s.* manifesto.

to **placate** *vt.* placare.

placatory *agg.* conciliante.

place *s.* **1.** posto **2.** brano || *to take* —, aver luogo, accadere.

to **place** vt. mettere, porre, situare.
placement s. collocamento.
placid agg. placido.
placidity s. placidità.
placing s. sistemazione.
plagiarism s. plagio.
plagiarist s. plagiario.
to **plagiarize** vt. plagiare.
plagiary s. 1. plagio 2. plagiario.
plague s. peste.
to **plague** vt. affliggere.
plaguer s. tormentatore.
plaid s. 1. mantello scozzese 2. tessuto a quadri.
plain agg. 1. piano, chiaro, evidente 2. semplice 3. comune, scialbo. ♦ **plain** s. pianura. ♦ **plain** avv. 1. chiaramente 2. semplicemente.
plain-clothes s. pl. abiti borghesi.
plainness s. 1. chiarezza 2. semplicità 3. aspetto scialbo.
plaint s. 1. lamento, lagnanza 2. (giur.) querela.
plaintiff s. (giur.) attore (nei processi civili).
plaintive agg. lamentoso.
plait s. 1. piega (di abiti) 2. treccia.
to **plait** vt. 1. pieghettare 2. intrecciare.
plan s. 1. piano, progetto 2. pianta (di una città).
to **plan** vt. progettare.
plane[1] agg. piano. ♦ **plane** s. 1. piano 2. aereo.
plane[2] s. pialla.
plane[3] s. — -tree, platano.
to **plane**[1] vi. volare.
to **plane**[2] vt. piallare.
planer s. (mecc.) piallatrice.
planet s. (astr.) pianeta.
planetary agg. planetario.
planimetric(al) agg. planimetrico.
planimetry s. planimetria.
planisphere s. planisfero.
plank s. tavola, asse.
to **plank** vt. coprire di tavole.
planking s. tavolato.
plankton s. plancton.
planner s. progettista.
planning s. progettazione.
plant s. 1. pianta 2. impianto, apparato 3. fabbrica, stabilimento.
to **plant** vt. (im)piantare.
plantation s. piantagione.
planter s. 1. piantatore 2. colonizzatore.
plantigrade agg. e s. plantigrado.
plaque s. placca.
plash s. pozzanghera.

plaster s. 1. cerotto 2. gesso 3. intonaco.
to **plaster** vt. 1. incerottare 2. ingessare 3. intonacare 4. ricoprire.
plastering s. 1. intonacatura 2. ingessatura.
plastic agg. plastico, malleabile.
plasticine s. plastilina.
plasticity s. plasticità.
to **plasticize** vt. rendere plastico.
plastics s. pl. materie plastiche.
plate s. 1. lastra, lamina 2. piatto 3. tavola fuori testo 4. targa 5. squama 6. vasellame.
to **plate** vt. 1. placcare 2. rivestire di piastre.
plateau s. altipiano.
platen s. 1. piastra metallica 2. rullo di macchina da scrivere.
platform s. 1. piattaforma 2. (ferr.) marciapiede 3. impalcatura 4. (amer.) programma politico.
plating s. 1. placcatura 2. rivestimento metallico.
to **platinize** vt. platinare.
platinum s. platino.
platitude s. banalità.
Platonic agg. platonico.
Platonism s. platonismo.
platoon s. plotone.
plausibility s. plausibilità.
plausible agg. plausibile.
play s. 1. gioco 2. dramma 3. (mus.) esecuzione 4. azione || — bill, cartellone teatrale; — -time, ricreazione.
to **play** vt. e vi. 1. giocare 2. recitare 3. agire 4. suonare || to — down, dare poca importanza a.
playboy s. (fam.) gaudente.
player s. 1. giocatore 2. attore 3. suonatore.
playful agg. giocoso.
playfulness s. allegria.
playground s. terreno di giochi.
playhouse s. teatro.
playing s. 1. gioco 2. rappresentazione 3. (mus.) esecuzione.
plaything s. giocattolo.
playwright, playwriter s. commediografo.
plea s. 1. giustificazione 2. (giur.) eccezione difensiva.
to **plead** vt. 1. patrocinare 2. addurre a pretesto 3. (giur.) perorare (una causa). ♦ to **plead** vi. 1. difendersi 2. supplicare.
pleader s. patrocinatore.
pleading agg. supplichevole. ♦

pleading s. difesa. ♦ **pleadings** s. pl. comparse.

pleasant agg. piacevole.

pleasantry s. piacevolezza.

to **please** vt. e vi. piacere (a) || — God, a Dio piacendo.

pleased agg. lieto.

pleasing agg. piacevole.

pleasure s. piacere.

pleat s. piega (di abiti ecc.).

to **pleat** vt. pieghettare.

plebeian agg. e s. plebeo.

plebiscitary agg. plebiscitario.

plebiscite s. plebiscito.

plectrum s. plettro.

pledge s. 1. pegno 2. promessa 3. brindisi.

to **pledge** vt. 1. impegnare 2. brindare a.

pledgee s. (giur.) creditore pignoratizio.

plenary agg. plenario || — session, seduta plenaria.

plenilune s. plenilunio.

plenipotentiary agg. e s. plenipotenziario.

plentiful agg. abbondante.

plenty s. abbondanza, quantità.

pleonasm s. pleonasma.

pleonastic agg. pleonastico.

plethora s. pletora.

plethoric agg. pletorico.

pleurisy s. pleurite.

plexus s. plesso.

pliability s. pieghevolezza.

pliable agg. pieghevole.

pliancy s. V. pliability.

pliant s. V. pliable.

pliers s. pl. pinze.

plight[1] s. situazione critica.

plight[2] s. impegno, promessa.

to **plight** vt. impegnare, promettere.

plod s. 1. passo pesante 2. lavoro faticoso.

to **plod** vt. e vi. 1. camminare faticosamente 2. sgobbare.

plodder s. 1. chi cammina faticosamente 2. sgobbone.

plot s. 1. appezzamento 2. trama 3. congiura.

to **plot** vt. e vi. 1. fare la pianta di 2. tramare.

plotter s. cospiratore.

plough s. aratro.

to **plough** vt. e vi. 1. arare 2. solcare.

ploughing s. aratura.

ploughman s. aratore.

ploughshare s. vomere.

plover s. piviere.

pluck s. 1. strappo 2. coraggio.

to **pluck** vt. 1. strappare 2. spennare 3. tirare || to — up, sradicare.

plucky agg. coraggioso.

plug s. 1. tappo (di lavandino ecc.) 2. (elettr.; tel.) spina || spark(ing)- — (mecc.), candela.

to **plug** vt. 1. tappare 2. tamponare || to — in, inserire la corrente; to — away, sgobbare.

plugging s. chiusura.

plum s. 1. prugna, susina 2. uva passa 3. (fig.) il meglio.

plumage s. piumaggio.

plumb agg. 1. a piombo 2. completo. ♦ **plumb** s. 1. filo a piombo 2. scandaglio. ♦ **plumb** avv. 1. a piombo 2. esattamente.

to **plumb** vt. 1. rendere verticale 2. scandagliare 3. impiombare.

plumber s. idraulico.

plumbery s. negozio di idraulico.

plumbing s. 1. piombatura 2. lavori idraulici.

plumbum s. piombo.

plume s. piuma, penna.

plummet s. piombino.

plump[1] agg. grassottello.

plump[2] agg. brusco, netto.
♦ **plump** avv. 1. improvvisamente 2. direttamente.

to **plump** vt. 1. ingrassare 2. far cadere. ♦ to **plump** vi. 1. ingrassare 2. cadere.

to **plunder** v. depredare.

plunderer s. saccheggiatore.

plunge s. tuffo.

to **plunge** vt. tuffare. ♦ to **plunge** vi. tuffarsi.

plunger s. 1. tuffatore 2. stantuffo.

plunk s. colpo metallico.

to **plunk** vt. far cadere pesantemente. ♦ to **plunk** vi. cadere pesantemente.

plural agg. e s. plurale.

pluralism s. pluralismo.

plurality s. pluralità.

plus agg. 1. in più 2. (elettr.) positivo || — value, plusvalore. ♦ **plus** s. 1. più 2. quantità positiva. ♦ **plus** prep. più.

plush s. « peluche », felpa.

plutocracy s. plutocrazia.

plutocrat s. plutocrate.

ply s. piega || — -wood, compensato.

to **ply** vt. 1. maneggiare 2. importunare. ♦ to **ply** vi. 1. lavorare as-

siduamente **2.** fare la spola.
pneumatic *agg.* e *s.* pneumatico.
pneumonia *s.* polmonite.
pneumothorax *s.* pneumotorace.
to **poach** *vt.* **1.** calpestare **2.** cacciare di frodo **3.** interferire.
poacher *s.* bracconiere.
poaching *s.* bracconaggio.
pocket *s.* **1.** tasca **2.** buca (*di biliardo*) ǁ — *-book*, libro tascabile.
to **pocket** *vt.* **1.** intascare **2.** nascondere, soffocare (*sentimenti ecc.*).
pocketful *s.* tascata.
pod *s.* **1.** baccello **2.** gruppetto.
poem *s.* **1.** poesia **2.** poema.
poet *s.* poeta.
poetic(al) *agg.* poetico.
poetic(s) *s.* poetica.
poetry *s.* poesia.
poignant *agg.* **1.** pungente **2.** commovente.
point *s.* **1.** punto **2.** punta, estremità **3.** caratteristica.
to **point** *vt.* **1.** indicare, segnare a dito **2.** appuntire **3.** dirigere ǁ *to* — *out*, indicare, porre in rilievo.
point-blank *agg.* diretto. ♦ **point-blank** *avv.* direttamente.
pointed *agg.* **1.** appuntito **2.** mordace **3.** evidente.
pointer *s.* **1.** indicatore **2.** lancetta (*di orologio*).
pointless *agg.* **1.** spuntato **2.** inutile, senza scopo.
pointsman *s.* (*ferr.*) deviatore.
poise *s.* equilibrio.
to **poise** *vt.* bilanciare. ♦ to **poise** *vi.* bilanciarsi.
poison *s.* veleno.
to **poison** *vt.* avvelenare.
poisoning *agg.* velenoso. ♦ **poisoning** *s.* avvelenamento.
poisonous *agg.* velenoso (*anche fig.*).
poke *s.* spinta, urto.
to **poke** *vt.* e *vi.* **1.** spingere **2.** andare a tastoni.
poker *s.* attizzatoio.
poky *agg.* meschino.
polar *agg.* polare.
polarity *s.* polarità.
polarization *s.* polarizzazione.
to **polarize** *vt.* polarizzare.
pole[1] *s.* palo
pole[2] *s.* polo.
Pole[3] *s.* polacco.
polecat *s.* puzzola.
polemic *s.* **1.** polemica **2.** polemista.
polemic(al) *agg.* polemico.

polemi(ci)st *s.* polemista.
to **polemize** *vi.* polemizzare.
police *s.* polizia ǁ — *-force*, corpo di polizia.
police court *s.* pretura.
policeman *s.* poliziotto.
policy[1] *s.* **1.** linea di condotta **2.** sagacia.
policy[2] *s.* polizza.
polio(myelitis) *s.* poliomielite.
Polish[1] *agg.* polacco.
polish[2] *s.* **1.** lucidatura **2.** lucido **3.** raffinatezza ǁ *shoe* —, lucido per le scarpe.
to **polish** *vt.* **1.** lucidare **2.** raffinare. ♦ to **polish** *vi.* **1.** divenire lucido **2.** raffinarsi.
polisher *s.* **1.** lucidatore **2.** lucido.
polishing *s.* lucidatura.
polite *agg.* cortese.
politeness *s.* cortesia.
politic *agg.* abile.
political *agg.* politico.
politician *s.* uomo politico.
politics *s.* politica.
poll *s.* **1.** votazione, scrutinio **2.** referendum.
to **poll** *vt.* radere. ♦ to **poll** *vi.* votare, raccogliere voti.
pollen *s.* polline.
to **pollinate** *vt.* impollinare.
pollination *s.* impollinazione.
to **pollute** *vt.* contaminare.
pollution *s.* contaminazione.
polyandry *s.* poliandria.
polychrome *agg.* policromo.
polychromy *s.* policromia.
polyclinic *s.* policlinico.
polygamist *s.* poligamo.
polygamous *agg.* poligamo.
polygamy *s.* poligamia.
polyglot *agg.* e *s.* poliglotta.
polygon *s.* poligono.
polyhedral *agg.* poliedrico.
polyhedron *s.* poliedro.
polymerization *s.* polimerizzazione.
polymorphic *agg.* polimorfo.
polymorphism *s.* polimorfismo.
polyp *s.* polipo.
polyphonic *agg.* polifonico.
polyphony *s.* polifonia.
polysyllabic(al) *agg.* polisillabico.
polysyllable *s.* polisillabo.
polytechnic *agg.* e *s.* politecnico.
polytheism *s.* politeismo.
polytheist *s.* politeista.
polytheistic(al) *agg.* politeistico.
polyvalent *agg.* polivalente.

pomade s. pomata.
to pomade vt. impomatare.
pomegranate s. 1. melagrana 2. melograno.
pomp s. pompa, fasto.
pomposity s. pomposità.
pompous agg. pomposo.
pond s. stagno.
to pond vt. e vi. stagnare.
to ponder vt. e vi. ponderare.
ponderable agg. ponderabile.
ponderous agg. ponderoso.
pontiff s. pontefice.
pontifical agg. pontificio. ♦ **pontifical** s. pontificato.
pontificate s. pontificato.
to pontificate vi. pontificare.
pontoon s. pontone.
pony s. « pony », piccolo cavallo.
poodle s. barboncino.
pool[1] s. 1. stagno 2. pozza || *swimming* —, piscina.
pool[2] s. (*comm.*) 1. fondo comune 2. (*comm.*) consorzio, sindacato.
poor agg. povero.
poorly avv. male.
poorness s. povertà.
pop s. scoppio.
to pop vi. scoppiare. ♦ **to pop** vt. 1. far scoppiare 2. ficcare.
popcorn s. fiocco di granoturco.
pope s. papa.
popery s. papismo.
poplar s. pioppo.
poppied agg. coperto di papaveri.
poppy s. papavero.
populace s. plebaglia.
popular agg. popolare.
popularity s. popolarità.
popularization s. popolarizzazione.
to popularize vt. popolarizzare.
to populate vt. popolare.
population s. popolazione.
Populism s. populismo.
Populist s. populista.
populous agg. popoloso.
porch s. portico.
porcupine s. porcospino.
pore s. poro.
to pore vi. esaminare.
pork s. carne di maiale.
pornographic agg. pornografico.
pornography s. pornografia.
porosity s. porosità.
porous agg. poroso.
porphyry s. porfido.
port[1] s. porto.
port[2] s. 1. (*mecc.*) apertura, foro 2. (*mar.*) portello.

port[3] s. fianco sinistro di nave.
portable agg. portatile.
portal s. portale.
portcullis s. saracinesca (*di fortezza*).
to portend vt. preannunciare.
portent s. 1. presagio 2. portento.
portentous agg. 1. sinistro 2. portentoso.
porter[1] s. facchino.
porter[2] s. custode, portiere.
porter[3] s. birra scura.
portfolio s. 1. cartella, busta 2. (*pol.*) portafoglio.
porthole s. 1. (*mar.*) portello 2. feritoia.
portion s. porzione, parte.
to portion vt. dividere, distribuire.
portrait s. ritratto.
portraitist s. ritrattista.
to portray vt. ritrarre.
portrayal s. ritratto.
portrayer s. ritrattista.
Portuguese agg. e s. portoghese.
pose s. posa.
to pose[1] vt. proporre.
to pose[2] vi. posare.
poser s. posatore.
position s. posizione.
positive agg. 1. positivo 2. sicuro. ♦ **positive** s. 1. realtà 2. (*foto*) positiva.
positivism s. positivismo.
positivist s. positivista.
positivistic agg. positivistico.
posology s. posologia.
to possess vt. possedere.
possessed agg. indemoniato.
possession s. possesso.
possessive agg. possessivo.
possessor s. possessore.
possibility s. possibilità.
possible agg. possibile.
possibly avv. possibilmente.
post[1] s. posta, corrispondenza || — *card*, cartolina; *by return of* —, a giro di posta.
post[2] s. 1. palo, sostegno, puntello 2. stipite || *sign*- —, indicatore stradale.
to post[1] vt. imbucare, inviare per posta.
to post[2] vt. affiggere.
postage s. spese postali (*pl.*).
postage stamp s. francobollo.
postal agg. postale.
to postdate vt. posdatare.
poster s. 1. affisso 2. attacchino.
poste-restante s. fermo posta.

posterior *agg.* posteriore.
posterity *s.* posterità.
postern *s.* postierla.
post-free *agg.* franco di porto.
posthumous *agg.* postumo.
postil(l)ion *s.* postiglione.
postman *s.* postino.
postmark *s.* timbro postale.
postmaster *s.* direttore di ufficio postale.
to **postpone** *vt.* rimandare.
postponement *s.* rinvio.
to **post-score** *vt.* (*cine*) sonorizzare.
postscript *s.* poscritto.
postulate *s.* postulato.
to **postulate** *vt.* **1.** porre come postulato **2.** chiedere.
postulator *s.* postulante.
posture *s.* posizione.
to **posture** *vi.* assumere una posizione.
post-war *agg.* postbellico.
posy *s.* mazzolino di fiori.
pot *s.* **1.** recipiente **2.** pentola || — -*bellied*, panciuto.
to **pot** *vt.* conservare (*in vaso*).
potable *agg.* potabile.
potash *s.* potassa.
potassic *agg.* potassico.
potassium *s.* potassio.
potato *s.* patata.
potent *agg.* potente.
potential *agg.* e *s.* potenziale.
potentiality *s.* potenzialità.
potion *s.* pozione.
potter *s.* vasaio.
pottery *s.* **1.** terraglie **2.** fabbrica di terraglie.
pouch *s.* borsa.
to **pouch** *vt.* intascare.
poulterer *s.* pollivendolo.
poultry *s.* pollame.
pounce *s.* balzo.
to **pounce** *vi.* avventarsi su, contro.
pound[1] *s.* **1.** libbra **2.** sterlina.
pound[2] *s.* recinto.
to **pound**[1] *vt.* e *vi.* pestare.
to **pound**[2] *vt.* rinchiudere.
pour *s.* acquazzone.
to **pour** *vt.* versare. ♦ to **pour** *vi.* **1.** versarsi **2.** diluviare.
pout *s.* broncio.
to **pout** *vi.* fare il broncio.
poverty *s.* povertà.
powder *s.* **1.** polvere **2.** cipria, talco.
to **powder** *vt.* **1.** polverizzare **2.** incipriare. ♦ to **powder** *vi.* **1.** pol-

verizzarsi **2.** incipriarsi.
powdery *agg.* **1.** friabile **2.** polveroso.
power *s.* potenza, potere || *horse* —, cavallo vapore; — -*station*, centrale elettrica.
to **power** *vt.* motorizzare.
powerful *agg.* potente.
powerless *agg.* debole.
pox *s.* sifilide || *chicken*- —, varicella, *small*- —, vaiolo.
practicability *s.* praticabilità.
practicable *agg.* **1.** praticabile **2.** fattibile.
practical *agg.* pratico.
practicality *s.* praticità.
practice *s.* **1.** pratica **2.** abitudine, regola **3.** esercizio **4.** professione **5.** (*coll.*) clienti (*di medico ecc.*).
to **practise** *vt.* **1.** praticare **2.** esercitare. ♦ to **practise** *vi.* esercitarsi.
practitioner *s.* professionista.
praetorian *s.* pretoriano.
pragmatic(al) *agg.* prammatico.
pragmatism *s.* pragmatismo.
pragmatist *agg.* e *s.* pragmatista.
prairie *s.* prateria.
praise *s.* lode.
to **praise** *vt.* lodare.
praiser *s.* lodatore.
praiseworthy *agg.* lodevole.
prance *s.* impennata.
prank *s.* monelleria.
to **prank** *vt.* ornare, agghindare vistosamente. ♦ to **prank** *vi.* mettersi in mostra.
prate *s.* chiacchiera, sproloquio.
to **prate** *vi.* chiacchierare, proferire parole senza senso.
prattle *s.* balbettio.
to **prattle** *vt.* e *vi.* balbettare.
praxis *s.* prassi.
to **pray** *vt.* e *vi.* pregare.
prayer *s.* preghiera.
to **preach** *vt.* e *vi.* predicare.
preacher *s.* predicatore.
to **preachify** *vi.* predicare in modo noioso.
preaching *s.* predicazione.
preachy *agg.* (*fam.*) incline a far prediche.
to **pre-announce** *vt.* preannunziare.
to **prearrange** *vt.* predisporre.
prearrangement *s.* predisposizione.
prebend *s.* prebenda.
prebendary *s.* prebendario.
precarious *agg.* precario.

precariousness s. precarietà.
precatory agg. supplichevole.
precaution s. precauzione.
precautional agg. precauzionale.
to **precede** vt. e vi. precedere.
precedence s. precedenza.
precedent agg. e s. precedente.
preceding agg. precedente.
precept s. precetto.
preceptive agg. istruttivo.
preceptor s. precettore.
precession s. precessione.
precinct s. 1. recinto 2. limiti 3. vicinanze (pl.).
preciosity s. preziosità.
precious agg. prezioso.
preciousness s. preziosità.
precipice s. precipizio.
precipitate agg. e s. precipitato.
to **precipitate** vt. e vi. precipitare.
precipitation s. precipitazione.
precipitous agg. ripido.
précis s. riassunto.
precise agg. preciso.
precision s. precisione.
to **preclude** vt. precludere.
precocious agg. precoce.
precociousness, precocity s. precocità.
preconceived agg. preconcetto.
precursor s. precursore, predecessore.
precursory agg. 1. preliminare 2. premonitore.
predaceous agg. rapace.
to **predate** vt. predatare.
predatory agg. rapace.
to **predecease** vt. premorire a.
predecessor s. predecessore.
to **predesignate** vt. predesignare.
predestination s. predestinazione.
to **predestine** vt. predestinare.
predetermination s. predeterminazione.
to **predetermine** vt. predeterminare.
predicable agg. asseribile.
predicament s. situazione scabrosa.
predicate agg. e s. predicato.
to **predicate** vt. 1. asserire 2. implicare.
predication s. affermazione.
predicative agg. 1. predicativo 2. affermativo.
predicatory agg. predicatorio.
to **predict** vt. e vi. predire.
prediction s. predizione.
predilection s. predilezione.

to **predispose** vt. predisporre.
predisposition s. predisposizione.
predominance s. predominanza.
to **predominate** vi. predominare.
pre-eminence s. preminenza.
pre-eminent agg. preminente.
pre-emption s. prelazione, priorità.
to **pre-engage** vt. impegnare in anticipo.
to **pre-establish** vt. prestabilire.
to **pre-exist** vi. preesistere.
pre-existence s. preesistenza.
to **prefabricate** vt. prefabbricare.
prefabricated agg. — house, casa prefabbricata.
preface s. prefazione.
to **preface** vt. 1. fare una prefazione a 2. iniziare.
prefatory agg. introduttivo.
prefect s. prefetto.
prefecture s. prefettura.
to **prefer** vt. 1. preferire 2. promuovere, elevare.
preferable agg. preferibile.
preference s. preferenza.
preferential agg. preferenziale.
preferment s. avanzamento, promozione.
prefiguration s. prefigurazione.
to **prefigure** vt. prefigurare.
prefix s. prefisso.
pregnancy s. 1. gravidanza 2. (fig.) significato, importanza.
pregnant agg. 1. incinta 2. significativo, importante 3. fecondo.
prehension s. 1. prensione 2. apprendimento.
prehistoric(al) agg. preistorico.
prehistory s. preistoria.
prejudice s. pregiudizio.
to **prejudice** vt. 1. pregiudicare 2. influenzare.
prejudicial agg. pregiudizievole.
prelate s. prelato.
prelatic(al) agg. prelatizio.
preliminary agg. preliminare. ♦ **preliminaries** s. pl. preliminari.
prelude s. preludio.
to **prelude** vt. preludere. ♦ to **prelude** vi. eseguire un preludio.
premature agg. prematuro.
to **premeditate** vt. premeditare.
premeditation s. premeditazione.
premier s. primo ministro.
premise s. 1. premessa 2. stabile con terreni annessi.
to **premise** vt. premettere.
premolar agg. e s. premolare.
premonitory agg. premonitore.

preoccupation s. preoccupazione.

to **preoccupy** vt. 1. preoccupare 2. occupare in precedenza.

preparation s. preparazione, preparativo.

preparative, preparatory agg. preparatorio.

to **prepare** vt. preparare. ♦ to **prepare** vi. prepararsi.

preponderance s. preponderanza.

preponderant agg. preponderante.

preposition s. preposizione.

prepositional agg. di preposizione.

to **prepossess** vt. 1. occupare in precedenza 2. influenzare.

prepossessing agg. attraente.

prepossession s. prevenzione.

preposterous agg. assurdo.

prepotence s. predominio.

prepotent agg. predominante.

Pre-Raphaeli(ti)sm s. preraffaellismo.

prerogative agg. privilegiato. ♦ **prerogative** s. prerogativa.

presage s. presagio.

presbyope s. presbite.

presbyopic agg. presbite.

Presbyterian agg. e s. presbiteriano.

Presbyterianism s. presbiterianismo.

presbytery s. presbiterio.

prescience s. prescienza.

to **prescribe** vt. prescrivere.

prescript s. ordinanza.

prescription s. prescrizione.

presence s. presenza.

present[1] agg. presente || — -day, contemporaneo. ♦ **present** s. presente, tempo presente || at —, attualmente. ♦ **presents** s. pl. (giur.) documento (sing.).

present[2] s. dono, regalo.

to **present** vt. 1. presentare 2. regalare.

presentable agg. presentabile.

presentation s. 1. presentazione 2. dono.

presenter s. 1. presentatore 2. donatore.

presentiment s. presentimento.

presently avv. presto, quanto prima.

presentment s. presentazione.

preservable agg. conservabile.

preservation s. conservazione.

preservative agg. e s. preservativo.

preserve s. 1. riserva 2. conserva (di pomodoro, frutta ecc.).

to **preserve** vt. 1. preservare 2. conservare 3. mettere in conserva.

to **preside** vi. presiedere.

presidency s. presidenza.

president s. presidente.

presidential agg. presidenziale.

press s. 1. stretta, pressione 2. pressa 3. (fig.) stampa 4. calca, ressa || — conference, conferenza stampa.

to **press** vt. 1. premere, comprimere 2. costringere. ♦ to **press** vi. affollarsi.

pressing agg. 1. urgente 2. insistente.

pressman s. 1. cronista (di giornale) 2. (tip.) stampatore.

pressure s. pressione || — -cooker, pentola a pressione.

to **pressurize** vt. pressurizzare.

prestige s. prestigio.

presumable agg. presumibile.

to **presume** vt. e vi. 1. presumere 2. avere la presunzione di.

presuming agg. presuntuoso.

presumption s. 1. presunzione 2. supposizione.

presumptive agg. presunto.

presumptuous agg. presuntuoso.

presumptuousness s. presunzione.

to **presuppose** vt. presupporre.

presupposition s. presupposizione.

pretence s. 1. pretesa 2. pretesto 3. simulazione.

to **pretend** vi. 1. pretendere 2. fingere.

pretender s. 1. pretendente 2. simulatore.

pretension s. 1. pretesa 2. presunzione.

pretentious agg. pretenzioso.

preternatural agg. soprannaturale.

pretext s. pretesto.

prettiness s. grazia.

pretty agg. grazioso. ♦ **pretty** avv. abbastanza.

to **prevail** vi. prevalere.

prevailing agg. 1. prevalente 2. efficace.

prevalence s. prevalenza.

to **prevaricate** vi. 1. tergiversare 2. mentire.

prevarication s. 1. tergiversazione 2. menzogna.

prevaricator s. 1. chi tergiversa 2. mentitore.

to **prevent** vt. impedire.

prevention s. 1. impedimento 2. prevenzione.

preventive agg. preventivo.

preview s. anteprima.
previous agg. precedente.
prevision s. previsione.
pre-war agg. prebellico.
prey s. preda.
to **prey** vi. **1.** (de)predare **2.** (fig.) consumare.
price s. prezzo, costo.
to **price** vt. fissare il prezzo di.
priceless agg. inestimabile.
prick s. **1.** punta **2.** puntura **3.** (fig.) pungolo, rimorso.
to **prick** vt. **1.** pungere **2.** segnare **3.** rizzare le orecchie. ♦ to **prick** vi. **1.** formicolare **2.** pungersi.
prickle s. **1.** spina **2.** pungiglione.
prickly agg. pungente.
pride s. orgoglio.
to **pride** vt. to — oneself upon, essere orgoglioso di.
priest s. prete.
priesthood s. **1.** clero **2.** sacerdozio.
prig s. presuntuoso.
prim agg. affettato.
primary agg. primo, primario.
primate s. (eccl.) primate.
prime agg. **1.** primo **2.** di prima qualità. ♦ **prime** s. **1.** principio **2.** (fig.) fiore.
to **prime** vt. caricare, innescare.
primer[1] s. sillabario.
primer[2] s. innesco.
primeval agg. primordiale.
primigenial agg. primigenio.
priming s. **1.** innesco **2.** prima mano (di vernice ecc.).
primitive agg. e s. primitivo.
primitiveness s. primitività.
primogeniture s. primogenitura.
primordial agg. primordiale.
primrose s. primula.
prince s. principe.
princely agg. principesco.
princess s. principessa.
principal agg. principale. ♦ **principal** s. **1.** principale, direttore **2.** (edil.) trave maestra **3.** (comm.) mandante.
principality s. principato.
principle s. principio.
print s. **1.** impronta **2.** stampa **3.** stampatello **4.** (foto) copia.
to **print** vt. **1.** stampare **2.** scrivere a stampatello **3.** imprimere.
printer s. **1.** tipografo **2.** (mecc.) stampatrice.
printing s. **1.** stampa **2.** tiratura ‖ — -press, pressa tipografica.
prior agg. precedente. ♦ **prior** s.

priore. ♦ **prior** avv. prima.
priorate s. priorato.
prioress s. priora.
priority s. priorità.
prism s. prisma.
prismatic(al) agg. prismatico.
prison s. prigione.
prisoner s. prigioniero.
privacy s. **1.** intimità **2.** riserbo.
private agg. **1.** privato **2.** appartato **3.** segreto, riservato, personale. ♦ **private** s. soldato semplice.
privation s. privazione.
privative agg. privativo.
privilege s. privilegio.
to **privilege** vt. privilegiare.
privy agg. **1.** nascosto **2.** al corrente di.
prize s. premio.
to **prize** vt. stimare.
probabilism s. probabilismo.
probability s. probabilità.
probable agg. probabile.
probate s. omologazione.
probation s. prova.
probative agg. probativo.
probatory agg. probatorio.
probe s. sonda.
to **probe** vt. sondare.
probity s. probità.
problem s. problema.
problematic(al) agg. problematico.
procedural agg. procedurale.
procedure s. **1.** procedimento **2.** procedura.
to **proceed** vi. **1.** procedere **2.** provenire.
proceeding s. V. procedure.
proceeds s. pl. profitto (sing.).
process s. **1.** procedimento **2.** processo.
to **process** vt. **1.** processare **2.** (chim.) trattare.
procession s. processione.
processionary s. (zool.) processionaria.
proclaim s. proclama.
to **proclaim** vt. proclamare.
proclamation s. proclama(zione).
proconsul s. proconsole.
to **procrastinate** vt. e vi. procrastinare.
procrastination s. procrastinazione.
to **procreate** vt. procreare.
procreation s. procreazione.
procreator s. procreatore.
proctor s. **1.** censore **2.** (giur.) procuratore.

procurator s. procuratore.
to **procure** vt. **1.** procurare, procurarsi **2.** adescare.
procurer s. mezzano.
prod s. pungolo.
to **prod** vt. pungolare.
prodigal agg. e s. prodigo.
prodigality s. prodigalità.
prodigious agg. **1.** prodigioso **2.** enorme.
prodigiousness s. prodigiosità.
prodigy s. prodigio.
produce s. prodotto || farm —, prodotto agricolo; raw —, materia prima.
to **produce** vt. **1.** produrre **2.** presentare.
producer s. **1.** produttore **2.** (teat.) regista.
product s. prodotto.
production s. **1.** esibizione **2.** produzione.
productive agg. produttivo.
productivity s. produttività.
proem s. proemio.
profanation s. profanazione.
profane agg. **1.** profano **2.** empio.
to **profane** vt. profanare.
profaner s. profanatore.
profanity s. **1.** profanità **2.** empietà.
to **profess** vt. **1.** professare **2.** pretendere.
profession s. professione.
professional agg. professionale || — man, professionista. ♦ **professional** s. professionista.
professionalism s. professionismo.
professor s. professore (d'università).
professorial agg. professorale.
proficiency s. competenza || — in English, buona conoscenza dell'inglese.
proficient agg. e s. esperto, competente.
profile s. profilo.
to **profile** vt. **1.** profilare **2.** tracciare il profilo di.
profit s. profitto, guadagno.
to **profit** vt. giovare. ♦ to **profit** vi. approfittare.
profitable agg. vantaggioso.
profiteer s. profittatore.
profligacy s. **1.** sregolatezza **2.** sperpero.
profligate agg. e s. **1.** dissoluto **2.** scialacquatore.
profound agg. profondo.

profuse agg. **1.** abbondante **2.** prodigo.
profusion s. **1.** profusione **2.** prodigalità.
progenitor s. progenitore.
progeny s. progenie.
prognathism s. prognatismo.
prognathous agg. prognato.
prognosis s. (pl. -ses) prognosi.
prognostic agg. rivelatore. ♦ **prognostic** s. **1.** pronostico **2.** sintomo.
prognostication s. **1.** pronostico **2.** prognosi.
program(me) s. programma.
to **program(me)** vt. programmare.
programming s. programmazione.
programmist s. programmista.
progress s. **1.** progresso **2.** avanzata **3.** sviluppo **4.** andamento, corso.
to **progress** vi. **1.** progredire **2.** avanzare **3.** svilupparsi.
progression s. **1.** progressione **2.** avanzamento.
progressive agg. progressivo, progressista. ♦ **progressive** s. progressista.
to **prohibit** vt. proibire.
prohibition s. **1.** proibizione **2.** proibizionismo.
prohibitionist s. proibizionista.
prohibitive agg. proibitivo.
project s. progetto.
to **project** vt. **1.** progettare **2.** proiettare. ♦ to **project** vi. sporgere.
projectile s. proiettile.
projection s. **1.** progetto **2.** proiezione.
projector s. **1.** progettista **2.** proiettore.
proletarian agg. e s. proletario.
proletariat s. proletariato.
to **proliferate** vt. proliferare. ♦ to **proliferate** vi. moltiplicarsi.
proliferation s. proliferazione.
prolific agg. prolifico.
prolix agg. prolisso.
prolixity s. prolissità.
prologue s. prologo.
to **prolong** vt. **1.** prolungare **2.** (comm.) prorogare.
promenade s. passeggiata, passeggio pubblico, lungomare.
prominence s. prominenza.
prominent agg. prominente.
promiscuity s. promiscuità.
promiscuous agg. promiscuo.
promise s. promessa.
to **promise** vt. e vi. promettere.

promissory *agg.* contenente una promessa || — *note* (*comm.*), pagherò cambiario.

promontory *s.* promontorio.

to **promote** *vt.* **1.** promuovere **2.** dare impulso, favorire.

promoter *s.* promotore.

promotion *s.* **1.** promozione **2.** incoraggiamento.

prompt *agg.* **1.** sollecito **2.** (*comm.*) in contanti. ♦ **prompt** *s.* **1.** (*comm.*) termine di pagamento **2.** suggerimento.

to **prompt** *vt.* **1.** spingere **2.** suggerire.

prompter *s.* suggeritore.

promptness *s.* prontezza.

to **promulgate** *vt.* promulgare.

promulgation *s.* promulgazione.

promulgator *s.* promulgatore.

prone *agg.* prono.

prong *s.* **1.** dente (*di forca*) **2.** forca.

pronominal *agg.* pronominale.

pronoun *s.* pronome.

to **pronounce** *vt.* **1.** pronunciare **2.** dichiarare. ♦ to **pronounce** *vi.* pronunciarsi.

pronouncement *s.* dichiarazione.

pronouncing, pronunciation *s.* pronuncia.

proof *agg.* a prova di. ♦ **proof** *s.* **1.** prova **2.** bozza **3.** gradazione alcoolica || — -*reader*, correttore di bozze; *burden of* — (*giur.*), onere della prova.

prop *s.* puntello.

to **prop** *vt.* **1.** sostenere **2.** appoggiare.

propaedeutic(al) *agg.* propedeutico.

propaedeutics *s.* propedeutica.

propagandist *s.* propagandista.

to **propagandize** *vt.* propagandare.

to **propagate** *vt.* propagare. ♦ to **propagate** *vi.* propagarsi.

propagation *s.* **1.** propagazione **2.** (*bot.; zool.*) riproduzione.

propagator *s.* propagatore.

propane *s.* propano.

to **propel** *vt.* spingere avanti.

propellent *agg.* e *s.* propulsore, propellente.

propeller *s.* propulsore || (*screw-*) —, elica.

propensity *s.* propensione.

proper *agg.* **1.** proprio **2.** adatto **3.** corretto **4.** propriamente detto.

property *s.* **1.** proprietà **2.** (*teat.*) costumi, arredi per la scena (*pl.*) ||

real —, beni immobili (*pl.*).

prophecy *s.* profezia.

to **prophesy** *vt.* e *vi.* profetizzare.

prophet *s.* profeta.

prophetic(al) *agg.* profetico.

prophylactic *agg.* e *s.* profilattico.

prophylaxis *s.* profilassi.

to **propitiate** *vt.* propiziare.

propitiation *s.* propiziazione.

propitiator *s.* propiziatore.

propitiatory *agg.* propiziatorio.

propitious *agg.* propizio.

proportion *s.* **1.** proporzione **2.** parte. ♦ **proportions** *s. pl.* dimensioni.

to **proportion** *vt.* **1.** proporzionare **2.** dividere in parti proporzionate.

proportional *agg.* proporzionale.

proportionality *s.* proporzionalità.

proportionate *agg.* proporzionato.

to **proportionate** V. *to proportion.*

proportioning *s.* proporzionamento.

proposal *s.* proposta.

to **propose** *vt.* proporre. ♦ to **propose** *vi.* **1.** prefiggersi, intendere **2.** fare richiesta di matrimonio || *to* — *the health of so.*, bere alla salute di qu.

proposition *s.* **1.** proposta **2.** proposizione **3.** asserzione **4.** problema.

proprietary *agg.* di proprietà. ♦ **proprietary** *s.* proprietario || — *rights*, diritti di proprietà.

proprietor *s.* proprietario.

propriety *s.* **1.** proprietà **2.** opportunità **3.** decoro, decenza. ♦ **proprieties** *s. pl.* convenienze.

propulsion *s.* propulsione.

propulsive *agg.* propulsivo.

propylaeum *s.* (*pl.* -laea) propileo.

propylene *s.* propilene.

prosaic *agg.* prosaico.

prosaism *s.* prosaicità.

proscenium *s.* (*pl.* -nia) proscenio.

to **proscribe** *vt.* **1.** bandire **2.** vietare.

proscription *s.* **1.** proscrizione **2.** proibizione.

prose *s.* **1.** prosa **2.** prosaicità || — *writer*, prosatore.

prosecutable *agg.* perseguibile.

to **prosecute** *vt.* **1.** proseguire **2.** perseguire.

prosecution *s.* **1.** proseguimento **2.** processo **3.** (*giur.*) accusa.

prosecutor *s.* **1.** prosecutore **2.** accusatore || *Public* — (*giur.*), l'accusa pubblica.

proselyte s. proselito.
proselytism s. proselitismo.
prosiness s. 1. prosaicità 2. banalità.
prosody s. prosodia.
prospect s. 1. panorama 2. prospettiva 3. speranza, aspettativa.
to **prospect** vt. 1. esplorare 2. ricercare.
prospecting s. ricerca.
prospective agg. 1. futuro 2. eventuale.
to **prosper** vt. far prosperare. ♦ to **prosper** vi. prosperare.
prosperity s. prosperità.
prosperous agg. prospero.
prostate s. prostata.
prostatic agg. prostatico.
prosthesis s. (med.) protesi.
prostitute s. prostituta.
to **prostitute** vt. prostituire.
prostitution s. prostituzione.
prostrate agg. prostrato.
to **prostrate** vt. prostrare.
prostration s. 1. prostrazione 2. prosternazione.
prostyle agg. e s. prostilo.
prosy agg. 1. prosaico 2. noioso.
protagonist s. protagonista.
to **protect** vt. proteggere.
protection s. 1. protezione 2. salvacondotto.
protectionism s. protezionismo.
protectionist s. protezionista.
protective agg. protettivo.
protector s. protettore.
protectorate s. protettorato.
protectory s. patronato.
protein s. proteina.
protest s. 1. protesta 2. (comm.) protesto.
to **protest** vt. e vi. protestare.
protestant agg. e s. protestante.
Protestantism s. protestantesimo.
protestation s. dichiarazione.
protocol s. protocollo.
proton s. protone.
protoplasm s. protoplasma.
prototype s. prototipo.
Protozoa s. pl. protozoi.
to **protract** vt. 1. protrarre 2. rilevare.
protraction s. 1. protrazione 2. rilievo.
protractor s. 1. protrattore 2. goniometro.
to **protrude** vt. 1. sporgere 2. imporre. ♦ to **protrude** vi. 1. sporgersi 2. imporsi.

protrusion, protuberance s. protuberanza.
proud agg. orgoglioso, superbo.
to **prove** vt. 1. provare, verificare 2. omologare. ♦ to **prove** vi. risultare.
provender s. foraggio, biada.
proverb s. proverbio.
proverbial agg. proverbiale.
to **provide** vi. 1. provvedere 2. premunirsi 3. stabilire (di leggi). ♦ to **provide** vt. 1. procurare 2. rifornire.
provided cong. purché, a patto che.
providence s. 1. provvidenza 2. previdenza.
provident agg. 1. provvido 2. previdente.
providential agg. provvidenziale.
province s. 1. provincia 2. (fig.) sfera, campo d'attività.
provincial agg. e s. provinciale.
provincialism s. provincialismo.
provision s. 1. preparativo 2. provvedimento 3. clausola 4. (giur.) disposizione. ♦ **provisions** s. pl. provviste.
to **provision** vt. approvvigionare.
provisional agg. provvisorio.
provisioning s. approvvigionamento.
provocation s. provocazione.
provocative agg. 1. provocante 2. stimolante.
provocativeness s. provocazione.
to **provoke** vt. 1. provocare 2. irritare.
provoker s. provocatore.
provost s. prevosto.
prow s. prora.
prowess s. prodezza, valore.
proximity s. prossimità.
proxy s. 1. procura 2. procuratore.
prude s. persona eccessivamente pudica.
prudence s. prudenza.
prudent agg. prudente.
prudential agg. prudenziale.
prudentials s. pl. provvedimenti precauzionali.
prudery s. ritrosia eccessiva.
prudish agg. pudibondo.
prune s. prugna secca.
to **prune** vt. potare.
pruner s. potatore.
pruning s. potatura || — -hook, falcetto.
prussic agg. prussico.
pry[1] s. ficcanaso.

pry² s. leva.
to pry¹ vi. indagare.
to pry² vt. muovere con una leva.
psalm s. salmo.
psalmody s. salmodia.
pseudonym s. pseudonimo.
psyche s. psiche.
psychiatric(al) agg. psichiatrico.
psychiatrist s. psichiatra.
psychiatry s. psichiatria.
psychic s. 1. medium 2. psicologia.
psychic(al) agg. psichico.
psychoanalysis s. psicanalisi.
psychoanalyst s. psicanalista.
psychoanalytic(al) agg. psicanalitico.
to psychoanalyze vt. psicanalizzare.
psychologic(al) agg. psicologico.
psychologist s. psicologo.
psychology s. psicologia.
psychometry s. psicometria.
psychopathic agg. e s. psicopatico.
psychopathology s. psicopatologia.
psychopathy s. psicopatia.
psychosis s. psicosi.
psychotherapy s. psicoterapia.
ptisan s. tisana.
pub s. bar (in Gran Bretagna).
puberty s. pubertà.
pubis s. (pl. -bes) pube.
public agg. e s. pubblico || the reading —, i lettori (pl.).
publican s. 1. oste 2. (stor.) pubblicano.
publication s. pubblicazione.
publicity s. pubblicità.
to publish vt. 1. pubblicare 2. divulgare.
publishable agg. pubblicabile.
publisher s. editore.
pucker s. ruga, grinza.
to pucker vt. raggrinzare, corrugare. ♦ to pucker vi. raggrinzarsi, corrugarsi.
pudding s. 1. budino 2. pasticcio || black —, sanguinaccio.
puddle s. 1. pozzanghera 2. malta.
to puddle vt. 1. infangare 2. coprire di malta.
puerility s. puerilità.
Puerto Rican agg. e s. portoricano.
puff s. 1. soffio, sbuffo 2. piumino.
to puff vi. 1. sbuffare 2. gonfiarsi. ♦ to puff vt. 1. soffiare 2. gonfiare.
puffy agg. 1. gonfio 2. ansimante 3. paffuto, grasso.
pugilist s. pugile.

pugnacious agg. pugnace.
pugnacity s. combattività.
puke s. vomito.
to puke vt. e vi. vomitare.
pull s. 1. strappo 2. sforzo, tensione 3. maniglia (di cassetto).
to pull vt. 1. tirare 2. strappare || to — down, demolire. ♦ to pull vi. 1. trascinarsi 2. remare || to — back, ritirarsi; to — up, fermarsi.
puller s. (mecc.) estrattore.
pulley s. puleggia.
pulmonary agg. polmonare.
pulp s. polpa.
to pulp vt. ridurre in polpa. ♦ to pulp vi. diventare polposo.
pulpit s. pulpito.
pulpy agg. polposo.
pulsation s. pulsazione.
pulsatory agg. pulsante.
pulse s. 1. pulsazione, polso, battito 2. (radio) impulso.
to pulse vi. pulsare.
to pulverize vt. polverizzare. ♦ to pulverize vi. polverizzarsi.
pumice s. pomice.
pump s. pompa || petrol —, distributore di benzina.
to pump vt. e vi. pompare || to — up, gonfiare.
pumpkin s. zucca.
pun s. gioco di parole.
punch¹ s. punzone.
punch² s. pugno.
punch³ s. « punch » (bevanda alcoolica).
to punch¹ vt. (per)forare.
to punch² vt. prendere a pugni.
punching s. perforazione.
punctilio s. meticolosità.
punctilious agg. meticoloso.
punctual agg. puntuale.
punctuality s. puntualità.
punctually avv. puntualmente.
to punctuate vt. 1. punteggiare 2. (fig.) sottolineare.
punctuation s. punteggiatura.
puncture s. 1. puntura 2. foratura.
to puncture vt. 1. pungere 2. forare.
pungency s. 1. asprezza 2. acutezza (di dolore).
pungent agg. 1. pungente 2. acuto, cocente 3. piccante.
to punish vt. punire.
punishable agg. punibile.
punishment s. punizione.
punitive, punitory agg. punitivo.
punt s. chiatta.

punter s. puntatore (*di corse ecc.*).
puny *agg.* sparuto.
pup s. cucciolo.
pupil[1] s. **1.** allievo **2.** (*giur.*) pupillo.
pupil[2] s. pupilla.
pupil(l)age s. (*giur.*) minorità: *child in* —, bambino sotto tutela.
pupil(l)ary *agg.* (*giur.*) pupillare.
puppet s. burattino || — *show*, spettacolo di burattini; — *player*, burattinaio.
puppy s. cucciolo.
purchase s. acquisto.
to **purchase** *vt.* acquistare.
purchaser s. acquirente.
purchasing s. acquisto || — *power*, potere di acquisto.
pure *agg.* puro, schietto, casto.
purely *avv.* puramente, semplicemente.
purgative *agg.* purgativo. ♦ **purgative** s. purgante.
purgatory s. purgatorio.
purge s. **1.** purga **2.** epurazione.
to **purge** *vt.* **1.** purgare **2.** epurare. ♦ to **purge** *vi.* purgarsi.
purification s. purificazione.
purificatory *agg.* purificatore.
to **purify** *vt.* purificare.
purism s. purismo.
purist s. purista.
Puritan *agg.* e s. puritano.
Puritanism s. puritanismo.
purity s. purezza.
to **purloin** *vt.* rubare.
purloiner s. frodatore.
purple *agg.* **1.** purpureo, paonazzo **2.** ornato. ♦ **purple** s. porpora.
to **purple** *vt.* imporporare. ♦ to **purple** *vi.* imporpòrarsi.
purport s. significato.
to **purport** *vt.* **1.** significare **2.** pretendere.
purpose s. **1.** intenzione, scopo **2.** fermezza || *on* —, di proposito.
to **purpose** *vi.* proporsi (*di*).
purposeful *agg.* **1.** premeditato **2.** avveduto.
purposefully *avv.* intenzionalmente, espressamente.
purposeless *agg.* **1.** inutile **2.** senza intenzione.
purpurin s. porporina.
to **purr** *vi.* fare le fusa.
purse s. borsellino.
to **purse** *vt.* contrarre. ♦ to **purse** *vi.* incresparsi, contrarsi.
purser s. commissario di bordo.
pursuant *agg.* conforme.

to **pursue** *vt.* **1.** (in)seguire **2.** continuare.
pursuer s. **1.** inseguitore **2.** continuatore.
pursuit s. **1.** inseguimento **2.** occupazione, impiego.
purulence s. suppurazione.
purulent *agg.* purulento.
push s. **1.** spinta, influenza, pressione **2.** bisogno **3.** (*elettr.*) pulsante.
to **push** *vt.* **1.** spingere, incalzare, fare pressione **2.** lanciare (*una moda, un articolo ecc.*) ♦ to **push** *vi.* spingersi.
pusher s. chi, ciò che spinge.
pusillanimity s. pusillanimità.
pusillanimous *agg.* pusillanime.
puss(y) s. micino.
pustule s. pustola.
to **put (put, put)** *vt.* **1.** mettere, porre **2.** esporre, sottoporre || *to* — *off*, rimandare, togliere (*vestiti ecc.*); *to* — *on*, indossare, accendere; *to* — *through*, mettere in comunicazione telefonica; *to* — *up*, alzare. ♦ to **put (put, put)** *vi.* dirigersi.
putative *agg.* putativo.
putrefaction s. putrefazione.
to **putrefy** *vt.* putrefare. ♦ to **putrefy** *vi.* putrefarsi.
putrescence s. putrescenza.
putrescible *agg.* putrescibile.
putrid *agg.* putrido.
putridness s. putridità.
puttees s. *pl.* mollettiere.
putty s. mastice, stucco.
puzzle s. **1.** enigma **2.** imbarazzo **3.** intrigo.
to **puzzle** *vt.* imbarazzare. ♦ to **puzzle** *vi.* essere imbarazzato.
pygmy *agg.* e s. pigmeo.
pyjamas s. *pl.* pigiama (*sing.*).
pylon s. pilone || *steel* —, traliccio.
pylorus s. piloro.
pyorrh(o)ea s. piorrea.
pyramid s. piramide.
pyramidal *agg.* piramidale.
pyre s. pira.
pyrites s. pirite.
pyrography s. pirografia.
pyromancy s. piromanzia.
pyromaniac s. piromane.
pyrope s. piropo.
pyrotechnic(al) *agg.* pirotecnico.
pyrotechnics s. pirotecnica.
Pythagorean *agg.* e s. pitagorico.
python s. pitone.
pyx s. pisside.

Q

quack[1] s. ciarlatano.
quack[2] s. schiamazzare (di anitra).
to quack[1] vi. fare il ciarlatano.
to quack[2] vi. schiamazzare (di anitra).
quadrangle s. quadrangolo.
quadrangular agg. quadrangolare.
quadrant s. quadrante.
quadrennial agg. quadriennale.
quadrilateral agg. e s. quadrilatero.
quadrille s. quadriglia.
quadrumane s. quadrumane.
quadrumanous agg. quadrumane.
quadruped agg. e s. quadrupede.
quadruple agg. e s. quadruplo.
to quadruple vt. quadruplicare. ♦
to quadruple vi. quadruplicarsi.
quagmire s. pantano.
quail s. quaglia.
to quail vi. avvilirsi, sgomentarsi.
quaint agg. strano, bizzarro.
quake s. scossa, tremito.
to quake vi. 1. avere i brividi 2. tremare (anche di terra).
Quaker s. Quacchero.
quaky agg. tremante.
qualifiable agg. qualificabile.
qualification s. 1. qualificazione, capacità, requisito 2. condizione, riserva 3. qualifica.
qualified agg. 1. qualificato, competente 2. limitato || — acceptance (comm.), accettazione con riserva.
qualifier s. (gramm.) parola che modifica.
to qualify vt. 1. qualificare, definire 2. abilitare 3. (giur.) autorizzare. ♦ to qualify vi. 1. qualificarsi 2. abilitarsi.
qualitative agg. qualitativo.
quality s. qualità, caratteristica.
qualm s. 1. nausea 2. scrupolo.
qualmish agg. 1. soggetto a nausee 2. nauseante 3. scrupoloso.
quantitative agg. quantitativo.
quantity s. quantità.
quarantine s. quarantena.
quarrel s. lite, contesa.
to quarrel vi. litigare, venire a contesa.
quarreller s. attaccabrighe, contendente.
quarrelsome agg. attaccabrighe, rissoso.
quarry[1] s. 1. cava 2. (fig.) fonte d'informazione.

quarry[2] s. selvaggina, preda.
to quarry vt. 1. cavare (pietre, marmo ecc.) 2. ricavare informazioni da.
quarter s. 1. quarto: a — of an hour, un quarto d'ora 2. quartiere, rione. ♦ quarters s. pl. 1. alloggio 2. (mil.) acquartieramento.
to quarter vt. e vi. 1. dividere in quattro parti 2. alloggiare 3. (mil.) acquartierarsi.
quarterly agg. trimestrale. ♦ quarterly s. pubblicazione trimestrale. ♦ quarterly avv. trimestralmente.
quartermaster s. 1. commissario 2. quartiermastro.
quartet s. quartetto.
quartz s. quarzo.
to quash vt. (giur.) annullare.
quaternary agg. quaternario.
quatrain s. quartina.
quaver s. trillo, vibrazione.
to quaver vt. e vi. 1. vibrare, tremare (di voce) 2. gorgheggiare.
quay s. banchina, molo.
queasy agg. 1. nauseabondo 2. schizzinoso.
queen s. regina.
queenlike agg. regale.
queenly agg. regale, da regina.
queer agg. strano, eccentrico.
to queer vt. mettere in ridicolo.
queerly avv. stranamente.
to quench vt. 1. spegnere, estinguere 2. calmare.
quencher s. estintore.
quenchless agg. inestinguibile.
querulous agg. querulo, gemebondo.
query s. domanda, quesito.
to query vt. e vi. 1. chiedere, indagare 2. mettere in dubbio.
quest s. ricerca.
to quest vt. e vi. cercare, far ricerche.
question s. 1. domanda, interrogazione 2. dubbio, obiezione 3. questione, problema || — mark, punto interrogativo.
to question vt. 1. interrogare 2. mettere in dubbio.
questionable agg. incerto, discutibile.
questionably avv. discutibilmente.
questionary s. questionario.
queue s. 1. coda 2. fila di persone: to stand in a —, fare la coda.
to queue vt. e vi. fare la coda, mettere in coda.

quibble *s.* giuoco di parole, doppio senso.

to quibble *vi.* **1.** fare giuochi di parole **2.** cavillare.

quibbling *agg.* a doppio senso.

quick *agg.* **1.** rapido, veloce **2.** pronto, intelligente, acuto ‖ — -*eyed*, dagli occhi penetranti; — -*eared*, dall'orecchio fino; — -*lime*, calce viva; — -*sighted*, dalla vista acuta; — -*tempered*, irascibile.

to quicken *vt.* **1.** affrettare **2.** animare. ♦ **to quicken** *vi.* **1.** affrettarsi **2.** animarsi.

quickly *avv.* rapidamente, prontamente.

quickness *s.* **1.** rapidità **2.** vivacità, acutezza.

quicksand *s.* sabbia mobile.

quickset *s.* siepe di sempreverdi.

quicksilver *s.* mercurio, argento vivo (*anche fig.*).

quickstep *s.* passo cadenzato.

quickthorn *s.* biancospino.

quiescence *s.* quiescenza.

quiescent *agg.* quiescente.

quiescently *avv.* tranquillamente.

quiet *agg.* **1.** quieto, tranquillo **2.** sobrio, tenue (*di colore*) **3.** docile, dolce.

to quiet *vt.* acquietare. ♦ **to quiet** *vi.* acquietarsi.

quietism *s.* quietismo.

quietist *s.* quietista.

quietly *avv.* tranquillamente, con calma.

quietness *s.* quiete, tranquillità.

quill *s.* **1.** penna, penna d'oca **2.** piccolo galleggiante (*per canna da pesca*).

to quill *vt.* pieghettare, increspare.

quilt *s.* trapunta.

to quilt *vt.* trapuntare.

quince *s.* cotogna ‖ — *jam,* marmellata di cotogne.

quinine *s.* chinino.

quinquennial *agg.* quinquennale.

quintal *s.* quintale.

quintessence *s.* quintessenza.

quintet *s.* quintetto.

quintuple *agg.* e *s.* quintuplo.

to quintuple *vt.* quintuplicare. ♦ **to quintuple** *vi.* quintuplicarsi.

quisling *s.* collaborazionista.

to quit *vt.* **1.** abbandonare, lasciare **2.** quietanzare, saldare.

quite *avv.* **1.** completamente, interamente **2.** piuttosto, abbastanza ‖ — *young,* giovanissimo; *to be*

— *well,* stare proprio bene.

quiver *s.* fremito, brivido.

to quiver *vt.* e *vi.* **1.** tremare, fremere **2.** palpitare.

quivering *agg.* fremente, tremolante. ♦ **quivering** *s.* tremolio.

quixotic *agg.* donchisciottesco.

quiz *s.* (*pl.* quizzes) burlone.

to quiz *vt.* burlare.

quotation *s.* **1.** citazione **2.** (*comm.*) quotazione.

quote *s.* (*fam.*) citazione. ♦ **quotes** *s. pl.* virgolette.

to quote *vt.* **1.** citare **2.** (*comm.*) quotare (*in borsa*).

quotidian *agg.* quotidiano.

quotient *s.* quoziente.

R

rabbi *s.* rabbino.

rabbit *s.* coniglio.

rabble *s.* plebaglia.

to rabble *vt.* assaltare, linciare.

rabid *agg.* **1.** rabbioso **2.** irragionevole **3.** idrofobo.

rabidity *s.* **1.** rabbia **2.** fanatismo.

rabies *s.* idrofobia.

race¹ *s.* **1.** corso **2.** corsa ‖ — -*meeting,* concorso ippico.

race² *s.* razza.

to race *vi.* **1.** correre **2.** imballarsi (*di motori*) **3.** prendere parte a una corsa **4.** allevare cavalli da corsa.

racecourse *s.* ippodromo.

racehorse *s.* cavallo da corsa.

racer *s.* **1.** corridore **2.** cavallo da corsa **3.** mezzo da corsa.

racial *agg.* razziale.

racialism *s.* razzismo.

racialist *s.* razzista.

racially *avv.* dal punto di vista razziale.

racily *avv.* vivacemente.

raciness *s.* vivacità.

racing *s.* corsa ‖ — *car,* automobile da corsa.

racism *s.* razzismo.

racist *s.* razzista.

rack¹ *s.* **1.** rastrelliera **2.** reticella portabagagli **3.** (*mecc.*) cremagliera ‖ *clothes* —, attaccapanni.

rack² *s.* ruota, strumento di tortura.

rack³ *s.* nembo, nuvolaglia.

rack⁴ *s.* rovina, distruzione.

to **rack**[1] *vt.* **1.** torturare **2.** pretendere troppo.

to **rack**[2] *vi.* fuggire (*di nubi*).

racket[1] *s.* racchetta.

racket[2] *s.* **1.** fracasso **2.** baldoria **3.** (*gergo*) associazione a delinquere.

racy *agg.* **1.** genuino **2.** vivace, pungente.

radial *agg.* radiale.

radiance *s.* radiosità.

radiant *agg.* **1.** radiante **2.** raggiante.

to **radiate** *vt.* e *vi.* irradiare.

radiation *s.* (ir)radiazione.

radiator *s.* radiatore.

radical *agg.* e *s.* radicale.

radicalism *s.* radicalismo.

radio *s.* radio || — *-beacon,* radiofaro; — *-control,* radiocomando; — *-operator,* radiotelegrafista.

radioactive *agg.* radioattivo.

radioactivity *s.* radioattività.

radioengineering *s.* radiotecnica.

radiogoniometer *s.* radiogoniometro.

radiogram *s.* **1.** marconigramma **2.** radiogrammofono.

radiograph *s.* radiografia.

radiography *s.* radiografia.

radiologist *s.* radiologo.

radiology *s.* radiologia.

radioscopy *s.* radioscopia.

radiostatics *s. pl.* disturbi atmosferici.

radiotelegraphy *s.* radiotelegrafia.

radiotelephony *s.* radiotelefonia.

radiotherapeutics *s.* radioterapia.

radish *s.* ravanello.

radium *s.* radio.

radius *s.* raggio.

raffia *s.* rafia.

raft *s.* zattera || — *-bridge,* ponte di barche.

rag *s.* straccio.

ragamuffin *s.* pezzente.

rage *s.* **1.** furore **2.** passione.

to **rage** *vi.* infuriare || *the plague raged,* la peste infieriva.

ragged *agg.* **1.** lacero **2.** frastagliato **3.** spettinato **4.** rozzo.

raggedly *avv.* **1.** a brandelli **2.** in modo non uniforme.

raggedness *s.* **1.** cenciosità **2.** ineguaglianza.

raging *agg.* furioso.

raid *s.* incursione, scorreria.

to **raid** *vt.* e *vi.* fare un'incursione.

rail, railing *s.* **1.** sbarra **2.** ringhiera **3.** rotaia || *to go by* —, viaggiare per ferrovia.

raillery *s.* canzonatura.

railroad, railway *s.* ferrovia || — *companies,* società ferroviarie.

railwayman *s.* ferroviere.

rain *s.* pioggia || *it looks like* —, vuol piovere; *to be drenched with* —, essere inzuppato || — *-glass,* barometro.

to **rain** *v. imp.* piovere. ♦ to **rain** *vt.* far piovere.

rainbow *s.* arcobaleno.

raincoat *s.* impermeabile.

rainfall *s.* **1.** piovosità **2.** scroscio di pioggia.

rainproof *agg.* impermeabile.

rainy *agg.* piovoso.

raise *s.* aumento.

to **raise** *vt.* **1.** alzare **2.** innalzare **3.** allevare **4.** coltivare **5.** (*mil.*) arruolare.

raisin *s.* uva passa.

raising *s.* **1.** innalzamento **2.** aumento **3.** allevamento **4.** coltivazione **5.** educazione.

rake[1] *s.* rastrello.

rake[2] *s.* inclinazione.

rake[3] *s.* libertino.

to **rake**[1] *vt.* **1.** rastrellare **2.** raschiare || *to* — *up,* ammucchiare.

to **rake**[2] *vi.* essere inclinato.

rally[1] *s.* riunione, raduno.

rally[2] *s.* canzonatura.

to **rally**[1] *vt.* raccogliere. ♦ to **rally** *vi.* rianimarsi.

to **rally**[2] *vt.* canzonare.

ram *s.* **1.** ariete **2.** (*mar.*) sperone.

to **ram** *vt.* **1.** (*mar.*) speronare **2.** conficcare **3.** comprimere.

ramble *s.* vagabondaggio.

to **ramble** *vi.* **1.** vagare **2.** divagare.

rambler *s.* **1.** vagabondo **2.** rampicante.

rambling *agg.* **1.** errante **2.** sconnesso || — *thoughts,* divagazioni.

ramification *s.* ramificazione.

to **ramify** *vt.* ramificare. ♦ to **ramify** *vi.* ramificarsi.

rammer *s.* (*mil.*) pestello.

ramp[1] *s.* rampa.

ramp[2] *s.* (*gergo*) truffa.

rampage *s.* contegno iroso.

rampant *agg.* **1.** rampante **2.** violento **3.** predominante **4.** lussureggiante.

rampart *s.* bastione.

to **rampart** *vt.* fortificare.

ramshackle *agg.* sgangherato, che cade in rovina.

ran V. *to run.*
rancid *agg.* rancido.
rancour *s.* rancore.
rand *s.* soletta (*di scarpa*).
random *agg.* fatto a caso || *at —,* a casaccio.
rang V. *to ring.*
range *s.* 1. fila 2. catena (*di monti*) 3. spazio 4. sfera, raggio 5. gamma 6. fornello 7. (*aer.*) autonomia.
to range *vt.* 1. allineare 2. classificare 3. puntare. ♦ **to range** *vi.* 1. vagare 2. avere una portata di 3. oscillare (*di prezzi*).
ranger *s.* 1. guardia forestale 2. vagabondo.
rank *agg.* 1. rigoglioso 2. volgare 3. puzzolente. ♦ **rank** *s.* 1. fila 2. rango, grado 3. truppa.
to rank *vi.* 1. schierarsi 2. essere classificato.
to ransack *vt.* 1. frugare 2. saccheggiare.
ransom *s.* riscatto.
to ransom *vt.* riscattare.
to rant *vt.* e *vi.* declamare.
rap *s.* colpo.
to rap *vt.* e *vi.* 1. battere 2. bussare.
rapacious *agg.* rapace.
rapacity *s.* rapacità.
rape[1] *s.* violenza carnale.
rape[2] *s.* rapa.
to rape *vt.* violentare.
rapid *agg.* rapido. ♦ **rapid** *s.* rapida.
rapidity *s.* rapidità.
rapt *agg.* rapito.
raptorial *agg.* rapace.
rapture *s.* rapimento.
rare *agg.* 1. raro 2. rarefatto.
rarefaction *s.* rarefazione.
to rarefy *vt.* 1. rarefare 2. raffinare. ♦ **to rarefy** *vi.* rarefarsi.
rarely *avv.* 1. raramente 2. in modo eccellente.
rareness, rarity *s.* 1. rarità 2. rarefazione.
rascal *s.* furfante.
rascalism, rascality *s.* furfanteria.
rash *agg.* avventato. ♦ **rash** *s.* eruzione cutanea.
rashness *s.* avventatezza.
rasp *s.* 1. raspa 2. stridore.
to rasp *vt.* 1. raspare 2. irritare.
raspberry *s.* lampone.
rasping *agg.* stridente.
rat *s.* 1. topo 2. (*fig.*) traditore.
rate *s.* 1. tasso, quota 2. tassa 3. prezzo, tariffa 4. ritmo, andamento

|| *first —,* di prim'ordine; *— of discount,* tasso di sconto.
to rate[1] *vt.* 1. stimare 2. tassare 3. classificare.
to rate[2] *vt.* redarguire.
rateable *agg.* soggetto ad imposta.
ratepayer *s.* contribuente.
rather *avv.* piuttosto || *I had —,* preferirei; *I would — not,* non ci tengo.
ratification *s.* ratifica.
to ratify *vt.* ratificare.
rating[1] *s.* 1. stima 2. tassa 3. classificazione.
rating[2] *s.* sgridata.
ratio *s.* rapporto.
ration *s.* razione.
to ration *vt.* razionare.
rational *agg.* razionale.
rationalism *s.* razionalismo.
rationalist *s.* razionalista.
rationality *s.* razionalità.
to rationalize *vt.* 1. razionalizzare 2. spiegare razionalmente.
rationally *avv.* razionalmente.
rattle *s.* 1. sonaglio 2. rantolo 3. tintinnio.
to rattle *vt.* far risuonare. ♦ **to rattle** *vi.* 1. risuonare 2. cianciare.
rattling *agg.* 1. vivace 2. tintinnante.
ravage *s.* rovina.
to ravage *vt.* devastare.
rave *s.* delirio.
to rave *vt.* declamare. ♦ **to rave** *vi.* delirare || *to — about sthg.,* andar pazzo per qc.
ravel *s.* 1. groviglio 2. lembo sfilacciato.
to ravel *vt.* ingarbugliare. ♦ **to ravel** *vi.* sfilacciarsi.
raven *s.* corvo.
to raven *vt.* e *vi.* saccheggiare.
ravenous *agg.* vorace.
ravine *s.* burrone.
raving *agg.* delirante. ♦ **raving** *s.* delirio.
to ravish *vt.* 1. rapire 2. violentare.
ravisher *s.* rapitore.
ravishing *agg.* (*fig.*) affascinante.
ravishment *s.* 1. rapimento 2. stupro.
raw *agg.* 1. crudo 2. greggio 3. inesperto 4. a nudo. ♦ **raw** *s.* punto vivo.
rawness *s.* 1. crudezza 2. rozzezza 3. inesperienza 4. escoriazione.
ray[1] *s.* 1. raggio 2. lampo.

ray² *s.* (*zool.*) razza.
to **ray** *vt.* irradiare. ♦ to **ray** *vi.* irradiarsi.
to **raze** *vt.* radere al suolo.
razor *s.* rasoio || — -*blade*, lametta.
to **reabsorb** *vt.* riassorbire.
reach *s.* **1.** portata **2.** penetrazione || *beyond my* —, irraggiungibile.
to **reach** *vt.* **1.** raggiungere **2.** porgere. ♦ to **reach** *vi.* estendersi.
to **react** *vi.* reagire.
reaction *s.* reazione.
reactionary *agg. e s.* reazionario.
reactive *agg.* reattivo.
read *agg.* colto. ♦ **read** *s.* lettura.
to **read** (**read, read**) *vt.* **1.** leggere **2.** interpretare **3.** segnare || *to* — *over*, rileggere; *to* — *through*, esaminare.
readable *agg.* **1.** leggibile **2.** interessante.
reader *s.* **1.** lettore **2.** libro di lettura.
readily *avv.* prontamente.
readiness *s.* prontezza.
reading *s.* **1.** lettura **2.** interpretazione || — -*desk*, leggio.
to **readjust** *vt.* riaggiustare.
readjustment *s.* riordinamento.
to **readmit** *vt.* riammettere.
readmittance *s.* riammissione.
ready *agg.* pronto || — -*made*, confezionato; — *money*, contanti; — -*made clothes*, abito preconfezionato; — -*built*, prefabbricato.
to **ready** *vt.* preparare.
to **reaffirm** *vt.* riaffermare.
reafforestation *s.* rimboschimento.
reagent *s.* reagente.
real *agg. e s.* reale || — *estate*, beni immobili (*pl.*).
realism *s.* realismo.
realist *s.* realista.
realistic *agg.* realistico.
reality *s.* **1.** realtà **2.** realismo.
realizable *agg.* realizzabile.
realization *s.* **1.** realizzazione **2.** percezione.
to **realize** *vt.* **1.** accorgersi di **2.** realizzare **3.** capire.
really *avv.* realmente.
realm *s.* reame.
realty *s.* beni immobili (*pl.*).
ream *s.* (*tip.*) risma.
to **reap** *vt.* **1.** mietere **2.** fare il raccolto (*anche fig.*).
reaper *s.* mietitore.
reaping *s.* mietitura.

to **reappear** *vi.* riapparire.
to **reappoint** *vt.* rinominare.
rear *agg.* posteriore. ♦ **rear** *s.* **1.** retroguardia **2.** retro.
to **rear** *vt.* **1.** alzare, innalzare **2.** allevare **3.** coltivare.
to **rearm** *vt.* riarmare.
rearmament *s.* riarmo.
to **rearrange** *vt.* riordinare.
rearrangement *s.* riordinamento.
reason *s.* **1.** ragione **2.** causa, motivo **3.** raziocinio.
to **reason** *vt. e vi.* **1.** ragionare **2.** persuadere || *to* — *about a subject*, discutere di un argomento.
reasonable *agg.* ragionevole.
reasonableness *s.* ragionevolezza.
reasonably *avv.* ragionevolmente.
reasoning *s.* ragionamento.
to **reassert** *vt.* riasserire.
reassurance *s.* rassicurazione.
to **reassure** *vt.* rassicurare.
to **reawaken** *vt.* risvegliare. ♦ to **reawaken** *vi.* risvegliarsi.
rebate *s.* riduzione, sconto.
rebel *agg. e s.* ribelle.
to **rebel** *vi.* ribellarsi.
rebellion *s.* ribellione.
rebellious *agg.* ribelle.
to **rebind** (**rebound, rebound**) *vt.* rilegare (*un libro*).
rebirth *s.* rinascita.
reborn *agg.* rinato.
rebound¹ V. *to rebind*.
rebound² *s.* rimbalzo.
to **rebound** *vi.* rimbalzare.
rebuff *s.* diniego, mortificazione.
to **rebuild** (**rebuilt, rebuilt**) *vt.* ricostruire.
rebuke *s.* rimprovero.
to **rebuke** *vt.* rimproverare.
to **rebut** *vt.* respingere, rifiutare.
recalcitrant *agg.* recalcitrante.
to **recalcitrate** *vi.* recalcitrare.
recall *s.* **1.** richiamo **2.** revoca.
to **recall** *vt.* **1.** richiamare **2.** rievocare, far tornare alla memoria.
to **recant** *vt. e vi.* ritrattare.
recantation *s.* ritrattazione.
to **recapitulate** *vt. e vi.* ricapitolare.
recapitulation *s.* ricapitolazione.
recapture *s.* riconquista.
to **recapture** *vt.* riconquistare.
recast *s.* nuova forma.
to **recast** (**recast, recast**) *vt.* **1.** rifondere **2.** rimaneggiare.
to **recede** *vi.* **1.** indietreggiare **2.** diminuire.

receding *agg.* **1.** rientrante **2.** sfuggente.
receipt *s.* **1.** ricevimento **2.** ricevuta **3.** ricetta.
to receipt *vt.* quietanzare.
to receive *vt.* **1.** ricevere **2.** accettare.
receiver *s.* **1.** ricevitore **2.** (*giur.*) ricettatore.
receiving *s.* ricezione.
recension *s.* revisione.
recent *agg.* recente.
receptacle *s.* ricettacolo.
reception *s.* **1.** ricevimento **2.** ricezione **3.** accoglienza.
receptive *agg.* ricettivo.
receptivity *s.* ricettività.
recess *s.* **1.** intervallo **2.** rientranza **3.** recesso.
recession *s.* **1.** ritiro **2.** recessione.
recessive *agg.* retrocedente.
recharge *s.* ricarica.
to recharge *vt.* ricaricare.
to rechristen *vt.* ribattezzare.
recidivism *s.* recidività.
recipe *s.* ricetta.
recipient *agg. e s.* ricevente.
reciprocal *agg.* reciproco. ♦ **reciprocal** *s.* (*mat.*) numero reciproco.
to reciprocate *vt.* **1.** contraccambiare **2.** muovere alternativamente. ♦ **to reciprocate** *vi.* muoversi alternativamente.
reciprocating *agg.* (*mecc.*) alternativo.
reciprocation *s.* **1.** moto alterno **2.** scambio.
reciprocity *s.* reciprocità.
recital *s.* **1.** relazione **2.** recitazione.
recitation *s.* **1.** recitazione **2.** recita **3.** narrazione.
recitative *agg. e s.* recitativo.
to recite *vt.* **1.** recitare **2.** riferire.
reckless *agg.* incurante.
recklessness *s.* noncuranza.
to reckon *vt.* **1.** contare, computare **2.** considerare.
reckoner *s.* calcolatore.
reckoning *s.* conto.
reclaim *s.* rivendicazione.
to reclaim *vt.* **1.** redimere **2.** bonificare **3.** rivendicare.
reclamation *s.* **1.** redenzione **2.** bonifica **3.** rivendicazione.
to recline *vt.* chinare. ♦ **to recline** *vi.* chinarsi.
reclining *agg.* chinato.
recluse *agg.* recluso. ♦ **recluse** *s.* eremita.

reclusion *s.* **1.** reclusione **2.** eremo.
recognition *s.* riconoscimento.
recognizable *agg.* riconoscibile.
to recognize *vt.* riconoscere.
recoil *s.* **1.** il ritrarsi **2.** rinculo.
to recoil *vi.* **1.** ritrarsi **2.** ricadere **3.** rinculare.
to recollect *vt.* **1.** raccogliere **2.** ricordare ‖ *to — oneself,* riaversi.
recollection *s.* ricordo.
to recommence *vt. e vi.* ricominciare.
to recommend *vt.* raccomandare.
recommendation *s.* raccomandazione.
recommendatory *agg.* raccomandatorio.
recompense *s.* **1.** ricompensa **2.** risarcimento.
to recompense *vt.* **1.** ricompensare **2.** risarcire.
to recompose *vt.* ricomporre.
recomposition *s.* ricomposizione.
to reconcile *vt.* (ri)conciliare ‖ *to — oneself,* rassegnarsi.
reconcilement *s.* **1.** riconciliazione **2.** rassegnazione.
reconnaissance *s.* ricognizione.
to reconnoitre *vt. e vi.* perlustrare.
to reconquer *vt.* riconquistare.
reconquest *s.* riconquista.
to reconsider *vt.* riconsiderare.
reconsideration *s.* revisione.
reconstitute *vt.* ricostituire.
to reconstruct *vt.* ricostruire.
reconstruction *s.* ricostruzione.
reconversion *s.* riconversione.
to reconvert *vt.* riconvertire.
record *s.* **1.** registrazione **2.** documento **3.** passato **4.** disco ‖ *— player,* giradischi.
to record *vt.* registrare.
recorder *s.* **1.** cancelliere **2.** registratore **3.** archivista ‖ *tape —,* magnetofono.
recording *s.* registrazione.
recordist *s.* (*cine*) tecnico del suono.
recourse *s.* ricorso.
to recover *vt.* ricuperare, riacquistare, riscoprire. ♦ **to recover** *vi.* ristabilirsi.
recoverable *agg.* **1.** ricuperabile **2.** guaribile.
recovery *s.* **1.** recupero **2.** guarigione **3.** (*giur.*) rivendicazione.
to recreate *vt.* divertire. ♦ **to recreate** *vi.* divertirsi.
to re-create *vt.* ricreare.
recreation *s.* ricreazione.

recreative *agg.* ricreativo.
to recriminate *vi.* recriminare.
recrimination *s.* recriminazione.
recrudescence *s.* recrudescenza.
recrudescent *agg.* che rincrudisce.
recruit *s.* recluta.
to recruit *vt.* **1.** reclutare **2.** rinforzare. ♦ **to recruit** *vi.* ristabilirsi.
recruitment *s.* reclutamento.
rectangle *s.* rettangolo.
rectangular *agg.* rettangolare.
rectification *s.* rettificazione.
rectifier *s.* (*mecc.*) rettificatrice.
to rectify *vt.* rettificare.
rectilineal *agg.* rettilineo.
rectitude *s.* rettitudine.
rector *s.* **1.** rettore **2.** parroco.
rectorate *s.* rettorato.
rectorship *s.* rettorato.
rectory *s.* **1.** presbiterio **2.** (*eccl.*) beneficio.
to recur *vi.* ritornare.
recurrence *s.* ricorso.
recurrent *agg.* ricorrente.
recusant *agg.* e *s.* dissidente.
red *agg.* e *s.* rosso || — -*hot*, rovente; — -*lead*, minio; — -*letter day*, giorno festivo. ♦ **Reds** *s. pl.* comunisti.
to redact *vt.* **1.** redigere **2.** revisionare.
redactor *s.* redattore.
to redden *vt.* arrossare. ♦ **to redden** *vi.* arrossire.
reddish *agg.* rossiccio.
to redeem *vt.* **1.** riscattare **2.** ricuperare **3.** estinguere: *to — a mortgage*, estinguere un'ipoteca.
redeemable *agg.* **1.** riscattabile **2.** ricuperabile.
redeemer *s.* redentore.
redemption *s.* **1.** redenzione **2.** (*comm.*) rimborso **3.** (*giur.*) riscatto.
redness *s.* rossore.
to redouble *vt.* e *vi.* raddoppiare.
redress *s.* riparazione.
to redress *vt.* riparare, rimediare.
redskin *agg.* e *s.* pellerossa.
to reduce *vt.* **1.** ridurre **2.** degradare.
reduced *agg.* ridotto.
reducer *s.* riduttore.
reduction *s.* **1.** riduzione **2.** degradazione.
redundance *s.* sovrabbondanza.
redundant *agg.* ridondante.
redwood *s.* sequoia.
to re-echo *vt.* e *vi.* riecheggiare.
reed *s.* canna || *broken* —, perso-

na infida; — -*pipe*, zampogna.
re-edification *s.* riedificazione.
to re-edify *vt.* riedificare.
to re-educate *vt.* rieducare.
reef *s.* secca || *coral-* —, banco di coralli.
to reek *vi.* puzzare. ♦ **to reek** *vt.* trasudare.
reel *s.* **1.** bobina **2.** giro vorticoso || *news-* —, cinegiornale.
to reel *vt.* avvolgere || *to* — *off*, snocciolare. ♦ **to reel** *vi.* girare.
to re-elect *vt.* rieleggere.
to re-emerge *vi.* riemergere.
to re-enact *vt.* richiamare in vigore (*una legge*).
to re-enter *vt.* rientrare.
re-entrance *s.* rientro.
re-entry *s.* **1.** rientro **2.** nuova registrazione.
to re-establish *vt.* ristabilire.
re-establishment *s.* ristabilimento.
re-examination *s.* riesame.
to re-examine *vt.* riesaminare.
refectory *s.* refettorio.
to refer *vt.* **1.** attribuire **2.** rimandare. ♦ **to refer** *vi.* **1.** riferirsi **2.** rivolgersi.
referable *agg.* riferibile.
referee *s.* arbitro.
to referee *vt.* e *vi.* arbitrare.
reference *s.* **1.** riferimento **2.** consultazione **3.** referenza **4.** (*giur.*) rinvio.
referential *agg.* riferentesi a.
refill *s.* ricambio.
to refill *vt.* riempire di nuovo.
to refine *vt.* raffinare. ♦ **to refine** *vi.* raffinarsi.
refined *agg.* **1.** raffinato **2.** colto.
refinement *s.* **1.** raffinamento **2.** raffinatezza.
refiner *s.* raffinatore.
refinery *s.* raffineria.
refit *s.* riparazione.
to refit *vt.* riparare.
to reflect *vt.* e *vi* **1.** riflettere **2.** meditare.
reflection *s.* **1.** riflessione, riflesso **2.** biasimo || *to cast reflections on so.*, criticare qu.
reflective *agg.* riflessivo.
reflector *s.* riflettore.
reflex *agg.* e *s.* riflesso.
reflorescence *s.* rifioritura.
reflux *s.* riflusso.
reform *s.* riforma.
to reform *vt.* riformare.
reformation *s.* riforma.

reformational *agg.* di riforma.
reformatory *agg.* riformativo. ◆ **reformatory** *s.* riformatorio.
reformer *s.* riformatore.
to **refract** *vt.* rifrangere.
refraction *s.* rifrazione.
refractivity *s.* rifrangibilità.
refractor *s.* rifrattore.
refractory *agg.* **1.** refrattario **2.** ostinato.
refrain *s.* ritornello.
to **refrain** *vi.* trattenersi, astenersi.
to **refresh** *vt.* **1.** rinfrescare **2.** rinvigorire. ◆ to **refresh** *vi.* **1.** rinvigorirsi **2.** rifornirsi.
refreshment *s.* ristoro. ◆ **refreshments** *s. pl.* cibo, bevanda (*sing.*).
refrigerant *agg.* e *s.* refrigerante.
to **refrigerate** *vt.* refrigerare.
refrigeration *s.* refrigerazione.
refrigerator *s.* frigorifero.
refrigeratory *agg.* refrigerante.
to **refuel** *vt.* rifornire di carburante. ◆ to **refuel** *vi.* rifornirsi di carburante.
refuge *s.* rifugio.
refugee *s.* rifugiato, profugo.
refulgence *s.* fulgore.
refulgent *agg.* rifulgente.
refund *s.* rimborso.
to **refund** *vt.* rimborsare.
refusable *agg.* rifiutabile.
refusal *s.* **1.** rifiuto **2.** diritto di opzione.
refuse *s.* rifiuto.
to **refuse** *vt.* rifiutare. ◆ to **refuse** *vi.* rifiutarsi.
refuser *s.* ricusante.
refutal *s.* confutazione.
to **refute** *vt.* confutare.
to **regain** *vt.* riguadagnare.
regal *agg.* regale.
regality *s.* regalità.
regally *avv.* regalmente.
regard *s.* **1.** considerazione **2.** sguardo || *with — to*, riguardo a. ◆ **regards** *s. pl.* saluti.
to **regard** *vt.* **1.** considerare **2.** riguardare **3.** osservare.
regardful *agg.* **1.** attento **2.** rispettoso.
regardless *agg.* senza riguardo. ◆ **regardless** *avv.* senza riguardo a, senza badare a.
regatta *s.* regata.
regelation *s.* ricongelamento.
regency *s.* reggenza.
to **regenerate** *vt.* rigenerare. ◆ to **regenerate** *vi.* rigenerarsi.

regeneration *s.* rigenerazione.
regenerative *agg.* rigeneratore.
regenerator *s.* rigeneratore.
regent *agg.* e *s.* reggente.
regicide *s.* **1.** regicida **2.** regicidio.
regimen *s.* regime.
regiment *s.* reggimento.
to **regiment** *vt.* **1.** irreggimentare **2.** disciplinare.
regimental *agg.* reggimentale.
regimentals *s. pl.* (*mil.*) uniforme (*sing.*).
region *s.* regione.
regional *agg.* regionale.
register *s.* registro.
to **register** *vt.* registrare, iscrivere. ◆ to **register** *vi.* iscriversi.
registrar *s.* **1.** segretario **2.** ufficiale di stato civile.
registration *s.* registrazione, iscrizione.
registry *s.* **1.** registrazione **2.** ufficio del Registro.
regnant *agg.* regnante.
regress *s.* retrocessione.
to **regress** *vi.* retrocedere.
regression *s.* regresso.
regressive *agg.* regressivo.
regret *s.* rammarico.
to **regret** *vt.* **1.** rimpiangere **2.** rammaricarsi di.
regretful *agg.* pieno di rammarico.
regular *agg.* e *s.* regolare.
regularity *s.* regolarità.
regularization *s.* regolarizzazione.
to **regularize** *vt.* regolarizzare.
regularly *avv.* regolarmente.
to **regulate** *vt.* regolare.
regulation *s.* **1.** regolamento **2.** regolazione.
regulative *agg.* e *s.* regolatore.
regulator *s.* regolatore.
to **rehabilitate** *vt.* **1.** riabilitare **2.** ripristinare.
rehabilitation *s.* **1.** riabilitazione **2.** ripristino.
rehearsal *s.* **1.** ripetizione **2.** (*teat.*) prova.
to **rehearse** *vt.* **1.** ripetere **2.** provare.
reign *s.* regno.
to **reign** *vi.* regnare.
to **reimburse** *vt.* rimborsare.
reimbursement *s.* rimborso.
rein *s.* redine.
to **rein** *vt.* tenere a freno.
to **reincarnate** *vt.* reincarnare.
reincarnation *s.* reincarnazione.
reindeer *s.* renna.

to **reinforce** vt. rinforzare.
reinforce(ment) s. rinforzo.
to **reinstate** vt. ristabilire.
to **reintegrate** vt. reintegrare.
reinvestment s. nuovo investimento.
to **reinvigorate** vt. rinvigorire.
reinvigoration s. rinvigorimento.
to **reiterate** vt. reiterare.
reiteration s. reiterazione.
reject s. persona, cosa rifiutata.
to **reject** vt. rifiutare.
rejection s. rifiuto.
to **rejoice** vt. rallegrare. ♦ to **rejoice** vi. rallegrarsi.
rejoicing s. 1. allegria 2. festa.
rejuvenation s. ringiovanimento.
relapse s. ricaduta.
to **relapse** vi. 1. ricadere 2. avere una ricaduta.
to **relate** vt. 1. narrare 2. mettere in relazione. ♦ to **relate** vi. aver rapporto con.
relater s. narratore.
relation s. 1. relazione 2. parente.
relationship s. 1. relazione 2. parentela.
relative agg. relativo. ♦ **relative** s. parente.
relativism s. relativismo.
relativity s. relatività.
to **relax** vt. 1. rilassare 2. allentare. ♦ to **relax** vi. rilassarsi.
relaxation s. 1. rilassamento 2. svago 3. mitigazione.
relay s. 1. turno 2. ricambio 3. (radio) collegamento.
to **relay** vt. (radio) collegare.
release s. 1. liberazione 2. quietanza 3. cessione 4. scarico.
to **release** vt. 1. liberare 2. cedere.
releasee s. cessionario.
to **relegate** vt. 1. relegare 2. rimettere.
relegation s. relegazione.
relentless agg. inflessibile.
to **relent** vi. impietosirsi.
relevance s. 1. relazione 2. pertinenza.
relevant agg. 1. relativo 2. pertinente.
reliability s. attendibilità.
reliable agg. attendibile, fidato.
reliance s. 1. fede 2. persona, cosa di fiducia.
relic s. reliquia.
relief[1] s. 1. sollievo 2. aiuto 3. esenzione 4. cambio.
relief[2] s. 1. rilievo 2. (pitt.) prospettiva.

to **relieve** vt. 1. alleviare, sollevare 2. aiutare 3. dare il cambio a 4. dare rilievo a.
reliever s. soccorritore.
relieving agg. 1. che allevia, soccorre 2. (mil.) che dà il cambio.
religion s. religione.
religiosity s. religiosità.
religious agg. e s. religioso.
to **relinquish** vt. abbandonare.
relinquishment s. abbandono.
reliquary s. reliquario.
reliques s. pl. resti.
relish s. 1. gusto 2. sapore, profumo, aroma 3. condimento.
to **relish** vt. 1. gustare 2. insaporire.
to **relive** vt. e vi. rivivere.
to **reload** vt. ricaricare.
to **reluct** vi. essere riluttante.
reluctance s. riluttanza.
reluctant agg. riluttante.
reluctantly avv. con riluttanza.
to **rely** vi. fidarsi.
remade V. to remake.
to **remain** vi. rimanere, restare.
remainder s. resto, avanzo, rimanenza.
remains s. pl. resti.
to **remake (remade, remade)** vt. rifare.
remark s. nota, osservazione, commento.
to **remark** vt. e vi. osservare.
remarkable agg. notevole.
remarkableness s. ragguardevolezza.
remarkably avv. notevolmente.
to **remarry** vt. risposare. ♦ to **remarry** vi. risposarsi.
remediable agg. rimediabile.
remedy s. rimedio, cura.
to **remedy** vt. rimediare.
to **remember** vt. ricordare. ♦ to **remember** vi. ricordarsi.
remembrance s. ricordo.
to **remind** vt. ricordare (qc. a qu.), far ricordare, rammentare.
reminder s. ricordo, promemoria.
remindful agg. 1. memore 2. che fa ricordare.
reminiscence s. ricordo.
reminiscent agg. che ricorda.
remise s. (giur.) cessione.
to **remise** vt. (giur.) rinunciare a, cedere (diritti ecc.).
remiss agg. negligente.
remissible agg. remissibile.

remission s. 1. remissione 2. esonero, annullamento 3. (*med.*) remissione.

remissive agg. indulgente.

to **remit** vt. rimettere. ♦ to **remit** vi. diminuire, mitigarsi.

remittal s. (*giur.*) remissione (*condono*).

remittance s. rimessa (*di denaro*).

remittent agg. (*med.*) intermittente.

remnant agg. rimanente. ♦ **remnant** s. resto, rimanenza, avanzo.

to **remodel** vt. rimodellare.

remonstrance s. rimostranza.

to **remonstrate** vi. protestare.

remonstration s. rimostranza.

remorse s. rimorso.

remorseful agg. pieno di rimorso.

remorseless agg. senza rimorsi.

remote agg. remoto.

remoteness s. distanza, lontananza.

remotion s. rimozione, allontanamento.

remount s. rimonta (*di cavalli*).

to **remount** vt. e vi. 1. rimontare (*a cavallo, in bicicletta*) 2. risalire.

removable agg. rimovibile.

removal s. 1. rimozione 2. trasferimento, trasloco.

remove s. 1. trasferimento 2. grado (*di parentela*).

to **remove** vt. rimuovere. ♦ to **remove** vi. trasferirsi.

removed agg. lontano.

remover s. chi, ciò che toglie.

to **remunerate** vt. rimunerare.

remuneration s. rimunerazione.

remunerative agg. rimunerativo.

renaissance s. rinascimento.

renal agg. renale.

to **rename** vt. rinominare.

to **rend (rent, rent)** vt. lacerare. ♦ to **rend (rent, rent)** vi. lacerarsi.

to **render** vt. 1. rendere 2. consegnare.

rendering s. 1. restituzione 2. resa.

renegade s. rinnegato.

to **renew** vt. rinnovare. ♦ to **renew** vi. rinnovarsi.

renewable agg. rinnovabile.

renewal s. 1. rinnovo 2. ripresa.

renewer s. rinnovatore.

renitency s. riluttanza.

renitent agg. renitente, riluttante.

rennet s. ranetta.

to **renounce** vt. 1. rinunciare a 2. ripudiare.

renouncement s. rinuncia.

to **renovate** vt. rinnovare.

renown s. rinomanza, fama.

renowned agg. rinomato, famoso.

rent[1] s. affitto.

rent[2] s. 1. strappo, squarcio 2. spaccatura.

rent[3] V. to rend.

to **rent** vt. affittare. ♦ to **rent** vi. essere affittato.

rental s. affitto.

renunciation s. rinuncia.

to **reoccupy** vt. rioccupare.

to **reopen** vt. riaprire. ♦ to **reopen** vi. riaprirsi.

reopening s. riapertura.

reorganization s. riassetto, riorganizzazione.

repaid V. to repay.

repair s. 1. riparazione, restaurazione 2. stato, condizione.

to **repair** vt. riparare, restaurare.

repairer s. riparatore.

reparation s. riparazione.

repartee s. replica arguta.

repartition s. ripartizione.

to **repatriate** vt. e vi. rimpatriare.

repatriation s. rimpatrio.

to **repay (repaid, repaid)** vt. ripagare.

repayable agg. ripagabile.

repeal s. revoca.

to **repeal** vt. revocare.

repealer s. revocatore.

repeat s. ripetizione.

to **repeat** vt. ripetere. ♦ to **repeat** vi. ripetersi.

repeater s. 1. ripetitore 2. ripetente 3. arma a ripetizione.

repeating agg. 1. a ripetizione 2. periodico (*di numero*).

to **repel** vt. respingere.

repellent agg. repellente.

to **repent** vt. e vi. pentirsi.

repentance s. pentimento.

repentant agg. pentito.

repenter s. penitente.

repercussion s. ripercussione.

repercussive agg. ripercussivo.

repertoire s. repertorio.

repertory s. 1. repertorio 2. raccolta.

repetition s. ripetizione.

to **repine** vi. lamentarsi.

to **replace** vt. 1. ricollocare 2. rimpiazzare, sostituire.

replaceable agg. sostituibile.

replacement s. 1. ricollocamento 2. sostituzione.

replete *agg.* pieno.

repletion *s.* pienezza.

replication *s.* replica.

reply *s.* risposta.

to **reply** *vi.* rispondere.

report *s.* **1.** diceria **2.** reputazione **3.** rapporto **4.** scoppio.

to **report** *vt.* riportare. ♦ to **report** *vi.* **1.** stendere rapporto **2.** fare il cronista **3.** presentarsi.

reporter *s.* cronista (*di giornale*).

to **repose** *vt.* porre. ♦ to **repose** *vi.* riposare.

to **reprehend** *vt.* rimproverare.

reprehensible *agg.* biasimevole.

reprehension *s.* biasimo.

to **represent** *vt.* rappresentare, raffigurare.

representation *s.* **1.** rappresentazione **2.** rappresentanza.

representative *agg.* rappresentativo. ♦ **representative** *s.* rappresentante.

to **repress** *vt.* reprimere.

repressed *agg.* represso.

repressible *agg.* reprimibile.

repression *s.* repressione.

repressive *agg.* repressivo.

reprimand *s.* rimprovero.

reprint *s.* ristampa.

to **reprint** *vt.* ristampare.

reprisal *s.* rappresaglia.

reproach *s.* **1.** rimprovero **2.** discredito.

to **reproach** *vt.* **1.** rimproverare **2.** discreditare.

reproachable *agg.* riprovevole.

reproachful *agg.* di rimprovero.

reprobate *agg.* corrotto. ♦ **reprobate** *s.* reprobo.

to **reprobate** *vt.* **1.** riprovare **2.** dannare.

reprobation *s.* **1.** riprovazione **2.** dannazione.

to **reproduce** *vt.* riprodurre. ♦ to **reproduce** *vi.* riprodursi.

reproducer *s.* riproduttore.

reproducible *agg.* riproducibile.

reproduction *s.* riproduzione.

reproductive *agg.* riproduttivo.

reproof *s.* rimprovero.

to **reprove** *vt.* rimproverare.

reptile *agg.* strisciante. ♦ **reptile** *s.* rettile.

republic *s.* repubblica.

republican *agg.* e *s.* repubblicano.

republication *s.* ripubblicazione.

to **republish** *vt.* ripubblicare.

to **repudiate** *vt.* ripudiare.

repudiation *s.* ripudio.

repugnance *s.* **1.** ripugnanza **2.** incompatibilità.

repugnant *agg.* **1.** ripugnante **2.** incompatibile.

repulse *s.* ripulsa, rifiuto.

to **repulse** *vt.* respingere.

repulsion *s.* repulsione.

repulsive *agg.* ripulsivo.

reputable *agg.* onorato.

reputation *s.* reputazione.

repute *s.* fama.

to **repute** *vt.* reputare.

reputed *agg.* **1.** supposto **2.** putativo.

request *s.* richiesta.

to **request** *vt.* (ri)chiedere.

to **require** *vt.* **1.** richiedere **2.** ordinare, obbligare.

requirement *s.* **1.** richiesta **2.** requisito.

requisite *agg.* richiesto. ♦ **requisite** *s.* requisito.

requisition *s.* **1.** richiesta **2.** requisito **3.** requisizione.

to **requisition** *vt.* requisire.

requital *s.* **1.** contraccambio **2.** ricompensa.

to **requite** *vt.* **1.** ricompensare **2.** contraccambiare.

to **reread** (**reread, reread**) *vt.* rileggere.

to **rescind** *vt.* rescindere.

rescission *s.* rescissione.

rescue *s.* **1.** liberazione **2.** soccorso.

to **rescue** *vt.* **1.** liberare **2.** riacquistare **3.** soccorrere.

research *s.* ricerca ‖ — *work*, lavoro di ricerca.

to **research** *vi.* fare ricerche.

researcher *s.* ricercatore.

to **resell** (**resold, resold**) *vt.* rivendere.

resemblance *s.* rassomiglianza.

to **resemble** *vt.* assomigliare a.

to **resent** *vt.* risentirsi di.

resentful *agg.* **1.** risentito **2.** permaloso.

resentment *s.* risentimento.

reservation *s.* **1.** riserva **2.** prenotazione.

reserve *s.* **1.** riserva **2.** riserbo.

to **reserve** *vt.* riservare.

reservoir *s.* serbatoio.

to **reset** (**reset, reset**) *vt.* **1.** rimettere a posto **2.** (*tip.*) ricomporre.

to **resettle** *vt.* risistemare. ♦ to **resettle** *vi.* risistemarsi.

resettlement *s.* risistemazione.

to **reshape** vt. dare nuova forma a.
to **reside** vi. risiedere.
residence s. residenza.
resident agg. e s. residente.
residential agg. residenziale.
residual agg. residuo. ♦ **residual** s. 1. residuo 2. resto.
residue s. residuo, avanzo.
to **resign** vt. 1. consegnare 2. rinunciare ‖ to — oneself, rassegnarsi. ♦ to **resign** vi. dimettersi.
resignation s. 1. dimissioni (pl.) 2. rinuncia 3. rassegnazione.
resigned agg. rassegnato.
resilience, resiliency s. elasticità.
resilient agg. elastico.
resin s. resina.
resinous agg. resinoso.
resipiscence s. resipiscenza.
resipiscent agg. resipiscente.
resist s. sostanza protettiva.
to **resist** vt. e vi. resistere.
resistance s. resistenza.
resistant, resistent agg. resistente.
resistive agg. resistente.
resold V. to resell.
to **resole** vt. risolare.
resolubile agg. (ri)solubile.
resolute agg. risoluto.
resoluteness s. risolutezza.
resolution s. 1. risolutezza 2. risoluzione 3. scissione.
resolutive agg. risolutivo.
resolvable agg. risolvibile.
resolve s. risoluzione.
to **resolve** vt. 1. risolvere 2. scindere. ♦ to **resolve** vi. risolversi.
resolvent agg. e s. solvente.
resonance s. risonanza.
resonant agg. risonante.
to **resorb** vt. riassorbire.
resorbent agg. riassorbente.
resort s. 1. ricorso 2. risorsa 3. ritrovo 4. luogo di soggiorno.
to **resort** vi. 1. ricorrere 2. recarsi.
to **resound** vi. risonare. ♦ to **resound** vt. proclamare.
resource s. risorsa.
resourceful agg. pieno di risorse.
resourceless agg. senza risorse.
respect s. 1. rispetto, stima 2. aspetto 3. punto di vista.
to **respect** vt. rispettare.
respectability s. 1. rispettabilità 2. convenzioni sociali (pl.).
respectable agg. rispettabile.
respectful agg. rispettoso.
respecting prep. rispetto a. ↘
respective agg. rispettivo.

respiration s. respirazione.
respirator s. respiratore.
respiratory agg. respiratorio.
respite s. 1. dilazione 2. tregua.
to **respite** vt. concedere una dilazione, una tregua a.
resplendent agg. risplendente.
respond s. responsorio.
to **respond** vi. rispondere.
respondence s. rispondenza.
respondent agg. 1. rispondente 2. sensibile. ♦ **respondent** s. (giur.) convenuto.
response s. risposta.
responsibility s. responsabilità.
responsible agg. 1. responsabile 2. di responsabilità.
responsive agg. rispondente.
responsory s. responsorio.
rest[1] s. 1. riposo 2. appoggio.
rest[2] s. resto, residuo.
to **rest** vt. 1. riposare 2. appoggiare. ♦ to **rest** vi. 1. riposarsi 2. appoggiarsi.
to **restate** vt. riesporre.
restaurant s. ristorante ‖ — -car, vagone ristorante.
restful agg. tranquillo.
restfulness s. tranquillità.
resting-place s. luogo di riposo.
restitution s. restituzione.
restive agg. 1. restio 2. irrequieto.
restless agg. 1. irrequieto 2. incessante.
restlessness s. irrequietezza.
restorable agg. 1. restituibile 2. restaurabile.
restoration s. 1. restituzione 2. restauro 3. restaurazione 4. ricostruzione.
to **restore** vt. 1. restituire 2. restaurare 3. ricostruire 4. ristabilire.
to **restrain** vt. 1. trattenere 2. confinare.
restrainable agg. reprimibile.
restraint s. 1. freno 2. detenzione.
to **restrict** vt. limitare.
restrictedly avv. limitatamente.
restriction s. restrizione.
restrictive agg. restrittivo.
result s. risultato.
to **result** vi. 1. risultare 2. risolversi.
resultant agg. e s. risultante.
resultful agg. utile, efficace.
resultless agg. inutile, inefficace.
to **resume** vt. riprendere.
resummons s. nuova convocazione.
resumption s. ripresa.

resurgent *agg.* risorgente.
to **resurrect** *vt.* (*fam.*) risuscitare.
resurrection *s.* risurrezione.
resurrectional *agg.* di risurrezione.
to **resuscitate** *vt.* e *vi.* risuscitare.
resuscitation *s.* risuscitamento.
to **ret** *vt.* macerare.
retail *s.* vendita al minuto || *by* —, al minuto.
to **retail** *vt.* e *vi.* vendere al minuto.
retailer *s.* dettagliante.
to **retain** *vt.* trattenere, conservare.
retainable *agg.* trattenibile, conservabile.
retainer *s.* caparra, anticipo.
retaining *agg.* — *wall*, muro di sostegno.
retake *s.* (*cine*) replica di una ripresa.
to **retake** (**retook, retaken**) *vt.* 1. riprendere 2. (*cine*) ripetere una ripresa.
to **retaliate** *vi.* far rappresaglia.
retaliation *s.* rappresaglia.
retaliative, retaliatory *agg.* vendicativo.
retard *s.* ritardo.
to **retard** *vt.* e *vi.* ritardare.
to **retaste** *vt.* riassaggiare.
to **retch** *vi.* avere conati di vomito.
to **retell** (**retold, retold**) *vt.* ripetere.
retention *s.* 1. ritenzione 2. memoria.
retentive *agg.* 1. che trattiene 2. tenace (*di memoria*).
reticence, reticency *s.* reticenza.
reticent *agg.* reticente.
reticle *s.* (*ott.*) reticolo.
reticular *agg.* reticolare.
reticulate *agg.* reticolato.
reticulum *s.* (*pl.* -la) reticolo.
retinue *s.* seguito.
to **retire** *vt.* ritirare. ◆ to **retire** *vi.* ritirarsi.
retired *agg.* 1. ritirato 2. a riposo, in ritiro.
retirement *s.* 1. ritiro 2. collocamento a riposo 3. (*mil.*) ritirata.
retiring *agg.* 1. riservato 2. che si ritira, uscente.
retold V. *to retell.*
retook V. *to retake.*
retorsion *s.* ritorsione.
retort *s.* storta.
to **retort** *vt.* ritorcere. ◆ to **retort** *vi.* ribattere.
retort(ion) *s.* ritorsione.
retouch *s.* ritocco.

to **retouch** *vt.* ritoccare.
to **retrace** *vt.* ripercorrere, risalire.
to **retract** *vt.* 1. ritrarre 2. ritrattare. ◆ to **retract** *vi.* ritrarsi.
retractable *agg.* ritraibile 2. ritrattabile.
retractation *s.* ritrattazione.
retractile *agg.* retrattile.
retractor *s.* (*med.*) divaricatore.
to **retread** (**retrod, retrodden**) *vt.* ripercorrere.
retreat *s.* eremo, luogo appartato.
to **retreat** *vi.* ritirarsi, retrocedere.
retreating *agg.* sfuggente. ◆ **retreating** *s.* (*mil.*) ritirata.
retribution *s.* punizione.
retrievable *agg.* 1. ricuperabile 2. riparabile.
retrieval *s.* 1. ricupero (*di beni*) 2. riparazione.
to **retrieve** *vt.* 1. ricuperare 2. riparare.
retroaction *s.* 1. reazione 2. azione retroattiva.
retroactive *agg.* retroattivo.
to **retrocede**[1] *vi.* retrocedere.
to **retrocede**[2] *vt.* restituire.
retrocession[1] *s.* retrocessione.
retrocession[2] *s.* restituzione.
retrod V. *to retread.*
retrodden V. *to retread.*
retrospect(ion) *s.* sguardo retrospettivo.
retrospective *agg.* retrospettivo.
retroversion *s.* retroversione.
return *s.* 1. ritorno 2. restituzione 3. guadagno, profitto 4. relazione || — *journey*, viaggio di ritorno; *election returns*, risultati elettorali.
to **return** *vi.* 1. ritornare 2. rispondere, ricambiare, replicare. ◆ to **return** *vt.* 1. restituire, rimandare 2. produrre, fruttare 3. (*pol.*) eleggere.
reunion *s.* riunione.
to **reunite** *vt.* riunire. ◆ to **reunite** *vi.* riunirsi.
revaluation *s.* rivalutazione.
to **revalue** *vt.* rivalutare.
to **reveal** *vt.* rivelare.
revel *s.* baldoria.
to **revel** *vi.* far baldoria.
revelation *s.* rivelazione.
reveller *s.* chi fa baldoria.
revelry *s.* baldoria.
revenge *s.* vendetta.
to **revenge** *vt.* vendicare. ◆ to **revenge** *vi.* vendicarsi.
revengeful *agg.* vendicativo.

revenger s. vendicatore.
revenue s. 1. entrata 2. fisco.
to **reverberate** vt. e vi. riverberare.
reverberation s. riverberazione, riverbero.
to **revere** vt. riverire.
reverence s. riverenza.
to **reverence** vt. riverire.
reverend agg. reverendo.
reverent(ial) agg. riverente.
reverie s. fantasticheria.
reversal s. 1. rovesciamento 2. (giur.) annullamento.
reverse agg. e s. rovescio || — gear, retromarcia.
to **reverse** vt. rovesciare. ♦ to **reverse** vi. innestare la retromarcia.
reversibility s. reversibilità.
reversible agg. reversibile, rovesciabile.
reversion s. reversione.
to **revert** vi. ritornare.
review s. 1. revisione 2. recensione 3. rivista, periodico 4. (mil.) rivista.
to **review** vt. 1. rivedere 2. recensire 3. (mil.) passare in rivista.
reviewal s. revisione, recensione.
reviewer s. recensore, revisore.
to **revile** vt. e vi. ingiuriare.
to **revise** vt. rivedere, modificare.
reviser s. revisore.
revision s. revisione, correzione.
revival s. 1. ripristino 2. ripresa 3. rinascita.
to **revive** vt. e vi. resuscitare.
reviver s. chi, ciò che rinvigorisce.
revivification s. rinascita.
to **revivify** vt. ravvivare.
revocable agg. revocabile.
revocation s. revoca.
revocatory agg. revocatorio.
to **revoke** vt. revocare.
revolt s. rivolta.
to **revolt** vt. disgustare. ♦ to **revolt** vi. rivoltarsi.
revolution s. rivoluzione.
revolutionary agg. e s. rivoluzionario.
to **revolutionize** vt. rivoluzionare.
to **revolve** vt. meditare. ♦ to **revolve** vi. girare, rotare.
revolver s. rivoltella.
revolving agg. 1. rotante 2. rotativo.
revulsion s. 1. revulsione 2. mutamento.
revulsive agg. revulsivo.

reward s. ricompensa.
to **reward** vt. ricompensare.
rewarding agg. rimunerativo. ♦ **rewarding** s. rimunerazione.
to **rewrite** (**rewrote, rewritten**) vt. riscrivere.
rhagades s. pl. ragadi.
rhapsody s. rapsodia.
rheostat s. reostato.
rhetoric s. retorica.
rhetorical agg. retorico.
rhetorician s. retore.
rheumatic agg. e s. reumatico.
rheumatism s. reumatismo.
rhinitis s. rinite.
rhinoceros s. rinoceronte.
rhizome s. rizoma.
rhododendron s. rododendro.
rhomb s. rombo.
rhombic(al) agg. rombico.
rhombohedron s. (pl. -dra) romboedro.
rhomboid agg. e s. romboide.
rhubarb s. rabarbaro.
rhyme s. rima.
to **rhyme** vt. far rimare. ♦ to **rhyme** vi. rimare.
rhymer s. rimatore.
Rhynchota s. pl. rincoti.
rhythm s. ritmo.
rhythmic(al) agg. ritmico.
rib s. 1. costola 2. costa, nervatura 3. stecca.
to **rib** vt. 1. munire (di coste ecc.) 2. scanalare.
ribbing s. 1. nervatura 2. rigatura.
ribbon s. nastro.
rice s. riso || — -field (o — -swamp), risaia.
rich agg. ricco.
richly avv. riccamente.
richness s. ricchezza.
rick s. bica.
ricket(s) s. rachitismo.
rickety agg. 1. rachitico 2. malsicuro.
to **rid** (**rid, rid**) vt. liberare || to get — of, sbarazzarsi di.
ridden V. to ride.
riddle[1] s. indovinello.
riddle[2] s. vaglio, crivello.
to **riddle**[1] vt. risolvere.
to **riddle**[2] vt. 1. vagliare 2. setacciare.
ride s. passeggiata, percorso (a cavallo, su un veicolo).
to **ride** (**rode, ridden**) vt. 1. montare (cavallo, bicicletta) 2. percorrere (a cavallo, su un veicolo) 3.

(*fig.*) opprimere. ♦ **to ride (rode, ridden)** *vi.* andare (*a cavallo, su un veicolo*).

rider *s.* cavaliere, fantino.

ridge *s.* cresta, catena di monti.

ridicule *s.* ridicolo.

to ridicule *vt.* schernire.

ridiculous *agg.* ridicolo.

riding *s.* corsa (*a cavallo, in veicolo*).

rifle *s.* fucile.

rifleman *s.* fuciliere.

rift *s.* crepa.

rigging *s.* attrezzatura.

right[1] *agg.* **1.** giusto **2.** (*geom.*) retto **3.** destro.

right[2] *s.* **1.** il giusto, il bene **2.** diritto **3.** destra, mano destra, lato destro.

right[3] *avv.* **1.** giustamente, bene **2.** direttamente **3.** proprio **4.** a destra.

righteous *agg.* giusto.

righteousness *s.* rettitudine.

rightful *agg.* **1.** legittimo **2.** giusto.

rightly *avv.* **1.** rettamente **2.** esattamente.

rigid *agg.* rigido.

rigidity, rigor *s.* rigidità.

rigorism *s.* rigorismo.

rigorist *s.* rigorista.

rigorous *agg.* rigido.

rigour *s.* rigore.

rim *s.* bordo, orlo.

to rim *vt.* bordare, cerchiare.

rind *s.* **1.** buccia **2.** corteccia **3.** crosta **4.** cotenna.

to rind *vt.* **1.** sbucciare **2.** scortecciare.

ring[1] *s.* **1.** anello, cerchio **2.** pista.

ring[2] *s.* **1.** scampanellata **2.** (*fig.*) accento, tono.

to ring[1] *vt.* circondare.

to ring[2] **(rang, rung)** *vt.* suonare || *to — up*, telefonare. ♦ **to ring (rang, rung)** *vi.* risuonare.

ringleader *s.* capobanda.

rink *s.* pista di pattinaggio.

to rinse *vt.* sciacquare.

rinsing *s.* risciacquatura.

riot *s.* **1.** rivolta **2.** gazzarra.

to riot *vi.* **1.** tumultuare **2.** gozzovigliare.

rioter *s.* rivoltoso.

riotous *agg.* **1.** tumultuante **2.** sregolato.

rip *s.* lacerazione, scucitura, strappo.

to rip *vt.* lacerare. ♦ **to rip** *vi.* lacerarsi.

ripe *agg.* maturo.

to ripen *vt.* e *vi.* maturare.

ripeness *s.* maturità.

ripple *s.* **1.** increspatura, ondulatura **2.** gorgoglio.

to ripple *vt.* increspare, ondulare. ♦ **to ripple** *vi.* incresparsi, ondularsi.

rise *s.* **1.** il sorgere **2.** salita, ascesa **3.** aumento **4.** sorgente.

to rise (rose, risen) *vi.* **1.** sorgere **2.** aumentare.

riser *s.* chi si alza.

risible *agg.* risibile.

rising *s.* **1.** sorgere **2.** salita, ascesa **3.** aumento **4.** rivolta.

risk *s.* rischio.

to risk *vt.* rischiare.

risky *agg.* rischioso.

rissole *s.* polpetta.

rite *s.* rito.

ritual *agg.* e *s.* rituale.

rival *agg.* e *s.* rivale.

to rival *vt.* rivaleggiare.

rivality, rivalry *s.* rivalità.

river *s.* fiume.

riverside *s.* lungofiume.

to rivet *vt.* **1.** ribadire **2.** fissare.

rivulet *s.* fiumicello.

road *s.* strada || *— -bed*, fondo stradale; *— sign*, cartello stradale.

roadstead *s.* (*mar.*) rada.

roadway *s.* carreggiata.

to roam *vt.* e *vi.* vagare (*per*).

roar *s.* **1.** ruggito **2.** rombo.

to roar *vt.* e *vi.* **1.** ruggire **2.** tuonare || *— with laughter*, ridere fragorosamente.

roaring *agg.* **1.** rumoroso **2.** ruggente, mugghiante. ♦ **roaring** *s.* V. *roar*.

roast *agg.* e *s.* arrosto.

to roast *vt.* **1.** arrostire **2.** tostare. ♦ **to roast** *vi.* arrostirsi.

roasting *agg.* rovente. ♦ **roasting** *s.* **1.** arrostimento **2.** torrefazione.

to rob *vt.* derubare. ♦ **to rob** *vi.* rubare.

robber *s.* ladro.

robbery *s.* furto.

robe *s.* **1.** toga **2.** vestiti (*pl.*).

to robe *vt.* vestire. ♦ **to robe** *vi.* vestirsi.

robin *s.* pettirosso.

robust *agg.* **1.** robusto **2.** faticoso.

robustness *s.* robustezza.

rock[1] *s.* **1.** roccia **2.** rocca.

rock[2] *s.* dondolio.

to rock *vt.* cullare, dondolare. ♦

to **rock** vi. dondolarsi, oscillare, barcollare.

rocker s. **1.** chi culla, dondola **2.** dondolo (di sedia ecc.) **3.** (mecc.) bilanciere.

rocket s. razzo.

rocking agg. **1.** a dondolo **2.** vacillante. ♦ **rocking** s. oscillazione, dondolio.

rocky agg. roccioso.

rod s. verga || fishing- —, canna da pesca.

rode V. to ride.

rodent agg. e s. roditore.

roe[1] s. capriolo maschio.

roe[2] s. uova di pesce.

rogue s. briccone.

roguery s. bricconeria.

roguish agg. bricconesco.

role s. **1.** (teat.) ruolo, parte **2.** funzione.

roll[1] s. **1.** rotolo **2.** elenco, lista **3.** rullo, cilindro.

roll[2] s. **1.** (mar.; aer.) rollio **2.** rullo (di tamburo).

to **roll** vt. **1.** far rotolare **2.** arrotolare **3.** spianare. ♦ to **roll** vi. **1.** rotolare **2.** arrotolarsi **3.** ruotare **4.** rollare **5.** rullare.

roller s. **1.** rullo, cilindro **2.** cavallone || — skates, schettini.

rolling s. (ar)rotolamento || — -mill, laminatoio; — pin, matterello.

Roman agg. e s. romano.

Romance agg. romanzo, neolatino.

romance s. **1.** poema cavalleresco, racconto fantastico **2.** avventura romanzesca **3.** idillio **4.** poesia **5.** (mus.) romanza.

Romanesque agg. e s. romanico.

Romanian agg. e s. romeno.

Romanic agg. romanico.

Romanist s. romanista.

Romansh agg. e s. ladino.

romantic agg. e s. romantico.

romanticism s. romanticismo.

to **romanticize** vt. romanzare.

to **romp** vi. giocare rumorosamente.

rompish agg. chiassoso.

rood s. croce.

roof s. tetto || — -garden, giardino pensile.

to **roof** vt. **1.** coprire con un tetto **2.** ospitare.

rook s. cornacchia.

room s. **1.** stanza **2.** spazio **3.** possibilità.

to **room** vt. e vi. (amer.) alloggiare.

roomy agg. spazioso.

root s. radice.

to **root**[1] vt. piantare || to — away, out, up, sradicare. ♦ to **root** vi. mettere radice.

to **root**[2] vt. e vi. grufolare.

rope s. fune, corda || — -dancer, funambolo.

to **rope** vt. legare.

rosary s. **1.** roseto **2.** (eccl.) rosario.

rose agg. e s. rosa || — -bush, rosaio; — -diamond, rosetta; — -window, rosone.

rose V. to rise.

rosemary s. rosmarino.

roseola s. rosolia.

rosery s. roseto.

rosette s. **1.** rosetta **2.** (arch.) rosone **3.** coccarda.

rosewood s. palissandro.

rosin s. pece greca.

rostrum s. (pl. rostra o rostrums) rostro.

rosy agg. roseo.

rot s. putrefazione.

to **rot** vt. e vi. imputridire.

rotary agg. rotante. ♦ **rotary** s. — (press), rotativa.

to **rotate** vt. e vi. rotare.

rotation s. rotazione.

rotative, rotatory agg. rotatorio.

rote s. abitudine, memoria meccanica.

rotogravure s. rotocalco.

rotor s. rotore.

rotten agg. marcio.

rottenness s. marciume.

rotund agg. **1.** rotondo **2.** enfatico.

rouble s. rublo.

rouge agg. rossetto.

rough agg. **1.** irregolare, ruvido, scabro **2.** tempestoso **3.** rozzo.

to **rough** vt. irruvidire || to — il (fam.), vivere primitivamente.

to **roughen** vt. irruvidire. ♦ to **roughen** vi. irruvidirsi.

to **rough-hew** vt. abbozzare.

roughly avv. ruvidamente.

roughness s. **1.** ruvidezza **2.** rudezza **3.** inclemenza (di tempo).

round agg. **1.** rotondo **2.** intero **3.** franco **4.** vigoroso **5.** considerevole. ♦ **round** s. **1.** cerchio **2.** sfera **3.** ciclo **4.** giro, ronda.

round avv. intorno. ♦ **round** prep. intorno a.

to **round** vt. arrotondare. ♦ to **round** vi. **1.** arrotondarsi **2.** girare

3. svilupparsi.

roundabout *agg.* indiretto. ♦ **roundabout** *s.* giostra.

roundly *avv.* 1. vigorosamente 2. francamente.

roundness *s.* 1. rotondità 2. scorrevolezza 3. franchezza.

to **rouse** *vt.* (ri)svegliare (*anche fig.*). ♦ to **rouse** *vi.* (ri)svegliarsi.

rouser *s.* ridestatore.

rousing *agg.* stimolante.

rout *s.* 1. plebaglia 2. tumulto 3. rotta.

to **rout** *vt.* sconfiggere.

route *s.* via, rotta.

routinist *s.* abitudinario.

rove *s.* vagabondaggio.

to **rove** *vt.* e *vi.* vagare.

rover *s.* 1. vagabondo 2. pirata.

roving *s.* vagabondaggio.

row[1] *s.* fila.

row[2] *s.* remata, gita in barca.

to **row** *vt.* trasportare (*remando*). ♦ to **row** *vi.* remare.

rowdy *agg.* e *s.* turbolento.

rower *s.* rematore.

rowlock *s.* scalmo.

royal *agg.* regale, reale.

royalist *s.* realista.

royalty *s.* 1. regalità 2. i reali 3. diritto d'autore.

rub *s.* 1. fregata, grattata 2. ineguaglianza 3. ostacolo, difficoltà.

to **rub** *vt.* fregare. ♦ to **rub** *vi.* fregarsi.

rubber *s.* 1. massaggiatore 2. strofinaccio 3. gomma || — *-solution*, mastice.

rubbish *s.* rifiuti (*pl.*).

rubble *s.* pietrisco.

ruby *s.* rubino.

rucksack *s.* zaino.

rudder *s.* timone.

ruddy *agg.* rosso, rubicondo.

rude *agg.* 1. rude, violento 2. rudimentale 3. grezzo.

rudeness *s.* 1. rozzezza 2. violenza.

rudiment *s.* rudimento.

rudimentary *agg.* rudimentale.

ruffian *agg.* brutale. ♦ **ruffian** *s.* ribaldo.

ruffle *s.* 1. increspatura 2. sconvolgimento 3. tumulto.

to **ruffle** *vt.* 1. increspare 2. arruffare 3. agitare.

rug *s.* 1. coperta 2. tappetino.

rugged *agg.* 1. ruvido 2. scompigliato 3. austero 4. rozzo.

ruggedness *s.* 1. ruvidezza 2. auste-

rità 3. rudezza.

ruin *s.* rovina.

to **ruin** *vt.* e *vi.* rovinare.

ruinous *agg.* 1. rovinoso 2. in rovina.

rule *s.* 1. regola 2. dominio 3. riga da disegno.

to **rule** *vt.* 1. governare, dominare 2. rigare.

ruler *s.* 1. dominatore 2. regolo.

ruling *s.* 1. governo 2. decisione.

Rumanian *agg.* e *s.* romeno.

rumble *s.* 1. rombo 2. brontolio.

to **rumble** *vt.* e *vi.* 1. rombare 2. brontolare.

rumbling *s.* V. *rumble.*

rumen *s.* rumine.

ruminant *agg.* e *s.* ruminante.

to **ruminate** *vt.* e *vi.* ruminare.

rummage *s.* ricerca, perquisizione.

to **rummage** *vt.* e *vi.* 1. rovistare 2. perquisire.

rumour *s.* diceria.

to **rumour** *vt.* far correre la voce.

rump *s.* 1. posteriore 2. resto.

to **rumple** *vt.* 1. spiegazzare 2. arruffare.

run *s.* 1. corsa 2. percorso, giro 3. andamento 4. periodo 5. richiesta.

to **run** (**ran**, **run**) *vi.* 1. correre 2. colare 3. diventare 4. estendersi 5. essere in vigore, durare. ♦ to **run** (**ran**, **run**) *vt.* 1. far funzionare 2. dirigere 3. seguire 4. passare || *to — in*, rodare; *to — over*, investire.

runaway *agg.* 1. fuggitivo 2. decisivo. ♦ **runaway** *s.* 1. fuggitivo 2. fuga.

rung[1] *s.* 1. piolo 2. raggio (*di ruota*).

rung[2] V. *to ring.*

runnel *s.* ruscello.

runner *s.* 1. corridore 2. messo 3. passatoia 4. pattino 5. carrello.

running *s.* 1. corsa 2. esercizio 3. flusso || — *-in*, rodaggio.

runway *s.* pista.

rupture *s.* rottura.

rural *agg.* rurale.

rush[1] *s.* giunco.

rush[2] 1. attacco 2. impeto 3. afflusso || — *-hours*, ore di punta.

to **rush** *vt.* spingere. ♦ to **rush** *vi.* precipitarsi.

rushy *agg.* 1. di giunchi 2. folto di giunchi.

Russian *agg.* e *s.* russo.

rust *s.* ruggine.

to **rust** *vt*. arrugginire. ♦ to **rust** *vi*. arrugginirsi.
rustic(al) *agg*. rustico. ♦ **rustic(al)** *s*. campagnolo.
rustle *s*. fruscio, stormire (*di foglie*).
to **rustle** *vt*. far frusciare. ♦ to **rustle** *vi*. frusciare.
rusty *agg*. **1.** rugginoso **2.** (*fig.*) ombroso.
ruthless *agg*. spietato.
ruthlessness *s*. crudeltà.
rye *s*. segale.

S

Sabbath *s*. il giorno della settimana dedicato al riposo.
sable *s*. zibellino.
sabot *s*. zoccolo.
sabotage *s*. sabotaggio.
to **sabotage** *vt*. e *vi*. sabotare.
saboteur *s*. sabotatore.
sabre *s*. sciabola || — *-cut*, sciabolata.
to **sabre** *vt*. sciabolare.
saccharin(e) *s*. saccarina.
saccharose *s*. saccarosio.
sacerdotal *agg*. sacerdotale.
sack[1] *s*. **1.** sacco **2.** (*gergo*) licenziamento.
sack[2] *s*. (*mil.*) sacco, saccheggio.
sack[3] *s*. vino bianco delle Canarie.
to **sack**[1] *vt*. **1.** insaccare **2.** (*gergo*) licenziare.
to **sack**[2] *vt*. (*mil.*) saccheggiare.
sacking[1] *s*. tela da sacco.
sacking[2] *s*. saccheggio.
sacral[1] *agg*. (*anat.*) sacro.
sacral[2] *agg*. rituale.
sacrament *s*. sacramento.
sacramental *agg*. sacramentale.
sacred *agg*. **1.** sacro, religioso **2.** consacrato, dedicato.
sacrifice *s*. **1.** sacrificio **2.** abnegazione.
to **sacrifice** *vt*. e *vi*. **1.** sacrificare, immolare **2.** rinunziare.
sacrilege *s*. sacrilegio.
sacrist *s*. sagrestano.
sacristy *s*. sagrestia.
sacrosanct *agg*. sacrosanto.
sad *agg*. triste, mesto || *to make so.* —, rattristare qu.
to **sadden** *vt*. rattristare. ♦ to **sadden** *vi*. rattristarsi.

saddle *s*. **1.** sella, sellino **2.** giogaia.
to **saddle** *vt*. sellare, mettere in sella.
saddler *s*. sellaio.
sadism *s*. sadismo.
sadist *s*. sadico.
sadistic *agg*. sadico.
sadly *avv*. tristemente, mestamente.
sadness *s*. tristezza, mestizia.
safe *agg*. **1.** sicuro, al riparo **2.** salvo, intatto **3.** innocuo || — *and sound*, sano e salvo; — *-conduct*, salvacondotto; — *-deposit*, cassetta di sicurezza. ♦ **safe** *s*. **1.** cassaforte **2.** sicura (*di armi*).
safeguard *s*. salvaguardia.
to **safeguard** *vt*. salvaguardare, difendere.
safekeeping *s*. custodia.
safety *s*. sicurezza, salvezza, scampo || — *belt*, cintura di sicurezza; — *device*, dispositivo di sicurezza; — *-pin*, spilla di sicurezza.
saffron *s*. zafferano.
sag *s*. **1.** abbassamento, cedimento **2.** (*mar.*) scarroccio.
sagacious *agg*. acuto, sagace.
sagaciousness, **sagacity** *s*. sagacia, perspicacia.
sage[1] *s*. salvia.
sage[2] *s*. saggio, dotto.
said V. to *say*.
sail[1] *s*. vela, velatura || *to set* (*v. irr.*) —, spiegare le vele, salpare; *to strike* (*v. irr.*) —, ammainare le vele.
sail[2] *s*. gita su imbarcazione a vela.
to **sail** *vt*. e *vi*. **1.** veleggiare, navigare, costeggiare **2.** salpare **3.** volare, veleggiare (*di uccelli, nuvole ecc.*).
sailer *s*. veliero.
sailing *s*. **1.** navigazione, traversata **2.** partenza (*di navi*).
sailor *s*. marinaio.
sailplane *s*. veleggiatore.
saint *agg*. e *s*. santo.
to **saint** *vt*. canonizzare, santificare.
sainthood, **saintliness** *s*. santità.
saintly *agg*. santo, di santo.
sake *s*. **1.** amore, interesse **2.** riguardo, rispetto || *for God's* —, per l'amor di Dio.
salaam *s*. riverenza, salamelecco.
salacious *agg*. salace, lascivo.
salad *s*. insalata || *fruit* —, macedonia di frutta.
salamander *s*. salamandra.

salariat s. categorie salariate.

salary s. stipendio.

sale s. **1.** vendita || *bill of* —, fattura; *on* —, in vendita **2.** asta: — *by auction*, vendita all'asta **3.** liquidazione, svendita.

sal(e)able agg. vendibile, commerciabile.

salesman s. venditore, commesso.

saleswoman s. venditrice, commessa.

salicylate s. salicilato.

salient agg. **1.** sporgente, prominente **2.** saliente, notevole.

saline agg. salino, salso.

salinity s. salsedine, salinità.

saliva s. saliva.

salivary agg. salivare.

salivation s. salivazione.

sallow agg. giallastro.

sally s. **1.** (*mil.*) sortita **2.** escursione.

to sally vi. fare una sortita || *to* — *forth*, uscire (*per una passeggiata*).

salmon s. salmone.

saloon s. salone || *dancing* —, sala da ballo.

salt s. sale. ♦ **salt** agg. **1.** salato **2.** sotto sale **3.** (*fig.*) amaro, piccante || — *-cellar*, saliera; — *-mine*, salina.

to salt vt. **1.** salare, cospargere di sale **2.** rendere piccante (*anche fig.*).

salting s. palude costiera.

saltish agg. salmastro, salaticcio.

saltness s. salsedine.

saltpetre s. salnitro.

salty agg. **1.** salato, salmastro **2.** piccante (*anche fig.*).

salubrious agg. salubre.

salutary agg. salutare.

salutation s. saluto.

salute s. saluto, gesto di saluto || *to fire a* —, salutare a salve.

to salute vt. salutare, dare il benvenuto.

salvage s. salvataggio (*di navi, carico ecc.*).

salvation s. salvezza (*anche relig.*).

salve s. unguento, balsamo.

same agg. medesimo, stesso, uguale || *at the* — *time*, allo stesso tempo. ♦ **same** pron. lo stesso, il medesimo.

samely agg. monotono, uniforme.

sameness s. **1.** somiglianza **2.** monotonia.

sample s. campione, modello, esemplare || — *book*, campionario.

sanatorium s. sanatorio.

sanatory agg. curativo.

sanctification s. santificazione.

to sanctify vt. santificare.

sanction s. **1.** autorizzazione, approvazione **2.** (*giur.*) ratifica **3.** sanzione.

to sanction vt. **1.** autorizzare **2.** (*giur.*) ratificare **3.** aggiungere sanzioni penali (*ad una legge*).

sanctity s. santità.

sanctuary s. **1.** santuario **2.** asilo, rifugio.

sand s. sabbia, rena || — *-bath*, bagno di sabbia. ♦ **sands** s. *pl.* spiaggia (*sing.*).

to sand vt. **1.** coprire di sabbia **2.** arenare **3.** smerigliare.

sandal s. sandalo.

sandpaper s. carta vetrata.

sandstone s. arenaria.

sandy agg. sabbioso.

sane agg. sano di mente, sensato.

saneness, sanity s. sanità (*di mente*), equilibrio.

sang V. *to sing*.

sanguinary agg. sanguinario, crudele.

sanguine agg. sanguigno.

sanguineous agg. del sangue, sanguigno.

sanitarian s. igienista. ♦ **sanitarian** agg. igienico.

sanitarist s. igienista.

sanitary agg. igienico, sanitario.

sanity s. V. *saneness*.

sank V. *to sink*.

Sanscrit, Sanskrit agg. e s. Sanscrito.

santon s. santone.

sap s. **1.** linfa, succo **2.** (*fig.*) vigore.

sapful agg. **1.** succoso **2.** vigoroso.

sapid agg. sapido, gustoso (*anche fig.*).

sapient agg. pedante.

sapless agg. **1.** secco, avvizzito **2.** fiacco.

saponification s. saponificazione.

to saponify vt. saponificare.

Sapphic agg. saffico.

sapphire s. zaffiro.

saraband s. sarabanda.

Saracen agg. e s. saraceno.

sarcasm s. sarcasmo.

sarcastic agg. sarcastico.

sarcophagus s. (*pl.* -gi) sarcofago.

sardine s. sardina.
sardonic agg. sardonico.
sash[1] s. fascia, cintura.
sash[2] s. telaio scorrevole (di fine-stra).
sat V. to sit.
satanic(al) agg. satanico.
satchel s. cartella (di scolaro).
to **sate** vt. saziare.
satellite s. satellite.
satiable agg. saziabile.
to **satiate** vt. saziare, satollare.
satiety s. sazietà.
satin s. raso.
satire s. satira.
satiric(al) agg. satirico.
satirist s. autore di satire.
to **satirize** vt. satireggiare.
satisfaction s. 1. soddisfazione 2. riparazione 3. (giur.) estinzione.
satisfactory agg. soddisfacente.
satisfiable agg. che può essere sod-disfatto.
to **satisfy** vt. soddisfare, appagare || to — a claim, accogliere un re-clamo. ♦ to **satisfy** vi. fare am-menda.
satrap s. satrapo.
saturate agg. saturo.
to **saturate** vt. saturare, impregnare.
saturation s. saturazione.
Saturday s. sabato.
satyr s. satiro.
satyric agg. satiresco.
sauce s. salsa, intingolo.
saucepan s. casseruola.
saucer s. piattino, sottocoppa.
saucily avv. sfacciatamente.
saucy agg. sfacciato, insolente.
sauerkraut s. crauti.
to **saunter** vi. bighellonare.
saunterer s. bighellone.
sausage s. salsiccia, salame.
savage agg. 1. selvaggio, barbaro 2. feroce, crudele. ♦ **savage** s. sel-vaggio.
savagely avv. selvaggiamente, barba-ramente.
savannah s. savana.
save prep. salvo, tranne, eccetto.
to **save** vt. e vi. 1. salvare, difendere 2. conservare, risparmiare.
saving s. liberazione, salvezza. ♦ **savings** s. pl. risparmi.
saviour s. salvatore, redentore.
to **savour** vi. aver sapore.
savoury agg. saporito, piccante.
saw s. sega || — -mill, segheria.
to **saw (sawed, sawn)** vt. e vi.

segare.
saw V. to see.
sawdust s. segatura.
sawn V. to saw.
sawyer s. segatore.
Saxon agg. e s. sassone.
saxophone s. sassofono.
say s. il dire, detto, parola.
to **say (said, said)** vt. e vi. 1. di-re, affermare 2. esprimere un'o-pinione || to — out, dire aperta-mente.
saying s. proverbio, massima: as the — goes, come dice il proverbio.
scabbard s. fodero.
scabby agg. coperto di croste.
scabies s. scabbia.
scaffold s. 1. impalcatura 2. patibo-lo, forca.
to **scaffold** vt. erigere impalcature.
scaffolding s. impalcatura.
scald s. scottatura.
to **scald** vt. 1. scottare 2. steriliz-zare con acqua bollente. ♦ to **scald** vi. scottarsi.
scale[1] s. piatto (di bilancia). ♦ **scales** s. pl. bilancia (sing.).
scale[2] s. scaglia.
scale[3] s. scala, misura, gradazione.
to **scale**[1] vt. e vi. pesare.
to **scale**[2] vt. squamare, scrostare. ♦ to **scale** vi. squamarsi, scrostarsi.
to **scale**[3] vt. 1. scalare 2. graduare || to — down, diminuire; to — up, aumentare.
scalene agg. e s. scaleno.
scallop s. 1. conchiglia 2. dentella-tura, festone, smerlo (di stoffa).
to **scallop** vt. 1. tagliare a festone 2. cuocere pesce in conchiglia.
scalp s. 1. cranio, cuoio capelluto 2. scalpo.
to **scalp** vt. 1. scalpare 2. criticare aspramente.
scalpel s. bisturi.
to **scan** vt. e vi. 1. scandire (versi) 2. esaminare, scrutare.
scandal s. 1. scandalo 2. maldicenza 3. (giur.) diffamazione.
to **scandalize** vt. scandalizzare.
scandalous agg. scandaloso.
Scandinavian agg. e s. scandinavo.
scanning s. 1. scansione (di versi) 2. osservazione || — -line, (tv), li-nea di scansione.
scansion s. scansione.
scantily avv. debolmente, scarsa-mente.
scantiness s. insufficienza, scarsezza.

scanty *agg.* **1.** scarso, insufficiente **2.** esiguo, angusto.

scapegoat *s.* capro espiatorio.

scapegrace *s.* **1.** scapestrato **2.** monello.

scapular *agg.* scapolare.

scar *s.* cicatrice, sfregio.

to scar *vt.* **1.** cicatrizzare **2.** sfregiare. ♦ **to scar** *vi.* cicatrizzarsi.

scarab *s.* scarabeo.

scarce *agg.* insufficiente, scarso.

scarcely *avv.* appena, a fatica, a malapena.

scare *s.* terrore, sgomento.

to scare *vt.* spaventare, sgomentare.

scarecrow *s.* **1.** spaventapasseri **2.** spauracchio.

scarf *s.* sciarpa, fascia.

to scarify *vt.* scarificare.

scarlet *agg.* scarlatto, porporino || — -*fever*, scarlattina.

scarp(e) *s.* scarpata.

to scatter *vt.* **1.** spargere **2.** mettere in fuga, disperdere. ♦ **to scatter** *vi.* spargersi, diffondersi.

scattered *agg.* sparso, disseminato.

scattering *s.* sparpagliamento, dispersione.

scenario *s.* sceneggiatura || — *writer*, sceneggiatore.

scene *s.* **1.** scena **2.** episodio **3.** scenario, quinta **4.** vista, panorama || — -*painter*, scenografo.

scenery *s.* **1.** scenario **2.** prospettiva, veduta.

scenographer *s.* scenografo.

scenographic *agg.* scenografico.

scenography *s.* scenografia.

scent *s.* **1.** odore, profumo **2.** traccia, pista (*anche fig.*).

to scent *vt.* **1.** fiutare, seguire la traccia **2.** profumare.

scented *agg.* profumato.

scentless *agg.* inodoro.

sceptical *agg.* scettico.

scepticism *s.* scetticismo.

sceptre *s.* scettro.

schedule *s.* **1.** catalogo, distinta, elenco **2.** (*amer.*) orario **3.** inventario.

to schedule *vt.* comporre una lista, un catalogo.

schematic(al) *agg.* schematico.

schematism *s.* schematismo.

scheme *s.* **1.** schema **2.** piano, progetto.

to scheme *vt.* e *vi.* **1.** progettare, fare un piano **2.** tramare.

schism *s.* scisma.

schismatic(al) *s.* scismatico.

schizophrenic *agg.* e *s.* schizofrenico.

scholar *s.* studioso, letterato.

scholarly *agg.* dotto, istruito.

scholarship *s.* **1.** dottrina, sapere **2.** borsa di studio.

scholastic *agg.* **1.** scolastico, pedante **2.** (*fil.*) scolastico.

scholastically *avv.* scolasticamente, secondo la scolastica.

scholasticism *s.* (*fil.*) scolastica.

school *s.* **1.** scuola, classe **2.** lezione, ora di lezione || — -*book*, libro di testo; — -*mate*, compagno di scuola; — -*report*, pagella; — -*term*, trimestre; — -*time*, periodo scolastico; *boarding*- —, collegio; *grammar*- —, ginnasio; *night*- —, serale.

to school *vt.* **1.** istruire **2.** controllare, disciplinare.

schoolboy *s.* scolaro.

schoolfellow *s.* compagno di scuola.

schoolmaster *s.* maestro, insegnante.

schoolmistress *s.* maestra, insegnante.

schoolroom *s.* aula scolastica.

schooner *s.* (*mar.*) goletta.

science *s.* scienza || — *fiction*, fantascienza; *man of* —, scienziato.

scientific *agg.* scientifico.

scientifically *avv.* scientificamente.

scientism *s.* scientismo.

scientist *s.* scienziato.

scimitar *s.* scimitarra.

scion *s.* **1.** germoglio **2.** rampollo, discendente.

scission *s.* scissione, divisione.

scissors *s. pl.* forbici, cesoie.

sclerosis *s.* (*pl.* -ses) sclerosi.

sclerotic *s.* sclerotico.

scoff *s.* derisione, scherno.

to scoff *vt.* e *vi.* deridere, schernire || *to* — *at so.*, farsi beffe di qu.

scold *s.* donna bisbetica.

to scold *vt.* sgridare, rimproverare. ♦ **to scold** *vi.* essere adirato.

scolding *s.* sgridata, rimprovero.

scoliosis *s.* scoliosi.

scooter *s.* **1.** monopattino **2.** motoretta.

scope *s.* **1.** portata, possibilità **2.** prospettiva, sfera, campo.

scorbutic *agg.* e *s.* scorbutico.

scorch *s.* bruciatura, scottatura.

to scorch *vt.* e *vi.* **1.** bruciacchiare **2.** inaridire (*di sole, gelo ecc.*).

scorching *agg.* **1.** bruciante, ardente **2.** (*fig.*) caustico, mordace.

score *s.* **1.** tacca, scanalatura **2.** linea, segno, linea di partenza, limite (*in corse, giuochi ecc.*) **3.** (*sport*) punteggio **4.** (*mus.*) spartito.

to score *vt. e vi.* **1.** intaccare, intagliare **2.** marcare, segnare **3.** (*sport*) segnare il punteggio **4.** (*mus.*) orchestrare ‖ *to — up*, mettere in conto.

scorer *s.* (*sport*) marcatore.

scorn *s.* **1.** disprezzo, disdegno **2.** scherno.

to scorn *vt.* disprezzare, disdegnare.

scornful *agg.* sprezzante, sdegnoso.

scorpion *s.* scorpione ‖ *— -fish*, scorfano.

Scot *s.* scozzese.

Scotch *agg.* scozzese.

Scotsman *s.* (*uomo*) scozzese.

Scottish *agg.* scozzese.

scoundrel *s.* furfante, farabutto.

scourge *s.* (*fig.*) flagello.

to scourge *vt.* sferzare, flagellare.

scout *s.* esploratore, ricognitore.

to scout *vi.* andare in esplorazione, in ricognizione. ♦ **to scout** *vt.* perlustrare.

scowl *s.* cipiglio, sguardo torvo.

to scowl *vt. e vi.* aggrottare le ciglia, guardare torvamente.

scramble *s.* **1.** arrampicata **2.** contesa, gara.

to scramble *vt.* **1.** arraffare **2.** mescolare alla rinfusa. ♦ **to scramble** *vi.* **1.** inerpicarsi **2.** gareggiare **3.** (*cuc.*) strapazzare (*le uova*).

scrap *s.* pezzetto, frammento ‖ *-heap*, mucchio di rifiuti. ♦ **scraps** *s. pl.* rimasugli, scarti.

scrape *s.* **1.** graffio, scalfittura **2.** raschio.

to scrape *vt. e vi.* **1.** raschiare, grattare **2.** levigare **3.** sfregare, strisciare ‖ *to — a living*, sbarcare il lunario.

scraper *s.* **1.** raschietto **2.** strimpellatore.

scraping *s.* raschiatura.

scratch *s.* **1.** graffiatura, graffio **2.** grattata **3.** colpo fortunato (*al giuoco*).

to scratch *vt. e vi.* **1.** graffiare **2.** (*fig.*) scalfire **3.** grattare.

scrawl *s.* scarabocchio, sgorbio.

to scrawl *vt. e vi.* **1.** scarabocchiare **2.** scribacchiare.

scrawler *s.* chi scarabocchia.

scrawly *agg.* scarabocchiato ‖ *— writing* (*fam.*), scritto a zampe di gallina.

scream *s.* grido acuto, strillo.

to scream *vt. e vi.* **1.** gridare, strillare **2.** fischiare (*di locomotiva*).

screamer *s.* strillone.

screaming *agg.* **1.** strillante, urlante **2.** sguaiato.

screech *s.* **1.** grido, strillo acuto **2.** stridore.

screen *s.* **1.** paravento **2.** (*cine; tv*) schermo **3.** (*mil.*) scorta.

to screen *vt. e vi.* **1.** riparare, schermare **2.** vagliare.

screenings *s. pl.* materiale vagliato (*sing.*).

screenplay *s.* (*cine*) sceneggiatura.

screenwriter *s.* sceneggiatore.

screw *s.* **1.** vite **2.** cavatappi, succhiello **3.** elica.

to screw *vt.* **1.** avvitare, stringere **2.** torcere. ♦ **to screw** *vi.* torcersi ‖ *to — out*, svitare.

screwdriver *s.* cacciavite.

screwy *agg.* **1.** brillo **2.** tirchio, spilorcio.

scribble *s.* sgorbio, scarabocchio (*anche fig.*).

to scribble *vt. e vi.* scarabocchiare.

scribe *s.* copista.

scriber *s.* punta a tracciare.

scrip¹ *s.* **1.** pezzo di carta **2.** frammento di uno scritto.

scrip² *s.* certificato provvisorio, cedola.

scripture *s.* la sacra Scrittura.

to scrounge *vt. e vi.* rubacchiare.

scrounger *s.* ladruncolo, scroccone.

scrub *s.* **1.** boscaglia **2.** povero diavolo (*fam.*).

to scrub *vt. e vi.* sfregare.

scrubby *agg.* esile, debole.

scruff *s.* nuca, collottola.

scruple *s.* scrupolo.

scrupolosity *s.* scrupolosità.

scrupulous *agg.* scrupoloso.

to scrutinize *vt.* scrutinare, esaminare.

scrutiny *s.* **1.** esame minuzioso **2.** scrutinio **3.** esame (*di una legge*).

scuffle *s.* zuffa, tafferuglio.

to scuffle *vi.* azzuffarsi.

scullery *s.* retrocucina ‖ *— -boy*, *-maid*, sguattero, sguattera.

sculptor *s.* scultore.

sculptress *s.* scultrice.

sculptural *agg.* scultorio, statuario.

sculpture *s.* scultura.

to sculpture *vt.* e *vi.* scolpire.

scum *s.* **1.** schiuma, spuma **2.** feccia (*anche fig.*).

to scum *vt.* e *vi.* **1.** schiumare, far schiuma **2.** produrre feccia.

scummer *s.* schiumarola.

scurf *s.* **1.** squama, forfora **2.** incrostazioni (*pl.*).

scurrility *s.* scurrilità, volgarità.

scurrilous *agg.* scurrile, triviale.

to scurry *vi.* precipitarsi.

scurvy *agg.* spregevole, meschino.

scuttle[1] *s.* recipiente per carbone.

scuttle[2] *s.* **1.** (*mar.*) portellino **2.** botola.

scuttle[3] *s.* fuga precipitosa.

to scuttle[1] *vt.* produrre falle (*in una nave*).

to scuttle[2] *vi.* correre via precipitosamente.

sea *s.* mare || — *-bear*, orso polare; — *-biscuit*, galletta; — *calf*, foca; — *fight*, battaglia navale; — *food*, frutti di mare; — *front*, lungomare; — *quake*, maremoto; — *storm*, mareggiata.

seacoast *s.* costa, spiaggia.

seafarer *s.* navigante, navigatore.

seafaring *s.* viaggi per mare.

seahorse *s.* ippocampo.

seal[1] *s.* foca.

seal[2] *s.* **1.** sigillo, timbro **2.** (*fig.*) suggello, vincolo.

to seal[1] *vi.* andare a caccia di foche.

to seal[2] *vt.* **1.** sigillare **2.** suggellare || *to* — *one's fate*, decidere la propria sorte.

sealing *s.* suggellamento || — *-wax*, ceralacca.

seam *s.* **1.** cucitura **2.** sutura.

to seam *vt.* **1.** unire con cucitura **2.** rigare, segnare.

seamen *s. pl.* equipaggio (*di una nave*).

seamanship *s.* arte della navigazione.

seamless *agg.* senza cucitura.

seamstress *s.* cucitrice.

seaplane *s.* idrovolante.

seaport *s.* porto marittimo.

search *s.* **1.** ricerca, indagine **2.** perquisizione, visita doganale || — *warrant*, mandato di perquisizione.

to search *vt.* e *vi.* cercare, perlustrare, perquisire || *to* — *out*, rinvenire, scovare.

searcher *s.* ricercatore.

searching *agg.* indagatore, inquisitorio. ♦ **searching** *s.* **1.** ricerca, esame **2.** sondaggio.

searchlight *s.* riflettore.

seashore *s.* spiaggia, lido.

seasickness *s.* mal di mare.

seaside *s.* spiaggia, riva.

season *s.* stagione, epoca || — *bill* (*teat.*), cartellone; — *ticket*, abbonamento stagionale.

to season *vt.* **1.** stagionare **2.** acclimatare **3.** condire. ♦ **to season** *vi.* **1.** stagionarsi **2.** invecchiarsi (*di vino*).

seasonable *agg.* **1.** di stagione **2.** opportuno.

seasonal *agg.* stagionale.

seasoned *agg.* **1.** stagionato **2.** condito.

seasoning *s.* **1.** stagionatura **2.** condimento.

seat *s.* **1.** sedile, posto **2.** seggio **3.** sede.

to seat *vt.* **1.** mettere a sedere **2.** insediare, collocare.

seaward *agg.* che va verso il mare.

seaweed *s.* alga marina.

sebaceous *agg.* sebaceo.

secant *agg.* e *s.* secante.

to secede *vi.* separarsi, ritirarsi.

seceder *s.* secessionista, separatista.

secession *s.* secessione, scissione.

secessionism *s.* secessionismo.

to seclude *vt.* **1.** appartare, isolare **2.** rinchiudere.

secluded *agg.* appartato, isolato, solitario.

seclusion *s.* **1.** isolamento **2.** solitudine.

seclusive *agg.* che serve ad isolare.

second[1] *s.* minuto secondo.

second[2] *agg.* secondo.

secondary *agg.* secondario.

secrecy *s.* **1.** segretezza **2.** riserbo.

secret *agg.* **1.** segreto **2.** nascosto, intimo. ♦ **secret** *s.* segreto.

secretariat(e) *s.* **1.** segretariato **2.** segreteria.

secretary *s.* **1.** segretario **2.** ministro (*preposto ad un dicastero*).

to secrete[1] *vt.* secernere.

to secrete[2] *vt.* occultare, nascondere.

secretion *s.* secrezione.

secretly *avv.* **1.** segretamente **2.** in modo reticente.

sect *s.* setta.

sectarian *s.* settario.

sectarianism *s.* spirito di setta.

sectary *s.* settario.

section s. 1. sezione, parte 2. paragrafo 3. regione, quartiere.
to **section** vt. sezionare.
sectional agg. 1. parziale, di classe 2. a sezioni.
sector s. settore.
secular agg. 1. secolare 2. laico 3. mondano, profano. ♦ **secular** s. laico.
secularism s. secolarismo.
secularist agg. e s. laico.
to **secularize** vt. laicizzare.
secure agg. 1. sicuro, certo 2. salvo.
to **secure** vt. 1. assicurare, salvaguardare 2. (giur.; comm.) garantire 3. mettere al sicuro.
security s. 1. sicurezza, protezione 2. certezza 3. garanzia, cauzione. ♦ **securities** s. pl. titoli, valori.
sedan s. — (-chair), portantina.
sedate agg. 1. posato, composto 2. grave, serio.
sedative agg. e s. sedativo.
sedentary agg. e s. sedentario.
sediment s. sedimento.
sedimentary agg. sedimentario.
sedimentation s. sedimentazione.
sedition s. sedizione.
seditious agg. sedizioso.
to **seduce** vt. sedurre, corrompere.
seduction s. seduzione.
sedulous agg. assiduo.
to **see (saw, seen)** vt. e vi. 1. vedere, scorgere 2. capire, rendersi conto di 3. esaminare, giudicare 4. fare in modo che || to — about, assumersi l'incarico di; to — off, accompagnare (alla partenza); to — over, ispezionare; to — through (fig.), indovinare, penetrare.
see s. (eccl.) sede, diocesi.
seed s. 1. seme, semenza 2. (fig.) principio, germe 3. stirpe.
seedy agg. pieno di semi.
to **seek (sought, sought)** vt. e vi. 1. cercare, andare alla ricerca di 2. ottenere 3. chiedere, ricorrere a || to — for sthg., ricercare qc.
seeker s. cercatore.
to **seem** vi. sembrare, apparire.
seeming agg. apparente, esteriore.
seemliness s. decenza, decoro.
seemly agg. decoroso, decente.
seen V. to see.
segment s. segmento, sezione.
segmentation s. segmentazione.
to **segregate** vt. segregare, separare. ♦ to **segregate** vi. separarsi, scindersi.

segregation s. segregazione.
seismograph s. sismografo.
seismologist s. sismologo.
seismology s. sismologia.
seizable agg. afferrabile.
to **seize** vt. e vi. 1. afferrare, prendere 2. capire, comprendere 3. (giur.) avere in possesso, sequestrare.
seizing s. 1. atto dell'afferrare 2. conquista, cattura.
seizure s. 1. (giur.) confisca, sequestro 2. conquista, cattura.
seldom avv. raramente.
select agg. 1. scelto, selezionato 2. schizzinoso.
to **select** vt. selezionare.
selection s. selezione, scelta.
selective agg. selettivo.
selectivity s. selettività.
selector s. selettore.
self s. (pl. selves) l'io, l'individuo. ♦ **self** agg. 1. della stessa materia 2. uniforme.
self-conceit s. presunzione.
self-control s. autocontrollo.
self-defence s. legittima difesa.
self-denial s. abnegazione.
self-determination s. autodeterminazione.
self-educated agg. autodidatta.
self-examination s. esame di coscienza.
self-government s. (pol.) autogoverno.
self-help s. (giur.) legittima difesa.
selfish agg. egoistico.
selfishness s. egoismo.
self-portrait s. autoritratto.
sell s. (fam.) delusione.
to **sell (sold, sold)** vt. e vi. 1. vendere 2. (fig.) vendere, tradire || to — off (comm.), liquidare.
seller s. 1. venditore 2. articolo che si vende.
selling s. vendita, smercio || — up, vendita fallimentare.
selves V. self.
semantic agg. semantico.
semantics s. semantica.
semester s. semestre.
semi prefisso semi, mezzo, metà.
semicircle s. semicerchio.
semicircular agg. semicircolare.
semicolon s. punto e virgola.
semifinal agg. e s. semifinale.
seminar s. seminario (d'università).
seminarist s. seminarista.
seminary s. seminario.
semination s. semina.

Semite agg. e s. semita.
Semitic agg. semitico.
Semitism s. semitismo.
semitone s. semitono.
semivowel s. semivocale.
senate s. senato.
senator s. senatore.
senatorial agg. senatoriale.
to send (sent, sent) vt. e vi. mandare, inviare, spedire || to — away, congedare; to — back, rinviare; to — for, mandare a chiamare; to — off, inviare (per lettera); to — out, emettere.
sender s. **1.** mandante, mittente **2.** (comm.) spedizioniere **3.** (radio, tv.) emittente.
sending s. **1.** invio **2.** (comm.) spedizione **3.** (radio, tv.) trasmissione.
senescence s. senescenza.
senile agg. senile.
senility s. senilità.
senior agg. **1.** più vecchio, più anziano **2.** più ragguardevole, che ha più anzianità. ◆ **senior** s. **1.** decano, anziano **2.** il superiore.
seniority s. anzianità (d'anni, di grado).
sensation s. **1.** senso, sensazione **2.** colpo, impressione.
sensational agg. **1.** che dipende dai sensi **2.** sensazionale.
sense s. **1.** senso, sensazione, impressione **2.** conoscenza **3.** significato || common —, buon senso. ◆ **senses** s. pl. facoltà mentale (sing.).
senseful agg. significativo.
senseless agg. **1.** inanimato **2.** insensato.
sensibility s. **1.** sensibilità, sensitività **2.** emotività.
sensible agg. **1.** sensato, giudizioso **2.** percettibile **3.** notevole, considerevole **4.** consapevole.
sensibly avv. **1.** assennatamente **2.** percettibilmente.
sensism s. sensismo.
sensist s. sensista.
sensitive agg. **1.** sensitivo, sensibile **2.** suscettibile, impressionabile.
sensitively avv. sensibilmente.
sensitiveness s. **1.** sensibilità **2.** suscettibilità.
to sensitize vt. sensibilizzare.
sensitizer s. (foto) sensibilizzatore.
sensorial agg. sensorio.
sensory agg. sensoriale.
sensual agg. sensuale.

sensualism s. sensualismo.
sensuality s. sensualità.
sensually avv. sensualmente, voluttuosamente.
sensuous agg. sensoriale, voluttuoso.
sent V. to send.
sentence s. **1.** giudizio, sentenza **2.** (gramm.) frase || to pass a —, pronunciare una sentenza.
to sentence vt. giudicare, pronunciare una sentenza contro.
sententious agg. sentenzioso.
sententiously avv. sentenziosamente.
sentient agg. senziente, sensibile.
sentiment s. **1.** sentimento **2.** opinione, parere.
sentimental agg. sentimentale, romantico.
sentimentalism s. sentimentalismo.
sentimentalist s. persona sentimentale.
sentimentality s. sentimentalità.
sentinel s. sentinella, guardia.
sentry s. sentinella, guardia, scolta || — box, garitta.
separate agg. separato, staccato.
to separate vt. separare. ◆ **to separate** vi. separarsi.
separately avv. separatamente.
separation s. separazione, divisione.
separatism s. separatismo.
September s. settembre.
septicaemia s. setticemia.
septuagenarian agg. e s. settuagenario.
septuagenary agg. settuagenario.
septum s. (pl. -ta) diaframma.
sepulchral agg. sepolcrale.
sepulchre s. sepolcro.
sequacious agg. pedissequo, servile.
sequel s. **1.** conseguenza **2.** seguito.
sequence s. **1.** successione, sequela **2.** sequenza.
to sequestrate vt. sequestrare, confiscare.
sequestration s. sequestro, confisca.
sequin s. lustrino.
seraphic(al) agg. serafico.
serenade s. serenata.
serene agg. **1.** sereno, senza nubi **2.** calmo, tranquillo.
serenely avv. serenamente.
serenity s. **1.** serenità, limpidezza **2.** tranquillità.
sergeant s. **1.** sergente **2.** brigadiere.
serial s. romanzo a puntate, pubblicazione periodica.

serially *avv.* **1.** in serie **2.** periodicamente.

sericulture *s.* sericoltura.

sericulturist *s.* sericoltore.

series *s.* serie, successione.

serigraphy *s.* serigrafia.

serious *agg.* **1.** serio, pensieroso **2.** grave, importante.

seriousness *s.* **1.** serietà **2.** gravità.

sermon *s.* sermone, predica.

serotherapy *s.* sieroterapia.

serous *agg.* sieroso.

serpent *s.* serpente.

serum *s.* siero.

servant *s.* servo, servitore.

to serve *vt. e vi.* **1.** servire, essere al servizio di **2.** servire, essere utile **3.** essere sotto le armi **4.** (*giur.*) notificare (*di atti*) || *to —out*, distribuire.

server *s.* **1.** chi serve **2.** chierico **3.** vassoio.

service *s.* **1.** servizio (*anche militare*) **2.** servigio, favore **3.** funzione religiosa **4.** (*giur.*) notifica. ♦ **Services** *s. pl.* forze armate.

serviceable *agg.* utile, pratico.

serviette *s.* tovagliolo.

servile *agg.* servile.

servilism *s.* servilismo.

servility *s.* servilità.

serving *s.* **1.** il servire **2.** servizio (*di tavola*).

servitude *s.* servitù, schiavitù.

session *s.* sessione, seduta. ♦ **sessions** *s. pl.* (*giur.*) udienze.

set¹ *agg.* **1.** fermo, fisso **2.** stabilito, prestabilito **3.** studiato, preparato. ♦ **set** *s.* **1.** il solidificarsi **2.** forma, serie **3.** gruppo **4.** direzione, corso **5.** (*poet.*) tramonto **6.** serie completa, insieme: *a — of teeth*, una dentiera; *the complete — of Shakespeare's works*, la raccolta completa delle opere di Shakespeare.

to set (set, set) *vt. e vi.* **1.** mettere, porre, collocare **2.** sistemare, mettere a punto **3.** tramontare (*anche fig.*) || *to — about*, accingersi; *to — back*, impedire; *to — in*, incominciare; *to — out*, esporre; *to — up*, fissare, installare; *to — aside* (*giur.*), annullare; *to — off*, compensare.

set-back *s.* contrattempo.

set-down *s.* rimprovero.

set-off *s.* **1.** contrasto **2.** compensazione.

setting *s.* **1.** messa in opera, montaggio **2.** ambiente **3.** scenario, messa in scena **4.** incastonatura.

to settle *vt. e vi.* **1.** fissare, decidere, determinare **2.** saldare, liquidare (*conti, questioni ecc.*) **3.** sistemare, sistemarsi **4.** stabilire **5.** calmare, calmarsi **6.** depositare, depositarsi (*di sedimenti ecc.*) || *to — down*, stabilirsi (*in un luogo*).

settled *agg.* fissato, stabilito.

settlement *s.* **1.** determinazione **2.** saldo, liquidazione **3.** sistemazione **4.** lo stabilirsi (*in un luogo*) **5.** colonia, distretto **6.** (*giur.*) transazione || *financial —*, regolamento di conti.

settler *s.* **1.** chi decide **2.** colonizzatore.

settling *s.* **1.** stabilizzazione **2.** saldo, pagamento.

set-to *s.* zuffa.

setup *s.* disposizione, organizzazione.

seven *agg.* sette.

sevenfold *agg.* settuplo. ♦ **sevenfold** *avv.* sette volte tanto.

seventeen *agg.* diciassette.

seventeenth *agg.* diciassettesimo.

seventh *agg.* settimo.

seventieth *agg.* settantesimo.

seventy *agg.* settanta.

to sever *vt.* staccare, dividere. ♦ **to sever** *vi.* staccarsi, dividersi.

several *agg.* **1.** parecchi, diversi (*pl.*) **2.** separato, distinto. ♦ **several** *pron.* alcuni, diversi (*pl.*) || *— of them*, alcuni di loro.

severally *avv.* separatamente, individualmente.

severe *agg.* **1.** severo, austero **2.** violento, forte **3.** rigido (*di clima*).

severely *avv.* **1.** severamente **2.** violentemente.

severity *s.* **1.** severità, durezza **2.** violenza.

to sew (sewed, sewn) *vt. e vi.* cucire.

sewage *s.* acque di scolatura.

sewer¹ *s.* chi cuce, cucitrice.

sewer² *s.* **1.** canale artificiale di drenaggio **2.** fogna.

sewing *s.* **1.** il cucire **2.** lavoro di cucito.

sewn V. *to sew.*

sex *s.* sesso.

sexagenarian *agg. e s.* sessagenario.

sextet(te) *s.* sestetto.

sexton *s.* sagrestano.

sextuple *agg. e s.* sestuplo.

sexual *agg.* sessuale.

shabbiness s. 1. l'essere male in arnese 2. meschinità.

shabby agg. 1. male in arnese, cencioso 2. meschino, gretto.

shackles s. pl. 1. manette, ceppi 2. (fig.) impedimenti.

shade s. 1. ombra (anche fig.) 2. sfumatura (di colore, significato ecc.) 3. spirito, ombra 4. schermo, riparo || eye — —, visiera.

to shade vt. e vi. 1. ombreggiare, riparare (da luce, calore) 2. velare, oscurare (anche fig.).

shadiness s. ombrosità.

shading s. 1. l'ombreggiare 2. ombreggiatura, sfumatura.

shadow s. ombra (anche fig.). ♦ **shadows** s. pl. oscurità.

to shadow vt. pedinare, seguire come un'ombra.

shadowy agg. 1. ombroso, ombreggiato 2. indistinto, vago.

shady agg. ombreggiato, all'ombra.

shaft[1] s. 1. lancia, giavellotto 2. fulmine 3. gambo, stelo 4. asta, bastone 5. (mecc.) albero.

shaft[2] s. sfiatatoio, condotto.

shaggy agg. 1. ispido, irsuto 2. peloso (di tessuto) 3. incolto.

Shah s. scià.

shake s. 1. scossa, scuotimento 2. tremore, tremito 3. frullato.

to shake (shook, shaken) vt. e vi. 1. scuotere, agitare (liquidi) 2. tremare, far tremare 3. turbare 4. indebolire.

shakily avv. instabilmente.

shaking agg. tremante, vacillante. ♦ **shaking** s. scossa, scuotimento.

shaky agg. 1. instabile, tremolante 2. malsicuro.

shall v. dif. 1. (aus. per le prime pers. del fut. predicente) I — go to England next summer, andrò in Inghilterra l'estate prossima; we — work next week, lavoreremo la prossima settimana 2. (aus. per le seconde e terze pers. del fut. volitivo) you — go to bed!, andrai a letto! 3. dovere: you — wait for me, devi aspettarmi.

shallow agg. 1. poco profondo, basso 2. (fig.) superficiale.

sham s. 1. finta, inganno 2. ipocrita.

shaman s. sciamano.

shambles s. pl. 1. mattatoio (sing.) 2. carneficina (sing.).

shame s. 1. vergogna, pudore 2. disonore.

to shame vt. 1. svergognare, far arrossire 2. disonorare.

shamefaced agg. 1. vergognoso 2. timido.

shameful agg. vergognoso, disonorevole.

shameless agg. svergognato, sfacciato.

shamelessly avv. sfacciatamente.

shank s. 1. gamba, stinco 2. gambo, stelo 3. fusto (di colonna) || — -bone, tibia.

shape s. forma, figura.

to shape vt. e vi. creare, dar forma a.

shapeless agg. informe.

shapely agg. ben fatto.

share s. 1. parte, porzione 2. (comm.) azione, titolo.

to share vt. dividere, spartire. ♦ **to share** vi. partecipare, condividere.

shareholder s. azionista.

share-out s. distribuzione.

shark s. 1. squalo, pescecane 2. (fig.) profittatore.

sharp agg. 1. tagliente, affilato 2. aguzzo 3. scosceso, ripido 4. netto, chiaro 5. intelligente, acuto.

sharp avv. puntualmente, in punto.

to sharpen vt. 1. affilare, aguzzare 2. (fig.) rendere più acuto.

sharper s. imbroglione.

sharply avv. acutamente.

sharpness s. 1. filo, affilatura 2. acutezza 3. vivacità, intelligenza.

sharp-sighted agg. dalla vista acuta.

to shatter vt. frantumare. ♦ **to shatter** vi. frantumarsi.

shattering s. disintegrazione.

shave[1] s. il radersi, rasatura.

shave[2] s. pialla.

to shave[1] vt. radere. ♦ **to shave** vi. radersi.

to shave[2] vt. piallare.

shaven agg. 1. rasato 2. (eccl.) tonsurato.

shaving s. 1. il radersi 2. truciolo.

shawl s. scialle.

she pron. pers. f. ella, lei, colei. ♦ **she** attr. indicante il sesso degli animali: a — -bear, un'orsa.

sheaf s. (pl. sheaves) 1. fascio, covone 2. (geom.) fascio (di rette ecc.).

to shear (sheared, shorn) vt. 1. cesoiare, tranciare 2. tosare.

shearing s. recisione, taglio.

shears s. pl. cesoie, forbici.

sheath s. guaina, fodero.

to **sheathe** vt. **1.** mettere nel fodero **2.** rivestire di.

sheaves V. sheaf.

to **shed (shed, shed)** vt. **1.** versare, spandere **2.** lasciar cadere.

shed s. tettoia, capannone.

shedding s. **1.** spargimento **2.** perdita, caduta (di foglie ecc.).

sheen s. splendore, lucentezza.

sheep s. (anche pl.) **1.** pecora, ovino **2.** (fig.) persona debole, timorosa.

sheepish agg. timido, impacciato.

sheepskin s. **1.** pelle di pecora **2.** cartapecora.

sheer[1] agg. **1.** puro, semplice, mero **2.** liscio, non diluito (di bevande).

sheer[2] s. virata, cambiamento di rotta.

sheet s. **1.** lenzuolo **2.** foglio **3.** lamina, lamiera.

sheik(h) s. sceicco.

shelf s. (pl. shelves) mensola, scaffale.

shell s. **1.** conchiglia, guscio **2.** involucro, carcassa **3.** bossolo (di cartuccia) **4.** (fig.) apparenza.

to **shell** vt. e vi. sgusciare, sgranare.

shelter s. **1.** riparo, rifugio **2.** pensilina.

to **shelter** vt. riparare. ♦ to **shelter** vi. ripararsi.

to **shelve** vt. **1.** provvedere di scaffali **2.** mettere negli scaffali.

shelves V. shelf.

shelving s. scaffalatura.

shepherd s. pastore, pecoraio.

sherbet s. sorbetto.

shield s. **1.** scudo **2.** (fig.) protezione.

to **shield** vt. proteggere, difendere.

shift s. **1.** cambiamento, sostituzione **2.** risorsa, espediente **3.** turno (di lavoro).

to **shift** vt. **1.** spostare **2.** cambiare. ♦ to **shift** vi. **1.** spostarsi **2.** arrangiarsi.

shilling s. scellino.

to **shilly-shally** vi. tentennare.

to **shimmer** vi. luccicare, mandare bagliori.

to **shine (shone, shone)** vt. e vi. **1.** splendere, brillare (anche fig.) **2.** essere brillante.

shine s. **1.** splendore, luminosità **2.** luce del sole.

Shintoist s. scintoista.

shiny agg. splendente, rilucente.

ship s. nave, bastimento || convoy- —, nave scorta; flag- —, nave ammiraglia; landing- —, nave da sbarco.

to **ship** vt. **1.** imbarcare **2.** (comm.) spedire. ♦ to **ship** vi. imbarcarsi.

shipboard s. bordo.

shipboy s. mozzo.

shipbuilder s. costruttore navale.

shipmate s. compagno di bordo.

shipment s. imbarco, spedizione di merci.

shipping s. **1.** forze navali (pl.) **2.** imbarco, spedizione.

shipwreck s. naufragio.

to **shipwreck** vi. naufragare.

shipyard s. cantiere navale.

shirker s. scansafatiche.

shirt s. camicia (da uomo).

shiver[1] s. scheggia.

shiver[2] s. brivido, fremito.

to **shiver**[1] vt. frantumare. ♦ to **shiver** vi. frantumarsi.

to **shiver**[2] vt. e vi. rabbrividire, tremare.

shivering s. V. shiver.

shivery agg. **1.** fragile **2.** tremante.

shoal[1] s. secca, bassofondo.

shoal[2] s. banco (di pesci).

shock s. **1.** urto, collisione **2.** forte impressione, violenta emozione.

to **shock** vt. **1.** colpire, disgustare **2.** provocare un collasso. ♦ to **shock** vi. **1.** scandalizzarsi **2.** scontrarsi.

shocking agg. **1.** che colpisce **2.** disgustoso.

shoe s. scarpa, calzatura || horse- —, ferro di cavallo.

shoeblack s. lustrascarpe.

shoemaker s. calzolaio.

shoe-string s. laccio (da scarpe).

shone V. to shine.

shook V. to shake.

shoot s. **1.** spedizione di caccia **2.** virgulto **3.** puntura, fitta.

to **shoot (shot, shot)** vt. e vi. **1.** lanciare **2.** sparare, uccidere sparando **3.** cacciare **4.** fare un'istantanea.

shooter s. cacciatore.

shooting s. **1.** tiro, sparo **2.** caccia **3.** il fotografare, il girare un film.

shop s. **1.** bottega, negozio **2.** officina, laboratorio || — -assistant, commesso; — -book, libro dei conti; — -lifter, taccheggiatore; — -window, vetrina.

shopkeeper s. negoziante.
shopman s. commesso di negozio.
shopping s. compere, acquisti (pl.).
shore s. spiaggia, lido.
shorn V. to shear.
short agg. 1. corto, breve 2. basso, piccolo (di statura) 3. conciso 4. brusco, rude. ♦ **short** s. 1. compendio 2. (cine) cortometraggio.
short avv. 1. bruscamente, improvvisamente 2. (comm.) allo scoperto.
shortage s. mancanza, carenza.
short-circuit s. corto circuito.
short-cut s. scorciatoia.
short-dated agg. (comm.) a breve scadenza.
to **shorten** vt. accorciare, abbreviare.
shortening s. accorciamento, abbreviazione.
shorthand s. stenografia.
shortly avv. 1. fra breve 2. brevemente.
shortness s. brevità.
short-sighted agg. miope.
shot[1] V. to shoot.
shot[2] s. 1. sparo, colpo 2. proiettile 3. ripresa cinematografica.
shotgun s. fucile da caccia.
should s. dif. 1. (aus. per le prime pers. del condiz.) I — be very happy, sarei felicissimo 2. dovere: it — be so, dovrebbe essere così.
shoulder s. spalla.
to **shoulder** vt. e vi. 1. spingere con le spalle 2. portare sulle spalle.
shout s. grido, chiasso.
to **shout** vt. e vi. gridare, urlare.
shove s. spinta, urto.
to **shove** vt. spingere. ♦ to **shove** vi. spingersi.
shovel s. pala.
to **shovel** vt. spalare.
shoveller s. spalatore.
show s. 1. mostra, esibizione 2. apparenza 3. pompa, ostentazione || — case, bacheca; — down, chiarificazione; — -off, esibizionismo.
to **show (showed, shown)** vt. e vi. 1. mostrare, far vedere 2. rappresentare, indicare 3. dimostrare, provare 4. apparire, farsi vedere || to — down, mettere le carte in tavola; to — off, darsi delle arie.
shower s. acquazzone, rovescio.
showman s. presentatore.
shown V. to show.

showy agg. fastoso, appariscente.
shrank V. to shrink.
shred s. brandello, frammento.
shrew s. bisbetica.
shrewd agg. sagace, accorto.
shrewdly avv. sagacemente.
shrewdness s. sagacia, accortezza.
shrewish agg. brontolone.
shriek s. grido, strillo, suono lacerante.
to **shriek** vt. e vi. gridare, stridere.
shrill agg. stridulo, acuto.
to **shrill** vt. e vi. strillare, stridere.
shrimp s. gamberetto.
shrine s. reliquiario.
shrink s. restringimento.
to **shrink (shrank, shrunk)** vt. e vi. 1. restringere, restringersi, contrarre 2. indietreggiare.
shrinkable agg. restringibile.
shrinkage s. 1. diminuzione, restringimento 2. (comm.) deprezzamento.
shrinking s. contrazione, ritiro.
shroud s. sudario.
shrub s. arbusto, cespuglio.
shrubbery s. boscaglia d'arbusti.
shrug s. spallucciata.
to **shrug** vi. alzare le spalle.
shrunk V. to shrink.
shudder s. brivido.
to **shudder** vi. rabbrividire.
shuffle s. 1. passo strascicato 2. scompiglio 3. il mescolare (le carte).
to **shuffle** vt. e vi. 1. muoversi a fatica 2. mescolare, scompigliare.
to **shun** vt. sfuggire, scansare.
shunt s. 1. (elett.) derivazione 2. (ferr.) scambio.
to **shunt** vt. e vi. 1. (elett.) inserire in derivazione 2. (ferr.) smistare, smistarsi.
shut agg. ben chiuso.
to **shut (shut, shut)** vt. e vi. chiudere, serrare || shut up!, taci!
shutter s. imposta, persiana.
shuttle s. spola, navetta.
shy agg. riservato, timido.
to **shy** vt. spaventare. ♦ to **shy** vi. scartare (di cavallo).
shyly avv. timidamente.
shyness s. timidezza, scontrosità.
Siberian agg. e s. siberiano.
sibilant agg. e s. sibilante.
Sibylline agg. sibillino.
Sicilian agg. e s. siciliano.
sick agg. 1. ammalato 2. nauseato || to fall —, ammalarsi.

to **sicken** *vt.* e *vi.* **1.** far ammalare, ammalarsi **2.** sfiorire **3.** sentir nausea.

sickening *agg.* nauseabondo, rivoltante.

sickle *s.* falce.

sickly *agg.* **1.** malaticcio **2.** pallido, debole **3.** nauseante.

sickness *s.* malattia.

side *s.* **1.** lato, fianco **2.** parte, partito, fazione **3.** discendenza || — -door, porta laterale; — -face, profilo; — -look, occhiata in tralice; — -note, nota marginale; — -post, stipite.

sideboard *s.* credenza.

sidecar *s.* motocarrozzetta.

sidelong *agg.* laterale, obliquo.

sidereal *agg.* sidereo.

sideways *avv.* lateralmente, obliquamente.

to **sidle** *vi.* camminare di fianco, andare a sghembo || *to — up to so.*, avvicinarsi furtivamente a qu.

siege *s.* assedio.

sieve *s.* setaccio, crivello.

to **sieve** *vt.* setacciare, crivellare.

to **sift** *vt.* e *vi.* setacciare **2.** filtrare (*di luce, polvere ecc.*).

sigh *s.* sospiro.

to **sigh** *vt.* e *vi.* **1.** sospirare **2.** sibilare.

sight *s.* **1.** vista, visione **2.** veduta, panorama **3.** colpo d'occhio **4.** mirino.

to **sight** *vt.* e *vi.* **1.** avvistare **2.** prendere la mira.

sighted *agg.* **1.** fornito di vista || *long- —*, presbite; *short- —*, miope.

sightless *agg.* senza vista.

sign *s.* **1.** segno, cenno **2.** indicazione, traccia || *traffic —*, segnale stradale.

to **sign** *vt.* e *vi.* firmare, segnare, sottoscrivere.

signal *s.* segnale, segno.

to **signal** *vt.* segnalare. ♦ to **signal** *vi.* far segnali.

signalman *s.* segnalatore.

signatory *s.* firmatario.

signature *s.* **1.** firma, sigla **2.** (*tip.*) segnatura.

signboard *s.* insegna (*di albergo, negozio ecc.*).

significant *agg.* espressivo, significativo.

to **signify** *vt.* e *vi.* **1.** significare, voler dire **2.** denotare, indicare, presagire **3.** importare.

silence *s.* silenzio.

to **silence** *vt.* far tacere, imporre il silenzio.

silencer *s.* silenziatore.

silent *agg.* **1.** silenzioso, taciturno **2.** muto.

silently *avv.* silenziosamente.

silhouette *s.* profilo, contorno.

silica *s.* silice.

silicate *s.* silicato.

silicon *s.* silicio.

silicosis *s.* silicosi.

silk *s.* seta.

silken *agg.* serico, di seta.

silkworm *s.* baco da seta || — *breeding*, sericoltura.

silky *agg.* di seta, serico.

sill *s.* basamento, soglia.

silliness *s.* stupidità, sciocchezza.

silly *agg.* sciocco, stupido.

to **silo** *vt.* conservare, mettere in silo.

silt *s.* melma.

silver *s.* argento, argenteria || — -plate, argenteria; — -plating, argentatura || *quick —*, mercurio.

to **silver** *vt.* inargentare. ♦ to **silver** *vi.* inargentarsi.

silverware *s.* oggetti d'argento.

silvery *agg.* argenteo.

similar *agg.* simile, analogo.

similarity *s.* somiglianza, similitudine.

similitude *s.* **1.** similitudine **2.** somiglianza.

simoniac *agg.* e *s.* simoniaco.

simony *s.* simonia.

to **simper** *vi.* parlare in modo affettato.

simple *agg.* **1.** semplice, elementare **2.** sincero **3.** autentico.

simpleton *s.* sempliciotto.

simplicity *s.* semplicità, candore.

simplification *s.* semplificazione.

to **simplify** *vt.* semplificare.

simply *avv.* semplicemente.

simulation *s.* simulazione.

simulator *s.* simulatore.

simultaneity *s.* simultaneità.

simultaneous *agg.* simultaneo.

sin *s.* **1.** peccato, colpa **2.** offesa.

to **sin** *vi.* peccare.

since *avv.* da allora, da allora in poi || *long —*, molto tempo fa. ♦ **since** *cong.* **1.** da quando **2.** poiché. ♦ **since** *prep.* da, fin da.

sincere *agg.* sincero, schietto.

sincerely *avv.* sinceramente || *yours —*, cordialmente vostro (*nelle lettere*).

sincerity s. sincerità.
sinew s. **1.** tendine, nervo **2.** (fig.) vigore, nerbo.
sinful agg. peccaminoso, colpevole.
sinfully avv. peccaminosamente.
to **sing (sang, sung)** vt. e vi. cantare.
to **singe** vt. bruciacchiare, strinare (anche fig.). ♦ to **singe** vi. bruciarsi.
singer s. cantante.
singing s. **1.** canto **2.** fischio (del vento ecc.).
single agg. **1.** solo, unico **2.** individuale, particolare **3.** celibe || every — day, tutti i giorni.
to **single** vt. distinguere, scegliere: to — out sthg., scegliere qc.
singleness s. **1.** unicità **2.** sincerità.
singly avv. **1.** separatamente, ad uno ad uno **2.** da solo, senza aiuto.
singsong s. cantilena, canto monotono.
singular agg. **1.** singolare, solo **2.** eccezionale **3.** bizzarro, strano.
singularity s. **1.** singolarità, rarità **2.** particolarità **3.** stranezza.
singularly avv. singolarmente.
sinister agg. sinistro, funesto, di cattivo augurio.
sink s. **1.** lavandino, acquaio **2.** scolo.
to **sink (sank, sunk)** vi. **1.** affondare, andare a fondo **2.** sprofondare **3.** abbassare, abbassarsi, calare **4.** cadere, cedere (di terreno, muro ecc.).
sinner s. peccatore.
sinuous agg. sinuoso.
sinus s. **1.** cavità **2.** seno.
sip s. sorso.
to **sip** vt. e vi. sorseggiare.
siphon s. sifone.
sir s. **1.** (vocativo) signore **2.** « sir » (titolo).
siren s. sirena.
siroc s. scirocco.
sirup s. sciroppo.
sister s. **1.** sorella **2.** suora || — -in- -law, cognata.
sisterhood s. congregazione religiosa di suore.
sisterly avv. da sorella, amorevolmente.
to **sit (sat, sat)** vt. e vi. **1.** sedere, stare seduto, far sedere **2.** essere in seduta **3.** appollaiarsi, posare **4.** covare || to — out, rimanere fino alla fine; to — up, rimanere al-

zato.
site s. area fabbricabile.
sitting s. **1.** posa, seduta **2.** adunanza || — -room, stanza di soggiorno. ♦ **sittings** s. pl. sessioni (di una Corte).
situated agg. **1.** situato, collocato **2.** in una certa situazione (di persona).
situation s. **1.** situazione, posizione **2.** stato, circostanza **3.** posto, impiego: to apply for a —, fare una domanda di impiego.
six agg. sei.
sixfold agg. sestuplo. ♦ **sixfold** avv. sei volte tanto.
sixpence s. moneta da sei « pence », mezzo scellino.
sixpenny agg. del valore di sei « pence ».
sixteen agg. sedici.
sixteenth agg. sedicesimo.
sixth agg. sesto.
sixtieth agg. sessantesimo.
sixty agg. sessanta.
size s. **1.** grandezza, misura, dimensione **2.** formato, taglia **3.** colla.
to **size** vt. allineare || to — up, valutare.
sizzle s. sfrigolio.
skate s. pattino || roller —, pattino a rotelle.
to **skate** vi. pattinare.
skating s. pattinaggio.
skein s. matassa.
skeleton s. scheletro (anche fig.).
to **skeletonize** vt. scheletrire. ♦ to **skeletonize** vi. scheletrirsi (anche fig.).
skeptic agg. e s. scettico.
skeptical agg. scettico.
skepticism s. scetticismo.
sketch s. **1.** schizzo, abbozzo **2.** scenetta.
to **sketch** vt. abbozzare, schizzare.
skewness s. asimmetria.
ski s. sci || — -lift, sciovia.
to **ski** vi. sciare.
skier s. sciatore.
skiff s. (mar.) schifo.
skilful agg. abile, esperto.
skilfully avv. abilmente.
skilfulness s. abilità.
skill s. abilità, destrezza.
skilled agg. esperto, abile, versato || — worker, operaio specializzato.
to **skim** vt. e vi. **1.** schiumare, scremare **2.** rasentare, sfiorare.
skimmer s. schiumarola.

skimming s. scrematura.

skin s. pelle, cute.

to **skin** vt. e vi. scuoiare || to — over, rimarginarsi (di ferite).

skinny agg. magro, scarno.

to **skip** vt. e vi. fare un balzo, saltare alla corda || to — a few pages, saltare qualche pagina.

skirmish s. scaramuccia.

skirt s. 1. sottana, gonna 2. orlo, lembo.

to **skirt** vt. e vi. orlare, costeggiare.

skittish agg. capriccioso, frivolo.

skittles s. pl. birilli.

skull s. cranio, teschio || — -cap, papalina.

sky s. cielo, firmamento.

skylark s. allodola.

skylight s. lucernario.

skyline s. linea, profilo (di montagne ecc.).

skyman s. paracadutista.

skyscraper s. grattacielo.

skyward agg. e avv. verso il cielo.

slab s. 1. lastra, piastra 2. pezzo, fetta.

slack agg. 1. molle, allentato 2. debole, fiacco 3. (comm.) calmo, stagnante, debole. ♦ **slack** s. (comm.) stagione morta.

to **slacken** vt. 1. allentare, mollare 2. diminuire. ♦ to **slacken** vi. 1. allentarsi 2. smorzarsi.

slacker s. fannullone.

slain V. to slay.

slam s. sbatacchiamento.

to **slam** vt. sbattere, chiudere violentemente. ♦ to **slam** vi. chiudersi violentemente.

slander s. 1. calunnia 2. (giur.) diffamazione.

to **slander** vt. 1. calunniare 2. (giur.) diffamare.

slanderer s. 1. calunniatore 2. (giur.) diffamatore.

slanderous agg. calunnioso, maldicente.

slang s. gergo.

slant s. pendenza, inclinazione.

to **slant** vt. e vi. essere in pendenza, inclinare.

slanting agg. inclinato, obliquo, sghembo.

slap s. schiaffo, ceffone.

to **slap** vt. 1. schiaffeggiare 2. sbattere.

slash s. 1. taglio, sfregio 2. frustata.

to **slash** vt. tagliare, fendere.

slate s. ardesia, tegola d'ardesia.

slaughter s. 1. macello 2. carneficina, massacro.

to **slaughter** vt. 1. macellare 2. massacrare.

slaughterer s. 1. macellatore 2. massacratore.

slaughterhouse s. mattatoio.

Slav agg. e s. slavo.

slave s. schiavo.

slaver[1] s. schiavista.

slaver[2] s. saliva, bava.

slavery s. schiavitù.

to **slay** (**slew, slain**) vt. ammazzare.

sleek agg. lucido, levigato.

sleep s. sonno, dormita || — walker, sonnambulo.

to **sleep** (**slept, slept**) vt. e vi. 1. dormire, riposare 2. passare la notte.

sleeper s. 1. dormiente, dormiglione 2. (ferr.) traversina 3. (ferr.) vettura letto.

sleepily avv. con aria assonnata.

sleeping agg. dormiente, addormentato || — bag, sacco a pelo; — -berth, cuccetta; — -car, vagone letto; — -draught, sonnifero.

sleepless agg. insonne.

sleeplessness s. insonnia.

sleepy agg. assonnato, sonnolento.

sleet s. nevischio.

sleeve s. manica.

sleeved agg. con maniche.

sleigh s. slitta.

slender agg. 1. magro, snello 2. debole, fiacco.

slenderness s. 1. snellezza, magrezza 2. debolezza.

slept V. to sleep.

slew V. to slay.

slice s. pezzo, fetta, porzione.

to **slice** vt. affettare.

slicer s. affettatrice.

slid V. to slide.

slide s. 1. scivolata 2. pendenza 3. scivolo 4. (mecc.) carrello, pattino.

to **slide** (**slid, slid**) vt. e vi. 1. scivolare, far scivolare, scorrere, far scorrere 2. sfuggire.

sliding agg. scorrevole.

slight agg. 1. esile, minuto, magro 2. leggero, scarso.

slim agg. 1. magro, sottile 2. debole.

slime s. melma, limo.

slimy agg. fangoso, viscoso.

sling[1] s. fionda.

sling[2] *s.* cinghia.

to sling[1] **(slung, slung)** *vt.* scagliare con la fionda.

to sling[2] *vt.* sospendere, appendere.

to slink (slunk, slunk) *vi.* sgattaiolare.

slip[1] *s.* **1.** innesto **2.** (*tip.*) bozza in colonna.

slip[2] *s.* **1.** scalo, molo **2.** guinzaglio **3.** sottoveste **4.** scivolone **5.** papera, lapsus.

to slip *vt. e vi.* **1.** scivolare, inciampare **2.** entrare, uscire furtivamente **3.** sgusciare, liberarsi || *to — away*, scorrere (*di tempo*).

slipper *s.* pantofola.

slippery *agg.* sdrucciolevole, viscido (*anche fig.*).

slipshod *agg.* **1.** scalcagnato **2.** trasandato.

slit *s.* fessura, fenditura.

to slit (slit, slit) *vt.* fendere.

slope *s.* pendenza, pendio.

to slope *vi.* essere in pendenza, inclinarsi.

sloping *agg.* inclinato, obliquo.

slot *s.* fessura, scanalatura || *— -machine,* distributore automatico a gettoni.

sloth *s.* pigrizia, indolenza.

slothful *agg.* pigro, indolente.

slouch *s.* andatura dinoccolata.

slouching *agg.* dinoccolato, goffo.

slovenliness *s.* sciatteria, sporcizia.

slovenly *agg.* sciatto, sudicio.

slow *agg.* **1.** lento **2.** tardo, ottuso || *— -down,* rallentamento; *— -match,* miccia.

to slow *vt. e vi.* to — *up* o *down,* rallentare.

slowly *avv.* lentamente.

slowness *s.* lentezza, pigrizia.

sluggish *agg.* pigro, tardo, indolente.

sluggishness *s.* pigrizia, indolenza.

slum *s.* vicolo, tugurio. ♦ **slums** *s. pl.* quartieri poveri (*di una città*).

slumber *s.* dormiveglia, assopimento.

to slumber *vt. e vi.* dormire, dormicchiare.

slung V. *to sling.*

slunk V. *to slink.*

slush *s.* poltiglia, fango.

sly *agg.* **1.** astuto, malizioso **2.** infido.

smack *s.* **1.** sapore, aroma **2.** schiocco **3.** schiaffo.

to smack *vt. e vi.* **1.** schioccare **2.** schioccare baci **3.** schiaffeggiare.

small *agg.* **1.** piccolo, minuto **2.** leggero, debole **3.** poco, scarso **4.** di poca importanza.

small-arms *s. pl.* armi portatili.

smallness *s.* piccolezza.

smallpox *s.* vaiolo.

smart *agg.* **1.** acuto, pungente **2.** vivace, sveglio **3.** elegante.

to smarten *vt. e vi.* abbellire || *to — up,* rianimarsi, farsi bello.

smartness *s.* **1.** acutezza, vivacità, brio **2.** eleganza.

smash *s.* **1.** urto, scontro **2.** rovina.

to smash *vt.* **1.** frantumare, fracassare **2.** sconfiggere, annientare. ♦ **to smash** *vi.* **1.** frantumarsi **2.** sfasciarsi **3.** crollare.

smasher *s.* **1.** chi frantuma **2.** (*fam.*) caso eccezionale.

smear *s.* macchia, imbrattatura.

to smear *vt.* macchiare, imbrattare.

smell *s.* **1.** odorato, olfatto **2.** odore.

to smell (smelt, smelt) *vt. e vi.* **1.** fiutare, sentire l'odore **2.** avere odore || *to — of,* sapere di; *to — out,* scovare.

smile *s.* sorriso.

to smile *vt. e vi.* sorridere || *fortune smil'ed on you,* la fortuna ti fu favorevole.

smiling *agg.* sorridente, sereno.

smirch *s.* onta, macchia.

to smite (smote, smitten) *vt. e vi.* **1.** colpire, percuotere **2.** sconfiggere, sgominare || *to — down,* abbattere.

smith *s.* fabbro.

smitten V. *to smite.*

smoke *s.* **1.** fumo **2.** fumata || *— -stack,* fumaiolo.

to smoke *vt. e vi.* **1.** fumare **2.** affumicare.

smoker *s.* fumatore, fumatrice.

smoking *s.* il fumare. ♦ **smoking** *agg.* fumante.

smoky *agg.* **1.** fumoso **2.** affumicato, annerito dal fumo **3.** che sa di fumo.

smooth *agg.* **1.** liscio, levigato **2.** omogeneo **3.** armonioso (*di suono*) **4.** mellifluo **5.** calmo, tranquillo (*di mare*).

to smooth *vt.* **1.** lisciare, spianare **2.** appianare.

smoothing *s.* lisciatura, spianatura.

smoothly *avv.* **1.** pianamente **2.** armonicamente **3.** in modo mellifluo.

smoothness *s.* **1.** levigatezza **2.** armonia (*di verso, suono*) **3.** affabilità.

smote V. *to smite.*

to **smother** *vt.* e *vi.* **1.** soffocare, opprimere **2.** ricoprire.

to **smoulder** *vi.* ardere sotto la cenere.

to **smuggle** *vt.* e *vi.* contrabbandare.

smuggler *s.* contrabbandiere.

smuggling *s.* contrabbando.

smut *s.* fuliggine.

snack *s.* **1.** boccone, porzione **2.** spuntino || — -*bar,* tavola calda.

snail *s.* chiocciola, lumaca.

snake *s.* serpente.

snakily *avv.* **1.** tortuosamente **2.** (*fig.*) slealmente.

snaky *agg.* serpentino.

snap *s.* **1.** colpo secco, morso, schiocco **2.** scatto **3.** fermaglio, fibbia.

to **snap** *vt.* e *vi.* **1.** schioccare, far schioccare **2.** aprirsi di colpo, spezzare con un colpo secco **3.** (*foto*) scattare un'istantanea.

snapshot *s.* (*foto*) istantanea.

snare *s.* **1.** trappola, rete **2.** insidia, tentazione.

to **snare** *vt.* prendere in trappola, al laccio (*anche fig.*).

snarl *s.* ringhio.

to **snarl** *vi.* ringhiare.

snatch *s.* **1.** strappo, strattone **2.** brano, frammento.

to **snatch** *vt.* e *vi.* afferrare, ghermire || *to* — *off,* strappare.

sneak *s.* persona malfida.

sneer *s.* sogghigno beffardo.

to **sneer** *vt.* e *vi.* sorridere beffardamente, schernire.

sneeze *s.* starnuto.

to **sneeze** *vi.* starnutire.

to **sniff** *vt.* e *vi.* fiutare || *to* — *at sthg.* annusare qc.

snip *s.* **1.** ritaglio, scampolo **2.** forbiciata.

to **snip** *vt.* tagliuzzare.

snobbery *s.* snobismo.

to **snore** *vi.* russare.

snort *s.* sbuffo, rumore sbuffante.

to **snort** *vt.* e *vi.* sbuffare.

snout *s.* muso, grugno.

snow *s.* neve, nevicata || — *plough,* spazzaneve; — -*slide,* valanga.

to **snow** *v. imp.* nevicare || *it is snowing,* nevica.

snowfall *s.* nevicata.

snowflake *s.* fiocco di neve.

snowy *agg.* **1.** nevoso, coperto di neve **2.** niveo.

snuff *s.* **1.** l'aspirare col naso **2.** tabacco da fiuto || — -*box,* tabacchiera.

to **snuff**[1] *vt.* e *vi.* **1.** annusare aspirando **2.** fiutare tabacco.

to **snuff**[2] *vt.* e *vi.* smoccolare (*una candela*).

to **snuffle** *vt.* e *vi.* pronunciare con tono nasale.

snug *agg.* **1.** comodo **2.** confortevole **3.** nascosto.

to **snuggle** *vi.* **1.** rannicchiarsi **2.** accoccolarsi.

so *avv.* così, tanto, talmente || — *far,* fino ad ora; — *long as,* a patto che; *if* —, in tal caso; *that being* —, stando così le cose.

to **soak** *vt.* **1.** immergere **2.** bagnare. ♦ to **soak** *vi.* **1.** inzupparsi, imbeversi **2.** bagnarsi.

soaking *agg.* **1.** che bagna, che inzuppa **2.** bagnato. ♦ **soaking** *s.* immersione, bagnatura.

soap *s.* sapone || — *dish,* portasapone.

to **soap** *vt.* insaponare. ♦ to **soap** *vi.* insaponarsi.

soapbox *s.* **1.** cassa per sapone **2.** (*fam.*) palco improvvisato per oratori (*da strada*).

soapsuds *s. pl.* saponata (*sing.*).

soapwort *s.* saponaria.

sob *s.* singhiozzo.

to **sob** *vt.* e *vi.* singhiozzare.

sober *agg.* **1.** sobrio (*nel bere*) **2.** calmo, composto.

sobriety *s.* **1.** sobrietà (*nel bere*) **2.** moderazione, calma.

so-called *agg.* cosiddetto.

sociability *s.* socievolezza.

sociable *agg.* socievole.

social *agg.* **1.** sociale **2.** socievole.

socialism *s.* socialismo.

socialist *s.* socialista.

sociality *s.* socievolezza.

to **socialize** *vt.* socializzare.

society *s.* **1.** società, compagnia **2.** strato sociale **3.** associazione.

sociological *agg.* sociologico.

sociologist *s.* sociologo.

sociology *s.* sociologia.

sock *s.* **1.** calzino, calza corta **2.** soletta.

socket *s.* **1.** cavità **2.** (*elett.*) presa di corrente, portalampada **3.** (*anat.*) orbita.

Socratic *agg.* e *s.* socratico.

sod *s.* zolla erbosa.

soda *s.* carbonato di sodio.

sodium s. sodio.

soft agg. **1.** molle, tenero **2.** liscio, morbido, soffice **3.** dolce, mite || — -boiled (egg), uovo alla coque.

to **soften** vt. **1.** ammollire, ammorbidire **2.** calmare, raddolcire. ◆ to **soften** vi. **1.** ammorbidirsi **2.** intenerirsi.

softening agg. che rende molle. ◆ **softening** s. **1.** ammorbidimento **2.** intenerimento.

softly avv. **1.** teneramente **2.** sommessamente **3.** pian piano.

softness s. **1.** morbidezza **2.** dolcezza, mitezza.

soil s. **1.** suolo, terreno **2.** macchia (anche fig.).

to **soil** vt. macchiare. ◆ to **soil** vi. macchiarsi.

sojourn s. soggiorno.

to **sojourn** vi. soggiornare.

solace s. sollievo, conforto.

to **solace** vt. consolare.

solar agg. solare.

sold V. to sell.

solder s. lega per saldatura.

to **solder** vt. saldare.

soldering s. saldatura.

soldier s. **1.** soldato **2.** stratega || foot- —, soldato di fanteria; horse- —, soldato di cavalleria.

soldierlike agg. militaresco.

soldiery s. coll. soldatesca, truppe.

sole[1] agg. solo, unico.

sole[2] s. suola, pianta del piede.

sole[3] s. sogliola.

solecism s. solecismo.

solely avv. solamente.

solemn agg. solenne, serio, grave.

solemnity s. solennità.

to **solemnize** vt. solennizzare.

solemnly avv. solennemente.

sol-fa s. solfeggio.

to **sol-fa** vt. e vi. solfeggiare.

to **solicit** vt. **1.** sollecitare **2.** adescare. ◆ to **solicit** vi. fare sollecitazioni.

solicitation s. **1.** sollecitazione **2.** invito, adescamento.

solicitor s. **1.** sollecitatore **2.** procuratore legale.

solicitous agg. **1.** sollecito **2.** ansioso, desideroso.

solid agg. **1.** solido, compatto **2.** reale, fondato. ◆ **solid** s. solido.

solidarity s. solidarietà.

solidary agg. solidale.

solidification s. solidificazione.

to **solidify** vt. solidificare. ◆ to **so-**

lidify vi. solidificarsi.

solidity s. **1.** solidità **2.** (comm.) solvenza.

solidly avv. **1.** solidamente **2.** all'unanimità.

soliloquy s. soliloquio.

solitaire s. solitario (pietra preziosa e giuoco delle carte).

solitary agg. **1.** solo, unico **2.** solitario **3.** isolato, romito.

solitude s. solitudine, isolamento.

soloist s. solista.

solstice s. solstizio.

solubility s. solubilità.

soluble agg. **1.** solubile **2.** scomponibile **3.** risolubile.

solution s. **1.** (chim.) soluzione **2.** risoluzione.

solvability s. **1.** (comm.) solvibilità **2.** solubilità **3.** risolubilità.

solvable agg. **1.** (comm.) solvibile **2.** solubile **3.** risolubile.

to **solve** vt. risolvere, chiarire.

solvency s. (comm.) solvibilità.

solvent agg. **1.** (comm.) solvibile **2.** solvente. ◆ **solvent** s. solvente.

somatic(al) agg. somatico.

somatology s. somatologia.

sombre agg. **1.** fosco, scuro **2.** (fig.) tetro, triste.

some agg. **1.** qualche, alcuni, certi **2.** un certo, qualsiasi **3.** (partitivo) un po' di, del, della, dei, degli, delle. ◆ **some** pron. **1.** alcuni, alcune **2.** un po'. ◆ **some** avv. circa.

somebody pron. indef. qualcuno.

somehow avv. in qualche modo, in un modo o nell'altro.

someone pron. indef. qualcuno: — else, qualcun altro.

somersault s. **1.** salto mortale, capriola **2.** (aer.) capottamento **3.** (auto) ribaltamento.

to **somersault**, to **somerset** vi. **1.** fare salti mortali **2.** (aer.) capottare **3.** (auto.) ribaltare.

something pron. indef. qualche cosa.

sometime avv. **1.** un tempo **2.** presto o tardi, un giorno o l'altro.

sometimes avv. qualche volta, alcune volte.

someway avv. in un modo o nell'altro.

somewhat pron. ind. un poco.

somewhere avv. in qualche luogo.

somnambulism s. sonnambulismo.

somnambulist s. sonnambulo.

somnolent *agg.* **1.** sonnolento **2.** assopito.

son *s.* figlio, figliolo || — *-in-law,* genèro.

song *s.* canto, canzone.

songbook *s.* canzoniere.

songful *agg.* **1.** melodioso **2.** che ama cantare.

songster *s.* cantante (*uomo*).

sonnet *s.* sonetto.

sonority *s.* sonorità.

sonorous *agg.* sonoro, risonante.

sonorously *avv.* sonoramente.

soon (*comp. di* sooner) *avv.* presto, tra poco || *the sooner the better,* prima è meglio è; *sooner or later,* presto o tardi; *I had sooner,* preferirei; *as — as,* non appena.

soot *s.* fuliggine.

to soot *vt.* macchiare, sporcare di fuliggine.

to soothe *vt.* calmare, placare.

soothsayer *s.* indovino.

sooty *agg.* fuligginoso.

sophism *s.* sofisma.

sophist *s.* sofista (*anche fig.*).

sophistic(al) *agg.* sofistico, pedante.

sophisticated *agg.* **1.** sofisticato, raffinato **2.** adulterato.

sophistry *s.* sofisma.

sorcerer *s.* stregone, mago.

sorceress *s.* strega, maga.

sorcery *s.* stregoneria, sortilegio.

sordid *agg.* **1.** sordido, avaro **2.** vile, meschino.

sore *agg.* **1.** doloroso, dolorante, infiammato **2.** triste, addolorato **3.** estremo, intenso.

sorrel *s.* sauro.

sorrow *s.* **1.** dispiacere, dolore **2.** rincrescimento **3.** sventura.

to sorrow *vi.* affliggersi, addolorarsi.

sorrowful *agg.* **1.** triste, infelice **2.** penoso, doloroso.

sorry *agg.* spiacente, dolente || *sorry!,* scusate!; *to be —,* dispiacersi.

sort *s.* sorta, specie.

to sort *vt.* raggruppare, selezionare.
♦ **to sort** *vi.* accordarsi, adattarsi.

sought *V. to seek.*

soul *s.* **1.** anima, animo, spirito **2.** essenza, personificazione.

sound[1] *avv.* profondamente.

sound[2] *agg.* **1.** sano, intero, in buono stato **2.** buono, solido **3.** profondo, completo || — *-headed* equilibra-

to, — *-minded,* di buon senso.

sound[3] *s.* suono, rumore || — *wave,* onda sonora.

sound[4] *s.* sondaggio.

sound[5] *s.* braccio di mare, stretto.

to sound[1] *vt. e vi.* **1.** suonare, risuonare **2.** sembrare, aver l'aria di.

to sound[2] *vt. e vi.* sondare, scandagliare.

sounding *agg.* sonoro, sonante, risonante.

soundless *agg.* muto, senza suono.

soundly *avv.* **1.** sanamente **2.** profondamente.

soundness *s.* **1.** buona condizione (*di salute*) **2.** solidità (*di argomento*).

soup *s.* zuppa, minestra.

sour *agg.* **1.** acido, aspro, acerbo **2.** bisbetico.

to sour *vt. e vi.* **1.** inacidire **2.** inasprire, esacerbare.

source *s.* **1.** fonte, sorgente **2.** origine.

sourdine *s.* (*mus.*) sordina.

sourish *agg.* acidulo.

sourness *s.* acidità.

south *s.* sud, mezzogiorno.

southern *agg.* del sud, meridionale.

southerner *s.* abitante del sud, meridionale.

southward *avv.* verso sud.

sovereign *s.* sovrano.

sovereignty *s.* sovranità.

sow *s.* scrofa.

to sow (**sowed, sown**) *vt. e vi.* seminare, piantare.

sowing *s.* seminagione.

sown *V. to sow.*

spa *s.* sorgente minerale.

space *s.* spazio || — *-ship,* astronave.

to space *vt.* spaziare, disporre ad intervalli.

spaceman *s.* astronauta.

spacesuit *s.* tuta spaziale.

spacial *agg.* spaziale.

spacing *s.* spaziatura, interlineatura.

spacious *agg.* spazioso, ampio.

spade *s.* vanga, badile.

span *V. to spin.*

span *s.* **1.** spanna, palmo **2.** breve spazio di tempo.

to span *vt.* **1.** misurare a spanne **2.** attraversare.

spangle *s.* lustrino.

Spaniard *s.* spagnolo.

Spanish *agg.* spagnolo.

to spank *vt.* (*fam.*) sculacciare.

spar[1] *s.* (*mar.*) antenna.

spar[2] *s.* incontro di pugilato.

spare *agg.* **1.** parco, frugale **2.** d'avanzo, disponibile, in più || — *room*, camera in più (*per gli ospiti*); — *time*, tempo disponibile; — *wheel*, ruota di scorta.

to **spare** *vt.* **1.** economizzare, risparmiare **2.** privarsi, fare a meno di. ♦ to **spare** *vi.* essere frugale.

sparing *agg.* **1.** parco, frugale **2.** limitato, moderato.

spark *s.* **1.** scintilla, favilla **2.** (*fig.*) lampo, barlume.

to **spark** *vi.* scintillare, emettere scintille.

sparkle *s.* scintilla, favilla.

to **sparkle** *vi.* **1.** emettere scintille (*di fuoco*) **2.** sfavillare, brillare, risplendere (*anche fig.*).

sparkler *s.* stella filante.

sparkling *agg.* scintillante, vivace (*anche fig.*).

sparrow *s.* passero || — -*hawk*, sparviero.

Spartan *agg.* e *s.* spartano.

spasm *s.* **1.** spasmo **2.** attacco, spasimo (*anche fig.*).

spasmodic(al) *agg.* spasmodico.

spastic *agg.* spastico.

spat V. *to spit.*

spatial *agg.* spaziale.

spatiality *s.* spazialità.

spatter *s.* **1.** schizzo **2.** sgocciolio.

to **spatter** *vt.* e *vi.* **1.** schizzare, inzaccherare **2.** gocciolare.

to **speak (spoke, spoken)** *vt.* e *vi.* **1.** parlare **2.** esprimere, rivelare || *to* — *at*, alludere a; *to* — *out*, parlare francamente; *to* — *to*, garantire; *to* — *up*, alzare la voce.

speaker *s.* parlatore, oratore, annunciatore || *the* — *of the House of Commons*, il Presidente della Camera dei Comuni.

speaking *agg.* parlante, espressivo, eloquente. ♦ **speaking** *s.* **1.** il parlare, discorso **2.** eloquenza, declamazione.

spear *s.* **1.** lancia, alabarda, asta **2.** fiocina.

to **spear** *vt.* **1.** trafiggere (*con lancia*) **2.** fiocinare.

special *agg.* **1.** speciale, particolare **2.** eccezionale, straordinario.

specialist *s.* specialista.

speciality *s.* specialità, particolarità.

to **specialize** *vt.* specializzare. ♦ to

specialize *vi.* specializzarsi.

specially *avv.* specialmente, soprattutto.

specialty *s.* **1.** (*comm.*) specialità **2.** (*giur.*) contratto sigillato.

species *s.* **1.** specie, classe **2.** sorta, genere, tipo.

specific *agg.* specifico, particolare.

specification *s.* **1.** specificazione **2.** descrizione dettagliata.

to **specify** *vt.* specificare, precisare.

specimen *s.* modello, esemplare.

speck *s.* **1.** macchiolina, punto **2.** granello (*di polvere ecc.*).

speckled *agg.* macchiato, screziato.

speckless *agg.* senza macchia (*anche fig.*).

spectacle *s.* spettacolo, vista. ♦ **spectacles** *s. pl.* occhiali: *to put on one's* —, mettersi gli occhiali.

spectacled *agg.* che porta gli occhiali.

spectacular *agg.* spettacolare.

spectator *s.* spettatore.

spectral *agg.* spettrale.

spectre *s.* spettro, fantasma.

specular *agg.* speculare.

to **speculate** *vt.* e *vi.* **1.** meditare, considerare **2.** (*comm.*) speculare.

speculation *s.* **1.** speculazione, meditazione **2.** (*comm.*) speculazione.

speculative *agg.* contemplativo, speculativo (*anche comm.*).

speculator *s.* **1.** spirito speculatore **2.** (*comm.*) speculatore.

sped V. *to speed.*

speech *s.* **1.** parola, favella **2.** discorso, arringa **3.** linguaggio.

speechless *agg.* senza parola, muto (*anche fig.*).

speed *s.* velocità, rapidità.

to **speed** *vi.* affrettarsi. ♦ to **speed (sped, sped)** *vt.* **1.** aiutare **2.** affrettare **3.** regolare la velocità || *to* — *up the work*, affrettare i lavori.

speedometer *s.* tachimetro.

speedway *s.* pista, circuito (*di autodromo*).

speedy *agg.* rapido, pronto.

spell[1] *s.* incantesimo.

spell[2] *s.* **1.** turno di lavoro **2.** intervallo.

to **spell (spelt, spelt)** (*anche reg.*) *vt.* e *vi.* compitare, sillabare.

to **spellbind (spellbound, spellbound)** *vt.* incantare, affascinare.

spelling *s.* **1.** compitazione **2.** ortografia.

spelt V. *to spell.*

to spend (spent, spent) *vt.* e *vi.*
1. spendere, sborsare **2.** dedicare,
impiegare **3.** passare, trascorrere.

sperm *s.* sperma.

sphenoid *agg.* e *s.* sfenoide.

sphere *s.* sfera, globo.

spheric(al) *agg.* sferico.

sphericity *s.* sfericità.

sphincter *s.* sfintere.

Sphinx *s.* sfinge (*anche fig.*).

spice *s.* **1.** aroma **2.** (*fig.*) sapore,
gusto **3.** spezie (*pl.*).

to spice *vt.* **1.** condire con spezie
2. (*fig.*) dar gusto a, rendere interessante.

spicery *s.* spezie, aromi (*pl.*).

spicily *avv.* **1.** aromaticamente **2.**
(*fig.*) gustosamente.

spiciness *s.* **1.** aroma, profumo **2.**
(*fam.*) arguzia.

spick-and-span *agg.* (*fam.*) lindo,
lucente.

spicy *agg.* **1.** aromatico, piccante **2.**
(*fig.*) arguto, mordace.

spider *s.* ragno.

spidery *agg.* **1.** simile a ragno **2.**
infestato da ragni.

spike¹ *s.* punta, aculeo.

spike² *s.* spiga.

to spike *vt.* inchiodare || *to —
so.'s guns,* guastare i piani di qu.

to spill (spilt, spilt) *vt.* **1.** versare **2.** disarcionare. ♦ **to spill
(spilt, spilt)** *vi.* versarsi, traboccare.

spin *s.* (*aer.*) avvitamento.

to spin (span, spun) *vt.* e *vi.* **1.**
filare (*cotone ecc.*) **2.** (*mecc.*) lavorare al tornio **3.** girare, far girare.

spinach *s.* spinacio.

spinal *agg.* spinale.

spindle *s.* **1.** fuso, fusello **2.** (*mecc.*)
asse, mandrino.

spine *s.* **1.** spina, lisca **2.** spina dorsale.

spineless *agg.* **1.** senza spine **2.** senza spina dorsale **3.** (*fam.*) debole,
molle.

spinner *s.* **1.** ragno filatore **2.** (*aer.*)
ogiva **3.** filatore.

spinning *s.* **1.** filatura, filato **2.** mo-
vimento rotatorio || *— -mill,* fi-
landa.

spinster *s.* **1.** filatrice **2.** donna nu-
bile, zitella.

spiral *agg.* spirale, a spirale. ♦
spiral *s.* spirale.

spire¹ *s.* guglia, cuspide.

spire² *s.* spira, spirale.

spirit *s.* **1.** spirito, anima **2.** folletto, fantasma **3.** genio, intelletto
4. coraggio, vigore.

spirits¹ *s. pl.* umore, stato d'animo
(*sing.*).

spirits² *s. pl.* bevande fortemente
alcooliche.

spirited *agg.* brioso, vivace || *high-
- —,* fiero; *poor- —,* depresso.

spiritism *s.* spiritismo.

spiritual *agg.* spirituale.

spiritualism *s.* **1.** spiritualismo **2.**
spiritismo.

spiritualist *s.* **1.** spiritualista **2.** spiritista.

spirituality *s.* spiritualità.

spit *s.* sputo, saliva.

to spit (spat, spat) *vi.* sputare.

spite *s.* dispetto, ripicco: *out of
—,* per dispetto; *in — of,* a dispetto di.

spiteful *agg.* dispettoso.

spittle V. *spit.*

spittoon *s.* sputacchiera.

splash *s.* **1.** schizzo, spruzzo **2.** tonfo.

to splash *vt.* e *vi.* **1.** schizzare,
spruzzare **2.** inzaccherare, infangare. ♦ **to splash** *vi.* **1.** spruzzare
2. cadere con un tonfo.

splashy *agg.* bagnato, fangoso.

splay *agg.* largo e piatto. ♦ **splay**
s. (*arch.*) strombatura.

to splay *vt.* (*arch.*) strombare. ♦
to splay *vi.* essere in posizione
obliqua.

spleen *s.* **1.** milza **2.** (*fig.*) malumore, umore nero.

splendid *agg.* splendido, magnifico.

splendour *s.* splendore, lustro.

splenetic *agg.* e *s.* splenetico, bilioso.

splinter *s.* scheggia, frantume.

split *agg.* spaccato, diviso. ♦ **split**
s. **1.** fessura, crepaccio **2.** scissione.

to split (split, split) *vt.* **1.** fen-
dere **2.** spaccare, frazionare || *to
— hairs,* spaccare un capello in
quattro; *to — one's sides (with
laughing),* ridere a crepapelle. ♦
to split (split, split) *vi.* fen-
dersi.

splitting *agg.* che si fende, che fende. ♦ **splitting** *s.* fessura, spaccatura.

spoil(s) *s.* spoglia, preda.

to **spoil** (**spoilt**, **spoilt**) (*anche reg.*) *vt.* e *vi.* **1.** rovinare, alterare, sciupare, viziare **2.** saccheggiare, predare.

spoilt *agg.* **1.** guasto, avariato **2.** viziato.

spoke *s.* **1.** raggio (*di ruota*) **2.** piolo (*di scala*).

spoke V. *to speak*.

spoken V. *to speak*.

spokesman *s.* portavoce.

spoliation *s.* ruberia, saccheggio.

sponge *s.* spugna, colpo di spugna.

to **sponge** *vt.* **1.** pulire, lavare con la spugna **2.** fare spugnature **3.** (*fig.; fam.*) scroccare.

sponger *s.* **1.** pescatore di spugne **2.** scroccone.

spongy *agg.* spugnoso, poroso.

sponsor *s.* **1.** padrino, madrina **2.** (*giur.*) garante, mallevadore.

to **sponsor** *vt.* **1.** essere garante di **2.** offrire (*programmi radio, tv*).

sponsorial *agg.* **1.** di garanzia **2.** di padrino, di madrina.

sponsorship *s.* **1.** garanzia **2.** qualità di padrino, di madrina.

spontaneity *s.* spontaneità.

spontaneous *agg.* spontaneo.

spontaneously *avv.* spontaneamente.

spool *s.* rocchetto, bobina.

spoon *s.* cucchiaio.

to **spoon** *vt.* prendere con un cucchiaio.

spoon-fed *agg.* coccolato, viziato.

spoonful *s.* cucchiaiata.

sporadic *agg.* sporadico, raro.

sport *s.* **1.** giuoco, divertimento **2.** scherzo **3.** sport. ♦ **sports** *s. pl* gare, incontri.

to **sport** *vi.* **1.** scherzare **2.** giocare **3.** fare dello sport.

sporting *agg.* sportivo.

sportive *agg.* **1.** gioviale **2.** sportivo.

sportsman *s.* **1.** sportivo **2.** uomo animato da spirito sportivo.

sportsmanlike *agg.* caratteristico di uno sportivo.

sportswoman *s.* donna sportiva.

spot *s.* **1.** luogo, località **2.** macchia (*anche fig.*) || *on the* —, sul colpo.

to **spot** *vt.* macchiare, punteggiare. ♦ to **spot** *vi.* macchiarsi.

spotless *agg.* senza macchia, immacolato (*anche fig.*).

spotlight *s.* riflettore, luce della ribalta.

spotty *agg.* macchiato, chiazzato.

spout *s.* **1.** tubo di scarico, grondaia **2.** getto, colonna (*d'acqua*).

to **spout** *vt.* scaricare, emettere. ♦ to **spout** *vi.* scaturire, zampillare.

sprain *s.* distorsione, strappo muscolare.

to **sprain** *vt.* storcere, slogare.

sprang V. *to spring*.

to **sprawl** *vi.* sdraiarsi in modo scomposto.

spray *s.* **1.** spruzzo, schiuma **2.** getto vaporizzato (*di acqua ecc.*) **3.** spruzzatore.

to **spray** *vt.* **1.** polverizzare, vaporizzare **2.** aspergere, spruzzare.

sprayer *s.* spruzzatore.

spread *agg.* steso, aperto, spiegato.

to **spread** (**spread**, **spread**) *vt.* **1.** stendere, spiegare, spalmare **2.** (*fig.*) spargere, diffondere. ♦ to **spread** (**spread**, **spread**) *vi.* stendersi, spiegarsi.

spreader *s.* spruzzatore.

spreading *agg.* che si propaga. ♦ **spreading** *s.* (*fig.*) propagazione.

spree *s.* baldoria.

sprig *s.* **1.** ramoscello **2.** (*fig.*) rampollo.

spring *s.* **1.** sorgente, fonte **2.** primavera **3.** salto, balzo **4.** molla, elasticità || — *-board*, trampolino; — *-head*, fontana; — *-mattress*, materasso a molle.

to **spring** (**sprang**, **sprung**) *vi.* **1.** nascere, discendere, scaturire (*di acqua*) **2.** saltare **3.** scattare || *to* — *up*, crescere (*di piante*). ♦ to **spring** (**sprang**, **sprung**) *vt.* **1.** far scattare (*con una molla*) **2.** far brillare (*una mina*) **3.** saltare.

springiness *s.* elasticità.

springy *agg.* **1.** pieno di sorgenti **2.** elastico.

sprinkle *s.* aspersione, spruzzatina.

to **sprinkle** *vt.* e *vi.* spruzzare, aspergere.

sprinkler *s.* **1.** spruzzatore, innaffiatoio **2.** aspersorio.

sprint *s.* (*sport*) scatto finale.

to **sprout** *vi.* germogliare. ♦ to **sprout** *vt.* far germogliare.

to **spruce** *vt.* adornare, agghindare.

sprung V. *to spring*. ♦ **sprung** *agg.* **1.** a molla **2.** spaccato.

spun V. *to spin*.

spur *s.* **1.** sperone **2.** (*fig.*) sprone.

to **spur** *vt.* **1.** spronare **2.** (*fig.*) incitare.

to **spurn** vt. e vi. disdegnare, trattare con disprezzo.

s**p**urt s. getto, vampata.

spy s. spia.

to **spy** vt. e vi. spiare, fare la spia.

squabble s. battibecco, lite.

to **squabble** vi. accapigliarsi, venire a parole.

sq**u**ad s. squadra, plotone.

squalid agg. squallido, miserabile.

squall s. urlo, strepito.

squalor s. squallore.

to **squander** vt. sprecare, scialacquare.

squanderer s. sciupone, sperperatore.

square agg. 1. quadrato 2. robusto, massiccio 3. perpendicolare. ♦ **square** s. 1. quadrato 2. piazza 3. squadra || -built, tarchiato; — -root, radice quadrata; — -shouldered, dalle spalle larghe e diritte. ♦ **square** avv. ad angolo retto, in squadra.

to **square** vt. e vi. 1. quadrare, squadrare 2. pareggiare un conto 3. elevare al quadrato.

squared agg. 1. squadrato, quadrato 2. elevato al quadrato.

squash s. 1. cosa schiacciata 2. spremuta (di frutta): orange- —, spremuta d'arancio.

to **squash** vt. 1. schiacciare, spiaccicare 2. spremere.

squat agg. rannicchiato, accoccolato.

to **squat** vi. accovacciarsi, accoccolarsi.

squatter s. pioniere.

squeak s. 1. grido acuto 2. pigolio, squittio, guaito 3. cigolio.

to **squeak** vt. e vi. 1. strillare in tono acuto 2. squittire, guaire 3. cigolare.

squeaky agg. 1. che strilla 2. che guaisce, squittisce 3. cigolante.

squeamish agg. 1. soggetto a nausee 2. schizzinoso.

squeeze s. 1. compressione 2. spremitura 3. stretta, abbraccio.

to **squeeze** vt. 1. spremere 2. stringere, abbracciare. ♦ to **squeeze** vi. accalcarsi.

squeezer s. 1. ciò che preme 2. (mecc.) torchio.

squid s. seppia.

squint agg. strabico. ♦ **squint** s. strabismo.

to **squint** vi. essere strabico. ♦ to **squint** vt. guardare di traverso.

squire s. gentiluomo, nobiluomo (di campagna).

squirrel s. scoiattolo.

stab s. coltellata, pugnalata.

to **stab** vt. pugnalare, accoltellare.

to **stabilize** vt. stabilizzare.

stabilizer s. stabilizzatore.

stable[1] agg. stabile, permanente.

stable[2] s. scuderia, stalla.

stack s. mucchio, cumulo || chimney- —, ciminiera.

to **stack** vt. ammucchiare, accumulare.

staff s. 1. bastone, sostegno (anche fig.) 2. stato maggiore 3. personale (di ufficio ecc.) || editorial —, corpo redazionale; flag —, asta della bandiera.

stag s. cervo.

stage s. 1. piattaforma 2. palcoscenico 3. (fig.) campo d'azione, scena 4. stadio, grado 5. tappa || -direction, didascalia; —-director, regista (teat.); —-effect, effetto scenico; —-name, nome d'arte; landing- —, (mar.), pontile.

to **stage** vt. 1. mettere in scena 2. inscenare (una dimostrazione ecc.).

stagger s. barcollamento, andatura a zig-zag.

to **stagger** vi. 1. vacillare 2. dubitare, esitare. ♦ to **stagger** vt. far vacillare.

staginess s. teatralità.

staging s. 1. (teat.) messa in scena 2. (edil.) impalcatura.

stagnancy s. ristagno.

stagnant agg. stagnante.

to **stagnate** vi. ristagnare.

stagnation s. ristagno, stasi.

staid agg. posato, serio.

stain s. 1. scolorimento, macchia 2. (fig.) taccia, onta.

to **stain** vt. 1. macchiare 2. tingere. ♦ to **stain** vi. macchiarsi, sporcarsi.

stained agg. macchiato, sporco.

stainless agg. senza macchia.

stair s. scalino, gradino. ♦ **stairs** s. pl. scale || winding- —, scala a chiocciola; flight of —, rampa di scale.

staircase s. 1. scala, scalone 2. tromba delle scale.

stairway s. scalinata.

stake[1] s. 1. palo, paletto 2. piccola incudine.

stake[2] s. posta, scommessa || at —, in giuoco. ♦ **stakes** s. pl. (ippica) premio, corsa.

to **stake**[1] vt. cintare, chiudere (con una palizzata).

to **stake**[2] vt. mettere in giuoco, scommettere.

stale agg. 1. vecchio, stantio 2. (fig.) trito, caduto in disuso.

stalk[1] s. stelo, gambo.

stalk[2] s. andatura rigida e maestosa.

stall s. 1. stalla 2. bancarella, chiosco.

stammer s. balbuzie, balbettamento.

to **stammer** vt. e vi. 1. balbettare 2. farfugliare.

stammering agg. balbuziente. ♦ **stammering** s. balbuzie.

stamp s. 1. impronta, segno 2. francobollo, bollo 3. stampo || — -collector, filatelico; — -paper, carta bollata.

to **stamp** vt. 1. imprimere, incidere 2. (fig.) dare l'impronta 3. timbrare || to — down, calpestare. ♦ to **stamp** vi. battere i piedi.

stamping s. 1. scalpitio 2. timbratura.

stand s. 1. pausa, fermata 2. punto di vista 3. posizione, luogo (d'appostamento) 4. palco, tribuna 5. bancarella, chiosco || test- —, banco di prova.

to **stand** (stood, stood) vi. 1. essere, stare in piedi 2. stare, trovarsi 3. fermarsi, indugiare 4. conservarsi, rimaner valido || to — by, stare accanto, restare fedele a; to — for, significare, implicare; to — out, resistere, tener duro, spiccare. ♦ to **stand** (stood, stood) vt. sopportare, resistere.

standard s. 1. stendardo, bandiera 2. modello, campione 3. livello, qualità 4. supporto, base 5. tipo.

standardization s. standardizzazione.

stand-by s. scorta, riserva.

standing agg. 1. eretto, che sta in piedi 2. fermo, inattivo 3. fisso, immutabile. ♦ **standing** s. 1. posizione eretta 2. posizione, rango 3. periodo di tempo.

standoffish agg. riservato, altezzoso.

standpoint s. 1. luogo di osservazione 2. punto di vista.

standstill agg. in riposo, fermo. ♦ **standstill** s. arresto, fermata.

stank V. to stink.

staple s. 1. prodotto principale (di un paese ecc.) 2. (fig.) argomento principale (di una conversazione).

star s. 1. stella, astro 2. (fig.) fortuna, destino 3. (tip.) asterisco.

to **star** vt. 1. costellare 2. segnare con un asterisco. ♦ to **star** vi. (cine, teat.) avere il ruolo di protagonista.

starboard agg. di dritta. ♦ **starboard** s. (mar.) dritta.

starch s. 1. amido 2. (fig.) rigidezza, formalismo.

to **starch** vt. 1. inamidare 2. (fig.) rendere formale.

starchiness s. 1. inamidatura 2. (fig.) formalismo, rigidità.

stardom s. divismo.

stare s. sguardo fisso.

to **stare** vt. guardare intensamente, fissare. ♦ to **stare** vi. sgranare gli occhi.

starfish s. stella di mare.

staring agg. 1. fisso, stupefatto 2. sgargiante, vistoso.

staringly avv. fissamente, con occhi sbarrati.

stark agg. 1. rigido, duro 2. completo, vero e proprio.

starless agg. senza stelle.

starlet s. 1. piccola stella 2. (cine) stellina.

starlight agg. stellato, stellare. ♦ **starlight** s. luce stellare.

starlike agg. simile a stella.

starlit agg. illuminato dalle stelle.

starred agg. 1. stellato, adorno di stelle 2. a stella.

starry agg. stellato, trapunto di stelle, brillante come una stella.

start s. 1. inizio, partenza 2. soprassalto || by fits and starts, irregolarmente 3. vantaggio dato all'inizio di una corsa 4. (mecc.) avviamento.

to **start** vi. 1. partire, mettersi in viaggio 2. cominciare 3. trasalire || to — out, aver intenzione di; to — up, spuntare all'improvviso. ♦ to **start** vt. 1. cominciare 2. far trasalire.

starter s. 1. iniziatore, fondatore 2. (sport) "starter", mossiere.

starting s. 1. inizio, partenza 2. debutto 3. (mecc.) messa in moto, avviamento.

startle s. trasalimento.

to **startle** vt. spaventare, far trasalire. ♦ to **startle** vi. spaventarsi, trasalire.

startling agg. impressionante, sorprendente.

starvation s. inedia, fame.

to starve vi. **1.** morire di fame **2.** (fig.) bramare. ♦ **to starve** vt. far morire di fame.

state s. **1.** stato, condizione **2.** governo, nazione **3.** rango, dignità || — -control, statalizzazione; — -documents, documenti ufficiali; — -prisoner, prigioniero politico; — -trial, processo politico.

to state vt. **1.** affermare, dichiarare **2.** stabilire.

stateless agg. **1.** senza patria **2.** senza pompa **3.** apolide.

stately agg. nobile, signorile.

statement s. **1.** esposto, relazione **2.** asserzione, affermazione **3.** (giur.) deposizione, esposizione dei fatti.

statesman s. statista.

static(al) agg. statico.

statics s. statica.

station s. **1.** posto, luogo, base **2.** stazione **3.** condizione sociale || petrol —, stazione di rifornimento; through —, stazione di transito.

stationary agg. stazionario.

stationer s. cartolaio || —'s (shop), cartoleria.

stationery s. articoli di cancelleria.

station house s. guardina.

stationmaster s. capostazione.

statist s. statista.

statistic(al) agg. statistico.

statistically avv. statisticamente.

statistics s. **1.** scienza della statistica **2.** statistiche (pl.).

statuary agg. statuario, scultorio.

statue s. statua.

statuesque agg. statuario.

stature s. statura.

status s. **1.** stato, condizione sociale **2.** situazione.

statute s. statuto, regolamento.

statutory agg. statutario.

to staunch vt. **1.** arrestare **2.** stagnare. ♦ **to staunch** vi. stagnarsi.

stave s. **1.** doga (di botte) **2.** piolo (di scala) **3.** strofa.

stay[1] s. **1.** soggiorno **2.** pausa.

stay[2] s. **1.** sostegno, supporto **2.** (mecc.) puntello.

to stay[1] vi. **1.** fermarsi, sostare, soggiornare **2.** resistere || to — away, essere assente; to — in, stare in casa, (mil.) essere consegnato; to

— up, vegliare. ♦ **to stay** vt. **1.** arrestare, fermare **2.** resistere.

to stay[2] vt. (mecc.) puntellare.

steadfast agg. fermo, risoluto.

steadfastly avv. stabilmente, fermamente.

steadfastness s. fermezza, tenacia.

steadily avv. **1.** saldamente, fermamente **2.** costantemente.

steadiness s. **1.** fermezza, sicurezza **2.** assiduità, perseveranza.

steading s. tenuta agricola.

steady agg. **1.** fermo, saldo **2.** equilibrato **3.** continuo, regolare **4.** fedele, assiduo.

to steady vt. rafforzare, rendere fermo, equilibrato. ♦ **to steady** vi. rafforzarsi.

steak s. bistecca.

to steal (stole, stolen) vt. e vi. rubare || to — along, camminare furtivamente; to — away, svignarsela; to — upon, avvicinarsi pian piano.

stealing s. furto || cattle (o horse)- -—, abigeato.

stealthily avv. furtivamente.

stealthy agg. furtivo.

steam s. vapore: — -engine, macchina a vapore.

to steam vt. **1.** esporre al vapore **2.** cucinare al vapore. ♦ **to steam** vi. emettere vapore.

steamboat s. imbarcazione a vapore.

steamer s. nave a vapore.

steamship s. piroscafo.

steamtight agg. a tenuta di vapore.

steamy agg. **1.** che esala vapore **2.** appannato, umido.

stearic agg. stearico.

steel s. **1.** acciaio **2.** arma, spada **3.** acciarino || — cap, elmetto; — company, acciaieria || stainless —, acciaio inossidabile.

steelwork s. lavoro, struttura in acciaio.

steelwork s. pl. acciaieria (sing.).

steely agg. **1.** di acciaio, simile ad acciaio **2.** (fig.) severissimo.

steelyard s. stadera.

steep[1] agg. **1.** ripido, scosceso **2.** (fig.) ambizioso, arduo **3.** esorbitante (di prezzi).

steep[2] s. macerazione, l'inzuppare.

to steep vt. immergere (anche fig.), inzuppare.

steeple s. guglia, campanile.

steeplechase s. (ippica) corsa ad

ostacoli.

steer *s.* bue giovane, manzo.

to steer *vt.* **1.** governare, manovrare **2.** dirigere. ♦ **to steer** *vi.* **1.** dirigersi **2.** (*auto*) sterzare.

steering *s.* guida, governo (*dello sterzo, del timone*).

stem *s.* **1.** tronco, gambo, stelo **2.** cannello (*di pipa*) **3.** (*mar.*) prua.

to stem *vt.* arrestare, arginare.

stench *s.* puzzo, tanfo.

step *s.* **1.** passo (*anche fig.*), andatura **2.** orma, impronta **3.** provvedimento **4.** gradino || *to be in — with so.*, tenere il passo con qu.; *— by —*, gradualmente; *in —* (*elett.*), in fase.

to step *vi.* camminare || *to — aside*, farsi da parte; *to — forward*, avanzare; *to — in*, montare (*su un veicolo*). ♦ **to step** *vt.* misurare a passi.

stepbrother *s.* fratellastro.

stepchild *s.* (*pl.* -children) figliastro.

stepdaughter *s.* figliastra.

stepfather *s.* patrigno.

stepmother *s.* matrigna.

stepsister *s.* sorellastra.

stepson *s.* figliastro.

stereophonic *agg.* stereofonico.

stereophony *s.* stereofonia.

stereoscope *s.* stereoscopio.

stereotype *s.* stereotipo.

sterile *agg.* sterile.

sterility *s.* sterilità.

to sterilize *vt.* rendere sterile, sterilizzare.

stern[1] *agg.* severo, austero.

stern[2] *s.* (*mar.*) poppa.

sternly *avv.* severamente.

sternness *s.* severità, austerità.

stethoscope *s.* stetoscopio.

stevedore *s.* scaricatore (*di porto*).

stew *s.* (*cuc.*) umido, stufato.

to stew *vt.* e *vi.* cuocere in umido.

steward *s.* **1.** amministratore, intendente **2.** (*aer., mar.*) cameriere di bordo.

stewardess *s.* **1.** dispensiere **2.** (*aer., mar.*) cameriera di bordo.

stick *s.* **1.** bastone **2.** bastoncino **3.** barra, stecca.

to stick (**stuck, stuck**) *vt.* **1.** ficcare, conficcare **2.** infilare **3.** incollare, appiccicare. ♦ **to stick** (**stuck, stuck**) *vi.* **1.** fissarsi, conficcarsi **2.** incollarsi.

stickiness *s.* viscosità, adesività.

sticky *agg.* **1.** appiccicaticcio, visco-

so **2.** poco accomodante.

stiff *agg.* **1.** rigido, duro **2.** (*fig.*) inflessibile **3.** indolenzito, intorpidito **4.** freddo, riservato || *— collar*, colletto duro; *— -neck*, torcicollo.

to stiffen *vt.* **1.** indurire **2.** indolenzire, intorpidire **3.** rassodare. ♦ **to stiffen** *vi.* **1.** indurirsi, irrigidirsi (*anche fig.*) **2.** rassodarsi.

stiffness *s.* **1.** durezza, rigidezza **2.** intorpidimento.

to stifle *vt.* **1.** soffocare **2.** (*fig.*) reprimere. ♦ **to stifle** *vi.* sentirsi soffocare.

stifling *agg.* soffocante.

to stigmatize *vt.* **1.** marchiare **2.** stigmatizzare.

stile *s.* scaletta.

still[1] *agg.* tranquillo, calmo, silenzioso || *— -life* (*pitt.*), natura morta.

still[2] *avv.* **1.** ancora, tuttora **2.** tuttavia, nondimeno.

still[3] *s.* alambicco.

to still *vt.* acquietare, calmare. ♦ **to still** *vi.* acquietarsi, calmarsi.

stillness *s.* calma, quiete.

stilt *s.* trampolo.

stimulant *s.* **1.** stimolante **2.** bevanda alcolica.

to stimulate *vt.* stimolare, incitare.

stimulus *s.* (*pl.*- li) stimolo, incentivo.

sting *s.* **1.** pungiglione, aculeo **2.** puntura d'insetto **3.** dolore acuto **4.** pungolo, stimolo.

to sting (**stung, stung**) *vt.* e *vi.* **1.** pungere **2.** colpire, ferire (*anche fig.*).

stinginess *s.* avarizia, spilorceria.

stinging *agg.* pungente, mordace.

stingy *agg.* avaro, taccagno.

stink *s.* puzzo, fetore.

to stink (**stank, stunk**) *vt.* e *vi.* puzzare, riempire di puzzo.

stinking *agg.* puzzolente, fetido.

to stipulate *vt.* e *vi.* stipulare.

stipulation *s.* stipulazione, patto.

stir *s.* **1.** il rimescolare, l'attizzare || *to give a —*, dare una rimescolata **2.** animazione, tumulto.

to stir *vt.* **1.** rimescolare **2.** muovere, agitare. ♦ **to stir** *vi.* muoversi, agitarsi.

stirabout *agg.* indaffarato.

stirrer *s.* incitatore, istigatore.

stirring *agg.* eccitante.

stirrup *s.* staffa.

stitch *s.* **1.** punto **2.** maglia.

stock s. **1.** rifornimento, provvista || to be out of —, essere sprovvisto **2.** titoli, azioni (pl.) **3.** tronco, ceppo **4.** (fig.) stirpe.

to stock vt. **1.** approvvigionare **2.** tenere in magazzino.

stockbroker s. agente di cambio.

stockbroking s. professione dell'agente di cambio.

stock company s. società per azioni.

Stock Exchange s. Borsa valori.

stockfish s. stoccafisso.

stockholder s. azionista.

stocking s. calza lunga.

stoic agg. e s. stoico.

stoicism s. stoicismo.

stoker s. fuochista.

stole V. to steal.

stolen V. to steal.

stolid agg. **1.** imperturbabile **2.** sciocco.

stolidity s. flemma.

stomach s. stomaco: — -ache, mal di stomaco.

stomatitis s. stomatite.

stomatology s. stomatologia.

stone s. **1.** pietra, ciottolo, sasso **2.** nocciolo **3.** (med.) calcolo || — -blind, completamente cieco; — -breaker, spaccapietre; — cutter, tagliapietre.

to stone vt. **1.** lapidare **2.** rivestire di pietra **3.** snocciolare.

stoneless agg. senza nocciolo.

stoneware s. ceramica.

stony agg. **1.** pietroso, sassoso **2.** (fig.) duro, insensibile.

stood V. to stand.

stool s. sgabello, seggiolino.

stoop s. curvatura, inchino.

to stoop vi. **1.** curvare, inchinarsi **2.** (fig.) accondiscendere, abbassarsi.

stop s. **1.** sosta, arresto **2.** segno di punteggiatura || — watch, cronometro.

to stop vt. **1.** fermare **2.** turare, otturare **3.** impedire. ♦ to **stop** vi. fermarsi.

stopper s. **1.** tappo, turacciolo **2.** otturatore.

stopping s. **1.** otturazione **2.** (comm.) cessazione, sospensione (di pagamenti ecc.).

storage s. **1.** immagazzinamento **2.** deposito, magazzino.

store s. **1.** provvista, riserva **2.** magazzino || — -keeper, magazzinie-

re; — -ship, nave da carico.

to store vt. **1.** fornire, rifornire **2.** immagazzinare, mettere da parte (anche fig.).

storehouse s. magazzino, deposito.

storey s. piano (di edificio).

stork s. cicogna.

storm s. **1.** tempesta, temporale **2.** tumulto, agitazione.

to storm vi. **1.** infuriare, scatenarsi **2.** (fam.) adirarsi. ♦ to **storm** vt. attaccare.

stormy agg. tempestoso, burrascoso.

story s. storia, racconto, novella, favola || to tell stories, contar frottole.

stoup s. acquasantiera.

stout agg. **1.** forte, robusto, resistente **2.** fermo, risoluto **3.** grosso, tozzo.

stove s. **1.** stufa **2.** cucina economica: gas- —, cucina a gas.

to stove vt. mettere in forno, stufa.

to stow vt. stivare, riempire.

stowage s. (mar.) stivaggio.

straddle s. posizione a gambe divaricate, il mettersi a cavalcioni.

to straddle vt. stare a cavalcioni di. ♦ to **straddle** vi. mettersi a gambe divaricate.

straight[1] agg. **1.** diritto, rettilineo **2.** onesto, retto **3.** ordinato || a — whisky, un whisky liscio.

straight[2] s. **1.** posizione diritta **2.** (fig.) condotta onesta.

straight[3] avv. **1.** diritto, in linea retta **2.** direttamente.

to straighten vt. raddrizzare. ♦ to **straighten** vi. raddrizzarsi.

straightforward agg. **1.** diritto, diretto **2.** schietto, leale.

straightforwardly avv. **1.** in linea retta **2.** francamente, schiettamente.

strain s. **1.** tensione (anche fig.) **2.** sforzo, fatica **3.** distorsione, strappo muscolare.

to strain vt. **1.** sottoporre a tensione **2.** sforzare. ♦ to **strain** vi. sforzarsi.

strained agg. **1.** teso **2.** indebolito **3.** non spontaneo, forzato.

strainer s. colino, filtro.

strait s. (geogr.) stretto. ♦ to **strand** vi. incagliarsi.

stranding s. incagliamento (di una nave).

strange agg. **1.** strano, bizzarro **2.** estraneo, sconosciuto.

stranger s. estraneo, sconosciuto, forestiero.

to strangle vt. strangolare.

strangling s. strangolamento.

strap s. 1. cinghia, correggia 2. maniglia a pendaglio (su tram ecc.).

to strap vt. legare con cinghia.

stratagem s. stratagemma.

strategic(al) agg. strategico.

strategist s. stratega.

strategy s. strategia.

stratification s. stratificazione.

to stratify vt. stratificare.

stratosphere s. stratosfera.

stratospheric agg. stratosferico.

stratum s. (pl. -ta) 1. strato 2. strato sociale.

straw s. 1. paglia 2. fuscello, cannuccia || — (-hat), paglietta; —-colour, giallo paglierino.

strawberry s. fragola.

stray agg. 1. smarrito, randagio 2. casuale. ♦ **stray** s. animale domestico smarrito.

to stray vi. vagare, vagabondare (anche fig.).

streak s. 1. striscia, striatura 2. vena (anche fig.).

to streak vt. striare 2. venare.

stream s. 1. corso d'acqua, ruscello 2. flusso, fiotto 3. corrente (anche fig.).

to stream vi. 1. scorrere, fluire 2. ondeggiare || to — out, effondersi. ♦ **to stream** vt. far scorrere.

street s. via, strada || one-way —, strada a senso unico.

streetwalker s. passeggiatrice.

strength s. 1. forza, vigore 2. solidità, tenacia.

to strengthen vt. rafforzare, irrobustire. ♦ **to strengthen** vi. rafforzarsi, irrobustirsi.

strengthening agg. fortificante.

strenuous agg. strenuo, energico.

strenuously avv. strenuamente.

strenuousness s. vigore.

streptococcus s. (pl. -cci) streptococco.

streptomycin s. streptomicina.

stress s. 1. sforzo, pressione 2. enfasi 3. accento tonico.

to stress vt. 1. forzare 2. accentuare 3. porre in rilievo.

stretch s. 1. stiramento, tensione 2. spazio di tempo 3. distesa, estensione.

to stretch vt. tirare, tendere, stendere. ♦ **to stretch** vi. estendersi.

stretcher s. 1. tenditore 2. lettiga.

to strew (strewed, strewn) vt. spargere, sparpagliare.

strict agg. 1. preciso, esatto 2. (fig.) severo, rigido.

strictly avv. 1. esattamente 2. severamente.

stridden V. to stride.

stride s. passo lungo, andatura || to make great strides, avanzare a grandi passi.

to stride (strode, stridden) vi. camminare a grandi passi.

strident agg. stridente.

strife s. contesa, lotta.

strike s. 1. sciopero 2. scoperta (di giacimento) 3. attacco aereo.

to strike (struck, struck) vt. e vi. 1. battere, colpire 2. (fig.) impressionare, colpire 3. suonare le ore 4. accendere (un fiammifero) 5. scioperare || to — down, abbattere; to — in, frapporsi.

striker s. 1. scioperante 2. (mecc.) percussore.

striking agg. sorprendente.

string s. 1. spago, cordicella 2. laccio 3. (mus.) corda.

to string (strung, strung) vt. e vi. 1. legare con corde 2. accordare (uno strumento) || to — up, impiccare.

strip s. striscia, nastro.

to strip vt. svestire. ♦ **to strip** vi. svestirsi.

stripe s. striscia, lista.

to stripe vt. rigare, listare.

striped agg. a righe, a strisce.

to strive (strove, striven) vi. sforzarsi.

strode V. to stride.

stroke s. 1. colpo, percossa 2. movimento 3. bracciata (al nuoto), remata, battuta (al tennis) 4. tratto (di penna ecc.) 5. rintocco (d'orologio) 6. (med.) colpo 7. carezza.

to stroke¹ vi. vogare in cadenza.

to stroke² vt. accarezzare, lisciare.

stroll s. passeggiatina, quattro passi.

to stroll vi. gironzolare.

strolling agg. errante, girovago.

strong agg. forte, robusto, energico.

stronghold s. roccaforte.

strontium s. stronzio.

strove V. to strive.

struck V. to strike.

structural agg. strutturale.

structure s. 1. struttura 2. costruzione.

struggle s. 1. lotta, combattimento 2. sforzo || *hand-to-hand* —, lotta corpo a corpo.

to **struggle** vi. 1. lottare, divincolarsi 2. (*fig.*) sforzarsi.

struggler s. contendente, chi lotta.

to **strum** vt. e vi. strimpellare.

strumpet s. prostituta.

strung V. *to string*.

strut s. andatura solenne.

to **strut** vi. incedere con sussiego.

stub s. 1. ceppo 2. mozzicone.

stubble s. stoppia.

stubborn agg. ostinato, cocciuto, tenace, ribelle.

stubbornness s. caparbietà, tenacia.

to **stucco** vt. stuccare.

stuck V. *to stick*.

stud s. 1. chiodo a capocchia larga 2. bottoncino (*da camicia*).

to **stud** vt. guarnire di borchie.

student s. studente.

studentship s. borsa di studio.

studied agg. 1. studiato, ricercato 2. colto.

studio s. 1. studio (*d'artista*) 2. teatro di posa.

studious agg. studioso, diligente.

study s. 1. studio 2. esame attento, investigazione.

to **study** vt. e vi. 1. studiare 2. esaminare attentamente.

stuff s. 1. sostanza, materia prima 2. cosa, roba 3. stoffa, tessuto.

to **stuff** vt. 1. imbottire 2. (*cuc.*) farcire 3. rimpinzare.

stuffing s. 1. imbottitura 2. (*cuc.*) ripieno.

stuffy agg. afoso || — *air*, aria viziata.

to **stumble** vi. 1. inciampare 2. (*fig.*) fare passi falsi.

stump s. 1. ceppo, tronco 2. radice (*di dente*) 3. piattaforma, podio.

to **stun** vt. stordire, tramortire.

stung V. *to sting*.

stunk V. *to stink*.

stunt s. (*gergo*) 1. bravata, esibizione 2. trovata pubblicitaria, notizia sensazionale.

stupefaction s. 1. stupore 2. torpore provocato da stupefacenti.

to **stupefy** vt. 1. istupidire 2. abbrutire. ♦ to **stupefy** vi. 1. istupidirsi 2. abbrutirsi.

stupendous agg. splendido, stupendo.

stupid agg. stupido, ottuso.

stupidity s. stupidità.

stupidly avv. stupidamente.

sturdy agg. 1. vigoroso, forte 2. risoluto.

to **stutter** vt. e vi. balbettare.

stuttering s. balbuzie.

sty s. porcile.

style s. 1. stile (*anche fig.*) 2. modello, genere 3. moda.

to **style** vt. chiamare, denominare.

stylist s. stilista.

stylistic agg. stilistico.

stylization s. stilizzazione.

to **stylize** vt. stilizzare.

stylographic agg. stilografico.

stylus s. stilo.

subalpine agg. subalpino.

subaltern s. subalterno.

subaquatic agg. subacqueo.

subclass s. sottoclasse.

subcommission s. sottocommissione.

subcommissioner s. vice-commissario.

subcommittee s. sottocomitato.

subconscious agg. e s. subcosciente.

subcutaneous agg. sottocutaneo.

subdeacon s. suddiacono.

to **subdivide** vt. suddividere. ♦ to **subdivide** vi. suddividersi.

subdivisible agg. suddivisibile.

subdivision s. suddivisione.

subdual s. 1. soggiogamento 2. attenuazione.

to **subdue** vt. 1. conquistare, soggiogare 2. ridurre, attenuare.

subgovernor s. vicegovernatore.

subject[1] agg. 1. soggetto, assoggettato 2. sottoposto, esposto a.

subject[2] 1. argomento, materia di studio 2. (*gramm.*) soggetto 3. suddito.

to **subject** vt. 1. assoggettare 2. esporre.

subjection s. 1. assoggettamento 2. dipendenza.

subjective agg. soggettivo.

subjectivism s. soggettivismo.

subjunctive s. congiuntivo.

sublease s. subaffitto.

to **sublease** vt. subaffittare.

to **sublet (sublet, sublet)** vt. subaffittare.

sublieutenancy s. grado di sottotenente.

sublieutenant s. sottotenente.

sublimate agg. e s. sublimato.

to **sublimate** vt. sublimare.

sublime agg. e s. sublime.

sublimity s. sublimità.
submarine agg. subacqueo. ♦ **submarine** s. sommergibile.
submariner s. sommergibilista.
to **submerge** vt. immergere, sommergere. ♦ to **submerge** vi. immergersi.
submergence s. sommersione.
submersible agg. affondabile.
submersion s. immersione.
submission s. sottomissione, docilità.
submissive agg. remissivo, docile.
submissively avv. in modo remissivo.
submissiveness s. sottomissione.
to **submit** vt. sottomettere, sottoporre. ♦ to **submit** vi. sottomettersi, assoggettarsi.
submultiple agg. e s. sottomultiplo.
subnormal agg. al di sotto della norma.
subordinacy s. subordinazione.
subordinate agg. subordinato. ♦ **subordinate** s. subalterno, inferiore.
to **subordinate** vt. subordinare.
subordination s. subordinazione.
to **suborn** vt. subornare, corrompere.
subornation s. subornazione.
subplot s. trama secondaria.
to **subscribe** vt. e vi. **1.** sottoscrivere, firmare **2.** aderire, trovarsi d'accordo **3.** abbonarsi.
subscriber s. **1.** the —, il sottoscritto **2.** abbonato.
subscription s. **1.** sottoscrizione **2.** abbonamento **3.** consenso.
subsequence s. susseguenza.
subsequent agg. successivo, ulteriore.
subsequently avv. successivamente.
to **subside** vi. **1.** calare, decrescere **2.** quietarsi **3.** cadere (sul fondo), depositare (di liquidi).
subsidiary agg. sussidiario, supplementare, ausiliario.
to **subsidize** vt. sussidiare.
subsidy s. sussidio.
to **subsist** vt. e vi. sussistere.
subsistence s. esistenza, sussistenza.
subsistent agg. sussistente.
subsoil s. sottosuolo.
subspecies s. sottospecie.
substance s. **1.** sostanza, essenza **2.** contenuto, l'essenziale **3.** solidità, fondamento.
substantial agg. **1.** sostanzioso, so-

lido **2.** importante, notevole.
substantialism s. sostanzialismo.
substantiality s. **1.** sostanzialità **2.** concretezza.
substantially avv. sostanzialmente.
substantive agg. considerevole, reale. ♦ **substantive** s. (gramm.) sostantivo.
substitute s. **1.** sostituto **2.** surrogato, imitazione.
to **substitute** vt. e vi. sostituire.
substitution s. sostituzione.
substratum s. (pl. -ta) **1.** sostrato (anche fig.).
subtenancy s. subaffitto.
subtenant s. subaffittuario.
subterfuge s. sotterfugio.
subterranean agg. sotterraneo.
sub-title s. sottotitolo, didascalia.
subtle agg. **1.** penetrante, acuto, sottile **2.** elusivo, indefinibile.
subtleness s. **1.** sottigliezza, acutezza **2.** carattere elusivo.
subtlety s. sottigliezza.
subtly avv. **1.** acutamente, sottilmente **2.** elusivamente.
to **subtract** vt. sottrarre, detrarre.
subtraction s. sottrazione.
subtractive agg. sottrattivo.
subtrahend s. sottraendo.
suburb s. sobborgo. ♦ **suburbs** s. pl. periferia (sing.).
suburban agg. suburbano, periferico.
subversion s. sovversione.
subversive agg. sovversivo.
to **subvert** vt. sovvertire.
subway s. **1.** sottopassaggio **2.** (amer.) metropolitana.
to **succeed** vt. succedere a, seguire, subentrare a. ♦ to **succeed** vi. **1.** succedere, seguire **2.** riuscire, aver successo.
success s. successo, riuscita.
successful agg. che ha successo.
successfully avv. con successo.
succession s. successione, serie.
successive agg. successivo, seguente.
successively avv. successivamente.
successor s. successore.
succint agg. succinto, conciso.
succulent agg. succulento.
to **succumb** vi. soccombere, soggiacere.
succursal s. succursale.
such agg. tale, simile: — that, — as, tale che, tale da. ♦ **such** pron. tale, tali, questo, quello, questa,

quella, questi, quelli, queste, quelle.

suchlike *agg.* simile, dello stesso genere.

suck *s.* succhiata, poppata.

to suck *vt.* e *vi.* **1.** succhiare, poppare **2.** assorbire.

sucker *s.* **1.** (*mecc.*) pistone **2.** ventosa.

to suckle *vt.* allattare.

suckling *s.* lattante.

sudden *agg.* improvviso, inaspettato. ♦ **sudden** *s.* evento improvviso.

suddenly *avv.* inaspettatamente.

suddenness *s.* subitaneità.

to sue *vt.* e *vi.* **1.** ricorrere in giudizio **2.** sollecitare.

to suffer *vt.* e *vi.* **1.** subire, patire **2.** tollerare **3.** soffrire.

suffering *s.* **1.** sofferenza, pena **2.** tolleranza.

sufficiency *s.* sufficienza.

sufficient *agg.* sufficiente.

suffix *s.* (*gramm.*) suffisso.

to suffocate *vt.* e *vi.* soffocare.

suffocation *s.* soffocamento.

suffrage *s.* **1.** suffragio, diritto di voto **2.** preghiera.

to suffuse *vt.* coprire, cospargere.

sugar *s.* **1.** zucchero **2.** (*fig.*) atteggiamento mellifluo || — *-beet*, barbabietola da zucchero; — *-cane*, canna da zucchero; — *-tongs*, mollette per lo zucchero; *lump* —, zucchero in zollette.

to sugar *vt.* **1.** inzuccherare **2.** (*fig.*) addolcire, adulare.

sugariness *s.* **1.** dolcezza **2.** mellifluità.

sugary *agg.* **1.** zuccheroso, zuccherino **2.** (*fig.*) mellifluo.

to suggest *vt.* **1.** suggerire **2.** far nascere un'idea **3.** insinuare.

suggestible *agg.* suggeribile, suggestionabile.

suggestion *s.* **1.** suggerimento **2.** suggestione **3.** associazione di idee.

suggestive *agg.* stimolante, che ispira.

suggestiveness *s.* carattere allusivo.

suicidal *agg.* suicida, che ha tendenze al suicidio.

suicide *s.* **1.** suicidio **2.** suicida.

suit *s.* **1.** domanda, preghiera **2.** (*giur.*) causa **3.** abito completo (*da uomo*) || — *-case*, valigia.

to suit *vt.* adattare, convenire a, far comodo a. ♦ **to suit** *vi.* essere conveniente, accordarsi, adattarsi.

suitability *s.* convenienza.

suitable *agg.* adatto, idoneo.

suitably *avv.* appropriatamente.

suite *s.* **1.** seguito, corteo **2.** serie.

suitor *s.* **1.** postulante **2.** corteggiatore.

sulkiness *s.* malumore.

sulks *s. pl.* malumore, broncio (*sing.*).

sulky[1] *agg.* **1.** imbronciato, scontroso **2.** tetro.

sulky[2] *s.* "sulky", sediolo.

sullen *agg.* **1.** accigliato **2.** tetro.

sullenly *avv.* accigliato, di malumore.

sulphate *s.* solfato.

sulphide *s.* solfuro.

sulphite *s.* solfito.

sulphonamide *s.* sulfamidico.

sulphur *s.* zolfo || — *-mine* (*o* — *-pit*), solfatara.

to sulphur, to sulphurate *vt.* solforare.

sulphuric *agg.* solforico.

sulphurous *agg.* solforoso.

sultan *s.* sultano.

sultanate *s.* sultanato.

sultriness *s.* afa, caldo soffocante.

sultry *agg.* afoso, soffocante.

sum *s.* **1.** somma, quantità (*di denaro*) **2.** addizione.

to sum *vt.* e *vi.* sommare, addizionare || *to* — *up*, riassumere.

summarily *avv.* sommariamente.

to summarize *vt.* e *vi.* riassumere.

summary *s.* sommario, ricapitolazione.

summer *s.* estate.

to summer *vi.* trascorrere l'estate.

summertime *s.* stagione estiva.

summit *s.* **1.** cima, vetta **2.** (*fig.*) culmine || *at the* — (*pol.*), al vertice.

to summon *vt.* **1.** chiamare, mandare a chiamare **2.** convocare **3.** (*giur.*) citare.

summons *s.* **1.** (*giur.*) citazione, ingiunzione **2.** convocazione.

sumptuous *agg.* sontuoso.

sumptuously *avv.* sontuosamente.

sumptuousness *s.* sontuosità.

sun *s.* sole || — *-bath*, bagno di sole; — *-glasses*, occhiali da sole.

to sun *vt.* esporre al sole. ♦ **to sun** *vi.* esporsi al sole.

to sun-bathe *vi.* fare i bagni di sole.

sunbeam *s.* raggio di sole.

sunbow *s.* arcobaleno.

sunburn *s.* **1.** abbronzatura **2.** scottatura (solare).

sunburnt *agg.* **1.** abbronzato **2.** scottato dal sole.

sunburst *s.* sprazzo di sole.

Sunday *s.* domenica.

to **sunder** *vt.* separare, recidere. ◆ to **sunder** *vi.* separarsi, scindersi.

sundry *agg.* parecchi, vari.

sunflower *s.* girasole.

sung V. *to sing.*

sunk V. *to sink.*

sunlight *s.* luce del sole.

sunlit *agg.* soleggiato.

sunny *agg.* luminoso, soleggiato.

sunproof *agg.* inalterabile al sole.

sunrise *s.* il sorgere del sole.

sunset *s.* tramonto (*anche fig.*).

sunshade *s.* parasole.

sunshine *s.* luce del sole.

sunspot *s.* macchia solare.

sunstroke *s.* insolazione.

sun-worship *s.* culto del Sole.

sup *s.* sorso, goccia.

to **sup**¹ *vt. e vi.* sorseggiare.

to **sup**² *vi.* cenare.

superable *agg.* superabile.

to **superabound** *vi.* sovrabbondare.

superabundance *s.* sovrabbondanza.

superabundant *agg.* sovrabbondante.

superb *agg.* superbo, magnifico.

superciliary *agg.* sopracciliare.

supercilious *agg.* altero.

superelevation *s.* sopraelevazione.

superficial *agg.* superficiale, poco profondo.

superficiality *s.* superficialità.

superfluous *agg.* superfluo.

superhuman *agg.* sovrumano.

to **superimpose** *vt.* sovrapporre.

superintendence *s.* sovrintendenza.

superintendent *s.* sovrintendente.

superior *agg.* superiore.

superiority *s.* superiorità.

superlative *agg.* superlativo.

superman *s.* superuomo.

supermarket *s.* supermercato.

supermundane *agg.* ultraterreno.

supernatural *agg.* soprannaturale.

supernutrition *s.* supernutrizione.

to **supersede** *vt.* rimpiazzare.

supersensitive *agg.* ipersensibile.

supersensitiveness *s.* ipersensibilità.

supersession *s.* sostituzione.

supersonic *agg.* ultrasonoro, supersonico.

superstition *s.* superstizione.

superstitious *agg.* superstizioso.

superstructure *s.* sovrastruttura.

supertax *s.* soprattassa.

superterrestrial *agg.* ultraterreno.

to **supervise** *vt. e vi.* sovrintendere.

supervision *s.* sorveglianza, sovrintendenza.

supervisor *s.* sovrintendente.

supervisory *agg.* di controllo.

supine *agg.* supino (*anche fig.*).

supinely *avv.* supinamente.

supper *s.* cena || *to have —,* cenare; *— -time,* ora di cena.

to **supplant** *vt.* soppiantare.

supple *agg.* **1.** pieghevole, flessibile **2.** elastico (*anche fig.*).

supplement *s.* supplemento.

supplementary *agg.* supplementare.

suppliant *agg.* supplichevole. ◆ **suppliant** *s.* supplicante.

supply *s.* **1.** rifornimento, approvvigionamento **2.** (*comm.*) fornitura **3.** sostituto, supplente.

to **supply** *vt.* fornire, rifornire. ◆ to **supply** *vi.* fare da sostituto.

support *s.* sostegno, appoggio || *in — of,* in favore di.

to **support** *vt.* **1.** sostenere, reggere **2.** dare appoggio a **3.** mantenere.

supportable *agg.* sostenibile, sopportabile.

supporter *s.* **1.** sostegno **2.** fautore, sostenitore.

to **suppose** *vt.* supporre, presupporre, presumere.

supposed *agg.* presunto, supposto.

supposition *s.* supposizione, ipotesi.

suppository *s.* (*med.*) supposta.

to **suppress** *vt.* **1.** sopprimere, reprimere **2.** (*fig.*) soffocare, trattenere.

suppression *s.* **1.** soppressione **2.** il mettere a tacere.

to **suppurate** *vi.* suppurare.

suppuration *s.* suppurazione.

suprarenal *agg.* surrenale.

supremacy *s.* supremazia.

supreme *agg.* sommo, supremo.

surcharge *s.* **1.** sovraccarico **2.** soprattassa **3.** sovrapprezzo.

sure *agg.* sicuro, certo, fidato.

surely *avv.* sicuramente, certamente.

surety *s.* garanzia, pegno.

suretyship *s.* garanzia.

surf *s.* **1.** risacca **2.** spuma dei marosi.

surface *s.* superficie (*anche fig.*).

surfeit *s.* **1.** eccesso **2.** sazietà. ◆ to **surfeit** *vt.* saziare. ◆ to **sur-**

feit *vi.* saziarsi.

surge *s.* **1.** maroso, cavallone **2.** (*fig.*) impeto.

to **surge** *vi.* gonfiarsi, sollevarsi, tumultuare.

surgeon *s.* chirurgo.

surgery *s.* chirurgia.

surgical *agg.* chirurgico.

surlily *avv.* sgarbatamente.

surly *agg.* sgarbato.

to **surmount** *vt.* sormontare, superare.

surname *s.* **1.** cognome **2.** soprannome.

to **surname** *vt.* soprannominare.

to **surpass** *vt.* sorpassare, superare.

surpassing *agg.* superiore, eccellente.

surpassingly *avv.* straordinariamente.

surplus *s.* **1.** sovrappiù, eccedenza **2.** residuati di guerra.

surprise *s.* **1.** sorpresa **2.** stupore, meraviglia.

to **surprise** *vt.* **1.** sorprendere, cogliere all'improvviso **2.** stupire.

surprisedly *avv.* con sorpresa.

surprising *agg.* sorprendente.

surrealism *s.* surrealismo.

surrealist *agg.* e *s.* surrealista.

surrender *s.* **1.** resa, capitolazione **2.** abbandono, cessione.

to **surrender** *vt.* cedere, consegnare. ♦ to **surrender** *vi.* arrendersi.

surreptitious *agg.* clandestino, furtivo.

surrogate *s.* sostituto, supplente.

surround *s.* bordura, bordo.

to **surround** *vt.* **1.** circondare **2.** accerchiare.

surrounding *agg.* circostante. ♦ **surroundings** *s. pl.* dintorni.

survey *s.* esame, sguardo generale.

to **survey** *vt.* e *vi.* esaminare, fare rivelazioni.

surveyor *s.* ispettore.

survival *s.* **1.** sopravvivenza **2.** avanzo, reliquia.

to **survive** *vi.* sopravvivere. ♦ to **survive** *vt.* vivere più a lungo di.

survivor *s.* superstite.

susceptibility *s.* suscettibilità.

susceptible *agg.* **1.** suscettibile **2.** impressionabile.

suspect *agg.* sospetto. ♦ **suspect** *s.* persona sospetta.

to **suspect** *vt.* sospettare. ♦ to **suspect** *vi.* essere sospettoso.

to **suspend** *vt.* **1.** appendere, tenere

sospeso **2.** sospendere.

suspender *s.* giarrettiera, bretella.

suspense *s.* incertezza, attesa ansiosa.

suspension *s.* sospensione.

suspensive *agg.* sospensivo.

suspicion *s.* sospetto, dubbio.

suspicious *agg.* sospettoso, diffidente.

suspiciously *avv.* sospettosamente.

to **sustain** *vt.* **1.** mantenere, sostenere **2.** prolungare **3.** reggere.

sustainable *agg.* sostenibile.

sustenance *s.* mezzi di sussistenza (*pl.*).

suture *s.* sutura.

to **suture** *vt.* suturare.

swab *s.* **1.** strofinaccio **2.** (*mar.*) radazza **3.** (*med.*) tampone.

to **swab** *vt.* pulire, strofinare.

swag *s.* movimento ondeggiante.

swagger *agg.* sgargiante.

to **swagger** *vi.* **1.** pavoneggiarsi **2.** gloriarsi.

swallow[1] *s.* rondine.

swallow[2] *s.* **1.** baratro **2.** deglutizione.

to **swallow** *vt.* e *vi.* **1.** deglutire, inghiottire **2.** (*fig.*) ingoiare.

swam V. *to swim*.

swamp *s.* palude || — -*fever,* febbre malarica.

to **swamp** *vt.* inondare, inzuppare. ♦ to **swamp** *vi.* affondare (*anche fig.*).

swan *s.* cigno || — *song,* canto del cigno.

swarm *s.* sciame, folla.

to **swarm** *vi.* **1.** sciamare **2.** pullulare, brulicare, essere affollato.

swash *s.* **1.** sciacquio **2.** gradassata.

to **swash** *vi.* **1.** spruzzare, sguazzare **2.** turbinare, infrangersi. ♦ to **swash** *vt.* far sguazzare.

to **swat** *vt.* colpire, schiacciare (*mosche ecc.*).

swathe *s.* benda, fascia.

to **swathe** *vt.* bendare, fasciare.

sway *s.* **1.** oscillazione **2.** potere, potenza, preponderanza.

to **sway** *vt.* **1.** sballottolare **2.** dominare, influenzare **3.** maneggiare, impugnare **4.** (*mar.*) issare. ♦ to **sway** *vi.* **1.** ondeggiare **2.** propendere **3.** predominare.

swear *s.* bestemmia, imprecazione.

to **swear (swore, sworn)** *vt.* e *vi.* **1.** giurare, far giurare **2.** imprecare, bestemmiare.

sweat s. sudore, traspirazione.

to sweat vt. e vi. traspirare, sudare, sfacchinare.

sweater s. **1.** chi suda **2.** maglione di lana.

sweating s. sudore || — -bath, bagno turco.

sweaty agg. **1.** sudato **2.** che fa sudare.

Swede s. svedese.

Swedish agg. svedese.

sweep s. **1.** scopata **2.** movimento circolare **3.** curva, distesa.

to sweep (swept, swept) vi. **1.** spazzare, scopare **2.** muoversi rapidamente **3.** estendersi. ♦ **to sweep (swept, swept)** vt. **1.** spazzare **2.** sfiorare.

sweeping agg. **1.** vasto **2.** completo **3.** rapido, impetuoso (di corrente). ♦ **sweepings** s. pl. rifiuti.

sweet agg. **1.** dolce, amabile **2.** piacevole, gentile. ♦ **sweet** s. **1.** dolce, torta **2.** caramella.

to sweeten vt. **1.** zuccherare **2.** addolcire. ♦ **to sweeten** vi. addolcirsi.

sweetening s. **1.** addolcimento **2.** sostanza che addolcisce.

sweetheart s. innamorato.

sweetly avv. dolcemente.

sweetmeat s. dolciumi, frutta candita.

sweetness s. **1.** sapore dolce **2.** dolcezza, amabilità.

swell s. **1.** rigonfiamento **2.** il gonfiarsi (dell'acqua ecc.).

to swell (swelled, swollen) vi. **1.** gonfiarsi **2.** crescere, aumentare. ♦ **to swell (swelled, swollen)** vt. gonfiare.

swelling s. rigonfiamento, ingrossamento.

swept V. to sweep.

to swerve vt. deviare. ♦ **to swerve** vi. fare uno scarto.

swift agg. rapido, veloce.

swim s. nuotata.

to swim (swam, swum) vi. nuotare. ♦ **to swim (swam, swum)** vt. attraversare a nuoto.

swimmer s. nuotatore.

swimming s. nuoto || — -belt, salvagente; — -pool, piscina.

swindle s. truffa, frode.

to swindle vt. e vi. truffare.

swindler s. truffatore.

swine s. maiale, porco || — -herd, porcaro.

swing s. **1.** oscillazione **2.** libertà d'azione **3.** altalena.

to swing (swung, swung) vt. **1.** dondolare, oscillare **2.** ruotare **3.** camminare dondolandosi. ♦ **to swing (swung, swung)** vt. **1.** far dondolare **2.** far ruotare.

swinging s. dondolio.

swish s. **1.** sibilo **2.** sferzata.

Swiss agg. svizzero.

switch s. **1.** verga, frustino **2.** (elett.) interruttore.

to switch vt. e vi. **1.** colpire con un frustino **2.** muovere bruscamente **3.** (ferr.) smistare || to — off, spegnere (la luce); to — on, accendere (la luce).

swollen V. to swell.

swoon s. svenimento.

to swoon vi. svenire.

to swoop vi. calare improvvisamente, abbattersi.

sword s. spada.

swore V. to swear.

sworn V. to swear.

swum V. to swim.

swung V. to swing.

sycamore s. sicomoro.

syllable s. sillaba.

syllogism s. sillogismo.

syllogistic agg. sillogistico.

to syllogize vt. e vi. sillogizzare.

sylph s. silfo, silfide.

sylvan agg. silvano, silvestre.

symbiosis s. simbiosi.

symbol s. simbolo.

symbolic(al) agg. simbolico.

symbolism s. simbolismo.

to symbolize vt. simboleggiare.

symmetric(al) agg. simmetrico.

symmetry s. simmetria.

sympathetic agg. **1.** sensibile, comprensivo **2.** congeniale, adatto.

to sympathize vi. condividere i sentimenti altrui.

sympathizer s. **1.** chi è comprensivo **2.** simpatizzante (di un partito ecc.).

sympathy s. **1.** comprensione, partecipazione **2.** condoglianze (pl.).

symphonic agg. sinfonico.

symphony s. sinfonia.

symposium s. simposio, banchetto.

symptom s. sintomo.

symptomatic(al) agg. sintomatico.

synagogue s. sinagoga.

synchronism s. sincronismo.

synchronization s. sincronizzazione.

to **synchronize** *vt.* e *vi.* sincronizzare.

to **syncopate** *vt.* sincopare.

syncope *s.* sincope.

syndicalism *s.* sindacalismo.

syndicate *s.* sindacato.

synod *s.* sinodo.

synonym *s.* sinonimo.

synonymous *agg.* sinonimo.

synonymy *s.* sinonimia.

synovitis *s.* sinovite.

syntactic(al) *agg.* sintattico.

syntax *s.* sintassi.

synthesis *s.* (*pl.* -ses) sintesi.

to **synthesize** *vt.* sintetizzare.

synthetic(al) *agg.* sintetico.

syntony *s.* sintonia.

syphilis *s.* sifilide.

syphilitic *agg.* sifilitico.

Syrian *agg.* e *s.* siriano.

syringe *s.* siringa.

syrup *s.* sciroppo.

syrupy *agg.* sciropposo.

system *s.* **1.** sistema **2.** metodo || *railway* —, rete ferroviaria.

systematic(al) *agg.* sistematico, metodico.

systematically *avv.* sistematicamente, metodicamente.

systematization *s.* sistemazione.

to **systematize** *vt.* ridurre a sistema.

T

tab *s.* **1.** linguetta (*di scarpa*) **2.** (*mil.*) mostrina **3.** talloncino.

tabernacle *s.* **1.** tabernacolo **2.** tempio.

table *s.* **1.** tavola **2.** tavolata **3.** tabella || —*cloth*, tovaglia; *time*—, orario.

tablet *s.* **1.** tavoletta **2.** pastiglia. compressa.

tabloid *s.* pasticca.

taboo *agg.* e *s.* tabù.

tabular *agg.* **1.** a forma di tabella **2.** catalogato **3.** piano, piatto.

tabulate *agg.* piano.

to **tabulate** *vt.* disporre in tabelle.

tabulation *s.* classificazione.

tabulator *s.* tabulatore.

tachometer *s.* tachimetro.

tachycardia *s.* tachicardia.

tacit *agg.* tacito.

taciturn *agg.* taciturno.

tack *s.* **1.** chiodo **2.** imbastitura **3.** bordata **4.** (*fig.*) linea di condotta.

to **tack** *vt.* **1.** inchiodare **2.** imbastire. ◆ to **tack** *vi.* **1.** bordeggiare **2.** virare.

tacking *s.* **1.** l'inchiodare **2.** imbastitura **3.** bordeggio.

tackle *s.* **1.** arnesi (*pl.*) **2.** (*mar.*) paranco.

to **tackle** *vt.* **1.** afferrare **2.** affrontare (*difficoltà ecc.*).

tacky *agg.* viscoso.

tact *s.* tatto.

tactful *agg.* pieno di tatto.

tactical *agg.* tattico.

tactician *s.* tattico.

tactics *s.* tattica.

tactile *agg.* **1.** tattile **2.** tangibile.

tactility *s.* **1.** tattilità **2.** tangibilità.

tactless *agg.* senza tatto.

tactlessness *s.* mancanza di tatto.

tactual *agg.* tattile.

tadpole *s.* (*zool.*) girino.

tag *s.* **1.** lembo pendente **2.** cartellino **3.** aggiunta **4.** luogo comune || *licence* —, bollo di circolazione.

to **tag** *vt.* mettere cartellini a.

tail *s.* coda || — -*coat*, marsina.

to **tail** *vt.* munire di coda. ◆ to **tail** *vi.* **1.** essere in coda **2.** seguire da presso || *to* — *away*, affievolirsi.

tailor *s.* sarto || — -*made costume*, tailleur.

to **tailor** *vi.* fare il sarto. ◆ to **tailor** *vt.* fare un abito.

taint *s.* **1.** infezione **2.** tara **3.** marchio.

to **taint** *vt.* guastare. ◆ to **taint** *vi.* guastarsi.

taintless *agg.* incontaminato.

take *s.* **1.** presa **2.** incasso **3.** (*cine*) ripresa.

to **take** (**took, taken**) *vt.* **1.** prendere **2.** portare **3.** accompagnare **4.** necessitare || *to* — *after*, assomigliare; *to* — *in*, ricevere, ridurre, capire; *to* — *off*, togliere, decollare; *to* — *on*, assumere; *to* — *to*, darsi a.

take-off *s.* (*aer.*) decollo.

taking *agg.* **1.** attraente **2.** contagioso. ◆ **taking** *s.* **1.** presa **2.** incasso.

talc(um) *s.* talco || *talcum powder*, talco in polvere.

tale s. racconto, storia, novella.
talent s. talento.
talented agg. che ha talento.
talentless agg. senza talento.
tales s. pl. (giur.) giudici supplenti.
talisman s. talismano.
talk s. 1. conversazione 2. chiacchiera.
to talk vt. e vi. parlare, conversare, discutere || to — out, discutere a fondo.
talkative agg. loquace.
talkativeness s. loquacità.
talker s. 1. parlatore 2. chiacchierone.
talkies s. pl. (gergo) film sonoro (sing.).
talking s. conversazione.
talky agg. loquace.
tall agg. 1. alto 2. incredibile.
tallness s. altezza, statura.
tallow s. sego.
tally s. 1. tacca 2. cartellino, talloncino, etichetta.
to tally vt. registrare. ♦ **to tally** vi. combaciare.
tallyshop s. negozio che vende a rate.
talon s. 1. artiglio 2. (mecc.) dente 3. (comm.) matrice.
tamarind s. tamarindo.
tambourine s. tamburello.
tame agg. 1. addomesticato 2. mansueto 3. insipido, banale.
to tame vt. domare, addomesticare. ♦ **to tame** vi. ammansirsi.
tameable agg. addomesticabile.
tameless agg. indomito.
tamely avv. docilmente.
tameness s. 1. docilità 2. banalità.
tamer s. domatore.
taming s. addomesticamento.
to tamp vt. pigiare.
tamper s. pestello.
to tamper vi. 1. manomettere 2. immischiarsi: to — with, immischiarsi in 3. corrompere.
tamperer s. 1. falsificatore 2. corruttore 3. ficcanaso.
tampering s. 1. manomissione 2. corruzione.
tampon s. tampone.
tan agg. marrone rossiccio. ♦ **tan** s. 1. tannino 2. concia 3. abbronzatura.
to tan vt. 1. conciare 2. abbronzare. ♦ **to tan** vi. abbronzarsi.
tanning s. abbronzatura.

tang¹ s. 1. punta 2. odore, sapore penetrante.
tang² s. suono acuto.
to tang vt. far risuonare. ♦ **to tang** vi. risuonare.
tangency s. tangenza.
tangent agg. e s. tangente.
tangential agg. tangenziale.
tangerine s. mandarino.
tangibility s. tangibilità.
tangible agg. tangibile.
tangle s. groviglio.
to tangle vt. 1. aggrovigliare 2. intrappolare. ♦ **to tangle** vi. aggrovigliarsi.
tanglesome, tangly agg. ingarbugliato.
tank s. 1. serbatoio, cisterna 2. carro armato || — -truck, autobotte.
tankard s. boccale.
tanker s. nave cisterna || air —, aerocisterna; oil —, petroliera.
tanner s. conciatore.
tannery s. conceria.
tannin s. tannino.
tanning s. concia.
to tantalize vt. tormentare.
tantalizing agg. allettante.
tantamount agg. equivalente.
tap¹ rubinetto, spina.
tap² s. colpetto.
to tap¹ vt. 1. spillare 2. forare.
to tap² vt. battere leggermente.
tape s. nastro || — -recorder, magnetofono; recording —, nastro magnetico.
to tape vt. 1. legare con un nastro 2. misurare con un nastro 3. incidere su nastro magnetico.
taper agg. conico, rastremato ♦ **taper** s. 1. candela 2. conicità, rastremazione.
to taper vt. assottigliare. ♦ **to taper** vi. assottigliarsi, restringersi.
tapestry s. arazzo.
tapeworm s. tenia.
tapir s. tapiro.
tar s. catrame.
to tar vt. incatramare.
tardiness s. 1. lentezza 2. indolenza.
tardy agg. 1. lento 2. svogliato.
tare s. tara.
target s. bersaglio.
tariff s. tariffa.
tarnish s. 1. appannamento 2. macchia.
to tarnish vi. 1. appannarsi 2. macchiarsi. ♦ **to tarnish** vt. 1. mac-

chiare **2.** inquinare.
tarpaulin s. telone impermeabile.
tarry agg. **1.** catramato **2.** simile a c^trame.
to **tarry** vi. indugiare.
tart agg. aspro.
tart s. torta di frutta, crostata.
tartan[1] s. tessuto scozzese.
tartan[2] s. (mar.) tartana.
tartar agg. e s. tartaro.
tartaric agg. tartarico.
tartlet s. pasticcino.
tartly avv. in modo acido.
task s. compito, dovere, impresa.
to **task** vt. **1.** assegnare un compito a **2.** affaticare.
task-work s. lavoro a cottimo.
tassel s. **1.** nappa **2.** segnalibro.
to **tassel** vt. adornare di nappe.
taste s. **1.** gusto **2.** assaggio.
to **taste** vt. **1.** gustare **2.** assaggiare. ♦ to **taste** vi. sapere di.
tasteful agg. raffinato.
tastefulness s. buon gusto.
tasteless agg. **1.** insipido **2.** di cattivo gusto.
tastelessness s. **1.** scipitezza **2.** mancanza di gusto.
taster s. assaggiatore.
tasty agg. **1.** saporito **2.** (gergo) di buon gusto.
tatter s. cencio.
to **tatter** vt. stracciare. ♦ to **tatter** vi. cadere a pezzi.
tattery agg. stracciato.
tattle s. chiacchiera.
to **tattle** vi. chiacchierare.
tattler s. chiacchierone.
tattoo[1] s. tatuaggio.
tattoo[2] s. (mil.) **1.** ritirata **2.** carosello militare.
to **tattoo**[1] vt. tatuare.
to **tattoo**[2] vi. tamburellare.
taught V. to **teach**.
taunt s. sarcasmo.
to **taunt** vt. **1.** rimproverare **2.** schernire.
taunting agg. beffardo. ♦ **taunting** s. rimprovero sarcastico.
taut agg. **1.** teso **2.** in ordine.
to **tauten** vt. tendere. ♦ to **tauten** vi. tendersi.
tautness s. tensione.
tautologic(al) agg. tautologico.
tautology s. tautologia.
tavern s. taverna || — -keeper, oste.
taw s. biglia.
tawdry agg. sgargiante.
tawny agg. bruno fulvo.

tax s. **1.** tassa **2.** peso || — -payer, contribuente.
to **tax** vt. **1.** tassare **2.** accusare.
taxability s. tassabilità.
taxable agg. tassabile.
taxation s. tassazione.
taxi s. tassì || — -driver, tassista; (aer.) — track, pista di rullaggio.
to **taxi** vi. (aer.) rullare.
taxicab s. autopubblica.
taximeter s. tassametro.
tea s. tè || — -pot, teiera; high —, cena fredda; — -set, servizio da tè.
to **teach (taught, taught)** vt. insegnare.
teachable agg. **1.** che apprende facilmente **2.** che si insegna facilmente.
teacher s. insegnante.
teachership s. insegnamento.
teaching agg. che insegna. ♦ **teaching** s. insegnamento.
teacup s. tazza da tè.
team s. **1.** squadra **2.** tiro (di cavalli).
to **team** vt. aggiogare, accoppiarsi, raggrupparsi. ♦ to **team** vi. accoppiarsi, associarsi.
tear[1] s. **1.** lacrima **2.** goccia || — -gas, gas lacrimogeno.
tear[2] s. strappo, lacerazione.
to **tear (tore, torn)** vt. strappare, lacerare. ♦ to **tear (tore, torn)** vi. strapparsi.
tearful agg. lacrimoso.
tearing agg. violento. ♦ **tearing** s. strappo, lacerazione.
tear-off s. parte da staccare.
tease s. chi stuzzica.
to **tease** vt. **1.** stuzzicare **2.** cardare (lana ecc.).
teaser s. **1.** seccatore **2.** cardatore **3.** questione difficile.
teaspoon s. cucchiaino da tè.
technical agg. tecnico.
technicality s. tecnicismo.
technician s. tecnico.
technique s. tecnica.
technological agg. tecnologico.
technology s. tecnologia.
tectonics s. **1.** edilizia **2.** tettonica.
tedious agg. tedioso.
tediousness s. tedio.
to **teem** vi. brulicare.
teen-ager s. adolescente.
teens s. pl. età da tredici a diciannove anni.
teeth V. **tooth**.
teething s. dentizione.

teetotal(l)er s. astemio.

telecast s. teletrasmissione || — *news*, telegiornale.

to **telecast** (telecast, telecast) vt. teletrasmettere.

telecommunication s. telecomunicazione.

telecontrol s. telecomando.

telegram s. telegramma.

telegraph s. telegrafo.

to **telegraph** vt. e vi. telegrafare.

telegraphic agg. telegrafico.

telegraphist s. telegrafista.

telegraphy s. telegrafia.

telemeter s. telemetro.

telepathy s. telepatia.

telephone s. telefono || — *booth*, cabina telefonica; — *-book*, elenco telefonico.

to **telephone** vt. e vi. telefonare.

telephonist s. telefonista.

telephony s. telefonia.

telephoto s. telefoto.

telephotograph s. telefotografia.

telescope s. telescopio.

to **telescope** vi. incastrarsi.

teletype s. telescrivente.

teletyper s. telescriventista.

teletypewriter s. telescrivente.

to **teleview** vt. e vi. guardare la televisione.

televiewer s. telespettatore.

to **televise** vt. riprendere con la televisione.

television s. televisione || — *set*, televisore.

televisional agg. televisivo.

to **tell** (told, told) vt. e vi. **1.** dire **2.** raccontare **3.** distinguere.

teller s. **1.** narratore **2.** (*comm.*) cassiere.

telling agg. efficace. ♦ **telling** s. **1.** il raccontare **2.** rivelazione.

telltale s. **1.** chiacchierone **2.** (*tec.*) controllore.

telluric agg. tellurico.

telpher s. cabina di funivia.

telpherage s. trasporto per teleferica.

temper s. **1.** indole **2.** umore **3.** collera **4.** moderazione.

to **temper** vt. temperare.

temperament s. temperamento.

temperamental agg. capriccioso.

temperance s. temperanza.

temperate agg. **1.** temperato (*di clima*) **2.** moderato.

temperature s. temperatura || *to have a* —, avere la febbre.

tempered agg. **1.** temprato **2.** moderato **3.** di indole, umore || *quick* —, irritabile.

tempest s. tempesta.

temple[1] s. tempio.

temple[2] s. (*anat.*) tempia.

temporal agg. temporale.

temporariness s. temporaneità.

temporary agg. temporaneo.

temporization s. temporeggiamento.

to **temporize** vi. temporeggiare.

to **tempt** vt. tentare.

temptation s. tentazione.

tempter s. tentatore.

tempting agg. seducente.

ten agg. e s. dieci.

tenacious agg. **1.** tenace **2.** viscoso.

tenacity s. tenacia.

tenancy s. locazione.

tenant s. **1.** proprietario **2.** locatario.

to **tend**[1] vt. curare, badare a, custodire.

to **tend**[2] vi. tendere.

tendency s. tendenza.

tendential, tendentious agg. tendenzioso.

tender[1] agg. tenero || — *of*, sollecito verso.

tender[2] s. **1.** guardiano, custode **2.** nave di appoggio.

tender[3] s. offerta, proposta.

to **tender** vt. offrire, presentare.

tenderness s. **1.** tenerezza **2.** delicatezza.

tendon s. (*anat.*) tendine.

tendril s. viticcio.

tenebrous agg. tenebroso.

tenement s. **1.** podere **2.** abitazione.

tenor s. **1.** tenore (*di vita ecc.*) **2.** (*giur.*) copia esatta **3.** (*mus.*) tenore.

tense[1] agg. teso.

tense[2] s. (*gramm.*) tempo.

to **tense** vt. tendere. ♦ to **tense** vi. tendersi.

tension s. tensione.

tent s. tenda.

tentacle s. tentacolo.

tentative agg. sperimentale. ♦ **tentative** s. tentativo, prova.

tenth agg. e s. decimo.

tenuity s. **1.** tenuità **2.** rarefazione **3.** fluidità.

tenuous agg. **1.** tenue **2.** rarefatto **3.** fluido.

tenure s. **1.** possesso **2.** gestione.

tepid agg. tiepido.
tepidity s. tepidezza.
tercet s. terzina.
tergal agg. dorsale.
to **tergiversate** vi. tergiversare.
tergiversation s. tergiversazione.
term s. 1. termine 2. (scol.) trimestre 3. (giur.) sessione 4. condizione. ♦ **terms** s. pl. rapporti.
to **term** vt. definire.
terminable agg. terminabile.
terminal agg. estremo. ♦ **terminal** s. 1. estremità 2. stazione di testa, capolinea 3. (elettr.) morsetto.
to **terminate** vt. 1. limitare 2. terminare. ♦ to **terminate** vi. 1. essere limitato 2. terminare.
termination s. 1. termine 2. (gramm.) desinenza.
terminator s. 1. chi termina 2. limite.
terminology s. terminologia.
terminus s. (pl. -ni) 1. capolinea 2. meta.
termite s. (zool.) termite.
tern s. terno.
ternary agg. ternario.
terrace s. 1. terrapieno 2. terrazzo (sul tetto) 3. fila di case.
terraqueous agg. terracqueo.
terrestrial agg. e s. terrestre.
terrible agg. terribile.
terrific agg. 1. spaventoso 2. (fam.) straordinario.
to **terrify** vt. atterrire.
territorial agg. territoriale.
territory s. territorio.
terror s. terrore.
terrorism s. terrorismo.
terrorist s. terrorista.
terroristic agg. terroristico.
to **terrorize** vt. terrorizzare.
terse agg. conciso.
terseness s. concisione.
tertiary agg. e s. terziario.
test s. 1. prova, esperimento, saggio 2. "test", reattivo psicologico || — driver, collaudatore; — film, provino; — -tube, provetta.
to **test** vt. 1. controllare 2. mettere alla prova 3. analizzare.
testament s. testamento.
testamentary agg. testamentario.
tester s. 1. collaudatore 2. apparecchio di misura 3. baldacchino.
testicle s. testicolo.
to **testify** vt. e vi. testimoniare.
testimonial s. 1. benservito 2. dono.
testimony s. testimonianza.

testing s. collaudo, prova.
tetanic(al) agg. tetanico.
tetanus s. tetano.
tetchy agg. stizzoso.
tetrahedron s. tetraedro.
tetralogy s. tetralogia.
Teutonic agg. teutonico.
text s. 1. testo 2. argomento.
textile agg. e s. tessile.
textual agg. testuale.
texture s. trama, tessuto.
thallium s. tallio.
than cong. che, di, di quello che (non), di quanto (non): he is older — you, è più vecchio di te.
to **thank** vt. ringraziare || — you!, grazie!
thankful agg. riconoscente.
thankfulness s. riconoscenza.
thankless agg. ingrato.
thanks s. pl. grazie, ringraziamenti.
thanksgiving s. ringraziamento.
that agg. (pl. those) quello, quella. ♦ **that** pron. dimostr. quello, questo, ciò. ♦ **that** pron. rel. che, il quale, la quale, i quali, le quali.
that cong. 1. che 2. affinché 3. purché.
thatch s. copertura di paglia (per tetti).
to **thatch** vt. coprire con paglia.
thaumaturge s. taumaturgo.
thaumaturgic(al) agg. taumaturgico.
thaw s. sgelo, disgelo.
to **thaw** vt. sgelare. ♦ to **thaw** vi. sgelarsi.
the art. il, lo, la, i, gli, le.
theatre s. teatro.
theatrical agg. teatrale.
theft s. furto.
their agg. poss. loro.
theirs pron. poss. il, la loro; i, le loro.
theism s. teismo.
them pron. loro, li, le, sé.
thematic agg. tematico.
theme s. tema.
themselves pron. r. 1. se stessi, se stesse, sé, si 2. essi stessi, esse stesse.
then avv. 1. allora 2. poi.
theocracy s. teocrazia.
theocratic(al) agg. teocratico.
theologian s. teologo.
theologic(al) agg. teologico.
theology s. teologia.
theorem s. teorema.

theoretic(al) *agg.* teorico.

theoretics *s.* teoretica.

theorist *s.* teorico.

to **theorize** *vi.* teorizzare.

theory *s.* teoria.

therapeutic(al) *agg.* terapeutico.

therapeutics *s.* terapeutica.

therapy *s.* terapia.

there *avv.* **1.** là, lì **2.** ci, vi **3.** in ciò. ♦ **there** *inter.* ecco! su!

thereabout(s) *avv.* **1.** là vicino **2.** all'incirca.

thereby *avv.* per mezzo di, perciò.

therefore *avv.* quindi, dunque.

thereupon *avv.* al che, tosto.

thermal *agg.* termico, termale.

thermic *agg.* termico.

thermionic *agg.* termoionico.

thermodynamics *s.* termodinamica.

thermoelectric *agg.* termoelettrico.

thermometer *s.* termometro.

thermonuclear *agg.* termonucleare.

thermostat *s.* termostato.

these (*pl. di* this), questi, queste.

thesis *s.* (*pl.* -ses) tesi, dissertazione.

thews *s. pl.* muscoli.

they *pron. pers.* **1.** essi, esse, loro **2.** (*in costruzioni impersonali*) si: — *say,* si dice.

thick *agg.* **1.** spesso, grosso: *a — book,* un grosso libro **2.** fitto, folto **3.** denso, torbido.

to **thicken** *vt.* ispessire, addensare. ♦ to **thicken** *vi.* ispessirsi, addensarsi.

thickening *s.* ispessimento.

thicket *s.* boschetto.

thickly *avv.* fittamente, densamente.

thickness *s.* **1.** spessore, grossezza **2.** densità **3.** strato.

thickset *agg.* **1.** fitto, spesso **2.** tarchiato.

thief *s.* (*pl.* thieves) ladro.

to **thieve** *vt.* e *vi.* rubare, essere ladro.

thievish *agg.* ladresco.

thigh *s.* coscia || — *bone,* femore.

thimble *s.* ditale.

thin *agg.* **1.** sottile **2.** magro, snello **3.** rado, raro **4.** fluido, rarefatto **5.** debole, fiacco.

to **thin** *vt.* e *vi.* **1.** assottigliare, assottigliarsi, dimagrire **2.** diradare, sfoltire. ♦ to **thin** *vt.* **1.** assottigliare **2.** diradare, sfoltire. ♦ to **thin** *vi.* **1.** assottigliarsi **2.** diradarsi.

thing *s.* **1.** cosa, oggetto **2.** argomento, soggetto.

to **think** (**thought, thought**) *vt.* e *vi.* **1.** pensare, riflettere **2.** ritenere, considerare **3.** credere, aspettarsi || *to — of,* pensare, avere in animo di; *to — ill of so.,* avere una cattiva opinione di qu.; *to — out,* escogitare; *to — over,* riflettere.

thinkable *agg.* concepibile, immaginabile.

thinker *s.* pensatore.

thinking *agg.* pensante, ragionevole ♦ **thinking** *s.* pensiero, riflessione, opinione.

thinness *s.* sottigliezza, tenuità, magrezza, radezza.

third *agg.* e *s.* terzo.

thirdly *avv.* in terzo luogo.

third-rate *agg.* di terz'ordine.

thirst *s.* **1.** sete, arsura **2.** (*fig.*) avidità.

thirsty *agg.* assetato || *to be —,* aver sete; *to be — for* (*fig.*), bramare.

thirteen *agg.* tredici.

thirteenth *agg.* tredicesimo.

thirtieth *agg.* trentesimo.

thirty *agg.* trenta.

this *agg.* e *pron. dimostr.* (*pl.* these) questo, questa.

Thomism *s.* tomismo.

thomist *s.* tomista.

thorax *s.* torace.

thorn *s.* spina (*anche fig.*).

thorny *agg.* spinoso (*anche fig.*).

thorough *agg.* **1.** completo, totale **2.** perfetto, esperto **3.** meticoloso.

thoroughbred *agg.* **1.** purosangue (*di cavallo*) **2.** di antico lignaggio. ♦ **thoroughbred** *s.* purosangue.

thoroughfare *s.* arteria di grande traffico || *no —,* passaggio vietato.

those (*pl. di* that) quelli, quelle.

though *avv.* comunque, tuttavia. ♦ **though** *cong.* benché, sebbene.

thought V. to **think**.

thought *s.* **1.** pensiero, riflessione **2.** idea, parere **3.** concezione.

thoughtful *agg.* **1.** pensoso, pensieroso **2.** sollecito.

thoughtless *agg.* sconsiderato, sventato, negligente.

thoughtlessness *s.* sconsideratezza, negligenza.

thousand *agg.* mille. ♦ **thousand** *s.* migliaio.

thrall *s.* schiavo.

to **thrash** *vt.* e *vi.* **1.** battere, sferzare 2. (*mar.*) navigare contro vento 3. trebbiare 4. bastonare || to — out, dibattere.

thrasher *s.* trebbiatore.

thrashing machine *s.* trebbiatrice.

thread *s.* 1. filo (*anche fig.*) 2. vena, filone.

to **thread** *vt.* 1. infilare 2. far passare attraverso.

threadbare *agg.* 1. consumato, consunto 2. (*fig.*) vieto, trito.

threading *s.* filettatura.

threadlike *agg.* filiforme.

threat *s.* minaccia.

to **threaten** *vt.* e *vi.* minacciare.

threatening *agg.* minaccioso.

three *agg.* e *s.* tre.

threescore *agg.* sessanta.

to **thresh** *vt.* e *vi.* trebbiare.

threshold *s.* 1. soglia, limitare 2. (*fig.*) esordio, inizio.

threw *V.* to *throw*.

thrice *avv.* tre volte.

thriftiness *s.* economia, parsimonia.

thrifty *agg.* frugale, economo.

thrill *s.* brivido, palpito.

to **thrill** *vt.* far fremere, elettrizzare. ◆ to **thrill** *vi.* fremere, vibrare, emozionarsi.

thriller *s.* (*gergo*) storia, film sensazionale, poliziesco.

thrilling *agg.* 1. sensazionale, emozionante 2. penetrante.

to **thrive** (**throve**, **thriven**) *vi.* 1. prosperare, fiorire 2. crescere vigorosamente.

thriving *agg.* 1. prospero, fiorente 2. rigoglioso.

throat *s.* gola || — *wash*, gargarismo; *sore* —, mal di gola.

throaty *agg.* gutturale.

throb *s.* battito, pulsazione, fremito.

to **throb** *vi.* battere, pulsare, fremere.

throbbing *agg.* palpitante, vibrante (*anche fig.*).

thrombosis *s.* trombosi.

throne *s.* trono.

throng *s.* folla, moltitudine.

to **throng** *vt.* affollare, stipare. ◆ to **throng** *vi.* affollarsi, affluire.

to **throttle** *vt.* strozzare, strangolare.

through *avv.* 1. attraverso, da una parte all'altra 2. (*ferr.*) direttamente || — *train*, treno diretto. ◆ **through** *prep.* 1. attraverso, per 2. durante, per tutta la durata di 3. per mezzo.

throughout *avv.* da un capo all'altro, dal principio alla fine. ◆ **throughout** *prep.* in ogni parte di, durante tutto il, dal principio alla fine di.

throve *V.* to *thrive*.

throw *s.* lancio, gittata (*di missile ecc.*), tiro.

to **throw** (**threw**, **thrown**) *vt.* e *vi.* 1. gettare, scagliare, proiettare 2. atterrare, rovesciare || to — *away*, buttar via; to — *off*, buttar fuori; to — *out* espellere.

throwback *s.* 1. movimento brusco all'indietro 2. ostacolo.

thrown *V.* to *throw*.

thrush *s.* tordo.

thrust *s.* 1. colpo, botta 2. colpo con arma appuntita.

to **thrust** (**thrust**, **thrust**) *vt.* e *vi.* 1. spingere, ficcare 2. frapporre 3. forzare.

thud *s.* tonfo, rumore sordo.

to **thud** *vi.* fare un rumore sordo.

thumb *s.* pollice.

to **thumb** *vt.* 1. lasciare ditate su (*un foglio ecc.*) 2. strimpellare.

thump *s.* rumore sordo.

to **thump** *vt.* battere, percuotere, dar pugni.

thumping *agg.* pesante.

thunder *s.* 1. tuono: *a peal of* —, un colpo di tuono 2. scoppio, rombo 3. fulmine (*anche fig.*).

to **thunder** *vt.* e *vi.* 1. tuonare, rimbombare 2. minacciare.

thunderbolt *s.* fulmine, saetta (*anche fig.*).

thundering *agg.* 1. tonante, fulminante 2. (*fam.*) straordinario.

thundery *agg.* minaccioso.

Thursday *s.* giovedì.

thus *avv.* così, in questo modo.

to **thwart** *vt.* opporsi a, ostacolare.

thyme *s.* timo.

thyroid *s.* tiroide.

tibia *s.* tibia.

tick *s.* tic-tac, ticchettio (*di orologio*).

to **tick** *vt.* e *vi.* ticchettare.

ticket *s.* 1. biglietto, tessera, scontrino 2. (*mil.*) congedo || — *-collector*, bigliettario; — *-inspector*, controllore; *single* —, biglietto di andata.

to **ticket** *vt.* 1. mettere il cartellino del prezzo a 2. fornire di biglietto.

ticking s. traliccio.

tickle s. solletico.

to tickle vt. fare il solletico, solleticare (anche fig.). ♦ **to tickle** vi. prudere.

tickler s. 1. chi solletica 2. questione delicata.

ticklish agg. 1. sensibile al solletico 2. scabroso.

tide s. 1. marea 2. (fig.) corrente, corso || — -gauge, mareografo.

to tide vi. salire, crescere come la marea.

tidily avv. lindamente.

tidings s. pl. novità.

tidy agg. ordinato, preciso, pulito.

to tidy vt. riordinare, mettere in ordine.

tie s. 1. laccio, legaccio 2. cravatta 3. (fig.) legame 4. (ferr.) traversina.

to tie vt. 1. legare, allacciare, congiungere (anche fig.) 2. annodare.

tied agg. vincolato, schiavo.

tier s. ordine, fila (di posti).

to tier vt. allineare.

tiff s. stizza, bisticcio || to be in a —, essere in collera.

to tiff vi. essere stizzito.

tiger s. tigre.

tight agg. 1. impermeabile, a perfetta tenuta 2. teso, tirato 3. stretto, aderente, attillato 4. scarso, a corto di denaro 5. (gergo) ubriaco. ♦ **tight** avv. 1. ermeticamente 2. in maniera tesa.

to tighten vt. 1. serrare 2. tirare, tendere. ♦ **to tighten** vi. 1. serrarsi 2. tendersi.

tightly avv. ermeticamente, strettamente.

tightness s. 1. impermeabilità, tenuta 2. tensione 3. (gergo) ubriachezza.

tights s. pl. calzamaglia.

tigress s. tigre (femmina).

tile s. 1. tegola, mattonella, piastrella 2. (fam.) cappello a cilindro.

to tile vt. coprire di tegole, piastrelle.

tilemaking s. fabbricazione di tegole.

tilery s. fabbrica di tegole.

tiling s. tegolato, piastrellatura.

till¹ prep. fino a: — now, fino ad ora. ♦ **till** cong. finché, fino al momento in cui.

till² s. cassetto in cui si custodisce il denaro.

to till vt. dissodare, arare.

tillage s. 1. dissodamento, aratura 2. terreno coltivato.

tiller s. 1. aratore 2. (mar.) barra del timone.

tilt¹ s. tenda, tendone.

tilt² s. 1. torneo, giostra 2. contesa, disputa 3. inclinazione, pendenza.

to tilt vt. 1. inclinare 2. rovesciare. ♦ **to tilt** vi. 1. oscillare 2. (mar.) beccheggiare.

timber s. 1. legname da costruzione 2. bosco con alberi d'alto fusto 3. trave 4. (fig.) tempra, carattere 5. (mar.) costola || — -work, costruzione in legno.

to timber vt. rivestire di legno.

timbre s. timbro (di suoni).

time s. 1. tempo, periodo di tempo, circostanza, epoca, età 2. volta, volte 3. orario, ora || with —, col passar del tempo; from — to —, di tanto in tanto; as times go, coi tempi che corrono; at times, a volte; in good —, per tempo; what — is it?, che ore sono?

to time vt. fissare l'orario di. ♦ **to time** vi. tenere il tempo.

timekeeper s. 1. cronometro 2. cronometrista.

timeliness s. tempestività.

timely agg. opportuno, tempestivo.

timepiece s. orologio (da tavolo).

timer s. cronometrista.

time-study agg. — engineer, analista tempi.

timid agg. timido.

timidity s. timidezza.

timing s. 1. calcolo del tempo (di pose fotografiche ecc.) 2. (mecc.) messa in fase.

timorous agg. timoroso.

tin s. 1. stagno, latta 2. recipiente.

to tin vt. 1. stagnare 2. conservare in scatola.

tincture s. 1. (chim.) tintura, soluzione alcoolica 2. tinta 3. sfumatura, traccia 4. gusto, aroma.

to tincture vt. 1. tingere, colorare 2. aromatizzare.

tinder s. esca (per fuoco).

tinge s. 1. sfumatura, tocco 2. (fig.) pizzico.

to tinge vt. dare una sfumatura a (anche fig.).

to tingle vt. 1. pizzicare 2. far tintinnare. ♦ **to tingle** vi. arrossire (di guance).

tink s. tintinnio.

tinker s. calderaio (*ambulante*), stagnino.

to **tinker** vt. rabberciare, riparare.

tinkle s. tintinnio.

to **tinkle** vt. far tintinnare. ♦ to **tinkle** vi. tintinnare.

tinkling s. tintinnio.

tinsel agg. vistoso, sgargiante. ♦ **tinsel** s. orpello (*anche fig.*).

tint s. tinta, colore delicato, sfumatura.

to **tint** vt. colorire, tinteggiare.

tiny agg. minuscolo.

tip[1] s. 1. punta, cima 2. puntale.

tip[2] s. 1. immondezzaio 2. inclinazione.

tip[3] s. mancia.

to **tip**[1] vt. toccare, battere leggermente.

to **tip**[2] vt. 1. rovesciare 2. inclinare. ♦ to **tip** vi. 1: rovesciarsi 2. inclinarsi.

to **tip**[3] vt. e vi. 1. dare la mancia 2. (*gergo*) dare, passare.

tippet s. mantellina.

tipsy agg. ubriaco.

tiptoe s. punta dei piedi: *on* —, in punta di piedi.

to **tiptoe** vi. camminare in punta di piedi.

tire s. 1. cerchione di ruota 2. pneumatico || *flat* —, gomma a terra.

to **tire**[1] vt. stancare, annoiare. ♦ to **tire** vi. stancarsi, annoiarsi.

to **tire**[2] vt. fornire di cerchione, di pneumatico.

tired agg. stanco, affaticato, esausto || *to be* — *out*, essere stanco morto.

tireless agg. instancabile.

tiresome agg. faticoso, stancante, noioso.

tissue s. tessuto || — *paper*, carta velina.

Titan s. titano, gigante.

titanic agg. titanico (*anche fig.*).

title s. 1. titolo 2. titolo, grado, qualifica.

to **title** vt. 1. intitolare, intestare 2. conferire un titolo.

titular s. titolare.

to prep. 1. (*con verbo di moto*) a, in, da 2. verso, per 3. (*di tempo*) fino a 4. (*paragone, rapporto*) contro a 5. riguardo a || — *all appearances*, stando alle apparenze; — *my despair*, con mia disperazione; — *this end*, a questo scopo.

toad s. rospo.

toady s. adulatore.

to **toady** vt. adulare, comportarsi servilmente.

toast[1] s. pane abbrustolito, crostino.

toast[2] s. brindisi.

to **toast**[1] vt. abbrustolire, tostare.

to **toast**[2] vt. e vi. fare un brindisi.

toaster s. tostapane.

tobacco s. tabacco || — *box*, tabacchiera.

tobacconist s. tabaccaio || — *'s shop*, tabaccheria.

tocsin s. segnale d'allarme.

today s. oggi. ♦ **today** avv. oggigiorno.

toddle s. andatura incerta, vacillante.

to **toddle** vi. camminare a passi incerti, passeggiare.

toe s. dito del piede.

together avv. assieme, insieme, unitamente.

toil[1] s. fatica, duro lavoro || — *worn*, sfinito dalla fatica.

toil[2] s. laccio, trappola (*anche fig.*).

to **toil**[1] vi. faticare, lavorare duramente.

to **toil**[2] vt. prendere in trappola (*anche fig.*).

toilet s. 1. toletta, pulizia 2. abbigliamento 3. bagno, gabinetto || — *paper*, carta igienica.

toilsome agg. faticoso, laborioso.

token s. 1. segno, simbolo 2. prova, pegno, ricordo.

tolerable agg. 1. tollerabile 2. discreto.

tolerance s. tolleranza.

tolerant agg. tollerante.

to **tolerate** vt. tollerare, sopportare.

toleration s. tolleranza.

toll[1] s. pedaggio, dazio, gabella.

toll[2] s. rintocco (*di campana*).

to **toll** vt. suonare. ♦ to **toll** vi. rintoccare.

tomato s. pomodoro.

tomb s. tomba.

tomboy s. ragazza indiavolata.

tome s. tomo, volume.

tomfool agg. e s. sciocco, banale.

tommy s. 1. pane, pagnotta 2. provviste (*che l'operaio porta da casa*) (*pl.*).

tommy-gun s. fucile mitragliatore, mitra.

tomorrow s. e avv. domani.

ton s. tonnellata.

tonality s. tonalità.

tone s. tono, timbro, accento.

to **tone** vt. e vi. 1. (mus.) dare il tono, intonare, accordare 2. (pitt.) sfumare.

toneless agg. inespressivo, privo di colore, senza vigore.

tongs s. pl. pinze, molle, tenaglie.

tongue s. 1. lingua 2. lingua, linguaggio 3. lingua (di terra, fuoco) || — -tied, muto, taciturno; — -twister, scioglilingua.

to **tongue** vt. leccare, lambire.

tonic agg. tonico, corroborante. ♦ **tonic** s. (med.) tonico, energetico.

tonight avv. e s. stanotte, stasera.

tonnage s. tonnellaggio, stazza.

tonsil s. tonsilla.

tonsillitis s. tonsillite.

tonsure s. tonsura.

to **tonsure** vt. tonsurare.

too avv. 1. troppo 2. anche, pure 3. inoltre.

took V. to take.

tool s. 1. arnese, attrezzo, utensile 2. (fig.) strumento.

tooth s. (pl. teeth) 1. dente, zanna 2. dente (di pettine, forchetta ecc.) || — -paste, dentifricio; — -pick, stuzzicadenti.

toothache s. mal di denti.

toothbrush s. spazzolino da denti.

toothing s. dentatura, dentellatura.

toothless agg. sdentato.

toothy agg. dai denti sporgenti.

top[1] s. 1. cima, sommità 2. (fig.) apice 3. parte superiore, "capote" di automobile.

top[2] s. trottola.

topaz s. topazio.

topic s. argomento, soggetto.

topical agg. d'attualità.

topographer s. topografo.

topographic(al) agg. topografico.

topography s. topografia.

topology s. topologia.

toponymy s. toponomastica.

topsail s. vela di gabbia.

topsyturvy agg. sottosopra, capovolto. ♦ **topsyturvy** s. capovolgimento, disordine, scompiglio. ♦ **topsyturvy** avv. sottosopra.

to **topsyturvy** vt. mettere sossopra.

toque s. berretto, tocco.

torch s. torcia, fiaccola || electric —, lampadina tascabile.

torchlight s. luce di fiaccole, torce || — procession, fiaccolata.

tore V. to tear.

torment s. tormento, tortura.

to **torment** vt. tormentare.

torn V. to tear.

tornado s. ciclone.

torpedo s. 1. (zool.) torpedine 2. (mar.) siluro || — -boat, torpediniera; — boat destroyer, cacciatorpediniere.

to **torpedo** vt. silurare.

torpid agg. torpido, apatico.

torpor s. torpore.

torrefaction s. torrefazione.

to **torrefy** vt. torrefare.

torrent s. torrente (anche fig.).

torrential agg. torrenziale.

torrid agg. torrido.

torsion s. torsione.

tortoise s. tartaruga.

torture s. tortura, tormento (anche fig.).

to **torture** vt. torturare, tormentare.

torturous agg. tormentoso.

toss s. 1. lancio 2. movimento del capo.

to **toss** vt. 1. gettare, lanciare 2. agitare, scuotere 3. disarcionare. ♦ to **toss** vi. 1. agitarsi, smaniare 2. tirare a sorte 3. (mar.) beccheggiare.

total agg. totale, completo. ♦ **total** s. totale.

totalitarian agg. totalitario.

totalitarianism s. totalitarismo.

totality s. totalità.

totalizator s. totalizzatore.

to **totalize** vt. e vi. totalizzare.

totalizer s. totalizzatore.

to **totter** vi. camminare barcollando.

tottering agg. vacillante, malsicuro.

touch s. 1. tocco, colpetto 2. tatto 3. contatto, rapporto.

to **touch** vt. 1. toccare 2. sfiorare 3. (fig.) colpire, commuovere. ♦ to **touch** vi. essere in contatto, confinare.

touchiness s. suscettibilità.

touching agg. toccante, commovente. ♦ **touching** prep. riguardo a.

touchstone s. pietra di paragone.

touchwood s. esca (per accendere il fuoco).

touchy agg. permaloso.

tough agg. 1. duro 2. forte, robusto 3. (fig.) inflessibile 4. difficile 5. violento.

to **toughen** vt. indurire. ♦ to **toughen** vi. indurirsi.

toughness s. 1. durezza 2. inflessibilità.

tour s. giro, viaggio, escursione.

to **tour** vt. e vi. fare un viaggio.

tourism *s.* turismo.

tourist *s.* turista.

tourmalin(e) *s.* tormalina.

tournament *s.* torneo.

to **tousle** *vt.* scompigliare, arruffare.

tow *s.* rimorchio.

toward(s) *prep.* **1.** verso, in direzione di **2.** riguardo a **3.** verso, circa (*di tempo*).

towel *s.* asciugamano || — -*horse*, porta-asciugamano.

tower *s.* torre.

to **tower** *vi.* torreggiare.

towing *s.* rimorchio.

town *s.* **1.** città **2.** cittadinanza || — -*council*, consiglio comunale; — -*planning*, piano regolatore; *chief* —, capoluogo.

townhall *s.* municipio.

townhouse *s.* residenza di città.

townscape *s.* veduta (*di città*).

townsfolk *s.* abitanti di una città.

township *s.* territorio, giurisdizione di una città.

townsman *s.* cittadino.

townspeople *s.* cittadinanza.

townward(s) *avv.* verso la città.

toxic(al) *agg.* tossico.

toxicity *s.* tossicità.

toxicologist *s.* tossicologo.

toxicology *s.* tossicologia.

toxin *s.* tossina.

toy *s.* **1.** giocattolo **2.** bazzecola, storiella.

to **toy** *vi.* giocherellare, trastullarsi.

toyish *agg.* **1.** simile a giocattolo **2.** insignificante.

toyshop *s.* negozio di giocattoli.

trabeation *s.* trabeazione.

trace *s.* traccia, orma.

to **trace** *vt.* **1.** tracciare **2.** seguire le tracce **3.** rintracciare || *to* — *back*, risalire.

traceable *agg.* **1.** rintracciabile **2.** che si può tracciare.

trachea *s.* trachea.

tracheal *agg.* tracheale.

tracheitis *s.* tracheite.

trachyte *s.* trachite.

tracing *s.* **1.** tracciato **2.** calco, ricalco.

track *s.* **1.** traccia, orma **2.** sentiero, corso (*anche fig.*) **3.** (*sport*) pista **4.** (*ferr.*) binario || *sound* — (*cine*), colonna sonora.

to **track** *vt.* **1.** inseguire, pedinare **2.** tracciare un sentiero. ♦ to **track** *vi.* posare i binari.

tract¹ *s.* periodo, tratto, spazio.

tract² *s.* opuscolo.

tractability *s.* arrendevolezza.

tractable *agg.* arrendevole.

traction *s.* **1.** trazione **2.** contrazione.

tractor *s.* trattore.

trade *s.* **1.** mestiere **2.** commercio, traffico **3.** commercianti (*pl.*) || — *bank*, banca commerciale; — *dispute*, vertenza sindacale; — -*mark*, marchio di fabbrica; — -*show* (*cine*), anteprima per la critica; *free*—, libero scambio.

to **trade** *vt.* e *vi.* commerciare, negoziare.

trader *s.* **1.** commerciante **2.** nave mercantile.

trading *s.* commercio.

tradition *s.* tradizione.

traditional *agg.* tradizionale.

traditionalism *s.* tradizionalismo.

traditionalist *s.* tradizionalista.

to **traduce** *vt.* calunniare.

traffic *s.* **1.** traffico, commercio **2.** traffico, circolazione || — *lights*, semaforo; — *jam*, ingorgo stradale.

tragedian *s.* **1.** tragediografo **2.** attore tragico.

tragedy *s.* tragedia.

tragic(al) *agg.* tragico.

tragicomedy *s.* tragicommedia.

tragicomic(al) *agg.* tragicomico.

trail *s.* **1.** traccia, striscia **2.** pista, orma **3.** cammino, sentiero.

to **trail** *vt.* **1.** trascinare **2.** seguire le tracce di. ♦ to **trail** *vi.* trascinarsi.

trailer *s.* **1.** inseguitore, cacciatore **2.** rimorchio **3.** (*cine*) film di prossima programmazione.

train *s.* **1.** treno: *express* — (o *fast* —), rapido; *slow* —, accelerato **2.** seguito, corteo **3.** serie, successione, fila.

to **train** *vt.* **1.** allevare, educare **2.** esercitare, allenare, addestrare. ♦ to **train** *vi.* **1.** esercitarsi, allenarsi **2.** viaggiare in ferrovia.

trainer *s.* istruttore, allenatore.

training *s.* educazione, ammaestramento, allenamento.

trait *s.* tratto, fattezza, caratteristica.

traitor *s.* traditore.

trajectory *s.* traiettoria.

tram *s.* **1.** tram **2.** carrello da miniera || — -*conductor*, tranviere.

trammel *s.* **1.** tramaglio **2.** intoppo.

tramp *s.* **1.** calpestio **2.** viaggio a piedi.

to **tramp** vt. 1. camminare pesantemente 2. viaggiare a piedi 3. vagabondare.

trample s. calpestio.

to **trample** vt. 1. calpestare 2. (fig.) offendere. ♦ to **trample** vi. camminare pesantemente.

tramway s. tranvia.

to **tranquillize** vt. tranquillizzare.

tranquillizer s. (med.) tranquillante.

to **transact** vt. e vi. negoziare, trattare affari.

transaction s. 1. affare, operazione 2. (giur.) transazione 3. atti (di congresso ecc.) (pl.).

transactor s. negoziatore.

transalpine agg. e s. transalpino.

transatlantic agg. transatlantico.

to **transcend** vt. trascendere, superare.

transcendence s. trascendenza.

transcendent agg. trascendente.

transcendental agg. trascendentale.

transcendentalism s. trascendentalismo.

transcontinental agg. transcontinentale.

to **transcribe** vt. trascrivere.

transcript s. riproduzione, copia.

transcription s. trascrizione.

transept s. transetto.

transfer s. 1. trasferimento, cessione 2. (giur.) trapasso 3. decalcomania.

to **transfer** vt. trasferire, cedere.

transferable agg. trasferibile.

transfiguration s. trasfigurazione.

to **transfigure** vt. trasfigurare.

to **transfix** vt. trafiggere.

transfocator s. (cine) teleobiettivo.

to **transform** vt. trasformare.

transformable agg. trasformabile.

transformation s. trasformazione.

transformer s. trasformatore.

transformism s. trasformismo.

to **transfuse** vt. 1. travasare 2. fare una trasfusione (di sangue).

transfusion s. trasfusione.

to **transgress** vt. trasgredire. ♦ to **transgress** vi. commettere una violenza, peccare.

transgression s. trasgressione.

transgressor s. trasgressore.

transient agg. passeggero, transitorio.

transistor s. (radio) transistor.

transit s. 1. transito, passaggio 2. trasporto.

transition s. transizione.

transitive agg. transitivo.

transitory agg. transitorio.

translatable agg. traducibile.

to **translate** vt. tradurre.

translation s. 1. traduzione 2. trasferimento, assunzione (al cielo).

translator s. traduttore.

translucent agg. traslucido, diafano, trasparente.

to **transmigrate** vi. trasmigrare.

transmigration s. trasmigrazione.

transmissible agg. trasmissibile.

transmission s. trasmissione.

to **transmit** vt. trasmettere.

transmitter s. trasmettitore.

transoceanic agg. transoceanico.

transparence s. trasparenza.

transparent agg. 1. trasparente, limpido 2. chiaro, evidente.

to **transpire** vt. e vi. traspirare.

to **transplant** vt. trapiantare.

transplantation s. trapianto.

transport s. 1. trasporto (anche fig.) 2. mezzo di trasporto.

transportable agg. trasportabile.

transposal s. trasposizione.

transposition s. trasposizione (di parole, cifre ecc.).

transubstantiation s. transustanziazione.

transversal agg. e s. trasversale.

trap s. trappola || — -door, botola.

to **trap** vt. prendere in trappola.

trapezium s. trapezio.

trapper s. chi tende trappole.

trash[1] s. rifiuto.

trash[2] s. guinzaglio.

to **trash** vt. sfrondare.

trashy agg. senza valore.

traumatic agg. traumatico.

travel s. 1. viaggi (pl.): — agency, agenzia di viaggi 2. (mecc.) corsa.

to **travel** vi. viaggiare.

traveller s. viaggiatore.

travelling agg. 1. viaggiante 2. di, da viaggio 3. mobile. ♦ **travelling** s. il viaggiare.

traverse agg. trasversale. ♦ **traverse** s. 1. trasversale 2. traversata.

to **traverse** vt. 1. traversare 2. muovere lateralmente. ♦ to **traverse** vi. 1. fare una traversata 2. muoversi lateralmente 3. girare su un perno.

travertin(e) s. travertino.

travesty s. parodia.

trawl s. (mar.) strascico.

trawler s. peschereccio a strascico.
tray s. vassoio || *ash-* —, portacenere.
treacherous agg. traditore, sleale.
treacherousness, treachery s. tradimento, slealtà.
tread s. 1. passo 2. suola 3. battistrada.
to tread (trod, trodden) vt. e vi. camminare. ♦ **to tread (trod, trodden)** vt. 1. percorrere 2. calpestare.
treadle s. pedale.
treason s. tradimento.
treasure s. tesoro.
to treasure vt. 1. ammassare 2. custodire gelosamente.
treasurer s. tesoriere.
treasury s. 1. tesoreria 2. Ministero del Tesoro.
treat s. festa.
to treat vt. 1. trattare 2. offrire.
treatise s. trattato.
treatment s. 1. trattamento 2. (*med.*) cura.
treaty s. trattato.
treble agg. 1. triplo, triplice 2. (*mus.*) di soprano, parte di soprano.
to treble vt. triplicare. ♦ **to treble** vi. triplicarsi.
tree s. 1. albero 2. trave || — *-frog*, raganella.
trefoil s. trifoglio.
trellis s. graticcio.
tremble s. tremito.
to tremble vi. tremare.
trembling agg. tremante, tremolante. ♦ **trembling** s. tremito.
tremendous agg. tremendo.
tremor s. tremore.
tremulous agg. tremulo.
trench s. 1. fosso 2. trincea.
to trench vt. e vi. scavare, solcare, scavare trincee.
trenchant agg. tagliente, incisivo, efficace.
trencher s. tagliere.
trend s. direzione, orientamento, tendenza.
to trend vi. tendere.
trepan s. trapano.
to trepan vt. trapanare.
trepidation s. 1. tremito 2. trepidazione.
trespass s. 1. trasgressione 2. violazione.
to trespass vi. 1. commettere una violazione 2. peccare.

trespasser s. 1. trasgressore 2. peccatore.
trestle s. 1. cavalletto 2. intelaiatura.
trial s. 1. processo 2. prova, esperimento.
triangle s. triangolo.
triangular agg. triangolare.
triangulation s. triangolazione.
tribal agg. tribale.
tribe s. tribù.
tribune[1] s. tribuno.
tribune[2] s. tribuna.
tributary agg. e s. tributario.
tribute s. tributo.
trichromatic agg. tricromico.
trick s. 1. trucco 2. imbroglio 3. mania.
to trick vt. ingannare.
trickery s. inganno.
trickish agg. scaltro.
trickle s. gocciolio.
to trickle vi. gocciolare.
tricky agg. 1. scaltro 2. intricato.
tricolour agg. e s. tricolore.
tricycle s. triciclo.
trident s. tridente.
tridimensional agg. tridimensionale.
triennial agg. triennale.
trifle s. sciocchezza.
to trifle vi. scherzare.
trifler s. persona leggera.
trifling agg. 1. insignificante 2. frivolo.
trigeminal agg. e s. trigemino.
trigeminus s. trigemino.
trigger s. grilletto.
trigonometry s. trigonometria.
trihedron s. triedro.
trill s. trillo.
to trill vt. e vi. trillare.
trillion s. 1. trilione 2. (*amer.*) bilione.
trilogy s. trilogia.
trim agg. ordinato. ♦ **trim** s. 1. ordine 2. assetto 3. (*cine*) taglio.
to trim vt. 1. ordinare 2. tagliare.
trimester s. trimestre.
trimmer s. decoratore.
trimming s. 1. guarnizione 2. bastonatura.
trinity s. trinità.
trinket s. ninnolo.
trinomial s. trinomio.
trip s. 1. gita, viaggio 2. passo agile 3. passo falso.
to trip vi. 1. saltellare 2. inciampare. ♦ **to trip** vt. 1. far inciam-

pare **2.** (*mecc.*) liberare.
tripartite *agg.* tripartito.
tripartition *s.* tripartizione.
tripe *s.* **1.** trippa **2.** (*gergo*) ciarpame, sciocchezze (*pl.*).
triple *agg.* triplo.
to **triple** *vt.* triplicare. ♦ to **triple** *vi.* triplicarsi.
triplicate *agg.* triplicato. ♦ **triplicate** *s.* triplice copia.
to **triplicate** *vt.* triplicare.
tripod *s.* **1.** treppiede **2.** tripode.
tripper *s.* gitante.
triptych *s.* trittico.
trisyllabic(al) *agg.* trisillabico.
trite *agg.* trito.
to **triturate** *vt.* triturare.
triumph *s.* trionfo.
to **triumph** *vi.* trionfare.
triumphant *agg.* trionfante.
triumvir *s.* triumviro.
triumvirate *s.* triumvirato.
trivalent *agg.* trivalente.
trivial *agg.* banale.
triviality *s.* banalità.
trod V. *to tread.*
trodden V. *to tread.*
troglodyte *s.* troglodita.
troglodytic(al) *agg.* trogloditico.
trolley *s.* carrello || — *bus*, filobus; — *line*, linea tranviaria.
troop *s.* **1.** gruppo **2.** truppe (*pl.*).
to **troop** *vi.* **1.** radunarsi **2.** sfilare.
trophy *s.* trofeo.
tropic *agg.* tropico.
tropical *agg.* tropicale.
tropism *s.* tropismo.
troposphere *s.* troposfera.
trot *s.* trotto.
to **trot** *vt.* far trottare. ♦ to **trot** *vi.* trottare.
trotter *s.* trottatore.
trouble *s.* guaio, disturbo.
to **trouble** *vt.* disturbare. ♦ to **trouble** *vi.* preoccuparsi.
troublesome *agg.* fastidioso.
trough *s.* **1.** truogolo **2.** condotto, solco **3.** depressione (*atmosferica*).
trousers *s. pl.* calzoni
trout *s.* trota.
trowel *s.* cazzuola.
truce *s.* tregua.
truck[1] *s.* baratto, scambio.
truck[1] *s.* **1.** carrello **2.** (*amer.*) autocarro.
to **truck**[1] *vt.* barattare.
to **truck**[2] *vt.* trasportare (*su carrello*).
trucker *s.* camionista.
truculent *agg.* truculento.

to **trudge** *vi.* camminare faticosamente.
true *agg.* vero, esatto || *ouf of* —, sfasato.
truffle *s.* tartufo.
truly *avv.* **1.** veramente **2.** esattamente.
to **trump** *vt.* ingannare || *to* — *up a charge,* inventare un'accusa.
trumpery *agg.* illusorio. ♦ **trumpery** *s.* orpello.
trumpet *s.* tromba.
to **trumpet** *vi.* **1.** suonare la tromba **2.** barrire. ♦ to **trumpet** *vt.* strombazzare.
trumpeter *s.* trombettiere.
truncate *agg.* tronco, troncato.
truncheon *s.* manganello.
trunk *s.* **1.** tronco **2.** baule **3.** proboscide || — -*call,* comunicazione interurbana. ♦ **trunks** *s. pl.* calzoni corti.
truss *s.* **1.** fascio **2.** (*arch.*) capriata.
trust *s.* **1.** fede, fiducia **2.** incarico di fiducia **3.** (*econ.*) "trust", consorzio monopolistico.
to **trust** *vt.* e *vi.* confidare, fidarsi di, dar credito || *to* — *so. with sthg.,* affidare qc. a qu.
trustee *s.* **1.** (*comm.*) fiduciario **2.** (*giur.*) curatore.
truster *s.* chi si fida.
trustful *agg.* fiducioso.
trustworthy *agg.* degno di fiducia.
truth *s.* verità.
truthful *agg.* **1.** vero **2.** fedele.
try *s.* tentativo || — -*on,* prova (*di abiti*); — -*out* (*mecc.*), prova.
to **try** *vt.* provare, tentare || *to* — *for sthg.,* cercare di ottenere qc.; *to* — *on,* provare (*di abiti*); *to* — *out,* sottoporre a dura prova.
trying *agg.* **1.** difficile **2.** difficilmente sopportabile.
tub *s.* tinozza, vasca.
tube *s.* **1.** tubo **2.** camera d'aria **3.** (*fam.*) ferrovia sotterranea.
tuber *s.* **1.** tubero **2.** tubercolo.
tubercular *agg.* **1.** tubercolare **2.** tubercoloso.
tuberculosis *s.* tubercolosi.
tuberculous *agg.* tubercoloso.
tubing *s.* tubatura.
tubular, tubulous *agg.* tubolare.
tuck *s.* piega (*di abito*).
to **tuck** *vt.* **1.** (ri)piegare **2.** pigiare || *to* — *up,* rimboccare.
Tuesday *s.* martedì.
tuff *s.* tufo vulcanico.

tuft s. 1. ciuffo 2. fiocco 3. cespuglio.

tug s. strappo || — -of-war, tiro alla fune.

to **tug** vt. e vi. 1. tirare 2. dare strattoni.

tugboat s. (mar.) rimorchiatore.

tuition s. istruzione.

tulip s. tulipano.

tumble s. 1. caduta 2. confusione.

to **tumble** vi. 1. cadere 2. agitarsi 3. precipitarsi 4. fare acrobazie. ♦ to **tumble** vt. 1. far cadere 2. scompigliare.

tumble-down agg. in rovina.

tumbler s. 1. acrobata 2. bicchiere (senza piede).

tumefaction s. tumefazione.

to **tumefy** vt. tumefare. ♦ to **tumefy** vi. tumefarsi.

tumescence s. tumescenza.

tumescent agg. gonfio.

tumid agg. tumido.

tumidity s. gonfiore.

tumour s. tumore.

tumult s. tumulto.

tumultuous agg. tumultuoso.

tumulus s. (pl. -li) tumulo.

tun s. botte.

tuna s. tonno.

tune s. 1. tono 2. accordo 3. motivo || in —, intonato; out of —, stonato.

to **tune** vt. (mus.) accordare || to — up, mettere a punto. ♦ to **tune** vi. essere in armonia.

tuneful agg. armonioso.

tuner s. 1. (mus.) accordatore 2. (radio) sintonizzatore.

tungsten s. tungsteno.

tunic s. tunica.

Tunisian agg. e s. tunisino.

to **tunnel** vi. costruire un tunnel. ♦ to **tunnel** vt. perforare.

tunny s. tonno.

turban s. turbante.

turbid agg. torbido.

turbidity s. torbidezza.

turbine s. turbina.

turbojet s. turbogetto || — engine, turboreattore.

turbulence s. turbolenza.

turbulent agg. turbolento.

tureen s. zuppiera.

turf s. 1. zolla erbosa 2. torba 3. campo da corse || — -accountant, allibratore.

turgid agg. turgido.

turgidity s. turgidezza.

Turk agg. e s. turco.

turkey s. tacchino.

Turkish agg. turco.

turmoil s. agitazione.

turn s. 1. giro 2. curva 3. turno 4. servizio 5. attitudine || — -out, assemblea, sciopero, produzione; — -table, piattaforma girevole, giradischi.

to **turn** vi. 1. girarsi, volgersi 2. diventare. ♦ to **turn** vt. 1. girare, volgere 2. mutare 3. tornire || to — off, chiudere, spegnere; to — on, aprire, accendere; to — down, abbassare; to — out, scacciare, produrre, spegnere, risultare; to — over, rovesciare.

turnabout s. 1. giostra 2. inversione (di rotta).

turncoat s. voltagabbana.

turner s. tornitore.

turning s. 1. giro, svolta 2. tornitura.

turning-point s. svolta decisiva, momento critico.

turnip s. rapa.

turnkey s. secondino.

turnout s. 1. folla 2. equipaggio.

turnover s. 1. rovesciamento 2. (comm.) giro 3. torta.

turnpike s. strada a pedaggio.

turnspit s. girarrosto.

turpentine s. trementina.

turpitude s. turpitudine.

turquoise s. turchese.

turret s. torretta.

turtle s. 1. tartaruga 2. — (-dove), tortora.

Tuscan agg. e s. toscano.

tusk s. zanna.

tussle s. zuffa.

to **tussle** vi. azzuffarsi.

tutelar(y) agg. tutelare.

tutor s. istitutore.

to **tutor** vt. 1. istruire 2. controllare.

tutorial agg. di istitutore.

tutorship s. mansione di istitutore.

twang s. 1. suono acuto 2. suono nasale.

to **twang** vi. 1. avere un suono acuto 2. parlare con voce nasale.

tweet s. cinguettio.

to **tweet** vi. cinguettare.

tweezers s. pl. pinzette.

twelfth agg. e s. dodicesimo.

twelve agg. e s. dodici.

twentieth agg. e s. ventesimo.

twenty agg. e s. venti.

twice *avv.* due volte.

twig *s.* ramoscello.

twilight *s.* **1.** crepuscolo **2.** luce fioca.

twin *agg.* e *s.* gemello.

to twin *vt.* accoppiare. ♦ **to twin** *vi.* accoppiarsi.

twine *s.* **1.** spago, corda **2.** groviglio.

twinge *s.* fitta, dolore.

twinkle *s.* **1.** scintillio **2.** ammicco ‖ *in a* —, in un batter d'occhio.

to twinkle *vi.* **1.** scintillare **2.** ammiccare.

twinkling *s.* balenio.

twirl *s.* piroetta, rotazione.

to twirl *vt.* e *vi.* girare, roteare.

twist *s.* **1.** filo ritorto **2.** torsione **3.** curva.

to twist *vt.* **1.** torcere **2.** travisare. ♦ **to twist** *vi.* **1.** torcersi **2.** serpeggiare.

twister *s.* **1.** torcitore **2.** truffatore.

twisty *agg.* **1.** tortuoso **2.** disonesto.

to twit *vt.* biasimare.

twitch *s.* **1.** strattone **2.** tic nervoso.

twitter *s.* **1.** pigolio **2.** agitazione.

to twitter *vi.* **1.** pigolare **2.** essere ansioso.

two *agg.* e *s.* due.

twofold *agg.* doppio. ♦ **twofold** *avv.* doppiamente.

twopence *s.* due penny (*valore*).

tycoon *s.* (*amer.*) magnate.

type *s.* **1.** tipo **2.** simbolo **3.** (*tip.*) carattere tipografico ‖ — *-setting* (*tip.*), composizione.

to type *vt.* **1.** rappresentare **2.** dattilografare.

written) *vt.* e *vi.* dattilografare.

to typewrite (typewrote, typewritten *V. to typewrite.*

typewriter *s.* dattilografo.

typewriting *s.* dattilografia.

typewritten V. *to typewrite.*

typewrote V. *to typewrite.*

typhoon *s.* tifone.

typhus *s.* tifo.

typic(al) *agg.* tipico.

to typify *vt.* **1.** incarnare **2.** esemplificare.

typist *s.* dattilografo.

typographer *s.* tipografo.

typographic(al) *agg.* tipografico.

typography *s.* tipografia.

tyrannic(al) *agg.* tirannico.

tyrannicide *s.* **1.** tirannicida **2.** tirannicidio.

to tyrannize *vt.* e *vi.* tiranneggiare.

tyrannous *agg.* tirannico.

tyranny *s.* tirannia.

tyrant *s.* tiranno.

tyre *s.* V. *tire.*

Tyrrhene, Tyrrhenian *agg.* e *s.* tirreno.

Tzigane *agg.* e *s.* tzigano.

U

ubication *s.* ubicazione.

ugliness *s.* bruttezza.

ugly *agg.* **1.** brutto **2.** vile, turpe.

ulcer *s.* ulcera, piaga (*anche fig.*).

to ulcerate *vt.* ulcerare. ♦ **to ulcerate** *vi.* ulcerarsi.

ulceration *s.* ulcerazione.

ulcerous *agg.* ulceroso.

ulna *s.* (*pl.* -ae) (*anat.*) ulna.

ultimate *agg.* ultimo, finale, definitivo.

ultra *agg.* ultra, estremo, eccessivo. ♦ **ultra** *s.* estremista.

ultramarine *agg.* oltremarino.

ultramontane *agg.* e *s.* oltremontano.

ultramundane *agg.* oltremondano.

ultra-red *agg.* infrarosso.

ultrasonic *agg.* ultrasonico.

ultraviolet *agg.* ultravioletto.

umbilical *agg.* ombelicale.

umbrella *s.* ombrello ‖ — *-stand*, portaombrelli.

umpire *s.* (*giur.; sport*) arbitro.

unabashed *agg.* imperturbato.

unabated *agg.* non diminuito, non scemato.

unable *agg.* incapace, inabile.

unabridged *agg.* non abbreviato, completo ‖ — *edition*, edizione integrale.

unacceptable *agg.* inaccettabile.

unaccomplished *agg.* incompleto, incompiuto.

unaccountability *s.* inesplicabilità.

unaccountable *agg.* inesplicabile.

unaccustomed *agg.* non abituale, insolito.

unachievable *agg.* ineseguibile.

unacquainted *agg.* **1.** ignaro di, non al corrente di **2.** sconosciuto, poco familiare.

unacquired *agg.* non acquisito, innato.

unactive *agg.* inattivo.

unadapted *agg.* inadatto.

unadorned *agg.* disadorno.
unadvisable *agg.* non consigliabile, inopportuno.
unaffected *agg.* **1.** senza affettazione, semplice **2.** insensibile.
unafraid *agg.* impavido.
unalienable *agg.* inalienabile.
unallied *agg.* senza relazione, senza connessione.
unalterable *agg.* inalterabile.
unamendable *agg.* incorreggibile.
to **unanchor** *vi.* toglier l'ancora.
♦ to **unanchor** *vt.* disancorare.
unanimated *agg.* inanimato.
unanimity *s.* unanimità.
unanimous *agg.* unanime.
unannounced *agg.* non annunciato, imprevisto.
unanswerable *agg.* **1.** a cui non si può rispondere **2.** irrefutabile.
unanswered *agg.* senza risposta.
unappealable *agg.* inappellabile.
unappeasable *agg.* implacabile.
unappeased *agg.* insoddisfatto.
unapplied *agg.* non impiegato, inapplicato.
unappreciated *agg.* non apprezzato, incompreso.
unapprehensive *agg.* **1.** lento nell'apprendere **2.** non apprensivo.
unapproachable *agg.* inaccessibile.
unapt *agg.* **1.** inadatto **2.** inetto.
unargued *agg.* indiscusso.
to **unarm** *vt.* disarmare.
unarmed *agg.* disarmato, inerme.
unartful *agg.* privo di artifici, ingenuo.
unascertainable *agg.* non verificabile.
unascertained *agg.* sconosciuto, non accertato.
unasked *agg.* non richiesto.
unaspiring *agg.* senza ambizione.
unassailable *agg.* inattaccabile.
unassailed *agg.* inattaccato.
unasserted *agg.* non asserito.
unassuming *agg.* modesto, senza pretese.
unattackable *agg.* inattaccabile.
unattainable *agg.* inaccessibile.
unattempted *agg.* intentato.
unauthorized *agg.* **1.** non autorizzato **2.** illecito.
unavailable *agg.* **1.** inutile, vano **2.** non disponibile.
unavenged *agg.* impunito.
unavoidable *agg.* inevitabile.
unaware *agg.* inconsapevole, inconscio.

unawareness *s.* inconsapevolezza.
unawares *avv.* inconsapevolmente, inconsciamente.
unbalance *s.* squilibrio.
to **unbalance** *vt.* sbilanciare.
to **unbandage** *vt.* sbendare.
unbearable *agg.* insopportabile.
unbeaten *agg.* **1.** insuperato, non battuto **2.** non frequentato.
unbecoming *agg.* disdicevole.
unbelief *s.* incredulità, scetticismo.
unbelievable *agg.* incredibile.
unbelieving *agg.* incredulo, scettico.
to **unbend** (**unbent, unbent**) *vt.* **1.** raddrizzare **2.** allentare, slegare.
♦ to **unbend** (**unbent, unbent**) *vi.* raddrizzarsi.
unbias(s)ed *agg.* imparziale, senza preconcetti.
to **unbind** (**unbound, unbound**) *vt.* sciogliere, slegare.
to **unbolt** *vt.* disserrare, aprire.
unborn *agg.* non nato, nascituro, che deve venire.
to **unbosom** *vt.* rivelare, confidare.
♦ to **unbosom** *vi.* sfogarsi: *to — oneself to so.,* aprirsi con qu.
unbound V. to *unbind*.
unbreakable *agg.* infrangibile.
unbreathable *agg.* irrespirabile.
to **unbreech** *vt.* togliere i calzoni.
to **unbridle** *vt.* sbrigliare, dare libero corso a *(anche fig.)*.
unbridled *agg.* incontrollato, senza briglia.
unbroken *agg.* **1.** intatto, intero, inviolato **2.** incessante.
unbruised *agg.* non ammaccato, illeso.
to **unbuckle** *vt.* sfibbiare, slacciare.
to **unburden** *vt.* **1.** scaricare, alleggerire **2.** *(fig.)* alleviare.
unburied *agg.* insepolto.
to **unbury** *vt.* disseppellire.
to **unbutton** *vt.* sbottonare. ♦ to **unbutton** *vi.* sbottonarsi.
uncalled *agg.* non chiamato, non invitato: — *for,* superfluo, gratuito.
uncanny *agg.* misterioso, irreale.
uncared-for *agg.* negletto, abbandonato.
unceasing *agg.* incessante.
uncensurable *agg.* incensurabile.
uncertain *agg.* **1.** incerto, malsicuro **2.** irresoluto.
uncertainty *s.* **1.** incertezza **2.** irresolutezza.
to **unchain** *vt.* sciogliere da catene.

unchanged *agg.* immutato.
uncharged *agg.* **1.** non carico **2.** non incriminato.
uncharitable *agg.* poco caritatevole.
to uncharm *vt.* liberare da un incantesimo.
unchaste *agg.* impuro.
unchecked *agg.* sfrenato.
uncivil *agg.* **1.** scortese, maleducato **2.** indecoroso.
uncivilized *agg.* non civilizzato.
to unclasp *vt.* slacciare. ♦ **to unclasp** *vi.* allentare la stretta.
uncle *s.* zio.
uncombed *agg.* spettinato.
uncomely *agg.* **1.** sgraziato **2.** sconveniente.
uncomfortable *agg.* **1.** scomodo, a disagio **2.** spiacevole.
uncommon *agg.* insolito, raro.
uncompared *agg.* incomparato.
uncompelled *agg.* non costretto, spontaneo.
unconcerned *agg.* indifferente, noncurante.
unconcerning *agg.* irrilevante, che non interessa.
unconditional *agg.* incondizionato.
uncongenial *agg.* **1.** antipatico, spiacevole **2.** non congeniale.
unconquerable *agg.* invincibile, indomabile.
unconquered *agg.* invitto, indomito.
unconscionable *agg.* **1.** irragionevole **2.** senza scrupoli.
unconscious *agg.* **1.** inconscio, ignaro **2.** privo di sensi. ♦ **unconscious** *s.* inconscio.
unconsciousness *s.* **1.** inconsapevolezza **2.** stato di incoscienza.
unconsolable *agg.* inconsolabile.
unconstitutional *agg.* incostituzionale.
unconstrained *agg.* **1.** non costretto, libero **2.** disinvolto.
unconstraint *s.* **1.** assenza di costrizione, libertà **2.** spontaneità.
uncontrollable *agg.* incontrollabile.
uncontrolled *agg.* senza controllo, sfrenato.
unconventional *agg.* non convenzionale, disinvolto.
unconvertible *agg.* inconvertibile.
unconvincing *agg.* non convincente.
to uncork *vt.* sturare, stappare.

uncountable *agg.* innumerevole.
to uncouple *vt.* **1.** sguinzagliare **2.** staccare.
uncouth *agg.* **1.** ordinario, rozzo **2.** desolato.
to uncover *vt.* **1.** scoprire **2.** spogliare. ♦ **to uncover** *vi.* togliersi il cappello.
uncovered *agg.* **1.** scoperto, senza tetto **2.** spogliato **3.** senza cappello.
unction *s.* **1.** unzione **2.** unguento.
unctuous *agg.* grasso, untuoso (*anche fig.*).
uncultivable *agg.* non coltivabile.
uncultivated *agg.* incolto, non coltivato.
uncut *agg.* intonso, non tagliato.
undaunted *agg.* intrepido, impavido.
to undeceive *vt.* disingannare.
undecided *agg.* **1.** indeciso, non risolto **2.** indefinito **3.** irresoluto.
undeclinable *agg.* indeclinabile.
undecomposable *agg.* indecomponibile.
undefended *agg.* **1.** indifeso **2.** (*giur.*) non assistito da difesa legale.
undeniable *agg.* innegabile.
under *prep.* **1.** sotto, al di sotto di **2.** in corso di **3.** meno di. ♦ **under** *avv.* sotto, al di sotto || —*-age*, minorenne.
underbrush *s.* sottobosco.
to undercharge *vt.* far pagare troppo poco.
underclothes *s. pl.* biancheria intima (*sing.*).
undercover *agg.* segreto.
undercurrent *s.* **1.** corrente sottomarina **2.** (*fig.*) attività, tendenza nascosta.
to underdo (underdid, underdone) *vt. e vi.* **1.** agire in modo insufficiente **2.** cuocere poco.
underdone V. *to underdo.* ♦ **underdone** *agg.* poco cotto.
to underestimate *vt.* sottovalutare.
underfed *agg.* denutrito.
to underfeed (underfed, underfed) *vt.* nutrire insufficientemente.
to undergo (underwent, undergone) *vt.* **1.** subire, essere sottoposto a **2.** sopportare.
undergraduate *s.* studente universitario.
underground *agg.* sotterraneo. ♦ **underground** *s.* **1.** sottosuolo **2.** metropolitana.

underground *avv.* **1.** sottoterra **2.** (*pol.*) clandestinamente.

underhand *agg.* **1.** clandestino, segreto **2.** furbo, astuto. ♦ **underhand** *avv.* segretamente, clandestinamente.

to **underline** *vt.* sottolineare.

underlining *s.* sottolineatura.

undermentioned *agg.* sottoindicato.

to **undermine** *vt.* **1.** minare, scalzare **2.** (*fig.*) indebolire, insidiare.

underneath *avv.* di sotto, al di sotto.

to **underpay (underpaid, underpaid)** *vt.* pagare inadeguatamente.

to **underrate** *vt.* sottovalutare.

underscriber *s.* sottoscrittore.

undersea *agg.* sottomarino.

to **undersell (undersold, undersold)** *vt.* svendere.

undershrub *s.* sottobosco.

undersignature *s.* firma in calce.

undersold V. *to undersell.*

to **understand (understood, understood)** *vt.* e *vi.* **1.** capire, comprendere **2.** dedurre, supporre **3.** sentir dire.

understandable *agg.* comprensibile.

understanding *s.* **1.** comprensione **2.** patto, intesa || *on this —,* a queste condizioni.

to **understate** *vt.* minimizzare.

understatement *s.* attenuazione del vero.

understood V. *to understand.*

to **undertake (undertook, undertaken)** *vt.* e *vi.* **1.** intraprendere **2.** incaricarsi di **3.** prendere in appalto.

undertaker *s.* **1.** impresario **2.** imprenditore di pompe funebri.

undertaking *s.* **1.** l'intraprendere **2.** (*comm.*) impresa **3.** (*giur.*) promessa, obbligazione.

undertook V. *to undertake.*

undervaluation *s.* **1.** scarsa stima **2.** svalutazione.

to **undervalue** *vt.* sottovalutare.

underwater *agg.* subacqueo || *fishing —,* pesca subacquea.

underwent V. *to undergo.*

underworld *s.* **1.** bassifondi (*pl.*) **2.** oltretomba.

to **underwrite (underwrote, underwritten)** *vt.* e *vi.* **1.** sottoscrivere, firmare **2.** (*comm.*) assicurare.

undeserved *agg.* immeritato.

undeserving *agg.* immeritevole.

undesirable *agg.* indesiderabile.

undestroyable *agg.* indistruttibile.

undetected *agg.* non scoperto.

undetermined *agg.* **1.** indeterminato **2.** indeciso.

undid V. *to undo.*

undies *s. pl.* biancheria intima (*sing.*).

undine *s.* ondina.

undisciplined *agg.* indisciplinato.

undiscriminating *agg.* che non distingue, che non fa distinzioni.

undiscussed *agg.* indiscusso.

indisputed *agg.* incontestato.

undissembled *agg.* non dissimulato.

undistinguished *agg.* indistinto.

undisturbed *agg.* indisturbato.

undividable *agg.* indivisibile.

to **undo (undid, undone)** *vt.* **1.** disfare, sciogliere **2.** annullare, rovinare.

undoing *s.* **1.** disfacimento **2.** rovina.

undone[1] V. *to undo.* ♦ **undone** *agg.* disfatto, rovinato.

undone[2] *agg.* incompiuto.

undoubtable *agg.* indubitabile.

undoubted *agg.* indubbio.

undreamed *agg.* non sognato, impensato.

to **undress** *vt.* svestire. ♦ to **undress** *vi.* svestirsi.

undue *agg.* **1.** non dovuto, indebito **2.** inadatto.

to **undulate** *vi.* **1.** ondeggiare **2.** essere ondulato.

undulation *s.* ondulazione.

undulatory *agg.* ondulatorio.

unduly *avv.* indebitamente.

to **unearth** *vt.* **1.** dissotterrare, portare alla luce **2.** far uscire dalla tana (*un animale*).

unearthly *agg.* ultraterreno || *— hour,* ora impossibile.

uneasily *avv.* **1.** a disagio, con difficoltà **2.** con ansia.

uneasiness *s.* **1.** disagio, pena **2.** ansia.

uneasy *agg.* **1.** a disagio **2.** ansioso, inquieto.

uneatable *agg.* immangiabile.

uneducated *agg.* rozzo, ignorante.

uneffected *agg.* non effettuato.

unembarrassed *agg.* a proprio agio, disinvolto.

unemployed *agg.* **1.** disoccupato **2.** non usato.

unemployment *s.* disoccupazione

|| — *benefit,* sussidio di disoccupazione.

unending *agg.* eterno, senza fine.

unequal *agg.* **1.** ineguale **2.** inadeguato, incapace.

unequalled *agg.* ineguagliato.

unerring *agg.* infallibile, sicuro.

uneven *agg.* **1.** ineguale, irregolare **2.** ruvido, non livellato.

unevenness *s.* **1.** disuguaglianza, irregolarità **2.** dislivello.

uneventful *agg.* pacifico, senza avvenimenti importanti.

unexceptionable *agg.* ineccepibile.

unexhausted *agg.* inesausto.

unexpected *agg.* inatteso.

unexpensive *agg.* poco costoso.

unexplored *agg.* inesplorato.

unextinguishable *agg.* inestinguibile.

unfadable *agg.* **1.** che non può appassire **2.** solido (*di colore*).

unfading *agg.* **1.** che non appassisce **2.** che non sbiadisce.

unfailing *agg.* **1.** infallibile, sicuro **2.** immancabile.

unfair *agg.* sleale: — *competition,* concorrenza sleale.

unfairness *s.* slealtà, ingiustizia.

unfaithful *agg.* **1.** infedele, sleale **2.** inesatto.

unfaithfulness *s.* **1.** infedeltà **2.** inesattezza.

unfaltering *agg.* fermo, non esitante.

unfamiliar *agg.* poco familiare.

unfashionable *agg.* fuori moda.

to **unfasten** *vt.* slacciare, slegare. ◆ to **unfasten** *vi.* slacciarsi, slegarsi.

unfathomable *agg.* insondabile.

unfavourable *agg.* sfavorevole.

unfeeling *agg.* insensibile, spietato.

unfinished *agg.* **1.** incompleto **2.** non rifinito.

unfit *agg.* **1.** inadatto, disadatto **2.** inabile.

unfitness *s.* **1.** inidoneità **2.** debole costituzione.

to **unfold** *vt.* **1.** aprire, schiudere **2.** svelare. ◆ to **unfold** *vi.* **1.** aprirsi, schiudersi **2.** svelarsi.

unforbearing *agg.* insofferente, impaziente.

unforeseeing *agg.* imprevidente.

unforeseen *agg.* imprevisto.

unforgettable *agg.* indimenticabile.

unforgiving *agg.* senza misericordia.

unforgotten *agg.* inobliato.

unfortunate *agg.* sfortunato.

unfortunately *avv.* sfortunatamente.

unfounded *agg.* infondato.

to **unfreeze (unfroze, unfrozen)** *vt.* disgelare, scongelare. ◆ to **unfreeze (unfroze, unfrozen)** *vi.* disgelarsi.

unfrequent *agg.* infrequente.

unfriendly *agg.* poco amichevole.

to **unfrock** *vt.* spretare.

unfroze V. to *unfreeze.*

unfrozen V. to *unfreeze.*

unfruitful *agg.* infruttuoso.

unfruitfulness *s.* infruttuosità.

to **unfurl** *vt.* e *vi.* spiegare, spiegarsi (*di bandiere ecc.*).

unfurnished *agg.* **1.** non ammobiliato **2.** sfornito.

ungainly *agg.* goffo, maldestro.

ungentlemanlike *agg.* indegno di un gentiluomo.

ungirt *agg.* senza cintura.

to **unglue** *vt.* scollare. ◆ to **unglue** *vi.* scollarsi.

ungodly *agg.* **1.** empio **2.** malvagio.

ungraceful *agg.* sgraziato.

ungrammatical *agg.* sgrammaticato.

ungrateful *agg.* ingrato.

ungrounded *agg.* **1.** infondato **2.** senza preparazione.

unguarded *agg.* sguarnito, senza difesa.

unguent *s.* unguento.

unhandy *agg.* **1.** maldestro **2.** poco maneggevole.

unhappiness *s.* infelicità.

unhappy *agg.* infelice, triste.

unharmed *agg.* intatto, illeso.

unharmful *agg.* innocuo.

unhealthily *avv.* in modo malsano, poco igienicamente.

unhealthy *agg.* **1.** malsano, insalubre **2.** (*fig.*) dannoso **3.** malaticcio.

unheard *agg.* **1.** non udito **2.** non ascoltato **3.** sconosciuto, strano || — *-of,* inaudito.

to **unhinge** *vt.* scardinare.

unholy *agg.* profano, empio.

to **unhook** *vt.* sganciare. ◆ to **unhook** *vi.* sganciarsi.

unhoped *agg.* insperato, inatteso.

to **unhorse** *vt.* **1.** disarcionare **2.** staccare i cavalli da.

unhuman *agg.* sovrumano.

unhurt *agg.* illeso, incolume.

unhurtful *agg.* innocuo.

unicellular *agg.* unicellulare.
unification *s.* unificazione.
uniform *agg.* uniforme, costante. ♦
   uniform *s.* uniforme, divisa.
to **uniform** *vt.* uniformare.
uniformity *s.* uniformità.
to **unify** *vt.* unificare.
unilateral *agg.* unilaterale.
unilaterally *avv.* unilateralmente.
unimaginable *agg.* inimmaginabile.
unimpaired *agg.* inalterato, intatto.
unimpassioned *agg.* spassionato, calmo.
unimpeachable *agg.* incensurabile.
unimportance *s.* scarsa importanza.
unimportant *agg.* privo d'importanza.
unimposing *agg.* poco imponente, che non fa soggezione.
uninhabitable *agg.* inabitabile.
uninhabited *agg.* disabitato.
uninominal *agg.* uninominale.
unintelligent *agg.* stupido.
unintelligible *agg.* inintelligibile.
unintended *agg.* **1.** involontario **2.** (*giur.*) non intenzionale.
uninteresting *agg.* non interessante.
uninviting *agg.* poco attraente.
union *s.* unione, associazione, lega || (*trade*) —, sindacato; *the Union Jack*, la bandiera del Regno Unito.
unionism *s.* tendenza ad unirsi.
unionist *s.* unionista.
uniparous *agg.* uniparo.
unique *agg.* **1.** unico, solo **2.** eccezionale.
uniqueness *s.* unicità.
unisexual *agg.* unisessuale.
unison *s.* **1.** (*mus.*) unisono **2.** (*fig.*) concordia.
unit *s.* **1.** unità, unità di misura **2.** complesso, insieme.
unitary *agg.* unitario.
to **unite** *vt.* unire. ♦ to **unite** *vi.* **1.** unirsi **2.** mettersi d'accordo.
united *agg.* unito, collegato.
unity *s.* **1.** unità **2.** armonia.
universal *agg.* universale.
universality *s.* universalità.
to **universalize** *vt.* universalizzare.
universe *s.* universo.
university *s.* università.
univocal *agg.* univoco, non ambiguo.
to **unjoint** *vt.* disgiungere.
unjust *agg.* ingiusto.
unjustifiable *agg.* ingiustificabile.
unjustified *agg.* ingiustificato.
unkempt *agg.* trascurato, sciatto.

unkind *agg.* **1.** sgarbato, scortese **2.** crudele.
unkindness *s.* scortesia.
unknown *agg.* sconosciuto, ignoto.
unlawful *agg.* illegale.
to **unlearn (unlearnt, unlearnt)** (*anche reg.*) *vt.* disimparare.
unleavened *agg.* non lievitato || — *bread,* pane azzimo.
unless *cong.* a meno che, salvo che.
unlike *agg.* dissimile, diverso. ♦
   unlike *avv.* diversamente. ♦ **unlike** *prep.* diversamente da.
unlikelihood *s.* inverosimiglianza, improbabilità.
unlikely *agg.* inverosimile, improbabile.
unlimited *agg.* illimitato, sconfinato.
to **unline** *vt.* sfoderare.
unlined[1] *agg.* senza fodera.
unlined[2] *agg.* senza rughe.
unliterary *agg.* non letterario.
to **unload** *vt.* **1.** scaricare **2.** (*fig.*) alleggerire.
to **unlock** *vt.* aprire (*con chiave*).
unlooked-for *agg.* imprevisto.
to **unloose** *vt.* slegare.
unlosable *agg.* che non può essere perso.
unlovable *agg.* poco amabile, antipatico.
unlucky *agg.* **1.** sfortunato **2.** di cattivo augurio.
to **unman** *vt.* **1.** evirare **2.** abbrutire **3.** togliere forza.
unmarred *agg.* non sciupato.
unmarried *agg.* non coniugato.
to **unmask** *vt.* togliere la maschera (*anche fig.*). ♦ to **unmask** *vi.* togliersi la maschera.
unmatched *agg.* senza rivali.
unmentionable *agg.* innominabile, irripetibile.
unmerciful *agg.* spietato.
unmethodical *agg.* non metodico.
unminded *agg.* negletto.
unmindful *agg.* **1.** immemore **2.** incurante.
unmistakable *agg.* indubbio, inequivocabile.
to **unmoor** *vt. e vi.* togliere gli ormeggi a.
to **unnail** *vt.* schiodare.
unnatural *agg.* innaturale, contro natura.
unnavigable *agg.* non navigabile.
unnecessary *agg.* non necessario.
unneeded *agg.* inutile, non neces-

sario.

to **unnerve** *vt.* snervare.

unnoticed *agg.* inosservato.

unobjectionable *agg.* ineccepibile.

unobliging *agg.* poco compiacente.

unobservant *agg.* **1.** inosservante **2.** distratto.

unobserved *agg.* inosservato.

unobtrusive *agg.* discreto, modesto.

unoffending *agg.* inoffensivo.

unofficial *agg.* ufficioso.

to **unpack** *vt.* e *vi.* **1.** disfare (*le valigie*) **2.** disimballare.

unpalatable *agg.* di gusto sgradevole.

unpardonable *agg.* imperdonabile.

unpaved *agg.* non lastricato.

unperceivable *agg.* impercettibile.

unperceived *agg.* inavvertito.

unperishable *agg.* duraturo, imperituro.

unpleasant *agg.* spiacevole, sgradevole.

unpliable *agg.* poco piacevole.

unpoetic(al) *agg.* poco poetico.

to **unpoison** *vt.* svelenire.

unpolluted *agg.* incontaminato.

unpopular *agg.* impopolare.

unpopularity *s.* impopolarità.

unprecise *agg.* impreciso.

unpredictable *agg.* imprevedibile.

unpredicted *agg.* imprevisto.

unpremeditated *agg.* non premeditato.

unprepared *agg.* impreparato.

unpreparedness *s.* impreparazione.

unprepossessed *agg.* senza prevenzioni.

unprepossessing *agg.* senza attrattive, antipatico.

unpresentable *agg.* impresentabile.

unpriestly *agg.* che non si addice a un prete.

unprincely *agg.* che non si addice a un principe.

unprintable *agg.* non adatto ad essere pubblicato.

unproductive *agg.* improduttivo.

unprofitable *agg.* poco vantaggioso.

unprofitableness *s.* infruttuosità.

unpronounceable *agg.* impronunciabile.

unprovable *agg.* indimostrabile.

unpublished *agg.* inedito.

unqualified *agg.* **1.** incompetente **2.** non abilitato **3.** (*giur.*) senza restrizioni.

to **unqualify** *vt.* **1.** inabilitare **2.** squalificare.

unquenchable *agg.* inestinguibile, insaziabile (*anche fig.*).

unquestionable *agg.* incontestabile, indiscutibile.

unquestioned *agg.* indiscusso.

unquiet *agg.* inquieto.

unquoted *agg.* **1.** non citato **2.** (*comm.*) non quotato (*di titoli*).

to **unravel** *vt.* districare. ♦ to **unravel** *vi.* districarsi.

unreachable *agg.* irraggiungibile.

unready *agg.* **1.** impreparato **2.** tardo, lento.

unreal *agg.* irreale.

unreality *s.* irrealtà.

unrealizable *agg.* irrealizzabile.

unreasonable *agg.* irragionevole.

unrecognizable *agg.* irriconoscibile.

unredeemed *agg.* **1.** irredento **2.** non controbilanciato **3.** (*comm.*) non estinto.

unrelated *agg.* senza rapporti, senza legami.

unreliable *agg.* **1.** non fidato **2.** inattendibile.

unrepealed *agg.* (*giur.*) non abrogato.

unrequired *agg.* non richiesto.

unrest *s.* inquietudine.

unrestrained *agg.* non represso.

unrestricted *agg.* senza limitazioni.

unrevenged *agg.* invendicato.

unripe *agg.* immaturo, acerbo (*anche fig.*).

unrivalled *agg.* impareggiabile.

to **unroll** *vt.* svolgere. ♦ to **unroll** *vi.* svolgersi.

unruly *agg.* sregolato, indisciplinato.

to **unsaddle** *vt.* dissellare, disarcionare.

unsafe *agg.* malsicuro.

unsatisfied *agg.* **1.** insoddisfatto **2.** non convinto.

unsavoury *agg.* insipido, scipito.

unscholarly *agg.* **1.** indegno di un letterato **2.** non erudito.

to **unscrew** *vt.* svitare.

unscriptural *agg.* non conforme alle Sacre Scritture.

to **unseal** *vt.* dissigillare.

unseasonable *agg.* **1.** fuori stagione **2.** (*fig.*) intempestivo.

unseemliness *s.* indecenza

unseemly *agg.* sconveniente, indecente.

unseizable *agg.* inafferrabile.

unselfish *agg.* disinteressato.

unselfishness *s.* disinteresse.

unsettled *agg.* **1.** disordinato **2.** sconvolto, turbato **3.** mutevole, indeciso.

to **unsew (unsewed, unsewn)** *vt.* scucire.

unshaken *agg.* non scosso, fermo.

to **unsheathe** *vt.* sguainare.

to **unshoe (unshod, unshod)** *vt.* **1.** togliere le scarpe **2.** togliere i ferri a (*un cavallo*).

unshrinkable *agg.* irrestringibile.

unskilfulness *s.* incapacità, imperizia.

unskilled *agg.* inesperto, inabile.

unsocial *agg.* asociale.

unsold *agg.* invenduto.

to **unsolder** *vt.* dissaldare.

unsolved *agg.* insoluto.

unsound *agg.* **1.** malsano, malato **2.** guasto, avariato.

unspeakable *agg.* **1.** inesprimibile **2.** inqualificabile.

unstable *agg.* **1.** instabile **2.** (*fig.*) mutevole.

unsteadiness *agg.* incostanza, volubilità.

unsteady *agg.* instabile, incostante.

unsubstantial *agg.* **1.** inconsistente **2.** illusorio.

unsuccessful *agg.* mal riuscito, sfortunato.

unsuitable *agg.* inadatto, non appropriato.

unsure *agg.* **1.** malsicuro, precario **2.** incerto.

unsurpassed *agg.* insorpassato.

unsuspected *agg.* insospettato, non sospetto.

unsustainable *agg.* insostenibile.

untamable *agg.* indomabile.

untame *agg.* selvaggio, non addomesticato.

untaught *agg.* poco istruito, ignorante.

unteachable *agg.* **1.** difficile da insegnare **2.** non educabile.

unthinkable *agg.* inimmaginabile.

to **unthread** *vt.* sfilare, togliere il filo a.

untidily *avv.* disordinatamente.

untidy *agg.* disordinato, trasandato.

to **untie** *vt.* slegare. ♦ to **untie** *vi.* slegarsi.

until *prep.* fino a. ♦ **until** *cong.* finché.

untimeliness *s.* intempestività, inopportunità.

untimely *agg.* **1.** prematuro **2.** inopportuno. ♦ **untimely** *avv.* **1.** pre-

maturamente **2.** inopportunamente.

untiring *agg.* instancabile.

untitled *agg.* senza titolo.

to **untomb** *vt.* dissotterrare.

untouchable *agg.* **1.** intoccabile **2.** (*fig.*) irraggiungibile.

untouched *agg.* **1.** non toccato, intatto **2.** illeso, indenne.

untoward *agg.* **1.** restio, caparbio **2.** infausto.

untranslatable *agg.* intraducibile.

untravelled *agg.* che non ha viaggiato.

untrodden *agg.* non calpestato, non battuto.

untrue *agg.* **1.** falso, menzognero **2.** infedele.

untrustworthy *agg.* indegno di fiducia.

to **untune** *vt.* scordare (*uno strumento musicale*).

unusable *agg.* inutilizzabile.

unusual *agg.* insolito, inusitato.

unutterable *agg.* indescrivibile, impronunciabile.

unvarying *agg.* invariabile.

to **unveil** *vt.* **1.** togliere il velo a **2.** (*fig.*) rivelare.

unwary *agg.* incauto, sconsiderato.

unwatchful *agg.* non vigilante, disattento.

unweaned *agg.* non svezzato.

unweary *agg.* non stanco, indefesso.

unwell *agg.* indisposto, ammalato.

unwieldy *agg.* **1.** ingombrante **2.** impacciato.

unwilling *agg.* **1.** riluttante **2.** involontario.

unwillingly *avv.* malvolentieri.

unwillingness *s.* **1.** riluttanza **2.** malavoglia.

to **unwind (unwound, unwound)** *vt.* srotolare. ♦ to **unwind (unwound, unwound)** *vi.* srotolarsi.

unwise *agg.* malaccorto.

unwitting *agg.* inconsapevole.

unworldly *agg.* spirituale, non mondano.

unworthy *agg.* indegno, spregevole.

unwound *V.* to **unwind**.

to **unwrap** *vt.* disfare, svolgere.

unwritten *agg.* non scritto || — *law*, legge tramandata oralmente.

unwrought *agg.* **1.** non lavorato **2.** grezzo.

up[1] *avv.* **1.** su, in su, in alto **2.** in piedi || — *to*, fino a; *hurry* —, spicciati; *the game is —*, tutto è perduto. ◆ **up** *prep.* su, su per, in cima a ‖ *— now*, fino ad ora.

up² *agg.* ascendente, che va verso l'alto ‖ *— -train*, treno per Londra.

up-and-down *agg.* **1.** che va in su e in giù **2.** oscillante.

to upbraid *vt.* rimproverare.

upheaval *s.* **1.** sollevamento **2.** agitazione.

uphill *agg.* **1.** in salita **2.** (*fig.*) difficile. ◆ **uphill** *avv.* in salita. ◆ **uphill** *s.* salita.

to uphold (upheld, upheld) *vt.* **1.** sostenere, sorreggere **2.** (*fig.*) appoggiare, patrocinare.

to upholster *vt.* tappezzare, imbottire.

upholsterer *s.* tappezziere.

upholstery *s.* tappezzeria, imbottitura.

upkeep *s.* mantenimento, manutenzione.

upland *agg.* montuoso. ◆ **upland** *s.* zona montuosa.

upon *prep.* V. *on*.

upper *agg.* **1.** superiore, più alto **2.** più lontano (*dall'ingresso ecc.*) ‖ *the Upper House*, la Camera dei Lords.

uppercut *s.* (*sport*) "uppercut", colpo dal basso in alto.

upright *agg.* **1.** ritto, diritto, eretto **2.** retto, integro. ◆ **upright** *avv.* in piedi, perpendicolarmente.

uprightness *s.* **1.** perpendicolarità **2.** rettitudine.

uproar *s.* tumulto, chiasso.

uproarious *agg.* tumultuoso, chiassoso.

to uproot *vt.* sradicare, svellere.

ups and downs *s. pl.* **1.** ondulazioni (*del terreno*) **2.** (*fig.*) vicissitudini, alti e bassi.

to upset (upset, upset) *vt.* **1.** rovesciare **2.** disturbare, sconvolgere. ◆ **to upset (upset, upset)** *vi.* rovesciarsi, capovolgersi.

upset *agg.* **1.** rovesciato, capovolto **2.** (*fig.*) sconvolto, turbato. ◆ **upset** *s.* **1.** rovesciamento **2.** disordine.

upshot *s.* esito, risultato.

upside-down *avv.* capovolto, sottosopra.

upstairs *agg.* e *avv.* al piano superiore, di sopra.

upstanding *agg.* **1.** eretto, diritto **2.** (*fig.*) franco, leale.

up-to-date *agg.* aggiornato, all'ultima moda.

upward(s) *agg.* ascendente, rivolto verso l'alto. ◆ **upward** *avv.* **1.** in su, in alto **2.** al di sopra.

uranium *s.* uranio.

urban *agg.* urbano, di città.

urbane *agg.* urbano, cortese.

urbanity *s.* urbanità, cortesia.

urbanization *s.* urbanizzazione.

to urbanize *vt.* urbanizzare.

urchin *s.* monello.

uretic *agg.* e *s.* diuretico.

urge *s.* **1.** impulso, stimolo **2.** spinta, sprone.

to urge *vt.* e *vi.* **1.** spingere, stimolare **2.** consigliare, raccomandare.

urgency *s.* **1.** urgenza, premura **2.** bisogno urgente, necessità.

urgent *agg.* urgente, pressante.

uric *agg.* urico.

to urinate *vi.* orinare.

urine *s.* orina.

urn *s.* **1.** urna **2.** bricco.

us *pron. pers. compl. pl.* ci, noi: *three of —*, tre di noi.

usable *agg.* usabile, servibile.

usage *s.* **1.** uso, trattamento, impiego **2.** usanza.

use *s.* **1.** uso, impiego **2.** utilità, vantaggio **3.** (*giur.*) usufrutto.

to use *vt.* **1.** usare, adoperare **2.** trattare ‖ *to — up*, consumare.

used *agg.* **1.** usato, adoperato **2.** abituato ‖ *— -up*, esaurito.

useful *agg.* utile, pratico.

usefulness *s.* utilità, vantaggio.

useless *agg.* inutile, vano.

uselessness *s.* inutilità.

user *s.* **1.** utente **2.** (*giur.*) usufruttuario.

usher *s.* usciere.

to usher *vt.* precedere (*in qualità di usciere*).

usual *agg.* usuale, abituale ‖ *as —*, come al solito.

usually *avv.* di solito, abitualmente.

usufruct *s.* (*giur.*) usufrutto.

usufructuary *agg.* e *s.* usufruttuario.

usurer *s.* usuraio.

to usurp *vt.* usurpare.

usurpation *s.* usurpazione.

usurper *s.* usurpatore.

usury *s.* usura (*anche fig.*).

utensil *s.* utensile, arnese.

uterine *agg.* uterino.

uterus *s.* (*pl.* -ri) utero.

utilitarian *s.* utilitarista.

utilitarianism s. utilitarismo.
utility s. utilità, vantaggio.
utilizable agg. utilizzabile.
utilization s. utilizzazione.
to **utilize** vt. utilizzare.
utmost agg. e s. **1.** estremo, ultimo **2.** massimo, sommo || to do one's —, fare del proprio meglio.
Utopian s. utopista.
utter agg. completo, totale.
to **utter** vt. **1.** emettere **2.** esprimere, pronunciare.
utterable agg. esprimibile.
utterance s. espressione, sfogo.
uttering s. **1.** messa in circolazione **2.** spaccio (di assegni ecc.).
utterly avv. completamente, totalmente.
uttermost agg. e s. V. utmost.
uxoricide s. **1.** uxoricida **2.** uxoricidio.

V

vacancy s. **1.** vuoto, lacuna **2.** posto vacante || no —, completo (di alberghi ecc.).
vacant agg. **1.** vuoto, vacante **2.** non occupato.
to **vacate** vt. lasciar vacante, sgomberare || to — a seat, dare le dimissioni.
vacation s. **1.** il ritirarsi, il lasciar libero **2.** vacanze: long —, vacanze estive (pl.).
to **vaccinate** vt. e vi. vaccinare.
vaccination s. vaccinazione.
vaccine s. vaccino.
to **vacillate** vi. **1.** vacillare **2.** (fig.) esitare.
vacillating agg. **1.** vacillante **2.** incostante, irresoluto.
vacillation s. **1.** vacillamento **2.** esitazione.
vacillatory agg. V. vacillating.
vacuity s. vacuità (anche fig.).
vacuous agg. **1.** vacuo, vuoto **2.** sciocco, ozioso.
vacuum s. vuoto pneumatico || — cleaner, aspirapolvere.
vagabond s. viandante, vagabondo.
vagary s. fantasticheria, capriccio.
vagrancy s. vagabondaggio, accattonaggio.
vagrant agg. e s. vagabondo.

vague agg. vago, impreciso.
vaguely avv. vagamente.
vagueness s. indeterminatezza.
vain agg. **1.** vano, inutile **2.** vanitoso.
vainglorious agg. vanaglorioso.
vainglory s. vanagloria.
vainly avv. **1.** inutilmente **2.** vanitosamente.
valance s. **1.** drappeggio **2.** cortina (di un letto).
valediction s. addio, commiato.
valedictory agg. d'addio, di saluto.
♦ **valedictory** s. discorso d'addio.
valence s. (chim.) valenza.
valerian s. valeriana.
valet s. valletto.
valiant agg. valoroso, prode.
valid agg. valido, legittimo.
to **validate** vt. render valido, convalidare.
validity s. validità.
validly avv. validamente.
valley s. valle, vallata.
valorization s. valorizzazione.
to **valorize** vt. valorizzare.
valour s. valore.
valuable agg. **1.** di valore, prezioso **2.** valutabile.
valuation s. **1.** valutazione, stima **2.** considerazione.
value s. **1.** valore, prezzo **2.** (fig.) pregio, importanza || — in exchange, valore effettivo.
to **value** vt. **1.** valutare, stimare **2.** considerare, dar valore.
valueless agg. di nessun valore.
valuer s. estimatore.
valve s. **1.** valvola **2.** valva.
vamp¹ s. **1.** rappezzamento **2.** (mus.) accompagnamento.
vamp² s. (gergo) donna fatale.
vampire s. vampiro.
van s. **1.** furgone **2.** vagone ferroviario || luggage —, bagagliaio; prison —, cellulare.
Vandal agg. e s. vandalo.
Vandalic agg. vandalico.
vandalism s. vandalismo.
vane s. **1.** banderuola **2.** pala (di mulino a vento ecc.).
vanguard s. avanguardia (anche fig.).
vanilla s. vaniglia.
to **vanish** vi. svanire, sparire.
vanishing s. il dileguarsi, lo sparire.
vanity s. vanità || — -case, borsetta col necessario per il trucco.

to **vanquish** *vt.* vincere, conquistare.

vanquisher *s.* conquistatore

vantage *s.* vantaggio.

vapid *agg.* insulso.

vaporization *s.* evaporazione.

to **vaporize** *vt.* far evaporare. ♦ to **vaporize** *vi.* **1.** evaporare **2.** (*fig.*) volatilizzarsi.

vaporizer *s.* vaporizzatore.

vaporous *agg.* vaporoso.

vapour *s.* vapore, esalazione.

to **vapour** *vi.* **1.** evaporare **2.** (*fig.*) vantarsi.

vapouring *agg.* che evapora. ♦ **vapouring** *s.* vanteria.

vapourish *agg.* **1.** pieno di vapori **2.** depresso.

vapours *s. pl.* depressione (*sing.*), allucinazioni.

variability *s.* variabilità, mutevolezza.

variable *agg.* variabile, incostante.

variance *s.* **1.** variazione **2.** disaccordo.

variant *agg.* differente, contrastante. ♦ **variant** *s.* variante.

variation *s.* variazione, modificazione. ♦ **variations** *s. pl.* (*mat.*) variazioni.

varicoloured *agg.* variopinto.

varicose *agg.* varicoso.

varied *agg.* **1.** vario, variato **2.** variopinto.

to **variegate** *vt.* variegare, screziare.

variegated *agg.* variegato, screziato.

variegation *s.* screziatura.

variety *s.* varietà, diversità || — show (*teat.*), spettacolo di varietà.

various *agg.* alcuni, molti (*pl.*).

variously *avv.* variamente.

varnish *s.* **1.** vernice, lacca **2.** (*fig.*) apparenza, aspetto esteriore || *nail* —, smalto per unghie.

to **varnish** *vt.* **1.** verniciare, laccare **2.** (*fig.*) mascherare.

varnishing *s.* verniciatura, laccatura.

to **vary** *vt.* variare, cambiare. ♦ to **vary** *vi.* essere differente.

vase *s.* vaso.

vaseline *s.* vaselina.

vassal *s.* vassallo.

vassallage *s.* vassallaggio.

vast *agg.* ampio, immenso, vasto.

vastness *s.* vastità.

vat *s.* tino, tinozza.

vault[1] *s.* **1.** volta, soffitto a volta **2.** cantina **3.** sepolcro **4.** (*fig.*) volta celeste.

vault[2] *s.* volteggio.

to **vault** *vi.* volteggiare. ♦ to **vault** *vt.* saltare.

vaulting *s.* **1.** il costruire volte **2.** costruzione a volta.

to **vaunt** *vt.* vantare. ♦ to **vaunt** *vi.* vantarsi.

veal *s.* (*cuc.*) vitello.

vector *s.* vettore.

vectorial *agg.* vettoriale.

veer *s.* **1.** cambiamento di direzione **2.** (*mar.*) virata.

to **veer** *vi.* **1.** cambiare direzione **2.** (*mar.*) virare.

vegetable *agg.* vegetale. ♦ **vegetable** *s.* **1.** vegetale **2.** ortaggio. ♦ **vegetables** *s. pl.* verdura (*sing.*).

vegetal *agg.* vegetale.

vegetarian *agg.* e *s.* vegetariano.

to **vegetate** *vi.* vegetare (*anche fig.*).

vegetation *s.* **1.** vegetazione **2.** il vegetare.

vegetative *agg.* vegetativo.

vehemence *s.* veemenza.

vehement *agg.* veemente, impetuoso.

vehicle *s.* veicolo.

veil *s.* **1.** velo, cortina **2.** (*fig.*) apparenza, pretesto.

to **veil** *vt.* **1.** velare, coprire **2.** (*fig.*) dissimulare, nascondere.

veiling *s.* **1.** il velare **2.** velo, schermo.

vein *s.* **1.** (*anat.; geol.; fig.*) vena **2.** venatura, nervatura.

to **vein** *vt.* venare, coprire di venature.

veined *agg.* **1.** venato **2.** con venature, nervature.

velleity *s.* velleità.

velocipede *s.* velocipede.

velocity *s.* velocità.

velvet *agg.* di velluto, vellutato. ♦ **velvet** *s.* velluto.

velvety *agg.* vellutato, morbido.

venal *agg.* venale.

venality *s.* venalità.

to **vend** *vt.* vendere.

vendor *s.* venditore.

to **veneer** *vt.* **1.** impiallacciare **2.** (*fig.*) mascherare.

veneer, veneering *s.* **1.** impiallacciatura **2.** (*fig.*) maschera, vernice.

venerable *agg.* venerabile.

to **venerate** *vt.* venerare.

veneration *s.* venerazione.

venereal *agg.* venereo.

Venetian *agg.* e *s.* veneziano || —

blinds, shades, persiana alla veneziana.

vengeance *s.* vendetta || *to take — on so.,* vendicarsi di qu.

vengeful *agg.* vendicativo, vendicatore.

venial *agg.* veniale.

venom *s.* veleno (*di animali*).

venomous *agg.* velenoso.

venous *agg.* **1.** venoso **2.** con nervature.

vent[1] *s.* spacco, apertura (*di abito*).

vent[2] *s.* **1.** sbocco, apertura, foro **2.** (*fig.*) sfogo || *to give — to,* dar libero corso a.

to vent *vt.* **1.** svuotare, esalare **2.** (*fig.*) sfogare.

to ventilate *vt.* **1.** ventilare **2.** (*fig.*) discutere, rendere manifesto.

ventilation *s.* **1.** ventilazione **2.** discussione.

ventral *agg.* ventrale, addominale.

ventricle *s.* ventricolo.

ventriloquism *s.* ventriloquio.

ventriloquist *s.* ventriloquo.

venture *s.* **1.** avventura, azzardo **2.** (*comm.*) speculazione.

to venture *vt.* avventurare, arrischiare. ♦ **to venture** *vi.* avventurarsi, arrischiarsi.

venturer *s.* avventuriero.

venue *s.* sede giurisdizionale.

veracious *agg.* verace.

veracity *s.* veracità.

veranda(h) *s.* veranda.

verb *s.* verbo.

verbal *agg.* **1.** verbale **2.** orale, a parole.

verbally *avv.* verbalmente, oralmente.

verbiage *s.* verbosità.

verbose *agg.* verboso, prolisso

verdant *agg.* verdeggiante.

verdict *s.* verdetto.

verdigris *s.* verderame.

verge *s.* **1.** orlo, limite || *on the — of,* sul punto di **2.** bacchetta, verga.

to verge *vi.* **1.** confinare, essere contiguo, adiacente **2.** (*fig.*) rasentare: *to — on madness,* rasentare la pazzia.

verifiable *agg.* verificabile.

verification *s.* verifica.

verifier *s.* verificatore.

to verify *vt.* **1.** verificare, controllare **2.** (*giur.*) autenticare.

verily *avv.* in verità.

verisimilar *agg.* verosimile.

verisimilitude *s.* verosimiglianza.

verism *s.* verismo.

veritable *agg.* vero, genuino.

verity *s.* verità, realtà.

vermiform *s.* vermiforme.

vermin *s. coll.* insetti parassiti.

verminous *agg.* infestato da parassiti.

vernacular *s.* vernacolo, dialetto nativo. ♦ **vernacular** *agg.* vernacolo, nativo.

versatile *agg.* versatile, multiforme.

versatility *s.* versatilità.

verse *s.* **1.** verso **2.** strofa **3.** componimento in versi.

versification *s.* versificazione.

to versify *vt.* e *vi.* **1.** comporre in versi **2.** narrare in versi.

version *s.* versione, traduzione.

vertebra *s.* (*pl.* -ae) vertebra.

vertebral *agg.* vertebrale.

vertebrate *agg.* e *s.* vertebrato.

vertex *s.* (*pl.* -tices) vertice, apice, sommità.

vertical *agg.* verticale. ♦ **vertical** *s.* piano verticale, verticale.

verticality *s.* posizione verticale, perpendicolarità.

very *agg.* **1.** vero e proprio, autentico **2.** (*uso enfatico*) esatto, stesso: *at that — moment,* in quello stesso istante. ♦ **very** *avv.* molto, assai.

vessel *s.* **1.** vaso, recipiente **2.** nave, vascello.

vest *s.* **1.** panciotto **2.** camiciola, davantino.

to vest *vt.* **1.** conferire, investire **2.** (*giur.*) assegnare **3.** parare (*di altari ecc.*). ♦ **to vest** *vi.* passare per eredità.

vestal *s.* vestale.

vestibule *s.* vestibolo, entrata, portico di chiesa.

vestige *s.* vestigio, traccia.

vestment *s.* veste (*spec. liturgica*).

vestry *s.* **1.** sagrestia **2.** assemblea parrocchiale.

vesture *s.* rivestimento, veste.

veteran *agg.* e *s.* veterano.

veterinary *agg.* e *s.* veterinario.

to vex *vt.* **1.** vessare, opprimere **2.** irritare.

vexation *s.* **1.** vessazione, oppressione **2.** irritazione.

vexatious *agg.* **1.** irritante, fastidioso **2.** (*giur.*) vessatorio.

vexed *agg.* **1.** vessato, oppresso **2.** irritato.

via *prep.* per, via, attraverso: — *air mail*, per via aerea.

viability *s.* vitalità.

viable *agg.* vitale.

viaduct *s.* viadotto.

vial *s.* fiala.

viand *s.* vivanda, cibo.

vibrant *agg.* vibrante, tremante.

to vibrate *vi.* vibrare, risuonare. ♦ **to vibrate** *vt.* far vibrare.

vibration *s.* vibrazione, tremolio.

vibrator *s.* vibratore.

vibratory *agg.* **1.** vibratorio **2.** vibrante.

vicar *s.* **1.** curato (*nella Chiesa d'Inghilterra*) **2.** vicario (*Chiesa Cattolica*).

vicariate *s.* vicariato.

vice[1] *s.* **1.** immoralità, depravazione **2.** vizio.

vice[2] *s.* (*mecc.*) morsa.

vice[3] *s.* sostituto, vice.

vice[4] *prep.* in luogo di.

viceroy *s.* viceré.

vicinity *s.* **1.** vicinanza, prossimità **2.** affinità.

vicious *agg.* **1.** vizioso, immorale **2.** maligno **3.** bizzarro (*di animali*) **4.** difettoso, scorretto.

vicissitude *s.* vicissitudine.

victim *s.* vittima.

victor *s.* vincitore.

victorious *agg.* vittorioso.

victory *s.* vittoria.

to victual *vt.* vettovagliare, approvvigionare. ♦ **to victual** *vi.* approvvigionarsi.

victualling *s.* vettovagliamento, approvvigionamento.

victuals *s. pl.* vettovaglie, viveri.

to vie *vi.* gareggiare.

view *s.* **1.** vista, sguardo **2.** veduta, panorama **3.** opinione **4.** scopo, mira **5.** (*giur.*) sopralluogo || *point of* —, punto di vista; — *-finder* (*foto*), mirino.

to view *vt.* **1.** guardare attentamente **2.** esaminare.

viewer *s.* **1.** chi guarda **2.** telespettatore **3.** ispettore.

viewless *agg.* **1.** senza vista (*di casa ecc.*) **2.** invisibile.

viewpoint *s.* punto di vista.

vigil *s.* veglia.

vigilance *s.* vigilanza.

vigilant *agg.* vigilante, vigile.

vigorous *agg.* vigoroso, forte.

Viking *s.* vichingo.

vigour *s.* vigore, energia.

vigorously *avv.* vigorosamente.

vile *agg.* vile, spregevole.

vileness *s.* viltà, bassezza.

to vilify *vt.* diffamare.

villa *s.* villa.

village *s.* villaggio, paese.

villager *s.* abitante di villaggio.

villain *s.* furfante, scellerato.

villainous *agg.* scellerato, infame.

villainy *s.* scelleratezza.

to vindicate *vt.* **1.** rivendicare **2.** giustificare, difendere.

vindication *s.* **1.** rivendicazione **2.** giustificazione, difesa.

vindictive *agg.* vendicativo.

vine *s.* vite || — *-leaf*, pampino; — *-dresser*, vignaiuolo.

vinegar *s.* aceto.

vinery *s.* serra per viti.

vineyard *s.* vigneto, vigna.

vintage *s.* **1.** vendemmia **2.** annata.

vintager *s.* vendemmiatore.

vintner *s.* vinaio.

to violate *vt.* **1.** violare, trasgredire **2.** profanare.

violation *s.* **1.** violazione, trasgressione **2.** profanazione.

violator *s.* **1.** violatore, trasgressore **2.** profanatore.

violence *s.* violenza, veemenza.

violent *agg.* violento, impetuoso.

violet *agg.* violetto, viola. ♦ **violet** *s.* viola mammola.

violin *s.* violino.

violoncellist *s.* violoncellista.

viper *s.* vipera (*anche fig.*).

virgin *agg. e s.* vergine.

virginal *agg.* verginale.

virginity *s.* verginità.

virile *agg.* virile.

virility *s.* virilità.

virtual *agg.* virtuale, effettivo.

virtuality *s.* potenzialità, virtualità.

virtue *s.* **1.** virtù, moralità, forza d'animo **2.** qualità, merito.

virtuosity *s.* virtuosismo.

virtuous *agg.* virtuoso, morale.

virulence *s.* virulenza.

virulent *agg.* virulento.

virus *s.* virus.

visa *s.* visto consolare.

to visa *vt.* vistare (*un passaporto*).

visceral *agg.* viscerale.

viscid *agg.* viscido.

viscidity *s.* viscidità.

viscose *s.* viscosa.

viscosity *s.* viscosità.

viscount *s.* visconte.

viscous *agg.* viscoso.

visibility *s.* visibilità.

visible *agg.* visibile, evidente, manifesto.

vision *s.* **1.** visione, immaginazione **2.** vista, capacità visiva.

visional *agg.* irreale.

visionary *s.* visionario.

visit *s.* visita: *to pay a* —, fare una visita.

to visit *vt.* e *vi.* visitare, fare una visita.

visitation *s.* **1.** visita ufficiale **2.** castigo divino.

visitor *s.* visitatore, ospite.

visor *s.* visiera.

visual *agg.* visuale, visivo.

to visualize *vt.* **1.** rendere visibile **2.** prospettare. ♦ **to visualize** *vi.* diventare visibile.

vital *agg.* vitale, essenziale.

vifality *s.* vitalità.

to vitalize *vt.* vivificare.

vitals *s. pl.* organi vitali.

vitamin *s.* vitamina.

to vitiate *vt.* **1.** viziare **2.** (*giur.*) invalidare.

vitiation *s.* **1.** corruzione **2.** (*giur.*) l'invalidare.

viticulture *s.* viticoltura.

vitreous *agg.* vitreo.

vitrifiable *agg.* vetrificabile.

vitrification *s.* vetrificazione.

to vitrify *vt.* vetrificare. ♦ **to vitrify** *vi.* vetrificarsi.

vitriol *s.* vetriolo.

to vituperate *vt.* vituperare.

vituperation *s.* invettiva, biasimo.

vivacious *agg.* vivace, vispo.

vivacity *s.* vivacità, brio.

vivid *agg.* **1.** vivace, vigoroso **2.** vivido, colorito.

to vivify *vt.* vivificare, animare.

viviparous *agg.* viviparo.

vivisection *s.* vivisezione.

vixen *s.* **1.** volpe femmina **2.** megera.

vocabulary *s.* vocabolario.

vocal *agg.* vocale.

vocalization *s.* vocalizzazione.

to vocalize *vt.* e *vi.* vocalizzare.

vocation *s.* **1.** vocazione **2.** attitudine, inclinazione **3.** professione.

vocational *agg.* professionale.

vocative *agg.* e *s.* vocativo.

vociferous *agg.* clamoroso, vociferante.

vogue *s.* voga, moda.

voice *s.* voce || *with one* —, all'unanimità.

to voice *vt.* esprimere, dire.

voiced *agg.* **1.** dalla voce: *deep-* —, dalla voce profonda **2.** sonoro.

voiceless *agg.* senza voce, muto.

void *agg.* **1.** vuoto **2.** privo **3.** (*giur.*) nullo. ♦ **void** *s.* il vuoto.

to void *vt.* **1.** vuotare, liberare **2.** abrogare.

volatile *agg.* **1.** volatile, alato **2.** (*fig.*) incostante. ♦ **volatile** *s.* **1.** volatile **2.** (*chim.*) sostanza volatile.

to volatilize *vt.* volatilizzare. ♦ **to volatilize** *vi.* volatilizzarsi.

volcano *s.* vulcano.

volley *s.* **1.** scarica, raffica, salva || — *-ball*, palla a volo.

voltage *s.* (*elettr.*) voltaggio, tensione.

voltameter *s.* voltametro.

volubility *s.* speditezza (*di eloquio*), loquacità.

voluble *agg.* spedito (*di eloquio*), loquace.

volume *s.* **1.** volume **2.** tomo, libro **3.** massa.

volumetric(al) *agg.* volumetrico.

voluminous *agg.* **1.** in molti volumi **2.** (*fig.*) fecondo (*di scrittore*) **3.** voluminoso.

voluntarily *avv.* volontariamente.

voluntary *agg.* **1.** volontario, spontaneo **2.** voluto, fatto di proposito **3.** mantenuto da contributi non statali. ♦ **voluntary** *s.* azione volontaria.

volunteer *s.* volontario.

to volunteer *vi.* **1.** offrirsi volontariamente **2.** arruolarsi volontario.

voluptuary *agg.* **1.** voluttuario **2.** voluttuoso.

voluptuous *agg.* voluttuoso, sensuale.

voluptuousness *s.* voluttà, sensualità.

volute *s.* voluta, spirale.

vomit *s.* vomito.

to vomit *vt.* e *vi.* vomitare (*anche fig.*).

voracious *agg.* ingordo, vorace.

vortex *s.* vortice, gorgo.

vortical *agg.* vorticoso.

votary *s.* seguace, devoto.

vote *s.* voto, votazione.

to vote *vt.* e *vi.* votare.

voter *s.* elettore.

votive *agg.* votivo.

to vouch *vt.* e *vi.* **1.** attestare, garantire **2.** (*giur.*) citare come garante.

voucher s. 1. testimone 2. documento giustificativo.
to **vouchsafe** vt. concedere.
vow s. voto.
to **vow** vi. fare un voto.
vowel s. vocale.
voyage s. viaggio (spec. per via d'acqua) || outward —, viaggio di andata; home —, viaggio di ritorno.
to **voyage** vi. fare una traversata, navigare.
vulcanization s. vulcanizzazione.
vulgar agg. volgare, triviale.
vulgarism, vulgarity s. volgarità.
to **vulgarize** vt. 1. rendere volgare 2. divulgare.
vulnerability s. vulnerabilità.
vulnerable agg. vulnerabile.
vulture s. avvoltoio.

W

to **wabble** vi. vacillare, traballare.
wad s. 1. tampone 2. imbottitura 3. rotolo (di banconote).
to **wad** vt. 1. tamponare 2. imbottire.
wadable agg. guadabile.
wadding s. ovatta.
waddle s. andatura ondeggiante.
to **waddle** vi. camminare ondeggiando.
wade s. guado.
to **wade** vt. guadare. ♦ to **wade** vi. procedere faticosamente.
wader s. 1. chi passa a guado 2. (zool.) trampoliere. ♦ **waders** s. pl. stivaloni impermeabili.
wading s. il guadare.
wafer s. 1. cialda 2. disco adesivo.
waft s. soffio.
to **waft** vt. sospingere. ♦ to **waft** vi. fluttuare.
wag s. 1. cenno 2. scodinzolio.
to **wag** vt. scuotere. ♦ to **wag** vi. scuotersi || to have a wagging tongue, avere la lingua troppo lunga.
to **wage** vt. intraprendere (guerra).
to **wager** vt. e vi. scommettere.
wages s. pl. salario (sing.) || —-earner, salariato.
to **waggle** V. to wag.
wag(g)on s. carro || tea- —, car-

rello da tè.
waif s. relitto (anche fig.).
wail s. gemito.
to **wail** vt. e vi. gemere.
wainscot s. rivestimento in legno.
to **wainscot** vt. rivestire in legno.
waist s. cintola.
waistband s. cintura.
waistbelt s. cinturone.
waistcoat s. panciotto.
wait s. 1. attesa 2. agguato.
to **wait** vt. e vi. (for so., sthg.) aspettare (qu., qc.) || to — on, servire.
waiter s. 1. cameriere 2. vassoio.
waiting s. attesa || — -room, sala d'aspetto; to keep —, fare aspettare.
waitress s. cameriera.
to **waive** vt. rinunciare a, mettere da parte.
wake[1] s. 1. scia 2. pista.
wake[2] s. 1. risveglio 2. veglia (funebre).
to **wake** (waked e woke, waked, woke(n)) vt. svegliare. ♦ to **wake** (waked e woke, waked, woke(n)) vi. svegliarsi.
wakeful agg. sveglio.
wakefulness s. veglia.
to **waken** V. to wake.
wakening s. risveglio.
waking agg. sveglio. ♦ **waking** s. 1. risveglio 2. veglia.
walk s. 1. passeggiata 2. andatura 3. (fig.) rango || to take a —, fare una passeggiata.
to **walk** vi. passeggiare, andare a piedi || to — off, andarsene.
walker s. camminatore.
walkie-talkie s. (radio) trasmettitore-ricevitore portatile.
walking s. il camminare || — tour, escursione a piedi.
walkover s. facile vittoria.
wall s. muro || — paper, carta da parato; main —, muro maestro.
to **wall** vt. circondare di mura || to — up, murare.
wallet s. portafoglio.
wall-eye s. glaucoma.
Walloon agg. e s. vallone.
to **wallop** vt. 1. bastonare 2. percuotere, sculacciare.
wallow s. pantano.
to **wallow** vi. sguazzare.
walnut s. noce.
walrus s. tricheco.
waltz s. valzer.

to **waltz** *vi.* ballare il valzer.
wan *agg.* pallido.
to **wan** *vi.* impallidire.
wand *s.* bacchetta magica.
wander *s.* vagabondaggio.
to **wander** *vi.* **1.** vagare **2.** vaneggiare.
wanderer *s.* vagabondo.
wandering *agg.* **1.** errante **2.** delirante. ♦ **wandering** *s.* **1.** vagabondaggio **2.** delirio.
wane *s.* declino.
to **wane** *vi.* **1.** declinare **2.** decrescere **3.** essere in fase calante.
to **wangle** *vt.* ottenere con intrighi.
want *s.* **1.** mancanza **2.** bisogno: *to be in — of*, aver bisogno di.
to **want** *vt.* **1.** volere **2.** aver bisogno di **3.** mancare.
wanted *agg.* ricercato: *to be — by the police*, essere ricercato dalla polizia.
wanting *prep.* senza, in mancanza di.
wanton *agg.* **1.** licenzioso **2.** capriccioso **3.** arbitrario **4.** lascivo.
to **wanton** *vi.* **1.** scherzare **2.** comportarsi dissolutamente.
wantonness *s.* **1.** dissolutezza **2.** capriccio.
war *s.* guerra: *— Office*, Ministero della Guerra.
to **war** *vi.* guerreggiare.
warble *s.* trillo.
to **warble** *vt.* e *vi.* trillare.
warbling *agg.* melodioso. ♦ **warbling** *s.* gorgheggio.
ward *s.* **1.** guardia **2.** reparto **3.** rione **4.** tutela **5.** pupillo.
to **ward** *vt.* parare: *to — off a blow*, parare un colpo.
warden *s.* **1.** guardiano **2.** direttore **3.** governatore.
wardenship *s.* carica di direttore, governatore.
warder *s.* **1.** guardiano **2.** carceriere.
wardrobe *s.* guardaroba.
wardroom *s.* (*mar.*) quadrato ufficiali.
wardship *s.* tutela.
ware *agg.* conscio, circospetto.
to **ware** *vt.* fare attenzione a.
wares *s. pl.* **1.** articoli **2.** vasellame (*sing.*).
warehouse *s.* magazzino.
to **warehouse** *vt.* depositare in magazzino.
warehouseman *s.* **1.** magazziniere **2.** commerciante all'ingrosso.

warfare *s.* operazione bellica.
warfaring *agg.* bellicoso.
warily *avv.* cautamente.
wariness *s.* cautela.
warlike *agg.* guerriero.
warlikeness *s.* bellicosità.
warlock *s.* stregone.
warm *agg.* **1.** caldo **2.** animato.
to **warm** *vt.* **1.** scaldare **2.** animare. ♦ to **warm** *vi.* **1.** scaldarsi **2.** animarsi.
warmer *s.* riscaldatore.
warm-hearted *agg.* bonario, cordiale.
warming *s.* riscaldamento.
warmonger *s.* guerrafondaio.
warmth *s.* calore.
to **warn** *vt.* avvertire || *to — off*, invitare ad allontanarsi.
warning *s.* (pre)avviso || *— light*, spia luminosa.
warp *s.* **1.** ordito **2.** deformazione.
to **warp** *vt.* **1.** curvare **2.** (*fig.*) alterare. ♦ to **warp** *vi.* **1.** curvarsi **2.** (*fig.*) alterarsi.
warpath *s.* sentiero di guerra.
warping *s.* deformazione, pervertimento.
warrant *s.* **1.** garanzia, garante **2.** (*giur.; comm.*) ordine, autorizzazione.
to **warrant** *vt.* **1.** garantire **2.** giustificare.
warrantable *agg.* **1.** giustificabile **2.** legittimo.
warrantee *s.* chi riceve una garanzia.
warranter, -tor *s.* garante.
warranty *s.* **1.** garanzia **2.** autorizzazione.
warrior *s.* guerriero.
warship *s.* nave da guerra.
wart *s.* verruca.
wartime *s.* tempo di guerra.
wary *agg.* cauto.
was V. *to be.*
wash *s.* **1.** lavata **2.** bucato **3.** sciacquio **4.** brodaglia **5.** mano (*di colore*).
to **wash** *vt.* **1.** lavare **2.** bagnare **3.** gettare. ♦ to **wash** *vi.* **1.** lavarsi **2.** essere lavabile || *to — up*, rigovernare (*le stoviglie*); *to — over*, sommergere.
washable *agg.* lavabile.
washbasin *s.* catino.
washboard *s.* asse per lavare.
washer *s.* **1.** lavandaio **2.** (*mecc.*) lavatrice **3.** (*mecc.*) rondella.

washerwoman s. lavandaia.

washhouse s. lavanderia.

washing s. 1. lavaggio 2. bucato 3. risciacquatura || — -*machine*, lavatrice.

whashout s. erosione, dilatamento.

washroom s. 1. lavanderia 2. gabinetto.

washstand s. lavabo.

washy agg. 1. annacquato 2. scialbo.

wasp s. vespa.

waspish agg. pungente.

waspishness s. irascibilità.

wastage s. logorio.

waste agg. 1. deserto 2. di scarto. ♦ **waste** s. 1. spreco 2. scarto 3. deserto || — -*basket*, cestino per rifiuti; — -*paper*, carta straccia.

to waste vt. 1. consumare 2. sprecare 3. rovinare. ♦ **to waste** vi. 1. consumarsi 2. rovinarsi.

wasteful agg. 1. rovinoso 2. prodigo.

waster s. dissipatore.

wasting agg. 1. logorante 2. devastante. ♦ **wasting** s. 1. sciupio 2. deperimento 3. devastazione.

watch s. 1. orologio (*da polso*) 2. guardia || — -*fire*, fuoco di bivacco; *to be on the* —, stare in guardia.

to watch vt. 1. osservare 2. stare a guardia di. ♦ **to watch** vi. 1. vegliare 2. aspettare.

watcher s. 1. spettatore 2. sorvegliante.

watchful agg. attento.

watchfulness s. 1. vigilanza 2. cautela.

watchmaker s. orologiaio.

watchman s. guardia (*notturna*).

watchword s. parola d'ordine.

water s. acqua || *to hold* —, non fare acqua, (*fig.*) essere logico; — -*bottle*, borraccia; — -*colour*, acquarello; — -*colourist*, acquarellista; — -*closet*, gabinetto; — -*gate*, chiusa; — -*line*, linea di galleggiamento; — -*meadow*, marcita; — -*polo*, pallanuoto; *drinking* —, acqua potabile.

to water vt. 1. bagnare 2. diluire 3. abbeverare 4. secernere || *to make one's mouth* —, far venire l'acquolina in bocca. ♦ **to water** vi. 1. abbeverarsi 2. riempirsi di acqua.

waterfall s. cascata.

watering s. 1. annaffiamento 2. diluizione 3. abbeverarsi 4. rifornimento d'acqua 5. secrezione || — -*can*, — -*pot*, annaffiatoio.

waterman s. (*pl.* -men) barcaiolo.

watermark s. 1. filigrana 2. indicatore di livello 3. livello d'acqua.

watermelon s. anguria.

waterproof agg. e s. impermeabile.

to waterproof vt. impermeabilizzare.

watershed s. 1. spartiacque 2. bacino idrico.

watertight agg. stagno.

waterway s. canale navigabile.

waterworks s. pl. impianto idrico (*sing.*).

watery agg. 1. acquoso 2. lacrimoso.

wattle s. 1. fascina 2. vimine.

wave s. 1. onda, ondata 2. cenno (*della mano*).

to wave vi. 1. ondeggiare 2. far cenno (*con la mano*). ♦ **to wave** vt. 1. far ondeggiare 2. ondulare 3. chiamare (*con un cenno di mano*).

waved agg. ondulato.

wave-length s. lunghezza d'onda.

waveless agg. liscio.

wavelet s. piccola onda.

wavelike agg. ondeggiante.

to waver vi. vacillare.

wavering s. 1. oscillazione 2. esitazione.

wavily avv. a onde.

waviness s. ondulazione.

waving s. 1. ondeggiamento, ondulazione 2. sventolio 3. cenno.

wavy agg. 1. ondulato 2. ondeggiante.

wax s. 1. cera 2. paraffina.

to wax[1] vt. incerare.

to wax[2] vi. 1. crescere 2. aumentare.

waxen agg. di, come cera.

way s. 1. via 2. maniera 3. punto di vista 4. stato || *to make* —, far posto; *this* —, per di qua; *in a* —, in un certo senso; *by the* —, tra parentesi; *one-* —, senso unico; *out of the* —, fuori mano.

waybill s. lista dei passeggeri.

wayfarer s. viandante.

to waylay vt. tendere un agguato a.

wayside s. margine della strada.

wayward agg. 1. indocile 2. capriccioso.

waywardness s. ostinazione.

we pron. sogg. noi.

weak *agg.* **1.** debole **2.** diluito.

to **weaken** *vi.* indebolirsi. ♦ to **weaken** *vt.* indebolire.

weakling *s.* persona debole.

weakly *agg.* debole.

weakness *s.* debolezza.

weal[1] *s.* benessere, prosperità.

weal[2] *s.* livido.

wealth *s.* ricchezza.

wealthy *agg.* ricco.

to **wean** *vt.* **1.** svezzare **2.** togliere il vizio a.

weaning *s.* svezzamento.

weapon *s.* arma.

wear *s.* **1.** uso, usura **2.** durata **3.** abbigliamento.

to **wear** (**wore, worn**) *vt.* **1.** indossare **2.** logorare **3.** stancare || *to — out*, logorare, stancare. ♦ to **wear** (**wore, worn**) *vi.* **1.** logorarsi **2.** stancarsi **3.** durare || *to — out*, logorarsi, stancarsi.

wearily *avv.* stancamente.

weariness *s.* **1.** stanchezza **2.** tedio.

wearing *agg.* **1.** logorante **2.** da indossare. ♦ **wearing** *s.* **1.** logorio **2.** l'indossare.

wearisome *agg.* **1.** faticoso **2.** tedioso.

weary *agg.* **1.** stanco **2.** annoiato.

to **weary** *vt.* **1.** affaticare **2.** annoiare. ♦ to **weary** *vi.* **1.** affaticarsi **2.** annoiarsi.

weasel *s.* donnola.

weather *s.* tempo (*atmosferico*) || *— -glass*, barometro; *— -report*, bollettino meteorologico.

to **weather** *vt.* **1.** esporre all'aria **2.** superare || *to — a storm*, resistere a una burrasca. ♦ to **weather** *vi.* alterarsi.

weathercock *s.* banderuola.

weathering *s.* alterazione (*di tempo*).

weave *s.* tessuto.

to **weave** (**wove, woven**) *vt.* **1.** tessere, intrecciare **2.** (*fig.*) ideare.

weaver *s.* tessitore.

weaving *s.* **1.** tessitura **2.** orditura.

web *s.* **1.** tela **2.** (*fig.*) trama **3.** membrana || *cob— —*, ragnatela.

to **wed** *vt.* sposare. ♦ to **wed** *vi.* sposarsi.

wedding *s.* nozze (*pl.*) || *— -breakfast*, rinfresco di nozze; *— -ring*, fede nuziale.

wedge *s.* cuneo.

to **wedge** *vt.* **1.** incuneare **2.** fendere con cunei.

wedlock *s.* vincolo matrimoniale.

Wednesday *s.* mercoledì.

wee *agg.* minuscolo || *a — bit*, un tantino.

weed *s.* erbaccia. ♦ **weeds** *s. pl.* gramaglie.

to **weed** *vt.* **1.** sarchiare **2.** estirpare.

weeding *s.* sarchiatura.

week *s.* settimana || *today —*, oggi a otto; *— in — out*, una settimana dopo l'altra.

weekday *s.* giorno feriale.

week-end *s.* fine settimana.

weekly *agg.* e *s.* settimanale. ♦ **weekly** *avv.* settimanalmente.

weep *s.* pianto.

to **weep** (**wept, wept**) *vt.* e *vi.* **1.** piangere **2.** trasudare || *to — out*, piangere disperatamente.

weeper *s.* **1.** chi piange **2.** velo, nastro di lutto.

weeping *s.* **1.** pianto **2.** trasudamento.

weft *s.* trama (*di tessuto*).

to **weigh** *vt.* e *vi.* **1.** pesare **2.** (*fig.*) ponderare || *to — down*, piegare; *to — anchor* (*mar.*), levar l'ancora.

weigh-house *s.* pesa pubblica.

weighing *s.* pesatura || *— -machine*, pesa.

weight *s.* **1.** peso **2.** importanza || *to put on —*, ingrassare

to **weight** *vi.* appensantire, caricare.

weightiness *s.* **1.** pesantezza **2.** (*fig.*) importanza.

weightless *agg.* senza peso.

weighty *agg.* **1.** pesante **2.** (*fig.*) importante.

weir *s.* chiusa, diga.

weird *agg.* **1.** fatale **2.** misterioso.

welcome *agg.* gradito. ♦ **welcome** *s.* benvenuto.

to **welcome** *vt.* dare il benvenuto a, gradire.

to **weld** *vt.* saldare. ♦ to **weld** *vi.* saldarsi.

welding *s.* saldatura.

welfare *s.* benessere || *— contributions*, oneri previdenziali; *— state*, stato assistenziale; *— work*, assistenza sociale.

well[1] *s.* **1.** fonte, pozzo **2.** tromba delle scale.

well[2] *avv.* e *s.* bene || *as —*, pure; *as — as*, oltre a, oltre che; *to be —*, star bene; *to get —*, guarire.

to **well** *vi.* sgorgare.

well-advised *agg.* saggio.

well-being *s.* benessere.

well-bred *agg.* educato.

well-doing *s.* buona condotta.

well-done *agg.* (*cuc.*) ben cotto.

well-meaning *agg.* ben intenzionato.

well-off *agg.* agiato.

well-read *agg.* colto, ben educato.

well-timed *agg.* opportuno.

well-to-do *agg.* agiato.

Welsh *agg.* gallese.

Welshman *s.* gallese.

went V. *to go.*

wept V. *to weep.*

were V. *to be* || *as it* —, per così dire.

west *agg.* occidentale. ♦ **west** *avv.* a, verso ovest. ♦ **west** *s.* ovest.

westerly *agg.* 1. dall'ovest 2. verso ovest. ♦ **westerly** *avv.* verso ovest.

western *agg.* occidentale.

westerner *s.* occidentale.

to westernize *vt.* occidentalizzare. ♦ **to westernize** *vi.* occidentalizzarsi.

westward *agg. e avv.* verso ovest.

westwards *avv.* verso ovest.

wet *agg.* 1. umido 2. piovoso || — *blanket*, guastafeste. ♦ **wet** *s.* 1. umidità 2. tempo piovoso.

to wet *vt.* bagnare. ♦ **to wet** *vi.* bagnarsi.

wet-nurse *s.* nutrice.

wetting *s.* bagnatura.

whale *s.* balena || — *-boat*, baleniera.

to whale *vi.* andare a caccia di balene.

whalebone *s.* stecca di balena.

whaler *s.* 1. baleniere 2. baleniera.

wharf *s.* banchina.

to wharf *vt.* attraccare.

what *agg.* 1. (*int.*) quale? quali? che? 2. (*rel.*) (quello) ... che 3. (*escl.*) che! ♦ **what** *pron.* 1. (*int.*) che?, che cosa? 2. (*rel.*) ciò che 3. (*escl.*) quanto! || — *for?*, perché mai?; — *is he?*, che cosa fa? ♦ **what** *inter.* come!

whatever *agg.* qualunque. ♦ **whatever** *pron.* qualunque cosa. ♦ **whatever** *avv.* affatto.

whatsoever V. *whatever.*

wheat *s.* grano.

to wheedle *vt.* lusingare.

wheel *s.* 1. ruota 2. volante || *wheels within wheels*, retroscena.

to wheel *vt.* 1. far ruotare 2. spingere (*su un veicolo a ruote*). ♦

to wheel *vi.* ruotare.

wheelbarrow *s.* carriola.

wheeze *s.* respiro affannoso.

to wheeze *vi.* ansimare.

whelp *s.* cucciolo.

when *avv. e cong.* quando.

whence *avv.* da dove.

whenever *avv.* tutte le volte che.

where *avv.* dove.

whereabout(s) *avv. e cong.* dove. ♦ **whereabout(s)** *s.* luogo.

whereas *cong.* mentre.

whereby *avv.* 1. (*int.*) come? 2. (*rel.*) per cui.

wherefore *avv.* 1. (*int.*) perché 2. (*rel.*) perciò.

wherein *avv.* 1. (*int.*) come? dove? 2. (*rel.*) in cui.

whereof *avv.* 1. (*int.*) di che? 2. (*rel.*) di cui.

whereon *avv.* 1. (*int.*) su che? 2. (*rel.*) su cui.

whereto *avv.* 1. (*int.*) verso dove? a che scopo? 2. (*rel.*) a cui.

whereupon *avv.* 1. (*int.*) su che? 2. (*rel.*) dopo di che.

wherever *avv.* dovunque.

whet *s.* 1. affilatura 2. (*fig.*) stimolante.

to whet *vt.* 1. affilare 2. stimolare.

whether *cong.* se || — ... *or*, o...o.

whey *s.* siero (*del latte*).

which *agg.* 1. (*int.*) quale?, quali? 2. (*rel.*) il, la quale, i, le quali. ♦ **which** *pron.* 1. (*int.*) quale?, quali?, chi? 2. (*rel.*) il, la quale, i, le quali; il che || *I cannot tell* — *is* —, non so distinguerli l'uno dall'altro.

whichever *agg.* qualunque. ♦ **whichever** *pron.* qualunque cosa.

whiff *s.* 1. soffio 2. sbuffo.

to whiff *vt.* e *vi.* 1. soffiare 2. emettere sbuffi.

whig *agg. e s.* (*pol. inglese*) liberale.

while *cong.* 1. mentre 2. sebbene. ♦ **while** *s.* momento || *once in a* —, una volta tanto; *the* —, frattanto.

to while *vt. to* — *away the time*, ammazzare il tempo.

whilst V. *while.*

whim *s.* capriccio.

whimper *s.* 1. piagnucolio 2. uggiolio.

to whimper *vi.* 1. piagnucolare 2. uggiolare.

whimsical *agg.* stravagante.

whimsicality s. stravaganza.

whimsy agg. capriccioso. ◆ whimsy s. capriccio.

whine s. piagnisteo.

to whine v. to whimper.

whinny s. nitrito.

to whinny vi. nitrire.

whip s. frusta.

to whip vt. 1. frustare 2. frullare. ◆ to whip vi. precipitarsi || to — away, partire improvvisamente; to — out, pronunciare con violenza, tirar fuori.

whipper-snapper s. gradasso.

whirl s. 1. vortice 2. (fig.) confusione.

to whirl vt. 1. far roteare 2. trascinare. ◆ to whirl vi. 1. roteare 2. correr via 3. (fig.) esser confuso.

whirligig s. giostra.

whirlpool s. gorgo.

whirlwind s. turbine.

whir(r) s. 1. ronzio 2. frullio (d'ali) 3. rombo (di motore).

to whir(r) vi. 1. ronzare 2. frullare (d'ali) 3. rombare (di motore).

whisk s. 1. scopino 2. frullino 3. movimento rapido.

to whisk vt. 1. spazzare 2. (cuc.) frullare 3. agitare. ◆ to whisk vi. guizzare via.

whisker s. 1. basetta 2. baffo.

whisper s. 1. mormorio 2. diceria.

to whisper vt. e vi. mormorare, bisbigliare.

whistle s. fischio.

to whistle vt. e vi. 1. fischiare 2. chiamare con un fischio.

whistler s. 1. chi fischia 2. marmotta canadese.

whit s. 1. inezia 2. atomo.

Whit agg. di Pentecoste.

white agg. e s. bianco || — feather, viltà; — livered, codardo.

to whiten vt. e vi. imbiancare.

whitener s. 1. imbianchino 2. candeggiante.

whiteness s. bianchezza.

whitening s. 1. imbiancamento 2. candeggiamento.

whitesmith s. lattoniere.

whitethorn s. biancospino.

whitewash s. 1. calce 2. (fig.) riabilitazione.

to whitewash vt. 1. imbiancare 2. (fig.) riabilitare.

whitewasher s. imbianchino.

whitewashing s. 1. imbiancatura 2. riabilitazione.

whiting s. calce.

whitish agg. biancastro.

whitlow s. patereccio.

Whitsunday s. Pentecoste.

whiz s. sibilo

who pron. 1. (int.) chi? 2. (rel.) il, la quale, i, le quali.

whoever pron. chiunque.

whole agg. tutto, intero. ◆ whole s. 1. il tutto, l'intero 2. il complesso || as a —, nell'insieme; on the —, nel complesso.

wholeness s. totalità.

wholesale agg. e avv. all'ingrosso. ◆ wholesale s. vendita all'ingrosso.

to wholesale vt. e vi. vendere all'ingrosso.

wholesaler s. venditore all'ingrosso.

wholesome agg. salutare.

wholly avv. totalmente.

whom pron. compl. di who.

whomever pron. compl. chiunque.

whomsoever V. whomever.

whoop s. ululato.

whooping-cough s. pertosse.

whorl s. spirale.

whose pron. 1. (int.) di chi? 2. (rel.) del, della quale, dei, delle quali.

whosever pron. di chiunque.

whosoever V. whoever.

why avv. 1. (int.) perché? 2. (rel.) per cui. ◆ why cong. perché. ◆ why inter. perbacco.

wick s. lucignolo.

wicked agg. malvagio.

wickedness s. malvagità.

wicker s. vimine.

wicket s. 1. sportello 2. cancelletto.

wide agg. 1. largo 2. alto (di tessuto) 3. spalancato: — open, spalancato. ◆ wide avv. largamente.

wide-awake agg. 1. completamente sveglio 2. (fig.) vigilante.

widely avv. largamente.

to widen vt. allargare. ◆ to widen vi. allargarsi.

widespread agg. esteso.

widow s. vedova.

widower s. vedovo.

widowhood s. vedovanza.

width s. 1. larghezza 2. altezza (di stoffa).

to wield vt. 1. brandire 2. esercitare (autorità ecc.).

wife s. (pl. wives) moglie.

wig s. (fam.) sgridata.

wild *agg.* **1.** selvaggio, selvatico **2.** agitato **3.** pazzo **4.** avventato **5.** disordinato. ♦ **wild** *s.* deserto. ♦ **wild** *avv.* **1.** selvaggiamente **2.** impulsivamente **3.** sfrenatamente.

wilderness *s.* deserto.

wild-goose chase *s.* impresa vana, impossibile.

wildness *s.* **1.** selvatichezza **2.** furore.

wile *s.* astuzia.

wilful *agg.* **1.** ostinato **2.** premeditato.

wilfulness *s.* **1.** ostinazione **2.** premeditazione.

will *s.* **1.** volontà **2.** testamento || *free* —, libero arbitrio.

will *v. ausiliare* (*usato per il futuro*) *he* — *be*, egli sarà **2.** *v. dif.* volere: *I* — *go*, io voglio andare, io andrò (*futuro volitivo*).

to will *vt.* e *vi.* **1.** disporre **2.** lasciare per testamento.

willed *agg.* *strong* —, di forte volontà.

willing *agg.* **1.** volonteroso **2.** disposto || — *or not*, volente o nolente.

willingly *avv.* volentieri.

willow *s.* — -(*tree*), salice: *weeping* —, salice piangente.

willy-nilly *agg.* e *avv.* volente o nolente.

wily *agg.* astuto.

wimple *s.* **1.** soggolo **2.** arricciatura.

to win (won, won) *vt.* e *vi.* vincere || *to* — *back*, riconquistare.

wince *s.* sussulto.

to wince *vi.* trasalire.

winch *s.* **1.** argano **2.** manovella.

wind[1] *s.* **1.** vento **2.** respiro || *to get* — *of*, aver sentore di; — -*breaker*, giacca a vento; — -*cone*, manica a vento.

wind[2] *s.* **1.** svolta, curva **2.** giro di carica.

to wind[1] *vt.* **1.** fiutare **2.** sfiatare.

to wind[2] **(wound, wound)** *vt.* **1.** avvolgere **2.** (*una molla*) caricare **3.** girare || *to* — *off*, svolgere. ♦ **to wind (wound, wound)** *vi.* **1.** serpeggiare **2.** avvolgersi || *to* — *off*, svolgersi.

windbag *s.* **1.** otre (*di cornamusa*) **2.** (*fig.*) parolaio.

winder *s.* **1.** manovella **2.** avvolgitore.

winding *agg.* tortuoso. ♦ **winding** *s.* **1.** tortuosità **2.** tornante **3.** spira

4. caricamento **5.** ritorcitura.

windlass *s.* argano.

windmill *s.* mulino a vento.

window *s.* finestra, finestrino || — -*dresser*, vetrinista; *French*- —, porta finestra.

windpipe *s.* trachea.

windscreen *s.* parabrezza || — *wiper*, tergicristallo.

windshield *s.* (*amer.*) parabrezza.

windward *agg.* contro vento. ♦ **windward** *s.* sopravvento.

windy *agg.* **1.** ventoso **2.** verboso.

wine *s.* vino.

wing *s.* **1.** ala **2.** battente (*di porta*) **3.** (*teat.*) quinta || *on the* —, in volo; *to take* —, spiccare il volo.

winged *agg.* alato.

wink *s.* **1.** battito di palpebre **2.** ammicco **3.** (*fig.*) istante.

to wink *vi.* **1.** battere le palpebre **2.** ammiccare **3.** scintillare.

winner *s.* vincitore.

winning *agg.* **1.** vincitore **2.** suadente. ♦ **winning** *s.* vittoria.

to winnow *vt.* e *vi.* vagliare.

winsome *agg.* incantevole.

winter *s.* inverno. ♦ **winter** *agg.* invernale.

to winter *vi.* svernare.

wintered *agg.* gelato.

winterly *V.* *wintry*.

wintriness *s.* rigore invernale.

wintry *agg.* invernale, freddo.

wipe *s.* **1.** asciugatura **2.** spolverata.

to wipe *vt.* **1.** asciugare **2.** strofinare || *to* — *off*, cancellare.

wiper *s.* **1.** chi pulisce **2.** strofinaccio.

wire *s.* **1.** filo metallico **2.** telegramma || — *netting*, rete metallica; *barbed* —, filo spinato.

to wire *vt.* e *vi.* **1.** legare con filo metallico **2.** prendere in trappola **3.** telegrafare.

wired *agg.* munito di filo metallico, di rete metallica.

wireless *agg.* senza fili. ♦ **wireless** *s.* radiotelegrafia.

to wireless *vt.* e *vi.* radiotelegrafare.

wire-puller *s.* intrigante, eminenza grigia.

wiry *agg.* **1.** di, simile a filo metallico **2.** (*fig.*) resistente.

wisdom *s.* saggezza.

wise *agg.* **1.** saggio **2.** edotto, informato.

wise *s.* modo, maniera.

wiseacre *s.* saccente.

wisely *avv.* saggiamente.
wish *s.* **1.** desiderio **2.** augurio: *best wishes*, i migliori auguri.
to wish *vt.* e *vi.* **1.** desiderare **2.** augurare || *I wish I were*, vorrei essere; *I wish I had*, vorrei avere; *I wish I could*, vorrei potere.
wisher *s.* **1.** chi desidera **2.** chi augura.
wishful *agg.* desideroso.
wishing *agg.* desideroso. ♦ **wishing** *s.* desiderio.
wistaria *s.* glicine.
wistful *agg.* **1.** desideroso **2.** pensoso.
wistfully *avv.* **1.** con desiderio **2.** pensosamente.
wistfulness *s.* **1.** bramosia **2.** raccoglimento.
wit *s.* **1.** ingegno **2.** spirito **3.** persona di spirito || *to live by one's wits*, vivere di espedienti; *to be at one's wits' end*, non saper più cosa fare. .
witch *s.* strega.
to witch *vt.* stregare.
witchcraft *s.* **1.** stregoneria **2.** fascino.
witch-doctor *s.* stregone.
witchery *s.* V. *witchcraft*.
witching *agg.* magico.
with *prep.* **1.** con **2.** presso **3.** a causa di, per, da.
to withdraw (withdrew, withdrawn) *vt.* ritirare. ♦ **to withdraw (withdrew, withdrawn)** *vi.* ritirarsi.
withdrawal *s.* **1.** ritirata, ritiro **2** ritrattazione.
withdrawn V. *to withdraw*.
withdrew V. *to withdraw*.
withe *s.* vimine.
to wither *vt.* e *vi.* avvizzire.
withering *s.* avvizzimento.
to withhold (withheld, withheld) *vt.* **1.** trattenere **2.** rifiutare **3.** nascondere.
within *prep.* entro. ♦ **within** *avv.* dentro.
without *prep.* senza, senza di. ♦ **without** *cong.* senza (che). ♦ **without** *avv.* fuori.
to withstand (withstood, withstood) *vt.* resistere a, fronteggiare.
withstander *s.* oppositore.
withstood V. *to withstand*.
witness *s.* **1.** testimone: *eye- —*, testimone oculare **2.** testimonianza.

to witness *vt.* **1.** essere testimone a **2.** mostrare. ♦ **to witness** *vi.* testimoniare.
witticism *s.* arguzia.
wittily *avv.* spiritosamente.
wittiness *s.* spirito.
wittingly *avv.* consapevolmente.
witty *agg.* spiritoso.
wives V. *wife*.
wizard *s.* mago.
to wobble V. *to wabble*.
woe *s.* dolore.
woeful *agg.* doloroso.
woke V. *to wake*.
woken V. *to wake*.
wolf *s.* (*pl.* wolves) lupo || *she- —*, lupa.
to wolf *vt.* divorare.
wolfish *agg.* da lupo.
woman, *s.* (*pl.* women) donna.
womanhood *s.* **1.** femminilità **2.** maturità (*della donna*) **3.** condizione di donna.
womanish *agg.* **1.** effeminato **2.** femminile.
womankind *s.* le donne (*in genere*).
womanlike *agg.* femminile. ♦ **womanlike** *avv.* femminilmente.
womanliness *s.* femminilità.
womanly *agg.* femminile.
womb *s.* **1.** ventre **2.** grembo **3.** utero.
women V. *woman*.
won V. *to win*.
wonder *s.* **1.** prodigio **2.** meraviglia.
to wonder *vi.* **1.** domandarsi **2.** stupirsi.
wonderful *agg.* meraviglioso.
wonderingly *avv.* con meraviglia.
wonderland *s.* paese delle meraviglie.
wondrous *agg.* mirabile.
wont *agg.* abituato. ♦ **wont** *s.* abitudine.
wonted *agg.* abituato, abituale.
to woo *vt.* corteggiare.
wood *s.* **1.** bosco **2.** legno || *— -cutter*, boscaiolo.
woodcock *s.* beccaccia.
woodcut *s.* **1.** incisione su legno **2.** xilografia.
wooden *agg.* di legno.
woodiness *s.* **1.** boscosità **2.** legnosità.
woodland *s.* terreno boscoso.
woodman *s.* **1.** guardaboschi **2.** taglialegna.
woodpecker *s.* picchio.

woodwork s. lavoro in legno.
woody agg. 1. boscoso 2. legnoso.
wooer s. corteggiatore.
wool s. 1. lana 2. peluria di animale || *cotton* —, ovatta.
wool(l)en agg. di lana. ◆
  wool(l)en s. stoffa di lana.
woolly agg. 1. di lana, lanoso 2. (fig.) confuso.
word s. parola || *by* — *of mouth*, oralmente.
to word vt. esprimere.
wordiness s. verbosità.
wording s. espressione.
wordy agg. verboso.
wore V. to wear.
work s. lavoro || *out of* —, disoccupato. ◆ **works** s. pl. 1. meccanismo (sing.) 2. fabbrica, officina (sing.).
to work vt. 1. lavorare 2. far funzionare 3. dirigere || *to* — *in*, introdurre; *to* — *off*, liberarsi di; *to* — *out*, calcolare; *to* — *up*, elaborare. ◆ **to work** vi. 1. lavorare 2. funzionare 3. agitarsi.
workable agg. 1. eseguibile 2. lavorabile.
workaday agg. lavorativo.
workday s. giorno feriale.
worker s. lavoratore || *skilled* —, operaio qualificato.
workhouse s. ospizio di mendicità.
working agg. 1. laborioso 2. funzionante. ◆ **working** s. 1. lavorio 2. funzionamento 3. lavorazione || — *-clothes*, abiti da lavoro; — *expenses*, spese d'esercizio.
workless agg. senza lavoro.
workman s. operaio.
workmanship s. 1. abilità 2. fattura.
workroom s. laboratorio.
workshop s. officina.
workwoman s. operaia.
world s. mondo: *all over the* —, in tutto il mondo.
worldliness s. 1. condizione terrena 2. mondanità.
worldly agg. 1. terreno 2. mondano.
world-wide agg. diffuso, noto in tutto il mondo.
worm s. verme || — *-screw*, vite senza fine.
to worm vt. carpire || *to* — *one's way*, insinuarsi.
wormwood s. assenzio.
worn V. to wear. ◆ **worn** agg. 1.

consumato 2. indebolito || — *-out*, logoro, (fig.) esausto.
worried agg. 1. preoccupato 2. tormentato.
worrier s. seccatore.
worrisome agg. 1. irritante 2. preoccupato.
worry s. 1. ansia 2. guaio.
to worry vt. tormentare. ◆ **to worry** vi. preoccuparsi.
worrying agg. 1. preoccupante 2. tormentoso.
worse agg. (comp. di bad e ill) peggiore, peggio. ◆ **worse** avv. e s. peggio || *all the* —, tanto peggio; *so much the* — *for*, tanto peggio per; *none the* —, ugualmente; — *and* —, di male in peggio.
worship s. adorazione.
to worship vt. e vi. adorare, venerare.
worshipper s. 1. adoratore 2. fedele.
worst agg. (superl. di bad e ill) peggiore, pessimo. ◆ **worst** avv. e s. peggio || *at (the)* —, nella peggiore delle ipotesi.
worsted agg. di lana pettinata.
worth agg. degno. ◆ **worth** s. valore.
worthily avv. degnamente.
worthiness s. 1. valore 2. dignità.
worthless agg. 1. senza valore 2. indegno.
worthlessness s. 1. mancanza di valore 2. indegnità.
worthy agg. degno, meritevole. ◆ **worthy** s. persona illustre.
would v. dif. 1. (ausiliare del condiz.) *he* — *go*, egli andrebbe 2. (passato ind. imperfetto, congiuntivo, condiz.) volere 3. (imperfetto ind.) solere: *he* — *come every day*, soleva venire ogni giorno.
would-be agg. sedicente.
wound s. ferita.
to wound vt. ferire.
wound V. to wind.
wove V. to weave.
woven V. to weave.
wrack s. distruzione, rovina.
to wrangle vi. discutere.
wrangler s. attaccabrighe.
wrap s. sciarpa, coperta, mantello.
to wrap vt. avvolgere || *to* — *up*, impacchettare. ◆ **to wrap** vi. avvolgersi.
wrapper s. 1. imballatore 2. carta da imballo 3. copertina.

wrapping s. involucro || — *paper*, carta da imballaggio.
wrath s. ira.
wrathful agg. irato.
wrathfulness s. ira
wreath s. ghirlanda.
to **wreathe** vt. **1.** intrecciare 2. inghirlandare **3.** attorcigliare. ♦ to **wreathe** vi. innalzarsi in spire.
wreathy agg. **1.** inghirlandato **2.** a forma di ghirlanda.
wreck s. **1.** naufragio (anche fig.) **2.** relitto.
to **wreck** vt. rovinare. ♦ to **wreck** vi. naufragare.
wreckage V. *wreck.*
wren s. scricciolo.
wrench s. **1.** strappo **2.** (mecc.) chiave inglese.
to **wrench**, to **wrest** vt. **1.** strappare **2.** torcere.
wrestle s. lotta.
to **wrestle** vi. lottare.
wrestler s. lottatore.
wrestling s. (sport.) lotta.
wretch s. disgraziato.
wretched agg. **1.** disgraziato **2.** scadente.
wretchedness s. **1.** disgrazia **2.** squallore.
wriggle s. contorsione.
to **wriggle** vt. contorcere. ♦ to **wriggle** vi. **1.** contorcersi **2.** (fig.) dar risposte evasive.
wring s. **1.** torsione **2.** dolore acuto.
to **wring** (**wrung, wrung**) vt. **1.** torcere **2.** estorcere **3.** stringere || to — out, spremere, (fig.) strappare.
wringer s. **1.** torcitore **2.** torchio.
wringing agg. lancinante (di dolore). ♦ **wringing** s. torcitura.
wrinkle[1] s. **1.** ruga **2.** grinza.
wrinkle[2] s. stratagemma.
to **wrinkle** vt. **1.** corrugare **2.** spiegazzare. ♦ to **wrinkle** vi. corrugarsi.
wrinkled, wrinkly agg. **1.** corrugato **2.** rugoso.
wrinkledness s. rugosità.
wrist s. polso.
wristband s. polsino.
to **write** (**wrote, written**) vt. scrivere || to — back, rispondere; to — down, annotare, descrivere; to — off, cancellare; to — out, copiare, emettere un assegno.
writer s. scrittore.
writhe s. contorcimento.

to **writhe** vt. contorcere. ♦ to **writhe** vi. **1.** contorcersi **2.** (fig.) fremere.
writing s. **1.** lo scrivere **2.** scrittura **3.** scritto || — -desk, scrivania; — -paper, carta da lettere.
written V. *to write.*
wrong agg. **1.** sbagliato **2.** ingiusto **3.** illegale. ♦ **wrong** avv. **1.** erroneamente **2.** ingiustamente.
wrong s. **1.** torto **2.** male || — -doer, peccatore, offensore; — -doing, peccato, offesa.
to **wrong** vt. **1.** far torto a **2.** imbrogliare.
wrongful agg. V. *wrong.*
wrongfulness s. ingiustizia.
wrongly avv. V. *wrong.*
wrote V. *to write.*
wrought agg. lavorato || — -iron, ferro battuto.
wrung V. *to wring.*
wry agg. storto.
to **wry** vt. contorcere. ♦ to **wry** vi. contorcersi.
wryly avv. per traverso.

X

xenophobe s. xenofobo.
xenophobia s. xenofobia.
xerophilous agg. xerofilo.
Xmas s. Natale.
X-ray agg. attr. a, di raggi X.
to **X-ray** vt. sottoporre a raggi X.
X-rays s. pl. raggi X.
xylograph s. xilografia.
xylographer s. xilografo.
xylographic(al) agg. xilografico.
xylography s. xilografia.
xylophone s. xilofono.
xylophonist s. xilofonista.

Y

yacht s. panfilo.
to **yacht** vi. fare crociere su panfilo.
yachtsman s. (pl. -men) proprietario di panfilo.
to **yank** vt. e vi. strappare, dare uno

strattone.
yap s. guaito.
to **yap** vi. guaire.
yard s. 1. iarda 2. cortile 3. cantiere: ship- —, cantiere navale.
yarn s. 1. filo 2. (fig.) storia.
yawl s. (naut.) iole, piccola imbarcazione.
yawn s. 1. sbadiglio 2. apertura.
to **yawn** vi. 1. sbadigliare 2. aprirsi.
yawning agg. 1. sonnolento 2. spalancato.
yea avv. sì.
year s. anno: — by —, di anno in anno; all the — round, per tutto l'anno; New Year's Day, Capodanno.
yearbook s. annuario.
yearling agg. di un anno d'età. ♦
yearling s. animale di un anno.
yearlong agg. che dura un anno.
yearly agg. annuale. ♦ **yearly** avv. annualmente.
to **yearn** vi. languire || to — for, after sthg., bramare qc.
yearning s. brama. ♦ **yearning** agg. bramoso.
yeast s. 1. lievito 2. fermento.
to **yeast** vi. 1. lievitare 2. fermentare.
yell s. urlo.
to **yell** vt. e vi. urlare.
yeller s. urlatore.
yellow agg. e s. giallo.
to **yellow** vt. e vi. ingiallire.
yellowish agg. giallastro.
yelp s. guaito.
to **yelp** vi. guaire.
yeoman s. piccolo proprietario terriero.
yes avv. sì.
yesterday avv. e s. ieri: the day before —, l'altro ieri; — week, ieri a otto.
yet avv. 1. ancora 2. già || as —, finora. ♦ **yet** cong. tuttavia.
yew s. — (-tree) tasso.
yield s. 1. produzione 2. (comm.) rendita.
to **yield** vt. e vi. 1. produrre, rendere 2. cedere || to — oneself up, arrendersi.
yielding agg. 1. pieghevole 2. docile.
yoke s. 1. giogo 2. barra (del timone) 3. coppia (di animali).
to **yoke** vt. aggiogare.
yolk s. tuorlo.

yonder agg. quello là, di laggiù. ♦
yonder avv. là.
you pron. pers. 1. tu, te, ti 2. voi, ve, vi 3. (forma di cortesia) Lei, Loro.
young agg. giovane || — people, i giovani (in genere).
youngster s. giovanetto.
your agg. poss. 1. tuo 2. vostro 3. (forma di cortesia) Suo.
yours pron. poss. 1. tuo 2. vostro 3. (forma di cortesia) Suo, Loro || — truly, — faithfully, distinti saluti.
yourself pron. r. 1. tu stesso, ti, te, te stesso 2. (forma di cortesia) Lei stesso.
yourselves pron. r. 1. voi stessi, vi 2. (forma di cortesia) Loro stessi.
youth s. 1. gioventù 2. ragazzo.
youthful agg. 1. giovane 2. giovanile.
youthfulness s. aspetto giovanile.
Yugoslav agg. e s. iugoslavo.

Z

zeal s. zelo.
zealot s. fanatico.
zealous agg. zelante.
zed s. zeta.
zenith s. zenit.
zephyr s. zeffiro.
zero s. 1. zero 2. (fig.) nullità.
zest s. 1. gusto 2. aroma.
zigzag agg. e avv. a zigzag.
to **zigzag** vi. andare a zigzag.
zinc s. zinco.
to **zinc** vt. zincare.
zincking s. zincatura.
zincograph s. zincografia.
to **zincograph** vt. imprimere su lastre di zinco.
zincographer s. zincografo.
zincography s. zincografia.
Zionism s. sionismo.
Zionist s. e agg. sionista.
zip s. fischio || — (-fastener), cerniera lampo.
to **zip** vi. sibilare.
zipper s. cerniera lampo.
zircon s. zircone.
zirconium s. zirconio.
zodiac s. zodiaco.
zodiacal agg. zodiacale.

zonal, zonary *agg.* zonale.
zonate(d) *agg.* a zone.
zonation *s.* zonatura.
zone *s.* zona.
zoo *s.* zoo.
zoological *agg.* zoologico.
zoologist *s.* zoologo.
zoology *s.* zoologia.
zoom *s.* **1.** rombo **2.** (*aer.*) salita a candela.
to zoom *vi.* **1.** rombare **2.** (*aer.*) salire a candela.

zoomorphic *agg.* zoomorfo.
zoomorphism *s.* zoomorfismo.
zoophilist *s.* zoofilo.
zoophilous *agg.* zoofilo.
zoophily *s.* zoofilia.
zoophobia *s.* zoofobia.
zootechnic *agg.* zootecnico.
zootechnics, zootechny *s.* zootecnica.
zootomic(al) *agg.* zootomico.
zouave *s.* zuavo.
zygoma *s.* (*pl.* zygomata) zigomo.

NOMI PROPRI, STORICI E GEOGRAFICI

Abel Abele.
Abraham Abramo.
Abyssinia Abissinia.
Achilles Achille.
Adam Adamo.
Adolph Adolfo.
Adonis Adone.
Adriatic Sea Mar Adriatico.
Aegean Sea Mar Egeo
Aeneas Enea.
Aeschylus Eschilo.
Aesop Esopo.
Afghanistan Afganistan.
Agamemnon Agamennone.
Agatha Agata.
Agnes Agnese.
Ajax Aiace.
Albert Alberto
Aldous Aldo.
Alec, Alex *dim. di* Alexander.
Alexander Alessandro.
Alexandra Alessandra.
Alexis Alessio.
Alfred Alfredo.
Algiers Algeri.
Alps *pl.* Alpi.
Alsace Alsazia.
Amazon Rio delle Amazzoni.
Ambrose Ambrogio.
Andes *pl.* Ande.
Andrew Andrea.
Andy *dim. di* Andrew.
Angel Angelo.
Ann(e) Anna.
Annie *dim. di* Ann(e).
Antarctica Antartide.
Anthony Antonio.
Antoninus Antonino.
Antony Antonio.
Apennines *pl.* Appennini.
Aphrodite Afrodite.
Apulia Puglia.
Aragon Aragona.
Archimedes Archimede.
Ariadne Arianna.
Aristophanes Aristofane.
Aristotle Aristotele.
Armand Armando.
Arnold Arnaldo.
Arthur Arturo.
Athens Atene.
Atlantic Atlantico.

Augustin Agostino.
Augustus Augusto.
Azores *pl.* Azzorre.

Babel Babele.
Babylon Babilonia.
Bacchus Bacco.
Balearic Islands Baleari.
Balkans *pl.* Balcani.
Balthazar Baldassarre.
Baltic Sea Mar Baltico.
Baltimore Baltimora.
Baptist Battista.
Barcelona Barcellona.
Barnabas, Barnaby Barnaba.
Bartholomew Bartolomeo.
Basel Basilea.
Basil Basilio.
Beatrix Beatrice.
Belgium Belgio.
Belgrade Belgrado.
Benedict Benedetto.
Bengal Bengala.
Ben *dim. di* Benjamin.
Benjamin Beniamino.
Benny *dim. di* Benjamin.
Berlin Berlino.
Bermudas *pl.* Bermude.
Bern Berna.
Bernard Bernardo.
Bertha Berta.
Bess *dim. di* Elizabeth.
Bethlehem Betlemme.
Betty *dim. di* Elizabeth.
Bill(y) *dim. di* William.
Blanche Bianca.
Bob(by) *dim. di* Robert.
Bohemia Boemia.
Boniface Bonifacio.
Bosporus Bosforo.
Brandenburg Brandeburgo.
Brazil Brasile.
Brittany Bretagna.
Brutus Bruto.
Burma Birmania.

Cadiz Cadice.
Caesar Cesare.
Cain Caino.
Caius Caio.

Calvin Calvino.
Cambodia Cambogia.
Canada Canadà.
Capitol Campidoglio.
Caribbean Sea Mar dei Caraibi.
Caroline Carolina.
Carpathian Mountains *pl.* Carpazi.
Carthage Cartagine.
Cashmere Cascemir.
Caspian Sea Mar Caspio.
Cassiopeia Cassiopea.
Cassius Cassio.
Catherine Caterina.
Cato Catone.
Caucasus Caucaso.
Cecil Cecilio.
Channel (The) La Manica.
Charlemagne Carlomagno.
Charles Carlo.
Charlie *dim. di* Charles.
Charlotte Carlotta.
Chile Cile.
China Cina.
Christ Cristo.
Christine Cristina.
Christopher Cristoforo.
Cicero Cicerone.
Cinderella Cenerentola.
Clara Clara, Chiara.
Claude, Claudius Claudio.
Clement Clemente.
Clementine Clementina.
Clytemnestra Clitennestra.
Cologne Colonia.
Connie *dim. di* Constance.
Conrad Corrado.
Constance Costanza.
Constantine Costantino.
Constantinople Costantinopoli.
Corinth Corinto.
Cornelius Cornelio.
Cornwall Cornovaglia.
Crete Creta.
Cynthia Cinzia.
Cyprus Cipro.
Cyril Cirillo.
Cyrus Ciro.
Czechoslovakia Cecoslovacchia.

Daisy *dim. di* Margaret.
Damascus Damasco.
Damocles Damocle.
Dan *dim. di* Daniel.
Daniel Daniele.
Danny *dim. di* Daniel.
Danube Danubio.
Danzig Danzica.

Daphne Dafne.
Dardanelles *pl.* Dardanelli.
Darius Dario.
Dave *dim. di* David.
Deb(by) *dim. di* Deborah.
Deborah Debora.
Delphi Delfo.
Democritus Democrito.
Demosthenes Demostene.
Denmark Danimarca.
Dick *dim. di* Richard.
Dido Didone.
Diocletian Diocleziano.
Diogenes Diogene.
Dionysius Dionigi, Dionisio.
Dominic Domenico.
Domitian Domiziano.
Dorothy Dorotea.
Dublin Dublino.

Ed(dy) *dim. di* Edmund, Edward.
Edgar Edgardo.
Edinburgh Edimburgo.
Edmund Edmondo.
Edward Edoardo.
Egypt Egitto.
Eire (Stato Libero di) Irlanda.
Eleanor Eleonora.
Electra Elettra.
Elias, Elijah Elia.
Eliza Elisa.
Elizabeth Elisabetta.
Emanuel Emanuele.
Emily Emilia.
England Inghilterra.
Epaminondas Epaminonda.
Epicurus Epicuro.
Erasmus Erasmo.
Ernest Ernesto.
Esther Ester.
Ethiopia Etiopia.
Euclid Euclide.
Eugene Eugenio.
Euphrates Eufrate.
Euripides Euripide.
Europe Europa.
Eve Eva.
Evelyn Evelina.
Ezekiel Ezechiele.

Faust(us) Fausto.
Felix Felice.
Ferdinand Ferdinando.
Finland Finlandia.
Florence Firenze.
France Francia.
Frances Francesca.

Francis Francesco.
Frank Franco.
Frankfurt Francoforte.
Fred(dy) *dim. di* Frederic.
Frederic Federico.

Gabriel Gabriele.
Galilee Galilea.
Gascony Guascogna.
Gaule Gallia.
Geneva Ginevra.
Genoa Genova.
Geoffrey Goffredo.
George Giorgio.
Gerard Gerardo.
Germany Germania.
Gibraltar Gibilterra.
Gilbert Gilberto.
Golgotha Golgota.
Goliath Golia.
Grace Grazia.
Great Britain Gran Bretagna.
Greece Grecia.
Greenland Groenlandia.
Gregory Gregorio.
Guiana Guaiana.
Gustavus Gustavo.
Guy Guido.

Hadrian Adriano.
Hague (The) L'Aia.
Hamburg Amburgo.
Hamlet Amleto.
Hannibal Annibale.
Harold Aroldo.
Harriet Enrichetta.
Harry *dim. di* Harold, Henry.
Hebrides *pl.* Ebridi.
Hector Ettore.
Helen Elena.
Hellas Ellade.
Henrietta Enrichetta.
Henry Arrigo, Enrico.
Heraclitus Eraclito.
Herbert Erberto.
Hercules Ercole.
Hermes Ermete.
Herod Erode.
Herodotus Erodoto.
Hesiod Esiodo.
Hilary Ilario.
Himalaya Imalaia.
Hindustan Indostan.
Hippolytus Ippolito.
Holland Olanda.
Homer Omero.
Horace, Horatio Orazio.

Hubert Uberto.
Hugh Ugo.
Humbert Umberto.
Hungary Ungheria.

Icarus Icaro.
Iceland Islanda.
Ignatius Ignazio.
Innocent Innocente.
Ionian Sea Mar Ionio.
Ireland Irlanda.
Iris Iride.
Isaac Isacco.
Isabel Isabella.
Isaiah Isaia.
Ishmael Ismaele.
Isis Iside.
Israel Israele.
Italy Italia.

Jack(ie) *dim. di* John.
Jacob Giacobbe.
Jamaica Giamaica.
James Giacomo.
Jane Giovanna.
Janet *dim. di* Jane.
Japan Giappone.
Jason Giasone.
Java Giava.
Jean Giovanna.
Jeffrey Goffredo.
Jehovah Geova.
Jenny *dim. di* Jean.
Jeremiah Geremia.
Jericho Gerico.
Jerome Gerolamo.
Jerry *dim. di* Gerard, Jerome.
Jerusalem Gerusalemme.
Jesus Gesù.
Jim(my) *dim. di* James.
Jo *dim. di* Josephine.
Joan Giovanna.
Job Giobbe.
Joe *dim. di* Joseph.
John Giovanni.
Johnny *dim. di* John.
Jonah, Jonas Giona.
Jonathan Gionata.
Jordan Giordano.
Joseph Giuseppe.
Josephine Giuseppina.
Joshua Giosuè.
Jove Giove.
Judas, Jude Giuda.
Judea Giudea.
Judith Giuditta.
Judy *dim. di* Judith.

Julia Giulia.
Julian Giuliano.
Juliana Giuliana.
Julie Giulia.
Juliet Giulietta.
Julius Giulio.
Juno Giunone.
Jupiter Giove.
Juvenal Giovenale.

Kashmir Cascemir.
Kate, Kitty *dim. di* Catherine.
Korea Corea.

Lambert Lamberto.
Laocoon Laocoonte.
Lapland Lapponia.
Larry *dim. di* Lawrence.
Latium Lazio.
Launcelot Lancillotto.
Lausanne Losanna.
Lawrence Lorenzo.
Lazarus Lazzaro.
Leander Leandro.
Lebanon Libano.
Leghorn Livorno.
Leo(n) Leone.
Leonard Leonardo.
Leonidas Leonida.
Leopold Leopoldo.
Lethe Lete.
Letitia Letizia.
Lewis Luigi.
Libya Libia.
Liège Liegi.
Lisbon Lisbona
Livy Livio.
Liza, Lizzie, Liz(zy) *dim. di* Elizabeth.
Lombardy Lombardia.
London Londra.
Lou *dim. di* Louise.
Louis Luigi.
Louise Luigia, Luisa.
Louvain Lovanio.
Lucerne Lucerna.
Lucian Luciano.
Lucifer Lucifero.
Lucius Lucio.
Lucretius Lucrezio.
Lucy Lucia.
Luke Luca.
Luther Lutero.
Luxemburg Lussemburgo.
Lycurgus Licurgo.
Lydia Lidia.
Lyons Lione.

Magdalene Maddalena.
Mag(gie) *dim. di* Margaret.
Majorca Maiorca.
Malaya Malesia.
Manchuria Manciuria.
Manfred Manfredi.
Mantua Mantova.
Marathon Maratona.
Marcellus Marcello.
Margaret Margherita.
Margie *dim. di* Margaret.
Marianne Marianna.
Marius Mario.
Mark Marco.
Mars Marte.
Martha Marta.
Martial Marziale.
Martin Martino.
Mary Maria.
Matilda Matilde.
Matt *dim. di* Matthew.
Matthew Matteo.
Matty *dim. di* Martha, Matilda.
Maurice Maurizio.
Max *dim. di* Maximilian.
Maximilian Massimiliano.
May *dim. di* Mary.
Mediterranean Mediterraneo.
Meg *dim. di* Margaret.
Menelaus Menelao.
Mephistopheles Mefistofele.
Mercury Mercurio.
Merlin Merlino.
Methuselah Matusalemme.
Meuse Mosa.
Mexico Messico.
Michael Michele.
Mick(ey) *dim. di* Michael.
Midas Mida.
Mike *dim. di* Michael.
Milan Milano.
Minos Minosse.
Minotaur Minotauro.
Mithridates Mitridate.
Mohammed Maometto.
Moll(y) *dim. di* Mary.
Moluccas *pl.* Molucche.
Monaco (Principato di) Monaco.
Morocco Marocco.
Moscow Mosca.
Moses Mosè.
Mozambique Mozambico.
Munich Monaco di Baviera.
Mycenae Micene.

Naples Napoli.
Napoleon Napoleone.
Narcissus Narciso.

Nell(y) *dim. di* Helen.
Neptune Nettuno.
Nero Nerone.
Netherlands *pl.* Paesi Bassi.
Newfoundland Terranova.
New Zealand Nuova Zelanda.
Nice Nizza.
Nicholas Nicola.
Nick *dim. di* Nicholas.
Nile Nilo.
Noah Noè.
Normandy Normandia.
Norway Norvegia.

Oedipus Edipo.
Oliver Oliviero.
Olympus Olimpo.
Ophelia Ofelia.
Orestes Oreste.
Orion Orione.
Orkneys *pl.* Orcadi.
Orpheus Orfeo.
Osiris Osiride.
Oswald Osvaldo.
Othello Otello.
Ovid Ovidio.

Pacific Pacifico.
Paddy *dim. di* Patrick.
Padua Padova.
Palestine Palestina.
Pancras Pancrazio.
Papua Papuasia.
Paris[1] Paride.
Paris[2] Parigi.
Parnassus Parnaso.
Parthenon Partenone.
Pat *dim. di* Patricia, Patrick.
Patricia Patrizia.
Patrick Patrizio.
Paul Paolo.
Paula Paola.
Pauline Paolina.
Peg(gy) *dim.* di Margaret.
Peking Pechino.
Peloponnesus Peloponneso.
Pennsylvania Pensilvania.
Pericles Pericle.
Perseus Perseo.
Peru Perù.
Pete *dim. di* Peter.
Peter Pietro.
Phaedra Fedra.
Pharsalus Farsalo.
Philadelphia Filadelfia.
Philip Filippo.
Philippi Filippi.

Philippines *pl.* Filippine.
Piedmont Piemonte.
Pigmalion Pigmalione.
Pindar Pindaro.
Piraeus Pireo.
Pius Pio.
Plato Platone.
Pliny Plinio.
Plutarch Plutarco.
Poland Polonia.
Poll(y) *dim. di* Mary.
Polynesia Polinesia.
Pompey Pompeo.
Portugal Portogallo.
Prague Praga.
Prometheus Prometeo.
Ptolemy Tolomeo.
Pyrenees *pl.* Pirenei.
Pythagoras Pitagora.

Quentin Quintino.

Rachel Rachele.
Ramses Ramsete.
Raphael Raffaele, Raffaello.
Raymond Raimondo.
Remus Remo.
Rhine Reno.
Rhodes Rodi.
Rhone Rodano.
Richard Riccardo.
Rob *dim. di* Robert.
Robert Roberto.
Roderick Rodrigo.
Roger Ruggero.
Roland Orlando, Rolando.
Rome Roma.
Romulus Romolo.
Rosalie Rosalia.
Rosalind Rosalinda.
Rose Rosa.
Roumania Romania.
Roxana Rossana.
Rudolph Rodolfo.
Rudy *dim. di* Rudolph.

Sadie, Sally *dim. di* Sarah.
Sam *dim. di* Samuel.
Samson Sansone.
Samuel Samuele.
Sappho Saffo.
Sarah Sara.
Sardinia Sardegna.
Satan Satana.
Saturn Saturno.
Savoy Savoia.

Saxony Sassonia.
Scipion Scipione.
Scotland Scozia.
Sean Giovanni.
Sebastian Sebastiano.
Sibyl Sibilla.
Sicily Sicilia.
Silvester Silvestro.
Simeon Simeone.
Simon Simone.
Simplon Sempione.
Smyrna Smirne.
Socrates Socrate.
Sodom Sodoma.
Solomon Salomone.
Somaliland Somalia.
Sophia Sofia.
Sophocles Sofocle.
Soudan Sudan.
Spain Spagna.
Stephen Stefano.
Steve *dim. di* Stephen.
Stockholm Stoccolma.
Strasbourg Strasburgo.
Sue *dim. di* Susan(nah).
Sulla Silla.
Susy *dim. di* Susan(nah).
Susan(nah) Susanna.
Sweden Svezia.
Switzerland Svizzera.
Sylvia Silvia.
Syracuse Siracusa.
Syria Siria.

Tacitus Tacito.
Tangier(s) Tangeri.
Ted(dy) *dim. di* Edward.
Telemachus Telemaco.
Terence Terenzio.
Tess *dim. di* Theresa.
Thailand Tailandia.
Thames Tamigi.
Thebes Tebe.
Themistocles Temistocle.
Theodoric Teodorico.
Theresa Teresa.
Thermopylae *pl.* Termopili.
Theseus Teseo.
Thomas Tommaso.
Tiber Tevere.
Tiberius Tiberio.
Tirol Tirolo.
Titian Tiziano.
Titus Tito.
Tobias Tobia.
Toby *dim. di* Tobias.

Tom(my) *dim. di* Thomas.
Tonkin, Tonking Tonchino.
Tony *dim. di* Ant(h)ony.
Trajan Traiano.
Tristan, Tristram Tristano.
Troy Troia.
Tully Tullio.
Tunis Tunisi.
Turin Torino.
Turkey Turchia.
Tuscany Toscana.
Tyrol Tirolo.
Tyrrhenian Sea Mar Tirreno.

Ukraine Ucraina.
Ulysses Ulisse.
United States of America Stati
    Uniti d'America.
Urban Urbano.
Ursula Orsola.
USA Stati Uniti d'America.
USSR URSS (Unione Repubbliche
    Socialiste Sovietiche).

Valentine Valentino.
Valerius Valerio.
Vatican Vaticano.
Venetia Veneto.
Venice Venezia.
Venus Venere.
Vesuvius Vesuvio.
Victor Vittorio.
Victoria Vittoria.
Vincent Vincenzo.
Virgil Virgilio.
Vivian Viviana, Viviano.
Vulcan Vulcano.

Wales Galles.
Walter Gualtiero.
Warsaw Varsavia.
Will *dim. di* William.
William Guglielmo.
Willy *dim. di* William.

Xerxes Serse.

Yugoslavia Iugoslavia.

Zachary Zaccaria.
Zurich Zurigo.

SIGLE E ABBREVIAZIONI USATE NEI PAESI DI LINGUA INGLESE

a., 1. *about*: c., circa **2.** *acre*: acro **3.** *approved*: approvato, riconosciuto dallo Stato.

A.A., *Automobile Association*: A.C., Automobile Club.

A.A.R., *against all risks*: contro ogni rischio.

Abp., *Archbishop*: arcivescovo.

abr., 1. *abridged*: ridotto (*di edizione*) **2.** *abridgment*: compendio.

A.C., *alternating current*: c.a., corrente alternata.

a/c, ac., *account*: c., conto.

A.D., *Anno Domini* (= *dopo Cristo*): d.C., dopo Cristo.

adj., *adjourned*: aggiornato.

Adm., *Admiral*: ammiraglio.

adv., *advertisement*: inserzione.

A.E.C., *Atomic Energy Commission*: C.E.A., Commissione per l'energia atomica.

A.F., *Air Force*: A.M., Aeronautica Militare.

Ala., *Alabama*.

Alas., *Alaska*.

alt., 1. *alternate*: alternata **2.** *alternating*: alternata.

a.m., *ante meridiem, before noon*: antimeridiano.

Am(er)., *1. America*: Am., Amer., America **2.** *American*: am., amer., americano.

anon., *anonymous*: anonimo.

A.P., *Associated Press*: Stampa Associata.

app., *appendix*: app., appendice.

approx., *approximately*: appross., approssimativamente.

Apr., *April*: apr., aprile.

apt., *apartment*: appartamento.

Ariz., *Arizona*.

Ark., *Arkansas*.

arr., 1. *arrival*: arr., arrivo **2.** *arrived*: arr., arrivato.

ass., *association*: ass., associazione.

at. no., *atomic number*: n.a., numero atomico.

att(y)., *attorney*: proc., procuratore.

at. wt., *atomic weight*: p. at., peso atomico.

Aug., *August*: ago., agosto.

avdp., *avoirdupois*: avoirdupois.

ave., *avenue*: v.le, viale.

b., 1. *book*: l., libro **2.** *born*: n., nato.

B.A., *Bachelor of Arts*: diplomato in lettere.

Bap(t)., *Baptist*: Battista.

B.B.C., *British Broadcasting Corporation*: Ente Radiofonico Britannico.

B.C., *Before Christ*: a.C., avanti Cristo.

B/E, b.e., *bill of exchange*: cambiale.

B.E.A., *British European Airways*: Linee Aeree Europee Britanniche.

Beds., *Bedfordshire*.

Berks., *Berkshire*.

bet., *between*: fra.

B/L, *bill of lading*: polizza di carico.

blvd., *boulevard*: boulevard.

B.M., *British Museum*: Museo Britannico.

B.M.A., *British Medical Association*: Associazione Medica Britannica.

B.O.A.C., *British Overseas Airways Corporation*: Società aerea d'oltremare britannica.

B. of A., *Bank of America*: Banca d'America.

B. of E., *Bank of England*: Banca d'Inghilterra.

Bp, *Bishop*: vesc., vescovo.

bros., *brothers*: F.lli, Fratelli.

b.s., 1. *balance sheet*: bilancio di esercizio **2.** *bill of sale*: atto di vendita.

bsh., *bushel*: staio.

Bucks., *Buckinghamshire*.

bul(l)., *bulletin*: boll., bollettino.

c., 1. *centigrade*: c., centigrado **2.** *cent*: cent., centesimo **3.** *chapter*: cap., capitolo.

C/A, *current account*: c/c, conto corrente.

ca., 1. *cathode*: catodo 2. *about*: ca., circa.

Cal(if)., *California.*

Cam(b)., *Cambridge.*

Cambs., *Cambridgeshire.*

Can., 1. *Canada*: Canada 2. *Canadian*: canadese.

Cantab., *of Cambridge*: cantabrigense.

cap., 1. *chapter*: cap., capitolo 2. *capital*: capitale.

Capt., *Captain*: cap., capitano.

Card., *Cardinal*: card., cardinale.

cc., 1. *chapters*: capp., capitoli 2. *cubic centimetres*: cmc., centimetri cubi.

C.D., *Corps Diplomatique*: C.D., Corpo Diplomatico.

C.E.D., *Community for European Defence*: C.E.D., Comitato per la Difesa Europea.

Celt., *Celtic*: celtico.

cent., 1. *centigrade*: c., centigrado 2. *centimetre*: cm., centimetro 3. *central*: centrale 4. *century*: sec., secolo.

c.f., *cost and freight*: c.f., costo e nolo.

C.F.I., c.f.i., *cost, freight and insurance*: costo, nolo e assicurazione.

Ch., 1. *Church*: Chiesa 2. *China*: Cina 3. *Chinese*: cinese.

ch(ap)., *chapter*: cap., capitolo.

Ches(h)., *Cheshire.*

Chr., 1. *Christ*: Cristo 2. *Christian*: cristiano.

C.I.A., *Central Intelligence Agency*: Organizzazione centrale d'informazioni (Servizio segreto americano).

c.i.f., *cost, insurance, freight*: c.i.f., costo, assicurazione e nolo.

cm., *centimetre*: cm., centimetro.

Co., 1. *Company*: s., società 2. *County*: contea.

c/o, *care of*: c/o, presso.

C.O.D., c.o.d., *cash on delivery*: pagamento alla consegna.

Col., 1. *Colonel*: col., colonnello 2. *Colorado.*

coll., 1. *colleague*: collega 2. *college*: coll., collegio 3. *colloquial*: fam., familiare.

Colo., *Colorado.*

Conn., *Connecticut.*

Consol., *consolidated*: consolidato.

cont(d)., *continued*: continuo, ininterrotto.

coop., *co-operative*: coop., cooperativa.

corp., *corporation*: 1. corporazione 2. (*amer.*) s.r.l., società a responsabilità limitata.

Corn(w), *Cornwall.*

c.o.s., *cash on shipment*: pagamento alla spedizione.

C.P., *Communist Party*: P.C., Partito Comunista.

cp., *compare*: cfr., confrontare.

Ct., *Connecticut.*

cu., *cubic*: c., cubico.

Cumb., *Cumberland.*

C.U.P., *Cambridge University Press*: Edizioni dell'Università di Cambridge.

d., 1. *date*: data 2. *dead*: m., morto 3. *penny, pence*: penny, pence.

d.c., *direct current*: c.c., corrente continua.

D.A.B., *Dictionary of American Biography*: Dizionario della Biografia Americana.

Dak., *Dakota.*

D.C., *District of Columbia*: Distretto della Columbia.

D.D., *Doctor of Divinity*: dottore in teologia.

dd., d/d, *delivered*: consegnato.

Dec., *December*: dic., dicembre.

Del., *Delaware.*

dep., 1. *department*: reparto, ufficio; (*am.*) ministero 2. *deputy*: deputato.

Devon., *Devonshire.*

Dir., *director*: dirett., direttore.

disc., *discount*: sconto.

D. Lit., *Doctor of Literature*: dottore in letteratura.

D.N.B., *Dictionary of National Biography*: Dizionario della Biografia Nazionale.

dol., *dollar*: dollaro.

Dorset., *Dorsetshire.*

doz., *dozen*: dozz., dozzina.

D.P., *Displaced Person*: profugo.

Dr., 1. *Doctor*: dott., dottore 2. *Debtor*: debitore.

dz., *dozen*: dozz., dozzina.

E., 1. *East*: E, Est 2. *English*: inglese.

ea., *each*: cad., cadauno.

E.B., *Encyclopaedia Britannica*: Enciclopedia Britannica.

E.C.A., *Economic Co-operation Administration*: Amministrazione della cooperazione economica.

E.C.M., *European Common Market*: M.E.C., Mercato Comune Europeo.

ed., **1.** *edited*: ed., edito **2.** *edition*: ed., edizione.

E.D.C., *European Defence Community*: C.E.D., Comunità per la difesa europea.

edit., V. *ed*.

Edin., *Edinburgh*.

e.g., *for example*: p. es., per esempio.

Emp., *Emperor*: imperatore.

enc(l)., *enclosure*: all., allegato.

Eng., **1.** *England*: Inghilterra **2.** *English*: inglese.

esp(ec)., *especially*: spec., specialmente.

Esq., *Esquire (titolo di cortesia usato negli indirizzi)*: Egr., egregio.

etc., *and so on*: ecc., eccetera.

Eur., **1.** *Europe*: Europa **2.** *European*: europeo.

ex., **1.** *examined*: esaminato **2.** *example*: es., esempio **3.** *excepted*: eccetto **4.** *executive*: esecutivo.

exc., *except(ed)*: eccettuato.

F., *Fahrenheit*: F., Fahrenheit.

f., *frequency*: f., frequenza.

F.A.O., *Food and Agricultural Organization*: Organizzazione per l'agricoltura e l'alimentazione.

F.B.I., *Federal Bureau of Investigation*: Ufficio federale d'investigazione.

Feb., *February*: feb., febbraio.

Fed., **1.** *Federal*: fed., federale **2.** *Federation*: federazione.

Fla., **Flor.**, *Florida*.

F.O., *Foreign Office*: M.AA.EE., Ministero degli affari esteri.

F.O.B., **f.o.b.**, *free on board*: f.o.b., franco bordo.

fol., *folio*: folio.

fol(l)., *following*: seg., seguente.

Fr., **1.** *Father*: P., padre **2.** *France*: Francia **3.** *French*: francese **4.** *Friday*: ven., venerdì.

Fri., *Friday*: ven., venerdì.

ft., *foot, feet*: piede, piedi.

g., **1.** *conductance*: conduttanza **2.** *gender*: genere **3.** *gram*: g., grammo **4.** *guinea*: ghinea.

Ga., *Georgia*.

gal(l)., *gallon*: gallone.

G.B., *Great Britain*: Gran Bretagna.

Gen., *General*: gen., generale.

gen., **1.** *gender*: genere **2.** *generally*: gen., generalmente.

gent., *gentleman*: gentiluomo, signore.

G.H.Q., *General Headquarters*: Q.G., quartier generale.

G.I., *Government Issue*: promulgazione ministeriale.

Gloster., *Gloucestershire*.

G-Man., *Government Man*: soldato governativo.

G.O.P., *Grand Old Party (U.S. Republican Party)*: Partito Repubblicano Americano.

G.P.O., *General Post Office*: Posta centrale.

H, *hydrogen*: H., idrogeno.

h., **1.** *hour*: h., ora **2.** *high*: A., alto.

H.B.M., *His (Her) Britannic Majesty*: S.M.B., Sua Maestà Britannica.

H.C., *House of Commons*: Camera dei Comuni.

H.E., *His Excellency*: S.E., Sua Eccellenza.

Hereford., *Herefordshire*.

Herts., *Hertfordshire*.

hf., *half*: metà.

H.H., **1.** *His Holiness*: S.S., Sua Santità **2.** *His (Her) Highness*: S.A., Sua Altezza.

hhd., *hogshead*: hogshead *(misura di capacità l. 238,5)*.

H.L., *House of Lords*: Camera Alta.

H.M., *His (Her) Majesty*: V.M., Vostra Maestà.

H.M.S., *His (Her) Majesty's Service*: servizio di Sua Maestà.

Hon., *Honourable*: on., onorevole.

H.P., **1.** *high pressure*: alta pressione **2.** *horse power*: H.P., cavalli vapore.

hr., *hour*: h., ora.

H.S., *High School*: scuola media superiore.

Hunts., *Huntingdonshire*.

I(a)., *Iowa*.

ib(id)., *in the same place*: ibid., nello stesso luogo.

I.D., *Intelligence Department*: reparto informazioni.

id., *the same*: id., come sopra.

Id(a)., *Idaho*.

i.e., *that is*: cioè.

Ill., *Illinois*.

in., *inch*: pollice *(misura)*.

inc., **1.** *incorporated*: incorporato **2.** *including*: incluso.

inst., *instant (the present month)*: c.m., corrente mese.

I.O.U., *I owe you*: pagherò.

I.Q., *Intelligence Quotient*: Q.I., quoziente d'intelligenza.

Ire., *Ireland*.

Ja(n)., *January*: genn., gennaio.

J.P., *Justice of the Peace*: giudice di pace.

jr., jun., *junior*: iun., junior.

Kan(s)., *Kansas*.

kg., *kilogram*: kg., chilogrammo.

kilo., **1.** *kilogram*: chilogrammo **2.** *kilometre*: km., chilometro.

K.K.K., *Ku Klux Klan*: K.K.K., Ku Klux Klan.

km., *kilometre*: km., chilometro.

K.O., *knock out*: fuori combattimento.

kw., *kilowatt*: kw., chilowatt.

Ky., *Kentucky*.

L., *pound*: L.st., lira sterlina.

l., **1.** *litre*: l., litro **2.** *long*: lungo.

La., *Louisiana*.

Lancs., *Lancashire*.

Lat., *Latin*: latino.

lat., *latitude*: latitudine.

lb., *pound*: libbra.

L.C.D., *lowest common denominator*: m.c.d., minimo comun denominatore.

L.C.M., *least common multiple*: m.c.m., minimo comune multiplo.

Leics., *Leicestershire*.

L.F., *low frequency*: b.f., bassa frequenza.

Lieut., *Lieutenant*: luogotenente.

Lincs., *Lincolnshire*.

LL.D., *Doctor of Laws*: dottore in legge.

Lon., *London*: Londra.

lon(g)., *longitude*: longitudine.

L.P., **1.** *Labour Party*: Partito Laburista **2.** *Long Play*: microsolco.

L.R., *Lloyd's Register*: Registro dei Lloyd.

Ltd., *limited*: s.r.l., società a responsabilità limitata.

m., **1.** *male*: m., maschio **2.** *metre*: m., metro **3.** *mile*: miglio **4.** *minute*: m., minuto **5.** *month*: m., mese.

M.A., *Master of Arts*: laureato in lettere.

Mad., **Madm.**, *Madam*: sig.ra, signora.

Maj., *Major*: magg., maggiore.

Mar., *March*: mar., marzo.

Mass., *Massachusetts*.

max., *maximum*: mass., massimo.

M.C., *Member of Congress*: membro del Congresso.

Md., *Maryland*.

M.D., *Doctor of Medicine*: dottore in medicina.

Mdx., *Middlesex*.

Me., *Maine*.

M.F., *medium frequency*: m.f., media frequenza.

mg(m)., *milligram*: mg., milligrammo.

Mich., *Michigan*.

Minn., *Minnesota*.

Miss., *Mississippi*.

mm., *millimetre*: mm., millimetro.

Mo., **1.** *Missouri* **2.** *Monday*: lun., lunedì.

M.O., *money order*: ordine di pagamento.

Mon., *Monday*: lun., lunedì.

Mont., *Montana*.

M.P., **1.** *Military Police*: Polizia militare **2.** *Member of Parliament*: membro del Parlamento.

mph., *miles per hour*: miglia orarie.

Mr., *Mister*: sig., signor.

Mrs., *Mistress*: sig.ra, signora.

M/S, *motorship*: M/n, motonave.

MS., *manuscript*: ms., manoscritto.

MSS., *manuscripts*: mss., manoscritti.

Mt., *mount*: M., monte.

mus., **1.** *museum*: mus., museo **2.** *music*: musica.

N., *North*: N, Nord.

n., **1.** *born*: n., nato **2.** *number*: n., numero.

N.A.T.O., *North Atlantic Treaty Organization*: P.A., Patto atlantico.

N.B.C., *National Broadcasting Company*: Compagnia radiofonica nazionale.

N.C., *North Carolina*.

N.C.O., *non-commissioned officer*: s. uff., sottufficiale.

N. D(ak)., *North Dakota*.

Neb(r)., *Nebraska*.

Nev., *Nevada*.

New M., *New Mexico*.

N.H., *New Hampshire.*
N.J., *New Jersey.*
N. M(ex)., *New Mexico.*
no., *number*: n., numero.
Norf., *Norfolk.*
Northum(b)., *Northumberland*
nos., *numbers*: numeri.
Notts., *Nottinghamshire.*
Nov., *November*: nov., novembre.
N.Y., *New York*: Nuova York.

O., *Ohio.*
Oct., *October*: ott., ottobre.
O.E.D., *Oxford English Dictionary*: Dizionario Inglese Oxford.
Okla., *Oklahoma.*
op. cit., *in the work cited*: op. cit., opera citata.
Ore(g)., *Oregon.*
O.U.P., *Oxford University Press*: Edizioni dell'Università di Oxford.
Ox(f)., *Oxford.*
Oxon., **1.** *Oxford* **2.** *of Oxford*: ossoniese **3.** *Oxfordshire ounce*: oncia.

P., *(car-)park*: P., parcheggio.
p., **1.** *page*: p., pagina **2.** *past*: pass., passato.
Pa., *Pennsylvania.*
P.A.A., *Pan American Airways*: Linee aeree panamericane.
par., *paragraph*: parag., paragrafo.
pat., **1.** *patent*: brev., brevetto **2.** *patented*: brevettato.
P.A.Y.E., *pay as you earn (trattenuta di ricchezza mobile)*: R.M., ricchezza mobile.
pd., *paid*: pagato.
Penn(a). v. *Pa.*
Ph. D., *Doctor of Philosophy*: dottore in filosofia.
P.M., *Prime Minister*: Primo Ministro.
p.m., *post meridiem (after noon)*: pomeridiano.
P.O., p.o., **1.** *Post Office*: U.P., ficio postale **2.** *postal order*: V., vaglia.
P.O.B., *post office box*: C.P., casella postale.
p.o.d., *pay on delivery*: pagamento alla consegna.
pp., *pages*: pagg., pagine.
prep., *preparation*: preparazione.
Pres., *President*: pres., presidente.
Prof., *Professor*: prof., professore.
prox., *next*: prossimo.
P.S., *postscript*: P.S., poscritto.

p.t.o., *please turn over*: voltare pagina.

Q.M.G., *Quartermaster General*: capo dipartimento amministrazione e alloggi.
qu., **1.** *quart*: misura di capacità (l. 1.136) **2.** *quarter*: quarto.
quot., *quotation*: citazione.

R., r., **1.** *river*: f., fiume **2.** *road*: strada.
R.A.C., *Royal Automobile Club*: Regio Automobile Club.
R.A.D.I.A.C., *Radioactivity Detection Identification and Computation*: Rivelazione, identificazione e calcolo della radioattività.
R.A.F., *Royal Air Force*: Regia Aviazione militare.
R.C., **1.** *Red Cross*: C.R., Croce Rossa **2.** *Roman Catholic*: Cattolico Romano.
R.C.A., *Radio Corporation of America*: Associazione Radiofonica Americana.
re., *reference* **1.** ref., referenza **2.** riferimento.
rec., **1.** *receipt*: ricevuta **2.** *record*: record.
reg., **1.** *region*: regione **2.** *register*: reg., registro **3.** *regular*: regolare.
Rev., *Reverend*: rev., reverendo.
R.H., *Royal Highness*: A.R., Altezza Reale.
R.N., *Royal Navy*: Regia Marina.
Rt. Hon., *Right Honourable*: molto onorevole.
Rt. Rev., *Right Reverend*: molto reverendo.
Ry., *Railway*: ferrovia.

S., *South*: S, Sud.
s., **1.** *second*: secondo **2.** *shilling*: scellino.
Sat., *Saturday*: sab., sabato.
S.C., *South Carolina.*
sch., *school*: sc., scuola.
Scot., **1.** *Scotland*: Scozia **2.** *Scottish*: scozzese.
S. D(ak)., *South Dakota.*
sec., **1.** *second*: secondo **2.** *section*: sezione **3.** *secretary*: segr., segretario
Sen., **1.** *Senate*: senato **2.** *senator*: senatore **3.** *senior*: senior.
Sept., *September*: sett., settembre.
Sergt., *sergeant*: serg., sergente.
sh., *shilling*: scellino.

S.H.A.P.E., *Supreme Headquarters Allied Powers Europe*: quartier generale delle Forze alleate in Europa.

Shrops., *Shropshire.*

So., **1.** *South*: S, Sud **2.** *Southern*: sudista.

Soc., *society*: s., società.

Somerset., *Somersetshire.*

spec., **1.** *special*: spec., speciale **2.** *specification*: specificazione.

sp. gr., *specific gravity*: gravità specifica.

sq., *square*: p.za, piazza.

Sr., **1.** *senior*: senior **2.** *Sir*: Sir **3.** *sister*: sorella.

SS, S/S, *steamship*: piroscafo.

St., **1.** *Saint*: s., santo **2.** *street*: via.

st., *stone*: misura di peso (*Kg. 6,350*).

Staffs., *Staffordshire.*

ster., stg., *sterling*: L.st., lira sterlina.

St. Ex., *Stock Exchange*: Borsa valori.

Sun(d)., *Sunday*: dom., domenica.

Sup. Ct., *Supreme Court*: C.S., Corte suprema.

supp(l)., *supplement*: supplemento.

Sur., *Surrey.*

Sus., *Sussex.*

S.W., **1.** *South Wales*: Galles del sud **2.** *South West*: S.O., sud ovest.

Swit., Swtz., *Switzerland*: Svizzera.

syn., *synonym*: sinonimo

Sy., *Surrey.*

t., **1.** *ton*: t., tonnellata **2.** *volume*: v., volume.

T.B., *tuberculosis*: tbc, tubercolosi.

tel., **1.** *telegram*: telegramma **2.** *telegraph*: telegrafo **3.** *telephone*: tel., telefono.

Tenn., *Tennessee.*

Tex., *Texas.*

Thur(s)., *Thursday*: giov., giovedì.

T.O., *turn over*: voltare.

T.U., *Trade-Union*: Sindacato.

Tu(es)., *Tuesday*: mar., martedì.

TV., *television*: TV, televisione.

T.W.A., *Trans World Airlines*: linee aeree intercontinentali.

U., **1.** *Union*: U., unione **2.** *University*: Università.

U.K., *United Kingdom*: R.U., Regno Unito.

U.N., *United Nations*: N.U., Nazioni Unite.

U.N.E.S.C.O., *United Nations Educational Scientific and Cultural Organization*: Organizzazione culturale, scientifica e per l'educazione delle Nazioni Unite.

U.N.I.C.E.F., *United Nations International Children's Emergency Fund*: Fondo d'emergenza internazionale per l'infanzia delle Nazioni Unite.

U.N.O., *United Nations Organization*: O.N.U., Organizzazione delle Nazioni Unite.

U.P., *United Press*: Stampa associata.

U.S., *United States*: S.U., Stati Uniti.

U.S.A., **1.** *United States of America*: S.U.A., Stati Uniti d'America. **2.** *United States Army*: Esercito degli Stati Uniti.

U.S.A.E.C., *United States Atomic Energy Commission*: commissione per l'energia atomica degli Stati Uniti.

U.S.A.F., *United States Air Force*: Aviazione militare degli Stati Uniti.

U.S.I.S., *United States Information Service*: Servizio informazioni degli Stati Uniti.

U.S.N., *United States Navy*: Marina degli Stati Uniti.

U.S.S.R., *Union of Soviet Socialist Republics*: U.R.S.S., Unione delle repubbliche socialiste sovietiche.

U.S.S., *United States Ship*: nave degli Stati Uniti.

Ut., *Utah.*

v., *verse*: v., verso.

Va., *Virginia.*

Vat., *Vatican*: Vaticano.

Ven., *Venerable*: Ven., venerabile.

V.H.F., *very high frequency*: altissima frequenza.

Vic(t)., *Victoria.*

V.I.P., *Very Important Person*: Persona molto importante.

viz., *namely*: cioè.

vol., *volume*: vol., volume.

V.P., *Vice-President*: vicepresidente.

vs., *against*: contro.

Vt., *Vermont.*

Vul(g)., *Vulgate*: Vulgata.

vv., *verses*: vv., versi.

w., *watt*: W., watt.

W., 1. *West*: O, Ovest **2.** *Washington*.

w., 1. *week*: settimana **2.** *wife*: moglie **3.** *with*: con.

Warwick., *Warwickshire*.

Wash., *Washington*.

W.D., *War Department*: Ministero della Guerra.

Wed., *Wednesday*: mer., mercoledì.

Westm., *Westminster*.

Westmore., *Westmoreland*.

whf., *wharf*: pontile.

Wis(c)., *Wisconsin*.

wk., 1. *week*: settimana **2.** *work*: lavoro.

w.l., *wave length*: lunghezza d'onda.

Worcs., *Worcestershire*.

W.R.A.C., *Women's Royal Army Corps*: Regio corpo d'armata femminile.

wt., *weight*: peso.

W.Va., *West Virginia*: Virginia dell'ovest.

Wy(o)., *Wyoming*.

Xmas., *Christmas*: Natale.

y., 1. *yard*: iarda **2.** *year*: anno.

yd., *yard*: iarda.

Y.H.A., *Youth Hostels Association*: Associazione Ostelli per la gioventù.

Y.M.C.A., *Young men's Christian Association*: Associazione Cristiana per i giovani.

yr., 1. *year*: anno **2.** *your*: vostro.

Yorks., *Yorkshire*.

yrs., 1. *years*: anni **2.** *yours*: vostri.

Y.W.C.A., *Young Women's Christian Association*: Associazione Cristiana per le giovani.

Z., *atomic number*: n.a., numero atomico.

&, *and*: e.

&c., *and so forth*: etc., ecc., eccetera.

PREFACE TO THE ITALIAN-ENGLISH SECTION OF THE
PICCOLO DIZIONARIO ITALIANO-INGLESE

1. The first part of the English-Italian section of the **Compact Dictionary** contains information in Italian designed to help in its use. It gives rules of pronunciation, a list of irregular verbs, tables of comparison of the English and American units and metric system, information on the English and American currency, a list of cardinal and ordinal numbers, and an explanatory list of the abbreviations used.

A similar introduction is included here to help in the use of the Italian-English section.

2. Since Italian presents particular problems with its verbs we have provided a list of irregular verbs in general use. We have not included their compounds, as they are conjugated in the same way.

Those verbs which take *essere* as an auxiliary are indicated by means of a single star. Those which take *essere* when used intransitively and *avere* when used transitively have a double star.

With the past definite tense we have shown the 1st person singular only, since the 3rd person singular and the 3rd person plural follow the same pattern, while the 2nd person singular and plural are regular in form e.g.: *prendere* – **presi,** *prendesti,* **prese,** *prendemmo, prendeste,* **presero.**

3. There are two points concerning the current use of verbs which the student of Italian may well find helpful:

a) there is a tendency in modern Italian towards a more frequent use of the perfect tense to represent completed past action (though such irrefutable statements of the past as, for example, *Dante died in 1321* would still always be translated as *Dante morì . . .*);

b) though the polite form in the singular, with *Lei* and the 3rd person of the verb, is regularly used e.g.: *Lei scrive in inglese?* (Are you writing in English?), the plural form addressed to more than one person is now more frequently the 2nd person plural with *Voi* , instead of the 3rd person plural with *Loro* e.g.: *Voi scrivete in inglese?* rather than *Loro scrivono in inglese?*

4. As some Italian nouns have irregular plurals or do not change their form in the plural we have included a list of the more commonly used ones.

5. In illustrating the possible alternative translations for the Italian words listed, the following symbols have been adopted:

a) a double line (||) after the initial translation or translations indicates a grammatical change from, for example, an adjective to a noun or a pronoun to an adverb;

b) a lozenge (◆) indicates something more than just an alternative translation, showing, for example, a figurative or idiomatic use;

c) the numbers printed in large type (**1.**, **2.**, **3.**, etc.) indicate the various alternative meanings;

d) the small numbers ([1], [2], [3], etc.) indicate words of identical form but different meaning.

The Alphabet

The Italian alphabet consists of 21 letters only. j (*i lunga*), k (*cappa*), w (*doppio vu*), x (*ics*), y (*ipsilon*) do not occur in the alphabet, though they are used for the spelling of foreign words e.g.: *judo, kimono, watt, xenofobia, yacht*. In some cases y is replaced by i, e.g. *raion* for rayon. ch replaces k, e.g. *chilogramma* for kilogram. ph is represented by f, e.g. *fobia* for phobia. x occurs in certain expressions such as *ex-presidente, extraterritoriale*, etc.

Letter	Name	Letter	Name
a	*a*	m	*emme*
b	*bi*	n	*enne*
c	*ci*	o	*o*
d	*di*	p	*pi*
e	*e*	q	*cu*
f	*effe*	r	*erre*
g	*gi*	s	*esse*
h	*acca*	t	*ti*
i	*i*	u	*u*
l	*elle*	v	*vu*
		z	*zeta*

Pronunciation

Since Italian is a phonetic language, once the rules of pronunciation are learnt, it is possible to pronounce most words correctly, though it is not always easy to tell on which syllable the tonic stress falls.

The Vowels

Italian vowels are pure sounds and should be pronounced well forward in the mouth:

A	like a in far	*gala*
close E	like a in fate	*seta*
open E	like e in ten	*pelle*
I	like i in machine	*vino*
close O	like o in store	*corte*
open O	like o in spot	*motto*
U	like oo in spoon	*uso*

The Consonants

In the case of double consonants each consonant is sounded, with the voice rising on them and falling on the following vowel.

The consonants **B, D, F, L, M, N, P, Q, T** and **V** are pronounced very much as in English. The rest are as follows:

C   1. before **a, o, u**, and consonants, including **h**: like **c** in cat, as in *casa, crema, chilo*;

     2. before **e** or **i**: like **ch** in chip, as in *cena, cibo*.

G   1. before **a, o, u** and consonants, including **h** but not including **l** and **n**: like **g** in gap, as in *gala, grido, ghiro*;

     2. before **e** or **i**: like **g** in gem, as in *gente, gita*.

gli   like **lli** in billion, as in *figlia*; (a few exceptions have the **gli** pronounced as in English, e.g. *anglicano, negligente*).

gn   like **ni** in onion, as in *signore*.

H   is always silent and occurs in very few words, except as shown above to harden the **c** and **g** sounds before **e** and **i**.

Q   is always followed by **u**, like **qu** in quick, as in *quinto*.

R   is rolled, rather as in **rr** Scottish pronunciation, as in *pera, serra*.

S   1. is voiced, like **s** in rose, as in *rosa, esatto*, or when followed by **b, d, g, l, m, n, r, v**, the voiceless consonants, as in *sdegno, svelto*;

     2. is unvoiced like **s** in sap, at the beginning of a word, or when it is doubled, as in *sega, rosso*.

sc   1. before **e** or **i** is like **sh** in shot, as in *scena*;

     2. before **a, o** and **u** is like **sk** in skate, as in *scarpa, scopo, scudo*;

     3. an **h** after it and before **e** or **i** makes it like **sk**, as in *schema, schiena*;

     4. an **i** after it and before **a, o** or **u** makes it like **sh**, as in *scialle, sciocco, sciupare*.

Z   1. voiced like **ds** in treads, as in *zio*;

     2. unvoiced like **ts** in wits, as in *forza*.

Accentuation

In printed and written Italian an accent is used to indicate when the tonic stress falls on a final vowel such as in *città* or *caffè*. It is also used to distinguish between two words which are spelt and pronounced alike but have different meanings:

     è = is   *e* = and

     dà = he gives   *da* = from, by, of, etc.

It also occurs on some monosyllabic words as in *già* and *più*.

In print the acute accent is used to indicate a stress on a final **e** as in *perché* or *né*, though in handwriting the grave accent is more usual. In modern Italian the grave accent is normally used elsewhere and we have followed this practice.

As a general rule the tonic stress is on the penultimate syllable, but this is not by any means always so. The grave and acute accents have been

used to show where the stress falls when it does not fall on the penultimate syllable. The open and close e are distinguished in the accepted way
by means of è and é, e.g. *créscere, crédere, festival, fervido,* and the grave
accent is used everywhere else, e.g. *càndido, moltitùdine.*

IRREGULAR ITALIAN VERBS†

Accendere – *p. def.* accesi, *p.p.* acceso

Accludere – see alludere

Addurre – *pres.* adduco, *p. def.* addussi, *fut.* addurrò, *p.p.* addotto

Affliggere – *p. def.* afflissi, *p.p.* afflitto

Alludere – *p. def.* allusi, *p.p.* alluso

Andare* – *pres.* vado, vai, va, andiamo, andate, vanno *fut.* andrò

Annettere – *p. def.* annettei (annessi), *p.p.* annesso

Apparire* – *pres.* apparisco, *p. def.* apparii (apparvi, apparsi), *p.p.* apparso

Appendere – *p. def.* appesi, *p.p.* appeso

Ardere – *p. def.* arsi, *p.p.* arso

Aspergere – *p. def.* aspersi, *p.p.* asperso

Assalire – *pres.* assalgo (assalisco), assalgono

Assolvere – *p. def.* assolsi (assolvei, assolvetti), *p.p.* assolto

Assumere – *p. def.* assunsi, *p.p.* assunto

Bere – *pres.* bevo, *p. def.* bevvi, *fut.* berrò

Cadere* – *p. def.* caddi, *fut.* cadrò

Cedere – *p. def.* cedei (cedetti)

Chiedere – *p. def.* chiesi, *p.p.* chiesto

Chiudere – *p. def.* chiusi, *p.p.* chiuso

Cingere – *p. def.* cinsi, *p.p.* cinto

Cogliere – *pres.* colgo, colgono, *p. def.* colsi, *p.p.* colto

Comprimere – *p. def.* compressi, *p.p.* compresso

Conoscere – *p. def.* conobbi, *p.p.* conosciuto

Consumare – *p. def.* consumai (consunsi), *p.p.* consumato (consunto)

Correre** – *p. def.* corsi, *p.p.* corso

Costruire – *p.p.* costruito (costrutto)

Crescere* – *p. def.* crebbi, *p.p.* cresciuto

Cucire – *pres.* cucio

Cuocere – *pres.* cuocio, cuoci, cuoce, cociamo, cocete, cuociono, *p. def.* cossi, *p.p.* cotto

Dare – *pres.* do, dai, dà, diamo, date, danno, *p. def.* diedi (detti), desti, *fut.* darò, *p.p.* dato

† Verbs which take *essere* are indicated by one star.
  Those taking *avere* and *essere* have two stars.

Decidere – *p. def.* decisi, *p.p.* deciso
Difendere – *p. def.* difesi, *p.p.* difeso
Dipendere** – *p. def.* dipesi, *p.p.* dipeso
Dipingere – *p. def.* dipinsi, *p.p.* dipinto
Dire – *pres.* dico, dite, *p. def.* dissi, *fut.* dirò, *p.p.* detto
Dirigere – *p. def.* diressi, *p.p.* diretto
Discutere – *p. def.* discussi, *p.p.* discusso
Dissolvere – *p. def.* dissolsi (dissolvei), *p.p.* dissolto
Distinguere – *p. def.* distinsi, *p.p.* distinto
Dividere – *p. def.* divisi, *p.p.* diviso
Dolersi* – *pres.* mi dolgo, ti duoli, si duole, ci doliamo, vi dolete, si dolgono, *p. def.* mi dolsi, *fut.* mi dorrò
Dovere – *pres.* devo (debbo), devi, deve, dobbiamo, dovete, devono (debbono), *fut.* dovrò

Eccellere – *p. def.* eccelsi, *p.p.* eccelso
Emergere* – *p. def.* emersi, *p.p.* emerso
Ergere – *p. def.* ersi, *p.p.* erto
Erigere – *p. def.* eressi, *p.p.* eretto
Esigere – *p.p.* esatto
Espellere – *p. def.* espulsi, *p.p.* espulso
Esplodere** – *p. def.* esplosi, *p.p.* esploso
Evadere* – *p. def.* evasi, *p.p.* evaso

Fare – *pres.* faccio (fo), fai, fa, facciamo, fate, fanno, *imper.* facevo, *p. def.* feci, *fut.* farò, *p.p.* fatto
Fendere – *p. def.* fendei (fendetti), *p.p.* fesso (fenduto)
Figgere – *p. def.* fissi, *p.p.* fisso (fitto)
Fingere – *p. def.* finsi, *p.p.* finto
Fondere – *p. def.* fusi, *p.p.* fuso
Frangere – *p. def.* fransi, *p.p.* franto
Friggere – *p. def.* frissi, *p.p.* fritto

Giacere* – *pres.* giaccio, giacciono, *p. def.* giacqui, *p.p.* giaciuto
Giungere* – *p. def.* giunsi, *p.p.* giunto
Godere – *fut.* godrò

Incutere – *p. def.* incussi (incutei), *p.p.* incusso
Indulgere – *p. def.* indulsi, *p.p.* indulto
Intridere – *p. def.* intrisi, *p.p.* intriso
Invadere – *p. def.* invasi, *p.p.* invaso

Ledere – *p. def.* lesi, *p.p.* leso
Leggere – *p. def.* lessi, *p.p.* letto

Mettere – *p. def.* misi, *p.p.* messo

Mordere – *p. def.* morsi, *p.p.* morso

Morire* – *pres.* muoio, muori, muore, moriamo, morite, muoiono, *fut.* morrò, *p.p.* morto

Mungere – *p. def.* munsi, *p.p.* munto

Muovere – *pres.* moviamo, movete, *p. def.* mossi, *p.p.* mosso

Nascere* – *p. def.* nacqui, *p.p.* nato

Nascondere – *p. def.* nascosi, *p.p.* nascosto

Nuocere – *pres.* noccio, nociamo, nocete, nocciono, *p. def.* nocqui, *p.p.* nociuto

Offrire – *p. def.* offrii (offersi), *p.p.* offerto

Parere* – *pres.* paio, paiamo, paiono, *p. def.* parvi, *fut.* parrò, *p.p.* parso

Percuotere – *p.p.* percosso

Perdere – *p. def.* persi (perdei, perdetti), *p.p.* perduto (perso)

Persuadere – *p. def.* persuasi, *p.p.* persuaso

Piacere* – *pres.* piaccio, piaci, piace, piacciamo, piacete, piacciono, *p. def.* piacqui, *p.p.* piaciuto

Piangere – *p. def.* piansi, *p.p.* pianto

Piovere** – *p. def.* piovve, piovvero

Porgere – *p. def.* porsi, *p.p.* porto

Porre – *pres.* pongo, poni, pone, poniamo, ponete, pongono, *p. def.* posi, *fut.* porrò, *p.p.* posto

Potere – *pres.* posso, puoi, può, possiamo, potete, possono, *fut.* potrò

Prediligere – *p. def.* predilessi, *p.p.* prediletto

Prendere – *p. def.* presi, *p.p.* preso

Proteggere – *p. def.* protessi, *p.p.* protetto

Pungere – *p. def.* punsi, *p.p.* punto

Radere – *p. def.* rasi, *p.p.* raso

Redimere – *p. def.* redensi, *p.p.* redento

Reggere – *p. def.* ressi, *p.p.* retto

Rendere – *p. def.* resi, *p.p.* reso

Ridere – *p. def.* risi, *p.p.* riso

Rifulgere** – *p. def.* rifulsi, *p.p.* rifulso

Rispondere – *p. def.* risposi, *p.p.* risposto

Rodere – *p. def.* rosi, *p.p.* roso

Rompere – *p. def.* ruppi, *p.p.* rotto

Salire** – *pres.* salgo, salgono

Sapere – *pres.* so, sai, sa, sappiamo, sapete, sanno, *p. def.* seppi, *fut.* saprò

Scegliere – *pres.* scelgo, scelgono, *p. def.* scelsi, *p.p.* scelto

Scendere** – *p. def.* scesi, *p.p.* sceso

Scindere – *p. def.* scissi, *p.p.* scisso

Sciogliere – *pres.* sciolgo, sciolgono, *p. def.* sciolsi, *p.p.* sciolto

Scrivere – *p. def.* scrissi, *p.p.* scritto

Scuotere – *p. def.* scossi, *p.p.* scosso

Sedere* – *pres.* siedo (seggo), siedi, siede, sediamo, sedete, siedono (seggono)

Soddisfare – *pres.* soddisfo (soddisfaccio, soddisfò), soddisfi (soddisfai), soddisfa, soddisfiamo (soddisfacciamo), soddisfate, soddisfano (soddisfanno), *p. def.* soddisfeci, *p.p.* soddisfatto

Sorgere* – *p. def.* sorsi, *p.p.* sorto

Spargere – *p. def.* sparsi, *p.p.* sparso

Spegnere – *p. def.* spensi, *p.p.* spento

Spendere – *p. def.* spesi, *p.p.* speso

Spingere – *p. def.* spinsi, *p.p.* spinto

Stare* – *pres.* sto, stai, sta, stiamo, state, stanno, *imperf.* stavo, *p. def.* stetti, *p.p.* stato

Stringere – *p. def.* strinsi, *p.p.* stretto

Struggere – *p. def.* strussi, *p.p.* strutto

Svellere – *pres.* svello (svelgo), svellono (svelgono), *p. def.* svelsi, *p.p.* svelto

Svenire* – *p. def.* svenni

Tacere – *pres.* taccio, taci, tace, taciamo, tacete, tacciono, *p. def.* tacqui, *p.p.* taciuto

Tendere – *p. def.* tesi, *p.p.* teso

Tenere – *pres.* tengo, tieni, tiene, teniamo, tenete, tengono, *p. def.* tenni, *fut.* terrò

Tingere – *p. def.* tinsi, *p.p.* tinto

Togliere – *pres.* tolgo, tolgono, *p. def.* tolsi, *p.p.* tolto

Torcere – *p. def.* torsi, *p.p.* torto

Trarre – *pres.* traggo, trai, trae, traiamo, traete, traggono, *imperf.* traevo, *p. def.* trassi, *fut.* trarrò, *p.p.* tratto

Uccidere – *p. def.* uccisi, *p.p.* ucciso

Udire – *pres.* odo, odi, ode, udiamo, udite, odono, *fut.* udrò (udirò)

Ungere – *p. def.* unsi, *p.p.* unto

Uscire* – *pres.* esco, esci, esce, usciamo, uscite, escono

Valere** – *pres.* valgo, valgono, *p. def.* valsi, *fut.* varrò, *p.p.* valso

Vedere – *pres.* vedo (veggo), vedono (veggono), *p. def.* vidi, *fut.* vedrò, *p.p.* visto

Venire* – *pres.* vengo, vieni, viene, veniamo, venite, vengono, *p. def.* venni, *fut.* verrò

Vilipendere – *p. def.* vilipesi, *p.p.* vilipeso

Vincere – *p. def.* vinsi, *p.p.* vinto

Vivere** – *p. def.* vissi, *p.p.* vissuto

Volere – *pres.* voglio, vuoi, vuole, vogliamo, volete, vogliono, *p. def.* volli, *fut.* vorrò

Volgere – *p. def.* volsi, *p.p.* volto

IRREGULAR PLURALS OF NOUNS

l'autobus	gli autobus
il bar	i bar
il caffè	i caffè
la città	le città
la frutta	le frutta
il re	i re
il braccio	le braccia
il bue	i buoi
il centinaio	le centinaia
il dito	le dita
il ginocchio	le ginocchia
la guancia	le guance
il labbro	le labbra
il lenzuolo	le lenzuola
la mano	le mani
il migliaio	le migliaia
l'orecchio	le orecchie
il paio	le paia
l'uomo	gli uomini

ITALIAN MONEY

Italian bank notes are issued in the following denominations:

500 lire	10,000 lire
1000 lire	50,000 lire
2000 lire	100,000 lire.
5000 lire	

The one hundred thousand lire notes are not negotiable outside Italy.

Coins are issued in **five, ten, twenty, fifty, one hundred** and **five hundred** pieces.

NUMERALS

Cardinal		Cardinal cont.	
1	uno	3	tre
2	due	4	quattro

Cardinal		Cardinal cont.	
5	cinque	29	ventinove
6	sei	30	trenta
7	sette	31	trentuno
8	otto	32	trentadue
9	nove	38	trentotto
10	dieci	40	quaranta
11	undici	50	cinquanta
12	dodici	60	sessanta
13	tredici	70	settanta
14	quattordici	80	ottanta
15	quindici	90	novanta
16	sedici	100	cento
17	diciassette	101	centouno
18	diciotto	105	centocinque
19	diciannove	150	centocinquanta
20	venti	200	duecento
21	ventuno	300	trecento
22	ventidue	1000	mille
23	ventitré	1100	millecento
24	ventiquattro	1200	milleduecento
25	venticinque	2000	duemila
26	ventisei	100,000	centomila
27	ventisette	1,000,000	un milione
28	ventotto		

Ordinal

1st	primo
2nd	secondo
3rd	terzo
4th	quarto
5th	quinto
6th	sesto
7th	settimo
8th	ottavo
9th	nono
10th	decimo
11th	undicesimo *or* decimo primo
12th	dodicesimo *or* decimo secondo
20th	ventesimo
21st	ventunesimo *or* ventesimo primo
22nd	ventiduesimo *or* ventesimo secondo

30th	trentesimo
40th	quarantesimo
50th	cinquantesimo
101st	centunesimo
200th	duecentesimo
1000th	millesimo
1205th	milleduecentocinquesimo
1,000,000th	milionesimo

ABBREVIATIONS USED IN THE DICTIONARY

abbr.	abbreviation	*(dial.)*	dialect
(aer.)	aviation	*dif.*	defective
agg.	adjective	*dim.*	diminutive
(agr.)	agriculture	*dimostr.*	demonstrative
(amer.)	American		
amm.	administrative	*ecc., etc.*	etcetera
(anat.)	anatomy	*(eccl.)*	ecclesiastical
(ant.)	archaic	*(econ.)*	economics
(arch.)	architecture	*(edil.)*	building industry
art.	article	*(elettr.)*	electricity
(arte)	art	*escl.*	exclamation
assol.	absolute		
(astr.)	astronomy	*f.*	feminine
attr.	attribute	*(fam.)*	familiar
aus.	auxiliary	*(farm.)*	pharmaceutical
(auto)	motoring	*(ferr.)*	railway
avv.	adverb	*(fig.)*	figurative
		(fil.)	philosophy
(bot.)	botany	*(fis.)*	physics
(biol.)	biology	*(foto)*	photography
		fut.	future
(chim.)	chemistry		
(chir.)	surgery	*gen.*	genitive
(cine)	cinematography	*general.*	generally
coll.	collective	*(geogr.)*	geography
(comm.)	commerce	*(geol.)*	geology
comp.	comparative	*(geom.)*	geometry
compl.	complement	*ger.*	gerund
condiz.	conditional	*(gergo)*	jargon, slang
cong.	conjunction	*(giorn.)*	journalism
(costr.)	building	*(giur.)*	legal
(cuc.)	cooking	*(gramm.)*	grammar

i.	intransitive	*pl.*	plural
id.	idem	*(poet.)*	poetical
imp.	impersonal	*(pol.)*	political
imperat.	imperative	*(pop.)*	popular
imperf.	imperfect	*poss.*	possessive
ind.	indicative	*p.p.*	past participle
indef.	indefinite	*prep.*	preposition
inf.	infinitive	*pred.*	predicate
int.	interrogative	*pres.*	present
inter.	interjection	*pron.*	pronoun
(iron.)	ironic	*prov.*	proverbial
irr.	irregular	*(psicol.)*	psychology
(itt.)	ichthyology		
		qc.	something
(lat.)	Latin, Latinism	*qu.*	someone
loc. avv.	adverbial phrase		
loc. cong.	conjunctive	*r.*	reflexive
	phrase	*(radio)*	radio
loc. prep.	prepositional	*rec.*	reciprocal
	phrase	*reg.*	regular
(lett.)	literature	*rel.*	relative
		(relig.)	religion
m.	masculine		
(mar.)	naval, maritime	*s.*	masculine and
(mat.)	mathematics		feminine noun
(mecc.)	mechanics	*semidif.*	partly defective
(med.)	medicine	*sf.*	feminine noun
(metal.)	metallurgy	*sm.*	masculine noun
(mil.)	military	*(scherz.)*	humourous
(min.)	mineralogy	*(scol.)*	scolastic
(mit.)	mythology	*(scult.)*	sculpture
(mus.)	music	*sing.*	singular
		so	someone
neg.	negative	*sogg.*	subject
(neol.)	neologism	*sost.*	noun
		spec.	especially
		(spreg.)	pejorative
ogg.	object	*sthg.*	something
(ott.)	optics	*(stor.)*	history
		superl.	superlative
p.	participle		
pass.	past		
p. def.	past definite	*t.*	transitive
pers.	personal	*(teat.)*	theatre
(pitt.)	painting	*(tec.)*	technical

(tel.)	telephony	*v. dif.*	defective verb
(teol.)	theology	*vi.*	instransitive verb
(tip.)	typography	*(v. irr.)*	irregular verb
(tv.)	television	*(volg.)*	vulgar
		vr.	reflexive verb
(us.)	usage	*v. semidif.*	partially defective verb
v.	verb	*vt.*	transitive verb
V.	cf.		
(vezz.)	diminutive	*(zool.)*	zoology

A

a, ad *prep.* **1.** (*termine*) to: *l'ho dato a te*, I gave it to you **2.** (*moto a luogo*) *vado alla stazione*, I am going to the station **3.** (*stato in luogo*) in, at: *vivo a Milano*, I live in Milan; *sono a casa*, I am at home **4.** (*tempo determinato*) at, on, in: *al mio arrivo*, on my arrival **5.** (*iterativo*): *due, tre volte al giorno*, twice, three times a day.

àbaco (*arch.*) *sm.* abacus.
abate *sm.* abbot.
abbacchiare *vt.* (*di frutta*) to beat (*v. irr.*) down. ♦ **abbacchiarsi** *vr.* to feel (*v. irr.*) down-hearted.
abbacchiato *agg.* down-hearted.
abbacinare *vt.* to dazzle.
àbbaco *sm.* elementary arithmetic book.
abbagliante *agg.* dazzling: *fari abbaglianti*, dazzling beams.
abbagliare *vt.* to dazzle, to blind (with).
abbaglio *sm.* **1.** dazzling **2.** (*errore*) blunder.
abbaiare *vi.* to bark.
abbaino *sm.* garret.
abbandonare *vt.* **1.** to leave (*v. irr.*), to forsake (*v. irr.*), to abandon **2.** (*rinunciare*) to give (*v. irr.*) up.
abbandonato *agg.* **1.** (*trascurato*) neglected **2.** (*di casa*) deserted **3.** (*di persona*) forsaken.
abbandono *sm.* **1.** (*di persona che viene abbandonata*) forsaking **2.** (*rinuncia*) giving up.
abbarbicare *vi.* to take (*v. irr.*) root. ♦ **abbarbicarsi** *vr.* to cling (*v. irr.*) (*anche fig.*).
abbaruffarsi *vr.* to quarrel.
abbassamento *sm.* lowering || — *di temperatura*, fall (in temperature).
abbassare *vt.* **1.** to lower, to pull down || — *la .testa*, to bend (*v. irr.*) one's head **2.** (*ridurre*) to reduce. ♦ **abbassarsi** *vr.* to stoop (down).
abbasso *avv.* **1.** (*al di sotto*) below **2.** (*giù*) down **3.** (*al piano terreno, dopo aver sceso le scale*) downstairs. ♦ **abbasso!** *inter.* down with!
abbastanza *avv.* **1.** enough **2.** (*discretamente*) quite.

abbàttere *vt.* to pull down. ♦ **abbàttersi** *vr.* to be discouraged.
abbattimento *sm.* **1.** throwing down **2.** (*morale*) dejection.
abbattuto *agg.* disheartened.
abbazìa *sf.* abbey.
abbecedario *sm.* primer.
abbellimento *sm.* embellishment.
abbellire *vt.* to embellish.
abbeverare *vt.* to water. ♦ **abbeverarsi** *vr.* to water.
abbeveratoio *sm.* trough.
abbiccì *sm.* **1.** alphabet **2.** (*principi elementari*) primer.
abbiente *agg.* well-to-do, wealthy.
abbigliamento *sm.* clothes || *industria dell'*—, clothing industry.
abbigliare *vt.* to dress.
abbinare *vt.* to couple.
abbindolare *vt.* to cheat.
abbisognare *vi.* to need, to be necessary.
abboccamento *sm.* interview.
abboccare *vt. e vi.* **1.** to bite (*v. irr.*) **2.** (*fig.*) to be taken in. ♦ **abboccarsi** *vr.* to confer (with).
abbonacciarsi *vi.* **1.** (*di vento*) to drop **2.** (*di mare*) to smooth down.
abbonamento *sm.* **1.** subscription **2.** (*ferr.*) season-ticket.
abbonare *vt.* **1.** to make (*v. irr.*) (so.) a subscriber **2.** (*defalcare*) to make a discount. ♦ **abbonarsi** *vr.* to subscribe (to).
abbonato *sm.* **1.** subscriber **2.** (*ferr.*) season-ticket holder.
abbondante *agg.* plentiful.
abbondanza *sf.* plenty.
abbondare *vi.* to have plenty (of), to be plentiful.
abbonire *vt.* to calm.
abbordàbile *agg.* accessible.
abbordaggio *sm.* boarding.
abbordare *vt.* **1.** (*mar.*) to board **2.** (*una persona*) to open conversation (with).
abborracciare *vi.* to bungle.
abbottonare *vt.* to button (up). ♦ **abbottonarsi** *vr.* to button one's clothes (up).
abbottonatura *sf.* **1.** button-holes **2.** (*l'abbottonarsi*) buttoning.
abbozzare *vt.* to sketch || — *un sorriso*, to smile faintly.
abbozzo *sm.* sketch.
abbozzolarsi *vr.* to cocoon.
abbracciare *vt.* **1.** to embrace **2.** (*comprendere*) to include **3.** (*afferrare*) to grasp **4.** (*con lo sguardo*)

to take (*v. irr.*) in. ♦ **abbrac-ciarsi** *vr.* to embrace.

abbraccio *sm.* embrace.

abbrancare *vt.* to grasp. ♦ **abbrancarsi** *vr.* to cling (*v. irr.*) (to).

abbreviare *vt.* to shorten, to abridge.

abbreviazione *sf.* abbreviation.

abbrivare *vt.* to get (*v. irr.*) under way.

abbrivo *sm.* freshway.

abbronzare *vt.* **1.** to bronze **2.** (*al sole*) to tan. ♦ **abbronzarsi** *vr.* to get (*v. irr.*) tanned.

abbronzatura *sf.* tanning.

abbruciacchiare *vt.* to scorch.

abbrustolire *vt.* to toast, to roast.

abbrutimento *sm.* brutalization.

abbrutire *vt.* to brutalize.

abbuffarsi *vr.* to stuff oneself.

abbuiarsi *vr.* to get (*v. irr.*) dark.

abbuono *sm.* allowance.

abburattare *vt.* to sift.

abdicare *vi.* to abdicate.

abdicazione *sf.* abdication.

aberrare *vi.* to stray.

aberrazione *sf.* aberration.

abetaia *sf.* fir-wood.

abete *sm.* fir-tree.

abietto *agg.* abject, base.

abiezione *sf.* abjection.

abigeato *sm.* cattle-stealing.

àbile *agg.* **1.** able, skilful **2.** (*a fare qc.*) clever at.

abilità *sf.* ability, skill.

abilitare *vt.* to qualify.

abilitazione *sf.* qualification || *esame di* —, qualifying examination.

abisso *sm.* abyss.

abitàbile *agg.* inhabitable.

abitàcolo *sm.* (*aer.*) cockpit.

abitante *sm.* inhabitant.

abitare *vi.* to inhabit, to live in.

abitato *sm.* inhabited place.

abitazione *sf.* habitation, house.

àbito *sm.* **1.** (*da uomo*) suit **2.** (*da donna*) dress.

abituale *agg.* usual, customary.

abituare *vt.* to accustom. ♦ **abituarsi** *vr.* to get (*v. irr.*) used (to).

abitudinario *agg.* methodical. ♦ **abitudinario** *sm.* routinist.

abitùdine *sf.* habit, custom.

abituro *sm.* slum dwelling.

abiura *sf.* abjuration.

abiurare *vt.* to abjure.

ablazione *sf.* ablation.

abluzione *sf.* ablution.

abnegazione *sf.* self-denial.

abnorme *agg.* abnormal.

abolire *vt.* to abolish.

abolizione *sf.* abolition, repeal.

abominare *vt.* to loathe.

abominévole *agg.* abominable.

aborigeni *sm. pl.* the natives.

aborrimento *sm.* abhorrence.

aborrire *vt.* to hate, to loathe.

abortire *vi.* to miscarry.

aborto *sm.* miscarriage.

abrasione *sf.* abrasion.

abrogare *vt.* **1.** to abrogate **2.** (*giur.*) to repeal.

abrogazione *sf.* **1.** abrogation **2.** (*giur.*) repeal.

àbside *sf.* apse.

abulìa *sf.* (*fig.*) lack of will-power.

abùlico *agg.* (*fig.*) lacking in will-power.

abusare *vi.* to abuse.

abusivo *agg.* abusive.

abuso *sm.* abuse.

acacia *sf.* acacia.

acanto *sm.* acanthus.

acca *sf.* letter *H*.

accademia *sf.* academy.

accadèmico *agg.* academical. ♦ **accadèmico** *sm.* academician.

accademismo *sm.* academism.

accadere *vi.* to happen.

accaduto *sm.* event.

accagliarsi *vr.* **1.** to curdle **2.** (*del sangue*) to coagulate.

accalappiacani *sm.* dog-catcher.

accalappiare *vt.* **1.** to catch (*v. irr.*) **2.** (*fig.*) to ensnare.

accalcarsi *vr.* to crowd.

accaldarsi *vi.* **1.** to get (*v. irr.*) heated **2.** (*fig.*) to get excited.

accaldato *agg.* hot.

accalorarsi *vr.* to get (*v. irr.*) excited.

accampamento *sm.* camp.

accampare *vt.* to camp: — *diritti*, to lay (*v. irr.*) claims (to).

accanimento *sm.* **1.** fury **2.** (*tenacia*) tenacity.

accanirsi *vr.* **1.** (*infierire*) to rage **2.** (*ostinarsi*) to persist.

accanito *agg.* **1.** (*senza pietà*) relentless **2.** obstinate.

accanto *avv.* beside, near, by || *accanto a*, by, near, at the side of.

accantonare *vt.* to set (*v. irr.*) aside.

accaparrare *vt.* to buy (*v. irr.*) up.

accapigliarsi *vr.* to come (*v. irr.*) to blows, to quarrel.

accappatoio *sm.* bath-gown.

accapponarsi *vr.* to get (*v. irr.*) goose-flesh.

accarezzare *vt.* 1. to caress, to stroke 2. (*fig.*) to entertain.

accartocciare *vt.* 1. to wrap up 2. (*spiegazzare*) to crumple.

accasare *vt.* to marry, to give (*v. irr.*) in marriage. ♦ **accasarsi** *vr.* to get (*v. irr.*) married.

accasciarsi *vi.* 1. to fall (*v. irr.*) to the ground 2. (*fig.*) to lose (*v. irr.*) heart.

accatastare *vt.* to heap up.

accattivarsi *vi.* to win (*v. irr.*).

accattonaggio *sm.* begging.

accattone *sm.* beggar.

accavallare *vt.* to overlap: — le gambe, to cross one's legs.

accecamento *sm.* 1. blinding 2. (*fig.*) lack of perception.

accecare *vt.* to blind. ♦ **accecarsi** *vr.* to blind oneself.

accèdere *vi.* 1. to approach 2. (*entrare*) to enter 3. (*comm.*) to comply (with).

accelerare *vt.* 1. to quicken 2. (*di velocità*) to accelerate.

accelerato *sm.* (*ferr.*) slow train.

acceleratore *sm.* accelerator.

accelerazione *sf.* acceleration.

accèndere *vt.* 1. to light 2. (*di fiammiferi*) to strike (*v. irr.*) 3. (*di radio, luce ecc.*) to switch on 4. (*fig.*) to inflame. ♦ **accèndersi** *vr.* 1. to light up 2. (*prender fuoco*) to catch (*v. irr.*) fire || — in volto, to blush.

accendino *sm.* **accendisìgaro** *sm.* (cigarette)-lighter.

accennare *vi.* 1. to make (*v. irr.*) a sign 2. (*menzionare*) to mention 3. (*alludere*) to allude.

accenno *sm.* 1. sign 2. (*fig.*) hint.

accensione *sf.* 1. lighting 2. (*mecc.*) ignition || chiavetta d'—, ignition-key.

accentare *vt.* to accent, to stress.

accentazione *sf.* accentuation, stressing.

accento *sm.* 1. accent 2. (*tonico*) stress.

accentramento *sm.* centralization.

accentrare *vt.* to centralize.

accentuare *vt.* to accentuate, to stress. ♦ **accentuarsi** *vr.* to get (*v. irr.*) worse, to increase.

accerchiamento *sm.* surrounding.

accerchiare *vt.* to surround.

accertamento *sm.* 1. assurance 2. (*controllo*) verification.

accertare *vt.* 1. to assure 2. (*verificare*) to verify.

acceso *agg.* 1. lit up 2. (*in volto*) blushing 3. (*d'ira*) in a temper.

accessìbile *agg.* 1. open to 2. (*di persona*) approachable.

accesso *sm.* 1. admission 2. (*di malattia, passione*) fit.

accessorio *agg.* accessory. ♦ **accessori** *sm. pl.* fittings.

accetta *sf.* hatchet.

accettare *vt.* 1. to accept 2. (*consentire*) to consent.

accetto *agg.* welcome.

accezione *sf.* meaning.

acchiappare *vt.* to catch (*v. irr.*).

acchito *sm.* di primo —, at first sight, at once.

acciacco *sm.* infirmity.

acciaierìa *sf.* steel-mill.

acciaio *sm.* steel.

acciarino *sm.* 1. flint-lock 2. (*di fucile*) gun-lock.

accidentale *agg.* accidental.

accidentato *agg.* uneven.

accidente *sm.* chance, accident.

accidenti *inter.* damn.

accidia *sf.* sloth.

accigliarsi *vr.* to frown.

accìngersi *vr.* to set (*v. irr.*) about (doing).

acciottolare *vt.* to cobble.

acciottolato *sm.* cobbled paving.

acciottolìo *sm.* clatter.

acciuffare *vt.* to catch (*v. irr.*), to seize.

acciuga *sf.* anchovy.

acclamare *vt.* 1. to acclaim 2. (*applaudire*) to applaud.

acclamazione *sf.* acclamation, applause.

acclimatazione *sf.* acclimatization.

acclùdere *vt.* to enclose.

accluso *agg.* enclosed.

accoccolarsi *vr.* to squat down.

accodarsi *vr.* to follow.

accogliente *agg.* comfortable, hospitable.

accoglienza *sf.* reception, welcome.

accògliere *vt.* 1. to receive 2. (*fare buona accoglienza*) to welcome 3. (*una richiesta*) to grant.

accòlito *sm.* acolyte.

accollatura *sf.* neckline.

accoltellare *vt.* to stab.

accomiatare *vt.* **1.** to give (*v. irr.*) leave **2.** (*licenziare*) to dismiss. ♦ **accomiatarsi** *vr.* to take (*v. irr.*) leave (of).

accomodamento *sm.* **1.** adjustment **2.** (*conciliazione*) conciliation.

accomodante *agg.* yielding.

accomodare *vt.* **1.** (*riparare*) to repair **2.** (*sistemare*) to settle **3.** (*far comodo*) to suit.

accompagnamento *sm.* **1.** (*l'accompagnare*) accompanying **2.** (*seguito*) retinue **3.** (*mus.*) accompaniment.

accompagnare *vt.* **1.** to accompany **2.** (*— qu. alla stazione*) to see (*v. irr.*) so. off **3.** (*mus.*) to accompany.

accompagnatore *sm.* **1.** companion **2.** (*mus.*) accompanist.

accomunare *vt.* to join, to associate. ♦ **accomunarsi** *vr.* to join.

acconciare *vt.* **1.** to adjust, to adorn **2.** (*capelli*) to dress.

acconciatura *sf.* hair-style.

acconsentire *vi.* **1.** to consent **2.** (*annuire*) to assent.

accontentare *vt.* to satisfy. ♦ **accontentarsi** *vr.* to be content (with).

acconto *sm.* account.

accoppare *vt.* to kill.

accoppiamento *sm.* **1.** coupling **2.** (*di buoi al giogo*) yoking **3.** (*mecc.*) connection.

accoppiare *vt.* **1.** to couple **2.** (*fig.*) to match. ♦ **accoppiarsi** *vr.* to couple, to mate.

accoppiata *sf.* (*ippica*) fourecast.

accorato *agg.* sorrowful.

accorciare *vt.* to shorten.

accordare *vt.* **1.** to grant **2.** (*mus.*) to tune **3.** (*armonizzare*) to match. ♦ **accordarsi** *vr.* to agree (upon).

accordatore *sm.* tuner.

accordo *sm.* **1.** agreement ‖ *come d'—*, as agreed **2.** (*mus.*) chord **3.** (*fig.*) harmony.

accorgersi *vr.* **1.** (*percepire*) to perceive **2.** (*rendersi conto*) to realize.

accorgimento *sm.* **1.** sagacity **2.** (*stratagemma*) clever device.

accòrrere *vi.* to run (*v. irr.*), to hasten: *— in aiuto*, to rush to the help.

accortezza *sf.* sagacity.

accorto *agg.* shrewd.

accostare *vt.* **1.** to draw (*v. irr.*) near **2.** (*porte, finestre ecc.*) to set (*v. irr.*) ajar. ♦ **accostarsi** *vr.* to come (*v. irr.*) near.

accotonare *vt.* to raise.

accotonatura *sf.* raising.

accozzaglia *sf.* huddle: *un'— di gente*, a motley crowd.

accozzare *vt.* to huddle. ♦ **accozzarsi** *vr.* to huddle.

accreditamento *sm.* (*comm.*) crediting.

accreditare *vt.* to credit. ♦ **accreditarsi** *vr.* to gain credit.

accréscere *vt.* to increase.

accrescimento *sm.* increase.

accrescitivo *agg. e sm.* augmentative.

accucciarsi *vr.* to crouch.

accudire *vi.* to look after: *— alla casa*, to do (*v. irr.*) the housework.

accumulare *vt.* to heap up.

accumulatore *sm.* accumulator.

accuratezza *sf.* accuracy, care.

accurato *agg.* careful, precise.

accusa *sf.* charge.

accusàre *vt.* **1.** to accuse, to charge (with) **2.** (*sentire*) to feel (*v. irr.*) **3.** (*comm.*) to acknowledge.

accusativo *agg. e sm.* accusative.

accusato *agg.* accused.

accusatore *sm.* prosecutor: *pubblico —*, public prosecutor.

acerbo *agg.* **1.** unripe **2.** (*acido*) sour.

àcero *sm.* maple.

acetilene *sm.* acetylene.

aceto *sm.* vinegar.

acetone *sm.* acetone.

acidità *sf.* **1.** acidity **2.** (*di stomaco*) hyperchlorhydria.

àcido *agg.* sour. ♦ **àcido** *sm.* acid.

acidulo *agg.* acidulous.

àcino *sm.* (*di uva*) grape.

acme *sf.* **1.** acme **2.** (*di malattia*) crisis (*pl.* -ses).

acne *sf.* acne.

aconfessionale *agg.* nondenominational.

acqua *sf.* **1.** water: *— marina*, sea water; *— piovana*, rain water; *— potabile*, drinking water **2.** (*pioggia*) rain: *— a catinelle*, heavy rain.

acquaforte *sf.* etching.

acquaio *sm.* sink.

acquamarina *sf.* aquamarine.

acquaragia *sf.* turpentine.

acquario *sm.* aquarium.

acquasanta *sf.* holy water.

acquasantiera *sf.* stoup.
acquàtico *agg.* aquatic.
acquattarsi *vr.* **1.** to crouch **2.** (*nascondersi*) to hide (*v. irr.*).
acquavite *sf.* brandy.
acquazzone *sm.* downpour.
acquedotto *sm.* aqueduct.
acquerellista *sm.* water-colourist.
acquerello *sm.* water-colour.
acquerùgiola *sf.* drizzle.
acquiescente *agg.* acquiescent.
acquiescenza *sf.* acquiescence.
acquirente *sm.* buyer.
acquisire *vt.* to acquire.
acquistare *vt.* **1.** (*comperare*) to buy (*v. irr.*) **2.** (*ottenere*) to get (*v. irr.*) **3.** (*fig.*) to gain || — *terreno*, to make (*v. irr.*) progress.
acquisto *sm.* purchase || *fare acquisti*, to go (*v. irr.*) shopping.
acquitrino *sm.* marsh.
acquolina *sf.* drizzle: *far venire l'— in bocca*, to make (*v. irr.*) so.'s mouth water.
acre *agg.* **1.** sour **2.** (*fig.*) sarcastic **3.** (*pungente*) pungent.
acrèdine *sf.* **1.** acridity **2.** (*fig.*) acrimony.
acrimonia *sf.* acrimony.
acròbata *s.* acrobat.
acrobàtico *agg.* acrobatic.
acrobazìa *sf.* acrobatics (*pl.*) || *fare delle acrobazie*, to perform stunts.
acròpoli *sf.* acropolis.
acuire *vt.* to sharpen: — *l'interesse*, to stimulate interest.
acùleo *sm.* **1.** (*bot.*) prickle **2.** (*zool.*) sting.
acume *sm.* insight.
acuminare *vt.* to sharpen.
acùstica *sf.* acoustics.
acutezza *sf.* **1.** sharpness **2.** (*di mente*) perspicacity.
acutizzare *vt.* to make (*v. irr.*) acute. ♦ **acutizzarsi** *vr.* to grow (*v. irr.*) acute.
acuto *agg.* **1.** sharp **2.** (*di angoli, accenti*) acute **3.** (*intenso*) intense **4.** (*di suono*) shrill. ♦ **acuto** *sm.* (*mus.*) high note.
adagiare *vt.* to lay (*v. irr.*) down with care. ♦ **adagiarsi** *vr.* to lie (*v. irr.*) down.
adagio[1] *avv.* **1.** slowly **2.** (*con cautela*) cautiously **3.** (*con delicatezza*) gently.
adagio[2] *sm.* proverb, saying.
adamantino *agg.* adamantine.
adamìtico *agg.* adamic.

adattàbile *agg.* adaptable.
adattamento *sm.* **1.** adaptation **2.** (*assestamento*) adjustment.
adattare *vt.* to adapt, to fit. ♦ **adattarsi** *vr.* **1.** to adapt oneself **2.** (*attagliarsi*) to fit.
adatto *agg.* **1.** fit, proper **2.** (*che va bene*) suitable (for).
addebitare *vt.* to debit.
addébito *sm.* charge: *fare un — a qu. per qc.*, to charge so. with sthg.
addendo *sm.* addendum (*pl.* -da).
addensamento *sm.* **1.** thickening **2.** (*di persone*) crowding.
addensare *vt.* **1.** to thicken. ♦ **addensarsi** *vr.* **1.** to thicken **2.** (*di folla*) to crowd.
addentare *vt.* to bite (*v. irr.*).
addentellato *sm.* **1.** (*arch.*) toothing **2.** (*fig.*) stepping-stone.
addentrarsi *vr.* to penetrate: — *in una questione*, to probe a question.
addentro *avv.* inside.
addestramento *sm.* **1.** training **2.** (*mil.*) drilling.
addestrare *vt.* **1.** to train **2.** (*mil.*) to drill.
addetto *agg.* employed (in). ♦ **addetto** *sm.* attaché.
addietro *avv.* **1.** (*di spazio*) behind **2.** (*di tempo*) before, ago || *era venuto due giorni* —, he had come two days before.
addìo *inter.* good-bye.
addirittura *avv.* **1.** quite **2.** (*in esclamazioni*) really!
addirsi *vr.* to become (*v. irr.*).
additare *vt.* to point at.
addizionale *agg.* additional.
addizionare *vt.* to sum up.
addizionatrice *sf.* adding-machine, adder.
addizione *sf.* addition.
addobbare *vt.* to adorn.
addobbo *sm.* **1.** decoration **2.** (*eccl.*) sacred ornaments (*pl.*).
addolcire *vt.* **1.** (*di spazio*) to sweeten **2.** (*fig.*) to soften. ♦ **addolcirsi** *vr.* to become (*v. irr.*) soft(er).
addolorare *vt.* to grieve. ♦ **addolorarsi** *vr.* to be grieved.
addolorato *agg.* grieved, sorry.
addome *sm.* abdomen.
addomesticare *vt.* to tame.
addominale *agg.* abdominal.
addormentare *vt.* **1.** to send (*v. irr.*) to sleep **2.** (*med.*) to anaes-

thetize. ◆ **addormentarsi** *vr.* **1.** to fall (*v. irr.*) asleep **2.** (*fig.*) to go (*v. irr.*) to sleep.

addossare *vt.* **1.** to lean **2.** (*attribuire*) to lay (*v. irr.*). ◆ **addossarsi** *vr.* **1.** (*affollarsi*) to crowd **2.** (*prendere su di sé*) to take (*v. irr.*) upon oneself.

addosso *avv. prep.* **1.** on, upon: *mettere qc. —*, to put (*v. irr.*) sthg. on; *togliere qc. d'—*, to take (*v. irr.*) sthg. off **2.** (*vicino a*) close to: *la casa è — alla montagna*, the house is close to the mountain || *dare —*, to assault, to contradict.

addottrinare *vt.* to instruct. ◆ **addottrinarsi** *vr.* to instruct oneself.

addurre *vt.* **1.** to put (*v. irr.*) forward: *— una scusa*, to plead **2.** (*citare*) to quote.

adeguamento *sm.* **1.** proportionment **2.** (*adattamento*) adaptation.

adeguare *vt.* **1.** to proportionate **2.** (*adattare*) to conform. ◆ **adeguarsi** *vr.* to conform oneself, to adapt oneself.

adeguato *agg.* **1.** proportionate **2.** (*adatto*) convenient, fit **3.** (*giusto*) fair.

adémpiere *vt.* **1.** (*compiere*) to fulfil **2.** (*eseguire*) to carry out. ◆ **adémpiersi** *vr.* (*avverarsi*) to come (*v. irr.*) true.

adempimento *sm.* **1.** fulfilment **2.** (*esecuzione*) carrying out.

adenòidi *sf. pl.* adenoids.

adepto *sm.* **1.** adept **2.** (*seguace*) follower.

aderente *agg.* **1.** adherent **2.** (*di abito*) close-fitting.

aderenza *sf.* **1.** adherence **2.** (*med.*) adhesion **3.** (*pl.*) connections.

aderire *vi.* **1.** (*stare vicino e fig.*) to adhere, to stick **2.** (*consentire*) to comply with **3.** (*parteggiare per*) to take sides (with).

adescamento *sm.* **1.** enticement **2.** (*seduzione*) seduction.

adescare *vt.* **1.** to entice **2.** (*sedurre*) to seduce.

adesione *sf.* adhesion: *dare la propria — ad un partito*, to join a party.

adesivo *agg.* adhesive.

adesso *avv.* now, at present, at the moment.

adiacente *agg.* adjacent.

adibire *vt.* to use as.

àdipe *sm.* fat.

adiposo *agg.* adipose.

adirarsi *vr.* to get (*v. irr.*) angry.

adirato *agg.* angry.

adire *vt.* (*giur.*) to apply to: *— le vie legali*, to take (*v. irr.*) legal steps.

àdito *sm.* entry: *dare —*, to give (*v. irr.*) rise.

adocchiare *vt.* **1.** to glance **2.** (*scorgere*) to catch (*v. irr.*) sight of.

adolescente *agg.* teen-aged, adolescent. ◆ **adolescente** *sm.* teen-ager.

adolescenza *sf.* adolescence.

adombrare *vt.* **1.** to shade **2.** (*nascondere*) to conceal **3.** (*simboleggiare*) to symbolize. ◆ **adombrarsi** *vr.* **1.** to resent **2.** (*di cavallo*) to shy.

adoperare *vt.* to use. ◆ **adoperarsi** *vr.* to endeavour.

adoràbile *agg.* charming.

adorare *vt.* to adore, to worship.

adorazione *sf.* adoration, worship.

adornare *vt.* to adorn.

adorno *agg.* adorned.

adottare *vt.* to adopt.

adottivo *agg.* adoptive.

adozione *sf.* adoption: *patria d'—*, adopted country.

adrenalina *sf.* adrenalin.

adulare *vt.* to flatter.

adulatore *agg.* flattering. ◆ **adulatore** *sm.* flatterer.

adulazione *sf.* flattery.

adùltera *sf.* adulteress.

adulterare *vt.* **1.** to adulterate **2.** (*fig.*) to falsify.

adulterino *agg.* adulterine.

adulterio *sm.* adultery.

adùltero *agg.* adulterous. ◆ **adùltero** *sm.* adulterer.

adulto *agg. e sm.* grown-up, adult.

adunanza *sf.* meeting.

adunco *agg.* hooked.

aerare *vt.* **1.** to air **2.** (*chim.*) to aerate.

aerazione *sf.* **1.** airing **2.** (*chim.*) aeration.

aèreo *agg.* aerial || *per via aerea*, by air. ◆ **aèreo** *sm.* **1.** plane **2.** (*radio*) aerial.

aerodinàmica *sf.* aerodynamics.

aeròdromo *sm.* aerodrome.

aerolito *sm.* aerolite.

aeromodello *sm.* model aircraft.

aeronàuta *sm.* aeronaut.

aeronàutica *sf.* aeronautics.

aeronave *sf.* airship.

aeronavigazione *sf.* air navigation.

aeroplano *sm.* (aero)plane, aircraft || — *a razzo*, rocket plane; — *passeggeri*, passenger plane; — *da bombardamento*, bomber.

aeroporto *sm.* airport.

aerosòl *sm.* aerosol.

aerostàtica *sf.* aerostatics.

aeròstato *sm.* aerostat.

aerostazione *sf.* air-terminal.

aerotassì *sm.* airtaxi.

aerotrasportare *vt.* to air-bear.

afa *sf.* sultriness.

afasìa *sf.* aphasia.

affàbile *agg.* affable.

affabilità *sf.* affability, kindness.

affaccendarsi *vr.* to busy oneself.

affaccendato *agg.* busy.

affacciare *vt.* **1.** to show (*v. irr.*) **2.** (*un dubbio*) to raise. ♦ **affacciarsi** *vr.* **1.** to show oneself **2.** (*su un luogo*) to face.

affamare *vt.* to starve (out).

affamato *agg.* **1.** hungry **2.** (*fig.*) eager. ♦ **affamato** *sm.* starveling.

affamatore *sm.* starver.

affannare *vt.* to trouble, to worry. ♦ **affannarsi** *vr.* **1.** to worry oneself **2.** (*affaccendarsi*) to busy oneself.

affanno *sm.* **1.** breathlessness **2.** (*pena*) worry.

affannoso *agg.* **1.** breathless || *respiro* —, difficult breathing **2.** (*ansioso*) anxious.

affare *sm.* **1.** affair, business: — *di cuore*, love affair; *questo è* — *nostro*, this is our business **2.** (*comm.*) business: *fare affari*, to do (*v. irr.*) business || (*pol.*) *affari esteri*, foreign affairs; (*in Gran Bretagna*) *Ministero degli Affari Esteri*, Foreign Office.

affarista *sm.* speculator.

affascinante *agg.* charming.

affascinare *vt.* to charm.

affaticamento *sm.* weariness.

affaticare *vt.* to tire. ♦ **affaticarsi** *vr.* **1.** to get (*v. irr.*) tired **2.** (*lavorare molto*) to work hard.

affatto *avv.* **1.** completely, quite **2.** (*in frasi negative*) at all: *niente* —, not at all.

affatturare *vt.* to bewitch.

affermare *vt.* **1.** to affirm **2.** (*fig.*) to assert. ♦ **affermarsi** *vr.* to make (*v. irr.*) a name for oneself.

affermativo *agg.* affirmative.

affermazione *sf.* **1.** statement **2.** (*successo*) achievement.

afferrare *vt.* **1.** to grasp **2.** (*fig.*) to seize. ♦ **afferrarsi** *vr.* to grasp at, to clutch at.

affettare[1] *vt.* (*tagliare a fette*) to slice.

affettare[2] *vt.* (*ostentare*) to affect.

affettato[1] *agg.* sliced.

affettato[2] *agg.* (*ostentato*) affected.

affettatrice *sf.* slicing machine.

affettazione *sf.* affectation, show.

affettivo *agg.* emotional.

affetto[1] *sm.* affection: *portare* — *a qu.*, to set (*v. irr.*) one's affection on so.

affetto[2] *agg.* affected (with).

affettuosità *sf.* tenderness.

affettuoso *agg.* tender, affectionate.

affezionarsi *vr.* to grow (*v. irr.*) fond of.

affezione *sf.* **1.** affection **2.** (*med.*) affection, disease.

affiancare *vt.* to flank. ♦ **affiancarsi** *vr.* to line up (with).

affiatamento *sm.* concord.

affiatare *vt.* **1.** to bring (*v. irr.*) together **2.** (*mus.*) to tune. ♦ **affiatarsi** *vr.* to become (*v. irr.*) familiar (with).

affibbiare *vt.* **1.** to buckle **2.** (*fig.*) to shift (upon).

affidamento *sm.* trust, confidence: *dare* —, to inspire confidence.

affidare *vt.* **1.** to entrust **2.** (*consegnare*) to commit. ♦ **affidarsi** *vr.* to rely upon.

affievolire *vt.* to weaken. ♦ **affievolirsi** *vr.* to grow (*v. irr.*) weak.

affiggere *vt.* to post up: — *lo sguardo*, to fix one's eyes (on).

affilare *vt.* to sharpen. ♦ **affilarsi** *vr.* (*dimagrire*) to thin.

affilato *agg.* **1.** sharp **2.** (*di naso, viso*) thin.

affiliare *vt.* to affiliate.

affiliato *sm.* member, associate.

affiliazione *sf.* affiliation.

affinamento *sm.* **1.** refining **2.** (*fig.*) sharpening.

affinare *vt.* **1.** to refine **2.** (*assottigliare*) to make (*v. irr.*) thin. ♦ **affinarsi** *vr.* **1.** to refine, to improve **2.** (*assottigliarsi*) to become (*v. irr.*) thin.

affinché *cong.* so that, in order that.

affine *agg.* like, similar.

affinità *sf.* affinity.

affiorare *vi.* to appear on the surface.

affissare *vt.* to affix.

affissione *sf.* bill-posting.

affisso *sm.* 1. (*avviso*) bill 2. (*cartello*) placard 3. (*manifesto*) poster.

affittacàmere *sm. e sf.* landlord, landlady.

affittare *vt.* 1. (*dare in affitto*) to let (*v. irr.*) 2. (*prendere in affitto*) to rent 3. (*noleggiare*) to hire.

affitto *sm.* rent.

afflato *sm.* afflatus.

afflìggere *vt.* 1. to distress 2. (*di malattie*) to afflict. ♦ **afflìggersi** *vr.* to worry.

afflitto *agg.* sad, sorrowful.

afflizione *sf.* 1. affliction 2. (*flagello*) calamity.

afflosciarsi *vr.* 1. to become (*v. irr.*) flabby 2. (*fig.*) to weaken.

affluente *sm.* affluent.

affluenza *sf.* 1. (*di acque*) flow 2. (*di persone*) crowd 3. (*abbondanza*) plenty.

affluire *vi.* 1. (*di acque*) to flow 2. (*di persone*) to crowd 3. (*di cose*) to pour in.

afflusso *sm.* afflux.

affogamento *sm.* drowning.

affogare *vt.* 1. to drown 2. (*fig.*) to smother. ♦ **affogarsi** *vr.* to drown oneself.

affogato *agg.* 1. drowned 2. (*fig.*) oppressed || *uova affogate,* poached eggs.

affollamento *sm.* overcrowding, throng.

affollare *vt.* 1. to crowd 2. (*fig.*) to overwhelm. ♦ **affollarsi** *vr.* to press up.

affollato *agg.* crowded.

affondare *vt.* 1. (*sommergere*) to sink (*v. irr.*) 2. (*immergere*) to plunge.

affossamento *sm.* ditching.

affossare *vt.* to ditch. ♦ **affossarsi** *vr.* to become (*v. irr.*) hollow.

affrancamento *sm.* release.

affrancare *vt.* 1. to release 2. (*con francobollo*) to stamp. ♦ **affrancarsi** *vr.* to free oneself.

affrancato *agg.* 1. free 2. (*con francobollo*) stamped.

affrancatura *sf.* postage.

affranto *agg.* broken-hearted || (*dalla fatica*) worn out.

affratellarsi *vr.* to fraternize.

affresco *sm.* fresco.

affrettare *vt.* 1. to hasten 2. (*anticipare*) to anticipate. ♦ **affrettarsi** *vr.* to make (*v. irr.*) haste.

affrettatamente *avv.* hastily.

affrettato *agg.* 1. hasty 2. (*trascurato*) careless.

affrontare *vt.* 1. to face 2. (*fig.*) to deal (*v. irr.*) with. ♦ **affrontarsi** *vr.* (*venire alle mani*) to come (*v. irr.*) to blows.

affronto *sm.* insult.

affumicare *vt.* 1. to fill with smoke 2. (*cuc.*) to smoke.

affumicato *agg.* 1. blackened by smoke 2. (*cuc.*) smoked || *lenti affumicate,* sun-glasses.

affusolare *vt.* to taper.

afonìa *sf.* aphonia.

àfono *agg.* voiceless.

aforisma *sm.* aphorism.

afoso *agg.* sultry.

africano *agg. e sm.* African.

afroasiàtico *agg.* Afro-Asiatic.

afta *sf.* aphtha.

àgata *sf.* agate.

àgave *sf.* agave.

agenda *sf.* note-book.

agente *sm.* agent.

agenzìa *sf.* agency.

agevolare *vt.* to make (*v. irr.*) easy.

agevolazione *sf.* facilitation.

agévole *agg.* 1. easy 2. (*di strada*) smooth.

agevolmente *avv.* easily.

agganciare *vt.* 1. to hook 2. (*ferr.*) to couple up.

aggeggio *sm.* device.

aggettare *vi.* to jut out.

aggettivo *sm.* adjective.

agghiacciare *vt.* to freeze (*v. irr.*). ♦ **agghiacciarsi** *vr.* to freeze.

agghindare *vt.* to array. ♦ **agghindarsi** *vr.* to dress (oneself) up.

aggiogare *vt.* to yoke.

aggiornamento *sm.* 1. (*rinvio*) adjournment 2. (*di un libro*) revision.

aggiornare *vt.* 1. (*rinviare*) to adjourn 2. (*mettere al corrente*) to bring (*v. irr.*) up to date. ♦ **aggiornarsi** *vr.* to brush up one's knowledge.

aggiornato *agg.* up-to-date.

aggirare *vt.* to go (*v. irr.*) round || — *l'ostacolo,* to avoid an obstacle. ♦ **aggirarsi** *vr.* to wander about, to go about.

aggiudicare *vt.* to award. ♦ **ag-**

giudicarsi *vr.* to win (*v. irr.*).
aggiudicazione *sf.* award.
aggiùngere *vt.* to add. ♦ **aggiùngersi** *vr.* to join.
aggiunta *sf.* **1.** addition **2.** (*aumento*) increase.
aggiunto *agg.* added, joined. ♦ **aggiunto** *sm.* assistant.
aggiustare *vt.* **1.** (*riparare*) to mend **2.** (*sistemare*) to arrange. ♦ **aggiustarsi** *vr.* (*accomodarsi*) to make (*v. irr.*) oneself comfortable.
agglomerato *sm.* agglomerate.
agglutinare *vt.* to agglutinate.
aggraffare *vt.* to seize.
aggranchire *vt.* to benumb.
aggrapparsi *vr.* to cling (*v. irr.*) (to), to get (*v. irr.*) hold (of).
aggravante *agg.* aggravating. ♦ **aggravante** *sf.* (*giur.*) aggravating circumstance.
aggravare *vt.* to aggravate, to overburden. ♦ **aggravarsi** *vr.* to grow (*v. irr.*) worse.
aggravato *agg.* **1.** overburdened **2.** (*med.*) worse.
aggraziare *vt.* to make (*v. irr.*) graceful.
aggredire *vt.* to assault.
aggregare *vt.* to associate. ♦ **aggregarsi** *vr.* to join.
aggressione *sf.* aggression, assault.
aggressività *sf.* aggressiveness.
aggressivo *agg.* aggressive.
aggressore *sm.* aggressor.
aggrottare *vt.* to frown.
aggrovigliare *vt.* to entangle.
aggrovigliarsi *vr.* to get (*v. irr.*) entangled.
aggruppare *vt.* to group.
agguantare *vt.* to catch (*v. irr.*).
agguato *sm.* ambush.
agguerrire *vt.* to inure (for war). ♦ **agguerrirsi** *vr.* to get (*v. irr.*) inured.
agiatamente *avv.* in ease and comfort.
agiato *agg.* well-to-do.
àgile *agg.* nimble.
agilità *sf.* nimbleness.
agio *sm.* comfort, ease, leisure.
agiografia *sf.* hagiography.
agire *vi.* to act.
agitare *vt.* **1.** to agitate **2.** (*scuotere*) to shake (*v. irr.*) **3.** to stir (*anche fig.*). ♦ **agitarsi** *vr.* to be agitated.
agitatore *sm.* **1.** agitator **2.** (*mecc.*) stirrer.

agitazione *sf.* **1.** agitation **2.** (*eccitazione*) excitement **3.** (*di folla*) tumult.
aglio *sm.* garlic.
agnello *sm.* lamb.
agnosticismo *sm.* agnosticism.
ago *sm.* **1.** needle **2.** (*mecc.*) tongue.
agognare *vt.* to long (for sthg.).
agonìa *sf.* agony, pangs (*pl.*) of death.
agonismo *sm.* athletic spirit.
agonizzante *agg.* dying.
agonizzare *vi.* to be in one's death agony.
agorafobìa *sf.* agoraphobia.
agosto *sm.* August.
agraria *sf.* agriculture.
agrario *agg.* agrarian. ♦ **agrario** *sm.* **1.** land-owner **2.** (*esperto*) agriculturist.
agreste *agg.* agrestic, rustic.
agretto *agg.* sourish.
agrìcolo *agg.* agricultural.
agricoltore *sm.* farmer.
agricoltura *sf.* agriculture.
agrifoglio *sm.* holly.
agrimensore *sm.* land-surveyor.
agro *agg.* sour. ♦ **agro** *sm.* sourness.
agrodolce *agg.* bitter-sweet, sourish.
agronomìa *sf.* agronomy.
agronòmico *agg.* agronomical.
agrònomo *sm.* agronomist.
agrumi *sm. pl.* citrus fruit (*sing.*).
aguzzare *vt.* to sharpen.
aguzzino *sm.* **1.** gaoler, jailer **2.** (*fig.*) torturer.
aguzzo *agg.* sharp, pointed.
ahimè *inter.* alas.
aia *sf.* threshing-floor.
aio *sm.* tutor.
airone *sm.* heron.
aitante *agg.* vigorous, stout.
aiuola *sf.* flower-bed.
aiutante *sm.* **1.** assistant **2.** (*mil.*) adjutant: — *di campo*, aide-de-camp.
aiutare *vt.* to help. ♦ **aiutarsi** *vr.* (*ingegnarsi*) to make (*v. irr.*) shift. ♦ **aiutarsi** *vr. rec.* to help (one another).
aiuto *sm.* **1.** help: *chiedere* —, to call for help **2.** (*chi aiuta*) help, helper **3.** (*pl.*) (*mil.*) reinforcements.
aizzare *vt.* to incite, to rouse.
ala *sf.* wing.
alabarda *sf.* halberd.

alabastro *sm.* alabaster.

àlacre *agg.* brisk, industrious.

alacrità *sf.* alacrity.

alamaro *sm.* frog.

alambicco *sm.* still.

alano *sm.* Great Dane.

alba *sf.* dawn.

albanese *agg.* e *sm.* Albanian.

àlbatro *sm.* albatross.

albeggiare *vi.* to dawn.

alberare *vt.* **1.** to plant with trees **2.** (*mar.*) to mast.

alberato *agg.* planted with trees.

alberatura *sf.* (*mar.*) masting.

albergatore *sm.* hotel-keeper.

alberghiero *agg.* hotel (*attributivo*): *industria alberghiera.* hotel trade.

albergo *sm.* hotel.

àlbero *sm.* **1.** tree **2.** (*mar.*) mast **3.** (*mecc.*) shaft.

albicocca *sf.* apricot.

albino *agg.* e *sm.* albino.

albo *sm.* **1.** list, roll: — *degli avvocati,* Law List; — *d'onore,* roll of honour **2.** (*per fotografie ecc.*) album **3.** (*tavola per affissione*) notice-board.

album *sm.* album.

albume *sm.* albumen.

albumina *sf.* albumin.

alca *sf.* auk.

alcalino *agg.* e *sm.* alkaline.

alce *sm.* elk.

alchimìa *sf.* alchemy.

alcòlico *agg.* alcoholic.

alcolismo *sm.* alcoholism.

alcolizzato *agg.* e *sm.* alcoholic.

alcool *sm.* alcohol.

alcova *sf.* alcove.

alcunché *pron.* anything, something.

alcuno *agg.* **1.** (*frasi affermative*) some, a few **2.** (*frasi negative*) any. ♦ **alcuno** *pron.* **1.** (*frasi affermative*) somebody, someone **2.** (*frasi negative*) anybody, anyone.

aldilà *sm.* hereafter.

aleatorio *agg.* aleatory.

aleggiare *vi.* **1.** to flutter **2.** (*fig.*) to hover (about).

alettone *sm.* aileron.

alfa *sf.* alpha.

alfabeto *sm.* alphabet.

aliiere *sm.* **1.** ensign **2.** (*scacchi*) bishop.

alga *sf.* seaweed.

àlgebra *sf.* algebra.

algèbrico *agg.* algebraic, algebraical.

aliante *sm.* glider.

àlibi *sm.* alibi.

alienare *vt.* to alienate, to estrange. ♦ **alienarsi** *vr.* to alienate oneself, to become (*v. irr.*) estranged.

alienato *agg.* lunatic, mad; estranged, alienated. ♦ **alienato** *sm.* **1.** lunatic, madman (*pl.* -men) **2.** alienated person, estranged person.

alienazione *sf.* alienation, estrangement.

alienista *sm.* alienist, psychiatrist.

alieno *agg.* averse, opposed.

alimentare[1] *vt.* to feed (*v. irr.*), to nourish.

alimentare[2] *agg.* alimentary ‖ *generi alimentari,* foodstuffs; *negozio di generi alimentari,* grocery store.

alimentazione *sf.* nourishment, feeding.

alimento *sm.* food.

alìnea *sf.* paragraph.

alìquota *sf.* aliquot, rate.

aliscafo *sm.* hydrofoil boat.

aliseo *sm.* trade-wind.

àlito *sm.* breath.

allacciare *vt.* **1.** to lace, to connect **2.** (*fig.*) to establish. ♦ **allacciarsi** *vr.* **1.** (*abbracciarsi*) to embrace **2.** (*aggrovigliarsi*) to get (*v. irr.*) entangled, to be entangled.

allagare *vt.* to flood, to inundate.

allampanato *agg.* lean, lanky.

allargamento *sm.* widening, enlargement.

allargare *vt.* to widen, to enlarge, to extend. ♦ **allargarsi** *vr.* to widen, to extend, to spread (*v. irr.*).

allarmante *agg.* alarming.

allarmare *vt.* to alarm. ♦ **allarmarsi** *vr.* to get (*v. irr.*) frightened.

allarme *sm.* alarm, warning, alert.

allattamento *sm.* breast-feeding, nursing.

allattare *vt.* to suckle, to nurse.

alleanza *sf.* alliance.

allearsi *vr.* to ally, to become (*v. irr.*) allies.

alleato *agg.* allied. ♦ **alleato** *sm.* ally.

allegare *vt.* **1.** to allege **2.** (*accludere*) to enclose.

allegato *sm.* enclosure.

alleggerimento *sm.* lightening, relief.

alleggerire *vt.* to lighten, to re-

lieve, to unburden. ♦ **alleggerirsi** *vr.* to relieve oneself.
allegorìa *sf.* allegory.
allegòrico *agg.* allegoric(al).
allegramente *agg.* cheerfully, merrily.
allegrìa *sf.* cheerfulness, mirth.
allegro *agg.* merry, cheerful, jolly.
allegrone *sm.* jolly fellow.
allenamento *sm.* · training.
allenare *vt.* to train. ♦ **allenarsi** *vr.* to train (oneself).
allenatore *sm.* trainer; (*di squadre*) coach.
allentamento *sm.* **1.** loosening **2.** (*di velocità*) slackening.
allentare *vt.* to slacken, to loosen, to relax: — *il freno*, to release the brake. ♦ **allentarsi** *vr.* to slacken.
allergìa *sf.* allergy.
allèrgico *agg.* allergic.
allestimento *sm.* preparation, fitting out || — *scenico*, staging.
allestire *vt.* to prepare, to fit out.
allettamento *sm.* enticement, allurement.
allettante *agg.* alluring, enticing.
allettare *vt.* to allure, to entice.
allevamento *sm.* **1.** breeding, raising || (*di bambino*) bringing up **2.** (*luogo*) stock-farm || — *di cavalli*, stud-farm.
allevare *vt.* **1.** (*bambini*) to bring (*v. irr.*) up **2.** (*animali*) to breed (*v. irr.*), to rear.
allevatore *sm.* breeder.
alleviare *vt.* to relieve, to alleviate.
allibire *vi.* to be left speechless, to be struck dumb.
allibito *agg.* struck dumb, speechless.
allibratore *sm.* bookmaker.
allietare *vt.* to cheer. ♦ **allietarsi** *vr.* to cheer up.
allievo *sm.* **1.** pupil **2.** (*mil.*) cadet.
alligatore *sm.* alligator.
allineamento *sm.* **1.** alignment || (*tip.*) — *di caratteri*, ranging of characters **2.** (*mil.*) dressing.
allineare *vt.* **1.** to line up, to align: — *delle cifre*, to tabulate figures **2.** (*mil.*) to dress; (*in ordine di marcia*) to form up. ♦ **allinearsi** *vr.* **1.** to get (*v. irr.*) into line **2.** (*mil.*) to dress || *allineatevi*, draw up! **3.** (*pol.*) to be aligned with.
allocco *sm.* **1.** owl **2.** (*fig.*) fool.

allocuzione *sf.* allocution: *fare un'*—, to deliver a speech.
allòdola *sf.* skylark, lark.
allogare *vt.* to lodge.
allogazione *sf.* lease.
alloggiare *vt.* **1.** to lodge, to house, to put (*v. irr.*) up **2.** (*mil.*) to quarter; (*in casa privata*) to billet. ♦ **alloggiare** *vi.* **1.** to lodge, to live **2.** (*mil.*) to quarter; (*in casa privata*) to be billeted.
alloggio *sm.* · **1.** lodging || *indennità di* —, living-out allowance **2.** (*mil.*) quarters (*pl.*).
allontanamento *sm.* **1.** removal **2.** (*licenziamento*) dismissal.
allontanare *vt.* **1.** to remove, to drive (*v. irr.*) away: — *un pericolo*, to evert a danger **2.** (*licenziare*) to dismiss, to turn out. ♦ **allontanarsi** *vr.* to go (*v. irr.*) away, to depart.
allora *avv.* **1.** then **2.** (*quindi*) so.
allorché *cong.* when.
alloro *sm.* laurel.
àlluce *sm.* big toe.
allucinare *vt.* **1.** to dazzle **2.** (*dare allucinazioni*) to hallucinate.
allucinato *agg.* hallucinated.
allucinazione *sf.* hallucination.
allùdere *vi.* to allude (to), to hint (at).
alluminio *sm.* aluminium.
allunaggio *sm.* mooning.
allunare *vi.* to moon.
allungàbile *agg.* extensible.
allungamento *sm.* lengthening, stretching.
allungare *vt.* **1.** to lengthen, to extend, to stretch || — *il passo*, to quicken one's steps || — *il collo*, to stretch one's neck || — *gli orecchi*, to strain one's ears || (*fig.*) — *le mani su qc.*, to lay (*v. irr.*) hands on sthg. ♦ **allungarsi** *vr.* to lengthen, to grow (*v. irr.*) longer, to draw (*v. irr.*) out.
allusione *sf.* allusion, hint.
allusivo *agg.* allusive.
alluvionato *agg.* flooded || *zone alluvionate*, flood-areas. ♦ **alluvionato** *sm.* flood-victim.
alluvione *sf.* flood.
almanaccare *vi.* to fantasticate.
almanacco *sm.* almanac.
almeno *avv.* at least.
alno *sm.* alder-tree.
aloè *sm.* aloe.

alone sm. halo.

alpaca sm. alpaca.

alpe sf. alp.

alpestre agg. alpine.

alpinismo sm. (mountain-)climbing, mountaineering.

alpinista s. (mountain-)climber.

alpino agg. Alpine.

alquanto avv. somewhat, rather.

altalena sf. swing.

altana sf. roof-terrace.

altare sm. altar.

alterare vt. to alter; (salute) to impair; (cibo) to adulterate. ♦ **alterarsi** vr. 1. to alter, to change 2. (andare a male) to go (v. irr.) bad 3. (turbarsi) to be upset || la sua voce si alterò, his voice faltered.

alterazione sf. 1. alteration 2. (deteriorazione) deterioration 3. (turbamento) emotion; (della voce) faltering.

alterco sm. altercation.

alterigia sf. haughtiness.

alternanza sf. alternation.

alternare vt. to alternate. ♦ **alternarsi** vr. to alternate.

alternativa sf. alternative.

alterno agg. alternate.

altero agg. lofty, proud.

altezza sf. 1. height 2. (di tessuto) width 3. (di suono) pitch 4. (fig.) essere all'— di qc., to be equal to sthg.; to be up to sthg. 5. (titolo) highness.

altezzoso agg. haughty.

alticcio agg. tight, tipsy.

altimetro sm. altimeter.

altitùdine sf. altitude.

alto agg. 1. high, tall: un uomo —, a tall man || alta direzione, top management 2. (di suono) loud: ad alta voce, aloud, loudly 3. (profondo) deep: acqua alta, deep water 4. (geogr.) northern, upper 5. (stor.) early. ♦ **alto** sm. height || alti e bassi, ups and downs. ♦ **alto** avv. high, up || mani in —, hands up.

altoforno sm. blast-furnace.

altolocato agg. high-ranking, high-class.

altoparlante sm. loud-speaker.

altopiano sm. plateau.

altresì avv. likewise, also.

altrettanto agg. correlativo as much (...as); (pl.) as many (...as) || (neg.) as (o so) much (:..as); (pl.)

as (o so) many... (as): egli ha altrettante possibilità quanto me, he has as many chances as I. ♦ **altrettanto** pron. 1. as much; (pl.) as many 2. (lo stesso) the same: — a voi!, the same to you!. ♦ **altrettanto** avv. 1. (con agg. e avv.) as (...as); (neg.) as (o so) ...as) 2. (coi verbi) as much (as).

altrimenti avv. otherwise. ♦ **altrimenti** cong. otherwise, else.

altro agg. indef. 1. other || un —, another 2. (differente) different 3. (con pronomi int.) else: chi altro?, who else? 4. (in più) more: leggerò altri due libri, I shall read two more books 5. (susseguente) next: verrò l'altra domenica, I shall come next Sunday 6. (antecedente) last: andai l'altro mese, I went last month.

altronde 1. (nella loc. avv.) d'—, on the other hand 2. (tuttavia) however.

altrove avv. elsewhere, somewhere else.

altrùi agg. other people's, someone else's. ♦ **l'altrùi** sm. the property of others.

altruismo sm. unselfishness.

altruìstico agg. unselfish.

altura sf. height.

alunno sm. pupil.

alveare sm. beehive.

àlveo sm. river-bed.

alzaia sf. towing-line || strada d'—, towing-path.

alzare vt. 1. to lift, to raise 2. (erigere) to build (v. irr.) 3. (mar.) to hoist. ♦ **alzarsi** vr. (dal letto) to get (v. irr.) up 2. (in piedi) to stand (v. irr.) up 3. (in altezza) to grow (v. irr.) tall.

alzata sf. 1. raising 2. (l'alzarsi) rising.

amàbile agg. amiable.

amabilità sf. amiability.

amaca sf. hammock.

amàlgama sm. amalgam.

amalgamare vt. to amalgamate.

amante s. 1. lover 2. (fig.) fond.

amanuense sm. copyist.

amaranto sm. amaranth.

amare vt. 1. to love, to be fond of 2. (richiedere) to require.

amareggiare vt. 1. to make (v. irr.) bitter 2. (fig.) to sadden. ♦ **amareggiarsi** vr. to worry.

amarena sf. sour black cherry.

amaretto *sm.* macaroon.

amarezza *sf.* **1.** bitterness **2.** *(fig.)* sorrow.

amaro *agg.* bitter. ◆ **amaro** *sm.* *(liquore)* bitters *(pl.).*

amatore *sm.* **1.** lover **2.** *(chi si occupa d'arte per diletto)* amateur.

amàzzone *sf.* **1.** Amazon **2.** *(fig.)* masculine woman.

ambage *sf.* ambages *(pl.)* ‖ *senza ambagi,* plainly.

ambasciata *sf.* **1.** embassy **2.** *(messaggio)* message.

ambasciatore *sm.* ambassador.

ambedue *agg.* e *pron.* both.

ambientare *vt.* **1.** to acclimatize **2.** *(fatti, personaggi ecc.)* to place. ◆ **ambientarsi** *vr.* to get *(v. irr.)* accustomed.

ambiente *sm.* **1.** ambient **2.** *(fig.)* milieu **3.** *(stanza)* room.

ambiguità *sf.* ambiguity.

ambiguo *agg.* ambiguous.

ambio *sm.* amble.

ambire *vt.* to desire.

àmbito *sm.* ambit.

ambivalente *agg.* ambivalent.

ambivalenza *sf.* ambivalence.

ambizione *sf.* ambition.

ambizioso *agg.* ambitious.

ambo *sm.* ambo.

ambra *sf.* amber.

ambrosia *sf.* ambrosia.

ambulante *agg.* itinerant ‖ *venditore* —, pedlar.

ambulanza *sf.* ambulance.

ambulatorio *sm.* surgery.

ameba *sf.* amoeba.

amebìasi *sf.* amoebiasis *(pl.* -ses).

amenità *sf.* **1.** amenity **2.** *(facezia)* joke.

ameno *agg.* **1.** pleasant **2.** *(divertente)* funny: *un tipo* —, a funny chap.

americanismo *sm.* Americanism.

americano *agg.* e *sm.* American.

ametista *sf.* amethyst.

amianto *sm.* amianthus.

amichévole *agg.* friendly.

amicizia *sf.* friendship ‖ *fare* —, to make *(v. irr.)* friends with.

amico *sm.* friend.

amidatura *sf.* starching.

àmido *sm.* starch.

ammaccare *vt.* to bruise.

ammaccatura *sf.* bruise.

ammaestramento *sm.* **1.** *(addestramento)* training **2.** *(insegnamento)* teaching **3.** *(di animali)* taming.

ammaestrare *vt.* **1.** *(addestrare)* to train **2.** *(insegnare)* to teach *(v. irr.)* **3.** *(di animali)* to tame.

ammainare *vt.* to furl.

ammalarsi *vr.* to fall *(v. irr.)* ill.

ammalato *agg.* **1.** *(pred.)* ill **2.** *(attr.)* sick. ◆ **ammalato** *sm.* sick person, patient.

ammaliare *vt.* to bewitch.

ammaliatrice *sf.* bewitcher.

ammanco *sm.* shortage ‖ — *di cassa,* deficit.

ammanettare *vt.* to handcuff.

ammannire *vt.* to prepare.

ammansire *vt.* **1.** to tame **2.** *(fig.)* to calm. ◆ **ammansirsi** *vr.* **1.** to become *(v. irr.)* tamed **2.** to calm down.

ammarare *vi.* **1.** to alight (on water) **2.** *(di capsule spaziali)* to splash down.

ammassare *vt.* to heap. ◆ **ammassarsi** *vr.* to gather.

ammasso *sm.* heap.

ammattire *vi.* to get *(v. irr.)* mad.

ammazzare *vt.* to kill.

ammazzatoio *sm.* slaughter-house.

ammenda *sf.* amends *(pl.).*

amméttere *vt.* **1.** *(lasciar entrare)* to admit, to receive **2.** *(concedere, supporre)* to acknowledge, to suppose.

ammezzato *sm.* mezzanine.

ammezzire *vi.* to become *(v. irr.)* over-ripe.

ammiccare *vi.* to wink (at).

ammina *sf.* amine.

amministrare *vt.* **1.** to manage **2.** *(giur.; eccl.)* to administer.

amministrativo *agg.* administrative.

amministratore *sm.* manager.

amministrazione *sf.* management.

ammiràbile *agg.* admirable.

ammiraglio *sm.* admiral.

ammirare *vt.* to admire.

ammiratore *sm.* **1.** admirer **2.** *(di attori ecc.)* fan.

ammirazione *sf.* admiration.

ammirévole *agg.* admirable.

ammissìbile *agg.* admissible.

ammobiliamento *sm.* furnishing.

ammobiliare *vt.* to furnish.

ammodernare *vt.* to modernize.

ammodo *agg.* nice, proper.

ammogliare *vt.* to marry. ◆ **ammogliarsi** *vr.* to get *(v. irr.)* married.

ammollare *vt.* **1.** to soak **2.** (*ammorbidire*) to soften.

ammollire *vt.* to soften.

ammonìaca *sf.* ammonia.

ammonire *vt.* **1.** to admonish **2.** (*avvisare*) to warn.

ammonizione *sf.* **1.** admonition **2.** (*rimprovero*) reproof **3.** (*avvertimento*) warning.

ammontare *vi.* to amount.

ammonticchiare *vt.* to heap (up).

ammorbare *vt.* to taint.

ammorbidire *vt.* to soften.

ammortamento *sm.* redemption || *quota d'—*, depreciation allowance.

ammortire *vt.* to numb.

ammortizzare *vt.* to redeem.

ammosciare *vt.* to become (*v. irr.*) flabby.

ammucchiare *vt.* to heap (up).

ammuffire *vi.* **1.** to grow (*v. irr.*) musty **2.** (*fig.*) to languish: *— in casa*, to languish at home.

ammutinamento *sm.* mutiny.

ammutinarsi *vr.* to mutiny.

ammutinato *agg.* mutinous. ♦ **ammutinato** *sm.* mutineer.

ammutolire *vi.* **1.** to become (*v. irr.*) dumb **2.** (*essere ammutolito da altri*) to be struck dumb.

amnesìa *sf.* loss of memory.

amnistìa *sf.* amnesty.

amnistiare *vt.* to amnesty.

amo *sm.* fish-hook.

amorale *agg.* amoral.

amoralità *sf.* amorality.

amore *sm.* **1.** love || *— di sé*, selfishness **2.** (*persona o cosa amata*) beloved || *per amore di*, for the sake of.

amoreggiare *vi.* to flirt.

amoretto *sm.* flirtation.

amorévole *agg.* loving.

amorevolezza *sf.* lovingness.

amorfo *agg.* amorphous.

amorino *sm.* Cupid.

amoroso *agg.* **1.** loving **2.** (*fig.*) amorous: *poesia —*, amorous verse.

amovìbile *agg.* movable.

amperòmetro *sm.* amperometer.

ampiezza *sf.* width, (*anche fig.*) breadth.

ampio *agg.* **1.** wide **2.** (*di abito*) comfortable.

amplesso *sm.* embrace.

ampliamento *sm.* amplification.

ampliare *vt.* **1.** to amplify **2.** (*aumentare*) to increase. ♦ **ampliar-**

si *vr.* to widen.

amplificare *vt.* **1.** to enlarge **2.** (*fig.; fis.*) to amplify.

amplificatore *sm.* amplifier.

amplificazione *sf.* amplification.

ampolla *sf.* **1.** phial **2.** (*per olio, aceto ecc.*) cruet.

ampollosità *sf.* pomposity.

ampolloso *agg.* pompous: *stile —*, bombastic style.

amputare *vt.* to amputate.

amputazione *sf.* amputation.

amuleto *sm.* amulet.

anabbaglianti *sm. pl.* lower beams

anabolismo *sm.* anabolism.

anacoreta *sm.* anchorite.

anacronismo *sm.* anachronism.

anacronìstico *agg.* anachronistic.

anàgrafe *sf.* registry office.

anagramma *sm.* anagram.

analcòlico *agg.* soft.

anale *agg.* anal.

analfabeta *sm.* illiterate.

analfabetismo *sm.* illiteracy.

analgèsico *agg. e sm.* analgesic.

anàlisi *sf.* analysis (*pl.* -ses).

analìtico *agg.* analytical.

analizzare *vt.* to analyse.

analogamente *avv.* likewise.

analogìa *sf.* analogy.

anàlogo *agg.* similar.

ànanas *sf.* pine-apple.

anarchìa *sf.* anarchy.

anàrchico *agg.* anarchic. ♦ **anàrchico** *sm.* anarchist.

anatema *sm.* anathema.

anatomìa *sf.* anatomy.

anatòmico *agg.* anatomic.

anatomista *sm.* anatomist.

ànatra *sf.* duck.

anatròccolo *sm.* duckling.

anca *sf.* hip.

ancestrale *agg.* ancestral.

anche *avv.* **1.** (*pure*) also, too **2.** (*in frasi neg.*) either: *anch'io non verrò*, I will not come either **3.** (*con comp.*) even, still: *ciò è anche peggio*, it is still worse **4.** (*persino*) even. ♦ **anche** *cong.* (*anche se*) even if, even though

ancheggiare *vi.* to waddle.

anchilosato *agg.* ankylosed.

anchilosi *sf.* ankylosis.

àncora *sf.* **1.** anchor: *levar l'—*, to weigh anchor **2.** (*fig.*) hope: *— di salvezza*, last hope.

ancora *avv.* **1.** (*tuttora*) still **2.** (*in frasi neg.*) yet **3.** (*di nuovo*) again **4.** (*davanti a comp.*) still, even

5. (*con pron. e agg. quantitativi*) more: — *molte persone*, many more people **6.** (« *di più* » *in frasi affermative*) some more: *voglio ancora caffé*, I want some more coffee **7.** (« *di più* » *in frasi neg. e dubitative*) any more: *hai ancora caffé?*, have you any more coffee? **8.** (*più a lungo*) longer: *leggi ancora un po'*, read a little longer.

ancoraggio *sm.* anchorage.

ancorare *vt.* to anchor.

ancorché *cong.* even if, even though.

andamento *sm.* **1.** (*tendenza*) trend **2.** (*procedimento*) proceeding.

andante *agg.* **1.** (*scadente*) plain **2.** (*comm.*) current **3.** (*mus.*) andante.

andare *vi.* **1.** (*anche fig.*) to go (*v. irr.*): — *a cavallo*, to go on horseback; — *a far compere*, to go shopping; — *a piedi*, to go on foot; — *a zonzo*, to lounge about; — *e venire*, to come (*v. irr.*) and go; — *in bicicletta*, to ride (*v. irr.*) a bicycle; — *in treno*, to go by train; — *a male*, to go bad **2.** (*essere molto venduto*) to be in demand **3.** (— *bene, di indumento*) to fit || — *avanti* (*di orologi*), to be fast; — *indietro* (*di orologi*), to be slow. ♦ **andàrsene** *vr.* to go away.

andata *sf.* going: — *e ritorno*, going there and back || *biglietto di sola* —, single ticket || *biglietto di* — *e ritorno*, return ticket.

andatura *sf.* **1.** gait **2.** (*velocità*) pace.

andazzo *sm.* habit, custom.

andicappare *vt.* to handicap.

andirivieni *sm.* coming and going.

àndito *sm.* passage.

andrògino *agg.* androgynous. ♦ **andrògino** *sm.* androgyne.

androne *sm.* lobby.

aneddòtico *agg.* anecdotic.

anèddoto *sm.* anecdote.

anelare *vi.* **1.** to gasp **2.** (*fig.*) to long for.

anèlito *sm.* **1.** gasp **2.** (*fig.*) longing for.

anello *sm.* ring: — *di fidanzamento*, engagement ring; — *di matrimonio*, wedding ring || — *di catena*, link of a chain.

anemìa *sf.* anaemia.

anèmico *agg.* anaemic.

anèmone *sm.* anemone.

anestesìa *sf.* anaesthesia.

anestesista *s.* anaesthetist.

anestètico *agg. e sm.* anaesthetic.

anestetizzare *vt.* to anaesthetize.

anfibio *agg.* amphibious. ♦ **anfibio** *sm.* (*zool.*; *mil.*) amphibian.

anfiteatro *sm.* amphitheatre.

anfitrione *sm.* amphitryon.

ànfora *sf.* amphora (*pl.* -ae).

anfrattuoso *agg.* anfractuous.

angèlico *agg.* angelic(al).

àngelo *sm.* angel.

angherìa *sf.* vexation.

angina *sf.* angina.

angioma *sm.* angioma.

anglicano *agg. e sm.* Anglican.

angolare *agg.* angular.

àngolo *sm.* **1.** corner **2.** (*fis.*; *geom.*) angle.

angoloso *agg.* angular.

angoscia *sf.* anguish.

angosciare *vt.* to anguish.

angoscioso *agg.* **1.** (*che dà angoscia*) distressing **2.** (*pieno di angoscia*) full of anguish.

anguilla *sf.* **1.** eel **2.** (*fig.*) elusive person.

anguria *sf.* water-melon.

angustia *sf.* **1.** narrowness **2.** (*tribolazione*) distress.

angustiare *vt.* to afflict. ♦ **angustiarsi** *vr.* to worry.

angusto *agg.* **1.** narrow **2.** (*fig.*) mean.

ànice *sm.* anise.

anidride *sf.* anhydride.

anilina *sf.* aniline.

ànima *sf.* **1.** soul || *esalare l'*—, to die || *vender l'*— *a caro prezzo*, to sell (*v. irr.*) one's life dearly. **2.** (*parte centrale, nerbo*) soul, heart **3.** (*cuore, sentimento*) feeling, heart **4.** (*persona*) person: *Torino ha oltre un milione di anime*, Turin has over one million persons.

animale *sm. e agg.* animal.

animalesco *agg.* beastly.

animare *vt.* to enliven, to give (*v. irr.*) life. ♦ **animarsi** *vr.* to become (*v. irr.*) lively.

animatamente *avv.* animatedly.

animato *agg.* **1.** living **2.** (*vivace*) lively.

animatore *sm.* animator.

animazione *sf.* briskness.

animismo *sm.* animism.

ànimo *sm.* **1.** mind: *ho in animo di fare ciò*, I have a mind to do that **2.** (*coraggio*) courage **3.** (*inclinazione*) disposition.

animosità *sf.* animosity.
animoso *agg.* **1.** brave **2.** (*ostile*) malevolent.
anisetta *sf.* anisette.
ànitra *sf.* duck.
annacquare *vt.* **1.** to water **2.** (*fig.*) to moderate.
annaffiare *vt.* to water.
annaffiatoio *sm.* watering-can.
annali *sm. pl.* annals.
annaspare *vi.* to grope.
annaspìo *sm.* groping.
annata *sf.* **1.** year **2.** (*raccolto*) crop.
annebbiare *vt.* **1.** to dim **2.** (*fig.*) to dull. ♦ **annebbiarsi** *vr.* (*della vista*) to blur.
annegamento *sm.* drowning.
annegare *vt.* to drown. ♦ **annegarsi** *vr.* to drown oneself.
annegato *agg.* drowned.
annerimento *sm.* blackening.
annerire *vt.* to blacken.
annessione *sf.* annexation.
annesso *agg.* **1.** connected **2.** (*accluso*) enclosed.
annèttere *vt.* to annex.
annichilazione *sf.* annihilation.
annichilimento *sm.* annihilation.
annichilire *vt.* to annihilate.
annidarsi *vr.* **1.** to nestle **2.** (*nascondersi*) to hide (*v. irr.*).
annientamento *sm.* **1.** destruction **2.** (*di desideri*) frustration.
annientare *vt.* to destroy.
anniversario *agg. e sm.* anniversary.
anno *sm.* **1.** year: — *bisestile*, leap-year || *Capo d'*—, New Year's Day || *durante tutto l'*—, all the year round **2.** (*periodo lungo e indeterminato*) a long time **3.** (*nell'indicare l'età*) to be ... years old: *ho 10 anni*, I am 10 years old.
annodare *vt.* to knot: — *amicizie*, to make friends.
annoiare *vt.* to bore, to tire. ♦ **annoiarsi** *vr.* to be bored.
annoiato *agg.* bored.
annoiatore *sm.* tiresome person.
annoso *agg.* old.
annotare *vt.* **1.** (*corredare di note*) to annotate **2.** (*prendere nota*) to take (*v. irr.*) a note (of).
annotazione *sf.* note.
annottare *vi.* to grow (*v. irr.*) dark.
annuale *agg.* yearly.
annuario *sm.* year-book.
annuire *vi.* to nod.
annullamento *sm.* cancellation.

annullare *vt.* **1.** to annul **2.** (*comm.*) to cancel.
annunciare *vt.* **1.** to announce **2.** (*predire*) to foretell (*v. irr.*).
annunciatore *sm.* announcer.
annuncio *sm.* **1.** notice **2.** (*presagio*) presage.
ànnuo *agg.* yearly.
annusare *vt.* **1.** to smell **2.** (*tabacco*) to take (*v. irr.*) snuff.
annuvolarsi *vr.* **1.** to get (*v. irr.*) cloudy **2.** (*fig.*) to become (*v. irr.*) gloomy.
ano *sm.* anus.
anòdino *agg.* anodyne.
ànodo *sm.* anode.
anomalìa *sf.* anomaly.
anòmalo *agg.* anomalous.
anònima *sf.* joint-stock company.
anònimo *agg.* anonymous. ♦ **anònimo** *sm.* anonym.
anormale *agg.* abnormal.
anormalità *sf.* abnormality.
ansa *sf.* **1.** (*insenatura*) creek **2.** (*di fiume*) bend **3.** (*manico*) handle.
ansante *agg.* panting.
ansare *vi.* to pant.
ansia *sf.* anxiety.
ansietà *sf.* anxiety.
ansimare *vi.* to pant.
ansioso *agg.* **1.** anxious **2.** (*desideroso*) eager.
ànsito *sm.* panting.
anta *sf.* **1.** shutter **2.** (*di armadio*) door.
antagonismo *sm.* antagonism.
antagonista *s.* antagonist.
antàrtico *agg.* Antarctic.
antecedente *agg.* previous. ♦ **antecedente** *sm.* antecedent.
antecessore *sm.* predecessor.
antefatto *sm.* antecedent fact.
anteguerra *sm.* pre-war time.
antenato *sm.* ancestor.
antenna *sf.* **1.** (*zool.*) antenna (*pl.* -nae) **2.** (*radio*) aerial.
anteporre *vt.* to place before, to put (*v. irr.*) before.
anteprima *sf.* preview.
anteriore *agg.* **1.** (*nello spazio*) fore **2.** (*nel tempo*) previous, former.
antiabbaglianti *sm. pl.* anti-dazzle.
antiaèreo *agg.* anti-aircraft.
antibattèrico *agg. e sm.* antibacterial.
antibiòtico *agg. e sm.* antibiotic.
anticaglia *sf.* worthless antique.
anticamente *avv.* in ancient times.
anticàmera *sf.* ante-room || *fare* —,

to be kept waiting.

anticarro *agg.* anti-tank.

antichità *sf.* **1.** antiquity **2.** (*oggetti antichi*) antiques (*pl.*).

anticipare *vt.* **1.** to anticipate **2.** (*di danaro*) to pay in advance.

anticipatamente *avv.* in advance.

anticipato *agg.* **1.** advanced **2.** (*comm.*) in advance.

anticipazione *sf.* anticipation.

antìcipo *sm.* advance: *essere in* —, to be before time **2.** (*caparra*) earnest money.

anticlericale *agg. e s.* anticlerical.

anticlericalismo *sm.* anticlericalism.

antico *agg.* **1.** ancient **2.** (*all'antica*) old-fashioned.

anticonformista *s.* nonconformist.

anticongelante *sm.* anti-freeze.

anticorpo *sm.* antibody.

anticostituzionale *agg.* anticonstitutional.

antidatare *vt.* to antedate.

antidiluviano *agg. e sm.* antediluvian.

antìdoto *sm.* antidote.

antiestètico *agg.* antiaesthetic.

antifascismo *sm.* antifascism.

antifascista *s. e agg.* antifascist.

antifebbrile *sm.* febrifuge.

antifecondativo *sm.* anti-conceptive.

antìfona *sf.* antiphon: *capire l'*— to take (*v. irr.*) a hint.

antifurto *sm.* antitheft device.

antigàs *agg.* anti-gas: *maschera* —, gas-mask.

antigiènico *agg.* unhealthy.

antìlope *sf.* antelope.

antimilitarismo *sm.* antimilitarism.

antincendio *agg.* antifire: *pompa* —, fire-pump.

antinebbia *agg.* *faro* —, fog-light.

antinevràlgico *agg.* antineuralgic.

antinomìa *sf.* antinomy.

antiparticella *sf.* antiparticle.

antipasto *sm.* hors-d'oeuvre.

antipatìa *sf.* dislike.

antipàtico *agg.* disagreeable.

antìpodi *sm. pl.* antipodes.

antiquariato *sm.* antique-dealing.

antiquario *sm.* antique-dealer.

antiquato *agg.* old-fashioned.

antireumàtico *agg.* antirheumatic.

antirùggine *sf.* anti-rust.

antisemitismo *sm.* anti-Semitism.

ɛ ntisèttico *agg. e sm.* antiseptic.

antispàstico *agg.* antispasmodic.

antistante *agg.* before, in front of.

antìtesi *sf.* antithesis (*pl.* -ses).

antitètanico *agg.* antitetanic.

antitètico *agg.* antithetic(al).

antitòssico *agg.* antitoxic.

antivigilia *sf.* the day before the eve.

antologìa *sf.* anthology.

antològico *agg.* anthological.

antonomasia *sf.* antonomasia || *per* —, antonomastically.

antracite *sf.* anthracite.

antro *sm.* **1.** cave **2.** (*tana*) den.

antropocentrismo *sm.* anthropocentrism.

antropofagìa *sf.* anthropophagy.

antropòfago *agg.* anthropophagous.

  ♦ **antropòfago** *sm.* cannibal.

antropologìa *sf.* anthropology.

antropòlogo *sm.* anthropologist.

antropomorfo *agg.* anthropomorphous.

anulare *agg.* annular. ♦ **anulare** *sm.* ring-finger.

anzi *cong.* **1.** (*al contrario*) on the contrary **2.** (*in più*) moreover || — *che*, rather than; — *che no*, rather. ♦ **anzi** *avv.* before: — *tempo*, before time.

anzianità *sf.* seniority.

anziano *agg.* **1.** elderly **2.** (*in cariche, uffici ecc.*) senior.

anziché *cong.* **1.** rather than **2.** (*invece di*) instead of.

anzidetto *agg.* above-mentioned.

anzitempo *avv.* before time.

aorta *sf.* aorta.

apartìtico *agg.* non-sectarian.

apatìa *sf.* apathy, indifference.

apàtico *agg.* listless.

ape *sf.* bee.

aperitivo *sm.* aperitif.

apertamente *avv.* openly.

aperto *agg.* open.

apertura *sf.* **1.** opening **2.** (*di mente*) broad-mindedness **3.** (*ampiezza di un arco*) span: — *alare*, wing-span.

àpice *sm.* apex.

apicoltura *sf.* bee-keeping.

apnea *sf.* apnoea.

apocalisse *sf.* apocalypse.

apocalìttico *agg.* apocalyptic(al).

apòcrifo *agg.* apocryphal || *libri apocrifi*, Apocrypha.

apòfisi *sf.* apophysis.

apogeo *sm.* apogee.

apòlide *agg.* stateless. ♦ **apòlide** *sm.* stateless person.

apolìtico *agg.* non-political.
apologìa *sf.* apologia.
apologista *s.* apologist.
apòlogo *sm.* apologue.
apoplessìa *sf.* apoplexy.
apoplèttico *agg.* apoplectic: *colpo* —, apoplectic fit.
apostasìa *sf.* apostasy.
apòstata *sm.* apostate.
apòstolo *sm.* apostle.
apostrofare *vt.* to apostrophize.
apòstrofe *sf.* apostrophe.
apòstrofo *sm.* apostrophe.
apoteòsi *sf.* apotheosis.
appagare *vt.* **1.** to satisfy, to gratify **2.** (*la sete*) to quench one's thirst.
appaiare *vt.* **1.** to couple **2.** (*armonizzare colori, vestiario ecc.*) to match.
appallottolare *vt.* to roll into a ball.
appaltare *vt.* to give (*v. irr.*) out by contract.
appaltatore *sm.* contractor.
appalto *sm.* contract, bid.
appannaggio *sm.* apanage.
appannamento *sm.* **1.** (*di metalli*) tarnishing **2.** (*di vetri ecc.*) clouding **3.** (*di vista*) dimming.
appannare *vt.* **1.** (*di metalli*) to tarnish **2.** (*di vetri ecc.*) to cloud **3.** (*di vista*) to dim.
apparato *sm.* **1.** apparatus **2.** (*mostra*) display.
apparecchiare *vt.* to prepare: — *la tavola*, to lay (*v. irr.*) the table.
apparecchio *sm.* **1.** set **2.** (*aeroplano*) aeroplane || — *fotografico*, camera; — *telefonico*, telephone; — *radio*, radio set.
apparentare *vt.* to relate.
apparente *agg.* **1.** (*illusorio*) seeming **2.** (*chiaro*) apparent, obvious.
apparentemente *avv.* seemingly.
apparenza *sf.* **1.** appearance **2.** (*aspetto*) look **3.** (*pompa*) show.
apparire *vi.* **1.** to appear **2.** (*aver l'aspetto*) to look **3.** (*risultare*) to result.
appariscente *agg.* **1.** striking **2.** (*vistoso*) showy.
apparizione *sf.* apparition.
appartamento *sm.* flat.
appartarsi *vr.* to retire.
appartenenza *sf.* belonging.
appartenere *vi.* **1.** to belong (to) **2.** (*essere membro*) to be a member (of).

appassionare *vt.* to impassion. ♦ **appassionarsi** *vr.* to become (*v. irr.*) fond of.
appassionato *agg.* **1.** passionate **2.** (*di musica, arte ecc.*) keen (on).
appassire *vi.* to wither.
appellare *vt.* to name, to call. ♦ **appellarsi** *vr.* to appeal.
appellativo *sm.* appellative.
appello *sm.* **1.** (*giur.*) appeal **2.** (*chiamata*) call **3.** (*esortazione*) appeal.
appena *avv.* **1.** (*a fatica*) hardly **2.** (*molto poco*) very little **3.** (*da poco*) just: *ero* — *arrivato*, I had just arrived || *non* —, as soon as.
appèndere *vt.* to hang (*v. irr.*).
appendice *sf.* appendix || *romanzo d'*—, serial.
appendicite *sf.* appendicitis.
appesantire *vt.* to make (*v. irr.*) heavy. ♦ **appesantirsi** *vr.* to grow (*v. irr.*) heavy.
appestare *vt.* **1.** to infect **2.** (*spargere odore*) to stink (*v. irr.*).
appestato *agg.* **1.** plague-stricken **2.** (*fig.*) tainted. ♦ **appestato** *sm.* plague-stricken person.
appetenza *sf.* **1.** appetite **2.** (*desiderio*) longing (for sthg.).
appetibile *agg.* pleasing.
appetire *vt.* to desire.
appetito *sm.* appetite.
appezzamento *sm.* plot of land.
appianare *vt.* **1.** to level **2.** (*fig.*) to smooth.
appiattarsi *vr.* **1.** to crouch **2.** (*stare in agguato*) to lie (*v. irr.*) in wait **3.** (*nascondersi*) to hide (*v. irr.*).
appiattire *vt.* to flatten.
appiccare *vt.* (*il fuoco*) to set (*v. irr.*) fire.
appiccicare *vt.* **1.** to stick (*v. irr.*) **2.** (*appioppare*) to palm off.
appiccicoso *agg.* sticky.
appiè *prep.* **1.** (*al di sotto*) below **2.** (*ai piedi*) at the foot: — *del letto*, at the foot of the bed.
appiedare *vt.* to dismount.
appiedato *agg.* dismounted.
appieno *avv.* fully.
appigliarsi *vr.* to get (*v. irr.*) hold of: — *ad un pretesto*, to take (*v. irr.*) a pretext.
appiglio *sm.* **1.** support **2.** (*fig.*) pretext.
appiombo *sm.* perpendicularity.
appioppare *vt.* **1.** to give (*v. irr.*)

|| — *uno schiaffo*, to slap 2. (*affibbiare*) to palm off.

appisolarsi *vr.* to doze off.

applaudire *vt. e vi.* to applaud.

applauditore *sm.* applauder.

applàuso *sm.* 1. applause (*solo sing.*) 2. (*fig.*) praise.

applicare *vt.* 1. to apply 2. (*giur.*) to carry out 3. (*accostare*) to set (*v. irr.*). ♦ **applicarsi** *vr.* to apply oneself.

applicazione *sf.* 1. application 2. (*fig.*) care 3. (*guarnizione*) trimming.

appoggiare *vt.* 1. to lean (*v. irr.*) 2. (*posare*) to lay (*v. irr.*) 3. (*fig.*) to back. ♦ **appoggiarsi** *vr.* 1. to lean (*v. irr.*) 2. (*fig.*) to rely (on).

appoggio *sm.* 1. support 2. (*fig.*) assistance 3. (*colui che dà —*) supporter.

appollaiarsi *vr.* to perch.

apporre *vt.* to affix.

apportare *vt.* 1. to bring (*v. irr.*) 2. (*produrre*) to produce.

apporto *sm.* contribution.

appositamente *avv.* on purpose.

appòsito *agg.* 1. special 2. (*adatto*) fit.

apposizione *sf.* 1. (*gramm.*) apposition 2. (*l'apporre*) affixing.

apposta *avv.* expressly.

appostare *vt.* (*mil.*) to place. ♦ **appostarsi** *vr.* to lie (*v. irr.*) in ambush.

apprèndere *vt.* to learn (*v. irr.*).

apprendista *sm.* apprentice.

apprendistato *sm.* apprenticeship.

apprensione *sf.* 1. concern 2. (*l'apprendere*) learning.

appresso *avv.* near, close by. ♦ **appresso** *prep.* near, close to.

apprestamento *sm.* preparation.

apprestare *vt.* to prepare.

apprettare *vt.* to dress.

apprezzàbile *agg.* appreciable.

apprezzamento *sm.* 1. appreciation 2. (*giudizio*) opinion.

apprezzare *vt.* 1. to appreciate 2. (*valutare*) to value.

approdare *vi.* 1. to land 2. (*fig.*) to be of use.

approfittare *vi.* to profit (by). ♦ **approfittarsi** *vr.* 1. to avail oneself 2. (*abusare*) to take (*v. irr.*) undue advantage.

approfondire *vt.* 1. to make (*v. irr.*) deeper 2. (*fig.*) to examine closely.

approntare *vt.* to make (*v. irr.*) ready.

appropriarsi *vr.* to take (*v. irr.*) possession of.

appropriato *agg.* fit, suitable.

appropriazione *sf.* appropriation: — *indebita*, embezzlement.

approssimarsi *vr.* 1. to come (*v. irr.*) near 2. (*di tempo*) to draw (*v. irr.*) near.

approssimativamente *avv.* approximately.

approssimativo *agg.* approximative.

approssimazione *sf.* approximation.

approvare *vt.* 1. to approve (of) 2. (*promuovere*) to pass.

approvazione *sf.* approval.

approvvigionamento *sm.* 1. (*l'approvvigionare*) supplying 2. (*provviste*) supplies.

approvvigionare *vt.* to supply provisions (to).

appuntamento *sm.* appointment.

appuntare *vt.* 1. to sharpen 2. (*prender nota*) to note 3. (*biasimare*) to blame.

appuntellare *vt.* 1. to prop 2. (*fig.*) to support.

appuntino *avv.* nicely.

appuntito *agg.* pointed.

appunto[1] *sm.* 1. note 2. (*critica*) blame.

appunto[2] *avv.* exactly, just.

appurare *vt.* to verify.

apribottiglie *sm.* bottle-opener.

aprile *sm.* April: *pesce d'—*, April fool.

aprire *vt.* to open: — *le braccia a qc.*, to welcome so.

apriscàtole *sm.* tin-opener.

àquila *sf.* eagle.

aquilino *agg.* aquiline.

aquilone *sm.* 1. (*vento del nord*) north wind 2. (*giocattolo*) kite.

aquilotto *sm.* eaglet.

arabescare *vt.* to decorate with arabesques.

arabesco *sm.* arabesque.

aràbico *agg.* Arabic.

aràbile *agg.* arable.

àrabo *agg. e sm.* Arab.

aràchide *sf.* peanut.

aragosta *sf.* lobster.

aràldico *agg.* heraldic.

araldo *sm.* herald.

arancia *sf.* orange.

aranciata *sf.* orange squash.
aranciera *sf.* orangery.
arancio *agg.* (*colore*) orange. ♦
arancio *sm.* orange-tree.
arancione *agg.* orange-coloured.
arare *vt.* to plough.
aratore *sm.* ploughman (*pl.* -men).
aratro *sm.* plough.
aratura *sf.* ploughing.
arazzo *sm.* arras.
arbitraggio *sm.* **1.** (*sport*) umpirage **2.** (*comm.*) arbitrage.
arbitrare *vt.* **1.** to arbitrate **2.** (*calcio, boxe*) to referee.
arbitrario *agg.* arbitrary.
arbitrio *sm.* **1.** will: *libero —*, free will **1.** (*atto arbitrario*) arbitrary act.
àrbitro *sm.* **1.** (*sport*) umpire **2.** (*calcio, boxe*) referee **3.** (*giur.*) arbitrator.
arboricoltore *sm.* arboriculturist.
arboricoltura *sf.* arboriculture.
arboscello *sm.* shrub.
arbusto *sm.* shrub.
arca *sf.* ark || *— di scienza*, eminent scholar.
arcàdico *agg.* e *sm.* Arcadian.
arcàico *agg.* **1.** archaic **2.** (*di parole, stile*) obsolete.
arcaismo *sm.* **1.** archaism **2.** (*parola arcaica*) obsolete word.
arcàngelo *sm.* archangel.
arcano *agg.* mysterious.
archeologìa *sf.* archaeology.
archeològico *agg.* archaeologic(al).
archeòlogo *sm.* archaeologist.
archètipo *sm.* archetype.
archetto *sm.* **1.** small arch **2.** (*mus.*) bow.
architettare *vt.* **1.** to draw (*v. irr.*) the plans **2.** (*fig.*) to devise.
architetto *sm.* architect.
architettònico *agg.* architectonic.
architettura *sf.* architecture.
architrave *sm.* architrave.
archiviare *vt.* **1.** to place in the archives **2.** (*comm.*) to file.
archivio *sm.* **1.** archives (*pl.*) **2.** (*comm.*) file.
archivista *sm.* archivist.
arciduca *sm.* archduke.
arciere *sm.* archer.
arcigno *agg.* gruff.
arcimiliardario *sm.* multimillionaire.
arcipèlago *sm.* archipelago (*pl.* -goes).
arcivescovado *sm.* archbishopric.

arcivéscovo *sm.* archbishop.
arco *sm.* **1.** (*arma*) bow **2.** (*geom.*) arc **3.** (*arch.*) arch **4.** (*mus.*) bow.
arcobaleno *sm.* rainbow.
arcolaio *sm.* wool-winder.
arcuare *vt.* **1.** to arch **2.** (*piegare*) to bend (*v. irr.*).
ardente *agg.* **1.** burning **2.** (*fig.*) passionate.
ardentemente *avv.* ardently.
àrdere *vt.* to burn (*v. irr.*).
ardesia *sf.* slate.
ardire *vi.* **1.** to dare **2.** (*avere l'impudenza*) to have the impudence.
ardito *agg.* **1.** bold **2.** (*rischioso*) risky.
ardore *sm.* **1.** fierce heat **2.** (*fig.*) passion.
àrduo *agg.* **1.** hard **2.** (*erto*) steep.
àrea *sf.* **1.** area **2.** (*sfera d'azione*) sphere.
arena *sf.* **1.** (*sabbia*) sand **2.** (*arch.*) arena.
arenarsi *vr.* to get (*v. irr.*) stranded (*anche fig.*).
arengario *sm.* tribune.
areòpago *sm.* Areopagus.
àrgano *sm.* **1.** (*mar.*) capstan **2.** (*mecc.*) windlass.
argentare *vt.* to silver.
argènteo *agg.* silvery.
argenterìa *sf.* silver ware.
argentino *agg.* silvery.
argento *sm.* silver.
argilla *sf.* clay.
argilloso *agg.* clayey.
arginare *vt.* **1.** to dam **2.** (*fig.*) to check.
àrgine *sm.* bank.
argomentare *vt.* to infer. ♦ **argomentare** *vi.* to argue.
argomentazione *sf.* reasoning.
argomento *sm.* **1.** subject **2.** (*prova a sostegno*) argument.
arguire *vt.* to deduce.
argutezza *sf.* shrewdness.
arguto *agg.* **1.** sharp **2.** (*faceto*) witty.
arguzia *sf.* wit.
aria *sf.* **1.** air: *— condizionata*, air conditioning || *corrente d'—*, draught || *camera d'—*, inner tube || *andare all'—*, to fall (*v. irr.*) through **2.** (*aspetto*) look **3.** (*mus.*) tune.
ariano *agg.* e *sm.* Aryan.
aridità *sf.* **1.** aridity **2.** (*di cuore*) lack of feeling.
àrido *agg.* **1.** arid **2.** (*di cuore*)

lacking feeling.

arieggiare *vt.* **1.** to air **2.** (*rassomigliare*) to look like **3.** (*imitare*) to imitate.

arieggiato *agg.* aired.

ariete *sm.* ram.

aringa *sf.* herring.

arioso *agg.* airy.

aristocràtico *agg.* aristocratic. ◆ **aristocràtico** *sm.* aristocrat.

aristocrazìa *sf.* aristocracy.

aristotèlico *agg. e sm.* Aristotelian.

aritmètica *sf.* arithmetic.

aritmètico *agg.* arithmetic(al).

arlecchinata *sf.* harlequinade.

arlecchino *sm.* harlequin.

arma *sf.* weapon, arm: *armi bianche*, side-arms; *armi da fuoco*, fire-arms || *galleria d'armi*, armoury.

armadietto *sm.* **1.** (*per medicinali, strumenti ecc.*) cabinet **2.** (*per abiti*) locker.

armadio *sm.* **1.** (*per stoviglie*) cupboard **2.** (*per abiti*) wardrobe.

armaiolo *sm.* armourer.

armamentario *sm.* **1.** instruments (*pl.*) **2.** (*armeria*) armoury.

armamento *sm.* arming.

armare *vt.* to arm.

armata *sf.* army.

armatore *sm.* **1.** shipbuilder **2.** (*chi possiede una nave*) shipowner.

armatura *sf.* **1.** armour **2.** (*impalcatura*) scaffolding.

armeggiare *vi.* **1.** to handle arms **2.** (*darsi da fare*) to busy oneself **3.** (*tramare*) to manoeuvre.

armeggìo *sm.* **1.** handling of arms **2.** (*l'affaccendarsi*) bustling **3.** (*intrigo*) manoeuvre.

armento *sm.* herd.

armerìa *sf.* armoury.

armiere *sm.* gunsmith.

armistizio *sm.* armistice.

armonìa *sf.* harmony.

armònica *sf.* (*a bocca*) mouthorgan.

armònico *agg.* harmonic.

armonio *sm.* harmonium.

armonioso *agg.* harmonious.

armonista *s.* harmonist.

armonizzare *vt.* to harmonize. ◆ **armonizzare** *vi.* **1.** to harmonize **2.** (*di colori*) to match.

arnese *sm.* **1.** (*strumento*) tool **2.** (*aggeggio*) gadget.

arnia *sf.* beehive.

aroma *sm.* flavour.

aromàtico *agg.* aromatic.

aromatizzare *vt.* to flavour.

arpa *sf.* harp.

arpeggiare *vi.* to play the harp.

arpeggio *sm.* arpeggio.

arpista *s.* harpist.

arra *sf.* earnest.

arrabattarsi *vr.* to bestir oneself.

arrabbiare *vi.* **1.** to become (*v. irr.*) angry **2.** (*di cane*) to be affected with rabies. ◆ **arrabbiarsi** *vr.* to get (*v. irr.*) angry.

arrabbiato *agg.* **1.** angry **2.** (*di cane*) rabid.

arrabbiatura *sf.* rage.

arraffare *vt.* to grasp.

arrampicarsi *vr.* to climb.

arrampicata *sf.* climb.

arrampicatore *sm.* **1.** mountain climber **2.** (*fig.*) social climber.

arrancare *vi.* **1.** to plod along **2.** (*zoppicare*) to limp **3.** (*affaticarsi*) to get (*v. irr.*) tired.

arrangiamento *sm.* arrangement.

arrangiare *vt.* to arrange. ◆ **arrangiarsi** *vr.* to manage.

arrecare *vt.* **1.** to bring (*v. irr.*) **2.** (*causare*) to cause.

arredamento *sm.* furnishing.

arredare *vt.* to furnish.

arredatore *sm.* internal decorator.

arredo *sm.* piece of furniture.

arrèndersi *vr.* **1.** to surrender **2.** (*fig.*) to give (*v. irr.*) it up.

arrendévole *agg.* **1.** pliant **2.** (*fig.*) docile.

arrestare *vt.* **1.** to stop **2.** (*trarre in arresto*) to arrest. ◆ **arrestarsi** *vr.* to stop.

arresto *sm.* arrest.

arretrare *vt.* **1.** to pull back **2.** (*ritirare*) to withdraw (*v. irr.*).

arretrato *agg.* backward.

arricchimento *sm.* enrichment.

arricchire *vt.* to enrich. ◆ **arricchirsi** *vr.* to grow (*v. irr.*) rich.

arricciare *vt.* to curl: — *il naso*, to turn up one's nose.

arrìdere *vi.* to be favourable.

arringare *vt.* to harangue.

arringatore *sm.* haranguer.

arrischiare *vt.* to risk. ◆ **arrischiarsi** *vr.* to venture.

arrivare *vi.* **1.** to arrive (at), (in) **2.** (*fig.*) to attain.

arrivato *agg.* (*fig.*) successful.

arrivederci *inter.* goodbye.

arrivismo *sm.* social climbing.

arrivista *sm.* social climber.

arrivo *sm.* arrival.

arrogante *agg.* arrogant.
arroganza *sf.* arrogance.
arrogarsi *vr.* to arrogate to oneself.
arrossire *vi.* to blush.
arrostire *vt.* 1. to roast 2. (*di pane*) to toast.
arrosto *sm.* roast.
arrotare *vt.* to grind (*v. irr.*): — *i denti,* to grind one's teeth.
arrotino *sm.* knife-grinder.
arrotolare *vt.* to roll up.
arrotondare *vt.* 1. to round 2. (*di cifre*) to make (*v. irr.*) a round figure.
arrovellarsi *vr.* to worry.
arroventare *vt.* to make (*v. irr.*) red-hot.
arruffare *vt.* to ruffle.
arruffone *sm.* muddler
arrugginire *vi.* to rust.
arruolare *vt.* to enrol.
arsenale *sm.* 1. (*cantiere*) ship-yard 2. (*deposito di armi*) arsenal.
arsènico *sm.* arsenic.
arsura *sf.* 1. (*siccità*) drought 2. (*sete*) parching thirst.
arte *sf.* art || — *belle arti,* fine arts.
artefatto *agg.* adulterated.
artéfice *sm.* maker.
arteria *sf.* 1. artery 2. (*di traffico*) thoroughfare.
arteriosclerosi *sf.* arteriosclerosis.
artesiano *agg.* artesian.
àrtico *agg.* arctic.
articolare *vt.* to articulate.
articolazione *sf.* articulation.
artìcolo *sm.* 1. (*gramm.; di giornale*) article || — *di fondo,* editorial 2. (*comm.*) item.
artificiale *agg.* artificial.
artifìcio *sm.* 1. device 2. (*astuzia*) cunning.
artigianato *sm.* handicraft.
artigiano *sm.* craftsman (*pl.* -men).
artigliere *sm.* gunner.
artiglierìa *sf.* artillery.
artiglio *sm.* claw.
artista *sm.* artist.
artìstico *agg.* artistic(al).
arto *sm.* limb: — *artificiale,* artificial limb.
artrite *sf.* arthritis (*pl.* -ides).
artrosi *sf.* arthrosis.
arzigògolo *sm.* subtlety.
arzillo *agg.* lively, brisk.
ascella *sf.* armpit.
ascendente *sm.* 1. ascendancy 2. (*antenato*) ancestor.

ascendenza *sf.* ancestry.
ascéndere *vi.* (*anche fig.*) to rise (*v. irr.*).
ascensione *sf.* 1. ascension 2. (*scalata*) climb.
ascensore *sm.* lift.
ascesa *sf.* ascent.
ascesi *sf.* mystical practice.
ascesso *sm.* abscess.
asceta *sm.* ascetic.
ascètico *agg.* ascetical.
ascetismo *sm.* asceticism.
ascia *sf.* axe.
ascissa *sf.* abscissa (*pl.* -sae).
asciugacapelli *sm.* hair-drier.
asciugamano *sm.* towel.
asciugare *vt.* 1. to dry 2. (*con un panno*) to wipe. ♦ **asciugarsi** *vr.* to dry up.
asciugatoio *sm.* towel.
asciutto *agg.* 1. (*anche fig.*) dry 2. (*magro*) thin.
ascoltare *vt.* 1. to listen (to) 2. (*assistere*) to attend: — *le lezioni,* to attend classes.
ascolto *sm.* listening.
ascrìvere *vt.* 1. to count 2. (*attribuire*) to ascribe. ♦ **ascrìversi** *vr.* to claim.
asepsi *sf.* asepsis.
asessuale *agg.* asexual.
asèttico *agg.* aseptic.
asfaltare *vt.* to asphalt.
asfalto *sm.* asphalt.
asfissìa *sf.* 1. asphyxia 2. (*da gas*) gassing.
asfissiare *vt.* 1. to asphyxiate 2. (*con gas*) to gas.
asiàtico *agg.* e *sm.* Asiatic.
asilo *sm.* 1. shelter 2. (*scuola materna*) infant-school.
asimmetrìa *sf.* asymmetry.
asimmètrico *agg.* asymmetrical.
asinerìa *sf.* stupidity.
asinità *sf.* asininity.
àsino *sm.* 1. ass 2. (*fig.*) jackass.
asma *sf.* asthma.
asmàtico *agg.* asthmatical.
asociale *agg.* asocial.
àsola *sf.* buttonhole.
aspàrago *sm.* asparagus.
aspèrgere *vt.* to sprinkle.
asperità *sf.* 1. asperity 2. (*di superfici*) unevenness 3. (*di carattere*) harshness.
aspersorio *sm.* aspergillum.
aspettare *vt.* to wait (for). ♦ **aspettarsi** *vr.* to expect.
aspettativa *sf.* 1. expectation 2.

(*esonero temporaneo*) temporary retirement.

aspetto *sm.* look || *di bell'aspetto*, good-looking || *sala d'—*, waiting-room.

àspide *sm.* asp.

aspirante *agg.* aspirant. ♦ **aspirante** *sm.* candidate, applicant.

aspirapòlvere *sm.* vacuum cleaner, hoover.

aspirare *vt.* to inspire. ♦ **aspirare** *vi.* to aspire (to).

aspiratore *sm.* aspirator.

aspirazione *sf.* **1.** aspiration **2.** (*mecc.*) suction.

aspirina *sf.* aspirin.

asportare *vt.* **1.** to remove **2.** (*med.*) to extirpate.

asportazione *sf.* **1.** removal **2.** (*med.*) extirpation.

asprezza *sf.* **1.** sourness **2.** (*fig.*) harshness.

asprigno *agg.* sourish.

aspro *agg.* **1.** sour **2.** (*fig.*) harsh.

assaggiare *vt.* to taste.

assaggio *sm.* **1.** tasting **2.** (*campione*) sample.

assai *avv.* **1.** (*con agg. e avv.*) very **2.** (*con comp.*) much: *— meglio*, much better.

assalire *vt.* **1.** to assail **2.** (*di malattia*) to attack.

assalitore *sm.* assailer.

assaltare *vt.* to assault.

assalto *sm.* assault, attack.

assaporare *vt.* **1.** to savour **2.** (*fig.*) to enjoy.

assassinare *vt.* to murder.

assassinio *sm.* murder.

assassino *sm.* murderer.

asse *sf.* **1.** (*tavola di legno*) board **2.** (*geom.*) axis (*pl.* axes) **3.** (*stor.*) Axis.

assecondare *vt.* to favour.

assediare *vt.* to besiege.

assedio *sm.* siege.

assegnamento *sm.* assignment || *fare — su qualcuno*, to rely on so.

assegnare *vt.* **1.** to assign **2.** (*un premio*) to award.

assegno *sm.* cheque: *— al portatore*, cheque to bearer; *— circolare*, banker's draft; *— sbarrato*, crossed cheque.

assemblea *sf.* **1.** meeting **2.** (*corpo deliberante*) assembly.

assembramento *sm.* concourse of people.

assembrarsi *vr.* to assemble.

assennatezza *sf.* common sense.

assennato *agg.* sensible.

assenso *sm.* assent.

assentarsi *vr.* to go (*v. irr.*) away.

assente *agg.* absent.

assenteismo *sm.* absenteeism.

assentire *vi.* **1.** to assent (to) **2.** (*col capo*) to nod (in assent).

assenza *sf.* absence.

assenzio *sm.* absinth.

asserire *vt.* to affirm.

asserragliarsi *vr.* to barricade oneselt.

asserto *sm.* assertion.

assertore *sm.* **1.** assertor **2.** (*difensore*) defender, champion.

asservimento *sm.* enslavement.

asservire *vt.* to enslave, to subdue.

asserzione *sf.* statement.

assessorato *sm.* assessorship.

assessore *sm.* **1.** (*alle imposte*) assessor **2.** (*comunale*) councillor responsible for a municipal region.

assestamento *sm.* **1.** adjustment **2.** (*definitivo*) settlement **3.** (*del terreno*) settling.

assestare *vt.* to arrange: *— un colpo*, to deal (*v. irr.*) a blow. ♦ **assestarsi** *vr.* to settle (down).

assetato *agg.* **1.** thirsty **2.** (*fig.*) eager (for).

assetto *sm.* order.

assicurare *vt.* **1.** (*legare*) to fasten **2.** (*promettere*) to assure **3.** (*affermare*) to affirm **4.** (*comm.*) to insure.

assicurata *sf.* registered letter.

assicurato *agg.* insured, assured. ♦ **assicurato** *sm.* insurant.

assicuratore *sm.* insurer.

assicurazione *sf.* **1.** assurance **2.** (*comm.*) insurance.

assideramento *sm.* frost-bite.

assiduità *sf.* assiduity.

assiduo *agg.* assiduous.

assieme *avv.* V. *insieme*.

assieparsi *vr.* to crowd (round).

assillante *agg.* urging.

assillare *vt.* to urge.

assillo *sm.* **1.** urge **2.** (*fig.*) worry.

assimilàbile *agg.* assimilable.

assimilare *vt.* to assimilate, to absorb.

assimilazione *sf.* assimilation.

assioma *sm.* axiom.

assiomàtico *agg.* axiomatic.

assise *sf. pl.* assizes.

assistente *sm.* assistant.

assistenza *sf.* assistance.

assistenziale *agg.* charitable.
assistere *vt.* **1.** to assist **2.** (*curare*) to nurse. ♦ **assistere** *vi.* to attend (sthg.).
assito *sm.* **1.** wooden partition **2.** (*pavimento*) plank floor.
asso *sm.* **1.** (*carte*) ace **2.** (*sport*) champion || *piantare in —,* to leave (*v. irr.*) in the lurch.
associare *vt.* to join. ♦ **associarsi** *vr.* to associate.
associato *sm.* member.
associazione *sf.* association.
assodare *vt.* **1.** to consolidate **2.** (*accertare*) to ascertain.
assoggettare *vt.* to subject. ♦ **assoggettarsi** *vr.* to submit oneself.
assolato *agg.* sunny.
assoldare *vt.* to recruit.
assolo *sm.* (*mus.*) solo.
assolutamente *avv.* absolutely.
assolutismo *sm.* absolutism.
assolutista *agg. e sm.* absolutist.
assoluto *agg. e sm.* absolute.
assoluzione *sf.* **1.** (*eccl.*) absolution **2.** (*giur.*) discharge.
assolvere *vt.* **1.** (*teol.*) to absolve **2.** (*giur.*) to discharge **3.** (*eseguire*) to accomplish.
assomigliante *agg.* like.
assomigliare *vi.* to look like.
assommare *vt. e vi.* to add, to amount (to).
assonanza *sf.* assonance.
assonnarsi *vr.* to fall (*v. irr.*) asleep.
assonnato *agg.* sleepy.
assopimento *sm.* dozing.
assopire *vt.* to make (*v. irr.*) dozy. ♦ **assopirsi** *vr.* to doze off.
assorbente *agg.* absorbing || *carta —,* blotting-paper.
assorbimento *sm.* absorption.
assorbire *vt.* to absorb.
assordante *agg.* deafening.
assordare *vt.* to deafen.
assortimento *sm.* assortment.
assortire *vt.* **1.** to stock **2.** (*fig.*) to match.
assorto *agg.* absorbed.
assottigliamento *sm.* **1.** thinning **2.** (*riduzione*) reduction.
assottigliare *vt.* **1.** to thin **2.** (*diminuire*) to reduce. ♦ **assottigliarsi** *vr.* to grow (*v. irr.*) thin.
assuefare *vt.* to accustom. ♦ **assuefarsi** *vr.* to accustom oneself.
assuefazione *sf.* custom.
assumere *vt.* **1.** to assume **2.** (*in*

servizio) to employ **3.** (*informazioni*) to make (*v. irr.*) inquiries.
assunzione *sf.* **1.** (*ascesa*) accession **2.** (*impiego*) engagement **3.** (*teol.*) Assumption.
assurdamente *avv.* absurdly.
assurdità *sf.* absurdity.
assurdo *agg.* absurd. ♦ **assurdo** *sm.* absurdity.
assurgere *vi.* to rise (*v. irr.*).
asta *sf.* **1.** pole **2.** (*di bandiera*) flagstaff **3.** (*di occhiali*) bar **4.** (*di bilancia*) arm (of balance) **5.** (*vendita all'asta*) auction(-sale).
astante *agg.* present. ♦ **astante** *sm.* on-looker.
astemio *agg.* abstemious. ♦ **astemio** *sm.* teetotaller.
astenersi *vr.* to abstain.
astenìa *sf.* asthenia.
astensione *sf.* abstention.
astensionista *sm.* abstentionist.
asterisco *sm.* asterisk.
asteròide *sm.* asteroid.
asticciola *sf.* pothook.
astigmàtico *agg.* astigmatic.
astigmatismo *sm.* astigmatism.
astinenza *sf.* abstinence.
astio *sm.* resentment.
astiosamente *avv.* resentfully.
astioso *agg.* resentful.
astracàn *sm.* astrakhan.
astràgalo *sm.* **1.** (*bot.*) astragalus (*pl.* -li) **2.** (*arch.*) astragal.
astrale *agg.* astral.
astrarre *vt.* to abstract. ♦ **astrarsi** *vr.* to think (*v. irr.*) about sthg. else.
astrattismo *sm.* (*arte*) abstractionism.
astratto *agg.* abstract.
astrazione *sf.* abstraction.
astringente *agg. e sm.* astringent.
astro *sm.* star.
astrolabio *sm.* astrolabe.
astrologìa *sf.* astrology.
astròlogo *sm.* astrologer.
astronàuta *sm.* astronaut.
astronave *sf.* space-ship.
astronomìa *sf.* astronomy.
astronòmico *agg.* astronomic(al).
astrònomo *sm.* astronomer.
astrusità *sf.* abstruseness.
astruso *agg.* abstruse.
astuccio *sm.* case, box: — *per occhiali,* spectacle-case.
astuto *agg.* cunning.
astuzia *sf.* **1.** (*qualità*) cunning **2.** (*atto*) trick.

atassìa *sf.* ataxy.
atàvico *agg.* atavic.
atavismo *sm.* atavism.
ateismo *sm.* atheism.
àteo *agg.* atheistic. ♦ **àteo** *sm.* atheist.
atleta *sm.* athlete.
atlètica *sf.* athletics.
atlètico *agg.* athletic.
atmosfera *sf.* atmosphere.
atollo *sm.* atoll.
atòmico *agg.* atomic.
atomismo *sm.* atomism.
atomìstica *sf.* atomic theory.
atomizzatore *sm.* atomizer.
àtomo *sm.* (*anche fig.*) atom.
atonìa *sf.* atony.
àtono *agg.* atonic.
atrio *sm.* (entrance-)hall.
atroce *agg.* dreadful.
atrocità *sf.* atrocity.
atrofìa *sf.* atrophy.
atrofizzare *vt.* to atrophy.
atrofizzato *agg.* atrophic.
atropina *sf.* atropine.
attaccabottoni *sm.* buttonholer.
attaccabrighe *sm.* quarrelsome fellow.
attaccamento *sm.* attachment: *avere dell'—*, to entertain an attachment (for).
attaccante *sm.* attacker.
attaccapanni *sm.* cloak-stand.
attaccare *vt.* **1.** (*unire*) to attack **2.** (*appiccicare*) to stick (*v. irr.*) **3.** (*cucire*) to sew (*v. irr.*) **4.** (*assalire*) to attack **5.** (*mus.*) to open. ♦ **attaccarsi** *vr.* **1.** (*appigliarsi*) to cling (*v. irr.*) **2.** (*affezionarsi*) to become (*v. irr.*) fond of.
attaccatura *sf.* junction: *— della manica*, arm-hole.
attacchino *sm.* bill-poster.
attacco *sm.* **1.** (*mil.*) attack **2.** (*med.*) fit **3.** (*mecc.*) connection ‖ *— elettrico*, connecting plug.
attagliarsi *vr.* to suit.
attanagliare *vt.* to pinch.
attardarsi *vr.* to delay.
attecchire *vi.* **1.** to take (*v. irr.*) root **2.** (*aver fortuna*) to find (*v. irr.*) favour.
atteggiamento *sm.* attitude.
atteggiarsi *vr.* to assume an attitude: *— a vittima*, to pose as a victim.
attempato *agg.* elderly.
attendente *sm.* orderly.

attèndere *vt.* **1.** (*aspettare*) to wait for **2.** (*aspettarsi*) to expect **3.** (*accudire, frequentare*) to attend.
attendìbile *agg.* reliable.
attenere *vi.* to concern. ♦ **attenersi** *vr.* **1.** to cling (*v. irr.*) (on), (to) **2.** (*seguire*) to conform.
attentamente *avv.* **1.** attentively **2.** (*con cura*) carefully.
attentare *vi.* to attempt. ♦ **attentarsi** *vr.* to dare.
attentato *sm.* attempt (upon).
attenti *sm.* attention: *stare sull'—*, to stand (*v. irr.*) at attention.
attento *agg.* attentive, careful.
attenuante *agg.* extenuating.
attenuare *vt.* **1.** to attenuate **2.** (*giur.*) to extenuate.
attenuazione *sf.* **1.** attenuation **2.** (*di colpa*) extenuation.
attenzione *sf.* **1.** attention **2.** care: *fate —*, take care **3.** (*riguardo*) regard.
atterraggio *sm.* landing.
atterrare *vt.* to knock down. ♦ **atterrare** *vi.* (*aer.*) to land.
atterrire *vt.* to terrify. ♦ **atterrirsi** *vr.* to take (*v. irr.*) fright.
attesa *sf.* wait.
attestare *vt.* to attest.
attestato *sm.* **1.** certificate **2.** (*prova*) proof.
atticciato *agg.* sturdy.
àttico *sm.* attic.
attiguo *agg.* adjoining.
attillarsi *vr.* to spruce oneself up.
attillato *agg.* close-fitting.
àttimo *sm.* moment.
attinente *agg.* pertaining.
attinenza *sf.* relationship.
attìngere *vt.* to draw (*v. irr.*): *— acqua da un pozzo*, to draw water from a well; *— denaro da qu.*, to draw on so. for money.
attirare *vt.* to attract, to draw (*v. irr.*) (*anche fig.*).
attitùdine *sf.* turn, disposition.
attivare *vt.* to make (*v. irr.*) active.
attivista *s.* activist.
attività *sf.* **1.** activity **2.** (*comm.*) profit: *— e passività*, assets and liabilities.
attivizzare *vt.* to make (*v. irr.*) active.
attivo *agg.* active.
attizzare *vt.* to stir up.
attizzatoio *sm.* poker.
atto¹ *sm.* **1.** act **2.** (*azione*) action **3.** (*fatto*) deed: *un — buono*, a

good deed.

atto² *agg.* fit.

attònito *agg.* astonished.

attore *sm.* actor: — *cinematografico*, screen actor.

attorniare *vt.* to surround.

attorno *avv.* e *prep.* about, round, around: *non c'è nessuno* —, there is nobody about; — *alla tavola*, round the table; *le colline* — *al villaggio*, the hills around the village || *darsi d'*—, to busy oneself.

attraccaggio *sm.* mooring.

attraccare *vi.* to moor.

attraente *agg.* charming, attractive.

attrarre *vt.* to attract, to draw (*v. irr.*) (*anche fig.*).

attrattiva *sf.* attraction, appeal.

attraversamento *sm.* crossing.

attraversare *vt.* **1.** to cross **2.** (*ostacolare*) to thwart.

attraverso *avv.* **1.** (*di luogo*) across, through: — *il fiume*, across the river **2.** (*di tempo*) through.

attrazione *sf.* attraction, appeal.

attrezzare *vt.* to equip.

attrezzatura *sf.* equipment.

attrezzista *sm.* (*teat.*) property-man.

attrezzo *sm.* tool.

attribuire *vt.* **1.** to attribute **2.** (*assegnare*) to assign **3.** (*addossare*) to put (on).

attributo *sm.* attribute.

attribuzione *sf.* attribution.

attrice *sf.* actress: — *cinematografica*, screen actress.

attrito *sm.* **1.** friction **2.** (*fig.*) dissension.

attruppamento *sm.* trooping.

attrupparsi *vr.* to troop.

attuàbile *agg.* feasible.

attuale *agg.* present.

attualità *sf.* the moment: *cosa d'*—, topical question.

attualmente *avv.* at present.

attuare *vt.* to carry out.

attutire *vt.* to mitigate: — *un rumore*, to deaden a noise.

audace *agg.* bold.

audacia *sf.* boldness.

audiovisivo *agg.* audiovisual.

auditore *sm.* listener.

auditorio *sm.* **1.** auditorium **2.** (*pubblico*) audience.

audizione *sf.* **1.** (*fisiol.*) hearing **2.** (*teat.*) performance.

àuge *sm.* summit: *essere in* —, to enjoy great favour.

augurale *agg.* augural.

augurare *vt.* to wish.

augurio *sm.* wish || *auguri di Natale e Capodanno*, season's greetings.

augusto *agg.* august.

àula *sf.* hall, room: — *di scuola*, school-room.

aumentare *vt.* to increase.

aumento *sm.* increase.

àureo *agg.* **1.** gold **2.** (*dorato*) golden.

aurèola *sf.* halo.

auricola *sf.* auricle.

auricolare *agg.* auriculan.

aurifero *agg.* auriferous.

aurora *sf.* dawn (*anche fig.*).

auscultare *vt.* to auscultate.

auscultazione *sf.* auscultation.

ausiliare *agg.* auxiliary.

ausilio *sm.* **1.** help **2.** (*difesa*) defence.

auspicare *vt.* to augur.

auspicio *sm.* **1.** (*stor.*) auspice, omen: *di buon, cattivo* —, of good, ill omen **2.** (*augurio*) wish.

austerità *sf.* austerity.

austero *agg.* austere.

australe *agg.* austral.

australiano *agg.* e *sm.* Australian.

austrìaco *agg.* e *sm.* Austrian.

autarchìa *sf.* autarky.

autenticare *vt.* to certify.

autenticazione *sf.* authentication.

autenticità *sf.* authenticity.

autèntico *agg.* **1.** authentic **2.** (*genuino*) genuine.

autista *sm.* driver: — *di piazza*, taxi-driver.

àuto *sf.* car: — *da corsa*, racing car; — *aperta*, open car; — *di serie*, production-model car; — *fuori serie*, special-body car.

autoambulanza *sf.* ambulance.

auto-attrezzi *sf.* breakdown-lorry.

autobiografìa *sf.* autobiography.

autobiògrafo *sm.* autobiographer.

autoblinda *sf.* armoured car.

autobotte *sf.* tank truck.

àutobus *sm.* (motor-) bus.

autoclave *sf.* autoclave.

autocontrollo *sm.* self-control.

autòcrate *sm.* autocrat.

autocrazìa *sf.* autocracy.

autocrìtica *sf.* self-criticism.

autòctono *agg.* autochthonous. ◆ **autòctono** *sm.* native.

autodafé *sm.* auto-da-fé (*pl.* autos--da-fé).

autodeterminazione *sf.* self-determination.

autodidatta *s.* self-taught person.

autòdromo *sm.* motor-racing track.

autoeducazione *sf.* self-education.

autofinanziamento *sm.* self-financing.

autògeno *agg.* autogenous.

autogoverno *sm.* self-government.

autografare *vt.* to autograph.

autògrafo *agg.* autographic(al). ◆ **autògrafo** *sm.* autograph.

autolesione *sf.* self-injury.

autolesionismo *sm.* self-injuring.

autolettiga *sf.* ambulance.

autolìnea *sf.* bus line.

automa *sm.* automaton, robot.

automàtico *agg.* automatic: *pistola, fucile* —, automatic pistol, gun || *distributore* —, slot machine.

automatismo *sm.* automatism.

automazione *sf.* automation.

automòbile *sf.* V. *auto.*

automobilismo *sm.* motoring.

automobilista *sm.* motorist.

automotrice *sf.* rail-car.

autonoleggio *sm.* car rental.

autonomìa *sf.* autonomy: — *di volo,* flight range.

autonomismo *sm.* self-government.

autònomo *agg.* self-governing.

autoparco *sm.* car-park.

autopilota *sm.* automatic pilot.

autopompa *sf.* fire-engine.

autoposteggio *sm.* parking.

autopsìa *sf.* autopsy.

autoradio *sf.* car radio-set.

autore *sm.* author.

autorespiratore *sm.* aqualung.

autorévole *agg.* authoritative.

autorevolezza *sf.* authoritativeness.

autorimessa *sf.* garage.

autorità *sf.* authority.

autoritario *agg.* authoritative.

autoritratto *sm.* self-portrait.

autorizzare *vt.* **1.** (*dare autorità*) to empower **2.** (*permettere*) to permit.

autorizzazione *sf.* permission, consent.

autoscuola *sf.* driving school.

autostazione *sf.* filling station.

autostòp *sm.* hitch-hiking.

autostoppista *sm.* hitch-hiker.

autostrada *sf.* motor-way.

autosuggestione *sf.* auto-suggestion.

autotreno *sm.* motor-lorry.

autrice *sf.* authoress.

autunnale *agg.* autumnal.

autunno *sm.* autumn.

ava *sf.* **1.** grandmother **2.** (*antenata*) ancestress.

avallare *vt.* to guarantee.

avallo *sm.* guarantee.

avambraccio *sm.* forearm.

avamposto *sm.* outpost.

avanguardia *sf.* vanguard: *essere all'*—, to be in the van.

avannotto *sm.* fry.

avanscoperta *sf.* scouting party: *andare all'*—, to scout.

avanspettàcolo *sm.* introductory variety turn.

avanti *avv.* **1.** (*di luogo*) forward: *andare* —, to move forward **2.** (*a chi bussa*) « come in » **3.** (*di tempo*) before || (*di orologio*) fast: *il mio orologio è avanti di 20 minuti,* my watch is twenty minutes fast. ◆ **avanti** *prep.* before. ◆ **avanti che** *cong.* before (*con ger.*).

avantieri *avv.* the day before yesterday.

avanzamento *sm.* **1.** advancing **2.** (*progresso*) advancement **3.** (*promozione*) promotion.

avanzare *vt.* **1.** to advance **2.** (*fig.*) to put (*v. irr.*) forward **3.** (*promuovere*) to promote. ◆ **avanzare** *vi.* to advance. ◆ **avanzarsi** *vr.* to advance.

avanzata *sf.* advance.

avanzato *agg.* **1.** advanced **2.** (*promosso*) promoted.

avanzo *sm.* remnant || — *di galera,* jail-bird || — *di stoffa,* scrap of cloth.

avarìa *sf.* damage.

avariato *agg.* damaged.

avarizia *sf.* avarice.

avaro *agg.* avaricious.

avena *sf.* oats (*p*).

avere *vt.* **1.** (*general. e come v. ausiliare*) to have: *ho molti libri,* I have many books; *ho letto questo giornale,* I have read this newspaper **2.** (*possedere*) to own, to have got: *ha una grande casa,* he owns, has got a big house **3.** (*ottenere*) to get (*v. irr.*): *ebbi quell'impiego,* I got that job **4.** (*indossare*) to wear (*v. irr.*): *aveva (indosso) un abito rosso,* she was wearing a red dress **5.** (*dovere*) to have to: *ho molte cose da fare,*

I have many things to do **6.** (*di anni*) to be ... years old: *ho 10 anni*, I am ten years old.

aviatore *sm.* airman (*pl.* -men), pilot.

aviazione *sf.* **1.** aviation **2.** (*arma*) Air Force.

avicoltura *sf.* bird-rearing.

avidità *sf.* **1.** avidity **2.** (*ingordigia*) greed **3.** (*brama*) eagerness.

àvido *agg.* **1.** avid **2.** (*ingordo*) greedy **3.** (*desideroso*) eager.

aviere *sm.* airman (*pl.* -men).

aviogetto *sm.* jet(-plane).

aviolinea *sf.* airline.

aviotrasportare *vt.* to air-bear (*v. irr.*).

aviotrasporto *sm.* air-transport.

avitaminosi *sf.* avitaminosis.

avito *agg.* ancestral.

avo *sm.* **1.** grandfather **2.** (*antenato*) ancestor **3.** (*pl.*) forefathers.

avorio *sm.* ivory.

avulso *agg.* uprooted.

avvalersi *vr.* to avail oneself.

avvaloramento *sm.* strengthening.

avvalorare *vt.* **1.** to give (*v. irr.*) value to **2.** (*rafforzare*) to strengthen.

avvampare *vi.* to flare up (*anche fig.*).

avvantaggiare *vt.* to advantage, to better. ♦ **avvantaggiarsi** *vr.* to profit (by).

avvedersi *vr.* to perceive.

avvedutamente *avv.* shrewdly.

avvedutezza *sf.* shrewdness.

avveduto *agg.* shrewd.

avvelenamento *sm.* poisoning.

avvelenare *vt.* to poison.

avvelenatore *sm.* poisoner.

avvenente *agg.* charming, pretty.

avvenenza *sf.* charm, loveliness.

avvenimento *sm.* event.

avvenire[1] *vi. imp.* to happen.

avvenire[2] *sm.* future.

avventarsi *vr.* to throw (*v. irr.*) oneself.

avventatamente *avv.* rashly.

avventatezza *sf.* rashness.

avventato *agg.* rash.

avventizio *agg.* **1.** temporary **2.** (*giur.*) adventitious.

avvento *sm.* **1.** (*eccl.*) Advent **2.** arrival **3.** (*assunzione al trono*) accession.

avventore *sm.* customer.

avventura *sf.* adventure.

avventurarsi *vr.* to venture.

avventuriero *sm.* adventurer.

avventuroso *agg.* adventurous.

avverarsi *vr.* to come (*v. irr.*) true.

avverbiale *agg.* adverbial.

avverbio *sm.* adverb.

avversare *vt.* to oppose.

avversario *agg.* contrary. ♦ **avversario** *sm.* opponent.

avversione *sf.* aversion, dislike.

avversità *sf.* adversity, misfortune.

avverso *agg.* unfavourable.

avvertenza *sf.* **1.** (*avviso*) warning **2.** (*attenzione, cura*) attention, care.

avvertìbile *agg.* perceptible.

avvertimento *sm.* warning.

avvertire *vt.* **1.** (*avvisare*) to inform **2.** (*mettere in guardia*) to warn **3.** (*osservare*) to notice.

avvezzare *vt.* to accustom.

avvezzo *agg.* accustomed, used.

avviamento *sm.* starting.

avviare *vt.* to start.

avvicinamento *sm.* approach.

avvicinare *vt.* to approach. ♦ **avvicinarsi** *vr.* **1.** to approach **2.** (*essere simile*) to be similar.

avvicendare *vt.* to alternate. ♦ **avvicendarsi** *vr.* to alternate.

avvicendamento *sm.* alternation.

avvilente *agg.* **1.** discouraging **2.** (*umiliante*) humiliating.

avvilimento *sm.* **1.** dejection **2.** (*umiliazione*) humiliation.

avvilire *vt.* **1.** (*scoraggiare*) to dishearten **2.** (*umiliare*) to humiliate. ♦ **avvilirsi** *vr.* **1.** to lose heart **2.** (*umiliarsi*) to abase oneself.

avvilito *agg.* **1.** downcast **2.** (*umiliato*) humbled.

avviluppare *vt.* **1.** to wrap up **2.** (*aggrovigliare*) to entangle. ♦ **avvilupparsi** *vr.* **1.** to wrap oneself up **2.** (*aggrovigliarsi*) to get (*v. irr.*) entangled.

avvinazzarsi *vr.* to get (*v. irr.*) drunk.

avvinazzato *agg.* tipsy.

avvincente *agg.* engaging.

avvincere *vt.* to enthral.

avvinghiarsi *vr.* to cling (*v. irr.*).

avvìo *sm.* start: *prendere l'—*, to start off.

avvisaglia *sf.* (*primo segno*) foreshadowing.

avvisare *vt.* **1.** to inform, to let (*v. irr.*) know **2.** (*mettere in guardia*) to warn.

avviso *sm.* **1.** notice **2.** (*consiglio*) warning **3.** (*manifesto*) poster **4.**

(*opinione*) opinion.
avvistare *vt.* to sight.
avvitamento *sm.* spin.
avvitare *vt.* **1.** (*mecc.*) to screw **2.** (*aer.*) to spin.
avviticchiarsi *vr.* to twist round.
avvocato *sm.* **1.** lawyer **2.** (*civilista*) solicitor.
avvocatura *sf.* legal profession.
avvòlgere *vt.* **1.** to wrap (*anche* *fig.*) **2.** (*arrotolare*) to roll up.
avvolgimento *sm.* **1.** winding **2.** (*di pacchi*) wrapping up **3.** (*elettr.*) winding.
avvoltoio *sm.* vulture (*anche fig.*).
azalea *sf.* azalea.
azienda *sf.* firm, concern: — *industriale*, manufacturing concern; — *agricola*, farm.
aziendale *agg.* firm, concern.
àzimut *sm.* azimuth.
azimutale *agg.* azimuthal.
azionamento *sm.* working.
azionare *vt.* to set (*v. irr.*) in action, to work.
azionario *agg.* share: *capitale* —, share capital.
azione *sf.* **1.** action **2.** (*comm.*) share.
azionista *s.* shareholder.
azotare *vt.* to azotize.
azoto *sm.* azote.
azteco *agg. e sm.* Aztec.
azzannare *vt.* to seize in the jaws.
azzardare *vt.* to risk, to venture.
azzardo *sm.* hazard ‖ *gioco d'*—, game of chance.
azzeccare *vt.* to guess, to hit (*v. irr.*) the mark.
àzzimo *agg.* unleavened: *pane* —, unleavened bread.
azzoppare *vt.* to lame. ♦ **azzopparsi** *vr.* to become (*v. irr.*) lame.
azzuffarsi *vr.* to come (*v. irr.*) to blows.
azzurro *agg.* blue.
azzurrògnolo *agg.* bluish.

B

babbeo *sm.* blockhead.
babbo *sm.* father, daddy.
babbuccia *sf.* slipper.
babbuino *sm.* baboon.
babele *sf.* babel.
bacare *vi.* **bacarsi** *vr.* to rot.

bacato *agg.* rotten.
bacca *sf.* berry.
baccalà *sm.* stockfish.
baccanale *sm.* bacchanal.
baccano *sm.* uproar.
baccante *sf.* Bacchante.
baccarà *sm.* baccarat.
baccellierato *sm.* bachelorship.
baccelliere *sm.* bachelor.
baccello *sm.* pod.
bacchetta *sf.* **1.** rod **2.** (*di direttore d'orchestra*) baton **3.** (*di tamburo*) drumstick.
bacchettata *sf.* rod stroke.
bacchettone *sm.* bigot.
bacchiare *vt.* to beat (*v. irr.*) down.
bàcchico *agg.* Bacchic.
bacheca *sf.* show-case.
bachelite *sf.* bakelite.
bacherozzo *sm.* **1.** (*scarafaggio*) cockroach **2.** (*bruco*) maggot.
bachicoltura *sf.* silkworm breeding.
baciamano *sm.* hand-kissing.
baciapile *sm.* bigot.
baciare *vt.* to kiss. ♦ **baciarsi** *vr.* *rec.* to kiss each other.
bacile *sm.* basin.
bacillo *sm.* bacillus (*pl.* -li).
bacinella *sf.* basin.
bacino *sm.* **1.** basin **2.** (*anat.*) pelvis **3.** (*mar.*) dock: — *di carenaggio*, dry dock.
bacio *sm.* kiss.
baciucchiare *vt.* to kiss repeatedly.
baco *sm.* worm: — *da seta*, silkworm.
bada *sf.* (*nella loc.*) tenere a — *qu.*, to hold (*v. irr.*) so. at bay.
badare *vi.* to mind (so., sthg.): *senza* — *a spese*, regardless of expense.
badessa *sf.* abbess.
badìa *sf.* abbey.
badilante *sm.* navvy.
badile *sm.* shovel.
baffo *sm.* **1.** moustache: *portare i baffi*, to wear (*v. irr.*) a moustache ‖ *ridere sotto i baffi*, to laugh in one's sleeve **2.** (*sgorbio*) smear.
bagagliaio *sm.* luggage van.
bagaglio *sm.* luggage (*solo sing.*) ‖ *fare i bagagli*, to pack ‖ *disfare i bagagli*, to unpack.
bagarinaggio *sm.* cornering.
bagattella *sf.* trifle.
baggianata *sf.* **1.** (*azione*) foolish action **2.** (*discorso*) nonsense.
bagliore *sm.* flash.

bagnante *sm.* bather.
bagnare *vt.* 1. to wet 2. (*immergere*) to dip 3. (*di mare, fiume*) to wash. ♦ **bagnarsi** *vr.* 1. to get (*v. irr.*) wet 2. (*fare bagni in mare ecc.*) to bathe.
bagnato *agg.* wet.
bagnino *sm.* bathing attendant.
bagno *sm.* 1. bath: *far un —,* to take (*v. irr.*) a bath; *— di sole,* sun-bath 2. (*in mare ecc.*) bathe || *fare il —,* to bathe || *costume da —,* bathing-costume.
bagnomarìa *sm.* bain-marie.
bagordo *sm.* revelry.
baia[1] *sf.* (*scherzo*) joke || *dare la — a qu.,* to make (*v. irr.*) fun of so.
baia[2] *sf.* (*geogr.*) bay.
baionetta *sf.* bayonet.
bàita *sf.* Alpine hut.
balaustrata *sf.* balustrade.
balbettare *vt.* e *vi.* to stammer.
balbettìo *sm.* stammer.
balbuzie *sf.* stammer.
balbuziente *agg.* stammering. ♦ **balbuziente** *s.* stammerer.
balconata *sf.* balcony.
balcone *sm.* balcony.
baldacchino *sm.* canopy.
baldanza *sf.* boldness.
baldanzoso *agg.* bold.
baldo *agg.* bold.
baldoria *sf.* revel: *far —,* to make (*v. irr.*) merry.
balena *sf.* whale: *stecca di —,* whalebone.
balenare *vi.* 1. to lighten 2. (*di idea*) to flash.
baleno *sm.* lightning || *in un —,* in the twinkling of an eye.
balestra *sf.* 1. crossbow 2. (*mecc.*) leaf spring.
balia *sf.* wet nurse: *— asciutta,* dry-nurse.
balìa *sf.* mercy: *in — di,* at the mercy of.
balìstica *sf.* ballistics.
balla *sf.* 1. (*di cotone, di lana*) bale 2. (*volg.; fandonia*) tall story 3. (*fig.; mucchio*) heap.
ballare *vt.* e *vi.* to dance.
ballata *sf.* ballad.
ballatoio *sm.* gallery.
ballerina *sf.* 1. dancer 2. (*classica*) ballerina.
ballerino *sm.* 1. dancer 2. (*classico*) ballet-dancer.
balletto *sm.* ballet.

ballo *sm.* 1. dance 2. (*festa*) ball || *essere in —,* to be on the go; *tirare in —,* to call in question.
ballottaggio *sm.* second ballot.
balneare *agg.* bathing || *stazione —,* seaside resort.
balocco *sm.* toy.
balordàggine *sf.* 1. dullness 2. (*azione*) foolish action 3. (*discorso*) nonsense.
balordo *agg.* e *sm.* stupid.
balsàmico *agg.* balmy.
bàlsamo *sm.* balm.
baluardo *sm.* bulwark.
balza *sf.* 1. cliff 2. (*di vestito*) flounce.
balzano *agg.* 1. queer 2. (*di cavallo*) white-footed.
balzare *vi.* to jump.
balzo *sm.* jump: *cogliere la palla al —,* to seize an opportunity.
bambagia *sf.* cotton-wool.
bambina *sf.* 1. little girl, child (*pl.* children) 2. (*in fasce*) baby.
bambinaia *sf.* nurse.
bambino *sm.* 1. little boy, child (*pl.* children) 2. (*in fasce*) baby || *dare alla luce un —,* to bring (*v. irr.*) forth a child.
bamboccio *sm.* 1. (*bambola*) ragdoll 2. (*fig.*) simpleton.
bàmbola *sf.* doll.
bambù *sm.* bamboo.
banale *agg.* banal.
banalità *sf.* banality.
banana *sf.* banana.
banano *sm.* banana-tree.
banca *sf.* bank.
bancarella *sf.* stall.
bancario *agg.* bank: *libretto —,* passbook. ♦ **bancario** *sm.* bank clerk.
bancarotta *sf.* bankruptcy: *fare —,* to go (*v. irr.*) bankrupt.
banchetto *sm.* banquet.
banchiere *sm.* banker.
banchina *sf.* 1. (*molo*) wharf 2. (*terrapieno*) bank.
banchisa *sf.* ice-pack.
banco *sm.* 1. bench 2. (*di chiesa*) pew 3. (*di negozio*) counter 4. (*di nebbia, di sabbia, di gioco*) bank.
banconota *sf.* banknote.
banda *sf.* 1. (*lato*) side 2. (*mus.; striscia di stoffa*) band 3. (*di delinquenti*) gang.
banderuola *sf.* weathercock.
bandiera *sf.* flag, colours (*pl.*).
bandire *vt.* 1. to proclaim 2. (*esi-*

liare, eliminare) to banish.
bandito *sm.* outlaw.
bando *sm.* **1.** ban **2.** (*esilio*) banishment || *essere al* —, to be banished **3.** (*annunzio*) announcement.
bar *sm.* bar.
bara *sf.* coffin.
baracca *sf.* hut.
baraccone *sm.* booth.
baraonda *sf.* chaos.
barare *vi.* to cheat.
bàratro *sm.* abyss.
barattare *vt.* to exchange.
baratto *sm.* barter.
baràttolo *sm.* **1.** jar **2.** (*di metallo*) tin.
barba *sf.* beard: *fare, farsi la* —, to shave || (*fig.*) *in* — *a*, in spite of.
barbabiètola *sf.* beet-root.
barbarie *sf.* **1.** barbarousness **2.** (*crudeltà*) barbarity.
bàrbaro *agg. e sm.* barbarian.
barbiere *sm.* barber.
barbone *sm.* **1.** (*straccione*) tramp **2.** (*cane*) poodle.
barbuto *agg.* bearded.
barca *sf.* boat: *andare in* —, to go (*v. irr.*) boating.
barcaiolo *sm.* boatman (*pl.* -men).
barcamenarsi *vr.* to wangle.
barcollare *vi.* to stagger.
barcone *sm.* long boat.
bardare *vt.* to harness. ♦ **bardarsi** *vr.* to dress up.
barella *sf.* stretcher.
barile *sm.* barrel.
barista *sm.* barman (*pl.* -men). ♦ **barista** *sf.* barmaid.
baritonale *agg.* baritone.
barìtono *sm.* baritone.
barlume *sm.* glimmer.
baro *sm.* cheat.
barocco *agg. e sm.* baroque.
baromètrico *agg.* barometric(al).
baròmetro *sm.* barometer.
barone *sm.* baron.
baronessa *sf.* baroness.
barra *sf.* **1.** bar **2.** (*mar.*) helm.
barricare *vt.* to barricade.
barricata *sf.* barricade.
barriera *sf.* **1.** barrier **2.** (*fig.*) obstacle.
barrire *vi.* to trumpet.
barrito *sm.* trumpet.
barroccio *sm.* cart.
baruffa *sf.* quarrel.
barzelletta *sf.* joke.
basalto *sm.* basalt.

basamento *sm.* base.
basare *vt.* to base.
basco *agg. e sm.* Basque. ♦ **basco** *sm.* (*berretto*) beret.
base *sf.* base.
basette *sf. pl.* whiskers.
bàsico *agg.* basic.
basilare *agg.* basic.
basìlica *sf.* basilica.
basìlico *sm.* basil.
basilisco *sm.* basilisk.
bassezza *sf.* baseness.
basso *agg.* **1.** low **2.** (*di statura*) short **3.** (*abietto*) base. ♦ **basso** *avv.* low. ♦ **basso** *sm.* **1.** bottom **2.** (*mus.*) bass.
bassofondo *sm.* shallow || *i bassifondi della società*, the underworld.
bassopiano *sm.* lowland.
bassorilievo *sm.* bas-relief.
bassotto *agg.* thick-set. ♦ **bassotto** *sm.* (*cane*) dachshund.
bassoventre *sm.* belly.
basta *inter.* stop it!: — *con*, enough of.
bastardo *agg. e sm.* **1.** bastard **2.** (*di animali*) mongrel.
bastare *vi.* to be enough.
bastimento *sm.* ship.
bastione *sm.* **1.** rampart **2.** (*mil.*) bastion.
basto *sm.* pack-saddle.
bastonare *vt.* to cane.
bastonata *sf.* blow with a cane.
bastonatura *sf.* caning.
bastone *sm.* stick, staff.
batacchio *sm.* clapper.
batisfera *sf.* bathysphere.
batista *sf.* batiste.
batosta *sf.* blow.
batrace *sm.* batrachian.
battaglia *sf.* battle, fight || (*fig.*) *cavallo di* —, favourite subject, favourite piece.
battagliare *vi.* to battle, to fight (*v. irr.*), to struggle.
battagliero *agg.* **1.** warlike **2.** (*fig.*) fierce.
battaglione *sm.* battalion.
battelliere *sm.* boatman (*pl.* -men).
battello *sm.* boat.
battente *sm.* **1.** (*picchiotto*) knocker **2.** (*di porta*) wing.
bàttere *vt.* **1.** to beat (*v. irr.*), to strike (*v. irr.*) (*anche delle ore*) **2.** (*scrivere a macchina*) to type || — *le mani*, to clap hands; — *i piedi*, to stamp; *in un batter d'oc-*

chio, in the twinkling of an eye.
♦ **bàttere** *vi.* **1.** to knock **2.**
(*pulsare*) to throb. ♦ **bàttersi**
vr. to fight (*v. irr.*).

batterìa *sf.* **1.** battery **2.** (*da cucina*) kitchen utensils.

battèrio *sm.* bacterium (*pl.* -ia).

batteriologìa *sf.* bacteriology.

battésimo *sm.* baptism: *nome di* —, Christian name.

battezzare *vt.* to baptize.

battibaleno *sm.* (*nella loc. avv.*) *in un* —, in a twinkling.

battibecco *sm.* squabble.

batticuore *sm.* **1.** throb **2.** (*fig.*) fear.

battimano *sm.* clap.

battipanni *sm.* carpet-beater.

battistero *sm.* baptistery.

battistrada *sm.* **1.** outrider **2.** (*di pneumatico*) tread || *fare da* —, to lead (*v. irr.*) the way.

bàttito *sm.* **1.** beat **2.** (*mecc.*) knock.

battitore *sm.* **1.** beater **2.** (*cricket, baseball*) batsman (*pl.* -men).

battitura *sf.* thrashing.

battuta *sf.* **1.** beating: — *di caccia,* beating **2.** (*di spirito*) witty remark **3.** (*mus.*) bar **4.** (*teat.*) cue **5.** (*tennis*) service.

batùffolo *sm.* flock.

baule *sm.* trunk.

bauxite *sf.* bauxite.

bava *sf.* **1.** slaver **2.** (*di lumaca*) slime.

bavaglino *sm.* bib.

bavaglio *sm.* gag: *mettere il* — *a qu.* (*fig.*), to gag so.

bàvero *sm.* collar.

bazàr *sm.* bazaar.

bazza *sf.* slipper-chin.

bazzècola *sf.* trifle.

bazzicare *vt.* e *vi.* to frequent.

bazzotto *agg.* soft-boiled.

be' *inter.* well.

beare *vt.* to make (*v. irr.*) so. happy.
♦ **bearsi** *vr.* to rejoice (at).

beatificazione *sf.* beatification.

beatitùdine *sf.* beatitude.

beato *agg.* **1.** happy **2.** (*relig.*) blessed.

beccaccia *sf.* woodcock.

beccaccino *sm.* snipe.

beccare *vt.* **1.** to peck **2.** (*fam. per acchiappare*) to catch (*v. irr.*). ♦ **beccarsi** *vr.* **1.** (*procurarsi*) to get (*v. irr.*) **2.** (*litigare*) to quarrel.

beccata *sf.* peck.

beccheggiare *vi.* to pitch.

beccheggio *sm.* pitching.

becchime *sm.* birdseed.

becchino *sm.* grave-digger.

becco *sm.* **1.** beak **2.** (*caprone*) billy-goat **3.** (*fig.*) cuckold.

beccuccio *sm.* (*di teiera ecc.*) spout.

beduino *agg.* e *sm.* Bedouin.

befana *sf.* **1.** "befana" **2.** (*fig. fam.*) hag.

beffa *sf.* mockery: *farsi* — *di,* to laugh at; (*ingannare*) to make (*v. irr.*) a fool of.

beffardo *agg.* mocking. ♦ **beffardo** *sm.* mocker.

beffare *vt.* to mock. ♦ **beffarsi** *vr.* to laugh at.

beffeggiare *vt.* V. *beffare.*

bega *sf.* **1.** quarrel **2.** (*problema intricato*) entangled affair.

beghina *sf.* bigot.

begonia *sf.* (*bot.*) begonia.

belare *vi.* to bleat.

belato *sm.* bleat.

belga *agg.* e *sm.* Belgian.

bella *sf.* **1.** beauty **2.** (*innamorata*) sweetheart || *copiare in* —, to make (*v. irr.*) a fair copy.

belladonna *sf.* (*bot.; farm.*) belladonna.

belletto *sm.* rouge.

bellezza *sf.* beauty: *istituto di* —, beauty parlour.

bellicismo *sm.* warlikeness.

bèllico *agg.* **1.** war (*attributivo*) **2.** (*del tempo di guerra*) wartime.

bellicoso *agg.* warlike.

belligerante *agg.* e *sm.* belligerent.

belligeranza *sf.* belligerence.

bellimbusto *sm.* dandy.

bello *agg.* **1.** fine, beautiful **2.** (*di uomo*) handsome || *nel bel mezzo,* right in the middle. ♦ **bello** *sm.* **1.** (*la bellezza*) beauty **2.** (*innamorato*) sweetheart || *sul più* —, at the right moment; *ora viene il* —, now you'll hear the best of it.

belva *sf.* wild beast.

belvedere *sm.* **1.** observation post **2.** (*arch.*) belvedere.

bemolle *sm.* (*mus.*) flat.

benché *cong.* though.

benda *sf.* bandage.

bendaggio *sm.* bandage.

bendare *vt.* to bandage.

bene *sm.* good: *per il tuo* —, for your sake; *voler* —, to love. ♦

beni *sm. pl.* property || *— immo-bili*, real estate; *— di consumo*, consumer goods. ◆ **bene** *avv.* **1.** well **2.** (*molto*) very **3.** (*nientemeno*) no less than || *star —*, to be well; *andar —*, to suit.

benedetto *agg.* blessed.

benedire *vt.* to bless.

benedizione *sf.* blessing.

benefattore *sm.* benefactor.

beneficare *vt.* to help.

beneficenza *sf.* charity.

beneficiario *agg. e sm.* beneficiary.

beneficiata *sf.* benefit.

beneficio *sm.* **1.** benefit **2.** (*eccl.; giur.*) benefice.

benèfico *agg.* **1.** beneficent **2.** (*vantaggioso*) beneficial.

benemerenza *sf.* merit.

benemèrito *agg.* well-deserving.

beneplàcito *sm.* consent: *a tuo —*, as you like.

benèssere *sm.* welfare.

benestante *agg.* well-off. ◆ **benestante** *s.* well-to-do person.

benestare *sm.* assent.

benevolenza *sf.* benevolence.

benèvolo *agg.* benevolent.

bengala *sm.* Bengal light.

beniamino *sm.* darling.

benignità *sf.* **1.** benignity **2.** (*di clima*) mildness.

benigno *agg.* **1.** benign **2.** (*di clima*) mild.

beninteso *avv.* of course.

benpensante *agg.* sensible || *i benpensanti*, the right thinking.

benservito *sm.* testimonial.

bensì *cong.* but.

benvenuto *agg. sm. inter.* welcome || *dare il — a qu.*, to welcome so.

benvolere *vt.* to like: *farsi —*, to make (*v. irr.*) oneself liked.

benzina *sf.* petrol.

benzinaio *sm.* filling station attendant.

benzolo *sm.* benzol.

beone *sm.* drunkard.

beota *agg. e sm.* Boeotian.

bèrbero *agg. e sm.* Berber.

berciare *vi.* to bawl.

bere *vt.* to drink (*v. irr.*) || *darla a —* (*fig.*), to tell (*v. irr.*) tall stories.

bergamotto *sm.* (*bot.; farm.*) bergamot.

berillo *sm.* beryllium.

berlina *sf.* **1.** (*carrozza*) berline **2.** (*automobile*) limousine **3.** (*gogna*) pillory: *mettere alla —*, to pillory.

bernòccolo *sm.* bump.

berretta *sf.* cap.

berretto *sm.* cap.: *— con visiera*, peaked cap.

bersagliare *vt.* **1.** to shoot (*v. irr.*) (at) **2.** (*fig.*) to torment.

bersaglio *sm.* target: *tiro al —*, target-shooting || *colpire il —*, to hit (*v. irr.*) the mark.

besciamella *sf.* cream-sauce.

bestemmia *sf.* swear.

bestemmiare *vi.* to swear (*v. irr.*).

bestia *sf.* beast || *montare in —*, to lose (*v. irr.*) one's temper.

bestiale *agg.* beastly.

bestialità *sf.* **1.** beastliness **2.** (*fig.*) foolishness || *dire —*, to talk non-sense; *fare —*, to make (*v. irr.*) blunders.

bestiame *sm.* cattle.

béttola *sf.* tavern.

betulla *sf.* birch.

bevanda *sf.* drink.

beveraggio *sm.* beverage.

bevitore *sm.* drinker.

bevuta *sf.* **1.** draught **2.** (*il bere*) drinking.

biada *sf.* fodder.

biancastro *agg.* whitish.

biancheggiare *vi. e vt.* **1.** (*essere bianco*) to be white **2.** (*diventare, far diventare bianco*) to whiten.

biancherìa *sf.* linen.

bianco *agg.* white || *in —*, blank; *di punto in —*, suddenly.

biancore *sm.* whiteness.

biancospino *sm.* hawthorn.

biascicare *vt.* to mumble.

biasimare *vt.* to blame.

biasimévole *agg.* blamable.

biàsimo *sm.* blame.

Bibbia *sf.* Bible.

bìbita *sf.* drink.

bìblico *agg.* biblical.

bibliografìa *sf.* bibliography.

bibliogràfico *agg.* bibliographic(al).

biblioteca *sf.* **1.** library **2.** (*scaffale*) bookcase.

bibliotecario *sm.* librarian.

bica *sf.* stack.

bicamerale *agg.* (*pol.*) bicameral.

bicarbonato *sm.* bicarbonate.

bicchiere *sm.* glass.

bicèfalo *agg.* V. *bicipite*.

bicicletta *sf.* bicycle: *andare in —*, to cycle.

bicìpite *agg.* two-headed. ◆ **bicìpite** *sm.* biceps.

bicocca *sf.* hut.
bicolore *agg.* two-coloured.
bidè *sm.* bidet.
bidello *sm.* porter.
bidente *sm.* pitchfork.
bidone *sm.* **1.** can **2.** (*fam.*) swindle.
bieco *agg.* sinister.
biella *sf.* (*mecc.*) connecting rod.
biennale *agg.* biennial.
bietola *sf.* beet.
biennio *sm.* biennium (*pl.* -nia).
bifase *agg.* (*elettr.*) two-phase.
bifolco *sm.* boor.
biforcarsi *vr.* to fork.
biforcazione *sf.* fork.
biforcuto *agg.* forked.
bigamìa *sf.* bigamy.
bìgamo *agg.* bigamous. ♦ **bìgamo**
sm. bigamist.
bighellonare *vi.* to lounge.
bighellone *sm.* lounger.
bigio *agg.* grey.
bigiotterìa *sf.* trinkets (*pl.*).
biglia *sf.* (biliard-)ball.
bigliettaio *sm.* **1.** conductor **2.** (*di stazione*) booking-clerk.
biglietterìa *sf.* **1.** booking-office **2.** (*di teatro*) box-office.
biglietto *sm.* **1.** card: — *di visita*, visiting card **2.** (*di tram ecc.*) ticket: — *di andata e ritorno*, return ticket; *mezzo* —, half-fare ticket **3.** (*banconota*) bank-note.
bigodino *sm.* (hair-)curler.
bigotto *agg.* bigoted. ♦ **bigotto**
sm. bigot.
bikini *sm.* bikini.
bilancia *sf.* balance, scales (*pl.*).
bilanciare *vt.* to balance.
bilanciere *sm.* **1.** balance-wheel **2.** (*mar.*) outrigger.
bilancio *sm.* budget: *fare il* —, to strike (*v. irr.*) the balance.
bilaterale *agg.* bilateral.
bile *sf.* **1.** bile **2.** (*ira*) anger.
biliardo *sm.* billiards (*pl.*).
bìlico *sm.* **1.** balance **2.** (*fig.*) uncertainty ‖ *mettere in* —, to balance; *stare in* —, to be balanced.
bilingue *agg.* bilingual.
bilione *sm.* billion.
bilioso *agg.* bilious.
bimba *sf.* V. *bambina.*
bimbo *sm.* V. *bambino.*
bimensile *agg.* fortnightly.
bimestrale *agg.* bimestrial.
bimestre *sm.* (period of) two months.

bimotore *agg.* two-engined: *aereo*
—, two-engined plane.
binario *sm.* track: — *morto*, dead-end track.
binòcolo *sm.* binoculars (*pl.*).
binomio *sm.* binomial.
biòccolo *sm.* flock: — *di neve*, snow-flake.
biochìmica *sf.* biochemistry.
biofìsica *sf.* biophysics.
biografìa *sf.* biography.
biogràfico *agg.* biographic(al).
biògrafo *sm.* biographer.
biologìa *sf.* biology.
biològico *agg.* biologic(al).
biòlogo *sm.* biologist.
biondo *agg.* fair.
biosfera *sf.* biosphere.
biòssido *sm.* dioxide.
bipartizione *sf.* bipartition.
bìpede *agg. e sm.* biped.
biplano *sm.* biplane.
bipolare *agg.* bipolar.
birba *sf.* scapegrace.
birbante *s.* rogue.
birbonata *sf.* knavery.
birbone *sm.* rogue.
bireattore *sm.* two-engined jet.
birichino *sm.* urchin. ♦ **birichino**
agg. naughty.
birillo *sm.* skittle.
biro *sf.* ball-point pen.
biroccio *sm.* cart.
birra *sf.* beer.
birrerìa *sf.* **1.** beer-house **2.** (*fabbrica*) brewery.
bisaccia *sf.* packsack.
bisbètico *agg.* cantankerous.
bisbigliare *vt.* to whisper.
bisbiglio *sm.* whisper.
bisboccia *sf.* spree: *far* —, to revel.
bisca *sf.* gambling-house.
biscia *sf.* snake.
biscotto *sm.* biscuit.
bisessuale *agg.* bisexual.
bisestile *agg. anno* —, leap year.
bisettimanale *agg.* bi-weekly.
bisettrice *sf.* bisector.
bisìllabo *agg.* disyllabic. ♦ **bisìllabo**
sm. disyllable.
bislacco *agg.* odd.
bislungo *agg.* oblong.
bismuto *sm.* bismuth.
bisnipote *s.* great-grandchild (*pl.* -children).
bisnonna *sf.* great-grandmother.
bisnonno *sm.* great-grandfather.
bisognare *vi. imp.* to be necessary, must.

bisogno *sm.* **1.** need **2.** (*povertà*) necessity || *aver* —, to need.

bisognoso *agg.* needy.

bisonte *sm.* bison.

bissare *vt.* to give (*v. irr.*) an encore (of sthg.).

bistecca *sf.* beefsteak.

bisticciare *vi.* to squabble.

bisticcio *sm.* **1.** squabble **2.** (*gioco di parole*) pun.

bistrattare *vt.* to ill-treat.

bistro *sm.* bistre.

bisturi *sm.* lancet.

bitòrzolo *sm.* bump.

bitume *sm.* bitumen.

bivacco *sm.* bivouac.

bivalente *agg.* bivalent.

bivio *sm.* **1.** fork **2.** (*fig.*) alternative.

bizantino *agg. e sm.* Byzantine.

bizza *sf.* freak || *fare le bizze*, to be peevish.

bizzarria *sf.* **1.** peculiarity **2.** (*cosa*) curiosity **3.** (*atto, detto*) extravagance.

bizzarro *agg.* strange.

bizzoso *agg.* **1.** freakish **2.** (*irascibile*) irascible.

blandire *vt.* to soothe.

blandizia *sf.* blandishment.

blando *agg.* bland.

blasone *sm.* **1.** blazon **2.** (*nobiltà*) nobility.

blaterare *vi. e vt.* to prate.

bleso *agg.* lisping || *pronuncia blesa*, lisp. ♦ **bleso** *sm.* lisper.

blindare *vt.* (*mil.*) to armour.

bloccare *vt.* to block, to stop. ♦ **bloccarsi** *vr.* to jam.

blocco *sm.* **1.** block **2.** (*mil.*) blockade.

blu *agg. e sm.* blue.

bluff *sm.* bluff.

blusa *sf.* blouse.

boa[1] *sf.* (*mar.*) buoy.

boa[2] *sm.* (*zool.*) boa.

bobina *sf.* bobbin.

bocca *sf.* mouth: — *da incendio*, fire-plug; — *dello stomaco*, pit of the stomach; *chiudere la* — *a qu.*, to silence so.

boccaccia *sf.* grimace.

boccale *sm.* jug.

boccaporto *sm.* hatchway.

boccata *sf.* mouthful.

boccheggiare *vi.* to gasp.

bocchino *sm.* mouthpiece.

boccia *sf.* **1.** water-bottle **2.** (*sport*) bowl.

bocciare *vt.* **1.** (*respingere*) to reject **2.** (*agli esami*) to fail.

bocciatura *sf.* failure.

boccio *sm.* bud.

boccone *sm.* **1.** bit **2.** (*boccata*) mouthful **3.** (*esca*) bait.

bocconi *avv.* lying face downwards.

boia *sm.* executioner.

boicottare *vt.* to boycott.

bolgia *sf.* **1.** (*fig.*) bedlam **2.** (*di inferno*) pit.

bòlide *sm.* (*astr.*) bolide.

bolla *sf.* **1.** bubble **2.** (*vescica*) blister **3.** (*eccl.*) bull.

bollare *vt.* **1.** (*timbrare*) to stamp **2.** (*a fuoco e fig.*) to brand.

bollato *agg.* **1.** stamped: *carta bollata*, stamped paper **2.** (*a fuoco e fig.*) branded.

bollente *agg.* boiling.

bolletta *sf.* **1.** bill **2.** (*ricevuta*) receipt || *essere in* — (*fig.*), to be (*v. irr.*) penniless.

bollettario *sm.* counterfoil-book.

bollettino *sm.* **1.** bulletin **2.** (*comm.*) list, note.

bollire *vi. e vt.* to boil.

bollito *sm.* boiled meat.

bollitore *sm.* **1.** boiler **2.** (*bricco*) kettle.

bollitura *sf.* boiling.

bollo *sm.* stamp.

bollore *sm.* **1.** boil **2.** (*fig.*) excitement.

bolscevico *agg. e sm.* Bolshevist.

bolscevismo *sm.* Bolshevism.

boma *sf.* (*mar.*) boom.

bomba *sf.* bomb.

bombardamento *sm.* bombardment.

bombardare *vt.* to bombard; (*generalmente da aereo*) to bomb.

bombardiere *sm.* **1.** (*soldato*) bombardier **2.** (*aereo*) bomber.

bombetta *sf.* bowler.

bòmbola *sf.* bottle.

bomboniera *sf.* candy-box.

bonaccia *sf.* dead calm.

bonaccione *agg.* good-natured. ♦ **bonaccione** *sm.* good-natured man (*pl.* men).

bonarietà *sf.* good nature.

bonario *agg.* good-natured, friendly.

bonìfica *sf.* reclamation.

bonificare *vt.* **1.** to reclaim **2.** (*comm.*) to grant an allowance.

bonomìa *sf.* good nature.

bontà *sf.* goodness.

bonzo *sm.* bonze.

borbottare *vi. e vt.* **1.** to mumble

2. (*lamentarsi*) to grumble.
borbottìo *sm.* 1. mumbling 2. (*protesta*) grumbling.
bordare *vt.* to border.
bordeggiare *vi.* to tack.
bordello *sm.* bawdyhouse.
bordo *sm.* 1. edge 2. (*mar.*) board: *a* —, on board.
bordura *sf.* border.
bòrea *sf.* Boreas.
boreale *agg.* boreal: *aurora* —, aurora borealis.
borgata *sf.* village.
borghese *agg.* 1. middle-class 2. (*comune*) plain 3. (*civile*) civilian: *in* —, in civilian dress. ♦ **borghese** *s.* middle-class person.
borghesìa *sf.* middle class(es): *l'alta* —, the upper middle class(es); *la piccola* —, the lower middle class(es).
borgo *sm.* village.
borgomastro *sm.* burgomaster.
boria *sf.* arrogance.
bòrico *agg.* boric.
borioso *agg.* arrogant.
borotalco *sm.* talcum powder.
borraccia *sf.* flask.
borsa[1] *sf.* bag || — *per documenti*, brief case; — *di studio*, scholarship.
borsa[2] *sf.* (*comm.*) Stock Exchange.
borsaiolo *sm.* pickpocket.
borseggiare *vt.* to pick pockets.
borsellino *sm.* purse.
borsetta *sf.* (hand-)bag.
boscaglia *sf.* brushwood.
boscaiolo *sm.* woodman (*pl.* -men).
boschetto *sm.* grove.
bosco *sm.* wood.
boscoso *agg.* woody.
bòssolo *sm.* cartridge-case.
botànica *sf.* botany.
bòtola *sf.* trap-door.
botta *sf.* 1. blow 2. (*battuta*) sarcastic remark || *dare un sacco di botte a qu.*, to whack so.
botte *sf.* barrel.
bottega *sf.* shop.
bottegaio *sm.* shop-keeper.
bottiglia *sf.* bottle.
bottiglierìa *sf.* wine shop.
bottino *sm.* booty: *far* —, to plunder.
botto *sm.* blow || *di* —, suddenly.
bottone *sm.* button || *attaccare un* — (*fig.*), to buttonhole.
bovaro *sm.* cowherd.
bovini *sm. pl.* cattle (*sing.*).

bozza *sf.* 1. (*gonfiore*) swelling 2. (*tip.*) proof 3. (*abbozzo*) draft || *correggere le bozze*, to proofread.
bozzetto *sm.* sketch.
bòzzolo *sm.* cocoon.
braccare *vt.* to hunt.
braccetto (*nella loc. avv.*) *a* —, arm-in-arm.
bracciale *sm.* 1. (*fascia che si porta al braccio*) arm-band 2. (*braccialetto*) bracelet.
braccialetto *sm.* bracelet.
bracciante *sm.* labourer.
bracciata *sf.* 1. armful 2. (*di nuoto*) stroke.
braccio *sm.* arm: *essere in* — *a qu.*, to be in so.'s arms || — *di mare*, sound.
bracco *sm.* hound.
bracconaggio *sm.* poaching.
bracconiere *sm.* poacher.
brace *sf.* embers (*pl.*).
brache *sf. pl.* 1. trousers 2. (*mutande*) drawers.
brachicèfalo *agg.* brachycephalous.
braciere *sm.* brazier.
braciola *sf.* chop.
bradicardìa *sf.* (*med.*) bradycardia.
brado *agg.* wild.
brama *sf.* longing.
bramare *vt.* to long for (sthg.).
bramosìa *sf.* covetousness.
bramoso *agg.* eager for (sthg.).
branca *sf.* 1. claw 2. (*settore*) branch.
branchia *sf.* gill.
branco *sm.* 1. herd 2. (*di pecore*) flock 3. (*di pesci*) shoal 4. (*di lupi e fig.*) pack.
brancolare *vi.* to grope.
branda *sf.* 1. camp-bed 2. (*mar.*) bunk.
brandello *sm.* 1. rag 2. (*pezzetto*) bit || *coi vestiti a brandelli*, in rags; *fare a brandelli*, to tear (*v. irr.*) up.
brandire *vt.* to brandish.
brano *sm.* piece.
brasato *sm.* braised beef.
brasiliano *agg. e sm.* Brazilian.
bravata *sf.* bravado.
bravo *agg.* clever, good || —!, well done!; *su, da* —!, be a good boy!
bravura *sf.* 1. cleverness 2. (*coraggio*) bravery || (*mus.*) *pezzo di* —, bravura.
breccia *sf.* breach: *essere sulla* —, to stand (*v. irr.*) in the breach.
brefotrofio *sm.* foundling hospital.

bretella *sf.* brace.
breve *agg.* short.
brevettare *vt.* to patent.
brevetto *sm.* patent.
breviario *sm.* breviary.
brevità *sf.* brevity.
brezza *sf.* breeze.
bricco *sm.* kettle, pot.
bricconata *sf.* roguish trick.
briccone *sm.* rogue.
briciola *sf.* crumb.
briciolo *sm.* bit.
briga *sf.* 1. trouble 2. (*lite*) quarrel:
attaccar —, to pick a quarrel.
brigadiere *sm.* 1. « brigadiere » 2.
(*ufficiale nell'Esercito Britannico
assegnato al comando di brigata*)
brigadier.
brigante *sm.* robber.
brigantino *sm.* (*mar.*) brig.
brigare *vi.* to intrigue.
brigata *sf.* 1. party 2. (*mil.*) brigade.
briglia *sf.* bridle || *a* — *sciolta*, at
full gallop.
brillante *agg.* e *sm.* brilliant.
brillantina *sf.* brilliantine.
brillare *vi.* to shine (*v. irr.*). ♦
brillare *vt.* 1. (*riso ecc.*) to hull
2. (*una mina*) to blast.
brillo *agg.* tipsy.
brina *sf.* hoarfrost.
brinare *vi. imp.*: *ha brinato*, there
has been a frost.
brinata *sf.* hoarfrost.
brindare *vi.* to toast: — *a qu.*, to
toast so.
brindello *sm.* rag.
brindisi *sm.* toast.
brio *sm.* liveliness.
brioso *agg.* lively.
britànnico *agg.* British.
brìvido *sm.* 1. shiver 2. (*di paura,
orrore*) shudder.
brizzolato *agg.* grizzled.
brocca *sf.* jug.
broccato *sm.* brocade.
bròccolo *sm.* broccoli.
brodaglia *sf.* slops (*pl.*).
brodo *sm.* broth.
broglio *sm.* intrigue: — *elettorale*, gerry-mander.
bromo *sm.* bromine.
bromuro *sm.* bromide.
bronchiale *agg.* bronchial.
bronchite *sf.* bronchitis.
broncio *sm.* pout || *fare il* —, to
pout.
bronco *sm.* bronchus (*pl.* -chi).

broncopolmonite *sf.* bronchopneu-
monia.
brontolare *vi.* e *vt.* to grumble.
brontolìo *sm.* grumbling.
brontolone *sm.* grumbler.
brontosàuro *sm.* brontosaurus.
brònzeo *agg.* 1. bronze (*attributivo*)
2. (*simile a bronzo*) bronzy.
bronzo *sm.* bronze || *faccia di* —,
brazen-faced person.
brossura *sf.* paper-back binding ||
in —, paper-bound.
brucare *vt.* to browse (on).
bruciacchiare *vt.* to scorch.
bruciacchiatura *sf.* scorching.
bruciapelo (*nella loc. avv.*) *a* —,
point-blank.
bruciare *vt.* e *vi.* to burn (*v. irr.*).
bruciatore *sm.* burner.
bruciatura *sf.* burn.
bruciore *sm.* burning, smart (*anche
fig.*).
bruco *sm.* caterpillar.
brùffolo *sm.* pimple.
brughiera *sf.* heath.
brulicare *vi.* to swarm (with).
brulichìo *sm.* swarm.
brullo *agg.* bare.
bruma *sf.* mist.
brumoso *agg.* misty.
brunire *vt.* to burnish.
brunitura *sf.* burnishing.
bruno *agg.* brown.
bruscamente *avv.* roughly.
brusco *agg.* 1. rough 2. (*di sapore*)
sour.
brusìo *sm.* buzz.
brutale *agg.* brutal.
brutalità *sf.* brutality.
bruto *agg.* e *sm.* brute.
bruttezza *sf.* ugliness.
brutto *agg.* 1. ugly 2. (*cattivo*)
bad.
bruttura *sf.* 1. ugly thing 2. (*azione*) base action.
bùbbola *sf.* lie.
bubbone *sm.* bubo.
bubbònico *agg.* bubonic.
buca *sf.* hole: — *delle lettere*,
letter-box.
bucaneve *sm.* snowdrop.
bucaniere *sm.* buccaneer.
bucare *vt.* 1. to pierce 2. (*una gomma*) to puncture 3. (*biglietti*) to
punch.
bucato *sm.* 1. washing 2. (*i panni*)
laundry.
buccia *sf.* peel.
bucherellare *vt.* to riddle.

buco *sm.* hole.

bucòlico *agg.* bucolic.

buddismo *sm.* Buddhism.

buddista *s.* Buddhist.

budello *sm.* **1.** bowel **2.** (*strada stretta*) alley **3.** (*tubo*) narrow tube.

budino *sm.* pudding.

bue *sm.* ox (*pl.* oxen): *carne di —*, beef.

bùfalo *sm.* buffalo.

bufera *sf.* **1.** storm **2.** (*di vento*) gale.

buffetto *sm.* fillip: *dare un —*, to fillip.

buffo *agg.* funny || *opera buffa*, comic opera.

buffonata *sf.* buffoonery.

buffone *sm.* **1.** clown, fool **2.** (*di corte*) court jester **3.** (*fig.*) unreliable person.

bugìa *sf.* **1.** lie **2.** (*portacandela*) flat candlestick.

bugiardo *agg.* false. ♦ **bugiardo** *sm.* liar.

bugigàttolo *sm.* lumber-room.

buio *agg.* e *sm.* dark: *— pesto*, pitch dark.

bulbo *sm.* **1.** bulb **2.** (*di occhio*) eyeball.

bùlgaro *agg.* e *sm.* Bulgarian.

bulinare *vt.* to engrave.

bulino *sm.* burin.

bullonare *vt.* (*mecc.*) to bolt.

bullone *sm.* bolt.

buonanotte *sf.* good night.

buonasera *sf.* good evening.

buoncostume *sm.*: *squadra del —*, vice squad.

buongiorno *sm.* **1.** (*di mattina*) good morning **2.** (*di pomeriggio*) good afternoon **3.** (*a ogni ora incontrandosi, fam.*) hullo **4.** (*a ogni ora lasciandosi*) goodbye.

buongustaio *sm.* gourmet.

buongusto *sm.* good taste.

buono *agg.* **1.** good **2.** (*di tempo*) fine || *alla buona*, informal; *a buon diritto*, by right; *di buon grado*, willingly. ♦ **buono** *sm.* **1.** good **2.** (*persona*) good person **3.** (*comm.*) bond **4.** (*tagliando*) coupon.

buonsenso *sm.* (common) sense.

buontempone *sm.* merry fellow.

buonumore *sm.* V. *umore.*

buonuomo *sm.* **1.** good-natured man (*pl.* men) **2.** simple man (*pl.* men).

burattinaio *sm.* puppet showman (*pl.* -men).

burattino *sm.* puppet.

burbanzoso *agg.* haughty.

bùrbero *agg.* gruff.

burla *sf.* trick || *per —*, in fun.

burlare *vt.* to play a trick on (so.). ♦ **burlarsi** *vr.* to make (*v. irr.*) fun of.

burlesco *agg.* farcical.

burlone *sm.* joker.

buròcrate *sm.* bureaucrat.

burocràtico *agg.* bureaucratic.

burocrazìa *sf.* bureaucracy; (*in Inghilterra*) Civil Service.

burrasca *sf.* storm.

burrascoso *agg.* stormy

burrificio *sm.* dairy.

burro *sm.* butter.

burrone *sm.* ravine.

burroso *agg.* buttery.

buscarsi *vr.* to get (*v. irr.*) || *buscarle*, to get a thrashing.

bussare *vi.* to knock: *— alla porta*, to knock at the door.

busse *sf. pl.* blows: *prendere le —*, to get (*v. irr.*) a thrashing.

bùssola *sf.* compass: *perdere la —* (*fig.*), to lose (*v. irr.*) one's head.

bussolotto *sm.* dice-box || *fare il giuoco dei bussolotti* (*anche fig.*), to juggle.

busta *sf.* **1.** envelope **2.** (*astuccio*) case.

bustarella *sf.* bribe.

bustina *sf.* (*mil.*) service cap.

busto *sm.* **1.** bust **2.** (*indumento per donna*) corset.

butano *sm.* (*chim.*) butane.

buttare *vt.* **1.** to throw (*v. irr.*) **2.** (*sprecare*) to waste || *— all'aria*, to upset (*v. irr.*); *— a terra*, to knock down.

butterato *agg.* pitted.

buzzo *sm.* belly || *di — buono*, very eagerly.

C

càbala *sf.* cab(b)ala.

cabalìstico *agg.* cab(b)alistic(al).

cabina *sf.* **1.** box, hut: *— balneare*, bathing hut; *— telefonica*, telephone box **2.** (*aer.; mar.*) cabin.

cablogramma *sm.* cable.

cabotaggio *sm.* cabotage: *nave di piccolo —,* coasting vessel.

cacao *sm.* **1.** (*bot.*) cacao **2.** (*polvere, bevanda*) cocoa.

cacare *vi.* to evacuate one's bowels.

cacarella *sf.* diarrhoea.

cacatoa, cacatùa *sm.* cockatoo.

cacca *sf.* excrement.

caccia *sf.* hunt, hunting || *— grossa,* big game || *cane da —,* sporting dog; *stagione di —,* shooting season; *andare a —,* to go (*v. irr.*) hunting; *andare a — di uccelli,* to go shooting. ♦ **caccia** *sm.* (*aer.*) fighter.

cacciagione *sf.* game.

cacciare *vt.* **1.** to hunt **2.** (*mil.; mar.*) to chase **3.** (*scacciare*) to expel **4.** (*mettere*) to put (*v. irr.*).

cacciatore *sm.* hunter (*anche fig.*).

cacciatorpediniere *sf.* (torpedo--boat) destroyer.

cacciavite *sm.* screwdriver.

cachi *sm.* persimmon.

cacio *sm.* cheese || *essere alto come un soldo di —,* to be very short.

cacofonìa *sf.* cacophony.

cactus *sm.* cactus (*pl.* cacti).

cadauno *agg. e pron. indef.* each.

cadàvere *sm.* corpse.

cadavèrico *agg.* **1.** corpse-like **2.** (*pallido*) deadly pale.

cadente *agg.* **1.** falling **2.** (*di astri*) setting || *stella —,* shooting star || *età —,* decrepit old age.

cadenza *sf.* **1.** cadence **2.** (*ritmo*) rhythm **3.** (*accento*) accent.

cadere *vi.* **1.** to fall (*v. irr.*) (*anche fig.*): *— bocconi,* to fall flat on one's face; *— in mare,* to fall overboard; *— addormentato,* to fall asleep; *— a proposito,* to fall in the nick of time; *— dal sonno,* to be overcome by sleep; *— nell'errore,* to fall into error || *far —,* to knock down; (*fig.*) to bring (*v. irr.*) about the fall of **2.** (*tramontare, di astri*) to set (*v. irr.*) **3.** (*calare*) to drop **4.** (*far fiasco*) to fail.

cadetto *agg. e sm.* cadet.

caducità *sf.* caducity.

caduco *agg.* perishable, decaying.

caduta *sf.* **1.** fall, falling **2.** (*fig.*) downfall, ruin **3.** (*fis.*) drop.

caffè *sm.* **1.** coffee: *— macinato,* ground coffee; *— nero,* black coffee **2.** (*locale*) coffee-house.

caffeina *sf.* caffeine.

caffettiera *sf.* coffee-pot.

cafone *sm.* boor.

cagionévole *agg.* sickly, weak.

cagliarsi *vr.* to curdle.

cagna *sf.* bitch.

cagnara *sf.* **1.** furious barking **2.** (*fig.*) uproar.

cagnesco *agg.* *in —,* surlily || *guardare in —,* to scowl at.

cagnolino *s. z.* **1.** (*cucciolo*) puppy **2.** (*cane piccolo*) small dog.

caimano *sm.* cayman.

cala *sf.* **1.** creek **2.** (*mar.*) hold.

calabrone *sm.* hornet.

calamaio *sm.* ink-stand.

calamaro *sm.* calamary.

calamita *sf.* magnet (*anche fig.*).

calamità *sf.* calamity, misfortune.

calamitare *vt.* to magnetize (*anche fig.*).

calamitoso *agg.* calamitous.

calandra *sf.* **1.** (*zool.*) wood-lark **2.** (*mecc.*) calender.

calare *vt.* to lower, to drop || *cala la tela,* the curtain drops. ♦ **calare** *vi.* **1.** to descend **2.** (*di astri*) to set (*v. irr.*) **3.** (*di febbre*) to abate **4.** (*comm.*) to fall (*v. irr.*). ♦ **calarsi** *vr.* to let (*v. irr.*) oneself down.

calata *sf.* descent.

calca *sf.* crowd.

calcagno *sm.* heel || *stare alle calcagna di qu.,* to follow so. closely.

calcare[1] *vt.* **1.** to tread (*v. irr.*) **2.** (*premere*) to press down || *— la mano* (*fig.*), to exaggerate.

calcare[2] *sm.* limestone.

calcàreo *agg.* calcareous.

calce *sf.* lime || *in —* (*loc. avv.*), at the foot.

calcestruzzo *sm.* concrete.

calciare *vi.* to kick.

calciatore *sm.* footballer.

calcificare *vt.* to calcify.

calcificazione *sf.* calcification.

calcina *sf.* lime.

calcinaccio *sm.* debris (*solo sing.*).

calcinare *vt.* to calcine.

calcio[1] *sm.* **1.** kick **2.** (*giuoco*) football || *— d'inizio,* kick-off; *— di rigore,* penalty **3.** (*di arma*) butt.

calcio[2] *sm.* (*chim.*) calcium.

calco *sm.* **1.** (*scult.*) cast **2.** (*di disegno*) drawing.

calcolàbile *agg.* computable.

calcolare *vt.* **1.** to calculate, to compute **2.** (*prevedere*) to estimate.

calcolatore *sm.* (electronic) computer || *regolo —,* slide-rule.

calcolatrice *sf.* calculating machine.

càlcolo *sm.* 1. calculation 2. (*med.*) stone.

calcomanìa *sf.* transfer.

caldaia *sf.* 1. kier 2. (*per produzione di vapore*) boiler.

caldamente *avv.* warmly.

caldeggiare *vt.* to favour.

caldeggiatore *sm.* supporter.

calderaio *sm.* tinker.

calderone *sm.* 1. cauldron 2. (*fig.*) medley.

caldo *agg.* 1. warm; (*molto caldo*) hot 2. (*fig.*) ardent. ♦ **caldo** *sm.* heat || *far* —, to be warm, to be hot.

caleidoscopio *sm.* kaleidoscope.

calendario *sm.* calendar.

calende *sf. pl.* kalends || *rimandare alle — greche*, to put off till doomsday.

calesse *sf.* gig, calash.

calessino *sm.* gig.

calibrare *vt.* to calibrate.

calibratura *sf.* calibration.

càlibro *sm.* 1. calibre 2. (*di persona*) caliber, importance.

càlice *sm.* 1. (*eccl.*) chalice 2. (*bicchiere*) goblet, drinking-cup.

calìgine *sf.* thick fog, smog.

callifugo *sm.* corn-plaster.

calligrafìa *sf.* handwriting.

calligràfico *agg.* calligraphic.

calligrafo *sm.* calligrapher: *perito* —, handwriting expert.

callista *sm.* chiropodist.

callo *sm.* corn.

callosità *sf.* callosity.

calloso *agg.* callous.

calma *sf.* calm.

calmante *agg.* calming, soothing. ♦ **calmante** *sm.* (*farm.*) sedative.

calmare *vt.* 1. to calm 2. (*metter pace*) to appease.

calmo *agg.* calm, quiet.

calo *sm.* 1. shrinkage 2. (*comm.*) drop.

calore *sm.* 1. (*forte*) heat; (*moderato*) warmth 2. (*fig.*) warmth, eagerness.

calorìa *sf.* calory.

calorìfero *sm.* heating apparatus, radiator.

caloroso *agg.* 1. warm, hearty 2. (*che non sente freddo*) not feeling the cold.

calotta *sf.* 1. cap: — *cranica*, skull-cap 2. (*geom.*) bowl.

calpestare *vt.* to tread (*v. irr.*): *vietato — l'erba*, keep off the grass.

calpestìo *sm.* trampling (of feet).

calunnia *sf.* slander.

calunniare *vt.* to slander.

calunniatore *sm.* slanderer.

calvizie *sf.* baldness.

calvo *agg.* bald.

calza *sf.* 1. (*corta*) sock; (*da donna*) stocking 2. (*lavoro a maglia*) knitting || *fare la* —, to knit.

calzamaglia *sf.* tights (*pl.*).

calzare *vt.* to put (*v. irr.*) on. ♦ **calzare** *vi.* to fit.

calzatura *sf.* shoe || *negozio di calzature*, shoe-shop.

calzaturificio *sm.* boot factory.

calzettone *sm.* heavy sock.

calzino *sm.* sock.

calzolaio *sm.* shoemaker.

calzolerìa *sf.* shoemaker's shop.

calzoni *sm. pl.* trousers.

camaleonte *sm.* chameleon (*anche fig.*).

cambiale *sf.* bill (of exchange): — *a vista*, bill at sight; *emettere una* —, to issue a bill; *girare una* —, to endorse a bill; *protestare una* —, to note a bill || — *pagherò*, promissory note.

cambiamento *sm.* change.

cambiare *vt.* to change (*anche fig.*). ♦ **cambiarsi** *vr.* to change.

cambio *sm.* 1. change 2. (*econ.*) exchange 3. (*mecc.*) change-gear 4. (*auto*) gear || *in* —, in exchange for, instead of.

camelia *sf.* (*bot.*) camellia.

càmera *sf.* 1. room: — *da letto*, bedroom; — *dei bambini*, nursery; — *degli ospiti*, guest-room || *musica da* —, chamber music 2. (*pol.*) Chamber House: *camera dei deputati*, Chamber of Deputies 3. (*tec.*) chamber || — *oscura*, dark room; — *d'aria*, inner tube.

camerata[1] *sm.* comrade, mate.

camerata[2] *sf.* dormitory.

cameratismo *sm.* comradeship.

cameriera *sf.* 1. maid 2. (*di albergo*) chambermaid 3. (*di ristorante*) waitress.

cameriere *sm.* 1. man-servant (*pl.* men-) 2. (*di ristorante*) waiter.

càmice *sm.* 1. overall 2. (*eccl.*) surplice.

camicetta *sf.* blouse.

camicia *sf.* 1. (*da uomo*) shirt || — *da notte* (*da uomo*), night-shirt

2. (*da donna*) chemise || — *da notte* (*da donna*), night-dress **3.** (*tec.*) jacket || è *nato con la —*, he was born with a silver spoon in his mouth.

caminetto *sm.* fireplace.

camino *sm.* **1.** (*focolare*) fireplace **2.** (*comignolo*) chimney.

camion *sm.* lorry.

camioncino *sm.* van.

camionista *sm.* lorry-driver.

cammello *sm.* camel.

cammeo *sm.* cameo.

camminare *vi.* **1.** to walk || — *a grandi passi*, to stride (*v. irr.*) along; — *in punta di piedi*, to walk on tiptoe **2.** (*di meccanismi*) to go (*v. irr.*), to work **3.** (*discorsi, affari ecc.*) to proceed.

camminata *sf.* **1.** walk **2.** (*andatura*) gait.

camminatore *sm.* walker.

cammino *sm.* way.

camomilla *sf.* (*bot.*) camomile: *una tazza di —*, a cup of camomile-tea.

camoscio *sm.* chamois: *pelle di —*, chamois leather.

campagna *sf.* **1.** country: *casa di —*, country-house; *andare in —*, to go (*v. irr.*) into the country; *essere in —*, to be in the country **2.** (*tenuta*) estate **3.** (*mil.*) campaign **4.** (*villeggiatura*) holidays.

campana *sf.* bell.

campanaro *sm.* bell-ringer.

campanello *sm.* door-bell: — *d'allarme*, alarm-bell.

campanile *sm.* bell-tower.

campanilismo *sm.* parochialism.

campare *vi.* to live.

campeggiatore *sm.* camper.

campeggio *sm.* camping.

campestre *agg.* rural, rustic || *corsa —*, cross-country race.

campionario *sm.* set of samples, sample case || *fiera campionaria*, trade fair.

campionato *sm.* championship.

campione *sm.* **1.** champion **2.** (*comm.*) sample.

campo *sm.* **1.** (*mil.*) field **2.** (*sport*) sport ground **3.** (*a tennis*) tennis court **3.** (*terreno*) field || — *di battaglia*, battle-field.

camuffare *vt.* to disguise.

canadese *agg.* e *sm.* Canadian.

canaglia *sf.* **1.** rabble **2.** (*di persona malvagia*) rascal.

canale *sm.* **1.** canal **2.** (*braccio di mare*) channel **3.** (*condotto*) pipe **4.** (*tv.*) channel.

cànapa *sf.* hemp.

canarino *sm.* canary.

cancellare *vt.* **1.** (*a penna*) to cross out; (*con una gomma*) to rub out; (*con un panno*) to wipe out **2.** (*fig.*) efface.

cancellatura *sf.* **1.** erasure **2.** (*fig.*) effacement.

cancellerìa *sf.* **1.** (*pol.*) chancellery **2.** (*materiale di —*) stationery articles **3.** (*giur.*) record-office.

cancelliere *sm.* **1.** (*pol.*) chancellor **2.** (*giur.*) recorder.

cancello *sm.* gate.

cancrena *sf.* gangrene.

cancro *sm.* cancer.

candeggina *sf.* chloride.

candela *sf.* **1.** candle: — *di sego*, tallow candle; *al lume di —*, by candle-light **2.** (*auto*) sparking plug.

candelabro *sm.* branched candlestick.

candeliere *sm.* candlestick.

candelotto *sm.* short thick candle: — *fumogeno*, smoke candle.

candidato *sm.* candidate.

candidatura *sf.* candidature.

càndido *agg.* **1.** snow-white **2.** (*innocente*) innocent.

candito *agg.* candied. ♦ **candito** *sm.* sugar candy.

candore *sm.* **1.** whiteness **2.** (*innocenza*) innocence.

cane *sm.* **1.** dog: — *da caccia*, sporting dog; — *pastore*, sheep dog; — *da guardia*, watch-dog **2.** (*persona spietata*) brute **3.** (*di fucile*) cock.

cànfora *sf.* camphor.

canguro *sm.* kangaroo.

canìcola *sf.* the height of summer.

canile *sm.* kennel.

canino *agg.* canine: *dente —*, canine tooth.

canna *sf.* **1.** reed **2.** (*coltivata*) cane || — *da zucchero*, sugar cane **3.** (*tubo*) pipe **4.** (*di arma*) barrel **5.** (*da pesca*) (fishing-)rod.

cannella *sf.* **1.** (*bot.*) cinnamon **2.** (*di botte*) spout.

cannello *sm.* **1.** torch **2.** (*chim.*) pipe.

canneto *sm.* canebrake.

cannìbale *sm.* cannibal.

cannocchiale *sm.* binoculars (*pl.*) || — *da campagna*, field glasses; — *da teatro*, opera glasses.

cannone *sm.* **1.** gun: — *antiaereo,* anti-aircraft gun; — *anticarro,* anti-tank gun **2.** (*fig.*) ace.

cannuccia *sf.* **1.** thin cane: — *per sorbire bibite,* straw.

cànone *sm.* canon: — *d'affitto,* rent; — *della radio,* radio-licence fee.

canònica *sf.* rectory.

canònico *agg.* canonical || *diritti canonici,* canon law. ♦ **canònico** *sm.* canon.

canonizzare *vt.* to canonize.

canoro *agg.* singing.

canottaggio *sm.* **1.** rowing, boating **2.** (*come attività*) boating.

canottiera *sf.* vest.

canotto *sm.* small boat.

canovaccio *sm.* **1.** (*per asciugare stoviglie*) dish-cloth; **2.** (*per ricamo*) canvas **3.** (*trama di un'opera*) plot.

cantante *sm.* singer.

cantare *vt.* **1.** to sing (*v. irr.*) **2.** (*del gallo*) to crow **3.** (*fare la spia*) to squeal.

cantata *sf.* song.

canterellare *vt.* e *vi.* to sing (*v. irr.*) softly, to hum.

càntico *sm.* hymn.

cantiere *sm.* yard.

cantilena *sf.* sing-song.

cantina *sf.* cellar.

cantiniere *sm.* cellarman (*pl.* -men).

cantino *sm.* chanterelle.

canto[1] *sm.* singing.

canto[2] *sm.* (*angolo*) corner || *dal — mio,* for my part; *da un —,* on one hand.

cantonata *sf.* corner: *prendere una —,* to make (*v. irr.*) a blunder.

cantone *sm.* **1.** corner **2.** (*geogr.*) canton.

cantoniera *sf.* **1.** (*mobile*) corner cupboard **2.** (*casa*) roadman's house **3.** (*ferr.*) signalman's house.

cantoniere *sm.* signalman (*pl.* -men).

canuto *agg.* hoary.

canzonare *vt.* to make (*v. irr.*) fun of.

canzone *sf.* song.

canzonetta *sf.* **1.** short song **2.** (*poet.*) canzonet.

canzonettista *s.* **1.** music-hall singer **2.** (*autore di canzoni*) songwriter.

caolino *sm.* kaolin.

caos *sm.* chaos.

capace *agg.* **1.** able **2.** (*idoneo*) fit **3.** (*abile*) clever.

capacità *sf.* **1.** ability, cleverness **2.** (*capienza*) capacity.

capanna *sf.* hut.

capanno *sm.* **1.** (*da caccia*) shooting-box **2.** (*per bagnanti*) bathing-box.

caparbierìa *sf.* stubbornness.

caparbio *agg.* stubborn.

caparra *sf.* caution-money.

capeggiare *vt.* to lead (*v. irr.*).

capello *sm.* hair (*solo sing.*) || *acconciatura dei capelli,* hairdress; *farsi tagliare i capelli,* to have one's hair cut; *avere un diavolo per —,* to be furious.

capezzale *sm.* bolster.

capézzolo *sm.* nipple.

capienza *sf.* capacity.

capigliatura *sf.* hair.

capillare *agg.* capillary.

capillarità *sf.* capillarity.

capinera *sf.* blackcap.

capire *vt.* to understand (*v. irr.*).

capitale *sm.* capital. ♦ **capitale** *agg.* **1.** (*che riguarda la vita*) capital **2.** (*principale*) main.

capitalismo *sm.* capitalism.

capitalista *s.* capitalist.

capitalizzare *vt.* to capitalize. ♦ **capitalizzare** *vi.* (*accumulare denaro*) to save.

capitano *sm.* captain, leader.

capitare *vi.* **1.** (*giungere*) to arrive **2.** (*accadere*) to happen, to befall (*v. irr.*).

capitello *sm.* (*arch.*) capital.

capitolare *vi.* to capitulate.

capitolare *vt.* capitulary. ♦ **capitolare** *agg.* capitular.

capìtolo *sm.* chapter.

capitòmbolo *sm.* tumble.

capo *sm.* **1.** head || *avere mal di —,* to have a headache; *senza — né coda,* without rhyme or reason **2.** (*estremità*) end || *da un — all'altro,* from end to end; *andare a —,* new line; *in — a un anno,* within a year; *Capo d'Anno,* New Year's day **3.** (*geogr.*) cape **4.** (*chi comanda*) leader.

capobanda *sm.* **1.** (*mus.*) bandmaster **2.** (*di una banda di criminali*) ringleader.

capocuoco *sm.* head cook.

capocordata *sm.* first man on the rope.

capodanno *sm.* New Year's day.

capofamiglia *s.* head of a family.

capofila *sm.* file-leader.
capofitto (*nella loc. avv.*) *a* —, headlong ‖ *cadere, tuffarsi a* —, to fall (*v. irr.*), to dive head first.
capogiro *sm.* dizziness.
capolavoro *sm.* masterpiece.
capolinea *sm.* terminus (*pl.* -ni).
capolino *sm.* small head ‖ *far* —, to peep in.
capoluogo *sm.* main town.
caporale *sm.* corporal.
caporedattore *sm.* editor in chief.
caposaldo *sm.* **1.** datum point **2.** (*mil.*) stronghold **3.** (*fondamento*) main point.
caposcuola *sm.* leader of a movement.
capostazione *sm.* station-master.
capotare *vi.* **1.** (*di aerei*) to somersault **2.** (*di auto*) to turn over.
capoufficio *sm.* head-clerk.
capoverso *sm.* **1.** (*in poesia*) beginning of a line **2.** (*in prosa*) beginning of a paragraph.
capovòlgere *vt.* to turn upside down. ♦ **capovòlgersi** *vr.* to capsize.
cappa *sf.* **1.** (*mantello*) cloak **2.** (*di prete*) cape **3.** (*fig.*) vault ‖ — *del camino*, chimney.
cappella *sf.* chapel.
cappellano *sm.* chaplain.
cappello *sm.* **1.** hat: — *a cilindro*, top-hat; — *di paglia*, straw hat; **2.** (*introduzione*) preamble.
càppero *sm.* caper.
cappone *sm.* capon.
cappotto *sm.* **1.** coat **2.** (*di gioco*) capot.
cappuccino *sm.* **1.** (*eccl.*) capuchin **2.** (*bevanda*) white coffee.
cappuccio *sm.* hood.
capra *sf.* goat.
capretto *sm.* kid.
capriccio *sm.* whim: *fare i capricci*, to be naughty.
caprino *agg.* goatish.
capriola[1] *sf.* caper: *far capriole*, to cut (*v. irr.*) capers.
capriola[2] *sf.* (*femmina del capriolo*) doe.
capriolo *sm.* roe-deer.
càpsula *sf.* **1.** capsule **2.** (*di dente*) crown.
captare *vt.* (*radio*) to pick up.
capzioso *agg.* captious.
carabina *sf.* carabine.
carabiniere *sm.* carabineer.
caracollare *vi.* to caracole.

caraffa *sf.* **1.** (*per acqua*) carafe **2.** (*per vino*) decanter.
caràmbola *sf.* cannon: *far* —, to cannon.
carambolare *vi.* to cannon.
caramella *sf.* sugar-drop, toffee.
caramellare *vt.* to coat with burnt sugar.
caramello *sm.* caramel.
carato *sm.* carat.
caràttere *sm.* **1.** character, temper **2.** (*caratteristica*) character **3.** (*tip.*) type.
caratterista *s.* character actor (actress).
caratterìstico *agg.* characteristic. ♦ **caratterìstica** *sf.* characteristic.
caravella *sf.* caravel.
carbonaio *sm.* coal merchant.
carbone *sm.* coal ‖ — *di legna*, charcoal; — *fossile*, pit coal; *miniera di* —, coalmine.
carbonerìa *sf.* Carbonarist movement.
carbonìfero *agg.* carboniferous.
carbonio *sm.* carbon.
carbonizzare *vt.* **1.** to carbonize **2.** (*di legno*) to char.
carburante *sm.* fuel.
carburatore *sm.* carburettor.
carburazione *sf.* carburation.
carcassa *sf.* carcass.
carcerazione *sf.* imprisonment.
càrcere *sm.* prison, jail.
carceriere *sm.* jailer.
carciofo *sm.* artichoke.
cardano *sm.* (*mecc.*) cardan joint.
cardare *vt.* to card.
cardìaco *agg.* cardiac ‖ *disturbi cardiaci*, heart-disease.
cardinale *agg. e sm.* cardinal.
càrdine *sm.* **1.** hinge, pivot **2.** (*fig.*) foundation.
cardiòlogo *sm.* cardiologist.
cardiopatìa *sf.* cardiopathy.
cardo *sm.* **1.** (*bot.*) thistle **2.** (*cuc.*) cardoon **3.** (*mecc.*) carding machine.
carena *sf.* **1.** (*mar.*) keel **2.** (*aer.*) hull **3.** (*zool.*) càrina (*pl.* -nae).
carenza *sf.* want, lack.
carestìa *sf.* famine.
carezza *sf.* caress.
carezzévole *agg.* caressing.
cariàtide *sf.* caryatid.
cariato *agg.* decayed.
càrica *sf.* **1.** (*pubblico ufficio*) office: *entrare in* —, to take (*v.*

irr.) office **2.** (*mil.*) charge **3.** (*di arma da fuoco; elettr.*) charge **4.** (*di orologio*) winding up.

caricare *vt.* **1.** to load **2.** (*mil.; elettr.*) to charge **3.** (*di orologio*) to wind (*v. irr.*) up.

caricatore *sm.* **1.** loader **2.** (*di arma*) magazine.

caricatura *sf.* caricature.

càrico[1] *agg.* **1.** loaded, laden (*anche fig.*) **2.** (*di caffè*) strong **3.** (*elettr.*) charged.

càrico[2] *sm.* **1.** (*di nave*) freight; (*di veicolo*) load; (*di animale da soma*) burden **2.** (*fig.*) load, weight **3.** (*accusa*) charge || (*comm.*) essere a — di qu., to be charged to so.

carie *sf.* decay.

carino *agg.* pretty, nice.

carità *sf.* **1.** (*amore; teol.*) charity **2.** (*elemosina*) alms.

carlinga *sf.* cockpit.

carlona (*nella loc. avv.*) alla —, carelessly.

carminio *agg.* carmine.

carnagione *sf.* complexion.

carnale *agg.* carnal.

carne *sf.* **1.** flesh **2.** (*come alimento*) meat || — di manzo, beef; — di vitello, veal; — in scatola, tinned meat; — congelata, frozen meat.

carnéfice *sm.* executioner.

carneficina *sf.* slaughter.

carnevale *sm.* carnival.

carnìvoro *agg.* carnivorous.

caro *agg.* **1.** dear **2.** (*costoso*) dear, expensive.

carogna *sf.* carrion.

carosello *sm.* carousel.

carota *sf.* carrot.

caròtide *sf.* carotid.

carovana *sf.* caravan.

carovita *sm.* high cost of living.

carpa *sf.* carp.

carpentiere *sm.* carpenter.

carpire *vt.* **1.** to snatch **2.** (*con astuzia*) to swindle.

carponi *avv.* on all fours.

carràbile *agg.* cart: passo —, driveway.

carreggiata **1.** (*solco*) track **2.** (*strada*) cartway.

carrellata *sf.* dolly shot.

carrello *sm.* **1.** (*ferr.*) wag(g)on **2.** (*aer.*) landing gear **3.** (*cine; tv.*) dolly **4.** (*di macchina per scrivere*)

carriage.

carriera *sf.* career || di gran —, at full speed.

carriola *sf.* wheelbarrow.

carrista *sm.* (*mil.*) tankman (*pl.* -men).

carro *sm.* **1.** (*a due ruote*) cart **2.** (*a quattro ruote*) wag(g)on || — armato, tank.

carrozza *sf.* carriage: — diretta, through coach; — viaggiatori, passenger car.

carrozzàbile *agg.* practicable.

carrozzella *sf.* **1.** cab **2.** (*per bambini*) perambulator; (*fam.*) pram.

carrozzerìa *sf.* body.

carrozziere *sm.* body-maker.

carrozzone *sm.* **1.** lumbering coach **2.** (*di zingari*) caravan.

carruba *sf.*, **carrubo** *sm.* carob.

carrùcola *sf.* pulley.

carta *sf.* paper: — da lettere, writing-paper; — carbone, carbon paper; — d'identità, identity card; — stradale, road-map.

cartaio *sm.* paper-maker.

cartamodello *sm.* dressmaker's pattern.

cartamoneta *sf.* paper-money.

cartapesta *sf.* paper-pulp.

cartavetrata *sf.* sand-paper.

carteggio *sm.* **1.** correspondence **2.** (*collezione di lettere*) collection of letters.

cartella *sf.* **1.** (*da scuola*) satchel **2.** (*di cuoio*) brief-case.

cartello *sm.* **1.** bill **2.** (*pubblicitario*) poster **3.** (*stradale*) traffic sign **4.** (*econ.*) cartel.

cartellone *sm.* **1.** (*pubblicitario*) poster **2.** (*teat.*) bill.

cartellonista *sm.* commercial artist.

cartiera *sf.* paper-mill.

cartilàgine *sf.* cartilage.

cartoccio *sm.* paper-bag.

cartografìa *sf.* cartography.

cartolerìa *sf.* stationer's shop.

cartolina *sf.* postcard: — illustrata, picture postcard.

cartoncino *sm.* thin card.

cartone *sm.* cardboard || cartoni animati, cartoons.

cartuccia *sf.* cartridge || mezza — (*fig.*), shrimp.

casa *sf.* **1.** (*abitazione*) house **2.** (*ambiente familiare*) home || amico di —, family friend; donna di —, housewife; nostalgia di —, home-sickness; *andare a* —, to go (*v. irr.*) home; *restare a* —, to stay at home; *essere in* —, to be in **3.** (*stirpe*) house, dynasty, family.

casacca *sf.* coat.

casaccio (*nella loc. avv.*) *a* —, at random.

casalinga *sf.* housewife.

casalingo *agg.* homely: *cucina casalinga*, plain cooking.

casato *sm.* **1.** (*cognome*) surname **2.** (*origine, nascita*) birth.

cascame *sm.* waste.

cascamorto *sm.* spoon: *fare il* —, to run (*v. irr.*) after.

cascante *agg.* **1.** (*debole*) weak **2.** (*floscio*) flabby (*anche fig.*).

cascare *vi.* **1.** to fall (*v. irr.*) **2.** (*con rumore*) to crash ‖ — *dalle nuvole*, to be struck with amazement; — *dal sonno*, to be overcome with sleep.

cascata *sf.* **1.** (*caduta*) fall **2.** (*d'acqua*) waterfall **3.** (*fig.*) cascade.

cascina *sf.* **1.** dairy farm **2.** (*cascinale*) farmstead.

casco *sm.* **1.** helmet **2.** (*per asciugare i capelli*) dryer.

casella *sf.*: — *postale*, post-box.

casellante *sm.* **1.** (*ferr.*) signalman (*pl.* -men) **2.** (*di passaggio a livello*) crossing keeper.

casellario *sm.* **1.** set of pigeon-holes **2.** (*giur.*) — *penale*, records-office.

casereccio *agg.* homely: *pane* —, home-made bread.

caserma *sf.* barracks (*pl.*).

caso *sm.* **1.** chance **2.** (*fatto*) case **3.** (*possibilità*) way, possibility ‖ *a* —, at random; *per* —, by chance.

càspita *inter.* good gracious!

cassa *sf.* **1.** case, box **2.** (*comm.*) cash ‖ *libro di* —, cash-book; *pagamento per* —, cash-payment; *sportello di* —, cashier's window **3.** (*mus.*) case ‖ *gran* —, bass-drum.

cassaforte *sf.* safe.

cassapanca *sf.* chest.

cassazione *sf.* (*giur.*) cassation.

casseruola *sf.* saucepan.

cassetto *sm.* drawer.

cassettone *sm.* chest of drawers.

cassiere *sm.* cashier.

casta *sf.* caste.

castagna *sf.* chestnut.

castagnaccio *sm.* chestnut-tart.

castagno *sm.* chestnut-tree.

castano *agg.* nut-brown.

castellano *sm.* lord of a castle.

castello *sm.* castle.

castigare *vt.* to punish.

castigatezza *sf.* moderation.

castigato *agg.* **1.** (*casto*) chaste **2.** (*emendato*) castigated.

castigo *sm.* punishment.

castità *sf.* chastity.

casto *agg.* chaste.

castoro *sm.* beaver.

castrare *vt.* to castrate.

castrato *sm.* (*cuc.*) mutton.

castroneria *sf.* stupidity.

casuale *agg.* casual.

casualità *sf.* casualness.

cataclisma *sm.* cataclysm (*anche fig.*).

catacomba *sf.* catacomb.

catafalco *sm.* catafalque.

catafascio (*nella loc. avv.*) andare *a* —, to go (*v. irr.*) to rack and ruin; *a* —, topsyturvy.

catalessi *sf.* catalepsy.

catalizzatore *sm.* catalyst.

catalogare *vt.* to catalogue.

catàlogo *sm.* catalogue.

catapecchia *sf.* hovel.

catapulta *sf.* catapult.

catarifrangente *sm.* reflector.

catarro *sm.* catarrh.

catarsi *sf.* catharsis.

catasta *sf.* pile, heap.

catasto *sm.* cadastre.

catàstrofe *sf.* catastrophe.

catastròfico *agg.* catastrophic(al).

catechismo *sm.* catechism.

catechizzare *vt.* **1.** to catechize **2.** (*fig.*) to persuade.

catecùmeno *sm.* catechumen.

categoria *sf.* category, class.

categòrico *agg.* categorical, absolute.

catena *sf.* **1.** chain **2.** (*fig.*) bond.

catenaccio *sm.* bolt.

cateratta *sf.* cataract.

caterva *sf.* **1.** (*di persone*) crowd **2.** (*di cose*) great quantity.

catino *sm.* basin.

catione *sm.* (*fis.*) cation.

càtodo *sm.* cathode.

catramare *vt.* to tar.

catrame *sm.* tar.

càttedra *sf.* **1.** desk **2.** (*l'ufficio dell'insegnare*) teaching post **3.** (*di università*) chair.

cattedrale *sf.* cathedral.

cattiveria *sf.* wickedness.

cattività *sf.* captivity.

cattivo *agg.* e *sm.* bad || *— scritto-re,* poor writer.

cattolicésimo *sm.* catholicism.

cattòlico *agg.* catholic.

cattura *sf.* 1. capture 2. (*arresto*) arrest: *mandato di —,* warrant of arrest.

catturare *vt.* 1. to capture 2. (*arrestare*) to arrest.

cauccù *sm.* india-rubber.

càusa *sf* 1. cause 2. (*giur.*) law suit || *far — a qu.,* to sue so. (for).

causare *vt.* to cause.

càustico *agg.* caustic (*anche fig.*)

cautela *sf.* caution.

cautelare *vt.* to protect. ♦ **caute-larsi** *vr.* to take (*v. irr.*) precautions.

cauterizzare *vt.* to cauterize.

càuto *agg.* cautious, prudent.

cauzione *sf.* 1. guarantee 2. (*per essere rilasciato dalla polizia*) bail.

cava *sf.* quarry.

cavalcare *vt.* to ride (*v. irr.*). ♦ **cavalcare** *vi.* to ride on horseback.

cavalcavìa *sm.* fly-over bridge.

cavalcioni (a) *loc. avv.* astride.

cavaliere *sm.* 1. rider 2. (*di ordine cavalleresco*) knight.

cavalla *sf.* mare.

cavalleresco *agg.* knightly.

cavallerìa *sf.* 1. (*mil.*) cavalry 2. (*stor.*) chivalry.

cavalletta *sf.* grasshopper.

cavalletto *sm.* 1. trestle 2. (*foto*) tripod 3. (*per pittori*) easel.

cavallo *sm.* 1. horse: *— da corsa,* racehorse; *— a dondolo,* rocking-horse; *— da soma,* pack-horse; *ferro di —,* horse-shoe 2. (*ginnastica*) vaulting-horse 3. (*cavallo vapore*) horse-power (*abbr.* H.P.).

cavallone *sm.* (*maroso*) billow.

cavare *vt.* to take (*v. irr.*) off || *— un dente,* to pull out a tooth || *cavarsela,* to get (*v. irr.*) off.

cavatappi, cavaturàccioli *sm.* cork-screw.

caverna *sf.* cave.

cavernoso *agg.* cavernous || *voce cavernosa,* very deep voice.

cavezza *sf.* halter.

cavia *sf.* cavy.

caviale *sm.* caviar.

caviglia *sf.* ankle.

cavillare *vi.* to cavil (at).

cavillo *sm.* cavil.

cavità *sf.* cavity.

cavo *agg.* hollow, empty. ♦ **cavo** *sm.* cable, rope.

cavolfiore *sm.* cauliflower.

càvolo *sm.* cabbage.

cazzotto *sm.* punch || *fare a cazzot-ti,* to come (*v. irr.*) to blows.

cazzuola *sf.* trowel.

cece *sm.* chick-pea.

cecità *sf.* blindness (*anche fig.*).

cecoslovacco *agg.* e *sm.* Czechoslovak.

cèdere *vt.* e *vi.* 1. (*dare*) to give (*v. irr.*) 2. (*trasferire*) to hand over 3. (*vendere*) to dispose of. ♦ **cèdere** *vi.* 1. to surrender 2. (*venir meno*) to subside 3. (*essere inferiore*) to be second to.

cedimento *sm.* 1. yielding 2. (*fig.*) giving up.

cèdola *sf.* coupon.

cedrata *sf.* citron syrup.

cedrina *sf.* lemon-scented verbena.

cedro *sm.* 1. citron-tree 2. (*frutto*) citron.

cedrone *agg.* e *sm.* (*gallo*) capercaillie.

cefalea *sf.* cephalea.

cefalgìa *sf.* cephalalgy.

ceffone *sm.* slap in the face.

celare *vt.* to conceal, to hide (*v. irr.*).

celebrare *vt.* to celebrate || *— un anniversario,* to keep (*v. irr.*) an anniversary.

celebrazione *sf.* celebration.

cèlebre *agg.* celebrated.

celebrità *sf.* celebrity.

cèlere *agg.* quick, swift.

celerità *sf.* quickness.

celeste *agg.* 1. light-blue 2. (*del cielo*) heavenly.

celia *sf.* jest.

celiare *vi.* to jest.

celibato *sm.* bachelorhood.

cèlibe *agg.* e *sm.* single. ♦ **cèlibe** *sm.* bachelor.

cella *sf.* cell.

cèllula *sf.* cell.

cellulare *agg.* cellular || *segregazione —,* close confinement.

cellulite *sf.* cellulitis.

cellulòide *sf.* celluloid.

cellulosa *sf.* cellulose.

celta *sm.* Celt.

cèltico *agg.* Celtic.

cémbalo *sm.* 1. (*tamburello*) tambourine 2. (*spinetta*) spinet.

cementare *vt.* to cement (*anche fig.*).

cementazione *sf.* cementation.
cementificio *sm.* cement-factory.
cemento *sm.* cement: — *armato,* reinforced concrete.
cena *sf.* **1.** (*pasto serale leggero*) supper **2.** (*pranzo*) dinner || *far* —, to have supper.
cenàcolo *sm.* **1.** supper-room **2.** (*di artisti*) artistic coterie || *il — di Leonardo da Vinci,* Leonardo's Last Supper.
cenare *vi.* to have (*v. irr.*) supper.
cenciaio *sm.* ragman (*pl.* -men).
cencio *sm.* **1.** rag **2.** (*vestito logoro*) tatters (*pl.*).
cencioso *agg.* ragged, tattered.
cénere *sf.* ash (*general. al pl.*).
cenno *sm.* **1.** (*segno*) sign **2.** (*allusione*) hint **3.** (*breve notizia*) notice || *fare un — col capo,* to nod || *a un vostro —* (*comm.*), on hearing from you.
cenobio *sm.* coenobium (*pl.* -ia).
cenone *sm.* **1.** (*di Natale*) Christmas eve dinner **2.** (*di Capodanno*) New Year's eve dinner.
censimento *sm.* census.
censire *vt.* **1.** to take (*v. irr.*) a census of **2.** (*di proprietà*) to assess.
censo *sm.* **1.** (*stor.*) census **2.** (*ricchezza*) wealth.
censore *sm.* **1.** censor **2.** (*fig.*) critic.
censorio *agg.* censorial.
censura *sf.* **1.** (*ufficio di censore*) censorship **2.** (*azione di censura*) censure.
censurare *vt.* **1.** to censor **2.** (*fig.*) to censure.
centàuro *sm.* **1.** centaur **2.** (*fig., motociclista*) motorcyclist.
centellinare *vt.* to sip.
centenario *agg.* e *sm.* **1.** centennial **2.** (*di persona*) centenarian. ◆ **centenario** *sm.* (*commemorazione*) centenary.
centesimale *agg.* centesimal.
centèsimo *agg.* (the) hundredth. ◆ **centèsimo** *sm.* (one) hundredth (of sthg.) **2.** (*di dollaro*) cent **3.** (*di franco*) centime || *non avere un* —, to be penniless.
centìgrado *agg.* centigrade.
centigrammo *sm.* centigramme.
centìlitro *sm.* centilitre.
centìmetro *sm.* centimetre.
centinaio *sm.* hundred.
cento *agg.* e *num. card.* hundred || — *di questi giorni,* many happy

returns of the day.
centrale *agg.* central. ◆ **centrale** *sf.* **1.** — *elettrica,* power station **2.** — *telefonica,* exchange.
centralinista *s.* operator.
centralino *sm.* telephone exchange.
centralismo *sm.* centralism.
centrare *vt.* to hit (*v. irr.*) the centre.
centrìfuga *sf.* centrifuge.
centrìfugo *agg.* centrifugal.
centrino *sm.* doily.
centrìpeto *agg.* centripetal.
centrismo *sm.* centrism.
centro *sm.* **1.** centre **2.** (*istituto*) institute.
centuplicare *vt.* **1.** to centuplicate **2.** (*fig.*) to increase.
cèntuplo *agg.* e *sm.* centuple.
centuria *sf.* (*stor.*) century.
centurione *sm.* (*stor.*) centurion.
ceppo *sm.* **1.** stump **2.** (*fig.*) stock.
cera *sf.* **1.** wax **2.** (*aspetto*) look || *avere bella* —, to look well.
ceralacca *sf.* sealing-wax.
ceràmica *sf.* **1.** (*arte*) ceramics **2.** (*pezzo*) piece of pottery.
ceramista *sm.* ceramist.
cerato *agg.* waxed || *tela cerata,* wax-cloth.
cerbiatto *sm.* fawn.
cerbottana *sf.* **1.** blowgun **2.** (*giocattolo*) pea-shooter.
cercare *vt.* **1.** to look for **2.** (*per consultazione*) to look up **3.** (*a tentoni*) to fumble for **4.** (*chiedere*) to ask (for). ◆ **cercare** *vi.* to try.
cercatore *sm.* seeker: — *d'oro,* gold-digger; (*amer.*) prospector.
cerchia *sf.* circle.
cerchiare *vt.* to hoop.
cerchiatura *sf.* hooping.
cerchietto *sm.* **1.** small ring **2.** (*gioco*) quoit.
cerchio *sm.* **1.** circle **2.** (*gioco*) hoop.
cerchione *sm.* rim.
cereale *sm.* cereals (*pl.*).
cerebrale *agg.* cerebral.
cèreo *agg.* waxen.
ceretta *sf.* **1.** boot polish **2.** (*per depilare*) wax.
cerimonia *sf.* **1.** ceremony **2.** (*pompa*) pomp.
cerimoniale *sm.* ceremonial.
cerimoniere *sm.* Master of Ceremonies.
cerimonioso *agg.* ceremonious
cerino *sm.* match.

cerniera *sf.* **1.** (*di occhiali, porte, finestre*) hinge **2.** (*di borsetta*) clasp **3.** (*lampo*) zipper.

cèrnita *sf.* choice, selection.

cero *sm.* large candle.

cerone *sm.* make-up.

cerotto *sm.* plaster.

certamente *avv.* certainly, undoubtedly.

certezza *sf.* certainty.

certificare *vt.* to certify, to attest.

certificato *sm.* certificate.

certo[1] *agg. indef.* **1.** certain: *un — Mr. Smith*, a (certain) Mr. Smith **2.** (*qualche*) some: *certe persone lo riconobbero*, some people recognized him; *dopo un — tempo*, after some time **3.** (*tale, di tal genere*) such. ♦ **certi** *pron. indef. pl.* some people.

certo[2] *agg.* certain. ♦ **certo** *avv.* certainly.

certuni *pron. indef.* some.

cerùleo *agg.* sky-blue.

cerva *sf.* (*zool.*) hind.

cervella *sf.* brain.

cervelletto *sm.* cerebellum.

cervello *sm.* **1.** brain **2.** (*intelligenza, mente*) understanding, mind.

cervellòtico *agg.* far-fetched.

cervicale *agg.* cervical.

cervice *sf.* nape.

cèrvidi *sm. pl.* cervidae.

cervo *sm.* deer (*inv. al pl.*).

cesàreo *agg.* Caesarean ‖ *taglio —*, Caesarean operation.

cesarismo *sm.* Caesarism.

cesellare *vt.* to chisel (*anche fig.*).

cesellatura *sf.* chisel work.

cesello *sm.* chisel.

cesoia *sf.* shears (*pl.*).

cespuglio *sm.* bush, thicket.

cespuglioso *agg.* bushy.

cessare *vt.* e *vi.* to cease, to stop.

cessazione *sf.* cessation.

cessione *sf.* transfer.

cesso *sm.* lavatory.

cesta *sf.* basket.

cestaio *sm.* **1.** basket-maker **2.** (*chi vende*) basket-vendor.

cestinare *vt.* (*fig.*) to refuse.

cestino *sm.* small basket: *— da lavoro*, work-basket; *— da viaggio*, luncheon-basket; *— per la carta straccia*, waste-paper basket.

cesto *sm.* (*sport*) basket.

cesura *sf.* caesura.

cetàceo *agg.* e *sm.* cetacean.

ceto *sm.* class, rank.

cetra *sf.* cithern, lyre.

cetriolino *sm.* gherkin.

cetriolo *sm.* cucumber.

che[1] *pron. rel.* **1.** (*sogg., riferito a persone*) who, that: *l'uomo — mi parlò*, the man who (that) spoke to me **2.** (*sogg., riferito a cose e animali*) which, that: *ecco il cane — mi fu regalato*, here is the dog which (that) was given to me **3.** (*ogg., riferito a persone*) whom: *è la ragazza più graziosa — abbia mai incontrato*, she is the prettiest girl whom I ever met **4.** (*ogg., riferito a cose e animali*) which: *questo è il libro — le darò*, this is the book which I shall give her **5.** *il —*, which **6.** (*riferito a tempo*) when.

che[2] *agg. int.* **1.** what: *— musica preferisci?*, what music do you prefer? **2.** which: *— libro scegli?*, which book do you choose? ♦ **che** *pron. int.* what: *— è questo?*, what is this? ♦ **che** *agg. escl.* what, what a. ♦ **che** *pron. ind.* something.

che[3] *cong.* **1.** that **2.** (*comparativo*) than: *è più bella che intelligente*, she is more beautiful than intelligent **3.** (*correlativo*) whether: *— tu venga o no*, whether you come or not. ♦ **che** *inter.* what!

checché *pron. indef.* whatever.

checchessìa *pron. indef.* anything.

chepì *sm.* (*mil.*) kepi.

cherosene *sm.* kerosene.

cherubino *sm.* cherub.

chetamente *avv.* quietly, secretly.

chetare *vt.* to quiet. ♦ **chetarsi** *vr.* to quiet down.

chetichella (*nella loc. avv.*) *alla —*, on the sly, secretly.

cheto *agg.* quiet.

chi *pron. rel.* **1.** (*colui che*) he (*ogg.* him) who (*ogg.* whom) **2.** (*colei che*) she (*ogg.* her) who (*ogg.* whom) **3.** (*coloro che*) they (*ogg.* them) who (*ogg.* whom) **4.** (*gen.*) those, the person who(m). ♦ **chi** *pron. indef.* **1.** whoever, anyone **2.** (*qualcuno che*) someone who. ♦ **chi** *pron. int.* **1.** (*sogg.*) who **2.** (*ogg.*) whom **3.** which: *— di voi?*, which of you? **4.** (*specificazione poss.*) whose: *di — è questa casa?*, whose house is this?

chiàcchiera *sf.* chatter.

chiacchierare *vi.* to chat.

chiacchierata *sf.* chat.
chiacchierone *sm.* chatterbox.
chiamare *vt.* to call || *mandare a —*, to send (*v. irr.*) for; — *al telefono*, to call up. ◆ **chiamarsi** *vr.* to be called || *come ti chiami?*, what's your name?
chiamata *sf.* call, appeal.
chiara *sf.* — *d'uovo*, white (of an egg).
chiaretto *sm.* (*vino*) claret.
chiarezza *sf.* **1.** clearness **2.** (*fig.*) evidence.
chiarificare *vt.* to clarify.
chiarificazione *sf.* **1.** clarification **2.** (*fig.*) frank explanation.
chiarimento *sm.* explanation.
chiarire *vt.* **1.** to clarify, to clear up **2.** (*spiegare*) to explain.
chiaro *agg.* **1.** clear, evident **2.** (*di luce*) light.
chiarore *sm.* **1.** light **2.** (*luce tenue*) faint light.
chiaroscuro *sm.* light and shade.
chiaroveggente *agg.* **1.** clear-sighted **2.** (*che ha facoltà divinatorie*) clairvoyant.
chiassata *sf.* row.
chiasso *sm.* noise, uproar.
chiassone *sm.* noisy person.
chiassoso *agg.* **1.** noisy **2.** (*fig.*) showy.
chiatta *sf.* barge.
chiavarda *sf.* bolt.
chiave *sf.* **1.** key **2.** (*mus.*) clef.
chiavistello *sm.* latch, bolt.
chiazza *sf.* spot, stain.
chicchessìa *pron. indef.* anyone.
chicco *sm.* **1.** grain **2.** (*di grandine*) hailstone **3.** (*di caffè*) coffee-bean **4.** (*di uva*) grape.
chièdere *vt.* **1.** to ask: — *qc. a qu.*, (*per sapere*) to ask so. sthg., (*per avere*) to ask so. for sthg. **2.** (*riferito a un prezzo*) to charge.
chierichetto *sm.* altar boy.
chiesa *sf.* church.
chiglia *sf.* (*mar.*) keel.
chilo[1] *sm.* (*med.*) chyle || *fare il —*, to take (*v. irr.*) a nap.
chilo[2] *sm.* kilo.
chilogrammo *sm.* kilogram.
chilometraggio *sm.* distance in kilometres.
chilòmetro *sm.* kilometre.
chìlowatt *sm.* kilowatt.
chimera *sf.* chimera.
chìmica *sf.* chemistry.
chìmico *agg.* chemical. ◆ **chìmico**

sm. chemist.
china *sf.* slope.
chinare *vt.* to bend (*v. irr.*), to bow. ◆ **chinarsi** *vr.* to bend (*v. irr.*) down.
chincaglierìa *sf.* **1.** small fancy articles (*pl.*) **2.** (*negozio*) fancy goods shop.
chinino *sm.* quinine.
chioccia *sf.* brooding-hen.
chiòcciola *sf.* snail || *scala a —*, spiral staircase.
chiodato *agg.* nailed.
chiodo *sm.* **1.** nail **2.** (*fig.*) fixed idea.
chioma *sf.* hair.
chiosco *sm.* **1.** kiosk **2.** (*per giornali, frutta e verdura*) stand.
chiostro *sm.* cloister.
chiromante *s.* chiromancer.
chiromanzìa *sf.* chiromancy.
chirurgìa *sf.* surgery.
chirurgo *sm.* surgeon.
chissà *inter.* goodness knows.
chitarra *sf.* guitar.
chiùdere *vt.* **1.** to shut (*v. irr.*) || — *a chiave*, to lock **2.** (*terminare*) to close **3.** (*rinchiudere*) to shut (*v. irr.*) up.
chiunque *pron.* **1.** (*sogg.*) anyone who, whoever **2.** (*ogg.*) whomever, anyone **3.** (*specificazione possessiva*) *di —*, whosever.
chiuso *agg.* closed, shut || — *a chiave*, locked.
chiusura *sf.* closing.
ci *pron.* **1.** (*ogg.*) us: *essi — amano*, they love us **2.** (*riflessivo*) ourselves: *noi — laviamo*, we wash ourselves **3.** (*rec. fra due persone*) each other: *mia madre ed io — guardammo*, my mother and I looked at each other **4.** (*rec. fra più persone*) one another **5.** (*dimostrativo*) this, that, it: *non badarci*, pay no attention to it. ◆ **ci** *avv. di luogo* there (*là*), here (*qui*).
ciabatta *sf.* slipper.
ciambella *sf.* ring-shaped cake.
ciambellano *sm.* chamberlain.
ciancia *sf.* idle talk || *ciance!*, nonsense!
cianciare *vi.* to chatter.
cianografìa *sf.* blueprint.
cianuro *sm.* cyanide.
ciao *inter.* **1.** (*incontrandosi*) hullo **2.** (*congedandosi*) bye-bye.
ciarla *sf.* **1.** loquacity **2.** (*notizia*

falsa) false report.

ciarlare *vi.* to talk idly.

ciarlatano *sm.* charlatan.

ciascuno *agg.* every. ♦ **ciascuno** *pron.* **1.** (*con valore distributivo*) each **2.** (*tutti*) everybody, everyone.

cibernètica *sf.* cybernetics.

cibo *sm.* food.

ciborio *sm.* ciborium (*pl.* -ia).

cicala *sf.* cicada.

cicatrice *sf.* scar.

cicatrizzare *vt.* to cicatrize, to heal. ♦ **cicatrizzarsi** *vr.* to cicatrize, to heal.

cicerone *sm.* guide.

ciclamino *sm.* cyclamen.

cìclico *agg.* cyclic.

ciclismo *sm.* cycling.

ciclista *s.* cyclist.

ciclo *sm.* **1.** cycle **2.** (*di malattia*) course.

ciclone *sm.* hurricane.

ciclòpico *agg.* Cyclopean.

ciclostilare *vt.* to mimeograph.

ciclostile *sm.* cyclostyle.

ciclotrone *sm.* cyclotron.

cicogna *sf.* stork.

cicuta *sf.* hemlock.

cieco *agg.* blind (*anche fig.*). ♦ **cieco** *sm.* blind man.

cielo *sm.* **1.** sky **2.** (*aria*) air **3.** (*paradiso*) Heaven.

cifra *sf.* **1.** figure, number **2.** (*segno di cifrario*) cipher.

cifrare *vt.* **1.** to cipher **2.** (*ricamare in cifra*) to mark.

ciglio *sm.* **1.** eyelash **2.** (*bordo*) edge.

cigno *sm.* swan.

cilecca *sf.* failure || *far* —, to miss fire, (*fig.*) to fail.

cileno *agg.* Chilean.

cilicio *sm.* **1.** hairshirt **2.** (*relig.*) cilice.

ciliegia *sf.* cherry.

ciliegio *sm.* cherry-tree.

cilindrata *sf.* (*auto*) displacement.

cilindro *sm.* **1.** (*geom.; auto*) cylinder **2.** (*cappello*) top-hat.

cima *sf.* **1.** top, summit: *in* —, at the top **2.** (*fig.*) genius.

cìmbali *sm. pl.* essere in —, to be tipsy.

cimentare *vt.* to put (*v. irr.*) to the test. ♦ **cimentarsi** *vr.* to venture upon.

cimitero *sm.* cemetery, graveyard.

cinabro *sm.* cinnabar.

cincillà *sf.* chinchilla.

cineasta *sm.* cinematographer.

cinecàmera *sf.* cine-camera.

cinedilettante *sm.* film-amateur.

cinegiornale *sm.* news-reel.

cìnema *sm.* **1.** cinema, pictures (*pl.*) **2.** (*locale*) cinema **3.** (*amer.*) movies (*pl.*).

cinemàtica *sf.* kinematics.

cinematografìa *sf.* cinematography.

cinematògrafo *sm.* cinema.

cinèreo *agg.* cinereous, ashen-grey.

cinese *agg.* e *sm.* Chinese.

cineteca *sf.* film library.

cinètica *sf.* kinetics.

cìngere *vt.* **1.** to engird **2.** (*circondare*) to surround.

cinghia *sf.* **1.** strap **2.** (*mecc.*) belt.

cinghiale *sm.* (*zool.*) wild boar.

cìnico *agg.* cynical. ♦ **cìnico** *sm.* cynic.

cinismo *sm.* cynicism.

cinocèfalo *sm.* cynocephalus (*pl.* -ali).

cinòdromo *sm.* greyhound racing-track.

cinofilìa *sf.* dog-love.

cinquanta *agg.* fifty.

cinquantenario *sm.* fiftieth anniversary.

cinque *agg.* five.

cinquecento *agg.* five hundred.

cinta *sf.* town-walls (*pl.*): *muro di* —, boundary walls.

cinto *sm.* belt. ♦ **cinto** *agg.* surrounded.

cìntola *sf.* waist: *dalla* — *in giù*, below the waist; *dalla* — *in su*, above the waist.

cintura *sf.* belt.

cinturone *sm.* belt.

ciò *pron.* that, this, it.

ciocca *sf.* (*di capelli*) lock.

cioccolata *sf.* chocolate.

cioccolatino *sm.* chocolate.

cioccolato *sm.* chocolate.

cioè *cong.* that is.

ciondolare *vi.* **1.** to dangle **2.** (*fig.*) to lounge.

ciòndolo *sm.* pendant.

ciondoloni *avv.* dangling.

ciòtola *sf.* cup, bowl.

ciòttolo *sm.* pebble.

cipolla *sf.* onion.

cipresso *sm.* cypress.

cipria *sf.* powder: *piumino per* —, powder puff.

circa *prep.* e *avv.* about, nearly || — *a*, as to.

circo *sm.* circus.

circolante *agg.* circulating: *moneta* —, currency.

circolare[1] *agg.* circular. ♦ **circolare** *sf.* circular letter.

circolare[2] *vi.* to circulate.

circolatorio *agg.* circulatory.

circolazione *sf.* **1.** circulation **2.** (*traffico*) traffic **3.** (*comm.*) currency.

circolo *sm.* **1.** circle **2.** (*associazione*) club.

circoncidere *vt.* to circumcise.

circoncisione *sf.* circumcision.

circondare *vt.* to surround (*anche fig.*).

circonferenza *sf.* circumference.

circonflesso *agg.* circumflex.

circonlocuzione *sf.* circumlocution.

circonvallazione *sf.* ring-road.

circonvenire *vt.* to circumvent.

circonvoluzione *sf.* circumvolution.

circoscrivere *vt.* to circumscribe.

circoscrizione *sf.* **1.** circumscription **2.** (*territorio*) area.

circospetto *agg.* circumspect.

circospezione *sf.* circumspection.

circostante *agg.* **1.** surrounding **2.** (*attr.*) neighbouring.

circostanza *sf.* circumstance, occasion: *in queste circostanze*, under these circumstances; *in quella* —, on that occasion.

circostanziale *agg.* circumstantial.

circostanziare *vt.* to detail.

circuire *vt.* **1.** to surround **2.** (*fig.*) to circumvent.

circuito *sm.* circuit.

cirillico *agg.* cyrillic.

cirrosi *sf.* cirrhosis.

cisalpino *agg.* cisalpine.

cisposo *agg.* blear.

ciste *sf.* cyst.

cisterna *sf.* **1.** cistern **2.** (*serbatoio*) tank.

cistifellea *sf.* gall-bladder.

cistite *sf.* cystitis.

citare *vt.* **1.** (*menzionare*) to mention **2.** (*da un libro o da un discorso ecc.*) to quote **3.** (*giur.*) to summon.

citazione *sf.* **1.** (*da un discorso, un libro ecc.*) quotation **2.** (*giur.*) summons (*pl.*).

citofono *sm.* interphone.

citologia *sf.* (*biol.*) cytology.

citrato *sm.* citrate.

citrico *agg.* citric.

città *sf.* **1.** town: — *di provincia*, country town; — *natale*, home town; *gente di* —, townspeople; *vita di* —, town life **2.** (*metropoli*) city.

cittadella *sf.* **1.** citadel **2.** (*baluardo*) stronghold.

cittadina *sf.* **1.** small town **2.** (*donna che abita in città*) woman citizen.

cittadinanza *sf.* **1.** (*abitanti*) people of the city **2.** (*nazionalità*) citizenship: *diritto di* —, right of citizenship.

cittadino *sm.* **1.** (*che abita in città*) town-dweller **2.** (*che appartiene a uno stato*) citizen. ♦ **cittadino** *agg.* town.

ciuffo *sm.* **1.** forelock **2.** (*di penne, peli, erba*) tuft.

ciurma *sf.* crew.

civetta *sf.* **1.** owl **2.** (*fig.*) coquette.

civetteria *sf.* coquetry.

civico *agg.* civic.

civile *agg.* **1.** civil **2.** (*che riguarda la civiltà*) civilized **3.** (*gentile*) polite **4.** (*non ecclesiastico o non militare*) civilian.

civilizzare *vt.* to civilize.

civilizzazione *sf.* civilization.

civiltà *sf.* **1.** civilization **2.** (*cortesia*) politeness.

civismo *sm.* civic virtues (*pl.*).

clamore *sm.* uproar.

clamoroso *agg.* noisy.

clandestino *agg.* clandestine, secret.

clarinetto, clarino *sm.* clarinet.

classe *sf.* class ‖ *di* — (*qualità*), first-rate.

classicismo *sm.* classicism.

classico *agg.* classical. ♦ **classico** *sm.* classic.

classifica *sf.* **1.** classification **2.** (*sport*) position.

classificare *vt.* to classify.

classificazione *sf.* classification.

claudicare *vi.* to limp.

clausola *sf.* **1.** clause **2.** (*riserva*) reserve.

claustrofobia *sf.* claustrophobia.

clava *sf.* club.

clavicembalo *sm.* harpsichord.

clavicola *sf.* collar-bone.

clemente *agg.* clement, mild.

clemenza *sf.* clemency, mildness.

cleptomane *agg. e sm.* kleptomaniac.

cleptomania *sf.* kleptomania.

clericale *agg.* clerical.

clero *sm.* clergy.

cliente *sm.* **1.** customer **2.** (*di medico, avvocato*) client.

clientela *sf.* **1.** customers (*pl.*) **2.** (*di medico, avvocato*) practice **3.** (*comm.*) connection.

clima *sm.* climate.

clinica *sf.* nursing-home.

clinico *agg.* clinical. ♦ **clinico** *sm* clinician.

clistere *sm.* enema.

cloaca *sf.* cloaca.

cloro *sm.* chlorine.

clorofilla *sf.* chlorophyll.

cloroformio *sm.* chloroform.

cloruro *sm.* chloride.

coabitare *vi.* to cohabit.

coabitazione *sf.* cohabitation.

coadiuvante *agg.* coadjuvant.

coadiuvare *vt.* to help.

coagulare *vt.* **1.** to coagulate **2.** (*del latte*) to curdle.

coagulazione *sf.* coagulation.

coagulo *sm.* **1.** curd **2.** (*di sangue*) blood-clot.

coalizione *sf.* alliance, coalition.

coalizzare *vt.* to unite. ♦ **coalizzarsi** *vr.* to form a coalition.

coartare *vt.* to force.

coatto *agg.* forced: *domicilio —,* forced residence.

cobalto *sm.* cobalt.

cobelligerante *agg.* e *sm.* co-belligerent.

cobra *sm.* cobra.

cocaina *sf.* cocaine.

cocainòmane *s.* cocainist.

coccarda *sf.* cockade.

cocchiere *sm.* coachman (*pl.* -men).

cocchio *sm.* coach.

coccige *sm.* cocyx (*pl.* -yges).

coccinella *sf.* ladybird.

cocciniglia *sf.* cochineal.

coccio *sm.* **1.** (*terracotta*) crock, pot **2.** (*pezzo rotto*) fragment of pottery.

cocciutàggine *sf.* stubbornness.

cocciuto *agg.* stubborn.

cocco *sm.* **1.** (*frutto*) coconut **2.** (*albero*) coconut-tree **3.** (*fam. vezz.*) darling.

coccodrillo *sm.* crocodile.

coccolare *vt.* to pet, to fondle.

cocente *agg.* **1.** hot, scalding **2.** (*fig.*) deep, bitter.

cocòmero *sm.* water-melon.

cocùzzolo *sm.* **1.** crown **2.** (*vetta*) top.

coda *sf.* **1.** tail **2.** (*fila*) queue: *fare la —,* to queue up.

codardo *agg.* cowardly. ♦ **codardo** *sm.* coward.

codesto *agg.* **1.** that (*pl.* those) **2.** (*come « tale »*) such. ♦ **codesto** *pron.* that one (*pl.* those ones).

còdice *sm.* **1.** code: — *civile,* Civil Law **2.** (*manoscritto antico*) codex.

codificare *vt.* to codify.

coefficiente *sm.* coefficient.

coercitivo *agg.* coercive.

coercizione *sf.* compulsion.

coerente *agg.* coherent.

coerenza *sf.* coherence.

coesione *sf.* cohesion.

coesistenza *sf.* coexistence.

coesistere *vi.* to coexist.

coetàneo *agg.* e *sm.* contemporary || *Carlo ed io siamo coetanei,* Charles and I are the same age.

cofanetto *sm.* casket: — *di gioielli,* jewel box.

còfano *sm.* **1.** coffer **2.** (*auto*) bonnet.

cògliere *vt.* **1.** to pick up, to pluck **2.** (*sorprendere*) to catch (*v. irr.*) **3.** (*colpire*) to hit (*v. irr.*) **4.** (*afferrare*) to seize: — *la palla al balzo,* to seize the opportunity.

cognata *sf.* sister-in-law.

cognato *sm.* brother-in-law.

cognizione *sf.* **1.** knowledge **2.** (*giur.*) cognizance.

cognome *sm.* surname.

coincidenza *sf.* **1.** coincidence **2.** (*ferr.*) connection.

coincidere *vi.* to coincide, to clash.

coinvòlgere *vt.* to involve.

còito *sm.* coition.

colabrodo *sm.* strainer.

colaggio *sm.* **1.** (*di liquidi*) leakage **2.** (*metal.*) casting.

colare *vt.* **1.** to strain **2.** (*fondere*) to cast (*v. irr.*). ♦ **colare** *vi.* to drip.

colata *sf.* **1.** (*metal.*) casting **2.** (*quantità di metallo fuso*) cast **3.** (*di lava*) flow.

colato *agg.* strained, filtered.

colazione *sf.* **1.** (*del mattino*) breakfast **2.** (*di mezzogiorno*) lunch.

colbacco *sm.* busby.

colei *pron. dimostr.* **1.** (*sogg.*) she; (*ogg.*) her **2.** — *che,* she who, she whom (*sogg.*); her who, her whom (*ogg.*): — *che viene qui è mia sorella,* she who is coming here is my sister; — *che vedi è Maria,* she whom you see is Mary; *vedi — che viene?,* can you see her who is coming?; *sono stata aiutata da —*

che odiavo, I have been helped by her whom I hated.

coleòttero *sm.* coleopter.

colera *sm.* cholera.

colesterolo *sm.* cholesterol.

còlica *sf.* colic.

colino *sm.* strainer.

colite *sf.* colitis.

colla *sf.* glue || — *di farina,* paste.

collaborare *vi.* to collaborate.

collaboratore *sm.* collaborator.

collaborazione *sf.* collaboration.

collaborazionismo *sm.* collaborationism.

collaborazionista *sm.* collaborationist.

collana *sf.* **1.** necklace **2.** (*raccolta*) collection **3.** (*di libri*) series.

collare *sm.* collar.

collasso *sm.* breakdown: — *cardiaco,* heart failure.

collaterale *agg.* collateral.

collaudare *vt.* to test.

collaudatore *sm.* **1.** tester **2.** (*aer.*) test pilot **3.** (*auto*) test-driver.

collàudo *sm.* test: *fare un — di qc.,* to put (*v. irr.*) sthg. to the test.

collazionare *vt.* to collate.

colle *sm.* hill.

collega *sm.* colleague.

collegamento *sm.* **1.** connection **2.** (*mecc.*) linkwork || *essere in —,* to be in touch.

collegare *vt.* to connect, to link.

collegiale *agg.* collegial. ♦ **collegiale** *sm.* boarder.

collegio *sm.* **1.** college **2.** (*scuola con convitto*) boarding-school.

còllera *sf.* anger || *essere in —,* to be angry.

collèrico *agg.* hot-tempered.

colletta *sf.* collection.

collettivismo *sm.* collectivism.

collettività *sf.* collectivity.

collettivizzare *vt.* to collectivize.

collettivizzazione *sf.* collectivization.

collettivo *agg.* collective.

colletto *sm.* collar.

collettore *agg.* collecting. ♦ **collettore** *sm.* **1.** (*esattore; raccoglitore*) collector **2.** (*mecc.*) manifold **3.** (*elettr.*) commutator.

collezionare *vt.* to collect.

collezione *sf.* collection.

collezionista *sm.* collector.

collimare *vi.* **1.** (*essere d'accordo*) to agree (with) **2.** (*coincidere*) to coincide.

collina *sf.* hill.

collinoso *agg.* hilly.

collirio *sm.* eye-wash.

collisione *sf.* collision (*anche fig.*), impact.

collo *sm.* **1.** neck: *allungare il —,* to crane one's neck || *a rotta di —,* at breakneck speed; *tra capo e —,* unexpectedly **2.** (*pacco*) parcel, package.

collocamento *sm.* **1.** placing **2.** (*impiego*) employment || *agenzia di —,* employment bureau **3.** (*comm.*) disposal.

collocare *vt.* **1.** to place **2.** (*impiegare*) to employ **3.** (*comm.*) to sell (*v. irr.*), to dispose (of sthg.). ♦ **collocarsi** *vr.* **1.** to place oneself **2.** (*impiegarsi*) to get a situation.

collocazione *sf.* **1.** placing **2.** (*comm.*) sale **3.** (*di libri in biblioteche*) press-mark.

colloidale *agg.* colloidal.

colloquio *sm.* **1.** conversation, talk **2.** (*intervista*) interview.

collusione *sf.* collusion.

colluttazione *sf.* scuffle: *venire a —,* to come (*v. irr.*) to grips.

colmare *vt.* **1.** to fill up **2.** (*fig.*) to fill, to overwhelm.

colmo *agg.* full, brimful. ♦ **colmo** *sm.* top, summit, climax || *per — di sfortuna,* as a crowning misfortune; *è il —!,* that beats everything.

colomba *sf.* dove.

colombaia *sf.* dove-cot.

colombo *sm.* pigeon: — *viaggiatore,* carrier-pigeon.

colonia *sf.* colony.

coloniale *agg.* colonial.

colonialismo *sm.* colonialism.

colonialista *sm.* colonialist.

colonizzare *vt.* to colonize.

colonizzatore *sm.* colonizer.

colonizzazione *sf.* colonization.

colonna *sf.* column (*anche fig.*), pillar || — *d'acqua,* fall of water.

colonnato *sm.* colonnade.

colonnello *sm.* colonel.

colono *sm.* **1.** farmer **2.** (*abitante di una colonia*) settler.

colorante *agg.* colouring. ♦ **colorante** *sm.* dye.

colorare *vt.* to colour. ♦ **colorarsi** *vr.* **1.** to colour **2.** (*di persona*) to blush, to flush.

colorazione *sf.* colouring.

colore *sm.* **1.** colour || *biancheria di —*, coloured linen; *gente di —*, coloured people; *colori a olio*, oil-paints **2.** (*aspetto*) look.

colorire *vt.* to colour.

colorito *sm.* complexion.

coloritura *sf.* colouring.

coloro *pron. dimostr.* **1.** they (*sogg.*); them (*compl.*) **2.** *— che,* they who, they whom (*sogg.*); them who, them whom (*compl.*): *— studiano saranno premiati,* they who study will be given a prize; *— tu vedi sono i miei amici,* they whom you see are my friends; *amerò sempre — mi amano,* I shall always love them who love me; *ti presenterò a — hai visto ieri,* I shall introduce you to them whom you saw yesterday.

colossale *agg.* colossal.

colosso *sm.* colossus (*pl.* -si).

colpa *sf.* **1.** fault **2.** (*colpevolezza*) guilt.

colpévole *agg.* guilty.

colpevolezza *sf.* guilt, guiltiness.

colpire *vt.* **1.** to hit (*v. irr.*), to strike (*v. irr.; anche fig.*) **2.** (*di arma da fuoco*) to shoot (*v. irr.*).

colpo *sm.* **1.** blow, stroke (*anche fig.*): *— di fortuna,* stroke of luck; *— apoplettico,* stroke of apoplexy || *— d'aria,* draught; *a — d'occhio,* at a glance; *a — sicuro,* without any risk; *senza — ferire,* without resistance **2.** (*di arma da fuoco*) shot.

colposo *agg.* unpremeditated: *omicidio —,* manslaughter.

coltellata *sf.* stab.

coltello *sm.* knife: *— a serramanico,* jack-knife; *affilare un —,* to sharpen a knife.

coltivàbile *agg.* cultivable.

coltivare *vt.* to cultivate (*anche fig.*), to till, to farm.

coltivatore *sm.* **1.** tiller, farmer **2.** (*di patate, tabacco ecc.*) grower.

coltivazione *sf.* **1.** tilling, farming **2.** (*di patate, tabacco ecc.*) growing.

colto *agg.* (*istruito*) learned.

coltre *sf.* blanket, coverlet.

colui *pron. dimostr.* **1.** he (*sogg.*) him (*compl.*) **2.** *— che,* he who, he whom (*sogg.*); him who, him whom (*compl.*): *— che ti ha salutato è mio fratello,* he who has greeted you is my brother; *— che vedesti ieri è un mio vecchio ami-*co, he whom you saw yesterday is an old friend of mine; *daranno il premio a — che studierà,* they will give the prize to him who studies; *fui aiutata da — che avevo aiutato,* I was helped by him whom I had helped.

coma *sm.* coma.

comandamento *sm.* **1.** command, precept **2.** (*relig.*) commandment.

comandante *sm.* commander.

comandare *vt.* **1.** to order, to command **2.** (*essere al comando*) to command, to be in command of.

comando *sm.* **1.** (*ordine*) order **2.** (*autorità*) command **3.** (*sede del comandante*) headquarters (*pl.*).

comatoso *agg.* comatose.

combaciare *vi.* to fit together.

combattente *sm.* **1.** fighting man **2.** (*soldato*) soldier, service man.

combattentìstico *agg.* soldier (like) (*attr.*).

combàttere *vt. e vi.* to fight (*v. irr.*) (*anche fig.*).

combattimento *sm.* **1.** combat, fight, battle **2.** (*boxe*) match.

combattività *sf.* pugnacity.

combattivo *agg.* pugnacious.

combinare *vt.* **1.** to combine **2.** (*di colori*) to match **3.** (*concludere*) to conclude **4.** (*progettare*) to plan.

combinazione *sf.* **1.** combination **2.** (*sistemazione*) arrangement **3.** (*caso, coincidenza*) chance, coincidence.

combrìccola *sf.* **1.** band **2.** (*comitiva*) party.

combustìbile *agg.* combustible. ◆ **combustìbile** *sm.* fuel.

combustione *sf.* combustion.

combutta *sf.* **1.** gang: *essere in —,* to be hand in glove **2.** (*congiura*) plot.

come *avv.* **1.** (*simile a*) like: *è proprio — suo padre,* he is just like his father **2.** (*in qualità di, modale*) as: *ti parlo — amico,* I am speaking to you as a friend **3.** (*in comp.*) as ... as; so ... as: *Carlo è studioso — me,* Charles is as studious as I; *Carlo non è studioso — me,* Charles is not so studious as I **4.** (*int.*) how: *— va?,* How are you? **5.** (*escl.*) how: *— è interessante questo libro!,* How interesting this book is! ◆ **come** *prep.* **1.** (*tempo-*

rale) as, as soon as: — *sentii la sua voce lo riconobbi*, as soon as I heard his voice I recognized him **2.** (*come se*) as if: *mi guarda — se mi conoscesse*, he is looking at me as if he knew me || — *Dio volle*, in God's good time; — *segue*, as follows; — *d'accordo*, as agreed.

cometa *sf.* comet.

comicità *sf.* comicality.

còmico *agg.* comical, funny. ♦ **còmico** *sm.* comedian.

comìgnolo *sm.* chimney-pot.

cominciare *vt.* to begin (*v. irr.*), to start.

comitato *sm.* committee.

comitiva *sf.* party, company.

comizio *sm.* meeting.

comma *sm.* paragraph.

commedia *sf.* **1.** comedy, play **2.** (*fig.*) pretence || *recitare la —*, to play a part.

commediante *sm.* **1.** player **2.** (*fig.*) shammer.

commediògrafo *sm.* playwright.

commemorare *vt.* to commemorate.

commemorativo *agg.* memorial.

commemorazione *sf.* commemoration.

commendàbile *agg.* commendable.

commendatizia *sf.* letter of recommendation.

commensale *sm.* table-companion.

commentare *vt.* to comment (on).

commentario *sm.* (*lett.*) commentary.

commentatore *sm.* commentator.

commento *sm.* commentary.

commerciàbile *agg.* negotiable.

commerciale *agg.* commercial.

commercializzare *vt.* to commercialize.

commerciante *sm.* **1.** trader **2.** (*uomo d'affari*) business-man (*pl.* -men) || — *all'ingrosso*, wholesale dealer; — *al minuto*, retailer.

commerciare *vi.* to trade, to deal (*v. irr.*) (in).

commercio *sm.* **1.** commerce, trade **2.** (*affari*) business || — *all'ingrosso*, wholesale trade; — *al minuto*, retail trade; — *d'importazione, esportazione*, import, export trade; *essere in —*, to be on sale; *essere fuori —*, to be out of sale; *essere in — (di un commerciante)*, to be in business.

commessa *sf.* shop assistant, shop-girl.

commesso *sm.* clerk, shopman (*pl.* -men), shop assistant || — *viaggiatore*, commercial traveller.

commestìbile *agg.* eatable. ♦ **commestìbili** *sm. pl.* foodstuffs.

comméttere *vt.* **1.** to commit, to do (*v. irr.*), to make (*v. irr.*) **2.** (*ordinare*) to order.

commiato *sm.* **1.** (*preso*) leave **2.** (*dato*) dismissal.

commilitone *sm.* fellow-soldier.

comminatoria *sf.* commination.

comminatorio *agg.* comminatory.

commiserare *vt.* to pity.

commiserazione *sf.* pity.

commissariato *sm.* **1.** (*carica di commissario*) commissaryship **2.** (*ufficio*) commissary's office.

commissario *sm.* commissary.

commissionare *vt.* (*comm.*) to order.

commissionario *sm.* (*comm.*) commission agent.

commissione *sf.* **1.** errand: *fare una —*, to go (*v. irr.*) on an errand **2.** (*comm.*) commission, order **3.** (*comitato*) commission, committee.

commisurare *vt.* to compare.

committente *sm.* purchaser, buyer.

commosso *agg.* moved, affected.

commovente *agg.* moving, touching, affecting.

commozione *sf.* **1.** emotion **2.** (*med.*) concussion: — *cerebrale*, concussion of the brain.

commuòvere *vt.* to move, to touch. ♦ **commuòversi** *vr.* to be moved.

commutàbile *agg.* commutable.

commutare *vt.* to commute.

commutativo *agg.* commutative.

commutatore *sm.* commutator.

comò *sm.* chest of drawers.

comodino *sm.* night-table.

comodità *sf.* convenience, comfort.

còmodo *agg.* **1.** useful **2.** (*conveniente*) convenient **3.** (*confortevole*) comfortable **4.** (*maneggevole*) handy.

compagnìa *sf.* **1.** company: *tener —*, to keep (*v. irr.*) company **2.** (*gruppo di persone*) party **3.** (*società*) company.

compagno *sm.* companion, mate, comrade || — *di giuochi*, playmate; — *di stanza*, room-mate; — *di studi*, fellow-student.

compagnone *sm.* jolly good fellow.

comparàbile *agg.* comparable.

comparare *vt.* to compare.

comparativo *agg.* (*gramm.*) comparative.

comparato *agg.* comparative.

compare *sm.* **1.** (*compagno*) comrade, partner **2.** (*padrino*) godfather **3.** (*testimone di matrimonio*) witness **4.** (*complice*) accomplice.

comparire *vi.* **1.** to appear **2.** (*sembrare*) to show (*v. irr.*) oneself **3.** (*far bella mostra*) to show (*v. irr.*) off.

comparizione *sf.* appearance: (*giur.*) *mandato di —,* summons.

comparsa *sf.* **1.** appearance **2.** (*teat.; cine*) supernumerary **3.** (*giur.*) appearance.

compartecipare *vi.* to share in.

compartimento *sm.* **1.** compartment **2.** (*circoscrizione*) department.

compartizione *sf.* distribution.

compassato *agg.* **1.** stiff, formal **2.** (*di discorso*) restrained.

compassione *sf.* pity, commiseration.

compasso *sm.* compasses (*pl.*).

compatìbile *agg.* consistent.

compatibilità *sf.* consistency.

compatimento *sm.* pity, compassion.

compatire *vt.* to pity.

compatriota *sm.* fellow-countryman (*pl.* -men). ♦ **compatriota** *sf.* fellow-countrywoman (*pl.* -women).

compattezza *sf.* **1.** compactness **2.** (*di associazione, partito*) unity.

compatto *agg.* compact, solid.

compendiare *vt.* to abridge, to sum up.

compendio *sm.* **1.** abridgement, summary.

compenetrare *vt.* to penetrate.

compensàbile *agg.* remunerable.

compensare *vt.* **1.** to compensate **2.** (*ricompensare*) to reward.

compensato *sm.* ply-wood.

compensazione *sf.* **1.** compensation, indemnity **2.** (*comm.*) clearing.

compenso *sm.* **1.** compensation **2.** (*rimunerazione*) reward, retribution.

còmpera *sf.* purchase.

competente *agg.* competent.

competenza *sf.* **1.** competence **2.** (*onorario*) fee.

compètere *vi.* **1.** (*gareggiare*) to vie **2.** (*spettare*) to be due, to belong.

competitivo *agg.* competitive.

competitore *sm.* competitor, rival.

competizione *sf.* competition.

compiacente *agg.* obliging.

compiacenza *sf.* **1.** kindness **2.** (*soddisfazione*) satisfaction.

compiacere *vt.* to please, to gratify. ♦ **compiacersi** *vr.* **1.** to be pleased (with), to congratulate **2.** (*degnarsi*) to condescend.

compiacimento *sm.* **1.** satisfaction **2.** (*congratulazione*) congratulation.

compiàngere *vt.* **1.** to pity, to sympathize (with) **2.** (*disprezzare*) to despise.

compianto *agg.* regretted. ♦ **compianto** *sm.* regret.

còmpiere *vt.* **1.** (*finire*) to finish **2.** (*eseguire*) to accomplish **3.** (*adempiere*) to do (*v. irr.*): — *il proprio dovere,* to do one's duty **4.** (*di età*) *ho compiuto 30 anni,* I am now 30 years old.

compilare *vt.* to compile: — *un documento,* to draw (*v. irr.*) up a document; — *una lista,* to make (*v. irr.*) a list.

compilazione *sf.* **1.** compilation **2.** (*comm.*) drawing up.

compimento *sm.* **1.** (*il compire*) completion **2.** (*conclusione*) achievement.

compitare *vt.* to spell (*v. irr.*).

compitezza *sf.* politeness, refinement.

compito *agg.* polite.

còmpito *sm.* **1.** task, duty **2.** (*scolastico, a casa*) homework; (*a scuola*) class-work.

compiutamente *avv.* completely.

compiutezza *sf.* completeness.

compiuto *agg.* complete.

compleanno *sm.* birthday: *buon —!,* happy birthday!.

complementare *agg.* complementary.

complemento *sm.* **1.** complement **2.** (*gramm.*) — *indiretto,* indirect object **3.** (*mil.*) *truppe di —,* reserve.

complessato *agg.* neurotic.

complessione *sf.* constitution.

complessità *sf.* complexity.

complessivamente *avv.* on the whole.

complessivo *agg.* total, inclusive.

complesso *agg.* complex, complicated. ♦ **complesso** *sm.* **1.** whole **2.** (*industriale*) plant, set **3.** (*mus.*) band.

completamente *avv.* completely.

completare *vt.* to complete, to finish.

completezza *sf.* completeness.

completo *agg.* **1.** complete, whole **2.** (*pieno*) full. ♦ **completo** *sm.* (*vestito*) suit.

complicare *vt.* to complicate.

complicato *agg.* complicated.

complicazione *sf.* complication: *salvo complicazioni*, if no complications set in.

còmplice *s.* accomplice.

complicità *sf.* accomplicity.

complimentare *vt.* to compliment. ♦ **complimentarsi** *vr.* to congratulate (so.).

complimento *sm.* **1.** compliment **2.** (*congratulazione*) congratulation.

complottare *vi.* to plot.

complotto *sm.* plot, conspiracy.

compluvio *sm.* (*arch.*) compluvium (*pl.* -ia).

componente *agg.* component. ♦ **componente** *sm.* **1.** member **2.** (*chim.*) component.

componimento *sm.* **1.** (*lett.*; *mus.*; *scol.*) composition **2.** (*giur.*) settlement.

comporre *vt.* **1.** to compose: — *una poesia*, to write (*v. irr.*) a poem; — *un numero telefonico*, to dial a number **2.** (*chim.*) to compound **3.** (*assestare*) to arrange.

comportamento *sm.* behaviour.

comportare *vt.* to involve, to require. ♦ **comportarsi** *vr.* to behave (oneself).

compòsito *agg.* composite.

compositore *sm.* **1.** (*mus.*) composer **2.** (*tip.*) compositor.

composizione *sf.* **1.** composition **2.** (*conciliazione*) composition, agreement **3.** (*tip.*) composing.

composta *sf.* compote.

compostezza *sf.* **1.** composure **2.** (*dignità*) self-respect.

composto *agg.* **1.** compound **2.** (*ordinato*) tidy **3.** (*calmo*) calm ‖ *stare* —, to sit (*v. irr.*) still. ♦ **composto** *sm.* compound.

comprare *vt.* **1.** to buy (*v. irr.*): — *a credito*, to buy on credit; — *per contanti*, to buy for cash; — *all'ingrosso*, to buy wholesale **2.** (*corrompere*) to bribe.

compratore *sm.* buyer, purchaser.

compravéndita *sf.* marketing.

comprèndere *vt.* **1.** (*includere*) to include, to take (*v. irr.*) in **2.** (*capire*) to understand (*v. irr.*) **3.** (*rendersi conto*) to realize.

comprensìbile *agg.* intelligible.

comprensibilità *sf.* intelligibility.

comprensione *sf.* **1.** comprehension, understanding **2.** (*compassione*) sympathy.

comprensivo *agg.* **1.** comprehensive **2.** (*che capisce*) comprehending **3.** (*che prova simpatia*) sympathetic.

compressa *sf.* **1.** tablet **2.** (*di garza*) compress.

compressibilità *sf.* compressibility.

compressione *sf.* compression.

comprìmere *vt.* **1.** to compress **2.** (*fig.*) to restrain, to repress.

compromesso *sm.* compromise.

compromettente *agg.* compromising.

compromettère *vt.* to compromise, to involve.

comproprietà *sf.* joint ownership.

comproprietario *sm.* joint owner.

comprovare *vt.* to prove.

compunto *agg.* filled with compunction, contrite.

computare *vt.* to compute.

computisterìa *sf.* book-keeping.

còmputo *sm.* reckoning.

comunale *agg.* communal, municipal.

comunardo *sm.* (*stor.*) Communard.

comune[1] *agg.* **1.** common **2.** (*abituale*) frequent, usual.

comune[2] *sm.* **1.** commune **2.** (*edificio*) Town Hall.

comunella *sf.* cabal: *far — con qu.*, to consort.

comunemente *avv.* commonly, usually.

comunicàbile *agg.* communicable.

comunicabilità *sf.* communicability.

comunicante *agg.* communicating.

comunicare *vt.* **1.** to communicate, to transmit **2.** (*relig.*) to communicate. ♦ **comunicarsi** *vr.* to receive Holy Communion.

comunicativa *sf.* communicativeness.

comunicativo *agg.* communicative.

comunicato *sm.* bulletin.

comunicazione *sf.* communication.

comunione *sf.* **1.** communion: —

di idee, similarity of ideas **2.** (*relig.*) Holy Communion.

comunismo *sm.* communism.

comunista *s.* communist.

comunità *sf.* community.

comunque *avv.* however, anyhow.

con *prep.* **1.** (*compagnia, unione, strumento*) with: *venne — me*, he came with me; *scrivo — questa penna*, I write with this pen **2.** (*stato, condizione*) in: — *il freddo sto meglio*, in cold weather I feel better **3.** (*mezzo di trasporto*) by: *arriverò col treno delle 3*, I shall arrive by the three o'clock train **4.** (*per mezzo di*) by means of.

conato *sm.* effort ‖ *avere conati di vomito*, to feel (*v. irr.*) sick.

conca *sf.* **1.** basin, pot **2.** (*valle*) valley.

concatenamento *sm.* concatenation.

concatenare *vt.* to concatenate.

concatenazione *sf.* concatenation.

còncavo *agg.* concave, hollow.

concèdere *vt.* **1.** to grant, to bestow **2.** (*permettere*) to allow.

concentramento *sm.* concentration: *campo di —*, concentration camp.

concentrare *vt.* to concentrate. ♦ **concentrarsi** *vr.* to concentrate.

concentrato *agg.* concentrated. ♦ **concentrato** *sm.* concentrated food.

concentrazione *sf.* concentration.

concèntrico *agg.* concentric.

concepìbile *agg.* conceivable.

concepimento *sm.* conception.

concepire *vt.* **1.** to conceive **2.** (*nutrire speranze, timori*) to entertain **3.** (*formulare*) to express.

concerìa *sf.* tannery.

concèrnere *vt.* to concern, to relate to.

concertare *vt.* **1.** (*mus.*) to harmonize **2.** (*stabilire*) to plan, to arrange.

concertato *agg.* concerted (*anche mus.*), arranged.

concertista *s.* concert artist.

concertìstico *agg.* concert.

concerto *sm.* concert.

concessionario *sm.* concessionary agent.

concessione *sf.* **1.** concession **2.** (*permesso*) permission.

concetto *sm.* concept.

concettuale *agg.* conceptual.

concezionale *agg.* conceptional.

concezione *sf.* conception.

conchiglia *sf.* shell.

concia *sf.* **1.** (*di pelli*) tanning **2.** (*di tabacco*) curing.

conciare *vt.* **1.** (*pelli*) to tan **2.** (*tabacco*) to cure **3.** (*fig.*) to ill-treat **4.** (*insudiciare*) to soil. ♦ **conciarsi** *vr.* to get (*v. irr.*) dirty.

conciatore *sm.* tanner.

conciatura *sf.* tanning.

conciliàbile *agg.* compatible, consistent.

conciliabilità *sf.* compatibility.

conciliàbolo *sm.* conventicle, secret talk.

conciliante *agg.* conciliatory.

conciliare *vt.* **1.** to reconcile **2.** (*procacciare*) to win (*v. irr.*), to gain. ♦ **conciliarsi** *vr.* to win (*v. irr.*).

conciliare *agg.* conciliar.

conciliativo *agg.* conciliatory. ♦ **conciliatore** *sm.* peacemaker ‖ *giudice —*, Justice of the Peace.

conciliazione *sf.* conciliation.

concilio *sm.* Council.

concimaia *sf.* dung-hill, dung-pit.

concimare *vt.* to dung.

concimazione *sf.* dunging.

concime *sm.* **1.** (*organico*) dung **2.** (*chimico*) fertilizer.

concio *sm.* dung.

concionare *vi.* to harangue.

concione *sf.* harangue.

concisione *sf.* concision.

conciso *agg.* concise, brief.

concistoro *sm.* (*eccl.*) concistory.

concitare *vt.* to excite, to stir (up).

concitazione *sf.* excitement, agitation.

concittadino *sm.* fellow-citizen.

conclamare *vt.* to acclaim.

conclave *sm.* (*eccl.*) conclave.

concludente *agg.* **1.** conclusive **2.** (*di persona*) energetic.

conclùdere *vt.* **1.** to conclude, to finish **2.** (*dedurre*) to infer **3.** (*fare*) to do (*v. irr.*).

conclusionale *sf.* (*giur.*) pleadings (*pl.*).

conclusione *sf.* **1.** conclusion **2.** (*risultato*) issue, result.

conclusivo *agg.* conclusive.

concomitante *agg.* concomitant.

concomitanza *sf.* concomitance.

concordanza *sf.* agreement.

concordare *vi.* to agree. ♦ **concordare** *vt.* **1.** to agree upon **2.**

(*mettere d'accordo*) to reconcile **3.** (*gramm.*) to put (*v. irr.*) in concord.

concordatario *agg.* **1.** (*eccl.*) of concordat **2.** (*giur.; comm.*) composition.

concordato *sm.* **1.** convention **2.** (*eccl.*) concordat **3.** (*giur.; comm.*) agreement, composition.

concorde *agg.* concordant, agreeing: *volontà* —, unanimous will.

concordemente *avv.* concordantly.

concordia *sf.* concord, agreement.

concorrente *agg.* **1.** concurrent **2.** (*rivale*) competing. ◆ **concorrente** *sm.* **1.** candidate **2.** (*rivale*) competitor.

concorrenza *sf.* **1.** (*affluenza*) concourse **2.** (*comm.*) competition ‖ *fare* —, to compete with; — *sleale*, unfair competition.

concorrenziale *agg.* competitive.

concòrrere *vi.* **1.** to come (*v. irr.*) together **2.** (*contribuire*) to concur, to contribute **3.** (*partecipare*) to share in **4.** (*mettersi in gara*) to compete.

concorso *sm.* **1.** (*affluenza*) rush, crowd, concourse **2.** (*gara*) competition **3.** (*sport*) contest.

concretare *vt.* **1.** to make (*v. irr.*) concrete **2.** (*concludere*) to realize.

concretezza *sf.* concreteness.

concreto *agg.* **1.** concrete, real **2.** (*solido*) solid.

concrezione *sf.* concretion.

concubina *sf.* concubine.

concubinaggio, concubinato *sm.* concubinage.

conculcare *vt.* to trample on.

concupire *vt.* to covet, to lust after.

concupiscenza *sf.* concupiscence, lust.

concussione *sf.* (*giur.*) concussion.

condanna *sf.* **1.** condemnation **2.** (*sentenza*) sentence: — *a morte*, death sentence **3.** (*pena*) penalty.

condannàbile *agg.* condemnable.

condannare *vt.* **1.** to sentence **2.** (*fig.*) to condemn **3.** (*riprovare*) to blame.

condannato *agg.* sentenced. ◆ **condannato** *sm.* condemned man.

condensàbile *agg.* condensable.

condensabilità *vt.* condensability.

condensazione *sf.* condensation.

condensare *vt.* to condense.

condensatore *sm.* condenser.

condimento *sm.* seasoning, dressing.

condire *vt.* to season; (*anche fig.*) to flavour.

condirettore *sm.* joint manager.

condiscendente *agg.* complying.

condiscendenza *sf.* **1.** compliance **2.** (*degnazione*) condescension.

condiscèndere *vi.* **1.** to comply with **2.** (*degnarsi*) to condescend.

condiscépolo *sm.* schoolfellow.

condivìdere *vt.* to share (*anche fig.*).

condizionale *agg. e sm.* conditional. ◆ **condizionale** *sf.* (*giur.*) conditional sentence.

condizionamento *sm.* conditioning.

condizionare *vt.* to condition.

condizione *sf.* **1.** condition: *a* — *che*: on condition that **2.** (*ceto*) rank, station.

condoglianza *sf.* condolence.

condominio *sm.* joint ownership.

condòmino *sm.* joint-owner.

condonare *vt.* to remit.

condono *sm.* remission.

condotta *sf.* **1.** conduct, behaviour.

condotto *agg. medico* —, doctor employed by the local authority. ◆ **condotto** *sm.* **1.** conduit, pipeline **2.** (*anat.*) duct.

conducente *sm.* driver.

conducibilità *sf.* (*fis.*) conductibility.

condurre *vt.* **1.** (*guidare*) to lead (*v. irr.*) **2.** (*accompagnare*) to take (*v. irr.*) **3.** (*governare, trattare*) to manage: — *i propri affari*, to manage one's business **4.** (*vivere*) to lead (*v. irr.*): — *una vita triste*, to lead a sad life. ◆ **condurre** *vi.* to lead (*v. irr.*): *questa strada conduce a Milano*, this route leads to Milan. ◆ **condursi** *vr.* to behave.

conduttività *sf.* conductivity.

conduttivo *agg.* conducting.

conduttore *agg.* conducting. ◆ **conduttore** *sm.* **1.** leader, guide **2.** (*di veicoli*) driver **3.** (*fis.*) conductor.

conduttura *sf.* **1.** duct, conduit **2.** (*di tubazioni*) piping.

conduzione *sf.* **1.** management **2.** (*fis.*) conduction.

confabulare *vi.* to confabulate.

confacente *agg.* suitable, proper.

confarsi *vr.* to suit, to become (*v. irr.*).

confederale *agg.* confederal.

confederare *vt.* to confederate.

confederazione *sf.* **1.** Confederation **2.** (*alleanza*) confederacy.

conferenza *sf.* **1.** lecture **2.** (*assemblea*) conference.

conferenziere *sm.* lecturer.

conferimento *sm.* bestowal.

conferire *vt.* to confer, to bestow. ♦ **conferire** *vi.* **1.** to have an interview **2.** (*giovare*) to be useful.

conferma *sf.* confirmation.

confermare *vt.* to confirm. ♦ **confermarsi** *vr.* to prove oneself.

confermazione *sf.* confirmation.

confessare *vt.* **1.** to confess **2.** (*riconoscere, ammettere*) to admit. ♦ **confessarsi** *vr.* (*eccl.*) to go (*v. irr.*) to confession.

confessionale *agg.* confessional. ♦ **confessionale** *sm.* confessional.

confessione *sf.* **1.** confession **2.** (*ammissione*) admission **3.** (*memorie*) memoirs (*pl.*).

confessore *sm.* confessor.

confetterìa *sf.* confectionery.

confettiere *sm.* confectioner.

confetto *sm.* comfit.

confettura *sf.* **1.** (*confetti*) sweetmeats (*pl.*) **2.** (*marmellata*) jam ‖ — *d'arance*, marmalade.

confezionare *vt.* **1.** to make (*v. irr.*) up **2.** (*di piatti*) to prepare **3.** (*di pacchi*) to pack up.

confezione *sf.* **1.** manufacture **2.** (*preparazione*) preparation **3.** (*pl.*) (*abiti*) ready-to-wear clothes **4.** (*imballaggio*) packing.

conficcare *vt.* to hammer, to drive (*v. irr.*). ♦ **conficcarsi** *vr.* to run (*v. irr.*) into.

confidare *vt.* to confide. ♦ **confidare** *vi.* **1.** to confide, to trust **2.** (*fare assegnamento*) to rely (on).

confidente *agg.* trustful. ♦ **confidente** *sm.* **1.** confidant **2.** (*di polizia*) police spy.

confidenza *sf.* **1.** (*fiducia*) confidence **2.** (*cosa confidata*) secret **3.** (*familiarità*) familiarity ‖ *essere in* — *con qu.*, to be on familiar terms with so.

confidenziale *agg.* confidential: *strettamente* —, strictly confidential.

confidenzialmente *avv.* confidentially.

configgere *vt.* to drive (*v. irr.*) in.

configurare *vt.* to configure, to shape.

configurazione *sf.* configuration, shape.

confinante *agg.* **1.** neighbouring **2.** (*fig.*) bordering.

confinare *vi.* to border on. ♦ **confinare** *vt.* **1.** to banish **2.** (*fig.*) to confine.

confinario *agg.* border.

confinato *agg.* interned.

confine *sm.* **1.** border, frontier **2.** (*fig.*) limit, boundary.

confino *sm.* internment, political confinement.

confisca *sf.* confiscation.

confiscàbile *agg.* confiscable.

confiscare *vt.* to confiscate.

confitto *agg.* **1.** nailed, driven in **2.** (*fig.*) fixed.

conflagrare *vi.* to break (*v. irr.*) out.

conflagrazione *sf.* **1.** conflagration **2.** (*fig.*) sudden out-break (of war).

conflitto *sm.* **1.** conflict **2.** (*fig.*) clash.

confluente *sm.* confluent.

confluenza *sf.* confluence.

confluire *vi.* to flow together.

confòndere *vt.* **1.** to confuse **2.** (*scambiare una persona per un'altra*) to mistake (*v. irr.*) **3.** (*turbare*) to confound. ♦ **confòndersi** *vr.* **1.** to get (*v. irr.*) mixed up **2.** (*mescolarsi*) to mingle **3.** (*turbarsi*) to be disconcerted.

confondìbile *agg.* liable to be confused.

conformare *vt.* to conform. ♦ **conformarsi** *vr.* to conform.

conformato *agg.* shaped.

conformazione *sf.* conformation.

conforme *agg.* **1.** conforming **2.** (*simile*) similar **3.** (*fedele*) true ‖ — *a*, in conformity with. ♦ **conforme a·** *loc. avv.* in conformity with.

conformismo *sm.* time-serving.

conformista *s.* **1.** time-server **2.** (*relig.*) conformist.

conformìstico *agg.* conformist.

conformità *sf.* conformity.

confortàbile *agg.* consolable.

confortante *agg.* consoling.

confortare *vt.* **1.** to comfort **2.** (*incoraggiare*) to encourage.

confortatore *agg.* comforting. ♦ **confortatore** *sm.* comforter.

confortatorio *agg.* comforting.

confortévole *agg.* **1.** comforting **2.** (*comodo*) comfortable.

confortevolmente *avv.* comfortably.

conforto *sm.* **1.** comfort, solace **2.** (*incoraggiamento*) encouragement.

confratello *sm.* brother (*pl.* brethren).

confratèrnita *sf.* brotherhood.

confrontàbile *agg.* comparable.

confrontare *vt.* **1.** to compare **2.** (*giur.*) to confront.

confronto *sm.* **1.** comparison **2.** (*giur.*) confrontation || *nei confronti di,* to, towards; *in — a,* in comparison with.

confucianésimo *sm.* confucianism.

confusamente *avv.* confusedly.

confusionario *agg.* blundering, unmethodical. ◆ **confusionario** *sm.* bungler, muddler.

confusione *sf.* confusion, medley.

confusionismo *sm.* general confusion.

confuso *agg.* **1.** confused, mixed, vague **2.** (*indistinto*) indistinct **3.** (*imbarazzato*) embarrassed.

confutàbile *agg.* confutable.

confutare *vt.* to confute.

confutazione *sf.* confutation.

congedare *vt.* **1.** to dismiss **2.** (*mil.*) to discharge. ◆ **congedarsi** *vr.* to take (*v. irr.*) one's leave.

congedato *sm.* dischargee.

congedo *sm.* **1.** (*commiato*) leave **2.** (*mil.*) leave, discharge || *essere in —,* to be on leave.

congegnare *vt.* **1.** (*mecc.*) to assemble **2.** (*fig.*) to devise.

congegno *sm.* **1.** device, gear **2.** (*fig.*) device, scheme.

congelamento *sm.* **1.** freezing **2.** (*med.*) congelation.

congelare *vt.* to freeze (*v. irr.*), to congeal.

congelato *agg.* congealed, frozen (*anche comm.*).

congelatore *sm.* freezer.

congènere *agg.* **1.** akin (*attr.*) **2.** similar (*pred.*).

congeniale *agg.* congenial.

congènito *agg.* congenital, innate.

congestionare *vt.* to congest.

congestionato *agg.* congested: *viso —,* flushed face.

congestione *sf.* congestion.

congettura *sf.* conjecture, supposition.

congetturare *vt.* to conjecture.

congiùngere *vt.* **1.** to join **2.** (*collegare*) to connect.

congiuntiva *sf.* conjunctiva.

congiuntivite *sf.* conjunctivitis.

congiuntivo *agg.* conjunctive. ◆ **congiuntivo** *sm.* (*gramm.*) subjunctive.

congiunto *agg.* **1.** joined, united **2.** (*collegato*) connected. ◆ **congiunto** *sm.* relative.

congiunzione *sf.* **1.** point of junction **2.** (*circostanza, situazione*) circumstance, situation **3.** (*econ.*) trend, trade cycle.

congiunzione *sf.* **1.** connection **2.** (*gramm.; astr.*) conjunction.

congiura *sf.* conspiracy, plot.

congiurare *vi.* to conspire, to plot.

congiurato *sm.* conspirator, plotter.

conglobamento *sm.* conglobation.

conglobare *vt.* **1.** to conglobate **2.** (*di tasse, debiti ecc.*) to combine.

conglobazione *sf.* conglobation.

conglomerato *sm.* **1.** (*geol.*) conglomerate **2.** (*etnico; pol.*) grouping.

congratularsi *vr.* to congratulate.

congratulazione *sf.* congratulation.

congregazione *sf.* assembly, congregation (*anche eccl.*).

congressista *s.* member of a congress.

congresso *sm.* congress.

congruo *agg.* **1.** (*coerente*) congruous **2.** (*adeguato*) adequate.

conguagliare *vt.* **1.** to equalize **2.** (*comm.*) to balance.

coniare *vt.* to coin (*anche fig.*).

cònico *agg.* conic(al).

conifera *sf.* conifer.

coniglio *sm.* **1.** rabbit **2.** (*fig.*) faint-hearted.

conio *sm.* **1.** (*attrezzo per coniare*) minting die **2.** (*impronta*) coin, brand **3.** (*invenzione di nuove parole*) coinage.

coniugale *agg.* conjugal: *vita —,* married life.

coniugare *vt.* **1.** to conjugate **2.** (*unire in matrimonio*) to marry.

coniugato *agg.* married.

coniugazione *sf.* conjugation.

còniuge *sm.* husband. ◆ **còniuge** *sf.* wife.

connaturale *agg.* connatural, innate.

connaturato *agg.* deeply rooted.

connazionale *sm.* fellow-countryman (*pl.* -men). ◆ **connazionale** *sf.* fellow-countrywoman (*pl.* -women).

connessione *sf.* connection.
connesso *agg.* connected.
connèttere *vt.* **1.** (*unire*) to connect, to join **2.** (*fig.*) to associate, to link || *non connettere*, to talk at random.
connettivo *agg.* connective.
connivente *agg.* conniving (at).
connotato *sm.* description, feature || *i connotati*, description.
connubio *sm.* **1.** marriage **2.** (*fig.*) union.
cono *sm.* cone: — *gelato*, ice-cream cone.
conoscente *sm.* acquaintance.
conoscenza *sf.* **1.** knowledge || *venire a — di qc.*, to become (*v. irr.*) acquainted with sthg. **2.** (*persona*) acquaintance **3.** (*sensi*) consciousness.
conòscere *vt.* **1.** to know (*v. irr.*): — *di vista*, to know by sight; — *di fama*, to know by reputation; — *dalla voce*, to recognize by one's voice **2.** (*fare la conoscenza*) to meet (*v. irr.*).
conoscìbile *agg.* **1.** knowable **2.** (*riconoscibile*) recognizable.
conoscitivo *agg.* cognitive.
conoscitore *sm.* expert, good judge.
conosciuto *agg.* well-known, renowned.
conquista *sf.* conquest.
conquistare *vt.* **1.** to conquer **2.** (*fig.*) to win (*v. irr.*).
conquistatore *sm.* **1.** conqueror **2.** (*rubacuori*) lady-killer.
consacrare *vt.* **1.** (*eccl.*) to consecrate **2.** (*dedicare*) to devote.
consacrazione *sf.* consecration.
consanguineità *sf.* consanguinity.
consanguìneo *agg.* consanguine, akin. ♦ **consanguìneo** *sm.* kinsman (*pl.* -men).
consapévole *agg.* aware, conscious.
consapevolezza *sf.* **1.** consciousness **2.** (*conoscenza*) knowledge.
conscio *agg.* conscious.
consecutivo *agg.* **1.** following **2.** (*di seguito*) running: *per due giorni consecutivi*, for two days running **3.** (*gramm.*) consecutive.
consegna *sf.* **1.** (*comm.*) delivery: — *contro assegno*, cash on delivery; — *mancata*, nondelivery; *ordine di* —, delivery-note; *effettuare la* —, to effect delivery **2.** (*deposito*) consignment **3.** (*mil.*) orders (*pl.*) || — *in caserma*, confi-

nement to barracks.
consegnare *vt.* **1.** to deliver **2.** (*mil.*) to confine to barracks.
conseguente *agg.* consequent.
conseguenza *sf.* consequence.
conseguìbile *agg.* attainable.
conseguimento *sm.* attainment.
conseguire *vt.* to attain, to achieve, to get (*v. irr.*).
consenso *sm.* **1.** consent **2.** (*matrimoniale*) licence.
consensuale *agg.* by mutual consent.
consentire *vi.* to consent, to agree. ♦ **consentire** *vt.* to allow.
consenziente *agg.* consenting.
conserto *agg.* interwoven, folded: *a braccia conserte*, with folded arms.
conserva *sf.* preserve || — *di frutta*, jam; — *di pomodoro*, tomato sauce.
conservare *vt.* to preserve ♦ **conservarsi** *vr.* to keep (*v. irr.*).
conservativo *agg.* conservative.
conservatore *agg.* **1.** preserving **2.** (*pol.*) conservative. ♦ **conservatore** *sm.* **1.** preserver **2.** (*pol.*) conservative.
conservatorio *sm.* academy of music.
conservazione *sf.* preservation || *istinto di* —, instinct of self-preservation.
considerare *vt.* **1.** to consider, to think (*v. irr.*) of **2.** (*reputare*) to deem, to judge. ♦ **considerarsi** *vr.* to consider oneself.
considerato *agg.* considerate || — *che*, considering that.
considerazione *sf.* **1.** consideration **2.** (*stima*) esteem, regard || *avere — per qu.*, to have regard for so.
considerévole *agg.* considerable.
consigliare *vt.* to advise. ♦ **consigliarsi** *vr.* to ask so.'s advice, to consult (with).
consigliere *sm.* **1.** counsellor **2.** (*membro di un consiglio*) councillor.
consiglio *sm.* **1.** advice (*solo sing.*) **2.** (*corpo di persone*) council.
consiliare *agg.* of a council.
consìmile *agg.* similar.
consistente *agg.* firm, substantial.
consistenza *sf.* **1.** consistence **2.** (*comm.*) on hand: — *di cassa*, cash on hand.
consistere *vi.* to consist.

consociare *vt.* to associate.

consociato *agg.* associated.

consociazione *sf.* association.

consocio *sm.* co-partner.

consolante *agg.* cheering.

consolare[1] *vt.* to console, to comfort. ♦ **consolarsi** *vr.* to be comforted.

consolare[2] *agg.* consular.

consolato *sm.* consulate.

consolatore *agg.* consoling. ♦ **consolatore** *sm.* consoler.

consolazione *sf.* consolation, solace.

console *sm.* consul.

consolidamento *sm.* consolidation.

consolidare *vt.* to consolidate, to strengthen.

consolidato *agg.* consolidated.

consonante *sf.* consonant.

consonanza *sf.* consonance (*anche fig.*).

consono *agg.* in accordance (with).

consorella *sf.* (*eccl.*) sister.

consorte *sm.* consort, husband. ♦ **consorte** *sf.* consort, wife.

consorteria *sf.* faction.

consorzio *sm.* society: — *agrario*, agricultural union.

constare *vi.* 1. (*essere composto*) to consist 2. (*risultare*) to be within one's knowledge || *da quanto mi consta*, as far as I know.

constatare *vt.* V. *costatare*.

constatazione *sf.* V. *costatazione*.

consueto *agg.* usual, customary.

consuetudinario *agg.* customary, consuetudinary.

consuetudine *sf.* 1. custom, habit 2. (*comm.*) rule.

consulente *sm.* adviser.

consulenza *sf.* advice.

consulta *sf.* 1. consultation 2. (*corpo consultivo*) council.

consultare *vt.* 1. to consult 2. (*esaminare*) to examine.

consultazione *sf.* consultation: *libro di* —, reference book.

consultivo *agg.* consultative.

consulto *sm.* consultation.

consumare *vt.* 1. to consume 2. (*di abiti*) to wear (*v. irr.*) 3. (*dissipare*) to waste 4. (*compiere*) to commit.

consumato *agg.* 1. (*perfetto*) accomplished 2. (*logoro*) worn out 3. (*divorato*) consumed.

consumatore *sm.* consumer.

consumazione *sf.* 1. consumption 2. (*giur.*) consummation 3. (*bibi-*

ta) drink.

consumo *sm.* consumption || *per proprio uso e* —, for one's private use.

consuntivo *agg.* final: *bilancio* —, final balance.

consunzione *sf.* consumption.

contabile *agg.* bookkeeping. ♦ **contabile** *sm.* bookkeeper.

contabilità *sf.* bookkeeping.

contachilometri *sm.* speedometer.

contadino *sm.* countryman (*pl. -men*), peasant. ♦ **contadino** *agg.* rustic.

contado *sm.* countryside.

contagiare *vt.* to infect.

contagio *sm.* contagion (*anche fig.*), infection.

contagioso *agg.* contagious, infectious (*anche fig.*).

contagiri *sm.* revolution counter.

contagocce *sm.* dropper.

contaminare *vt.* 1. to pollute, to infect 2. (*un testo letterario*) to corrupt.

contaminazione *sf.* contamination (*anche fig.*), pollution.

contante *agg.* ready. ♦ **contante** *sm.* ready money || *pagare in contanti*, to pay cash.

contare *vt.* 1. to count, to number 2. (*considerare*) to consider 3. (*proporsi*) to think (*v. irr.*) of || *conto di andare a Milano domani*, I think of going to Milan tomorrow 4. (*aspettarsi*) to expect. ♦ **contare** *vi.* 1. (*avere importanza*) to count, to be important 2. (*fare assegnamento*) to rely on.

contatore *sm.* meter: — *del gas*, gas-meter; — *dell'acqua*, water-meter; — *della luce*, electric power-meter.

contatto *sm.* 1. contact, touch: *essere in* —, to be in touch 2. (*elettr.*) contact.

conte *sm.* 1. Count 2. (*in Gran Bretagna*) Earl.

contea *sf.* 1. earldom 2. (*divisione territoriale*) county.

conteggiare *vt.* to count.

conteggio *sm.* computation.

contegno *sm.* 1. behaviour 2. (*atteggiamento*) attitude.

contegnoso *agg.* 1. dignified 2. (*altero*) stiff.

contemperamento *sm.* adaptation.

contemperare *vt.* to adapt.

contemplare *vt.* 1. to behold (*v.*

irr.), to admire **2.** (*giur*.) to consider.

contemplativo *agg*. contemplative.

contemplatore *sm*. contemplator.

contemplazione *sf*. contemplation.

contempo (*nella loc. avv*.) **nel —**, in the meantime.

contemporaneamente *avv*. at the same time.

contemporaneità *sf*. contemporaneousness.

contemporàneo *agg*. e *sm*. contemporary.

contendente *agg*. contending, opposing. ♦ **contendente** *sm*. opponent, rival.

contèndere *vt*. to contend, to refuse. ♦ **contèndersi** *vr. rec.* to contend.

contenere *vt*. **1.** to contain, to hold (*v. irr*.) **2.** (*trattenere*) to repress. ♦ **contenersi** *vr*. **1.** (*comportarsi*) to behave **2.** (*dominarsi*) to contain oneself.

contenitore *sm*. container.

contentare *vt*. to content. ♦ **contentarsi** *vr*. to be content (with).

contentezza *sf*. pleasure, joy.

contento *agg*. content, pleased.

contenuto *sm*. contents (*pl*.).

contenzioso *agg*. contentious.

conterìe *sf. pl.* glass beads.

conterràneo *sm*. fellow-countryman (*pl*. -men) || (*femm*.) fellow-countrywoman (*pl*. -women).

contesa *sf*. **1.** contest **2.** (*litigio*) quarrel.

contessa *sf*. countess.

contestàbile *agg*. questionable.

contestare *vt*. **1.** to contest, to challenge, to deny **2.** (*notificare*) to declare.

contestazione *sf*. dispute, objection: *sollevare contestazioni*, to raise objections.

contesto *sm*. context.

contiguità *sf*. contiguity.

contiguo *agg*. neighbouring.

continentale *agg*. continental.

continente *agg*. moderate. ♦ **continente** *sm*. continent.

continenza *sf*. continence.

contingentamento *sm*. allotment.

contingentare *vt*. to allot.

contingenza *sf*. **1.** emergency **2.** (*circostanza*) circumstance **3.** (*fil*.) contingency.

continuamente *avv*. continuously.

continuare *vt*. e *vi*. **1.** to go on (*v.*

irr.) on (with) **2.** (*riprendere*) to resume.

continuativo *agg*. continuative.

continuato *agg*. **1.** (*ininterrotto*) continuous **2.** (*che si ripete*) continual.

continuatore *sm*. continuator.

continuazione *sf*. continuation.

continuità *sf*. continuity.

continuo *agg*. **1.** (*ininterrotto*) continuous **2.** (*che si ripete*) continual.

conto *sm*. **1.** (*anche comm.*) account: *fare i conti*, to make (*v. irr*.) up accounts **2.** (*di albergo ecc.*) bill **3.** (*assegnamento*) reliance: *far — su*, to rely on **4.** (*stima*) regard || *persona di poco —*, person of little account; *rendere — di*, to answer for; *rendersi —*, to realize; *mettersi per proprio —*, to set (*v. irr*.) for oneself.

contòrcere *vt*. to twist. ♦ **contòrcersi** *vr*. to twist.

contorcimento *sm*. twisting.

contornare *vt*. **1.** to surround **2.** (*con guarnizioni*) to trim.

contorno *sm*. **1.** outline **2.** (*orlo*) border **3.** (*cuc.*) vegetables (*pl*.).

contorsione *sf*. contortion.

contorsionismo *sm*. writhing.

contorsionista *s*. contorsionist.

contorto *agg*. twisted.

contrabbandare *vt*. to smuggle.

contrabbandiere *sm*. smuggler.

contrabbando *sm*. smuggling.

contrabbassista *sm*. double-bass player.

contrabbasso *sm*. double-bass.

contraccambiare *vt*. to return.

contraccambio *sm*. return || *rendere il —*, to retaliate (upon).

contraccolpo *sm*. **1.** counterblow **2.** (*fig.*) reaction.

contraccusa *sf*. countercharge.

contrada *sf*. **1.** quarter **2.** (*paese*) country.

contraddanza *sf*. country-dance.

contraddire *vt*. to contradict. ♦ **contraddirsi** *vr*. to contradict oneself. ♦ **contraddirsi** *v. rec.* to contradict one another, each other.

contraddistìnguere *vt*. to mark.

contraddittore *sm*. opposer.

contraddittorio *agg*. contradictory. ♦ **contraddittorio** *sm*. debate.

contraddizione *sf*. contradiction, discrepancy.

contraente *agg*. contracting. ♦

contraente *sm.* contractor.
contraèrea *sf.* anti-aircraft artillery.
contraèreo *agg.* anti-aircraft.
contraffare *vt.* to counterfeit.
contraffatto *agg.* counterfeit.
contraffattore *sm.* **1.** (*falsificatore*) counterfeiter **2.** (*imitatore*) imitator.
contrafforte *sm.* buttress.
contraggenio *sm.* dislike || *a* (*di*) —, unwillingly.
contràlbero *sm.* (*mecc.*) countershaft.
contralto *sm.* contralto.
contrammiraglio *sm.* rear-admiral.
contrappasso *sm.* retaliation.
contrappello *sm.* second roll-call.
contrappesare *vt.* to counterbalance.
contrappeso *sm.* counterbalance.
contrapporre *vt.* to oppose, to contrast || — *qc. a qu.*, to set (*v. irr.*) sthg. against so.
contrapposizione *sf.* contraposition.
contrapposto *agg.* opposite || *per* —, on the contrary. ♦ **contrapposto** *sm.* opposite.
contrappunto *sm.* counterpoint.
contrariamente *avv.* on the contrary || — *ad ogni aspettativa*, contrary to all expectation.
contrariare *vt.* **1.** to oppose **2.** (*irritare*) to annoy.
contrarietà *sf.* **1.** opposition **2.** (*avversità*) misfortune.
contrario *agg.* **1.** contrary, opposed **2.** (*nocivo*) harmful **3.** (*riluttante*) unwilling || *al* —, on the contrary. ♦ **contrario** *sm.* contrary.
contrarre *vt.* to contract.
contrassegnare *vt.* to mark.
contrassegno *sm.* **1.** countersign **2.** (*segno*) mark **3.** (*distintivo*) badge.
contrastare *vi.* to be in contrast. ♦ **contrastare** *vt.* to oppose.
contrastato *agg.* opposed.
contrasto *sm.* **1.** contrast **2.** (*dissidio*) conflict.
contrattaccare *vt.* to counterattack.
contrattacco *sm.* counterattack.
contrattare *vt.* to negotiate: — *il prezzo*, to haggle about the price.
contrattazione *sf.* dealing, negotiation.
contrattempo *sm.* **1.** (*incidente*) mishap **2.** (*inconveniente*) inconvenience.

contràttile *agg.* contractile.
contratto *sm.* contract.
contratto *agg.* contracted.
contrattuale *agg.* contractual.
contravveleno *sm.* antidote.
contravvenire *vi.* to infringe.
contravventore *sm.* transgressor.
contravvenzione *sf.* **1.** violation **2.** (*multa*) fine.
contrazione *sf.* contraction.
contribuente *sm.* taxpayer.
contribuire *vi.* to contribute.
contributo *sm.* contribution.
contribuzione *sf.* contribution.
contristarsi *vr.* to grieve.
contrito *agg.* contrite.
contrizione *sf.* contrition.
contro *prep.* **1.** against **2.** (*in opposizione a*) contrary to || — *assegno*, cash on delivery.
controbàttere *vt.* (*confutare*) to disprove, to confute.
controbilanciare *vt.* to counterbalance.
controcampo *sm.* (*cine*) reverse shot.
controcorrente *sf.* counter-current. ♦ **controcorrente** *loc. avv.* against the stream.
controffensiva *sf.* counter-offensive.
controfigura *sf.* double.
controfirmare *vt.* to countersign.
controindicare *vt.* (*med.*) to contra-indicate.
controindicazione *sf.* (*med.*) contra-indication.
controllare *vt.* **1.** to control **2.** (*verificare*) to verify, to check **3.** (*ispezionare*) to inspect **4.** (*comm.*) to audit.
controllo *sm.* **1.** control **2.** (*verifica*) check, verification **3.** (*ispezione*) inspection **4.** (*comm.*) audit.
controllore *sm.* **1.** controller **2.** (*ferr.*) ticket-inspector.
controluce *avv.* against the light. ♦ **controluce** *sf.* counterlight.
contromarca *sf.* pass-out check (ticket).
controparte *sf.* counter-party.
contropartita *sf.* **1.** (*comm.*) counter-item **2.** (*compenso*) compensation.
contropelo *sm.* wrong way of the hair || *fare il* —, to shave against the lie of the hair.
controproducente *agg.* having opposite effect.

controproposta sf. counter-proposal.

controprova sf. 1. countercheck 2. (giur.) counter-evidence.

contròrdine sm. counter-order: dare un —, to countermand an order.

controriforma sf. counter-reformation.

controrivoluzione sf. counter-revolution.

controsenso sm. self-contradiction, absurdity.

controspionaggio sm. counter-espionage.

controstòmaco avv. reluctantly.

controvelaccio sm. (mar.) main royal.

controvento avv. against the wind.

controversia sf. controversy.

controverso agg. controversial.

controvertìbile agg. controvertible.

controvoglia avv. unwillingly.

contumace agg. guilty of default.

contumacia sf. default.

contumaciale agg. (giur.) judge ment by default.

contumelia sf. insult, abuse.

contundente agg. blunt: corpo —, blunt instrument.

conturbare vt. 1. to perturb 2. (eccitare) to thrill.

contusione sf. bruise.

contuso agg. bruised.

convalescente agg. e sm. convalescent.

convalescenza sf. convalescence.

convalidare vt. to ratify, to confirm.

convegno sm. meeting.

convenévole agg. convenient, proper. ♦ **convenévoli** sm. pl. compliments.

conveniente agg. 1. convenient (for) 2. (economicamente vantaggioso) profitable.

convenienza sf. 1. convenience 2. (vantaggio economico) profit 3. (buona creanza) propriety.

convenire vi. 1. to convene 2. (essere d'accordo) to agree 3. (essere utile) to be convenient.

convento sm. 1. convent 2. (di suore) nunnery.

conventuale agg. conventual.

convenuto agg. agreed upon. ♦ **convenuto** sm. 1. agreement 2. i convenuti, the persons present.

convenzionale agg. conventional.

convenzionare vt. to make (v. irr.) an agreement.

convenzione sf. convention.

convergente agg. convergent.

convergenza sf. convergence.

convèrgere vi. to converge.

conversare vi. to talk.

conversatore sm. talker.

conversazione sf. conversation, talk.

conversione sf. 1. (anche fig.) conversion 2. (mil.) wheel.

convertìbile agg. convertible.

convertire vt. 1. (pol.; relig.) to convert 2. (mutare) to turn, to change. ♦ **convertirsi** vr. to be converted.

convessità sf. convexity.

convesso agg. convex.

convìncere vt. to convince, to persuade.

convinto agg. convinced, persuaded.

convinzione sf. persuasion, firm belief.

convitato sm. guest.

convito sm. banquet.

convitto sm. boarding-school.

convivente agg. cohabiting.

convivenza sf. cohabitation, life in common.

convìvere vi. to live together.

convocare vt. to convene, to summon.

convocazione sf. convocation, summoning.

convogliare vt. 1. (scortare) to escort 2. (trasportare) to carry away 3. (indirizzare) to address.

convoglio sm. 1. (treno) train 2. (mil.; mar.) convoy.

convolare vi. to fly (v. irr.) together: — a giuste nozze, to get (v. irr.) married.

convulsione sf. convulsion.

convulso agg. convulsive.

cooperare vi. to co-operate, to collaborate.

cooperativa sf. 1. co-operative society 2. (di consumo) co-operative store.

cooperativo agg. co-operative.

cooperatore sm. co-operator.

cooperazione sf. co-operation, collaboration.

coordinamento sm. co-ordination.

coordinare vt. to co-ordinate.

coordinata sf. co-ordinate.

coordinativo agg. co-ordinative.

coordinato agg. co-ordinate.

coordinatore *agg.* co-ordinative. ♦ **coordinatore** *sm.* co-ordinator.

coordinazione *sf.* co-ordination.

coorte *sf.* **1.** (*mil.*) cohort **2.** (*folla*) crowd.

copale *sf.* **1.** copal **2.** (*pelle*) patent leather.

copeco *sm.* copeck.

coperchio *sm.* lid, cover (*anche mecc.*).

coperta *sf.* **1.** blanket: — *da viaggio*, rug; — *scozzese*, plaid **2.** (*mar.*) deck.

copertina *sf.* cover: — *di libro*, book-cover.

coperto *agg.* **1.** (*riparato*) covered, sheltered ‖ — *di ferro*, iron-clad; *mettere al* —, to shelter from **2.** (*di cielo*) overcast **3.** (*nascosto*) hidden. ♦ **coperto** *sm.* cover.

copertone *sm.* tyre.

copertura *sf.* **1.** covering **2.** (*di mobili*) cover.

copia *sf.* **1.** copy **2.** (*foto*) print.

copiare *vt.* to copy.

copiativo *agg.* *matita copiativa*, copying pencil.

copiatura *sf.* copying.

copione *sm.* script.

copiosamente *avv.* plentifully.

copioso *agg.* plentiful.

copista *sm.* copyist.

coppa *sf.* **1.** cup **2.** (*auto*) pan.

coppella *sf.* (*metal.*) cupel.

coppellare *vt.* (*metal.*) to cupel.

coppia *sf.* **1.** (*di persone e cose*) couple **2.** (*di animali*) pair ‖ *una* — *di buoi*, a yoke.

copricapo *sm.* hat.

coprifuoco *sm.* curfew.

copriletto *sm.* coverlet.

coprire *vt.* **1.** to cover **2.** (*nascondere*) to conceal **3.** (*coprire un suono*) to drown.

copto *agg.* coptic. ♦ **copto** *sm.* copt.

copulativo *agg.* (*gramm.*) copulative.

copulazione *sf.* copulation.

coraggio *sm.* **1.** courage, bravery, heart **2.** (*sfrontatezza*) impudence.

coraggiosamente *avv.* bravely.

coraggioso *agg.* brave, bold.

corale *agg.* choral.

corallifero *agg.* coralliferous.

corallo *sm.* coral.

corazza *sf.* **1.** cuirass **2.** (*bot.; zool.*) armour, carapace.

corazzare *vt.* **1.** to armour **2.** (*fig.*)

to strengthen. ♦ **corazzarsi** *vr.* to harden oneself.

corazzata *sf.* (*mar.*) battleship.

corazziere *sm.* cuirassier.

corbellerìa *sf.* **1.** foolish action **2.** (*sciocchezza*) nonsense.

corda *sf.* **1.** rope **2.** (*mus.*) string.

cordaio *sm.* **1.** (*chi fabbrica corde*) rope-maker **2.** (*chi vende corde*) rope-seller.

cordame *sm.* cordage.

cordata *sf.* rope: *in* —, on the rope.

cordiale *agg.* cordial, hearty. ♦ **cordiale** *sm.* (*liquore*) cordial.

cordialità *sf.* cordiality.

cordialmente *avv.* cordially.

cordicella *sf.* string.

cordigliera *sf.* cordillera.

cordite *sf.* cordite.

cordoglio *sm.* deep sorrow.

cordone *sm.* **1.** cord **2.** (*mil.*) cordon.

coreano *agg. e sm.* Korean.

coreografìa *sf.* choreography.

coreogràfico *agg.* **1.** choreographic **2.** (*fig.*) spectacular.

coreògrafo *sm.* choreographer.

coriàceo *agg.* coriaceous, tough.

coriàndolo *sm.* confetti (*pl.*).

coricare *vt.* to lay (*v. irr.*) down. ♦ **coricarsi** *vr.* to lie (*v. irr.*) down.

corifeo *sm.* coryphaeus (*pl.* -aei).

corinzio *agg. e sm.* Corinthian.

corista *sm.* chorus-singer.

cormorano *sm.* (*zool.*) cormorant.

cornacchia *sf.* rook, crow.

cornamusa *sf.* bagpipe.

cornata *sf.* butt.

còrnea *sf.* cornea.

cornetta *sf.* cornet.

cornice *sf.* frame.

cornicione *sm.* **1.** (*arch.*) cornice **2.** (*di finestre, porte*) label **3.** (*di gronda*) eaves (*pl.*).

cornificare *vt.* **1.** (*di moglie*) to cuckold **2.** (*di marito*) to be unfaithful to.

corno *sm.* horn ‖ (*inter.*) *un* —, not at all.

cornuto *agg.* horned. ♦ **cornuto** *sm.* (*fig.*) cuckold.

coro *sm.* **1.** chorus **2.** (*eccl.*) choir.

corolla *sf.* corolla.

corollario *sm.* corollary.

corona *sf.* **1.** crown: — *del rosario*, rosary crown; — *del dente*, crown **2.** (*mecc.*) rim **3.** (*relig.*) (*tonsura*) tonsure.

coronamento *sm.* **1.** crowning **2.** (*completamento*) fulfilment.

coronare *vt.* to crown (*anche fig.*).

coronario *agg.* coronary.

corpo *sm.* **1.** body ‖ *a — morto*, desperately; *combattere a — a —*, to fight (*v. irr.*) hand to hand; *passare sul — di qu.*, to pass over so. **2.** (*cadavere*) corpse **3.** (*collettività*) corps ‖ *— insegnante*, teaching staff.

corporale *agg.* corporal.

corporativismo *sm.* (*econ.*) corporative system.

corporativo *agg.* (*econ.*) corporative.

corporatura *sf.* build, size.

corporazione *sf.* corporation.

corpòreo *agg.* corporeal.

corpulento *agg.* corpulent, stout.

corpulenza *sf.* stoutness.

corpuscolare *agg.* corpuscular.

corpùscolo *sm.* corpuscle.

corredare *vt.* **1.** to equip **2.** (*accompagnare*) to accompany.

corredino *sm.* baby's outfit.

corredo *sm.* **1.** outfit **2.** (*di sposa*) trousseau **3.** (*bagaglio*) wealth, store: *— di cultura*, store of knowledge.

corrèggere *vt.* **1.** to correct **2.** (*di bevande*) to lace. ♦ **corrèggersi** *vr.* to amend, to correct oneself.

correggia *sf.* leather strap.

correlativo *agg.* correlative.

correlazione *sf.* correlation.

corrente[1] *agg.* **1.** (*che scorre*) running **2.** (*circolante*) current **3.** (*comm.*) inst. (*abbrev. di* instant) ‖ *conto —*, current account **4.** (*andante*) common.

corrente[2] *sf.* **1.** current (*anche fig.*), stream **2.** (*di aria*) draught.

correntemente *avv.* fluently.

còrrere *vi.* **1.** to run (*v. irr.*): *— dietro a qu.*, to run after; *— a gambe levate*, to run as hard as one can ‖ *lasciar —*, to take (*v. irr.*) no notice of sthg. **2.** (*di tempo*) to pass **3.** (*di voci*) to be abroad.

corresponsàbile *agg.* jointly responsible.

corresponsione *sf.* payment.

correttezza *sf.* **1.** correctness **2.** (*onestà*) honesty **3.** (*decoro, educazione*) propriety, politeness.

correttivo *agg. e sm.* corrective.

corretto *agg.* **1.** correct, exact **2.** (*irreprensibile*) faultless **3.** (*di bevanda*) laced.

correttore *sm.* corrector ‖ *— di bozze*, proof-reader.

correzionale *agg.* correctional.

correzione *sf.* correction ‖ *— di bozze*, proof-reading; *casa di —*, house of correction.

corridoio *sm.* **1.** passage **2.** (*di treno*) corridor.

corridore *sm.* **1.** runner **2.** (*sport*) racer.

corriera *sf.* coach.

corriere *sm.* **1.** messenger **2.** (*chi trasporta merci*) carrier **3.** (*posta*) mail.

corrimano *sm.* handrail.

corrispettivo *agg.* correlative. ♦ **corrispettivo** *sm.* **1.** equivalent **2.** (*compenso*) compensation.

corrispondente *agg. e sm.* correspondent.

corrispondenza *sf.* correspondence.

corrispòndere *vi.* **1.** to correspond (with) **2.** (*ricambiare sentimenti ecc.*) to return. ♦ **corrispòndere** *vt.* to pay.

corrisposto *agg.* **1.** (*contraccambiato*) returned **2.** (*pagato*) paid.

corroborante *agg. e sm.* corroborant.

corroborare *vt.* to strengthen.

corròdere *vt.* to corrode.

corròmpere *vt.* **1.** to corrupt (*anche fig.*), to pollute **2.** (*con denaro*) to bribe.

corrosione *sf.* corrosion.

corrosivo *agg. e sm.* corrosive.

corrucciarsi *vr.* to get (*v. irr.*) angry.

corrucciato *agg.* angry, worried.

corruccio *sm.* anger, worry.

corrugamento *sm.* corrugation: *— della fronte*, wrinkling of the forehead.

corrugare *vt.* to wrinkle.

corruttìbile *agg.* corruptible.

corruttore *agg.* corrupting. ♦ **corruttore** *sm.* **1.** corrupter **2.** (*con denaro*) briber.

corruzione *sf.* **1.** corruption **2.** (*con denaro*) bribery.

corsa *sf.* **1.** run **2.** (*sport*) race **3.** (*su veicolo pubblico*) trip ‖ *prezzo della —*, fare; (*ferr.*) *perdere la —*, to miss the train.

corsaro *sm.* corsair.

corsetto *sm.* corset.

corsìa *sf.* **1.** passage **2.** (*di ospedale*) ward **3.** (*di strada*) lane.

corsiero *sm.* steed.

corsivo *agg.* cursive. ♦ corsivo *sm.* (*tip.*) italics (*pl.*).

corso *sm.* 1. course (*anche fig.*) 2. (*di acque*) water-course.

corte *sf.* 1. court 2. (*cortile*) court-yard 3. (*corteggiamento*) courtship.

corteccia *sf.* 1. bark 2. (*anat.*) cortex.

corteggiare *vt.* 1. to woo 2. (*adulare*) to flatter.

corteggiatore *sm.* suitor, lover.

corteo *sm.* train, procession: — *funebre*, funeral train.

cortese *agg.* kind.

cortesia *sf.* 1. kindness, politeness 2. (*favore*) favour || *per* —, please.

cortigiano *sm.* 1. courtier 2. (*adulatore*) flatterer.

cortile *sm.* courtyard || *animali da* —, poultry.

cortina *sf.* curtain: — *di ferro* (*pol.*), iron curtain.

cortisone *sm.* cortisone.

corto *agg.* short: *a — di*, short of.

cortocircùito *sm.* short circuit.

cortometraggio *sm.* short (film).

corvetta *sf.* (*mar.*) corvette.

corvino *agg.* 1. corvine 2. (*nero*) raven(-black).

corvo *sm.* raven.

cosa *sf.* 1. thing 2. (*faccenda*) matter || *nessuna* —, nothing; *ogni* —, everything; *che* —?, what?.

cosacco *agg.* e *sm.* Cossack.

coscia *sf.* 1. thigh 2. (*cuc.*) leg.

cosciente *agg.* 1. conscious 2. (*conscio*) aware.

coscienza *sf.* 1. conscience 2. (*consapevolezza*) consciousness.

coscienziosamente *avv.* conscientiously.

coscienzioso *agg.* conscientious.

cosciotto *sm.* leg: — *di manzo*, leg of beef.

coscritto *sm.* recruit.

coscrizione *sf.* conscription.

cosecante *sf.* cosecant.

coseno *sm.* (*mat.*) cosine.

così *avv.* so: *e — via*, and so on; — *come*, — *pure*, as well as; — ... *come*, — ... *quanto*, as ... as; — *da*, so ... as: *non è — sciocco da farlo*, he is not so foolish as to do that.

cosicché *cong.* so that.

cosiddetto *agg.* so-called.

cosiffatto *agg.* such, similar.

cosmesi *sf.* beauty culture.

cosmètico *agg.* e *sm.* cosmetic.

còsmico *agg.* cosmic.

cosmo *sm.* cosmos.

cosmogonìa *sf.* cosmogony.

cosmografìa *sf.* cosmography.

cosmògrafo *sm.* cosmographer.

cosmologìa *sf.* cosmology.

cosmonàuta *s.* astronaut.

cosmonàutica *sf.* astronautics.

cosmopolita *agg.* e *sm.* cosmopolitan.

cosmopolitismo *sm.* cosmopolitanism.

coso *sm.* (*fam.*) 1. (*cosa*) thing 2. (*individuo*) fellow.

cospàrgere *vt.* 1. to strew (*v. irr.*) 2. (*sale, zucchero ecc.*) to sprinkle.

cospetto *sm.* presence: *al — di*, in the presence of.

cospicuità *sf.* conspicuousness.

cospicuo *agg.* 1. (*visibile*) conspicuous 2. (*notevole*) remarkable.

cospirare *vi.* to plot.

cospiratore *sm.* plotter.

cospirazione *sf.* plot.

costa *sf.* 1. coast, shore 2. (*venatura*) rib 3. (*di monte*) side 4. (*di libro*) back.

costà *avv.* there.

costaggiù *avv.* down there.

costale *agg.* costal.

costante *agg.* steady. ♦ costante *sf.* constant.

costanza *sf.* 1. firmness 2. (*perseveranza*) perseverance || *con* —, steadily.

costare *vi.* to cost (*v. irr.*).

costassù *avv.* up there.

costata *sf.* chop.

costatare *vt.* 1. (*accertare*) to ascertain 2. (*notare*) to notice.

costatazione *sf.* 1. ascertainment 2. (*osservazione*) remark.

costato *sm.* chest.

costeggiare *vt.* 1. to follow the coast of 2. (*per terra*) to skirt. ♦ costeggiare *vi.* to coast along.

costei *pron.* 1. (*sogg.*) she 2. (*compl.*) her 3. this woman, that woman.

costellare *vt.* to scatter.

costellazione *sf.* constellation.

costernare *vt.* to dismay. ♦ costernarsi *vr.* to be dismayed (at).

costernazione *sf.* dismay.

costì *avv.* there.

costiera *sf.* stretch of coast.

costiero *agg.* coastal || *nave costiera*, coaster.

costipare vt. **1.** (un terreno) to tamp **2.** (ammassare) to amass. ♦ **costiparsi** vr. **1.** (raffreddarsi) to catch (v. irr.) a cold **2.** (di intestino) to become (v. irr.) constipated.

costipato agg. essere —, to have a cold.

costipazione sf. **1.** (raffreddore) cold **2.** (intestinale) constipation **3.** (di terreno) tamping.

costituente agg. constituent.

costituire vt. **1.** to constitute, to form **2.** (nominare) to appoint. ♦ **costituirsi** vr. (consegnarsi) to give (v. irr.) oneself up.

costituito agg. constituted.

costitutivo agg. constitutive.

costituto sm. (giur.) interrogation of the accused.

costituzionale agg. constitutional.

costituzionalismo sm. constitutionalism.

costituzionalità sf. constitutionality.

costituzione sf. **1.** establishment **2.** (pol.; med.) constitution.

costo sm. cost: ad ogni —, at all cost; a nessun —, in no case.

còstola sf. rib || stare alle costole, to watch over.

costoletta sf. cutlet.

costone sm. side.

costoro pron. **1.** (sogg.) they **2.** (compl.) them **3.** these people, those people.

costoso agg. expensive, dear.

costrìngere vt. **1.** (stringere) to press **2.** (obbligare) to compel.

costrizione sf. **1.** (restringimento) constriction **2.** (obbligo) compulsion.

costruire vt. to build (v. irr.).

costruttivo agg. constructive.

costruttore agg. building. ♦ **costruttore** sm. builder.

costruzione sf. construction, building.

costui pron. **1.** (sogg.) he **2.** (compl.) him **3.** this man, that man.

costumato agg. **1.** (virtuoso) virtuous **2.** (educato) polite.

costume sm. **1.** (usanza) custom **2.** (personale) habit **3.** (condotta) morals (pl.) **4.** (vestito) costume.

costumista sm. costume-designer.

cotangente sf. (mat.) cotangent.

cotenna sf. **1.** pigskin **2.** (del cranio) scalp **3.** (del lardo) rind.

còtica sf. V. cotenna.

cotogna sf. quince.

cotognata sf. quince jam.

cotoletta sf. cutlet.

cotone sm. cotton.

cotoniere sm. cotton-spinner.

cotoniero agg. cotton.

cotonificio sm. cotton-mill.

cotonina sf. calico.

cotta¹ sf. (eccl.) surplice.

cotta² sf. **1.** (cottura) cooking **2.** (infornata) batch **3.** (fam.) prendere una — per, to have a crush on.

cottimista sm. pieceworker.

còttimo sm. piecework: lavorare a —, to work by the job; lavoro a —, job-work; contratto a —, job contract.

cotto sm. brickwork.

cottura sf. **1.** cooking **2.** (in forno) baking.

coturno sm. cothurnus (pl. -ni).

cova sf. **1.** (il covare) brooding **2.** (nido) nest.

covare vt. **1.** to brood **2.** (fig.) to brood over **3.** (di fuoco; passioni) to smoulder **4.** (di malattia) to be latent.

covata sf. brood.

covo sm. den.

covone sm. sheaf (pl. sheaves).

cozza sf. mussel.

cozzare vi. **1.** to strike (v. irr.) **2.** (venire in collisione) to collide.

cozzo sm. **1.** clash, collision **2.** (conflitto) conflict.

crampo sm. cramp.

cranio sm. skull.

crasso agg. crass, gross: ignoranza crassa, gross ignorance.

cratere sm. crater.

cràuti sm. pl. sauerkraut (sing.)

cravatta sf. neck-tie.

creanza sf. politeness.

creare vt. **1.** to create **2.** (causare) to cause **3.** (nominare) to appoint **4.** (costituire) to form.

creativo agg. creative.

creato sm. creation.

creatore agg. creating. ♦ **creatore** sm. creator.

creatura sf. creature.

creazione sf. creation.

credente sm. believer.

credenza¹ sf. belief.

credenza² sf. (buffet) sideboard.

credenziale agg. credential: lettera —, credential.

crédere *vt.* e *vi.* **1.** (*pensare*) to think (*v. irr.*) **2.** (*prestar fede*) to believe. ♦ **crédersi** *vr.* to think (*v. irr.*) oneself.

credibile *agg.* **1.** credible **2.** (*di persona*) trustworthy.

credibilità *sf.* credibility.

creditizio *agg.* credit.

crédito *sm.* **1.** (*comm.*) credit: *a —*, on credit **2.** (*stima*) esteem.

creditore *sm.* creditor.

credo *sm.* creed.

credulità *sf.* credulity.

credulone *agg.* credulous.

crema *sf.* cream.

cremagliera *sf.* rack: *ferrovia a —*, rack-railway.

cremare *vt.* to cremate.

crematorio *agg.* crematory: *forno —*, crematory.

cremazione *sf.* cremation.

cremeria *sf.* creamery.

crèmisi *agg.* e *sm.* crimson.

crèolo *agg.* e *sm.* creole.

crepa *sf.* crack.

crepaccio *sm.* crevasse.

crepacuore *sm.* heart-break: *morire di —*, to die of a broken heart.

crepapelle (*nella loc. avv.*) *ridere a —*, to roar with laughter; *mangiare a —*, to eat to excess.

crepare *vi.* to crack.

crepella *sf.* crepoline.

crepitare *vi.* to crackle.

crepitìo *sm.* crackle.

crepuscolare *agg.* crepuscular.

crepùscolo *sm.* twilight.

crescente *agg.* growing.

crescenza *sf.* growth.

créscere *vi.* **1.** to grow (*v. irr.*) **2.** (*aumentare*) to increase.

crescione *sm.* (*bot.*) water-cress.

créscita *sf.* **1.** growth **2.** (*aumento*) increase.

crèsima *sf.* confirmation.

cresimare *vt.* to confirm.

creso *sm.* Croesus.

crespo *agg.* crisp.

cresta *sf.* **1.** crest **2.** (*di gallo*) comb.

crestina *sf.* maid-servant's cap.

creta *sf.* clay.

cretineria *sf.* **1.** idiocy **2.** (*azione*) foolish action **3.** (*detto*) nonsense.

cretinismo *sm.* idiocy.

cretino *agg.* e *sm.* idiot.

cricca *sf.* gang.

cricco *sm.* jack.

criminale *agg.* e *sm.* criminal.

criminalista *s.* **1.** (*avvocato*) criminal lawyer **2.** (*studioso*) criminologist.

criminalità *sf.* criminality.

crìmine *sm.* crime.

criminologìa *sf.* criminology.

criminosità *sf.* criminality.

criminoso *agg.* criminal.

crine *sm.* horse-hair.

criniera *sf.* mane.

crinolina *sf.* crinoline.

criolite *sf.* cryolite.

cripta *sf.* crypt.

crisàlide *sf.* chrysalid.

crisantemo *sm.* chrysanthemum.

crisi *sf.* **1.** crisis (*pl.* -ses) **2.** (*med.*) fit.

crisma *sm.* **1.** (*eccl.*) chrism **2.** (*fig.*) approval ‖ *con tutti i crismi*, approved, praised.

cristallerìa *sf.* **1.** crystal-ware **2.** (*fabbrica*) crystal manufactory.

cristalliera *sf.* glass case.

cristallino *agg.* e *sm.* crystalline.

cristallizzare *vt.* e *vi.*, **cristallizzarsi** *vr.* to crystallize.

cristallizzazione *sf.* crystallization.

cristallo *sm.* **1.** crystal **2.** (*lastra di vetro*) plate glass.

cristallografìa *sf.* crystallography.

cristianésimo *sm.* Christianity.

cristiania *sm.* (*sport*) Christiania.

cristianità *sf.* **1.** (*i cristiani*) Christendom **2.** (*cristianesimo*) Christianity.

cristiano *agg.* e *sm.* Christian.

criterio *sm.* **1.** principle **2.** opinion **3.** (*buon senso*) sense.

crìtica *sf.* **1.** criticism **2.** (*saggio*) critical essay **3.** (*i critici*) the critics (*pl.*).

criticamente *avv.* critically.

criticare *vt.* **1.** to criticize **2.** (*biasimare*) to blame.

criticismo *sm.* **1.** criticism **2.** (*stor.*) critical philosophy.

crìtico *agg.* critical. ♦ **crìtico** *sm.* critic.

criticone *sm.* fault-finder.

crittògama *sf.* (*bot.*) cryptogam.

crittografìa *sf.* cryptography.

crittogramma *sm.* cryptogram.

crivellare *vt.* to riddle.

crivellatura *sf.* riddling.

crivello *sm.* riddle.

croato *agg.* e *sm.* Croatian.

croccante *agg.* crisp. ♦ **croccante** *sm.* almond sweetmeat.

crocchetta *sf.* croquette.
crocchia *sf.* bun.
crocchio *sm.* group.
croce *sf.* cross.
crocerossina *sf.* Red Cross nurse.
crociata *sf.* crusade.
crociato *sm.* crusader.
crocicchio *sm.* cross-road.
crociera *sf.* **1.** cruise **2.** (*arch.*) cross-vault.
crocifiggere *vt.* to crucify.
crocifissione *sf.* crucifixion.
crocifisso *sm.* crucifix.
croco *sm.* (*bot.*) crocus.
crogiuolo *sm.* crucible.
crollare *vi.* to fall (*v. irr.*) down.
crollo *sm.* **1.** breakdown **2.** (*caduta*) falling down.
croma *sf.* (*mus.*) quaver.
cromare *vt.* to chromium-plate.
cromàtico *agg.* chromatic.
cromatismo *sm.* chromatism.
cromatografìa *sf.* chromatography.
cromatura *sf.* chromium plating.
cromo *sm.* chromium.
cromolitografìa *sf.* chromolithography.
cromosomo *sm.* chromosome.
crònaca *sf.* **1.** chronicle **2.** (*di giornale*) news.
crònico *agg.* chronic. ♦ **crònico** *sm.* chronic invalid.
cronista *sm.* reporter.
cronistoria *sf.* chronicle.
cronologìa *sf.* chronology.
cronològico *agg.* chronological.
cronometraggio *sm.* time-study.
cronometrare *vt.* to time.
cronometrìa *sf.* timing.
cronòmetro *sm.* stop watch.
crosta *sf.* **1.** crust **2.** (*tec.*) coating.
crostàcei *sm. pl.* Crustacea.
crostata *sf.* (*cuc.*) tart.
cròtalo *sm.* rattlesnake.
crucciare *vt.*, **crucciarsi** *vr.* to worry.
cruciale *agg.* crucial.
cruciverba *sm.* cross-word puzzle.
crudele *agg.* cruel.
crudeltà *sf.* cruelty.
crudezza *sf.* **1.** (*di stagione*) harshness **2.** (*di parole*) coarseness **3.** (*di cibo*) rawness.
crudo *agg.* **1.** raw **2.** (*poco cotto*) underdone **3.** (*aspro, rigido*) harsh **4.** (*rozzo*) coarse.
cruento *agg.* bloody.
crumiro *sm.* blackleg.
cruna *sf.* needle's eye.

crusca *sf.* bran.
cruscotto *sm.* dashboard.
cubaggio *sm.* cubage.
cubano *agg.* e *sm.* Cuban.
cubatura *sf.* cubature.
cubetto *sm.* — *di ghiaccio*, ice cube.
cùbico *agg.* cubic.
cubismo *sm.* cubism.
cubitale *agg.* *a caratteri cubitali*, in very large letters.
cùbito *sm.* **1.** (*misura*) cubit **2.** (*avambraccio*) forearm.
cubo *sm.* cube.
cuccagna *sf.* abundance ‖ *albero della* —, greasy pole.
cuccetta *sf.* berth.
cucchiaiata *sf.* spoonful.
cucchiaino *sm.* **1.** tea-spoon, coffee--spoon **2.** (*il contenuto*) tea-spoonful.
cucchiaio *sm.* spoon.
cuccia *sf.* dog-house.
cùcciolo *sm.* puppy.
cùccuma *sf.* kettle.
cucina *sf.* **1.** kitchen **2.** (*modo di cucinare*) cooking **3.** (*culinaria*) cookery **4.** (*stufa*) stove.
cucinare *vt.* to cook.
cuciniere *sm.* man-cook.
cucire *vt.* **1.** to sew (*v. irr.*) **2.** (*med.*) to stitch.
cucito *sm.* needlework.
cucitrice *sf.* **1.** seamstress **2.** (*macchinetta*) stapler.
cucitura *sf.* **1.** seam **2.** (*di fogli*) stapling.
cucù *sm.* (*zool.*) cuckoo.
cucùrbita *sf.* gourd.
cuffia *sf.* **1.** cap. **2.** (*radio*) headphone.
cugina *sf.* cousin.
cugino *sm.* cousin.
cui *pron. rel.* **1.** (*di possesso*) whose; (*di possesso, solo per animali e cose*) of which: *l'uomo la* — *casa*, the man whose house; *il libro le* — *pagine*, the book the pages of which **2.** (*altri casi, per persone*) whom; (*altri casi, per animali e cose*) which: *l'uomo con* — *parlai*, the man to whom I spoke; *il libro di* — *parlai*, the book about which I spoke ‖ *in* — (*dove*), where; *in* — (*quando*) when.
culaccio *sm.* rump.
culatta *sf.* breech.
culinaria *sf.* cookery.
culinario *agg.* culinary.

culla *sf.* cradle.

cullare *vt.* to rock, to lull (*anche fig.*).

culminante *agg.* culminant: *momento* —, climax.

culminare *vi.* to culminate.

culmine *sm.* **1.** summit **2.** (*fig.*) apex.

culo *sm.* bottom; (*volg.*) ass.

culto *sm.* **1.** cult **2.** (*religione*) religion **3.** (*adorazione*) worship.

cultore *sm.* lover.

cultura *sf.* culture.

culturale *agg.* cultural.

cumulare *vt.* to heap up.

cumulativo *agg.* cumulative.

cumulatore *sm.* hoarder.

cumulazione *sf.* hoarding.

cùmulo *sm.* **1.** heap **2.** (*nube*) cumulus (*pl.* -li).

cuna *sf.* cradle.

cuneiforme *agg.* cuneiform, wedge-shaped.

cùneo *sm.* wedge.

cunetta *sf.* **1.** (*stradale*) road bump **2.** (*scolo*) gutter.

cunìcolo *sm.* underground passage, shaft.

cuòcere *vt.* **1.** to cook **2.** (*in forno, fornace*) to bake.

cuoco *sm.* cook.

cuoiame *sm.* leather and hides.

cuoio *sm.* leather || — *capelluto*, scalp.

cuore *sm.* heart.

cupezza *sf.* **1.** darkness **2.** (*tristezza*) gloom.

cupidigia *sf.* cupidity, greed.

cùpido *agg.* greedy.

cupo *agg.* **1.** dark **2.** (*triste*) gloomy **3.** (*profondo*) deep.

cùpola *sf.* dome.

cùpreo *agg.* cupreous.

cùprico *agg.* cupric.

cura *sf.* **1.** care **2.** (*med.*) treatment || *casa di* —, nursing-home.

curàbile *agg.* curable.

curante *agg. medico* —, attending physician.

curare *vt.* **1.** (*aver cura di*) to take (*v. irr.*) care of **2.** (*med.*) to treat **3.** (*una pubblicazione*) to edit. ♦ **curarsi** *vr.* (*seguire una cura*) to follow a treatment.

curaro *sm.* curare.

curato *sm.* vicar.

curatore *sm.* trustee.

curdo *agg.* Kurdish. ♦ **curdo** *sm.* Kurd.

curia *sf.* **1.** (*eccl.*) see **2.** (*giur.*) court of justice.

curie *sm.* curie.

curiosare *vi.* to pry.

curiosità *sf.* **1.** curiosity **2.** (*stranezza*) oddity.

curioso *agg.* curious.

curriculum *sm.* curriculum (*pl.* -la).

cursore *sm.* **1.** messenger **2.** (*mecc.*) slider.

curva *sf.* bend.

curvare *vt.* to bend (*v. irr.*). ♦ **curvarsi** *vr.* **1.** to bend (*v. irr.*) **2.** (*inclinarsi*) to bow.

curvatura *sf.* **1.** bending **2.** (*arch.*) sweep.

curvilìneo *agg.* curvilinear.

curvo *agg.* bent.

cuscinetto *sm.* small cushion || — *a sfera*, ball bearing.

cuscino *sm.* **1.** cushion **2.** (*guanciale*) pillow **3.** (*mecc.*) pillow.

custode *sm.* keeper.

custodia *sf.* **1.** care **2.** (*tutela*) guardianship **3.** (*astuccio*) case.

custodire *vt.* **1.** to keep (*v. irr.*) **2.** (*aver cura di*) to look after.

cutàneo *agg.* skin: *malattia cutanea*, skin disease.

cute *sf.* skin.

D

da *prep.* **1.** (*provenienza*) from: *vengo* — *Milano*, I come from Milan **2.** (*moto a luogo*) to: *andremo* — *loro*, we shall go to their house **3.** (*stato in luogo*) at: *vivo* — *mia zia*, I live at my aunt's **4.** (*moto per luogo*) through: *passai* — *Roma*, I passed through Rome **5.** (*tempo, durata*) for: *siamo qui* — *due mesi*, we have been here for two months; (*a partire da*) since: *lo conosco dal 1955*, I have known him since 1955 **6.** (*agente*) by: *fu aiutato* — *sua sorella*, he was helped by his sister **7.** (*come*) like: *si comportano* — *bambini*, they are behaving like children || *fare* —, to act as.

dabbasso *avv.* **1.** below, down below **2.** (*al piano inferiore*) downstairs.

dabbenàggine sf. ingenuousness.
dabbene agg. honest.
daccapo avv. over again, from the beginning.
dacché cong. since.
dadaismo sm. dadaism.
dado sm. 1. die (pl. dice) 2. (cuc.) cube 3. (mecc.) nut.
daffare sm. work ‖ darsi —, to be on the go.
dagherrotipìa sf. daguerreotypy.
dagherròtipo sm. daguerreotype.
dàgli, dài inter. go on.
dàino sm. fallow-deer (invariato al pl.).
dalìa sf. dahlia.
daltònico agg. colour-blind.
daltonismo sm. colour-blindness.
d'altronde avv. on the other hand.
dama sf. 1. lady of rank 2. (al ballo) partner 3. (giuoco) draughts (pl.).
damasco sm. damask.
damerino sm. dandy.
damiere sm. draughtboard.
damigella sf. maid of honour.
damigiana sf. demijohn.
danaroso agg. wealthy.
danese agg. Danish. ♦ **danese** sm. Dane.
dannare vt. to damn ‖ far —, to drive (v. irr.) so. mad. ♦ **dannarsi** 1. to be damned 2. (fig.) to strive (v. irr.) hard.
dannato agg. damned. ♦ **dannato** sm. damned soul.
dannazione sf. damnation: —!, damn!
danneggiamento sm. damage.
danneggiare vt. 1. to damage 2. (di persone) to injure.
danno sm. 1. damage 2. (a persona) injury ‖ recare — a qu., to do (v. irr.) so. harm.
dànnoso agg. harmful.
dantesco agg. Dantesque.
danza sf. dance.
danzante agg. dancing: trattenimento —, dance.
danzare vt. e vi. to dance.
danzatore sm. dancer.
dappertutto avv. everywhere.
dappocàggine sf. ineptitude.
dappoco agg. inept.
dappresso avv. near-by.
dapprima avv. at first.
dardeggiare vt. e vi. to dart.
dardo sm. dart.
dare sm. debit. ♦ **dare** vt. to give

(v. irr.): — origine, luogo a qc., to give rise; — a bere a qu. che, to give so. to believe that; — ad intendere, to give to understand; — a pensare, to give food for thought ‖ — atto di qc., to acknowledge; può darsi, maybe; — alla testa, to go (v. irr.) to one's head; — nell'occhio, to stand (v. irr.) out. ♦ **darsi** vr. to devote oneself ‖ — al bere, to take (v. irr.) to drink; — ammalato, to pretend to be ill; — da fare, to busy oneself; darsela a gambe, to take (v. irr.) to one's heels.
dàrsena sf. wet dock.
darvinismo sm. Darwinism.
data sf. date: in — d'oggi, under to-day's date.
datare vt. to date.
dativo sm. dative.
dato agg. 1. given 2. (stabilito) stated 3. (dedito) addicted ‖ — e non concesso, supposing that. ♦ **dato** sm. datum (pl. -ta). ♦ **dato che** cong. since, as.
datore sm. giver ‖ — di lavoro, employer.
dàttero sm. 1. date 2. (albero) date-palm.
dattilografare vt. to typewrite.
dattilografìa sf. typewriting.
dattilògrafo sm. typist.
dattiloscritto agg. typewritten. ♦ **dattiloscritto** sm. typescript.
dattorno avv. round, about.
davanti avv. before, in front. ♦ **davanti** sm. front. ♦ **davanti** agg. front. ♦ **davanti a** (loc. prep.) before.
davantino sm. ruffle.
davanzale sm. window-sill.
davvero avv. really, indeed.
daziario agg. toll.
daziere sm. exciseman (pl. -men).
dazio sm. 1. toll, duty 2. (ufficio daziario) toll-house 3. (di consumo) excise.
dea sf. goddess.
deambulare vi. to walk about.
deambulatorio agg. e sm. deambulatory.
deambulazione sf. deambulation.
debellare vt. 1. to defeat 2. (fig.) to overcome (v. irr.).
debilitante agg. weakening.
debilitare vt. to weaken.
debilitazione debilitation.

debitamente avv. duly.
dèbito agg. due, proper. ♦ **dèbito** sm. debt: *fare un* —, to run (v. irr.) into debt.
debitore sm. debtor.
débole agg. weak.
debolezza sf. weakness.
debosciato agg. debauched.
debuttante sm. **1.** novice **2.** (di ragazza in società) debutante.
debuttare vi. **1.** to make (v. irr.) one's debut **2.** (di ragazza in società) to come (v. irr.) out.
debutto sm. **1.** debut **2.** (di ragazza in società) coming out.
dècade sf. **1.** (di giorni) ten days **2.** (di anni) ten years.
decadente agg. **1.** decaying **2.** (lett.) decadent.
decadenza sf. decay, decline.
decadere vi. to decline || — da un diritto, to lose (v. irr.) a right.
decaduto agg. impoverished.
decaedro sm. decahedron.
decagrammo sm. decagram.
decalcare vt. to transfer.
decalcificare vt. to decalcify.
decàlitro sm. decalitre.
decàlogo sm. decalogue.
decàmetro sm. decametre.
decampare vi. **1.** to decamp **2.** (fig.) to recede.
decano sm. **1.** senior **2.** (eccl.) dean.
decantare vt. **1.** to extol **2.** (chim.) to decant.
decantazione sf. (chim.) decantation.
decapitare vt. to behead.
decappottàbile agg. (auto) convertible.
decasìllabo agg. decasyllabic. ♦ **decasìllabo** sm. decasyllable.
decatissaggio sm. decatizing.
decèdere vi. to die.
decelerare vt. to decelerate.
decennale agg. decennial.
decenne agg. **1.** ten years old (predicativo) **2.** ten-year-old (attributivo).
decennio sm. ten-year period.
decente agg. decent, proper.
decentramento sm. decentralization.
decentrare vt. to decentralize.
decenza sf. decency.
decesso sm. death.
decìdere vt. to decide. ♦ **decìdersi** vr. to make (v. irr.) up one's mind.

decifrare vt. **1.** to decipher **2.** (fam.) to make (v. irr.) out.
decifrazione sf. deciphering.
decigrammo sm. decigram.
decìlitro sm. decilitre.
decimale agg. e sm. decimal.
decimare vt. to decimate.
decimazione sf. decimation.
decìmetro sm. decimetre.
dècimo agg. tenth.
decina sf. ten, half-a-score.
decisione sf. decision.
decisivo agg. decisive.
deciso agg. **1.** resolute, firm **2.** (definito) decided.
declamare vt. e vi. to declaim.
declamatorio agg. declamatory.
declamazione sf. declamation.
declassare vt. to degrade.
declinàbile agg. declinable.
declinante agg. declining.
declinare vt. **1.** to decline || — le proprie generalità, to say (v. irr.) one's name and surname. ♦ **declinare** vi. **1.** (del sole) to set (v. irr.) **2.** (degradare) to slope **3.** (venir meno) to decline.
declinazione sf. (gramm.) declension.
declino sm. decline.
declivio sm. declivity.
decollaggio sm. (aer.) take-off.
decollare vi. to take (v. irr.) off.
decollo sm. take-off.
decolorante agg. decolorating. ♦ **decolorante** sm. decolorant.
decolorare vt. to decolorate.
decolorazione sf. decoloration || — dei capelli, hair bleaching.
decomponìbile agg. decomposable.
decomporre vt. to decompose.
decomposizione sf. **1.** decomposition **2.** (putrefazione) putrefaction.
decongelare vt. to defrost.
decongestionare vt. to decongest.
decorare vt. to decorate: — al valore, to decorate for bravery.
decorativo agg. decorative.
decoratore sm. decorator.
decorazione sf. decoration.
decoro sm. dignity.
decoroso agg. decorous, proper.
decorrenza sf. expiration: con — da, beginning from.
decòrrere vi. **1.** to pass || a — da, to begin (v. irr.) from **2.** (comm.) to run (v. irr.), to have effect.
decorso sm. **1.** period **2.** (il passa-

re) passing.
decrepitezza *sf.* decrepitude.
decrèpito *agg.* decrepit.
decréscere *vi.* to decrease.
decretare *vt.* 1. to decree 2. (*concedere*) to confer.
decreto *sm.* decree: — *legge,* Order in Council.
decuplicare *vt.* to decuple.
dècuplo *sm.* decuple, ten times as much.
decurtare *vt.* to reduce.
dèdalo *sm.* maze.
dèdica *sf.* dedication.
dedicare *vt.* to dedicate. ♦ **dedicarsi** *vr.* to devote oneself.
dedicatorio *agg.* dedicatory.
dèdito *agg.* 1. given up 2. (*a vizio*) addicted.
dedizione *sf.* devotion.
dedurre *vt.* 1. to infer, to deduce 2. (*defalcare*) to deduct.
deduttivo *agg.* deductive.
deduzione *sf.* deduction.
defalcare *vt.* to deduct.
defalco *sm.* deduction.
defecare *vi.* to defecate.
defenestrare *vt.* 1. to throw (*v. irr.*) out of the window 2. (*fig.*) to dismiss.
defenestrazione *sf.* defenestration.
deferente *agg.* deferential.
deferenza *sf.* compliance, deference.
deferire *vt.* 1. to submit 2. (*giur.*) to remit.
defezionare *vi.* to desert.
defezione *sf.* 1. defection 2. (*mil.*) desertion.
deficiente *agg.* 1. insufficient 2. (*idiota*) mentally deficient. ♦ **deficiente** *sm.* idiot.
deficienza *sf.* 1. deficiency, lack 2. (*idiozia*) mental deficiency.
dèficit *sm.* deficit.
definìbile *agg.* definable.
definire *vt.* 1. to define 2. (*determinare, risolvere*) to determine.
definitivo *agg.* final.
definito *agg.* definite.
definizione *sf.* 1. definition 2. (*risoluzione*) settlement.
deflagrante *agg.* deflagrating.
deflagrare *vi.* to deflagrate.
deflagrazione *sf.* deflagration.
deflazione *sf.* deflation.
deflèttere *vi.* to deflect.
deflettore *sm.* baffle.
deflorare *vt.* to deflower.
deflorazione *sf.* defloration.

defluire *vi.* to flow down.
deflusso *sm.* 1. downflow 2. (*di marea*) ebb-tide.
deformante *agg.* deforming.
deformare *vt.* 1. to deform, to disfigure 2. (*alterare*) to alter. ♦ **deformarsi** *vr.* 1. (*mecc.*) to warp 2. to get (*v. irr.*) deformed.
deformazione *sf.* 1. deformation 2. (*mecc.*) buckling.
deforme *agg.* deformed.
deformità *sf.* deformity.
defraudare *vt.* to defraud.
defunto *agg.* e *sm.* dead.
degenerare *vi.* to degenerate.
degenerazione *sf.* degeneration.
degènere *agg.* degenerate.
degente *sm.* patient.
degenza *sf.* stay in hospital.
deglutizione *sf.* swallowing.
degnarsi *vr.* to condescend.
degnazione *sf.* condescension.
degno *agg.* worthy, deserving.
degradante *agg.* degrading.
degradare *vt.* to degrade.
degradazione *sf.* degradation.
degustare *vt.* to taste.
deiezione *sf.* dejection.
deificare *vt.* to deify.
deismo *sm.* deism.
deità *sf.* deity.
delatore *sm.* delator.
delazione *sf.* delation, informing.
delèbile *agg.* erasable.
dèlega *sf.* 1. delegation 2. (*procura*) proxy.
delegare *vt.* to delegate.
delegato *sm.* delegate.
delegazione *sf.* 1. delegation 2. (*commissione*) committee.
deleterio *agg.* harmful.
delfino *sm.* 1. (*zool.*) dolphin 2. (*fig.*) probable successor 3. (*stor.*) dauphin.
deliberare *vt.* to decide.
deliberazione *sf.* deliberation.
delicatezza *sf.* delicacy.
delicato *agg.* 1. delicate 2. (*scrupoloso*) scrupulous 3. (*discreto*) discreet, tactful.
delimitare *vt.* to delimit.
delimitazione *sf.* delimitation.
delineare *vt.* to outline.
delineazione *sf.* delineation.
delinquente *sm.* delinquent.
delinquenza *sf.* criminality.
delìnquere *vi.* to commit an offence.
deliquio *sm.* swoon.

delirare *vi.* to rave.
delirio *sm.* delirium, frenzy (*anche fig.*).
delitto *sm.* crime.
delittuoso *agg.* criminal.
delizia *sf.* delight.
deliziare *vt.* to delight.
delizioso *agg.* 1. delightful 2. (*di sapore, profumo*) delicious.
delta *sm.* delta.
deltòide *agg.* e *sm.* deltoid.
delucidare *vt.* to explain.
delucidazione *sf.* explanation.
delùdere *vt.* to disappoint.
delusione *sf.* disappointment.
demagogìa *sf.* demagogy.
demagògico *agg.* demagogic.
demagogo *sm.* demagogue.
demandare *vt.* to commit.
demaniale *agg.* (owned by the) State.
demanio *sm.* State property.
demarcare *vt.* to mark the boundaries of.
demarcazione *sf.* demarcation.
demente *agg.* insane. ♦ **demente** *sm.* madman (*pl.* -men).
demenza *sf.* insanity.
demeritare *vt.* to forfeit. ♦ **demeritare** *vi.* to deserve censure.
demèrito *sm.* demerit.
demiurgo *sm.* demiurge.
democràtico *agg.* democratic. ♦ **democràtico** *sm.* democrat.
democratizzare *vt.* to democratize.
democrazìa *sf.* democracy.
democristiano *sm.* christian-democrat.
demografìa *sf.* demography.
demogràfico *agg.* demographic(al).
demolire *vt.* to demolish.
demolitore *sm.* 1. demolisher 2. (*fig.*) iconoclast.
demolizione *sf.* 1. demolition 2. (*fig.*) destruction.
dèmone *sm.* 1. demon 2. (*diavolo*) devil.
demonìaco *agg.* demoniac(al).
demonio *sm.* 1. devil 2. (*fig.*) demon.
demonologìa *sf.* demonology.
demoralizzare *vt.* to demoralize. ♦ **demoralizzarsi** *vr.* to lose (*v. irr.*) heart.
demoralizzazione *sf.* demoralization.
denaro *sm.* 1. money 2. (*moneta antica*) denarius (*pl.* -rii).
denaturare *vt.* to denature.

dendrologìa *sf.* dendrology.
denegare *vt.* to deny.
denicotinizzare *vt.* to denicotinize.
denigrare *vt.* to denigrate.
denigratore *sm.* denigrator.
denigrazione *sf.* denigration.
denominare *vt.* to name.
denominativo *agg.* denominative.
denominatore *sm.* denominator.
denominazione *sf.* denomination.
denotare *vt.* to signify.
densità *sf.* density.
denso *agg.* thick.
dentale *agg.* dental.
dentario *agg.* dental, tooth (*attr.*).
dentato *agg.* toothed.
dentatura *sf.* 1. set of teeth 2. (*di ingranaggio*) toothing.
dente *sm.* tooth (*pl.* teeth).
dentellare *vt.* to indent.
dentellatura *sf.* indentation.
dentello *sm.* 1. (*mecc.*) tooth 2. (*arch.*) dentil 3. (*tacca*) notch.
dentiera *sf.* dental plate.
dentifricio *agg.* tooth (*attr.*) ♦ **dentifricio** *sm.* tooth-paste.
dentina *sf.* dentine.
dentista *sm.* dentist.
dentìstico *agg.* dental: *gabinetto* —, dentist's surgery.
dentizione *sf.* teething.
dentro *avv.* in, inside. ♦ **dentro** *prep.* 1. in, inside 2. (*di tempo*) (with)in.
denudare *vt.* 1. to strip 2. (*scoprire*) to lay (*v. irr.*) bare. ♦ **denudarsi** *vr.* to strip.
denudazione *sf.* denudation.
denuncia *sf.* 1. denunciation 2. (*dichiarazione*) statement: — *dei redditi*, statement of one's income.
denunciare *vt.* 1. to denounce 2. (*dichiarare*) to report 3. (*giur.*) — *qu.*, to inform against so.
denutrito *agg.* underfed.
denutrizione *sf.* underfeeding.
deodorante *agg.* deodorizing. ♦ **deodorante** *sm.* deodorant.
deodorare *vt.* to deodorize.
deontologìa *sf.* deontology.
depauperamento *sm.* impoverishment.
depauperare *vt.* to impoverish.
depennare *vt.* to cross out.
deperìbile *agg.* perishable.
deperimento *sm.* 1. (*di salute*) wasting away 2. (*per un dolore*) pining away 3. (*di cose*) deterioration.

deperire *vi.* **1.** (*di salute*) to waste away **2.** (*per un dolore*) to pine. away **3.** (*di cose*) to deteriorate.
depilare *vt.* to remove hair (from).
depilatore *sm.* hair-remover.
depilatorio *agg.* hair-removing.
depilazione *sf.* hair-removal.
deploràbile *agg.* deplorable.
deplorare *vt.* **1.** (*essere spiacenti*) to deplore **2.** (*lagnarsi di*) to complain of.
deplorazione *sf.* **1.** (*biasimo*) blame **2.** (*rimpianto*) regret.
deplorévole *agg.* **1.** deplorable **2.** (*biasimevole*) blamable.
deporre *vt.* **1.** to lay (*v. irr.*) **2.** (*da una carica*) to remove from (an) office **3.** (*depositare*) to deposit **4.** (*giur.*) to witness. ♦ **deporre** *vi.* (*giur.*) to give (*v. irr.*) evidence.
deportare *vt.* to deport.
deportato *agg.* deported. ♦ **deportato** *sm.* convict.
deportazione *sf.* deportation.
depositante *sm.* depositor.
depositare *vt.* to deposit: — *merci,* to store goods.
depositario *sm.* trustee.
depòsito *sm.* **1.** deposit **2.** (*luogo in cui depositare*) warehouse **3.** (*per bagagli*) left-luggage room.
deposizione *sf.* deposition.
depravare *vt.* to corrupt.
depravazione *sf.* corruption.
deprecàbile *agg.* deprecable.
deprecare *vt.* to deprecate.
deprecativo *agg.* deprecatory.
deprecazione *sf.* deprecation.
depredamento *sm.* plunder.
depredare *vt.* to plunder, to ravage.
depressione *sf.* depression.
depressivo *agg.* depressing.
depresso *agg.* depressed.
depressore *sm.* depressor.
deprezzamento *sm.* depreciation.
deprezzare *vt.* to depreciate.
deprimente *agg.* depressing.
deprimere *vt.* to depress.
depurare *vt.* to depurate.
depurativo *agg.* depurative.
depuratore *sm.* **1.** depurator **2.** (*mecc.*) cleaner.
depurazione *sf.* purification, depuration.
deputare *vt.* to depute.
deputato *sm.* deputy.
deputazione *sf.* deputation.

deragliamento *sm.* derailment.
deragliare *vi.* to go (*v. irr.*) off the rails.
derattizzare *vt.* to clear by deratization.
derattizzazione *sf.* deratization.
derelitto *agg.* forlorn.
deretano *sm.* posterior.
deridere *vt.* to laugh at, to make (*v. irr.*) fun of.
derisibile *agg.* laughable.
derisione *sf.* mockery.
derisorio *agg.* derisory.
deriva *sf.* drift.
derivare *vi.* **1.** to derive **2.** (*originarsi*) to rise (*v. irr.*). ♦ **derivare** *vt.* to derive.
derivativo *agg.* derivative.
derivato *agg.* derived. ♦ **derivato** *sm.* **1.** derivative **2.** (*sottoprodotto*) by-product.
derivazione *sf.* **1.** derivation **2.** (*elettr.*) shunt.
derma *sm.* derm.
dermatologìa *sf.* dermatology.
dermatològico *agg.* dermatological.
dermatòlogo *sm.* dermatologist.
dèroga *sf.* derogation.
derogare *vi.* to derogate.
derrata *sf.* **1.** victual **2.** (*alimentare*) food-stuff.
derubare *vt.* to rob (so. of).
desco *sm.* dinner table.
descrittivo *agg.* descriptive.
descrìvere *vt.* to describe.
descrivìbile *agg.* describable.
descrizione *sf.* description.
desèrtico *agg.* desert.
deserto *agg.* e *sm.* desert.
desideràbile *agg.* desirable.
desiderare *vt.* **1.** to wish **2.** (*desiderare di avere*) to wish for.
desiderio *sm.* wish.
desideroso *agg.* desirous, eager (for).
designare *vt.* to appoint.
designazione *sf.* designation.
desinare *vi.* to dine, to have dinner. ♦ **desinare** *sm.* dinner.
desinenza *sf.* ending.
desìstere *vi.* to cease, to leave (*v. irr.*) off.
desolare *vt.* **1.** to desolate **2.** (*addolorare*) to distress.
desolato *agg.* (*spiacente*) sorry.
desolazione *sf.* **1.** desolation **2.** (*dolore*) grief, sorrow.
dèspota *sm.* despot.
destare *vt.* **1.** to wake (*v. irr.*) **2.**

(*suscitare*) to rouse. ♦ **destarsi** *vr.*
to wake (*v. irr.*) up.
destinare *vt.* 1. to destine 2. (*devolvere*) to assign.
destinatario *sm.* addressee.
destinazione *sf.* destination.
destino *sm.* 1. destiny 2. (*sorte*) lot.
destituire *vt.* to dismiss.
destituzione *sf.* dismissal.
desto *agg.* awake.
destra *sf.* 1. right hand 2. (*parte destra*) right, right side: *alla tua —*, on your right; *tenere la —*, to keep (*v. irr.*) right.
destramente *avv.* skilfully.
destreggiarsi *vr.* to manage.
destrezza *sf.* dexterity.
destriero *sm.* steed.
destrina *sf.* dextrine.
destro *agg.* 1. right 2. (*abile*) clever. ♦ **destro** *sm.* opportunity.
desueto *agg.* unusual, obsolete.
desuetùdine *sf.* disuse.
desùmere *vt.* 1. to infer 2. (*trarre*) to draw (*v. irr.*).
detenere *vt.* 1. to hold (*v. irr.*) 2. (*tener prigioniero*) to keep (*v. irr.*) in prison.
detentore *sm.* holder.
detenuto *agg.* imprisoned. ♦ **detenuto** *sm.* prisoner.
detenzione *sf.* 1. possession 2. (*il detenere*) holding 3. (*galera*) detention.
detergente *agg. e sm.* detergent.
detèrgere *vt.* to cleanse.
deterioramento *sm.* deterioration.
deteriorare *vt.* 1. to deteriorate 2. (*danneggiare*) to damage.
deteriore *agg.* worse.
determinàbile *agg.* determinable.
determinante *agg.* determinant.
determinare *vt.* 1. to determine 2. (*causare*) to cause.
determinativo *agg.* determinative || *articolo —*, definite article.
determinato *agg.* 1. determinate 2. (*particolare*) special 3. (*deciso*) resolute.
determinazione *sf.* determination.
determinismo *sm.* determinism.
deterrente *sm.* deterrent.
detersivo *agg. e sm.* detersive.
detestàbile *agg.* detestable.
detestare *vt.* to loathe.
detettore *sm.* detector.
detonante *agg.* explosive.
detonare *vi.* to detonate.

detonatore *sm.* detonator.
detonazione *sf.* explosion.
detrarre *vt.* to deduct.
detrattore *sm.* detractor.
detrazione *sf.* 1. deduction 2. (*fig.*) detraction.
detrimento *sm.* detriment.
detrìtico *agg.* detrital.
detrito *sm.* rubble, debris.
detronizzare *vt.* to depose.
detronizzazione *sf.* dethronement.
detta (*nella loc. avv.*) *a — di qu.*, according to what so. says.
dettagliante *sm.* retailer.
dettagliare *vt.* to detail.
dettagliatamente *avv.* in detail.
dettaglio *sm.* 1. detail 2. (*comm.*) retail.
dettame *sm.* dictate.
dettare *vt.* 1. to dictate 2. (*suggerire*) to suggest || *— la legge*, to lay (*v. irr.*) down the law.
dettato *sm.* dictation.
detto *agg.* 1. called 2. (*sopraddetto*) said, above-mentioned. ♦ **detto** *sm.* saying.
deturpare *vt.* to disfigure.
deturpazione *sf.* disfigurement.
devalutazione *sf.* depreciation.
devastare *vt.* to ravage, to ruin.
devastatore *agg.* ravaging. ♦ **devastatore** *sm.* ravager.
devastazione *sf.* devastation.
deviare *vi.* to deviate || *non —!* (*non cambiare discorso*), stick to the point! ♦ **deviare** *vt.* to divert.
deviazione *sf.* 1. deviation 2. (*stradale*) detour || *— ferroviaria*, shunting.
deviazionismo *sm.* deviationism.
devoluzione *sf.* devolution.
devòlvere *vt.* 1. (*giur.*) to devolve, to assign 2. (*adoperare*) to employ.
devoto *agg.* 1. devout, affectionate 2. (*relig.*) pious, religious.
devozione *sf.* devotion, piety.
di *prep.* 1. of 2. (*partitivo*) some, any: *dammi del pane*, give me some bread; *hai dello zucchero?*, have you any sugar? 3. (*tempo*) in, during: *— mattina*, in the morning 4. (*argomento*) of, about 5. (*paragone coi comparativi*) than: *è più graziosa — sua sorella*, she is prettier than her sister 6. (*nei superl.*) of, in 7. (*modo*) with, in.
dì *sm.* day.
diabete *sm.* diabetes.
diabètico *agg. e sm.* diabetic.

diabòlico agg. diabolic(al).

diàcono sm. deacon.

diadema sm. diadem.

diàfano agg. diaphanous.

diaframma sm. diaphragm.

diàgnosi sf. diagnosis (pl. -ses).

diagnosticare vt. to diagnose.

diagnòstico agg. diagnostic.

diagonale agg. diagonal. ♦ **diagonale** sf. diagonal.

diagonalmente avv. diagonally.

diagramma sm. diagram.

dialettale agg. dialectal.

dialèttica sf. dialectics.

dialèttico agg. dialectic. ♦ **dialèttico** sm. dialectic.

dialetto sm. dialect.

diàlisi sf. dialysis (pl. -ses).

dialogare vi. to hold (v. irr.) a dialogue.

diàlogo sm. dialogue.

diamante sm. diamond.

diametralmente avv. diametrically.

diàmetro sm. diameter.

diàmine inter. good heavens!

dianzi avv. just, just now.

diapositiva sf. slide.

diarchìa sf. diarchy.

diario sm. diary.

diarrea sf. diarrhoea.

diaspro sm. jasper.

diatonìa sf. diatony.

diatriba sf. diatribe.

diavolerìa sf. 1. devilry 2. (fam.) trick.

diavoletto sm. imp.

diàvolo sm. devil.

dibàttere vt. to debate. ♦ **dibàttersi** vr. to struggle.

dibàttito sm. debate, discussion.

dibattuto agg. controversial.

diboscamento sm. deforestation.

diboscare vt. to deforest.

dicastero sm. office.

dicembre sm. December.

dicerìa sf. gossip, rumour.

dichiarare vt. to declare.

dichiarato agg. declared.

dichiarazione sf. declaration.

diciannove agg. nineteen.

diciannovenne agg. 1. nineteen years old (pred.) 2. nineteen-year-old (attr.).

diciannovèsimo agg. nineteenth.

diciassette agg. seventeen.

diciassettenne agg. 1. seventeen years old (pred.) 2. seventeen-year-old (attr.).

diciassettèsimo agg. seventeenth.

diciottenne agg. 1. eighteen years old (pred.) 2. eighteen-year-old (attr.).

diciottèsimo agg. eighteenth.

diciotto agg. eighteen.

dicitore sm. speaker.

dicitura sf. wording.

didascalìa sf. 1. explanation 2. (cine) subtitles (pl.).

didascàlico agg. didactic.

didàttica sf. didactics.

didàttico agg. didactic(al).

didentro sm. inside.

didietro sm. back.

dieci agg. ten.

diecina sf. ten, half a score.

diedro sm. dihedral.

dielèttrico agg. dielectric.

diesis sm. sharp.

dieta sf. diet.

dietètico agg. dietetic.

dietòlogo sm. dietician.

dietro avv. behind. ♦ **dietro** prep. behind, after. ♦ **dietro** sm. back, rear.

dietrofrònt sm. about turn!

difatti avv. as a matter of fact.

difèndere vt. to defend.

difendìbile agg. defensible.

difensiva sf. defensive.

difensivo agg. defensive.

difensore agg. defending. ♦ **difensore** sm. 1. defender 2. (giur.) defending counsel 3. (di un'idea ecc.) supporter.

difesa sf. defence.

difettare vi. to be wanting.

difettivo agg. defective.

difetto sm. defect.

difettoso agg. defective.

diffamare vt. to defame.

diffamatore sm. defamer.

diffamatorio agg. defamatory.

diffamazione sf. defamation.

differente agg. unlike, different.

differentemente avv. differently.

differenza sf. difference.

differenziale agg. e sm. differential.

differenziare vt. to differentiate.

differenziato agg. differentiated.

differenziazione sf. differentiation.

differìbile agg. that can be deferred.

differimento sm. deferment.

differire vi. (essere diverso) to differ (from). ♦ **differire** vt. to delay.

difficile *agg.* difficult.

difficilmente *avv.* with difficulty.

difficoltà *sf.* difficulty.

difficoltoso *agg.* difficult.

diffida *sf.* warning, intimation.

diffidare *vi.* to distrust. ♦ **diffidare** *vt.* to give (*v. irr.*) warning.

diffidente *agg.* suspicious.

diffidenza *sf.* **1.** distrust **2.** (*sospetto*) suspicion.

diffóndere *vt.* to diffuse, to spread (*v. irr.*). ♦ **diffóndersi** *vr.* to spread (*v. irr.*).

difforme *agg.* **1.** different **2.** shapeless.

difformità *sf.* difference, deformity.

difrazione *sf.* diffraction.

diffusamente *avv.* diffusely.

diffusione *sf.* **1.** diffusion, spreading **2.** (*di giornale*) circulation.

diffuso *agg.* diffuse.

diffusore *sm.* diffusor.

difilato *avv.* straight.

diftèrico *agg.* diphtheric.

difterite *sf.* diphtheria.

diga *sf.* dam.

digerente *agg.* digestive.

digerìbile *agg.* digestible.

digeribilità *sf.* digestibility.

digerire *vt.* to digest.

digestione *sf.* digestion.

digestivo *agg. e sm.* digestive.

digesto *sm.* digest.

digitale *agg.* digital ‖ *impronte digitali*, finger-prints. ♦ **digitale** *sf.* digitalis, (*fam.*) foxglove.

digiunare *vi.* to fast.

digiunatore *sm.* faster.

digiuno[1] *agg.* **1.** fasting **2.** (*fig.*) lacking (in).

digiuno[2] *sm.* fast.

dignità *sf.* dignity.

dignitario *sm.* dignitary.

dignitosamente *avv.* with dignity.

dignitoso *agg.* dignified.

digradante *agg.* **1.** sloping **2.** (*pitt.*) shading.

digradare *vi.* **1.** to slope down **2.** (*pitt.*) to shade off.

digressione *sf.* digression.

digressivo *agg.* digressive.

digrignare *vt.* to gnash.

digrossamento *sm.* **1.** reducing **2.** (*sbozzo*) rough-hewing.

digrossare *vt.* **1.** to reduce **2.** (*sbozzare*) to rough-hew.

dilacerare *vt.* to tear (*v. irr.*).

dilagare *vi.* to spread (*v. irr.*).

dilaniare *vt.* to tear (*v. irr.*) to pieces.

dilapidare *vt.* to squander.

dilapidatore *sm.* squanderer.

dilapidazione *sf.* squandering.

dilatàbile *agg.* dilatable.

dilatabilità *sf.* dilatability.

dilatare *vt.*, **dilatarsi** *vr.* **1.** to dilate **2.** (*fis.*) to expand.

dilatazione *sf.* dilatation.

dilatorio *agg.* dilatory.

dilavamento *sm.* washing away.

dilavare *vt.* to wash away.

dilazionare *vt.* to defer.

dilazione *sf.* delay, respite.

dileggiare *vt.* to mock.

dileggio *sm.* mockery.

dileguare *vt.* to disperse. ♦ **dileguarsi** *vr.* to disappear.

dilemma *sm.* dilemma.

dilettante *sm.* amateur.

dilettantismo *sm.* amateurism.

dilettare *vt.* to delight. ♦ **dilettarsi** *vr.* to take (*v. irr.*) delight (in).

dilettévole *agg.* delightful.

diletto *agg.* beloved. ♦ **diletto** *sm.* delight.

diligente *agg.* diligent.

diligenza *sf.* **1.** diligence **2.** (*carrozza*) stage-coach.

dilucidare *vt.* V. *delucidare.*

dilucidazione *sf.* V. *delucidazione.*

diluente *sm.* diluent.

diluire *vt.* **1.** to dilute **2.** (*fig.*) to water down.

diluizione *sf.* dilution.

dilungarsi *vr.* to speak (*v. irr.*) diffusely.

diluviale *agg.* **1.** torrential **2.** (*geol.*) diluvial.

diluviano *agg.* diluvial.

diluviare *vi.* **1.** to pour **2.** (*fig.*) to shower.

diluvio *sm.* deluge, flood.

dimagramento *sm.* thinning.

dimagrante *agg.* slimming.

dimagrare *vi.* to thin.

dimagrire *vi.* V. *dimagrare.*

dimenare *vt.* **1.** (*la coda*) to wag **2.** to wave. ♦ **dimenarsi** *vr.* to move about restlessly.

dimensione *sf.* dimension, size.

dimenticanza *sf.* **1.** (*svista*) oversight **2.** (*oblio*) oblivion.

dimenticare *vt.*, **dimenticarsi** *vr.* to forget (*v. irr.*).

diméntico *agg.* forgetful.

dimesso *agg.* **1.** modest **2.** (*trasandato*) shabby.

dimestichezza sf. familiarity.

dìmetro sm. dimeter.

diméttere vt. to dismiss || — dall'ospedale, to discharge. ♦ **diméttersi** vr. to resign.

dimezzamento sm. halving.

dimezzare vt. to halve.

diminuendo sm. 1. (mat.) minuend 2. (mus.) diminuendo.

diminuìbile agg. diminishable.

diminuire vt. e vi. to lessen, to diminish.

diminutivo agg. e sm. diminutive.

diminuzione sf. lessening, reduction.

dimissionare vt. to oblige (so.) to resign.

dimissionario agg. resigning.

dimissione sf. resignation || dare le dimissioni, to resign.

dimissoria sf. dimissory letter.

dimodoché cong. so that.

dimora sf. residence, lodgings (pl.).

dimorare vi. to stay, to live.

dimorfismo sm. dimorphism.

dimorfo agg. dimorphic.

dimostràbile agg. demonstrable.

dimostrabilità sf. demonstrability.

dimostrante sm. demonstrant.

dimostrare vt. 1. to show (v. irr.) 2. (provare) to demonstrate. ♦ **dimostrarsi** vr. to show oneself.

dimostrativo agg. e sm. demonstrative.

dimostratore sm. demonstrator.

dimostrazione sf. demonstration.

dina sf. dyne.

dinàmica sf. dynamics.

dinamicamente avv. dynamically.

dinamicità sf. dynamism, energy.

dinàmico agg. 1. dynamic 2. (fig.) energetic.

dinamismo sm. 1. dynamism 2. (fig.) energy.

dinamitardo sm. dynamiter.

dinamite sf. dynamite.

dìnamo sf. dynamo.

dinamòmetro sm. dynamometer.

dinanzi prep. before, in front of. ♦ **dinanzi** avv. before, in front, forward.

dìnaro sm. dinar.

dinasta sm. dynast.

dinastìa sf. dynasty.

dinàstico agg. dynastic(al).

dindo sm. turkey.

diniego sm. denial.

dinoccolato agg. slouching.

dinosàuro sm. dinosaur.

dintorni sm. pl. surroundings.

dintorno avv. e prep. 1. round, round about 2. (circa) about.

dio sm. god: Marte, il — della guerra, Mars, the god of war. ♦ **Dio** sm. God: — ci assista!, — non voglia!, God help us, God forbid.

diocesano agg. diocesan.

diòcesi sf. diocese.

dìodo sm. diode.

dionea sf. dionaea.

dionisìaco agg. Dionysiac.

diorama sm. diorama.

diorite sf. diorite.

diottrìa sf. diopter.

diòttrica sf. dioptrics.

diòttrico agg. dioptric.

dipanamento sm. winding into a ball.

dipanare vt. 1. to wind (v. irr.) into a ball 2. (fig.) to disentangle.

dipanatoio sm. skein-winder.

dipartimentale agg. departmental.

dipartimento sm. department.

dipartire vi. to depart. ♦ **dipartirsi** vr. 1. to go (v. irr.) away 2. (morire) to pass away.

dipartita sf. 1. departure 2. (morte) death.

dipendente agg. dependent (on). ♦ **dipendente** sm. employee.

dipendenza sf. dependence (on).

dipèndere vi. 1. (derivare) to be due 2. (essere subordinato, vivere a carico) to depend (on).

dipìngere vt. to paint.

dipinto agg. painted. ♦ **dipinto** sm. painting.

diplegìa sf. diplegia.

diplococco sm. diplococcus (pl. -ci).

diploma sm. diploma.

diplomare vt. to confer a diploma (upon so.). ♦ **diplomarsi** vr. to get (v. irr.) a diploma.

diplomàtica sf. diplomatics.

diplomaticamente avv. diplomatically.

diplomàtico agg. diplomatic. ♦ **diplomàtico** sm. diplomat.

diplomato agg. holding a diploma. ♦ **diplomato** sm. graduate.

diplomazìa sf. diplomacy.

diplopìa sf. diplopia.

dipnoi sm. pl. Dipnoi.

dipodìa sf. dipody.

dipoi avv. then.

diporto sm. recreation, diversion ||

viaggiare per —, to travel on pleasure.

dipresso (*nella loc. avv.*) *a un* —, approximately.

dìptero *agg.* dipteral.

diradamento *sm.* 1. thinning 2. (*di nebbia, gas*) rarefaction.

diradare *vt.* 1. to thin out 2. (*rendere meno frequente*) to do (*v. irr.*) less frequent. ♦ **diradarsi** *vr.* 1. to clear away 2. (*divenire meno frequente*) to become (*v. irr.*) less frequent.

diramare *vt.* to issue, to spread (*v. irr.*).

diramazione *sf.* 1. branching 2. (*diffusione*) diffusion 3. (*per radio*) broadcasting.

dire *vt.* 1. (*nel senso di enunciare e quando introduce il discorso diretto*) to say (*v. irr.*): *dice che ha sonno,* he says he is sleepy; *« venite »,* ci disse, « come », he said to us 2. (*nel senso di raccontare e quando è enunciata la persona cui si parla*) to tell (*v. irr.*): *gli dissi di venire,* I told him to come || *si dice,* they say; *mi si dice,* I am told; *inutile — che,* it goes without saying that; *vale a* —, that is to say; *sentir* —, to hear (*v. irr.*); *voler* —, to mean (*v. irr.*).

dire *sm.* words (*pl.*), speech.

direttamente *avv.* directly.

direttìssima *sf.* per —, summarily.

direttìssimo *sm.* (*ferr.*) fast train.

direttiva *sf.* directions (*pl.*).

direttivo *agg.* 1. leading 2. (*comm.*) managing.

diretto *agg.* direct, straight.

direttore *sm.* 1. (*comm.; amm.*) manager 2. (*di scuola*) headmaster.

direttoriale *agg.* directorial.

direttorio *sm.* executive board.

direttrice *sf.* 1. (*comm.; amm.*) manageress 2. (*di scuola*) headmistress.

direzionale *agg.* directional || *centro* —, office district.

direzione *sf.* 1. direction, course 2. (*di società*) management 3. (*di giornale*) editorship 4. (*di scuola*) headmastership 5. (*sede*) administrative office.

dirigente *agg.* directing, leading. ♦ **dirigente** *sm.* director, manager, leader.

dirìgere *vt.* 1. (*indirizzare*) to direct

2. (*guidare*) to lead (*v. irr.*) 3. (*sovraintendere*) to supervise. ♦ **dirìgersi** *vr.* to turn one's steps towards.

dirigìbile *sm.* airship.

dirigismo *sm.* state planning.

dirigista *sm.* supporter of state planning.

dirimente *agg.* diriment.

dirìmere *vt.* to settle.

dirimpettaio *sm.* person living just opposite.

dirimpetto *avv.* face to face, opposite.

diritta *sf.* right, right-hand: *a* —, on the right.

dirittamente *avv.* straight.

diritto *agg.* straight, upright || *rigare* —, to behave properly. ♦ **diritto** *sm.* 1. right 2. (*tassa, tributo*) due 3. (*legge*) law.

dirittura *sf.* 1. straight line 2. (*rettitudine*) uprightness 3. (*sport*) — *d'arrivo,* home stretch.

dirizzare *vt.* 1. to direct 2. (*erigere*) to raise 3. (*raddrizzare; fig.*) to put (*v. irr.*) right, to straighten.

dirizzone *sm.* inconsiderate action.

diroccamento *sm.* demolition.

diroccare *vt.* to demolish.

diroccato *agg.* 1. (*demolito*) dismantled 2. (*in rovina*) crumbled.

dirompente *agg.* disruptive.

diròmpere *vt.* 1. (*di lino, canapa ecc.*) to scutch 2. (*rompere*) to break (*v. irr.*).

dirottare *vt.* to divert. ♦ **dirottare** *vi.* to change course.

dirotto *agg.* excessive: *pianto* —, desperate crying; *piove a* —, it is pouring.

dirozzamento *sm.* 1. (*lo sbozzare*) rough-hewing 2. (*fig.*) refinement.

dirozzare *vt.* 1. (*sbozzare*) to rough-hew 2. (*fig.*) to refine.

dirugginire *vt.* to remove the rust from.

dirupamento *sm.* 1. falling down 2. (*di luogo*) abruptness.

dirupato *agg.* 1. abrupt 2. (*roccioso*) rocky.

dirupo *sm.* precipice.

disabbellire *vt.* to spoil the beauty of. ♦ **disabbellirsi** *vr.* to lose (*v. irr.*) one's beauty.

disabitato *agg.* 1. uninhabited 2. (*abbandonato*) deserted.

disabituare *vt.* to disaccustom. ♦ **disabituarsi** *vr.* to give (*v. irr.*)

up the habit of.

disaccordo *sm.* disagreement.

disacerbare *vt.* to appease.

disadatto *agg.* **1.** unfit **2.** (*che non si addice*) unbecoming.

disadornare *vt.* to disadorn.

disadorno *agg.* **1.** unadorned **2.** (*spoglio*) bare.

disaffezionarsi *vr.* to lose (*v. irr.*) one's affection (for).

disaffezionato *agg.* estranged.

disaffezione *sf.* estrangement.

disagévole *agg.* uncomfortable.

disagiatamente *avv.* uncomfortably.

disagiato *agg.* **1.** uncomfortable **2.** (*povero*) needy.

disagio *sm.* **1.** uneasiness || *essere a* —, to be uneasy **2.** (*disturbo*) inconvenience **3.** (*pl.; privazioni*) privations.

disamare *vt.* to cease to love.

disàmina *sf.* examination.

disaminare *vt.* to examine carefully.

disancorarsi *vr.* **1.** to weigh anchor **2.** (*fig.*) to break (*v. irr.*) all connections (with).

disanimarsi *vr.* to lose (*v. irr.*) heart.

disappetenza *sf.* lack of appetite.

disapprèndere *vt.* to forget (*v. irr.*).

disapprovare *vt.* to disapprove (of).

disapprovazione *sf.* disapproval.

disappunto *sm.* disappointment.

disarcionare *vt.* to unsaddle.

disarmare *vt.* to disarm.

disarmato *agg.* disarmed.

disarmo *sm.* disarmament.

disarmonìa *sf.* discord.

disarmonicamente *avv.* discordantly.

disarmònico *agg.* discordant.

disarmonizzare *vt.* to disharmonize.

disarticolare *vt.* to disjoint.

disarticolazione *sf.* disjointing.

disastro *sm.* disaster.

disastroso *agg.* disastrous.

disattento *agg.* inattentive.

disattenzione *sf.* inattention: *errore di* —, a slip of the pen.

disavanzo *sm.* deficit.

disavveduto *agg.* heedless.

disavventura *sf.* **1.** mishap **2.** (*sfortuna*) misfortune.

disavvertenza *sf.* inadvertence.

disavvezzo *agg.* unaccustomed.

disazotare *vt.* to remove nitrogen from.

disborso *sm.* disbursement.

disbrigo *sm.* dispatch.

disbrogliare *vt.* to disentangle.

discacciare *vt.* to turn out.

discapitare *vi.* to suffer damage.

discàpito *sm.* disadvantage.

discàrico *sm.* **1.** discharge **2.** (*scusa*) defence.

discendente *agg.* descending. ♦
discendente *sm.* descendant.

discendenza *sf.* **1.** descent **2.** (*discendenti*) offspring.

discéndere *vt.* **1.** to descend, to go (*v. irr.*) down **2.** (*di astri*) to sink (*v. irr.*) **3.** (*di prezzi*) to fall (*v. irr.*).

discépolo *sm.* disciple.

discèrnere *vt.* **1.** to discern **2.** (*distinguere*) to distinguish.

discernìbile *agg.* discernible.

discernimento *sm.* discernment.

discesa *sf.* **1.** descent **2.** (*declivio*) slope **3.** (*caduta*) fall **4.** (*invasione*) invasion.

dischiùdere *vt.* to disclose.

dischiuso *agg.* disclosed.

discinto *agg.* ungirt.

disciplina *sf.* **1.** (*materia di studio*) doctrine **2.** (*regola*) discipline.

disciplinàbile *agg.* disciplinable.

disciplinare[1] *vt.* to discipline.

disciplinare[2] *agg.* disciplinary.

disciplinarmente *avv.* with discipline.

disciplinatamente *avv.* with discipline.

disciplinato *agg.* disciplined.

disco *sm.* **1.** disk **2.** (*mus.*) record **3.** (*sport*) discus **4.** (*ferr.*) disk signal.

discòbolo *sm.* discus-thrower.

discòide *agg.* discoid.

dìscolo *sm.* wild boy, little scamp.

discolpa *sf.* excuse.

discolpare *vt.* to clear.

disconoscente *aff.* ungrateful.

disconoscenza *sf.* ungratitude.

disconòscere *vt.* to refuse to recognize.

disconoscimento *sm.* **1.** refusal to recognize **2.** (*ingratitudine*) ingratitude.

discontinuità *sf.* discontinuity.

discontinuo *agg.* discontinuous.

discordante *agg.* **1.** discordant **2.** (*diverso*) different **3.** (*di colori*)

clashing.
discordanza *sf.* discordance.
discordare *vi.* 1. to disagree 2. (*di colori*) to clash 3. (*di suoni*) to jar.
discorde *agg.* discordant (with).
discordemente *avv.* discordantly.
discordia *sf.* discord.
discòrrere *vi.* to talk.
discorsivo *agg.* talkative.
discorso *sm.* speech.
discostare *vt.* to shift.
discosto *agg.* far, distant. ♦ **discosto** *avv.* at some distance.
discoteca *sf.* record library.
discreditare *vt.* to discredit.
discrédito *sm.* discredit.
discrepante *agg.* differing.
discrepanza *sf.* discrepancy.
discretamente *avv.* 1. (*con discrezione*) discreetly 2. (*sufficientemente*) fairly 3. (*piuttosto*) rather.
discreto *agg.* 1. (*che ha discrezione*) discreet 2. (*moderato*) moderate 3. (*abbastanza buono*) fairly good.
discrezionale *agg.* discretionary.
discrezione *sf.* discretion.
discriminante *agg.* discriminating.
discriminare *vt.* to discriminate.
discriminazione *sf.* discrimination.
discussione *sf.* discussion.
discusso *agg.* discussed.
discùtere *vt.* to discuss.
discutìbile *agg.* questionable.
disdegnare *vt.* to disdain.
disdegno *sm.* disdain.
disdegnosamente *avv.* disdainfully.
disdegnoso *agg.* disdainful.
disdetta *sf.* 1. (*giur.*) notice of leave 2. (*sfortuna*) bad luck.
disdettare *vt.* to give (*v. irr.*) notice.
disdicévole *agg.* unbecoming.
disdire *vt.* 1. (*ritrattare*) to take (*v. irr.*) back, to retract 2. (*annullare*) to cancel.
disegnare *vt.* 1. to draw (*v. irr.*) 2. (*progettare*) to plan.
disegnatore *sm.* designer.
disegno *sm.* 1. drawing 2. (*di tessuto*) pattern 3. (*di edificio*) plan 4. (*schizzo*) sketch 5. (*fig.*) design, plan.
diseredare *vt.* to disinherit.
diseredato *agg.* 1. poor, destitute 2. (*privato di eredità*) disinherited.

disertare *vt.* 1. to desert 2. (*abbandonare*) to leave (*v. irr.*).
disertore *sm.* deserter.
diserzione *sf.* desertion.
disfacimento *sm.* 1. (*il disfare*) undoing 2. (*decadimento*) decay.
disfare *vt.* 1. to undo (*v. irr.*) 2. (*slegare*) to untie.
disfasia *sf.* dysphasia.
disfatta *sf.* defeat.
disfattismo *sm.* defeatism.
disfattista *agg. e s.* defeatist.
disfatto *agg.* 1. (*distrutto*) ruined 2. (*slegato*) undone 3. (*molto stanco*) worn out.
disfavore *sm.* disfavour.
disfida *sf.* challenge.
disfunzione *sf.* disorder.
disgelare *vt. e vi.* to thaw.
disgelo *sm.* thaw.
disgiùngere *vt.* to disjoin.
disgiungimento *sm.* disjoining.
disgiuntamente *avv.* separately.
disgiuntivamente *avv.* disjunctively.
disgiuntivo *agg.* disjunctive.
disgiunto *agg.* disjoined.
disgiunzione *sf.* disjunction.
disgrazia *sf.* 1. misfortune 2. (*sfavore*) disfavour || *cadere in* —, to lose (*v. irr.*) so.'s favour 3. (*fatto involontario*) accident.
disgraziatamente *avv.* unfortunately.
disgraziato *agg.* 1. unlucky, wretched 2. (*deforme*) misshapen.
disgregamento *sm.* disintegration.
disgregare *vt.* to disgregate, to break (*v. irr.*) up.
disgregazione *sf.* disgregation.
disguido *sm.* miscarriage.
disgustare *vt.* to disgust, to sicken. ♦ **disgustarsi** *vr.* to become (*v. irr.*) disgusted (with).
disgusto *sm.* 1. disgust 2. (*avversione*) dislike.
disgustoso *agg.* disgusting.
disidratare *vt.* to dehydrate.
disidratazione *sf.* dehydration.
disillùdere *vt.* to undeceive.
disillusione *sf.* disillusion.
disilluso *agg.* undeceived, disappointed.
disimballaggio *sm.* unpacking.
disimballare *vt.* to unpack.
disimpacciare *vt.* to disembarrass.
disimparare *vt.* to forget (*v. irr.*).
disimpegnare *vt.* 1. to redeem 2. (*liberare da un impegno*) to re-

lease. ♦ **disimpegnarsi** *vr.* **1.** to disengage oneself **2.** (*cavarsela*) to manage.

disimpegno *sm.* **1.** redemption **2.** (*il liberarsi da un impegno*) disengagement.

disincagliare *vt.* to get (*v. irr.*) afloat.

disincantare *vt.* to disenchant.

disincantato *agg.* disenchanted.

disincanto *sm.* disenchantment.

disinfestare *vt.* to disinfest.

disinfettante *sm.* disinfectant.

disinfettare *vt.* to disinfect.

disinfezione *sf.* disinfection.

disingannare *vt.* to undeceive.

disinganno *sm.* **1.** undeceiving **2.** (*delusione*) disappointment.

disinnescare *vt.* to defuse.

disinnestare *vt.* to disengage.

disinnesto *sm.* disengagement, release.

disinserire *vt.* to disconnect.

disintegrare *vt.* to disintegrate.

disintegratore *sm.* disintegrator.

disintegrazione *sf.* disintegration.

disinteressare *vt.* **1.** to disinterest **2.** (*comm.*) to buy (*v. irr.*) out. ♦ **disinteressarsi** *vr.* to take (*v. irr.*) no interest (in).

disinteressato *agg.* **1.** disinterested **2.** (*altruistico*) unselfish.

disinteresse *sm.* **1.** indifference **2.** (*altruismo*) unselfishness.

disintossicare *vt.* to unpoison.

disintossicazione *sf.* unpoisoning.

disinvolto *agg.* unconstrained, free-and-easy.

disinvoltura *sf.* unconstraint, free-and-easy way.

disistima *sf.* disesteem.

disistimare *vt.* to disesteem.

dislivello *sm.* **1.** difference of level **2.** (*di acque*) rise **3.** (*di strade*) gradient **4.** (*ineguaglianza*) inequality.

dislocamento *sm.* **1.** displacement **2.** (*mil.*) dislocation.

dislocare *vt.* **1.** to displace **2.** (*mil.*) to dislocate.

dislocazione *sf.* removal, dislocation.

dismisura *sf.* excess || *a* —, excessively.

disobbedire *vi.* V. *disubbidire*.

disobbligare *vt.* to release from duty. ♦ **disobbligarsi** *vr.* to free oneself from duty.

disoccupato *agg.* unemployed. ♦

disoccupato *sm.* unemployed person.

disoccupazione *sf.* unemployment.

disonestà *sf.* **1.** dishonesty **2.** (*atto disonesto*) fraud.

disonesto *agg.* dishonest, fraudulent.

disonorante *agg.* shameful.

disonorare *vt.* to dishonour.

disonore *sm.* dishonour, shame.

disonorévole *agg.* dishonourable.

disopra *avv.* **1.** above, over **2.** (*in cima*) on top **3.** (*ai piani superiori*) upstairs. ♦ **disopra** *sm.* top, upper part. ♦ **al disopra di, disopra a** *prep.* above.

disordinare *vt.* to disorder.

disordinatamente *avv.* untidily.

disordinato *agg.* untidy, disorderly.

disòrdine *sm.* **1.** disorder, untidiness **2.** (*sregolatezza*) disorderliness **3.** (*tumulto*) disorder, tumult.

disorgànico *agg.* inorganic.

disorganizzare *vt.* to disorganize.

disorganizzato *agg.* disorganized.

disorganizzazione *sf.* disorganization.

disorientamento *sm.* disorientation, confusion.

disorientare *vt.* **1.** to disorientate **2.** (*sconcertare*) to bewilder.

disorientato *agg.* bewildered, puzzled.

disormeggiare *vt.* to unmoor.

disossare *vt.* to bone.

disossidante *sm.* deoxidizer.

disossidare *vt.* to deoxidize.

disossidazione *sf.* deoxidation.

disotto *avv.* **1.** below, underneath **2.** (*al piano inferiore*) downstairs. ♦ **disotto** *sm.* underside, lower part. ♦ **al disotto di, disotto a** *prep.* under, beneath, below.

dispaccio *sm.* dispatch.

disparato *agg.* disparate.

disparere *sm.* difference of opinion.

dìspari *agg.* odd.

disparità *sf.* disparity.

disparte *avv.* aside, apart: *starsene in* —, to stand (*v. irr.*) aside; (*fig.*) to stand aloof; *mettere in* —, to put (*v. irr.*) aside; (*per uno scopo*) to put by.

dispendio *sm.* **1.** heavy expense **2.** (*di forza, tempo*) waste.

dispendioso *agg.* expensive.

dispensa *sf.* **1.** pantry **2.** (*mobile*) sideboard **3.** (*pubblicazione perio-*

dica) number **4.** (*esenzione; eccl.*) dispensation.

dispensare *vt.* **1.** (*distribuire*) to deal (*v. irr.*) out **2.** (*esentare*) to exempt, to dispense.

dispensario *sm.* dispensary.

dispensato *agg.* exempted.

dispensatore *sm.* distributor, dispenser.

dispepsìa *sf.* dyspepsia.

dispèptico *agg.* dyspeptic.

disperare *vi.* to despair, to lose (*v. irr.*) all hope. ♦ **disperarsi** *vr.* to give (*v. irr.*) oneself up to despair.

disperatamente *avv.* desperately.

disperato *agg.* **1.** despairing **2.** (*senza speranza*) hopeless || *essere* — (*di malato*), to be far gone. ♦ **disperato** *sm.* **1.** (*miserabile*) destitute **2.** (*forsennato*) madman (*pl.* -men).

disperazione *sf.* despair.

dispèrdere *vt.* to disperse **2.** (*consumare*) to waste.

dispersione *sf.* **1.** dispersion **2.** (*elettr.*) leak.

dispersivo *agg.* dispersive.

disperso *agg.* missing, lost.

dispetto *sm.* **1.** spite: *a — di,* in spite of **2.** (*stizza*) vexation.

dispettoso *agg.* spiteful.

dispiacere [1] *vi.* **1.** to dislike || *mi dispiace,* I am sorry; (*in espressioni di cortesia*) *se non vi dispiace,* if you please **2.** (*essere sgradevole*) to be disagreeable.

dispiacere [2] *sm.* **1.** regret **2.** (*disapprovazione*) displeasure **3.** (*fastidio*) tròuble.

dispiegare *vt.* **1.** (*allargare*) to spread (*v. irr.*) out **2.** (*le vele*) to unfurl.

displuvio *sm.* **1.** watershed || *linea di* —, ridge **2.** (*arch.*) hip.

disponìbile *agg.* available.

disponibilità *sf.* availability.

disporre *vt.* **1.** to arrange **2.** (*preparare*) to dispose **3.** (*deliberare*) to order.

dispositivo *sm.* (*mecc.*) device.

disposizione *sf.* **1.** disposition, arrangement **2.** (*ordine*) order, direction || *a —,* at one's disposal **3.** (*inclinazione*) bent.

disposto *agg.* **1.** ready, willing **2.** (*ben disposto fisicamente*) strong.

dispòtico *agg.* despotic.

dispotismo *sm.* despotism.

dispregiativamente *avv.* disparagingly.

dispregiativo *agg.* depreciative. ♦ **dispregiativo** *sm.* (*gramm.*) pejorative.

dispregiatore *sm.* contemner.

dispregio *sm.* contempt.

disprezzàbile *agg.* despicable.

disprezzare *vt.* **1.** to despise **2.** (*considerare di poco conto*) to look down on.

disprezzo *sm.* contempt.

dìsputa *sf.* discussion.

disputàbile *agg.* disputable.

disputare *vi* e *vt.* to discuss.

disquisizione *sf.* disquisition.

dissaldare *vt.* to unsolder.

dissanguamento *sm.* **1.** bleeding **2.** (*fig.*) impoverishment.

dissanguare *vt.* **1.** to bleed **2.** (*fig.*) to impoverish. ♦ **dissanguarsi** *vr.* (*fig.*) to become (*v. irr.*) impoverished.

dissanguato *agg.* **1.** bloodless **2.** (*fig.*) impoverished.

dissanguatore *sm.* (*fig.*) blood-sucker.

dissapore *sm.* disagreement.

dissecare *vt.* to dissect.

disseccamento *sm.* drying up.

disseccante *agg.* drying up. ♦ **disseccante** *sm.* desiccative.

disseccare *vt.* **1.** to dry up **2.** (*cibo*) to desiccate.

disselciare *vt.* to unpave.

disseminare *vt.* to disseminate.

disseminato *agg.* strewn.

disseminatore *agg.* disseminating. ♦ **disseminatore** *sm.* disseminator.

disseminazione *sf.* dissemination.

dissennatamente *avv.* madly.

dissennatezza *sf.* **1.** madness **2.** (*avventatezza*) rashness.

dissennato *agg.* **1.** mad **2.** (*avventato*) rash.

dissensione *sf.* dissension.

dissenso *sm.* dissent.

dissenterìa *sf.* dysentery.

dissentèrico *agg.* dysenteric.

dissentire *vi.* to dissent.

dissenziente *agg.* dissenting. ♦ **dissenziente** *sm.* dissenter.

disseppellimento *sm.* disinterment.

disseppellire *vt.* **1.** to disinter **2.** (*fig.*) to revive.

disserrare *vt.* to unfasten.

dissertare *vi.* to dissertate (on).

dissertatore *sm.* dissertator.

dissertazione *sf.* dissertation.

dissestare *vt.* **1.** (*finanziariamente*) to ruin **2.** (*mettere fuori posto*) to derange.

dissestato *agg.* (*di persona*) ruined.

dissesto *sm.* **1.** trouble **2.** (*fallimento*) bankruptcy.

dissetante *agg.* refreshing: *bibita* —, refreshing drink.

dissetare *vt.* to quench the thirst of. ♦ **dissetarsi** *vr.* **1.** to quench one's thirst **2.** (*bere*) to drink (*v. irr.*); (*di animali*) to water.

dissezione *sf.* dissection.

dissidente *agg.* e *sm.* dissident.

dissidenza *sf.* dissidence.

dissidio *sm.* **1.** dissension, disagreement **2.** (*litigio*) quarrel.

dissigillare *vt.* to unseal.

dissìmile *agg.* unlike.

dissimmetrìa *sf.* dissymmetry.

dissimulare *vt.* to dissemble.

dissimulatamente *avv.* dissemblingly.

dissimulatore *sm.* dissimulator.

dissimulazione *sf.* dissimulation.

dissipare *vt.* to dissipate. ♦ **dissiparsi** *vr.* to dissipate, to vanish.

dissipatezza *sf.* dissipation.

dissipatore *sm.* waster.

dissipazione *sf.* dissipation.

dissociàbile *agg.* dissociable.

dissociare *vt.* to dissociate.

dissociazione *sf.* dissociation.

dissodamento *sm.* tillage.

dissodare *vt.* to till.

dissolùbile *agg.* dissoluble.

dissolubilità *sf.* dissolubility.

dissolutezza *sf.* dissoluteness.

dissoluto *agg.* dissolute.

dissoluzione *sf.* dissolution.

dissolvente *agg.* e *sm.* dissolvent.

dissòlvere *vt.* **1.** to dissolve **2.** (*disperdere*) to dispel. ♦ **dissòlversi** *vr.* to dissolve.

dissolvimento *sm.* dissolution.

dissomigliante *agg.* dissimilar (to).

dissomiglianza *sf.* dissimilarity.

dissomigliare *vi.* to be unlike. ♦ **dissomigliarsi** *vr.* to differ from.

dissonante *agg.* dissonant.

dissonanza *sf.* **1.** dissonance **2.** (*fig.*) discordance.

dissonare *vi.* **1.** to be out of tune **2.** (*fig.*) to discord (with).

dissotterramento *sm.* disinterment.

dissotterrare *vt.* to disinter.

dissuadere *vt.* to dissuade.

dissuasione *sf.* dissuasion.

distaccamento *sm.* **1.** detaching **2.** (*mil.*) detachment.

distaccare *vt.* to detach. ♦ **distaccarsi** *vr.* to come (*v. irr.*) off.

distacco *sm.* **1.** detaching **2.** (*partenza*) leaving **3.** (*indifferenza*) unconcern.

distante *agg.* distant. ♦ **distante** *avv.* far, far off, far away.

distanza *sf.* distance.

distanziare *vt.* **1.** to space **2.** (*lasciare indietro*) to distance.

distanziato *agg.* **1.** spaced **2.** (*sport*) outdistanced.

distare *vi.* to be far: *quanto dista?*, how far is it?

distèndere *vt.* **1.** (*allungare*) to stretch **2.** (*spalmare*) to spread (*v. irr.*) **3.** (*porre, stendere*) to lay (*v. irr.*). ♦ **distèndersi** *vr.* **1.** to spread (*v. irr.*) **2.** (*sdraiarsi*) to lie (*v. irr.*) down **3.** (*rilassarsi*) to relax.

distensione *sf.* **1.** (*di nervi, tensione*) relaxation **2.** (*pol.*) distension.

distensivo *agg.* relaxing.

distesa *sf.* expanse || *a* —, continuously.

distesamente *avv.* diffusely.

disteso *agg.* **1.** (*teso*) extended **2.** (*giacente*) lying **3.** (*esteso*) extensive || *per* —, diffusely.

distico *sm.* couplet.

distillare *vt.* to distil.

distillato *agg.* distilled. ♦ **distillato** *sm.* distillate.

distillatoio *sm.* still.

distillatore *sm.* distiller.

distillazione *sf.* distillation.

distillerìa *sf.* distillery.

distinguere *vt.* **1.** to distinguish **2.** (*contrassegnare*) to mark.

distinta *sf.* list.

distintivo *agg.* distinctive. ♦ **distintivo** *sm.* badge.

distinto *agg.* **1.** distinct **2.** (*garbato*) distinguished.

distinzione *sf.* **1.** distinction **2.** (*riguardo*) regard **3.** (*raffinatezza*) refinement.

distògliere *vt.* **1.** (*dissuadere*) to dissuade **2.** (*distrarre*) to divert. ♦ **distògliersi** *vr.* to be distracted.

distorsione *sf.* distortion.

distrarre *vt.* **1.** (*distogliere*) to divert **2.** (*divertire*) to entertain.

distrattamente *avv.* **1.** absent-mindedly **2.** (*inavvertitamente*) inadvertently.

distratto *agg.* **1.** absent-minded **2.** (*disattento*) inattentive.

distrazione *sf.* **1.** absent-mindedness **2.** (*disattenzione*) inattention **3.** (*divertimento*) recreation.

distretta *sf.* urgent need.

distretto *sm.* district || — *militare*, recruiting centre.

distrettuale *agg.* district.

distribuibile *agg.* distributable.

distribuire *vt.* to distribute.

distributivo *agg.* e *sm.* distributive.

distributore *agg.* distributing. ◆ **distributore** *sm.* distributor || — *di benzina*, petrol pump.

distribuzione *sf.* distribution.

districare *vt.* to disentangle.

distrùggere *vt.* **1.** to destroy **2.** (*struggere*) to consume. ◆ **distrùggersi** *vr.* (*consumarsi*) to pine (away).

distruggìbile *agg.* destroyable.

distruttivo *agg.* destroying.

distrutto *agg.* destroyed.

distruttore *agg.* destroying. ◆ **distruttore** *sm.* destroyer.

distruzione *sf.* destruction.

disturbare *vt.* to disturb.

disturbato *agg.* **1.** disturbed **2.** (*indisposto*) unwell.

disturbatore *sm.* disturber.

disturbo *sm.* **1.** trouble, inconvenience **2.** (*malattia*) trouble, illness **3.** (*radio*) disturbance.

disubbidiente *agg.* disobedient.

disubbidienza *sf.* disobedience.

disubbidire *vi.* to disobey.

disuguaglianza *sf.* **1.** inequality **2.** (*di terreno*) unevenness.

disuguale *agg.* **1.** unequal **2.** (*irregolare*) irregular **3.** (*differente*) different.

disumanamente *avv.* inhumanly.

disumanare *vt.* to divest of humanity.

disumanità *sf.* inhumanity.

disumano *agg.* inhuman.

disumidire *vt.* to dry.

disunione *sf.* disunion.

disunire *vt.* to disunite. ◆ **disunirsi** *vr.* to become (*v. irr.*) disunited.

disunito *agg.* disunited.

disusare *vt.* to disuse.

disusato *agg.* disused.

disuso *sm.* disuse.

ditale *sm.* thimble.

ditata *sf.* finger-mark.

ditiràmbico *agg.* dithyrambic.

ditirambo *sm.* dithyramb.

dito *sm.* **1.** finger **2.** (*del piede*) toe.

ditta *sf.* firm.

dittàfono *sm.* dictaphone.

dittatore *sm.* dictator.

dittatoriale *agg.* dictatorial.

dittatorio *agg.* dictatorial.

dittatura *sf.* dictatorship.

dìttico *sm.* diptych.

dittongo *sm.* diphthong.

diuresi *sf.* diuresis.

diurètico *agg.* diuretic.

diurno *agg.* diurnal, daytime.

diuturnamente *avv.* for a long time.

diuturno *agg.* diuturnal.

diva *sf.* **1.** goddess **2.** (*cine*) star.

divagare *vi.* to wander **2.** (*divertire*) to amuse. ◆ **divagarsi** *vr.* **1.** to be distracted **2.** (*divertirsi*) to amuse oneself.

divagazione *sf.* digression.

divampare *vi.* to blaze.

divano *sm.* divan, sofa.

divaricamento *sm.* straddle.

divaricare *vt.* to open wide || — *le gambe*, to part one's legs wide.

divario *sm.* difference.

divedere *vt.* **1.** (*nella loc. avv.*) *dare a* —, to show (*v. irr.*) clearly **2.** (*dar a credere*) to make (*v. irr.*) believe.

divèllere *vt.* to uproot.

divenire[1] *vi.* **1.** to become (*v. irr.*) **2.** (*mutarsi lentamente*) to grow (*v. irr.*).

divenire[2] *sm.* becoming: *l'essere e il* —, being and becoming.

diverbio *sm.* quarrel.

divergente *agg.* divergent.

divergenza *sf.* divergence.

divèrgere *vi.* **1.** to diverge **2.** (*scostarsi*) to wander.

diversamente *avv.* **1.** differently **2.** (*altrimenti*) otherwise.

diversificare *vt.* to diversify. ◆ **diversificarsi** *vr.* to differ.

diversione *sf.* diversion.

diversità *sf.* diversity.

diversivo *agg.* **1.** deviating **2.** (*che distrae*) diverting. ◆ **diversivo** *sm.* diversion, distraction.

diverso *agg.* different.

divertente *agg.* amusing.

divertimento *sm.* amusement.
divertire *vt.* to amuse, to entertain
♦ **divertirsi** *vr.* to enjoy oneself, to have a good time.
divezzamento *sm.* weaning.
divezzare *vt.* to wean.
dividendo *sm.* dividend.
dividere *vt.* **1.** to divide **2.** (*condividere*) to share.
divieto *sm.* prohibition.
divinamente *avv.* divinely.
divinare *vt.* to divine.
divinatore *sm.* diviner.
divinatorio *agg.* divinatory.
divinazione *sf.* divination.
divincolarsi *vr.* to wriggle.
divinità *sf.* divinity.
divinizzare *vt.* to deify.
divino *agg.* divine.
divisa *sf.* **1.** uniform **2.** (*valuta*) currency.
divisare *vt.* to plan.
divisìbile *agg.* divisible.
divisibilità *sf.* divisibility.
divisionale *agg.* divisional.
divisione *sf.* **1.** division **2.** (*amm.*) department.
divisionismo *sm.* pointillism.
divisionista *s.* pointillist.
divismo *sm.* stardom, star worship.
diviso *agg.* **1.** divided **2.** (*separato*) separated **3.** (*condiviso*) shared.
divisore *sm.* divisor.
divisorio *agg.* dividing.
divo *sm.* **1.** deity **2.** (*cine*) star.
divorare *vt.* to devour.
divoratore *agg.* devouring.
divorziare *vi.* to divorce, to be divorced.
divorziato *agg.* divorced. ♦ **divorziato** *sm.* divorcee.
divorzio *sm.* divorce (*anche fig.*).
divulgàbile *agg.* that may be divulged.
divulgare *vt.* to spread (*v. irr.*).
divulgativo *agg.* divulging.
divulgatore *sm.* divulger.
divulgazione *sf.* divulgation, spreading.
dizionario *sm.* dictionary.
dizionarista *s.* lexicographer.
dizione *sf.* **1.** diction **2.** (*pronuncia*) pronunciation.
do *sm.* (*mus.*) C.
doccia *sf.* shower.
docente *agg.* teaching. ♦ **docente** *sm.* teacher || *libero* —, fully established university lecturer.
docenza *sf.* teaching.

dòcile *agg.* docile.
docilità *sf.* docility.
documentare *vt.* to document.
documentario *sm.* documentary.
documentarista *s.* documentary film-maker.
documentato *agg.* documented.
documentazione *sf.* **1.** documentation **2.** *pl.* (*documenti*) papers.
documento *sm.* document.
dodecaedro *sm.* dodecahedron.
dodecafonìa *sf.* dodecaphony.
dodecafònico *agg.* dodecaphonic.
dodecàgono *sm.* dodecagon.
dodecasìllabo *sm.* dodecasyllable.
dodicèsimo *agg.* twelfth.
dòdici *agg.* twelve.
doga *sf.* stave.
dogana *sf.* customs (*pl.*).
doganale *agg.* customs (*attr.*): *dichiarazione* —, customs entry.
doganiere *sm.* customs officer.
doge *sm.* doge.
doglia *sf.* **1.** sharp pains **2.** (*pl., med.*) throes.
dogma *sm.* dogma.
dogmàtico *agg.* dogmatic(al).
dogmatismo *sm.* dogmatism.
dolce *agg.* **1.** sweet **2.** (*mite*) mild **3.** (*tec.*) soft. ♦ **dolce** *sm.* **1.** sweet **2.** (*torta*) cake.
dolcezza *sf.* **1.** sweetness **2.** (*di clima*) mildness.
dolciario *agg.* confectionary.
dolciastro *agg.* sweetish.
dolcificare *vt.* **1.** to sweeten **2.** (*fig.*) to mitigate.
dolcificazione *sf.* sweetening.
dolciumi *sm. pl.* sweets.
dolente *agg.* **1.** afflicted, grieved **2.** (*spiacente*) sorry.
dolere *vi.* **1.** to ache **2.** (*rincrescere*) to regret. ♦ **dolersi** *vr.* to regret.
dolicocèfalo *agg.* dolichocephalic.
dòllaro *sm.* dollar.
dolmen *sm.* dolmen.
dolo *sm.* fraud.
dolomite *sf.* dolomite.
dolomìtico *agg.* dolomitic.
dolorante *agg.* aching.
dolore *sm.* **1.** pain, ache **2.** (*fig.*) sorrow, grief.
dolorosamente *avv.* **1.** painfully **2.** (*morale*) sadly.
doloroso *agg.* **1.** painful **2.** (*che causa dolore*) grievous.
doloso *agg.* fraudulent.
domàbile *agg.* tamable.
domanda *sf.* **1.** question, request

2. (*richiesta scritta*) application.
domandare *vt.* to ask (so. for sthg.). ♦ **domandarsi** *vr.* to wonder.
domani *avv.* tomorrow.
domare *vt.* **1.** to tame **2.** (*sottomettere*) to subdue.
domatore *sm.* tamer.
domattina *avv.* tomorrow morning.
doménica *sf.* Sunday.
domenicale *agg.* Sunday (*attr.*).
domenicano *agg.* dominican.
domèstica *sf.* maid.
domèstico *agg. e sm.* domestic ‖ *lavori domestici*, household duties.
domiciliare *agg.* domiciliary.
domiciliarsi *vr.* to settle (in).
domiciliato *agg.* resident, living.
domicilio *sm.* **1.** house, dwelling **2.** (*giur.*) domicile.
dominante *agg.* dominant.
dominare *vt.* to dominate.
dominatore *sm.* ruler.
dominazione *sf.* domination.
dominio *sm.* **1.** domination **2.** (*territorio*) dominion **3.** (*giur.*) domain ‖ *di — pubblico*, known to everybody.
dòmino *sm.* domino.
donare *vt.* to give (*v. irr.*) ♦ **donare** *vi.* (*addirsi*) to suit.
donatore *sm.* donor.
donazione *sf.* **1.** donation **2.** (*somma elargita per uno scopo*) grant.
donchisciottesco *agg.* quixotic.
donde *avv.* whence, from where ‖ *ne ha ben —*, he has good reason for it.
dondolamento *sm.* swinging.
dondolare *vt. e vi.* to swing (*v. irr.*). ♦ **dondolarsi** *vr.* to swing, to rock.
dondolìo *sm.* swinging.
dòndolo *sm.* **1.** (*altalena*) swing ‖ *a —*, rocking.
donna *sf.* woman (*pl.* women).
donnaiolo *sm.* ladies' man (*pl.* men).
.donnesco *agg.* womanlike.
dònnola *sf.* weasel.
dono *sm.* gift.
donzella *sf.* damsel.
dopo *avv.* **1.** (*di luogo*) after, next **2.** (*dietro*) behind **3.** (*di tempo*) after, then **4.** (*più tardi*) later. ♦ **dopo** *prep.* (*di luogo e tempo*) after.
dopodomani *avv.* the day after tomorrow.

dopoguerra *sm.* post-war period.
dopopranzo *sm.* afternoon.
dopotutto *avv.* after all.
doppiaggio *sm.* (*cine*) dubbing.
doppiamente *avv.* **1.** doubly **2.** (*con inganno*) deceitfully.
doppiare *vt.* **1.** to double **2.** (*cine*) to dub.
doppiato *agg.* **1.** doubled **2.** (*cine*) dubbed.
doppiatura *sf.* doubling.
doppietta *sf.* double-barrelled gun.
doppiezza *sf.* **1.** doubleness **2.** (*ambiguità*) double-dealing.
doppio *agg.* **1.** double **2.** (*ambiguo*) double-faced. ♦ **doppio** *sm.* twice as much, twice as many.
doppiofondo *sm.* double bottom.
doppione *sm.* **1.** double **2.** (*di parola*) doublet.
doppiopetto *sm.* double-breasted.
dorare *vt.* to gild.
dorato *agg.* **1.** gilded **2.** (*color oro*) golden.
doratore *sm.* gilder.
doratura *sf.* gilding.
dòrico *agg.* doric.
dorìfora *sf.* potato-beetle.
dormicchiare *vi.* to doze.
dormiente *agg.* sleeping. ♦ **dormiente** *sm.* sleeper.
dormiglione *sm.* sleepy-head.
dormire *vi.* **1.** to sleep (*v. irr.*) ‖ *— tra due guanciali*, to set (*v. irr.*) one's mind at rest **2.** (*fig.*) to remain inactive.
dormita *sf.* sleep.
dormitorio *sm.* dormitory.
dormiveglia *sm.* drowsiness.
dorsale *agg.* dorsal: *spina —*, backbone.
dorso *sm.* **1.** back **2.** (*di monte*) ridge.
dosàbile *agg.* measurable.
dosaggio *sm.* dosage.
dosare *vt.* to proportion: *— le parole*, to weigh one's words.
dosatura *sf.* dosage.
dose *sf.* dose: *una buona — di*, a good deal of.
dossale *sm.* dossal.
dosso *sm.* back: *togliersi di —*, to take (*v. irr.*) off.
dotare *vt.* **1.** to give (*v. irr.*) a dowry **2.** (*fornire di una rendita*) to endow **3.** (*fornire*) to provide (with).
dotato *agg.* **1.** gifted (with) **2.** (*e-*

quipaggiato) provided (with).
dotazione *sf.* endowment.
dote *sf.* **1.** dowry **2.** (*qualità*) endowment.
dotto[1] *agg.* learned. ♦ **dotto** *sm.* scholar.
dotto[2] *sm.* (*anat.*) duct.
dottorale *agg.* doctoral.
dottorato *sm.* doctorate.
dottore *sm.* **1.** doctor **2.** (*laureato*) graduate.
dottoressa *sf.* **1.** (*laureata*) graduate **2.** (*in medicina*) lady doctor.
dottrina *sf.* doctrine.
dottrinale *agg.* doctrinal.
dottrinario *sm.* doctrinaire.
dottrinarismo *sm.* doctrinairism.
dove *avv.* where.
dovere[1] *vi.* **1.** (*obbligo*) must (*v. dif.*): *devi lavorare*, you must work **2.** to have to **3.** (*possibilità, predestinazione*) to be to: *doveva diventare un grande scrittore*, he was to become a great writer **4.** (*devo?, dobbiamo?, nel senso di: vuoi che?*) shall (*v. dif.*): *devo aprire la finestra?*, shall I open the window? **5.** (*al condizionale*) ought to, should (*v. dif.*): *dovresti essere gentile*, you ought to be kind; *dovremmo partire*, we should leave **6.** (*al congiuntivo*) should, were to: *se dovesse venire*, if he should come, if he were to come **7.** (*essere obbligati*) to be obliged, to be forced **8.** (*essere da attribuire, dover arrivare*) to be due: *lo si deve al mio ritardo*, this is due to my being late; *il treno deve arrivare alle 4*, the train is due at 4 a.m. ♦ **dovere** *vt.* (*essere debitore in tutti i sensi*) to owe: *ti devo 1000 lire*, I owe you one thousand lire; *ti devo la vita*, I owe you my life.
dovere[2] *sm.* duty: *fare il proprio —*, to do (*v. irr.*) one's duty.
doverosamente *avv.* dutifully.
doveroso *agg.* dutiful.
dovizia *sf.* plenty.
dovizioso *agg.* abundant.
dovunque *avv.* **1.** everywhere **2.** (*seguito da verbo*) wherever.
dovuto *agg.* **1.** due **2.** (*equo*) fair. ♦ **dovuto** *sm.* due.
dozzina *sf.* dozen.
dozzinale *agg.* cheap, common.
draconiano *agg.* draconian.
draga *sf.* dredger.

dragaggio *sm.* dredging.
dragamine *sm.* mine-sweeper.
dragare *vt.* to dredge.
draglia *sf.* stay.
drago *sm.* dragon.
dragona *sf.* sword-knot.
dragone *sm.* dragon.
dramma *sm.* drama.
drammàtica *sf.* dramatics.
drammaticamente *avv.* dramatically.
drammaticità *sf.* tragicalness.
drammàtico *agg.* dramatic.
drammatizzare *vt.* to dramatise.
drammaturgìa *sf.* dramaturgy.
drammaturgo *sm.* dramatist.
drappeggiare *vt.* to drape.
drappeggio *sm.* draping.
drappello *sm.* squad.
drapperìa *sf.* drapery.
drappo *sm.* cloth.
dràstico *agg.* drastic.
drenaggio *sm.* drainage.
drenare *vt.* to drain.
drìade *sf.* **1.** (*mit.*) dryad **2.** (*bot.*) dryas (*pl.* -ades).
dribblare *vt.* to dribble.
dritta *sf.* **1.** right hand, right **2.** (*mar.*) starboard.
dritto *agg.* **1.** (*non storto*) straight **2.** (*eretto, onesto*) upright. ♦ **dritto** *sm.* right side.
drizza *sf.* halyard.
drizzare *vt.* to straighten.
droga *sf.* **1.** drug **2.** (*spezia*) spices (*pl.*).
drogare *vt.* **1.** to drug **2.** (*condire*) to spice.
drogherìa *sf.* grocery.
droghiere *sm.* grocer.
dromedario *sm.* dromedary.
drùido *sm.* druid.
drupa *sf.* drupe.
dualismo *sm.* dualism.
dualità *sf.* duality.
dubbiezza *sf.* dubiousness.
dubbio *sm.* doubt: *mettere in —*, to question. ♦ **dubbio** *agg.* dubious.
dubbioso *agg.* doubtful.
dubitare *vi.* to doubt.
dubitativo *agg.* dubitative.
duca *sm.* duke.
ducale *agg.* ducal.
ducato *sm.* **1.** dukedom **2.** (*moneta*) ducat.
duchessa *sf.* duchess.
due *agg.* two.
duecentèsimo *agg.* two hundredth.

duecentesco *agg.* thirteenth century (*attr.*).

duecento *sm.* two hundred || *il* —, the thirteenth century.

duellare *vi.* to duel.

duello *sm.* duel: — *all'ultimo sangue*, duel to the death.

duetto *sm.* duet.

duna *sf.* dune.

dunque *cong.* **1.** (*perciò*) therefore **2.** (*rafforzativo*) well, then. ◆ **dunque** *sm. venire al* —, to come (*v. irr.*) to the point.

duodenale *agg.* duodenal.

duodeno *sm.* duodenum.

duomo *sm.* cathedral.

duplicare *vt.* to duplicate.

duplicato *sm.* duplicate.

dùplice *agg.* twofold.

duplicità *sf.* double-dealing.

durabilità *sf.* durability.

duralluminio *sm.* duralumin.

durante *prep.* during.

durare *vi.* **1.** to last **2.** (*perseverare*) to persist **3.** (*resistere*) to hold (*v. irr.*) out. ◆ **durare** *vt.* to endure || *chi la dura la vince*, slow and steady wins the race.

durata *sf.* **1.** duration, length **2.** (*periodo*) term **3.** (*di un oggetto*) endurance.

duraturo *agg.* lasting.

durévole *agg.* durable.

durezza *sf.* **1.** hardness **2.** (*rigidità*) stiffness.

duro *agg.* **1.** hard **2.** (*di voce*) harsh || *avere il sonno* —, to sleep (*v. irr.*) like a log; *avere la testa dura*, to be a block-head, to be stubborn.

durone *sm.* hard skin.

dùttile *agg.* ductile.

duttilità *sf.* ductility.

E

e *cong.* and: *e... e*, both... and.

ebanista *sm.* cabinet-maker.

ebanisterìa *sf.* **1.** (*bottega*) cabinet-maker's shop **2.** (*arte*) cabinet-making.

ebanite *sf.* ebonite.

èbano *sm.* ebony.

ebbene *cong.* well: —?, what about it?

ebbrezza *sf.* **1.** drunkenness **2.** (*fig.*) elation.

ebbro *agg.* **1.** drunken **2.** (*fig.*) mad.

ebdomadario *agg.* weekly. ◆ **ebdomadario** *sm.* weekly paper.

èbete *agg.* idiotic. ◆ **èbete** *sm.* idiot.

ebollizione *sf.* boiling.

ebràico *agg.* Hebrew.

ebreo *agg.* Hebrew, Jewish. ◆ **ebreo** *sm.* Hebrew, Jew.

ecatombe *sf.* massacre.

eccedente *agg.* excessive, in excess (*pred.*). ◆ **eccedente** *sm.* (*comm.*) exceeding.

eccedenza *sf.* excess, surplus: — *di peso*, overweight.

eccèdere *vt.* to exceed. ◆ **eccèdere** *vi.* to go (*v. irr.*) too far.

eccellente *agg.* excellent.

eccellenza *sf.* **1.** excellence **2.** (*titolo*) excellency.

eccèllere *vi.* to excel.

eccelso *agg.* sublime.

eccentricità *sf.* eccentricity.

eccèntrico *agg.* eccentric.

eccepire *vi.* to object.

eccessivo *agg.* excessive.

eccesso *sm.* excess.

eccètera *sm.* et cetera (*abbr.* etc.), and so on.

eccetto *prep.* except, but, save. ◆ **eccetto che** *cong.* **1.** except that **2.** (*purché*) provided that.

eccettuare *vt.* to except.

eccettuato *agg.* excluded.

eccezionale *agg.* exceptional.

eccezione *sf.* exception.

ecchìmosi *sf.* bruise.

eccidio *sm.* bloodshed.

eccitàbile *agg.* excitable.

eccitabilità *sf.* excitability.

eccitamento *sm.* excitement.

eccitante *agg.* e *sm.* excitant.

eccitare *vt.* to excite. ◆ **eccitarsi** *vr.* to get (*v. irr.*) excited.

eccitatore *agg.* excitative. ◆ **eccitatore** *sm.* exciter.

eccitazione *sf.* excitement.

ecclesiàstico *agg.* ecclesiastical.

ecco *avv.* here, there (*in unione con le voci del verbo* to be *al pres. ind.*): — *il mio cappello!*, here is my hat! || — *tutto*, that's all; *quand'* —, when suddenly.

eccome *inter.* and how!

echeggiare *vi.* to echo (with sthg.).

echinoderma *sm.* echinoderm.

eclèttico *agg.* e *sm.* eclectic.

eclettismo *sm.* eclecticism.
eclissare *vt.* **1.** to eclipse **2.** (*fig.*) to overshadow.
eclisse, eclissi *sf.* eclipse.
eclìttica *sf.* ecliptic.
eclìttico *agg.* ecliptic.
eco *sf.* echo.
economato *sm.* **1.** steward's office **2.** (*in università*) bursar's office.
economìa *sf.* **1.** economy **2.** (*scienza*) economics.
econòmico *agg.* **1.** economic **2.** (*a buon prezzo*) cheap.
economista *s.* economist.
economizzare *vt.* to economize.
econòmo *agg.* economical. ♦ **ecònomo** *sm.* **1.** steward **2.** (*di università*) bursar.
ecumènico *agg.* ecumenical.
eczema *sm.* eczema.
edema *sm.* oedema.
eden *sm.* Eden.
èdera *sf.* ivy.
edìcola *sf.* newspaper kiosk.
edicolista *sm.* news-agent.
edificante *agg.* edifying.
edificare *vt.* **1.** to build (*v. irr.*) (up) **2.** (*fig.*) to edify.
edificatore *sm.* **1.** builder **2.** (*fig.*) edifier.
edificazione *sf.* **1.** building **2.** (*fig.*) edification.
edificio *sm.* building.
edile *agg.* building: *perito —,* master-builder. ♦ **edile** *sm.* (*stor. romana*) aedile.
edilizia *sf.* building industry.
edilizio *agg.* building (*attr.*).
èdito *agg.* published.
editore *sm.* publisher.
editorìa *sf.* book industry.
editoriale *agg.* e *sm.* editorial.
editrice *agg.:* *casa —,* publishing house.
editto *sm.* edict.
edizione *sf.* edition, issue.
edonismo *sm.* hedonism.
edonista *s.* hedonist.
edotto *agg.* aware: *rendere —,* to inform.
educanda *sf.* boarding-school girl.
educandato *sm.* girls' boarding--school.
educare *vt.* **1.** to educate **2.** (*allevare*) to bring (*v. irr.*) up.
educativo *agg.* educational.
educato *agg.* well-bred, polite.
educatore *sm.* educator.
educazione *sf.* **1.** education **2.**

(*buone maniere*) good manners (*pl.*).
edulcorare *vt.* to edulcorate.
efebo *sm.* ephebe.
efèlide *sf.* freckle.
effemèride *sf.* ephemeris (*pl.* -ides).
effeminare *vt.* to effeminate. ♦ **effeminarsi** *vr.* to become (*v. irr.*) effeminate.
effeminatezza *sf.* effeminacy.
efferatezza *sf.* brutality.
efferato *agg.* brutal.
effervescente *agg.* sparkling.
effervescenza *sf.* effervescence.
effettivamente *avv.* actually, indeed.
effettivo *agg.* actual.
effetto *sm.* **1.** effect, result ‖ *in effetti,* as a matter of fact **2.** (*comm.*) bill.
effettuàbile *agg.* feasible.
effettuare *vt.* to carry out: *— un piano,* to carry out a plan. ♦ **effettuarsi** *vr.* (*aver luogo*) to take (*v. irr.*) place.
effettuazione *sf.* accomplishment.
efficace *agg.* effective, efficacious.
efficacia *sf.* efficacy.
efficiente *agg.* efficient.
efficienza *sf.* efficiency.
effigiare *vt.* to portray.
effigie *sf.* image.
effìmera *sf.* (*fam.*) mayfly.
effìmero *agg.* ephemeral.
effluvio *sm.* exhalation.
effòndere *vt.* to pour forth. ♦ **effòndersi** *vr.* to spread (*v. irr.*) (about).
effrazione *sf.* (*giur.*) house-breaking, burglary.
effusione *sf.* **1.** shedding **2.** (*cordialità*) cordiality **3.** (*pl., manifestazioni*) effusions.
effusivo *agg.* effusive.
egemonìa *sf.* hegemony.
egemònico *agg.* hegemonic.
ègida *sf.* **1.** aegis **2.** (*fig.*) protection.
egiziano *agg.* e *sm.* Egyptian.
egli *pron.* he: *— stesso,* he himself.
ègloga *sf.* eclogue.
egocèntrico *agg.* egocentric. ♦ **egocèntrico** *sm.* egocentric man.
egocentrismo *sm.* egocentrism.
egoismo *sm.* selfishness.
egoista *agg.* e *sm.* egoist.
egotismo *sm.* self-conceit.
egregiamente *avv.* eminently.
egregio *agg.* eminent ‖ (*nelle lettere*) — *Signore,* Dear Sir.

eguaglianza, eguagliare, eguale ecc. V. *uguaglianza, uguagliare, uguale* ecc.

egualità *sf.* equality.

eiaculare *vi.* to ejaculate.

eiaculazione *sf.* ejaculation.

eiezione *sf.* ejection.

elaborare *vt.* to elaborate.

elaborato *agg.* elaborate.

elaborazione *sf.* 1. elaboration 2. (*di piano*) formulation.

elargire *vt.* to lavish.

elargizione *sf.* donation.

elasticità *sf.* 1. elasticity 2. (*agilità*) nimbleness.

elasticizzare *vt.* to make (*v. irr.*) elastic.

elàstico *agg.* 1. elastic 2. (*agile*) nimble. ♦ elàstico *sm.* rubber band.

elce *sm.* ilex.

elefante *sm.* elephant.

elefantesco *agg.* elephantine.

elefantìasi *sf.* elephantiasis.

elegante *agg.* elegant, smart.

eleganza *sf.* smartness.

elèggere *vt.* 1. to elect 2. (*nominare*) to appoint.

eleggìbile *agg.* eligible.

eleggibilità *sf.* eligibility.

elegìa *sf.* elegy.

elegìaco *agg.* elegiac.

elementare *agg.* elementary: scuola —, primary school.

elemento *sm.* 1. element 2. (*componente*) component 3. (*pl., rudimenti*) rudiments 4. (*persona*) person.

elemòsina *sf.* alms: *chiedere l'*—, to beg.

elemosinare *vt.* e *vi.* to beg (for).

elencare *vt.* to list.

elenco *sm.* list: — *telefonico,* telephone directory.

elettivo *agg.* elective.

eletto *agg.* elect, chosen.

elettorale *agg.* electoral.

elettorato *sm.* electorate.

elettore *sm.* voter.

elettràuto *sm.* 1. (*officina*) car electrical repairs (*pl.*) 2. (*meccanico*) car electrician.

elettricista *sm.* electrician.

elettricità *sf.* electricity.

elèttrico *agg.* electric.

elettrificare *vt.* to electrify.

elettrificazione *sf.* electrification.

elettrizzare *vt.* to electrify.

elettrocalamita *sf.* electro-magnet.

elettrocardiogramma *sm.* electro-cardiogram.

elettrodinàmica *sf.* electrodynamics.

elèttrodo *sm.* electrode.

elettrodomèstici *sm. pl.* electrical household appliances.

elettrògeno *agg.* generating electricity.

elettròlisi *sf.* electrolysis.

elettromagnètico *agg.* electro-magnetic.

elettromotore *sm.* dynamo.

elettromotrice *sf.* electric rail car.

elettrone *sm.* electron.

elettrònica *sf.* electronics.

elettrònico *agg.* electronic.

elettrotècnica *sf.* electrical technology.

elettrotreno *sm.* electric train.

elevamento *sm.* elevation.

elevare *vt.* 1. to elevate 2. (*erigere*) to erect 3. (*mat.*) to raise. ♦ elevarsi *vr.* to rise (*v. irr.*).

elevatezza *sf.* loftiness.

elevato *agg.* elevated, high.

elevatore *sm.* elevator.

elevazione *sf.* 1. elevation 2. (*l'elevare*) rising 3. (*mat.*) raising.

elezione *sf.* election.

èlica *sf.* 1. (*aer.*) propeller 2. (*mar.*) screw.

elicoidale *agg.* helicoidal.

elicòttero *sm.* helicopter.

elìdere *vt.* to annul. ♦ elìdersi *vr. rec.* to annul each other.

eliminare *vt.* to eliminate. ♦ eliminarsi *vr.* to be eliminated.

eliminatoria *sf.* preliminary heat.

eliminazione *sf.* elimination, expulsion.

elio *sm.* helium.

eliocèntrico *agg.* heliocentric.

eliografìa *sf.* heliography.

elioterapìa *sf.* heliotherapy.

eliotipìa *sf.* heliotypy.

eliporto *sm.* heliport.

elisione *sf.* elision.

elisìr *sm.* elixir.

èlitra *sf.* elytrum (*pl.* -ra).

ella *pron.* she: — *stessa,* she herself.

ellènico *agg.* Hellenic.

ellenismo *sm.* Hellenism.

ellenista *s.* Hellenist.

ellisse *sf.* ellipse.

ellissi *sf.* ellipsis (*pl.* -ses).

ellìttico *sm.* elliptic(al).

elmetto *sm.* helmet.

elmo *sm.* helmet.

elocuzione *sf.* elocution.

elogiàbile *agg.* praiseworthy.

elogiare *vt.* to eulogize, to praise.

elogiatore *sm.* eulogist.

elogio *sm.* eulogy, praise.

eloquente *agg.* eloquent.

eloquenza *sf.* eloquence.

elucubrare *vt.* to lucubrate: — *su, intorno a qc.*, to lucubrate on, about sthg.

elucubrazione *sf.* lucubration.

elùdere *vt.* to elude.

elusivo *agg.* elusive.

elvètico *agg.* Helvetic.

elzevir *sm.* 1. elzevir 2. *(giorn.)* leading literary article.

emaciare *vt.* to emaciate. ♦ **emaciarsi** *vr.* to become *(v. irr.)* emaciated.

emaciato *agg.* emaciated.

emanare *vt.* 1. to issue 2. *(vapori, profumi)* to exhale.

emanazione *sf.* emanation.

emancipare *vt.* to emancipate.

emancipato *agg.* emancipated.

emancipazione *sf.* emancipation.

emàtico *agg.* haematic.

ematoma *sm.* haematoma *(pl. -ata).*

ematosi *sf.* haematosis.

embargo *sm.* embargo.

emblema *sm.* 1. emblem 2. *(simbolo)* symbol.

emblemàtico *agg.* emblematic.

embolìa *sf.* embolism.

èmbolo *sm.* embolus *(pl. -li).*

embrionale *agg.* embryonic.

embrione *sm.* embryo.

emendamento *sm.* 1. amendment 2. *(correzione)* emendation.

emendare *vt.* 1. to amend 2. *(correggere)* to emend.

emergenza *sf.* emergency.

emèrgere *vi.* 1. to emerge 2. *(fig.)* to emerge, to appear.

emèrito *agg.* emeritus.

emeroteca *sf.* newspaper library.

emersione *sf.* emersion.

emèttere *vt.* 1. to emit 2. *(di suono)* to utter 3. *(emanare)* to deliver 4. *(banconote)* to issue.

emiciclo *sm.* hemicycle.

emicrania *sf.* headache.

emigrante *agg. e sm.* emigrant.

emigrare *vi.* to emigrate.

emigrato *sm.* emigrant.

emigrazione *sf.* emigration.

eminente *agg.* outstanding, eminent.

eminenza *sf.* eminence.

emiro *sm.* emir.

emisfèrico *agg.* hemispheric(al).

emisfero *sm.* hemisphere.

emissario *sm.* emissary.

emissione *sf.* 1. emission 2. *(econ.)* issue.

emistichio *sm.* hemistich.

emittente *agg.* issuing ‖ *stazione — (radio)*, broadcasting station.

emofìlia *sf.* haemophilia.

emoglobina *sf.* haemoglobin.

emolliente *agg.* emollient.

emolumento *sm.* emolument.

emorragìa *sf.* haemorrhage.

emorròidi *sf. pl.* haemorrhoids.

emòstasi *sf.* haemostasis.

emostàtico *agg.* haemostatic.

emoteca *sf.* blood bank.

emotività *sf.* emotionality.

emotivo *agg.* emotional.

emottisi *sf.* haemoptysis.

emozionante *agg.* touching, exciting, thrilling.

emozionare *vt.* to move. ♦ **emozionarsi** *vr.* to get *(v. irr.)* excited.

emozione *sf.* emotion, thrill.

empiastro *sm.* plaster.

empietà *sf.* impiety.

empio *agg.* impious.

empire *vt.* to fill.

empìrico *agg. e sm.* empiric.

empirismo *sm.* empiricism.

emporio *sm.* department store.

emulare *vt.* to emulate.

emulazione *sf.* emulation.

èmulo *sm.* rival.

emulsionare *vt.* to emulsify.

emulsione *sf.* emulsion.

encefalite *sf.* encephalitis.

encèfalo *sm.* encephalon *(pl. -ala).*

encìclica *sf.* encyclic.

enciclopedìa *sf.* encyclopaedia.

enciclopèdico *agg.* encyclopaedic.

enclìtico *agg.* enclitic.

encomiàbile *agg.* praiseworthy.

encomiare *vt.* to commend.

encomio *sm.* panegyric.

endecasìllabo *agg.* hendecasyllabic. ♦ **endecasìllabo** *sm.* hendecasyllable.

endèmico *agg.* endemic.

endocardio *sm.* endocardium.

endocardite *sf.* endocarditis.

endòcrino *agg.* endocrine.

endocrinologìa *sf.* endocrinology.

endovenoso *agg.* intravenous. ♦ **endovenosa** *sf.* intravenous injection.

energètico *agg. e sm.* tonic.
energìa *sf.* energy.
energicamente *avv.* energetically.
enèrgico *agg.* energetic(al).
energùmeno *sm.* energumen.
ènfasi *sf.* emphasis.
enfàtico *agg.* emphatic.
enfiagione *sf.* swelling.
enfisema *sm.* emphysema.
enfitèusi *sf.* emphyteusis.
enigma *sm.* enigma, puzzle.
enigmàtico *agg.* puzzling.
enigmista *sm.* enigmatographer.
enigmìstica *sf.* enigmatography.
enigmìstico *agg.* puzzle (*attr.*).
ennèsimo *agg.* nth: *ennesima potenza*, nth power.
enologìa *sf.* oenology.
enòlogo *sm.* oenologist.
enorme *agg.* huge.
enormità *sf.* **1.** hugeness **2.** (*fig.*) absurdity.
ente *sm.* **1.** being **2.** (*comm.*) body, corporation.
enterite *sf.* enteritis.
enteroclisma *sm.* enema.
enterocolite *sf.* enterocolitis.
entità *sf.* entity.
entomologìa *sf.* entomology.
entomòlogo *sm.* entomologist.
entrambi *pron. e agg.* both.
entrante *agg.* (*con espressioni di tempo*) next, coming.
entrare *vi.* to enter, to come (*v. irr.*) in, to go (*v. irr.*) in ‖ *non c'entra*, this has got nothing to do with it; — *correndo*, to run (*v. irr.*) in; — *in carica*, to come (*v. irr.*) into office; — *in società*, to go into partnership (with); — *precipitosamente*, to rush in; — *in giuoco*, to come into play; — *in vigore*, to come into force.
entrata *sf.* **1.** entrance, entry **2.** (*rendita*) income.
entratura *sf.* entrance.
entro *prep.* **1.** (*luogo*) inside **2.** (*tempo*) in, within, by: — *due giorni*, within two days; — *lunedì*, by Monday.
entrobordo *sm.* inboard.
entroterra *sm.* inland.
entusiasmante *agg.* exciting.
entusiasmare *vt.* to raise enthusiasm in. ♦ **entusiasmarsi** *vr.* to become (*v. irr.*) enthusiastic.
entusiasmo *sm.* enthusiasm.
entusiasta *agg.* enthusiast: *essere — di qc.*, to be crazy about sthg.

entusiàstico *agg.* enthusiastic(al).
enucleare *vt.* to enucleate.
enucleazione *sf.* enucleation.
enumerare *vt.* to enumerate.
enumerazione *sf.* enumeration.
enunciare *vt.* to state: — *un teorema*, to enunciate a theorem.
enunciato *sm.* proposition, terms (*pl.*).
enunciazione *sf.* enunciation.
enuresi *sf.* enuresis.
enzima *sm.* enzyme.
eòlico *agg.* Aeolian.
epàtico *agg.* hepatic.
epatite *sf.* hepatitis.
èpica *sf.* epic.
epicentro *sm.* epicentre.
èpico *agg.* epic.
epicureismo *sm.* **1.** epicurism **2.** (*fil.*) epicureanism.
epicureo *agg. e sm.* Epicurean.
epidemìa *sf.* epidemic.
epidèmico *agg.* epidemical.
epidèrmico *agg.* epidermic.
epidèrmide *sf.* epidermis, skin.
Epifanìa *sf.* Epiphany, Twelfth Night.
epìgono *sm.* imitator, follower.
epìgrafe *sf.* epigraph.
epigrafìa *sf.* epigraphy.
epigramma *sm.* epigram.
epigrammista *s.* epigrammatist.
epilessìa *sf.* epilepsy.
epilèttico *agg. e sm.* epileptic.
epìlogo *sm.* epilogue.
episcopale *agg.* episcopal.
episcopato *sm.* episcopacy.
episòdico *agg.* episodic(al).
episodio *sm.* episode.
epìstola *sf.* epistle.
epistolare *agg.* epistolary.
epistolario *sm.* letters (*pl.*).
epitaffio *sm.* epitaph.
epitalamio *sm.* epithalamium (*pl.* -ia).
epitelio *sm.* epithelium.
epìteto *sm.* epithet.
epìtome *sf.* epitome.
època *sf.* **1.** epoch **2.** (*età*) age **3.** (*data*) date ‖ *far —*, to mark an epoch.
epopea *sf.* **1.** epopee **2.** (*serie di fatti eroici*) epos.
eppure *cong.* yet.
epulone *sm.* glutton.
epurare *vt.* to purge.
epurazione *sf.* purge.
equamente *avv.* fairly.
equànime *agg.* equanimous.

equanimità sf. equanimity, impartiality.

equatore sm. equator.

equatoriale agg. equatorial.

equazione sf. equation.

equestre agg. equestrian.

equidistante agg. equidistant.

equidistanza sf. equidistance.

equilàtero agg. equilateral.

equilibrare vt. to balance.

equilibrato agg. 1. balanced 2. (fig.) well-balanced.

equilibrio sm. balance, equilibrium.

equilibrismo sm. acrobatics (pl.).

equilibrista s. acrobat.

equino agg. equine.

equinozio sm. equinox.

equipaggiamento sm. equipment, outfit.

equipaggiare vt. to equip, to fit out.

equipaggio sm. (mar.; aer.) crew.

equiparàbile agg. comparable.

equiparare vt. to equalize.

equiparazione sf. equalization.

equipollente agg. equipollent.

equipollenza sf. equipollence.

equità sf. equity, fairness.

equitazione sf. riding.

equivalente agg. equivalent.

equivalenza sf. equivalence.

equivalere vi. to be equivalent. ♦ **equivalersi** vr. to be equivalent.

equivocàbile agg. mistakable.

equivocare vi. to misunderstand (v. irr.).

equìvoco agg. equivocal, ambiguous. ♦ **equivoco** sm. equivocation.

equo agg. fair.

era sf. era, epoch.

erariale agg. fiscal.

erario sm. Treasury.

erba sf. grass || in —, green; (fig.) budding: un poeta in —, a budding poet.

erbaccia sf. weed.

erbàceo agg. herbaceous.

erbaggio sm. vegetable.

erbario sm. herbarium.

erbetta sf. new grass.

erbivéndolo sm. greengrocer.

erbìvoro agg. herbivorous.

erborista s. herborist.

erboso agg. grassy.

èrcole sm. Hercules.

ercùleo agg. Herculean.

erede sm. heir. ♦ **erede** sf. heiress.

eredità sf. inheritance.

ereditare vt. to inherit.

ereditarietà sf. hereditariness.

ereditario agg. hereditary.

ereditiera sf. heiress.

eremita sm. hermit.

eremitaggio sm. hermitage.

èremo sm. hermitage.

eresia sf. heresy.

erètico agg. heretical.

erèttile agg. erectile.

eretto agg. 1. upright 2. (costruito) built.

erezione sf. 1. erection 2. (costruzione) building.

ergastolano sm. convict (serving a life sentence).

ergàstolo sm. life imprisonment.

èrgere vt. to raise. ♦ **èrgersi** vr. to rise (v. irr.).

èrica sf. heather.

erìgere vt. to erect, to build (v. irr.). ♦ **erìgersi** vr. to set up (for).

erma sf. herma (pl. -ae).

ermafrodito agg. hermaphrodite.

ermellino sm. ermine.

ermenèuta sm. hermeneut.

ermenèutica sf. hermeneutics.

ermètico agg. 1. (tec.) airtight 2. (oscuro) obscure.

ermetismo sm. obscurity.

ernia sf. hernia.

erniario agg. hernial.

erodere vt. to wear (v. irr.) away.

eroe sm. hero.

erogare vt. 1. to distribute 2. (elett.; idraulica) to deliver.

erogazione sf. 1. distribution 2. (elett.; idraulica) delivery.

eròico agg. heroic.

eroina sf. 1. heroine 2. (farm.) heroin.

eroismo sm. heroism.

eròmpere vi. to burst (v. irr.) forth.

erosione sf. erosion.

erosivo agg. erosive.

eròtico agg. erotic.

erotismo sm. eroticism.

erotòmane s. erotomaniac.

èrpete sm. herpes.

érpice sm. harrow.

errabondo agg. wandering.

errante agg. errant.

errare vi. 1. (vagare) to wander 2. (sbagliare) to err.

erràtico agg. erratic.

errato agg. wrong.

erròneo agg. erroneous.

errore *sm.* error, mistake.

erta *sf.* steep || *stare all'—*, to be on the look-out.

erto *agg.* steep.

erudire *vt.* to teach (*v. irr.*). ♦ **erudirsi** *vr.* to get (*v. irr.*) educated.

erudito *agg.* learned. ♦ **erudito** *sm.* scholar.

erudizione *sf.* erudition, learning.

eruttare *vt.* to erupt.

eruttivo *agg.* eruptive.

eruzione *sf.* eruption.

esacerbare *vt.* to embitter.

esacerbazione *sf.* embitterment.

esaedro *sm.* hexahedron.

esagerare *vt.* to exaggerate. ♦ **esagerare** *vi.* to go (*v. irr.*) too far, to exceed.

esagerato *agg.* **1.** exaggerated **2.** (*di prezzo*) exorbitant.

esagerazione *sf.* exaggeration.

esagitare *vt.* to stir violently.

esagonale *agg.* hexagonal.

esàgono *sm.* hexagon.

esalare *vt.* to exhale. ♦ **esalare** *vi.* to exhale, to rise (*v. irr.*).

esalazione *sf.* exhalation.

esaltare *vt.* to exalt. ♦ **esaltarsi** *vr.* **1.** (*vantarsi*) to boast **2.** (*infervorarsi*) to become (*v. irr.*) excited.

esaltato *agg.* excited. ♦ **esaltato** *sm.* hot-head.

esaltazione *sf.* **1.** exaltation **2.** (*eccitazione*) excitement.

esame *sm.* examination: *dare un —*, to take (*v. irr.*) an examination; *essere respinto ad un —*, to fail in an examination.

esàmetro *sm.* hexameter.

esaminando *sm.* candidate.

esaminare *vt.* to examine.

esaminatore *sm.* examiner.

esangue *agg.* bloodless.

esànime *agg.* lifeless.

esasperare *vt.* to exasperate. ♦ **esasperarsi** *vr.* to become (*v. irr.*) irritated.

esasperato *agg.* exasperated.

esasperazione *sf.* exasperation.

esattamente *avv.* exactly, just.

esattezza *sf.* exactitude.

esatto *agg.* exact, right.

esattore *sm.* collector.

esattorìa *sf.* collector's office.

esaudimento *sm.* satisfaction.

esaudire *vt.* to grant.

esauriente *agg.* exhaustive.

esaurimento *sm.* exhaustion.

esaurire *vt.* to exhaust. ♦ **esaurirsi** *vr.* to get (*v. irr.*) exhausted.

esaurito *agg.* **1.** exhausted **2.** (*di persona*) worn out **3.** (*che ha l'esaurimento nervoso*) suffering from a nervous breakdown **4.** (*di libro*) out of print.

esàusto *agg.* exhausted.

esautorare *vt.* to deprive of authority.

esazione *sf.* collection.

esborso *sm.* outlay.

esca *sf.* **1.** bait **2.** (*materiale infiammabile*) tinder **3.** (*di esplosivo*) fuse.

escandescenza *sf.* outburst of rage || *dare in escandescenze*, to lose (*v. irr.*) one's temper.

escatologìa *sf.* eschatology.

escavatore *sm.* digger.

escavatrice *sf.* digger.

escavazione *sf.* digging out.

eschimese *agg. e sm.* Eskimo.

esclamare *vi.* to exclaim.

esclamativo *agg.* exclamatory: *punto —*, exclamation mark.

esclamazione *sf.* exclamation.

esclùdere *vt.* to exclude, to leave (*v. irr.*) out.

esclusione *sf.* exclusion || *ad — di*, except.

esclusiva *sf.* **1.** patent **2.** (*diritto esclusivo*) sole right.

esclusività *sf.* exclusiveness.

esclusivo *agg.* exclusive, sole.

escluso *agg.* **1.** excluded **2.** (*eccettuato*) excepted.

escogitare *vt.* to contrive.

escoriare *vt.* to graze.

escoriazione *sf.* abrasion.

escremento *sm.* excrement.

escrescenza *sf.* excrescence.

escursione *sf.* excursion, trip.

escursionista *s.* excursionist.

escussione *sf.* examination.

esecràbile *agg.* execrable.

esecrare *vt.* to execrate.

esecrazione *sf.* execration.

esecutivo *agg.* executive.

esecutore *sm.* **1.** executor **2.** (*di musica*) performer **3.** (*carnefice*) executioner.

esecuzione *sf.* **1.** execution **2.** (*mus.*) performance.

esedra *sf.* exedra (*pl.* -ae).

esegesi *sf.* exegesis (*pl.* -ses).

esegeta *s.* exegete.

eseguìbile *agg.* feasible.

eseguire *vt.* **1.** to execute, to carry out **2.** (*mus.*) to perform.

esempio *sm.* **1.** example, instance **2.** (*modello perfetto*) pattern.

esemplare *agg.* exemplary. ◆ **esemplare** *sm.* **1.** pattern, specimen **2.** (*di libro*) copy.

esemplificare *vt.* to exemplify.

esemplificazione *sf.* exemplification.

esentare *vt.* to exempt.

esente *agg.* exempt, free.

esenzione *sf.* exemption.

esequie *sf. pl.* exequies.

esercente *sm.* shop-keeper.

esercire *vt.* to manage (a business) || — un negozio, to keep (*v. irr.*) a shop.

esercitare *vt.* **1.** to exercise **2.** (*una professione*) to practice **3.** (*addestrare*) to train. ◆ **esercitarsi** *vr.* to practice.

esercitazione *sf.* **1.** exercise **2.** (*allenamento*) training **3.** (*mil.*) drill.

esercito *sm.* army.

esercizio *sm.* **1.** exercise **2.** (*negozio*) shop **3.** (*comm.*) — finanziario, financial year.

esibire *vt.* to exhibit, to show (*v. irr.*).

esibizione *sf.* exhibition, show.

esibizionismo *sm.* exhibitionism, showing-off.

esibizionista *s.* exhibitionist.

esigente *agg.* exacting.

esigenza *sf.* **1.** demand, exigence **2.** (*pretesa*) pretension.

esigere *vt.* **1.** (*comm.*) to collect **2.** (*richiedere con autorità*) to insist on **3.** (*pretendere*) to exact.

esigibile *agg.* **1.** exigible **2.** (*riscuotibile*) collectable.

esiguità *sf.* exiguity.

esiguo *agg.* exiguous, scanty.

esilarante *agg.* exhilarating.

esilarare *vt.* to exhilarate.

èsile *agg.* slender.

esiliare *vt.* to exile. ◆ **esiliarsi** *vr.* to go (*v. irr.*) into exile.

esiliato *agg.* banished. ◆ **esiliato** *sm.* exile.

esilio *sm.* exile.

esimere *vt.* to free, to excuse. ◆ **esimersi** *vr.* to evade (sthg.).

esimio *agg.* excellent.

esistente *agg.* **1.** existing **2.** (*di cose*) extant.

esistenza *sf.* existence.

esistenziale *agg.* existential.

esistenzialismo *sm.* existentialism.

esistenzialista *agg. e s.* existentialist.

esìstere *vi.* to exist.

esitante *agg.* hesitating: voce —, faltering voice.

esitare *vi.* **1.** to hesitate **2.** (*di voce*) to falter.

esitazione *sf.* hesitation: senza —, unhesitatingly.

èsito *sm.* result, outcome.

esiziale *agg.* ruinous.

èsodo *sm.* exodus.

esòfago *sm.* oesophagus.

esògeno *agg.* exogenous.

esonerare *vt.* to exonerate.

esònero *sm.* exoneration.

esorbitante *agg.* exorbitant.

esorbitanza *sf.* exorbitance.

esorbitare *vi.* to exceed.

esorcismo *sm.* exorcism.

esorcista *sm.* exorcist.

esorcizzare *vt.* to exorcize.

esorcizzatore *sm.* exorcizer.

esordiente *agg.* beginning. ◆ **esordiente** *sm.* beginner.

esordio *sm.* preamble, beginning.

esordire *vi.* **1.** to begin (*v. irr.*) **2.** (*in arte*) to make (*v. irr.*) one's debut.

esortare *vt.* to exhort.

esortativo *agg.* exhortative.

esortazione *sf.* exhortation.

esosità *sf.* greediness.

esoso *agg.* greedy.

esotèrico *agg.* esoteric.

esotèrmico *agg.* exothermic.

esòtico *agg.* exotic.

esotismo *sm.* exoticism.

espàndere *vt.* to spread (*v. irr.*) (out). ◆ **espàndersi** *vr.* to spread.

espansione *sf.* expansion.

espansionismo *sm.* expansionism.

espansività *sf.* effusiveness.

espansivo *agg.* effusive.

espatriare *vi.* to emigrate.

espatrio *sm.* expatriation.

espediente *sm.* expedient.

espèllere *vt.* to expel.

esperanto *sm.* Esperanto.

esperienza *sf.* experience.

esperimento *sm.* **1.** experiment **2.** (*esame*) test **3.** (*tentativo*) trial.

esperire *vt.* to try.

esperto *agg. e sm.* expert.

espettorante *agg. e sm.* expectorant.

espettorare *vt.* to expectorate.

espettorazione *sf.* expectoration.
espiare *vt.* to expiate.
espiatorio *agg.* expiatory: *capro* —, scapegoat.
espiazione *sf.* expiation.
espirare *vt.* e *vi.* to expire.
espirazione *sf.* expiration.
espletare *vt.* to dispatch.
espletazione *sf.* dispatching.
esplicare *vt.* to explicate: — *un'attività*, to have an activity.
esplicativo *agg.* explanatory.
esplicazione *sf.* explication.
esplicito *agg.* explicit.
esplòdere *vi.* to explode, to burst (*v. irr.*).
esplorare *vt.* 1. to explore 2. (*mil.*) to scout.
esploratore *sm.* 1. explorer 2. (*mil.*) scout.
esplorazione *sf.* 1. exploration 2. (*mil.*) scouting expedition.
esplosione *sf.* 1. explosion, blast 2. (*fig.*) outbreak.
esplosivo *agg.* e *sm.* explosive.
esponente *sm.* exponent.
esporre *vt.* 1. to show (*v. irr.*) 2. (*a rischio*) to venture 3. (*spiegare*) to expound 4. (*mettere in vista*) to display. ♦ **esporsi** *vr.* to expose oneself.
esportare *vt.* to export.
esportatore *agg.* exporting. ♦ **esportatore** *sm.* exporter.
esportazione *sf.* export, exportation.
esposimetro *sm.* exposure-meter.
espositore *sm.* exhibitor.
esposizione *sf.* 1. exposure 2. (*mostra*) exhibition 3. (*eloquio*) exposition.
esposto *sm.* petition.
espressamente *avv.* 1. expressly 2. (*appositamente*) on purpose.
espressione *sf.* expression.
espressionismo *sm.* expressionism.
espressionista *s.* expressionist.
espressivo *agg.* expressive.
espresso *agg.* express.
esprìmere *vt.* to express.
esprimìbile *agg.* expressible.
espropriare *vt.* to dispossess.
espropriazione *sf.* expropriation.
espugnare *vt.* to conquer.
espugnatore *sm.* conqueror.
espugnazione *sf.* conquest.
espulsione *sf.* expulsion.
espulsivo *agg.* e *sm.* expulsive.

espulsore *sm.* ejector.
espùngere *vt.* to expunge.
espurgare *vt.* 1. to expurgate 2. (*un libro*) to bowdlerize.
espurgazione *sf.* 1. expurgation 2. (*un libro*) to bowdlerize.
essa *pron.* 1. (*sogg.*) she, (*compl.*) her 2. (*riferito a cose o animali*) it.
esse *sf.* letter S.: *a* —, S-shaped.
essenza *sf.* essence.
essenziale *agg.* essential.
essenzialità *sf.* essentiality.
èssere *vi.* to be ‖ *c'è, ci sono*, there is, there are.
èssere *sm.* 1. being 2. (*esistenza*) existence.
essi *pron.* (*sogg.*) they, (*compl.*) them.
essiccare *vt.* to dry.
essiccatoio *sm.* drier.
essiccazione *sf.* drying process.
esso *pron.* 1. (*sogg.*) he, (*compl.*) him 2. (*per cose o animali*) it.
essudato *sm.* exudate.
essudazione *sf.* exudation.
est *sm.* east.
èstasi *sf.* ecstasy: *andare in* —, to go (*v. irr.*) into ecstasies; *mandare in* —, to throw (*v. irr.*) into ecstasies.
estasiare *vt.* to enrapture. ♦ **estasiarsi** *vr.* to be enraptured.
estate *sf.* summer.
estàtico *agg.* ecstatic.
estemporàneo *agg.* extempore.
estèndere *vt.* to extend.
estendìbile *agg.* extensible.
estensione *sf.* 1. extension 2. (*distesa*) expanse, extent 3. (*mus.*) range.
estensivo *agg.* extensive.
estensore *sm.* 1. compiler 2. (*giur.*) drafts-man (*pl.* -men) 3. (*sport*) chest-expander.
estenuante *agg.* exhausting.
estenuare *vt.* to tire out.
estenuazione *sf.* exhaustion.
esteriore *agg.* outward. ♦ **esteriore** *sm.* exterior, outside.
esteriorità *sf.* outward appearance.
esternamente *avv.* externally, outside.
esternare *vt.* to express, to utter.
esterno *agg.* outer, external.
èstero *agg.* foreign. ♦ **èstero** *sm.* foreign countries (*pl.*) ‖ *all'*—, abroad.
esterofilìa *sf.* xenomania.

esterrefatto *agg.* aghast, amazed.

esteso *agg.* large, wide || *per —*, in detail.

esteta *s.* aesthete.

estètica *sf.* aesthetics.

estètico *agg.* aesthetic.

estetismo *sm.* aestheticism.

èstimo *sm.* estimate.

estinguere *vt.* **1.** to put (*v. irr.*) out **2.** (*saldare*) to extinguish || — *la propria sete*, to slake one's thirst. ♦ **estìnguersi** *vr.* (*finire*) to die.

estinguìbile *agg.* extinguishable.

estinto *agg.* **1.** extinct **2.** (*morto*) dead. ♦ **estinto** *sm.* deceased man.

estintore *sm.* extinguisher.

estinzione *sf.* **1.** extinction **2.** (*di sete*) quenching **3.** (*di debito*) paying off.

estirpare *vt.* **1.** to extirpate **2.** (*di denti*) to pull out.

estirpazione *sf.* **1.** extirpation **2.** (*di denti*) extraction.

estivo *agg.* summer (*attr.*).

estòrcere *vt.* to extort.

estorsione *sf.* extortion.

estradare *vt.* to extradite.

estradizione *sf.* extradition.

estràneo *agg.* extraneous, alien. ♦ **estràneo** *sm.* stranger.

estraniare *vt.* to estrange. ♦ **estraniarsi** *vr.* to get (*v. irr.*) estranged.

estrarre *vt.* to draw (*v. irr.*) out: — *a sorte*, to draw by lot.

estrattivo *agg.* extractive.

estratto *sm.* **1.** extract **2.** (*riassunto*) excerpt **3.** (*comm.*) — *conto*, statement of account.

estrattore *sm.* extractor.

estrazione *sf.* **1.** extraction **2.** (*di lotteria*) drawing.

estremamente *avv.* extremely.

estremismo *sm.* extremism.

estremista *s.* extremist: — *di destra*, extreme rightist; — *di sinistra*, extreme leftist.

estremità *sf.* extremity, end.

estremo *agg.* **1.** utmost **2.** (*eccessivo*) intense **3.** (*drastico*) drastic. ♦ **estremo** *sm.* extreme.

estrinsecare *vt.* to express. ♦ **estrinsecarsi** *vr.* to be expressed.

estrinsecazione *sf.* expression.

estrìnseco *agg.* extrinsic(al).

estro *sm.* **1.** inspiration **2.** (*capriccio*) whim.

estrométtere *vt.* to turn out.

estromissione *sf.* expulsion.

estroso *agg.* **1.** (*ispirato*) inspired **2.** freakish.

estroverso *agg.* extroverted.

estuario *sm.* estuary.

esuberante *agg.* exuberant.

esuberanza *sf.* exuberance.

esulare *vi.* **1.** to go (*v. irr.*) into exile **2.** (*fig.*) to be beyond.

esulcerare *vt.* to exulcerate.

esulcerazione *sf.* exulceration.

èsule *sm.* **1.** exile **2.** (*profugo*) refugee.

esultante *agg.* rejoicing.

esultanza *sf.* exultation.

esultare *vi.* to rejoice.

esumare *vt.* to exhume.

esumazione *sf.* exhumation.

età *sf.* age || *che — hai?*, how old are you?; *avere la stessa —*, to be the same age; *una persona di mezza —*, a middle-aged person.

ètere *sm.* ether.

etèreo *agg.* ethereal.

eternare *vt.* to make (*v. irr.*) eternal.

eternità *sf.* eternity.

eterno *agg.* eternal, everlasting.

eteròclito *agg.* **1.** heteroclite **2.** (*fig.*) irregular.

eterodossìa *sf.* heterodoxy.

eterodosso *agg.* heterodox.

eterogeneità *sf.* heterogeneity.

eterogèneo *agg.* heterogeneous.

ètica *sf.* ethics.

etichetta *sf.* **1.** label **2.** (*galateo*) etiquette.

etichettare *vt.* to stick (*v. irr.*) a label (on).

ètico *agg.* ethical.

etilene *sm.* ethylene.

etìlico *agg.* ethylic.

etilismo *sm.* alcoholism.

etimologìa *sf.* etymology.

etimològico *agg.* etymologic(al).

ètnico *agg.* ethnic(al).

etnografìa *sf.* ethnography.

etnologìa *sf.* ethnology.

etnòlogo *sm.* ethnologist.

etrusco *agg. e sm.* Etruscan.

ettàgono *sm.* heptagon.

èttaro *sm.* hectare.

etto *sm.* hectogram.

ettòlitro *sm.* hectolitre.

ettòmetro *sm.* hectometre.

eucalipto *sm.* eucalyptus.

eucaristìa *sf.* Eucharist, Holy Communion.

eucarìstico *agg.* Eucharistic.
eufemismo *sm.* euphemism.
eufonìa *sf.* euphony.
eufònico *agg.* euphonic(al).
euforbia *sf.* Euphorbia.
euforìa *sf.* euphoria.
eufòrico *agg.* euphoric.
eunuco *sm.* eunuch.
euritmìa *sf.* eurhythmy.
europeismo *sm.* Europeanism.
europeo *agg.* e *sm.* European.
eurovisione *sf.* Eurovision.
eutanasìa *sf.* euthanasia.
evacuare *vt.* to evacuate.
evacuazione *sf.* evacuation.
evàdere *vi.* to escape. ♦ **evàdere**
vt. (*burocratico*) **1.** to dispatch **2.**
(*eludere*) to evade.
evanescente *agg.* vanishing.
evangèlico *agg.* evangelic(al).
evangelista *sm.* evangelist.
evangelizzare *vt.* to evangelize.
evaporare *vi.* to evaporate.
evaporazione *sf.* evaporation.
evasione *sf.* **1.** escape **2.** (*comm.*)
dare — a una pratica, to dispatch
a business.
evasivo *agg.* evasive.
evaso *sm.* runaway.
evasore *sm.* evader: *— fiscale*, tax
evader.
evenienza *sf.* event, occurrence:
per ogni —, for any occasion.
evento *sm.* event.
eventuale *agg.* possible.
eventualità *sf.* eventuality.
eventualmente *avv.* in case.
evidente *agg.* evident, obvious,
clear.
evidenza *sf.* evidence.
evìncere *vt.* (*giur.*) to evict.
evirare *vt.* to evirate.
evitàbile *agg.* avoidable.
evitare *vt.* **1.** to avoid **2.** (*sfuggire*)
to escape.
evo *sm.* age: *il Medio Evo*, the
Middle Ages.
evocare *vt.* to evoke, to recall.
evocativo *agg.* evocative.
evocazione *sf.* evocation.
evolutivo *agg.* evolutive.
evoluto *agg.* well-developed, modern.
evoluzione *sf.* evolution.
evoluzionismo *sm.* evolutionism.
evòlvere *vt.* to evolve.
evviva *inter.* hurray.
ex libris *sm.* ex libris.
extra *agg.* extra.

extraterritoriale *agg.* extraterritorial.
eziologìa *sf.* aetiology.

F

fa¹ *sm.* (*mus.*) F.
fa² *avv.* ago: *un anno —*, a year ago.
fabbisogno *sm.* needs (*pl.*).
fàbbrica *sf.* **1.** factory || *— di au-
tomobili*, motor works; *— di
mattoni*, brickyard; *— di carta*,
paper-mill; *capo —*, fore-man (*pl.*
-men); *marchio di —*, trade-mark
2. (*fabbricazione*) manufacture.
fabbricàbile *agg.* manufacturable ||
area —, housing area.
fabbricante *sm.* manufacturer.
fabbricare *vt.* **1.** (*produrre*) to
manufacture **2.** (*costruire*) to build
(*v. irr.*). **3.** (*fare*) to make (*v. irr.*).
fabbricato *sm.* building || *imposta
sui fabbricati*, house tax.
fabbricazione *sf.* **1.** manufacture,
make **2.** (*costruzione*) building.
fabbro *sm.* blacksmith.
fabbroferraio *sm.* blacksmith.
faccenda *sf.* matter; business (*solo
sing.*) || *— di stato*, state affair
2. (*lavori domestici*) housework
(*solo sing.*).
faccendiere *sm.* busybody.
faccetta *sf.* little face **2.** (*geom.*)
facet.
facchinaggio *sm.* porterage.
facchino *sm.* porter.
faccia *sf.* **1.** face: *che — tosta!*,
what a face!; *a — a —*, face to face
2. (*aspetto*) look, expression **3.** (*lato, superficie*) face, side.
facciale *agg.* facial.
facciata *sf.* **1.** front, façade **2.** (*pagina*) page.
face *sf.* torch.
faceto *agg.* facetious, witty.
facezia *sf.* witty remark, joke: *dire delle facezie*, to crack jokes.
fachiro *sm.* fakir.
fàcile *agg.* **1.** easy **2.** (*trattabile*)
docile **3.** (*pronto*) ready **4.** (*incline*) inclined **3.** (*probabile*) likely.
facilità *sf.* **1.** facility **2.** (*attitudine*) aptitude.
facilitare *vt.* to make (*v. irr.*)
easier

facilitazione *sf.* **1.** facilitation **2.** (*agevolazione*) facility.

facilone *sm.* slipshod fellow.

facinoroso *agg.* lawless. ♦ **facinoroso** *sm.* lawless man.

facoltà *sf.* faculty.

facoltativo *agg.* facultative: *fermata facoltativa*, request stop.

facoltoso *agg.* wealthy.

facondia *sf.* eloquence.

facondo *agg.* eloquent.

facsìmile *sm.* facsimile.

factotum *sm.* factotum

faggeto *sm.* beech-wood.

faggio *sm.* beech.

fagiano *sm.* pheasant.

fagiolino *sm.* French bean.

fagiolo *sm.* bean.

fagocita, **fagocito** *sm.* phagocyte.

fagocitare *vt.* **1.** to phagocyte **2.** (*fig.*) to absorb.

fagocitosi *sf.* phagocytosis.

fagotto[1] *sm.* bundle.

fagotto[2] *sm.* (*mus.*) bassoon.

faina *sf.* beech-marten.

falange *sf.* phalanx (*pl.* -nges).

falcata *sf.* **1.** curvet **2.** (*di persona*) stride.

falce *sf.* **1.** sickle **2.** (*da fieno*) scythe **3.** (*di luna*) crescent.

falciare *vt.* **1.** to mow (*v. irr.*) **2.** (*fig.*) to mow down.

falciatore *sm.* mower.

falciatrice *sf.* mowing-machine.

falciatura *sf.* mowing.

falcidiare *vt.* to reduce.

falco *sm.* hawk: *avere occhi di* —, to be hawk-eyed.

falconerìa *sf.* falconry.

falconiere *sm.* hawker.

falda *sf.* **1.** (*strato*) stratum (*pl.* -ta) **2.** (*di neve*) flake **3.** (*di cappello*) brim **4.** (*di monte*) slope.

falegname *sm.* joiner.

falegnamerìa *sf.* **1.** joinery **2.** (*bottega*) joiner's shop.

falena *sf.* moth.

falla *sf.* leak.

fallace *agg.* false, disappointing.

fallacia *sf.* fallacy.

fallibile *agg.* liable to make mistakes.

fàllico *agg.* phallic.

fallimentare *agg.* bankruptcy.

fallimento *sm.* **1.** bankruptcy **2.** (*fig.*) failure.

fallire *vi.* **1.** to fail **2.** (*comm.*) to go (*v. irr.*) bankrupt **3.** (*fam.*) to go under.

fallito *agg.* **1.** (*comm.*) bankrupt **2.** (*fig.*) unsuccessful. ♦ **fallito** *sm.* **1.** (*comm.*) bankrupt **2.** (*fig.*) failure.

fallo *sm.* **1.** fault: *senza* —, without fail **2.** (*anat.*) phallus (*pl.* -li).

falò *sm.* bonfire.

falpalà *sm.* furbelow.

falsare *vt.* **1.** to misrepresent **2.** (*falsificare*) to falsify.

falsariga *sf.* **1.** ruling paper **2.** (*fig.*) pattern, model.

falsario *sm.* **1.** forger **2.** (*di monete*) coiner.

falsetto *sm.* falsetto.

falsificàbile *agg.* falsifiable.

falsificare *vt.* to falsify, to counterfeit.

falsificatore *sm.* **1.** falsifier **2.** (*di monete*) coiner.

falsificazione *sf.* falsification, forgery.

falsità *sf.* **1.** falseness **2.** (*menzogna*) falsehood **3.** (*ipocrisia*) insincerity.

falso *agg.* **1.** false **2.** (*falsificato*) forged.

fama *sf.* fame, renown, reputation: *acquistarsi* —, to win (*v. irr.*) fame; *avere cattiva* —, to have a bad reputation.

fame *sf.* **1.** hunger: *avere* —, to be hungry; *far morire di* —, to starve **2.** (*carestia*) famine.

famèlico *agg.* ravenous.

famigerato *agg.* ill-famed.

famiglia *sf.* family.

familiare *agg.* **1.** domestic, homely **2.** (*intimo, anche fig.*) familiar **3.** (*senza cerimonie*) informal. ♦ **familiare** *sm.* relative.

familiarità *sf.* familiarity: *avere — con qu.*, to be familiar with so.

famoso *agg.* famous, celebrated.

fanale *sm.* **1.** lamp **2.** (*auto*) light: *— anteriore*, head-light; *— di coda*, (*aer.*) tail light, (*auto*) rear lamp; *— di posizione*, parking lights (*pl.*).

fanàtico *agg.* fanatical. ♦ **fanàtico** *sm.* **1.** fanatic **2.** (*fam.*) fan.

fanatismo *sm.* fanaticism.

fanatizzare *vt.* to fanaticize.

fanciulla *sf.* young girl.

fanciullàggine *sf.* **1.** childishness **2.** (*azione infantile*) childish action.

fanciullesco *agg.* childish.

fanciullezza *sf.* childhood.

fanciullo *sm.* young boy, child (*pl.* children).

fandonia *sf.* lie.

fanello *sm.* linnet.

fanfara *sf.* **1.** brass band **2.** (*suono di trombe*) fanfare.

fanfaronata *sf.* boasting.

fanfarone *sm.* boaster.

fangaia *sf.* muddy road.

fanghiglia *sf.* slush.

fango *sm.* **1.** mud: *gettare del — addosso a qu.*, to throw (*v. irr.*) mud at so.; *cadere nel —*, to fall (*v. irr.*) very low **2.** (*med.*) mud-baths (*pl.*).

fangoso *agg.* muddy.

fannullone *sm.* idler.

fanone *sm.* whalebone.

fantaccino *sm.* foot-soldier.

fantascienza *sf.* science fiction.

fantasìa *sf.* **1.** imagination, fancy **2.** (*inventiva*) inventiveness **3.** (*articoli fantasia*) fancy goods.

fantasioso *agg.* fanciful.

fantasma *sm.* ghost.

fantasmagorìa *sf.* phantasmagoria.

fantasmagòrico *agg.* phantasmagoric.

fantasticare *vt.* to daydream.

fantasticherìa *sf.* daydream.

fantàstico *agg.* **1.** fanciful **2.** (*bizzarro*) queer **3.** (*fam.*) extraordinary.

fante *sm.* **1.** infantryman (*pl.* -men) **2.** (*delle carte*) knave, jack.

fanterìa *sf.* infantry.

fantesca *sf.* maid-servant.

fantino *sm.* jockey.

fantoccio *sm.* puppet (*anche fig.*).

fantomàtico *agg.* mysterious.

farabutto *sm.* blackguard.

faraona *sf.* guinea-hen.

faraone *sm.* Pharaoh.

farcire *vt.* to stuff.

farcito *agg.* stuffed.

fardello *sm.* **1.** bundle **2.** (*fig.*) burden.

fare *vt.* **1.** (*in senso generale*) to do (*v. irr.*): *cosa fai?*, what are you doing?; *ecco fatto!*, that's done!; *— del proprio meglio*, to do one's best; **2.** (*fabbricare, produrre*) to make (*v. irr.*): *— amicizia*, to make friends; *— un errore*, to make a mistake; *— in fretta*, to make haste **3.** (*essere, esercitare una professione*) to be: *faccio l'insegnante*, I am a teacher **4.** (*reputare*) to think (*v. irr.*): *la facevo*

più intelligente, I thought she was more intelligent **5.** (*segnare le ore*): *che ora fa il tuo orologio?*, what time is it by your watch? **6.** (*praticare*) to go (*v. irr.*) in for || *— le carte*, to shuffle; *— fagotto*, to pack up; *— una passeggiata*, to go for a walk; *— colazione*, to have breakfast; *— bella, brutta figura*, to cut (*v. irr.*) a fine, a poor figure; *— compassione*, to rouse compassion; *— aspettare qu.*, to keep (*v. irr.*) so. waiting; *— avere, sapere, vedere a qu.*, to let (*v. irr.*) so. have, know, see. ♦ **fare** *vi.* **1.** (*di condizioni atmosferiche*): *che tempo fa?*, what is the weather like? **2.** (*far caldo, freddo*) to be hot, cold **3.** (*essere adatto*) to suit. ♦ **farsi** *vr.* to become (*v. irr.*), to grow (*v. irr.*) || *— animo*, to take (*v. irr.*) courage.

fare *sm.* manners (*pl*).

faretra *sf.* quiver.

farfalla *sf.* butterfly.

farfugliare *vt.* to mumble.

farina *sf.* meal, flour.

farinàceo *agg.* farinaceous.

faringe *sf.* pharynx (*pl.* -nges).

faringite *sf.* pharyngitis.

farinoso *agg.* mealy, floury.

fariseo *agg.* e *sm.* Pharisee.

farmacèutico *agg.* pharmaceutic.

farmacìa *sf.* **1.** pharmacy **2.** (*negozio*) chemist's shop.

farmacista *sm.* chemist.

fàrmaco *sm.* medicine, remedy (*anche fig.*).

farmacologìa *sf.* pharmacology.

farmacopea *sf.* pharmacopoeia.

farneticare *vi.* to rave.

faro *sm.* **1.** lighthouse **2.** (*auto*) headlight.

farràgine *sf.* medley, mixture.

farraginoso *agg.* confused.

farsa *sf.* farce.

farsesco *agg.* farcical.

fascetta *sf.* **1.** small band **2.** (*med.*) bandage **3.** (*edit.*) wrapper.

fascia *sf.* **1.** band **2.** (*med.*) bandage **3.** (*dei bambini*) swaddling-band.

fasciame *sm.* planking.

fasciare *vt.* **1.** to bind (*v. irr.*) (up) **2.** (*dei neonati*) to swaddle.

fasciatura *sf.* **1.** dressing **2.** (*di neonato*) swaddling.

fascìcolo *sm.* booklet.

fascina *sf.* faggot.

fàscino *sm.* charm, fascination.

fascio *sm.* **1.** bundle **2.** (*geom.*) sheaf **3.** (*di luce*) beam.

fascismo *sm.* Fascism.

fascista *agg.* e *s.* Fascist.

fase *sf.* **1.** stage **2.** (*elettr.*) phase **3.** (*auto*) stroke.

fastello *sm.* faggot.

fastidio *sm.* **1.** trouble: *dare — a qu.*, to give (*v. irr.*) so. trouble **2.** (*contrarietà*) annoyance.

fastidioso *agg.* tiresome.

fastigio *sm.* **1.** pediment **2.** (*fig.*) height.

fasto *sm.* pomp.

fastosità *sf.* pomp, splendour.

fastoso *agg.* magnificent.

fasullo *agg.* false.

fata *sf.* fairy.

fatale *agg.* fatal, inevitable.

fatalismo *sm.* fatalism.

fatalista *agg.* e *s.* fatalist.

fatalità *sf.* fatality.

fatica *sf.* weariness, fatigue.

faticare *vi.* to toil, to work hard.

faticata *sf.* drudgery.

faticoso *agg.* hard, tiring.

fatìdico *agg.* fatidical.

fato *sm.* **1.** fate, destiny **2.** (*sorte*) lot.

fatta *sf.* kind, sort.

fattìbile *agg.* practicable.

fattispecie *sf.* case in point: *nella —*, in this case.

fattivo *agg.* **1.** effective **2.** (*attivo*) busy.

fatto *sm.* **1.** fact **2.** (*azione*) deed **3.** (*avvenimento*) event || *sapere il — proprio*, to know (*v. irr.*) one's business; *venire al`—*, to go (*v. irr.*) to the point; *in — di*, as regards.

fattore *sm.* **1.** factor **2.** (*agr.*) farmer.

fattorìa *sf.* farm.

fattorino *sm.* errand-boy.

fattucchiere *sm.* wizard.

fattura *sf.* **1.** making **2.** (*lavorazione*) work **3.** (*comm.*) invoice **4.** (*stregoneria*) sorcery.

fatturare *vt.* **1.** to adulterate **2.** (*comm.*) to invoice.

fatturazione *sf.* (*comm.*) invoicing.

fatuità *sf.* fatuity.

fatuo *agg.* **1.** fatuous **2.** (*vanitoso*) vain || *fuoco —*, will-o'-the-wisp.

fàuci *sf. pl.* **1.** jaws **2.** (*di persona*) throat (*sing.*).

fàuna *sf.* fauna.

fàuno *sm.* faun.

fàusto *agg.* propitious.

fautore *sm.* supporter.

fava *sf.* broad bean || *pigliare due piccioni con una —*, to kill two birds with one stone.

favella *sf.* speech.

favellare *vi.* to speak (*v. irr.*).

favilla *sf.* spark (*anche fig.*).

favo *sm.* **1.** honeycomb **2.** (*med.*) favus.

fàvola *sf.* **1.** fable **2.** (*frottola*) idle story **3.** (*oggetto di pettegolezzo*) byword.

favoloso *agg.* fabulous.

favore *sm.* favour.

favoreggiamento *sm.* favouring.

favoreggiare *vt.* to favour.

favoreggiatore *sm.* abettor.

favorévole *agg.* favourable.

favorire *vt.* **1.** to favour **2.** (*aiutare*) to help **3.** (*promuovere*) to foster.

favoritismo *sm.* favouritism.

favorito *agg.* e *sm.* favourite.

fazione *sf.* faction.

fazioso *agg.* factious.

fazzoletto *sm.* **1.** handkerchief **2.** (*da collo*) neckerchief.

febbraio *sm.* February.

febbre *sf.* fever.

febbricitante *agg.* feverish.

febbrìfugo *agg.* febrifugal. ♦ **febbrìfugo** *sm.* febrifuge.

febbrile *agg.* feverish.

fecale *agg.* fecal.

feccia *sf.* dregs (*pl.*) (*anche fig.*).

feci *sf. pl.* excrement (*sing.*).

fècola *sf.* starch.

fecondare *vt.* to fecundate.

fecondazione *sf.* fecundation.

fecondità *sf.* fecundity.

fecondo *agg.* fecund.

fede *sf.* **1.** faith, belief **2.** (*fiducia*) trust.

fedele *agg.* faithful.

fedeltà *sf.* fidelity.

fèdera *sf.* pillow-case.

federale *agg.* federal.

federalismo *sm.* federalism.

federativo *agg.* federative.

federato *agg.* federate.

federazione *sf.* federation.

fedìfrago *sm.* traitor.

fedina *sf.* criminal record.

fègato *sm.* **1.** liver **2.** (*fig.*) courage.

fegatoso *agg.* **1.** bilious **2.** (*fig.*) irritable.

felce *sf.* fern.

feldspato *sm.* felspar.

felice *agg.* **1.** happy **2.** (*fortunato*) lucky **3.** (*piacevole*) pleasant.

felicità *sf.* happiness.

felicitarsi *vr.* to congratulate (so. on sthg.).

felicitazioni *sf. pl.* congratulation (*sing.*).

felino *agg.* e *sm.* feline.

fellone *sm.* villain, traitor.

fellonìa *sf.* felony, treason.

felpato *agg.* **1.** plushy **2.** (*fig.*) soft || *a passi felpati*, stealthily.

feltro *sm.* felt.

feluca *sf.* **1.** (*mar.*) felucca **2.** (*cappello*) cocked hat.

fémmina *sf.* female || *mala —*, bad woman.

femminile *agg.* **1.** female **2.** (*da donna*) feminine.

femminilità *sf.* womanliness.

femminismo *sm.* feminism.

femminuccia *sf.* **1.** simple woman **2.** (*uomo senza coraggio*) coward.

fèmore *sm.* thigh-bone.

fendente *sm.* cutting blow.

fèndere *vt.* to rend (*v. irr.*).

fenditura *sf.* cleft, fissure.

fenice *sf.* phoenix.

fènico *agg.* phenic.

fenolo *sm.* phenol.

fenomenale *agg.* phenomenal.

fenomenismo *sm.* phenomenalism.

fenòmeno *sm.* phenomenon (*pl.* -na).

fenomenologìa *sf.* phenomenology.

ferace *agg.* fruitful, rich (*anche fig.*).

ferale *agg.* feral, deadly.

fèretro *sm.* coffin.

ferie *sf. pl.* holidays.

feriale *agg.* working: *giorno —*, working-day.

ferimento *sm.* wounding.

ferino *agg.* ferine, wild.

ferire *vt.* to wound, to hurt (*v. irr.*).

ferita *sf.* wound (*anche fig.*).

ferito *agg.* wounded, injured.

feritoia *sf.* loophole.

ferma *sf.* **1.** (*mil.*) service **2.** (*caccia*) pointing.

fermacarte *sm.* paper-weight.

fermaglio *sm.* **1.** clasp **2.** (*per gioielli*) brooch **3.** (*per carte*) clip.

fermare *vt.* **1.** to stop, to arrest **2.** (*fissare*) to fix (*anche fig.*) **3.** (*giur.*) to hold (*v. irr.*). ♦ **fermarsi** *vr.* **1.** to stop **2.** (*soggiornare*) to stay **3.** (*fare una pausa*) to pause.

fermata *sf.* **1.** stop **2.** (*pausa*) pause.

fermentare *vi.* to ferment (*anche fig.*).

fermentazione *sf.* fermentation.

fermento *sm.* **1.** ferment **2.** (*fig.*) turmoil, ferment.

fermezza *sf.* firmness, strength.

fermo *agg.* **1.** still **2.** (*irremovibile*) steady, firm || *mano ferma*, firm hand; *volontà ferma*, unfaltering will. ♦ **fermo** *sm.* **1.** (*mecc.*) lock, catch, stop **2.** (*giur.*) provisional arrest.

fermoposta *sm.* poste-restante.

feroce *agg.* fierce, cruel.

ferocia *sf.* fierceness.

ferraglia *sf.* scrap-iron.

ferragosto *sm.* **1.** August holiday **2.** (*in Inghilterra*) August Bank holiday.

ferraio *sm.* blacksmith.

ferramenta *sf. pl.* hardware (*sing.*).

ferramento *sm.* iron tool.

ferrare *vt.* **1.** to fit with iron **2.** (*di cavalli*) to shoe.

ferrato *agg.* **1.** ironshod **2.** (*di scarpe*) hobnailed **3.** (*strada ferrata*) railway **4.** (*fig.*) well read.

ferratura *sf.* shoeing.

fèrreo *agg.* iron (*attr.*).

ferriera *sf.* iron-foundry.

ferro *sm.* iron: *— battuto*, wrought iron; *— da stiro*, flat-iron; *— da calza*, knitting needle || *i ferri del mestiere*, the tools of the trade; *tocca —!*, touch wood!

ferroso *agg.* ferrous.

ferrovìa *sf.* railway.

ferroviario *agg.* railway (*attr.*).

ferroviere *sm.* railwayman (*pl.* -men).

ferruginoso *agg.* ferruginous.

fèrtile *agg.* fertile (*anche fig.*).

fertilità *sf.* fertility.

fertilizzante *agg.* fertilizing. ♦ **fertilizzante** *sm.* fertilizer.

fertilizzare *vt.* to fertilize.

fèrula *sf.* rod.

fervente *agg.* burning, ardent (*anche fig.*).

fèrvido *agg.* fervid, ardent || *fervidi auguri*, best wishes.

fervore *sm.* fervour, heat.

fessura *sf.* **1.** crack **2.** (*per liquidi*) leak.

festa *sf.* **1.** (*giorno di riposo*) holiday **2.** (*religiosa*) feast **3.** (*anniversario*) birthday **4.** (*onomasti-*

co) Saint's day **5.** (*banchetto, ballo*) feast, ball || *giorno di —,* festal day.

festaiolo *sm.* reveller.

festante *agg.* rejoicing.

festeggiamento *sm.* celebration.

festeggiare *vt.* **1.** to celebrate **2.** (*accogliere festosamente*) to give (*v. irr.*) a hearty welcome.

festévole *agg.* festive.

festino *sm.* feast.

fèstival *sm.* festival.

festività *sf.* festivity.

festivo *agg.* **1.** festive **2.** (*domenicale*) Sunday (*attr.*).

festone *sm.* festoon.

festoso *agg.* joyous.

festuca *sf.* straw.

feticcio *sm.* fetish.

feticismo *sm.* fetishism.

feticista *s.* fetishist.

fètido *agg.* foetid, foul.

feto *sm.* foetus.

fetore *sm.* stink.

fetta *sf.* **1.** slice **2.** (*piccolo pezzo*) piece.

fettuccia *sf.* tape.

feudale *agg.* feudal.

feudalésimo *sm.* feudalism.

feudatario *sm.* feudatory.

fèudo *sm.* feud.

fiaba *sf.* **1.** fable **2.** (*falsità*) falsehood.

fiabesco *agg.* fairy-like.

fiacca *sf.* weariness || *battere la —* (*fam.*), to be sluggish.

fiaccare *vt.* to exhaust. ♦ **fiaccarsi** *vr.* to break (*v. irr.*) down.

fiacchezza *sf.* weakness, weariness.

fiacco *agg.* weak, exhausted.

fiàccola *sf.* torch.

fiaccolata *sf.* torchlight procession.

fiala *sf.* phial.

fiamma *sf.* **1.** flame **2.** (*molto viva*) blaze.

fiammante *agg.* **1.** flaming **2.** (*fig.*) bright || *nuovo —,* brand-new.

fiammata *sf.* blaze.

fiammeggiante *agg.* blazing, burning.

fiammeggiare *vi.* to blaze, to flame, to burn.

fiammifero *sm.* match: *accendere un —,* to strike (*v. irr.*) a match.

fiammingo *agg.* Flemish. ♦ **fiammingo** *sm.* Fleming.

fiancata *sf.* **1.** side **2.** (*mar.*) broadside.

fiancheggiare *vt.* **1.** to flank **2.** (*fig.*) to support.

fiancheggiatore *sm.* flanker, supporter.

fianco *sm.* **1.** hip, side (*anche fig.*) **2.** (*di animali; mil.*) flank.

fiasca *sf.* flask.

fiasco *sm.* flask || *fare —,* to fail utterly.

fiatare *vi.* to breathe: *senza —,* without speaking.

fiato *sm.* breath.

fibbia *sf.* buckle.

fibra *sf.* **1.** fibre **2.** (*costituzione*) constitution.

fibroma *sm.* fibroma (*pl.* -ata).

fibroso *agg.* fibrous.

fìbula *sf.* **1.** fibula **2.** (*med.*) splint-bone.

ficcanaso *sm.* meddler.

ficcare *vt.* to thrust (*v. irr.*); to drive (*v. irr.*) (in). ♦ **ficcarsi** *vr.* to interfere || *— in testa qc.,* to get (*v. irr.*) sthg. into one's head.

fico *sm.* fig.

fidanzamento *sm.* engagement.

fidanzare *vt.* to engage. ♦ **fidanzarsi** *vr.* to become (*v. irr.*) engaged (to so.).

fidanzata *sf.* fiancée.

fidanzato *sm.* fiancé.

fidare *vi.* to trust. ♦ **fidarsi** *vr.* to trust (upon so., sthg.).

fidato *agg.* reliable.

fideiussione *sf.* suretyship.

fidente *agg.* confiding.

fido *agg.* faithful. ♦ **fido** *sm.* **1.** devoted follower **2.** (*comm.*) credit.

fiducia *sf.* trust, confidence: *— in se stessi,* self-confidence.

fiduciario *agg.* fiduciary. ♦ **fiduciario** *sm.* fiduciary, trustee.

fiducioso *agg.* trusting, hopeful.

fiele *sm.* **1.** gall **2.** (*fig.*) hatred.

fienagione *sf.* haymaking.

fienile *sm.* hay-loft.

fieno *sm.* hay: *asma da —,* hay-asthma.

fiera *sf.* **1.** fair **2.** (*esposizione*) exhibition || *— campionaria,* samples fair.

fierezza *sf.* fierceness.

fiero *agg.* proud.

fièvole *agg.* **1.** feeble **2.** (*di luce, suono*) dim.

fìggere *vt.* to fix.

figlia *sf.* daughter.

figliare *vt.* to bring (*v. irr.*) forth.

figliastra sf. step-daughter.
figliastro sm. step-son.
figlio sm. son.
figlioccia sf. goddaughter.
figlioccio sm. godson.
figliolanza sf. children (pl.), family.
figliolo sm. son.
figura sf. 1. figure 2. (illustrazione) illustration, picture 3. (personaggio di romanzi, opere teatrali ecc.) character || fare una bella, brutta —, to cut (v. irr.) a fine, poor figure.
figurare vt. 1. to represent 2. (far figura) to look smart 3. (apparire) to appear.
figurativo agg. figurative.
figurato agg. 1. (illustrato) illustrated 2. (di linguaggio, senso) figurative.
figurazione sf. figuration.
figurinista s. dress-designer.
figurino sm. fashion-plate.
figuro sm. scoundrel.
fila sf. 1. row, file 2. (coda) queue: fare la —, to queue (up).
filaccia sf. lint.
filamento sm. filament.
filamentoso agg. filamentous.
filanda sf. spinning-mill.
filandaia sf. spinner.
filante agg.: stella — 1. (astr.) falling-star 2. (di carta) (paper) streamer.
filantropìa sf. philanthropy.
filàntropo sm. philanthrope.
filare[1] vt. 1. to spin (v. irr.) 2. (correre) to run (v. irr.) 3. (amoreggiare) to flirt.
filare[2] sm. row, line.
filarmònico agg. e sm. philharmonic.
filastrocca sf. nursery rhyme.
filatelìa sf. stamp-collecting.
filatèlico agg. philatelic. ♦ **filatèlico** sm. philatelist.
filato agg. 1. spun 2. (di seguito) running.
filatura sf. spinning.
filettare vt. (mecc.) to thread.
filettatura sf. (mecc.) threading.
filetto sm. 1. (filo sottile) thin thread 2. (mecc.) thread || — della lingua, fraenum.
filiale agg. filial. ♦ **filiale** sf. branch house.
filiazione sf. filiation.
filibustiere sm. 1. filibuster 2. (fig.) adventurer, rascal.

filiera sf. 1. (mecc.) screw cutting die 2. (ind. tess.) spinneret.
filiforme agg. threadlike.
filigrana sf. 1. filigree 2. (di carta) watermark.
filìppica sf. philippic.
fillòssera sf. phylloxera.
film sm. picture || girare un —, to shoot (v. irr.) a picture.
filmare vt. to film.
filo sm. 1. thread 2. (ind. tessile) yarn 3. (tec.) wire || un — d'acqua, a fine stream of water; un — d'aria, a breath of air.
filobus sm. trolley-bus.
filologìa sf. philology.
filòlogo sm. philologist.
filone sm. 1. (di pane) long loaf 2. (min.) vein.
filosofare vi. to philosophize.
filosofìa sf. philosophy.
filòsofo sm. philosopher.
filovìa sf. trolley-bus line.
filtrare vt. to filter, to strain.
filtro sm. 1. filter 2. (colino) strainer.
filza sf. 1. string 2. (fig.) series (pl.) 3. (cucito) running stitch.
finale agg. last, final.
finalità sf. aim, end.
finalmente avv. 1. at last 2. (in conclusione) finally.
finanche avv. even.
finanza sf. finance.
finanziamento sm. financing.
finanziare vt. to finance.
finanziario agg. financial.
finanziatore sm. financing capitalist.
finanziere sm. financier.
finché cong. 1. till, until 2. (per tutto il tempo che) as long as.
fine[1] sf. end || alla fin —, after all. ♦ **fine** sm. (scopo) purpose.
fine[2] agg. fine, thin.
finestra sf. window.
finestrino sm. window.
finezza sf. 1. thinness 2. (acume) subtlety 3. (raffinatezza) refinement 4. (gentilezza) kindness.
fìngere vt. to pretend. ♦ **fìngersi** vr. to feign oneself.
finimenti sm. pl. harness (sing.).
finimondo sm. 1. end of the world 2. (fig.) catastrophe.
finire vi. 1. to finish, to end 2. (interrompersi) to stop || — con, to end by: finii con l'andare, I ended by going.
finitezza sf. perfection.

finìtimo *agg.* bordering.

finito *agg.* **1.** finished, ended **2.** (*rovinato*) done for.

finitura *sf.* finishing.

fino *prep.* **1.** (*di tempo*) till, until, up to: — *a dicembre*, till December **2.** (*di spazio*) as far as: *andammo fino a Roma*, we went as far as Rome **3.** (*fino da*) from **4.** (*a partire da*) since.

finocchio *sm.* fennel.

finora *avv.* till now, so far.

finta *sf.* **1.** sham **2.** (*scherma*) feint.

fintantoché *avv.* V. **finché**.

finto *agg.* false.

finzione *sf.* pretence, duplicity.

fio *sm.* penalty: *pagare il* —, to pay (*v. irr.*) the penalty (of).

fioccare *vi.* **1.** to snow **2.** (*fig.*) to shower.

fiocco *sm.* **1.** ribbon **2.** (*di lana*) staple **3.** (*falda*) flake **4.** (*di neve*) snowflake.

fiòcina *sf.* harpoon.

fioco *agg.* **1.** (*rauco*) hoarse **2.** (*debole*) weak **3.** (*di luce*) dim **4.** (*di voce*) faint.

fionda *sf.* sling.

fioraio *sm.* florist.

fiorame *sm.* floral design.

fiordaliso *sm.* bluebottle.

fiordo *sm.* fjord.

fiore *sm.* **1.** flower **2.** (*fioritura*) bloom: *essere in* — (*anche fig.*), to be in bloom **3.** (*parte scelta*) the best part **4.** (*nelle carte*) clubs (*pl.*).

fiorente *agg.* **1.** blooming **2.** (*fig.*) flourishing.

fioretto *sm.* **1.** little flower **2.** (*relig.*) act of mortification **3.** (*scherma*) foil.

fioricultore *sm.* floriculturist.

fiorino *sm.* florin.

fiorire *vi.* **1.** to flower, to bloom, to blossom **2.** (*fig.*) to flourish.

fiorista *s.* florist.

fiorito *agg.* **1.** flowery **2.** (*in fiore*) in bloom.

fioritura *sf.* **1.** flowering **2.** (*fig.*) flourishing.

fiotto *sm.* wave, stream: *a fiotti*, in streams.

firma *sf.* signature.

firmamento *sm.* firmament.

firmare *vt.* to sign.

firmatario *sm.* **1.** signatory **2.** (*comm.*) signer.

fisarmònica *sf.* accordion.

fisarmonìcista *s.* accordionist.

fiscale *agg.* **1.** fiscal **2.** (*inquisitorio*) strict.

fiscalismo *sm.* rigorism.

fischiare *vi.* **1.** to whistle **2.** (*di segnale acustico*) to hoot **3.** (*di serpente; per disapprovare*) to hiss **4.** (*nelle orecchie*) to buzz **5.** (*di proiettili*) to whiz.

fischiata *sf.* **1.** whistling **2.** (*di disapprovazione*) hissing.

fischiettare *vt.* to whistle softly.

fischietto *sm.* whistle.

fischio *sm.* **1.** whistle **2.** (*di serpente; di disapprovazione*) hiss **3.** (*segnali acustici*) hoot **4.** (*nelle orecchie*) buzzing.

fisco *sm.* public treasury.

fìsica *sf.* physics.

fìsico *agg.* physical, bodily. ♦ **fìsico** *sm.* **1.** (*scienziato*) physicist **2.** (*costituzione*) physique.

fìsima *sf.* caprice, whim.

fisiologìa *sf.* physiology.

fisiològico *agg.* physiologic(al).

fisiòlogo *sm.* physiologist.

fisionomìa *sf.* **1.** features (*pl.*) **2.** (*carattere*) character.

fisionomista *sm.* physiognomist.

fisioterapìa *sf.* physiotherapy.

fissaggio *sm.* fixing.

fissare *vt.* **1.** to fix **2.** (*guardare fisso*) to gaze **3.** (*prenotare*) to book. ♦ **fissarsi** *vr.* **1.** to be fixed **2.** (*stabilirsi*) to settle down.

fissato *agg.* **1.** fixed **2.** (*fam.*) obsessed.

fissatore *sm.* **1.** fixer **2.** (*foto*) fixing bath.

fissazione *sf.* fixed idea.

fissione *sf.* fission.

fissità *sf.* fixity.

fisso *agg.* fixed.

fistola *sf.* **1.** Pan-pipe **2.** (*patol.*) fistula.

fitologìa *sf.* phytology.

fitta *sf.* stitch.

fittàvolo *sm.* tenant farmer.

fittizio *agg.* fictitious.

fitto¹ *agg.* **1.** (*conficcato*) driven in **2.** (*denso*) thick.

fitto² *sm.* rent.

fiumana *sf.* **1.** broad stream **2.** (*fig.*) crowd, stream.

fiume *sm.* **1.** river **2.** (*fig.*) flood.

fiutare *vt.* **1.** to smell (*v. irr.*) **2.** (*fig.*) to guess.

fiuto *sm.* **1.** scent, smell **2.** (*fig.*) intuition.

flàccido *agg.* flabby.

flacone *sm.* vial.

flagellare *vt.* 1. to flagellate 2. (*fig.*) to scourge.

flagellazione *sf.* flagellation.

flagello *sm.* 1. scourge, whip 2. (*fig.*) scourge, plague.

flagrante *agg.* flagrant || *cogliere qu. in* —, to catch (*v. irr.*) so. in the open act.

flagranza *sf.* flagrancy.

flanella *sf.* flannel.

flato *sm.* flatus.

flatulenza *sf.* flatulence.

flautato *agg.* fluted.

flautista *sm.* flute-player.

flàuto *sm.* flute.

flèbile *agg.* plaintive, feeble.

flebite *sf.* phlebitis.

fleboclisi *sf.* phleboclysis.

flebòtomo *sm.* phlebotomist.

flemma *sf.* coolness, phlegm.

flemmàtico *agg.* phlegmatic.

flèmmone *sm.* phlegmon.

flessibile *agg.* flexible, pliant (*anche fig.*).

flessibilità *sf.* flexibility.

flessione *sf.* flexion, bending.

flessuosità *sf.* 1. flexuosity 2. (*di corpo*) suppleness.

flessuoso *agg.* 1. flexuous 2. (*di corpo*) supple.

flèttere *vt.* to bend (*v. irr.*).

flirtare *vi.* to flirt.

flogìstico *agg.* (*med.*) phlogistic.

flora *sf.* flora.

floreale *agg.* floral.

floricoltore *sm.* floriculturist.

floricoltura *sf.* floriculture.

floridezza *sf.* prosperity.

flòrido *agg.* 1. prosperous 2. (*fig.*) buxom 3. (*di colorito*) ruddy.

florilegio *sm.* florilegium (*pl.* -ia).

floscio *agg.* flabby.

flotta *sf.* fleet: — *metropolitana* (*in Gran Bretagna*), the Home Fleet.

flottante *agg.* floating.

flottiglia *sf.* flotilla.

fluente *agg.* fluent (*anche fig.*).

fluidità *sf.* fluency.

flùido *agg.* e *sm.* fluid.

fluire *vi.* to flow.

fluorescente *agg.* fluorescent.

fluorescenza *sf.* 1. (*fig.*) fluorescence 2. (*elettr.*) glow.

fluorìdrico *agg.* hydrofluoric.

fluorite *sf.* fluorite.

fluoro *sm.* fluorine.

fluoruro *sm.* fluoride.

flussione *sf.* fluxion.

flusso *sm.* 1. (*di marea*) flood(-tide) 2. (*fig.*) flux.

flutto *sm.* wave.

fluttuante *agg.* 1. fluctuating, floating 2. (*incerto*) irresolute.

fluttuare *vi.* to fluctuate, to waver.

fluttuazione *sf.* fluctuation.

fluviale *agg.* river (*attr.*).

fobìa *sf.* phobia, aversion.

foca *sf.* seal.

focaccia *sf.* cake || *rendere pan per* —, to give (*v. irr.*) tit for tat.

focaia *sf.* *pietra* —, flint.

focale *agg.* focal.

foce *sf.* mouth.

focolaio *sm.* centre of infection.

focolare *sm.* 1. hearth 2. (*caminetto*) fireplace 3. (*fig.*) home.

focoso *agg.* hot, fiery.

fòdera *sf.* lining.

foderare *vt.* to line.

fòdero *sm.* scabbard, sheath.

foga *sf.* impetuosity.

foggia *sf.* 1. (*moda*) fashion 2. (*maniera*) way 3. (*forma*) shape.

foggiare *vt.* to shape.

foglia *sf.* leaf (*pl.* leaves) || *mangiare la* —, to take (*v. irr.*) the hint.

fogliame *sm.* foliage, leafage.

foglio *sm.* sheet.

fogna *sf.* sewer.

fognatura *sf.* sewage.

foia *sf.* lust.

fola *sf.* 1. fable 2. (*fandonia*) fib.

folata *sf.* (*di vento*) gust.

folclore *sm.* folklore.

folclorìstico *agg.* folkloristic.

folgorante *agg.* flashing, dazzling.

folgorare *vt.* to strike (*v. irr.*) with lightning.

folgorazione *sf.* 1. (*elettr.*) electrocution 2. (*fig.*) fulmination.

fòlgore *sf.* thunderbolt.

folla *sf.* crowd.

folle *agg.* 1. mad 2. (*mecc.*) idle 3. (*auto*) neutral.

folleggiare *vi.* 1. to behave foolishly 2. (*divertirsi*) to make (*v. irr.*) merry.

folletto *sm.* 1. imp 2. (*ragazzo*) restless child.

follìa *sf.* madness || *amare qu. alla* —, to be madly in love with so.

folto *agg.* thick. ♦ **folto** *sm.* thick.

fomentare *vt.* to foster.

fomentatore *sm.* fomenter.

fomento *sm.* fomentation.

fonda sf. anchorage || nave alla —, ship at anchor.

fòndaco sm. draper's shop.

fondale sm. 1. (teat.) background 2. (mar.) depth.

fondamentale agg. fundamental.

fondamento sm. 1. foundation: gettare le fondamenta, to lay (v. irr.) the foundation 2. (fig.) basis, ground.

fondare vt. to found. ♦ **fondarsi** vr. to base oneself on.

fondatezza sf. foundation, ground.

fondato agg. well-grounded.

fondatore sm. founder.

fondazione sf. 1. foundation 2. (istituzione) institution.

fòndere vt. 1. to melt 2. (fondere in forma) to cast (v. irr.) 3. (unire) to blend.

fonderìa sf. foundry.

fondiario agg. land (attr.).

fondista sm. long-distance runner.

fonditore sm. melter, caster.

fonditura sf. 1. melting 2. (colata) casting.

fondo agg. deep. ♦ **fondo** sm. 1. (parte inferiore) bottom 2. (estremità) end 3. (indole) nature 4. (possedimento) estate 5. (capitale) fund || articolo di —, leading article.

fonema sm. phoneme.

fonètica sf. phonetics.

fonogramma sm. phonogram.

fonologìa sf. phonology.

fontana sf. fountain.

fontanella sf. (anat.) fontanel.

fonte sf. spring, source (anche fig.).

foraggio sm. forage.

foràneo agg. 1. rural 2. (mar.) outer.

forare vt. 1. to pierce 2. (di pneumatico) to puncture 3. (di biglietti) to punch.

foratura sf. 1. piercing 2. (di pneumatico) puncture.

fòrbici sf. pl. scissors.

forbire vt. 1. to clean 2. (di stile) to polish.

forbito agg. 1. elegant 2. (di stile) polished.

forca sf. 1. fork 2. (patibolo) gallows.

forcella sf. 1. forked stick 2. (mecc.) fork 3. (per capelli) hairpin.

forchetta sf. fork.

forcina sf. hairpin.

fòrcipe sm. forceps (pl.).

forcuto agg. forked.

forense agg. forensic.

foresta sf. forest (anche fig.), wood.

forestale agg. forestal: guardia —, forester.

foresterìa sf. guest-rooms (pl.).

forestiero agg. foreign. ♦ **forestiero** sm. foreigner.

fòrfora sf. dandruff, scurf.

forgiare vt. 1. to forge 2. (modellare) to shape.

forma sf. 1. form, shape 2. (tec.) mould.

formaggio sm. cheese.

formale agg. 1. formal 2. (solenne) solemn.

formalismo sm. formalism.

formalista agg. e s. formalist.

formalità sf. formality.

formalizzarsi vr. to be shocked (at, by).

formare vt. 1. to form 2. (fare) to make (v. irr.), to create 3. (modellare) to shape 4. (addestrare) to train. ♦ **formarsi** vr. 1. to form 2. (crescere, affinarsi) to grow (v. irr.), to develop.

formativo agg. formative.

formato sm. 1. form 2. (misura) size 3. (di libro) format.

formazione sf. formation.

formica sf. ant.

formichiere sm. ant-eater.

formicolare vi. 1. to swarm 2. (sentire un formicolio) to tingle.

formicolìo sm. 1. swarming 2. (intorpidimento) tingling.

formidàbile agg. formidable.

fòrmula sf. formula (pl. -ae).

formulare vt. to formulate.

fornace sf. furnace.

fornaio sm. 1. baker 2. (negozio) baker's shop.

fornello sm. stove.

fornire vt. 1. to supply (with), to provide (with) 2. (equipaggiare) to equip (with).

fornito agg. 1. furnished (with), supplied (with) 2. (equipaggiato) equipped (with).

fornitore sm. furnisher, supplier.

fornitura sf. 1. (il fornire) supplying 2. (attrezzatura) furniture, fitting.

forno sm. 1. (da cucina) oven 2. (metal.) furnace.

foro[1] sm. hole.

foro[2] sm. 1. court of justice 2. (gli avvocati) the Bar 3. (stor.) forum.

forse *avv.* **1.** perhaps, maybe **2.** (*circa*) about.

forsennato *agg.* mad, frantic.

forte *agg.* **1.** strong (*anche fig.*) **2.** (*di mali*) severe **3.** (*violento*) heavy **4.** (*di suono*) loud. ♦ **forte** *sm.* **1.** strong man **2.** (*punto di forza*) strong point **3.** (*fortezza*) fortress. ♦ **forte** *avv.* strongly.

fortezza *sf.* stronghold, fortress.

fortificare *vt.* to strengthen, to fortify (*anche fig.*).

fortificazione *sf.* fortification.

fortino *sm.* block-house.

fortùito *agg.* fortuitous, accidental.

fortuna *sf.* **1.** luck **2.** (*ricchezza*) fortune, wealth **3.** (*riuscita*) success **4.** (*emergenza*) emergency.

fortunale *sm.* storm.

fortunato *agg.* lucky.

fortunoso *agg.* **1.** stormy **2.** (*fig.*) eventful.

forùncolo *sm.* boil.

foruncolosi *sf.* furunculosis.

forviare *vt.* to lead (*v. irr.*) astray.

forza *sf.* **1.** strength **2.** (*fig.*) power || — *di volontà*, will-power; *a — di*, by dint of **3.** (*mil.*) force.

forzare *vt.* **1.** to force, to compel **2.** (*scassinare*) to pick the lock of. ♦ **forzato** *agg.* forced. ♦ **forzato** *sm.* convict.

forziere *sm.* coffer.

forzoso *agg.* forced.

foschìa *sf.* haze, mist.

fosco *agg.* **1.** dark, hazy **2.** (*di aspetto*) gloomy.

fosfato *sm.* phosphate.

fosforescente *agg.* phosphorescent.

fosforescenza *sf.* phosphorescence.

fòsforo *sm.* **1.** phosphorus **2.** (*fig.*) intelligence.

fossa *sf.* **1.** ditch **2.** (*cavità*) hollow **3.** (*tomba*) grave.

fossato *sm.* ditch.

fòssile *agg.* e *sm.* fossil || *carbon —*, pit-coal.

fosso *sm.* ditch.

foto *sf.* photo.

fotocèllula *sf.* photoelectric cell.

fotocopia *sf.* photocopy.

fotogènico *agg.* photogenic.

fotografare *vt.* to photograph.

fotografìa *sf.* **1.** (*arte fotografica*) photography **2.** (*immagine fotografica*) photograph || — *istantanea*, snapshot; *fare una —*, to take (*v. irr.*) a photograph.

fotògrafo *sm.* photographer.

fotomontaggio *sm.* photomontage.

fra *prep.* V. *tra*.

fra' *sm.* (*relig.*) Brother.

frac *sm.* tail-coat.

fracassare *vt.* to smash, to shatter.

fracasso *sm.* **1.** noise, hubbub **2.** (*di cose rotte*) crash.

fracco *sm.* **1.** a great deal **2.** (*di botte*) a good thrashing.

fràdicio *agg.* **1.** rotten **2.** (*bagnato*) wet through.

fràgile *agg.* **1.** fragile **2.** (*fig.*) frail.

fragilità *sf.* fragility (*anche fig.*).

fràgola *sf.* strawberry.

fragore *sm.* loud noise.

fragoroso *agg.* noisy.

fragrante *agg.* fragrant.

fragranza *sf.* fragrance.

fraintèndere *vt.* to misunderstand (*v. irr.*).

frammassone *sm.* freemason.

frammassonerìa *sf.* freemasonry.

frammentario *agg.* fragmentary.

frammento *sm.* fragment.

framméttere *vt.* to interpose. ♦ **framméttersi** *vr.* to interpose, to intrude.

frammezzare *vt.* to intersperse.

frammezzo *prep.* V. *tra*.

frammischiare *vt.* to intermingle. ♦ **frammischiarsi** *vr.* to intermingle.

frana *sf.* landslide.

franare *vi.* **1.** (*di terreno*) to slide (*v. irr.*) down **2.** (*di casa*) to fall (*v. irr.*) in.

francescano *agg.* e *sm.* Franciscan.

francese *agg.* French. ♦ **francese** *sm.* Frenchman (*pl.* -men).

francesismo *sm.* Gallicism.

franchezza *sf.* frankness, outspokenness.

franchigia *sf.* **1.** immunity **2.** (*postale*) post-free **3.** (*mar.*) furlough.

franco¹ *agg.* **1.** frank, outspoken **2.** (*libero; comm.*) free: *un porto —*, a free port; — *a bordo*, free on board; — *di spese*, free of charge.

franco² *sm.* franc.

francobollo *sm.* stamp.

francotiratore *sm.* sharp-shooter.

frangente *sm.* **1.** (*mar.*) breaker **2.** (*situazione difficile*) emergency.

fràngere *vt.* **1.** to break (*v. irr.*) **2.** (*schiacciare*) to crush.

frangetta *sf.* fringe.

frangia *sf.* **1.** fringe **2.** (*fig.*) embellishment.

frangiare *vt.* to fringe.
frangìbile *agg.* frangible.
frangibilità *sf.* frangibility.
frangiflutti *agg. e sm.* breakwater.
frangizolle *sm.* (*agr.*) clod-smasher.
franoso *agg.* crumbling.
frantoio *sm.* oil-mill.
frantumare *vt.* to shatter.
frantume *sm.* fragment || *andare in frantumi*, to break (*v. irr.*) into fragments.
frappé *sm.* shake.
frapporre *vt.* to interpose. ♦ **frapporsi** *vr.* to interpose.
frasario *sm.* jargon.
frasca *sf.* 1. leafy branch 2. (*donna leggera*) coquette.
frascheggiare *vi.* 1. to rustle 2. (*civettare*) to flirt.
fraschetta *sf.* 1. twig 2. (*fig.*) frivolous girl.
frase *sf.* sentence.
fraseggiare *vi.* to phrase.
fraseologìa *sf.* phraseology.
fràssino *sm.* ash-tree.
frastagliare *vt.* to indent.
frastagliato *agg.* indented.
frastaglio *sm.* indentation.
frastornare *vt.* to disturb.
frastuono *sm.* noise, uproar, hubbub.
frate *sm.* 1. friar 2. (*come appellativo*) Brother.
fratellanza *sf.* brotherhood, fraternity.
fratellastro *sm.* half-brother.
fratello *sm.* brother || *fratelli siamesi*, Siamese twins.
fraternità *sf.* brotherhood, fraternity.
fraternizzare *vi.* to fraternize.
fraternizzazione *sf.* fraternization.
fraterno *agg.* brotherly.
fratricida *agg.* fratricidal. ♦ **fratricida** *s.* fratricide.
fratricidio *sm.* fratricide.
fratta *sf.* thicket.
frattaglie *sf. pl.* chitterlings.
frattanto *avv.* meantime, meanwhile.
frattempo (*nella loc. avv.*) *nel —*, in the meanwhile.
fratto *agg.* broken, crushed.
frattura *sf.* fracture.
fratturare *vt.* to fracture, to break (*v. irr.*). ♦ **fratturarsi** *vr.* to fracture, to break.
fraudolento *agg.* fraudulent.
fraudolenza *sf.* fraudulence.

frazionamento *sm.* division.
frazionare *vt.* to divide.
frazionario *agg.* fractional.
frazione *sf.* fraction.
freccia *sf.* arrow.
frecciata *sf.* (*fig.*) gibe.
freddare *vt.* 1. to cool 2. (*ammazzare*) to kill.
freddezza *sf.* coldness, coldheartedness.
freddo *agg.* cold. ♦ **freddo** *sm.* cold: *avere —*, to be cold; *tremare di —*, to shiver with cold.
freddoloso *agg.* sensitive to cold.
freddura *sf.* pun.
fregagione *sf.* massage.
fregare *vt.* 1. to rub 2. (*imbrogliare; volg.*) to swindle.
fregata[1] *sf.* rubbing.
fregata[2] *sf.* (*nave*) frigate.
fregatura *sf.* swindle.
fregiare *vt.* to decorate, to adorn.
fregio *sm.* 1. ornament 2. (*arch.*) frieze.
frego *sm.* stroke: *tirare un — su qc.*, to cross sthg. out.
frègola *sf.* heat.
fremente *agg.* quivering: *— d'ira*, fuming.
frèmere *vi.* to quiver, to tremble.
frèmito *sm.* quiver, thrill.
frenare *vt.* 1. to brake 2. (*trattenere*) to restrain.
frenata *sf.* braking.
frenesìa *sf.* 1. frenzy 2. (*desiderio sfrenato*) immoderate desire.
frenètico *agg.* 1. frantic 2. (*entusiastico*) enthusiastic.
freno *sm.* 1. brake || *bloccare i freni*, to jam the brakes; *togliere il —*, to release the brake 2. (*ritegno*) check restraint || *mordere il —*, to fret under restraint; *stringere i freni*, to shorten the reins 3. (*di cavallo*) bit.
frenologìa *sf.* phrenology.
frequentare *vt.* 1. to frequent 2. (*di scuola*) to attend 3. (*di luogo pubblico*) to patronize.
frequentato *agg.* 1. frequented 2. (*di scuola*) attended 3. (*di luogo pubblico*) patronized.
frequentatore *sm.* 1. frequenter 2. (*cliente assiduo*) regular customer.
frequente *agg.* frequent.
frequenza *sf.* 1. frequency 2. (*affluenza*) concourse 3. (*assiduità*) attendance.

fresa sf. milling machine.
fresatrice sf. milling machine.
freschezza sf. freshness (anche fig.), coolness.
fresco agg. 1. fresh 2. (di temperatura) cool.
frescura sf. coolness.
fretta sf. haste, hurry: avere —. to be in a hurry.
frettoloso agg. hurried.
freudiano agg. Freudian.
friàbile agg. crumbly.
friabilità sf. friability.
fricassea sf. fricassee.
frìggere vt. to fry || andare a farsi —, to go (v. irr.) to the devil.
friggitorìa sf. fried food shop.
frigidezza, frigidità sf. frigidity.
frìgido agg. frigid (anche fig.).
frignare vi. to whimper.
frigorìfero agg. refrigerant. ♦ **frigorìfero** sm. 1. refrigerator 2. (fam.) fridge.
fringuello sm. finch.
frittata sf. omelette.
frittella sf. pancake.
fritto agg. fried.
frittura sf. fry.
frivolezza sf. 1. frivolity 2. (cosa frivola) trifle.
frìvolo agg. frivolous.
frizionare vt. to rub, to massage.
frizione sf. 1. rub, rubbing, massage 2. (auto) clutch.
frizzante agg. 1. biting 2. (di bevanda) sparkling.
frizzare vi. 1. to tingle 2. (di bevanda) to sparkle.
frizzo sm. 1. witticism 2. (scherno) gibe.
frodare vt. to defraud.
frodatore sm. defrauder.
frode sf. fraud, swindle.
frodo sm. smuggling || cacciare di —, to poach; cacciatore di —, poacher.
frollare vt. to hang. ♦ **frollare** vi. to become (v. irr.) tender.
frollatura sf. hanging.
frollo agg. tender, high || pasta frolla, pastry.
fronda[1] sf. leafy branch.
fronda[2] sf. (rivolta) rebellion: vento di —, trouble brewing.
frondoso agg. leafy.
frontale agg. frontal.
fronte sf. 1. forehead: — ampia, sfuggente, broad, receding forehead 2. (arch.) front || di — a, in front

of; far — a, to face. ♦ **fronte** sm. 1. (mil.) front 2. (pol.) union.
fronteggiare vt. to face.
frontespizio sm. 1. (arch.) frontispiece 2. (di libro) title page.
frontiera sf. frontier, border.
frontone sm. 1. pediment 2. (di porta, finestra) gable.
frònzolo sm. frill || senza fronzoli, plain.
frotta sf. 1. crowd 2. (di animali) flock.
fròttola sf. fib.
frugacchiare vi. to rummage.
frugale agg. frugal.
frugalità sf. frugality.
frugare vi. to search, to rummage.
frùgolo sm. lively child.
fruire vi. to enjoy, to avail oneself of.
fruizione sf. fruition.
frullare vi. 1. to whip, to beat (v. irr.) up 2. (di ali) to whir.
frullato sm. — di frutta, fruit-shake.
frullatore sm. mill.
frullino sm. whisk.
frullìo sm. whirring.
frullo sm. whir.
frumento sm. wheat.
frusciare vi. to rustle.
fruscìo sm. rustle.
frusta sf. 1. whip 2. (cuc.) whisk.
frustare vt. to whip, to lash.
frustata sf. lash.
frustino sm. riding-whip.
frusto agg. worn-out, thread-bare.
frustrare vt. to frustrate.
frutta sf. fruit: — candita, candied fruit; — sciroppata, fruit in syrup; — cotta, compote.
fruttare vi. 1. to bear (v. irr.) fruit, to pay (v. irr.) 2. (comm.) to yield.
frutteto sm. orchard.
frutticultura sf. fruit-growing.
fruttiera sf. fruit-dish.
fruttifero agg. 1. fruitful 2. (econ.) interest-bearing: buono —, interest-bearing security.
fruttificare vi. to bear (v. irr.) fruit.
fruttivéndolo sm. greengrocer.
frutto sm. fruit || frutti di mare, edible mussels.
fruttuoso agg. fruitful, profitable.
fu agg. late.
fucilare vt. to shoot (v. irr.).
fucilata sf. shot.
fucilazione sf. shooting.

fucile sm. rifle, gun: — ad aria compressa, air-gun; — da caccia, shotgun; calcio del —, butt; canna del —, gun-barrel; caricare un —, to load a gun.

fucilerìa sf. 1. rifle fire 2. (insieme di fucili) musketry.

fuciliere sm. rifleman (pl. -men).

fucina sf. forge.

fucinare vt. to forge.

fuco sm. 1. drone 2. (bot.) fucus.

fucsia sf. fuchsia.

fuga sf. 1. flight, escape 2. (di innamorati) elopement 3. (falla, apertura) escape, leak 4. (mus.) fugue.

fugace agg. short-lived, transient.

fugacità sf. fugacity.

fugare vt. 1. to put (v. irr.) to flight, to disperse 2. (scacciare) to dispel.

fuggévole agg. flying, ephemeral.

fuggiasco agg. e sm. runaway.

fuggire vi. 1. to run (v. irr.) away, to flee (v. irr.) 2. (di innamorati) to elope. ♦ **fuggire** vt. to shun.

fuggitivo agg. e sm. fugitive.

fulcro sm. fulcrum (pl. -ra).

fùlgido agg. shining.

fulgore sm. brightness.

fulìggine sf. soot.

fuligginoso agg. sooty.

fulminante agg. fulminant. ♦ **fulminante** sm. 1. (chim.) fulminate 2. (di arma) primer.

fulminare vt. 1. to strike (v. irr.) by lightning 2. (colpire) to strike.

fulminato agg. 1. struck by lightning 2. (fig.) thunder-struck.

fùlmine sm. lightning.

fulmìneo agg. flashing.

fulvo agg. tawny.

fumaiolo sm. smoke-stack.

fumante agg. smoking, steaming.

fumare vt. e vi. to smoke.

fumarola sf. fumarole.

fumata sf. 1. smoke 2. (segnale) smoke signal.

fumatore sm. smoker.

fumetto sm. strip cartoon || giornali a fumetti, comics.

fumista s. stove-repairer.

fumo sm. 1. smoke || venditore di —, windbag; andare in —, to end in smoke 2. (vapore) fume (anche fig.) 3. (di pentole) steam.

fumògeno agg. smoke-producing.

fumoso agg. smoky.

funàmbolo sm. rope-dancer.

fune sf. 1. rope 2. (cavo) cable.

fùnebre agg. 1. funeral: canto —, dirge; carro —, hearse 2. (cupo) gloomy.

funerale sm. funeral || i funerali, the obsequies.

funerario agg. funerary.

funèreo agg. funereal.

funestare vt. to afflict.

funesto agg. baneful, woeful.

fungaia sf. mushroom-bed.

fùngere vi. to act (as).

fungo sm. mushroom.

funicolare sf. funicular.

funivìa sf. telpherage.

funzionale agg. functional.

funzionamento sm. working.

funzionare vi. 1. to act (as) 2. (andar bene) to work.

funzionario sm. official.

funzione sf. 1. function 2. (carica) office 3. (relig.) service.

fuochista sm. stoker.

fuoco sm. 1. fire 2. (cine; foto; mat.) focus: mettere a —, to focus.

fuorché cong. except, but.

fuori avv. 1. out, outdoors 2. (all'estero) abroad. ♦ **fuori (di)** prep. out of, outside.

fuoribordo sm. outboard motor.

fuoriclasse sm. first-rater.

fuorigioco sm., agg. e avv. off-side.

fuorilegge sm. outlaw.

fuoriserie agg. e sm. special body car.

fuoruscito sm. exile, refugee.

fuorviare vt. to lead (v. irr.) astray.

furberìa sf. cunning.

furbo agg. cunning, shrewd.

furente agg. furious, mad.

furerìa sf. orderly room.

furetto sm. ferret.

furfante sm. rascal, scamp.

furgoncino sm. small van.

furgone sm. van.

furia sf. fury: montare su tutte le furie, to fly (v. irr.) into a fury.

furibondo agg. furious.

furioso agg. 1. furious 2. (violento) violent.

furore sm. fury: far —, to be a hit.

furoreggiare vi. to be all the rage.

furtivo agg. stealthy.

furto sm. theft.

fuscello sm. 1. twig, straw 2. (fig.) thin person.

fusìbile sm. fuse.

fusione sf. 1. fusion 2. (di società comm.) merging.

fuso *sm.* spindle || — *orario*, time zone.
fusoliera *sf.* fuselage.
fustigare *vt.* to flog.
fusto *sm.* **1.** (*bot.*) stalk **2.** (*tronco umano*) trunk **3.** (*per benzina*) drum **4.** (*di legno per liquori*) barrel **5.** (*giovane prestante*) muscle-man (*pl.* -men) **6.** (*di colonna*) shaft.
fùtile *agg.* trifling.
futilità *sf.* trifle.
futurismo *sm.* futurism.
futurista *agg. e sm.* futurist.
futuro *agg. e sm.* future.

G

gabbamondo *sm.* swindler.
gabbare *vt.* to swindle.
gabbia *sf.* **1.** cage **2.** (*per imballaggio*) crate.
gabbiano *sm.* sea-gull.
gabellare *vt.* (*far credere*) to pass off as.
gabinetto *sm.* **1.** (*studio*) study **2.** (*pol.*) cabinet **3.** (*latrina*) water-closet, toilet.
gagà *sm.* dandy.
gagliardamente *avv.* vigorously.
gagliardetto *sm.* pennon.
gagliardo *agg.* vigorous.
gaglioffo *sm.* rascal.
gaiezza *sf.* **1.** cheerfulness **2.** (*di colore*) brightness.
gaio *agg.* **1.** cheerful **2.** (*di colore*) bright.
gala *sf.* **1.** (*trina*) frill **2.** (*festa*) gala: *abito di* —, gala dress.
galante *agg. e sm.* gallant || *lettera* —, love letter; *fare il* —, to flirt.
galanterìa *sf.* **1.** gallantry **2.** (*complimento*) compliment.
galantina *sf.* galantine.
galantuomo *sm.* honest man.
galassia *sf.* galaxy.
galateo *sm.* **1.** good manners (*pl.*) **2.** (*libro*) book of manners.
galena *sf.* galena.
galeone *sm.* galleon.
galeotto *sm.* **1.** convict **2.** (*mezzano*) pander **3.** (*mar.*) galley-slave.
galera *sf.* **1.** jail **2.** (*mar.*) galley.
galileo *agg. e sm.* Galilean.

galla[1] (*nella loc. avv.*) *a* —, afloat || *stare a* —, to float; *venire a* —, to come (*v. irr.*) to the surface; (*fig.*) to come to light.
galla[2] *sf.* (*bot.*) gall.
galleggiamento *sm.* floating: *linea di* —, water-line.
galleggiante *agg.* floating, afloat (*pred.*). ♦ **galleggiante** *sm.* **1.** float **2.** (*boa*) buoy.
galleggiare *vi.* to float.
gallerìa *sf.* **1.** tunnel **2.** (*d'arte, in teatro*) gallery.
gallese *agg.* Welsh. ♦ **gallese** *sm.* Welshman (*pl.* -men).
galletta *sf.* biscuit.
gallina *sf.* **1.** hen **2.** (*cibo*) chicken.
gallinàceo *agg. e sm.* gallinacean.
gallio *sm.* gallium.
gallismo *sm.* cocksure behaviour (towards women).
gallo *sm.* **1.** cock **2.** (*stor.*) Gaul.
gallonato *agg.* gallooned.
gallone *sm.* **1.** braid, galloon **2.** (*mil.*) chevron stripes (*pl.*) **3.** (*misura*) gallon.
galoppante *agg.* galloping.
galoppare *vi.* to gallop.
galoppata *sf.* gallop.
galoppatoio *sm.* riding-track.
galoppino *sm.* **1.** errand-boy **2.** (*tirapiedi*) drudge.
galoppo *sm.* gallop: *al* —, at a gallop, (*fig.*) at full speed; *andare al gran* —, to ride (*v. irr.*) full gallop.
galoscia *sf.* galosh.
galvànico *agg.* galvanic.
galvanizzare *vt.* **1.** to galvanize **2.** (*rivestire di metallo*) to electro-plate.
galvanizzazione *sf.* **1.** galvanization **2.** (*rivestitura di metallo*) electro-plating.
galvanoplàstica *sf.* galvanoplastics.
gamba *sf.* leg || *avere le gambe lunghe*, to be long-legged; *male in* —, down at heel; *in* — (*fig.*), smart.
gambale *sm.* **1.** legging **2.** (*di armatura*) jamb.
gamberetto *sm.* shrimp.
gàmbero *sm.* **1.** (*di mare*) lobster **2.** (*d'acqua dolce*) crayfish || *andare come un* —, to go (*v. irr.*) backwards.
gambo *sm.* stem.
gamma *sf.* range: — *di lunghezza d'onda*, waveband.

ganascia *sf.* jaw || *mangiare a quattro ganasce*, to eat (*v. irr.*) voraciously.

gancio *sm.* hook.

ganga *sf.* gang.

gànghero *sm.* hinge || *andare fuori dai gangheri*, to lose (*v. irr.*) one's temper.

ganglio *sm.* ganglion (*pl.* -ia).

gangsterismo *sm.* gangsterism.

ganimede *sm.* dandy.

gara *sf.* competition.

garagista *sm.* garage keeper.

garante *sm.* 1. warranter 2. (*per un imputato*) bail || *essere —*, to answer for.

garantire *vt.* 1. to warrant 2. (*farsi garante per*) to answer for 3. (*un imputato*) to go (*v. irr.*) bail for.

garanzìa *sf.* 1. warranty, guarantee 2. (*somma di —*) security 3. (*cauzione*) bail || *dare, non dare —*, to be reliable, unreliable; *a — di*, as a guarantee for.

garbare *vi.* to like.

garbatamente *avv.* politely.

garbatezza *sf.* politeness.

garbato *agg.* polite.

garbo *sm.* politeness || *con bel —*, with a good grace.

garbuglio *sm.* entanglement.

gardenia *sf.* gardenia.

gareggiare *vi.* to compete.

garganella (*nella loc. avv.*) *bere a —*, to gulp down.

gargarismo *sm.* gargle.

gargarizzare *vi.* to gargle.

garibaldino *agg. e sm.* Garibaldian.

garitta *sf.* 1. sentry-box 2. (*torretta*) look-out turret 3. (*di guardiano*) cabin.

garòfano *sm.* carnation || *chiodo di —*, clove.

garrese *sm.* withers (*pl.*).

garretto *sm.* 1. back of heel 2. (*di animale*) hock.

garrire *vi.* 1. (*di bandiere*) to flutter, to flap 2. (*di uccelli*) to chirp.

gàrrulo *agg.* talkative.

garza *sf.* gauze.

garzone *sm.* shop-boy, apprentice.

gas *sm.* gas.

gasolio *sm.* gas oil.

gasometro *sm.* gasholder.

gassare *vt.* to gas.

gassato *agg.* aerated || *acqua gassata*, soda-water.

gassista *sm.* gas-fitter.

gassògeno *sm.* gas producer.

gassoso *agg.* 1. gaseous 2. (*gassato*) aerated.

gàstrico *agg.* gastric.

gastrite *sf.* gastritis.

gastroenterite *sf.* gastroenteritis.

gastronomìa *sf.* gastronomy.

gastronòmico *agg.* gastronomic(al).

gatta *sf.* she-cat.

gattabuia *sf.* jail.

gatto *sm.* cat.

gattopardo *sm.* leopard.

gaudente *agg.* 1. jolly 2. (*dissipato*) fast. ♦ **gaudente** *sm.* fast person.

gàudio *sm.* joy.

gavetta *sf.* mess-tin.

gavitello *sm.* buoy.

gazza *sf.* magpie.

gazzarra *sf.* din.

gazzella *sf.* gazelle.

gazzetta *sf.* gazette.

gelare *vt. e vi.* to freeze (*v. irr.*).

gelata *sf.* frost.

gelataio *sm.* ice-cream vendor.

gelaterìa *sf.* ice-cream shop.

gelatina *sf.* 1. (*cuc.*) jelly 2. (*chim.*) gelatine.

gelatinoso *agg.* gelatinous.

gelato *agg.* frozen, icy. ♦ **gelato** *sm.* ice-cream.

gèlido *agg.* icy (*anche fig.*).

gelo *sm.* 1. intense cold 2. (*fig.*) chill 3. (*ghiaccio*) ice 4. (*brina*) frost.

gelone *sm.* chilblain.

gelosìa *sf.* 1. jealousy 2. (*cura*) care 3. (*persiana*) shutter.

geloso *agg.* jealous.

gelso *sm.* mulberry(-tree).

gelsomino *sm.* jasmine.

gemebondo *agg.* groaning.

gemelli *sm. pl.* (*di polsino*) cuff-links.

gemello *agg. e sm.* twin.

gèmere *vi.* to groan.

gèmito *sm.* groan.

gemma *sf.* 1. gem 2. (*bot.*) bud.

gemmare *vi.* (*bot.*) to bud.

gendarme *sm.* policeman (*pl.* -men).

gendarmerìa *sf.* 1. police-force 2. (*caserma*) police-station.

genealogìa *sf.* genealogy.

genealògico *agg.* genealogical.

generàbile *agg.* generable.

generale[1] *agg.* general || *quartier —*, headquarters (*pl.*).

generale² *sm.* general.
generalità *sf.* generality || *dare le proprie —*, to give (*v. irr.*) one's particulars.
generalizzare *vt.* to generalize.
generalizzazione *sf.* generalization.
generare *vt.* **1.** to beget (*v. irr.*) **2.** (*produrre, anche tec.*) to produce. ◆ **generarsi** *vr.* to be born.
generatore *agg.* generative. ◆ **generatore** *sm.* generator.
generazione *sf.* generation.
gènere *sm.* **1.** kind **2.** (*gramm.*) gender **3.** (*letterario*) genre **4.** (*prodotto*) product || *generi alimentari*, foodstuffs; *generi di prima necessità*, commodities.
genèrico *agg.* generic, vague.
gènero *sm.* son-in-law.
generosità *sf.* generosity.
generoso *agg.* generous.
gènesi *sf.* genesis (*pl.* -ses).
genètica *sf.* genetics.
genètico *agg.* genetic.
genetlìaco *sm.* birthday.
gengiva *sf.* gum.
genìa *sf.* **1.** race **2.** (*spreg.*) tribe.
geniale *agg.* clever.
genialità *sf.* **1.** cleverness **2.** (*genio*) genius.
genio *sm.* genius || *andare a —*, to please.
genitale *agg. e sm.* genital.
genitivo *sm.* genitive.
genitore *sm.* **1.** parent **2.** (*padre*) father.
genitrice *sf.* mother.
gennaio *sm.* January.
genocidio *sm.* genocide.
gentaglia *sf.* rabble.
gente *sf.* people: *c'è molta —*, there are a lot of people; *le genti dell'Asia*, the peoples of Asia.
gentildonna *sf.* lady.
gentile *agg.* **1.** kind **2.** (*cortese*) polite || *è — da parte sua*, it is kind of him.
gentilezza *sf.* **1.** kindness **2.** (*cortesia*) politeness **3.** (*favore*) favour.
gentilizio *agg.* noble: *stemma —*, coat of arms.
gentiluomo *sm.* gentleman (*pl.* -men).
genuflessione *sf.* genuflection.
genuflèttersi *vr.* to kneel down.
genuinità *sf.* genuineness.
genuino *agg.* genuine.
genziana *sf.* gentian.
geodesìa *sf.* geodesy.

geofìsica *sf.* geophysics.
geografìa *sf.* geography.
geogràfico *agg.* geographic(al) || *carta geografica*, map.
geògrafo *sm.* geographer.
geologìa *sf.* geology.
geològico *agg.* geologic(al).
geòlogo *sm.* geologist.
geòmetra *sm.* **1.** geometer **2.** (*agrimensore*) land-surveyor.
geometrìa *sf.* geometry.
geomètrico *agg.* geometric(al).
geopolìtica *sf.* geopolitics.
geòrgico *agg.* georgic.
geranio *sm.* geranium.
gerarca *sm.* leader.
gerarchìa *sf.* hierarchy.
gerente *sm.* manager.
gerenza *sf.* management.
gergo *sm.* **1.** slang **2.** (*di una classe professionale*) jargon.
germànico *agg.* Germanic.
germanio *sm.* germanium.
germanismo *sm.* Germanism.
germanista *s.* Germanist.
germanìstica *sf.* Germanic studies.
germano¹ *agg. e sm.* German.
germano² *agg.* german: *fratello —*, brother-german.
germe *sm.* germ.
germicida *agg.* germicidal. ◆ **germicida** *sm.* germicide.
germinare *vi.* V. *germogliare.*
germinazione *sf.* germination.
germogliare *vi.* **1.** to sprout **2.** (*fig.*) to spring (*v. irr.*) (up).
germoglio *sm.* germ.
geroglìfico *sm.* hieroglyphic.
gerontologìa *sf.* gerontology.
gerundio *sm.* gerund.
gessetto *sm.* chalk.
gesso *sm.* **1.** chalk **2.** (*med.; scult.; edil.*) plaster.
gesta *sf. pl.* deeds.
gestante *sf.* pregnant woman.
gestazione *sf.* gestation.
gesticolare *vi.* to gesticulate.
gestione *sf.* management.
gestire¹ *vt.* to manage.
gestire² *vi.* to gesture.
gesto *sm.* gesture || *un bel —*, a noble deed.
gestore *sm.* manager.
gesuita *sm.* Jesuit.
gesuìtico *agg.* Jesuitic(al).
gettare *vt.* **1.** to throw (*v. irr.*), (*anche metal.; edil.*) to cast (*v. irr.*) **2.** (*bot.*) to sprout **3.** (*fruttare*) to yield || *— le fondamenta,*

to lay (v. irr.) the foundations; — un grido, to utter a cry. ♦ gettarsi vr. (di fiume) to flow.

gettata sf. 1. throw 2. (edil.; metal.) cast 3. (di arma) range 4. (molo) jetty.

gèttito sm. (delle imposte) yield.

getto sm. 1. throw 2. (mecc.; di liquidi) jet 3. (bot.) sprout 4. (metal.; edil.) casting || di —, effortlessly; a — continuo, continuously.

gettone sm. 1. counter: — telefonico, telephone counter 2. (contromarca) check || macchina a —, slot-machine.

geyser sm. geyser.

gheriglio sm. kernel.

gherminella sf. trick: fare una —, to play a trick (on).

ghermire vt. to clutch.

ghette sf. pl. spats.

ghetto sm. 1. ghetto 2. (insieme degli ebrei) Jewry.

ghiacciaia sf. 1. ice-box 2. (stanza) ice-house.

ghiacciaio sm. glacier.

ghiacciare vi e vt. to freeze (v. irr.).

ghiacciato agg. 1. frozen 2. (molto freddo) icy.

ghiaccio sm. ice.

ghiacciolo sm. icicle.

ghiaia sf. gravel.

ghiaioso agg. gravelly.

ghianda sf. acorn.

ghiàndola sf. gland.

ghibellino agg. e sm. Ghibelline.

ghigliottina sf. guillotine.

ghigliottinare vt. to guillotine.

ghignare vi. to grin.

ghigno sm. grin.

ghìngheri (nella loc. avv.) mettersi in —, to dress up.

ghiotto agg. 1. greedy 2. (appetitoso) dainty.

ghiottone sm. glutton.

ghiottonerìa sf. 1. gluttony 2. (cibo prelibato) dainty.

ghiribizzo sm. whim.

ghirigoro sm. doodle.

ghirlanda sf. wreath.

ghiro sm. dormouse (pl. dormice) || dormire come un —, to sleep (v. irr.) like a log.

ghisa sf. cast iron.

già avv. 1. already 2. (un tempo) once 3. (certamente) of course.

giacca sf. coat, jacket.

giacché cong. as, since.

giacente agg. 1. lying 2. (di capitale) uninvested 3. (di posta) unclaimed.

giacenza sf. lying || capitale in —, uninvested capital; lettera in —, unclaimed letter; merci in —, goods in stock.

giacere vi. to lie (v. irr.).

giaciglio sm. couch.

giacimento sm. (min.) deposit: — di petrolio, oil-field.

giacinto sm. hyacinth.

giacobino sm. e agg. Jacobin.

giada sf. jade.

giaggiolo sm. iris.

giaguaro sm. jaguar.

giallastro agg. yellowish.

giallo agg. yellow || romanzo, film, dramma —, thriller.

giammai avv. never.

giansenismo sm. Jansenism.

giansenista s. Jansenist.

giapponese agg. e sm. Japanese (invariato al pl.).

giara sf. jar.

giardinaggio sm. gardening.

giardinetta sf. station wagon.

giardiniere sm. gardener.

giardino sm. garden || — d'infanzia, nursery-school.

giarrettiera sf. garter.

giavellotto sm. javelin: lancio del —, javelin throwing.

gibbosità sf. hump.

giberna sf. cartridge-pouch.

gigante sm. giant || fare passi da —, to make (v. irr.) rapid progress.

giganteggiare vi. to tower.

gigantesco agg. gigantic.

gigantismo sm. giantism.

gigione sm. ham.

giglio sm. lily.

gilè sm. waistcoat.

gincana sf. gymkhana.

gineceo sm. gynaeceum (pl. -ea).

ginecologìa sf. gynaecology.

ginecològico agg. gynaecological.

ginecòlogo sm. gynaecologist.

ginepraio sm. 1. juniper thicket 2. (fig.) fix: ficcarsi in un —, to get (v. irr.) into a scrape.

ginepro sm. juniper.

ginestra sf. broom.

gingillarsi vr. to dawdle.

gingillo sm. 1. knick-knack 2. (balocco) plaything.

ginnasio sm. 1. grammar school 2.

(*in Italia e stor.*) gymnasium (*pl.* -ia).

ginnasta *sm.* athlete.

ginnàstica *sf.* gymnastics.

gìnnico *agg.* gymnastic, athletic.

ginocchiata *sf.* blow with the knee.

ginocchiera *sf.* **1.** knee-guard **2.** (*mecc.*) toggle.

ginocchio *sm.* **1.** knee: *in* —, on one's knees **2.** (*mecc.*) bend.

ginocchioni *avv.* on one's knees.

giocare *vi.* **1.** to play **2.** (*d'azzardo*) to gamble **3.** (*scommettere*) to bet (*v. irr.*) **4.** (*in borsa*) to speculate. ♦ **giocare** *vt.* **1.** to play **2.** (*ingannare*) to deceive. ♦ **giocarsi** *vr.* (*beffarsi*) to trifle (with).

giocata *sf.* **1.** game **2.** (*puntata*) stake.

giocatore *sm.* **1.** player **2.** (*d'azzardo*) gambler **3.** (*in borsa*) stock-jobber.

giocàttolo *sm.* toy.

giocherellare *vi.* to toy.

gioco *sm.* **1.** play **2.** (*regolato da norme*) game **3.** (*d'azzardo*) gambling **4.** (*scherzo*) joke || *per* —, for fun; — *di pazienza*, puzzle; — *di parole*, pun; *essere in* —, to be involved.

giocoforza *sm.* necessary: *è* —, it is absolutely necessary.

giocoliere *sm.* juggler.

giocondità *sf.* gaiety.

giocondo *agg.* gay.

giocosità *sf.* playfulness.

giocoso *agg.* playful.

giogaia *sf.* mountain range.

giogo *sm.* **1.** yoke **2.** (*di monte*) summit.

gioia *sf.* **1.** joy **2.** (*gioiello*) jewel.

gioiellerìa *sf.* **1.** jewelry **2.** (*negozio*) jeweller's shop.

gioielliere *sm.* jeweller

gioiello *sm.* jewel

gioioso *agg.* joyful.

gioire *vi.* to rejoice (at).

giornalaio *sm.* newsman (*pl.* -men).

giornale *sm.* **1.** newspaper **2.** (*comm.*) journal || — *radio*, news bulletin; *cine* —, news-reel.

giornaliero *agg.* daily.

giornalismo *sm.* **1.** journalism **2.** (*la stampa*) press.

giornalista *s.* journalist, reporter.

giornalìstico *agg.* journalistic || *ambiente* —, press.

giornalmente *avv.* daily.

giornata *sf.* day: *lavorare a* —, to work by the day || *donna a* —, charwoman (*pl.* -women).

giorno *sm.* day: *di* —, by day; *a giorni*, in a few days' time; *due volte al* —, twice a day; *un* — (*avv.*), one day || — *festivo*, holiday.

giovamento *sm.* benefit || *trarre* — *da*, to benefit by.

giòvane *agg.* young. ♦ **giòvane** *sm.* young man (*pl.* -men). ♦ **giòvane** *sf.* young woman (*pl.* women).

giovanetta *sf.* girl.

giovanetto *sm.* boy.

giovanile *agg.* **1.** juvenile **2.** (*da giovane*) youthful.

giovanotto *sm.* young man (*pl.* men).

giovare *vi.* to be of use. ♦ **giovare** *vt.* to be good (for). ♦ **giovarsi** *vr.* to benefit (by).

giovedì *sm.* Thursday.

giovenca *sf.* heifer.

gioventù *sf.* youth.

gioviale *agg.* jolly.

giovialità *sf.* jollity.

giovinastro *sm.* hooligan.

giovincello *sm.* lad.

giovinezza *sf.* youth.

giràbile *agg.* endorsable.

giradischi *sm.* record player.

giradito *sm.* whitlow.

giraffa *sf.* giraffe.

giramento *sm.* turning: — *di capo*, giddiness; *avere un* —, to feel (*v. irr.*) giddy.

giramondo *sm.* **1.** wanderer **2.** (*turista*) globe-trotter.

giràndola *sf.* **1.** (*fuoco d'artificio*) Catherine-wheel **2.** (*fig.*) fickle person.

girandolare *vi.* to saunter.

girandolone *sm.* saunterer.

girante *sm.* **1.** (*comm.*) endorser **2.** (*mecc.*) impeller (*di pompa*), wheel (*di turbina*).

girare *vi. e vt.* **1.** to turn **2.** (*evitare*) to avoid **3.** (*viaggiare*) to tour **4.** (*vagare*) to stroll **5.** (*comm.*) to endorse **6.** (*riprendere un film*) to shoot (*v. irr.*). ♦ **girarsi** *vr.* to turn.

girarrosto *sm.* spit.

girasole *sm.* sunflower.

girata *sf.* **1.** turn **2.** (*comm.*) endorsement.

giratario *sm.* (*comm.*) endorsee.

giravolta *sf.* **1.** turning **2.** (*fig.*) shift || *fare una —*, to turn round.

girello *sm.* **1.** (*per bambini*) go-cart **2.** (*parte di bue*) rump.

giretto *sm.* stroll: *fare un —*, to take (*v. irr.*) a short walk.

girévole *agg.* revolving.

girino *sm.* tadpole.

giro *sm.* **1.** turn **2.** (*viaggio*) tour **3.** (*passeggiata*) stroll **4.** (*percorso*) round || *a — di posta*, by return of post; *— d'affari*, turnover; *nel — di pochi giorni*, in a few days' time; *fare un — in auto*, to go (*v. irr.*) for a drive in a car; *fare un — in bicicletta*, to take (*v. irr.*) a ride on a bicycle.

girondino *agg. e sm.* Girondist

gironzolare *vi.* to stroll.

giroscopio *sm.* gyroscope.

girotondo *sm.* round dance.

girovagare *vi.* to wander.

giròvago *agg.* wandering. ♦ **giròvago** *sm.* tramp || *venditore —*, pedlar.

gita *sf.* trip: *fare una —*, to take (*v. irr.*) a trip.

gitano *sm.* Spanish gipsy.

gitante *s.* tripper.

giù *avv.* **1.** down **2.** (*dabbasso*) downstairs || *— per*, down; *su per —*, approximately.

giubba *sf.* coat.

giubbetto *sm.* **1.** jacket **2.** (*da donna*) bodice.

giubbotto *sm.* (heavy) coat.

giubilare *vi.* to exult.

giubileo *sm.* jubilee.

giùbilo *sm.* rejoicing.

giudàico *agg.* Judaic.

giudaismo *sm.* Judaism.

giudeo *agg.* Jewish. ♦ **giudeo** *sm.* Jew. ♦ **giudea** *sf.* Jewess.

giudicare *vt.* **1.** to judge **2.** (*pensare*) to think (*v. irr.*).

giùdice *sm.* judge || *i giudici*, the Bench.

giudiziario *agg.* judicial.

giudizio *sm.* **1.** judgement **2.** (*causa*) trial **3.** (*sentenza*) sentence **4.** (*buon senso*) common sense || *far —*, to behave oneself; *rinviare a —*, to commit for trial.

giudizioso *agg.* sensible.

giùggiola *sf.* jujube || *andare in brodo di giuggiole*, to be extremely pleased.

giuggiolone *sm.* simpleton.

giugno *sm.* June.

giugulare *agg.* jugular.

giuliano *agg.* Julian.

giulivo *agg.* cheerful.

giullare *sm.* jester.

giumenta *sf.* (*cavalla*) mare.

giunca *sf.* junk.

giunco *sm.* reed.

giùngere *vi.* **1.** to arrive (at), to reach (sthg.) **2.** (*riuscire*) to succeed (in). ♦ **giùngere** *vt.* (*congiungere*) to join.

giungla *sf.* jungle.

giunta[1] *sf.* **1.** addition: *per —*, in addition **2.** (*di peso*) make-weight.

giunta[2] *sf.* *— comunale*, town council.

giunto *sm.* (*mecc.*) joint.

giuntura *sf.* juncture.

giunzione *sf.* **1.** connection **2.** (*giunto*) joint || *fare una —*, to joint.

giuramento *sm.* oath: *sotto —*, on oath.

giurare *vt.* to swear (*v. irr.*).

giurato *sm.* juryman (*pl.* -men) || *i giurati*, the jury (*sing.*).

giuria *sf.* jury.

giurìdico *agg.* juridical: *stato —*, legal status.

giurisdizione *sf.* jurisdiction.

giurisprudenza *sf.* law.

giurista *sm.* jurist.

giustezza *sf.* **1.** exactness **2.** (*tip.*) measure.

giustificàbile *agg.* justifiable.

giustificare *vt.* to justify.

giustificazione *sf.* justification.

giustizia *sf.* justice.

giustiziare *vt.* to execute.

giustiziato *sm.* executed man.

giustiziere *sm.* **1.** executioner **2.** (*vendicatore*) avenger.

giusto *agg.* **1.** just **2.** (*esatto*) right **3.** (*legittimo*) legitimate.

glabro *agg.* hairless.

glaciale *agg.* icy: *regione —*, ice region.

glaciazione *sf.* glaciation.

gladiatore *sm.* gladiator.

gladiolo *sm.* gladiolus.

glande *sm.* glans (*pl.* -ndes).

glàndola *sf.* V. *ghiandola*.

glandolare *agg.* glandular.

glassare *vt.* **1.** (*con zucchero*) to ice **2.** (*con gelatina*) to glaze.

glàuco *agg.* glaucous.

glaucoma *sm.* glaucoma.

gleba *sf.* clod || *servo della —*, serf.

gli¹ *art.* **1.** the **2.** (*in senso generico non si traduce*): — *stranieri amano l'Italia*, foreigners love Italy **3.** (*si traduce col possessivo coi capi di vestiario ecc.*): *si tolse* — *occhiali*, he took off his glasses.

gli² *pron.* **1.** (*per persona*) him, to him **2.** (*per cosa*) it, to it || — *mandai un libro*, I sent him a book, I sent a book to him.

glicerina *sf.* glycerine.

glicine *sm.* wisteria.

glicògeno *sm.* glycogen.

glielo *pron.* it (to) him; it (to) her; him to him; him to her; it to it.

globale *agg.* total.

globo *sm.* globe.

globulare *agg.* globular.

glòbulo *sm.* (*biol.*) corpuscle.

gloria *sf.* glory.

gloriarsi *vr.* to glory (in).

glorificare *vt.* to glorify.

glorificazione *sf.* glorification.

glorioso *agg.* glorious.

glossa *sf.* gloss.

glossario *sm.* glossary.

glòttide *sf.* glottis.

glottologìa *sf.* glottology.

glottològico *agg.* glottological.

glottòlogo *sm.* glottologist.

glucosio *sm.* glucose.

glùteo *sm.* gluteus (*pl.* -ei).

glutinato *sm.* gluten (*attr.*).

glùtine *sm.* gluten.

gnomo *sm.* gnome.

gnosticismo *sm.* gnosticism.

gnòstico *agg.* e *sm.* gnostic.

gobba *sf.* **1.** hump (*anche fig.*) **2.** (*donna* —) humpbacked woman.

gobbo *agg.* **1.** humpbacked **2.** (*curvo*) bent. ♦ **gobbo** *sm.* humpback.

goccia *sf.* **goccio** *sm.* drop.

gocciolare *vi.* e *vt.* to drip.

gocciolìo *sm.* dripping.

godere *vi.* e *vt.* to enjoy || *godersela*, to have a good time.

godereccio *agg.* **1.** (*amante dei godimenti*) pleasure-loving **2.** (*che dà godimento*) pleasant.

godimento *sm.* enjoyment.

goffàggine *sf.* **1.** clumsiness **2.** (*atto goffo*) clumsy action.

goffo *agg.* clumsy.

gogna *sf.* pillory: *mettere alla* —, to pillory.

ɜola *sf.* **1.** throat: *aver mal di* —, to have a sorethroat **2.** (*golosità*) gluttony: *far* —, to tempt **3.** (*geogr.*) gorge.

goletta *sf.* (*mar.*) schooner.

golf *sm.* **1.** jersey **2.** (*gioco*) golf.

golfo *sm.* gulf.

goliàrdico *agg.* of students.

goliardo *sm.* university student.

golosità *sf.* **1.** greediness **2.** (*cibo prelibato*) dainty.

goloso *agg.* greedy. ♦ **goloso** *sm.* glutton.

gòmena *sf.* rope.

gomitata *sf.* nudge || *farsi avanti a gomitate*, to elbow one's way.

gòmito *sm.* **1.** elbow **2.** (*di strada*) sharp bend || — *a* —, side by side.

gomìtolo *sm.* clew.

gomma *sf.* **1.** rubber **2.** (*sostanza resinosa*) gum **3.** (*pneumatico*) tyre.

gommapiuma *sf.* foam rubber.

gòndola *sf.* gondola.

gonfalone *sm.* standard.

gonfiare *vt.* **1.** to swell (*v. irr.*) **2.** (*esagerare*) to exaggerate. ♦ **gonfiarsi** *vr.* to swell (*anche fig.*).

gonfiatura *sf.* **1.** swelling **2.** (*esagerazione*) exaggeration.

gonfio *agg.* **1.** swollen **2.** (*di stile*) bombastic.

gonfiore *sm.* swelling.

gong *sm.* gong.

gongolante *agg.* rejoicing (at).

gongolare *vi.* to rejoice (at).

goniòmetro *sm.* goniometer.

gonna *sf.* **1.** skirt **2.** (*di costume storico anche maschile*) gown.

gonnellino *sm.* — *scozzese*, kilt.

gonzo *sm.* blockhead.

gorgheggiare *vi.* to trill.

gorgheggio *sm.* trill.

gorgo *sm.* whirlpool.

gorgogliare *vi.* to gurgle.

gorgoglio *sm.* gurgling.

gorilla *sm.* gorilla.

gota *sf.* cheek.

gòtico *agg.* Gothic.

gotta *sf.* gout.

governàbile *agg.* governable.

governante *sm.* **1.** ruler **2.** (*statista*) statesman (*pl.* -men). ♦ **governante** *sf.* **1.** housekeeper **2.** (*bambinaia*) nurse.

governare *vt.* **1.** to govern, to rule **2.** (*badare a*) to look after **3.** (*mar.*) to steer.

governativo *agg.* government (*attributivo*).

governatore *sm.* governor.

governo *sm.* **1.** government **2.** (*dominio*) rule **3.** (*comm.*) management **4.** (*mar.*) steerage || — *della*

casa, housekeeping.
gozzo *sm.* **1.** goitre **2.** (*di uccello*) crop.
gozzoviglia *sf.* revelry.
gozzovigliare *vi.* to revel.
gozzuto *agg.* goitrous.
gracchiare *vi.* to croak.
gracidare *vi.* to croak.
gracidìo *sm.* croaking.
gràcile *agg.* frail.
gracilità *sf.* frailty.
gradassata *sf.* boastfulness, brag.
gradasso *sm.* boaster, braggart.
gradatamente *avv.* gradually.
gradazione *sf.* **1.** gradation **2.** (*sfumatura*) shade.
gradévole *agg.* agreeable.
gradimento *sm.* **1.** pleasure **2.** satisfaction **3.** (*approvazione*) approval.
gradinata *sf.* **1.** flight of steps **2.** (*negli stadi*) tiers of seats.
gradino *sm.* **1.** step **2.** (*di stadio*) stage.
gradire *vt.* **1.** to like **2.** (*accettare*) to accept.
gradito *agg.* **1.** (*piacevole*) pleasant **2.** (*ben accetto*) welcome.
grado *sm.* **1.** degree **2.** (*mil.*) rank || *essere in* —, to be able; *di buon* —, willingly.
graduale *agg.* gradual.
gradualità *sf.* graduality.
graduare *vt.* to graduate.
graduato *agg.* **1.** graded **2.** (*di strumento*) graduated. ♦ **graduato** *sm.* non-commissioned officer.
graduatoria *sf.* **1.** classification **2.** (*sport*) position.
graduazione *sf.* graduation.
graffa *sf.* clip.
graffiare *vt.* to scratch.
graffiatura *sf.* scratch.
graffio *sm.* scratch.
graffito *sm.* graffito (*pl.* -ti).
grafia *sf.* **1.** writing **2.** (*ortografia*) spelling.
gràfico *agg.* graphic. ♦ **gràfico** *sm.* graph.
grafite *sf.* graphite.
grafologìa *sf.* graphology.
grafòlogo *sm.* graphologist.
grafòmane *s.* graphomaniac.
grafomanìa *sf.* graphomania.
gragnuola *sf.* **1.** hail **2.** (*fig.*) shower.
gramaglie *sf. pl.* mourning (*sing.*): *mettersi in* —, to go (*v. irr.*) into mourning.

gramigna *sf.* couch-grass.
graminàcee *sf. pl.* Gramineae.
grammàtica *sf.* grammar.
grammaticale *agg.* grammatical.
grammàtico *sm.* grammarian.
grammo *sm.* gram.
grammòfono *sm.* gramophone.
gramo *agg.* **1.** miserable **2.** (*scarso*) scanty.
grana *sf.* **1.** grain **2.** (*noia*) trouble **3.** (*denaro*) dough.
granaglie *sf. pl.* corn (*sing.*).
granaio *sm.* barn.
granata[1] *sf.* (*scopa*) broom.
granata[2] *sf.* (*mil.*) grenade.
granatiere *sm.* grenadier.
granatina *sf.* grenadine.
granato *agg.* **1.** garnet red **2.** (*fatto a grani*) grainy.
grancassa *sf.* big drum.
granchio *sm.* crab || *prendere un* —, to make (*v. irr.*) a blunder.
grande *agg.* **1.** great **2.** (*esteso*) large **3.** (*grosso*) big **4.** (*alto*) high; (*di statura*) tall **5.** (*adulto*) grownup.
grandeggiare *vi.* **1.** to tower **2.** (*ostentare*) to show (*v. irr.*) off.
grandezza *sf.* **1.** greatness **2.** (*dimensione*) size **3.** (*estensione*) largeness **4.** (*grandiosità*) grandeur **5.** (*liberalità*) liberality **6.** (*mat.*) quantity.
grandiloquenza *sf.* magniloquence.
grandinare *vi.* to hail (*anche fig.*).
grandinata *sf.* hail-storm.
gràndine *sf.* hail.
grandiosità *sf.* grandeur.
grandioso *agg.* grand.
granduca *sm.* Grand Duke.
granducato *sm.* Grand Duchy.
granduchessa *sf.* Grand Duchess.
granello *sm.* grain.
granita *sf.* grated-ice drink.
granìtico *agg.* granitic.
granito *sm.* granite.
granìvoro *agg.* granivorous.
grano *sm.* **1.** grain **2.** (*frumento*) wheat **3.** (*ogni cereale*) corn.
granturco *sm.* maize.
granulare *agg.* granular.
granuloma *sm.* granuloma.
granuloso *agg.* granulose.
grappa[1] *sf.* (*per unire blocchi di legno ecc.*) cramp.
grappa[2] *sf.* (*liquore*) "grappa".
gràppolo *sm.* cluster.
grassaggio *sm.* greasing.
grassatore *sm.* robber.

grassazione *sf.* robbery.
grassetto *sm.* (*tip.*) heavytype.
grassezza *sf.* fatness.
grasso *agg.* fat. ♦ **grasso** *sm.* **1.** fat **2.** (*lubrificante*) grease.
grassoccio *agg.* plump.
grata *sf.* grating.
graticciata *sf.* trellis-work.
graticola *sf.* **1.** grill **2.** (*di forno*) grate.
graticolato *sm.* **1.** trellis **2.** (*inferriata*) grating.
gratifica *sf.* bonus.
gratificare *vt.* to gratify.
gratificazione *sf.* gratuity.
gratis *avv.* free.
gratitùdine *sf.* gratitude.
grato *agg.* **1.** grateful **2.** (*gradito*) welcome **3.** (*piacevole*) pleasant.
grattacapo *sm.* trouble.
grattacielo *sm.* skyscraper.
grattare *vt.* **1.** to scratch **2.** (*grattugiare*) to grate.
grattugia *sf.* grater.
grattugiare *vt.* to grate.
gratùito *agg.* **1.** free **2.** (*ingiustificato*) gratuitous.
gravame *sm.* **1.** burden **2.** (*ipoteca*) mortgage.
gravare *vi.* to weigh. ♦ **gravare** *vt.* to burden.
grave *agg.* **1.** grave **2.** (*pesante*) heavy **3.** (*importante, pericoloso*) serious.
gravezza *sf.* **1.** (*pesantezza*) heaviness **2.** (*serietà*) gravity **3.** (*stanchezza*) weariness.
gravidanza *sf.* pregnancy.
gràvido *agg.* **1.** (*di femmina*) pregnant **2.** (*fig.*) fraught (with).
gravità *sf.* **1.** gravity **2.** (*severità*) severity.
gravitare *vi.* to gravitate.
gravitazionale *agg.* gravitational.
gravitazione *sf.* gravitation.
gravosità *sf.* heaviness.
gravoso *agg.* heavy.
grazia *sf.* **1.** grace **2.** (*favore*) favour **3.** (*clemenza*) mercy **4.** (*teol.*) grace **5.** *Sua, Vostra Grazia*, His, Her, Your Grace ‖ *in — di*, owing to.
graziare *vt.* to pardon.
grazie *inter.* thank you!, thanks! *— tante,* many thanks!
grazioso *agg.* pretty, graceful.
greca *sf.* **1.** (*disegno*) Greek fret **2.** (*mil.*) zig-zag braid.
grecale *sm.* north-east wind.

grecismo *sm.* Hellenism.
grecista *s.* Hellenist.
greco *agg.* e *sm.* Greek.
greco-romano *agg.* Graeco-Roman.
gregario *sm.* **1.** follower **2.** (*aiutante*) helper.
gregge *sm.* flock.
greggio *agg.* **1.** raw **2.** (*di tessuto*) unbleached **3.** (*di metallo e fig.*) unrefined.
gregoriano *agg.* Gregorian.
grembiale, grembiule *sm.* apron.
grembo *sm.* **1.** lap **2.** (*ventre materno*) womb **3.** (*fig.*) bosom.
gremire *vt.* to fill.
gremito *agg.* filled (with).
greppia *sf.* crib.
gres *sm.* stoneware.
greto *sm.* **1.** (*di fiume*) gravel bank **2.** (*di mare*) shingly shore.
grettezza *sf.* meanness.
gretto *agg.* mean, narrow-minded.
greve *agg.* heavy.
grezzo *agg.* V. greggio.
gridare *vt.* e *vi.* **1.** to cry **2.** (*gridare forte, protestare*) to cry out: *gridò per il dolore,* he cried out with pain.
grido *sm.* cry ‖ *di —,* famous.
grifagno *agg.* **1.** rapacious **2.** (*fig.*) fierce.
grifo *sm.* snout.
grifone *sm.* griffin.
grigiastro *agg.* greyish.
grigio *agg.* grey: *— perla,* pearl grey.
grigiore *sm.* greyness.
griglia *sf.* **1.** (*di finestra*) shutter **2.** (*di forno*) grate **3.** (*grata, graticola*) grill ‖ *cuocere alla —,* to grill.
grilletto *sm.* trigger.
grillo *sm.* **1.** cricket **2.** (*fig.*) fancy.
grillotalpa *sm.* mole-cricket.
grimaldello *sm.* picklock.
grinfia *sf.* clutch.
grinta *sf.* grim face.
grinza *sf.* **1.** (*di pelle*) wrinkle **2.** (*di stoffa*) crease ‖ (*fig.*) *non fa una —,* it is quite correct.
grinzoso *agg.* **1.** (*di pelle*) wrinkly **2.** (*di stoffa*) creasy.
grisù *sm.* fire-damp.
gronda *sf.* eaves (*pl.*).
grondaia *sf.* **1.** gutter **2.** (*tubo di discesa*) gutter pipe.
grondante *agg.* dripping.
grondare *vi.* to drip ‖ *— sangue,* to bleed (*v. irr.*).
groppa *sf.* back.

groppo *sm.* knot: *avere un — in gola*, to have a lump in one's throat.

groppone *sm.* back: *piegare il —*, to submit.

grossa *sf. dormire della —*, to sleep (*v. irr.*) soundly.

grossezza *sf.* **1.** bigness **2.** (*dimensione*) size **3.** (*spessore*) thickness.

grossista *s.* wholesaler.

grosso *agg.* **1.** (*anche fig.*) big **2.** (*denso*) thick.

grossolanità *sf.* coarseness.

grossolano *agg.* coarse: *errore —*, blunder.

grotta *sf.* cave.

grottesco *agg.* grotesque.

groviera *sf.* gruyère.

groviglio *sm.* tangle.

gru *sf.* (*zool.; mecc.*) crane.

gruccia *sf.* **1.** crutch **2.** (*per abiti*) dress-hanger **3.** (*per uccelli*) perch.

grufolare *vi.* to root.

grugnire *vi.* to grunt.

grugnito *sm.* grunt.

grugno *sm.* snout.

grumo *sm.* clot.

grumoso *agg.* clotted.

gruppo *sm.* group.

grùzzolo *sm.* hoard; (*risparmi*) savings (*pl.*).

guadàbile *agg.* fordable.

guadagnare *vt.* **1.** to gain **2.** (*col lavoro*) to earn.

guadagno *sm.* **1.** earnings (*pl.*) **2.** (*comm.*) profits (*pl.*) **3.** (*fig.*) gain.

guadare *vt.* to ford.

guado *sm.* ford.

guai *inter.* woe!

guaina *sf.* **1.** (*bot.; fodero per armi*) sheath **2.** (*custodia, astuccio*) case **3.** (*anat.*) theca (*pl. -ae*).

guaio *sm.* trouble.

guaire *vi.* to yelp.

guaito *sm.* yelp.

gualcire *vt.* to rumple.

gualdrappa *sf.* saddle-cloth.

guancia *sf.* cheek.

guanciale *sm.* pillow || *dormire fra due guanciali*, to have no worries.

guantaio *sm.* glover.

guantiera *sf.* **1.** (*scatola per guanti*) glove-box **2.** (*vassoio*) tray.

guantificio *sm.* glove-factory.

guanto *sm.* glove.

guantone *sm.* boxing-glove.

guardabarriere *sm.* gate-keeper.

guardaboschi *sm.* forester.

guardacaccia *sm.* gamekeeper.

guardacoste *sm.* coastguard.

guardalìnee *sm.* (*sport*) linesman (*pl. -men*).

guardamano *sm.* (*di scala*) hand-rail.

guardapesca *sm.* fishing warden.

guardaportone *sm.* doorkeeper.

guardare *vt.* **1.** to look (at) **2.** (*proteggere*) to protect. ♦ **guardare** *vi.* **1.** (*tentare*) to try **2.** (*essere orientato*) to face. ♦ **guardarsi** *vr.* (*da*), to beware (of).

guardaroba *sm.* **1.** wardrobe **2.** (*in teatro ecc.*) cloak-room.

guardarobiera *sf.* **1.** (*nei locali pubblici*) cloak-room attendant **2.** (*in alberghi e case private*) linen maid.

guardarobiere *sm.* (*nei locali pubblici*) cloak-room attendant.

guardasala *sm.* ticket-collector.

guardasigilli *sm.* keeper of the seals.

guardavìa *sm.* guard-rail.

guardia *sf.* guard || *— medica*, first-aid station; *fare la — a*, to guard; *mettere in —*, to warn.

guardiamarina *sm.* midshipman (*pl. -men*).

guardiano *sm.* **1.** keeper **2.** (*di armenti*) herdsman (*pl. -men*) || *— notturno*, night watchman (*pl. -men*).

guardina *sf.* guard-room.

guardingo *agg.* wary.

guardiola *sf.* guard-room.

guarìbile *agg.* **1.** curable **2.** (*di ferita*) healable.

guarigione *sf.* recovery.

guarire *vt.* **1.** to cure **2.** (*una ferita*) to heal. ♦ **guarire** *vi.* **1.** to recover **2.** (*di ferita*) to heal.

guaritore *sm.* healer.

guarnigione *sf.* garrison.

guarnire *vt.* **1.** to trim **2.** (*cuc.*) to garnish **3.** (*fornire*) to furnish **4.** (*mecc.*) to pack.

guarnitura, guarnizione *sf.* **1.** trimming **2.** (*cuc.*) garniture **3.** (*mecc.*) packing.

gusconata *sf.* gasconade.

guascone *agg. e sm.* (*anche fig.*) Gascon.

guastafeste *s.* kill-joy.

guastamestieri *sm.* bungler.

guastare *vt.* **1.** to spoil (*v. irr.*) **2.** (*danneggiare*) to damage.

guastatore *sm.* **1.** destroyer **2.** (*mil.*) sapper.

guasto *agg.* **1.** damaged **2.** (*marcio*) rotten **3.** (*corrotto*) tainted **4.** (*mecc.*) out of order.

guasto *sm.* **1.** damage **2.** (*mecc.*) breakdown || *ci deve essere un —,* there must be something wrong.

guatare *vt.* to gaze (at).

guazzabuglio *sm.* mess.

guazzare *vi.* **1.** to paddle **2.** (*rotolarsi*) to wallow **3.** (*di liquidi in recipienti*) to splash about.

guazzo *sm.* (*pitt.*) gouache.

guelfo *agg. e sm.* Guelph.

guercio *agg.* squinting. ♦ **guercio** *sm.* squinter.

guerra *sf.* war.

guerrafondaio *sm.* warmonger.

guerreggiante *agg. e sm.* belligerent.

guerreggiare *vi.* to fight (*v. irr.*), to war.

guerresco *agg.* **1.** war (*attr.*) **2.** (*bellicoso*) warlike.

guerriero *agg.* warlike. ♦ **guerriero** *sm.* warrior.

guerriglia *sf.* guerrilla.

guerrigliero *sm.* **1.** guerrilla **2.** partisan.

gufo *sm.* owl.

guglia *sf.* spire.

gugliata *sf.* needleful.

guida *sf.* **1.** guide **2.** (*auto*) drive || *patente di —,* driving licence; *— telefonica,* telephone book.

guidare *vt.* **1.** to guide **2.** (*auto*) to drive (*v. irr.*).

guidatore *sm.* driver.

guidoslitta *sf.* bobsleigh.

guinzaglio *sm.* leash: *mettere al —,* to leash.

guisa *sf.* manner || *a — di,* like.

guitto *sm.* strolling player.

guizzante *agg.* **1.** darting **2.** (*di luce*) flashing **3.** (*di pesci*) wriggling.

guizzare *vi.* **1.** to dart **2.** (*di luce*) to flash **3.** (*di pesci*) to wriggle.

guizzo *sm.* **1.** dart **2.** (*di luce*) flash **3.** (*di pesci*) wriggle.

guscio *sm.* shell.

gustare *vt.* **1.** to enjoy **2.** (*assaggiare*) to taste.

gustativo *agg.* gustative.

gustatore *sm.* taster.

gusto *sm.* **1.** taste **2.** (*gradimento*) liking || *di, con —,* with relish.

gustoso *agg.* **1.** (*saporito*) tasty **2.** (*piacevole*) pleasant.

guttaperca *sf.* gutta-percha.

gutturale *agg.* guttural.

H

harem *sm.* harem.

hascisc *sm.* hashish.

hawaiano *agg. e sm.* Hawaiian.

hurrà *inter.* hurrah.

i *art.* the.

iarda *sf.* yard.

iato *sm.* hiatus.

iattanza *sf.* boastfulness.

iattura *sf.* misfortune.

ibèrico *agg. e sm.* Iberian.

ibernazione *sf.* hibernation.

ibisco *sm.* hibiscus.

ibridazione *sf.* hybridization.

ibridismo *sm.* hybridism.

ìbrido *agg. e sm.* hybrid.

icona *sf.* icon.

iconoclasta *sm.* iconoclast.

idea *sf.* idea.

ideàbile *agg.* imaginable.

ideale *agg. e sm.* ideal.

idealismo *sm.* idealism.

idealista *s.* idealist.

idealìstico *agg.* idealistic.

idealizzare *vt.* to idealize.

idealizzazione *sf.* idealization.

ideare *vt.* to conceive, to devise.

ideatore *sm.* inventor, deviser.

ideazione *sf.* ideation.

idèntico *agg.* identic.

identificàbile *agg.* identifiable.

identificare *vt.* to identify.

identificazione *sf.* identification.

identità *sf.* identity.

ideografìa *sf.* ideography.

ideogramma *sm.* ideogram.

ideologìa *sf.* ideology.

ideològico *agg.* ideologic(al).

ideologismo *sm.* ideology.

ideòlogo *sm.* ideologist.

idillìaco *agg.* idyllic.

idillio *sm.* idyl.

idioma *sm.* language.

idiomàtico *agg.* idiomatic.

idiosincrasìa *sf.* idiosyncrasy.

idiota *sm.* idiot. ♦ **idiota** *agg.* idiotic.

idiotismo *sm.* idiom.

idiozìa *sf.* idiocy.

idolatra *sm.* idolater.

ìdolatrare *vt.* to worship.
idolatrìa *sf.* idolatry.
ìdolo *sm.* idol.
idoneità *sf.* fitness.
idòneo *agg.* fit.
idrante *sm.* hydrant.
idratare *vt.* to hydrate.
idrato *sm.* hydrate.
idràulica *sf.* hydraulics.
idràulico *agg.* hydraulic. ♦ **idràulico** *sm.* plumber.
ìdrico *agg.* water.
idrocarburo *sm.* hydrocarbon.
idrocefalìa *sf.* hydrocephalus.
idrocèfalo *sm.* hydrocephalus.
idroelèttrico *agg.* hydroelectric.
idròfilo *agg.* absorbent: *cotone* —, cotton wool.
idrofobìa *sf.* rabies.
idròfobo *agg.* 1. rabid 2. (*fig.*) furious.
idrògeno *sm.* hydrogen.
idrografìa *sf.* hydrography.
idròlisi *sf.* hydrolysis (*pl.* -ses).
idrologìa *sf.* hydrology.
idròpico *agg.* dropsical.
idropisìa *sf.* dropsy.
idroscalo *sm.* seaplane station.
idrostàtica *sf.* hydrostatics.
idrovolante *sm.* seaplane.
idròvora *sf.* water-scooping machine.
iella *sf.* bad luck.
iena *sf.* 1. hyaena 2. (*fig.*) vixen.
ieràtico *agg.* hieratic(al).
ieri *avv.* yesterday.
iettatore *sm.* evil-eyed man.
iettatura *sf.* evil-eye.
igiene *sf.* 1. hygiene 2. (*sistema sanitario*) sanitation.
igiènico *agg.* sanitary.
igienista *s.* hygienist.
ignaro *agg.* ignorant.
ignavia *sf.* laziness.
ignavo *agg.* lazy.
igneo *agg.* igneous.
ignòbile *agg.* mean.
ignominia *sf.* ignominy.
ignominioso *agg.* ignominious.
ignorante *agg.* e *sm.* ignorant.
ignoranza *sf.* ignorance.
ignorare *vt.* to ignore.
ignoto *agg.* unknown.
ignudo *agg.* naked.
igrometrìa *sf.* hygrometry.
iguana *sf.* iguana.
il *art.* the.
ìlare *agg.* cheerful.
ilarità *sf.* hilarity.

ilìaco *agg.* iliac.
illanguidire *vt.* to weaken.
illazione *sf.* illation.
illécito *agg.* illicit.
illegale *agg.* illegal.
illegalità *sf.* illegality.
illeggìbile *agg.* illegible.
illegittimità *sf.* illegitimacy.
illegìttimo *agg.* illegitimate.
illeso *agg.* unhurt.
illibatezza *sf.* purity.
illibato *agg.* pure.
illiberale *agg.* illiberal.
illimitato *agg.* unlimited.
illividire *vt.* to make (*v. irr.*) livid. ♦ **illividire** *vi.* to turn livid.
illogicità *sf.* illogicality.
illogico *agg.* illogical.
illùdere *vt.* to delude. ♦ **illùdersi** *vr.* to delude oneself.
illuminante *agg.* illuminating.
illuminare *vt.* to light up.
illuminazione *sf.* lighting.
illuminismo *sm.* Illuminism.
illusione *sf.* illusion.
illusionismo *sm.* illusionism.
illusionista *s.* conjurer.
illuso *agg.* deluded. ♦ **illuso** *sm.* day-dreamer.
illusorio *agg.* illusory.
illustrare *vt.* to illustrate.
illustrativo *agg.* illustrative.
illustrato *agg.* illustrated ‖ *cartolina illustrata*, picture post-card.
illustrazione *sf.* illustration.
illustre *agg.* renowned.
imbacuccare *vt.* to muffle up.
imbaldanzire *vt.* to embolden. ♦ **imbaldanzirsi** *vr.* to grow (*v. irr.*) bold.
'mballaggio *sm.* packing.
imballare *vt.* to pack (up). ♦ **imballarsi** *vr.* (*di motori*) to race.
imbalsamare *vt.* 1. to embalm 2. (*di animali*) to stuff.
imbalsamatore *sm.* 1. embalmer 2. (*di animali*) stuffer.
imbalsamazione *sf.* 1. embalming 2. (*di animali*) stuffing.
imbambolato *agg.* dull.
imbandierare *vt.* to deck with flags.
imbandire *vt.* 1. (*la tavola*) to lay (*v. irr.*) 2. to prepare.
imbarazzante *agg.* embarrassing.
imbarazzare *vt.* to embarrass. ♦ **imbarazzarsi** *vr.* to meddle.
imbarazzato *agg.* embarrassed.
imbarazzo *sm.* embarrassment.

imbarcadero *sm.* landing-stage.
imbarcare *vt.* to take (*v. irr.*) on board. ♦ **imbarcarsi** *vr.* to embark.
imbarcazione *sf.* boat.
imbarco *sm.* embarkation.
imbastardire *vt.* to debase.
imbastardito *agg.* debased.
imbastire *vt.* **1.** to tack **2.** (*fig.*) to put (*v. irr.*) together.
imbastitura *sf.* tacking.
imbàttersi *vr.* to meet (*v. irr.*) (with).
imbattìbile *agg.* invincible.
imbattibilità *sf.* invincibility.
imbavagliare *vt.* to gag.
imbeccare *vt.* **1.** to feed (*v. irr.*) **2.** (*fig.*) to prompt.
imbeccata *sf.* **1.** beakful **2.** (*fig.*) prompting.
imbecille *agg. e sm.* imbecile.
imbecillità *sf.* imbecility.
imbelle *agg.* weak.
imbellettare *vt.* to make (*v. irr.*) up.
imbellire *vt.* to embellish.
imberbe *agg.* beardless.
imbestialire *vi.* to get (*v. irr.*) furious. ♦ **imbestialirsi** *vr.* to get furious.
imbévere *vt.* to imbue with.
imbiancamento *sm.* whitening.
imbiancare *vt.* **1.** to whiten **2.** (*i muri*) to whitewash.
imbiancatura *sf.* **1.** (*di muri*) whitewashing **2.** (*di tessuti*) bleaching.
imbianchino *sm.* house painter.
imbiondire *vt.* to make (*v. irr.*) fair. ♦ **imbiondire** *vi.* to become (*v. irr.*) fair.
imbizzarrirsi *vr.* **1.** to become (*v. irr.*) restive **2.** (*adirarsi*) to fire up.
imboccare *vt.* **1.** to feed (*v. irr.*) **2.** (*di strada*) to enter.
imboccatura *sf.* **1.** mouth **2.** (*di strumento*) mouthpiece.
imbonimento *sm.* sales talk.
imbonire *vt.* to allure.
imbonitore *sm.* charlatan.
imborghesimento *sm.* getting into middle-class habits.
imborghesire *vt.* to give (*v. irr.*) middle-class habits. ♦ **imborghesirsi** *vr.* to acquire middle-class habits.
imboscare *vt.* **1.** to put (*v. irr.*) into safe keeping **2.** (*mil.*) to help to evade military service. ♦ **im-**

boscarsi *vr.* **1.** to lie (*v. irr.*) in ambush **2.** (*mil.*) to evade military service.
imboscata *sf.* ambush.
imboscato *sm.* shirker.
imboschimento *sm.* afforestation.
imboschire *vt.* to afforest.
imbottigliamento *sm.* bottling ‖ — *stradale*, traffic jam.
imbottigliare *vt.* **1.** to bottle **2.** (*fig.*) to block.
imbottire *vt.* **1.** to stuff **2.** (*di vestiti*) to wad **3.** (*fig.*) — *la testa*, to cram. ♦ **imbottirsi** *vr.* **1.** to fill oneself (with), to stuff oneself (with) **2.** (*coprirsi*) to wrap oneself (into).
imbottita *sf.* quilt.
imbottito *agg.* stuffed, filled ‖ *panino* —, sandwich.
imbottitura *sf.* **1.** stuffing **2.** (*di vestiti*) wadding.
imbracciare *vt.* **1.** to put (*v. irr.*) sthg. on one's hands **2.** (*di fucile*) to bring (*v. irr.*) to firing position.
imbrancare *vt.* to herd.
imbrattacarte *sm.* scribbler.
imbrattamento *sm.* soiling.
imbrattare *vt.* to soil.
imbrattatele *sm.* dauber.
imbrigliamento *sm.* bridling.
imbrigliare *vt.* to bridle.
imbrigliatura *sf.* bridling.
imbroccare *vt.* **1.** to hit (*v. irr.*) **2.** (*fig.*) to guess.
imbrogliare *vt.* **1.** to cheat **2.** (*confondere*) to confuse.
imbroglio *sm.* cheat, swindle.
imbroglione *sm.* cheat, swindler.
imbronciarsi *vr.* to pout.
imbronciato *agg.* sulky.
imbrunire *vi.* **1.** to brown **2.** (*farsi sera*) to get (*v. irr.*) dark.
imbrunire *sm.* nightfall.
imbruttire *vt.* to make (*v. irr.*) ugly. ♦ **imbruttirsi** *vr.* to become (*v. irr.*) ugly.
imbucare *vt.* to post.
imburrare *vt.* to butter.
imbuto *sm.* funnel.
imene *sm.* hymen.
imeneo *sm.* wedding.
imenòttero *sm.* hymenopteron (*pl.* -ra).
imitare *vt.* to imitate.
imitativo *agg.* imitative.
imitatore *sm.* imitator.
imitazione *sf.* imitation.

immacolato *agg.* spotless.
immagazzinare *vt.* to store (up).
immaginàbile *agg.* imaginable.
immaginare *vt.* to imagine.
immaginario *agg.* imaginary.
immaginativa *sf.* imagination.
immaginativo *agg.* imaginative.
immaginazione *sf.* imagination.
immàgine *sf.* image.
immalinconire *vt.* to make (*v. irr.*) melancholy. ♦ **immalinconire** *vi.* to grow (*v. irr.*) sad.
immancàbile *agg.* unfailing.
immane *agg.* 1. huge 2. (*fig.*) frightful.
immanente *agg.* immanent.
immanenza *sf.* immanence.
immangiàbile *agg.* uneatable.
immarcescìbile *agg.* incorruptible.
immateriale *agg.* immaterial.
immaterialità *sf.* immateriality.
immatricolare *vt.* to matriculate. ♦ **immatricolarsi** *vr.* to matriculate.
immatricolazione *sf.* matriculation.
immaturità *sf.* immaturity.
immaturo *agg.* 1. (*di frutto*) unripe 2. (*di persona*) immature.
immedesimare *vt.* 1. to unify. ♦ **immedesimarsi** *vr.* to identify oneself (with).
immedesimazione *sf.* unifying.
immediatamente *avv.* at once.
immediatezza *sf.* immediateness.
immediato *agg.* immediate.
immemoràbile *agg.* immemorial.
immèmore *agg.* forgetful.
immensità *sf.* immensity.
immenso *agg.* immense.
immèrgere *vt.* to immerse. ♦ **immèrgersi** *vr.* to immerse oneself.
immeritato *agg.* undeserved.
immeritévole *agg.* undeserving.
immersione *sf.* immersion.
immèttere *vt.* to let (*v. irr.*) in. ♦ **immèttersi** *vr.* to penetrate.
immigrante *agg.* e *sm.* immigrant.
immigrare *vi.* to immigrate.
immigrato *agg.* immigrated. ♦ **immigrato** *sm.* immigrant.
immigrazione *sf.* immigration.
imminente *agg.* impending.
imminenza *sf.* imminence.
immischiare *vt.* to involve. ♦ **immischiarsi** *vr.* to meddle (with).
immiserimento *sm.* impoverishing.
immiserire *vt.* to impoverish. ♦

immiserirsi *vr.* 1. to become (*v. irr.*) poor 2. (*fig.*) to weaken.
immissario *sm.* affluent.
immissione *sf.* letting in.
immòbile *agg.* immobile || *beni immòbili,* immovables.
immobiliare *agg.* immovable.
immobilismo *sm.* ultra-conservatism.
immobilità *sf.* immobility.
immobilizzare *vt.* 1. to immobilize 2. (*comm.*) to lock up.
immobilizzazione *sf.* 1. immobilization 2. (*comm.*) locking up.
immoderato *agg.* immoderate.
immodestia *sf.* immodesty.
immodesto *agg.* immodest.
immolare *vt.* to immolate.
immondezza *sf.* dirtiness.
immondezzaio *sm.* garbage heap.
immondizia *sf.* 1. filth 2. (*spazzatura*) garbage.
immondo *agg.* dirty.
immorale *agg.* immoral.
immoralità *sf.* immorality.
immortalare *vt.* to immortalize.
immortale *agg.* immortal.
immortalità *sf.* immortality.
immoto *agg.* motionless.
immune *agg.* immune.
immunità *sf.* immunity.
immunizzare *vt.* to immunize.
immunizzazione *sf.* immunization.
immusonirsi *vr.* to sulk.
immusonito *agg.* sulky.
immutàbile *agg.* immutable.
immutabilità *sf.* immutability.
impacchettare *vt.* to package.
impacciare *vt.* to hamper.
impacciato *agg.* 1. embarrassed 2. (*goffo*) awkward.
impaccio *sm.* hindrance.
impacco *sm.* compress.
impadronirsi *vr.* to take (*v. irr.*) possession (of).
impagàbile *agg.* priceless.
impaginare *vt.* to make-up.
impaginatore *sm.* maker-up.
impaginazione *sf.* making-up.
impagliare *vt.* 1. to cover with straw 2. (*di animali*) to stuff with straw.
impagliatore *sm.* 1. chair-mender 2. (*di animali*) stuffer.
impagliatura *sf.* 1. chair-mending 2. (*di animali*) stuffing.
impalare *vt.* to impale.
impalato *agg.* stiff.
impalcatura *sf.* 1. scaffolding 2.

(*di corna di cervo*) antlers (*pl.*).
impallidire *vi.* to turn pale.
impallinare *vt.* to shot.
impalmare *vt.* to marry.
impalpàbile *agg.* impalpable.
impalpabilità *sf.* impalpability.
impanare *vt.* **1.** (*cuc.*) to bread **2.** (*mecc.*) to thread.
impantanare *vt.* to swamp. ♦ **impantanarsi** *vr.* to swamp (*anche fig.*).
impaperarsi *vr.* to slip up.
impappinarsi *vr.* to stammer. ·
imparagonàbile *agg.* incomparable.
imparare *vt.* to learn (*v. irr.*).
impareggiàbile *agg.* unparalleled.
imparentare *vt.* to relate. ♦ **imparentarsi** *vr.* to become (*v. irr.*) related (to).
ìmpari *agg.* unequal.
imparisìllabo *agg.* e *sm.* imparisyllabic.
imparruccato *agg.* bewigged.
impartire *vt.* to impart.
imparziale *agg.* impartial.
imparzialità *sf.* impartiality.
impassìbile *agg.* impassive, unmoved.
impassibilità *sf.* impassibility.
impastare *vt.* to knead || — *i colori*, to impaste.
impastato *agg.* **1.** kneaded **2.** (*fig.*) full.
impastatore *sm.* kneader.
impastatrice *sf.* kneading-machine.
impasto *sm.* **1.** dough **2.** (*miscuglio*) mixture.
impastoiare *vt.* (*fig.*) to impede.
impatto *sm.* impact.
impaurire *vt.* to frighten. ♦ **impaurirsi** *vr.* to get (*v. irr.*) scared.
impaurito *agg.* afraid: *sguardo* —, fearful look.
impàvido *agg.* fearless.
impaziente *agg.* impatient.
impazientirsi *vr.* to lose (*v. irr.*) one's patience.
impazienza *sf.* impatience.
impazzare *vi.* to be at one's height.
impazzata (*nella loc. avv.*) all'—, madly.
impazzire *vi.* to go·(*v. irr.*) mad.
impeccàbile *agg.* faultless.
impeciare *vt.* to pitch.
impedimento *sm.* obstacle.
impedire *vt.* to prevent (from).
impegnare *vt.* **1.** (*dare in pegno*) to pawn **2.** (*prenotare*) to reserve,

to book. ♦ **impegnarsi** *vr.* to engage (oneself).
impegnativo *agg.* binding || *lavoro* —, exacting job.
impegno *sm.* engagement.
impegolarsi *vr.* (*fig.*) to get (*v. irr.*) involved.
impelagarsi *vr.* to get (*v. irr.*) in trouble.
impellente *agg.* urgent.
impellicciare *vt.* to fur.
impellicciatura *sf.* veneering.
impenetràbile *agg.* impenetrable.
impenetrabilità *sf.* impenetrableness.
impenitente *agg.* impenitent.
impennacchiare *vt.* to plume.
impennarsi *vr.* **1.** (*di cavallo*) to rear **2.** (*fig.*) to rear up.
impennata *sf.* (*di cavallo*) rearing **2.** (*fig.*) bristling.
impensàbile *agg.* unthinkable.
impensato *agg.* unexpected.
impensierire *vt.* to worry.
imperante *agg.* ruling.
imperare *vi.* to rule (over).
imperativo *agg.* imperative.
imperatore *sm.* emperor.
imperatrice *sf.* empress.
impercettìbile *agg.* imperceptible.
impercettibilità *sf.* imperceptibility.
imperdonàbile *agg.* unpardonable.
imperfetto *agg.* **1.** (*gramm.*) imperfect **2.** (*fig.*) faulty.
imperfezione *sf.* imperfection.
imperiale[1] *agg.* imperial.
imperiale[2] *sm.* imperial.
imperialismo *sm.* imperialism.
imperialista *s.* imperialist.
imperialìstico *agg.* imperialistic
imperio *sm.* command, authority.
imperioso *agg.* imperious.
imperito *agg.* unskilful.
imperituro *agg.* everlasting.
imperizia *sf.* unskilfulness.
imperlare *vt.* to bead. ♦ **imperlarsi** *vr.* to bead.
impermalirsi *vr.* to resent (sthg.).
impermeàbile *agg.* impermeable. ♦ **impermeàbile** *sm.* raincoat.
impermeabilità *sf.* impermeability.
impermeabilizzare *vt.* to waterproof.
impermeabilizzazione *sf.* waterproofing.
imperniare *vt.* to pivot (upon).
impero *sm.* empire.
imperscrutàbile *agg.* inscrutable.

imperscrutabilità *sf.* inscrutableness.

impersonale *agg.* impersonal.

impersonalità *sf.* impersonality.

impersonare *vt.* to impersonate. ♦ **impersonarsi** *vr.* to materialize.

imperterrito *agg.* undaunted.

impertinente *agg.* impertinent.

impertinenza *sf.* impertinence.

imperturbàbile *agg.* impassive.

imperturbabilità *sf.* imperturbability.

imperturbato *agg.* imperturbed.

imperversare *vi.* to rage.

impervio *agg.* inaccessible.

impeto *sm.* **1.** rush, impetus **2.** (*impulso*) impulse.

impetrare *vt.* to impetrate.

impettito *agg.* stiff.

impetuosità *sf.* impetuosity.

impetuoso *agg.* impetuous.

impiantare *vt.* to found.

impiantito *sm.* **1.** (*di legno*) parquet floor **2.** (*di piastrelle*) tiled floor.

impianto *sm.* plant, installation.

impiastricciare *vt.* to daub.

impiastro *sm.* **1.** plaster **2.** (*fig.*) bore.

impiccagione *sf.* hanging.

impiccare *vt.* to hang.

impiccato *agg.* hanged. ♦ **impiccato** *sm.* hanged man.

impicciare *vt.* to hinder. ♦ **impicciarsi** *vr.* to meddle (in).

impiccio *sm.* hindrance.

impiccolire *vt.* to make (*v. irr.*) smaller.

impiegare *vt.* **1.** to employ **2.** (*spendere*) to spend (*v. irr.*) **3.** (*comm.*) to invest.

impiegatizio *agg.* white-collar (*attributivo*).

impiegato *agg.* employed. ♦ **impiegato** *sm.* employee, clerk.

impiego *sm.* **1.** employment **2.** (*uso*) use.

impietosire *vt.* to move to pity. ♦ **impietosirsi** *vr.* to feel (*v. irr.*) sorry (for).

impietrire *vt.* to petrify.

impigliare *vt.* to entangle.

impigrire *vt.* to make (*v. irr.*) lazy.

impinguare *vt.* **1.** to fatten **2.** (*fig.*) to enrich.

impiombare *vt.* **1.** to plumb **2.** (*otturare*) to fill **3.** (*coprire di piombo*) to lead.

impiombatura *sf.* **1.** plumbing **2.** (*otturazione*) filling **3.** (*copertura di piombo*) leading.

implacàbile *agg.* implacable.

implacabilità *sf.* implacability.

implicare *vt.* to involve.

implìcito *agg.* implicit.

implorare *vt.* to implore.

implorazione *sf.* entreaty.

implume *agg.* featherless.

impolìtico *agg.* impolitic.

impollinare *vt.* to pollinate.

impollinazione *sf.* pollination.

impoltronire *vt.* to make (*v. irr.*) lazy. ♦ **impoltronirsi** *vr.* to grow (*v. irr.*) lazy.

impolverare *vt.* to cover with dust.

impolverato *agg.* dusty.

impomatare *vt.* to pomade. ♦ **impomatarsi** *vr.* to pomade oneself.

imponderàbile *agg.* imponderable.

imponderabilità *sf.* imponderability.

imponente *agg.* imposing.

imponenza *sf.* grandeur, majesty.

imponìbile *agg.* taxable.

imponibilità *sf.* taxability.

impopolare *agg.* unpopular.

impopolarità *sf.* unpopularity.

imporporarsi *vr.* to purple.

imporre *vt.* to impose: — *un nome*, to give (*v. irr.*) a name. ♦ **imporsi** *vr.* **1.** to impose oneself **2.** (*avere successo*) to become (*v. irr.*) popular.

importante *agg.* important.

importanza *sf.* importance.

importare *vi. imp.* to matter, to care. ♦ **importare** *vt.* (*comm.*) to import.

importatore *sm.* importer.

importazione *sf.* import.

importo *sm.* amount.

importunare *vt.* to importune, to bother.

importunità *sf.* importunity.

importuno *agg.* boring. ♦ **importuno** *sm.* bore.

imposizione *sf.* imposition.

impossessarsi *vr.* to take (*v. irr.*) possession (of).

impossìbile *agg.* impossible.

impossibilità *sf.* impossibility.

impossibilitato *agg.* unable.

imposta *sf.* **1.** tax **2.** (*edil.*) shutter.

impostare *vt.* **1.** to start **2.** (*di lettera*) to post.

impostazione *sf.* general lines (*pl.*).

impostore *sm.* impostor.

impostura *sf.* **1.** imposture **2.** (*frode*) fraud.

impotente *agg.* powerless. ♦ **impotente** *agg.* e *sm.* (*med.*) impotent.

impotenza *sf.* impotence.

impoverimento *sm.* impoverishment.

impoverire *vt.* to impoverish. ♦ **impoverirsi** *vr.* to become (*v. irr.*) poor.

impraticàbile *agg.* impracticable: *strada —,* impassable road.

impraticabilità *sf.* impracticability.

impratichire *vt.* to train. ♦ **impratichirsi** *vr.* to get (*v. irr.*) trained.

imprecare *vi.* to curse.

imprecazione *sf.* curse.

imprecisàbile *agg.* indeterminable.

imprecisato *agg.* undetermined.

imprecisione *sf.* **1.** vagueness **2.** (*inesattezza*) inaccuracy.

impreciso *agg.* inaccurate.

impregnare *vt.* to impregnate (with). ♦ **impregnarsi** *vr.* to become (*v. irr.*) imbued (with).

imprèndere *vt.* to undertake (*v. irr.*).

imprendìbile *agg.* elusive, invincible.

imprenditore *sm.* **1.** entrepreneur **2.** (*edil.*) contractor.

impreparato *agg.* unprepared.

impreparazione *sf.* unpreparedness.

impresa *sf.* **1.** (*iniziativa*) undertaking **2.** (*gesta*) deed **3.** (*azienda*) firm, company.

impresario *sm.* **1.** contractor **2.** (*teat.*) manager.

imprescindìbile *agg.* unavoidable.

imprescrittìbile *agg.* indefeasible.

impressionàbile *agg.* impressionable.

impressionabilità *sf.* impressionability.

impressionante *agg.* frightening.

impressionare *vt.* **1.** to impress **2.** (*foto*) to expose.

impressione *sf.* impression.

impressionismo *sm.* impressionism.

impressionista *s.* impressionist.

impresso *agg.* printed.

imprestare *vt.* to lend (*v. irr.*).

imprevedìbile *agg.* unforeseeable.

impreveduto *agg.* unforeseen.

imprevidente *agg.* improvident.

imprevidenza *sf.* improvidence.

imprevisto *agg.* unexpected. ♦ **imprevisto** *sm.* unforeseen event.

impreziosire *vt.* to make (*v. irr.*) precious. ♦ **impreziosirsi** *vr.* to become (*v. irr.*) precious.

imprigionamento *sm.* imprisonment.

imprigionare *vt.* to imprison.

imprìmere *vt.* to impress.

improbàbile *agg.* improbable.

improbabilità *sf.* improbability.

ìmprobo *agg.* **1.** dishonest **2.** (*faticoso*) hard.

improduttività *sf.* unproductiveness.

improduttivo *agg.* unproductive.

impronta *sf.* **1.** impression: — *del piede, digitale,* footprint, fingerprint **2.** (*fig.*) mark.

improntare *vt.* **1.** to prepare **2.** (*fig.*) to mark.

improntitùdine *sf.* impudence.

impronunciàbile *agg.* unpronounceable.

improperio *sm.* insult.

improprietà *sf.* impropriety.

improprio *agg.* improper.

improrogàbile *agg.* undelayable.

improvvido *agg.* improvident.

improvvisamente *avv.* suddenly.

improvvisare *vt.* e *vi.* to improvise. ♦ **improvvisarsi** *vr.* to act.

improvvisata *sf.* surprise.

improvvisatore *sm.* improviser.

improvvisazione *sf.* improvisation.

improvviso *agg.* sudden.

imprudente *agg.* imprudent.

imprudenza *sf.* imprudence.

impudente *agg.* impudent.

impudenza *sf.* impudence.

impudicizia *sf.* immodesty.

impudico *agg.* shameless, immodest.

impugnàbile *agg.* (*giur.*) impugnable.

impugnabilità *sf.* (*giur.*) impugnment.

impugnare *vt.* **1.** to grasp, to hold **2.** (*giur.*) to impugn.

impugnatura *sf.* hilt.

impulsività *sf.* impulsiveness.

impulsivo *agg.* impulsive.

impulso *sm.* impulse.

impunemente *avv.* safely.

impunità *sf.* impunity.

impunito *agg.* unpunished.

impuntare *vi.* to stumble (over).

♦ **impuntarsi** *vr.* **1.** to jib **2.** (*ostinarsi*) to stick (*v. irr.*) (to).
impuntura *sf.* stitching.
impurità *sf.* impurity.
impuro *agg.* impure.
imputàbile *agg.* **1.** imputable **2.** (*giur.*) chargeable (with).
imputare *vt.* **1.** to impute **2.** (*giur.*) to charge (with).
imputato *sm.* defendant.
imputazione *sf.* imputation.
imputridimento *sm.* putrefaction.
imputridire *vi.* to rot.
in *prep.* (*stato in luogo*) in, at: *essere — campagna, — città*, to be in the country, in town; *essere — casa, — chiesa*, to be at home, at church **2.** (*moto a luogo*) to: *andò — America*, he went to America **3.** (*moto dentro luogo*) into: *va' nello studio*, go into the study **4.** (*coi mezzi di trasporto*) by: *sono venuto — treno*, I came by train.
inàbile *agg.* **1.** unable **2.** (*non idoneo*) unfit.
inabilità *sf.* **1.** inability **2.** (*inidoneità*) unfitness.
inabilitare *vt.* to disable.
inabilitazione *sf.* disability.
inabissamento *sm.* sinking.
inabissarsi *vr.* to sink (*v. irr.*).
inabitàbile *agg.* uninhabitable.
inabitabilità *sf.* uninhabitableness.
inabitato *agg.* **1.** uninhabited **2.** (*deserto*) deserted.
inaccessìbile *agg.* inaccessible.
inaccessibilità *sf.* inaccessibility.
inaccettàbile *agg.* unacceptable.
inaccettabilità *sf.* unacceptableness.
inacerbire *vt.* to exacerbate. ♦ **inacerbirsi** *vr.* to grow (*v. irr.*) bitter.
inacidire *vt.* to sour. ♦ **inacidirsi** *vr.* to turn sour.
inacidito *agg.* sour.
inadattàbile *agg.* unadaptable.
inadattabilità *sf.* inadaptability.
inadatto *agg.* **1.** unfit (for) **2.** (*sconveniente*) unbecoming.
inadeguato *agg.* inadequate.
inadempìbile *agg.* unfulfillable.
inadempiente *agg.* defaulting.
inadempienza *sf.* non-execution.
inafferràbile *agg.* unseizable.
inalare *vt.* to inhale.
inalatore *sm.* inhaler.
inalazione *sf.* inhalation.

inalberare *vt.* to hoist. ♦ **inalberarsi** *vr.* **1.** to rear up **2.** (*fig.*) to lose (*v. irr.*) one's temper.
inalienàbile *agg.* inalienable.
inalienabilità *sf.* inalienability.
inalteràbile *agg.* inalterable.
inalterabilità *sf.* inalterability.
inalterato *agg.* unaltered.
inalveare *vt.* to canalize.
inamidare *vt.* to starch.
inammissìbile *agg.* inadmissible.
inammissibilità *sf.* inadmissibility.
inamovìbile *agg.* irremovable.
inamovibilità *sf.* irremovability.
inane *agg.* inane.
inanellare *vt.* to curl.
inanimato *agg.* lifeless.
inanità *sf.* inanity.
inappagàbile *agg.* unsatisfiable.
inappagato *agg.* unsatisfied.
inappellàbile *agg.* inappellable.
inappetenza *sf.* inappetence.
inapplicàbile *agg.* inapplicable.
inapprezzàbile *agg.* priceless.
inappuntàbile *agg.* **1.** irreproachable **2.** (*nel vestire*) faultlessly dressed.
inarcamento *sm.* bending, arching.
inarcare *vt.* to bend (*v. irr.*) || *le sopracciglia*, to raise one's brows. ♦ **inarcarsi** *vr.* to arch.
inargentare *vt.* to silver.
inaridire *vt.* to dry. ♦ **inaridirsi** *vr.* to dry up.
inarticolato *agg.* inarticulate.
inascoltato *agg.* unheard.
inaspettato *agg.* unexpected.
inasprimento *sm.* embitterment.
inasprire *vt.* to embitter. ♦ **inasprirsi** *vr.* to become (*v. irr.*) embittered.
inattaccàbile *agg.* unassailable.
inattendìbile *agg.* unreliable.
inatteso *agg.* unexpected.
inattività *sf.* inactivity.
inattivo *agg.* inactive.
inattuàbile *agg.* impracticable.
inattuale *agg.* outdated.
inaudito *agg.* unheard of.
inaugurale *agg.* inaugural.
inaugurare *vt.* to inaugurate.
inaugurazione *sf.* inauguration.
inavvedutezza *sf.* carelessness.
inavveduto *agg.* careless.
inavvertenza *sf.* inadvertence.
inavvertito *agg.* unperceived.
inazione *sf.* inaction.
incagliare *vt.* to hinder. ♦ **incagliarsi** *vr.* to strand.

incaglio *sm.* 1. stranding 2. (*fig.*) obstacle.

incalcolàbile *agg.* incalculable.

incallire *vi.* to harden. ♦ **incallirsi** *vr.* to harden.

incallito *agg.* hardened.

incalzante *agg.* 1. pursuing 2. (*fig.*) pressing.

incalzare *vt.* 1. to pursue 2. (*fig.*) to urge.

incameramento *sm.* confiscation.

incamerare *vt.* to confiscate.

incamminare *vt.* to set (*v. irr.*) going. ♦ **incamminarsi** *vr.* to set out (for).

incanalamento *sm.* canalization.

incanalare *vt.* to canalize.

incancellàbile *agg.* indelible.

incancrenire *vi.* to become (*v. irr.*) gangrenous.

incandescente *agg.* white-hot.

incandescenza *sf.* incandescence.

incantamento *sm.* charm.

incantare *vt.* to charm. ♦ **incantarsi** *vr.* to be charmed.

incantato *agg.* enchanted.

incantatore *agg.* enchanting. ♦ **incantatore** *sm.* enchanter.

incantésimo *sm.* spell.

incantévole *agg.* charming.

incanto[1] *sm.* enchantment.

incanto[2] *sm.* (*comm.*) auction: *vendere all'—*, to sell (*v. irr.*) by auction.

incanutire *vi.* to grow (*v. irr.*) hoary.

incapace *agg.* unable.

incapacità *sf.* incapacity.

incaparbirsi *vr.* to become (*v. irr.*) obstinate.

incappare *vi.* to get (*v. irr.*) into, to stumble.

incappucciare *vt.* to hood. ♦ **incappucciarsi** *vr.* to put (*v. irr.*) on one's hood.

incapricciarsi *vr.* to take (*v. irr.*) a fancy (to).

incapsulare *vt.* to capsule.

incarcerare *vt.* to imprison.

incarcerazione *sf.* imprisonment.

incaricare *vt.* to charge (so. with). ♦ **incaricarsi** *vr.* to charge oneself (with).

incaricato *agg.* charged (with). ♦ **incaricato** *sm.* appointee.

incàrico *sm.* task, duty.

incarnare *vt.* to embody. ♦ **incarnarsi** *vr.* to take (*v. irr.*) body.

incarnato *sm.* complexion.

incarnazione *sf.* incarnation.

incarnire *vi.* to grow (*v. irr.*) into flesh.

incartamento *sm.* dossier.

incartapecorire *vi.* to wrinkle.

incartapecorito *agg.* 'wrinkled with age.

incartare *vt.* to wrap in paper.

incarto *sm.* set of papers.

incartocciare *vt.* to wrap up in a cornet.

incasèllare *vt.* to put (*v. irr.*) in squares.

incassamento *sm.* 1. boxing 2. (*mecc.; arch.*) embedding.

incassare *vt.* 1. to box 2. (*riscuotere*) to cash.

incassatura *sf.* hollow.

incasso *sm.* 1. collection 2. (*di spettacoli*) receipts (*pl.*).

incastellamento *sm.* 1. fortifications (*pl.*) 2. (*arch.*) scaffolding.

incastellare *vt.* to fortify with battlements.

incastellatura *sf.* 1. frame 2. (*arch.*) scaffolding.

incastonare *vt.* to set (*v. irr.*).

incastonatura *sf.* setting.

incastrare *vt.* 1. to embed 2. (*adattare*) to fit in. ♦ **incastrarsi** *vr.* 1. to fit 2. (*impigliarsi*) to get (*v. irr.*) stuck.

incastro *sm.* joint.

incatenamento *sm.* chaining.

incatenare *vt.* to chain. ♦ **incatenarsi** *vr.* to be linked (with).

incatramare *vt.* to tar.

incattivire *vt.* to exasperate. ♦ **incattivirsi** *vr.* to get (*v. irr.*) crossed.

incàuto *agg.* rash.

incavare *vt.* to hollow out.

incavatura *sf.* hollowness.

incavo *sm.* hollow.

incèdere *vi.* to advance.

incendiare *vt.* to set (*v. irr.*) on fire.

incendiario *agg. e sm.* incendiary.

incendio *sm.* fire.

incenerire *vt.* to reduce to ashes.

incensamento *sm.* 1. incensation 2. (*fig.*) flattery.

incensare *vt.* 1. to incense 2. (*fig.*) to flatter.

incenso *sm.* incense.

incensuràbile *agg.* irreproachable.

incensurato *agg.* blameless: *essere —*, to be a first-offender.

incentivo *sm.* incentive.

inceppamento *sm.* 1. obstacle 2. (*mecc.*) jam.

inceppare *vt.* 1. to clog 2. (*ostacolare*) to encumber. ♦ **incepparsi** *vr.* to jam.

incerare *vt.* to wax.

incertezza *sf.* uncertainty, doubt.

incerto *agg.* uncertain. ♦ **incerto** *sm.* uncertainty.

incespicare *vi.* to stumble.

incessante *agg.* unceasing.

incesto *sm.* incest.

incestuoso *agg.* incestuous.

incetta *sf.* cornering: *fare — di*, to make (*v. irr.*) a corner in.

incettare *vt.* to corner.

incettatore *sm.* cornerer.

inchiesta *sf.* inquiry, investigation.

inchinare *vt.* to bow. ♦ **inchinarsi** *vr.* to bow (down).

inchino *sm.* bow.

inchiodare *vt.* to nail.

inchiodatura *sf.* nailing.

inchiostro *sm.* ink.

inciampare *vi.* to stumble.

inciampo *sm.* obstacle.

incidentale *agg.* 1. incidental 2. (*gramm.*) parenthetic.

incidente *agg.* incident. ♦ **incidente** *sm.* accident.

incidenza *sf.* incidence.

incìdere[1] *vt.* 1. to cut (*v. irr.*) 2. (*intagliare*) to engrave 3. (*su disco, nastro ecc.*) to record.

incìdere[2] *vi.* to weigh heavily: *— sul bilancio*, to weigh heavily on one's budget.

incinta *agg. f.* pregnant.

incipiente *agg.* incipient.

incipriare *vt.* to powder. ♦ **incipriarsi** *vr.* to powder (oneself).

incirca (*nella loc. avv.*) *all'—*, about.

incisione *sf.* 1. cut 2. (*arte*) engraving 3. (*su disco, nastro ecc.*) recording.

incisività *sf.* sharpness.

incisivo *agg.* incisive. ♦ **incisivo** *sm.* (*anat.*) incisor.

inciso *sm.* parenthetic clause: *per —*, incidentally.

incisore *sm.* engraver.

incitamento *sm.* urge.

incitare *vt.* to urge, to stimulate.

incitrullire *vi.* to become (*v. irr.*) silly.

incivile *agg.* 1. uncivilized 2. (*scortese*) rude.

incivilimento *sm.* civilization.

incivilire *vt.* to civilize. ♦ **incivilirsi** *vr.* to become (*v. irr.*) civilized.

inciviltà *sf.* 1. barbarism 2. (*fig.*) rudeness.

inclassificàbile *agg.* unclassifiable.

inclemente *agg.* 1. inclement: *tempo —*, inclement weather 2. (*spietato*) merciless.

inclemenza *sf.* 1. (*di tempo*) inclemency 2. (*crudeltà*) mercilessness.

inclinare *vt.* to incline, to bend (*v. irr.*).

inclinato *agg.* inclined (*anche fig.*).

inclinazione *sf.* 1. inclination 2. (*attitudine*) bent.

incline *agg.* disposed.

inclito *agg.* famous.

inclùdere *vt.* to include.

inclusione *sf.* inclusion.

inclusivo *agg.* inclusive.

incluso *agg.* 1. included 2. (*accluso*) enclosed.

incoccare *vt.* to nock.

incoercìbile *agg.* irrepressible.

incoercibilità *sf.* irrepressibleness.

incoerente *agg.* incoherent.

incoerenza *sf.* incoherence.

incògnita *sf.* 1. (*mat.*) unknown quantity 2. (*fig.*) uncertainty.

incògnito *agg.* unknown. ♦ **incògnito** *sm.* incognito (*pl.* -tos).

incollamento *sm.* pasting.

incollare *vt.* to stick (*v. irr.*). ♦ **incollarsi** *vr.* to stick.

incollatrice *sf.* sizing-machine.

incollatura[1] *sf.* sticking.

incollatura[2] *sf.* (*ippica*) neck.

incollerire *vi.* to get (*v. irr.*) angry. ♦ **incollerirsi** *vr.* to get angry.

incollerito *agg.* angry.

incolonnamento *sm.* column formation.

incolonnare *vt.* to form into columns. ♦ **incolonnarsi** *vr.* to rank.

incolore *agg.* colourless.

incolpàbile *agg.* accusable.

incolpare *vt.* to charge (with), to accuse (of). ♦ **incolparsi** *vr.* to accuse oneself.

incolpévole *agg.* blameless.

incolto *agg.* uncultivated.

incòlume *agg.* unhurt.

incolumità *sf.* safety.

incombente *agg.* impending.

incombenza *sf.* errand, task.

incòmbere *vi.* 1. (*spettare*) to be

one's job **2.** (*sovrastare*) to impend (over).

incombustìbile *agg.* incombustible.

incominciare *vt.* e *vi.* V. *cominciare.*

incommensuràbile *agg.* incommensurable.

incommensurabilità *sf.* incommensurability.

incommerciàbile *agg.* not negotiable.

incommutàbile *agg.* incommutable.

incomodare *vt.* to annoy. ♦ **incomodarsi** *vr.* to trouble.

incomodità *sf.* uncomfortableness.

incomodo *agg.* uncomfortable || *essere d' —*, to be in the way.

incomparàbile *agg.* incomparable.

incompatìbile *agg.* incompatible.

incompatibilità *sf.* incompatibility.

incompetente *agg.* incompetent.

incompetenza *sf.* incompetence.

incompiuto *agg.* unfinished.

incompletezza *sf.* incompleteness.

incompleto *agg.* incomplete.

incompostezza *sf.* disorder.

incomposto *agg.* disorderly.

incomprensìbile *agg.* incomprehensible.

incomprensibilità *sf.* incomprehensibility.

incomprensione *sf.* incomprehension.

incompreso *agg.* **1.** not understood **2.** (*non apprezzato*) unappreciated.

incomputàbile *agg.* incalculable.

incomunicàbile *agg.* incommunicable.

incomunicabilità *sf.* incommunicability.

inconcepìbile *agg.* inconceivable.

inconciliàbile *agg.* irreconcilable.

inconciliabilità *sf.* irreconcilability.

inconcludente *agg.* **1.** inconclusive **2.** (*di persona*) good-for-nothing.

inconcusso *agg.* unshaken.

incondizionato *agg.* unconditional.

inconfessàbile *agg.* unavowable.

inconfessato *agg.* unconfessed.

inconfondìbile *agg.* unmistakable.

inconfutàbile *agg.* irrefutable.

incongruente *agg.* incongruous.

incongruenza *sf.* incongruity.

incòngruo *agg.* incongruous.

inconsapévole *agg.* unconscious, unaware.

inconsapevolezza *sf.* unconsciousness, unawareness.

inconscio *agg.* e *sm.* unconscious.

inconseguente *agg.* inconsequent.

inconseguenza *sf.* inconsequence.

inconsideratezza *sf.* rashness.

inconsiderato *agg.* rash.

inconsistente *agg.* insubstantial.

inconsistenza *sf.* insubstantiality.

inconsolàbile *agg.* inconsolable.

inconsueto *agg.* unusual.

inconsulto *agg.* unadvised, rash.

incontaminato *agg.* unpolluted.

incontentàbile *agg.* insatiable.

incontentabilità *sf.* insatiability.

incontestàbile *agg.* incontestable.

incontinente *agg.* incontinent.

incontinenza *sf.* incontinence.

incontrare *vt.* to meet (*v. irr.*). ♦ **incontrarsi** *vr.* to meet || *i nostri gusti non si incontrano*, our tastes do not agree.

incontrastàbile *agg.* incontestable.

incontrastato *agg.* uncontested.

incontro[1] *sm.* **1.** meeting **2.** (*sport*) match.

incontro[2] *prep. — a,* towards, to.

incontrollàbile *agg.* uncontrollable.

incontrollato *agg.* uncontrolled.

incontrovertìbile *agg.* indisputable.

inconveniente *sm.* inconvenience, drawback.

inconvertìbile *agg.* inconvertible.

inconvertibilità *sf.* inconvertibility.

incoraggiamento *sm.* encouragement.

incoraggiante *agg.* encouraging.

incoraggiare *vt.* to encourage.

incorniciare *vt.* to frame.

incorniciatura *sf.* framing.

incoronamento *sm.* V. *coronamento.*

incoronare *vt.* V. *coronare.*

incoronazione *sf.* coronation.

incorporare *vt.* to incorporate.

incorporazione *sf.* incorporation.

incorpòreo *agg.* incorporeal.

incorreggìbile *agg.* incorrigible.

incòrrere *vi.* to incur, to suffer (sthg.).

incorretto *agg.* incorrect.

incorrotto *agg.* incorrupt.

incorruttìbile *agg.* incorruptible.

incorruttibilità *sf.* incorruptibility.

incosciente *agg.* **1.** unconscious **2.** (*irresponsabile*) reckless. ♦ **incosciente** *sm.* irresponsible.

incoscienza *sf.* **1.** unconsciousness **2.** (*spericolatezza*) rashness.

incostante *agg.* inconstant: *tempo* —, changeable weather.

incostituzionale *agg.* unconstitutional.

incostituzionalità *sf.* unconstitutionality.

incredìbile *agg.* incredible.

incredibilità *sf.* incredibility.

incredulità *sf.* incredulity.

incrèdulo *agg.* incredulous.

incrementare *vt.* to increase.

incremento *sm.* increase.

increscioso *agg.* unpleasant.

increspamento *sm.* 1. (*di acque*) rippling 2. (*di capelli*) ruffling.

increspare *vt.*, **incresparsi** *vr.* 1. (*di acque*) to ripple 2. (*di capelli*) to ruffle.

incretinire *vt.* to make (*v. irr.*) stupid. ♦ **incretinirsi** *vr.* to dull.

incriminàbile *agg.* impeachable.

incriminare *vt.* to impeach.

incriminazione *sf.* 1. (*l'accusare*) crimination 2. (*atto d'accusa*) indictment.

incrinare *vt.* to crack. ♦ **incrinarsi** *vr.* to crack.

incrinatura *sf.* crack.

incriticàbile *agg.* uncensurable.

incrociare *vt.* to cross. ♦ **incrociarsi** *vr.* to cross.

incrociatore *sm.* cruiser.

incrocio *sm.* 1. crossing || — *stradale*, cross-road 2. (*di razze*) crossbreed.

incrollàbile *agg.* unshakable.

incrostare *vt.* to incrust. ♦ **incrostarsi** *vr.* to become (*v. irr.*) incrusted.

incrostazione *sf.* incrustation.

incrudelimento *sm.* toughening.

incrudelire *vi.* to become (*v. irr.*) cruel || — *contro qu.*, to be pitiless towards so.

incrudire *vi.* to grow (*v. irr.*) worse.

incruento *agg.* bloodless.

incubatrice *sf.* incubator.

incubazione *sf.* incubation.

ìncubo *sm.* nightmare.

incùdine *sf.* anvil.

inculcare *vt.* to inculcate.

incunàbolo *sm.* incunabulum.

incuneare *vt.* to wedge. ♦ **incunearsi** *vr.* to wedge oneself.

incupire *vt.* e *vi.* to darken. ♦ **incupirsi** *vr.* to become (*v. irr.*) gloomy.

incuràbile *agg.* e *sm.* incurable.

incurabilità *sf.* incurability.

incurante *agg.* careless, heedless.

incuria *sf.* heedlessness.

incuriosire *vt.* to make (*v. irr.*) curious. ♦ **incuriosirsi** *vr.* to become (*v. irr.*) curious.

incuriosito *agg.* made curious.

incursione *sf.* raid.

incurvare *vt.* e **incurvarsi** *vr.* to bend (*v. irr.*), to curve.

incurvatura *sf.* bend.

incustodito *agg.* unguarded.

incùtere *vt.* to rouse.

ìndaco *sm.* indigo.

indaffarato *agg.* busy.

indagare *vt.* to investigate.

indagatore *agg.* investigating.

indàgine *sf.* 1. research, investigation 2. (*giur.*) inquiry.

indebitare *vt.* to involve in debt. ♦ **indebitarsi** *vr.* to run (*v. irr.*) into debt.

indébito *agg.* undue.

indebolimento *sm.* weakening.

indebolire *vt.* to weaken. ♦ **indebolirsi** *vr.* to weaken.

indecente *agg.* indecent.

indecenza *sf.* indecency.

indecifràbile *agg.* 1. indecipherable 2. (*di calligrafia*) illegible.

indecisione *sf.* indecision.

indeciso *agg.* 1. irresolute 2. (*di cose*) undecided.

indeclinàbile *agg.* 1. indeclinable 2. (*che non si può eludere*) unavoidable.

indecoroso *agg.* unseemly.

indefesso *agg.* indefatigable.

indefinìbile *agg.* indefinable.

indefinito *agg.* indefinite.

indeformàbile *agg.* indeformable.

indegno *agg.* 1. unworthy 2. (*spregevole*) disgraceful.

indelèbile *agg.* indelible.

indelicatezza *sf.* indelicacy.

indelicato *agg.* tactless.

indemoniato *agg.* 1. possessed 2. (*fig.*) frantic. ♦ **indemoniato** *sm.* demoniac.

indenne *agg.* undamaged.

indennità *sf.* allowance.

indennizzare *vt.* to indemnify.

indennizzo *sm.* indemnity.

inderogàbile *agg.* intransgressible.

indescrivìbile *agg.* indescribable.

indesideràbile *agg.* undesirable.

indeterminàbile *agg.* indeterminable.

indeterminatezza *sf.* vagueness.

indeterminativo *agg.* (*gramm.*) indefinite.

indeterminato *agg.* indeterminate.

indeterminazione *sf.* indetermination.

indi *avv.* **1.** (*di tempo*) then **2.** (*di luogo*) (from) thence.

indiano *agg.* Indian: — *d'America*, Red Indian; *in fila indiana*, in Indian file.

indiavolato *agg.* frenzied, furious.

indicare *vt.* **1.** to show (*v. irr.*) **2.** (*col dito*) to point at.

indicativo *agg.* indicative.

indicato *agg.* **1.** (*adatto*) suitable **2.** (*consigliabile*) advisable.

indicatore *agg.* indicatory. ♦ **indicatore** *sm.* indicator.

indicazione *sf.* indication.

indice *sm.* **1.** (*dito della mano*) forefinger **2.** (*di libro, statistica ecc.*) index.

indicìbile *agg.* inexpressible.

indietreggiare *vi.* to withdraw (*v. irr.*).

indietro *avv.* (*di spazio, tempo*) back, behind.

indifendìbile *agg.* indefensible.

indifeso *agg.* undefended.

indifferente *agg.* indifferent.

indifferenza *sf.* indifference.

indifferìbile *agg.* undelayable.

indìgeno *agg. e sm.* native.

indigente *agg.* indigent, poor.

indigenza *sf.* indigence.

indigestione *sf.* indigestion.

indigesto *agg.* **1.** indigestible **2.** (*fig.*) heavy.

indignare *vt.* to make (*v. irr.*) indignant. ♦ **indignarsi** *vr.* to get (*v. irr.*) angry.

indignazione *sf.* indignation.

indimenticàbile *agg.* unforgettable.

indimostràbile *agg.* indemonstrable.

indipendente *agg.* independent (of). ♦ **indipendente** *sm.* (*pol.*) independent.

indipendenza *sf.* independence.

indire *vt.* to call, to announce.

indiretto *agg.* indirect.

indirizzare *vt.* to address. ♦ **indirizzarsi** *vr.* **1.** (*dirigersi*) to set (*v. irr.*) out (for) **2.** (*rivolgersi*) to address oneself (to).

indirizzo *sm.* **1.** address **2.** (*linea di condotta*) trend.

indisciplina *sf.* indiscipline.

indisciplinato *agg.* undisciplined.

indiscretezza *sf.* indiscretion.

indiscreto *agg.* indiscreet.

indiscrezione *sf.* indiscretion.

indiscriminato *agg.* indiscriminate.

indiscusso *agg.* undiscussed.

indiscutìbile *agg.* unquestionable.

indispensàbile *agg.* indispensable.

indispettire *vt.* to vex. ♦ **indispettirsi** *vr.* to become (*v. irr.*) vexed.

indispettito *agg.* vexed.

indisponente *agg.* irritating.

indisporre *vt.* to irritate.

indisposizione *sf.* indisposition.

indisposto *agg.* unwell (*pred.*).

indissolùbile *agg.* indissoluble.

indissolubilità *sf.* indissolubility.

indistinto *agg.* indistinct.

indistruttìbile *agg.* indestructible.

indisturbato *agg.* undisturbed.

individuale *agg.* individual.

individualismo *sm.* individualism

individualista *s.* individualist.

individualìstico *agg.* individualistic.

individuare *vt.* to single out.

individuo *sm.* individual.

indivisìbile *agg.* indivisible.

indivisibilità *sf.* indivisibility.

indiviso *agg.* undivided.

indiziare *vt.* to make (*v. irr.*) suspect.

indiziario *agg.* presumptive.

indiziato *agg. e sm.* suspect.

indizio *sm.* **1.** indication **2.** (*giur.*) circumstantial proof.

indòcile *agg.* indocile.

indocilità *sf.* indocility.

indoeuropeo *agg. e sm.* Indo-European.

indole *sf.* nature, disposition ‖ *un ragazzo di buona —*, a good-natured boy.

indolente *agg.* indolent.

indolenza *sf.* indolence.

idolenzimento *sm.* numbness.

indolenzire *vt.* to numb. ♦ **indolenzirsi** *vr.* to become (*v. irr.*) numb.

indolenzito *agg.* numb.

indolore *agg.* painless.

indomàbile *agg.* untamable.

indomani *sm.* next day ‖ *all' —*, on the day after.

indòmito *agg.* indomitable.

indorare *vt.* V. *dorare*.

indossare *vt.* **1.** (*avere indosso*) to wear (*v. irr.*) **2.** (*mettere indosso*) to put (*v. irr.*) on.

indossatrice *sf.* mannequin.
indosso *avv.* on.
indotto *agg.* (*spinto*) driven.
indovinare *vt.* to guess.
indovinello *sm.* riddle.
indovino *sm.* soothsayer.
indubbio *agg.* undoubted.
indubitàbile *agg.* indubitable.
indugiare *vi.* to delay, to hesitate.
indugio *sm.* delay.
indulgente *agg.* indulgent.
indulgenza *sf.* indulgence.
indùlgere *vi.* to indulge (in).
indulto *sm.* **1.** (*eccl.*) indult **2.** (*giur.*) free pardon.
indumento *sm.* garment.
indurimento *sm.* hardening.
indurire *vt.* e *vi.* to harden. ♦ **indurirsi** *vr.* to harden.
indurre *vt.* to induce, to get (*v. irr.*) || — *in errore,* to mislead (*v. irr.*). ♦ **indursi** *vr.* to bring (*v. irr.*) oneself (to).
industria *sf.* industry.
industriale *agg.* industrial. ♦ **industriale** *sm.* industrialist, manufacturer.
industrialismo *sm.* industrialism.
industrializzare *vt.* to industrialize.
industrializzazione *sf.* industrialization.
industriarsi *vr.* to do (*v. irr.*) one's best.
industrioso *agg.* industrious.
induttivo *agg.* inductive.
induttore *agg.* inductor.
induzione *sf.* induction.
inebetire *vt.* e *vi.* to dull.
inebetito *agg.* dull.
inebriante *agg.* inebriating.
inebriare *vt.* **1.** to make (*v. irr.*) drunk **2.** (*fig.*) to inebriate. ♦ **inebriarsi** *vr.* **1.** to get (*v. irr.*) drunk **2.** (*fig.*) to go (*v. irr.*) into raptures.
ineccepìbile *agg.* unexceptionable.
inedia *sf.* starvation.
inèdito *agg.* unpublished.
ineducato *agg.* ill-bred.
ineffàbile *agg.* ineffable.
inefficace *agg.* ineffective.
inefficacia *sf.* inefficacy.
inefficiente *agg.* inefficient.
inefficienza *sf.* ineffectiveness.
ineguaglianza *sf.* inequality.
ineguale *agg.* **1.** unlike **2.** (*irregolare*) irregular **3.** (*di superficie*) uneven.

ineleggìbile *agg.* ineligible.
ineleggibilità *sf.* ineligibility.
ineluttàbile *agg.* ineluctable.
ineluttabilità *sf.* inevitableness.
inenarràbile *agg.* unutterable.
inequivocàbile *agg.* unmistakable
'nerente *agg.* concerning.
inerme *agg.* unarmed.
inerpicarsi *vr.* to climb (up).
inerte *agg.* inert.
inerzia *sf.* inertness.
inesattezza *sf.* inaccuracy.
inesatto *agg.* incorrect.
inesaudito *agg.* ungranted.
inesaurìbile *agg.* inexhaustible.
inesàusto *agg.* unexhausted.
ineseguìbile *agg.* inexecutable.
inesigìbile *agg.* **1.** uncollectable **2.** (*di assegno*) worthless.
inesistente *agg.* inexistent.
inesistenza *sf.* inexistence.
inesoràbile *agg.* inexorable.
inesorabilità *sf.* inexorability.
inesperienza *sf.* inexperience.
inesperto *agg.* unskilled.
inespiàbile *agg.* inexpiable.
inesplicàbile *agg.* inexplicable.
inesploràbile *agg.* inexplorable.
inesplorato *agg.* unexplored.
inespressivo *agg.* inexpressive.
inespresso *agg.* implied.
inesprimìbile *agg.* inexpressible.
inespugnàbile *agg.* inexpugnable.
inespugnabilità *sf.* inexpugnability.
inestimàbile *agg.* inestimable.
inestinguìbile *agg.* unquenchable.
inestirpàbile *agg.* ineradicable.
inestricàbile *agg.* inextricable.
inettitùdine *sf.* unfitness.
inetto *agg.* **1.** unapt **2.** (*dappoco*) good-for-nothing.
inevaso *agg.* outstanding, unanswered.
inevitàbile *agg.* inevitable.
inezia *sf.* trifle.
infagottare *vt.* to muffle up. ♦ **infagottarsi** *vr.* to muffle oneself up.
infallìbile *agg.* infallible.
infallibilità *sf.* infallibility.
infamante *agg.* shameful.
infamare *vt.* to defame, to disgrace.
infame *agg.* wicked.
infamia *sf.* infamy.
infangare *vt.* to muddy. ♦ **infangarsi** *vr.* to become (*v. irr.*) muddy.
infanticida *s.* child-murderer.

infanticidio sm. child-murder.

infantile agg. childlike, childish.

infantilismo sm. infantilism.

infanzia sf. 1. infancy 2. (coll.) children (pl.).

infarcire vt. V. farcire.

infarinare vt. to flour. ♦ **infarinarsi** vr. to get (v. irr.) covered with flour.

infarinatura sf. 1. flouring 2. (fig.) smattering.

infarto sm. infarct.

infastidire vt. to annoy. ♦ **infastidirsi** vr. to get (v. irr.) bored.

infaticàbile agg. tireless.

infatti cong. in fact.

infatuare vt. to infatuate. ♦ **infatuarsi** vr. to get (v. irr.) crazy (about).

infatuato agg. crazy (about).

infatuazione sf. infatuation.

infàusto agg. unlucky.

infecondità sf. sterility.

infecondo agg. steril.

infedele agg. unfaithful. ♦ **infedele** sm. infidel.

infedeltà sf. unfaithfulness.

infelice agg. 1. unhappy 2. (non appropriato) ill-timed. ♦ **infelice** s. wretch.

infelicità sf. unhappiness.

inferiore agg. 1. inferior 2. (più basso) lower 3. (al di sotto) below. ♦ **inferiore** sm. inferior.

inferiorità sf. inferiority.

inferire vt. 1. (dedurre) to infer 2. (dare) to inflict.

infermerìa sf. infirmary.

infermiera sf. nurse.

infermiere sm. hospital attendant.

infermità sf. infirmity.

infermo agg. e sm. invalid.

infernale agg. 1. infernal 2. (fig.) awful.

inferno sm. hell.

inferocire vt. to enrage. ♦ **inferocire** vi. to get (v. irr.) fierce.

inferriata sf. grating.

infervorare vt. to excite. ♦ **infervorarsi** vr. to get (v. irr.) excited.

infervorato agg. fervent.

infestare vt. to infest.

infestazione sf. infestation.

infettare vt. to infect. ♦ **infettarsi** vr. to become (v. irr.) infected.

infettivo agg. contagious.

infetto agg. infected.

infezione sf. infection.

infiacchimento sm. weakening.

infiacchire vt. e vi. to weaken. ♦ **infiacchirsi** vr. to become (v. irr.) weak.

infiammàbile agg. inflammable.

infiammabilità sf. inflammability.

infiammare vt. 1. to set (v. irr.) on fire 2. (fig.) to inflame. ♦ **infiammarsi** vr. 1. to take (v. irr.) fire 2. (fig.) to get (v. irr.) excited.

infiammato agg. inflamed (with).

infiammatorio agg. inflammatory.

infiammazione sf. inflammation.

infiascare vt. to put (v. irr.) into flasks.

inficiare vt. 1. to invalidate 2. (giur.) to impugn.

infido agg. false.

infierire vi. to be pitiless.

infìggere vt. 1. to infix 2. (conficcare) to drive (v. irr.) (into).

infilare vt. 1. to thread 2. (introdurre) to insert 3. (passare per) to enter. ♦ **infilarsi** vr. to slip into.

infilata sf. row.

infiltrarsi vr. to penetrate.

infiltrazione sf. infiltration.

infilzare vt. 1. to transfix 2. (conficcare) to stick (v. irr.). ♦ **infilzarsi** vr. 1. to run (v. irr.) oneself through 2. (conficcarsi) to get (v. irr.) stuck.

infilzata sf. string.

ìnfimo agg. lowest.

infine avv. at last.

infingardàggine sf. laziness.

infingardo agg. lazy.

infinità sf. infinity.

infinitamente avv. infinitely.

infinitesimale agg. infinitesimal.

infinito agg. boundless. ♦ **infinito** sm. 1. infinite 2. (gramm.) infinitive.

infioccare vt. to tassel.

infiorare vt. to flower.

infirmare vt. to invalidate.

infischiarsi vr. not to care (about).

infittire vi. to thicken. ♦ **infittirsi** vr. to thicken.

inflazione sf. inflation.

inflazionìstico agg. inflationary.

inflessìbile agg. inflexible.

inflessibilità sf. inflexibility.

inflessione sf. inflexion.

inflìggere vt. to inflict.

influente agg. influential.

influenza sf. 1. influence 2. (med.) (fam.) 'flu.

influenzare vt. to influence.

influire *vi.* to exert influence (on, upon, over).

influsso *sm.* influence.

infocare *vt.* **1.** to heat up **2.** to inflame.

infocato *agg.* **1.** red hot **2.** (*fig.*) inflamed.

infoltire *vi.* to thicken.

infondatezza *sf.* groundlessness.

infondato *agg.* groundless.

infóndere *vt.* to infuse.

inforcare *vt.* **1.** to pitchfork **2.** (*montare a cavalcioni*) to get (*v. irr.*) on ‖ — *gli occhiali*, to put (*v. irr.*) on one's glasses.

informale *agg.* informal.

informare *vt.* **1.** to inform **2.** (*dare forma*) to shape. ♦ **informarsi** *vr.* to inquire (about).

informativo *agg.* informative.

informato *agg.* informed.

informatore *sm.* informer.

informazione *sf.* information (*solo sing.*), news (*pl.*).

informe *agg.* shapeless.

infornare *vt.* to put (*v. irr.*) into an oven.

infornata *sf.* batch.

infortunarsi *vr.* to get (*v. irr.*) injured.

infortunato *agg.* injured.

infortunio *sm.* accident.

infortunìstica *sf.* industrial accident research.

infossamento *sm.* hollow.

infossare *vt.* to hollow. ♦ **infossarsi** *vr.* to become (*v. irr.*) hollow.

infradiciare *vt.* **1.** to drench **2.** (*marcire*) to rot (*v. irr.*).

inframmettenza *sf.* interference.

inframméttere *vt.* to interpose. ♦ **inframméttersi** *vr.* to meddle (with).

infràngere *vt.* **1.** to shatter **2.** (*trasgredire*) to infringe. ♦ **infràngersi** *vr.* to break (*v. irr.*) (up).

infrangìbile *agg.* unbreakable: *vetro* —, shatter-proof glass.

infranto *agg.* **1.** shattered, broken **2.** (*di legge*) infringed.

infrarosso *agg.* infrared.

infrasettimanale *agg.* midweek.

infrastruttura *sf.* infrastructure.

infrazione *sf.* infraction.

infreddolirsi *vr.* to feel (*v. irr.*) cold.

infreddolito *agg.* chilly.

infrequente *agg.* infrequent.

infrollirsi *vr.* **1.** to become (*v. irr.*) tender **2.** (*di selvaggina*) to become (*v. irr.*) high.

infruttifero *agg.* unfruitful.

infruttuoso *agg.* **1.** unfruitful **2.** (*fig.*) useless.

infuori (*loc. prep.*) all'—, except.

infuriare *vi.* to enrage. ♦ **infuriarsi** *vr.* to flare up.

infusione *sf.* infusion.

infuso *agg.* infused. ♦ **infuso** *sm.* infusion.

infusorio *sm.* infusorial.

ingabbiare *vt.* **1.** to cage **2.** (*fig.*) to lock up.

ingaggiare *vt.* to engage.

ingaggio *sm.* engagement.

ingagliardire *vt.* to strengthen. ♦ **ingagliardirsi** *vr.* to strengthen.

ingannare *vt.* to deceive ‖ — *il tempo*, to while away the time. ♦ **ingannarsi** *vr.* to be mistaken.

ingannatore *agg.* deceiving. ♦ **ingannatore** *sm.* deceiver.

ingannévole *agg.* deceitful.

inganno *sm.* deception, fraud.

ingarbugliare *vt.* to entangle. ♦ **ingarbugliarsi** *vr.* to get (*v. irr.*) mixed up.

ingegnarsi *vr.* to contrive (to).

ingegnere *sm.* engineer.

ingegnerìa *sf.* engineering.

ingegno *sm.* talent.

ingegnosità *sf.* ingeniousness.

ingegnoso *agg.* ingenious.

ingelosire *vt.* to make (*v. irr.*) jealous. ♦ **ingelosirsi** *vr.* to become (*v. irr.*) jealous.

ingenerare *vt.* to engender.

ingeneroso *agg.* selfish.

ingente *agg.* huge.

ingentilire *vt.* to refine.

ingenuità *sf.* naïveness.

ingenuo *agg.* naïve.

ingerenza *sf.* interference.

ingerimento *sm.* swallowing.

ingerire *vt.* to swallow.

ingessare *vt.* to plaster.

ingessatura *sf.* **1.** plastering **2.** (*med.*) plaster cast.

inghiaiare *vt.* to gravel.

inghiottire *vt.* **1.** to swallow **2.** (*di acque ecc.*) to engulf **3.** (*sopportare*) to lump.

inghirlandare *vt.* to wreathe.

ingiallire *vt.* e *vi.* to yellow.

ingigantire *vt.* to magnify. ♦ **ingigantire** *vi.* to become (*v. irr.*) gigantic.

inginocchiarsi *vr.* to kneel (*v. irr.*) (down).

inginocchiatoio *sm.* kneeler.

ingioiellare *vt.* to bejewel.

ingiù *avv.* down, downwards.

ingiùngere *vt.* to order.

ingiuntivo *agg.* injunctive.

ingiunzione *sf.* injunction.

ingiuria *sf.* insult.

ingiuriare *vt.* to insult.

ingiurioso *agg.* insulting.

ingiustamente *avv.* unjustly.

ingiustificàbile *agg.* unjustifiable.

ingiustificato *agg.* unjustified.

ingiustizia *sf.* unjustice.

ingiusto *agg.* unjust.

inglese *agg.* English. ♦ **inglese** *sm.* Englishman (*pl.* -men) ‖ *gli Inglesi*, the English (people).

inglobare *vt.* to inglobe.

inglorioso *agg.* inglorious.

ingobbire *vi.* to become (*v. irr.*) humpbacked. ♦ **ingobbirsi** *vr.* to become humpbacked.

ingoiare *vt.* to swallow.

ingolfarsi *vr.* (*fig.*) to throw (*v. irr.*) oneself (into).

ingollare *vt.* to gulp down.

ingolosire *vt.* to make (*v. irr.*) greedy.

ingombrante *agg.* cumbersome.

ingombrare *vt.* to encumber.

ingombro *agg.* encumbered (with). ♦ **ingombro** *sm.* encumbrance.

ingommare *vt.* 1. to gum 2. (*incollare*) to stick (*v. irr.*).

ingordigia *sf.* greed.

ingordo *agg.* greedy.

ingorgare *vt.* to choke. ♦ **ingorgarsi** *vr.* to become (*v. irr.*) choked.

ingorgo *sm.* 1. obstruction 2. (*del traffico*) traffic jam.

ingozzare *vt.* to gulp.

ingranaggio *sm.* 1. gear 2. (*fig.*) mechanism.

ingranare *vt.* 1. to put (*v. irr.*) into gear 2. (*auto*) — *una marcia*, to engage a gear. ♦ **ingranare** *vi.* (*fam.*) to get (*v. irr.*) along (with).

ingrandimento *sm.* 1. enlargement 2. (*ott.*) magnification.

ingrandire *vt.* 1. to enlarge 2. (*ott.*) to magnify. ♦ **ingrandirsi** *vr.* to become (*v. irr.*) larger.

ingrassare *vt.* 1. to fatten 2. (*lubrificare*) to grease. ♦ **ingrassare** *vi.* to grow (*v. irr.*) fat.

ingrasso *sm.* fattening.

ingratitùdine *sf.* ingratitude.

ingrato *agg.* ungrateful. ♦ **ingrato** *sm.* ingrate.

ingravidare *vt.* to make (*v. irr.*) pregnant. ♦ **ingravidare** *vi.* to become (*v. irr.*) pregnant.

ingraziarsi *vr.* to get (*v. irr.*) into so.'s good graces.

ingrediente *sm.* ingredient.

ingresso *sm.* 1. entry 2. (*entrata*) entrance 3. (*accesso*) admittance.

ingrossamento *sm.* enlargement.

ingrossare *vt.* e *vi.* to enlarge. ♦ **ingrossarsi** *vr.* to become (*v. irr.*) bigger.

ingrosso (*nella loc. avv.*) all'—, wholesale.

ingualcìbile *agg.* crease-resistant.

inguarìbile *agg.* incurable.

inguinale *agg.* inguinal.

inguine *sm.* inguen.

ingurgitare *vt.* to swallow.

inibire *vt.* to inhibit.

inibito *agg.* inhibited.

inibizione *sf.* inhibition.

iniettare *vt.* to inject.

iniezione *sf.* injection.

inimicare *vt.* to alienate. ♦ **inimicarsi** *vr.* to estrange from oneself.

inimicizia *sf.* enmity.

inimitàbile *agg.* incomparable, inimitable.

inimmaginàbile *agg.* unimaginable.

inintelligìbile *agg.* unintelligible.

ininterrotto *agg.* continuous, unceasing.

iniquità *sf.* iniquity.

iniquo *agg.* 1. unfair 2. (*malvagio*) wicked.

iniziale *agg.* initial, starting. ♦ **iniziale** *sf.* initial.

iniziare *vt.* 1. to begin (*v. irr.*), to start 2. (*introdurre*) to initiate.

iniziativa *sf.* initiative.

iniziato *agg.* e *sm.* initiate.

iniziazione *sf.* initiation.

inizio *sm.* beginning.

innaffiare *vt.* to water.

innaffiatoio *sm.* watering-pot.

innalzamento *sm.* elevation.

innalzare *vt.* 1. to raise 2. (*rendere più alto*) to heighten. ♦ **innalzarsi** *vr.* to rise (*v. irr.*).

innamoramento *sm.* falling in love.

innamorare *vt.* to charm. ♦ **innamorarsi** *vr.* to fall (*v. irr.*) in love (with).

innamorato *agg.* in love (with). ♦ **innamorato** *sm.* lover.

innanzi *avv.* **1.** forward, on **2.** (*di fronte*) in front of **3.** (*più avanti*) further || *d'ora* —, from now on. ♦ **innanzi** *prep.* before.

innato *agg.* inborn.

innaturale *agg.* unnatural.

innegàbile *agg.* undeniable.

inneggiare *vi.* **1.** to exalt **2.** (*acclamare*) to cheer.

innervare *vt.* to innervate.

innervosire *vt.* to get (*v. irr.*) on so.'s nerves. ♦ **innervosirsi** *vr.* to get nervous.

innescamento *sm.* priming.

innescare *vt.* to prime.

innesco *sm.* primer.

innestare *vt.* **1.** (*agr.; med.*) to graft **2.** (*mecc.*) to engage.

innesto *sm.* **1.** (*agr.; med.*) graft **2.** (*mecc.*) clutch.

inno *sm.* hymn || — *nazionale*, national anthem.

innocente *agg. e sm.* innocent.

innocenza *sf.* innocence.

innocuità *sf.* innocuousness.

innocuo *agg.* harmless.

innominàbile *agg.* unmentionable.

innovare *vt.* to innovate.

innovatore *agg.* innovating. ♦ **innovatore** *sm.* innovator.

innovazione *sf.* innovation.

innumerévole *agg.* numberless.

inoculare *vt.* to inoculate.

inoculazione *sf.* inoculation.

inodoro *agg.* odourless.

inoffensivo *agg.* harmless.

inoltrare *vt.* to forward. ♦ **inoltrarsi** *vr.* to advance.

inoltrato *agg.* advanced, late.

inoltre *avv.* moreover, besides.

inoltro *sm.* **1.** (*di merci*) forwarding **2.** (*di documenti*) sending on.

inondare *vt.* to flood.

inondazione *sf.* flood.

inoperosità *sf.* inactivity.

inoperoso *agg.* inactive.

inopinàbile *agg.* inconceivable.

inopinato *agg.* unexpected.

inopportunità *sf.* inopportunity.

inopportuno *agg.* inopportune.

inoppugnàbile *agg.* incontestable.

inoppugnabilità *sf.* incontestability.

inorgànico *agg.* inorganic.

inorgoglire *vt.* to make (*v. irr.*) proud. ♦ **inorgoglirsi** *vr.* to become (*v. irr.*) proud.

inorridire *vt.* to horrify. ♦ **inorridire** *vi.* to be horrified.

inospitale *agg.* inhospitable.

inosservanza *sf.* inobservance.

inosservato *agg.* unobserved.

inossidàbile *agg.* rust-proof || *acciaio* —, stainless steel.

inquadramento *sm.* framing.

inquadrare *vt.* **1.** to frame **2.** (*fig.*) to set (*v. irr.*) **3.** (*mil.*) to rank **4.** (*foto, cine*) to frame.

inquadratura *sf.* (*cine*) shot.

inqualificàbile *agg.* despicable.

inquietante *agg.* worrying.

inquietare *vt.* to worry. ♦ **inquietarsi** *vr.* to get (*v. irr.*) angry.

inquieto *agg.* **1.** restless **2.** (*preoccupato*) worried **3.** (*arrabbiato*) angry.

inquietùdine *sf.* **1.** restlessness **2.** (*preoccupazione*) anxiety.

inquilino *sm.* tenant.

inquinamento *sm.* defilement.

inquinare *vt.* to defile.

inquirente *agg.* investigating.

inquisire *vt.* to investigate. ♦ **inquisire** *vi.* to inquire.

inquisitore *agg.* inquiring. ♦ **inquisitore** *sm.* inquisitor.

inquisizione *sf.* inquisition.

insabbiamento *sm.* (*fig.*) hindering.

insabbiare *vt.* **1.** to sand **2.** (*fig.*) to hinder.

insaccare *vt.* to sack.

insalata *sf.* salad.

insalatiera *sf.* salad-bowl.

insalubre *agg.* unhealthy.

insalubrità *sf.* insalubrity.

insanàbile *agg.* incurable.

insanguinare *vt.* to cover (with blood). ♦ **insanguinarsi** *vr.* to become (*v. irr.*) bloodstained.

insano *agg.* insane.

insaponare *vt.* to soap.

insaponatura *sf.* soaping.

insaporire *vt.* to flavour.

insaporo *agg.* flavourless.

insaputa *sf.* (*nella loc. avv.*) *all'— di*, unknown (to).

insaziàbile *agg.* insatiable.

insaziabilità *sf.* insatiability.

insaziato *agg.* unappeased.

inscatolare *vt.* to tin.

inscenare *vt.* to stage.

inscindìbile *agg.* inseparable.

inscrìvere *vt.* **1.** (*a una scuola, esame ecc.*) to enrol **2.** (*scrivere, scolpire; geom.*) to inscribe.

insediamento *sm.* installation.
insediare *vt.* to install. ♦ **insediarsi** *vr.* to install oneself.
insegna *sf.* **1.** insignia (*pl.*) **2.** (*bandiera*) flag **3.** (*di negozio*) sign-board.
insegnamento *sm.* **1.** teaching **2.** (*precetto, lezione*) precept, lesson.
insegnante *agg.* teaching. ♦ **insegnante** *s.* teacher.
insegnare *vt.* to teach (*v. irr.*).
inseguimento *sm.* pursuit.
inseguire *vt.* to pursue.
inseguitore *sm.* pursuer.
insellare *vt.* to saddle.
inselvatichire *vi.* to grow (*v. irr.*) wild.
insenatura *sf.* inlet, creek.
insensatezza *sf.* **1.** craziness **2.** (*atto insensato*) foolish action.
insensato *agg.* foolish, crazy.
insensìbile *agg.* **1.** insensible **2.** (*indifferente*) indifferent **3.** (*frigido*) unfeeling.
insensibilità *sf.* **1.** insensibility **2.** (*indifferenza*) indifference.
insensibilmente *avv.* **1.** (*impercettibilmente*) imperceptibly, slightly **2.** (*senza sentimento*) insensibly.
inseparàbile *agg.* inseparable.
insepolto *agg.* unburied.
inserimento *sm.* insertion.
inserire *vt.* **1.** to insert **2.** (*elettr.*) to connect.
inserto *sm.* **1.** file, dossier **2.** (*cine, stampa*) insert.
inservìbile *agg.* useless.
inserviente *sm.* attendant.
inserzione *sf.* **1.** insertion **2.** (*pubblicitaria*) advertisement.
inserzionista *sm.* advertiser.
insetticida *agg.* e *sm.* insecticide.
insettìvoro *agg.* insectivorous. ♦ **insettìvoro** *sm.* insectivore.
insetto *sm.* insect.
insicurezza *sf.* insecurity.
insidia *sf.* **1.** snare **2.** (*pericolo*) danger.
insidiare *vt.* to endanger || — *la vita di una persona*, to attempt a person's life.
insidioso *agg.* insidious.
insieme *avv.* **1.** together **2.** (*allo stesso tempo*) at the same time. ♦ **insieme** *prep.* together (with). ♦ **insieme** *sm.* whole: *nell'—*, as a whole || *sguardo d'—*, comprehensive view.
insigne *agg.* famous.

insignificante *agg.* insignificant.
insignire *vt.* to confer (sthg. upon).
insincerità *sf.* insincerity.
insincero *agg.* insincere.
insindacàbile *agg.* undisputable.
insinuante *agg.* insinuating.
insinuare *vt.* to hint. ♦ **insinuarsi** *vr.* to insinuate oneself.
insinuazione *sf.* hint, insinuation.
insipidezza *sf.* insipidness.
insìpido *agg.* **1.** tasteless **2.** (*fig.*) insipid.
insistente *agg.* **1.** insistent, steady **2.** (*molesto*) irritating.
insistenza *sf.* insistence.
insìstere *vi.* to insist (on).
insito *agg.* inborn, inherent.
insoddisfatto *agg.* dissatisfied (with).
insoddisfazione *sf.* dissatisfaction (with).
insofferente *agg.* intolerant.
insofferenza *sf.* intolerance.
insoffrìbile *agg.* unbearable.
insolazione *sf.* sunstroke.
insolente *agg.* e *sm.* insolent.
insolentire *vt.* to insult.
insolenza *sf.* insolence.
insòlito *agg.* unusual.
insolùbile *agg.* insoluble.
insolubilità *sf.* insolubility.
insoluto *agg.* **1.** unsolved **2.** (*non pagato*) unpaid.
insolvente *agg.* insolvent.
insolvenza *sf.* insolvency.
insolvìbile *agg.* **1.** (*di debito*) unpayable **2.** (*di persona*) insolvent.
insolvibilità *sf.* insolvency.
insomma *avv.* finally, in short.
insondàbile *agg.* unfathomable.
insonne *agg.* sleepless.
insonnia *sf.* insomnia.
insonnolito *agg.* drowsy, sleepy.
insopportàbile *agg.* unbearable.
insopprimìbile *agg.* insuppressible.
insòrgere *vi.* **1.** to rise (*v. irr.*) **2.** (*protestare*) to protest, to rebel **3.** (*manifestarsi*) to arise (*v. irr.*).
insormontàbile *agg.* insurmountable.
insorto *sm.* rebel.
insospettàbile *agg.* beyond suspicion.
insospettato *agg.* unsuspected.
insospettire *vt.* to make (*v. irr.*) suspicious. ♦ **insospettirsi** *vr.* to grow (*v. irr.*) suspicious.
insostenìbile *agg.* unsustainable.
insostituìbile *agg.* irreplaceable.

insozzare *vt.* **1.** to soil **2.** (*fig.*) to disgrace.
insperàbile *agg.* beyond hope.
insperato *agg.* unhoped for.
inspiegàbile *agg.* inexplicable.
inspirare *vt.* to breathe in.
inspirazione *sf.* breathing in, inhalation.
instàbile *agg.* unstable || *tempo* —, unsettled weather.
instabilità *sf.* **1.** instability **2.** (*fig.*) fickleness.
installare *vt.* to install. ◆ **installarsi** *vr.* to settle.
installazione *sf.* installation.
instancàbile *agg.* untiring.
instaurare *vt.* to set (*v. irr.*) up.
instaurazione *sf.* establishment.
instradare *vt.* to direct, to coach.
insú *avv.* up, upwards.
insubordinatezza *sf.* insubordination.
insubordinato *agg.* insubordinate.
insubordinazione *sf.* insubordination.
insuccesso *sm.* failure.
insudiciare *vt.* to soil.
insufficiente *agg.* insufficient.
insufficienza *sf.* **1.** insufficiency **2.** (*scol.*) low mark.
insulare *agg.* insular.
insulina *sf.* insulin.
insulsàggine *sf.* **1.** silliness **2.** (*cosa insulsa*) nonsense.
insulso *agg.* silly.
insultare *vt.* to insult.
insulto *sm.* insult.
insuperàbile *agg.* insuperable.
insuperato *agg.* unsurpassed.
insuperbire *vt.* to elate. ◆ **insuperbirsi** *vr.* to pride oneself (on).
insurrezionale *agg.* insurrectional.
insurrezione *sf.* insurrection.
insussistente *agg.* unfounded.
intaccare *vt.* **1.** to notch **2.** (*chim.*) to etch **3.** (*fig.*) to injure.
intacco *sm.* notch.
intagliare *vt.* **1.** to carve **2.** (*incidere*) to engrave.
intaglio *sm.* **1.** carving **2.** (*incisione*) engraving.
intangìbile *agg.* intangible.
intanto *avv.* meanwhile.
intarsiare *vt.* to inlay.
intarsio *sm.* inlay.
intasamento *sm.* obstruction.
intasare *vt.* to obstruct.
intascare *vt.* to pocket.

intatto *agg.* intact.
intavolare *vt.* **1.** to plank **2.** (*iniziare*) to begin (*v. irr.*), to start.
integèrrimo *agg.* strictly honest.
integràbile *agg.* integrable.
integrale *agg.* integral: (*mat.*) *calcolo* —, integral calculus.
integrante *agg.* integrant.
integrare *vt.* to integrate.
integrazione *sf.* integration.
integrità *sf.* integrity.
integro *agg.* **1.** integral **2.** (*onesto*) honest.
intelaiatura *sf.* **1.** framework **2.** (*di finestre*) sash.
intellettivo *agg.* intellective.
intelletto *sm.* intellect.
intellettuale *agg. e sm.* intellectual.
intellettualismo *sm.* intellectualism.
intelligente *agg.* intelligent.
intelligenza *sf.* intelligence.
intelligìbile *agg.* intelligible.
intelligibilità *sf.* intelligibility.
intemerata *sf.* reprimand.
intemerato *agg.* faultless.
intemperante *agg.* intemperate.
intemperanza *sf.* intemperance.
intemperie *sf. pl.* inclemency of the weather (*sing.*).
intempestività *sf.* untimeliness.
intempestivo *agg.* untimely.
intendente *agg.* expert. ◆ **intendente** *sm.* superintendent.
intendenza *sf.* superintendence.
intèndere *vt.* **1.** (*capire*) to understand (*v. irr.*) **2.** (*significare*) to mean (*v. irr.*) **3.** (*avere intenzione di*) to intend to. ◆ **intèndersi** *vr.* **1.** (*avere cognizione*) to be a good judge **2.** (*mettersi d'accordo*) to come (*v. irr.*) to an agreement.
intendimento *sm.* **1.** understanding **2.** (*intenzione*) intention.
intenditore *sm.* **1.** good judge **2.** (*d'arte*) connoisseur.
intenerimento *sm.* **1.** softening **2.** (*fig.*) tenderness.
intenerire *vt.* **1.** to soften **2.** (*fig.*) to move to pity. ◆ **intenerirsi** *vr.* to be moved to pity.
intensificare *vt.* to intensify.
intensificazione *sf.* intensification.
intensità *sf.* intensity.
intensivo *agg.* intensive.
intenso *agg.* intense.
intentàbile *agg.* **1.** unattemptable **2.** (*giur.*) suable.

intentare vt. to bring (v. irr.).
intento agg. intent. ♦ **intento** sm. aim, purpose.
intenzionale agg. deliberate.
intenzionato agg. disposed.
intenzione sf. intention.
intepidire vt. to warm, to make (v. irr.) tepid. ♦ **intepidirsi** vr. to get (v. irr.) tepid.
interamente avv. wholly, entirely.
intercalare agg. intercalary. ♦ **intercalare** sm. pet phrase.
intercalare vt. to intercalate.
intercambiàbile agg. interchangeable.
intercèdere vi. to intercede, to plead.
intercessione sf. intercession.
intercessore sm. intercessor.
intercettare vt. to intercept.
intercettatore sm. interceptor.
intercettazione sf. interception.
intercomunale sf. (tel.) long-distance call.
intercontinentale agg. intercontinental.
intercòrrere vi. 1. to pass 2. (accadere) to happen.
intercostale agg. intercostal.
interdetto agg. 1. prohibited 2. (giur.) interdicted. ♦ **interdetto** sm. interdict.
interdipendente agg. interdependent.
interdipendenza sf. interdependence.
interdire vt. to interdict.
interdizione sf. interdiction.
interessamento sm. concern.
interessante agg. interesting.
interessare vt. 1. to interest 2. (riguardare) to concern. ♦ **interessarsi** vr. 1. to be interested (in) 2. (provvedere) to take (v. irr.) care (of).
interessato agg. interested.
interesse sm. interest.
interessenza sf. share, profit.
interezza sf. wholeness.
interferenza sf. interference.
interferire vi. to interfere.
interiezione sf. interjection.
interinale agg. temporary.
interiora sf. pl. entrails.
interiore agg. inner. ♦ **interiore** sm. interior, inside.
interiorità sf. inwardness.
interiormente avv. 1. (intimamente) innerly 2. (nell'interno) inside.

interlìnea sf. 1. interline 2. (tip.) lead.
interlineare vt. 1. to interline 2. (tip.) to lead (v. irr.).
interlineare vt. to interline.
interlocutore sm. interlocutor.
interlocutorio agg. interlocutory.
interloquire vi. to join in the conversation.
interludio sm. interlude.
intermediario agg. intermediary. ♦ **intermediario** sm. 1. go-between 2. (comm.) middleman (pl. -men).
intermedio agg. intermediate, middle.
intermezzo sm. 1. intermission 2. (mus.) intermezzo.
interminàbile agg. endless.
intermittente agg. intermittent.
intermittenza sf. intermittence.
internamento sm. internment.
internare vt. to intern.
internato agg. interned. ♦ **internato** sm. (scol.) boarding-school.
internazionale agg. international.
internazionalismo sm. internationalism.
internazionalizzare vt. to internationalize.
interno agg. 1. internal, interior 2. (interiore) inner. ♦ **interno** sm. interior.
intero agg. 1. whole 2. (intatto) intact.
interpellanza sf. interrogation.
interpellare vt. 1. (pol.) to interpellate 2. (giur.) to summon 3. (chiedere) to ask.
interplanetario agg. interplanetary.
interpolare vt. to interpolate.
interpolazione sf. interpolation.
interporre vt. to interpose.
interpretare vt. 1. to interpret, to render 2. (teat.) to play.
interpretativo agg. interpretative.
interpretazione sf. 1. interpretation 2. (cine) starring 3. (mus.) performance 4. (teat.) acting.
intèrprete s. 1. interpreter 2. (teat.; cine) actor, player.
interpunzione sf. punctuation.
interramento sm. burial.
interrare vt. 1. to bury 2. (riempire di terra) to fill up with earth.
interrogare vt. to question.
interrogativo agg. interrogative || punto —, question mark. ♦ **interrogativo** sm. interrogative.

interrogatore *agg.* interrogating. ◆
  interrogatore *sm.* examiner.
interrogatorio *sm.* examination.
interrogazione *sf.* **1.** interrogation
  2. (*scol.*) oral test.
interròmpere *vt.* to interrupt. ◆
  interròmpersi *vr.* to stop.
interrotto *agg.* interrupted || *stra-
da interrotta*, blocked road.
interruttore *sm.* (*elettr.*) switch.
interruzione *sf.* interruption.
intersecare *vt.* to intersect.
intersezione *sf.* intersection.
interstizio *sm.* interstice.
intervallare *vt.* to space.
intervallo *sm.* **1.** interval **2.** (*spazio*) space.
intervenire *vi.* **1.** to intervene **2.**
  (*essere presenti*) to be present.
interventismo *sm.* intervention-
ism.
interventista *s.* interventionist.
intervento *sm.* **1.** intervention **2.**
  (*presenza*) presence **3.** (*chir.*) operation.
intervenuto *agg.* present. ◆ **intervenuto** *sm.* person present.
intervista *sf.* interview.
intervistare *vt.* to interview.
intesa *sf.* agreement.
inteso *agg.* **1.** agreed (upon) **2.** (*mi-
rante*) aiming (at).
intèssere *vt.* to interweave (*v. irr.*).
intestare *vt.* to head, to register. ◆
  intestarsi *vr.* to be determinated.
intestatario *sm.* holder.
intestato *agg.* **1.** headed **2.** (*giur.*)
registered **3.** (*senza testamento*)
intestate **4.** (*ostinato*) stubborn.
intestazione *sf.* **1.** title **2.** (*di lettera ecc.*) heading.
intestinale *agg.* intestinal.
intestino *sm.* intestine.
intimare *vt.* **1.** (*ordinare*) to order
2. (*ingiungere*) to summon.
intimazione *sf.* **1.** order **2.** (*ingiunzione*) summons.
intimidatorio *agg.* intimidatory.
intimidazione *sf.* intimidation.
intimidire *vt.* **1.** to make (*v. irr.*)
shy **2.** (*impaurire*) to intimidate.
intimità *sf.* **1.** privacy **2.** (*familiarità*) familiarity.
ìntimo *agg.* **1.** intimate **2.** (*profondo*) deep. ◆ **ìntimo** *sm.* **1.** (*ami-
co*) intimate **2.** (*animo*) soul ||
nell'—, at heart.
intimorire *vt.* to frighten. ◆ **in-
timorirsi** *vr.* to get (*v. irr.*)

frightened.
intìngere *vt.* to dip.
intìngolo *sm.* **1.** gravy **2.** (*salsa*)
sauce.
intirizzire *vt.* to benumb.
intitolare *vt.* **1.** to entitle **2.** (*dedicare*) to dedicate.
intoccàbile *agg. e sm.* untouchable.
intolleràbile *agg.* intolerable.
intollerante *agg.* intolerant.
intolleranza *sf.* intolerance.
intonacare *vt.* to plaster.
intonacatura *sf.* plastering.
intònaco *sm.* plaster.
intonare *vt.* **1.** to tune **2.** (*cantile-
nare*) to intone. ◆ **intonarsi** *vr.*
1. to harmonize (with) **2.** (*di colori*) to match.
intonato *agg.* **1.** in tune **2.** (*di colori*) matching.
intonazione *sf.* **1.** intonation **2.** (*di
strumenti*) tuning **3.** (*di colori, voce*) tone.
intonso *agg.* (*di libri*) uncut.
intontimento *sm.* stunning.
intontire *vt.* to stun.
intoppare *vt.* to stumble (on).
intoppo *sm.* **1.** obstacle **2.** (*fig.*)
hitch.
intorbidare *vt.* to make (*v. irr.*)
muddy. ◆ **intorbidarsi** *vr.* to become (*v. irr.*) muddy.
intorno *avv.* round, around. ◆ **intorno a** *prep.* **1.** round, around
2. (*circa, su di*) about.
intorpidimento *sm.* numbness.
intorpidire *vt.* to benumb. ◆ **intorpidirsi** *vr.* to grow (*v. irr.*)
numb.
intossicare *vt.* to poison.
intossicazione *sf.* poisoning.
intraducìbile *agg.* untranslatable.
intralciare *vt.* to hinder, to interfere.
intralcio *sm.* hindrance.
intrallazzo *sm.* **1.** plotting **2.** (*imbroglio*) swindle.
intramezzare *vt.* to interpose, to
alternate.
intramontàbile *agg.* everlasting.
intramuscolare *agg.* intermuscu-
lar.
intransigente *agg.* strict, intransigent.
intransigenza *sf.* intransigence.
intransitivo *agg. e sm.* intransitive.
intrappolare *vt.* to entrap.
intraprendente *agg.* enterprising.
intraprendenza *sf.* enterprise.

intraprèndere vt. **1.** to undertake (v. irr.), to start **2.** (una professione) to go (v. irr.) in for.

intrattàbile agg. intractable.

intrattenere vt. to entertain. ♦ **intrattenersi** vr. **1.** to linger **2.** (dilungarsi) to dwell (v. irr.).

intravedere vt. **1.** (vedere di sfuggita) to catch (v. irr.) a glimpse of **2.** (vedere indistintamente) to see (v. irr.) indistinctly.

intrecciare vt. **1.** to interlace || — danze, to dance **2.** (capelli, nastri) to plait.

intreccio sm. **1.** interlacement **2.** (di romanzi) plot.

intrèpido agg. brave, fearless.

intricare vt. to tangle. ♦ **intricarsi** vr. to get (v. irr.) entangled.

intrico sm. tangle.

intrìdere vt. to soak.

intrigante agg. crafty. ♦ **intrigante** sm. intriguer.

intrigare vi. to intrigue. ♦ **intrigarsi** vr. to meddle (with).

intrigo sm. intrigue, plot.

intrìnseco agg. intrinsic.

intristire vi. **1.** to pine away **2.** (incattivire) to grow (v. irr.) wicked.

introdotto agg. **1.** (importato) imported **2.** (conosciuto) well-known.

intriso agg. soaked (with), imbrued.

introdurre vt. **1.** to introduce **2.** (far entrare) to show (v. irr.) in. ♦ **introdursi** vr. to get (v. irr.) into, to slip into.

introduttivo agg. introductory.

introduzione sf. introduction.

introitare vt. to cash.

intròito sm. profit.

introméttere vt. to introduce. ♦ **introméttersi** vr. to interfere.

intromissione sf. intrusion.

intronare vt. to stun.

introspettivo agg. introspective.

introspezione sf. introspection.

introvàbile agg. not to be found.

introversione sf. introversion.

introverso agg. introverted. ♦ **introverso** sm. introvert.

intrufolarsi vr. to intrude (in).

intruglio sm. bad mixture.

intruppamento sm. trooping.

intrupparsi vr. to troop.

intrusione sf. intrusion.

intruso sm. intruder.

intuìbile agg. guessable.

intuire vt. to guess, to perceive.

intuitivo agg. intuitive.

intùito sm. intuition, insight.

intuizione sf. intuition.

inturgidimento sm. swelling.

inturgidire vi. to swell (up). **inturgidirsi** vr. to swell (up).

inuguale agg. unlike.

inumanità sf. inhumanity.

inumano agg. inhuman.

inumare vt. to inter.

inumazione sf. interment.

inumidire vt. to moisten. ♦ **inumidirsi** vr. to moisten.

inurbanità sf. incivility.

inurbano agg. uncivil.

inurbarsi vr. to inurbate.

inusitato agg. unusual.

inùtile agg. useless.

inutilità sf. uselessness.

inutilizzàbile agg. unusable.

invadente agg. intrusive.

invadenza sf. intrusiveness.

invàdere vt. to invade.

invaghimento sm. fancy (for).

invaghirsi vr. to take (v. irr.) a fancy (for), to fall (v. irr.) in love (with).

invaghito agg. fond (of), infatuated.

invalere vi. to prevail.

invalicàbile agg. impassable.

invalidare vt. to invalidate.

invalidazione sf. invalidation.

invalidità sf. invalidity.

invàlido agg. e sm. invalid.

invalso agg. prevailed.

invano avv. in vain.

invariàbile agg. **1.** invariable **2.** (di tempo) unchangeable.

invariabilità sf. invariability.

invariato agg. unchanged.

invasamento sm. obsession.

invasare vt. to possess.

invasato agg. possessed. ♦ **invasato** sm. possessed person.

invasione sf. invasion.

invasore sm. invader.

invecchiamento sm. ageing.

invecchiare vt. to make (v. irr.) old. ♦ **invecchiare** vi. to grow (v. irr.) old.

invece avv. on the contrary || — di, instead of.

inveire vi. to rail (at).

invelenire vt. to embitter.

invendìbile agg. unsaleable.

invendicato agg. unavenged.

invenduto agg. unsold.

inventare vt. to invent.

inventariare vt. to inventory.

inventario sm. inventory || con beneficio d'—, with reservation.

inventiva sf. inventiveness.

inventivo agg. inventive.

inventore sm. inventor.

invenzione sf. invention.

inverdire vi. to turn green.

inverecondia sf. immodesty.

inverecondo agg. immodest.

inverificàbile agg. unverifiable.

invernale agg. 1. winter (attr.) 2. (da inverno) wintry.

invernata sf. wintertime.

inverno sm. winter.

invero avv. indeed.

inverosimiglianza sf. unlikelihood.

inverosìmile agg. unlikely.

inversione sf. inversion.

inverso agg. 1. (mat.) inverse 2. opposite, contrary. ♦ **inverso** sm. opposite, contrary.

invertebrato agg. e sm. invertebrate.

invertìbile agg. invertible.

invertire vt. to invert || — la marcia, to reverse.

invertito sm. invert.

invertitore sm. reverse gear.

investigare vt. to inquire.

investigativo agg. investigative.

investigatore sm. detective.

investigazione sf. investigation.

investimento sm. 1. investment 2. collision 3. (stradale) running down.

investire vt. 1. to invest (with) 2. (comm.) to invest 3. (assalire) to assail 4. (auto) to run (v. irr.) down.

investitore sm. (comm.) investor.

investitura sf. investiture.

inveterato agg. inveterate.

invetriata sf. glass window.

invettiva sf. invective.

inviare vt. to send (v. irr.).

inviato sm. 1. messenger 2. (in diplomazia) envoy 3. (in giornalismo) correspondent.

invidia sf. envy: per —, out of envy.

invidiàbile agg. enviable.

invidiare vt. to envy.

invidioso agg. envious.

invigorire vt. to strengthen. ♦ **invigorirsi** vr. to strengthen.

inviluppare vt. to envelop, to wrap up.

invincìbile agg. invincible.

invincibilità sf. invincibility.

invìo sm. 1. (per posta) mailing 2. (di merci) forwarding 3. (per nave) shipment 4. (di danaro) remittance.

inviolàbile agg. inviolable.

inviolabilità sf. inviolability.

inviperirsi vr. to become (v. irr.) furious.

inviperito agg. furious.

invischiare vt. 1. to lime 2. (fig.) to entangle. ♦ **invischiarsi** vr. to get (v. irr.) entangled.

invisìbile agg. invisible.

invisibilità sf. invisibility.

inviso agg. disliked.

invitante agg. inviting.

invitare vt. 1. to invite 2. (domandare) to request.

invitato agg. invited. ♦ **invitato** sm. guest.

invito sm. invitation.

invitto agg. unconquered.

invocare vt. to invoke.

invocazione sf. invocation.

invogliare vt. to tempt.

involare vt. to abduct. ♦ **involarsi** vr. to flee, to run (v. irr.) away.

involontario agg. unintentional.

involto sm. bundle, parcel.

invòlucro sm. 1. envelope 2. (bot.) involucre.

involutivo agg. involutionary.

involuto agg. involved.

involuzione sf. 1. involution 2. (decadenza) decline.

invulneràbile agg. invulnerable.

invulnerabilità sf. invulnerability.

inzaccherare vt. to muddy. ♦ **inzaccherarsi** vr. to get (v. irr.) muddy.

inzuppare vt. 1. to soak 2. (intingere) to dip.

io pron. I: — stesso, I myself.

iodato agg. iodized. ♦ **iodato** sm. iodate.

iodio sm. iodine.

iole sf. gig.

ione sm. ion.

iònico agg. Ionic.

ionizzazione sf. ionization.

ionosfera sf. ionosphere.

iosa (nella loc. avv.) a —, in plenty.

iperalimentazione sf. hypernutrition.

ipèrbole sf. hyperbole.

iperbòlico agg. hyperbolic(al).

iperbòreo agg. hyperborean.

ipercrìtico *agg.* hypercritical.
ipermetropìa *sf.* hypermetropia.
ipermètrope *agg.* hypermetropic.
ipernutrizione *sf.* hypernutrition.
ipersensìbile *agg.* hypersensitive.
ipersensibilità *sf.* hypersensitivity.
ipertensione *sf.* hypertension.
iperteso *agg. e sm.* hypertensive.
ipertrofìa *sf.* hypertrophy.
ipnosi *sf.* hypnosis.
ipnòtico *agg.* hypnotic.
ipnotismo *sm.* hypnotism.
ipnotizzare *vt.* to hypnotize.
ipnotizzatore *sm.* hypnotizer.
ipocondrìa *sf.* hypochondria.
ipocondrìaco *agg. e sm.* hypochon-
    driac.
ipocrisìa *sf.* hypocrisy.
ipòcrita *agg.* hypocritical. ♦ ipò-
    crita *sm.* hypocrite.
ipodèrmico *agg.* hypodermic.
ipodermoclisi *sf.* hypodermoclysis.
ipòfisi *sf.* hypophysis.
ipoteca *sf.* mortgage.
ipotecare *vt.* to mortgage.
ipotenusa *sf.* hypotenuse.
ipòtesi *sf.* **1.** hypothesis (*pl.* -ses) **2.**
    (*supposizione*) supposition.
ipotètico *agg.* hypothetical.
ìppica *sf.* horse-racing.
ìppico *agg.* horse (*attr.*).
ippocampo *sm.* hippocampus (*pl.*
    -pi).
ippocastano *sm.* horse-chestnut.
ippòdromo *sm.* race-course.
ippopòtamo *sm.* hippopotamus.
ira *sf.* anger, rage.
iracondo *agg.* irascible.
irascìbile *agg.* irritable.
irascibilità *sf.* irritability.
irato *agg.* angry.
iridato *agg.* iridescent.
ìride *sf.* iris.
iridescente *agg.* iridescent.
iridescenza *sf.* iridescence.
irlandese *agg.* Irish.
ironìa *sf.* irony.
irònico *agg.* ironic(al).
ironizzare *vi.* to make (*v. irr.*)
    ironical remarks.
iroso *agg.* wrathful.
irradiamento *sm.* irradiation.
irradiare *vt.* to irradiate.
irradiazione *sf.* V. irradiamento.
irraggiare *vt.* V. irradiare.
irraggiungìbile *agg.* unreachable.
irragionévole *agg.* unreasonable.
irrancidire *vi.* to grow (*v. irr.*)
    rank.

irrazionale *agg.* irrational.
irrazionalità *sf.* irrationality.
irreale *agg.* unreal.
irrealizzàbile *agg.* unrealizable.
irrealtà *sf.* unreality.
irreconciliàbile *agg.* irreconcilable.
irrecuperàbile *agg.* irrecoverable.
irrefrenàbile *agg.* unrestrainable.
irrefutàbile *agg.* irrefutable.
irregolare *agg.* irregular.
irregolarità *sf.* irregularity.
irremovìbile *agg.* **1.** immovable **2.**
    (*inflessibile*) inflexible.
irreparàbile *agg.* irreparable.
irreperìbile *agg.* elusive: *render-
    si* —, to hide (*v. irr.*) oneself.
irreprensìbile *agg.* irreproachable.
irrequietezza *sf.* restlessness.
irrequieto *agg.* restless.
irresistìbile *agg.* irresistible.
irresolutezza *sf.* irresolution.
irresoluto *agg.* hesitating.
irrespiràbile *agg.* unbreathable.
irresponsàbile *agg.* irresponsible.
irresponsabilità *sf.* irresponsibi-
    lity.
irrestringìbile *agg.* unshrinkable.
irretire *vt.* to snare.
irreversìbile *agg.* irreversible.
irreversibilità *sf.* irreversibility.
irrevocàbile *agg.* irrevocable.
irriconoscìbile *agg.* unrecognizable.
irrìdere *vt.* to laugh at.
irriducìbile *agg.* irreducible.
irriflessione *sf.* thoughtlessness.
irriflessivo *agg.* thoughtless.
irrigàbile *agg.* irrigable.
irrigare *vt.* to irrigate.
irrigazione *sf.* irrigation.
irrigidimento *sm.* stiffening.
irrigidire *vt.* to stiffen. ♦ irrigi-
    dirsi *vr.* to stiffen.
irriguo *agg.* well-watered.
irrilevante *agg.* insignificant.
irrimediàbile *agg.* irremediable.
irrisione *sf.* mockery.
irrisorio *agg.* derisory, paltry.
irrispettoso *agg.* disrespectful.
irritàbile *agg.* **1.** (*di persona*) irri-
    table **2.** (*di pelle*) sensitive.
irritabilità *sf.* **1.** (*di persona*) irri-
    tability **2.** (*di pelle*) sensitiveness.
irritante *agg.* irritating.
irritare *vt.* to irritate. ♦ irritarsi
    vr. **1.** to grow (*v. irr.*) angry **2.**
    (*di pelle*) to become (*v. irr.*) irri-
    tated.
irritazione *sf.* **1.** irritation **2.** (*di
    pelle*) inflammation.

irriverente *agg.* disrespectful.

irriverenza *sf.* irreverence.

irrobustire *vt.* to strengthen. ♦ **irrobustirsi** *vr.* to strengthen.

irròmpere *vi.* **1.** to break (*v. irr.*) into **2.** (*di acque*) to overflow.

irrorare *vt.* to sprinkle.

irroratrice *sf.* sprayer.

irruente *agg.* impetuous.

irruenza *sf.* impetuosity.

irruvidire *vt.* to roughen.

irruzione *sf.* irruption: *fare* —, to rush into.

irsuto *agg.* shaggy.

irto *agg.* bristling (with).

iscritto *sm.* member.

iscrìvere *vt.* **1.** (*a scuola, esami ecc.*) to enrol **2.** (*registrare*) to record **3.** (*scolpire*) to engrave. ♦ **iscrìversi** *vr.* to enter, to join.

iscrizione *sf.* **1.** inscription **2.** (*a scuola, esami ecc.*) entry || *domanda d'*—, application.

islàmico *agg.* Islamic.

islamismo *sm.* Islamism.

isocronismo *sm.* isochronism.

ìsola *sf.* island.

isolamento *sm.* **1.** isolation **2.** (*elettr.*) insulation || — *acustico*, sound-proofing.

ìsolano *agg.* insular. ♦ **isolano** *sm.* islander.

isolante *agg.* insulating. ♦ **isolante** *sm.* insulator.

isolare *vt.* **1.** to isolate **2.** (*elettr.*) to insulate || — *acusticamente*, to soundproof. ♦ **isolarsi** *vr.* to seclude oneself.

isolato *agg.* **1.** isolated **2.** (*elettr.*) insulated. ♦ **isolato** *sm.* (*edil.*) block.

isolatore *sm.* insulator.

isolazionismo *sm.* isolationism.

isolazionista *s.* isolationist.

isolotto *sm.* islet.

isomorfismo *sm.* isomorphism.

isomorfo *agg.* isomorphous.

isòscele *agg.* isosceles.

isotèrmico *agg.* isothermal.

isòtopo *sm.* isotope.

isòtropo *sm.* isotrope.

ispànico *agg.* Hispanic.

ispanismo *sm.* Hispanicism.

ispanista *s.* Hispanist.

ispettorato *sm.* inspectorate.

ispettore *sm.* inspector.

ispezionare *vt.* to inspect.

ispezione *sf.* inspection.

ìspido *agg.* hispid.

ispirare *vt.* to inspire (with). ♦ **ispirarsi** *vr.* to draw (*v. irr.*) one's inspiration (from).

ispirato *agg.* **1.** inspired **2.** (*basato*) imbued (with).

ispiratore *agg.* inspiring. ♦ **ispiratore** *sm.* inspirer.

ispirazione *sf.* inspiration.

israeliano *agg.* e *sm.* Israeli.

israelita *agg.* e *s.* Israelite.

issare *vt.* to hoist.

istantànea *sf.* snapshot: *fare un'*—, to snapshot.

istantaneità *sf.* instantaneousness.

istantàneo *agg.* instantaneous.

istante *sm.* instant || *all'*—, *sull'*—, instantly.

istanza *sf.* **1.** request, instance **2.** (*supplica*) entreaty **3.** (*domanda scritta*) application.

istèrico *agg.* hysteric(al). ♦ **istèrico** *sm.* hysterical man (*pl.* -men).

isterilire *vt.* to sterilize. ♦ **isterilirsi** *vr.* to become (*v. irr.*) barren.

isterismo *sm.* hysteria.

istigare *vt.* to instigate.

istigatore *sm.* instigator.

istigazione *sf.* instigation.

istintivo *agg.* instinctive.

istinto *sm.* instinct.

istituire *vt.* **1.** to institute **2.** (*fondare*) to found **3.** (*giur.*) to appoint.

istituto *sm.* **1.** institute **2.** (*istituzione*) institution **3.** (*scuola*) school.

istitutore *sm.* tutor.

istitutrice *sf.* governess.

istituzionale *agg.* institutional.

istituzione *sf.* institution.

istmo *sm.* isthmus (*pl.* -mi).

istologìa *sf.* histology.

ìstrice *sm.* hedgehog.

istrione *sm.* **1.** (*teat.*) histrion **2.** (*ciarlatano*) quack.

istriònico *agg.* histrionic.

istruire *vt.* **1.** to teach (*v. irr.*) **2.** (*dare istruzioni*) to instruct, to direct **3.** (*giur.*) to institute. ♦ **istruirsi** *vr.* to educate oneself.

istruito *agg.* learned.

istruttivo *agg.* instructive.

istruttore *sm.* instructor: *giudice* —, examining magistrate.

istruttoria *sf.* examination || *aprire l'*—, to open proceedings.

istruzione *sf.* **1.** education **2.** (*cultura*) learning **3.** (*insegnamento*) teaching **4.** (*ordine*) instruction.

istupidire *vt.* to make (*v. irr.*) stupid. ♦ **istupidirsi** *v.r.* to become (*v. irr.*) stupid.

italiano *agg. e sm.* Italian.

itinerario *sm.* itinerary.

itterizia *sf.* jaundice.

ittiologìa *sf.* ichthyology.

ittiòlogo *sm.* ichthyologist.

iugoslavo *agg. e sm.* Yugoslav.

iugulare *agg.* jugular.

iuta *sf.* jute.

ivi *avv.* there.

L

la[1] *art.* the. ♦ **la** *pron.* **1.** (*per donna*) her **2.** (*per animale e cosa*) it **3.** (*forma di cortesia*) you.

la[2] *sm.* (*mus.*) A.

là *avv.* there || *l'al di —*, the hereafter; *— per —*, on the spot; *al di — di*, beyond; *più in —*, (*spazio*) further on, (*tempo*) later on.

labbro *sm.* lip.

labiale *agg.* labial.

làbile *agg.* fleeting: *memoria —*, weak memory.

labirinto *sm.* labyrinth.

laboratorio *sm.* **1.** laboratory **2.** (*artigianale*) workshop.

laboriosità *sf.* laboriousness.

laborioso *agg.* laborious.

laburismo *sm.* labourism.

laburista *agg.* labour || *partito —*, Labour Party. ♦ **laburista** *s.* Labourite.

lacca *sf.* lacquer.

laccare *vt.* to lacquer.

laccatura *sf.* lacquering.

laccio *sm.* **1.** string || *lacci da scarpe*, shoe-laces **2.** (*trappola*) snare || *prendere al —* (*fig.*), to ensnare.

laceramento *sm.* tearing.

lacerante *agg.* rending.

lacerare *vt.* to tear (*v. irr.*) (up), to rend (*v. irr.*) (*anche fig.*). ♦ **lacerarsi** *v.r.* to tear.

lacerazione *sf.* laceration.

làcero *agg.* **1.** torn **2.** (*med.*) lacerated.

laconicità *sf.* laconicism.

lacònico *agg.* laconic(al).

làcrima *sf.* tear.

lacrimale *agg.* lachrymal.

lacrimare *vi.* to weep (*v. irr.*).

lacrimazione *sf.* lachrymation.

lacrimévole *agg.* tearful.

lacrimògeno *agg.* lachrymatory: *gas —*, tear-gas.

lacrimoso *agg.* tearful.

lacuna *sf.* gap.

lacunoso *agg.* lacunous.

lacustre *agg.* lacustrine.

laddove *cong.* whereas. ♦ **laddove** *avv.* (there) where.

ladra *sf.* woman thief.

ladro *agg.* thieving. ♦ **ladro** *sm.* thief: *al —!*, stop thief!

ladrocinio *sm.* theft.

ladrone *sm.* robber.

ladronerìa *sf.* robbery.

laggiù *avv.* down there.

lagna *sf.* lament.

lagnanza *sf.* complaint.

lagnarsi *vr.* to complain (of).

lago *sm.* lake.

laguna *sf.* lagoon.

lagunare *agg.* lagoon (*attr.*).

laicato *sm.* laity.

laicismo *sm.* laicism.

laicizzare *vt.* to laicize.

làico *agg.* laic. ♦ **làico** *sm.* layman (*pl.* -men).

laidezza *sf.* ugliness, foulness.

làido *agg.* **1.** dirty **2.** (*brutto*) ugly.

lama[1] *sf.* blade.

lama[2] *sm.* (*zool.*) llama.

lama[3] *sm.* (*monaco buddista*) lama.

lambiccare *vt.* to distil || *lambiccarsi il cervello*, to rack one's brains.

lambiccato *agg.* **1.** distilled **2.** (*ricercato*) over-elaborate.

lambicco *sm.* alembic.

lambire *vt.* to lick.

lamella *sf.* lamella (*pl.* -lae).

lamentare *vt.* to lament. ♦ **lamentarsi** *vr.* to moan.

lamentazione *sf.* lamentation.

lamentela *sf.* complaint.

lamentévole *agg.* mournful.

lamento *sm.* moan.

lamentoso *agg.* mournful.

lametta *sf.* razor-blade.

lamiera *sf.* sheet.

làmina *sf.* lamina (*pl.* -nae).

laminare *vt.* to laminate.

laminato *sm.* **1.** (*tessuto*) lamé **2.** (*metallo*) rolled section.

laminatoio *sm.* rolling-mill.

làmpada *sf.* lamp.

lampadario *sm.* chandelier, lamp holder.

lampadina *sf.* bulb.

lampante *agg.* glaring, evident.

lampeggiamento *sm.* **1.** flashing, lightning **2.** (*di fari, semafori ecc.*) winking **3.** (*di auto*) to blink.

lampeggiare *vi.* **1.** to flash, to lighten **2.** (*di fari, semafori ecc.*) to wink.

lampeggiatore *sm.* **1.** winking light **2.** (*di auto*) blinker.

lampione *sm.* street-lamp.

lampo *sm.* **1.** lightning **2.** (*luce istantanea, anche fig.*) flash || *chiusura* —, zip-fastener.

lampone *sm.* raspberry.

lampreda *sf.* lamprey.

lana *sf.* wool.

lancetta *sf.* **1.** (*di quadrante*) hand **2.** (*di chirurgo*) lancet.

lancia[1] *sf.* lance.

lancia[2] *sf.* (*mar.*) launch || — *di salvataggio*, lifeboat.

lanciafiamme *sm.* flame-thrower.

lanciare *vt.* **1.** to throw (*v. irr.*) **2.** (*fig.*) to launch || — *un'occhiata*, to cast (*v. irr.*) a glance. ♦ **lanciarsi** *vr.* to dash.

lanciatore *sm.* thrower.

lanciere *sm.* lancer.

lancinante *agg.* piercing.

lancio *sm.* **1.** throwing **2.** (*pubblicitario*) launching.

landa *sf.* moor.

lànguido *agg.* languid.

languire *vi.* to languish.

languore *sm.* languor.

laniero *agg.* woollen.

lanificio *sm.* wool factory.

lanolina *sf.* lanolin.

lanoso *agg.* woolly.

lanterna *sf.* lantern.

lanùgine *sf.* down.

laparatomìa *sf.* laparotomy.

lapidare *vt.* to stone.

lapidario *agg.* lapidary.

lapidazione *sf.* lapidation.

làpide *sf.* **1.** tablet **2.** (*sepolcrale*) tombstone.

lapis *sm.* pencil.

lardellare *vt.* to lard.

lardo *sm.* lard, bacon.

larga (*nella loc. avv.*) *alla* —, **away** (from).

largheggiare *vi.* to abound (with).

larghezza *sf.* **1.** breadth **2.** (*liberalità*) liberality **3.** (*abbondanza*) plenty.

largire *vt.* to bestow (upon).

largitore *sm.* bestower.

largizione *sf.* bestowal.

largo *agg.* broad, wide. ♦ **largo** *sm.* **1.** (*mar.*) open sea **2.** (*piazza*) square || *prendere il* —, to set (*v. irr.*) sail; (*fig.*) to run (*v. irr.*) away; *andare al* —, to take (*v. irr.*) to the open sea; *fare* —, to make (*v. irr.*) room.

làrice *sm.* larch.

laringe *sf.* larynx.

laringite *sf.* laryngitis.

larva *sf.* larva (*pl.* -ae).

lasciapassare *sm.* pass.

lasciare *vt.* **1.** to leave (*v. irr.*) **2.** (*permettere*) to let (*v. irr.*), to allow. ♦ **lasciarsi** *vr. rec.* (*separarsi*) to part.

làscito *sm.* legacy.

lascivia *sf.* lust.

lascivo *agg.* lustful.

lassativo *agg. e sm.* laxative.

lasso *sm.* lapse: *dopo un certo* — *di tempo*, after a lapse of time.

lassù *avv.* up there.

lastra *sf.* **1.** (*vetro*) glass' sheet **2.** (*di pietra*) slab **3.** (*di metallo, foto*) plate.

lastricare *vt.* to pave.

lastricatura *sf.* paving.

làstrico *sm.* pavement || *essere sul* — (*fig.*), to be destitute.

latente *agg.* latent.

laterale *agg.* side: *via* —, by-street.

lateralmente *avv.* sideways.

laterizi *sm. pl.* bricks.

làtice *sm.* latex.

latifondista *sm.* landowner.

latifondo *sm.* large landed estate.

latinismo *sm.* Latinism.

latinista *s.* Latinist.

latinità *sf.* Latinity.

latino *agg. e sm.* Latin.

latitante *agg.* absconding: *essere* —, to be in hiding. ♦ **latitante** *s.* absconder.

latitanza *sf.* hiding: *darsi alla* —, to evade arrest.

latitùdine *sf.* latitude.

lato[1] *sm.* **1.** side **2.** (*fig.*) point of view || *d'altro* —, on the other hand; *da un* —, on the one hand.

lato[2] *agg.* wide || *in senso* —, in a broad sense.

latore *sm.* bearer.

latrare *vi.* to bark.

latrato *sm.* barking.

latrina *sf.* lavatory.

latta *sf.* tin.

lattaio *sm.* milkman (*pl.* -men).
lattante *agg.* unweaned. ♦ **lattante** *s.* suckling (baby).
latte *sm.* milk.
làtteo *agg.* milky.
latterìa *sf.* dairy.
latticini *sm. pl.* dairy products.
lattiera *sf.* milk-jug.
lattiginoso *agg.* **1.** milky **2.** (*bot.*) lactescent.
lattoniere *sm.* tinker.
lattosio *sm.* lactose.
lattuga *sf.* lettuce.
laudativo *agg.* laudatory.
làurea *sf.* degree.
laureare *vt.* to confer a degree (on). ♦ **laurearsi** *vr.* to graduate.
laureato *agg.* graduated. ♦ **laureato** *sm.* graduate || — *in lettere,* Doctor of Literature Degree.
làuro *sm.* laurel.
làuto *agg.* sumptuous || *lauti guadagni,* large profits.
lavà *sf.* lava.
lavàbile *agg.* washable.
lavabo *sm.* washbowl.
lavaggio *sm.* washing: — *a secco,* dry cleaning.
lavagna *sf.* **1.** blackboard **2.** (*ardesia*) slate.
lavanda[1] *sf.* **1.** washing **2.** (*med.*) lavage.
lavanda[2] *sf.* (*bot.*) lavender.
lavandaia *sf.* laundress.
lavanderìa *sf.* laundry.
lavandino *sm.* sink.
lavapiatti *s.* dish-washer.
lavare *vt.* to wash: — *a secco,* to dry-clean. ♦ **lavarsi** *vr.* to wash (oneself).
lavata *sf.* wash || *dare una — di capo* (*fig.*), to scold.
lavativo *sm.* **1.** (*med.*) enema **2.** (*fig.*) lazy-bones.
lavatoio *sm.* **1.** wash-house **2.** (*asse per lavare*) wash-board.
lavatrice *sf.* **1.** washer **2.** (*lavabiancheria*) washing machine.
lavatura *sf.* washing.
lavina *sf.* landslip.
lavorante *sm.* worker.
lavorare *vi. e vt.* to work.
lavorativo *agg.* working || *ora lavorativa,* man-hour.
lavoratore *agg.* working. ♦ **lavoratore** *sm.* worker || — *a giornata,* day-labourer.
lavorazione *sf.* **1.** processing **2.** (*fattura*) work **3.** (*agr.*) tilling || —

a mano, handwork.
lavorìo *sm.* intense activity.
lavoro *sm.* **1.** work **2.** (*occupazione*) job || — *a ore,* work by the hour; *lavori di casa,* housework; — *su ordinazione,* work to order; *eccesso di —,* overwork; — *in proprio,* self-employment.
lazzaretto *sm.* lazaretto.
lazzarone *sm.* slacker.
lazzo *sm.* joke.
le *art.* the. ♦ **le** *pron.* **1.** (*sing.*) her, to her **2.** (*pl.*) them **3.** (*forma di cortesia*) you, to you.
leale *agg.* **1.** loyal **2.** (*corretto*) fair.
lealtà *sf.* **1.** loyalty **2.** (*correttezza*) fairness.
lebbra *sf.* leprosy.
lebbrosario *sm.* leper hospital.
lebbroso *agg.* leprous. ♦ **lebbroso** *sm.* leper.
leccapiedi *sm.* bootlicker.
leccare *vt.* to lick. ♦ **leccarsi** *vr.* to lick (oneself).
leccata *sf.* licking.
leccornìa *sf.* dainty.
lécito *agg.* **1.** lawful **2.** (*giusto*) right **3.** (*permesso*) allowed. ♦ **lécito** *sm.* right.
lèdere *vt.* **1.** to injure **2.** (*danneggiare*) to damage.
lega *sf.* **1.** league **2.** (*di metalli*) alloy || *di buona —,* genuine; *di cattiva —,* low.
legaccio *sm.* string.
legale *agg.* legal, lawful || *procedere per vie legali,* to have recourse to the law. ♦ **legale** *sm.* lawyer.
legalità *sf.* legality.
legalizzare *vt.* **1.** to legalize **2.** (*autenticare*) to authenticate.
legalizzazione *sf.* **1.** legalization **2.** (*autenticazione*) authentication.
legame *sm.* **1.** string **2.** (*vincolo*) tie **3.** (*connessione*) link.
legamento *sm.* **1.** string **2.** (*anat.*) ligament.
legare[1] *vt.* **1.** to tie **2.** (*di metalli*) to alloy (with) **3.** (*aver connessione*) to be connected. ♦ **legarsi** *vr.* to bind (*v. irr.*) oneself.
legare[2] *vt.* (*giur.*) to bequeath.
legatario *sm.* legatee.
legato[1] *sm.* **1.** ambassador **2.** (*eccl.*) legate.
legato[2] *sm.* (*giur.*) legacy.
legatore *sm.* binder.
legatorìa *sf.* bookbinder's establishment.

legatura *sf.* **1.** binding **2.** (*mus.; med.*) ligature.

legazione *sf.* legation.

legge *sf.* **1.** law **2.** (*singola*) act **3.** (*regola*) rule || *progetto di —*, bill; *a norma di —*, according to the law; *a termini di —*, as by law enacted.

leggenda *sf.* legend.

leggendario *agg.* legendary.

lèggere *vt.* to read (*v. irr.*).

leggerezza *sf.* lightness.

leggero *agg.* light.

leggiadrìa *sf.* loveliness.

leggiadro *agg.* lovely.

leggìbile *agg.* readable.

leggìo *sm.* **1.** reading-desk **2.** (*mus.*) music-stand.

legiferare *vi.* to legislate.

legionario *agg. e sm.* legionary.

legione *sf.* legion.

legislativo *agg.* legislative.

legislatore *sm.* legislator.

legislatura *sf.* legislature.

legislazione *sf.* legislation.

legittimare *vt.* to legitimate.

legittimazione *sf.* legitimation.

legittimità *sf.* legitimacy.

legìttimo *agg.* legitimate.

legna *sf.* wood || *— da ardere*, firewood.

legnaia *sf.* wood-store.

legname *sm.* **1.** wood **2.** (*da costruzione*) timber.

legnata *sf.* blow with a cudgel.

legno *sm.* wood || *di —*, wooden.

legnosità *sf.* woodiness.

legnoso *agg.* **1.** woody **2.** (*duro*) tough.

legume *sm.* legume.

leguminoso *agg.* leguminous.

lei *pron.* **1.** (*sogg.*) she, (*compl.*) her **2.** (*forma di cortesia*) you.

lembo *sm.* **1.** edge **2.** (*pezzo*) strip.

lemma *sm.* lemma.

lèmure *sm.* lemur. ♦ **lèmuri** *sm. pl.* (*mit.*) lemures.

lena *sf.* **1.** energy **2.** (*respiro*) breath.

lenire *vt.* to soothe.

lenone *sm.* pander.

lente *sf.* lens: *— d'ingrandimento*, magnifying lens || *lenti*, glasses.

lentezza *sf.* slowness.

lenticchia *sf.* lentil.

lentìggine *sf.* freckle.

lentigginoso *agg.* freckly.

lento *agg.* **1.** slow **2.** (*non teso*) loose.

lenza *sf.* fishing-line.

lenzuolo *sm.* sheet.

leone *sm.* lion.

leonessa *sf.* lioness.

leonino *agg.* leonine.

leopardo *sm.* leopard.

lèpido *agg.* witty.

lepidòttero *sm.* lepidopteron (*pl.* -era).

leporino *agg.* leporine || *labbro —*, hare-lip.

lepre *sf.* hare.

lercio *agg.* filthy.

lèsbica *e sf.* Lesbian.

lésina *sf.* awl.

lesinare *vi.* to be stingy. ♦ **lesinare** *vt.* to grudge.

lesionare *vt.* to damage, to injure.

lesione *sf.* **1.** lesion, injury **2.** (*danno*) damage.

lesivo *agg.* harmful.

leso *agg.* **1.** injured **2.** (*danneggiato*) damaged.

lessare *vt.* to boil.

lessicale *agg.* lexical.

lèssico *sm.* lexicon.

lessicografìa *sf.* lexicography.

lessicologìa *sf.* lexicology.

lesso *agg.* boiled. ♦ **lesso** *sm.* boiled meat.

lestezza *sf.* quickness.

lesto *agg.* quick.

lestofante *sm.* swindler.

letale *agg.* lethal.

letamaio *sm.* dunghill.

letame *sm.* dung.

letàrgico *agg.* **1.** lethargic **2.** (*di animali, in inverno*) hibernating; (*id., in estate*) estivating.

letargo *sm.* **1.** lethargy **2.** (*di animali, in inverno*) hibernation; (*id., in estate*) estivation.

letizia *sf.* joy.

lèttera *sf.* letter || *alla —*, literally.

letterale *agg.* literal.

letterario *agg.* literary.

letterato *agg.* lettered. ♦ **letterato** *sm.* literary man.

letteratura *sf.* literature.

lettiga *sf.* stretcher.

letto *sm.* bed || *camera da —*, bedroom; *vagone —*, sleeping-car.

lettore *sm.* reader.

lettura *sf.* reading.

leucemìa *sf.* leukaemia.

leucociti *sm. pl.* leucocytes.

leucoma *sm.* leucoma.

leva[1] *sf.* **1.** lever **2.** (*fig.*) stimulus || *far — sui sentimenti di qu.*, to play on so.'s feelings.

leva² *sf.* (*mil.*) draft: *essere di —*, to be due for draft.

levante *sm.* **1.** east **2.** (*vento*) levanter.

levare *vt.* **1.** (*sollevare*) to raise **2.** (*togliere*) to take (*v. irr.*) off. ♦ **levarsi** *vr.* **1.** to rise (*v. irr.*) **2.** (*togliersi*) to take off.

levata *sf.* **1.** (*di sole*) rising **2.** (*di posta*) collection || *— di scudi* rebellion.

levataccia *sf.* early rising.

levatoio *agg.* ponte *—*, drawbridge.

levatrice *sf.* midwife (*pl.* -wives).

levatura *sf.* intelligence.

levigare *vt.* to smooth.

levigatezza *sf.* smoothness.

levigato *agg.* smooth.

levitazione *sf.* levitation.

levriere *sm.* greyhound.

lezione *sf.* **1.** lesson **2.** (*universitaria*) lecture **3.** (*lett.*) reading.

leziosàggine *sf.* affectation.

lezioso *agg.* affected.

lezzo *sm.* stench.

li *pron.* them.

lì *avv.* there: *— vicino*, near there; *— dentro*, in there || *— per —*, at first; *di — a poco*, soon after; *giù di —* (*press'a poco*), thereabouts; *essere — per*, to be on the point of.

liana *sf.* liana.

libagione *sf.* libation.

libbra *sf.* pound.

libeccio *sm.* Southwest wind.

libello *sm.* libel.

libèllula *sf.* dragonfly.

liberale *agg.* e *sm.* liberal.

liberalismo *sm.* liberalism.

liberalità *sf.* generosity.

liberalizzare *vt.* to liberalize.

liberare *vt.* **1.** to free **2.** (*da pericoli*) to rescue **3.** (*sbarazzare*) to rid (*v. irr.*) (of). ♦ **liberarsi** *vr.* (*sbarazzarsi*) to get (*v. irr.*) rid (of).

liberatore *agg.* liberating. ♦ **liberatore** *sm.* deliverer.

liberazione *sf.* liberation.

libero *agg.* free.

liberoscambista *agg.* e *sm.* free-trader.

libertà *sf.* liberty, freedom.

libertario *agg.* e *sm.* libertarian.

liberticida *agg.* e *s.* liberticide.

libertinaggio *sm.* libertinage.

libertino *agg.* e *sm.* libertine.

libìdine *sf.* lust.

libidinoso *agg.* lustful.

libido *sf.* lustfulness.

libraio *sm.* bookseller.

librarsi *vr.* to hover.

librerìa *sf.* **1.** bookshop **2.** (*mobile*) bookcase.

libresco *agg.* bookish.

libretto *sm.* **1.** booklet **2.** (*d'opera*) libretto || *— di assegni*, cheque-book; *— di risparmio*, savings-book; *— personale*, record-book.

libro *sm.* book.

licenza *sf.* **1.** (*abuso*) licence **2.** (*permesso*) permission, leave **3.** (*documento*) licence.

licenziamento *sm.* dismissal.

licenziare *vt.* to dismiss. ♦ **licenziarsi** *vr.* to give (*v. irr.*) up one's job.

licenziosità *sf.* licentiousness.

licenzioso *agg.* licentious.

lichene *sm.* lichen.

licitazione *sf.* sale by auction.

lido *sm.* shore.

lieto *agg.* glad.

lieve *agg.* slight.

lievitare *vi.* to rise (*v. irr.*). ♦ **lievitare** *vt.* to leaven.

lievitazione *sf.* leavening.

lièvito *sm.* **1.** yeast **2.** (*fermento*) ferment.

ligio *agg.* faithful, observant (of).

lignaggio *sm.* lineage.

ligneo *agg.* wooden.

lignite *sf.* lignite.

lillà *sm.* lilac.

lillipuziano *agg.* e *sm.* Lilliputian.

lima *sf.* file.

limaccioso *agg.* slimy.

limare *vt.* **1.** to file **2.** (*fig.*) to polish.

limatrice *sf.* (*mecc.*) shaping-machine.

limatura *sf.* filing.

limbo *sm.* limbo.

limitare *vt.* to limit. ♦ **limitarsi** *vr.* (*controllarsi*) to check oneself.

limitatezza *sf.* limitation.

limitativo *agg.* limitative.

limitato *agg.* limited.

limitazione *sf.* limitation: *— delle nascite*, birth-control.

lìmite *sm.* limit: *— di velocità*, speed-limit || *— di rottura*, breaking-point.

limìtrofo *agg.* neighbouring.

limo *sm.* slime.

limonata *sf.* lemonade.

limone sm. lemon.
limpidezza sf. clearness.
limpido agg. limpid, clear.
lince sf. lynx.
linciaggio sm. lynching
linciare vt. to lynch.
lindo agg. neat.
linea sf. line ‖ aereo di —, air-liner; mantenere la —, to keep (v. irr.) one's figure.
lineamenti sm. pl. 1. features 2. (linee essenziali) outlines.
lineare agg. 1. linear 2. (fig.) unswerving.
lineetta sf. 1. dash 2. (trattino d'unione) hyphen.
linfa sf. (biol.) lymph.
linfàtico agg. lymphatic.
linfatismo sm. lymphatism.
lingotto sm. ingot.
lingua sf. 1. tongue 2. (linguaggio) language.
linguacciuto agg. talkative.
linguaggio sm. language.
linguetta sf. 1. flap 2. (mecc.; di scarpe) tongue.
linguista s. linguist.
linguìstica sf. linguistics.
linguìstico agg. linguistic.
linimento sm. liniment.
lino sm. flax.
linòleum sm. linoleum.
linone sm. lawn.
linotipìa sf. linotyping.
linotipista s. linotypist.
liquefare vt. to liquefy. ♦ **lique farsi** vr. to liquefy.
liquefazione sf. liquefaction.
liquidare vt. 1. to liquidate 2. (comm.) to sell (v. irr.) off, to settle ‖ — una questione, to settle a question.
liquidatore sm. liquidator.
liquidazione sf. liquidation, sale.
liquido agg. e sm. liquid ‖ denaro —, cash.
liquirizia sf. liquorice.
liquore sm. liqueur ‖ i liquori, spirits.
liquoroso agg. liqueur-like.
lira sf. 1. (moneta) lira 2. (mus.) lyre.
lìrica sf. 1. lyric poetry 2. (teatro lirico) opera.
lìrico agg. lyric(al). ♦ **lìrico** sm. lyrist.
lirismo sm. lyrism.
lisciare vt. 1. to smooth 2. (adulare) to flatter. ♦ **lisciarsi** vr. to sleek oneself.
liscio agg. 1. smooth 2. (di bevanda) undiluted 3. (semplice) plain 4. (di capelli) sleek.
lisciva sf. lye.
liso agg. threadbare.
lista sf. 1. (elenco) list, note 2. (striscia) stripe.
listare vt. 1. to stripe 2. (bordare) to border.
listino sm. list.
litanìa sf. litany.
lite sf. 1. quarrel, wrangle 2. (giur.) lawsuit.
litigante sm. 1. wrangler 2. (giur.) litigant.
litigare vi. 1. to quarrel 2. (giur.) to litigate.
litigio sm. quarrel.
litigioso agg. quarrelsome.
litografìa sf. 1. lithography 2. (pezzo singolo) lithograph.
litogràfico agg. lithographic.
litorale agg. littoral. ♦ **litorale** sm. coast.
litro sm. litre.
liturgìa sf. liturgy.
litùrgico agg. liturgic(al).
liuto sm. lute.
livellamento sm. levelling.
livellare vt. to level.
livellatrice sf. bulldozer.
livello sm. level: a — del mare, at sea-level; passaggio a —, level-crossing; essere allo stesso — di, to be on a level with.
lìvido agg. livid. ♦ **lìvido** sm. bruise.
livore sm. 1. (invidia) envy 2. (odio) hatred.
livrea sf. livery.
lizza sf. competition, lists (pl.) ‖ essere in — (fig.), to be competing.
lo art. the. ♦ **lo** pron. 1. (per uomo) him 2. (per animale, cosa) it ‖ — credo, I think so.
lobo sm. lobe.
locale agg. local. ♦ **locale** sm. 1. room 2. (ritrovo) place.
località sf. locality, spot.
localizzare vt. to localize.
localizzazione sf. localization.
locanda sf. inn.
locandiere sm. innkeeper.
locandina sf. play-bill.
locare vt. to rent.
locatario sm. tenant.
locativo agg. locative ‖ valore —, rental value.

locatore *sm.* lessor.
locazione *sf.* lease.
locomotiva *sf.* locomotive.
locomotore *agg. e sm.* locomotive.
locomozione *sf.* locomotion.
locusta *sf.* locust.
locuzione *sf.* locution.
lodàbile *agg.* laudable.
lodare *vt.* to praise.
lodatore *sm.* praiser.
lode *sf.* praise.
lodévole *agg.* praiseworthy.
logaritmo *sm.* logarithm.
loggia *sf.* **1.** (*arch.*) loggia **2.** (*massonica*) lodge.
loggione *sm.* gallery.
lògica *sf.* logic.
logicità *sf.* logicality.
lògico *agg.* logical. ◆ **lògico** *sm.* logician.
logìstica *sf.* logistics.
logìstico *agg.* logistic(al).
loglio *sm.* darnel.
logomachìa *sf.* logomachy.
logoramento *sm.* **1.** wear **2.** (*fig.*) wasting away.
logorante *agg.* wearing.
logorare *vt.* to wear (*v. irr.*) (out, down). ◆ **logorarsi** *vr.* to wear (out, down).
logorìo *sm.* wear and tear.
lògoro *agg.* worn (out, down).
lombàggine *sf.* lumbago.
lombardo *agg. e sm.* Lombard.
lombare *agg.* lumbar.
lombi *sm. pl.* loins.
lombrico *sm.* earth-worm.
longànime *agg.* forbearing.
longanimità *sf.* forbearance.
longevità *sf.* longevity.
longevo *agg.* longevous.
longitudinale *agg.* longitudinal.
longitùdine *sf.* longitude.
lontananza *sf.* distance: *in* —, in the distance.
lontano *agg.* **1.** far **2.** (*nel tempo*) far off, distant **3.** (*vago*) vague. ◆ **lontano** *avv.* far || *da* —, from afar.
lontra *sf.* otter.
loquace *agg.* talkative.
loquacità *sf.* talkativeness.
loquela *sf.* glibness.
lordare *vt.* to soil. ◆ **lordarsi** *vr.* to get (*v. irr.*) dirty.
lordo *agg.* **1.** (*sporco*) filthy **2.** (*di peso*) gross.
loro *agg. poss.* their. ◆ **loro** *pron. poss.* theirs. ◆ **loro** *pron. pers.*

1. (*sogg.*) they, (*compl.*) them **2.** (*forma di cortesia*) you.
losanga *sf.* lozenge.
losco *agg.* **1.** (*bieco*) sinister **2.** (*sospetto*) suspicious.
loto *sm.* **1.** (*fango*) mud **2.** (*bot.*) lotus.
lotta *sf.* **1.** struggle **2.** (*sport*) wrestling.
lottare *vi.* **1.** to struggle **2.** (*sport*) to wrestle.
lottatore *sm.* **1.** struggler **2.** (*sport*) wrestler.
lotterìa *sf.* lottery.
lottizzare *vt.* to lot.
lottizzazione *sf.* division into lots.
lotto *sm.* **1.** lot **2.** (*gioco*) state lottery.
lozione *sf.* lotion.
lubricità *sf.* lubricity.
lùbrico *agg.* **1.** lubricous **2.** (*fig.*) lascivious.
lubrificante *agg.* lubricating. ◆ **lubrificante** *sm.* lubricant.
lubrificare *vt.* to lubricate.
lubrificazione *sf.* lubrication.
lucchetto *sm.* padlock.
luccicante *agg.* glittering.
luccicare *vi.* to glitter.
luccichìo *sm.* glitter.
lùcciola *sf.* **1.** firefly **2.** (*senz'ali*) glow-worm.
luce *sf.* light || *alla* — *del sole* (*fig.*), openly; *dare alla* — *un bambino*, to give (*v. irr.*) birth to a child; *mettere in* —, to show (*v. irr.*); *venire alla* — (*nascere*), to be born.
lucente *agg.* bright.
lucentezza *sf.* brightness.
lucerna *sf.* oil-lamp.
lucernario *sm.* skylight.
lucèrtola *sf.* lizard.
lucidare *vt.* to polish.
lucidatrice *sf.* **1.** floor-polisher **2.** (*mecc.*) polishing machine.
lucidatura *sf.* polishing.
lucidezza *sf.* **1.** brightness **2.** (*di mente*) lucidness.
lucidità *sf.* lucidity.
lùcido *agg.* **1.** lucid **2.** (*lucidato*) glossy. ◆ **lùcido** *sm.* **1.** (*per scarpe*) shoe-polish **2.** (*lucidezza*) shine.
lucìgnolo *sm.* wick.
lucrare *vt.* to profit.
lucrativo *agg.* profitable.
lucro *sm.* profit: *a scopo di* —, for the sake of gain.
ludibrio *sm.* mockery

luglio *sm.* July.
lùgubre *agg.* lugubrious.
lui *pron.* **1.** (*sogg.*) he **2.** (*compl.*) him.
lumaca *sf.* snail.
lume *sm.* light || *al — di candela,* by candle-light; *perdere il — della ragione,* to be blinded by anger.
lumeggiare *vt.* (*fig.*) to put (*v. irr.*) in evidence.
luminare *sm.* luminary.
luminescenza *sf.* luminescence.
luminosità *sf.* brightness.
luminoso *agg.* bright.
luna *sf.* moon: *— calante,* waning moon; *— crescente,* waxing moon || *chiaro di —,* moonlight; *— di miele,* honeymoon; *avere la —* (*fig.*), to be in the sulks.
lunare *agg.* lunar.
lunario *sm.* almanac || *sbarcare il —,* to make (*v. irr.*) both ends meet.
lunàtico *agg.* moody.
lunazione *sf.* lunation.
lunedì *sm.* Monday.
lunetta *sf.* lunette.
lungàggine *sf.* slowness, delay.
lunghezza *sf.* length.
lungimirante *agg.* far-sighted.
lungo *agg.* **1.** long: *a —,* long; *a — andare,* in the long run **2.** (*lento*) slow || *in — e in largo,* far and wide; *di gran lunga,* by far. ♦ **lungo** *prep.* **1.** along **2.** (*durante*) during.
lungofiume *sm.* embankment.
lungolago *sm.* lake-front.
lungomare *sm.* sea-front.
lungometraggio *sm.* feature film.
luogo *sm.* place: *— di nascita,* birthplace; *sul —,* on the spot; *aver —,* to take (*v. irr.*) place; *dar —,* to cause.
luogotenente *sm.* lieutenant.
lupa *sf.* she-wolf.
lupanare *sm.* brothel.
lupara *sf.* shotgun.
lupino *sm.* (*bot.*) lupine.
lupo *sm.* wolf || *— di mare,* sea-dog; *in bocca al —!,* good luck!
lùppolo *sm.* hop.
lùrido *agg.* dirty.
luridume *sm.* dirt.
lusinga *sf.* allurement, flattery.
lusingare *vt.* to allure, to flatter.
lusinghiero *agg.* alluring, flattering.
lussare *vt.* to dislocate.
lussazione *sf.* dislocation.

lusso *sm.* luxury.
lussuoso *agg.* luxurious, rich.
lussureggiante *agg.* luxuriant.
lussureggiare *vi.* to thrive (*v. irr.*).
lussuria *sf.* lust.
lussurioso *agg.* lustful.
lustrale *agg.* lustral.
lustrare *vt.* to polish.
lustrascarpe *sm.* shoeblack.
lustratura *sf.* polish.
lustrino *sm.* spangle.
lustro *agg.* shining, shiny. ♦ **lustro** *sm.* lustre.
luteranésimo *sm.* Lutheranism.
luterano *agg. e sm.* Lutheran.
lutto *sm.* mourning: *mettere il —,* to go (*v. irr.*) into mourning.
luttuoso *agg.* mournful.

M

ma *cong.* **1.** but **2.** (*tuttavia*) however, still.
màcabro *agg.* macabre.
macaco *sm.* **1.** macaque **2.** (*fig.*) runt.
macché *inter.* you don't say it!
maccheroni *sm. pl.* macaroni (*sing.*).
macchia[1] *sf.* spot, stain.
macchia[2] *sf.* (*boscaglia*) bush: *darsi alla —,* to take (*v. irr.*) to the bush.
macchiare *vt.* to stain. ♦ **macchiarsi** *vr.* **1.** to get (*v. irr.*) stained **2.** (*fig.*) to soil oneself.
macchiato *agg.* spotted.
macchietta *sf.* **1.** caricature **2.** (*di persona*) character.
màcchina *sf.* **1.** engine, machine: *— calcolatrice,* calculating machine; *— per cucire,* sewing-machine; *— da presa,* cine-camera; *— per scrivere,* typewriter; *— fotografica,* camera; *fatto a —,* machine-made; *andare in —* (*di giornali*), to go (*v. irr.*) to press **2.** (*automobile*) car.
macchinale *agg.* mechanical.
macchinare *vt.* to plot.
macchinario *sm.* machinery.
macchinazione *sf.* machination.
macchinista *sm.* **1.** (*ferr.*) engine-driver **2.** (*teat.*) scene-shifter.
macchinoso *agg.* complicated.

macedonia *sf.* (*cuc.*) fruit-salad.

macellaio *sm.* butcher.

macellare *vt.* to slaughter.

macellerìa *sf.* butcher's shop.

macello *sm.* 1. (*luogo dove si macella*) slaughter-house 2. (*massacro*) slaughter.

macerare *vt.* 1. to soak 2. (*di lino, canapa*) to ret. ♦ **macerarsi** *vr.* (*fig.*) to waste (away).

maceratoio *sm.* rettery.

macerazione *sf.* 1. soaking 2. (*industria tessile*) retting.

macerie *sf. pl.* rubble (*sing.*), ruins.

màcero *sm.* (*per canapa e lino*) retting-ground: *carta da —*, wastepaper.

machiavèllico *agg.* Machiavellian.

machiavellismo *sm.* Machiavellism.

macigno *sm.* boulder.

macilento *agg.* emaciated.

macilenza *sf.* emaciation.

màcina *sf.* grindstone.

macinacaffè *sm.* coffee-mill.

macinapepe *sm.* pepper-mill.

macinare *vt.* 1. to grind (*v. irr.*), to mince.

macinino *sm.* grinder.

maciullare *vt.* to crush.

macrocèfalo *agg.* macrocephalous.

macrocosmo *sm.* macrocosm.

macromolècola *sf.* macromolecule.

macroscòpico *agg.* macroscopic.

maculato *agg.* spotted.

madia *sf.* 1. kitchen cupboard 2. (*per pane*) kneading trough.

màdido *agg.* wet: — *di sudore*, bathed in sweat.

madonna *sf.* 1. (*titolo*) Lady, My Lady 2. (*relig.*) The Virgin Mary, Our Lady 3. (*pitt.*) Madonna.

madornale *agg.* huge.

madre *sf.* mother.

madrepatria *sf.* mother-country.

madreperla *sf.* mother-of-pearl.

madreperlàceo *agg.* pearly.

madrèpora *sf.* madrepore.

madrepòrico *agg.* madreporic.

madrevite *sf.* 1. nut screw 2. (*utensile*) die.

madrigale *sm.* madrigal.

madrina *sf.* godmother.

maestà *sf.* majesty.

maestosità *sf.* majesty.

maestoso *agg.* majestic.

maestra *sf.* (*scol.*) teacher.

maestrale *sm.* mistral.

maestranza *sf.* skilled workers (*pl.*).

maestrìa *sf.* skill, ability.

maestro *sm.* 1. (*scol.*) teacher 2. (*uomo dotto*) master 3. (*mus.*) conductor, "maestro" ‖ *albero —*, mainmast.

mafia *sf.* "Mafia".

maga *sf.* sorceress.

magagna *sf.* flaw, imperfection.

magari *inter.* if only! ♦ **magari** *avv.* (*forse*) perhaps, maybe. ♦ **magari** *cong.* even if.

magazzinaggio *sm.* storage.

magazziniere *sm.* store-keeper.

magazzino *sm.* warehouse ‖ *fondi di —*, unsold stock.

maggese *sm.* fallow land.

maggio *sm.* May.

maggiolino *sm.* May-bug.

maggiorana *sf.* marjoram.

maggioranza *sf.* majority, most (of).

maggiorare *vt.* to increase.

maggiorazione *sf.* increase, charge.

maggiordomo *sm.* butler.

maggiore *agg.* 1. (*più grande, ampio*) greater, larger 2. (*più vecchio*) older: *il —*, the oldest 3. (*di fratelli*) elder (*fra due*), eldest (*fra molti*). ♦ **maggiore** *sm.* 1. (*mil.*) major 2. (*superiore*) superior.

maggiorenne *agg.* of age: *diventare —*, to come (*v. irr.*) of age. ♦ **maggiorenne** *sm.* major.

maggiorente *sm.* notable.

maggioritario *agg.* majority (*attr.*).

maggiormente *avv.* more, much more.

magìa *sf.* magic.

màgiaro *agg.* e *sm.* Magyar.

magicamente *avv.* magically.

màgico *agg.* magical.

magistrale *agg.* 1. magisteral ‖ *scuola —*, teachers' institute 2. (*eccellente*) masterly.

magistralmente *avv.* skilfully.

magistrato *sm.* Magistrate.

magistratura *sf.* magistracy.

maglia *sf.* 1. (*di lavoro a maglia*) stitch ‖ *lavorare a —*, to knit (*v. irr.*) 2. (*indumento*) vest 3. (*di catena*) link.

magliaia *sf.* knitter.

maglierìa *sf.* hosiery.

maglificio *sm.* hosiery.

maglio *sm.* 1. mallet 2. (*mecc.*) hammer.

maglione *sm.* sweater.

magma *sm.* magma.

magnanimità *sf.* magnanimity.

magnànimo *agg.* magnanimous.
magnate *sm.* magnate.
magnesia *sf.* magnesia.
magnesio *sm.* magnesium. *lampo al —*, flash.
magnete *sm.* magnet.
magnètico *agg.* magnetic.
magnetismo *sm.* magnetism.
magnetite *sf.* magnetite.
magnetizzare *vt.* to magnetize.
magnetizzatore *sm.* magnetizer.
magnetizzazione *sf.* magnetization.
magnetòfono *sm.* tape-recorder.
magnetòmetro *sm.* magnetometer.
magnificamente *avv.* magnificent-ly.
magnificare *vt.* to extol, to glorify.
magnificenza *sf.* magnificence.
magnìfico *agg.* magnificent.
magniloquente *agg.* magniloquent.
magniloquenza *sf.* magniloquence.
magnolia *sf.* magnolia.
mago *sm.* wizard.
magra *sf.* (*di fiumi*) low water.
magrezza *sf.* thinness.
magro *agg.* 1. thin 2. (*di carni*) lean.
mah *inter.* who knows!
mai *avv.* 1. ever 2. (*non mai*) never: *— e poi —*, never never; *— più*, never more; *caso —*, if; *non si sa —*, you never can tell; *meglio tardi che —*, better late than never.
maiale *sm.* 1. pig 2. (*carne*) pork.
maièutica *sf.* maieutics.
maiòlica *sf.* majolica.
maionese *sf.* mayonnaise
mais *sm.* maize.
maiùscola *sf.* capital letter.
maiuscoletto *sm.* small capitals.
maiùscolo *agg.* capital.
malaccorto *agg.* ill-advised
malachite *sf.* malachite.
malacreanza *sf.* rudeness.
malafede *sf.* bad faith.
malaffare *sm.* 1. *donna di —*, whore 2. *gente di —*, crooks (*pl.*).
malagévole *agg.* difficult, hard.
malagrazia *sf.* bad grace.
malalingua *sf.* backbiter.
malamente *avv.* badly.
malandato *agg.* in bad condition.
malandrino *sm.* 1. brigand 2. (*fam.*) rogue.
malànimo *sm.* malevolence.
malanno *sm.* 1. calamity 2. (*malattia*) illness.

malapena (*nella loc. avv.*) *a —*, hardly.
malaria *sf.* malaria.
malaticcio *agg.* sickly.
malato *agg.* sick, ill. ♦ **malato** *sm.* patient.
malattìa *sf.* sickness, disease.
malauguratamente *avv.* unluckily.
malaugurato *agg.* ill-fated.
malaugurio *sm.* ill-omen.
malavita *sf.* underworld.
malavoglia *sf.* unwillingness || *di —*, reluctantly.
malcapitato *agg.* unlucky. ♦ **malcapitato** *sm.* victim.
malconcio *agg.* 1. battered 2. (*contuso*) bruised.
malcontento *agg.* dissatisfied (with). ♦ **malcontento** *sm.* discontent.
malcostume *sm.* immorality, corruption.
maldestro *agg.* awkward.
maldicente *agg.* disparaging. ♦ **maldicente** *sm.* slanderer.
maldicenza *sf.* backbiting.
maldisposto *agg.* ill-disposed, hostile.
male *sm.* 1. evil 2. (*malattia*) illness, disease 3. (*dolore fisico*) pain || *— di testa*, headache. ♦ **male** *avv.* badly, ill.
maledettamente *avv.* awfully.
maledetto *agg.* cursed.
maledico *agg.* slanderous.
maledire *vt.* to curse.
maledizione *sf.* curse, malediction || *—! (inter.)*, damn!
maleducato *agg.* rude, impolite.
maleducazione *sf.* rudeness.
malefatta *sf.* mischief.
maleficio *sm.* sorcery.
malèfico *agg.* harmful.
malerba *sf.* weed.
malese *agg.* e *sm.* Malay.
malèssere *sm.* 1. malaise 2. (*disagio*) uneasiness.
malestro *sm.* mischief.
malevolenza *sf.* malevolence.
malèvolo *agg.* malevolent.
malfamato *agg.* ill-famed.
malfatto *agg.* 1. ill-shaped 2. (*di abito*) ill-fitting.
malfattore *sm.* evil-doer.
malfermo *agg.* shaky || *salute malferma*, poor health.
malfido *agg.* unreliable.
malfondato *agg.* ill-grounded.

malformato *agg.* malformed.

malformazione *sf.* malformation.

malgarbo *sm.* bad grace.

malgoverno *sm.* misgovernment, misrule.

malgrado *prep.* e *avv.* in spite of.
♦ **malgrado (che)** *cong.* though, although.

malìa *sf.* (*fascino*) fascination.

maliarda *sf.* **1.** (*donna affascinante*) fascinating woman **2.** (*maga*) witch.

malignamente *avv.* maliciously.

malignare *vi.* to speak (*v. irr.*) ill (of).

malignità *sf.* malice.

maligno *agg.* malicious: *tumore* —, malignant tumor.

malinconìa *sf.* melancholy.

malinconicamente *avv.* sadly.

malincònico *agg.* melancholy.

malincuore (*nella loc. avv.*) a —, unwillingly.

malintenzionato *agg.* ill-disposed.

malinteso *agg.* misplaced. ♦ **malinteso** *sm.* misunderstanding.

malizia *sf.* **1.** malice **2.** (*astuzia*) cunning.

maliziosamente *avv.* artfully.

malizioso *agg.* malicious, mischievous.

malleàbile *agg.* malleable.

malleabilità *sf.* malleability.

malleverìa *sf.* bail.

malloppo *sm.* swag.

malmenare *vt.* to manhandle.

malmesso *ag.* poorly dressed.

malnato *agg.* ill-bred.

malocchio *sm.* evil eye.

malora *sf.* ruin || *va alla* —!, go to the devil!

malore *sm.* illness.

malpensante *agg.* wrong-thinking.

malsano *agg.* unhealthy.

malsicuro *agg.* unsafe.

malta *sf.* mortar.

maltempo *sm.* bad weather.

maltenuto *agg.* untidy.

maltese *agg.* e *sm.* Maltese.

malto *sm.* malt.

maltolto *agg.* ill-gotten. ♦ **maltolto** *sm.* ill-gotten property.

maltosio *sm.* maltose.

maltrattamento *sm.* maltreatment.

maltrattare *vt.* to maltreat.

maltusianismo *sm.* Malthusianism.

maltusiano *agg.* e *sm.* Malthusian.

malumore *sm.* ill-humour.

malva *sf.* mallow.

malvagio *agg.* wicked.

malvagità *sf.* wickedness.

malversatore *sm.* embezzler.

malversazione *sf.* embezzlement.

malvisto *agg.* unpopular (with).

malvivente *sm.* gangster.

malvivenza *sf.* delinquency.

malvolentieri *avv.* unwillingly.

malvolere *sm.* ill-will.

malvolere *vi.* to dislike.

mamma *sf.* mama, mummy.

mammalucco *sm.* (*fam.*) simpleton.

mammella *sf.* **1.** mamma (*pl.* -ae) **2.** (*di animali da latte*) udder.

mammìfero *agg.* mammiferous. ♦ **mammìfero** *sm.* mammal.

màmmola *sf.* sweet-smelling violet.

mammùt *sm.* mammoth.

manata *sf.* slap.

manca *sf.* **1.** left hand **2.** (*parte sinistra*) left || *a dritta e a* —, on all sides.

mancante *agg.* incomplete.

mancanza *sf.* **1.** lack, shortage **2.** (*fallo*) fault || *sentire la* — *di qu.*, to miss so.

mancare *vi.* **1.** to be lacking (in) **2.** (*non esserci*) to be missing **3.** (*venir meno*) to fail **4.** (*agire scorrettamente*) to wrong (so.).

mancato *agg.* unsuccessful.

manchévole *agg.* defective.

manchevolezza *sf.* defect, fault.

mancia *sf.* tip || *dare la* — *a qu.*, to tip so.

manciata *sf.* handful.

mancina *sf.* left-hand.

mancino *agg.* left-handed. ♦ **mancino** *sm.* left-hander.

manco *avv.* not even.

mandamento *sm.* district.

mandante *sm.* **1.** instigator **2.** (*giur.*) principal.

mandare *vt.* **1.** to send (*v. irr.*) **2.** (*spedire*) to forward **3.** (*emettere*) to give (*v. irr.*) out.

mandarino *sm.* mandarin.

mandata *sf.* batch || — *di chiave*, turn.

mandatario *sm.* mandatary.

mandato *sm.* **1.** mandate **2.** (*comm.* agency **3.** (*giur.*) warrant.

mandìbola *sf.* mandible.

mandola *sf.* mandola.

mandolinista *s.* mandolinist.

mandolino *sm.* mandolin.

màndorla *sf.* almond.

màndorlo *sm.* almond-tree.

mandràgora *sf.* mandrake.
mandria *sf.* herd.
mandriano *sm.* herdsman (*pl.* -men).
maneggévole *agg.* handy.
maneggiare *vt.* to handle.
maneggio *sm.* **1.** (*equitazione*) riding-ground **2.** (*uso*) use **3.** (*intrigo*) plot.
manesco *agg.* rough, aggressive.
manette *sf. pl.* handcuff (*sing.*).
manforte *sf.* help.
manganellare *vt.* to cudgel.
manganello *sm.* cudgel.
manganese *sm.* manganese.
mangereccio *agg.* eatable.
mangiàbile *agg.* eatable.
mangiare *vt.* to eat (*v. irr.*).
mangiata *sf.* square meal.
mangiatoia *sf.* manger.
mangime *sm.* fodder.
mangiucchiare *vt.* to nibble (at).
manìa *sf.* mania.
manìaco *agg.* **1.** maniac **2.** (*fig.*) crazy. ♦ **manìaco** *sm.* maniac.
mànica *sf.* sleeve || *essere di — larga, stretta*, to be indulgent, strict.
manicheìsmo *sm.* Manicheism.
manicheo *agg. e sm.* Manichean.
manichino *sm.* manikin.
mànico *sm.* handle.
manicomio *sm.* mental hospital.
manicotto *sm.* **1.** muff **2.** (*mecc.*) sleeve.
maniera *sf.* manner, way.
manierato *agg.* affected.
manierismo *sm.* mannerism.
maniero *sm.* castle.
manifattura *sf.* manufacture.
manifatturiero *agg.* manufacturing.
manifestante *s.* demonstrator.
manifestare *vt.* **1.** to manifest, to show (*v. irr.*) **2.** (*pol.*) to demonstrate.
manifestazione *sf.* **1.** manifestation **2.** (*pol.*) demonstration.
manifesto *agg.* manifest, clear, obvious. ♦ **manifesto** *sm.* **1.** (*affisso*) poster **2.** (*volantino*) leaflet **3.** (*dichiarazione*) manifesto.
maniglia *sf.* handle.
manigoldo *sm.* scoundrel.
manioca *sf.* manioc.
manipolare *vt.* to manipulate.
manipolatore *sm.* manipulator.
manipolazione *sf.* manipulation.
manìpolo *sm.* (*eccl.; stor.*) maniple.
maniscalco *sm.* blacksmith.

manna *sf.* **1.** manna **2.** (*fig.*) blessing.
mannaia *sf.* **1.** axe **2.** (*della ghigliottina*) knife.
mannaro *agg. lupo —*, werewolf.
mano *sf.* hand: *fatto a —*, hand-made; *stringere la —*, to shake (*v. irr.*) hands with || *a — armata*, by force of arms; *sotto —*, underhand.
manodòpera *sf.* labour.
manòmetro *sm.* manometer.
manométtere *vt.* to tamper with.
manomissione *sf.* tampering.
manòpola *sf.* **1.** knob **2.** (*impugnatura*) handle.
manoscritto *agg.* handwritten. ♦ **manoscritto** *sm.* manuscript.
manovale *sm.* hodman (*pl.* -men).
manovella *sf.* crank.
manovra *sf.* manoeuvre, operation.
manovràbile *agg.* manoeuvrable.
manovrare *vt.* **1.** to manoeuvre **2.** (*mecc.*) to operate.
manovratore *sm.* operator, driver.
manrovescio *sm.* back-handed slap.
mansarda *sf.* mansard.
mansione *sf.* function.
mansuefare *vt.* to tame.
mansueto *agg.* meek, mild.
mansuetùdine *sf.* meekness.
mantella *sf.* cape.
mantello *sm.* cloak.
mantenere *vt.* to keep (*v. irr.*), to maintain: *— la parola*, to keep one's word.
mantenimento *sm.* maintenance.
màntice *sm.* bellows (*pl.*).
manto *sm.* cloak.
manuale *agg.* manual. ♦ **manuale** *sm.* handbook.
manubrio *sm.* **1.** handle **2.** (*di bicicletta ecc.*) handle-bar.
manufatto *agg.* hand-made. ♦ **manufatto** *sm.* hand-manufactured article.
manutèngolo *sm.* abettor.
manutenzione *sf.* maintenance, servicing.
manzo *sm.* **1.** (*zool.*) steer **2.** (*carne*) beef.
maomettano *agg. e sm.* Mohammedan.
mappa *sf.* map.
mappamondo *sm.* globe.
marachella *sf.* trick.
marasma *sm.* **1.** (*med.*) marasmus **2.** (*fig.*) decadence.
maratona *sf.* marathon race.

marca *sf.* brand: — *di fabbrica*, trade mark.

marcare *vt.* **1.** to mark **2.** (*sport*) to score.

marcato *agg.* marked, branded.

marcatore *sm.* **1.** marker **2.** (*sport*) scorer.

marcatura *sf.* **1.** marking **2.** (*sport*) scoring.

marchesa *sf.* **1.** marchioness **2.** (*se non è inglese*) marquise.

marchesato *sm.* marquisate.

marchese *sm.* marquis.

marchiano *agg.* enormous, glaring.

marchiare *vt.* to brand.

marchiatura *sf.* branding.

marchio *sm.* **1.** stamp **2.** (*a fuoco*) brand **3.** (*fig.; comm.*) mark.

marcia *sf.* **1.** (*auto*) gear **2.** (*mil.; mus.*) march.

marciapiede *sm.* **1.** pavement **2.** (*ferr.*) platform.

marciare *vi.* to march.

marciatore *sm.* (*sport*) road-walker.

marcio *agg.* **1.** rotten **2.** (*fig.*) corrupted. ♦ **marcio** *sm.* (*fig.*) corruption.

marcire *vi.* **1.** (*guastarsi*) to go (*v. irr.*) bad **2.** (*decomporsi*) to rot (*v. irr.*).

marciume *sm.* rottenness.

marco *sm.* mark.

marconigrafia *sf.* marconigraphy.

mare *sm.* sea.

marea *sf.* tide.

mareggiata *sf.* sea-storm.

maremma *sf.* maremma (*pl.* -me).

maremoto *sm.* seaquake.

mareògrafo *sm.* tide-gauge.

maresciallo *sm.* marshal.

margarina *sf.* margarine.

margherita *sf.* daisy.

marginale *agg.* marginal.

marginare *vt.* **1.** to border **2.** (*tip.*) to margin.

marginatura *sf.* **1.** edging **2.** (*tip.*) furniture.

màrgine *sm.* **1.** border, edge **2.** (*fig.*) margin.

marina *sf.* **1.** navy **2.** (*costa*) seashore **3.** (*pitt.*) sea-scape.

marinaio *sm.* sailor.

marinara *sf.* **1.** (*cappotto*) duffle coat **2.** (*cappello*) sailor hat.

marinare *vt.* (*cuc.*) to pickle || — *la scuola*, to play truant.

marinaresco *agg.* sailor-like.

marinaro *agg.* **1.** maritime **2.** sailor-like. ♦ **marinaro** *sm.* sailor.

marinerìa *sf.* **1.** seamanship **2.** (*marina*) navy.

marino *agg.* sea (*attr.*).

mariolo *sm.* rogue.

marionetta *sf.* puppet.

maritale *agg.* marital.

maritare *vt.* to marry. ♦ **maritarsi** *vr.* to get (*v. irr.*) married.

marito *sm.* husband.

marìttimo *agg.* maritime || *città marittima*, sea-town; *commercio* —, shipping business. ♦ **marìttimo** *sm.* seafarer || *i marittimi*, seafolk (*sing.*).

marmaglia *sf.* rabble.

marmellata *sf.* **1.** jam **2.** (*d'arance*) marmalade.

marmista *sm.* marble-cutter.

marmitta *sf.* **1.** (*cuc.*) stock-pot **2.** (*auto*) silencer's muffler.

marmo *sm.* marble.

marmocchio *sm.* kid.

marmòreo *agg.* marble.

marmotta *sf.* **1.** marmot **2.** (*di persona*) lazy-bones.

marna *sf.* marl.

marocchino *agg.* Moroccan. ♦ **marocchino** *sm.* **1.** (*persona*) Moroccan **2.** (*cuoio*) Morocco leather.

maroso *sm.* billow.

marra *sf.* **1.** (*agr.*) hoe **2.** (*mar.*) fluke.

marrone *agg.* brown. ♦ **marrone** *sm.* chestnut.

martedì *sm.* Tuesday.

martellamento *sm.* hammering.

martellare *vt.* **1.** to hammer **2.** (*mil.*) to pound **3.** (*pulsare*) to throb.

martellata *sf.* hammer-blow.

martello *sm.* hammer.

martinetto *sm.* jack.

martingala *sf.* half-belt.

màrtire *sm.* martyr.

martirio *sm.* martyrdom.

martirizzare *vt.* to martyrize.

martirologio *sm.* martyrology.

màrtora *sf.* marten.

martoriare *vt.* to torture.

marxismo *sm.* Marxism.

marxista *agg. e s.* Marxist.

marzapane *sm.* marzipan.

marziale *agg.* martial.

marziano *sm.* Martian.

marzo *sm.* March.

mascalzonata *sf.* knavery.

mascalzone *sm.* rascal.

mascella *sf.* jaw.

mascellare *agg.* jaw (*attr.*).

màschera *sf.* **1.** mask **2.** (*figura mascherata*) masker **3.** (*cosmesi*) face-pack **4.** (*inserviente di cinema, teatro*) usher.

mascheramento *sm.* masking.

mascherare *vt.* to mask.

mascherata *sf.* masquerade.

maschietto *sm.* male.

maschile *agg.* male.

maschio¹ *agg.* **1.** male **2.** (*virile*) manly. ♦ **maschio** *sm.* **1.** (*di animale*) (*uccelli*) cock, (*mammiferi*) bull (*attributivi*) **2.** (*di uomo*) male **3.** (*bambino*) boy.

maschio² *sm.* (*torre*) donjon.

mascolinità *sf.* masculinity.

masnada *sf.* gang.

masnadiere *sm.* highwayman (*pl.* -men).

masochismo *sm.* masochism.

masonite *sf.* masonite.

massa *sf.* mass, heap.

massacrante *agg.* exhausting.

massacrare *vt.* to massacre.

massacratore *sm.* slaughterer.

massacro *sm.* massacre.

massaggiare *vt.* to massage.

massaggiatore *sm.* masseur.

massaggiatrice *sf.* masseuse.

massaggio *sm.* massage.

massaia *sf.* housewife (*pl.* -wives).

massello *sm.* ingot.

masserìa *sf.* farm.

masserizie *sf. pl.* household goods.

massicciata *sf.* road-bed.

massiccio *agg.* solid. ♦ **massiccio** *sm.* massif.

màssima *sf.* maxim, rule ‖ *in linea di* —, on the whole; *accordo di* —, general agreement.

massimalismo *sm.* Maximalism.

massimalista *s.* Maximalist.

màssimo *agg.* **1.** greatest, highest **2.** (*l'estremo*) utmost **3.** (*il più lungo*) longest. ♦ **màssimo** *sm.* **1.** most **2.** (*il meglio*) best **3.** (*mat.; fis.*) maximum.

masso *sm.* boulder.

massone *sm.* freemason.

massonerìa *sf.* freemasonry.

mastello *sm.* tub.

masticare *vt.* to chew.

masticazione *sf.* mastication.

màstice *sm.* rubber.

mastino *sm.* mastiff.

mastite *sf.* mastitis.

mastodonte *sm.* **1.** (*zool.*) mastodon **2.** (*fig.*) giant.

mastodòntico *agg.* colossal.

mastòide *sf.* mastoid.

mastoidite *sf.* mastoiditis.

mastro *sm.* **1.** (*libro*) ledger **2.** (*appellativo*) Master.

masturbazione *sf.* masturbation.

matassa *sf.* **1.** hank **2.** (*fig.*) tangle.

matemàtica *sf.* mathematics.

matemàtico *agg.* mathematical. ♦ **matemàtico** *sm.* mathematician.

materasso *sm.* mattress.

materia *sf.* matter, subject.

materiale *agg.* **1.** material **2.** (*rozzo*) rough. ♦ **materiale** *sm.* material.

materialismo *sm.* materialism.

materialista *s.* materialist.

materialìstico *agg.* materialistic.

materializzare *vt.* to materialize.

maternità *sf.* maternity.

materno *agg.* motherly, maternal ‖ *scuola materna*, nursery-school.

matita *sf.* pencil.

matriarcato *sm.* matriarchy.

matrice *sf.* **1.** matrix (*pl.* matrices) **2.** (*comm.*) counterfoil.

matricida *s.* matricide.

matricidio *sm.* matricide.

matrìcola *sf.* **1.** matricula, register ‖ *numero di* —, matriculation number **2.** (*scol.*) freshman (*pl.* -men).

matricolato *agg.* matriculated ‖ *briccone* —, arrant knave.

matrigna *sf.* stepmother.

matrimoniale *agg.* matrimonial.

matrimonio *sm.* **1.** marriage **2.** (*cerimonia nuziale*) wedding.

matrona *sf.* matron.

matta *sf.* **1.** mad woman (*pl.* women) **2.** (*al gioco*) jolly joker.

mattacchione *sm.* joker.

mattatoio *sm.* slaughter-house.

matterello *sm.* rolling-pin.

mattina *sf.* morning.

mattinata *sf.* **1.** morning **2.** (*teat.*) matinée.

mattiniero *agg.* early-rising.

mattino *sm.* morning.

matto¹ *agg.* mad, crazy. ♦ **matto** *sm.* madman (*pl.* -men).

matto² *agg.* **1.** (*non lucido*) mat **2.** (*di gioielli*) false.

mattone *sm.* **1.** brick **2.** (*fig.*) bore.

mattonella *sf.* tile.

mattutino *agg.* morning (*attr.*). ♦ **mattutino** *sm.* (*eccl.*) matins (*pl.*).

maturare *vi. e vt.* to ripen, to mature (*anche fig.*).

maturazione *sf.* maturation, ripening (*anche fig.*).

maturità *sf.* ripening, maturity (*anche fig.*).

maturo *agg.* ripe, mature (*anche fig.*).

mausoleo *sm.* mausoleum.

mazurca *sf.* mazurka.

mazza *sf.* **1.** (*clava*) club **2.** (*martello di legno*) mallet.

mazzata *sf.* heavy blow (*anche fig.*).

mazziere *sm.* **1.** mace-bearer **2.** (*di carte*) dealer.

mazzo *sm.* **1.** bunch **2.** (*di carte*) pack || *fare il —*, to shuffle **3.** (*di fiori*) bouquet.

mazzolino *sm.* (*di fiori*) posy.

mazzuolo *sm.* mallet.

me *pron.* **1.** me **2.** (*me stesso*) myself.

meandro *sm.* **1.** meander **2.** (*labirinto*) maze.

meato *sm.* meatus.

meccànica *sf.* mechanics.

meccànico *agg.* mechanical. ♦ **meccànico** *sm.* mechanic.

meccanismo *sm.* **1.** gear **2.** (*movimento*) motion.

meccanizzare *vt.* to mechanize.

meccanizzazione *sf.* mechanization.

meccanografia *sf.* mechanography.

meccanogràfico *agg.* mechanographic.

mecenate *sm.* Maecenas.

mecenatismo *sm.* patronage.

medaglia *sf.* medal.

medaglione *sm.* **1.** locket **2.** (*arch.*) medallion.

medaglista *sm.* **1.** (*incisore*) medallist **2.** (*collezionista*) collector of medals.

medésimo *agg. e pron.* V. *stesso.*

media *sf.* **1.** average: *alla — di*, at an average of **2.** (*mat.*) mean.

mediana *sf.* median line.

mediànico *agg.* mediumistic.

mediano *agg.* **1.** medial, middle (*attr.*) **2.** (*geom.; anat; bot.*) median. ♦ **mediano** *sm.* (*sport*) half-back.

mediante *prep.* by, by means of, through.

mediato *agg.* indirect.

mediatore *sm.* **1.** mediator **2.** (*comm.*) broker.

mediazione *sf.* **1.** mediation **2.** (*comm.*) brokerage.

medicamento *sm.* medicament.

medicare *vt.* to dress.

medicastro *sm.* quack (doctor).

medicazione *sf.* **1.** medication **2.** (*di ferita*) dressing.

medicina *sf.* medicine.

medicinale *sm.* medicinal.

mèdico *agg.* medical. ♦ **mèdico** *sm.* physician, doctor.

medievale *agg.* medieval.

medio *sm.* **1.** (*dito*) middle finger **2.** (*mat.*) mean. ♦ **medio** *agg.* **1.** middle **2.** (*normale, che risulta da una media*) average.

mediocre *agg.* second-rate.

mediocrità *sf.* mediocrity.

medioevo *sm.* Middle Ages (*pl.*).

meditabondo *agg.* thoughtful.

meditare *vt.* **1.** to ponder **2.** (*avere un'intenzione*) to meditate.

meditativo *agg.* meditative.

meditazione *sf.* meditation.

mediterràneo *agg.* **1.** inland **2.** Mediterranean.

medium *sm.* medium.

medusa *sf.* medusa (*pl.* -ae).

mefistofèlico *agg.* satanic.

mefìtico *agg.* poisonous.

megaciclo *sm.* megacycle.

megàfono *sm.* megaphone.

megalòmane *sm.* megalomaniac.

megalomanìa *sf.* megalomania.

megatone *sm.* megaton.

meglio *avv.* **1.** (*comp.*) better **2.** (*superl. rel.*) best. ♦ **meglio** *agg.* **1.** (*comp.*) better: *questo vestito è — di quello*, this dress is better than that **2.** (*superl. rel.*) best. ♦ **meglio** *sm.* best, best thing || *in mancanza di —*, for lack of anything better. ♦ **meglio** *sf.* *avere la —*, to have the better || *alla —*, as well as possible.

mela *sf.* apple.

melacotogna *sf.* quince.

melagrana *sf.* pomegranate.

melanismo *sm.* melanism.

melanzana *sf.* aubergine.

melassa *sf.* molasses (*pl.*).

melato *agg.* **1.** sweetened with honey **2.** (*fig.*) honeyed.

melenso *agg.* dull, silly.

mellifluo *agg.* honeyed.

melma *sf.* slime.

melmoso *agg.* slimy.

melo *sm.* apple-tree.

melodìa *sf.* melody.

melòdico *agg.* melodic.

melodioso *agg.* melodious.

melodramma *sm.* **1.** opera **2.** (*fig.*) melodrama.

melodrammàtico *agg.* **1.** operatic **2.** (*fig.*) melodramatic.

melograno *sm.* pomegranate-tree.

melòmane *s.* melomaniac.

melomanìa *sf.* melomania.

melone *sm.* melon.

membra *sf. pl.* limbs.

membrana *sf.* membrane.

membratura *sf* structure.

membro *sm.* **1.** member **2.** (*anat.*) limb.

memoràbile *agg.* memorable.

memorandum *sm.* memorandum (*pl.* -da).

mèmore *agg.* mindful.

memoria *sf.* **1.** memory: — *di ferro*, cast-iron memory || *a* —, by heart **2.** (*ricordo*) memory, recollection.

memoriale *sm.* **1.** (*petizione*) memorial **2.** (*libro di memorie*) memoirs (*pl.*).

memorialista *s.* memorialist.

menabò *sm.* dummy.

menadito (*nella loc. avv.*) *a* —, perfectly || *sapere qc. a* —, to have sthg. at one's finger-tips.

menagramo *sm.* bearer of ill-luck.

menare *vt.* (*condurre*) to lead (*v. irr.*) || — *vanto*, to boast; — *il can per l'aia*, to beat (*v. irr.*) about the bush; — *buono, gramo*, to bring (*v. irr.*) good, bad luck.

mendace *agg.* mendacious, false.

mendacia *sf.* mendacity.

mendicante *sm.* beggar.

mendicare *vi.* to beg.

mendicità *sf.* mendicity.

mendico *agg.* e *sm.* mendicant.

menestrello *sm.* minstrel.

meninge *sf.* meninx (*pl.* meninges).

menisco *sm.* meniscus.

meno *avv.* **1.** (*comp.*) less **2.** (*superl. rel.*) least || *fare a* —, to do (*v. irr.*) without; *non poter fare a* —, cannot help: *non posso fare a* — *di andare*, I cannot help going **3.** (*mat.*) minus. ◆ **meno** *prep.* but for || *a* — *che* (*non*), unless. ◆ **meno** *agg.* **1.** (*comp. sing.*) less: *è* — *bella di sua sorella*, she is less beautiful than her sister **2.** (*comp. con s. pl.*) fewer: *ho* — *libri di te*, I have fewer books than you **3.** (*superl. rel. sing.*) the least: *è il* — *intelligente dei miei amici*, he is the least intelligent of my friends **4.** (*superl. rel. con s. pl.*) the fewest (*raro*).

◆ **meno** *sm.* **1.** (*comp.*) less **2.** (*superl. rel.*) the least.

menomare *vt.* to lessen.

menomato *agg.* **1.** lessened **2.** (*di vista, udito*) impaired.

menomazione *sf.* **1.** lessening **2.** (*di arti, sensi*) impairment **3.** (*di persona*) disablement.

menopàusa *sf.* menopause.

mensa *sf.* table.

mensile *agg.* monthly. ◆ **mensile** *sm.* **1.** (*salario*) month's salary **2.** (*pubblicazione*) monthly.

mensilità *sf.* monthly instalment || *tredicesima* —, Christmas bonus.

mensilmente *avv.* monthly, once a month.

mènsola *sf.* **1.** bracket **2.** (*scaffale*) shelf (*pl.* -lves).

menta *sf.* mint.

mentale *agg.* mental.

mentalità *sf.* mentality.

mente *sf.* mind: *persona dalla* — *ristretta*, narrow-minded person; *aguzzare la* —, to sharpen one's wits.

mentecatto *agg.* insane. ◆ **mentecatto** *sm.* madman (*pl.* -men).

mentina *sf.* peppermint-drop.

mentire *vi.* to lie.

mentito *agg.* false: *sotto mentite spoglie*, under false pretences.

mentitore *sm.* liar.

mento *sm.* chin.

mentolo *sm.* menthol.

mèntore *sm.* mentor.

mentre *cong.* **1.** (*temporale*) while, as, when **2.** (*avversativo*) whereas, while **3.** (*finché*) as long as, while. ◆ **mentre** *sm.* moment: *in quel* —, at that moment.

menzionare *vt.* to mention.

menzione *sf.* mention.

menzogna *sf.* falsehood.

menzognero *agg.* **1.** (*di persona*) mendacious **2.** (*di cosa*) false.

meraviglia *sf.* wonder: *sopraffatto dalla* —, wonder-struck; *non fa* — *che, nessuna* — *che*, no wonder.

meravigliare *vt.* to astonish. ◆ **meravigliarsi** *vr.* to be astonished (at).

meravigliato *agg.* astonished.

meraviglioso *agg.* wonderful.

mercante *sm.* merchant.

mercanteggiare *vi.* (*tirare sul prezzo*) to bargain, to haggle.

mercantile *agg.* mercantile. ◆ **mercantile** *sm.* cargo boat.

mercantilismo sm. mercantilism.
mercanzia sf. merchandise.
mercato sm. market || a buon —, cheap.
merce sf. goods (pl.).
mercé sf. mercy.
mercede sf. pay, reward.
mercenario agg. e sm. mercenary.
merceologìa sf. technology of marketable goods.
mercerìa sf. 1. haberdashery 2. (negozio) haberdasher's shop.
mercerizzato agg. mercerized.
merciaio sm. haberdasher.
mercoledì sm. Wednesday: — delle Ceneri, Ash Wednesday.
mercurio sm. mercury, quicksilver.
merenda sf. afternoon snack.
meretrice sf. prostitute.
meretricio sm. prostitution.
meridiana sf. sun-dial.
meridiano agg. e sm. meridian.
meridionale agg. Southern. ♦ **meridionale** sm. Southerner.
meridione sm. south.
meringa sf. meringue.
merino sm. merino.
meritare vt. to deserve.
meritévole agg. deserving.
mèrito sm. merit || in — a, as to.
meritorio agg. meritorious, deserving.
merletto sm. lace.
merlo sm. 1. blackbird 2. (sciocco) simpleton.
merluzzo sm. codfish.
mero agg. 1. pure 2. (fig.) mere.
mesata sf. 1. month 2. (paga di un mese) month's pay.
méscere vt. to pour (out).
meschinità sf. meanness.
meschino agg. mean. ♦ **meschino** sm. wretch.
méscita sf. pouring (out).
mescolanza sf. 1. mixing 2. (miscuglio) mixture.
mescolare vt. 1. to mix 2. (tè, caffè, liquori, tabacco) to blend. ♦ **mescolarsi** vr. to mingle.
mescolatrice sf. mixer.
mese sm. month.
messa sf. 1. (eccl.) Mass 2. (azione del mettere) putting, setting: — a punto, setting up || — a fuoco, focusing.
messaggero sm. messenger.
messaggio sm. 1. message 2. (allocuzione) address.
messale sm. missal.

messe sf. crop, harvest.
messìa sm. Messiah.
messiànico agg. Messianic.
messianismo sm. Messianism.
messicano agg. e sm. Mexican.
messinscena sf. staging.
mestare vt. to stir.
mestiere sm. 1. trade 2. (perizia) skill 3. (lavoro) work.
mestizia sf. sadness.
méstola sf. ladle.
méstolo sm. ladle.
mestruazione sf. menstruation.
meta sf. 1. destination 2. (scopo) aim, purpose: senza —, aimless.
metà sf. 1. half (pl. halves) 2. (parte mediana) middle 3. (coniuge) la mia —, my better half.
metabolismo sm. metabolism.
metafìsica sf. metaphysics.
metàfora sf. metaphor.
metafòrico agg. metaphoric(al).
metàllico agg. metallic.
metallo sm. metal.
metallurgìa sf. metallurgy.
metallùrgico agg. metallurgic(al). ♦ **metallùrgico** sm. metallurgist.
metalmeccànico sm. metallurgist and mechanic.
metamòrfico agg. metamorphic.
metamorfismo sm. metamorphism.
metamòrfosi sf. metamorphosis (pl. -ses).
metano sm. methane.
metapsìchica sf. metapsychics.
metapsìchico agg. metapsychic(al).
metàstasi sf. metastasis (pl. -ses).
metempsicosi sf. metempsychosis (pl. -ses).
metèora sf. meteor.
meteòrico agg. meteoric.
meteorite sm. meteorite.
meteorologìa sf. meteorology.
meteorològico agg. meteorological || previsioni meteorologiche, weather-forecast (sing.).
meteoròlogo sm. meteorologist.
meticcio agg. e sm. mestizo (pl. -za).
meticoloso agg. meticulous.
metodicità sf. methodicalness.
metòdico agg. methodical.
metodista agg. e s. Methodist.
mètodo sm. method.
metodologìa sf. methodology.
metodològico agg. methodological.
mètopa sf. metope.
metraggio sm. 1. length (in metres) 2. (cine) corto, lungo —, short, full-length film.

mètrica sf. prosody.
mètrico agg. metric.
metrite sf. metritis.
metro sm. 1. metre 2. (strumento per misurare) rule.
metrònomo sm. metronome.
metronotte sm. night-watch.
metròpoli sf. metropolis (pl. -ses).
metropolitana sf. underground.
metropolitano agg. metropolitan.
méttere vt. 1. to put (v. irr.) || — in chiaro qc., to make (v. irr.) sthg. clear; — in dubbio qc., to doubt sthg.; — in serbo, to lay (v. irr.) aside; — in moto, to start; — in luce, to emphasize; — in guardia qu., to put so. on his guard; — le mani su qc., to take (v. irr.) possession of; — le mani sul fuoco per qu., to speak (v. irr.) for so. 2. (impiegare, di tempo) to take 3. (indossare) to put on 4. (paragonare) to compare. ♦ **mettersi** vr. 1. to put oneself || — in contatto con qu., to get (v. irr.) in touch with so.; — in testa di fare qc., to take into one's head to do sthg.; — sotto, to get down to it 2. (incominciare) to begin (v. irr.) 3. (indossare) to put (v. irr.) on.
mettifoglio sm. (tip.) feeder.
mezzadrìa sf. métayage.
mezzadro sm. métayer.
mezzaluna sf. 1. half-moon 2. (emblema islamico) crescent 3. (cuc.) mincing-knife.
mezzana[1] sf. (mar.) mizzen sail.
mezzana[2] sf. procuress.
mezzano agg. middle. ♦ **mezzano** sm. go-between.
mezzanotte sf. midnight.
mezzatinta sf. half-tone.
mezzo[1] agg. 1. half 2. (medio) middle. ♦ **mezzo** avv. half. ♦ **in mezzo a** prep. 1. in the middle of 2. (fra molti) among 3. (fra due) between.
mezzo[2] sm. 1. means 2. (fis.) medium.
mezzo[3] agg. (marcio) rotten.
mezzobusto sm. bust.
mezzocerchio sm. semicircle.
mezzodì sm. midday, noon.
mezzofondo sm. middle-distance race.
mezzogiorno sm. 1. midday 2. (Sud) South.
mezzosoprano sm. mezzo-soprano.

mi[1] pron. 1. me 2. (me stesso) myself 3. (a me) to me.
mi[2] sm. (mus.) E, mi.
miagolare vi. to mew
miagolìo sm. mewing
miasma sm. miasma.
mica sf. mica.
miccia sf. fuse.
michetta sf. roll.
micidiale agg. lethal, deadly.
micino sm. kitten, pussy.
micosi sf. mycosis (pl. -ses).
microbio sm. microbe.
microbiologìa sf. microbiology.
microcosmo sm. microcosm.
microfilm sm. microfilm.
micròfono sm. microphone.
microfotografìa sf. microphotography.
micrometrìa sf. micrometry.
micròmetro sm. micrometer.
micron sm. micron.
microrganismo sm. microorganism.
microscopìa sf. microscopy.
microscòpico agg. microscopic(al).
microscopio sm. microscope.
microsolco sm. long-playing record.
microtelèfono sm. microtelephone.
midolla sf. crumb.
midollare agg. medullar.
midollo sm. marrow: — spinale, spinal cord.
miele sm. honey.
mietere vt. to reap.
mietitrice sf. reaper.
mietitura sf. reaping.
migliaio sm. thousand.
miglio[1] sm. (bot.) millet.
miglio[2] sm. (misura di lunghezza) mile.
miglioramento sm. improvement.
migliorare vt. to better, to improve.
migliore agg. 1. (comp.) better: questo libro è — di quello, this book is better than that 2. (superl.) the best: è il — alunno della classe, he is the best pupil in his class.
migliorìa sf. improvement.
mignatta sf. leech.
mignolo sm. little finger.
migrare vi. to migrate.
migratore agg. migratory. ♦ **migratore** sm. migrant.
migratorio agg. migratory.
migrazione sf. migration.
miliardario sm. multi-millionaire.

miliardo *sm.* a thousand millions.
miliare *agg. pietra —,* milestone.
milionario *sm.* millionaire.
milione *sm.* million.
milionèsimo *agg.* millionth.
militante *agg.* militant.
militare[1] *agg.* military. ♦ **militare** *sm.* soldier.
militare[2] *vi.* **1.** to be a soldier **2.** (*lavorare a favore di*) to support.
militaresco *agg.* soldierlike.
militarismo *sm.* militarism.
militarista *sm.* militarist.
militarizzare *vt.* to militarize.
militarizzazione *sf.* militarization.
militarmente *avv.* militarily.
mìlite *sm.* militiaman (*pl.* -men).
milizia *sf.* Army.
miliziano *sm.* militiaman (*pl.* -men).
millantare *vt.* to boast of. ♦ **millantarsi** *vr.* to boast.
millantatore *sm.* boaster.
millanterìa *sf.* boasting.
mille *agg.* one thousand.
millenario *agg.* e *sm.* millenary.
millennio *sm.* millennium.
millepiedi *sm.* millepede.
millèsimo *agg.* thousandth.
milligrammo *sm.* milligram.
millìmetro *sm.* millimetre.
milza *sf.* spleen.
mimare *vt.* e *vi.* to mime.
mimètico *agg.* mimetic.
mimetismo *sm.* **1.** (*di animali*) mimicry **2.** (*mil.*) camouflage.
mimetizzare *vt.* to camouflage.
mimetizzazione *sf.* camouflage.
mìmica *sf.* **1.** (*teat.*) mimic art **2.** (*di gesti*) gesticulation.
mìmico *agg.* miming, mimic.
mimo *sm.* mime.
mimosa *sf.* mimosa.
mina *sf.* mine.
minaccia *sf.* threat.
minacciare *vt.* to threaten.
minaccioso *agg.* threatening.
minare *vt.* **1.** to mine **2.** (*fig.*) undermine.
minareto *sm.* minaret.
minatore *sm.* miner.
minatorio *agg.* threatening.
minchione *sm.* simpleton.
minerale *agg.* mineral. ♦ **minerale** *sm.* mineral.
mineralizzare *vt.* to mineralize.
mineralogìa *sf.* mineralogy.
minerario *agg.* mining (*attr.*).
mìnestra *sf.* soup.
mingherlino *agg.* slim.

miniare *vt.* **1.** to paint in miniature **2.** (*di manoscritti*) to illuminate.
miniato *agg.* illuminated.
miniatura *sf.* miniature.
miniaturista *sm.* miniaturist.
miniera *sf.* mine.
minigonna *sf.* miniskirt.
minimamente *avv.* not in the least.
minimizzare *vt.* to minimize.
mìnimo *agg.* least, slightest, smallest. ♦ **mìnimo** *sm.* minimum..
minio *sm.* red lead.
ministeriale *agg.* ministerial.
ministero *sm.* ministry: *— dell'Istruzione,* ministry of Education || *— degli Esteri, dell'Interno,* Foreign, Home Office; *— del Tesoro,* Treasury.
ministro *sm.* minister.
minoranza *sf.* minority.
minorare *vt.* to diminish.
minorato *agg.* disabled.
minorazione *sf.* **1.** (*diminuzione*) reduction **2.** (*invalidità*) disablement.
minore *agg.* **1.** (*comp.*) (*più piccolo*) smaller, less; (*più basso*) lower; (*più corto*) shorter; (*più giovane*) younger **2.** (*superl.*) the smallest, least, lowest, shortest, youngest.
minorile *agg.* juvenile.
minorenne *agg.* under age. ♦ **minorenne** *s.* minor.
minorile *agg.* juvenile.
minorità *sf.* minority.
minoritario *agg.* minority (*attr.*).
minuetto *sm.* minuet.
minugia *sf.* gut.
minùscolo *agg.* small letter.
minuta *sf.* rough copy.
minutaglia *sf.* bits and pieces (*pl.*).
minuto[1] *agg.* **1.** minute **2.** (*dettagliato*) detailed.
minuto[2] *sm.* minute.
minuto[3] *sm.* (*comm.*) retail.
minuzia *sf.* trifle.
minuziosamente *avv.* minutely.
minuziosità *sf.* minuteness.
minuzioso *agg.* minute, detailed.
minùzzolo *sm.* crumb.
mio *agg.* my. ♦ **mio** *pron.* mine.
miocardìa *sf.* myocardia.
miocardio *sm.* myocardium.
miocardite *sf.* myocarditis.
miocene *sm.* miocene.
mìope *agg.* short-sighted.
miopìa *sf.* myopia.

mira sf. **1.** aim: *prendere la* —, to take (*v. irr.*) aim **2.** (*fig.*) aim, design.
miràbile agg. admirable.
mirabilia sf. pl. wonders.
mirabolante agg. astonishing.
miràcolo sm. miracle: *fare miracoli*, to do (*v. irr.*) miracles, (*fig.*) to work wonders.
miracoloso agg. miraculous.
miraggio sm. mirage.
mirare vt. to look at. ♦ **mirare** vi. to aim (at).
mirìade sf. myriad.
miriagrammo sm. myriagram.
miriàmetro sm. myriametre.
miriàpodi sm. pl. Myriapoda.
mirìfico agg. wondrous.
mirino sm. **1.** sight **2.** (*foto*) view-finder.
mirra sf. myrrh.
mirtillo sm. bilberry.
mirto sm. myrtle.
misantropìa sf. misanthropy.
misàntropo sm. misanthrope.
miscela sf. **1.** mixture **2.** (*di caffè, tè, liquori, tabacco*) blend.
miscelare vt. **1.** to mix **2.** (*di caffè, tabacco, liquori ecc.*) to blend.
miscellànea sf. miscellany.
mischia sf. fray.
mischiare vt. to mix, to mingle.
mischiatura sf. **1.** (*il mischiare*) mixing **2.** (*miscuglio*) mixture.
misconòscere vt. not to acknowledge.
miscredente agg. misbelieving. ♦ **miscredente** sm. misbeliever.
miscredenza sf. misbelief.
miscuglio sm. **1.** mixture **2.** (*amalgama*) blend.
miseràbile agg. **1.** miserable **2.** (*scarso*) poor **3.** (*vile*) despicable, mean. ♦ **miseràbile** sm. wretch.
miserando agg. miserable.
miserévole agg. miserable, pitiable.
miseria sf. **1.** misery, poverty **2.** (*scarsità*) lack **3.** (*inezia*) trifle.
misericordia sf. mercy.
misericordioso agg. merciful.
misero agg. **1.** poor, scanty **2.** (*meschino*) wretched.
misfatto sm. misdeed.
misoginìa sf. misogyny.
misògino agg. misogynous. ♦ **misògino** sm. misogynist.
misoneismo sm. misoneism.
missaggio sm. mixing.
missile sm. missile.

missionario sm. missionary.
missione sf. mission.
missiva sf. letter.
misteriosamente avv. mysteriously.
misterioso agg. mysterious.
mistero sm. mystery.
mìstica sf. mysticism.
misticismo sm. mysticism.
mìstico agg. mystic.
mistificare vt. to mystify.
mistificatore sm. mystifier.
mistificazione sf. mystification.
misto agg. mixed.
mistura sf. mixture.
misura sf. **1.** (*misurazione, precauzione*) measure **2.** (*taglia*) size **3.** (*limite*) limit.
misuràbile agg. measurable.
misurare vt. **1.** to measure **2.** (*tec.*) to gauge **3.** (*limitare*) to limit. ♦ **misurarsi** vr. to compete.
misurato agg. measured.
misuratore sm. **1.** (*persona che misura*) measurer **2.** (*strumento*) gauge.
misurazione sf. measurement.
misurino sm. small measure.
mite agg. gentle, meek.
mitezza sf. gentleness, meekness.
mìtico agg. mythical.
mitigare vt. **1.** to mitigate **2.** (*passioni*) to appease **3.** (*dolori*) to relieve. ♦ **mitigarsi** vr. to be appeased.
mitigazione sf. **1.** mitigation **2.** (*di passioni*) appeasement **3.** (*di dolore*) relief.
mìtilo sm. mussel.
mito sm. myth.
mitologìa sf. mythology.
mitològico agg. mythological.
mitòmane s. mythomaniac.
mitomanìa sf. mythomania.
mitra[1] sf. (*eccl.*) mitre.
mitra[2] sm. (*mil.*) tommy-gun.
mitraglia sf. grape-shot.
mitragliare vt. to machine-gun.
mitragliatore sm. machine-gunner.
mitragliatrice sf. machine-gun.
mitragliere sm. machine-gunner.
mitrale agg. mitral.
mitrato agg. mitred.
mitridàtico agg. mithridatic.
mitridatismo sm. mithridatism.
mittente sm. sender.
mnemònica sf. mnemonics.
mnemònico agg. mnemonic.
mo' (*nella loc. prep.*) *a* — *di*, like.

mòbile *agg.* **1.** movable || *scala —*, escalator; *beni mobili*, personal property **2.** (*mutevole*) inconstant. ◆ **mòbile** *sm.* piece of furniture.

mobilia *sf.* furniture.

mobiliare[1] *agg.* movable, personal.

mobiliare[2] *vt.* to furnish.

mobilità *sf.* **1.** mobility **2.** (*fig.*) inconstancy.

mobilitare *vt.* to mobilize.

mobilitazione *sf.* mobilization.

mocassino *sm.* moccasin.

moccioso *agg.* snivelling. ◆ **moccioso** *sm.* young scoundrel, brat.

mòccolo *sm.* **1.** candle-end **2.** (*bestemmia*) curse.

moda *sf.* **1.** fashion: *di —*, in fashion; *fuori —*, out of fashion || *alla —*, fashionable **2.** (*abitudine, modo*) manner, way: *alla — di*, after the manner of.

modale *agg.* modal.

modalità *sf.* modality.

modanatura *sf.* moulding.

mòdano *sm.* model.

modella *sf.* model.

modellare *vt.* to model, to shape.

modellatore *sm.* modeller.

modellazione *sf.* modelling.

modello *sm.* **1.** model, pattern **2.** (*stampo*) mould.

moderare *vt.* to moderate, to check.

moderato *agg.* moderate.

moderatore *agg.* moderating. ◆ **moderatore** *sm.* moderator.

moderazione *sf.* moderation.

modernismo *sm.* modernism.

modernità *sf.* modernity.

modernizzare *vt.* to modernize.

moderno *agg.* modern, up-to-date (*attr.*).

modestia *sf.* modesty: *— a parte*, modesty apart.

modesto *agg.* modest.

modicità *sf.* **1.** moderateness **2.** (*di prezzi*) cheapness.

mòdico *agg.* moderate: *a prezzo —*, cheap.

modìfica *sf.* alteration, change.

modificare *vt.* to modify.

modificazione *sf.* V. *modifica*.

modista *sf.* milliner.

modisterìa *sf.* milliner's shop.

modo *sm.* **1.** way, manner **2.** (*gramm.*) mood **3.** (*mezzo*) means: *in nessun —*, by no means || *di — che*, so (that); *in — da*, so as to; *in che —*, how; *in qualche —*, anyhow; *oltre —*, beyond measure.

modulare *vt.* to modulate.

modulato *agg.* modulated.

modulazione *sf.* modulation

mòdulo *sm.* form.

moffetta *sf.* skunk.

mògano *sm.* mahogany.

moggio *sm.* bushel.

mogio *agg.* depressed.

moglie *sf.* wife (*pl.* wives).

moina *sf.* simpering.

mola[1] *sf.* **1.** (*di mulino*) millstone **2.** (*per arrotare*) grindstone.

mola[2] *sf.* (*itt.*) sun-fish.

molare[1] *vt.* to grind (*v. irr.*).

molare[2] *agg.* molar. ◆ **molare** *sm.* (*dente*) molar (tooth).

molatura *sf.* grinding.

molazza *sf.* muller.

mole *sf.* **1.** mass, bulk **2.** (*dimensione*) size.

molècola *sf.* molecule.

molecolare *agg.* molecular.

molestare *vt.* to molest, to tease.

molestatore *agg.* molesting. ◆ **molestatore** *sm.* molester.

molestia *sf.* nuisance, trouble.

molesto *agg.* troublesome.

molibdeno *sm.* molybdenum.

molitorio *agg.* molinary.

molla *sf.* **1.** spring **2.** (*incentivo*) spur.

mollare *vt.* **1.** (*allentare*) to slacken **2.** (*mar.*) to let (*v. irr.*) go. ◆ **mollare** *vi.* to give (*v. irr.*) in.

molle *agg.* **1.** soft **2.** (*floscio*) flabby **3.** (*debole*) weak **4.** (*inzuppato*) soaking wet. ◆ **molle** *sf. pl.* tongs.

molleggiamento *sm.* **1.** (*elasticità*) springiness **2.** (*di veicoli*) springing system.

molleggiare *vi.* to be springy.

molleggiato *agg.* sprung.

molleggio *sm.* (*di veicoli*) suspension.

molletta *sf.* **1.** (*per il bucato*) clothes-peg **2.** (*per i capelli*) hair-pin.

mollettiere *sf. pl.* puttees.

mollettone *sm.* thick flannel.

mollezza *sf.* **1.** (*morbidezza*) softness **2.** (*debolezza*) weakness.

mollica *sf.* crumb.

mollo *agg.* damp: *mettere a —*, to steep.

mollusco *sm.* mollusc.

molo *sm.* pier, wharf.

moltéplice *agg.* manifold.

molteplicità *sf.* multiplicity.

moltìplica *sf.* (*mecc.*) chain gearing.
moltiplicando *sm.* multiplicand.
moltiplicare *vt.* to multiply.
moltiplicatore *sm.* multiplier.
moltiplicazione *sf.* multiplication.
moltìssimo *agg. indef.* **1.** very much (*pl.* very many) **2.** (*di tempo*) very long. ◆ **moltìssimo** *avv.* a great deal, very much.
moltitùdine *sf.* multitude.
molto *agg. indef.* **1.** (*sing.*) much, a great deal of, a lot of, plenty of **2.** (*pl.*) many, a good many, a lot of, plenty of **3.** (*di tempo*) long. ◆ **molto** *avv.* **1.** very **2.** (*con comp.*) much, far **3.** (*di tempo*) long, a long time.
momentaneamente *avv.* at the moment.
momentàneo *agg.* momentary.
momento *sm.* **1.** moment || *dal — che*, since **2.** (*tempo, circostanza*) time **3.** (*opportunità*) chance.
mònaca *sf.* nun.
monacale *agg.* monastic.
mònaco *sm.* monk.
mònade *sf.* monad.
monarca *sm.* monarch.
monarchìa *sf.* monarchy.
monàrchico *agg.* monarchic.
monastero *sm.* monastery.
monàstico *agg.* monastic.
moncherino *sm.* stump.
monco *agg.* **1.** maimed **2.** (*fig.*) incomplete.
moncone *sm.* stump.
mondanità *sf.* **1.** society life **2.** worldliness.
mondano *agg.* worldly.
mondare *vt.* **1.** to clean || *— il grano*, to winnow the corn **2.** (*fig.*) to cleanse.
mondiale *agg.* world-wide, world (*attr.*).
mondina *sf.* rice-weeder.
mondo[1] *sm.* world: *fare il giro del —*, to go (*v. irr.*) round the world; *da che — è —*, since the world began.
mondo[2] *agg.* clean.
monelleria *sf.* prank.
monello *sm.* little rascal, urchin.
moneta *sf.* **1.** money (*solo sing.*) **2.** (*ogni singolo pezzo*) coin **3.** (*spiccioli*) change.
monetario *agg.* monetary.
monetizzare *vt.* to monetize.
mongolfiera *sf.* montgolfier.
mongolismo *sm.* mongolism.

mòngolo *agg.* Mongolian. ◆ **mòngolo** *sm.* Mongol.
mongolòide *agg. e sm.* mongoloid.
monile *sm.* jewel.
monismo *sm.* monism.
mònito *sm.* warning.
monoblocco *sm.* monobloc.
monòcolo *sm.* monocle.
monocromàtico *agg.* monochromatic.
monòcromo *agg.* monochrome.
monodìa *sf.* monody.
monogamìa *sf.* monogamy.
monògamo *agg.* monogamous. ◆ **monògamo** *sm.* monogamist.
monografìa *sf.* monograph.
monogràfico *agg.* monographic.
monogramma *sm.* monogram.
monolìtico *agg.* monolithic.
monòlogo *sm.* monologue, soliloquy.
monometallismo *sm.* monometallism.
monomio *sm.* monomial.
monopàttino *sm.* scooter.
monoplano *sm.* monoplane.
monopolio *sm.* monopoly.
monopolista *sm.* monopolist.
monopolizzare *vt.* to monopolize.
monoposto *agg. e sm.* single-seater.
monorotaia *sf.* monorail.
monosillàbico *agg.* monosyllabic.
monosìllabo *sm.* monosyllable.
monoteismo *sm.* monotheism.
monoteista *s.* monotheist.
monoteìstico *agg.* monotheistic.
monotipo *sm.* monotype.
monotonìa *sf.* monotony.
monòtono *agg.* monotonous.
monovalente *agg.* monovalent.
monsignore *sm.* monsignor (*pl.* -ri).
monsone *sm.* monsoon.
montacàrichi *sm.* goods-lift.
montaggio *sm.* **1.** assembly: *linea di —*, assembly line **2.** (*cine*) editing **3.** (*foto*) montage.
montagna *sf.* mountain.
montagnoso *agg.* mountainous.
montanaro *agg.* mountain (*attr.*). ◆ **montanaro** *sm.* mountaineer.
montante *sm.* **1.** (*boxe*) uppercut **2.** (*mecc.; edil.*) vertical rod.
montare *vt.* **1.** (*mettere insieme*) to assemble **2.** (*cavalcare*) to ride (*v. irr.*) **3.** (*di panna*) to whip. ◆ **montare** *vi.* **1.** to climb **2.** (*alzarsi, aumentare*) to rise (*v. irr.*). ◆ **montarsi** *vr.* to get (*v. irr.*) excited.

montatore *sm.* assembler.
montatura *sf.* **1.** fitting **2.** (*fig.*) hot hair.
montavivande *sm.* dumb-waiter.
monte *sm.* **1.** mount (*seguito dal nome*) **2.** mountain || *andare a* —, to come (*v. irr.*) to nothing; *mandare a* —, to cause to fail.
montone *sm.* **1.** ram **2.** (*carne*) mutton.
montuosità *sf.* hilliness.
montuoso *agg.* hilly.
monumentale *agg.* monumental.
monumento *sm.* monument.
mora¹ *sf.* (*bot.*) mulberry.
mora² *sf.* (*giur.*) delay.
morale *agg.* moral. ♦ **morale** *sm.* morale. ♦ **morale** *sf.* **1.** morals (*pl.*) **2.** (*fil.*) ethics **3.** (*conclusione*) moral.
moralismo *sm.* moralism.
moralista *s.* moralist.
moralistico *agg.* moralistic.
moralità *sf.* morality.
moralizzare *vt.* to moralize.
moralizzazione *sf.* moralization.
moratorio *agg.* moratory.
morbidezza *sf.* softness.
mòrbido *agg.* soft.
morbillo *sm.* measles (*pl.*).
morbo *sm.* disease, plague.
morbosità *sf.* morbidity.
morboso *agg.* morbid.
mordace *agg.* biting, pungent.
mordacità *sf.* mordacity.
mordente *sm.* **1.** (*mus.*) mordent **2.** (*spirito aggressivo*) bite.
mòrdere *vt.* **1.** to bite (*v. irr.*) **2.** (*tormentare*) to torment || — *il freno*, to strain at the leash; — *la polvere*, to bite the dust.
morena *sf.* moraine.
morènico *agg.* morainic.
morente *agg.* dying. ♦ **morente** *sm.* dying man.
moresco *agg.* Moorish.
morfina *sf.* morphine.
morfinòmane *s.* morphinomaniac
morfologìa *sf.* morphology.
morfològico *agg.* morphologic(al).
morganàtico *agg.* morganatic.
moribondo *agg.* dying. ♦ **moribondo** *sm.* dying man.
morigeratezza *sf.* moderation.
morigerato *agg.* moderate, sober.
morire *vi.* **1.** to die **2.** (*di luci e colori*) to fade **3.** (*di suoni*) to die out **4.** (*tramontare*) to set (*v. irr.*) ♦ **morire** *sm.* death.

mormone *agg. e sm.* Mormon.
mormorare *vt.* to murmur. ♦ **mormorare** *vi.* (*parlar male*) to gossip.
mormorìo *sm.* **1.** murmur **2.** (*lamento*) complaining **3.** (*malignità*) evil gossip.
moro *agg.* dark. ♦ **moro** *sm.* **1.** moor **2.** (*bot.*) mulberry-tree.
morra *sf.* "morra".
morsa *sf.* vice.
morsetto *sm.* (*mecc.*) clamp.
morsicare *vt.* to bite (*v. irr.*).
morsicatura *sf.* bite.
morsicchiare *vt.* to nibble.
morso *sm.* **1.** bite **2.** (*puntura, stimolo*) sting, pang **3.** (*del cavallo*) bit **4.** (*boccone*) morsel, bit.
mortaio *sm.* mortar.
mortale *agg.* mortal, deadly.
mortalità *sf.* mortality.
mortalmente *avv.* mortally.
mortaretto *sm.* cracker.
morte *sf.* death || *pena di* —, capital punishment; *dar la* — *a qu.*, to kill so.; *odiare a* — *qu.*, to hate so. like poison.
mortella *sf.* myrtle.
mortifero *agg.* lethal.
mortificare *vt.* **1.** to humiliate **2.** (*reprimere*) to mortify.
mortificato *agg.* humiliated.
mortificazione *sf.* mortification.
morto *agg.* **1.** dead || *natura morta* (*pitt.*), still life; *stanco* —, dead tired **2.** (*senza vivacità*) dull. ♦ **morto** *sm.* dead man.
mortorio *sm.* funeral.
mortuario *agg.* mortuary.
mosaicista *s.* mosaicist.
mosàico *sm.* mosaic.
mosca *sf.* fly.
moscatello *sm.* muscatel.
moscato *sm.* (*vino*) muscatel. ♦ **moscato** *agg. noce moscata*, nutmeg.
moscerino *sm.* gnat.
moschea *sf.* mosque.
moschettiere *sm.* musketeer.
moschetto *sm.* musket.
moscio *agg.* flabby.
moscone *sm.* blue-bottle.
mossa *sf.* **1.** movement **2.** (*spostamento al gioco; fig.*) move **3.** (*sport*) starting post.
mossiere *sm.* (*sport*) starter.
mosso *agg.* **1.** (*di mare*) rough **2.** (*di capelli*) wavy.
mosto *sm.* must.

mostra sf. **1.** (esposizione) show, exhibition **2.** (vetrina) shop-window **3.** (ostentazione) display.

mostrare vt. **1.** to show (v. irr.) **2.** (ostentare) to show (v. irr.) off **3.** (dimostrare) to prove **4.** (fingere) to pretend.

mostrina sf. collar badge.

mostro sm. monster.

mostruosamente avv. monstrously.

mostruosità sf. monstrosity.

mostruoso agg. monstrous. for **2.** (giur.) to allege.

mota sf. mud, mire.

motivare vt. **1.** to state the reason

motivazione sf. **1.** motivation **2.** (giur.) opinion.

motivo sm. **1.** reason || a — di, owing to; senza —, groundless **2.** (mus.) theme.

moto sm. **1.** motion, movement **2.** (esercizio fisico) exercise **3.** (impulso) impulse. ♦ **moto** sf. motor-cycle.

motobarca sf. motor-boat.

motocarrozzetta sf. side-car.

motocicletta sf. motor-cycle.

motociclismo sm. motor-cycling.

motociclista s. motor-cyclist.

motofurgone sm. van.

motore agg. motor, driving. ♦ **motore** sm. engine, motor.

motorista sm. engineer.

motorizzare vt. to motorize. ♦ **motorizzarsi** vr. to buy (v. irr.) a car, a motor-cycle.

motorizzazione sf. motorization.

motoscafo sm. motor-boat.

motoveicolo sm. motòr vehicle.

motrice sf. **1.** tractor **2.** (ferr.) engine.

motteggiare vt. to make (v. irr.) fun of. ♦ **motteggiare** vi. to joke.

motteggiatore agg. joking. ♦ **motteggiatore** sm. joker.

motteggio sm. **1.** (il motteggiare) raillery **2.** (detto arguto) joke.

mottetto sm. motet.

motto sm. **1.** word **2.** (proverbio) saying **3.** (facezia) witticism.

movente sm. motive, cause.

movenza sf. movements (pl.).

movìbile agg. movable.

movimentare vt. to enliven.

movimentato agg. **1.** lively **2.** (pieno di movimento) eventful.

movimento sm. **1.** movement **2.**

(traffico, trambusto) traffic, bustle.

moviola sf. film-editing machine.

mozione sf. motion.

mozzare vt. to cut (v. irr.) off.

mozzicone sm. **1.** stump **2.** (di sigaretta) butt.

mozzo¹ agg. cut (off).

mozzo² sm. **1.** (di ruota) hub **2.** (mar.) ship-boy.

mucca sf. cow.

mucchio sm. heap, mass.

mùcido agg. mouldy. ♦ **mùcido** sm. mould.

muco sm. mucus.

mucosa sf. mucous membrane.

mucoso agg. mucous.

muffa sf. mould.

muffire vi. to mildew.

muflone sm. moufflon.

mugghiare vi. **1.** to bellow **2.** (fig.) to roar **3.** (del vento) to howl.

mugghio sm. **1.** bellow **2.** (fig.) roar **3.** (del vento) howl.

muggire vi. V. mugghiare.

muggito sm. V. mugghio.

mughetto sm. lily of the valley.

mugnaio sm. miller.

mugolare vi. **1.** to howl **2.** (piagnucolare) to whimper.

mugolìo sm. **1.** howling **2.** (piagnucolio) whimpering.

mugugnare vi. to mumble.

mulattiera sf. mule-track.

mulattiere sm. mule-driver.

mulatto sm. mulatto.

mulìebre agg. feminine, womanly.

mulinare vt. **1.** to whirl **2.** (fig.) to brood (over).

mulinello sm. **1.** (d'acqua) whirlpool **2.** (d'aria) whirlwind **3.** (rapido movimento) twirl.

mulino sm. mill.

mulo sm. mule.

multa sf. fine.

multare vt. to fine.

multicolore agg. many-coloured.

multiforme agg. multiform.

mùltiplo agg. e sm. multiple.

mummia sf. mummy.

mummificare vt. to mummify.

mummificazione sf. mummification.

mùngere vt. to milk.

mungitore sm. milker.

mungitura sf. milking.

municipale agg. municipal.

municipalità sf. municipality.

municipalizzare vt. to municipalize.

municipalizzazione *sf.* municipalization.

municipio *sm.* **1.** municipality **2.** (*palazzo*) townhall **3.** (*stor.*) municipium (*pl.* -ia).

munificenza *sf.* munificence.

munifico *agg.* munificent.

munire *vt.* **1.** (*fortificare*) to fortify **2.** (*provvedere*) to supply (with).

munizione *sf.* munition.

muòvere *vt.* to move. ♦ **muòversi** *vr.* to move, to stir || *muoviti!* hurry up!

mura[1] *sf.* (*mar.*) tack.

mura[2] *sf. pl.* walls.

muraglia *sf.* wall.

muraglione *sm.* massive wall.

murale *agg.* mural.

murare *vt.* **1.** to wall up **2.** (*cingere di mura*) to wall.

murario *agg.* building (*attr.*).

murata *sf.* ship's side.

muratore *sm.* bricklayer.

muratura *sf.* masonry || *lavoro in* —, brickwork.

murena *sf.* moray.

muriàtico *agg.* muriatic.

muricciolo *sm.* low wall.

murice *sm.* murex.

muro *sm.* wall || *armadio a* —, built-in cupboard; — *del suono*, sound barrier.

musa *sf.* muse.

muschiato *agg.* musky.

muschio[1] *sm.* (*sostanza odorosa*) musk.

muschio[2] *sm.* (*bot.*) moss.

muscolare *agg.* muscular.

muscolatura *sf.* musculature.

mùscolo *sm.* muscle.

muscoloso *agg.* muscular.

muscoso *agg.* mossy.

museo *sm.* museum.

museruola *sf.* muzzle.

mùsica *sf.* music.

musicale *agg.* musical.

musicalità *sf.* musicality.

musicante *sm.* musician.

musicare *vt.* to set (*v. irr.*) to music.

musicista *sm.* musician.

mùsico *sm.* musician.

musicologia *sf.* musicology.

musicòlogo *sm.* musicologist.

musivo *agg.* mosaic (*attr.*).

muso *sm.* **1.** muzzle **2.** (*broncio*) long face: *fare il* —, to pull a long face.

musone *sm.* **1.** large muzzle **2.** (*per-* *sona che tiene il broncio*) sulky person.

musonerìa *sf.* sulkiness.

mussare *vi.* to froth.

mussolina *sf.* muslin.

mustèlidi *sm. pl.* mustelidae.

musulmano *agg. e sm.* Muslim.

muta *sf.* **1.** (*di cani*) pack of hounds **2.** (*della guardia*) change **3.** (*biol.*) moult.

mutàbile *agg.* changeable.

mutabilità *sf.* **1.** (*di cosa*) changeability **2.** (*di persona*) fickleness.

mutamento *sm.* change.

mutande *sf. pl.* drawers.

mutandine *sf. pl.* trunks.

mutare *vt.* **1.** to change **2.** (*di animali*) to shed (*v. irr.*), to moult. ♦ **mutarsi** *vr.* to change.

mutazione *sf.* change.

mutévole *agg.* changeable.

mutilare *vt.* **1.** to maim **2.** (*fig.*) to mutilate.

mutilato *agg.* **1.** maimed **2.** (*fig.*) mutilated. ♦ **mutilato** *sm.* cripple.

mutilazione *sf.* **1.** maiming **2.** (*fig.*) mutilation.

mùtilo *agg.* mutilated.

mutismo *sm.* dumbness.

muto *agg.* **1.** dumb || *carta geografica muta*, blank map **2.** (*fonetica*) mute.

mutria *sf.* stand-offishness.

mutua *sf.* national insurance || *medico della* —, panel doctor.

mutualistico *agg.* insurance (*attr.*).

mutualità *sf.* mutual help.

mutuare *vt.* **1.** (*dare in mutuo*) to lend (*v. irr.*) **2.** (*prendere a mutuo*) to borrow.

mutuatario *sm.* borrower.

mutuato *agg.* insured.

mutuo *agg.* mutual. ♦ **mutuo** *sm.* loan.

N

nababbo *sm.* nabob.

nàcchera *sf.* castanet.

nafta *sf.* **1.** oil **2.** (*chim.*) naphtha.

naftalina *sf.* moth-balls (*pl.*).

naia[1] *sf.* (*zool.*) cobra.

naia[2] *sf.* (*mil.*) *fare la* —, to do (*v. irr.*) one's bit.

nàiade *sf.* naiad.
nàilon *sm.* nylon.
nandù *sm.* nandu.
nanismo *sm.* nanism.
nano *sm.* dwarf.
nappa *sf.* tassel.
narcisismo *sm.* narcissism.
narcisista *sm.* narcissist.
narciso *sm.* narcissus.
narcosi *sf.* narcosis (*pl.* -ses).
narcòtico *agg. e sm.* narcotic.
narcotizzare *vt.* to narcotize.
narice *sf.* nostril.
narrare *vt.* to tell (*v. irr.*).
narrativa *sf.* fiction.
narrativo *agg.* narrative.
narratore *sm.* **1.** story-teller **2.** (*scrittore*) writer.
narrazione *sf.* narration.
narvalo *sm.* narwhal.
nasale *agg.* nasal.
nascente *agg.* rising.
nàscere *vi.* **1.** to be born **2.** (*di piante*) to spring (*v. irr.*) up **3.** (*di fiume; sorgere*) to rise (*v. irr.*) **4.** (*avere origine*) to originate || *far —*, to give (*v. irr.*) rise to.
nàscita *sf.* **1.** birth **2.** (*origine*) origin.
nascituro *sm.* unborn child.
nascòndere *vt.* to hide (*v. irr.*). ♦ **nascòndersi** *vr.* to hide (oneself).
nascondiglio *sm.* hiding-place.
nascosto *agg.* hidden || *di —*, secretly.
nasello *sm.* (*itt.*) whiting.
naso *sm.* nose || *a lume di —*, by guesswork; *ficcare il — in qc.*, to poke one's nose into sthg.; *avere buon —*, to be shrewd.
nassa *sf.* bow-net.
nastro *sm.* **1.** ribbon **2.** (*tec.*) tape.
natale *agg.* native. ♦ **Natale** *sm.* Christmas.
natalità *sf.* birth-rate.
natalizio *agg.* Christmas (*attr.*).
natante *agg.* floating. ♦ **natante** *sm.* watercraft.
natatoia *sf.* fin.
natatorio *agg.* swimming (*attr.*).
nàtica *sf.* buttock.
natività *sf.* nativity.
nativo *agg.* **1.** native **2.** (*innato*) inborn.
nato *agg.* born.
natura *sf.* nature.
naturale *agg.* natural.
naturalezza *sf.* naturalness, simplicity.

naturalismo *sm.* naturalism.
naturalista *s.* naturalist.
naturalizzare *vt.* to naturalize.
naturalizzazione *sf.* naturalization.
naturalmente *avv.* naturally, of course.
naturismo *sm.* naturism.
naturista *s.* naturist.
naufragare *vi.* **1.** to be shipwrecked **2.** (*fig.*) to be wrecked.
naufragio *sm.* **1.** shipwreck **2.** (*fig.*) wreck.
nàufrago *sm.* shipwrecked person.
nàusea *sf.* disgust, nausea || *avere la —*, to feel (*v. irr.*) sick.
nauseabondo *agg.* nauseating.
nauseare *vt.* to make (*v. irr.*) sick.
nàutica *sf.* navigation.
nàutico *agg.* nautical.
navale *agg.* naval.
navata *sf.* **1.** (*centrale*) nave **2.** (*laterale*) aisle.
nave *sf.* ship.
navetta *sf.* shuttle.
navicella *sf.* (*aer.*) nacelle.
navigàbile *agg.* navigable.
navigabilità *sf.* navigability.
navigare *vi.* to sail.
navigato *agg.* (*fig.*) cunning.
navigatore *sm.* navigator.
navigazione *sf.* navigation.
naviglio *sm.* **1.** fleet **2.** (*nave*) craft.
nazionale *agg.* national.
nazionalismo *sm.* nationalism.
nazionalista *s.* nationalist.
nazionalità *sf.* nationality.
nazionalizzare *vt.* to nationalize.
nazionalizzazione *sf.* nationalization.
nazionalsocialismo *sm.* National Socialism.
nazione *sf.* nation.
nazismo *sm.* Nazism.
nazista *agg. e sm.* Nazi.
nazzareno *agg. e sm.* Nazarene.
ne *pron.* **1.** of him, about him; of her, about her; of it, about it; of them, about them; of this, about this; of that, about that **2.** (*partitivo*) some: *— ho*, I have some; any: *non — ho*, I haven't any. ♦ **ne** (*particella avv. di moto da luogo*) from there.
né *cong.* **1.** neither, nor **2.** (*né... né...*) neither... nor; (*in presenza di altra negazione*) either... or.
neanche *avv.* not even. ♦ **neanche** *cong.* neither, nor: *essi non anda-*

rono e — io, they did not go and neither did I.

nebbia *sf.* fog.

nebbioso *agg.* foggy.

nebulizzare *vt.* to nebulize.

nebulizzatore *sm.* nebulizer.

nebulosa *sf.* nebula (*pl.* -ae).

nebulosità *sf.* **1.** nebulosity **2.** (*fig.*) haziness.

nebuloso *agg.* **1.** nebulous **2.** (*fig.*) vague.

necessario *agg.* necessary. ♦ **necessario** *sm.* **1.** necessary **2.** (*l'indispensabile*) necessities (*pl.*).

necessità *sf.* **1.** necessity **2.** (*bisogno*) need.

necessitare *vi.* to need.

necrologìa *sf.* obituary-notice.

necrologio *sm.* **1.** necrology **2.** (*annuncio*) obituary.

necròpoli *sf.* necropolis.

necrosi *sf.* necrosis (*pl.* -ses).

necrotizzare *vt.* to necrotize.

nefandezza *sf.* wickedness.

nefando *agg.* wicked.

nefasto *agg.* ill-omened.

nefrite *sf.* nephritis.

nefrìtico *agg.* nephritic. ♦ **nefrìtico** *sm.* nephritic subject.

negare *vt.* **1.** to deny **2.** (*rifiutare*) to refuse.

negativa *sf.* (*anche foto*) negative.

negativo *agg.* negative.

negato *agg.* **1.** refused, denied **2.** (*inadatto*) unfit (for).

negatore *agg.* negatory. ♦ **negatore** *sm.* denier.

negazione *sf.* **1.** denial **2.** (*gramm.*) negative **3.** (*cosa diametralmente opposta all'altra*) negation.

neghittoso *agg.* slothful.

negletto *agg.* **1.** neglected **2.** (*di aspetto*) slovenly.

negligente *agg.* negligent, careless.

negligenza *sf.* negligence, carelessness.

negoziàbile *agg.* negotiable.

negoziante *sm.* **1.** merchant, trader **2.** (*chi ha negozio*) shopkeeper.

negoziare *vt.* to negotiate.

negoziato *agg.* negotiated. ♦ **negoziato** *sm.* negotiation.

negozio *sm.* **1.** shop **2.** (*commercio*) trade **3.** (*faccenda*) affair.

negriero *agg.* slave (*attr.*). ♦ **negriero** *sm.* slave-trader.

negro *agg. e sm.* **1.** negro **2.** (*spreg.*) nigger.

negròide *agg. e s.* negroid.

negromante *sm.* necromancer.

negromanzìa *sf.* necromancy.

nembo *sm.* **1.** raincloud **2.** (*fig.*) multitude.

nèmesi *sf.* nemesis (*pl.* -ses).

nemico *agg.* **1.** adverse **2.** (*del nemico*) enemy (*attr.*). ♦ **nemico** *sm.* enemy.

neo[1] *sm.* **1.** mole **2.** (*fig.*) flaw.

neo[2] *agg.* neo.

neocapitalismo *sm.* neo-capitalism.

neocapitalista *agg. e sm.* neo--capitalist.

neocapitalìstico *agg.* neo-capitalistic.

neoclassicismo *sm.* neo-classicism.

neoclàssico *agg.* neo-classic.

neofascismo *sm.* neofascism.

neofascista *agg. e s.* neofascist.

neòfita *sm.* **1.** neophyte **2.** (*fig.*) beginner.

neolìtico *agg.* .Neolithic.

neologismo *sm.* neologism.

neon *sm.* neon: *insegna al —,* neon sign.

neonato *agg.* new-born. ♦ **neonato** *sm.* (new-born) baby.

neorealismo *sm.* Neorealism.

neorealista *agg. e sm.* neorealist.

neozelandese *agg.* New Zealand (*attr.*). ♦ **neozelandese** *s.* New Zealander.

nepotismo *sm.* 'nepotism.

nerastro *agg.* blackish.

nerbo *sm.* **1.** sinew **2.** (*fig.*) strength, vigour.

nerboruto *agg.* brawny.

neretto *sm.* (*tip.*) boldface.

nerezza *sf.* blackness.

nero *agg.* black.

nerofumo *sm.* lamp-black.

nerògnolo *agg.* blackish.

nerume *sm.* mass of black.

nervatura *sf.* ribbing.

nervo *sm.* nerve.

nervosamente *agg.* nervously.

nervosismo *sm.* nervousness.

nervoso *agg.* nervous, irritable.

nèspola *sf.* medlar.

nèspolo *sm.* medlar(-tree).

nesso *sm.* connection.

nessuno *agg.* **1.** no **2.** (*in presenza di altra neg.*) any. ♦ **nessuno** *pron.* **1.** (*per persone*) nobody, no one; (*per cose*) none **2.** (*in presenza di altra neg.*) anybody (*solo per persone*), anyone, any || *— di,* none of, (*in presenza di altra neg.*) any of.

nèttare sm. nectar.

nettare vt. to clean.

nettezza sf. cleanness: — urbana, municipal street cleansing.

netto agg. 1. clean, spotless (anche fig.) 2. (comm.) net.

nettunio sm. neptunium.

neurite sf. neuritis.

neurochirurgìa sf. neurosurgery.

neurologìa sf. neurology.

neuròlogo sm. neurologist.

neuropàtico agg. neuropathic. ♦ **neuropàtico** sm. neuropath.

neuropatologìa sf. neuropathology.

neurosi sf. neurosis (pl. -ses).

neurovegetativo agg. vegetative nervous.

neutrale agg. neutral.

neutralismo sm. neutralism.

neutralista s. neutralist.

neutralità sf. neutrality.

neutralizzare vt. to neutralize.

neutralizzazione sf. neutralization.

nèutro agg. 1. neutral 2. (gramm.; bot.; zool.) neuter.

neutrone sm. neutron.

neve sf. snow.

nevicare vi. to snow: nevica, it is snowing.

nevicata sf. snowfall.

nevischio sm. sleet.

nevoso agg. snowy.

nevralgìa sf. neuralgia.

nevràlgico agg. neuralgic.

nevrastenìa sf. neurasthenia.

nevrastènico agg. neurasthenic.

nevròtico agg. e sm. neurotic.

nibbio sm. kite.

nicchia sf. niche.

nicchiare vi. to shilly-shally.

nichel sm. nickel.

nichelare vt. to nickel.

nichelatura sf. nickel-plating.

nichelino sm. nickel coin.

nichilismo sm. nihilism.

nichilista s. nihilist.

nicotina sf. nicotine.

nidiata sf. 1. nest 2. (covata) brood || una — di bambini, a swarm of children.

nidificare vi. to nest.

nido sm. nest.

niente pron. 1. nothing 2. (in presenza di altre negazioni) anything.

nimbo sm. halo.

ninfa sf. nymph.

ninfea sf. water-lily.

ninfòmane sf. nymphomaniac.

ninnananna sf. lullaby.

nìnnolo sm. 1. knick-knack 2. (balocco) plaything.

nipote sm. 1. (di nonno) grand-son 2. (di zio) nephew. ♦ **nipote** sf. 1. (di nonno) grand-daughter 2. (di zio) niece.

nippònico agg. e sm. Japanese.

nirvana sm. nirvana.

nitidezza sf. neatness.

nìtido agg. neat, clear.

nitrato sm. nitrate.

nìtrico agg. nitric.

nitrire vi. to whinny.

nitrito[1] sm. (di cavallo) whinny.

nitrito[2] sm. (chim.) nitrite.

nitroglicerina sf. nitroglycerin.

nìveo agg. snowy.

no avv. no.

nòbile agg. e sm. noble.

nobiliare agg. nobiliary.

nobilitare vt. to ennoble.

nobilitazione sf. ennobling.

nobilmente avv. nobly.

nobiltà sf. nobility.

nocca sf. knuckle.

nocchiere sm. helmsman (pl. -men).

nocciola sf. hazel-nut.

nòcciolo sm. 1. stone 2. (ciò che è essenziale) heart.

nocciolo sm. (bot.) hazel-tree.

noce sm. walnut-tree. ♦ **noce** sf. walnut || guscio di — (barchetta), cockle-shell; — moscata, nutmeg.

nocivo agg. noxious, harmful.

nodo sm. knot.

nodoso agg. knotty.

noi pron. 1. (sogg.) we 2. (compl.) us.

noia sf. 1. boredom 2. (fastidio) worry, nuisance.

noioso agg. 1. boring 2. (molesto) annoying.

noleggiante sm. (mar.) charterer.

noleggiare vt. 1. to hire 2. (di navi) to charter.

noleggiatore sm. hirer.

noleggio sm. 1. hire 2. (mar.) freight.

nolente agg. unwilling || volente o —, willy-nilly.

nolo sm. 1. hire 2. (mar.) freight.

nòmade agg. e s. nomad.

nomadismo sm. nomadism.

nome sm. 1. name 2. (di battesimo) Christian name || senza —, nameless; a — di, on behalf of; per —, by name 3. (gramm.) noun.

nomea sf. notoriety.

nomenclatura *sf.* nomenclature.
nomìgnolo *sm.* nickname.
nòmina *sf.* appointment.
nominale *agg.* nominal.
nominalismo *sm.* nominalism.
nominalista *s.* nominalist.
nominalmente *avv.* nominally.
nominare *vt.* 1. to name 2. (*eleggere*) to appoint.
nominativo *agg.* 1. nominative 2. (*comm.*) registered. ♦ **nominativo** *sm.* name.
non *avv.* not.
nona *sf.* 1. (*eccl.*) Nones (*pl.*) 2. (*mus.*) ninth.
nonagenario *agg.* ninety years old (*pred.*); ninety-year-old (*attr.*). ♦ **nonagenario** *sm.* nonagenarian.
nonconformista *s.* non-conformist.
noncurante *agg.* careless.
noncuranza *sf.* carelessness.
nondimeno *avv.* nevertheless.
nonna *sf.* grandmother.
nonno *sm.* grandfather: *i miei nonni*, my grandparents.
nonnulla *sm.* trifle.
nono *agg.* ninth.
nonostante *prep.* notwithstanding || — *che*, though, although.
nonsenso *sm.* nonsense.
non-ti-scordar-di-me *sm.* forget--me-not.
nord *sm.* north.
nordamericano *agg.* e *sm.* North American.
nòrdico *agg.* 1. northern 2. (*dell'Europa settentrionale*) Nordic. ♦ **nòrdico** *sm.* 1. Northerner 2. (*dell'Europa settentrionale*) Nordic.
nordista *sm.* (*stor. amer.*) Federal.
norma *sf.* 1. rule, norm 2. (*istruzioni*) instruction, direction || *a — di legge*, according to law.
normale *agg.* e *sm.* 1. normal 2. (*che dà una norma*) standard.
normalità *sf.* normality.
normalizzare *vt.* to normalize.
normalizzazione *sf.* normalization.
normalmente *avv.* usually.
normanno *agg.* e *sm.* Norman: *anglo-—*, (*stor.*) Anglo-Norman.
normativo *agg.* normative.
normògrafo *sm.* stencil.
norvegese *agg.* e *sm.* Norwegian.
nosocòmio *sm.* hospital.
nostalgìa *sf.* home-sickness.
nostàlgico *agg.* homesick.
nostrano *agg.* home (*attr.*), national.

nostro *agg.* our: *i nostri amici*, our friends. ♦ **nostro** *pron.* ours: *questa casa è nostra*, this house is ours. ♦ **nostro** *sm.* 1. *viviamo del —*, we live on our own income 2. *il Nostro* (*di autore*), the Author 3. *i nostri*, our family.
nostromo *sm.* boatswain.
nota *sf.* 1. note 2. (*lista*) list.
notàbile *agg.* notable.
notaio *sm.* notary.
notare *vt.* to note.
notariato *sm.* profession of notary.
notarile *agg.* notarial.
notazione *sf.* notation.
notévole *agg.* remarkable, notable.
notevolmente *avv.* remarkably.
notìfica *sf.* 1. notification 2. (*giur.*) service.
notificare *vt.* 1. to notify 2. (*informare*) to inform 3. (*giur.*) to serve.
notizia *sf.* 1. news (*pl. con costruzione sing.*), piece of news (*solo sing.*) 2. (*informazione*) information (*solo sing.*) 3. (*dato*) note: *notizie biografiche*, biographical notes.
notiziario *sm.* news (*pl.*, con costruzione sing.).
noto *agg.* well-known. ♦ **noto** *sm.* the known.
notoriamente *avv.* notoriously.
notorietà *sf.* notoriety.
notorio *agg.* 1. (*in senso sfavorevole*) notorious 2. well-known.
nottàmbulo *agg.* noctambulous. ♦ **nottàmbulo** *sm.* night-bird.
nottata *sf.* night.
notte *sf.* night.
nottetempo *avv.* by night.
notturno *agg.* night (*attr.*). ♦ **notturno** *sm.* (*mus.*) nocturne.
novanta *agg.* ninety.
novantenne *agg.* 1. ninety years old (*pred.*) 2. ninety-year-old (*attr.*).
novantèsimo *agg.* ninetieth.
novatore *sm.* innovator.
nove *agg.* nine.
novecento *agg.* nine hundred.
novella *sf.* short story, tale.
novellino *agg.* inexperienced. ♦ **novellino** *sm.* beginner.
novellista *s.* short-story writer.
novellìstica *sf.* story-telling.
novello *agg.* 1. new, spring (*attr.*) 2. (*nuovo*) second: *un — Raffaello*, a second Raffaello.

novembre *sm.* November.
novena *sf.* novena (*pl.* -ae).
nòvero *sm.* number **2.** (*categoria*) class.
novilunio *sm.* new moon.
novità *sf.* **1.** novelty **2.** (*notizia*) news (*pl. con costruzione sing.*), piece of news (*solo sing.*).
noviziato *sm.* novitiate.
novizio *sm.* novice.
nozione *sf.* notion.
nozze *sf. pl.* wedding (*sing.*).
nube *sf.* cloud.
nubifragio *sm.* downpour.
nùbile *agg.* unmarried, single. ♦ **nùbile** *sf.* single woman.
nuca *sf.* nape.
nucleare *agg.* nuclear.
nucleina *sf.* nuclein.
nùcleo *sm.* nucleus (*pl.* -ei).
nudismo *sm.* nudism.
nudista *s.* nudist.
nudità *sf.* nakedness.
nudo *agg.* naked, bare.
nùgolo *sm.* cloud.
nulla *pron.* V. *niente*.
nullaosta *sm.* permit.
nullatenente *agg.* without property. ♦ **nullatenente** *s.* person without property.
nullità *sf.* **1.** (*di cose*) nullity **2.** (*di persone*) nonentity.
nullo *agg.* (*giur.*) null, void.
nume *sm.* numen, deity.
numeràbile *agg.* numerable.
numerabilità *sf.* numerability.
numerale *agg.* numeral.
numerare *vt.* **1.** to count **2.** (*segnare con numero*) to number.
numerato *agg.* **1.** counted **2.** (*segnato con un numero*) numbered.
numerario *agg.* numerary. ♦ **numerario** *sm.* (*comm.*) ready cash.
numeratore *sm.* (*mat.*) numerator.
numerazione *sf.* **1.** numbering **2.** (*mat.*) numeration.
numericamente *avv.* numerically.
numèrico *agg.* numerical.
nùmero *sm.* number.
numeroso *agg.* numerous.
numismàtica *sf.* numismatics.
numismàtico *agg.* numismatic. ♦ **numismàtico** *sm.* numismatist.
nunziatura *sf.* (*eccl.*) nunciature.
nunzio *sm.* nuncio.
nuòcere *vi.* to damage, to harm.
nuora *sf.* daughter-in-law.
nuotare *vi.* to swim (*v. irr.*).
nuotata *sf.* swim.

nuotatore *sm.* swimmer.
nuoto *sm.* swimming: *gara di* —, swimming-race.
nuova *sf.* news (*pl. con costruzione sing.*), piece of news (*solo sing.*).
nuovamente *avv.* again.
nuovo *agg.* new: — *di zecca, fiammante*, brand-new.
nutazione *sf.* nutation.
nutrice *sf.* wet-nurse.
nutriente *agg.* nourishing.
nutrimento *sm.* **1.** feeding **2.** (*fig.*) nourishment.
nutrire *vt.* **1.** to feed (*v. irr.*) **2.** (*mantenere*) to maintain **3.** (*di sentimenti, passioni*) to foster. ♦ **nutrirsi** *vr.* to feed (on).
nutritivo *agg.* nourishing.
nutrito *agg.* fed, nourished.
nutrizione *sf.* **1.** feeding **2.** (*fig.*) nourishment.
nùvola *sf.* cloud.
nuvoloso *agg.* overcast, cloudy.
nuziale *agg.* wedding (*attr.*).

O

o *cong.* or ‖ *o* ... *o*, either ... or: — *tu* — *tua madre dovete venire*, either you or your mother must come; — *l'uno* — *l'altro*, either: *prendi* — *l'uno* — *l'altro*, take either.
òasi *sf.* oasis (*pl.* -ses).
obbligare *vt.* to compel. ♦ **obbligarsi** *vr.* to bind (*v. irr.*) oneself.
obbligatorietà *sf.* compulsoriness.
obbligatorio *agg.* compulsory.
obbligazione *sf.* **1.** obligation **2.** (*comm.*) bond.
obbligazionista *sm.* bond-holder.
òbbligo *sm.* obligation: *assumersi l'*—, to undertake (*v. irr.*).
obbrobrio *sm.* disgrace.
obbrobrioso *agg.* disgraceful.
obelisco *sm.* obelisk.
oberare *vt.* to burden.
obesità *sf.* obesity.
obeso *agg.* obese.
òbice *sm.* howitzer.
obiettare *vt.* to object.
obiettivamente *avv.* objectively.
obiettivismo *sm.* objectivism.
obiettività *sf.* objectivity.

obiettivo *agg.* objective. ♦ **obiettivo** *sm.* **1.** (*mil.*) objective **2.** (*scopo*) aim **3.** (*foto*) lens.
obiettore *sm.* objector: — *di coscienza*, conscentious objector.
obiezione *sf.* objection.
obitorio *sm.* morgue.
oblatore *sm.* donor.
oblazione *sf.* donation.
obliare *vt.* to forget (*v. irr.*).
oblìo *sm.* oblivion.
obliquamente *avv.* obliquely.
obliquità *sf.* obliquity.
obliquo *agg.* oblique.
obliterare *vt.* to obliterate.
obliterazione *sf.* obliteration.
oblò *sm.* porthole.
oblungo *agg.* oblong.
òboe *sm.* oboe.
òbolo *sm.* offering.
obsoleto *agg.* obsolete.
oca *sf.* goose (*pl.* geese): *pelle d'*—, goose flesh; *penna d'*—, goose-quill.
occasionale *agg.* occasional.
occasionalismo *sm.* occasionalism.
occasionalmente *avv.* occasionally.
occasione *sf.* occasion.
occhiaia *sf.* eye-socket || *avere le occhiaie*, to have rings under one's eyes.
occhiali *sm. pl.* spectacles, glasses.
occhialuto *agg.* spectacled, wearing spectacles (*pred.*).
occhiata *sf.* look, glance.
occhiataccia *sf.* glare.
occhieggiare *vt.* to cast (*v. irr.*) glances (at). ♦ **occhieggiare** *vi.* to peep (at).
occhiello *sm.* **1.** button-hole **2.** (*mecc.*) eye.
occhietto *sm. fare l'*— *a qu.*, to wink at so.
occhio *sm.* eye || *costare un* —, to be terribly expensive; *chiudere un* — *su*, to turn a blind eye to; *dare nell'*—, to strike (*v. irr.*) the eye; *tenere d'*—, to keep (*v. irr.*) an eye on; *in un batter d'*—, in the twinkling of an eye.
occidentale *agg.* west, western. ♦ **occidentale** *s.* westerner.
occidentalizzare *vt.* to occidentalize.
occidente *sm.* west.
occipitale *agg.* occipital.
occìpite *sm.* occiput (*pl.* occipita).
occlusione *sf.* occlusion.
occlusivo *agg.* occlusive.

occorrente *agg.* necessary. ♦ **occorrente** *sm.* the necessary.
occorrenza *sf.* all'—, in case of need.
occòrrere *vi.* **1.** (*imp.*) to be necessary **2.** (*abbisognare*) to need.
occultamento *sm.* concealment.
occultare *vt.* to hide (*v. irr.*), to conceal. ♦ **occultarsi** *vr.* to hide.
occultatore *sm.* hider.
occultismo *sm.* occultism.
occulto *agg.* **1.** occult **2.** (*nascosto*) hidden.
occupante *agg.* occupying. ♦ **occupante** *s.* occupant.
occupare *vt.* **1.** to occupy **2.** (*ingaggiare*) to employ. ♦ **occuparsi** *vr.* **1.** (*impiegarsi*) to find (*v. irr.*) a job **2.** (*badare*) to attend (to).
occupato *agg.* engaged || *essere* — (*fare un lavoro*), to work.
occupazione *sf.* **1.** occupation **2.** (*lavoro*) job.
oceànico *agg.* oceanic.
ocèano *sm.* ocean.
oceanografia *sf.* oceanography.
ocello *sm.* ocellus (*pl.* -li).
ocra *sf.* ochre.
oculare *agg.* ocular, eye (*attr.*). ♦ **oculare** *sm.* (*fis.*) eyepiece.
oculatezza *sf.* shrewdness.
oculato *agg.* prudent.
oculista *sm.* oculist.
oculìstica *sf.* ophthalmology.
odalisca *sf.* odalisque.
ode *sf.* ode.
odiare *vt.* to hate.
odierno *agg.* of today, today's.
odio *sm.* hatred.
odioso *agg.* hateful.
odontàlgico *agg.* odontalgic.
odontoiatra *s.* odontologist, dentist.
odontoiatrìa *sf.* odontology.
odontoiàtrico *agg.* odontological.
odorare *vt.* e *vi.* to smell (*v. irr.*).
odorato *sm.* smell.
odore *sm.* smell.
odorìfero *agg.* odoriferous.
odoroso *agg.* fragrant.
offèndere *vt.* to offend. ♦ **offèndersi** *vr.* to be offended (at, by); to feel (*v. irr.*) hurt (by).
offensiva *sf.* offensive.
offensivo *agg.* offensive.
offensore *sm.* offender.
offerente *s.* **1.** offerer **2.** (*a un'asta*) bidder.

offerta *sf.* offer, donation.
offesa *sf.* offence.
offeso *agg.* offended, injured.
officiare *vi.* to officiate.
officina *sf.* workshop.
officinale *agg.* officinal.
offrire *vt.* to offer. ♦ **offrirsi** *vr.* to offer (oneself).
offuscamento *sm.* **1.** dimming **2.** (*oscurità*) dimness.
offuscare *vt.* to dim. ♦ **offuscarsi** *vr.* to grow (*v. irr.*) dim.
oftalmìa *sf.* ophthalmia.
oftàlmico *agg.* ophthalmic.
oftalmologìa *sf.* ophthalmology.
oftalmoscopìa *sf.* ophthalmoscopy.
oftalmoscopio *sm.* ophthalmoscope.
oggettivamente *avv.* objectively.
oggettivare *vt.* to objectify.
oggettivazione *sf.* objectification.
oggettivismo *sm.* objectivism.
oggettività *sf.* objectivity.
oggettivo *agg.* objective.
oggetto *sm.* object.
oggi *avv.* today.
ogiva *sf.* ogive.
ogivale *agg.* ogival.
ogni *agg.* every, each || *in — modo*, anyhow; *in — luogo*, everywhere.
ogniqualvolta *cong.* whenever.
ognuno *pron.* everybody, everyone || *— di*, each of.
oleandro *sm.* oleander.
oleario *agg.* oil (*attr.*).
oleato *agg.* oiled || *carta oleata*, grease-proof paper.
oleificio *sm.* oil mill.
oleodotto *sm.* oil pipeline.
oleografìa *sf.* **1.** oleography **2.** (*pezzo singolo*) oleograph.
oleoso *agg.* oily.
olezzare *vi.* to smell (*v. irr.*) sweetly.
olezzo *sm.* fragrance.
olfattivo *agg.* olfactory.
olfatto *sm.* smell.
oliare *vt.* to oil.
oliatore *sm.* oil-can.
oliera *sf.* cruet.
oligarca *sm.* oligarch.
oligarchìa *sf.* oligarchy.
oligàrchico *agg.* oligarchic(al).
oligocene *sm.* Oligocene.
olimpìaco *agg.* V. *olimpico*.
olimpìade *sf.* Olympiad || *le Olimpiadi*, Olympic games.
olimpico *agg.* Olympic.
olimpiònico *agg.* Olympic games (*attr.*). ♦ **olimpiònico** *sm.*

Olympic champion.
olio *sm.* oil.
oliva *sf.* olive.
olivastro *agg.* olive.
oliveto *sm.* olive-grove.
olivo *sm.* olive.
olmo *sm.* elm.
olocàusto *sm.* holocaust.
ològrafo *agg.* holograph.
oltraggiare *vt.* to outrage.
oltraggio *sm.* outrage.
oltraggioso *agg.* outrageous.
oltramontano *agg.* e *sm.* ultramontane.
oltranza *sf.* (*nella loc. avv.*) *a —*, to the bitter end.
oltranzista *sm.* extremist.
oltre *avv.* **1.** (*di luogo*) further, farther **2.** (*di tempo*) longer. ♦ **oltre** *prep.* **1.** (*di luogo*) beyond **2.** (*più di*) over **3.** (*in aggiunta*) in addition to. ♦ **oltre a, che** *cong.* besides.
oltrecortina *avv.* beyond the Iron Curtain.
oltremare *avv.* overseas: *d'—*, overseas (*attr.*).
oltremodo *avv.* extremely.
oltrepassare *vt.* to go (*v. irr.*) beyond || *— i limiti* (*fig.*), to go (*v. irr.*) too far.
oltretomba *sm.* hereafter.
omaccione *sm.* burly man (*pl.* men).
omaggio *sm.* **1.** homage **2.** (*offerta*) gift.
ombelicale *agg.* umbilical.
ombelico *sm.* navel.
ombra *sf.* **1.** shade (*anche spettro*) **2.** (*immagine proiettata, parvenza*) shadow || *dar — a qu.*, to overshadow so.
ombreggiare *vt.* to shade.
ombreggiatura *sf.* shading.
ombrella *sf.* (*bot.*) umbel.
ombrellìfero *agg.* umbelliferous.
ombrellino *sm.* parasol.
ombrello *sm.* umbrella.
ombrellone *sm.* sunshade.
ombretto *sm.* eye shadow.
ombrina *sf.* umbrina.
ombrosità *sf.* **1.** shadiness **2.** (*di persona*) touchiness **3.** (*di cavallo*) skittishness.
ombroso *agg.* **1.** shady **2.** (*di persona*) touchy **3.** (*di cavallo*) skittish.
omega *sm.* omega.
omelìa *sf.* homily.
omeopatìa *sf.* homeopathy.

omeopàtico *agg.* homeopathic. ♦
  omeopàtico *sm.* homeopath
omèrico *agg.* Homeric.
òmero *sm.* humerus (*pl.* -ri).
omertà *sf.* silence.
omesso *agg.* omitted.
ométtere *vt.* to omit, to leave out.
omicida *agg.* homicidal. ♦ **omicida** *s.* homicide.
omicidio *sm.* homicide.
omissione *sf.* omission.
òmnibus *sm.* bus.
omogeneità *sf.* homogeneity.
omogeneizzare *vt.* to homogenize.
omogèneo *agg.* homogeneous.
omologare *vt.* **1.** to homologate **2.** (*sport*) to ratify.
omologazione *sf.* **1.** homologation **2.** (*sport*) ratification.
omòlogo *agg.* homologous.
omonimìa *sf.* homonymy.
omònimo *agg.* homonymous. ♦
  omònimo *sm.* homonym.
omosessuale *agg. e s.* homosexual.
omosessualità *sf.* homosexuality.
oncia *sf.* ounce.
onda *sf.* wave || *mettere in —* (*radio*), to broadcast (*v. irr.*).
ondata *sf.* wave: *a ondate*, in waves.
onde *avv.* **1.** whence **2.** (*affinché*) so that **3.** (*cosicché*) therefore **4.** (*da, con cui*) from, by, with which.
ondeggiamento *sm.* **1.** waving **2.** (*di barca*) rolling **3.** (*esitazione*) wavering.
ondeggiante *agg.* **1.** waving **2.** (*di barca*) rolling **3.** (*esitante*) wavering.
ondeggiare *vi.* **1.** to wave **2.** (*di barca*) to roll **3.** (*esitare*) to waver.
ondina *sf.* undine.
ondoso *agg.* undulatory.
ondulare *vt.* to wave.
ondulato *agg.* **1.** wavy **2.** (*tec.*) corrugated.
ondulatorio *agg.* undulatory.
ondulazione *sf.* **1.** undulation **2.** (*di capelli*) wave.
onerare *vt.* to burden.
ònere *sm.* burden || *— fiscale*, tax.
oneroso *agg.* burdensome.
onestà *sf.* **1.** honesty **2.** (*castità*) chastity.
onesto *agg.* **1.** honest **2.** (*casto*) chaste.
ònice *sf.* onyx.
onìrico *agg.* oneiric.

onnipotente *agg.* omnipotent. ♦
  Onnipotente (l') *sm.* the Almighty.
onnipotenza *sf.* omnipotence.
onnipresente *agg.* omnipresent.
onnisciente *agg.* omniscient.
onniscienza *sf.* omniscience.
onniveggente *agg.* omnipercipient.
onnìvoro *agg.* omnivorous. ♦ **onnìvoro** *sm.* omnivore.
onomàstico *agg.* onomastic. ♦
  onomàstico *sm.* name-day.
onomatopea *sf.* onomatopoeia.
onomatopèico *agg.* onomatopoeic.
onoràbile *agg.* honourable.
onorabilità *sf.* honourableness.
onoranza *sf.* honour.
onorare *vt.* to honour. ♦ **onorarsi** *vr.* to be proud (of).
onorario *agg.* honorary. ♦ **onorario** *sm.* fee.
onorato *agg.* **1.** honoured **2.** (*onesto*) honourable.
onore *sm.* honour || *farsi —*, to excel; *a onor del vero*, to tell (*v. irr.*) the truth; *serata d'—*, gala night.
onorévole *agg.* honourable.
onorificenza *sf.* **1.** honour **2.** (*decorazione*) decoration.
onorìfico *agg.* honorific(al).
onta *sf.* **1.** shame **2.** (*offesa*) insult || *ad — di*, in spite of.
ontano *sm.* alder.
ontologìa *sf.* ontology.
ontològico *agg.* ontological.
opacità *sf.* opacity.
opaco *agg.* **1.** opaque **2.** (*di suoni, colori*) dull.
opale *sm.* opal.
opalescente *agg.* opalescent.
opalino *agg.* opaline.
òpera *sf.* **1.** work **2.** (*melodramma*) opera **3.** (*istituto*) institution.
operàbile *agg.* **1.** workable. **2.** (*chir.*) operable.
operaio *agg.* working. ♦ **operaio** *sm.* worker: *— specializzato*, skilled worker.
operante *agg.* operating.
operare *vi.* to work, to operate (*anche med.*).
operativo *agg.* operative.
operato *agg.* (*di tessuto*) diapered. ♦ **operato** *sm.* **1.** (*condotta*) behaviour **2.** (*chi ha subito un'operazione*) operated patient.
operatore *sm.* **1.** operator **2.** (*cine*) cameraman (*pl.* -men).

operatorio *agg.* operating.
operazione *sf.* operation: *fare un'— a qu.*, to perform an operation on so.; *subire un'—*, to undergo (*v. irr.*) an operation.
operetta *sf.* operetta.
operìstico *agg.* opera (*attr.*).
operosità *sf.* industry.
operoso *agg.* industrious.
opificio *sm.* factory.
opimo *agg.* fertile.
opinàbile *agg.* thinkable.
opinare *vi.* to think (*v. irr.*).
opinione *sf.* opinion: *secondo l'— di qu.*, in so.'s opinion.
opossum *sm.* opossum.
oppiare *vt.* to opiate.
oppiato *agg. e sm.* opiate.
oppio *sm.* opium.
oppiòmane *s.* opium-addict.
opponente *agg. e sm.* opponent.
opponìbile *agg.* opposable.
opporre *vt.* 1. to oppose 2. (*obiettare*) to object. ♦ **opporsi** *vr.* to object (to), to be opposed.
opportunismo *sm.* opportunism.
opportunista *s.* opportunist.
opportunìstico *agg.* opportunistic.
opportunità *sf.* 1. (*occasione*) opportunity 2. (*l'essere opportuno*) timeliness.
opportuno *agg.* 1. opportune 2. (*giusto*) right.
oppositore *sm.* opponent.
opposizione *sf.* opposition || *fare — (a qu., qc.)*, to oppose (so., sthg.).
opposto *agg. e sm.* opposite.
oppressione *sf.* oppression.
oppressivo *agg.* oppressive.
oppresso *agg.* oppressed.
oppressore *sm.* oppressor.
opprimente *agg.* oppressive.
opprimere *vt.* to oppress.
oppugnare *vt.* to assail.
oppure *cong.* 1. or 2. (*altrimenti*) or else.
optare *vi.* to opt.
opulento *agg.* opulent.
opulenza *sf.* opulence.
opùscolo *sm.* pamphlet.
opzione *sf.* option.
ora[1] *sf.* 1. hour 2. (*tempo*) time: *che — è?*, what time is it?; *— di punta*, rush hour; *all'—*, by the hour; *di — in —*, hourly; *di buon'—*, early; *— legale*, summer time; *non veder l'— di*, to look forward to.

ora[2] *avv.* now || *— come —*, at the moment; *d'— in poi*, from now on; *fino ad —*, so far; *sin d'—*, now; *prima d'—*, before; *or —*, just. ♦ **ora che** *cong.* now (that).
oràcolo *sm.* oracle.
òrafo *sm.* goldsmith.
orale *agg. e sm.* oral.
oralmente *avv.* orally.
oramai *avv.* V. *ormai*.
orango *sm.* orang-outang.
orario *agg.* 1. time (*attr.*) 2. (*all'ora*) per hour. ♦ **orario** *sm.* 1. hours (*pl.*) 2. (*tabella*) time-table || *in —*, on time.
orata *sf.* dory.
oratore *sm.* orator.
oratoria *sf.* oratory.
oratorio *sm.* oratory.
orazione *sf.* 1. oration 2. (*preghiera*) prayer.
orbare *vt.* to bereave (*v. irr.*).
orbene *avv.* well.
òrbita *sf.* orbit.
orbitale *agg.* orbital.
orbo *agg.* (*di un occhio*) one-eyed.
orchestra *sf.* orchestra.
orchestrale *agg.* orchestral. ♦ **orchestrale** *s.* member of an orchestra.
orchestrare *vt.* to orchestrate.
orchestrazione *sf.* orchestration.
orchestrina *sf.* band.
orchidea *sf.* orchid.
orcio *sm.* pitcher.
orco *sm.* ogre.
orda *sf.* horde.
ordigno *sm.* device.
ordinale *agg. e sm.* ordinal.
ordinamento *sm.* 1. arrangement 2. (*regolamento*) code, system.
ordinanza *sf.* 1. order 2. (*attendente mil.*) batman (*pl.* -men).
ordinare *vt.* 1. to order 2. (*mettere in ordine*) to put (*v. irr.*) in order 3. (*eccl.*) to ordain 4. (*med.*) to prescribe. ♦ **ordinarsi** *vr.* 1. to straighten up 2. (*mil.*) to draw (*v. irr.*) up.
ordinario *agg. e sm.* ordinary.
ordinata *sf.* 1. (*mat.*) ordinate 2. (*aer.; mar.*) frame.
ordinatamente *avv.* tidily.
ordinato *agg.* tidy, orderly.
ordinazione *sf.* 1. order 2. (*med.*) prescription 3. (*eccl.*) ordination.
òrdine *sm.* order || *— d'idee*, scheme of things; *all'— del giorno*,

on the agenda; *per — di*, by order of; *parola d'—*, password; *di primʹ—*, firstclass (*attr.*).

ordire *vt.* **1.** to warp **2.** (*fig.*) to plot.

ordito *sm.* warp.

orecchiàbile *agg.* catchy.

orecchino *sm.* earring.

orecchio *sm.* ear.

orecchioni *sm. pl.* mumps.

oréfice *sm.* jeweller.

orefìcerìa *sf.* **1.** jeweller's art **2.** (*negozio*) jeweller's shop.

òrfano *agg. e sm.* orphan.

orfanotrofio *sm.* orphanage.

organetto *sm.* barrel-organ ‖ *suonatore di —*, organ-grinder.

organicità *sf.* organic unity.

orgaǹico[1] *agg.* organic.

orgaǹico[2] *sm.* staff.

organismo *sm.* **1.** organism **2.** (*ente*) body.

organista *s.* organist.

organizzàbile *agg.* organizable.

organizzare *vt.* to organize.

organizzatore *sm.* organizer.

organizzazione *sf.* organization.

òrgano *sm.* organ.

organza *sf.* organza.

organzino *sm.* organzine.

orgasmo *sm.* orgasm.

orgia *sf.* orgy.

orgiàstico *agg.* orgiastic.

orgoglio *sm.* pride.

orgoglioso *agg.* proud.

orientale *agg.* eastern.

orientalista *s.* orientalist.

orientamento *sm.* orientation ‖ *perdere l'—*, to lose (*v. irr.*) one's bearings.

orientare *vt.* to orient. ♦ **orientarsi** *vr.* **1.** to find (*v. irr.*) one's bearings **2.** (*tendere*) to tend.

oriente *sm.* east.

orifiamma *sf.* oriflamme.

orifizio *sm.* orifice.

orìgano *sm.* origan.

originale *agg.* **1.** original **2.** (*strano*) odd. ♦ **originale** *sm.* **1.** original **2.** (*persona eccentrica*) eccentric.

originalità *sf.* **1.** originality **2.** (*stranezza*) oddity.

originare *vt. e vi.* to originate.

originariamente *avv.* originally.

originario *agg.* original.

orìgine *sf.* origin ‖ *avere —*, to originate; *dare —*, to cause.

origliare *vi.* to eavesdrop.

orina *sf.* urine.

orinale *sm.* chamber pot.

orinare *vi.* to urinate.

orinatoio *sm.* public lavatory.

orizzontale *agg.* horizontal.

orizzontalmente *avv.* horizontally.

orizzontare *vt.*, **orizzontarsi** *vr.* V. *orientare, orientarsi*.

orizzonte *sm.* horizon.

orlare *vt.* **1.** (*bordare*) to edge **2.** (*fare l'orlo*) to hem.

orlatura *sf.* hemming.

orlo *sm.* **1.** (*di abito ecc.*) hem **2.** (*bordatura*) border **3.** (*estremità*) edge **4.** (*di oggetto rotondo*) rim ‖ *— a giorno*, hem-stitch; *sull'— della rovina*, on the verge of ruin.

orma *sf.* **1.** mark **2.** (*traccia*) trace **3.** (*di piede*) footprint ‖ *seguire le orme di qu.*, to follow in so.'s footsteps; *tornare sulle proprie orme*, to go (*v. irr.*) back on one's tracks.

ormai *avv.* **1.** (by) now **2.** (*al passato*) (by) then.

ormeggiare *vt.* to moor. ♦ **ormeggiarsi** *vr.* to moor.

ormeggio *sm.* mooring.

ormone *sm.* hormone.

ormònico *agg.* hormonic.

ornamentale *agg.* ornamental.

ornamentazione *sf.* ornamentation.

ornamento *sm.* ornament.

ornare *vt.* to adorn.

ornato *agg.* **1.** adorned (with) **2.** (*di stile*) ornate.

ornitologìa *sf.* ornithology.

ornitològico *agg.* ornithological.

ornitòlogo *sm.* ornithologist.

oro *sm.* gold ‖ *d'—*, golden.

orografìa *sf.* orography.

orogràfico *agg.* orographic(al).

orologerìa *sf.* **1.** (*arte*) horology **2.** (*negozio*) watchmaker's shop ‖ *movimento d'—*, clock movement.

orologiaio *sm.* watchmaker.

orologio *sm.* **1.** watch **2.** (*a muro, da tavolo*) clock.

oròscopo *sm.* horoscope.

orpello *sm.* tinsel.

orrendamente *avv.* dreadfully.

orrendo *agg.* dreadful.

orrìbile *agg.* horrible.

orribilmente *avv.* horribly.

òrrido *agg.* frightful.

orripilante *agg.* terrifying.

orrore *sm.* horror.

orsa *sf.* she-bear: *— Maggiore*,

Great Bear; — *Minore*, Little Bear.

orsacchiotto *sm.* **1.** young bear **2.** (*giocattolo*) Teddy bear.

orso *sm.* bear.

ortaggio *sm.* vegetable.

ortensia *sf.* hydrangea.

ortica *sf.* nettle.

orticaria *sf.* nettle-rash.

orticultore *sm.* horticulturist.

orticultura *sf.* horticulture.

orto *sm.* **1.** kitchen garden **2.** (*di orticoltore*) market garden.

ortodossìa *sf.* orthodoxy.

ortodosso *agg.* orthodox.

ortofrutticolo *agg.* horticultural.

ortogonale *agg.* orthogonal.

ortografìa *sf.* orthography, spelling.

ortogràfico *agg.* orthographic(al).

ortolano *sm.* **1.** market-gardener **2.** (*negoziante*) greengrocer.

ortopedìa *sf.* orthopedics.

ortopèdico *agg.* orthopedic. ♦ **ortopèdico** *sm.* orthopedist.

orzaiolo *sm.* sty.

orzata *sf.* (*bibita*) orgeat.

orzo *sm.* barley.

osanna *sf.* hosanna.

osare *vi.* to dare (*v. semidif.*). ♦ **osare** *vt.* (*tentare*) to attempt.

oscenità *sf.* obscenity.

osceno *agg.* obscene.

oscillare *vi.* **1.** to swing (*v. irr.*) **2.** (*di fiamma; opinioni*) to waver **3.** (*elettr.*) to oscillate **4.** (*di prezzi*) to fluctuate.

oscillatore *sm.* oscillator.

oscillatorio *agg.* oscillatory.

oscillazione *sf.* **1.** swing **2.** (*di fiamma; opinioni*) wavering **3.** (*elettr.*) oscillation **4.** (*di prezzi*) fluctuation.

oscillògrafo *sm.* oscillograph.

oscurantismo *sm.* obscurantism.

oscurantista *agg. e s.* obscurantist.

oscurare *vt.* **1.** to darken **2.** (*fig.*) to overshadow. ♦ **oscurarsi** *vr.* to darken.

oscurità *sf.* **1.** darkness **2.** (*fig.*) obscurity.

oscuro *agg.* **1.** dark **2.** (*sconosciuto, umile*) obscure **3.** (*difficile*) hard, difficult **4.** (*sconosciuto*) unknown.

osmosi *sf.* osmosis (*pl.* -ses).

ospedale *sm.* hospital.

ospedaliero *agg.* hospital (*attr.*).

ospitale *agg.* hospitable.

ospitalità *sf.* hospitality.

ospitare *vt.* to entertain.

òspite *s.* **1.** (*chi ospita, uomo*) host; (*id., donna*) hostess **2.** (*chi è ospitato*) guest.

ospizio *sm.* **1.** (*per poveri*) alms-house **2.** (*per trovatelli*) foundling hospital **3.** (*per vecchi ecc.*) home (for the old etc.).

ossario *sm.* charnel-house, ossuary.

ossatura *sf.* **1.** skeleton **2.** (*di edificio, discorso*) framework.

òsseo *agg.* bony.

ossequente *agg.* respectful.

ossequio *sm.* **1.** homage **2.** (*obbedienza*) obedience **3.** (*saluti*) regards (*pl.*).

ossequiosità *sf.* deference.

ossequioso *agg.* deferential.

osservàbile *agg.* observable.

osservante *agg.* observant.

osservanza *sf.* **1.** observance **2.** (*ossequio*) regards (*pl.*).

osservare *vt.* **1.** to observe **2.** (*esaminare*) to examine.

osservatore *agg.* observing. ♦ **osservatore** *sm.* observer.

osservatorio *sm.* observatory.

osservazione *sf.* **1.** observation: *in —*, under observation **2.** (*rimprovero*) reproach.

ossessionante *agg.* haunting.

ossessionare *vt.* to haunt.

ossessione *sf.* obsession.

ossessivo *agg.* haunting.

ossesso *sm.* person possessed.

ossìa *cong.* (*cioè*) that is.

ossidàbile *agg.* oxidizable.

ossidare *vt.* to oxidize. ♦ **ossidarsi** *vr.* to oxidize.

ossidazione *sf.* oxidation.

òssido *sm.* oxide.

ossìdrico *agg.* oxyhydrogen.

ossificare *vt.* to ossify. ♦ **ossificarsi** *vr.* to ossify.

ossificazione *sf.* ossification.

ossigenare *vt.* **1.** to oxygenate **2.** (*di capelli*) to peroxide.

ossigenato *agg.* **1.** oxygenated **2.** (*di capelli*) peroxided || *acqua ossigenata*, hydrogen peroxide.

ossìgeno *sm.* oxygen.

osso *sm.* bone || *in carne e ossa*, in flesh and blood; *avere le ossa rotte*, to be aching all over.

ossuto *agg.* bony.

ostacolare *vt.* to hamper.

ostàcolo *sm.* **1.** obstacle **2.** (*sport*) hurdle || *corsa ippica ad ostacoli*, steeple-chase.

ostaggio *sm.* hostage.

oste sm. innkeeper.
osteggiare vt. to oppose.
ostello sm. — della gioventù, (youth) hostel.
ostensorio sm. monstrance.
ostentare vt. 1. to show (v. irr.) off 2. (fingere) to feign.
ostentatamente avv. ostentatiously.
ostentazione sf. ostentation.
osteologìa sf. osteology.
osterìa sf. pub.
ostètrica sf. midwife (pl. -wives).
ostetricia sf. obstetrics.
ostètrico sm. obstetrician.
ostia sf. 1. wafer 2. (eccl.) host.
òstico agg. 1. irksome 2. (di sapore) unpalatable 3. (fig.) difficult.
ostile agg. hostile.
ostilità sf. hostility.
ostinarsi vr. to persist (in).
ostinato agg. stubborn.
ostinazione sf. obstinacy.
ostracismo sm. ostracism.
òstrica sf. oyster.
ostricaio sm. oyster-seller.
ostricultura sf. oyster-breeding.
ostruire vt. to obstruct.
ostruzione sf. obstruction.
ostruzionismo sm. obstructionism.
ostruzionista s. obstructionist.
otaria sf. otary.
otite sf. otitis.
otorinolaringoiatra s. otorhino-laryngologist.
otorinolaringolatrìa sf. otorhino-laryngology.
ottaedro sm. octahedron.
ottagonale agg. octagonal.
ottàgono sm. octagon.
ottanta agg. eighty.
ottantenne agg. eighty years old, eighty-year-old (attr.).
ottantèsimo agg. eightieth.
ottava sf. octave.
ottavo agg. e sm. eighth.
ottemperanza sf. compliance.
ottemperare vi. to comply (with).
ottenebrare vt. to cloud.
ottenere vt. to obtain, to get (v. irr.).
ottetto sm. octet.
òttica sf. optics.
òttico agg. optic(al). ♦ **òttico** sm. optician.
ottimismo sm. optimism.
ottimista s. optimist.
ottimìstico agg. optimistic.
òttimo agg. best, very good. ♦ **òttimo** sm. optimum (pl. -ma).

otto agg. eight.
ottobre sm. October.
ottocento agg. eight hundred. ♦ **ottocento** sm. l'—, the nineteenth century.
ottomana sf. ottoman.
ottomano agg. e sm. Ottoman.
ottone sm. brass.
ottuagenario agg. e sm. octogenarian.
otturare vt. to stop. ♦ **otturarsi** vr. to stop.
otturatore sm. (foto) shutter.
otturazione sf. stopping.
ottusità sf. obtuseness.
ottuso agg. obtuse.
ovaia sf. ovary.
ovale agg. e sm. oval.
ovatta sf. 1. wadding 2. (cotone idrofilo) cotton-wool.
ovattare vt. to stuff with wadding.
ovazione sf. ovation.
ove avv. where.
ovest sm. west.
ovile sm. fold.
ovino agg. ovine. ♦ **ovino** sm. sheep (invariato al pl.).
ovìparo agg. oviparous.
ovòide agg. egg-shaped.
òvolo sm. (fungo) agaric.
ovulazione sf. ovulation.
òvulo sm. ovule.
ovunque avv. 1. everywhere 2. (in qualsiasi posto) anywhere. ♦ **o-vunque** cong. wherever.
ovvero cong. or.
ovviare vi. to obviate (sthg.).
ovvio agg. obvious.
oziare vi. to loaf, to idle.
ozio sm. idleness.
oziosamente avv. idly.
ozono sm. ozone.

P

pacare vt. to calm.
pacatezza sf. calmness.
pacato agg. calm.
pacca sf. slap.
pacchetto sm. packet.
pacchia sf. godsend.
pacchianata sf. coarse action.
pacchiano agg. coarse.
pacco sm. 1. (postale) parcel 2. (collo) package.

paccottiglia *sf.* cheap stuff.
pace *sf.* peace ‖ *darsi —*, to set (*v. irr.*) one's mind at rest.
pachiderma *sm.* pachyderm.
pachistano *agg. e sm.* Pakistani.
pacificare *vt.* 1. to pacify 2. (*riconciliare*) to reconcile. ◆ **pacificarsi** *vr.* to become (*v. irr.*) reconciled.
pacificazione *sf.* 1. pacification 2. (*riconciliazione*) reconciliation.
pacifico *agg.* 1. pacific 2. (*evidente*) self-evident.
pacifismo *sm.* pacifism.
pacifista *s.* pacifist.
pacioccone *sm.* easy-going person.
padella *sf.* frying-pan.
padiglione *sm.* pavilion.
padre *sm.* father.
padrino *sm.* godfather.
padronale *agg.* (*privato*) private ‖ *casa —*, manor-house.
padronanza *sf.* mastery: *— di sé*, self-control.
padrone *sm.* 1. master 2. (*proprietario*) owner 3. (*di casa, albergo*) landlord ‖ *essere — di sé*, to have self-control; *padronissimo!*, do as you like!
paesaggio *sm.* landscape.
paesano *agg.* rural. ◆ **paesano** *sm.* peasant.
paese *sm.* 1. (*nazione, territorio*) country 2. (*villaggio*) village.
paesista *s.* landscape painter.
paffuto *agg.* chubby.
paga *sf.* pay, wages (*pl.*): *libro —*, wages book; *giorno di —*, pay day.
pagàbile *agg.* payable.
pagaia *sf.* paddle.
pagamento *sm.* payment.
paganésimo *sm.* paganism.
pagano *agg. e sm.* pagan.
pagare *vt.* to pay (*v. irr.*).
pagella *sf.* schoolreport.
paggio *sm.* page.
pagherò *sm.* promissory note.
pàgina *sf.* page.
paglia *sf.* straw.
pagliacciata *sf.* buffoonery.
pagliaccio *sm.* clown.
pagliaio *sm.* strawstack.
pagliericcio *sm.* paillasse.
paglierino *agg.* straw-coloured.
vaglietta *sf.* 1. (*cappello*) straw-hat 2. (*paglia di ferro*) steel-wool 3. (*trucioli per imballaggio*) wood-shavings (*pl.*) 4. (*trucioli, di carta*) paper-wool.

pagnotta *sf.* round loaf (*pl.* -aves).
pagoda *sf.* pagoda.
paio *sm.* 1. (*di cose necessariamente unite*) pair 2. (*due*) couple.
pala *sf.* 1. shovel 2. (*di remo, elica*) blade 3. (*di ruota*) paddle ‖ *— d'altare*, altar-piece.
paladino *sm.* 1. paladin 2. (*fig.*) champion.
palafitta *sf.* 1. pile 2. (*abitazione*) pile-dwelling.
palafreniere *sm.* groom.
palafreno *sm.* palfrey.
palanchino *sm.* palanquin.
palata *sf.* 1. shovelful 2. (*colpo*) blow with a shovel ‖ *a palate* (*fig.*), in plenty.
palatale *agg.* palatal.
palatino *agg.* palatine.
palato *sm.* palate.
palazzo *sm.* palace.
palco *sm.* 1. (*di teatro*) box 2. (*pedana*) stand.
palcoscènico *sm.* stage.
paleocristiano *agg.* paleo-christian.
paleografìa *sf.* paleography.
paleògrafo *sm.* paleographer.
paleontologìa *sf.* paleontology.
paleontològico *agg.* paleontologic(al).
paleontòlogo *sm.* paleontologist.
palesare *vt.* to reveal.
palese *agg.* evident.
palestra *sf.* gymnasium.
paletta *sf.* (*di capostazione*) signal stick.
palinodìa *sf.* palinode.
palissandro *sm.* rosewood.
palizzata *sf.* palisade.
palla *sf.* 1. ball 2. (*pallottola*) bullet.
pallacanestro *sf.* basket-ball.
pallanuoto *sf.* water-polo.
pallavolo *sf.* volley-ball.
palleggiare *vi.* (*calcio*) to dribble. ◆ **palleggiare** *vt.* to toss. ◆ **palleggiarsi** *vr. rec.* to shift on one another.
palleggio *sm.* 1. (*calcio*) dribbling 2. (*tennis*) tossing.
palliativo *agg. e sm.* palliative.
pallidezza *sf.* paleness.
pàllido *agg.* pale.
pallino *sm.* 1. (*di fucile*) shot 2. (*mania*) craze.
palloncino *sm.* 1. balloon 2. (*lampioncino*) Chinese lantern.
pallone *sm.* ball ‖ *gioco del —*, football.

pallore *sm.* pallor.
pallòttola *sf.* **1.** pellet **2.** (*mil.*) bullet.
pallottoliere *sm.* abacus (*pl.* -ci).
palma[1] *sf.* (*della mano*) palm.
palma[2] *sf.* (*albero*) palm(-tree).
palmare *agg.* **1.** (*anat.*) palmar **2.** (*evidente*) clear.
palmato *agg.* **1.** (*bot.*) palmate **2.** (*zool.*) webbed.
palmeto *sm.* palm-grove.
palmìpede *agg. e sm.* palmiped.
palmo *sm.* palm.
palo *sm.* **1.** pole **2.** (*per fondamenta, ormeggio*) pile ‖ — *indicatore,* signpost; *fare il* —, to be on the lookout.
palombaro *sm.* diver.
palpàbile *agg.* tangible.
palpare *vt.* **1.** to finger **2.** (*med.*) to palpate.
pàlpebra *sf.* eyelid ‖ *battere le palpebre,* to blink.
palpitante *agg.* **1.** throbbing **2.** (*fig.*) fascinating.
palpitare *vi.* to throb (with sthg.).
palpitazione *sf.* **1.** throbbing **2.** (*med.*) palpitation.
pàlpito *sm.* throb.
paltò *sm.* overcoat.
palude *sf.* marsh.
paludoso *agg.* marshy.
pàmpino *sm.* vine-leaf (*pl.* -leaves).
panacea *sf.* panacea.
panare *vt.* to bread.
panca *sf.* bench.
pancetta *sf.* **1.** (*cu persona*) pot-belly.
panchina *sf.* bench.
pancia *sf.* belly.
panciera *sf.* body-belt.
panciotto *sm.* waistcoat.
panciuto *agg.* pot-bellied.
pancotto *sm.* panada.
pàncreas *sm.* pancreas.
pancreàtico *agg.* pancreatic.
pandemonio *sm.* pandemonium.
pane *sm.* bread.
panegìrico *sm.* panegyric.
panetterìa *sf.* bakery.
panettiere *sm.* baker.
pànfilo *sm.* yacht.
pangermanismo *sm.* Pan-Germanism.
pànico *agg. e sm.* panic.
panico *sm.* (*bot.*) millet.
paniere *sm.* basket.
panificare *vi.* to make (*v. irr.*) bread.

panificazione *sf.* bread-making.
panificio *sm.* bakery.
panino *sm.* roll: — *imbottito,* sandwich.
panna[1] *sf.* cream: — *montata,* whipped cream.
panna[2] *sf. restare in* —, to have a breakdown.
pannello *sm.* **1.** (*edil.*) panel **2.** (*di stoffa*) light panel.
panno *sm.* **1.** cloth (*pl.* cloths) **2.** *pl.* (*vestiti*) clothes.
pannocchia *sf.* cob.
pannolino *sm.* **1.** (*per bambini*) napkin **2.** (*assorbente igienico*) sanitary towel.
panorama *sm.* view.
panslavismo *sm.* Pan-slavism.
pantagruèlico *agg.* Pantagruelian.
pantaloni *sm. pl.* trousers ‖ — *corti,* shorts.
pantano *sm.* **1.** mire **2.** (*luogo pantanoso; fig.*) quagmire.
panteismo *sm.* pantheism.
panteista *s.* pantheist.
panteìstico *agg.* pantheistic(al).
pantera *sf.* panther.
pantòfola *sf.* slipper.
pantògrafo *sm.* pantograph.
pantomima *sf.* pantomime.
panzana *sf.* fib.
paonazzo *agg.* purple.
papa *sm.* pope.
papà *sm.* daddy.
papale *agg.* papal.
papalina *sf.* skull-cap.
papato *sm.* papacy.
papàvero *sm.* poppy ‖ *alto* —, (*fig.*) bigwig.
pàpera *sf.* **1.** (*zool.*) duckling **2.** (*errore*) slip **3.** (*teat.*) fluff.
papilla *sf.* papilla (*pl.* -ae).
papillare *agg.* papillary.
papiro *sm.* papyrus (*pl.* -ri).
papirologìa *sf.* papyrology.
papismo *sm.* popery.
papista *s.* papist.
pappa *sf.* pap.
pappagallo *sm.* parrot ‖ *ripetere a* —, to parrot.
pappagorgia *sf.* double chin.
pappare *vt.* to gorge. ♦ **papparsi** *vr.* to eat up.
pàprica *sf.* paprika.
paràbola *sf.* **1.** parable **2.** (*geom.; mil.*) parabola.
parabòlico *agg.* parabolic.
parabrezza *sm.* windscreen.
paracadutare *vt.* to parachute. ♦

paracadutarsi *vr.* to bail out.
paracadute *sm.* parachute.
paracadutismo *sm.* parachutism.
paracadutista *sm.* **1.** parachutist **2.** (*mil.*) paratrooper.
paracarro *sm.* wayside post.
paradigma *sm.* paradigm.
paradisìaco *agg.* paradisiac(al).
paradiso *sm.* paradise.
paradossale *agg.* paradoxical.
paradosso *sm.* paradox.
parafango *sm.* mudguard.
paraffina *sf.* paraffin.
parafrasare *vt.* to paraphrase.
paràfrasi *sf.* paraphrase.
parafùlmine *sm.* lightning-rod.
paragonàbile *agg.* comparable.
paragonare *vt.* to compare.
paragone *sm.* comparison: *a — di*, in comparison with.
paràgrafo *sm.* paragraph.
paràlisi *sf.* palsy.
paralìtico *agg. e sm.* paralytic.
paralizzare *vt.* to paralyze.
parallela *sf.* parallel: *le parallele* (*sport*), parallel bars.
parallelepìpedo *sm.* parallelepiped (*pl.* -da).
parallelismo *sm.* parallelism.
parallelo *agg. e sm.* parallel.
parallelogrammo *sm.* parallelogram.
paralume *sm.* lamp-shade.
paramento *sm.* **1.** hanging **2.** (*eccl.*) vestment.
paràmetro *sm.* parameter.
paraninfo *sm.* paranymph.
paranoia *sf.* paranoia.
paranòico *agg. e sm.* paranoiac.
paraocchi *sm. pl.* blinkers.
parapetto *sm.* **1.** parapet **2.** (*davanzale*) sill.
parapiglia *sm.* turmoil.
parapioggia *sm.* umbrella.
parare *vt.* **1.** (*riparare*) to shield **2.** (*evitare*) to parry **3.** (*ornare*) to decorate || *andare a —*, to drive (*v. irr.*) at. ♦ **pararsi** *vr.* **1.** (*comparire*) to appear **2.** (*adornarsi*) to deck oneself.
parasole *sm.* parasol.
parassita *agg.* parasitic. ♦ **parassita** *s.* parasite.
parassitismo *sm.* parasitism.
parastatale *agg.* State controlled || *ente —*, semi-governmental body.
parata *sf.* **1.** parade **2.** (*sport*) parry || *fare una —* (*sport*), to parry.
paratìa *sf.* bulkhead.

paratifo *sm.* paratyphoid.
parato *sm.* hanging || *carta da parati*, wallpaper.
paratoia *sf.* cataract.
paraurti *sm.* bumper.
paravento *sm.* screen.
parcella *sf.* fee.
parcheggiare *vt.* to park.
parcheggio *sm.* **1.** parking **2.** (*luogo*) car park.
parco[1] *sm.* park: *— di divertimenti*, fun-fair.
parco[2] *agg.* sparing.
parecchio *agg.* quite a lot of. ♦ **parecchio** *avv.* quite a lot, quite (+ *agg.*). ♦ **parecchio** *pron.* a good deal of it, several (*pl.*).
pareggiare *vt.* **1.** (*livellare*) to level **2.** (*comm.*) to balance **3.** (*parificare una scuola*) to recognize officially. ♦ **pareggiare** *vi.* (*sport*) to draw (*v. irr.*).
pareggio *sm.* **1.** (*comm.*) balance **2.** (*sport*) draw, tie.
parentado *sm.* V. *parentela.*
parente *sm.* relative.
parentela *sf.* **1.** relationship **2.** (*i parenti*) relatives.
parèntesi *sf.* **1.** parenthesis (*pl.* -ses) **2.** (*segno grafico*) bracket.
parere[1] *vi.* **1.** to seem **2.** (*essere simile a*) to look like **3.** (*pensare*) to think (*v. irr.*) (of).
parere[2] *sm.* opinion.
paresi *sf.* paresis.
parete *sf.* wall: *— divisoria*, partition.
pàrgolo *sm.* little child (*pl.* children).
pari *agg.* **1.** equal, same **2.** (*simile*) like **3.** (*divisibile per due*) even. ♦ **pari** *sm.* equal, peer.
paria *sm.* pariah.
parietale *agg.* parietal.
parificazione *sf.* **1.** (*comm.*) balance **2.** (*scuola*) official recognition **3.** (*livellamento*) levelling.
parigino *agg. e sm.* Parisian
pariglia *sf.* pair.
parimenti *avv.* likewise.
parità *sf.* equality.
paritario *agg.* equalitarian.
parlamentare[1] *agg.* parliamentary. ♦ **parlamentare** *sm.* Member of Parliament.
parlamentare[2] *vi.* to parley.
parlamentarismo *sm.* parliamentarianism.

parlamento *sm.* parliament.

parlantina *sf.* talkativeness || *aver buona* —, to be a glib talker.

parlare *vi.* to speak (*v. irr.*), to talk.

parlare *sm.* **1.** (*discorso*) speech **2.** (*chiacchiere*) talk **3.** (*idioma*) language.

parlato *agg.* cinema —, talkies (*pl.*).

parlatore *sm.* speaker.

parlatorio *sm.* parlour.

parlottare *vi.* to mutter.

parodìa *sf.* parody.

parodiare *vt.* to parody.

parodista *s.* parodist.

parola *sf.* **1.** word **2.** (*facoltà di parlare; discorso*) speech || *parole incrociate*, crosswords; *gioco di parole*, pun; *far* —, to mention; *restare senza* —, to be left speechless; *venire a parole con*, to have words with; *rivolgere la* — *a qu.*, to address so.; *avere la* — *facile*, to be a glib talker.

parolaccia *sf.* nasty word: *dire parolacce*, to swear (*v. irr.*).

parolaio *sm.* **1.** chatterbox **2.** (*di scrittore*) word-monger.

paroliere *sm.* « lyrics » writer.

parossismo *sm.* paroxysm.

paròtide *sf.* parotid.

parricida *s.* parricide.

parricidio *sm.* parricide.

parrocchia *sf.* parish.

parrocchiale *agg.* parish (*attr.*).

parrocchiano *sm.* parishioner.

pàrroco *sm.* **1.** (*cattolico*) parish priest **2.** (*protestante*) parson.

parrucca *sf.* wig.

parrucchiere *sm.* hairdresser.

parsimonia *sf.* thriftiness.

parsimonioso *agg.* thrifty.

parte *sf.* **1.** part **2.** (*lato*) side **3.** (*porzione*) share **4.** (*pol.; comm.; giur.*) party || *da* —, aside: *da* — *di*, from; *da* — *a* —, right through; *da una* — ... *dall'altra*, on one hand ... on the other; *la maggior* — *di*, most (of); *a* — *ciò*, apart from that; *farsi da* —, to get (*v. irr.*) out of the way; *fare la* — *di*, to play.

partecipante *s.* **1.** sharer **2.** (*chi annuncia*) spokesman (*pl.* -men) **3.** (*chi presenzia*) the bystander.

partecipare *vi.* **1.** to share (in) **2.** (*esser presente*) to be present. ♦ **partecipare** *vt.* to announce.

partecipazione *sf.* **1.** sharing **2.**

(*esser presente*) presence **3.** (*annuncio*) announcement **4.** (*biglietto*) card.

partécipe *agg.* **1.** sharing **2.** (*informato*) acquainted || *rendere* — *qu. di qc.*, to acquaint so. with sthg.

parteggiare *vi.* to take (*v. irr.*) sides (with).

partenogènesi *sf.* parthenogenesis.

partenza *sf.* **1.** departure, leaving **2.** (*sport*) start || *punto di* —, starting-point; *essere in* —, to be leaving.

particella *sf.* particle.

participiale *agg.* participial.

participio *sm.* participle.

particolare *agg.* particular. ♦ **particolare** *sm.* detail.

particolareggiato *agg.* detailed.

particolarismo *sm.* particularism.

particolarità *sf.* **1.** particularity **2.** (*dettaglio*) detail.

partigiano *agg. e sm.* partisan.

partire[1] *vi.* **1.** to leave (*v. irr.*) **2.** (*muoversi, iniziare, anche fig.*) to start || *a* — *da*, (beginning) from.

partire[2] *vt.* to separate.

partita *sf.* **1.** (*giocata*) game, match **2.** (*di merce*) lot **3.** (*in contabilità*) entry || *dar* — *vinta* (*fig.*), to give (*v. irr.*) in.

partitivo *agg. e sm.* partitive.

partito *sm.* party.

partitura *sf.* (*mus.*) score.

partizione *sf.* division.

parto *sm.* **1.** delivery **2.** (*fig.*) product.

partoriente *agg.* parturient. ♦ **partoriente** *sf.* lying-in woman.

partorire *vt.* to bring (*v. irr.*) forth, to beget (*v. irr.*) (*anche fig.*).

parvenza *sf.* **1.** appearance **2.** (*ombra*) shadow.

parziale *agg.* partial.

parzialità *sf.* partiality.

parzialmente *avv.* partially.

pàscere *vt. e vi.* **1.** to feed (*v. irr.*) **2.** (*al pascolo*) to graze. ♦ **pàscersi** *vr.* to feed (on).

pascià *sm.* pasha.

pasciuto *agg.* fed.

pascolare *vt. e vi.* to pasture.

pàscolo *sm.* pasture || *essere al* —, to be grazing.

Pasqua *sf.* Easter.

pasquale *agg.* Easter (*attr.*).

passàbile *agg.* passabl▪

passabilmente *avv.* passably.
passaggio *sm.* **1.** passage **2.** (*traversata*) crossing || *dare un — in macchina*, to give (*v. irr.*) a lift; *vietato il —*, no thoroughfare; *di —*, of transition; (*incidentalmente*) incidentally.
passamanerìa *sf.* passementerie.
passamano *sm.* (*fettuccia*) braid.
passamontagna *sm.* snow-cap.
passante *sm.* **1.** (*di cinghia ecc.*) loop **2.** (*persona*) passer-by.
passaporto *sm.* passport.
passare *vi.* **1.** to pass **2.** (*andare*) to call (on so., at sthg.). ♦ **passare** *vt.* **1.** to pass **2.** (*di tempo*) to spend (*v. irr.*) **3.** (*sopportare, trafiggere*) to pass through.
passatempo *sm.* pastime.
passatista *s.* traditionalist.
passato *agg.* **1.** past **2.** (*scorso*) last. ♦ **passato** *sm.* **1.** past **2.** (*cuc.*) mash.
passaverdura *sm.* vegetable masher.
passeggero *agg.* passing. ♦ **passeggero** *sm.* passenger.
passeggiare *vi.* to walk, to take (*v. irr.*) a walk.
passeggiata *sf.* **1.** walk **2.** (*in auto*) drive **3.** (*in bicicletta, a cavallo*) ride **4.** (*lungomare*) promenade.
passeggino *sm.* perambulator.
passeggio *sm.* **1.** walk **2.** (*gente che passeggia*) promenaders (*pl.*) || *andare a —*, to go (*v. irr.*) for a walk.
passeràceo *sm. e agg.* passerine.
passerella *sf.* **1.** (*ponte pedonale*) footbridge **2.** (*provvisoria*) trestle-bridge **3.** (*mar.; edil.*) gangway **4.** (*teat.*) parade.
pàssero *sm.* sparrow.
passìbile *agg.* liable (to).
passiflora *sf.* passion-flower.
passino *sm.* strainer.
passionale *agg.* **1.** passional **2.** (*appassionato*) passionate.
passione *sf.* passion.
passivamente *avv.* passively.
passività *sf.* **1.** passivity **2.** (*comm.*) liabilities (*pl.*).
passivo *agg.* passive. ♦ **passivo** *sm.* **1.** passive **2.** (*comm.*) liabilities (*pl.*).
passo *sm.* **1.** step **2.** (*andatura*) pace **3.** (*di montagna*) pass **4.** (*brano, passaggio*) passage **5.** (*cine*)

gauge **6.** (*tec.*) pitch || *passo passo*, very slowly; *segnare il —*, to mark time; *camminare a grandi passi*, to stride (*v. irr.*).
pasta *sf.* **1.** paste **2.** (*pasticcino*) cake **3.** (*per minestre*) "pasta".
pasteggiare *vi.* to feed (*v. irr.*) (on).
pastella *sf.* (*cuc.*) batter.
pastello *sm.* pastel: *matita, disegno a —*, pastel.
pasticca *sf.* tablet.
pasticcerìa *sf.* confectionery.
pasticciare *vt. e vi.* to make (*v. irr.*) a mess (of).
pasticciere *sm.* confectioner.
pasticcino *sm.* cake.
pasticcio *sm.* **1.** (*cuc.*) pie **2.** (*fig.*) mess || *essere nei pasticci*, to be in trouble.
pasticcione *sm.* bungler.
pastificio *sm.* « pasta » factory.
pastiglia *sf.* tablet.
pasto *sm.* meal.
pastoia *sf.* hobble.
pastone *sm.* mash.
pastorale *agg.* pastoral.
pastore *sm.* **1.** shepherd **2.** (*relig.*) parson.
pastorizia *sf.* stock-raising.
pastorizzare *vt.* to pasteurize.
pastorizzazione *sf.* pasteurization.
pastosità *sf.* **1.** mellowness **2.** (*morbidezza*) doughiness.
pastoso *agg.* **1.** mellow **2.** (*morbido*) doughy.
pastrano *sm.* overcoat.
pastura *sf.* pasture.
patacca *sf.* **1.** (*macchia*) spot **2.** (*cosa senza valore*) worthless object.
patata *sf.* potato: *— americana*, sweet potato || *— fritta*, chip; (*id.*, *croccante*) crisp.
patema *sm.* worry.
patentato *agg.* licenced.
patente *agg.* patent. ♦ **patente** *sf.* licence.
patereccio *sm.* whitlow.
paternale *sf.* scolding || *fare una — a qu.*, to lecture so.
paternalismo *sm.* paternalism.
paternalìstico *agg.* paternalistic.
paternità *sf.* paternity.
paterno *agg.* paternal.
pateticamente *avv.* pathetically.
patètico *agg. e sm.* pathetic.
patibolare *agg.* sinister.
patìbolo *sm.* scaffold.
patimento *sm.* pain.
pàtina *sf.* **1.** patina **2.** (*di vernice*)

coat of varnish **3.** (*sulla lingua*) coat **4.** (*su carta, terracotta*) glaze.
patinare *vt.* **1.** to varnish **2.** (*carta, terracotta*) to glaze.
patire *vt. e vi.* to suffer: — *il freddo,* to suffer from the cold || — *la fame,* to starve.
patito *agg.* sickly. ♦ **patito** *sm.* (*fig.*) fan.
patògeno *agg.* pathogenic.
patologìa *sf.* pathology.
patològico *agg.* pathologic(al).
patòlogo *sm.* pathologist.
patria *sf.* **1.** country, fatherland **2.** (*luogo natale*) birthplace.
patriarca *sm.* patriarch.
patriarcale *agg.* patriarchal.
patriarcato *sm.* patriarchate.
patricida *s.* V. *parricida.*
patrigno *sm.* stepfather.
patrimoniale *agg.* patrimonial.
patrimonio *sm.* patrimony.
patrio *agg.* **1.** native **2.** (*paterno*) paternal.
patriota *s.* patriot.
patriottardo *sm. e agg.* jingoist.
patriòttico *agg.* patriotic.
patriottismo *sm.* patriotism.
patriziato *sm.* patriciate.
patrizio *sm. e agg.* patrician.
patrocinante *sm.* pleader.
patrocinare *vt.* **1.** (*sostenere*) to support **2.** (*giur.*) to plead.
patrocinio *sm.* **1.** support **2.** (*giur.*) pleading.
patronato *sm.* **1.** patronage **2.** (*istituto benefico*) charitable institution.
patronessa *sf.* patroness.
patrono *sm.* **1.** patron **2.** (*giur.*) counsel for the defence.
patteggiare *vi.* to come (*v. irr.*) to terms.
pattinaggio *sm.* skating.
pattinare *vi.* to skate.
pattinatore *sm.* skater.
pàttino *sm.* **1.** (*a rotelle*) roller-skate **2.** (*da ghiaccio*) ice-skate **3.** (*di slitta*) shoe **4.** (*aer.*) skid **5.** (*mecc.*) sliding-block.
patto *sm.* **1.** agreement, pact **2.** (*condizione*) term || *a — che,* provided that; *a nessun —,* by no means.
pattuglia *sf.* patrol.
pattugliare *vi.* to patrol.
pattuire *vi.* to reach an agreement (upon). ♦ **pattuire** *vt.* to agree (on).
pattume *sm.* rubbish.

pattumiera *sf.* dust-bin.
pauperismo *sm.* pauperism.
paura *sf.* **1.** fear, dread **2.** (*spavento*) fright, scare.
pauroso *agg.* fearful.
pàusa *sf.* pause.
pavesare *vt.* to dress (with flags).
pavese *sm.* (*mar.*) hoist.
pavimentare *vt.* **1.** to pave **2.** (*una stanza*) to floor.
pavimento *sm.* floor.
pavone *sm.* peacock.
pavoneggiarsi *vr.* to show (*v. irr.*) off.
pazientare *vi.* to have patience.
paziente *agg. e sm.* patient.
pazienza *sf.* patience || —*!,* never mind!
pazzesco *agg.* foolish.
pazzìa *sf.* **1.** madness **2.** (*azione, idea pazza*) folly || *fare pazzie,* to act like a fool.
pazzo *agg.* mad. ♦ **pazzo** *sm.* madman (*pl.* -men).
pecca *sf.* fault || *senza —,* faultless.
peccaminoso *agg.* sinful.
peccare *vi.* **1.** to sin **2.** (*errare*) to err **3.** (*esser manchevole*) to lack (sthg.).
peccato *sm.* sin || *che —!,* what a pity!; *è un — che,* it is a pity that.
peccatore *sm.* sinner.
pece *sf.* pitch.
pècora *sf.* **1.** sheep (*pl. invariato*) **2.** (*femmina*) ewe.
pecoraio *sm.* shepherd.
peculato *sm.* peculation.
peculiare *agg.* peculiar.
peculiarità *sf.* peculiarity.
peculio *sm.* money.
pecuniario *agg.* pecuniary.
pedaggio *sm.* toll.
pedagogìa *sf.* pedagogy.
pedagògico *agg.* pedagogic(al).
pedagogista *s.* pedagogist.
pedagogo *sm.* pedagogue.
pedalare *vi.* to pedal.
pedale *sm.* pedal.
pedaliera *sf.* **1.** (*aer.*) rudder-bar **2.** (*mus.*) pedal keyboard.
pedana *sf.* **1.** (*sport*) spring-board **2.** (*piedistallo*) stand.
pedante *agg.* pedantic. ♦ **pedante** *s.* pedant.
pedanterìa *sf.* pedantry.
pedantesco *agg.* pedantic.
pedata *sf.* **1.** kick **2.** (*impronta*) footprint.

pedemontano *agg.* piedmont.

pederasta *sm.* homosexual.

pederastìa *sf.* homosexuality.

pedestre *agg.* pedestrian.

pediatra *s.* pediatrist.

pediatrìa *sf.* pediatrics.

pedicure *s.* chiropodist.

pediluvio *sm.* foot-bath.

pedina *sf.* **1.** (*alla dama*) piece **2.** (*agli scacchi*) pawn ‖ *muovere una — (anche fig.),* to make (*v. irr.*) a move.

pedinare *vt.* to shadow.

pedonale *agg.* pedestrian (*attr.*): *passaggio —,* pedestrian crossing.

pedone *sm.* pedestrian ‖ *strada riservata ai pedoni,* footpath.

pedùncolo *sm.* stalk.

peggio *agg.* (*comp.*) worse. ♦ **peggio** *sm.* the worst. ♦ **peggio** *avv.* **1.** (*comp.*) worse **2.** (*superl. rel.*) the worst ‖ *— per lui,* so much the worse for him; *alla —,* at worst; *avere la —,* to get (*v. irr.*) the worst of it.

peggioramento *sm.* aggravation.

peggiorare *vt.* to make (*v. irr.*) worse. ♦ **peggiorare** *vi.* to get (*v. irr.*) worse.

peggiorativo *agg. e sm.* pejorative.

peggiore *agg.* **1.** (*comp.*) worse: *questo libro è — di quello,* this book is worse than that **2.** (*superl. rel.*) the worst: *era il suo — nemico,* he was his worst enemy.

pegno *sm.* pledge ‖ *dare qc. in —,* to pledge sthg.; *polizza di —,* pawn-ticket; *agenzia di pegni,* pawnshop.

pelàgico *agg.* pelagic.

pelame *sm.* hair.

pelapatate *sm.* potato peeler.

pelare *vt.* **1.** to unhair **2.** (*sbucciare*) to peel **3.** (*spellare*) to skin **4.** (*far pagare caro*) to fleece. ♦ **pelarsi** *vr.* to lose (*v. irr.*) one's hair.

pelato *agg.* bald.

pelatura *sf.* **1.** unhairing **2.** (*sbucciatura*) peeling.

pellaio *sm.* furrier.

pellame *sm.* hides (*pl.*).

pelle *sf.* skin; (*di animale grosso*) hide ‖ *articoli in —,* leather articles; *amici per la —,* bosom friends.

pellegrina *sf.* (*mantella*) tippet.

pellegrinaggio *sm.* pilgrimage: *in —,* on a pilgrimage.

pellegrinare *vi.* to wander, to roam.

pellegrino *sm.* pilgrim.

pellerossa *agg. e sm.* redskin.

pelletterìa *sf.* **1.** leather goods **2.** (*negozio*) leather goods shop.

pellicano *sm.* pelican.

pelliccerìa *sf.* **1.** furriery **2.** (*negozio*) furrier's shop

pelliccia *sf.* fur.

pellicciaio *sm.* furrier.

pellìcola *sf.* film: *— a passo ridotto,* substandard film.

pelo *sm.* hair: *per un —,* by a hair's breadth; *cercare il — nell'uovo,* to split (*v. irr.*) hairs ‖ *non avere peli sulla lingua,* to be outspoken.

peloso *agg.* hairy.

pelota *sf.* pelota.

peltro *sm.* pewter.

peluria *sf.* down ‖ *coperto di —,* downy.

pelvi *sf.* pelvis.

pèlvico *agg.* pelvic.

pena *sf.* **1.** (*punizione*) punishment **2.** (*dolore*) pain **3.** (*disturbo*) trouble ‖ *essere in —,* to worry; *aver — di,* to pity; *a mala —,* hardly; *non ne vale la —,* it is not worth while.

penale *agg.* **1.** criminal **2.** (*relativo alla pena*) penal.

penalista *sm.* criminal lawyer.

penalità *sf.* penalty.

penalizzare *vt.* to penalize.

penare *vi.* **1.** to suffer **2.** (*far fatica*) to be hardly able.

pendaglio *sm.* pendant.

pendente *agg.* **1.** pendent **2.** (*inclinato*) leaning. ♦ **pendente** *sm.* pendant.

pendenza *sf.* **1.** slope **2.** (*grado d'inclinazione*) gradient **3.** (*giur.*) pending suit **4.** (*comm.*) outstanding account.

pèndere *vi.* **1.** to hang (*v. irr.*) **2.** (*inclinare*) to lean (*v. irr.*) **3.** (*essere in declino*) to slope **4.** (*incombere*) to overhang (*v. irr.*) **5.** (*essere incerto*) to waver.

pendìo *sm.* slope.

pèndola *sf.* pendulum-clock.

pendolare *agg.* pendular.

pèndolo *sm.* pendulum.

pèndulo *agg.* pendulous.

pene *sm.* penis.

penetràbile *agg.* penetrable.

penetrabilità *sf.* penetrability.

penetrante *agg.* piercing.
penetrare *vi.* e *vt.* 1. to penetrate 2. (*con fatica; di freddo, suono*) to pierce 3. (*furtivamente*) to steal (*v. irr.*) (into).
penetrazione *sf.* penetration.
penicillina *sf.* penicillin.
peninsulare *agg.* peninsular.
penìsola *sf.* peninsula.
penitente *agg.* e *s.* penitent.
penitenza *sf.* 1. (*teol.*) penance 2. (*pentimento*) repentance 3. (*nei giochi*) forfeit.
penitenziale *agg.* penitential.
penitenziario *agg.* penitentiary. ♦ **penitenziario** *sm.* jail.
penna *sf.* 1. pen 2. (*di uccello*) feather.
pennacchio *sm.* 1. plume 2. (*mil.*) panache.
pennecchio *sm.* wool on the distaff.
pennellare *vi.* 1. to brush 2. (*med.*) to paint.
pennellata *sf.* touch (of the brush).
pennellessa *sf.* flat brush.
pennello *sm.* brush.
pennino *sm.* nib.
pennone *sm.* (*mar.*) yard.
pennuto *agg.* feathered. ♦ **pennuto** *sm.* bird.
penombra *sf.* half-light
penoso *agg.* painful.
pensare *vi.* e *vt.* 1. to think (*v. irr.*) (of) 2. (*badare*) to look after || *pensa ai fatti tuoi*, mind your own business.
pensata *sf.* thought, idea.
pensatore *sm.* thinker.
pensiero *sm.* 1. thought 2. (*opinione*) mind, opinion 3. (*ansia*) worry.
pensieroso *agg.* thoughtful.
pènsile *agg.* hanging || *giardino —*, roof garden.
pensilina *sf.* 1. penthouse 2. (*di attesa*) shelter.
pensionàbile *agg.* pensionable.
pensionante *s.* boarder.
pensionato¹ *agg.* retired. ♦ **pensionato** *sm.* pensioner, retired person.
pensionato² *sm.* (*istituto*) hostel.
pensione *sf.* 1. (*assegno vitalizio*) pension || *essere in —*, to be retired; *mettere in —*, to pension off 2. (*albergo*) boarding-house || *essere a —*, to be boarding (at); *— completa*, full board.

pensoso *agg.* pensive.
pentaedro *sm.* pentahedron.
pentàgono *sm.* pentagon.
pentagramma *sm.* (*mus.*) pentagram.
pentàmetro *sm.* pentameter.
pentano *sm.* pentane.
Pentecoste *sf.* Pentecost, Whitsunday.
pentimento *sm.* repentance.
pentirsi *vr.* 1. to repent 2. (*rimpiangere*) to regret.
pèntodo *sm.* pentode.
pèntola *sf.* pot.
penùltimo *agg.* e *sm.* last but one.
penuria *sf.* shortage, penury.
penzolare *vi.* to dangle.
penzoloni *agg.* 1. (*dondolante*) dangling 2. (*pèndente*) hanging.
peocio *sm.* mussel.
peonia *sf.* peony.
pepaiola *sf.* pepper-box.
pepare *vt.* to pepper.
pepato *agg.* peppery (*anche fig.*).
pepe *sm.* pepper.
peperone *sm.* pepper: *peperoni sott'aceto*, pickled peppers.
pepita *sf.* nugget.
peplo *sm.* peplum.
pepsina *sf.* pepsin.
peptone *sm.* peptone.
per *prep.* 1. for: *fallo — me*, do it for me 2. (*moto per luogo*) through: *passai per Roma*, I passed through Rome 3. (*entro, per mezzo di*) by: *devo farlo — la fine dell'anno*, I have to do it by the end of the year; *— telegramma*, by telegram 4. (*causa*) owing to, because of: *non potemmo andare — la nebbia*, we couldn't go owing to (because of) fog || *— l'addietro*, in the past; *— caso*, by chance; *— nulla*, not at all; *— sempre*, for ever; *— tempo*, early. ♦ **per** *cong.* 1. (*finale*) to, in order to 2. (*causale*) for.
pera *sf.* pear.
peràcido *sm.* peracid.
perbacco *inter.* by Jove.
perbene *agg.* respectable.
percalle *sm.* percale.
percentuale *agg.* per cent. ♦ **percentuale** *sf.* percentage.
percepìbile *agg.* 1. perceptible 2. (*di somme*) receivable.
percepire *vt.* 1. to perceive 2. (*di stipendio*) to receive.

percettìbile agg. perceptible.
percettivo agg. perceptive.
percezione sf. perception.
perché cong. 1. (int.) why 2. (nelle risposte) because 3. (affinché) so that. ♦ **perché** sm. reason, why: chiedersi il —, to wonder why.
perciò cong. therefore, so.
perclorato sm. perchlorate.
percòrrere vt. 1. to cover 2. (attraversare) to run (v. irr.) through.
percorso sm. 1. (distanza) distance 2. (tragitto) way 3. (tracciato) course.
percossa sf. blow.
percuòtere vt. to strike (v. irr.).
percussione sf. percussion.
percussore sm. percussion-pin.
perdente agg. losing. ♦ **perdente** s. loser.
pèrdere vt. 1. to lose (v. irr.) 2. (di treno, occasione) to miss 3. (far acqua) to leak. ♦ **pèrdersi** vr. 1. to get (v. irr.) lost 2. (svanire) to fade 3. (rovinarsi) to be ruined || — d'animo, to lose heart.
perdifiato (nella loc. avv.) a —, with all one's strength.
perdigiorno sm. idler.
pèrdita sf. 1. loss 2. (falla, fuga) leak.
perditempo sm. waste of time.
perdizione sf. perdition.
perdonàbile agg. pardonable.
perdonare vt. 1. to forgive (v. irr.) 2. (risparmiare) to spare. ♦ **perdonarsi** vr. to forgive oneself. ♦ **perdonarsi** v. rec. to forgive each other (one another).
perdono sm. forgiveness || chiedere —, to beg one's pardon.
perdurare vi. to continue.
perdutamente avv. desperately.
perduto agg. lost.
peregrinare vi. to wander, to roam.
peregrinazione sf. wandering, roaming.
peregrino agg. rare.
perenne agg. 1. perennial 2. (eterno) everlasting.
perennemente avv. 1. perennially 2. (per sempre) for ever.
perentorio agg. peremptory.
perequazione sf. equalization.
perfettamente avv. perfectly.
perfettìbile agg. perfectible.
perfettibilità sf. perfectibility.
perfetto agg. perfect. ‹ **perfetto**

sm. (gramm.) perfect.
perfezionamento sm. perfecting.
perfezionare vt. 1. to perfect 2. (migliorare) to improve. ♦ **perfezionarsi** vr. to improve.
perfezione sf. perfection: alla —, to perfection.
perfidamente avv. wickedly.
perfidia sf. wickedness.
pèrfido agg. wicked.
perfino avv. even.
perforare vt. 1. to pierce 2. (d biglietti, schede) to punch 3. (mecc.) to drill, to bore.
perforatore agg. perforating. ♦ **perforatore** sm. perforator.
perforatrice sf. (macchina) drill, punch.
perforazione sf. 1. perforation 2. (mecc.) drilling 3. (di biglietti, schede) punching.
pergamena sf. parchment.
pèrgola sf. bower.
pergolato sm. arbour.
pericardio sm. pericardium (pl. -ia).
pericolante agg. tottering.
perìcolo sm. danger || mettere in —, to endanger; correre un —, to be in danger.
pericolosamente avv. dangerously.
pericoloso agg. dangerous.
periferìa sf. 1. periphery 2. (di città) suburbs (pl.).
perifèrico agg. 1. peripheral 2. (suburbano) suburban.
perìfrasi sf. periphrasis (pl. -ses).
perifràstico agg. periphrastic.
perigeo sm. perigee.
perìmetro sm. perimeter.
periodicità sf. periodicity.
periòdico agg. e sm. periodical.
perìodo sm. period.
peripezìa sf. vicissitude.
pèriplo sm. circumnavigation.
perire vi. to perish.
periscopio sm. periscope.
peristilio sm. peristyle.
perito sm. 1. expert 2. (comm.) estimator.
peritonite sf. peritonitis.
perituro agg. perishable.
perizia sf. 1. (abilità) skill 2. (valutazione) survey.
perla sf. pearl.
perlàceo agg. pearly.
perlìfero agg. pearl (attr.).
perlomeno avv. at least.
perlustrare vt. 1. to reconnoitre 2. (di polizia) to patrol.

perlustratore *sm.* scout.
perlustrazione *sf.* **1.** reconnaissance **2.** (*di polizia*) patrol || *essere in* —, to be on a reconnaissance.
permalosità *sf.* touchiness.
permaloso *agg.* touchy.
permanente *agg.* permanent. ♦ **permanente** *sf.* permanent wave.
permanentemente *avv.* permanently.
permanenza *sf.* **1.** permanence **2.** (*soggiorno*) stay.
permanere *vi.* **1.** to remain **2.** (*durare*) to last.
permanganato *sm.* permanganate.
permeàbile *agg.* permeable.
permeabilità *sf.* permeability.
permeare *vt.* to permeate.
permesso *agg.* allowed. ♦ **permesso** *sm.* **1.** leave: *in* —, on leave **2.** (*autorizzazione*) licence || *documento di* —, permit.
perméttere *vt.* to allow || *permettete?*, may I? ♦ **perméttersi** *vr.* (*prendersi la libertà*) to take (*v. irr.*) the liberty (of) || — *il lusso*, to afford.
pèrmuta *sf.* exchange.
permutàbile *agg.* exchangeable.
permutare *vt.* to exchange.
permutazione *sf.* permutation.
pernice *sf.* partridge.
pernicioso *agg.* pernicious.
perno *sm.* pivot.
pernottamento *sm.* overnight stay.
pernottare *vi.* to stay overnight.
pero *sm.* pear-tree.
però *cong.* but.
peronòspora *sf.* mildew.
perorare *vt.* to plead.
perorazione *sf.* pleading.
peròssido *sm.* peroxide.
perpendicolare *agg.* e *sf.* perpendicular.
perpetrare *vt.* to perpetrate.
perpetuamente *avv.* perpetually.
perpetuare *vt.* to perpetuate. ♦ **perpetuarsi** *vr.* to last.
perpetuità *sf.* perpetuity.
perpetuo *agg.* perpetual: *in* —, perpetually.
perplessità *sf.* perplexity.
perplesso *agg.* perplexed: *rendere* —, to perplex.
perquisire *vt.* to search.
perquisizione *sf.* search.
persecutore *sm.* persecutor.
persecuzione *sf.* persecution.
perseguìbile *agg.* (*giur.*) prosecu-

table.
perseguire *vt.* **1.** to pursue **2.** (*giur.*) to prosecute.
perseguitare *vt.* to persecute.
perseguitato *sm.* persecuted person.
perseverante *agg.* persevering.
perseveranza *sf.* perseverance.
perseverare *vi.* to persevere.
persiana *sf.* shutter.
persiano *agg.* e *sm.* Persian.
persistente *agg.* persistent.
persistenza *sf.* persistence.
persistere *vi.* to persist.
persona *sf.* person: *di* —, personally; — *giuridica*, artificial person.
personaggio *sm.* **1.** personage **2.** (*di romanzo ecc.*) character.
personale *agg.* personal. ♦ **personale** *sm.* **1.** staff **2.** (*corporatura*) figure.
personalità *sf.* personality: — *giuridica*, legal status.
personalmente *avv.* personally.
personificare *vt.* **1.** to personify **2.** (*teat.*) to play.
personificazione *sf.* personification.
perspicace *agg.* shrewd.
perspicacia *sf.* shrewdness
perspicuo *agg.* perspicuous.
persuadere *vt.* to persuade. ♦ **persuadersi** *vr.* to convince oneself.
persuasione *sf.* persuasion.
persuasivo *agg.* persuasive.
pertanto *cong.* therefore.
pèrtica *sf.* perch.
pertinace *agg.* pertinacious.
pertinacia *sf.* pertinacity.
pertinente *agg.* pertinent.
pertinenza *sf.* pertinence.
pertosse *sf.* whooping cough.
pertugio *sm.* hole.
perturbare *vt.* to disturb.
perturbatore *agg.* disturbing. ♦ **perturbatore** *sm.* disturber.
perturbazione *sf.* disturbance.
pervàdere *vt.* to pervade.
pervenire *vi.* to arrive (at).
perversione *sf.* perversion.
perversità *sf.* perversity.
perverso *agg.* perverse.
pervertire *vt.* to pervert. ♦ **pervertirsi** *vr.* to go (*v. irr.*) astray.
pervicace *agg.* obstinate.
pervicacia *sf.* obstinacy.
pervinca *sf.* periwinkle.
pesa *sf.* **1.** (*luogo*) weigh-house **2.** (*apparecchio*) weighing-machine.
pesante *agg.* heavy.

pesantezza *sf.* heaviness.

pesare *vt.* to weigh. ♦ **pesare** *vi.*
1. to weigh 2. (*fig.*) to lie (*v. irr.*)
heavy.

pesata *sf.* weighing.

pesca[1] *sf.* (*bot.*) peach.

pesca[2] *sf.* 1. (*il pescare*) fishing 2.
(*industria*) fishery 3. (*il pescato*)
catch.

pescaggio *sm.* (*mar.*) draught.

pescare *vt.* 1. to fish 2. (*fig.*) to
fish out 3. (*cogliere sul fatto*) to
catch (*v. irr.*) red-handed 4. (*carte*)
to draw (*v. irr.*). ♦ **pescare** *vi.*
to draw.

pescatore *sm.* 1. fisher 2. (*con lenza*) angler.

pesce *sm.* fish: — *rosso*, goldfish;
— *persico*, perch.

pescecane *sm.* shark.

peschereccio *agg.* fishing. ♦ **peschereccio** *sm.* fishing-boat.

pescherìa *sf.* 1. fish-shop 2. (*mercato*) fish-market.

peschiera *sf.* fish-pond.

pesciaiola *sf.* (*cuc.*) fish-kettle.

pesco *sm.* peach-tree.

pescoso *agg.* fishy.

pesista *sm.* weight thrower.

peso *sm.* weight: *a* —, by weight.

pessimismo *sm.* pessimism.

pessimista *agg.* pessimistic. ♦ **pessimista** *s.* pessimist.

pessimìstico *agg.* pessimistic.

pèssimo *agg.* worst, very bad.

pesta *sf.* 1. track 2. (*difficoltà*) difficulty.

pestaggio *sm.* scuffle.

pestare *vt.* 1. to pound 2. (*picchiare*) to beat (*v. irr.*) 3. (*calpestare*) to tread (*v. irr.*) on.

pestata *sf.* 1. (*lo schiacciare*) pounding 2. (*il calpestare*) treading.

peste *sf.* plague.

pestello *sm.* pestle.

pestìfero *agg.* pestiferous.

pestilenza *sf.* plague.

pestilenziale *agg.* pestilential.

pesto *agg.* pounded: *buio* —, pitch
dark; *avere gli occhi pesti*, to have
rings under one's eyes.

pètalo *sm.* petal.

petardo *sm.* petard.

petizione *sf.* petition.

petraia *sf.* 1. (*cava*) quarry 2. (*mucchio di pietre*) heap of stones.

petrografìa *sf.* petrography.

petroliera *sf.* tanker.

petrolìfero *agg.* oil (*attr.*).

petrolio *sm.* oil.

pettégola *sf.* gossiper.

pettegolare *vi.* to gossip.

pettegolezzo *sm.* gossip.

pettégolo *agg.* gossipy. ♦ **pettégolo** *sm.* gossiper.

pettinare *vt.* to comb. ♦ **pettinar-
si** *vr.* to comb one's hair.

pettinato *sm.* worsted.

pettinatrice *sf.* 1. hairdresser 2.
(*industria tessile*) comber.

pettinatura *sf.* 1. hairdo 2. (*industria tessile*) combing.

pèttine *sm.* comb.

pettirosso *sm.* robin.

petto *sm.* 1. breast 2. (*torace*) chest
|| — *a* —, face to face; *prendere
di* —, to face.

pettorale *agg. e sm.* pectoral.

pettorina *sf.* stomacher.

pettoruto *agg.* 1. full-breasted 2.
(*fig.*) haughty.

petulante *agg.* pert.

petulanza *sf.* pertness.

petunia *sf.* petunia.

pezza *sf.* 1. patch 2. (*macchia*) spot
|| — *di stoffa*, roll.

pezzato *agg.* spotted.

pezzente *agg.* beggarly. ♦ **pezzente** *s.* ragamuffin.

pezzo *sm.* piece: *fare a pezzi*, to
tear (*v. irr.*) to pieces; *a pezzi e
bocconi*, piecemeal; — *grosso* (*fig.*),
bigwig; — *di ricambio*, spare part.

pezzuola *sf.* handkerchief.

piacente *agg.* pleasant.

piacere[1] *sm.* 1. pleasure 2. (*favore*)
favour || *per* —, please; —! (*nelle
presentazioni*), how do you do!

piacere[2] *vi.* to like: *gli piace leggere*, he likes reading, he likes to
read; *come pare e piace*, as one
pleases.

piacévole *agg.* pleasant.

piacimento *sm.* pleasure, liking: *a*
—, as much as one likes.

piaga *sf.* 1. sore 2. (*calamità*)
plague 3. (*fig.*) nuisance.

piagnisteo *sm.* moaning.

piagnucolare *vi.* to whimper.

piagnucolìo *sm.* whimper.

piagnucoloso *agg.* whimpering.

pialla *sf.* plane.

piallare *vt.* to plane.

piallatrice *sf.* planer.

piallatura *sf.* 1. planing 2. (*trucioli*) shavings (*pl.*).

piana *sf.* plane.

pianeggiante *agg.* level.

pianella *sf.* **1.** (*pantofola*) slipper **2.** (*mattonella*) flat tile.

pianeròttolo *sm.* landing.

pianeta *sm.* planet.

piangente *agg.* weeping, crying.

piàngere *vi.* to cry, to weep (*v. irr.*). ♦ **piàngere** *vt.* to weep **2.** (*un lutto*) to mourn || — *a calde lacrime*, to weep one's heart out.

pianificare *vt.* to plan.

pianificazione *sf.* planning.

pianista *s.* pianist.

piano[1] *agg.* **1.** flat **2.** (*chiaro*) clear **3.** (*semplice*) simple.

piano[2] *sm.* **1.** plain **2.** (*di casa*) floor, storey **3.** (*strato*) layer **4.** (*superficie piana, livello*) plane **5.** (*progetto*) plan **6.** (*cine*) primo —, close up || — *stradale*, roadway; *in primo* —, in the foreground.

piano[3] *avv.* **1.** (*lentamente*) slowly **2.** (*sommessamente*) softly **3.** (*con cautela*) gently.

pianoforte *sm.* piano.

pianola *sf.* barrel-organ.

pianta *sf.* **1.** plant **2.** (*carta topografica*) map **3.** (*del piede*) sole || *di sana* — (*completamente*), completely; (*di nuovo*) anew.

piantagione *sf.* plantation.

piantare *vt.* **1.** to plant **2.** (*conficcare*) to drive (*v. irr.*) **3.** (*lasciare*) to leave (*v. irr.*) || *piantarla*, to stop.

piantatore *sm.* planter.

pianterreno *sm.* ground-floor.

pianto *sm.* **1.** tears (*pl.*): *scoppiare in* —, to burst (*v. irr.*) into tears **2.** (*dolore*) grief.

piantonamento *sm.* guarding.

piantonare *vt.* to guard.

piantone[1] *sm.* soldier on guard.

piantone[2] *sm.* (*agr.*) shoot.

pianura *sf.* plain.

piastra *sf.* **1.** plate **2.** (*di marmo*) slab **3.** (*moneta*) piastre.

piastrella *sf.* tile.

piastrellare *vt.* to tile.

piastrellatura *sf.* tiling.

piastrina *sf.* plaque.

piattaforma *sf.* platform.

piattello *sm.* pan || *tiro al* —, trap-shooting.

piattino *sm.* saucer.

piatto[1] *agg.* flat.

piatto[2] *sm.* **1.** dish **2.** (*portata*) course **3.** (*di lama*) flat **4.** (*di grammofono*) turn-table.

piazza *sf.* **1.** square **2.** (*comm.*) market || *mettere qc. in* —, to make (*v. irr.*) sthg. public.

piazzaforte *sf.* stronghold.

piazzale *sm.* large square.

piazzamento *sm.* place.

piazzare *vt.* to place. ♦ **piazzarsi** *vr.* (*sport*) to be placed.

piazzista *sm.* salesman (*pl.* -men).

picaresco *agg.* picaresque.

picca *sf.* pike || *picche* (*alle carte*), spades (*pl.*).

piccante *agg.* **1.** piquant **2.** (*salace*) spicy.

piccarsi *vr.* to plume oneself (on).

piccato *agg.* resentful.

picchettare *vt.* **1.** to peg out **2.** (*mil.*) to picket.

picchetto *sm.* **1.** peg **2.** (*mil.*) picket: *essere di* —, to be on picket.

picchiare *vt. e vi.* **1.** (*percuòtere*) to beat (*v. irr.*) **2.** (*battere*) to strike (*v. irr.*) **3.** (*bussare*) to knock **4.** (*aer.*) to pitch || — *in testa* (*di motore*), to ping. ♦ **picchiarsi** *vr. rec.* to fight (*v. irr.*).

picchiata *sf.* **1.** beating **2.** (*aer.*) dive || *scendere in* —, to dive.

picchiatello *agg.* slightly crazy.

picchiettare *vt.* **1.** (*battere*) to tap **2.** (*chiazzare*) to spot.

picchiettato *agg.* spotted.

picchiettìo *sm.* tapping.

picchio[1] *sm.* **1.** (*colpo*) blow **2.** (*alla porta*) knock.

picchio[2] *sm.* (*zool.*) woodpecker.

picchiotto *sm.* door-knocker.

piccinerìa *sf.* meanness.

piccino *agg.* **1.** little **2.** (*fig.*) mean.

piccionaia *sf.* **1.** pigeon-house **2.** (*teat.*) gallery.

piccione *sm.* pigeon.

picco *sm.* peak || *a* —, vertically; *colare a* —, *mandare a* —, to sink (*v. irr.*).

piccolezza *sf.* **1.** smallness **2.** (*meschinità*) meanness **3.** (*inezia*) trifle.

pìccolo *agg.* **1.** small, little **2.** (*di statura, breve*) short **3.** (*giovane*) young **4.** (*meschino*) mean **5.** (*leggero*) light.

piccone *sm.* pick(axe).

piccozza *sf.* axe.

pidocchieria *sf.* meanness.

pidocchio *sm.* **1.** louse (*pl.* lice) **2.** (*fig.*) miser.

pidocchioso *agg.* **1.** lousy **2.** (*fig.*) stingy.

piede *sm.* foot (*pl.* feet): *a piedi,* on foot || *a — libero,* on bail; *prender —,* to get (*v. irr.*) a footing.

piedistallo *sm.* pedestal.

piega *sf.* 1. fold 2. (*fatta ad arte*) pleat 3. (*segno*) crease || *messa in — (di capelli),* set.

piegàbile *agg.* folding.

piegamento *sm.* 1. folding 2. (*flessione*) flexing.

piegare *vt.* 1. to fold 2. (*flettere, anche fig.*) to bend (*v. irr.*). ♦ **piegare** *vi.* 1. (*voltare*) to turn 2. (*curvarsi*) to bend. ♦ **piegarsi** *vr.* to bend.

piegatrice *sf.* (*mecc.*) bending-machine.

pieghettare *vt.* to pleat.

pieghévole *agg.* 1. pliable 2. (*atto a essere piegato*) folding. ♦ **pieghévole** *sm.* folder.

pieghevolezza *sf.* pliability.

piena *sf.* 1. flood, spate 2. (*folla*) crowd.

pienamente *avv.* fully.

pienezza *sf.* 1. fullness 2. (*massimo grado*) height.

pieno *agg.* full: *— zeppo,* full up; *in — (completamente),* fully, (*esattamente, (nel mezzo)* in the middle; *in — giorno,* in broad daylight. ♦ **pieno** *sm.* (*il colmo*) middle || *fare il — (auto),* to fill up.

pietà *sf.* 1. pity 2. (*relig.*) piety || *aver — di,* to have mercy on; *far —,* to arouse pity; *per —!,* for pity's sake!

pietanza *sf.* 1. main course 2. (*piatto*) dish.

pietismo *sm.* pietism.

pietosamente *avv.* pitifully.

pietoso *agg.* pitiful.

pietra *sf.* stone: *posare la prima —,* to lay the foundation stone.

pietraia *sf.* V. petraia.

pietrificare *vt.* to petrify. ♦ **pietrificarsi** *vr.* to petrify.

pietrina *sf.* flint.

pietrisco *sm.* rubble.

pietroso *agg.* stony.

pìffero *sm.* pipe.

pigiama *sm.* pyjamas (*pl.*).

pigia pigia *sm.* awful crush.

pigiare *vt.* to press. ♦ **pigiarsi** *vr.* to crowd.

pigione *sf.* rent: *stare a — presso,* to lodge with.

pigmentato *agg.* pigmented.

pigmentazione *sf.* pigmentation.

pigmento *sm.* pigment.

pigmeo *sm.* pigmy.

pigna *sf.* pinecone.

pignatta *sf.* pot.

pignolerìa *sf.* faultfinding.

pignolo *sm.* 1. (*bot.*) pine-seed 2. (*fig.*) faultfinder.

pignoramento *sm.* attachment.

pignorare *vt.* to distrain.

pigolare *vi.* to peep.

pigolìo *sm.* peep.

pigramente *avv.* 1. lazily 2. (*lentamente*) sluggishly.

pigrizia *sf.* 1. laziness 2. (*lentezza*) sluggishness.

pigro *agg.* 1. lazy 2. (*lento*) sluggish.

pila *sf.* pile: *— a secco,* dry battery.

pilastro *sm.* pillar.

pìllola *sf.* pill: *— anticoncezionale,* contraceptive (pill), the "pill".

pilone *sm.* 1. pylon 2. (*di ponte*) pier || *— d'ormeggio,* mooring-mast.

piloro *sm.* pylorus (*pl.* -ri).

pilota *sm.* 1. pilot 2. (*di auto*) driver.

pilotaggio *sm.* pilotage: *scuola di —,* flying-school.

pilotare *vt.* 1. to pilot 2. (*un'auto*) to drive (*v. irr.*).

piluccare *vt.* to nibble.

piluccone *sm.* nibbler.

pinacoteca *sf.* picture-gallery.

pinastro *sm.* pinaster.

pindàrico *agg.* Pindaric.

pineta *sf.* pinewood.

pingue *agg.* 1. fat 2. (*ricco*) rich.

pinguèdine *sf.* fatness.

pinguino *sm.* penguin.

pinna *sf.* 1. fin 2. (*sport*) flipper.

pinnàcolo[1] *sm.* pinnacle.

pinnàcolo[2] *sm.* (*gioco*) pinochle.

pino *sm.* pine (-tree).

pinolo *sm.* pine-seed.

pinta *sf.* pint.

pinza *sf.* pliers (*pl.*), pincers (*pl.*).

pinzetta *sf.* tweezers (*pl.*).

pio *agg.* pious || *opera pia,* charitable organization.

pioggia *sf.* rain: *sotto la —,* in the rain.

piolo *sm.* V. piuolo.

piombare *vt.* 1. to plumb 2. (*tip.*) to lead || *— un dente,* to stop a tooth. ♦ **piombare** *vi.* 1. (*cade-*

re) to fall (*v. irr.*) heavily 2. (*assalire*) to assail 3. (*precipitarsi*) to rush.

piombatura *sf.* sealing, leading.

piombino *sm.* 1. plummet 2. (*sigillo*) leaden seal.

piombo *sm.* 1 lead 2. (*sigillo*) leaden seal 3. (*pallottola*) bullet || *filo a —*, plumb line; *a —*, perpendicularly; *di —*, leaden; *andare coi piedi di —*, to proceed very cautiously.

pioniere *sm.* pioneer.

pioppeto *sm.* poplargrove.

pioppo *sm.* poplar.

piorrea *sf.* pyorrhoea.

piovano *agg.* rain (*attr.*).

piovasco *sm.* shower.

piòvere *vi.* to rain, to pour (*anche fig.*).

piovigginare *vi.* to drizzle.

piovigginoso *agg.* drizzly, rainy.

piovoso *agg.* rainy.

piovra *sf.* octopus.

pipa *sf.* pipe.

pipetta *sf.* (*chim.*) pipette.

pipistrello *sm.* bat.

pipita *sf.* agnail.

pira *sf.* pyre.

piramidale *ag.* pyramidal.

piràmide *sf.* pyramid.

pirata *sm.* pirate || *— della strada*, hit-and-run driver.

piraterìa *sf.* piracy.

pìrico *agg. polvere pirica*, gunpowder.

pirite *sf.* pyrite(s).

piroetta *sf.* pirouette.

piroettare *vi.* to pirouette.

piroga *sf.* pirogue.

pirografìa *sf.* pyrography.

piròscafo *sm.* steamer.

pirotècnica *sf.* pyrotechnics.

pirotècnico *agg.* pyrotechnic(al): *spèttacolo —*, fireworks. ♦ **pirotècnico** *sm.* pyrotechnist.

piscia *sf.* piss.

pisciare *vi.* to piss.

pisciata *sf.* piss.

pisciatoio *sm.* urinal.

piscicoltura *sf.* pisciculture.

piscina *sf.* swimming-pool.

pisello *sm.* pea.

pisolino *sm.* nap.

pista *sf.* 1. (*traccia*) track 2. (*di animale*) trail 3. (*aer.*) strip.

pistacchio *sm.* pistachio.

pistillo *sm.* pistil.

pistola *sf.* pistol

pistone *sm.* piston.

pitagòrico *agg. e sm.* Pythagorean: *tavola pitagorica*, multiplication table.

pitale *sm.* chamber pot.

pitocco *agg.* 1. mean 2. (*fig.*) stingy. ♦ **pitocco** *sm.* 1. beggar 2. (*fig.*) mean person.

pitone *sm.* python.

pitonessa *sf.* pythoness.

pittore *sm.* painter.

pittoresco *agg.* picturesque.

pittòrico *agg.* pictorial.

pittrice *sf.* paintress.

pittura *sf.* 1. painting 2. (*dipinto, descrizione*) picture 3. (*vernice*) paint.

pitturare *vt.* to paint.

più *avv.* 1. (*comp. di maggioranza con agg. polisillabi, con s., v. e avv.*) more: *questo libro è — costoso di quello*, this book is more expensive than that; *ho — libri di te*, I have more books than you; *lavoro — di te*, I work more than you 2. (*comp. di maggioranza con agg. e avv. monosillabi e bisillabi terminanti in y, er, ow*) ...er: *è — gentile di lui*, he is kinder than he is 3. (*superl. rel., corrispondente a "more"*) the most, the more (*fra due*): *è il libro — costoso di tutti*, it is the most expensive book of all; *la — bella delle due sorelle*, the more beautiful of the two sisters 4. (*superl. rel., corrispondente a " ...er"*) the ...est, the ...er (*fra due*): *è la persona — felice che conosca*, she is the happiest person I know; *è la — graziosa delle due sorelle*, she is the prettier of the sisters 4. (*di tempo*) no longer, no more, not again || *mai —*, never again. ♦ **più** *agg.* 1. more 2. (*diversi*) several. ♦ **più** *sm.* most: *il — è fatto*, most of it is done || *i —*, most people (*al sing.*).

piuma *sf.* 1. feather, down 2. (*ornamento*) plume.

piumaggio *sm.* plumage.

piumino *sm.* 1. down 2. (*copriletto*) eiderdown 3. (*per la cipria*) powder-puff 4. (*per spolverare*) duster.

piuttosto *avv.* rather. ♦ **piuttosto che**, **di** *cong.* rather than.

piuolo *sm.* 1. peg: *scala a piuoli*, ladder 2. (*paletto*) post.

piva *sf.* bagpipe.

pivello *sm.* greenhorn.

piviere *sm.* plover.

pizzicàgnolo *sm.* delicatessen seller.

pizzicare *vt.* **1.** to pinch, to nip **2.** (*di insetti*) to bite (*v. irr.*) **3.** (*di sostanza acre*) to burn (*v. irr.*) **4.** (*con parole*) to tease **5.** (*sorprendere*) to catch (*v. irr.*). ◆ **pizzicare** *vi.* (*prudere*) to itch, to tingle.

pizzicherìa *sf.* **1.** delicatessen shop **2.** (*merci*) delicatessen.

pìzzico *sm.* **1.** pinch **2.** (*pizzicore*) itch **3.** (*fig.*) bit.

pizzicore *sm.* itch.

pizzicotto *sm.* pinch.

pizzo *sm.* **1.** lace (*solo sing.*) **2.** (*di montagna*) peak **3.** (*barba*) pointed beard.

placare *vt.* to appease: — *la fame di qu.*, to satisfy so.'s hunger; — *la sete di qu.*, to quench so.'s thirst. ◆ **placarsi** *vr.* to calm down.

placca *sf.* plaque.

placcare *vt.* to plate (sthg. with).

placcatura *sf.* plating.

placenta *sf.* placenta.

placidità *sf.* placidity.

plàcido *agg.* placid.

plaga *sf.* region.

plagiare *vt. e vi.* to plagiarize.

plagiario *agg.* plagiaristic. ◆ **plagiario** *sm.* plagiarist.

plagio *sm.* plagiarism.

planare *vi.* to glide down.

planata *sf.* glide.

plancia *sf.* (*mar.*) deck.

plancton *sm.* plankton.

planetario *agg.* planetary. ◆ **planetario** *sm.* planetarium (*pl.* -ia).

planimetrìa *sf.* planimetry, plan.

planimètrico *agg.* planimetric(al).

planisfero *sm.* planisphere.

plantìgrado *agg. e sm.* plantigrade.

plasma *sm.* plasma.

plasmare *vt.* to mould.

plàstica *sf.* **1.** (*operazione*) plastic operation **2.** (*materiale*) plastic.

plasticare *vt.* to plasticize.

plasticità *sf.* plasticity.

plàstico *agg.* plastic. ◆ **plàstico** *sm.* **1.** plastic model **2.** (*carta topografica*) relief map.

plastilina *sf.* plasticine.

plàtano *sm.* plane (-tree).

platea *sf.* pit: *poltrona di* —, stall.

plateale *agg.* coarse.

platinare *vt.* **1.** to platinize **2.** (*di capelli*) to bleach.

plàtino *sm.* platinum.

platònico *agg.* Platonic.

plaudente *agg.* applauding.

plausìbile *agg.* plausible.

plàuso *sm.* **1.** applause **2.** (*lode*) praise.

plebaglia *sf.* mob.

plebe *sf.* populace.

plebeo *agg. e sm.* plebeian.

plebiscitario *agg.* plebiscitary.

plebiscito *sm.* plebiscite.

plenario *agg.* plenary.

plenilunio *sm.* plenilune.

plenipotenziario *agg. e sm.* plenipotentiary.

pleonasmo *sm.* pleonasm.

pleonàstico *agg.* pleonastic.

plesso *sm.* plexus.

plètora *sf.* plethora.

pletòrico *agg.* plethoric.

plettro *sm.* plectrum (*pl.* -ra).

plèura *sf.* pleura (*pl.* -rae).

pleurite *sf.* pleurisy.

plico *sm.* **1.** packet **2.** (*busta*) cover: *in* — *separato*, under separate cover.

plotone *sm.* platoon.

plùmbeo *agg.* leaden.

plurale *agg. e sm.* plural.

pluralismo *sm.* pluralism.

pluralità *sf.* plurality.

pluricellulare *agg.* multicellular.

plusvalore *sm.* plus value.

plutòcrate *sm.* plutocrat.

plutocrazìa *sf.* plutocracy.

pneumàtico *agg.* pneumatic, inflatable. ◆ **pneumàtico** *sm.* (*di auto*) tyre.

pneumatorace *sm.* pneumothorax.

pochezza *sf.* (*scarsità, ristrettezza*) scantiness, insufficiency.

pochìssimo *agg. e avv.* **1.** very little **2.** (*rarissimamente*) very seldom. ◆ **pochìssimi** *sm. pl.* very few.

poco *avv.* **1.** not very (*con agg. e avv.*), little (*con comp., p. passati, verbi*): *a* — *a* —, little by little; — *per volta*, a little at a time **2.** (*di tempo*) a short time || *fra* —, soon. ◆ **poco** *agg.* **1.** little (*pl.* few) **2.** (*di tempo*) short. ◆ **poco** *pron. e sm.* little (*pl.* few): *un* — *di*, a little.

podere *sm.* farm.

poderoso *agg.* powerful.

podio *sm.* platform.

podismo *sm.* **1.** walking **2.** (*sport*) foot-racing.

podista *sm.* (*sport*) foot-racer.

podìstico *agg.* foot (*attr.*).

poema *sm.* poem.

poesìa *sf.* **1.** poetry **2.** (*composizione poetica*) poem.

poeta *sm.* poet.

poetare *vi.* to write (*v. irr.*) poetry.

poètico *agg.* poetic(al).

poggiapiedi *sm.* footstool.

poggiare *vi. e vt.* to rest. ♦ **poggiarsi** *vr.* to lean (*v. irr.*) against.

poggio *sm.* hillock.

poi *avv.* **1.** then **2.** (*più tardi*) later || *d'ora in* —, from now on.

poiché *cong.* since, as.

polacca *sf.* (*mus.*) polonaise.

polacco *agg.* Polish. ♦ **polacco** *sm.* Pole.

polare *agg.* polar || *stella* —, pole-star.

polarità *sf.* polarity.

polarizzare *vt.* to polarize.

polarizzatore *agg.* polarizing. ♦ **polarizzatore** *sm.* polarizer.

polarizzazione *sf.* polarization.

polca *sf.* polka.

polèmica *sf.* polemic.

polèmico *agg. e sm.* polemic.

polemista *s.* polemist.

polemizzare *vi.* to polemize.

poliandrìa *sf.* polyandry.

policlìnico *sm.* polyclinic.

policromìa *sf.* polychromy.

policromo *agg.* polychrome.

polièdrico *agg.* **1.** polyhedral **2.** (*fig.*) versatile.

poliedro *sm.* polyhedron.

polifonìa *sf.* polyphony.

polifònico *agg.* polyphonic.

poligamìa *sf.* polygamy.

polìgamo *agg.* polygamous. ♦ **polìgamo** *sm.* polygamist.

poliglotta *s.* polyglot.

polìgono *sm.* polygon || — *di tiro*, shooting-range.

polimerizzazione *sf.* polymerization.

polìmero *agg.* polymeric. ♦ **polìmero** *sm.* polymer.

polimorfismo *sm.* polymorphism.

poliomielite *sf.* poliomyelitis.

poliomielìtico *agg.* polio (*attr.*). ♦ **poliomielìtico** *sm.* person who has had polio.

pòlipo *sm.* polyp.

polisìllabo *agg.* polysyllabic(al). ♦ **polisìllabo** *sm.* polysyllable.

politècnico *agg. e sm.* polytechnic.

politeismo *sm.* polytheism.

politeista *agg.* polytheistic. ♦ **politeista** *s.* polytheist.

polìtica *sf.* **1.** politics **2.** (*linea di condotta*) policy.

politicante *sm.* petty politician.

polìtico *agg.* **1.** political **2.** (*sagace*) politic || *uomo* —, politician.

polivalente *agg.* polyvalent.

polizìa *sf.* police (*us. al pl.*).

poliziesco *agg.* **1.** police (*attr.*) **2.** (*di film ecc.*) detective (*attr.*).

poliziotto *sm.* policeman (*pl.* -men).

pòlizza *sf.* **1.** policy **2.** (*ricevuta*) bill.

polla *sf.* spring.

pollaio *sm.* hen-house.

pollame *sm.* poultry.

pollastra *sf.* pullet.

pollastro *sm.* cockerel.

pòllice *sm.* **1.** thumb **2.** (*del piede*) big toe **3.** (*misura*) inch.

pollicoltore *sm.* poultryman (*pl.* -men).

pollicoltura *sf.* poultry-farming.

pòlline *sm.* pollen.

pollivéndolo *sm.* poulterer.

pollo *sm.* **1.** chicken **2.** (*fig.*) dupe.

polmonare *agg.* pulmonary.

polmone *sm.* lung; — *d'acciaio*, iron lung.

polmonite *sf.* pneumonia.

polo[1] *sm.* pole.

polo[2] *sm.* (*sport*) polo.

polpa *sf.* **1.** (*di frutta*) pulp **2.** (*carne*) lean meat.

polpaccio *sm.* calf (*pl.* calves).

polpastrello *sm.* finger-tip.

polpetta *sf.* meat-ball, croquette.

polposo *agg.* pulpy.

polsino *sm.* cuff.

polso *sm.* **1.** wrist **2.** (*fig.*) energy **3.** (*pulsazione*) pulse **4.** (*polsino*) cuff || *tastare il* — *a qu.*, to feel (*v. irr.*) so.'s pulse; *uomo di* —, energetic man.

poltiglia *sf.* **1.** pulp **2.** (*fanghiglia*) mud.

poltrire *vi.* to idle.

poltrona *sf.* **1.** armchair **2.** (*teat.*) stall.

poltrone *agg.* idle. ♦ **poltrone** *sm.* idler.

poltronerìa *sf.* idleness.

pòlvere *sf.* **1.** dust **2.** (*sostanza polverizzata*) powder || *toglierle.la* —, to dust.

polveriera *sf.* powder-magazine.

polverizzare vt. to pulverize. ♦
polverizzarsi vr. to pulverize.
polverone sm. cloud of dust.
polveroso agg. dusty.
pomata sf. salve.
pomello sm. 1. (di porta ecc.) knob
2. (di guancia) cheek-bone.
pomeridiano agg. 1. afternoon
(attr.) 2. (con le ore) p. m. (post
meridiem): alle 5 pomeridiane,
at five o'clock.
pomeriggio sm. afternoon.
pòmice sf. pumice.
pomo sm. 1. (mela) apple 2. (di
porta ecc.) knob.
pomodoro sm. tomato.
pompa sf. 1. pump 2. (fasto) pomp
3. (ostentazione) display || impresa
di pompe funebri, undertaker's
business; far — di sé, to show (v.
irr.) off.
pompare vt. 1. to pump 2. (fig.)
to puff up.
pompelmo sm. grapefruit.
pompiere sm. fireman (pl. -men).
pomposità sf. pomposity.
pomposo agg. pompous.
ponderàbile agg. ponderable.
ponderabilità sf. ponderability.
ponderare vt. to ponder.
ponderatamente avv. after reflection.
ponderatezza sf. circumspection.
ponderato agg. pondered.
ponderazione sf. consideration.
ponderoso agg. ponderous.
ponente sm. west.
ponte sm. 1. bridge: — girevole,
swing bridge 2. (mar.) deck 3.
(impalcatura) scaffold || rompere i
ponti con (fig.), to break (v. irr.)
with.
pontéfice sm. pope.
pontificale agg. pontifical.
pontificare vi. to pontificate.
pontificato sm. pontificate.
pontificio agg. papal.
pontile sm. landing-stage.
pontone sm. pontoon.
ponzare vi. to rack one's brains.
popolamento sm. peopling.
popolano agg. common. ♦ **popola-
no** sm. man of the people || i
popolani, the common people.
popolare[1] vt. to people. ♦ **popo-
larsi** vr. to become (v. irr.) pop-
ulated.
popolare[2] agg. 1. popular 2. (tradizionale) folk (attr.).

popolaresco agg. popular-like.
popolarità sf. popularity.
popolarizzare vt. to popularize.
popolazione sf. population.
pòpolo sm. 1. (gente) people (pl.)
2. (nazione) people.
popoloso agg. populous.
popone sm. melon.
poppa[1] sf. 1. (mar.) stern || avere il
vento in —, to sail before the
wind; a —, astern.
poppa[2] sf. breast.
poppante s. suckling.
poppare vt. to suck.
poppata sf. suck: ora della —,
feeding-time.
poppatoio sm. feeding-bottle.
populismo sm. populism.
populista agg. populistic. ♦ **populista** s. populist.
porcaro sm. swineherd.
porcellana sf. china (solo sing.).
porcherìa sf. 1. dirt 2. (azione di-
sonesta) dirty trick 3. (detto indecente) obscene word 4. (atto indecente) obscene act 5. (cibo cattivo) revolting stuff 6. (cose senza
valore) rubbish.
porcile sm. pigsty.
porcino agg. pig (attr.). ♦ **porcino** sm. (fungo) boletus.
porco sm. 1. pig 2. (cuc.) pork.
porcospino sm. porcupine.
pòrfido sm. porphyry.
pòrgere vt. 1. to hand 2. (offrire)
to offer.
pornografia sf. pornography.
pornogràfico agg. pornographic
poro sm. pore.
porosità sf. porosity.
poroso agg. porous.
pòrpora sf. purple.
porporato sm. Cardinal.
porre vt. 1. to put (v. irr.) 2. (sup-
porre) to suppose || — le fonda-
menta, to lay (v. irr.) the foundations; — mano, to begin (v. irr.).
porro sm. 1. leek 2. (med.) wart.
porta sf. 1. door 2. (di mura ecc.)
gate 3. (sport) goal.
portabagagli sm. 1. luggage-rack
2. (facchino) porter.
portabandiera sm. ensign.
portacarte sm. portfolio.
portacénere sm. ash-tray.
portachiavi sm. key-holder.
portacipria sm. compact.
portaèrei sf. aircraft carrier.
portaferiti sm. stretcher-bearer.

portafiori sm. flower-holder.
portafoglio sm. 1. wallet 2. (pol.) portfolio.
portafortuna sm. mascot.
portagioielli sm. jewel-case.
portalèttere sm. postman (pl. -men).
portamento sm. 1. gait 2. (condotta) behaviour.
portamonete sm. purse.
portantina sf. sedan-chair.
portaombrelli sm. umbrella-stand.
portaòrdini sm. messenger.
portapacchi sm. carrier.
portapenne sm. penholder.
portare vt. 1. (verso chi parla o ascolta) to bring (v. irr.) 2. (lontano da chi parla, accompagnare) to take (v. irr.) 3. (trasportare) to carry 4. (condurre) to lead (v. irr.) 5. (indossare) to wear (v. irr.) 6. (avere) to have.
portasapone sm. soap-dish.
portasigarette sm. cigarette-case.
portaspilli sm. pincushion.
portata sf. 1. (di pranzo) course 2. (di arma, strumento ottico) range 3. (di fiume) flow 4. (di ponte, auto ecc.) capacity 5. (stazza) tonnage 6. (fig.) importance.
portàtile agg. portable.
portatore sm. bearer.
portauovo sm. egg-cup.
portavoce sm. spokesman (pl. -men).
portello sm. hatch.
portento sm. prodigy.
portentosamente avv. prodigiously.
portentoso agg. prodigious.
porticato sm. arcade.
pòrtico sm. 1. (loggia) porch 2. (porticato) arcade.
portiera[1] sf. (porta) door.
portiera[2] sf. doorkeeper.
portiere sm. 1. (sport) goal-keeper 2. porter.
portinaio sm. door keeper.
portinerìa sf. porter's lodge.
porto[1] sm. 1. port (anche fig.) 2. (bacino) harbour (anche fig.).
porto[2] sm. (trasporto) carriage: franco di —, carriage paid || — d'armi, shooting licence; condurre in — (fig.), to carry out.
portoghese agg. e sm. Portuguese.
portone sm. main door.
portuale agg. harbour (attr.): città —, port. ♦ **portuale** sm. docker.

porzione sf. portion.
posa sf. 1. (il porre) laying 2. (posizione) posture 3. (affettazione) pose 4. (pausa) pause 5. (foto) exposure || mettersi in —, to pose; senza —, incessantly.
posare vt. to lay (v. irr.). ♦ **posare** vi. 1. (aver fondamento) to rest 2. (assumere un atteggiamento non spontaneo) to pose 3. (di liquido) to stand (v. irr.). ♦ **posarsi** vr. 1. to settle 2. (aer.; di uccello) to alight.
posata sf. 1. (coltello) knife (pl. knives) 2. (forchetta) fork 3. (cucchiaio) spoon.
posato agg. staid.
poscritto sm. postscript.
positiva sf. (foto) positive.
positivamente avv. positively.
positivismo sm. positivism.
positivista s. positivist.
positivo agg. positive.
posizione sf. position.
posologìa sf. posology.
posporre vt. 1. to place after 2. (posticipare) to postpone.
possedere vt. to possess.
possedimento sm. V. possesso.
possente agg. powerful.
possessivo agg. possessive.
possesso sm. 1. possession 2. (proprietà) property.
possessore sm. possessor, owner.
possìbile agg. possible: il più presto —, as soon as possible; fare il —, to do (v. irr.) one's best.
possibilità sf. 1. possibility 2. (potere) power || finanziarie, means.
possidente sm. 1. man (pl. -men) of property 2. (terriero) landowner.
posta sf. 1. post, mail 2. (ufficio postale) post-office || fermo —, poste restante; a giro di —, by return of post; per —, by mail 3. (al gioco) stake.
postale agg. postal, post (attr.), mail (attr.): per pacco —, by parcel post; spese postali, postage.
postazione sf. stationing.
postbèllico agg. post-war (attr.).
postdatare vt. to postdate.
posteggiare vt. to park.
posteggiatore sm. 1. car-park attendant 2. (venditore) stall-keeper.
posteggio sm. car-park || — di taxi, taxi rank.
postelegrafònico agg. postal telegraph and telephone (attr.). ♦

postelegrafònico *sm.* post-office clerk.

postema *sf.* aposteme.

pòsteri *sm. pl.* descendants.

posteriore *agg.* **1.** (*nel tempo*) following **2.** (*nello spazio*) back, rear.

posterità *sf.* posterity.

posticcio *agg.* false. ♦ **posticcio** *sm.* toupee.

posticipare *vt.* to postpone.

posticipazione *sf.* deferment.

postiglione *sm.* postilion.

postilla *sf.* (*marginal*) note.

postillare *vt.* to annotate.

postino *sm.* postman (*pl.* -men).

posto *sm.* **1.** place **2.** (*spazio*) room **3.** (*lavoro*) job **4.** (*posto a sedere*) seat **5.** (*stazione*) station ‖ *al — di*, instead of.

postoperatorio *agg.* postoperative.

postrìbolo *sm.* brothel.

postulante *sm.* **1.** petitioner **2.** (*eccl.*) postulant.

postulare *vt.* to petition (for sthg.).

postulato *sm.* postulate.

pòstumo *agg.* posthumous.

potàbile *agg.* drinkable.

potare *vt.* to prune.

potassa *sf.* potash.

potàssico *agg.* potassic.

potassio *sm.* potassium.

potatore *sm.* pruner.

potatura *sf.* pruning.

potente *agg.* powerful.

potenza *sf.* power ‖ *in —* (*avv.*), potentially, (*agg.*) potential.

potenziale *agg.* e *sm.* potential.

potenzialità *sf.* potentiality.

potenziamento *sm.* **1.** (*rafforzamento*) strengthening **2.** (*sviluppo*) development.

potenziare *vt.* **1.** (*rafforzare*) to strengthen **2.** (*sviluppare*) to develop.

potere[1] *vi.* **1.** can (*pres.*), could (*pass., condiz.*), to be able: *non può venire*, he cannot come **2.** (*eventualità, augurio, permesso*) may (*pres.*), might (*pass., condiz.*), to be allowed to: *può darsi*, maybe; *può darsi che venga*, he may come.

potere[2] *sm.* power.

potestà *sf.* power, authority.

poveraccio *sm.* poor devil.

pòvero *agg.* poor.

povertà *sf.* poverty.

pozione *sf.* potion.

pozza *sf.* pool.

pozzànghera *sf.* puddle.

pozzetto *sm.* **1.** (*di motore*) sump **2.** (*di fognatura*) drain well.

pozzo *sm.* well: *— nero*, cesspool; *— carbonifero*, coal-pit.

pragmatismo *sm.* pragmatism.

pragmatista *s.* pragmatist.

pragmatìstico *agg.* pragmatist.

prammàtica *sf.* custom: *di —*, customary.

prammàtico *agg.* pragmatic.

pranzare *vi.* to dine.

pranzo *sm.* **1.** dinner **2.** (*di mezzogiorno*) lunch.

prassi *sf.* praxis.

prataiolo *agg.* field (*attr.*).

praterìa *sf.* prairie.

pràtica *sf.* **1.** practice **2.** (*affare*) matter **3.** (*esperienza*) experience **4.** (*incartamento*) file **5.** (*trattativa*) dealing **6.** (*passo presso un'autorità*) step ‖ *far —*, to practise; *aver — di*, to be familiar with.

praticàbile *agg.* practicable.

praticabilità *sf.* practicability.

praticaccia *sf.* practical knowledge.

praticante *agg.* practising.

praticare *vt.* **1.** to practise **2.** (*frequentare*) to frequent **3.** (*fare*) to make (*v. irr.*).

praticità *sf.* practicality.

pràtico *agg.* **1.** practical **2.** (*esperto*) skilled ‖ *esser — di*, to be familiar with.

prativo *agg.* grass (*attr.*).

prato *sm.* **1.** meadow **2.** (*artificiale*) lawn.

pratolina *sf.* daisy.

pravo *agg.* perverse.

preallarme *sm.* prewarning.

preàmbolo *sm.* preface.

preannunziare *vt.* to portend.

preavvertire *vt.* to forewarn.

preavvisare *vt.* to forewarn.

preavviso *sm.* **1.** forewarning **2.** (*disdetta*) notice.

prebèllico *agg.* pre-war (*attr.*).

prebenda *sf.* **1.** (*eccl.*) prebend **2.** (*salario*) salary.

precarietà *sf.* precariousness.

precario *agg.* precarious.

precauzionale *agg.* precautionary.

precauzione *sf.* **1.** precaution **2.** (*cautela*) caution.

precedente *agg.* previous. ♦ **precedente** *sm.* precedent ‖ *i precedenti* (*condotta*), record.

precedenza *sf.* precedence ‖ *in —*, previously.

precèdere *vt.* to precede. ♦ precèdere *vi.* to come (*v. irr.*) first.

precessione *sf.* precession.

precettare *vt.* 1. (*giur.*) to summon 2. (*mil.*) to call to arms.

precetto *sm.* 1. precept 2. (*mil.*) call-up notice.

precettore *sm.* tutor.

precipitare *vt.* to precipitate. ♦ precipitare *vi.* 1. to fall (*v. irr.*) 2. (*chim.*) to precipitate. ♦ precipitarsi *vr.* to dash.

precipitato *agg.* e *sm.* precipitate.

precipitazione *sf.* 1. (*atmosferica*) precipitation 2. (*furia*) haste.

precipitoso *agg.* 1. (*impetuoso*) headlong 2. (*frettoloso*) hasty 3. (*scosceso*) precipitous.

precipizio *sm.* precipice: *a — (precipitosamente)*, headlong; (*a picco*) perpendicularly.

precipuo *agg.* principal.

precisare *vt.* to specify.

precisazione *sf.* specification.

precisione *sf.* 1. precision 2. (*chiarezza*) clarity.

preciso *agg.* 1. precise 2. (*accurato*) careful 3. (*definito*) definite 4. (*identico*) identical 5. (*di ore*) sharp.

preclaro *agg.* prominent.

preclùdere *vt.* to preclude.

precoce *agg.* 1. precocious 2. (*di frutto, stagione*) early 3. (*prematuro*) premature.

precocità *sf.* precociousness.

preconcetto *agg.* preconceived. ♦ preconcetto *sm.* prejudice.

preconizzare *vt.* to foretell (*v. irr.*).

precordi *sm. pl.* praecordia.

precòrrere *vt.* to anticipate.

precursore *agg.* precursory. ♦ precursore *sm.* forerunner.

preda *sf.* 1. prey 2. (*bottino*) booty ‖ *cadere in — a*, to fall (*v. irr.*) a prey to; *far — di*, to plunder.

predace *agg.* predacious.

predare *vt.* to plunder.

predatore *agg.* predatory. ♦ predatore *sm.* plunderer.

predatorio *agg.* predatory.

predecessore *sm.* forerunner.

predella *sf.* 1. platform 2. (*sgabello*) stool.

predellino *sm.* 1. (*di vettura*) footboard 2. (*poggiapiedi*) footstool.

predestinare *vt.* to predestine.

predestinazione *sf.* 1. predestina-

tion 2. (*destino*) destiny.

predeterminare *vt.* to predetermine.

predeterminazione *sf.* predetermination.

predetto *agg.* 1. (*suddetto*) above mentioned 2. (*presagito*) foretold (*pred.*).

prediale *agg.* praedial.

prèdica *sf.* sermon: *fare la — a qu.*, to lecture so.

predicàbile *agg.* predicable.

predicare *vt.* e *vi.* to preach.

predicativo *agg.* predicate.

predicato *sm.* predicate: *essere in — per*, to be considered for.

predicatore *sm.* preacher.

predicatorio *agg.* preachifying.

predicazione *sf.* preaching.

predicozzo *sm.* lecture.

predigestione *sf.* preliminary digestion.

prediletto *agg.* favourite. ♦ prediletto *sm.* pet.

predilezione *sf.* predilection.

predilìgere *vt.* to prefer.

predire *vt.* to foretell (*v. irr.*).

predisporre *vi.* 1. to predispose 2. (*provvedere*) to arrange. ♦ predisporsi *vr.* to prepare oneself.

predisposizione *sf.* 1. (*med.*) predisposition 2. (*inclinazione*) bent.

predizione *sf.* prediction.

predominante *agg.* prevailing.

predominanza *sf.* prevalence.

predominare *vi.* to prevail.

predominio *sm.* predominance.

predone *sm.* plunderer.

preesistente *agg.* pre-existing.

preesistenza *sf.* pre-existence.

preesìstere *vi.* to pre-exist.

prefabbricare *vt.* to prefabricate.

prefazio *sm.* preface.

prefazione *sf.* preface.

preferenza *sf.* preference: *di —*, generally.

preferenziale *agg.* preferential.

preferìbile *agg.* preferable.

preferire *vt.* to prefer.

preferito *agg.* e *sm.* V. *prediletto*.

prefettizio *agg.* prefectorial.

prefetto *sm.* prefect.

prefettura *sf.* prefecture.

prefìggere *vt.* to (pre-)establish. ♦ prefìggersi *vr.* to be resolved: *— uno scopo*, to propose an aim to oneself.

prefigurare *vt.* to prefigure.

prefigurazione *sf.* prefiguration.

prefisso sm. prefix.

preformare vt. to preform.

pregare vt. 1. to pray 2. (chiedere) to beg.

pregévole agg. valuable.

preghiera sf. 1. prayer 2. (domanda) request.

pregiare vt. to esteem. ♦ **pregiarsi** vr. to beg (to).

pregiato agg. valuable: vino —, vintage wine.

pregio sm. 1. (valore) value 2. (merito) merit || di —, valuable.

pregiudicare vt. to prejudice.

pregiudicato sm. previous offender.

pregiudiziale agg. prejudicial

pregiudizio sm. prejudice.

pregnante agg. pregnant.

pregno agg. 1. pregnant (with) 2. (pieno) full (of).

pregustare vt. to foretaste.

preistoria sf. prehistory.

preistòrico agg. prehistoric.

prelatizio agg. prelatic.

prelato sm. prelate.

prelazione sf. pre-emption.

prelevamento sm. drawing: fare un — (comm.), to draw (v. irr.).

prelevare vt. to draw (v. irr.).

prelibare vt. to foretaste.

prelibato agg. excellent.

prelievo sm. V. prelevamento.

preliminare agg. preliminary.

prelùdere vi. to prelude (sthg.), to foreshadow (sthg.).

preludiare vi. to prelude.

preludio sm. prelude.

prematuro agg. premature.

premeditare vt. to premeditate.

premeditato agg. premeditated.

premeditazione sf. premeditation.

prèmere vi. 1. to press 2. (importare) to interest 3. (essere urgente) to be urgent. ♦ **prèmere** vt. to press.

premessa sf. introduction.

premesso agg. previous.

preméttere vt. 1. to premise 2. (mettere prima) to put (v. irr.) before.

premiare vt. 1. to give (v. irr.) a prize 2. (ricompensare) to reward.

premiazione sf. awarding of prizes.

preminente agg. pre-eminent.

preminenza sf. pre-eminence.

premio sm. 1. prize 2. (ricompensa) reward 3. (comm.) premium.

prèmito sm. tenesmus.

premolare agg. e sm. premolar.

premonitore agg. premonitory.

premorire vi. to predecease.

premunire vt. to forearm. ♦ **premunirsi** vr. to secure.

premura sf. 1. (cura) care 2. (fretta) hurry 3. (gentilezza) kindness || aver —, to be in a hurry.

premuroso agg. 1. (servizievole) helpful 2. (gentile) obliging.

prèndere vt. 1. to take (v. irr.) 2. (sorprendere, afferrare) to catch (v. irr.) 3. (comprare, ottenere) to get (v. irr.). ♦ **prèndersi** vr. to take || che ti prende?, what's the matter with you?

prendisole sm. sun-suit.

prenome sm. praenomen (pl. -mina).

prenotare vt. to book. ♦ **prenotarsi** vr. to engage oneself.

prenotazione sf. booking.

prènsile agg. prehensile.

prensione sf. prehension.

preoccupante agg. worrying.

preoccupare vt. to worry. ♦ **preoccuparsi** vr. to be worried (about).

preoccupazione sf. worry.

preordinare vt. to prearrange.

preparare vt. to prepare. ♦ **prepararsi** vr. to get (v. irr.) ready.

preparativo sm. preparation.

preparato agg. ready. ♦ **preparato** sm. (med.) preparation.

preparatore sm. preparer.

preparatorio agg. preparatory.

preparazione sf. preparation.

preponderante agg. preponderant.

preponderanza sf. preponderance.

preporre vt. 1. to put (v. irr.) before 2. (preferire) to prefer 3. (mettere a capo) to put at the head.

prepositivo agg. prepositional.

preposizione sf. preposition.

preposto sm. 1. provost 2. (relig., prevosto) parish priest.

prepotente agg. overbearing.

prepotentemente avv. overbearingly.

prepotenza sf. 1. arrogance 2. (azione) overbearing action.

preraffaellismo sm. Pre-Raphaelitism.

preraffaellita agg. e s. Pre-Raphaelite.

prerogativa sf. 1. prerogative 2. (di persona) faculty 3. (di cosa) property.

presa sf. 1. taking 2. (stretta) grip

3. (*cattura*) capture **4.** (*elettr.*) plug **5.** (*pizzico*) pinch || *macchina da* —, camera; *far* — (*di cemento*), to set (*v. irr.*).

presagio *sm.* presage, omen.

presagire *vt.* **1.** to foresee (*v. irr.*) **2.** (*essere presagio di*) to forebode.

presago *agg.* essere — di (*prevedere*), to have a presentiment of.

presbiopìa *sf.* long-sightedness.

prèsbite *agg.* long-sighted.

presbiterianismo *sm.* Presbyterianism.

presbiteriano *agg.* e *sm.* Presbyterian.

presbiterio *sm.* presbytery.

prescégliere *vt.* to choose (*v. irr.*).

prescelto *agg.* chosen.

prescienza *sf.* prescience.

prescìndere *vi.* to leave (*v. irr.*) out of consideration: *a* — *da*, apart from.

prescritto *sm.* prescript.

prescrivere *vt.* to prescribe.

prescrizione *sf.* **1.** regulation **2.** (*med.; giur.*) prescription: *caduto in* —, invalidated by prescription.

presentàbile *agg.* presentable.

presentare *vt.* **1.** to present **2.** (*mostrare*) to show (*v. irr.*) **3.** (*far conoscere*) to introduce. ♦ **presentarsi** *vr.* **1.** to present oneself **2.** (*capitare*) to occur.

presentatore *sm.* **1.** announcer **2.** (*teat.*) showman (*pl.* -men).

presentazione *sf.* **1.** presentation **2.** (*di una persona*) introduction.

presente *agg.* e *s.* present || *i presenti*, the people present; *la* — (*lettera*), this letter.

presentemente *avv.* now.

presentimento *sm.* presentiment.

presentire *vt.* to foresee (*v. irr.*).

presenza *sf.* **1.** presence **2.** (*frequenza*) attendance.

presenziare *vt.* e *vi.* to be present (at).

presepio *sm.* crib.

preservare *vt.* to preserve.

preservativo *agg.* e *sm.* preservative.

preservazione *sf.* preservation.

prèside *sm.* headmaster. ♦ **prèside** *sf.* headmistress.

presidente *sm.* **1.** president **2.** (*di assemblea*) chairman (*pl.* -men).

presidenza *sf.* **1.** presidency **2.** (*di assemblea*) chairmanship **3.** (*di società*) management **4.** (*insieme di*

direttori) board of directors **5.** (*di scuola*) headmastership.

presidenziale *agg.* presidential.

presidiare *vt.* to garrison.

presidio *sm.* garrison.

presièdere *vt.* e *vi.* to preside (over, at).

pressa *sf.* press.

pressacarte *sm.* paper-weight.

pressante *agg.* pressing.

pressantemente *avv.* pressingly.

pressappoco *avv.* approximately.

pressare *vt.* to press.

pressi *sm. pl.* **1.** neighbourhood (*sing.*) **2.** (*sobborghi*) outskirts.

pressione *sf.* pressure: *fare* — *su qu.* (*fig.*), to put (*v. irr.*) pressure on so.

presso *avv.* nearly: *a un di* —, *press'a poco*, approximately; *da* —, closely. ♦ **presso** *prep.* **1.** near **2.** (*a casa di*) at **3.** (*nell'ufficio di*) with **4.** (*fra*) among **5.** (*negli indirizzi*) c/o (care of).

pressoché *avv.* almost.

pressurizzare *vt.* to pressurize.

pressurizzazione *sf.* pressurization.

prestabilire *vt.* to pre-arrange.

prestamente *avv.* quickly.

prestanome *sm.* man of straw.

prestante *agg.* good-looking.

prestanza *sf.* fine appearance.

prestare *vt.* V. imprestare. ♦ **prestarsi** *vr.* to volunteer.

prestatore *sm.* lender: — *d'opera*, workman (*pl.* -men).

prestazione *sf.* **1.** (*prestito*) loan **2.** (*servizio*) service **3.** (*sport*) performance.

prestezza *sf.* quickness.

prestidigitatore *sm.* conjurer.

prestigio *sm.* prestige || *gioco di* —, conjuring trick.

prestigioso *agg.* **1.** (*affascinante*) glamorous **2.** (*favoloso*) fabulous.

prèstito *sm.* loan: *prendere in* —, to borrow; *dare in* —, to lend (*v. irr.*).

presto[1] *agg.* — *di mano*, dexterous.

presto[2] *avv.* **1.** soon **2.** (*di buon'ora*) early **3.** (*in fretta*) quickly || — *o tardi*, sooner or later; *al più* —, as soon as possible. ♦ **presto!** *inter.* quick!

presùmere *vt.* to presume.

presumìbile *agg.* presumable.

presumibilmente *avv.* presumably.

presuntivo *agg.* presumptive.

presunto *agg.* supposed.

presuntuosamente *avv.* presumptuously.

presuntuosità *sf.* conceit.

presuntuoso *agg.* presumptuous.

presunzione *sf.* presumption.

presupporre *vt.* **1.** to presuppose **2.** (*supporre*) to suppose.

presupposizione *sf.* **1.** presupposition **2.** (*supposizione*) supposition.

presupposto *sm.* V. *presupposizione.*

prete *sm.* priest.

pretendente *sm.* **1.** pretender **2.** (*corteggiatore*) suitor.

pretèndere *vt.* **1.** to pretend **2.** (*esigere*) to want. ♦ **pretèndere** *vi.* to claim.

pretensione *sf.* pretension.

pretenzioso *agg.* **1.** pretentious **2.** (*presuntuoso*) conceited.

preterintenzionale *agg.* unintentional.

pretèrito *agg. e sm.* past.

pretesa *sf.* **1.** pretence **2.** (*richiesta*) claim || *avere molte pretese*, to be hard to please; *avanzare pretese su*, to claim rights over.

pretesto *sm.* **1.** pretext **2.** (*occasione*) occasion.

pretore *sm.* magistrate.

prettamente *avv.* purely.

pretto *agg.* pure.

pretura *sf.* magistrate's court.

prevalente *agg.* prevailing.

prevalenza *sf.* prevalence.

prevalere *vi.* to prevail.

prevaricare *vi.* **1.** to prevaricate **2.** (*abusare del potere*) to abuse one's office.

prevaricatore *sm.* prevaricator.

prevaricazione *sf.* **1.** prevarication **2.** (*abuso di potere*) abuse of office.

prevedere *vt.* **1.** to foresee (*v. irr.*) **2.** (*di legge, contratto*) to provide (for).

prevedìbile *agg.* foreseeable.

preveggente *agg.* foreseeing.

preveggenza *sf.* foresight.

prevenire *vt.* **1.** (*precedere*) to forestall **2.** (*evitare*) to prevent **3.** (*avvertire*) to warn.

preventivamente *avv.* **1.** beforehand **2.** (*in modo preventivo*) preventively.

preventivare *vt.* to estimate.

preventivo *agg.* **1.** preventive **2.** (*comm.*) estimated || *bilancio —*, budget. ♦ **preventivo** *sm.* estimate

preventorio *sm.* preventive sanatorium.

prevenuto *agg. essere — contro*, to have a prejudice against.

prevenzione *sf.* **1.** prejudice **2.** (*il prevenire*) prevention.

previdente *agg.* provident.

previdenza *sf.* providence: *— sociale*, social security.

previdenziale *agg.* social security (*attr.*).

previo *agg.* **1.** previous **2.** (*soggetto a*) subject to.

previsione *sf.* **1.** forecast **2.** (*comm.*) estimate.

previsto *agg.* **1.** foreseen **2.** (*comm.*) estimated **3.** (*giur.*) provided.

prevosto *sm.* V. *preposto.*

preziosismo *sm.* preciosity.

preziosità *sf.* preciousness.

prezioso *agg.* precious. ♦ **prezioso** *sm.* jewel.

prezzémolo *sm.* parsley.

prezzo *sm.* **1.** price, cost **2.** (*valore*) value || *a — di*, at the cost of.

prezzolare *vt.* to hire.

prezzolato *agg.* (*mercenario*) mercenary.

prigione *sf.* **1.** prison **2.** (*pena*) imprisonment.

prigionìa *sf.* imprisonment.

prigioniero *agg.* imprisoned. ♦ **prigioniero** *sm.* prisoner.

prillare *vi.* to twirl.

prima[1] *avv.* **1.** before **2.** (*in anticipo*) in advance **3.** (*un tempo*) once **4.** (*più presto*) earlier, sooner **5.** (*per prima cosa*) first || *— o poi*, sooner or later; *quanto —*, soon. ♦ **prima** *prep.* before. ♦ **prima che, di** *cong.* before.

prima[2] *sf.* **1.** (*ferr.; scuola*) first class **2.** (*teat.*) première.

primario *agg.* primary. ♦ **primario** *sm.* head physician.

primate *sm.* (*eccl.*) primate.

primati *sm. pl.* (*zool.*) Primates.

primaticcio *agg.* early.

primatista *s.* record-holder.

primato *sm.* **1.** supremacy **2.** (*sport*) record.

primavera *sf.* spring.

primaverile *agg.* spring (*attributivo*), springlike.

primeggiare *vi.* to excel.

primigenio *agg.* primigenial.

primìpara *sf.* primipara (*pl.* -ae).

primitivo *agg. e sm.* primitive.

primizia *sf.* **1.** (*frutta*) early fruit

2. (*verdura*) early vegetable **3.** (*novità*) novelty.

primo *agg.* **1.** first **2.** (*principale*) chief **3.** (*iniziale*) early **4.** (*prossimo*) next ‖ *in un — tempo*, at first.

primogènito *agg. e sm.* first-born.

primogenitura *sf.* primogeniture.

primordiale *agg.* primeval.

primordi *sm. pl.* beginnings.

prìmula *sf.* primrose.

principale *agg.* principal. ♦ **principale** *sm.* master, boss.

principato *sm.* principality.

prìncipe *sm.* prince.

principesco *agg.* princely.

principessa *sf.* princess.

principiante *sm.* beginner.

principiare *vt. e vi.* to begin (*v. irr.*).

princìpio *sm.* **1.** (*inizio*) beginning **2.** (*norma*) principle: *per —*, on principle.

priora *sf.* prioress.

priorato *sm.* priorate.

priore *sm.* prior.

priorità *sf.* priority.

prisma *sm.* prism.

prismàtico *agg.* prismatic(al).

prìstino *agg.* former.

privare *vt.* to deprive.

privatista *s.* external student.

privativa *sf.* **1.** (*esclusiva*) sole right **2.** (*monopolio*) monopoly **3.** (*tabaccheria*) tobacconist's shop.

privativo *agg.* privative.

privato *agg.* **1.** private **2.** (*privo*) deprived. ♦ **privato** *sm.* private citizen.

privazione *sf.* **1.** (*disagio*) privation **2.** (*perdita*) loss.

privilegiare *vt.* to privilege.

privilegiato *agg.* **1.** privileged **2.** (*comm.*) preferred.

privilegio *sm.* privilege.

privo *agg.* devoid: *— di padre*, fatherless; *— di madre*, motherless.

pro¹ *prep.* for.

pro² *sm. a che —?*, what is the use of?

proavo *sm.* great grandfather.

probàbile *agg.* probable.

probabilismo *sm.* probabilism.

probabilità *sf.* probability.

probante *agg.* probatory.

probativo *agg.* probative.

probità *sf.* uprightness.

probiviri *sm. pl.* arbiters.

problema *sm.* problem.

problematicità *sf.* problematic nature.

problemàtico *agg.* problematic(al).

probo *agg.* upright.

proboscidati *sm. pl.* Proboscidea.

probòscide *sf.* trunk.

procaccia *sm.* postman (*pl.* -men).

procacciare *vt.* to get (*v. irr.*). ♦ **procacciarsi** *vr.* to get.

procacciatore *sm.* procurer.

procace *agg.* **1.** (*provocante*) provoking **2.** (*inverecondo*) immodest.

procacità *sf.* **1.** provocativeness **2.** (*inverecondia*) immodesty.

pro capite *loc. avv.* each.

procèdere *vi.* **1.** to proceed, to go (*v. irr.*) on **2.** (*agire*) to act.

procedimento *sm.* **1.** (*progressione*) course **2.** (*condotta*) behaviour **3.** (*giur.*) proceedings (*pl.*) **4.** (*tec.*) process.

procedura *sf.* **1.** procedure **2.** (*giur.*) practice.

procedurale *agg.* procedural.

procella *sf.* storm.

procellaria *sf.* stormy-petrel.

procelloso *agg.* stormy.

processare *vt.* to try: *far —*, to prosecute.

processionaria *sf.* processioner.

processione *sf.* procession.

processo *sm.* **1.** (*giur.*) trial **2.** (*med.; chim.; tec.*) process ‖ *andare sotto —*, to be tried; *intentare un —*, to bring (*v. irr.*) an action.

processuale *agg.* trial (*attr.*).

procinto (*nella loc. avv.*) *in — di*, on the point of.

proclama *sm.* proclamation.

proclamare *vt.* to proclaim.

proclamatore *sm.* proclaimer.

proclamazione *sf.* proclamation.

proclive *agg.* inclined.

proclività *sf.* inclination.

procònsole *sm.* proconsul.

procrastinare *vt.* to postpone. ♦ **procrastinare** *vi.* to procrastinate.

procrastinazione *sf.* procrastination.

procreare *vt.* to procreate.

procreatore *sm.* procreator.

procreazione *sf.* procreation.

procura *sf.* **1.** proxy: *per —*, by proxy **2.** (*documento*) letter of attorney.

procurare *vt.* **1.** to get (*v. irr.*) **2.** (*causare*) to cause **3.** (*cercare*) to try. ♦ **procurarsi** *vr.* to get (*v. irr.*).

procuratore *sm.* attorney.

prode *agg.* brave.

prodezza *sf.* **1.** bravery **2.** (*azione*) brave deed.

prodiere *sm.* bowman (*pl.* -men).

prodiero *agg.* forward.

prodigalità *sf.* lavishness.

prodigare *vt.* to lavish. ♦ **prodigarsi** *vr.* to do (*v. irr.*) all one can.

prodigio *sm.* prodigy.

prodigiosità *sf.* prodigiousness.

prodigioso *agg.* prodigious.

pròdigo *agg.* lavish.

proditoriamente *avv.* treacherously.

proditorio *agg.* treacherous.

prodotto *sm.* **1.** product **2.** (*risultato*) result **3.** (*agr.*) produce.

pròdromo *sm.* **1.** warning sign **2.** (*med.*) symptom.

produrre *vt.* to produce. ♦ **prodursi** *vr.* **1.** (*causarsi*) to cause oneself **2.** (*accadere*) to happen **3.** (*esibirsi*) to perform (before).

produttività *sf.* productivity.

produttivo *agg.* productive.

produttore *agg.* productive. ♦ **produttore** *sm.* producer.

produzione *sf.* production.

proemio *sm.* proem.

profanamente *avv.* profanely.

profanare *vt.* to profane.

profanatore *agg.* profaning. ♦ **profanatore** *sm.* profaner.

profanazione *sf.* profanation.

profanità *sf.* profanity.

profano *agg.* profane. ♦ **profano** *sm.* (*persona inesperta*) layman (*pl.* -men) || *i profani*, the laity.

proferire *vt.* **1.** to pronounce **2.** (*dire*) to utter.

professare *vt.* to profess.

professionale *agg.* professional: *scuola —*, vocational school.

professione *sf.* profession.

professionismo *sm.* professionalism.

professionista *sm.* **1.** professional man **2.** (*sport*) professional.

professorale *agg.* professorial.

professore *sm.* **1.** teacher **2.** (*ordinario di università*) professor.

profeta *sm.* prophet.

profetare *vt.* to prophesy.

profètico *agg.* prophetic(al).

profetizzare *vt.* V. *profetare.*

profezìa *sf.* prophecy.

profferire *vt.* **1.** (*offrire*) to offer **2.** (*pronunciare*) to utter.

profferta *sf.* offer.

proficuo *agg.* profitable.

profilare *vt.* **1.** to profile **2.** (*orlare*) to edge. ♦ **profilarsi** *vr.* **1.** to be outlined **2.** (*apparire*) to loom.

profilassi *sf.* prophylaxis.

profilato *agg.* **1.** (*delineato*) outlined **2.** (*affilato*) sharp **3.** (*orlato*) edged. ♦ **profilato** *sm.* section.

profilàttico *agg. e sm.* prophylactic.

profilo *sm.* **1.** (*contorno*) outline **2.** (*di viso*) profile **3.** (*studio letterario*) monograph.

profittare *vi.* **1.** (*trar profitto*) to avail oneself (of) **2.** (*progredire*) to make (*v. irr.*) progress **3.** (*guadagnare*) to make profits.

profittatore *sm.* profiteer.

profittévole *agg.* profitable.

profitto *sm.* profit: *trar —*, to profit (by); *mettere qc. a —*, to make (*v. irr.*) good use of sthg.

profluvio *sm.* flood.

profondamente *avv.* deeply: *dormire —*, to sleep (*v. irr.*) soundly.

profòndere *vt.* to lavish. ♦ **profòndersi** *vr.* to be profuse (in, of).

profondità *sf.* depth.

profondo *agg.* deep. ♦ **profondo** *sm.* depth.

pròfugo *sm.* refugee.

profumare *vt.* to scent. ♦ **profumarsi** *vr.* to spray oneself with scent.

profumatamente *avv.* (*fig.*) dearly.

profumerìa *sf.* perfumery.

profumiere *sm.* perfumer.

profumo *sm.* perfume, scent.

profusamente *avv.* **1.** profusely **2.** (*lungamente*) at length.

profusione *sf.* profusion.

progenerare *vt.* to procreate.

progenie *sf.* progeny.

progenitore *sm.* ancestor.

progettare *vt.* to plan.

progettazione *sf.* planning.

progettista *s.* planner.

progetto *sm.* plan.

prognatismo *sm.* prognathism.

prognato *agg.* prognathous.

prògnosi *sf.* prognosis (*pl.* -ses).

programma *sm.* program(me).

programmare *vt.* to program(me).

programmatore *sm.* programmist.

programmazione *sf.* programming.

programmista *sm.* programmer.

progredire *vi.* **1.** to advance **2.** (*fig.*) to get (*v. irr.*) on **3.** (*far progressi*) to make (*v. irr.*) progress.

progressione *sf.* progression.

progressista *agg. e s.* progressive.

progressivamente *avv.* progressively.

progressivo *agg.* progressive.

progresso *sm.* progress.

proibire *vt.* **1.** to forbid (*v. irr.*) **2.** (*impedire*) to prevent.

proibitivo *agg.* prohibitive.

proibizione *sf.* prohibition.

proibizionismo *sm.* prohibitionism.

proibizionista *agg. e s.* prohibitionist.

proiettare *vt.* **1.** to project **2.** (*cine*) to show (*v. irr.*) ♦ **proiettare** *vi.* to project. ♦ **proiettarsi** *vr.* to be projected.

proièttile *sm.* shell.

proiettore *sm.* **1.** (*riflettore*) searchlight **2.** (*cine*) projector.

proiezione *sf.* **1.** projection **2.** (*cine*) movie show || *macchina da —*, projector; *sala di —*, projection room.

prole *sf.* issue.

proletariato *sm.* proletariat.

proletario *agg. e sm.* proletarian.

proliferare *vi.* to proliferate.

proliferazione *sf.* proliferation.

prolìfico *agg.* prolific.

prolissità *sf.* prolixity.

prolisso *agg.* prolix.

pròlogo *sm.* prologue.

prolungàbile *agg.* extendable.

prolungamento *sm.* extension.

prolungare *vt.* **1.** to extend **2.** (*differire*) to postpone. ♦ **prolungarsi** *vr.* **1.** to extend **2.** (*dilungarsi*) to dwell (*v. irr.*) (on).

prolusione *sf.* opening lecture.

promemoria *sm.* memorandum (*pl.* -da).

promessa *sf.* promise.

promettente *agg.* promising.

prométtere *vt.* to promise: *— bene*, to be full of promise.

prominente *agg.* prominent.

prominenza *sf.* prominence.

promiscuità *sf.* promiscuity.

promiscuo *agg.* mixed, promiscuous.

promontorio *sm.* promontory.

promosso *agg.* **1.** (*a scuola*) successful **2.** (*sostenuto*) promoted.

promotore *sm.* promoter.

promozione *sf.* promotion.

promulgare *vt.* to promulgate.

promulgatore *sm.* promulgator.

promulgazione *sf.* promulgation.

promuòvere *vt.* **1.** to promote **2.** (*a scuola*) to pass.

prònao *sm.* pronaos (*pl.* -aoi).

pronipote *sm.* **1.** (*di bisnonno*) great-grandson, great-grandchild (*pl.* -children) **2.** (*di prozio*) grandnephew || *i pronipoti* (*discendenti*), descendants. ♦ **pronipote** *sf.* **1.** (*di bisnonno*) great-granddaughter, great-grandchild **2.** (*di prozio*) grandniece.

prono *agg.* prone.

pronome *sm.* pronoun.

pronominale *agg.* pronominal.

pronosticare *vt.* **1.** to forecast (*v. irr.*) **2.** (*predire*) to foretell (*v. irr.*) **3.** (*far prevedere*) to portend.

pronòstico *sm.* forecast.

prontezza *sf.* readiness.

pronto *agg.* **1.** (*preparato*) ready **2.** (*veloce*) prompt **3.** (*al telefono*) hallo || *— soccorso*, first aid.

prontuario *sm.* handbook.

pronuncia *sf.* pronunciation.

pronunciamento *sm.* pronouncement.

pronunciare *vt.* **1.** to pronounce **2.** (*proferire*) to utter || *— un discorso*, to deliver a speech. ♦ **pronunciarsi** *vr.* to give (*v. irr.*) one's opinion.

pronunciato *agg.* pronounced.

propaganda *sf.* **1.** propaganda **2.** (*comm.*) advertising: *far — (comm.)*, to advertise **3.** (*pol.*) canvass.

propagandare *vt.* **1.** to propagandize **2.** (*comm.*) to advertise.

propagandista *s.* **1.** propagandist **2.** (*comm.*) advertiser.

propagandìstico *agg.* **1.** propagandist **2.** (*comm.*) advertising.

propagare *vt.* to propagate. ♦ **propagarsi** *vr.* to propagate.

propagatore *sm.* propagator.

propagazione *sf.* propagation.

propagginare *vt.* (*agr.*) to layer.

propàggine *sf.* **1.** (*agr.*) layer **2.** (*geogr.*) ramification **3.** (*discendenza*) offspring.

propalare *vt.* to spread (*v. irr.*).

propano *sm.* propane.

propedèutica *sf.* propaedeutics.

propedèutico *agg.* propaedeutic(al).

propellente *agg.* propellent. ♦
propellente *sm.* propellant.
propèndere *vi.* to be inclined. ,
propensione *sf.* propensity.
propenso *agg.* inclined.
propilene *sm.* propylene.
propileo *sm.* propylaeum (*pl.* -laea).
propina *sf.* examiner's fee.
propinare *vt.* to give (*v. irr.*).
propiziare *vt.* to propitiate. ♦
propiziarsi *vr.* to gain so.'s favour.
propiziatore *sm.* propitiator.
propiziatorio *agg.* propitiatory.
propiziazione *sf.* propitiation.
propizio *agg.* favourable.
proponimento *sm.* resolution: *far —*, to resolve.
proporre *vt.* 1. to propose 2. (*suggerire*) to suggest. ♦ **proporsi** *vr.* to intend, to mean (*v. irr.*).
proporzionale *agg.* proportional.
proporzionalità *sf.* proportionality.
proporzionare *vt.* to proportion.
proporzionato *agg.* (*adeguato*) proportionate: *ben —*, well-proportioned.
proporzione *sf.* 1. proportion 2. (*rapporto*) ratio.
proposito *sm.* 1. purpose 2. (*intenzione*) intention || *di —*, on purpose; *a — di*, with regard to; *a —* (*inter.*), by the way; *a —* (*al momento giusto*), at the right moment.
proposizione *sf.* sentence.
proposta *sf.* proposal.
proprietà *sf.* 1. property 2. (*l'essere proprietario*) ownership 3. (*correttezza*) propriety || *— letteraria*, copyright.
proprietario *agg.* proprietary. ♦
proprietario *sm.* 1. owner 2. (*di locanda*) landlord 3. (*possidente*) man of property || *— terriero*, landowner.
proprio *agg.* 1. (*rafforzativo del poss.*) own 2. (*adatto*) suitable 3. (*mat.; gramm.*) proper || *vero e —*, real. ♦ **proprio** *avv.* 1. (*esattamente*) exactly 2. (*veramente*) really || *— ora*, just now; *— così*, just like that.
propugnare *vt.* to support.
propugnatore *sm.* supporter.
propulsione *sf.* propulsion.
propulsivo *agg.* propulsive.
propulsore *sm.* propeller.
prora *sf.* bow.

proravìa (*nella loc. avv.*) *a —*, at the bow.
pròroga *sf.* 1. (*giur.*) adjournment 2. (*dilazione*) extension.
prorogàbile *agg.* 1. (*giur.*) adjournable 2. extensible.
prorogare *vt.* 1. to delay, to extend 2. (*giur.*) to postpone.
prorompente *agg.* bursting (out).
proròmpere *vi.* 1. to burst-(*v. irr.*) (out) 2. (*di liquidi*) to gush out.
prosa *sf.* prose || *teatro di —*, drama; *compagnia di —*, dramatic company.
prosaicità *sf.* prosaism.
prosàico *agg.* prosaic.
prosapia *sf.* race.
prosàstico *agg.* prose (*attr.*).
prosatore *sm.* prose-writer.
proscenio *sm.* proscenium.
proscimmie *sf. pl.* lemurs.
prosciògliere *vt.* 1. (*da un obbligo*) to release 2. (*giur.*) to acquit.
proscioglimento *sm.* 1. release 2. (*giur.*) acquittal.
prosciugamento *sm.* 1. drying up 2. (*artificiale*) draining.
prosciugare *vt.* 1. to dry up 2. (*artificialmente*) to drain. ♦ **prosciugarsi** *vr.* to dry up.
prosciutto *sm.* ham.
proscritto *sm.* exile.
proscrìvere *vt.* to banish.
proscrizione *sf.* banishment.
prosecuzione *sf.* prosecution.
proseguimento *sm.* continuation.
proseguire *vt.* to continue. ♦ **proseguire** *vi.* to go (*v. irr.*) on.
proselitismo *sm.* proselytism.
prosèlito *sm.* proselyte.
prosieguo *sm.* course.
prosodìa *sf.* prosody.
prosopopea *sf.* (*fig.*) haughtiness.
prosperare *vi.* to prosper.
prosperità *sf.* prosperity.
pròspero *agg.* prosperous.
prosperoso *agg.* 1. prosperous 2. (*in salute*) healthy.
prospettare *vt.* 1. (*indicare*) to point out 2. (*guardare*) to look on to.
prospèttico *agg.* perspective (*attr.*).
prospettiva *sf.* 1. perspective 2. (*possibilità*) prospect.
prospetto *sm.* 1. view 2. (*fronte*) front 3. (*specchietto, programma*) prospectus.
prospezione *sf.* prospecting.
prospiciente *agg.* facing.

prossimità *sf.* closeness: *in — di,* near.

pròssimo *agg.* **1.** (*vicino*) near **2.** (*seguente*) next. ♦ **pròssimo** *sm.* fellow creatures (*pl.*), neighbour.

pròstata *sf.* prostate.

prosternare *vt.* to prostrate.

prostituire *vt.* to prostitute.

prostituta *sf.* prostitute.

prostituzione *sf.* prostitution.

prostrare *vt.* to prostrate. ♦ **prostrarsi** *vr.* to bow down.

prostrazione *sf.* prostration.

protagonista *s.* protagonist.

protèggere *vt.* to protect.

protèico *agg.* protein (*attr.*).

proteina *sf.* protein.

protèndere *vt.* to stretch (out): *— lo sguardo,* to gaze. ♦ **protèndersi** *vr.* to stretch oneself.

protervia *sf.* insolence.

protervo *agg.* insolent.

pròtesi *sf.* prosthesis.

protesta *sf.* protest.

protestante *agg.* e *s.* protestant.

protestantésimo *sm.* Protestantism.

protestare *vt.* e *vi.* to protest.

protesto *sm.* protest: *in —,* under protest; *lasciar andare una cambiale in —,* to dishonour a bill.

protettivo *agg.* protective.

protetto *agg.* protected. ♦ **protetto** *sm.* favourite.

protettorato *sm.* protectorate.

protettore *sm.* **1.** protector **2.** (*patrono*) patron.

protezione *sf.* **1.** protection **2.** (*patronato*) patronage.

protezionismo *sm.* protectionism.

protezionista *s.* protectionist.

proto *sm.* overseer.

protocollare *agg.* protocol (*attr.*).

protocollo *sm.* **1.** protocol **2.** (*registro*) record ‖ *mettere a —,* to record; *carta —,* foolscap.

protone *sm.* proton.

protoplasma *sm.* protoplasm.

protòtipo *sm.* prototype.

protozoi *sm. pl.* Protozoa.

protrarre *vt.* **1.** to protract **2.** (*differire*) to defer. ♦ **protrarsi** *vr.* to go *(v. irr.)* on.

protrazione *sf.* **1.** protraction **2.** (*differimento*) deferment.

protuberanza *sf.* bulge.

prova *sf.* **1.** proof **2.** (*giur.*) evidence (*solo sing.*) **3.** (*esperimento, esame*) test **4.** (*tentativo*) try **5.**

(*sventura*) trial **6.** (*teat.*) rehearsal **7.** (*teat.*) on trial; *dar — di essere,* to prove to be; *superare una —,* to pass a test.

provare *vt.* **1.** to prove **2.** (*tentare, mettere alla prova*) to try **3.** (*sentire*) to feel *(v. irr.)* **4.** (*di abiti*) to try on **5.** (*teat.*) to rehearse **6.** (*collaudare*) to test. ♦ **provarsi** *vr.* **1.** (*tentare*) to try **2.** (*cimentarsi*) to engage (in).

provenienza *sf.* origin.

provenire *vi.* to come *(v. irr.)*.

provento *sm.* **1.** proceeds (*pl.*) **2.** (*reddito*) income.

proverbiale *agg.* proverbial

proverbio *sm.* proverb.

provetta *sf.* test-tube.

provetto *agg.* skilled.

provincia *sf.* province.

provinciale *agg.* e *s.* provincial: *strada —,* main road.

provincialismo *sm.* provincialism.

provino *sm.* **1.** (*teat.*) tryout **2.** (*cine*) test film.

provocante *agg.* **1.** provocative **2.** (*procace*) immodest.

provocare *vt.* **1.** to provoke **2.** (*causare*) to cause.

provocatore *sm.* provoker.

provocazione *sf.* provocation.

provvedere *vi.* **1.** to provide (for) **2.** (*badare a*) to see *(v. irr.)* (to) **3.** (*aver cura di*) to take *(v. irr.)* care of. ♦ **provvedere** *vt.* **1.** to provide **2.** (*preparare*) to prepare.

provvedimento *sm.* measure.

provveduto *agg.* **1.** provided (with) **2.** (*accorto*) wary.

provvidenza *sf.* providence: *essere una —,* to be providential.

provvidenziale *agg.* providential.

pròvvido *agg.* provident.

provvigione *sf.* **1.** (*comm.*) commission **2.** (*provvista*) supply.

provvisorietà *sf.* temporariness.

provvisorio *agg.* temporary: *in via provvisoria,* temporarily.

provvista *sf.* supply, provision (*specialmente di cibo*).

provvisto *agg.* **1.** supplied (with) **2.** (*fig.*) well-off.

prua *sf.* bow.

prudente *agg.* **1.** prudent **2.** (*cauto*) careful.

prudenza *sf.* **1.** prudence **2.** (*cautela*) care **3.** (*precauzione*) precaution.

prùdere *vi.* to itch.

prugna *sf.* plum.

prugno *sm.* plum-tree.

pruno *sm.* **1.** thorn-bush **2.** (*spina*) thorn.

pruriginoso *agg.* itching

prurito *sm.* itch.

prùssico *agg.* prussic.

pseudònimo *sm.* pseudonym.

psicanàlisi *sf.* psychoanalysis.

psicanalista *s.* psychoanalyst.

psicanalìtico *agg.* psychoanalytic(al).

psicanalizzare *vt.* to psychoanalyze.

psiche *sf.* psyche.

psichiatra *s.* psychiatrist.

psichiatrìa *sf.* psychiatry.

psichiàtrico *agg.* psychiatric(al).

psìchico *agg.* psychic(al).

psicologìa *sf.* psychology.

psicològico *agg.* psychological(al).

psicòlogo *sm.* psychologist.

psicometrìa *sf.* psychometry.

psicopatìa *sf.* psychopathy.

psicopàtico *agg.* e *sm.* psychopathic.

psicopatologìa *sf.* psychopathology.

psicosi *sf.* psychosis (*pl.* -ses).

psicoterapìa *sf.* psychotherapy.

psittacosi *sf.* psittacosis.

pubblicàbile *agg.* publishable.

pubblicano *sm.* publican.

pubblicare *vt.* **1.** to publish **2.** (*di leggi ecc.*) to issue.

pubblicazione *sf.* publication: *fare le pubblicazioni di matrimonio*, to put up the banns.

pubblicista *s.* journalist.

pubblicità *sf.* **1.** publicity **2.** (*propaganda*) advertising || *fare —*, to advertise.

pubblicitario *agg.* advertising.

pùbblico *agg.* public. ♦ **pùbblico** *sm.* **1.** public **2.** (*in teatro ecc.*) audience **3.** (*cine*) moviegoers (*pl.*).

pube *sm.* pubis (*pl.* -bes).

pubertà *sf.* puberty.

pudibondo *agg.* demure.

pudicizia *sf.* demureness.

pudico *agg.* demure.

pudore *sm.* decency.

puericoltura *sf.* puericulture.

puerile *agg.* childish.

puerilità *sf.* childishness.

puèrpera *sf.* childwife (*pl.* -wives)

pugilato *sm.* boxing: *fare del —*, to box

pùgile *sm.* boxer.

pugnalare *vt.* to stab.

pugnalata *sf.* **1.** stab **2.** (*fig.*) blow.

pugnale *sm.* dagger.

pugno *sm.* **1.** fist **2.** (*colpo*) punch **3.** (*manciata*) handful || *colpire col —*, to punch; *in —*, in one's hand; *di proprio —*, in one's own handwriting; *fare a pugni*, to fight (*v. irr.*), (*fig.*) to clash.

pula *sf.* chaff.

pulce *sf.* flea: *— in un orecchio*, suspicion.

pulcino *sm.* chick.

puledro *sm.* colt.

puleggia *sf.* pulley.

pulire *vt.* to clean: *pulirsi la bocca*, to wipe one's mouth.

pulito *agg.* clean.

pulitore *sm.* cleaner.

pulizìa *sf.* **1.** (*il pulire*) cleaning **2.** (*l'essere pulito*) cleanliness.

pullulare *vi.* to swarm (with).

pùlpito *sm.* pulpit.

pulsante *sm.* push button.

pulsare *vi.* to beat (*v. irr.*)

pulsazione *sf.* beat.

pulverulento *agg.* dusty.

pulvìscolo *sm.* dust: *— atmosferico*, motes (*pl.*).

puma *sm.* puma.

pungente *agg.* **1.** prickly **2.** (*fig.*) biting.

pùngere *vt.* **1.** to sting (*v. irr.*) **2.** (*di ago*) to prick **3.** (*fig.*) to tease. ♦ **pùngersi** *vr.* to prick oneself.

pungiglione *sm.* sting.

pungitopo *sm.* (*bot.*) butcher's broom.

pungolare *vt.* to goad.

pùngolo *sm.* goad.

punìbile *agg.* punishable.

punire *vt.* to punish: *— una offesa*, to revenge an insult.

punitivo *agg.* punitive.

punitore *agg.* punitory. ♦ **punitore** *sm.* punisher.

punizione *sf.* punishment.

punta *sf.* **1.** point **2.** (*estremità*) tip **3.** (*cima*) top **4.** (*un po'*) bit **5.** (*dolore, fitta*) twinge || *sulla — dei piedi*, on tiptoe; *avere qc. sulla — delle dita*, to have sthg. at one's finger-tips.

puntale *sm.* (*di bastone ecc.*) ferrule.

puntamento *sm.* aim.

puntare *vt.* **1.** to point (at) **2.** (*mirare*) to aim (at) **3.** (*spingere*) to push **4.** (*scommettere*) to bet (*v. irr.*) || — *i piedi* (fig.), to put (*v. irr.*) one's foot down. ♦ **puntare** *vi.* to head.

puntata *sf.* **1.** (*al gioco*) stake **2.** (*di romanzo*) instalment.

puntatore *sm.* **1.** (*mil.*) marksman (*pl.* -men) **2.** (*al gioco*) better.

punteggiare *vt.* **1.** to punctuate **2.** (*nel disegno*) to dot.

punteggiatura *sf.* **1.** punctuation **2.** (*nel disegno*) dotting.

punteggio *sm.* (*sport*) score.

puntellare *vt.* to prop.

puntellatura *sf.* propping.

puntello *sm.* prop.

punteruolo *sm.* punch.

puntiglio *sm.* **1.** punctilio **2.** (*ostinazione*) obstinacy || *per* —, out of pique.

puntigliosamente *avv.* **1.** punctiliously **2.** (*ostinatamente*) obstinately.

puntiglioso *agg.* **1.** punctilious **2.** (*ostinato*) obstinate.

puntina *sf.* **1.** (*da fonografo*) needle **2.** (*da disegno*) drawing-pin.

puntino *sm.* dot: *puntini di sospensione*, dots || *a* —, properly.

punto[1] *sm.* **1.** point **2.** (*di cucito*) stitch **3.** (*voto*) mark **4.** (*gramm.*) full stop **5.** (*macchiolina*) dot || *due punti*, colon; — *e virgola*, semicolon; *mettere a* —, to set (*v. irr.*) up.

punto[2] *avv.* not at all.

punto[3] *agg. e pron.* not ... any.

puntone *sm.* (*edil.*) strut.

puntuale *agg.* punctual.

puntualità *sf.* punctuality.

puntualizzare *vt.* to stress.

puntualmente *avv.* punctually.

puntura *sf.* **1.** (*di insetto*) sting **2.** (*di ago*) prick **3.** (*iniezione*) injection **4.** (*dolore, fitta*) pain.

puntuto *agg.* pointed.

punzecchiamento *sm.* **1.** (*d'insetto*) stinging **2.** (*d'ago*) pricking **3.** (*fig.*) teasing.

punzecchiare *vt.* **1.** (*di insetti*) to sting (*v. irr.*) **2.** (*fig.*) to tease.

punzonare *vt.* to punch.

punzonatrice *sf.* (*mecc.*) punch.

punzonatura *sf.* punching.

punzone *sm.* punch.

pupàttola *sf.* doll.

pupazzetto *sm.* (*disegno*) sketch.

pupazzo *sm.* puppet.

pupilla *sf.* pupil.

pupillo *sm.* pupil.

pupo *sm.* baby.

purché *cong.* provided (that).

pure *avv.* **1.** (*anche*) also, too **2.** (*eppure*) yet **3.** (*di concessione*) as you like, of course. ♦ **pure** *cong.* **1.** (*con frasi concessive*) even though **2.** (*tuttavia*) but, yet. ♦ **pure di** *cong.* if only.

purè *sm.* purée: — *di patate*, mashed potatoes; *fare un* — *di verdura*, to mash vegetables.

purezza *sf.* purity.

purga *sf.* purgative, purge.

purgante *sm.* purgative, purge.

purgare *vt.* **1.** to purge **2.** (*di scritti*) to expurgate.

purgativo *agg.* purgative.

purgatorio *sm.* purgatory.

purificare *vt.* to purify.

purificatore *agg.* purificatory.

purificazione *sf.* purification.

purismo *sm.* purism.

purista *s.* purist.

puritanésimo *sm.* Puritanism.

puritano *agg. e sm.* Puritan.

puro *agg.* **1.** pure **2.** (*mero*) mere.

purosangue *sm.* thoroughbred.

purpùreo *agg.* purple.

purpurina *sf.* purpurin.

purtroppo *avv.* unfortunately.

purulento *agg.* purulent.

pus *sm.* pus.

pusillànime *agg.* pusillanimous. ♦ **pusillànime** *s.* coward.

pusillanimità *sf.* pusillanimity.

pùstola *sf.* pustule.

putacaso *loc. avv.* supposing.

putativo *agg.* putative.

putiferio *sm.* uproar: *sollevare un* —, to make (*v. irr.*) an uproar.

putrèdine *sf.* **1.** putridness **2.** (*cosa putrefatta*) rot.

putrefare *vi.* to rot. ♦ **putrefarsi** *vr.* to rot.

putrefatto *agg.* rotten.

putrefazione *sf.* putrefaction.

putrella *sf.* iron beam.

putrescenza *sf.* putrescence.

putrescìbile *agg.* putrescible.

putridità *sf.* rottenness.

pùtrido *agg.* rotten.

putridume *sm.* rot.

putto *sm.* putto (*pl.* -ti).

puzza *sf.* V. *puzzo.*

puzzare *vi.* to stink (*v. irr.*).

puzzo *sm.* stench.

pùzzola *sf.* polecat.

puzzolente *agg.* stinking.

Q

qua *avv.* here: *di — di*, on this side of; *per di —*, this way; *da quando in —?*, since when?

quàcchero *agg. e sm.* Quaker.

quaderno *sm.* exercise-book.

quadrangolare *agg.* quadrangular.

quadràngolo *sm.* quadrangle.

quadrante *sm.* **1.** quadrant **2.** (*di orologio*) dial.

quadrare *vt.* **1.** (*geom.*) to square **2.** (*formare*) to shape. ♦ **quadrare** *vi.* (*corrispondere*) to suit.

quadrato *agg.* **1.** square **2.** (*fig.*) strong. ♦ **quadrato** *sm.* **1.** square **2.** (*sport*) ring.

quadratura *sf.* **1.** squaring **2.** (*mat.*) quadrature.

quadrettato *agg.* **1.** squared **2.** (*di tessuto*) chequered.

quadriennale *agg.* quadrennial.

quadriennio *sm.* quadrennium (*pl.* -ia).

quadrifoglio *sm.* four-leaved clover.

quadriglia *sf.* quadrille.

quadrilàtero *sm.* quadrilateral.

quadrimotore *sm.* four-engined aircraft.

quadrivio *sm.* cross-roads.

quadro *agg.* V. *quadrato.* ♦ **quadro** *sm.* **1.** picture **2.** (*tabella*) table **3.** (*teat.*) scene **4.** (*elettr.*) board **5.** (*mil.*) cadre ‖ *galleria di quadri*, picture-gallery; *— riassuntivo*, summary; *— degli interruttori*, switch board.

quadrumane *agg.* quadrumanous. ♦ **quadrùmane** *sm.* quadrumane.

quadrùpede *agg. e sm.* quadruped.

quadruplicare *vt.* to quadruple. ♦ **quadruplicarsi** *vr.* to quadruple.

quàdruplo *agg. e sm.* **1.** quadruple **2.** (*quattro volte tanto*) four times as much.

quaggiù *avv.* down here.

quaglia *sf.* quail.

qualche *agg.* (*in frasi affermative e interrogative che aspettano risposta affermativa*) some; (*in frasi interrogative, dubitative, condizionali*) any ‖ *— volta*, sometimes; *in — luogo*, somewhere; *in — modo*, somehow.

qualcosa *pron.* something, anything (*per l'uso* V. *qualche*).

qualcuno *pron.* **1.** somebody, someone **2.** (*alcuni*) some, any: *— di*, some, any of (*per l'uso* V. *qualche*).

quale *pron. rel.* **1.** (*per persone*) who (*sogg.*), whom (*altri casi*) **2.** (*per animali, cose*) which **3.** (*per tutti, solo sogg. e ogg.*) that ‖ *del — (poss.*), whose: *l'uomo la casa del —*, the man whose house. ♦ **quale** *agg. e pron. int.* **1.** (*di che tipo*) what **2.** (*scelta tra numero limitato*) which. ♦ **quale** *agg. escl.* what. ♦ **quale** *pron.* (*correlativo di "tale"*) as ‖ *è tale e — suo fratello*, he is just like his brother.

qualìfica *sf.* **1.** qualification **2.** (*titolo*) title.

qualificare *vt.* to qualify.

qualificativo *agg.* qualifying.

qualificato *agg.* qualified: *operaio —*, skilled worker.

qualificazione *sf.* qualification.

qualità *sf.* **1.** quality **2.** (*specie*) kind **3.** (*ufficio*) capacity.

qualitativo *agg.* qualitative.

qualora *cong.* in case.

qualsìasi *agg.* V. *qualunque.*

qualunque *agg.* **1.** any **2.** (*quale che sia*) whatever; (*riferito a numero limitato*) whichever **3.** (*comune*) ordinary ‖ *uno —*, anybody; *— cosa*, anything; *in — posto*, anywhere; *in — modo*, anyhow.

quando *avv. e cong.* when ‖ *da —*, since; *da —?*, since when?; *quand'anche*, even though; *di — in —*, now and then.

quantità *sf.* quantity: *una gran — di*, a great deal of.

quantitativo *agg.* quantitative. ♦ **quantitativo** *sm.* V. *quantità.*

quanto *agg.* how much (*pl.* how many) ‖ *tanto... —*, as much... as; *tanti... quanti*, as many... as; *— tempo?* how long? ♦ **quanto** *avv.* how, how much ‖ *tanto —*, as much as; *tanto... —*, as... as; *tanto... — (sia... sia)*, both ...and; *— più... tanto più*, the more... the more; *— più... tanto meno*, the more... the less; *— a*, as for; *— prima*, soon; *per —*, however; *— fa?*, how much is it?

quantunque *cong.* though, although.

quaranta *agg.* forty.

quarantena *sf.* quarantine.

quarantenne *agg.* forty years old, forty-year-old (*attr.*).

quarantèsimo *agg.* fortieth.

quarantina *sf.* about forty: *aver*

passato la —, to be over forty.

quarésima *sf.* Lent.

quartetto *sm.* quartet.

quartiere *sm.* 1. (*di una città*) quarter 2. (*rione amministrativo*) district || — *generale*, headquarters (*pl.*).

quartina *sf.* quatrain.

quarto *agg.* fourth. ♦ **quarto** *sm.* quarter.

quarzo *sm.* quartz.

quasi *avv.* almost: — *mai*, hardly ever.

quassù *avv.* up here.

quaterna *sf.* set of four numbers.

quaternario *agg.* quaternary. ♦ **quaternario** *sm.* (*verso di una poesia*) line of four syllables.

quatto *agg.* 1. squatting 2. (*silenzioso*) silent || — —, very quietly.

quattordicèsimo *agg.* fourteenth.

quattòrdici *agg.* fourteen.

quattrini *sm. pl.* money (*us. al sing.*): *star male a* —, to be hard up.

quattro *agg.* four || *in* — *e* — *otto*, in no time; *fare il diavolo a* —, to make (*v. irr.*) a hullabaloo; *farsi in* —, to do (*v. irr.*) one's utmost.

quattrocchi (*nella loc. avv.*) *a* —, privately.

quattrocento *agg.* four hundred. ♦ **quattrocento** *sm. il* —, the fifteenth century.

quattromila *agg.* four thousand.

quegli *agg.* V. *quelli*. ♦ **quegli** *pron.* V. *egli*.

quei *agg. e pron.* V. *quelli*.

quella *agg. e pron.* V. *quello*.

quelle *agg. e pron.* V. *quelli*.

quelli *agg.* those. ♦ **quelli** *pron.* those, the ones.

quello *agg.* that. ♦ **quello** *pron.* that, the one || — *che* (*ciò che*), what; *tutto* — *che*, all that.

quercia *sf.* oak.

querela *sf.* 1. complaint 2. (*giur.*) action; *sporger* —, to bring (*v. irr.*) an action.

querelante *s.* plaintiff.

querelare *vt.* to proceed (against).

querelato *sm.* defendant.

quèrulo *agg.* querulous.

quesito *sm.* question.

questa *agg. e pron.* V. *questo*.

queste *agg. e pron.* V. *questi*.

questi *agg.* these. ♦ **questi** *pron.* 1. these 2. (*sing.*) this (man).

questionare *vi.* to quarrel.

questionario *sm.* questionnaire.

questione *sf.* 1. question 2. (*lite*) quarrel.

questo *agg.* this. ♦ **questo** *pron.* this, that || — ...*quello* (*il primo... il secondo*) the former... the latter.

questore *sm.* questor.

questua *sf.* 1. begging 2. (*in chiesa*) collection.

questuante *agg.* begging. ♦ **questuante** *s.* beggar.

questuare *vi.* to beg.

questura *sf.* police-headquarters (*pl.*).

questurino *sm.* cop.

qui *avv.* here: *per di* —, this way; — *vicino*, close by; *da* — *innanzi*, from now on; *di* — *a un anno*, a year from now; *di* — *a otto giorni*, a week today; *fin* — (*di tempo*), so far.

quiescenza *sf.* quiescence.

quietanza *sf.* receipt.

quietare *vt.* to quiet. ♦ **quietarsi** *vr.* to quiet down.

quiete *sf.* quiet.

quietismo *sm.* quietism.

quieto *agg.* quiet || *star* — (*zitto*), to keep (*v. irr.*) quiet; *star* — (*fermo*), to keep (*v. irr.*) still; — —, very quietly.

quindi *avv.* 1. therefore 2. (*poi*) then.

quindicenne *agg.* fifteen years old, fifteen-year-old (*attr.*).

quindicèsimo *agg.* fifteenth.

quindici *agg.* fifteen.

quindicina *sf.* 1. about fifteen 2. (*salario*) a fortnight's wages || *una* — *di giorni*, about a fortnight.

quindicinale *agg.* fortnightly.

quinquennale *agg.* quinquennial.

quinta *sf.* (*teat.*) wing || *dietro le quinte*, behind the scenes.

quintale *sm.* quintal.

quinterno *sm.* five sheets (*pl.*).

quintessenza *sf.* quintessence.

quintetto *sm.* quintet(te).

quinto *agg.* fifth.

quintuplicare *vt.* to quintuple.

quìntuplo *agg. e sm.* quintuple.

quisquilia *sf.* trifle.

quivi *avv.* here.

quota *sf.* 1. share 2. (*aer.*) altitude 3. (*mar.*) depth || *perdere* —, to lose (*v. irr.*) height; *prender* —, to climb.

quotare *vt.* to quote. ♦ **quotarsi** *vr.* to subscribe.

quotato *agg.* 1. quoted 2. *(fig.)* esteemed.

quotazione *sf.* quotation.

quotidianamente *avv.* daily.

quotidiano *agg. e sm.* daily: *vita quotidiana,* everyday life.

quoziente *sm.* quotient.

R

rabàrbaro *sm.* rhubarb.

rabberciamento *sm.* patching (up).

rabberciare *vt.* to patch (up).

rabbia *sf.* 1. rage 2. *(idrofobia)* rabies || *far — a qu.,* to make (*v. irr.*) so. angry.

rabbino *sm.* rabbi.

rabbioso *agg.* 1. *(med.)* rabid 2. *(fig.)* angry.

rabbonire *vt.* to calm down.

rabbrividire *vi.* 1. *(di freddo)* to shiver 2. *(di paura ecc.)* to shudder.

rabbuffare *vt.* 1. to ruffle 2. *(rimproverare)* to reprimand.

rabbuffo *sm.* rebuke.

rabbuiarsi *vr.* to darken.

rabdomante *s.* dowser.

rabdomanzìa *sf.* dowsing.

rabesco *sm.* V. *arabesco.*

raccapezzare *vt.* 1. *(raccogliere)* to gather 2. *(capire)* to understand (*v. irr.*). ♦ **raccapezzarsi** *vr.* to see (*v. irr.*) one's way.

raccapricciante *agg.* horrifying.

raccapricciare *vt.* to horrify. ♦ **raccapricciarsi** *vr.* to be horrified.

raccapriccio *sm.* horror.

raccattare *vt.* to pick up.

racchétta *sf.* racket.

racchio *agg.* ugly.

racchiùdere *vt.* to contain.

raccògliere *vt.* 1. to pick (up) 2. *(radunare)* to gather 3. *(far collezione)* to collect 4. *(accogliere)* to shelter 5. *(agr.)* to reap. ♦ **raccògliersi** *vr.* 1. to gather 2. *(concentrarsi)* to collect one's thoughts.

raccoglimento *sm.* 1. concentration 2. *(meditazione)* meditation.

raccogliticcio *agg.* picked up at random.

raccoglitore *sm.* 1. picker 2. *(collezionista)* collector 3. *(cartella)* folder.

raccolta *sf.* 1. *(agr.)* harvest; *(di frutta, cotone)* picking 2. *(collezione)* collection 3. *(adunanza)* gathering || *fare la —,* to harvest; *chiamare a —,* to collect.

raccoltamente *avv.* intently

raccolto *sm.* harvest.

raccomandàbile *agg.* recommendable.

raccomandare *vt.* 1. to recommend 2. *(esortare)* to urge 3. *(di lettere, pacchi)* to register. ♦ **raccomandarsi** *vr.* to beg (so.).

raccomandata *sf.* registered letter: *fare una —,* to register a letter.

raccomandazione *sf.* 1. recommendation 2. *(consiglio)* advice 3. *(di lettere, pacchi)* registration.

raccomodare *vt.* to mend.

raccontare *vt.* to tell (*v. irr.*) || *si racconta,* it is said.

racconto *sm.* 1. tale 2. *(resoconto)* relation.

raccorciare *vt.* to shorten. ♦ **raccorciarsi** *vr.* to grow (*v. irr.*) shorter.

raccordare *vt.* to connect.

raccordo *sm.* 1. connection 2. *(mecc.)* union 3. *(ferr.)* siding.

ràchide *sf.* rachis (*pl.* -ides).

rachìtico *agg.* rickety.

rachitismo *sm.* rickets.

racimolare *vt.* to glean.

rada *sf.* roadstead.

radar *sm.* radar.

raddobbare *vt.* 1. *(mar.)* to repair 2. *(riparare)* to refit.

raddobbo *sm.* *(mar.)* repair.

raddolcimento *sm.* 1. sweetening 2. *(fig.)* softening.

raddolcire *vt.* 1. to sweeten 2. *(fig.)* to soften 3. *(alleviare)* to soothe. ♦ **raddolcirsi** *vr.* 1. to soften 2. *(alleviarsi)* to be soothed 3. *(mitigarsi)* to grow (*v. irr.*) milder.

raddoppiamento *sm.* doubling.

raddoppiare *vt.* to double. ♦ **raddoppiarsi** *vr.* to double.

raddoppio *sm.* doubling.

raddrizzamento *sm.* 1. straightening 2. *(correzione)* redressing.

raddrizzare *vt.* 1. to straighten 2. *(correggere)* to redress.

radente *agg.* 1. shaving 2. *(rasente)* grazing.

ràdere vt. 1. to shave 2. (sfiorare) to graze 3. (distruggere) to raze.

radezza sf. 1. thinness 2. (rarità) infrequency.

radiale agg. radial.

radiante agg. radiant.

radiare vt. 1. to radiate 2. (espellere) to expel 3. (un nome) to strike (v. irr.) off.

radiatore sm. radiator.

radiazione sf. 1. radiation 2. (espulsione) expulsion.

radicale agg. radical,

radicalismo sm. radicalism.

radicare vi. to root. ♦ **radicarsi** vr. to root.

radicato agg. deep-rooted.

radice sf. root.

radio¹ sm. (anat.) radius (pl. -dii).

radio² sm. (chim.) radium.

radio³ sf. radio, wireless: ponte —, radiolink; alla —, on the radio; — portatile ricevente e trasmittente, walkie-talkie.

radioattività sf. radioactivity.

radioattivo agg. radioactive.

radioaudizione sf. 1. broadcasting 2. (ascolto) listening.

radiocomunicazione sf. wireless communication.

radiocrònaca sf. running commentary, radio account.

radiocronista s. radio commentator, wireless commentator.

radiodiffusione sf. broadcast.

radioestesìa sf. sensitivity to radiation.

radiofaro sm. radio beacon.

radiogoniòmetro sm. radio compass.

radiografare vt. to radiograph.

radiografìa sf. 1. radiograph 2. (scienza) radiography.

radiogramma sm. radiogram.

radiogrammòfono sm. radio-gramophone.

radiologìa sf. radiology.

radiòlogo sm. radiologist.

radioscopìa sf. radioscopy.

radioscòpico agg. radioscopic.

radiosità sf. radiance.

radioso agg. bright.

radiotècnica sf. radioengineering.

radiotècnico sm. radioengineer.

radiotelefonìa sf. radiotelephony.

radiotelèfono sm. radiotelephone.

radiotelegrafìa sf. radiotelegraphy.

radiotelegràfico agg. radiotelegraphic, wireless (attr.).

radiotelegrafista s. telegraphist.

radiotelevisione sf. radio and television.

radioterapìa sf. radiotherapy.

radiotrasméttere vt. to broadcast (v. irr.).

rado agg. 1. thin 2. (non frequente) infrequent ‖ di —, seldom.

radunare vt. to gather. ♦ **radunarsi** vr. to gather.

raduno sm. gathering.

radura sf. glade.

raffazzonare vt. to patch up.

raffermo agg. stale.

ràffica sf. 1. gust 2. (di arma) burst 3. (fig.) hail.

raffigurare vt. to represent. ♦ **raffigurarsi** vr. (immaginare) to imagine.

raffinamento sm. 1. refining 2. (fig.) refinement.

raffinare vt. to refine. ♦ **raffinarsi** vr. to become (v. irr.) refined, to refine.

raffinatamente avv. refinedly.

raffinatezza sf. refinement.

raffinato agg. refined (anche fig.).

raffinazione sf. refining.

raffinerìa sf. refinery.

raffio sm. grapnel.

rafforzamento sm. strengthening.

rafforzare vt. to strengthen. ♦ **rafforzarsi** vr. to grow (v. irr.) stronger.

raffreddamento sm. 1. cooling 2. (fig.) coolness.

raffreddare vt. 1. to cool 2. (fig.) to lessen. ♦ **raffreddarsi** vr. 1. to cool 2. (fig.) to wane 3. (prendere un raffreddore) to catch (v. irr.) a cold.

raffreddato agg. essere —, to have a cold.

raffreddatore sm. cooler.

raffreddore sm. cold.

raffrenare vt. to restrain.

raffrontare vt. to compare.

raffronto sm. comparison.

rafia sf. raffia.

ràgadi sf. pl. rhagades.

raganella sf. 1. tree-frog 2. (strumento) rattle.

ragazza sf. girl.

ragazzaglia sf. crowd of youngsters.

ragazzata sf. escapade.

ragazzo sm. boy: da —, as a boy.

raggelare vt. to freeze (v. irr.). ♦ **raggelarsi** vr. to freeze.

raggiante agg. radiant (with).

raggiare *vi.* **1.** to shine (*v. irr.*) (with sthg.) **2.** (*fig.*) to beam (with sthg.). ♦ **raggiare** *vt.* to radiate.

raggiera *sf.* halo of rays: *a —*, radially.

raggio *sm.* **1.** ray **2.** (*geom.*) radius **3.** (*d'azione*) range **4.** (*di ruota*) spoke || — *di sole*, sunbeam.

raggirare *vt.* to cheat.

raggiro *sm.* cheat.

raggiùngere *vt.* to reach.

raggiungimento *sm.* reaching.

raggiustare *vt.* **1.** to repair **2.** (*riordinare*) to rearrange.

raggomitolare *vt.* to roll up. ♦ **raggomitolarsi** *vr.* to roll oneself up.

raggranellare *vt.* to scrape together.

raggrinzire *vt.* to wrinkle. ♦ **raggrinzirsi** *vr.* to wrinkle, to become (*v. irr.*) wrinkled.

raggrumare *vt.* to clot. ♦ **raggrumarsi** *vr.* to clot.

raggruppamento *sm.* **1.** grouping **2.** (*gruppo*) group.

raggruppare *vt.* to group. ♦ **raggrupparsi** *vr.* to gather.

ragguagliare *vt.* **1.** (*livellare*) to level **2.** (*informare*) to inform **3.** (*paragonare*) to compare **4.** (*comm.*) to balance.

ragguaglio *sm.* **1.** (*informazione*) information (*solo sing.*) **2.** (*paragone*) comparison **3.** (*comm.*) balance.

ragguardévole *agg.* considerable.

ragia *sf.* resin: *acqua —*, turpentine.

ragionamento *sm.* reasoning.

ragionare *vi.* **1.** to reason (about) **2.** (*discutere*) to discuss (sthg.).

ragionatore *sm.* reasoner.

ragione *sf.* **1.** reason **2.** (*diritto*) right **2.** (*rapporto*) rate || *la — per cui*, the reason why; *a — veduta*, after due consideration; *aver —*, to be right; *a maggior —*, all the more reason; *aver — di qu.*, to get (*v. irr.*) the better of so.; — *sociale* (*comm.*), style.

ragionerìa *sf.* bookkeeping.

ragionévole *agg.* **1.** reasonable **2.** (*di buon senso*) sensible.

ragionevolezza *sf.* reasonableness.

ragioniere *sm.* bookkeeper.

ragliare *vi.* to bray.

raglio *sm.* bray.

ragnatela *sf.* cobweb.

ragno *sm.* spider.

ragù *sm.* ragout.

raion *sm.* rayon.

rallegramenti *sm. pl.* congratulations.

rallegrare *vt.* to cheer (up). ♦ **rallegrarsi** *vr.* **1.** to rejoice (at) **2.** (*congratularsi*) to congratulate (so. on sthg.).

rallentamento *sm.* slowing down.

rallentare *vt.* to slacken. ♦ **rallentare** *vi.* **1.** to slacken **2.** (*di velocità*) to slow down. ♦ **rallentarsi** *vr.* to get (*v. irr.*) slack.

rallentatore *sm.* (*cine*) slow motion.

ramaiolo *sm.* ladle.

ramanzina *sf.* scolding.

ramare *vt.* to copper.

ramarro *sm.* green lizard.

ramazza *sf.* broom.

rame *sm.* copper.

ramifero *agg.* copper-bearing (*attr.*).

ramificare *vi.* to ramify. ♦ **ramificarsi** *vr.* to ramify.

ramificazione *sf.* ramification.

ramingo *agg.* roving.

rammagliare *vt.* to mend a run.

rammaricare *vt.* to afflict. ♦ **rammaricarsi** *vr.* **1.** to be sorry **2.** (*lamentarsi*) to complain (of).

rammàrico *sm.* sorrow.

rammendare *vt.* to darn.

rammendatrice *sf.* darner.

rammendo *sm.* **1.** darning **2.** (*parte rammendata*) darn.

rammentare *vt.* to remember: — *qc. a qu.*, to remind so. of sthg. ♦ **rammentarsi** *vr.* to remember.

rammollimento *sm.* softening.

rammollire *vt.* to soften. ♦ **rammollirsi** *vr.* to soften, to go (*v. irr.*) soft.

rammollito *agg.* soft: *un vecchio —*, a dotard. ♦ **rammollito** *sm.* imbecile.

ramo *sm.* branch.

ramoscello *sm.* twig.

ramoso *agg.* branched.

rampa *sf.* **1.** ramp **2.** (*di scale*) flight.

rampante *agg.* rampant.

rampicante *agg.* climbing: *pianta —*, creeper.

rampino *sm.* hook.

rampogna *sf.* reproach.

rampollare *vi.* to spring (*v. irr.*).

rampollo *sm.* **1.** (*d'acqua*) spring **2.** (*di albero*) shoot **3.** (*discendente*) offspring.

rampone *sm.* **1.** (*mar.*) harpoon **2.** (*da montagna*) crampon.

rana *sf.* frog: *uomo* —, frogman (*pl.* -men); *nuotare a* —, to swim (*v. irr.*) the breast stroke.

ràncido *agg.* **1.** rancid **2.** (*fig.*) trite || *sapere di* —, to have a rancid taste.

rancio *sm.* (*mil.*) mess.

rancore *sm.* grudge.

randagio *agg.* stray.

randellare *vt.* to cudgel.

randellata *sf.* blow with a cudgel.

randello *sm.* cudgel.

ranetta *sf.* rennet.

rango *sm.* rank.

rannicchiarsi *vr.* to crouch.

rannuvolamento *sm.* clouding over.

rannuvolare *vi.* to become (*v. irr.*) cloudy, to cloud over. ♦ **rannuvolarsi** *vr.* to get (*v. irr.*) cloudy.

ranocchio *sm.* frog.

rantolare *vi.* **1.** to wheeze **2.** (*in punto di morte*) to have the death-rattle.

ràntolo *sm.* **1.** wheeze **2.** (*di morte*) death-rattle.

ranùncolo *sm.* buttercup.

rapa *sf.* turnip.

rapace *agg.* greedy. ♦ **rapace** *sm.* bird of prey.

rapacità *sf.* greed.

rapare *vt.* to crop (so.'s hair).

rapato *agg.* shorn.

ràpida *sf.* rapid.

rapidità *sf.* swiftness.

ràpido *agg.* swift. ♦ **ràpido** *sm.* express (train).

rapimento *sm.* **1.** kidnapping **2.** (*di donna*) abduction **3.** (*fig.*) rapture.

rapina *sf.* robbery.

rapinare *vt.* to rob.

rapinatore *sm.* robber.

rapire *vt.* **1.** to kidnap **2.** (*una donna*) to abduct **3.** (*fig.*) to ravish.

rapitore *sm.* **1.** kidnapper **2.** (*di donna*) abductor.

rappacificare *vt.* to reconcile. ♦ **rappacificarsi** *vr.* to become (*v. irr.*) reconciled.

rappacificazione *sf.* reconciliation.

rappezzare *vt.* to patch.

rappezzatura *sf.* **1.** patching **2.** (*parte rappezzata*) patch.

rapporto *sm.* **1.** relation **2.** (*relazione*) report **3.** (*mat.*) ratio || *chiamare a* —, to summon; *andare a*

— *da*, to report to; *essere in buoni rapporti*, to be on good terms; *sotto tutti i rapporti*, in every respect.

rapprèndere *vi.* to coagulate. ♦ **rapprèndersi** *vr.* to coagulate.

rappresaglia *sf.* retaliation: *far* —, to retaliate.

rappresentàbile *agg.* performable.

rappresentante *s.* **1.** representative **2.** (*comm.*) agent.

rappresentanza *sf.* **1.** representation **2.** (*comm.*) agency || *in* — *di*, on behalf of.

rappresentare *vt.* **1.** to represent **2.** (*comm.*) to be agent (for) **3.** (*una parte*) to play **4.** (*un'opera teatrale*) to stage. ♦ **rappresentarsi** *vr.* to imagine.

rappresentativo *agg.* representative.

rappresentazione *sf.* **1.** representation **2.** (*teat.*) performance **3.** (*cine*) exhibition.

rapsodìa *sf.* rhapsody.

rarefare *vt.* to rarefy. ♦ **rarefarsi** *vr.* to rarefy.

rarefatto *agg.* rarefied.

rarefazione *sf.* rarefaction.

rarità *sf.* rarity.

raro *agg.* rare: *rare volte*, seldom; *una bestia rara* (*fig.*), a queer fish.

rasare *vt.* **1.** to shave **2.** (*un prato*) to mow (*v. irr.*) **3.** (*lisciare*) to smooth. ♦ **rasarsi** *vr.* to shave.

rasato *agg.* **1.** shaven **2.** (*liscio*) smooth **3.** (*simile a raso*) satin (*attributivo*).

rasatura *sf.* **1.** shave **2.** (*di prato*) mowing.

raschiamento *sm.* **1.** scraping **2.** (*med.*) curettage.

raschiare *vt.* **1.** to scrape **2.** (*med.*) to curette || *raschiarsi la gola*, to clear one's throat.

raschiata *sf.* scraping.

raschiatoio *sm.* **1.** scraper **2.** (*med.*) curette.

raschiatura *sf.* scraping.

raschietto *sm.* **1.** scraper **2.** (*per cancellare*) eraser.

rasciugare *vt.* to dry.

rasentare *vt.* **1.** to graze **2.** (*confinare*) to border (on).

rasente *prep.* close to: *passare* —, to skim.

raso *agg.* V. *rasato*. ♦ **raso** *sm.* satin.

rasoio *sm.* razor.

raspa *sf.* rasp.

raspamento *sm.* rasping.

raspare *vt.* **1.** to rasp **2.** (*con le unghie*) to scratch **3.** (*frugare*) to rummage.

rassegna *sf.* **1.** (*rivista, recensione*) review **2.** (*esame*) survey || *passare in* —, to inspect.

rassegnare *vt.* to hand in: — *le dimissioni*, to resign. ♦ **rassegnarsi** *vr.* to resign oneself.

rassegnato *agg.* resigned.

rassegnazione *sf.* resignation.

rasserenare *vt.* **1.** to clear **2.** (*fig.*) to cheer up. ♦ **rasserenarsi** *vr.* to clear up.

rassettare *vt.* **1.** to tidy **2.** (*riparare*) to mend.

rassicurante *agg.* reassuring.

rassicurare *vt.* to reassure. ♦ **rassicurarsi** *vr.* to be reassured.

rassicurazione *sf.* reassurance.

rassodamento *sm.* consolidation.

rassodare *vt.* **1.** to consolidate **2.** (*indurire*) to harden. ♦ **rassodarsi** *vr.* to harden.

rassomigliante *agg.* like, alike (*pred.*).

rassomiglianza *sf.* likeness.

rassomigliare *vi.* to be like. ♦ **rassomigliarsi** *vr. rec.* to be alike.

rassottigliare *vt.* V. *assottigliare*.

rastrellamento *sm.* **1.** raking **2.** (*mil.*) mopping up **3.** (*di polizia*) combing **4.** (*draggaggio*) dragging.

rastrellare *vt.* **1.** to rake **2.** (*mil.*) to mop up **3.** (*di polizia*) to comb **4.** (*dragare*) to drag.

rastrelliera *sf.* rack.

rastrello *sm.* rake.

rastremare *vt.* to taper. ♦ **rastremarsi** *vr.* to taper.

rata *sf.* instalment: *a rate*, by instalments.

rateale *agg.* by instalments.

rateare *vt.* to divide into instalments.

ratifica *sf.* ratification.

ratificare *vt.* to ratify.

ratificatore *sm.* ratifier.

ratificazione *sf.* V. *ratifica*.

ratto[1] *sm.* **1.** kidnapping **2.** (*di donna*) rape.

ratto[2] *sm.* (*topo*) rat.

rattoppare *vt.* to patch (up).

rattoppo *sm.* **1.** patching up **2.** (*toppa*) patch.

rattrappimento *sm.* **1.** (*intorpidi-*

mento) benumbing **2.** (*contrazione*) contraction.

rattrappire *vt.* **1.** (*contrarre*) to contract **2.** (*intorpidire*) to benumb.

rattristare *vt.* to grieve. ♦ **rattristarsi** *vr.* **1.** (*divenir triste*) to become (*v. irr.*) sad **2.** (*essere triste*) to be sad.

raucèdine *sf.* hoarseness: *avere la* —, to have a hoarse voice.

ràuco *agg.* hoarse.

ravanello *sm.* radish.

ravvedersi *vr.* to mend one's way.

ravvedimento *sm.* reformation.

ravviamento *sm.* tidying (up).

ravviare *vt.* to tidy (up).

ravvicinamento *sm.* **1.** approach **2.** (*conciliazione*) reconciliation.

ravvicinare *vt.* **1.** to bring (*v. irr.*) closer **2.** (*riconciliare*) to reconcile **3.** (*confrontare*) to compare. ♦ **ravvicinarsi** *vr.* **1.** to draw (*v. irr.*) closer **2.** (*riconciliarsi*) to become (*v. irr.*) reconciled.

ravvisàbile *agg.* recognizable.

ravvisare *vt.* to recognize.

ravvivamento *sm.* revival.

ravvivare *vt.* **1.** to revive **2.** (*rallegrare*) to brighten up || — *il fuoco*, to poke the fire. ♦ **ravvivarsi** *vr.* **1.** to revive **2.** (*rallegrarsi*) to brighten up.

raziocinante *agg.* reasoning.

raziocinio *sm.* **1.** reason **2.** (*buon senso*) common sense.

razionale *agg.* rational.

razionalismo *sm.* rationalism.

razionalista *s.* rationalist.

razionalità *sf.* rationality.

razionamento *sm.* rationing.

razionare *vt.* to ration.

razione *sf.* ration.

razza[1] *sf.* **1.** race **2.** (*di animali*) breed **3.** (*genere*) kind.

razza[2] *sf.* (*itt.*) ray.

razzìa *sf.* **1.** raid **2.** (*insetticida*) insecticide || *far* —, to plunder.

razziale *agg.* racial.

razziare *vt.* to plunder.

razziatore *sm.* plunderer.

razzismo *sm.* racialism.

razzista *s.* racialist.

razzo *sm.* rocket.

razzolare *vi.* to scratch about.

re[1] *sm.* king.

re[2] *sm.* (*mus.*) D, re.

reagente *sm.* reagent.

reagire *vi.* to react.

reale¹ agg. real.

reale² agg. (del re) royal.

realismo sm. realism.

realista¹ agg. e s. realist.

realista² agg. e s. (del re) royalist.

realìstico agg. realistic.

realizzàbile agg. realizable.

realizzare vt. to realize. ♦ **realizzarsi** vr. 1. to be realized 2. (avverarsi) to come (v. irr.) true.

realizzatore sm. realizer.

realizzazione sf. 1. realization 2. (teat.) staging 3. (cine) production.

realtà sf. reality.

reame sm. kingdom.

reato sm. 1. offence 2. (crimine) crime.

reattivo agg. reactive. ♦ **reattivo** sm. reagent.

reattore sm. 1. reactor 2. (aereo) jet.

reazionario agg. e sm. reactionary.

reazione sf. reaction: motore a —, jet engine; aereo a —,ˈ jet.

reboante agg. 1. thundering 2. (fig.) bombastic.

rebus sm. rebus.

recalcitrare vi. V. ricalcitrare.

recapitare vt. to deliver.

recàpito sm. 1. (consegna) delivery 2. (indirizzo) address.

recare vt. 1. to bring (v. irr.) 2. (fig.) to bear (v. irr.) 3. (causare) to cause. ♦ **recarsi** vr. to go (v. irr.).

recèdere vi. to withdraw (v. irr.).

recensione sf. review.

recensire vt. to review.

recensore sm. reviewer.

recente agg. recent.

recentemente avv. recently.

recentissime sf. pl. latest news.

recessione sf. recession.

recessivo agg. receding.

recesso sm. 1. recess 2. (recessione) recession 3. (giur.) withdrawal.

recettivo agg. V. ricettivo.

recezione sf. reception.

recìdere vt. to cut (v. irr.) off.

recidiva sf. relapse.

recidività sf. 1. (giur.) recidivism 2. (med.) relapse.

recidivo agg. 1. (giur.) recidivous 2. (med.) relapsing. ♦ **recidivo** sm. 1. (giur.) recidivist 2. (med.) relapser.

recintare vt. to fence.

recinto sm. enclosure.

recipiente sm. vessel.

reciprocamente avv. reciprocally.

reciprocità sf. reciprocity.

recìproco agg. reciprocal.

recisamente avv. resolutely.

recisione sf. excision.

reciso agg. 1. cut 2. (fig.) resolute.

rècita sf. performance.

recitare vt. 1. to recite 2. (teat.) to act || — una parte, to play a part.

recitativo sm. recitative.

recitazione sf. 1. recitation 2. (teat.) acting.

reclamante sm. claimant.

reclamare vt. to claim. ♦ **reclamare** vi. to complain.

reclamìstico agg. advertising.

reclamizzare vt. to advertise.

reclamo sm. complaint.

reclinare vt. to bow.

reclusione sf. 1. seclusion 2. (prigionia) imprisonment.

recluso agg. 1. secluded 2. (imprigionato) imprisoned. ♦ **recluso** sm. prisoner.

rècluta sf. 1. recruit 2. (fig.) novice.

reclutamento sm. enlistment.

reclutare vt. to enlist, to recruit.

recòndito agg. hidden.

recriminare vi. 1. to recriminate 2. (lamentarsi) to complain.

recriminazione sf. 1. recrimination 2. (lamentela) complaint.

recrudescente agg. recrudescent.

recrudescenza sf. recrudescence.

redarguire vt. to reproach.

redattore sm. 1. drawer 2. (di giornale) member of the editorial staff || — capo, editor.

redazionale agg. editorial.

redazione sf. 1. drawing up 2. (di giornale) editing 2. (i redattori) editorial staff 3. (ufficio) editorial office.

redditività sf. profitableness.

redditizio agg. profitable.

rèddito sm. 1. income 2. (dello Stato) revenue.

redento agg. redeemed.

redentore sm. redeemer.

redenzione sf. redemption.

redìgere vt. to draw (v. irr.) up.

redìmere vt. to redeem.

redimìbile agg. redeemable.

rèdini sf. pl. reins.

redivivo agg. 1. restored to life 2. (nuovo) new.

rèduce agg. back from. ♦ **rèduce** sm. veteran.

referendum *sm.* referendum.
referenza *sf.* reference.
referenziare *vt.* to give (*v. irr.*) references.
referto *sm.* report.
refettorio *sm.* refectory.
refezione *sf.* meal.
refrattario *agg.* refractory: *terra refrattaria,* fireclay.
refrigerante *agg.* e *sm.* refrigerant.
refrigerare *vt.* to refrigerate.
refrigeratore *sm.* refrigerator.
refrigerazione *sf.* refrigeration.
refrigerio *sm.* 1. cool 2. (*sollievo*) relief.
refurtiva *sf.* stolen goods (*pl.*).
refuso *sm.* misprint, wrong fount.
regalare *vt.* 1. to present (so. with sthg.) 2. (*vendere a poco prezzo*) to sell (*v. irr.*) cheap.
regalato *agg.* (*venduto a buon prezzo*) cheap.
regale *agg.* regal.
regalìa *sf.* (*mancia*) gratuity.
regalo *sm.* present: *in —,* as a present.
regata *sf.* regatta.
reggente *agg.* e *sm.* regent.
reggenza *sf.* regency.
règgere *vt.* 1. (*sorreggere*) to hold (*v. irr.*) 2. (*dirigere*) to run (*v. irr.*) 3. (*gramm.*) to govern || *— una prova,* to stand (*v. irr.*) a test. ♦ règgere *vi.* 1. (*resistere*) to hold (out) 2. (*stare in piedi, anche fig.*) to stand. ♦ règgersi *vr.* 1. (*sostenersi*) to stand 2. (*appoggiarsi a*) to hold (on, to).
reggia *sf.* royal palace.
reggicalze *sm.* girdle.
reggimento *sm.* (*mil.*) regiment.
reggipetto *sm.* bra.
reggiseno *sm.* V. *reggipetto.*
reggitore *sm.* ruler.
regìa *sf.* 1. (*teat.*) production 2. (*cine*) direction || *— di,* produced, directed by.
regicida *sm.* regicide.
regicidio *sm.* regicide.
regime *sm.* 1. regime 2. (*mecc.*) speed 3. (*dieta*) diet || *essere a —,* to be on a diet.
regina *sf.* queen.
regio *agg.* royal.
regionale *agg.* regional.
regionalismo *sm.* regionalism.
regionalista *s.* regionalist.
regione *sf.* 1. region 2. (*divisione amministrativa; fig.*) province.

regista *sm.* 1. (*teat.*) producer 2. (*cine*) director.
registràbile *agg.* registrable, recordable.
registrare *vt.* 1. to register 2. (*comm.*) to book 3. (*segnare; cine*) to record 4. (*su nastro*) to tape-record 5. (*mecc.*) to adjust.
registratore *sm.* 1. (*persona*) registrar 2. (*strumento*) register: *— di cassa,* cash-register 3. (*magnetofono*) taperecorder.
registrazione *sf.* 1. registration 2. (*comm.*) entry 3. (*di suoni*) recording.
registro *sm.* 1. register 2. (*comm.*) book 3. (*ufficio governativo*) registry.
regnante *agg.* reigning. ♦ regnante *s.* sovereign.
regnare *vi.* to reign.
regno *sm.* 1. reign 2. (*territorio; fig.*) kingdom.
règola *sf.* 1. rule 2. (*esempio*) example 3. (*misura*) moderation || *in —,* in order; *è di —,* it is the custom.
regolamentare *agg.* prescribed: *non essere —,* to be against the rules.
regolamentarmente *avv.* according to the rules.
regolamentazione *sf.* regulations (*pl.*).
regolamento *sm.* regulation: *— dei conti,* settlement.
regolare[1] *vt.* 1. to regulate 2. (*sistemare*) to settle 3. (*sintonizzare*) to tune (in). ♦ regolarsi *vr.* 1. to act 2. (*controllarsi*) to control oneself.
regolare[2] *agg.* regular.
regolarità *sf.* regularity.
regolarizzare *vt.* to regularize.
regolarizzazione *sf.* regularization.
regolatamente *avv.* 1. regularly 2. (*con moderazione*) moderately.
regolatezza *sf.* sobriety.
regolato *agg.* regular.
regolatore *agg.* regulating: *piano —,* townplan. ♦ regolatore *sm.* regulator.
regolazione *sf.* regulation.
règolo *sm.* rule: *— calcolatore,* slide rule.
regredire *vi.* to regress.
regressione *sf.* regression.
regressivo *agg.* regressive.
regresso *sm.* regress.

reietto agg. rejected. ♦ **reietto** sm. outcast.

reiezione sf. rejection.

reincarnare vt. to reincarnate. ♦ **reincarnarsi** vr. to be reincarnated.

reincarnazione sf. reincarnation.

reintegrare vt. 1. to restore 2. (risarcire) to indemnify.

reintegrazione sf. 1. restoration 2. (risarcimento) indemnification.

reità sf. 1. (colpevolezza) guiltiness 2. (malvagità) wickedness.

reiterare vt. to reiterate.

reiterazione sf. reiteration.

relativamente avv. comparatively: — a, as regards.

relativismo sm. relativism.

relativìstico agg. relativistic.

relatività sf. relativity.

relativo agg. 1. relative 2. (rispettivo) respective 3. (attinente) pertinent.

relatore sm. 1. relator 2. (di leggi) proposer.

relazionare vt. to relate.

relazione sf. 1. report 2. (legame) relation 3. (contatto) touch 4. (conoscenza) acquaintance || aver — con, to be connected with; essere in buone relazioni, to be on good terms; mettersi in — con, to get (v. irr.) into touch with; — amorosa, love affair.

relegare vt. to relegate.

relegazione sf. relegation.

religione sf. 1. religion 2. (culto) worship.

religiosità sf. piety.

religioso agg. e sm. religious.

reliquia sf. relic.

reliquario sm. reliquary.

relitto sm. 1. wreckage 2. (di persona) outcast.

remare vi. 1. to row 2. (con pagaia) to paddle.

remata sf. 1. row 2. (colpo di remo) stroke.

rematore sm. oarsman (pl. -men).

remiganti sf. pl. remiges.

remigare vi. 1. to row 2. (di ali) to flap.

reminiscenza sf. reminiscence.

remissione sf. (giur.) remission.

remissività sf. submissiveness.

remissivo agg. submissive.

remo sm. oar.

rèmora sf. 1. (ostacolo) obstacle 2. (indugio) delay 3. (zool.) remora.

remoto agg. remote: passato — (gramm.) past simple tense.

remunerare vt. to remunerate.

remunerativo agg. remunerative.

remunerazione sf. remuneration.

rena sf. sand.

renale agg. renal.

rèndere vt. 1. to render 2. (fruttare) to yield || — conto di, to account for; — giustizia a qu., to do (v. irr.) so. justice. ♦ **rèndersi** vr. to become (v. irr.) || — conto di, to realize.

rendiconto sm. 1. statement 2. (resoconto) report.

rendimento sm. 1. rendering 2. (resa) output 3. (efficienza) efficiency.

rèndita sf. 1. revenue 2. (privata) income.

rene sm. kidney.

renella sf. gravel.

reni sf. pl. back (sing.).

renitente agg. reluctant || essere — alla leva, to fail to appear at the draft.

renitenza sf. reluctance || — alla leva, failure to register for national service.

renna sf. reindeer (pl. invariato).

renoso agg. sandy.

reo agg. guilty. ♦ **reo** sm. culprit.

reòmetro sm. rheometer.

reòstato sm. rheostat.

reparto sm. 1. department 2. (mil.) detachment.

repellente agg. repulsive.

repentaglio sm. danger: a —, in danger.

repentino agg. sudden.

reperìbile agg. to be found (pred.).

reperire vt. to find (v. irr.).

reperto sm. 1. (giur.) evidence 2. (med.) report.

repertorio sm. (teat.) repertoire.

rèplica sf. 1. reply 2. (obiezione) objection 3. (copia) copy 4. (teat.) performance || avere molte repliche (teat.), to have a long run.

replicare vt. 1. to reply 2. (obiettare) to object 3. (ripetere) to repeat.

reprensìbile agg. reprehensible.

reprensione sf. reprehension.

repressione sf. repression.

repressivo agg. repressive.

represso agg. repressed.

reprimenda sf. reprimand.

reprìmere vt. to repress.

rèprobo agg. e sm. reprobate.
repùbblica sf. republic.
repubblicano agg. e sm. republican.
reputare vt. 1. to consider 2. (pensare) to think (v. irr.).
reputazione sf. reputation.
requie sf. rest.
requisire vt. to requisition.
requisito sm. qualification.
requisitoria sf. 1. indictment 2. (giur.) summing up.
requisizione sf. requisition.
resa sf. (rendimento) yield 2. (capitolazione) surrender || — dei conti, rendering of accounts.
rescìndere vt. to rescind.
rescindìbile agg. rescindable.
rescissione sf. rescission.
reseda sf. reseda.
resezione sf. resection.
residente agg. e sm. resident.
residenza sf. residence.
residenziale agg. residential.
residuare vi. to be left.
residuato agg. residual. ♦ **residuato** sm. — di guerra, war surplus.
residuo agg. remaining. ♦ **residuo** sm. residue: residui radioattivi, radioactive waste.
rèsina sf. resin.
resinoso agg. resinous.
resipiscenza sf. resipiscence.
resistente agg. 1. resistant 2. (forte) strong.
resistenza sf. resistance.
resìstere vi. 1. to resist 2. (sopportare) to endure.
resoconto sm. report.
respingente sm. buffer.
respìngere vt. 1. to repel 2. (rimandare) to return 3. (rifiutare) to reject 4. (scol.) to pluck.
respinta sf. V. parata.
respiràbile agg. breathable.
respirare vt. e vi. to breathe.
respiratore sm. respirator.
respiratorio agg. respiratory.
respirazione sf. respiration, breathing.
respiro sm. 1. breath 2. (riposo) respite.
responsàbile agg. responsible (for).
responsabilità sf. responsibility.
responso sm. 1. response 2. (opinione) opinion.
responsorio sm. responsory.
ressa sf. crowd: far — intorno a

qu., to crowd round so.
resta sf. 1. (di cipolla, aglio ecc.) string 2. (di lancia) rest.
restante agg. e sm. V. rimanente.
restare vi. V. rimanere.
restaurare vt. to restore.
restauratore sm. restorer.
restaurazione sf. restoration.
restàuro sm. restoration: in —, under repair.
restìo agg. loath, reluctant.
restituire vt. 1. to return 2. (reintegrare) to restore.
restituzione sf. 1. return 2. (reintegrazione) restoration.
resto sm. 1. rest 2. (mat.) remainder 3. (di denaro) change || resti, remains; del —, on the other hand.
restringente sm. astringent.
restrìngere vt. 1. (contrarre) to contract 2. (limitare) to limit 3. (un vestito) to tighten. ♦ **restrìngersi** vr. 1. to get (v. irr.) narrower 2. (contrarsi) to contract 3. (affollarsi) to close up 4. (di tessuti) to shrink (v. irr.).
restringimento sm. 1. narrowing 2. (contrazione) contraction 3. (limitazione) limitation 4. (di tessuto) shrinking 5. (di vestito) tightening.
restrittivo agg. restrictive.
restrizione sf. restriction.
retaggio sm. heritage.
retata sf. 1. haul 2. (di polizia) roundup.
rete sf. 1. net 2. (di letto) wire netting 3. (intreccio) network.
reticella sf. 1. (per capelli) hair-net 2. (per bagagli) luggage-rack.
reticente agg. reticent.
reticenza sf. reticence.
reticolato sm. 1. (mil.) barbed-wire entanglement 2. (tracciato di linee) network.
retìcolo sm. 1. (anat.) reticulum (pl. -la) 2. (ott.) reticle.
rètina sf. retina.
retina sf. V. reticella.
rètore sm. rhetorician.
retòrica sf. rhetoric.
retòrico agg. rhetorical.
retrarre vt. to retract.
retràttile agg. retractile.
retrattilità sf. retractility.
retribuire vt. to pay (v. irr.).
retribuzione sf. payment.
retrivo agg. reactionary.
retro sm. back.

retroattività sf. retroactivity.

retroattivo agg. retroactive.

retrobottega sm. back of the shop.

retrocèdere vi. to withdraw (v. irr.). ♦ retrocèdere vt. 1. (mil.) to degrade 2. to retrocede.

retrocessione sf. 1. retrocession 2. (mil.) degradation.

retrodatare vt. to date back.

retrògrado agg. 1. out-of-date 2. (reazionario) reactionary.

retroguardia sf. rear-guard.

retromarcia sf. reverse-gear.

retroscena sf. 1. back of the stage 2. (fig.) intrigue.

retrospettivo agg. retrospective.

retrostante agg. at the back.

retroterra sm. hinterland.

retroversione sf. 1. retroversion 2. (di traduzione) back version.

retrovìe sf. pl. zone behind the front (sing).

retrovisore sm. specchietto —, driving mirror.

retta¹ sf. (geom.) straight line.

retta² sf. (di pensione) terms (pl.).

retta³ sf. dar — a qu., to listen to so.

rettale agg. rectal.

rettamente avv. 1. (giustamente) rightly 2. (onestamente) honestly.

rettangolare agg. rectangular.

rettàngolo sm. rectangle.

rettìfica sf. 1. rectification 2. (mecc.) grinding.

rettificare vt. 1. to rectify 2. (mecc.) to grind (v. irr.).

rettificatrice sf. grinder.

rettificazione sf. V. rettìfica.

rettifilo sm. straight, stretch.

rèttile sm. reptile.

rettilìneo agg. rectilinear. ♦ rettilìneo sm. straight, stretch.

rettitùdine sf. righteousness, honesty.

retto agg. 1. straight 2. (geom.; giusto) right. ♦ retto sm. (anat.) rectum (pl. -ta).

rettorato sm. rectorship.

rettore sm. 1. rector 2. (di università) chancellor.

rèuma sm. rheumàtism.

reumàtico agg. e sm. rheumatic.

reumatismo sm. V. reuma.

reverendo agg. reverend. ♦ reverendo sm. clergyman (pl. -men).

reversìbile agg. reversible.

reversibilità sf. reversibility.

reversione sf. reversion.

revisionare vt. 1. (mecc.) to overhaul 2. (comm.) to audit.

revisione sf. 1. revision 2. (mecc.) overhaul 3. (comm.) audit.

revisionismo sm. revisionism.

revisore sm. 1. reviser 2. (comm.) auditor.

reviviscenza sf. reviviscence.

rèvoca sf. revocation.

revocàbile agg. revocable.

revocare vt. 1. (richiamare) to recall 2. (giur.) to revoke.

revocazione sf. revocation.

revolverata sf. revolver shot.

revulsione sf. revulsion.

revulsivo agg. revulsive.

riabbottonare vt. to button again.

riabilitare vt. to rehabilitate.

riabilitazione sf. rehabilitation.

riaccèndere vt. 1. to relight 2. (radio, luce ecc.) to turn on again. ♦ riaccèndersi vr. 1. to brighten again 2. (riprender fuoco) to catch (v. irr.) fire again.

riaccompagnare vt. to take (v. irr.) home.

riacquistare vt. 1. to buy (v. irr.) again 2. (riprendere) to recover.

riadattare vt. to adapt again. ♦ riadattarsi vr. (rassegnarsi) to resign oneself again.

riaddormentare vt. to send (v. irr.) to sleep again. ♦ riaddormentarsi vr. to fall (v. irr.) asleep again.

riaffacciare vt. to present again. ♦ riaffacciarsi vr. to reappear, to appear again.

riaffermare vt. to affirm again. ♦ riaffermarsi vr. to reaffirm oneself.

riafferrare vt. to grasp again. ♦ riafferrarsi vr. to catch (v. irr.) hold of (so., sth.) again.

riallacciare vt. 1. to fasten again 2. (riprendere) to resume.

riallargare vt. to widen again. ♦ riallargarsi vr. to widen again.

rialto sm. rise, height.

rialzamento sm. 1. raising 2. (rialzo) rise, height.

rialzare vt. 1. to raise 2. (rendere più alto) to make (v. irr.) higher. ♦ rialzarsi vr. to rise (v. irr.) again.

rialzato agg. piano —, ground floor.

rialzo sm. 1. rise 2. (di sostegno) support.

riamare vt. to love again.

riamméttere vt. to readmit.

rianimare vt. to revive. ♦ **rianimarsi** vr. 1. (riprendere allegria) to cheer up 2. (riprendere coraggio) to take (v. irr.) courage again.

riapertura sf. reopening.

riapparire vi. to reappear.

riaprire vt. to open again. ♦ **riaprirsi** vr. to open again.

riarmare vt. to rearm. ♦ **riarmarsi** vr. to rearm.

riarmo sm. rearmament.

riarso agg. parched.

riassestare vt. to readjust. ♦ **riassestarsi** vr. to readjust.

riassettare vt. to put (v. irr.) in order again.

riassetto sm. rearrangement.

riassorbire vt. to reabsorb.

riassùmere vt. 1. (assumere di nuovo) to take (v. irr.) on again 2. (riepilogare) to sum up 3. (riprendere) to resume.

riassuntivo agg. summarizing.

riassunto sm. summary.

riattaccare vt. 1. (con colla) to stick (v. irr.) again 2. (ricucire) to sew (v. irr.) 3. (riprendere) to begin (v. irr.) again 4. (mil.) to attack again 5. (tel.) to hang (v. irr.) up. ♦ **riattaccarsi** vr. to stick again.

riattamento sm. repair.

riattare vt. to repair.

riattivare vt. to restore.

riavere vt. 1. to have again 2. (ricuperare) to get (v. irr.) back. ♦ **riaversi** vr. to recover.

riavvicinare vt. 1. to approach again 2. (riconciliare) to reconcile. ♦ **riavvicinarsi** vr. to approach again 2. (riconciliarsi) to be reconciled.

ribadire vt. to rivet.

ribalderìa sf. rascality.

ribaldo sm. rascal.

ribalta sf. 1. (teat.) footlights (pl.) 2. (fig.) limelight.

ribaltàbile agg. overturnable.

ribaltare vt. to overturn. ♦ **ribaltarsi** vr. to capsize.

ribassare vt. to reduce. ♦ **ribassare** vi. to fall (v. irr.).

ribasso sm. 1. fall 2. (sconto) discount.

ribàttere vt. 1. to beat (v. irr.) again 2. (ribadire) to rivet 3. (confutare) to confute. ♦ **ribàttere** vi. to insist.

ribattezzare vt. to rename.

ribellarsi vr. to rebel.

ribelle agg. rebellious. ♦ **ribelle** s. rebel.

ribellione sf. rebellion.

ribes sm. gooseberry.

riboccante agg. overflowing (with).

riboccare vi. to overflow (with).

ribollimento sm. ebullition.

ribollire vi. to boil.

ribollitura sf. reboiling.

ribrezzo sm. disgust: fare —, to disgust.

ributtante agg. disgusting.

ributtare vt. 1. to throw (v. irr.) again 2. (respingere) to repel 3. (disgustare) to disgust.

ricacciare vt. 1. (respingere) to push (out, back) 2. (ficcare di nuovo) to thrust (v. irr.) again. ♦ **ricacciarsi** vr. to plunge again.

ricadere vi. 1. to fall (v. irr.) again 2. (avere una ricaduta) to relapse 3. (pendere) to hang (v. irr.).

ricaduta sf. relapse.

ricalcare vt. 1. to pull down 2. (un disegno) to transfer || — le orme di qu., to tread (v. irr.) in so.'s steps.

ricalcitrante agg. recalcitrant.

ricalcitrare vi. to recalcitrate.

ricamare vt. e vi. to embroider.

ricamatore sm. embroiderer.

ricamatrice sf. embroideress.

ricambiare vt. 1. to change again 2. (contraccambiare) to return.

ricambio sm. 1. replacement 2. (med.) metabolism || di —, spare (agg. attr.).

ricamo sm. embroidery: un —, a piece of embroidery.

ricapitolare vt. to summarize || ricapitolando, in short.

ricapitolazione sf. summary.

ricaricare vt. 1. to reload 2. (di batteria) to recharge 3. (di orologio) to wind (v. irr.) up again.

ricascare vi. V. ricadere.

ricattare vt. to blackmail.

ricattatore sm. blackmailer.

ricattatorio agg. blackmailing.

ricatto sm. blackmail.

ricavare vt. 1. to draw (v. irr.) 2. (ottenere) to get (v. irr.).

ricavato sm. proceeds (pl.).

ricavo sm. V. ricavato.

riccamente avv. richly.

ricchezza sf. wealth (solo sing.).

riccio[1] agg. curly.

riccio² *sm.* **1.** curl **2.** (*bot.*) chestnut husk **3.** (*zool.*) hedgehog **4.** (*di mare*) sea-urchin.

ricciuto *agg.* curly.

ricco *agg.* rich: — *di*, rich in.

ricerca *sf.* **1.** search **2.** (*scientifica*) research **3.** (*indagine*) investigation.

ricercare *vt.* **1.** (*cercare*) to seek (*v. irr.*) for **2.** (*investigare*) to investigate **3.** (*cercare di nuovo*) to look for (so., sthg.) again.

ricercatezza *sf.* refinement.

ricercato *agg.* **1.** (*richiesto*) sought--after **2.** (*raffinato*) refined **3.** (*insolito*) far-fetched **4.** (*dalla polizia*) wanted.

ricercatore *sm.* **1.** searcher **2.** (*scientifico*) researcher.

ricetta *sf.* **1.** (*med.*) prescription **2.** (*cuc.*) recipe.

ricettàcolo *sm.* receptacle.

ricettare *vt.* (*custodire cose rubate*) to receive.

ricettario *sm.* **1.** (*med.*) book of prescriptions **2.** (*cuc.*) book of recipes.

ricettatore *sm.* receiver.

ricettazione *sf.* receiving of stolen goods.

ricettività *sf.* receptivity.

ricettivo *agg.* receptive.

ricevente *agg.* receiving. ♦ **ricevente** *s.* receiver.

ricévere *vt.* to receive.

ricevimento *sm.* **1.** receipt **2.** (*festa*) party.

ricevitore *sm.* receiver.

ricevitorìa *sf.* receiving-office.

ricevuta *sf.* receipt: *accusare* —, to acknowledge receipt.

ricezione *vt.* reception.

richiamare *vt.* **1.** to call again **2.** (*far tornare*) to recall **3.** (*attirare*) to attract **4.** (*rimproverare*) to rebuke || — *all'ordine*, to call to order. ♦ **richiamarsi** *vr.* (*riferirsi*) to refer.

richiamata *sf.* recall.

richiamato *sm.* (*mil.*) re-drafted soldier.

richiamo *sm.* **1.** recall **2.** (*allettamento*) call.

richiedente *s.* applicant.

richièdere *vt.* **1.** to ask (for sthg., so.) again **2.** (*chiedere*) to ask for **3.** (*in restituzione*) to ask (for sthg.) back **4.** (*necessitare di*) to require.

richiesta *sf.* **1.** request: *dietro* —, at request **2.** (*comm.*) demand.

richiùdere *vt.* to close again. ♦ **richiùdersi** *vr.* to close again.

rìcino *sm.* castor-oil plant: *olio di* —, castor-oil.

ricognitore *sm.* (*mil.*) scout.

ricognizione *sf.* reconnaissance.

ricollegare *vt.* to connect. ♦ **ricollegarsi** *vr.* to be connected.

ricollocamento *sm.* replacement.

ricolmare *vt.* **1.** to fill up **2.** (*fig.*) to load.

ricolmo *agg.* **1.** full **2.** (*fig.*) loaded (with).

ricominciare *vt.* to begin (*v. irr.*) again.

ricomparire *vi.* to reappear.

ricompensa *sf.* reward: *in* —, as a reward.

ricompensare *vt.* to reward.

ricomperare *vt.* to buy (*v. irr.*) again.

ricomporre *vt.* to recompose.

ricomposizione *sf.* recomposition.

riconciliare *vt.* to reconcile. ♦ **riconciliarsi** *vr.* to be reconciled.

riconciliatore *sm.* reconciler.

riconciliazione *sf.* reconciliation.

ricondurre *vt.* to take (*v. irr.*) back, to bring (*v. irr.*) back.

riconferma *sf.* reconfirmation.

riconfermare *vt.* to reconfirm.

riconfortare *vt.* to cheer up. ♦ **riconfortarsi** *vr.* to cheer up.

ricongiùngere *vt.* to join again. ♦ **ricongiùngersi** *vr.* to join again.

ricongiungimento *sm.* reunion.

riconnèttere *vt.* to connect again.

riconoscente *agg.* grateful.

riconoscenza *sf.* gratitude.

riconòscere *vt.* to recognize.

riconoscìbile *agg.* recognizable.

riconoscimento *sm.* **1.** recognition **2.** (*ammissione*) admission.

riconquista *sf.* recapture.

riconquistare *vt.* to conquer again.

riconsegna *sf.* return.

riconsegnare *vt.* to redeliver.

riconsiderare *vt.* to reconsider.

riconversione *sf.* reconversion.

riconvocare *vt.* to resummon.

riconvocazione *sf.* resummons.

ricopiare *vt.* to copy.

ricopiatura *sf.* (re)copying.

ricoprire *vt.* **1.** to cover **2.** (*coprire di nuovo*) to cover again **3.** (*fig.*) to load.

ricordare *vt.* **1.** to remember **2.** (*chiamare alla memoria altrui*) to remind (so. of sthg.) **3.** (*nominare*) to mention. ♦ **ricordarsi** *vr.* to remember.

ricordo *sm.* **1.** memory **2.** (*oggetto ricordo*) souvenir **3.** (*memorie*) (*lett.*) memoirs (*pl.*).

ricorrente *agg.* recurrent.

ricorrenza *sf.* **1.** recurrence **2.** (*anniversario*) anniversary **3.** (*occasione*) occasion.

ricòrrere *vi.* **1.** (*ripetersi*) to recur **2.** (*rivolgersi*) to apply **3.** (*fare appello*) to appeal **4.** (*valersi*) to resort.

ricorso *sm.* **1.** (*ritorno*) return **2.** (*appello*) appeal || *su — di*, on a petition by.

ricostituente *agg. e sm.* tonic.

ricostituire *vt.* to form again. ♦ **ricostituirsi** *vr.* to form again.

ricostituzione *sf.* reconstitution.

ricostruire *vt.* to reconstruct.

ricostruttore *agg.* reconstructive. ♦ **ricostruttore** *sm.* reconstructor.

ricostruzione *sf.* reconstruction.

ricoverare *vt.* to shelter: *— in ospedale*, to hospitalize. ♦ **ricoverarsi** *vr.* to take (*v. irr.*) shelter.

ricòvero *sm.* **1.** sheltering **2.** (*in ospedale*) hospitalization **3.** (*ospizio*) home.

ricreare[1] *vt.* to re-create.

ricreare[2] *vt.* (*divertire*) to recreate. ♦ **ricrearsi** *vr.* to recreate.

ricreativo *agg.* recreative.

ricreazione *sf.* recreation: *ora della —*, playtime.

ricrédersi *vr.* to change one's mind.

ricréscere *vi.* to grow (*v. irr.*) again.

ricréscita *sf.* fresh growth.

ricucire *vt.* **1.** to sew (*v. irr.*) up **2.** (*cucire di nuovo*) to sew (*v. irr.*) again.

ricucitura *sf.* sewing up.

ricuòcere *vt. e vi.* **1.** to cook again **2.** (*al forno*) to bake again.

ricuperàbile *agg.* recoverable.

ricuperare *vt.* **1.** to recover **2.** (*di tempo*) to make (*v. irr.*) up for.

ricùpero *sm.* recovery.

ricurvare *vt.* **1.** to bend (*v. irr.*) **2.** (*curvare di nuovo*) to bend again.

ricurvo *agg.* bent.

ricusàbile *agg.* refusable.

ricusare *vt.* to refuse.

ridacchiare *vi.* to giggle.

ridanciano *agg.* jolly.

ridare *vt.* **1.** to give (*v. irr.*) again **2.** (*restituire*) to return.

ridda *sf.* turmoil.

ridente *agg.* **1.** smiling **2.** (*di luogo*) charming.

rìdere *vi.* to laugh (at): *per —*, for fun. ♦ **rìdersi** *vr.* to make (*v. irr.*) fun (of).

ridestare *vt.* **1.** to wake (*v. irr.*) (up) again **2.** (*destare*) to awaken. ♦ **ridestarsi** *vr.* **1.** to wake (up) again **2.** (*destarsi*) to awake.

ridicolàggine *sf.* nonsense (*solo sing.*).

ridìcolo *agg.* ridiculous. ♦ **ridìcolo** *sm.* ridicule.

ridimensionare *vt.* to reorganize.

ridire *vt.* **1.** to say (*v. irr.*) again, to tell (*v. irr.*) again **2.** (*riferire*) to repeat **3.** (*obiettare*) to object.

ridiscéndere *vi.* to come (*v. irr.*) down again, to go (*v. irr.*) down again.

ridiscòrrere *vi.* to talk again.

ridiventare *vi.* to become (*v. irr.*) again.

ridomandare *vt.* to ask again.

ridonare *vt.* **1.** to give (*v. irr.*) again **2.** (*restituire*) to give back.

ridondante *agg.* redundant.

ridondanza *sf.* redundancy.

ridondare *vi.* **1.** to be redundant **2.** (*risultare*) to redound.

ridosso (*nella loc. avv.*) *a — di*, close to.

ridotta *sf.* redoubt.

ridotto *agg.* **1.** reduced **2.** (*di libro*) abridged || *mal —*, in a sorry plight. ♦ **ridotto** *sm.* (*teat.*) foyer.

riducente *agg.* reducing. ♦ **riducente** *sm.* reducer.

riducìbile *agg.* reducible.

ridurre *vt.* **1.** to reduce **2.** (*adattare*) to adapt **3.** (*un libro*) to abridge. ♦ **ridursi** *vr.* **1.** to be reduced **2.** (*restringersi*) to shrink (*v. irr.*).

riduttore *agg. e sm.* V. *riducente*.

riduzione *sf.* **1.** reduction **2.** (*sconto*) discount **3.** (*cine; tv*) adaptation **4.** (*di libro*) abridgement.

riecheggiare *vt. e vi.* to re-echo.

riedificare *vt.* to rebuild (*v. irr.*).

riedificazione *sf.* rebuilding.

rieducare *vt.* to re-educate.

rieducazione *sf.* re-education.

rielaborare *vt.* to re-elaborate.

rielèggere vt. to re-elect.
rieleggìbile agg. re-elegible.
rielezione sf. re-election.
riemèrgere vi. to re-emerge.
riemersione sf. re-emergence.
riempire vt. to fill. ♦ **riempirsi** vr. to fill.
riempitivo sm. filling.
rientrante agg. receding.
rientranza sf. recess.
rientrare vi. 1. to re-enter 2. (tornare) to return 3. (far parte) to be part (of) 4. (piegare in dentro) to recede.
rientro sm. 1. recess 2. (astronautica) retro-firing 3. (ritorno) return.
riepilogare vt. to recapitulate.
riepìlogo sm. recapitulation.
riesame sm. re-examination.
riesaminare vt. to re-examine.
rièssere vi. to be again.
riesumare vt. 1. to exhume 2. (fig.) to bring (v. irr.) to light.
rievocare vt. to recall.
rievocazione sf. recalling.
rifacimento sm. 1. reconstruction 2. (adattamento) adaptation.
rifare vt. 1. to do (v. irr.) again, to make (v. irr.) again 2. (ripercorrere) to retrace 3. (riparare) to repair 4. (imitare) to imitate 5. (indennizzare) to indemnify. ♦ **rifarsi** vr. 1. to make up 2. (vendicarsi) to revenge oneself 3. (risalire) to go (v. irr.) back.
rifasciare vt. 1. to bandage again 2. (un bambino) to swaddle again.
riferìbile agg. 1. referable 2. (raccontabile) fit to be told.
riferimento sm. reference: linea, punto di —, datum-line, datum-point.
riferire vt. 1. to report 2. (attribuire) to ascribe. ♦ **riferirsi** vr. to refer.
rificcare vt. to thrust (v. irr.) again.
rifilare vt. 1. to spin again 2. (tagliare a filo) to trim 3. (appioppare) to palm off.
rifilatura sf. 1. trimming 2. (bordo) border.
rifinimento sm. finishing touch.
rifinire vt. to finish.
rifinitura sf. V. rifinimento.
rifiorire vi. 1. to blossom again 2. (fig.) to flourish again.
rifioritura sf. reflorescence.
rifiutàbile agg. refusable.

rifiutare vt. to refuse.
rifiuto sm. refusal || rifiuti, waste (solo sing.); i rifiuti della società, the dregs of society.
riflessione sf. reflection.
riflessivo agg. 1. reflective 2. (gramm.) reflexive.
riflesso agg. reflected, reflex (anche fig.). ♦ **riflesso** sm. 1. reflection 2. (di colore) tint 3. (med.) reflex || di —, as a consequence; per —, indirectly.
riflèttere vt. e vi. to reflect. ♦ **riflèttersi** vr. to be reflected.
riflettore sm. 1. reflector 2. (lampada) searchlight.
rifluire vi. 1. to flow again 2. (fluire indietro) to flow back.
riflusso sm. ebb.
rifocillare vt. to give (v. irr.) refreshment. ♦ **rifocillarsi** vr. to take (v. irr.) refreshment.
rifòndere vt. 1. to melt again 2. (rimborsare) to refund.
riforma sf. reformation.
riformare vt. 1. to reform 2. (mil.) to declare unfit for military service.
riformatore sm. reformer.
riformatorio sm. reformatory.
riformismo sm. reformism.
riformista s. reformist.
rifornimento sm. 1. supplying 2. (aer.; auto) refuelling 3. (scorta) supply || stazione di —, filling-station; far — di benzina, to fill up the tank.
rifornire vt. to supply (so. with).
rifornitore sm. supplier.
rifràngere vt. to refract. ♦ **rifràngersi** vr. to be refracted.
rifrangibilità sf. refrangibility.
rifrattore sm. refractor.
rifrazione sf. refraction.
rifritto agg. 1. fried again 2. (fig.) stale.
rifuggire vi. 1. to escape again 2. (essere alieno) to shrink (v. irr.).
rifugiarsi vr. to take (v. irr.) shelter.
rifugiato agg. e sm. refugee.
rifugio sm. 1. shelter 2. (di montagna) mountain hut.
rifùlgere vi. to shine (v. irr.) brightly (with sthg.).
rifusione sf. 1. re-melting 2. (rimborso) repayment.
riga sf. 1. line 2. (fila) row 3. (regolo) rule 4. (striscia) stripe 5. (scriminatura) parting 6. (mus.

stave || *mettersi in* —, to line up.

rigaglie *sf. pl.* giblets.

rigàgnolo *sm.* **1.** rivulet **2.** (*scolo*) gutter.

rigare *vt.* **1.** to rule **2.** (*solcare*) to furrow || — *diritto*, to behave well.

rigato *agg.* **1.** ruled **2.** (*a strisce*) striped **3.** (*solcato*) furrowed.

rigattiere *sm.* second-hand dealer.

rigatura *sf.* **1.** ruling **2.** (*di arma*) rifling.

rigenerare *vt.* **1.** to regenerate **2.** (*mecc.*) to repair.

rigeneratore *agg.* regenerative. ♦ **rigeneratore** *sm.* regenerator.

rigenerazione *sf.* regeneration.

rigettare *vt.* **1.** to throw (*v. irr.*) again **2.** (*gettare indietro*) to throw back **3.** (*vomitare*) to vomit **4.** (*respingere*) to reject.

rigetto *sm.* rejection.

righello *sm.* ruler.

rigidezza *sf.* **1.** stiffness **2.** (*di clima*) rigour.

rigidità *sf.* V. *rigidezza*.

rìgido *agg.* **1.** stiff **2.** (*di clima*) rigorous.

rigirare *vt.* **1.** to turn again **2.** (*cambiare*) to change. ♦ **rigirare** *vi.* to walk about. ♦ **rigirarsi** *vr.* to turn about.

rigiro *sm.* **1.** turning round **2.** (*di parole*) involved expression.

rigo *sm.* V. *riga*.

rigoglio *sm.* bloom.

rigogliosità *sf.* luxuriancy.

rigoglioso *agg.* flourishing.

rigonfiamento *sm.* swelling.

rigonfiare *vt.* to swell (*v. irr.*). ♦ **rigonfiarsi** *vr.* to swell.

rigonfio *agg.* swollen (with). ♦ **rigonfio** *sm.* swelling.

rigore *sm.* **1.** rigour **2.** (*esattezza*) exactness || *di* —, compulsory; *a* —, according to the rules; *a* — *di termini*, in the strict sense, *area di* — (*sport*), penalty-area.

rigorismo *sm.* rigorism.

rigorista *s.* rigorist.

rigorosità *sf.* **1.** rigour **2.** (*esattezza*) preciseness.

rigoroso *agg.* **1.** rigorous **2.** (*esatto*) exact.

rigovernare *vt.* **1.** to govern again **2.** (*di piatti*) to wash up.

rigovernatura *sf.* washing-up.

riguadagnare *vt.* **1.** to earn again **2.** (*ricuperare, raggiungere*) to regain.

riguardare *vt.* **1.** to look at (so., sthg.) again **2.** (*esaminare*) to examine **3.** (*considerare*) to regard. ♦ **riguardarsi** *vr.* to take (*v. irr.*) care of oneself.

riguardata *sf.* look.

riguardévole *agg.* **1.** considerable **2.** (*importante*) important.

riguardo *sm.* **1.** regard **2.** (*cura*) care || *persona di* —, person of consequence; — *a*, as regards; *a questo* —, in this connection.

riguardoso *agg.* respectful.

rigurgitare *vi.* **1.** to overflow **2.** (*di stomaco*) to regurgitate **3.** (*brulicare*) to swarm (with).

rigùrgito *sm.* **1.** overflow **2.** (*di stomaco*) regurgitation **3.** (*travaso*) extravasation **4.** (*gorgo*) eddy.

rilanciare *vt.* **1.** to throw (*v. irr.*) again **2.** (*lanciare indietro*) to throw back **3.** (*un'offerta*) to raise.

rilancio *sm.* **1.** new throw **2.** (*di offerta*) raising.

rilasciare *vt.* **1.** to release **2.** (*concedere*) to grant **3.** (*emettere*) to issue. ♦ **rilasciarsi** *vr.* **1.** to slacken **2.** (*med.*) to prolapse **3.** (*rilassarsi*) to relax.

rilascio *sm.* **1.** release **2.** (*concessione*) granting **3.** (*emissione*) issue.

rilassamento *sm.* **1.** slackening **2.** (*med.*) prolapse **3.** (*riposo*) relaxation.

rilassare *vt.* **1.** to slacken **2.** (*distendere*) to relax. ♦ **rilassarsi** *vr.* **1.** to slacken **2.** (*distendersi*) to relax.

rilassatezza *sf.* laxity.

rilegare *vt.* **1.** to tie again **2.** (*libri*) to bind (*v. irr.*).

rilegatura *sf.* binding.

rilèggere *vt.* to reread (*v. irr.*), to read (*v. irr.*) again.

rilento (*nella loc. avv.*) *a* —, slowly.

rilevamento *sm.* **1.** (*topografico*) survey **2.** (*mar.*) bearing **3.** (*cambio*) relieving.

rilevante *agg.* prominent.

rilevare *vt.* **1.** to take (*v. irr.*) off again **2.** (*notare*) to notice **3.** (*far notare*) to point out **4.** (*prendere*) to take **5.** (*topografia*) to survey **6.** (*sostituire*) to relieve **7.** (*comm.*) to take over.

rilevazione *sf.* V. *rilievo.*

rilievo *sm.* **1.** relief **2.** (*importanza*) importance **3.** (*osservazione*) remark **4.** (*topografico*) survey **5.** (*comm.*) taking over ‖ *mettere in —,* to stress.

rilucente *agg.* glittering.

rilùcere *vi.* to glitter.

riluttante *agg.* reluctant.

riluttanza *sf.* reluctance.

riluttare *vi.* to reluct (at).

rima *sf.* rhyme ‖ *rispondere per le rime,* to give (*v. irr.*) tit for tat.

rimandare *vt.* **1.** to send (*v. irr.*) again **2.** (*restituire*) to send back **3.** (*posporre*) to postpone **4.** (*far riferimento*) to refer **5.** (*agli esami*) to make (*v. irr.*) (so.) repeat (an exam).

rimando *sm.* **1.** returning **2.** (*differimento*) postponement **3.** (*segno di richiamo*) reference-mark.

rimaneggiamento *sm.* **1.** rearrangement **2.** (*di opera letteraria*) adaptation **3.** (*pol.*) shuffle.

rimaneggiare *vt.* **1.** to rearrange **2.** (*modificare*) to change **3.** (*pol.*) to shuffle.

rimanente *agg.* remaining. ♦ **rimanente** *sm.* rest.

rimanenza *sf.* remainder.

rimanere *vi.* **1.** to remain **2.** (*avanzare*) to be left **3.** (*essere sorpreso*) to be astonished.

rimangiare *vt.* to eat (*v. irr.*) again. ♦ **rimangiarsi** *vr.* to take (*v. irr.*) back.

rimarchévole *agg.* remarkable.

rimare *vt.* e *vi.* to rhyme.

rimarginare *vt.* to heal. ♦ **rimarginarsi** *vr.* to heal.

rimaritare *vt.* to marry again. ♦ **rimaritarsi** *vr.* to marry again.

rimasticare *vt.* **1.** to chew again **2.** (*fig.*) to muse.

rimasuglio *sm.* remains (*pl.*).

rimatore *sm.* rhymer.

rimbalzare *vi.* to rebound.

rimbalzello *sm.* ducks and drakes.

rimbalzo *sm.* rebound: *di —,* on the rebound.

rimbambimento *sm.* dotage.

rimbambire *vi.* to reach one's dotage.

rimbambito *agg.* in one's dotage (*pred.*): *un vecchio —,* a dotard.

rimbeccare *vt.* to retort.

rimbecco *sm.* retort.

rimbecillire *vi.* **1.** to grow (*v. irr.*) stupid **2.** (*per età*) to reach one's dotage.

rimbecillito *agg.* doting.

rimboccare *vt.* to tuck up. ♦ **rimboccarsi** *vr.* to tuck up.

rimbombante *agg.* thundering.

rimbombare *vi.* **1.** to thunder **2.** (*risuonare*) to resound.

rimbombo *sm.* roar.

rimborsàbile *agg.* repayable.

rimborsare *vt.* to reimburse.

rimborso *sm.* reimbursement.

rimboscare *vt.* V. *rimboschire.*

rimboschimento *sm.* reafforestation.

irr.) wooded again.

rimboschire *vt.* to reafforest. ♦ **rimboschirsi** *vr.* to become (*v. irr.*)

rimbrottare *vt.* to reproach.

rimbrotto *sm.* reproach.

rimediàbile *agg.* remediable.

rimediare *vi.* to find (*v. irr.*) a remedy (for).

rimedio *sm.* remedy.

rimembranza *sf.* memory.

rimembrare *vt.* to remember.

rimeritare *vt.* to reward.

rimescolamento *sm.* **1.** stir **2.** (*turbamento*) shock.

rimescolare *vt.* **1.** to stir again **2.** (*mescolare*) to stir. ♦ **rimescolarsi** *vr.* to be upset ‖ *gli si rimescolò il sangue* (*per rabbia*), his blood boiled, (*per paura*), his blood ran cold.

rimescolìo *sm.* confusion.

rimessa *sf.* **1.** replacing **2.** (*per auto*) garage **3.** (*di denaro*) remittance **4.** (*di merci*) consignment ‖ *— in gioco,* throw-in.

rimesso *agg.* **1.** (*falso*) false **2.** (*ristabilito*) well again **3.** (*perdonato*) forgiven.

rimestare *vt.* V. *rimescolare.*

riméttere *vt.* **1.** to put (*v. irr.*) again, to put back **2.** (*consegnare*) to hand **3.** (*mandare, perdonare*) to remit **4.** (*affidare*) to leave (*v. irr.*) **5.** (*vomitare*) to vomit ‖ *— in gioco,* to throw (*v. irr.*) in; *rimetterci,* to lose (*v. irr.*). ♦ **riméttersi** *vr.* **1.** (*affidarsi*) to rely on **2.** (*ristabilirsi*) to recover **3.** (*rasserenarsi*) to clear up.

rimirare *vt.* to gaze (at). ♦ **rimirarsi** *vr.* to admire oneself.

rimisurare *vt.* to measure again.

rimodellare *vt.* to remodel.

rimodernamento sm. modernization.

rimodernare vt. to modernize. ♦ **rimodernarsi** vr. to become up--to-date.

rimondare vt. to clean again.

rimonta sf. **1.** (mil.) remount **2.** (sport) catching up.

rimontare vt. **1.** to go (v. irr.) up **2.** (ricomporre) to reassemble. ♦ **rimontare** vi. **1.** to remount **2.** (fig.) to go back **3.** (sport) to catch (v. irr.) up || — in auto, to get (v. irr.) into a car again.

rimorchiare vt. to tow.

rimorchiatore sm. tug.

rimorchio sm. **1.** tow **2.** (veicolo) trailer.

rimòrdere vt. **1.** to bite (v. irr.) again **2.** (fig.) to prick.

rimorso sm. remorse.

rimosso agg. removed.

rimostranza sf. remonstrance: fare le proprie rimostranze, to remonstrate.

rimostrare vi. to remonstrate.

rimovibile agg. removable.

rimozione sf. removal.

rimpacchettare vt. to package again.

rimpadronirsi vr. to seize again.

rimpagliare vt. **1.** to re-cover with straw **2.** (imbottire) to re-stuff with straw.

rimpallo sm. counterblow.

rimpannucciarsi vr. (fig.) to improve one's financial position.

rimpastare vt. to knead again **2.** (fig.) to rearrange.

rimpasto sm. **1.** kneading again **2.** (fig.) rearrangement **3.** (pol.) reshuffle.

rimpatriare vt. to repatriate. ♦ **rimpatriare** vi. to return to one's country.

rimpatrio sm. repatriation.

rimpetto avv. opposite.

rimpiàngere vt. **1.** to regret **2.** (una perdita) to mourn.

rimpianto sm. regret.

rimpiattarsi vr. to hide (v. irr.) oneself.

rimpiattino sm. hide-and-seek.

rimpiazzare vt. to replace.

rimpiazzo sm. replacement.

rimpicciolire vt. to lessen. ♦ **rimpicciolirsi** vr. to lessen.

rimpiegare vt. to re-employ.

rimpiego sm. re-employment.

rimpinguare vt. **1.** to fatten **2.** (arricchire) to enrich. ♦ **rimpinguarsi** vr. **1.** to fatten **2.** (arricchirsi) to grow (v. irr.) rich.

rimpinzare vt. to stuff (with).

rimpolpare vt. V. rimpinguare.

rimproverare vt. to reproach.

rimpròvero sm. reproach: muovere un —, to reproach.

rimuginare vt. to brood over.

rimunerare vt. to remunerate.

rimuòvere vt. **1.** to remove **2.** (dissuadere) to dissuade **3.** (da una carica) to dismiss.

rimutare vt. to change again.

rinascenza sf. Renaissance.

rinàscere vi. to revive.

rinascimentale agg. Renaissance (attr.).

rinascimento sm. Renaissance.

rinàscita sf. **1.** rebirth **2.** (fig.) revival.

rincagnarsi vr. to frown.

rincagnato agg. pug (attr.).

rincalzare vt. **1.** (rimboccare) to tuck in **2.** (sostenere) to prop up.

rincalzo sm. support: a — di, in support of.

rincantucciare vt. to put (v. irr.) in a corner. ♦ **rincantucciarsi** vr. to hide (v. irr.) in a corner.

rincarare vt. **1.** to raise the price of **2.** (esagerare) to exaggerate. ♦ **rincarare** vi. to become (v. irr.) more expensive.

rincaro sm. rise in prices.

rincasare vi. to return home.

rinchiùdere vt. to shut (v. irr.) up.

rincitrullire vt. to make (v. irr.) silly. ♦ **rincitrullirsi** vr. to grow (v. irr.) silly.

rincivilire vt. to civilize. ♦ **rincivilirsi** vr. **1.** to become (v. irr.) civilized **2.** (raffinarsi) to become refined.

rincollare vt. to paste again.

rincominciare vt. to begin (v. irr.) again.

rincontrare vt. to meet (v. irr.) again. ♦ **rincontrarsi** vr. to meet again.

rincontro sm. meeting.

rincoramento sm. encouragement.

rincorare vt. to encourage. ♦ **rincorarsi** vr. to pluck up courage.

rincòrrere vt. to run (v. irr.) after.

rincorsa sf. run-up.

rincréscere vi. **1.** to be sorry: mi

rincresce, I am sorry **2.** (*dar noia*) to mind: *ti rincresce aprire la finestra?*, do you mind opening the window?

rincrescimento *sm.* regret: *con mio —*, to my regret.

rincrudimento *sm.* aggravation.

rincrudire *vi.* **1.** to aggravate **2.** (*esacerbare*) to embitter **3.** (*del tempo*) to get (*v. irr.*) worse.

rinculare *vi.* to recoil.

rinculo *sm.* recoil.

rinfacciare *vt.* to throw (*v. irr.*) (sthg.) in so.'s face.

rinfiancare *vt.* to support.

rinfilare *vt.* **1.** to thread again **2.** (*rinserire*) to insert again. ◆ **rinfilarsi** *vr.* **1.** (*introdursi*) to slip again **2.** (*rindossare*) to slip on again.

rinfiorare *vt.* to adorn with flowers again.

rinfittire *vt.* **1.** to thicken **2.** (*rendere più frequenti*) to make (*v. irr.*) more frequent. ◆ **rinfittirsi** *vr.* (*di lana*) to shrink (*v. irr.*).

rinfocolare *vt.* **1.** to poke **2.** (*fig.*) to stir up (again).

rinfoderare *vt.* to sheathe (again).

rinforzamento *sm.* strengthening.

rinforzare *vt.* **1.** to strengthen **2.** (*mecc.*) to stiffen. ◆ **rinforzarsi** *vr.* to become (*v. irr.*) stronger.

rinforzo *sm.* **1.** strengthening **2.** (*mil.*) reinforcements (*pl.*) **3.** (*fig.*) support **4.** (*mecc.*) stiffener.

rinfrancare *vt.* to encourage. ◆ **rinfrancarsi** *vr.* **1.** (*migliorare*) to improve **2.** (*riprendere coraggio*) to pluck up courage.

rinfrescamento *sm.* cooling.

rinfrescante *agg.* refreshing.

rinfrescare *vt.* **1.** to cool **2.** (*ristorare*) to refresh **3.** (*rinnovare*) to renovate. ◆ **rinfrescare** *vi.* to cool.

rinfresco *sm.* **1.** refreshments (*pl.*) **2.** (*ricevimento*) cocktail party.

rinfusa (*nella loc. avv.*) **alla —**, in confusion.

ringalluzzire *vt.* to make (*v. irr.*) cocky. ◆ **ringalluzzirsi** *vr.* to become (*v. irr.*) cocky.

ringentilire *vt.* to refine.

ringhiare *vi.* to snarl.

ringhiera *sf.* **1.** railing **2.** (*di scale*) banisters (*pl.*).

ringhio *sm.* snarl.

ringhioso *agg.* snarling

ringiovanimento *sm.* rejuvenation.

ringiovanire *vt.* **1.** to make (*v. irr.*) young again **2.** (*far sembrare più giovane*) to make (so.) look younger. ◆ **ringiovanire** *vi.* **1.** to grow (*v. irr.*) young again **2.** (*sembrare più giovane*) to look younger.

ringiovanito *agg.* young again.

ringoiare *vt.* to swallow up again.

ringranare *vt.* to re-engage.

ringraziamento *sm.* thanks (*pl.*).

ringraziare *vt.* to thank.

ringuainare *vt.* V. *rinfoderare*.

rinite *sf.* rhinitis.

rinnegàbile *agg.* deniable.

rinnegamento *sm.* disowning.

rinnegare *vt.* to disown.

rinnegato *agg. e sm.* renegade.

rinnegatore *sm.* disowner.

rinnestare *vt.* **1.** (*agr.*) to graft again **2.** (*mecc.*) to re-engage.

rinnesto *sm.* **1.** (*agr.*) new grafting **2.** (*mecc.*) re-engagement.

rinnovàbile *agg.* renewable.

rinnovamento *sm.* renewal.

rinnovare *vt.* to renew. ◆ **rinnovarsi** *vr.* (*riaccadere*) to happen again.

rinnovatore *sm.* renewer.

rinnovazione *sf.* renewal.

rinnovellare *vt.* to renew. ◆ **rinnovellarsi** *vr.* to be renewed.

rinnovo *sm.* renewal.

rinoceronte *sm.* rhinoceros.

rinolaringite *sf.* rhinolaryngitis.

rinologìa *sf.* rhinology.

rinomanza *sf.* renown.

rinomato *agg.* renowned.

rinominare *vt.* **1.** to name again **2.** (*designare di nuovo*) to reappoint.

rinoplàstica *sf.* rhinoplasty.

rinoscopìa *sf.* rhinoscopy.

rinoscopio *sm.* rhinoscope.

rinsaccare *vt.* to pack again. ◆ **rinsaccarsi** *vr.* to shrug one's shoulders.

rinsaldamento *sm.* consolidation.

rinsaldare *vt.* to consolidate.

rinsanguare *vt.* **1.** to supply with new blood **2.** (*fig.*) to reinvigorate. ◆ **rinsanguarsi** *vr.* **1.** to recover **2.** (*finanziariamente*) to re-establish one's financial condition.

rinsanire *vi.* **1.** to recover **2.** (*rinsavire*) to return to reason.

rinsavimento *sm.* return to reason.

rinsavire *vi.* to recover one's wits.

rinsecchire *vi.* **1.** to dry up **2.** (*di persone*) to get (*v. irr.*) thin **3.**

(*avvizzire*) to wither.

rinserrare *vt.* to shut (*v. irr.*) up (again).

rintanarsi *vr.* to shut (*v. irr.*) one-self up.

rintascare *vt.* to pocket again.

rintavolare *vt.* to start again.

rintoccare *vi.* **1.** (*di orologio*) to strike (*v. irr.*) **2.** (*di campana*) to toll.

rintocco *sm.* **1.** (*di orologio*) stroke **2.** (*di campana*) toll.

rintontire *vt.* to stun. ♦ **rinton-tirsi** *vr.* to be stunned.

rintracciare *vt.* **1.** to trace **2.** (*tro-vare*) to find (*v. irr.*) out.

rintronamento *sm.* booming.

rintronare *vt.* **1.** to deafen **2.** (*stor-dire*) to stun. ♦ **rintronare** *vi.* to boom.

rintuzzare *vt.* **1.** to blunt **2.** (*ri-battere*) to retort.

rinuncia *sf.* renouncement.

rinunciare *vi.* to renounce (sthg.).

rinunciatario *agg.* releasee.

rinvenimento *sm.* recovery.

rinvenire *vt.* to find (*v. irr.*). ♦ **rinvenire** *vi.* **1.** to recover one's senses **2.** (*riprendere freschezza*) to revive **3.** (*riprendere morbidezza*) to soften.

rinverdire *vt.* (*ravvivare*) to rea-waken. ♦ **rinverdire** *vi.* **1.** to turn green again **2.** (*ravvivarsi*) to revive.

rinvestimento *sm.* reinvestment.

rinvestire *vt.* **1.** to restore to the possession of **2.** (*comm.*) to rein-vest.

rinviare *vt.* **1.** to put (*v. irr.*) off **2.** (*mandare indietro*) to return.

rinvigorimento *sm.* reinvigoration.

rinvigorire *vt.* to reinvigorate. ♦ **rinvigorirsi** *vr.* to regain strength.

rinvilire *vt.* to lower. ♦ **rinvilire** *vi.* to become (*v. irr.*) cheaper.

rinvio *sm.* **1.** postponement **2.** (*il ri-mandare indietro*) returning.

rinvoltare *vt.* to wrap up again.

rinzaffare *vt.* **1.** to bung again **2.** (*arch.*) to rough in.

rinzaffatura *sf.* (*arch.*) roughing-in coat.

rio¹ *sm.* rivulet.

rio² *agg.* evil.

rioccupare *vt.* to reoccupy.

rioccupazione *sf.* reoccupation.

rionale *agg.* local, ward (*attr.*).

rione *sm.* ward, district.

riordinare *vt.* **1.** to tidy up **2.** (*rior-ganizzare*) to reorganize **3.** (*coman-dare di nuovo*) to order again.

riordinatore *sm.* **1.** rearranger **2.** (*riorganizzatore*) reorganizer.

riordinazione *sf.* **1.** rearrangement **2.** (*riorganizzazione*) reorganization **3.** (*nuova ordinazione*) new order.

riòrdino *sm.* V. riordinazione.

riorganizzare *vt.* to reorganize.

riorganizzatore *sm.* reorganizer.

riorganizzazione *sf.* reorganiza-tion.

riottosità *sf.* **1.** turbulence **2.** (*in-docilità*) indocility.

riottoso *agg.* **1.** turbulent **2.** (*indo-cile*) indocile.

ripa *sf.* **1.** bank **2.** (*scarpata*) scarp.

ripagare *vt.* **1.** to repay (*v. irr.*) **2.** (*pagare di nuovo*) to pay (*v. irr.*) again.

riparare *vt.* **1.** (*proteggere*) to shel-ter **2.** (*aggiustare*) to repair **3.** (*ri-sarcire*) to redress || — *un esame*, to repeat an exam. ♦ **riparare** *vi.* **1.** (*porre rimedio*) to remedy **2.** (*rifugiarsi*) to take (*v. irr.*) shel-ter. ♦ **ripararsi** *vr.* to take shelter.

riparatore *agg.* repairing. ♦ **ripa-ratore** *sm.* repairer.

riparazione *sf.* **1.** repair: *in —*, under repair **2.** (*fig.*) reparation.

riparlare *vi.* to speak (*v. irr.*) again.

riparo *sm.* **1.** shelter **2.** (*rimedio*) remedy **3.** (*mecc.*) guard.

ripartire¹ *vi.* to start again.

ripartire² *vt.* to divide.

ripartizione *sf.* division.

ripassare *vi.* **1.** to pass again **2.** (*far visita*) to call again. ♦ **ripas-sare** *vt.* **1.** (*riattraversare*) to cross again **2.** (*dare di nuovo*) to pass again **3.** (*rileggere, rivedere*) to go (*v. irr.*) through **4.** (*mecc.*) to overhaul.

ripassata *sf.* **1.** (*revisione*) revision **2.** (*mecc.*) overhauling **3.** (*pulita*) cleaning **4.** (*mano di vernice*) new coat.

ripasso *sf.* **1.** (*ritorno*) return **2.** (*revisione*) revision **3.** (*di lezioni*) review.

ripensamento *sm.* reflection: *avere un —*, to change one's mind.

ripensare *vi.* **1.** to think (*v. irr.*) (of sthg., so.) again **2.** (*riconside-*

rare) to think over **3.** (*cambiar parere*) to change one's mind: *ci ho ripensato,* I have changed my mind.

ripercòrrere *vt.* to travel over (sthg.) again.

ripercuòtere *vt.* to strike (*v. irr.*) again. ♦ **ripercuòtersi** *vr.* **1.** to reverberate **2.** (*fig.*) to influence (so., sthg.).

ripercussione *sf.* repercussion.

ripescare *vt.* **1.** to catch (*v. irr.*) again **2.** (*ritrovare*) to find (*v. irr.*) again.

ripetente *s.* repeater.

ripètere *vt.* to repeat.

ripetitore *sm.* **1.** repeater **2.** (*scol.*) private tutor.

ripetizione *sf.* **1.** (*rifacimento*) repetition **2.** (*ripasso*) revision **3.** (*lezione privata*) private lesson ‖ *arma a* —, repeater.

ripetuto *agg.* repeated.

ripiano *sm.* **1.** (*terreno*) terrace **2.** (*pianerottolo*) landing **3.** (*scaffale*) shelf (*pl.* -lves).

ripicco *sm.* spite: *per* —, out of spite.

ripidezza *sf.* steepness.

ripido *agg.* steep.

ripiegamento *sm.* **1.** folding **2.** (*il curvare*) bending **3.** (*mil.*) withdrawal.

ripiegare *vt.* **1.** to bend (*v. irr.*) again **2.** (*piegare*) to fold. ♦ **ripiegare** *vi.* **1.** to bend **2.** (*ritirarsi*) to withdraw (*v. irr.*). ♦ **ripiegarsi** *vr.* to bend.

ripiegatura *sf.* **1.** folding **2.** (*piega*) fold **2.** (*curva*) bend.

ripiego *sm.* **1.** expedient **2.** (*rimedio*) remedy.

ripienezza *sf.* fullness.

ripieno *agg.* **1.** full **2.** (*cuc.*) stuffed (with). ♦ **ripieno** *sm.* **1.** filling **2.** (*cuc.*) stuffing.

ripigliare *vt.* V. *riprendere.*

ripiombare *vt.* to plunge back. ♦ **ripiombare** *vi.* to fall (*v. irr.*) again.

ripopolamento *sm.* **1.** repeopling **2.** (*di animali*) restocking.

ripopolare *vt.* **1.** to repeople **2.** (*di animali*) to restock.

riporre *vt.* **1.** to replace **2.** (*metter via*) to put (*v. irr.*) away **3.** (*porre*) to place. ♦ **riporsi** *vr.* (*riprendere*) to resume.

riportare *vt.* **1.** to bring (*v. irr.*)

again, to take (*v. irr.*) again **2.** (*portare indietro*) to bring back, to take back **3.** (*riferire*) to report **4.** (*citare*) to quote **5.** (*ricevere*) to get (*v. irr.*) **6.** (*mat.*) to carry. ♦ **riportarsi** *vr.* (*tornare*) to go (*v. irr.*) back.

riporto *sm.* **1.** (*mat.*) carry over **2.** (*in borsa*) contango **3.** (*ornamento*) appliqué.

riposante *agg.* restful.

riposare *vt.* **1.** to rest **2.** (*posare di nuovo*) to place back. ♦ **riposare** *vi.* to rest. ♦ **riposarsi** *vr.* to rest.

riposato *agg.* **1.** (*fresco*) fresh **2.** (*tranquillo*) quiet.

riposo *sm.* rest: *andare a* —, to retire.

ripostiglio *sm.* cupboard.

riprèndere *vt.* **1.** to take (*v. irr.*) again **2.** (*riavere*) to take back **3.** (*riassumere, ricominciare*) to resume **4.** (*ricuperare*) to recover **5.** (*rimproverare*) to reprove **6.** (*teat.*) to revive **7.** (*cine*) to shoot (*v. irr.*). ♦ **riprèndersi** *vr.* **1.** to recover **2.** (*da turbamento*) to collect oneself **3.** (*correggersi*) to correct oneself.

riprensione *sf.* reprehension.

riprensivo *agg.* reprehensive.

ripresa *sf.* **1.** renewal **2.** (*teat.; rinascita*) revival **3.** (*riconquista*) recapture **4.** (*da malattia*) recovery **5.** (*cine*) shot **6.** (*auto*) acceleration **7.** (*registrazione*) recording **8.** (*di pugilato*) round **9.** (*sport*) second half.

ripresentare *vt.* to present again.

ripristinare *vt.* **1.** to restore **2.** (*rimettere in vigore*) to re-establish.

ripristino *sm.* **1.** restoration **2.** (*il rimettere in vigore*) re-establishment.

riproducìbile *agg.* reproducible.

riprodurre *vt.* to reproduce. ♦ **riprodursi** *vr.* to reproduce.

riproduttivo *agg.* reproductive.

riproduttore *agg.* reproducing. ♦ **riproduttore** *sm.* reproducer.

riproduzione *sf.* reproduction.

ripromèttere *vt.* to promise again. ♦ **ripromèttersi** *vr.* **1.** to intend **2.** (*aspettarsi*) to expect.

riproporre *vt.* to re-propose. ♦ **riproporsi** *vr.* to re-propose.

riprova *sf.* (new) proof.

riprovare *vt.* **1.** to try again **2.** (*sentire di nuovo*) to feel (*v. irr.*)

again **3.** (*disapprovare*) to criticize **4.** (*scol.*) to fail.

riprovazione *sf.* reprobation.

riprovévole *agg.* **1.** blamable **2.** (*spregevole*) despicable.

ripubblicare *vt.* to republish.

ripudiare *vt.* to repudiate.

ripudio *sm.* repudiation.

ripugnante *agg.* repugnant.

ripugnanza *sf.* repugnance.

ripugnare *vi.* **1.** (*disgustare*) to disgust **2.** (*essere contrario*) to be repugnant.

ripulire *vt.* **1.** to clean again **2.** (*pulire*) to clean **3.** (*fig.*) to polish **4.** (*saccheggiare*) to ransack.

ripulita *sf.* clean: *darsi una —,* to tidy oneself up.

ripulsa *sf.* repulse.

ripulsione *sf.* repulsion.

ripulsivo *agg.* repulsive.

riquadrare *vt.* **1.** to square **2.** (*una stanza*) to decorate.

riquadratura *sf.* **1.** square **2.** (*decorazione*) decoration.

riquadro *sm.* **1.** square **2.** (*su parete*) panel.

risacca *sf.* surf.

risaia *sf.* rice-field.

risalire *vt.* **1.** to go (*v. irr.*) up again **2.** (*contro corrente*) to go up: *— la corrente,* to go upstream. ♦ **risalire** *vi.* **1.** to go up again **2.** (*nel tempo*) to go back.

risaltare[1] *vi.* **1.** to show (*v. irr.*) up **2.** (*di persona*) to stand (*v. irr.*) out.

risaltare[2] *vt.* to jump again.

risalto *sm.* **1.** prominence **2.** (*rilievo*) relief.

risanàbile *agg.* **1.** curable **2.** (*bonificabile*) reclaimable.

risanamento *sm.* **1.** curing **2.** (*guarigione*) recovery **3.** (*bonifica*) reclamation **4.** (*fig.*) reformation || *— di quartiere,* slum-clearance.

risanare *vt.* **1.** to cure **2.** (*bonificare*) to reclaim **3.** (*un quartiere*) to clear (a slum). ♦ **risanare** *vi.* to recover.

risanatore *agg.* healing. ♦ **risanatore** *sm.* healer.

risapere *vt.* to come (*v. irr.*) to know.

risaputo *agg.* well-known.

risarcìbile *agg.* that can be indemnified.

risarcimento *sm.* indemnity.

risarcire *vt.* to indemnify.

risata *sf.* laugh: *scoppiare in una —,* to burst (*v. irr.*) out laughing.

riscaldamento *sm.* heating.

riscaldare *vt.* **1.** to warm (up) **2.** (*di casa*) to heat **3.** (*fig.*) to excite. ♦ **riscaldarsi** *vr.* to warm up.

riscaldo *sm.* inflammation.

riscattàbile *agg.* redeemable.

riscattare *vt.* to redeem.

riscatto *sm.* **1.** ransom **2.** (*redenzione*) redemption.

rischiaramento *sm.* brightening.

rischiarare *vt.* to light (*v. irr.*) (up). ♦ **rischiararsi** *vr.* **1.** to light up **2.** (*diventare più chiaro*) to get (*v. irr.*) clearer **3.** (*di cielo*) to clear up.

rischiare *vt.* to risk. ♦ **rischiare** *vi.* to run (*v. irr.*) the risk (of).

rischio *sm.* risk.

rischioso *agg.* risky.

risciacquare *vt.* to rinse. ♦ **risciacquarsi** *vr.* to rinse.

risciacquata *sf.* rinse.

risciacquatura *sf.* **1.** rinsing **2.** (*acqua*) dish-water.

riscontare *vt.* to rediscount.

risconto *sm.* rediscount.

riscontrare *vt.* **1.** (*controllare*) to check **2.** (*trovare*) to find (*v. irr.*) **3.** (*confrontare*) to compare.

riscontro *sm.* **1.** (*controllo*) checking **2.** (*confronto*) comparison **3.** (*risposta*) reply **4.** (*corrispondenza simmetrica*) pendant.

riscoprire *vt.* to discover again.

riscossa *sf.* **1.** (*rivolta*) revolt **2.** (*riscatto*) redemption || *andare alla —,* to counterattack.

riscossione *sf.* collection.

riscotìbile *agg.* collectable.

riscotimento *sm.* collection.

riscrìvere *vt.* **1.** to rewrite (*v. irr.*) **2.** (*in risposta*) to write (*v. irr.*) back.

riscuòtere *vt.* **1.** (*denaro*) to collect **2.** (*conseguire*) to win (*v. irr.*) **3.** (*scuotere*) to shake (*v. irr.*). ♦ **riscuòtersi** *vr.* (*trasalire*) to start.

riseccare *vt.* to dry up. ♦ **riseccarsi** *vr.* to dry up.

risedersi *vr.* to sit (*v. irr.*) down again.

risega *sf.* **1.** (*arch.*) offset **2.** (*della pelle*) fold.

riseminare *vt.* to sow (*v. irr.*) again.

risentimento *sm.* resentment: *con —,* resentfully.

risentire *vt.* **1.** (*sentire di nuovo*) to feel (*v. irr.*) again **2.** (*riudire*) to hear (*v. irr.*) again **3.** (*sentire*) to feel || — *di qc.*, to show (*v. irr.*) traces of sthg.; (*di persona*) to feel the effect of sthg. ♦ **risentirsi** *vr.* to take (*v. irr.*) offence (at).

risentito *agg.* (*sdegnato*) resentful.

riserbare *vt.* V. *riservare.*

riserbo *sm.* **1.** reserve **2.** (*discrezione*) discretion.

riserva *sf.* **1.** reserve **2.** (*di caccia, pesca*) preserve.

riservare *vt.* to reserve. ♦ **riservarsi** *vr.* (*ripromettersi*) to intend: — *la diagnosi*, to refuse to formulate a definite diagnosis.

riservatezza *sf.* reservedness.

riservato *agg.* **1.** reserved **2.** (*segreto*) private.

risìbile *agg.* laughable.

risicoltore *sm.* rice-grower.

risicoltura *sf.* rice-growing.

risièdere *vi.* to reside.

risma *sf.* **1.** ream **2.** (*fig.*) kind.

riso¹ *sm.* (*bot.*) rice.

riso² *sm.* laugh.

risolare *vt.* to resole.

risolatura *sf.* resoling.

risollevare *vt.* **1.** to raise again **2.** (*confortare*) to cheer up. ♦ **risollevarsi** *vr.* **1.** to rise again **2.** (*confortarsi*) to cheer up.

risolutezza *sf.* resolution.

risolutivo *agg.* resolutive.

risoluto *agg.* resolute.

risoluzione *sf.* **1.** resolution **2.** (*giur.*) cancellation.

risòlvere *vt.* **1.** to resolve **2.** (*rescindere*) to rescind. ♦ **risòlversi** *vr.* **1.** (*decidersi*) to make (*v. irr.*) up one's mind **2.** (*mutarsi*) to turn (into) **3.** (*di malattia*) to clear up.

risolvìbile *agg.* **1.** resolvable **2.** (*rescindibile*) rescindable.

risonante *agg.* resonant.

risonanza *sf.* resonance.

risonare *vt.* **1.** to play again **2.** (*un campanello*) to ring (*v. irr.*) again. ♦ **risonare** *vi.* to resound.

risòrgere *vi.* **1.** to rise (*v. irr.*) again **2.** (*rifiorire*) to revive || *far* —, to revive.

risorgimento *sm.* revival.

risorsa *sf.* resource.

risparmiare *vt.* **1.** to save **2.** (*evitare, salvare*) to spare.

risparmiatore *agg.* thrifty. ♦ **risparmiatore** *sm.* saver.

risparmio *sm.* saving: *senza* —, lavishly.

rispecchiare *vt.* to reflect. ♦ **rispecchiarsi** *vr.* to be reflected.

rispedire *vt.* **1.** to send (*v. irr.*) again **2.** (*spedire indietro*) to send back.

rispettàbile *agg.* respectable.

rispettabilità *sf.* respectability.

rispettare *vt.* **1.** to respect **2.** (*onorare*) to honour.

rispettivo *agg.* respective.

rispetto *sm.* respect: — *a*, as regards; *a* — *di*, in comparison to; *mancare di* — *a*, to be disrespectful to.

rispettoso *agg.* respectful.

risplendente *agg.* shining.

risplèndere *vi.* to shine (*v. irr.*).

rispolverare *vt.* **1.** to dust again **2.** (*fig.*) to brush up.

rispondente *agg.* answering (to).

rispondenza *sf.* correspondence.

rispòndere *vt.* e *vi.* **1.** to answer (so., sthg.) **2.** (*obbedire*) to respond || — *di qu.*, *qc.*, to answer for so., sthg.

risposare *vt.* V. *rimaritare.*

risposta *sf.* answer, reply.

rispuntare *vi.* **1.** to reappear **2.** (*risorgere*) to rise (*v. irr.*) again **3.** (*di germogli*) to sprout again.

rissa *sf.* brawl.

rissare *vi.* to brawl.

rissoso *agg.* quarrelsome.

ristabilimento *sm.* **1.** restoration **2.** (*di salute*) recovery.

ristabilire *vt.* to restore. ♦ **ristabilirsi** *vr.* **1.** to settle again **2.** (*rimettersi*) to recover.

ristagnamento *sm.* **1.** stagnation **2.** (*di sangue*) staunching.

ristagnare *vi.* to stagnate. ♦ **ristagnare** *vt.* to staunch.

ristagno *sm.* (*econ.*) slackness.

ristampa *sf.* reprint: *essere in* —, to be reprinting.

ristampare *vt.* to reprint.

ristare *vi.* **1.** (*cessare*) to stop **2.** (*rimanere*) to remain.

ristoràbile *agg.* restorable.

ristorante *sm.* restaurant.

ristorare *vt.* to refresh, to restore (*anche fig.*).

ristoratore *agg.* refreshing. ♦ **ristoratore** *sm.* restorer.

ristoro *sm.* **1.** relief **2.** (*cibo, be-*

vanda) refreshment || *luogo di —,* refreshment-room.

ristrettezza *sf.* 1. narrowness 2. (*insufficienza*) lack || *— di idee,* narrow-mindedness.

ristretto *agg.* 1. narrow 2. (*condensato*) condensed.

ristringere *vt.* 1. to tighten again 2. (*premere di nuovo*) to press again || *— la mano a qu.,* to shake (*v. irr.*) hands with so. again.

ristuccare *vt.* 1. (*edil.*) to replaster 2. (*nauseare*) to surfeit.

ristuccatura *sf.* (*edil.*) replastering.

ristudiare *vt.* to study again.

risucchiare *vt.* to suck (again).

risucchio *sm.* whirlpool.

risultante *agg. e sf.* resultant.

risultanza *sf.* result.

risultare *vi.* 1. to result 2. (*venire a sapere*) to turn out || *mi risulta,* I know.

risultato *sm.* result.

risurrezione *sf.* resurrection.

risuscitamento *sm.* resuscitation.

risuscitare *vt. e vi.* to resuscitate.

risvegliare *vt.* to wake (*v. irr.*) (up). ♦ **risvegliarsi** *vr.* to wake up.

risveglio *sm.* 1. awakening 2. (*fig.*) revival.

risvoltare *vt.* to turn up.

risvolto *sm.* 1. (*di giacca*) lapel 2. (*di calzoni*) turn-up.

ritagliare *vt.* 1. to cut (*v. irr.*) out 2. (*tagliare di nuovo*) to cut again.

ritaglio *sm.* 1. (*di stoffa*) remnant 2. (*di giornale*) clipping || *ritagli di tempo,* odd moments.

ritardare *vt.* to delay. ♦ **ritardare** *vi.* 1. to be late 2. (*di orologio*) to be slow.

ritardatario *sm.* late-comer.

ritardo *sm.* delay: *in —,* late.

ritegno *sm.* 1. reserve 2. (*freno*) restraint 3. (*riluttanza*) reluctance.

ritemprare *vt.* 1. to strengthen 2. (*metalli*) to harden again. ♦ **ritemprarsi** *vr.* to get (*v. irr.*) stronger.

ritenere *vt.* 1. to hold (*v. irr.*) 2. (*giudicare*) to consider 3. (*pensare*) to think (*v. irr.*).

ritentare *vt.* 1. to tempt again 2. (*riprovare*) to try again.

ritenuta *sf.* deduction.

ritenzione *sf.* retention.

ritingere *vt.* to dye again.

ritirare *vt.* 1. to withdraw (*v. irr.*)

2. (*farsi consegnare*) to collect. ♦ **ritirarsi** *vr.* 1. to retire 2. (*di stoffa*) to shrink (*v. irr.*).

ritirata *sf.* 1. retreat 2. (*latrina*) lavatory.

ritiro *sm.* 1. withdrawal 2. (*il ritirarsi*) retirement 3. (*luogo appartato*) retreat 4. (*il farsi consegnare*) collection.

ritmare *vt.* to mark.

ritmica *sf.* rhythmic(s).

ritmico *agg.* rhythmic(al).

ritmo *sm.* rhythm.

rito *sm.* rite: *essere di —,* to be customary.

ritoccare *vt.* to retouch.

ritoccatore *sm.* retoucher.

ritocco *sm.* retouch.

ritogliere *vt.* 1. to take (*v. irr.*) off again 2. (*riappropriarsi*) to take back. ♦ **ritogliersi** *vr.* to take off again.

ritorcere *vt.* 1. to twist again 2. (*torcere*) to twist 3. (*rivolgere*) to retort. ♦ **ritorcersi** *vr.* 1. to get (*v. irr.*) twisted 2. (*fig.*) to recoil (on, upon).

ritorcitura *sf.* twisting.

ritornare *vi.* to return.

ritornello *sm.* refrain.

ritorno *sm.* return: *— di fiamma,* backfire; *essere di —,* to be back.

ritorsione *sf.* retortion.

ritorto *agg.* twisted.

ritrarre *vt.* 1. to withdraw (*v. irr.*) 2. (*distogliere*) to turn away 3. (*rappresentare*) to represent 4. (*dedurre*) to understand (*v. irr.*). ♦ **ritrarsi** *vr.* to withdraw.

ritrattare *vt.* 1. to retract 2. (*trattare di nuovo*) to treat again.

ritrattazione *sf.* 1. retraction 2. (*nuova trattazione*) new treatment.

ritrattista *s.* portraitist.

ritrattistica *sf.* portraiture.

ritratto *sm.* portrait.

ritrazione *sf.* retraction.

ritrito *agg.* stale.

ritrosia *sf.* 1. (*riluttanza*) reluctance 2. (*timidezza*) shyness.

ritroso *agg.* 1. (*riluttante*) reluctant 2. (*timido*) shy || *a —,* backwards.

ritrovamento *sm.* finding.

ritrovare *vt.* 1. to find (*v. irr.*) again 2. (*ricuperare*) to recover 3. (*scoprire*) to discover. ♦ **ritrovarsi** *vr.* 1. to find oneself 2. (*rincontrarsi*) to meet (*v. irr.*) again.

ritrovato *sm.* **1.** invention **2.** (*scoperta*) discovery.

ritrovo *sm.* meeting-place, haunt.

ritto *agg.* upright.

rituale *agg.* e *sm.* ritual.

rituffare *vt.* to plunge again. ♦ **rituffarsi** *vr.* to plunge again.

riudire *vt.* to hear (*v. irr.*) again.

riunione *sf.* meeting.

riunire *vt.* **1.** to re-unite **2.** (*raccogliere*) to gather **3.** (*unire*) to join. ♦ **riunirsi** *vr.* **1.** to come (*v. irr.*) together again **2.** (*unirsi*) to unite **3.** (*incontrarsi*) to meet (*v. irr.*).

riuscire *vi.* **1.** to succeed (in), to be good (at) **2.** (*risultare*) to be **3.** (*uscire di nuovo*) to go (*v. irr.*) out again.

riuscita *sf.* **1.** issue **2.** (*successo*) success.

riutilizzare *vt.* to utilize again.

riva *sf.* **1.** (*di mare, lago*) shore **2.** (*di fiume*) bank.

rivale *agg.* e *sm.* rival.

rivaleggiare *vi.* to rival (so., sthg.).

rivalersi *vr.* **1.** to make (*v. irr.*) up for one's losses **2.** (*valersi di nuovo*) to make use again.

rivalicare *vt.* to recross.

rivalità *sf.* rivalry.

rivalsa *sf.* **1.** (*rivincita*) revenge **2.** (*risarcimento*) compensation **3.** (*comm.*) recourse.

rivalutare *vt.* **1.** to revalue **2.** (*elevare*) to raise.

rivalutazione *sf.* **1.** revaluation **2.** (*aumento*) rise.

rivangare *vt.* e *vi.* to dig (*v. irr.*) up again.

rivedere *vt.* **1.** to see (*v. irr.*) again **2.** (*revisionare*) to revise.

riveduta *sf.* look, revision.

rivelare *vt.* to reveal. ♦ **rivelarsi** *vr.* **1.** to reveal oneself **2.** (*dimostrarsi*) to prove.

rivelatore *agg.* revealing. ♦ **rivelatore** *sm.* **1.** revealer **2.** (*radio*) detector.

rivelazione *sf.* **1.** revelation **2.** (*fis.; radio*) detection.

rivéndere *vt.* **1.** to resell (*v. irr.*) **2.** (*al dettaglio*) to retail.

rivendicare *vt.* **1.** to claim **2.** (*vendicare*) to revenge.

rivendicatore *agg.* **1.** claiming **2.** (*vendicatore*) revenging. ♦ **rivendicatore** *sm.* **1.** claimant **2.** (*vendicatore*) revenger.

rivendicazione *sf.* claim.

rivéndita *sf.* **1.** resale **2.** (*spaccio*) shop.

rivenditore *sm.* retailer.

rivendùgliolo *sm.* V. *rigattiere.*

riverberare *vt.* to reverberate. ♦ **riverberarsi** *vr.* to reverberate.

rivèrbero *sm.* reverberation: *di —,* indirectly.

riverente *agg.* reverent.

riverenza *sf.* **1.** reverence **2.** (*inchino*) bow.

riverenziale *agg.* reverential.

riverire *vt.* **1.** to revere **2.** (*salutare*) to pay (*v. irr.*) one's respects (to).

riversare *vt.* **1.** to pour again **2.** (*versare*) to pour **3.** (*di fiume*) to flow. ♦ **riversarsi** *vr.* to flow.

riverso *avv.* on one's back.

rivestimento *sm.* **1.** covering **2.** (*interno*) lining.

rivestire *vt.* **1.** to dress again **2.** (*foderare*) to line (with sthg.) **3.** (*coprire*) to cover (with sthg.) **4.** (*fig.*) to hold (*v. irr.*).

riviera *sf.* coast ‖ *la Riviera,* the Riviera.

rivierasco *agg.* coast (*attr.*).

rivìncere *vt.* **1.** to win (*v. irr.*) again **2.** (*recuperare*) to win back.

rivìncita *sf.* **1.** (*vendetta*) revenge **2.** (*sport*) return match **3.** (*al gioco*) return game.

rivista *sf.* **1.** review **2.** (*teat.*) revue **3.** (*mil.*) parade ‖ *passare in —,* to review.

rivìvere *vi.* e *vt.* to live again.

rivo *sm.* stream.

rivolere *vt.* **1.** to want again **2.** (*volere indietro*) to want back.

rivòlgere *vt.* **1.** to turn **2.** (*indirizzare*) to address. ♦ **rivòlgersi** *vr.* **1.** to turn **2.** (*parlando*) to address (so.) **3.** (*ricorrere, riferirsi*) to apply (to).

rivolgimento *sm.* **1.** upheaval **2.** (*cambio*) change.

rìvolo *sm.* streamlet.

rivolta *sf.* revolt.

rivoltante *agg.* revolting.

rivoltare *vt.* **1.** to turn (over) again **2.** (*rovesciare*) to turn **3.** (*capovolgere*) to turn upside-down **4.** (*con l'interno all'esterno*) to turn inside out **5.** (*fig.*) to upset (*v. irr.*). ♦ **rivoltarsi** *vr.* **1.** to turn round **2.** (*rigirarsi*) to turn over **3.** (*ribellarsi*) to revolt **4.** (*fig.*) to turn.

rivoltella *sf.* revolver.

rivoltoso *agg. e sm.* rebel.
rivoluzionare *vt.* to revolutionize.
rivoluzionario *agg. e sm.* revolutionary.
rivoluzione *sf.* revolution.
rizoma *sm.* rhizome.
rizzare *vt.* to raise: — *le orecchie,* to prick one's ears. ♦ **rizzarsi** *vr.* 1. to stand (*v. irr.*) up 2. (*di capelli*) to stand on end.
roba *sf.* stuff, things (*pl.*).
robaccia *sf.* rubbish.
robinia *sf.* locust-tree.
robustezza *sf.* robustness.
robusto *agg.* robust.
rocambolesco *agg.* daring.
rocca[1] *sf.* 1. stronghold 2. (*roccia*) rock.
rocca[2] *sf.* (*conocchia*) distaff.
roccaforte *sf.* stronghold.
rocchetto *sm.* 1. spool 2. (*elettr.*) coil.
rocchio *sm.* 1. (*di tronco*) log 2. (*di colonna*) drum.
roccia *sf.* rock.
rocciatore *sm.* rock-climber.
roccioso *agg.* rocky.
roco *agg.* hoarse.
rodaggio *sm.* (*auto*) running in.
rodare *vt.* to run (*v. irr.*) in.
ròdere *vt.* 1. to gnaw 2. (*corrodere*) to corrode. ♦ **ròdersi** *vr.* 1. to worry 2. (*di rabbia ecc.*) to be consumed (with).
rodimento *sm.* 1. gnawing 2. (*fig.*) anxiety.
roditore *agg. e sm.* rodent.
rododendro *sm.* rhododendron.
rogare *vt.* to draw (*v. irr.*) up.
rogatoria *sf.* request.
rogazioni *sf. pl.* rogations.
roggia *sf.* irrigation ditch.
** rògito** *sm.* deed.
rogna *sf.* 1. scabies 2. (*fig.*) trouble.
rognone *sm.* kidney.
rognoso *agg.* scabby.
rogo *sm.* 1. fire 2. (*pira*) pyre 3. (*supplizio*) stake.
rollare *vi.* to roll.
rollìo *sm.* roll.
romancio *agg.* Romansh.
romànico *agg.* 1. (*arch.*) Romanesque 2. Romanic.
romano *agg. e sm.* Roman.
romanticherìa *sf.* 1. (*atteggiamento*) romantic attitude 2. (*azione*) romantic deed.
romanticismo *sm.* Romanticism.
romàntico *agg. e sm.* romantic.

romanza *sf.* romance.
romanzare *vt.* to romanticize.
romanzesco *agg.* romantic.
romanziere *sm.* novelist.
romanzo[1] *agg.* Romance.
romanzo[2] *sm.* 1. novel 2. (*storia incredibile*) romance || — *a puntate,* serial; — *a fumetti,* comics.
romba *sf.* roar.
rombare *vi.* to rumble.
ròmbico *agg.* rhombic(al).
rombo[1] *sm.* (*rumore*) rumble.
rombo[2] *sm.* (*geom.*) rhomb.
rombo[3] *sm.* (*itt.*) brill.
romboèdrico *agg.* rhombohedral.
romboedro *sm.* rhombohedron (*pl.* -ra).
romboidale *agg.* rhomboid(al).
rombòide *agg. e sm.* rhomboid.
romeno *agg. e sm.* Rumanian.
romeo *sm.* pilgrim.
romitaggio *sm.* hermitage.
ròmito *agg.* solitary. ♦ **romito** *sm.* hermit.
romitorio *sm.* hermitage.
ròmpere *vt.* to break (*v. irr.*): — *i ponti con qu.,* to break with so. ♦ **ròmpersi** *vr.* to break (up).
rompicapo *sm.* puzzle.
rompicollo *sm.* madcap: *a —,* headlong.
rompighiaccio *sm.* ice-breaker.
rompiscàtole *s.* nuisance.
rompitore *sm.* breaker.
ronca *sf.* pruning-knife (*pl.* -ives).
ronciglio *sm.* hook.
ròncola *sf.* pruning-hook.
ronda *sf.* 1. rounds (*pl.*) 2. (*pattuglia*) patrol.
rondella *sf.* washer.
ròndine *sf.* swallow: *a coda di —,* swallow-tailed.
rondinotto *sm.* young swallow.
rondò *sm.* 1. (*mus.*) rondo 2. (*poet.*) rondel 3. (*piazza circolare*) circus.
rondone *sm.* swift.
ronfare *vi.* to snore.
ronzare *vi.* 1. to buzz 2. (*fig.*) to hang (*v. irr.*) around.
ronzino *sm.* jade.
ronzìo *sm.* buzz.
ròrido *agg.* 1. (*bagnato*) wet 2. (*rugiadoso*) dewy.
rosa *sf.* rose || *all'acqua di rose* (*fig.*), moderate. ♦ **rosa** *agg. e sm.* pink.
rosàceo *agg.* rosy.
rosaio *sm.* rose-bush.
rosario *sm.* rosary.

rosato agg. rosy.

ròseo agg. rosy.

rosèola sf. roseola.

roseto sm. rose-garden.

rosetta sf. **1.** rosette **2.** (diamante) rose **3.** (mecc.) washer.

rosicchiare vt. to gnaw.

rosmarino sm. rosemary.

rosolare vt. to brown. ♦ **rosolarsi** vr. **1.** to get (v. irr.) brown **2.** (prendere il sole) to bask.

rosolìa sf. German measles (pl.).

rosolio sm. rosolio.

rosone sm. rose-window.

rospo sm. toad.

rossastro agg. reddish.

rosseggiare vi. to be reddish.

rossetto sm. **1.** (per labbra) lipstick **2.** (per guance) rouge.

rossiccio agg. ruddy.

rosso agg. e sm. red: — d'uovo, yolk; diventar —, to flush.

rossore sm. flush.

rosticcerìa sf. rotisserie.

rosticciere sm. owner of a rotisserie.

rostro sm. **1.** rostrum (pl. -ra) **2.** (becco) beak.

rotàbile agg. carriage (attr.).

rotaia sf. **1.** rail **2.** (solco) rut.

rotare vi. e vt. to rotate, to revolve.

rotativa sf. rotary press.

rotativo agg. rotary.

rotatorio agg. rotating.

rotazione sf. rotation.

roteare vt. **1.** to swing (v. irr.) **2.** (gli occhi) to roll. ♦ **roteare** vi. to wheel.

rotella sf. small wheel.

rotocalco sm. **1.** rotogravure **2.** (rivista) illustrated magazine.

rotolamento sm. rolling.

rotolare vt. e vi. to roll. ♦ **rotolarsi** vr. to roll.

ròtolo sm. roll || andare a rotoli, to go (v. irr.) to rack and ruin; mandare a rotoli, to ruin.

rotolone sm. V. ruzzolone.

rotonda sf. rotunda.

rotondità sf. roundness.

rotondo agg. **1.** round **2.** (grassoccio) plump.

rotore sm. rotor.

rotta sf. **1.** course **2.** (rottura) breach **3.** (sconfitta) rout || a — di collo, headlong; essere in — con, to be on bad terms with; mettere in —, to rout.

rottame sm. **1.** wreck **2.** (di scarto) scraps (pl.).

rotto agg. **1.** broken **2.** (stracciato) torn **3.** (avvezzo) accustomed.

rottura sf. break(ing).

ròtula sf. knee-cap.

rovente agg. red-hot.

ròvere sm. oak.

rovesciamento sm. **1.** overthrowing **2.** (cambiamento) reversal.

rovesciare vt. **1.** to overturn **2.** (capovolgere) to turn upside down **3.** (gettare) to throw (v. irr.) **4.** (rivoltare) to turn inside out **5.** (versare intenzionalmente) to pour **6.** (versare accidentalmente) to spill **7.** (abbattere) to overthrow (v. irr.). ♦ **rovesciarsi** vr. **1.** to overturn **2.** (riversarsi) to pour.

rovescio sm. **1.** reverse **2.** (opposto) opposite **3.** (di pioggia) heavy shower **4.** (di critiche ecc.) hail || a — (capovolto), upside down.

roveto sm. bramble-bush.

rovina sf. ruin.

rovinare vt. **1.** to ruin **2.** (sciupare) to spoil (v. irr.). ♦ **rovinare** vi. to crash.

rovinìo sm. **1.** downfall **2.** (rumore) crash.

rovinoso agg. ruinous.

rovistare vt. e vi. to rummage.

rovo sm. blackberry bush.

rozza sf. jade.

rozzezza sf. roughness.

rozzo agg. rough.

ruba sf. andare a —, to sell (v. irr.) like wildfire.

rubacchiare vt. to pilfer.

rubacuori agg. bewitching. ♦ **rubacuori** sm. lady-killer.

rubare vt. to steal (v. irr.).

ruberìa sf. theft.

rubicondo agg. ruddy.

rubinetterìa sf. plumbing fixtures (pl.).

rubinetto sm. tap.

rubino sm. ruby.

rubizzo agg. hale.

rublo sm. rouble.

rubrica sf. **1.** (di giornale) column **2.** (per indirizzi) addressbook.

rude agg. rough.

rùdere sm. ruin.

rudezza sf. roughness.

rudimentale agg. rudimentary.

rudimento sm. rudiment.

ruffiano sm. pander.

ruga sf. wrinkle.

ruggente agg. roaring.

rùggine *sf.* **1.** rust **2.** (*fig.*) grudge.
rugginoso *agg.* rusty.
ruggire *vi.* to roar.
ruggito *sm.* roar.
rugiada *sf.* dew: *goccia di —,* dew-drop.
rugiadoso *agg.* dewy.
rugosità *sf.* **1.** wrinkledness **2.** (*scabrosità*) ruggedness.
rugoso *agg.* **1.** wrinkled **2.** (*scabro*) rugged.
rullaggio *sm.* pista di —, taxi-track.
rullare *vi.* **1.** to roll **2.** (*di aereo*) to taxi.
rullino *sm.* roll.
rullìo *sm.* roll.
rullo *sm.* **1.** roll **2.** (*mecc.*) roller.
rum *sm.* rum.
ruminante *agg. e sm.* ruminant.
ruminare *vt.* to ruminate.
ruminazione *sf.* rumination.
rùmine *sm.* rumen.
rumore *sm.* **1.** noise **2.** (*diceria*) rumour || *far —* (*fig.*), to arouse great interest.
rumoreggiare *vi.* **1.** to rumble **2.** (*fig.*) to rumour.
rumorìo *sm.* noise.
rumorista *sm.* noise-maker.
rumoroso *agg.* noisy.
ruolino *sm.* (*di marcia*) time schedule.
ruolo *sm.* **1.** roll, list **2.** (*teat.*) role **3.** (*amm.*) roster.
ruota *sf.* wheel.
rupe *sf.* cliff.
rupestre *agg.* rocky.
rurale *agg.* rural || *i rurali,* country people.
ruscello *sm.* brook.
ruspa *sf.* scraper.
ruspare *vi.* (*razzolare*) to scratch about.
russare *vi.* to snore.
russo *agg. e sm.* Russian.
rusticità *sf.* rusticity.
rùstico *agg.* **1.** rustic **2.** (*ritroso*) unsociable.
ruta *sf.* rue.
rutilante *agg.* glowing.
ruttare *vi.* to belch.
rutto *sm.* belch.
rùvido *agg.* rough.
ruzzare *vi.* to romp.
ruzzolare *vt.* to roll. ♦ **ruzzolare** *vi.* **1.** to roll **2.** (*cadere*) to tumble down.
ruzzolone *sm.* tumble: *fare un —,* to tumble down.

S

sàbato *sm.* Saturday.
sabba *sm.* witches' Sabbath.
sabbia *sf.* sand.
sabbiare *vt.* to sand.
sabbiatura *sf.* sand-bath.
sabbioso *agg.* sandy.
sabotaggio *sm.* sabotage.
sabotare *vt.* to sabotage.
sabotatore *sm.* saboteur.
sacca *sf.* bag.
saccarina *sf.* saccharine.
saccarosio *sm.* saccharose.
saccente *agg.* pedantic. ♦ **saccente** *s.* pedant.
saccheggiare *vt.* to sack.
saccheggio *sm.* sack.
sacchetto *sm.* small bag.
sacco *sm.* **1.** sack, bag || *colazione al —,* picnic; *mettere qu. nel —,* to take (*v. irr.*) so. in **2.** (*grande quantità*) a lot of.
saccoccia *sf.* pocket.
saccone *sm.* palliasse.
sacerdotale *agg.* sacerdotal.
sacerdote *sm.* priest.
sacerdozio *sm.* priesthood.
sacrale *agg.* sacral.
sacramentale *agg.* sacramental.
sacramentare *vi.* (*fig.*) to swear (*v. irr.*).
sacramento *sm.* sacrament.
sacrario *sm.* shrine.
sacrificare *vt.* to sacrifice.
sacrificio *sm.* sacrifice.
sacrilegio *sm.* sacrilege.
sacrìlego *agg.* sacrilegious.
sacrista *sm.* sacristan.
sacro *agg.* sacred, holy.
sacrosanto *agg.* **1.** sacrosanct **2.** (*indiscutibile*) absolute.
sàdico *agg.* sadistic. ♦ **sàdico** *sm.* sadist.
sadismo *sm.* sadism.
saetta *sf.* **1.** arrow **2.** (*fulmine*) thunderbolt.
saettare *vt.* **1.** to shoot (*v. irr.*) arrows at **2.** (*fig.*) to dart. ♦ **saettare** *vi.* to dart.
sàffico *agg.* Sapphic.
sagace *agg.* sagacious.
sagacia *sf.* sagacity.
saggezza *sf.* wisdom.
saggiare *vt.* to assay, to test.
saggiatore *sm.* **1.** assayer **2.** (*bilancia*) assay balance.
saggina *sf.* sorghum.

saggio[1] *agg.* wise. ♦ **saggio** *sm.* wise man (*pl.* men).

saggio[2] *sm.* **1.** essay **2.** (*campione*) sample **3.** (*saggio ginnico*) display.

saggista *s.* essayist.

sagittario *sm.* **1.** archer **2.** (*astr.*) Sagittarius.

sàgoma *sf.* shape || è una —! (*fam.*), he is a character!

sagomare *vt.* to shape.

sagra *sf.* festival.

sagrato *sm.* church-square.

sagrestano *sm.* sacristan.

sagrestìa *sf.* sacristy.

saia *sf.* serge.

saio *sm.* habit.

sala *sf.* hall, room: — da pranzo, dining-room.

salace *agg.* salacious.

salacità *sf.* salacity.

salamandra *sf.* salamander.

salame *sm.* salami (*pl.*).

salamelecco *sm.* salaam.

salamoia *sf.* pickle.

salare *vt.* to salt.

salariale *agg.* salary (*attr.*).

salariato *agg.* wage-earning. ♦ **salariato** *sm.* wage-earner.

salario *sm.* wages (*pl.*).

salassare *vt.* to bleed (*v. irr.*).

salasso *sm.* **1.** bleeding **2.** (*fig.*) extortion.

salato *agg.* **1.** salty **2.** (*costoso*) dear **3.** (*salace*) keen.

salatura *sf.* salting.

salda *sf.* starch-water.

saldamente *avv.* firmly.

saldare *vt.* **1.** to solder, to weld **2.** (*un conto*) to settle.

saldatore *sm.* solderer, welder.

saldatrice *sf.* welding machine.

saldatura *sf.* soldering, welding.

saldezza *sf.* firmness.

saldo[1] *agg.* firm.

saldo[2] *sm.* balance: — attivo, passivo, credit, debit balance.

sale *sm.* salt.

salesiano *agg.* e *sm.* Salesian.

salgemma *sm.* rock-salt.

sàlice *sm.* willow.

salicilato *sm.* salicylate.

saliente *agg.* important.

saliera *sf.* salt-cellar.

salina *sf.* salt-pit.

salino *agg.* saline, salt (*attr.*).

salire *vi.* **1.** to rise (*v. irr.*), to go (*v. irr.*) up **2.** (*di prezzi*) to increase.

saliscendi *sm.* **1.** latch **2.** (*alter-*

narsi di salite e discese*) ups and downs (*pl.*).

salita *sf.* **1.** slope, ascent **2.** (*aumento*) rise.

saliva *sf.* saliva, spittle.

salivare *agg.* salivary.

salivare *vi.* to salivate.

salivazione *sf.* salivation.

salma *sf.* corpse.

salmastro *agg.* saltish.

salmo *sm.* psalm.

salmodìa *sf.* psalmody.

salmodiare *vi.* to sing (*v. irr.*) psalms.

salmone *sm.* salmon.

salnitro *sm.* saltpetre.

salone *sm.* large hall, reception--room.

salottiero *agg.* drawing-room (*attr.*).

salotto *sm.* sitting-room.

salpare *vi.* to set (*v. irr.*) sails.

salsa *sf.* sauce.

salsèdine *sf.* saltness.

salsiccia *sf.* sausage.

salsiera *sf.* sauce-boat.

salso *agg.* salt (*attr.*).

saltare *vt.* e *vi.* to jump, to leap (*v. irr.*): — di palo in frasca, to jump from one subject to another; far — una serratura, to break (*v. irr.*) a lock.

saltatore *agg.* jumping. ♦ **saltatore** *sm.* jumper.

saltellare *vi.* to hop.

saltimbanco *sm.* tumbler.

salto *sm.* jump, leap.

saltuario *agg.* desultory.

salubre *agg.* healthy.

salubrità *sf.* healthiness.

salume *sm.* salted meat.

salumiere *sm.* delicatessen seller.

salumerìa *sf.* delicatessen.

salutare[1] *agg.* healthy.

salutare[2] *vt.* to greet, to hail.

salute *sf.* health.

saluto *sm.* greeting, salute.

salva *sf.* volley (*anche fig.*): colpo a —, blank shot.

salvacondotto *sm.* safe-conduct.

salvadanaio *sm.* money-box.

salvagente *sm.* **1.** life-belt **2.** (*marciapiede*) traffic island.

salvaguardare *vt.* to safeguard.

salvaguardia *sf.* safeguard.

salvare *vt.* **1.** to save (*anche fig.*) **2.** (*trarre in salvo*) to rescue. ♦ **salvarsi** *vr.* to save oneself.

salvataggio *sm.* rescue.

salvatore *sm.* saviour, saver.

salve *inter.* hail.

salvezza *sf.* salvation.

salvia *sf.* sage.

salvietta *sf.* towel.

salvo *agg.* safe. ♦ **salvo** *prep.* except, save. ♦ **salvo che** *cong.* except that, unless.

sanàbile *agg.* curable, remediable.

sanare *vt.* to heal.

sanatorio *sm.* sanatorium (*pl.* -ia).

sancire *vt.* to sanction.

sanculotto *sm.* sansculotte.

sàndalo[1] *sm.* (*calzatura*) sandal.

sàndalo[2] *sm.* (*mar.*) punt.

sandolino *sm.* small canoe.

sangue *sm.* blood: *spargimento di* —, bloodshed; *perdita di* —, bleeding; — *freddo*, coolness; *a* — *freddo*, in cold blood; *farsi cattivo* —, to worry over; *buon* — *non mente*, blood will tell.

sanguigno *agg.* sanguineous, blood (*attr.*).

sanguinaccio *sm.* blood-sausage.

sanguinante *agg.* bleeding.

sanguinare *vi.* to bleed (*v. irr.*).

sanguinario *agg. e sm.* sanguinary: *uomo* —, bloodthirsty man.

sanguinoso *agg.* bloody.

sanguisuga *sf.* leech.

sanità *sf.* soundness, sanity.

sanitario *sm.* sanitary.

sano *agg.* **1.** healthy **2.** (*fig.*) sound **3.** (*intero, intatto*) intact.

sansa *sf.* husk.

sànscrito *sm.* Sanskrit.

santarellina *sf.* goody-goody.

santificante *agg.* sanctifying.

santificare *vt.* to canonize: — *le feste*, to observe holy days.

santificazione *sf.* sanctification.

santino *sm.* small holy picture.

santìssimo *agg.* most holy: *il* — *Sacramento*, the Blessed Sacrament.

santità *sf.* holiness.

santo *agg.* **1.** holy **2.** (*seguito da nome proprio*) saint. ♦ **santo** *sm.* saint.

santone *sm.* santon.

santuario *sm.* sanctuary.

sanzionare *vt.* to ratify.

sanzione *sf.* sanction.

sapere[1] *vt.* **1.** to know (*v. irr.*): *non* — *che fare*, to be at a loss what to do; *chi sa!*, who knows!; *non si sa mai*, you never know; *venire a* —, to hear (*v. irr.*) **2.** (*essere capace*) can, to be able: *sai parlare inglese?*, can you speak

English?; *non so farlo*, I am not able to do it. ♦ **sapere** *vi.* (*aver sapore*) to taste.

sapere[2] *sm.* **1.** knowledge **2.** (*cultura*) learning.

sàpido *agg.* sapid.

sapiente *agg.* wise. ♦ **sapiente** *sm.* sage.

sapienza *sf.* wisdom.

saponaria *sf.* soapwort.

saponata *sf.* lather (*solo sing.*).

sapone *sm.* soap: — *da barba*, shaving-soap; — *da bagno*, bath soap.

saponetta *sf.* cake of soap.

saponificare *vt.* to saponify.

saponificazione *sf.* saponification.

saponificio *sm.* soap-works (*pl. con costruzione sing.*).

sapore *sm.* taste, flavour (*anche fig.*).

saporire *vt.* to flavour.

saporitamente *avv.* savourily || *dormire* —, to sleep (*v. irr.*) soundly.

saporito *agg.* savoury, tasty.

saputello *sm.* wiseacre.

saputo *agg.* **1.** learned **2.** (*noto*) well-known.

sarabanda *sf.* saraband.

saraceno *sm.* saracen.

saracinesca *sf.* rolling-shutter.

sarcasmo *sm.* sarcasm.

sarcàstico *agg.* sarcastic.

sarchiare *vt.* to weed.

sarchiatore *agg.* weeding. ♦ **sarchiatore** *sm.* weeder.

sarchiatura *sf.* weeding.

sarchio *sm.* hoe.

sarcòfago *sm.* sarcophagus (*pl.* -gi).

sardina *sf.* sardine.

sardònico *agg.* sardonic.

sarmento *sm.* runner.

sarta *sf.* dressmaker.

sartie *sf. pl.* shrouds.

sartina *sf.* grisette.

sarto *sm.* tailor.

sartorìa *sf.* **1.** (*da uomo*) tailor's **2.** (*da donna*) dressmaker's.

sassaia *sf.* stony place.

sassaiuola *sf.* **1.** shower of stones **2.** (*battaglia di sassi*) stone-fight.

sassata *sf.* blow with a stone.

sasso *sm.* stone: *a un tiro di* — *da*, within a stone's throw of.

sassofonista *sm.* saxophonist

sassòfono *sm.* saxophone.

sassolino *sm.* pebble.

sàssone *agg. e sm.* Saxon.

sassoso *agg.* stony.
satànico *agg.* Satanic.
satèllite *sm.* satellite.
sàtira *sf.* satire.
satìrico *agg.* satirical.
sàtiro *sm.* satyr.
satollare *vt.* to satiate.
satollo *agg.* satiated.
sàtrapo *sm.* satrap.
saturare *vt.* to saturate.
saturazione *sf.* saturation.
saturnali *sm. pl.* saturnalia.
sàturo *agg.* saturated.
sàuro *agg.* sorrel.
savana *sf.* savannah.
savio *agg.* wise. ♦ **savio** *sm.* sage.
saziàbile *agg.* satiable.
saziare *vt.* to satisfy, to glut. ♦ **saziarsi** *vr.* to get (*v. irr.*) full.
sazietà *sf.* satiety: *mangiare, bere a —,* to eat (*v. irr.*), to drink (*v. irr.*) one's fill.
sazio *agg.* replete, full.
sbaciucchiare *vt.* to smother with kisses.
sbadatàggine *sf.* carelessness.
sbadato *agg.* careless.
sbadigliare *vi.* to yawn.
sbadiglio *sm.* yawn.
sbafare *vi.* to scrounge.
sbafatore *sm.* scrounger.
sbafo (*nella loc. avv.*) *prendere qc. a —,* to scrounge sthg.
sbagliare *vi.* to mistake (*v. irr.*). ♦ **sbagliarsi** *vr.* to make (*v. irr.*) a mistake.
sbagliato *agg.* wrong.
sbaglio *sm.* mistake.
sbalestrare *vt.* **1.** to send (*v. irr.*) **2.** (*fig.*) to flounder.
sballare *vt.* to unpack.
sballato *agg.* (*fig.*) foolhardy.
sballottamento *sm.* jolting.
sballottare *vt.* to jolt (about), to toss (about).
sbalordimento *sm.* amazement.
sbalordire *vt.* to amaze.
sbalorditivo *agg.* amazing.
sbalordito *agg.* amazed.
sbalzamento *sm.* **1.** overthrow **2.** (*fig.*) dismissal.
sbalzare[1] *vt.* to throw (*v. irr.*), to toss.
sbalzare[2] *vt.* (*arte*) to emboss.
sbalzato *agg.* (*arte*) embossed.
sbalzo *sm.* **1.** bound, jump **2.** (*cambio*) change.
sbancare *vt.* to leave (*v. irr.*) broke.

sbandamento *sm.* **1.** dispersal **2.** (*auto*) skid **3.** (*mar.*) list.
sbandare *vt.* **1.** to disperse **2.** (*auto*) to cause a skid.
sbandata *sf.* V. *sbandamento.*
sbandato *sm.* straggler.
sbandierare *vt.* (*fig.*) to display.
sbaragliare *vt.* to rout.
sbaraglio *sm.* jeopardy: *mettere allo —,* to jeopardize.
sbarazzare *vt.* to clear up. ♦ **sbarazzarsi** *vr.* to get (*v. irr.*) rid (of).
sbarazzino *agg.* free and easy. ♦ **sbarazzino** *sm.* little scamp.
sbarbare *vt.* to shave.
sbarbatello *sm.* young colt.
sbarcare *vt. e vi.* to land, to disembark.
sbarco *sm.* **1.** (*di passeggeri*) landing **2.** (*di merci*) unloading.
sbarra *sf.* **1.** bar **2.** (*del timone*) tiller.
sbarramento *sm.* **1.** barricade **2.** (*di acque*) dam **3.** (*mil.*) barrage.
sbarrare *vt.* **1.** to bar: *— un assegno,* to cross a cheque **2.** (*spalancare*) to open wide.
sbarrato *agg.* blocked || *occhi sbarrati,* wide open eyes.
sbatacchiamento *sm.* banging, slamming.
sbatacchiare *vt.* to bang, to slam.
sbàttere *vt.* **1.** (*urtare contro*) to knock **2.** (*scaraventare*) to throw (*v. irr.*) **3.** (*chiudere violentemente*) to slam **4.** (*di panna, uova*) to whip, to beat (*v. irr.*).
sbattezzare *vt.* to force to abjure Christianity.
sbattimento *sm.* banging.
sbattiuova *sm.* egg-whisk.
sbattuto *agg.* **1.** depressed: *viso —,* tired face **2.** (*di uova*) beaten.
sbavare *vi.* **1.** to dribble **2.** (*tip.*) to smudge.
sbavatura *sf.* **1.** dribble **2.** (*tip.*) smudge.
sbellicarsi *vr.* *— dalle risa,* to split (*v. irr.*) one's sides with laughter.
sbendare *vt.* to unbandage.
sberla *sf.* slap.
sberleffo *sm.* grimace.
sbertucciare *vt.* **1.** to mock **2.** (*sgualcire*) to crumple.
sbiadire *vi.* to fade.
sbiancare *vt.* to bleach. ♦ **sbiancare** *vi.* to turn white. ♦ **sbiancarsi** *vr.* to turn white.

sbieco *agg.* slanting: *guardare qu. di* —, to look askance at so.; *tagliare una stoffa di* —, to cut (*v. irr.*) a cloth on the bias.

sbigottimento *sm.* dismay.

sbigottire *vt.* to dismay. ♦ **sbigottirsi** *vr.* to be dismayed.

sbigottito *agg.* dismayed.

sbilanciare *vt.* to unbalance. ♦ **sbilanciarsi** *vr.* **1.** to lose (*v. irr.*) one's balance **2.** (*fig.*) to commit oneself.

sbilancio *sm.* lack of balance; disproportion.

sbilenco *agg.* crooked.

sbirciare *vt.* to cast (*v. irr.*) a sidelong glance.

sbirraglia *sf.* police (*us. al pl.*).

sbirro *sm.* policeman (*pl.* -men).

sbizzarrirsi *vr.* to satisfy one's whims.

sbloccare *vt.* to raise the blockade: — *gli affitti,* to decontrol rents.

sblocco *sm.* **1.** raising the blockade **2.** (*mecc.*) releasing the brake **3.** (*econ.*) decontrol.

sboccare *vi.* **1.** (*di corso d'acqua*) to flow **2.** (*di strada*) to lead (*v. irr.*).

sboccato *agg.* (*fig.*) coarse.

sbocciare *vi.* to open, to blossom.

sboccio *sm.* blooming.

sbocco *sm.* outlet, exit.

sbocconcellare *vt.* to nibble.

sbollire *vi.* (*fig.*) to cool down.

sbolognare *vt.* to palm off.

sbornia *sf.* drunkenness: *prendere la* —, to get (*v. irr.*) drunk.

sborsamento *sm.* paying out.

sborsare *vt.* to pay (*v. irr.*) out.

sborso *sm.* **1.** payment **2.** (*denaro sborsato*) outlay.

sbottare *vi.* to burst (*v. irr.*) out.

sbotto *sm.* outburst.

sbottonare *vt.* to unbutton. ♦ **sbottonarsi** *vr.* **1.** to undo (*v. irr.*) one's buttons **2.** (*fig.*) to disclose one's feelings.

sbozzare *vt.* to sketch out.

sbracare *vt.* to unbreech.

sbracato *agg.* (*fig.*) unseemly.

sbracciare *vi.* to gesticulate. ♦ **sbracciarsi** *vr.* **1.** to roll up one's sleeves **2.** (*agitarsi*) to strive (*v. irr.*).

sbracciato *agg.* (*di persona*) with bare arms.

sbraitare *vi.* to shout.

sbranamento *sm.* tearing to pieces.

sbranare *vt.* to tear (*v. irr.*) to pieces.

sbrancare *vt.* to separate. ♦ **sbrancarsi** *vr.* to scatter.

sbrattare *vt.* to clean.

sbriciolamento *sm.* crumbling.

sbriciolare *vt.* to crumble.

sbrigare *vt.* to finish off, to get (*v. irr.*) through. ♦ **sbrigarsi** *vr.* to hurry up.

sbrigativo *agg.* quick, hasty.

sbrigliare *vt.* to unbridle.

sbrinamento *sm.* defrosting.

sbrinare *vt.* to defrost.

sbrindellare *vt.* to tear (*v. irr.*) to ribbons.

sbrodolare *vt.* to spill (*v. irr.*).

sbrodolone *sm.* **1.** slovenly eater **2.** (*chi parla a lungo*) babbler.

sbrogliare *vt.* to disentangle. ♦ **sbrogliarsi** *vr.* to extricate oneself.

sbronza *sf.* V. *sbornia.*

sbronzarsi *vr.* to get (*v. irr.*) drunk.

sbronzo *agg.* drunk.

sbruffare *vt.* to besprinkle. ♦ **sbruffare** *vi.* (*fig.*) to brag.

sbruffo *sm.* sprinkle.

sbruffone *sm.* braggart.

sbucare *vi.* **1.** to come (*v. irr.*) out **2.** (*fig.*) to spring (*v. irr.*).

sbucciare *vt.* **1.** to peel **2.** (*sgranare*) to shell.

sbucciatura *sf.* **1.** peeling **2.** (*scalfittura*) scratch.

sbudellamento *sm.* stabbing.

sbudellare *vt.* to stab.

sbuffare *vi.* **1.** to pant, to puff **2.** (*per noia, ira*) to snort.

sbuffo *sm.* **1.** puff **2.** (*per noia, ira*) snort.

sbugiardare *vt.* to give (*v. irr.*) the lie to.

sbullonare *vt.* to unbolt.

scabbia *sf.* scabies.

scabbioso *agg.* scabby.

scabro *agg.* rough.

scabrosità *sf.* **1.** roughness **2.** (*fig.*) difficulty.

scabroso *agg.* **1.** rough **2.** (*fig.*) scabrous.

scacchiera *sf.* chess-board.

scacchiere *sm.* (*stor.*) Exchequer.

scacchista *sm.* chess-player.

scacciacani *sf.* dummy pistol.

scacciare *vt.* **1.** to drive (*v. irr.*) away **2.** (*da scuola*) to expel.

scacciata *sf.* expulsion.

scaccino sm. church cleaner.

scacco sm. 1. (quadratino) square 2. (disegno su tessuti) check 3. (giuoco) chess || — matto, checkmate.

scadente agg. 1. poor 2. (comm.) falling due.

scadenza sf. (comm.) maturity: a breve, lunga scadenza (comm.), at short, long maturity || a breve —, in a short time.

scadenzario sm. discount bill-book.

scadere vi. 1. to expire 2. (di pagamenti ecc.) to become (v. irr.) due 3. (peggiorare) to fall (v. irr.) off.

scadimento sm. decay.

scafandro sm. diving-suit.

scaffalare vt. to shelve.

scaffalatura sf. shelving.

scaffale sm. shelf (pl. shelves).

scafo sm. hull, body.

scagionare vt. to acquit. ♦ **scagionarsi** vr. to exculpate oneself.

scaglia sf. 1. scale 2. (di legno, pietra) chip.

scagliare vt. to fling (v. irr.), to throw (v. irr.).

scaglionare vt. to divide into groups.

scaglione sm. 1. group 2. (mil.) echelon.

scaglioso agg. scaly.

scala sf. 1. stairs (pl.) 2. (trasportabile) ladder 3. (scala graduata) scale || salire, scendere le scale, to go (v. irr.) upstairs, downstairs.

scalare[1] agg. gradual.

scalare[2] vt. 1. to climb (up) 2. (diminuire) to scale down.

scalata sf. climbing.

scalatore sm. climber.

scalcagnato agg. down-at-heel, shabby.

scalciare vi. to kick.

scalcinato agg. 1. unplastered 2. (sciatto) shabby.

scaldabagno sm. water-heater.

scaldaletto sm. bed-warmer.

scaldapiedi sm. foot-warmer.

scaldare vt. to heat, to warm. ♦ **scaldarsi** vr. to warm oneself, to get (v. irr.) warm.

scaldavivande sm. dish-warmer.

scaldino sm. hand-warmer.

scalea sf. flight of stairs.

scaleno agg. scalene.

scalfire vt. to scratch.

scalfittura sf. scratch.

scalinata sf. flight of steps.

scalino sm. step.

scalmanarsi vr. (fig.) to get (v. irr.) excited.

scalmanato agg. out of breath, excited.

scalmo sm. rowlock.

scalo sm. 1. (mar.; aer.) port of call: volo senza —, non-stop flight 2. (ferr.) goods station || fare — a, to touch at.

scalogna sf. bad luck.

scalognato agg. unlucky.

scalone sm. great staircase.

scaloppina sf. veal cutlet.

scalpellare vt. to chisel.

scalpellino sm. stone-cutter.

scalpello sm. chisel.

scalpicciare vi. to shuffle.

scalpiccìo sm. shuffling.

scalpitare vi. 1. to paw 2. (di persona) to stamp.

scalpitìo sm. 1. pawing 2. (di persona) stamping.

scalpore sm. fuss, noise.

scaltrezza sf. shrewdness.

scaltrire vt. to sharpen so.'s wits. ♦ **scaltrirsi** vr. to become (v. irr.) sharp.

scaltro agg. shrewd.

scalzacane sm. 1. (incompetente) botcher 2. (malridotto) down-and-out.

scalzare vt. 1. to take (v. irr.) so.'s shoes and socks off 2. (fig.) to undermine.

scalzo agg. barefoot.

scambiare vt. 1. to exchange 2. (sbagliarsi) to mistake (v. irr.).

scambiévole agg. reciprocal.

scambio sm. 1. exchange 2. (ferr.) points (pl.).

scambista sm. (ferr.) pointsman (pl. -men).

scamiciato agg. shirt-sleeved (attr.).

scamosciare vt. to chamois.

scamosciato agg. shammy.

scampagnata sf. trip into the country.

scampanare vt. to chime.

scampanellare vi. to ring (v. irr.) long and loudly.

scampanellata sf. loud long ring.

scampare vi. to escape || l'hai scampata bella!, you have had a narrow escape.

scampato sm. survivor.

scampo[1] sm. escape: via di —, escape.

scampo² *sm.* (*itt.*) shrimp.
scàmpolo *sm.* remnant.
scanalare *vt.* to channel.
scanalatura *sf.* groove.
scandagliare *vt.* to sound.
scandaglio *sm.* sounding-lead.
scandalizzare *vt.* to shock.
scandalizzato *agg.* shocked.
scàndalo *sm.* scandal: *fare uno —,* to stir up a scandal.
scandaloso *agg.* scandalous, shocking.
scandire *vt.* 1. to scan 2. (*parole*) to syllabize 3. (*mus.*) to stress.
scannare *vt.* 1. to cut (*v. irr.*) so.'s throat 2. (*uccidere crudelmente*) to slaughter.
scannatoio *sm.* slaughter-house.
scanno *sm.* seat.
scansafatiche *sm.* lazy-bones.
scansare *vt.* to avoid, to shun. ♦ **scansarsi** *vr.* to step aside.
scansìa *sf.* shelves (*pl.*).
scantinato *sm.* basement.
scantonamento *sm.* (*l'evitare*) avoiding.
scantonare *vt.* (*evitare*) to avoid. ♦ **scantonare** *vi.* to turn the corner.
scanzonato *agg.* unconventional.
scapaccione *sm.* slap.
scapatàggine *sf.* recklessness.
scapestrato *agg. e sm.* madcap.
scapigliare *vt.* to dishevel.
scapigliato *agg.* 1. dishevelled 2. (*fig.*) unruly.
scàpito *sm.* damage, detriment: *a — di,* to the detriment of.
scàpola *sf.* shoulder-blade.
scapolare *agg. e sm.* scapular.
scàpolo *agg.* single. ♦ **scàpolo** *sm.* bachelor.
scappamento *sm.* 1. escape 2. (*di motori*) exhaust.
scappare *vi.* to escape, to run (*v. irr.*) away || *lasciarsi —,* to miss.
scappata *sf.* 1. escape 2. (*breve visita*) call.
scappatella *sf.* prank.
scappatoia *sf.* loop-hole.
scappellarsi *vr.* to take (*v. irr.*) off one's hat.
scappellata *sf.* raising one's hat.
scappellotto *sm.* slap.
scarabeo *sm.* scarab.
scarabocchiare *vt. e vi.* to scribble.
scarabocchio *sm.* scribble.
scarafaggio *sm.* black-beetle.
scaramanzìa *sf. per —,* for luck.

scaramuccia *sf.* skirmish.
scaraventare *vt.* to hurl.
scarcerare *vt.* to release (from prison).
scarcerazione *sf.* release (from prison).
scardinare *vt.* to unhinge.
scàrica *sf.* 1. (*di armi da fuoco; elettr.*) discharge 2. (*di proiettili, frecce; fig.*) shower.
scaricabarili *sm. fare a —,* to lay (*v. irr.*) the blame on so. else.
scaricamento *sm.* unloading.
scaricare *vt.* to discharge.
scaricatoio *sm.* 1. wharf 2. (*tubo*) waste-pipe.
scaricatore *sm.* unloader: *— di porto,* docker.
scàrico *sm.* 1. (*scolo*) drain 2. (*di merci*) discharge. ♦ **scàrico** *agg.* 1. (*di arma*) unloaded 2. discharged.
scarlattina *sf.* scarlet fever.
scarlatto *agg.* scarlet.
scarmigliare *vt.* to dishevel.
scarnire *vt.* to take (*v. irr.*) flesh off.
scarno *agg.* thin, lean.
scarpa *sf.* shoe: *— col tacco alto,* high-heeled shoe; *lucido per scarpe,* shoe polish.
scarpata *sf.* scarp.
scarpone *sm.* boot.
scarroccio *sm.* (*mar.*) leeway.
scarrozzare *vt. e vi.* to drive (*v. irr.*) about.
scarsamente *avv.* scarcely.
scarseggiare *vi.* to be lacking (in).
scarsità *vt.* shortage, lack.
scarso *agg.* scanty, lacking in.
scartabellare *vt.* to look through.
scartafaccio *sm.* note-book.
scartamento *sm.* (*ferr.*) gauge: *— ridotto,* narrow gauge.
scartare¹ *vt.* (*mettere da parte*) to reject.
scartare² *vi.* to unwrap.
scartare³ *vt.* (*sport*) to swerve.
scarto¹ *sm.* 1. (*cosa scartata*) discard 2. (*lo scartare*) discarding.
scarto² *sm.* (*deviazione*) swerve.
scartocciare *vt.* to unwrap.
scartoffie *sf. pl.* heap of papers.
scassare *vt.* (*rompere*) to force open.
scassinare *vt.* to break (*v. irr.*) open.
scassinatore *sm.* 1. house-breaker 2. (*di notte*) burglar.

scasso sm. lock-picking, house--breaking: *furto con* — (*di giorno*), house-breaking; (*di notte*) burglary.

scatenamento sm. (*fig.*) outburst.

scatenare vt. 1. (*aizzare*) to stir up 2. (*suscitare*) to rouse. ♦ **scatenarsi** vr. 1. to break (*v. irr.*) loose 2. (*fig.*) to break out.

scàtola sf. 1. box 2. (*di latta*) tin.

scatolame sm. 1. tins (*pl.*) 2. (*cibo in scatola*) tinned food.

scattare vi. 1. (*adirarsi*) to lose (*v. irr.*) one's temper 2. to go (*v. irr.*) off; to spring (*v. irr.*). ♦ **scattare** vt. (*foto*) to shoot (*v. irr.*).

scatto sm. 1. (*d'ira*) outburst || *di* —, suddenly; *a scatti*, in jerks 2. (*rumore*) click 3. (*di stipendio*) increase.

scaturire vi. 1. to spring (*v. irr.*) 2. (*derivare*) to originate.

scavalcare vt. 1. (*gettare da cavallo*) to unhorse 2. (*fig.*) to supplant 3. (*passare sopra*) to step, to jump over.

scavare vt. 1. to dig (*v. irr.*) 2. (*archeologia*) to excavate.

scavatrice sf. excavator.

scavezzacollo sm. reckless fellow.

scavo sm. 1. digging 2. (*archeologia*) excavation.

scégliere vt. to choose (*v. irr.*), to pick out.

sceicco sm. sheik.

scelleratezza sf. 1. wickedness 2. (*atto scellerato*) misdeed.

scellerato agg. wicked. ♦ **scellerato** sm. wicked person.

scellino sm. shilling: *mezzo* —, sixpence.

scelta sf. choice.

scelto agg. choice, selected.

scemare vi. to diminish.

scemenza sf. stupidity.

scemo agg. e sm. stupid.

scempiare vt. to halve.

scempio[1] agg. stupid, foolish.

scempio[2] sm. havoc.

scena sf. 1. scene 2. (*palcoscenico*) stage: *colpo di* —, stage effect.

scenario sm. scenery.

scenata sf. row.

scéndere vi. 1. to go (*v. irr.*) down, to come (*v. irr.*) down 2. (*da un veicolo*) to get (*v. irr.*) off; (*da cavallo*), to dismount (from a horse) 3. (*declinare*) to slope down 4. (*di astri*) to sink (*v. irr.*) 5. (*avere origini*) to descend.

scendiletto sm. bedside-carpet.

sceneggiare vt. to arrange into scenes.

sceneggiatore sm. scenarist.

sceneggiatura sf. screenplay.

scenicamente avv. scenically.

scenografìa sf. scenography.

scèrnere vt. to choose (*v. irr.*).

scervellarsi vr. to rack one's brains.

scervellato agg. brainless. ♦ **scervellato** sm. brainless person.

scetticismo sm. scepticism.

scèttico agg. sceptical. ♦ **scèttico** sm. sceptic.

scettro sm. sceptre.

sceverare vt. to discern.

scevro agg. exempt.

scheda sf. card: — *elettorale*, voting-paper.

schedario sm. card-index.

scheggia sf. splinter, chip.

scheggiare vt. to chip, to splinter.

schelètrico agg. skeletal.

schèletro sm. skeleton.

schema sm. 1. scheme 2. (*tec.*) diagram.

schemàtico agg. schematic.

schematismo sm. schematism.

scherma sf. fencing.

schermaglia sf. skirmish.

schermare vt. 1. to screen 2. (*elettr.*) to shield.

schermirsi vr. to act coy.

schermitore sm. fencer.

schermo sm. 1. protection 2. (*cine*) screen 3. (*fis.*) shield 4. (*foto*) filter.

schernire vt. to laugh at.

scherno sm. mockery, derision.

scherzare vi. 1. to joke 2. (*considerare con leggerezza*) to trifle with.

scherzo sm. 1. joke: *per* —, for fun 2. (*effetto*) effects (*pl.*).

scherzosamente avv. playfully.

scherzoso agg. playful.

schettinare vi. to roller-skate.

schettini sm. pl. roller-skates.

schiaccianoci sm. nut-cracker.

schiacciante agg. (*decisivo*) overwhelming.

schiacciare vt. to crush, to squash.

schiàcciasassi sm. steam-roller.

schiaffare vt. to hurl.

schiaffeggiare vt. to slap.

schiaffo sm. 1. slap 2. (*affronto*) slap in the face.

schiamazzare vi. to make (*v. irr.*) a din.

schiamazzo sm. din, uproar.

schiantare *vt.* to break (*v. irr.*). ♦
schiantarsi *vr.* to break, to crash.
schiarimento *sm.* (*spiegazione*) explanation.
schiarire *vt.* to clear, to make (*v. irr.*) clear: — *i capelli*, to bleach one's hair. ♦ **schiarirsi** *vr.* (*fig.*) to brighten.
schiarita *sf.* **1.** clearing **2.** (*miglioramento*) improvement.
schiattare *vi.* to burst: — *di rabbia*, to burst with rage.
schiavista *sm.* **1.** anti-abolitionist **2.** (*mercante di schiavi*) slave-trader.
schiavitù *sf.* slavery.
schiavo *agg. e sm.* slave.
schidionata *sf.* spitful.
schidione *sm.* spit.
schiena *sf.* **1.** back **2.** (*di monte*) ridge.
schienale *sm.* back.
schiera *sf.* **1.** formation **2.** (*gruppo di persone*) group.
schieramento *sm.* array.
schierare *vt.* to array. ♦ **schierarsi** *vr.* **1.** to draw (*v. irr.*) up **2.** (*parteggiare*) to side with.
schiettezza *sf.* openness, purity.
schietto *agg.* pure, open.
schifare *vt.* to loathe. ♦ **schifarsi** *vr.* to feel (*v. irr.*) disgusted (at).
schifezza *sf.* disgusting thing.
schifiltoso *agg.* squeamish.
schifo¹ *sm.* disgust.
schifo² *sm.* (*mar.*) skiff.
schifoso *agg.* disgusting.
schioccare *vi.* **1.** to crack **2.** (*le dita*) to snap **3.** (*le labbra*) to smack.
schiocco *sm.* **1.** crack **2.** (*di labbra*) smack.
schiodare *vt.* to unnail.
schiodatura *sf.* unnailing.
schioppettata *sf.* shot.
schioppo *sm.* gun.
schiùdere *vt.* to open. ♦ **schiùdersi** *vr.* to open.
schiuma *sf.* **1.** foam **2.** (*di vino, birra*) froth **3.** (*di sapone*) lather.
schiumare *vt.* to skim. ♦ **schiumare** *vi.* **1.** to foam **2.** (*di bevande*) to froth.
schiumarola *sf.* skimmer.
schiumoso *agg.* **1.** (*di mare*) foamy **2.** (*di bevande*) frothy **3.** (*di sapone*) lathery.
schiuso *agg.* open.

schivare *vt.* to avoid.
schivata *sf.* dodge.
schivo *agg.* shy, bashful.
schizofrenìa *sf.* schizophrenia.
schizofrènico *agg.* schizophrenic. ♦ **schizofrènico** *sm.* schizophrene.
schizzare *vt.* **1.** to splash, to spatter **2.** (*abbozzare*) to sketch. ♦ **schizzare** *vi.* to spurt.
schizzata *sf.* splashing.
schizzatoio *sm.* spray.
schizzetto *sm.* spray.
schizzinoso *agg.* squeamish, fussy.
schizzo *sm.* **1.** splash, squirt **2.** (*pitt.*) sketch.
sci *sm.* ski.
scia *sf.* **1.** (*mar.*) wake **2.** (*traccia*) trail.
scià *sm.* shah.
sciàbica *sf.* trawl.
sciàbola *sf.* sabre.
sciabolata *sf.* sabre-cut.
sciabolatore *sm.* sabreur.
sciabordare *vi.* to wash.
sciabordìo *sm.* washing, lapping.
sciacallo *sm.* **1.** jackal **2.** (*fig.*) profiteer.
sciacquare *vt.* to rinse (out).
sciacquatura *sf.* **1.** rinsing **2.** (*acqua*) rinsing-water.
sciacquìo *sm.* rinsing.
sciacquone *sm.* flush.
sciagura *sf.* misfortune.
sciagurato *agg.* **1.** unlucky **2.** (*malvagio*) wicked. ♦ **sciagurato** *sm.* wretch.
scialacquare *vt.* to squander.
scialacquatore *sm.* squanderer.
scialacquìo *sm.* squandering.
scialare *vt.* to squander money.
scialbare *vt.* to plaster.
scialbo *agg.* pale, wan.
scialle *sm.* shawl.
scialo *sm.* waste.
scialuppa *sf.* boat.
sciamannato *agg.* slovenly.
sciamano *sm.* shaman.
sciamare *vi.* to swarm.
sciame *sm.* swarm.
sciancarsi *vr.* to become (*v. irr.*) lame.
sciancato *agg.* lame.
sciarada *sf.* charade.
sciare¹ *vi.* to ski.
sciare² *vi.* (*mar.*) to back water.
sciarpa *sf.* scarf.
sciàtica *sf.* sciatica.
sciàtico *agg.* sciatic.
sciatore *sm.* skier.

sciatterìa *sf.* slovenliness.
sciatto *agg.* **1.** slovenly, untidy **2.** (*di stile ecc.*) careless.
scìbile *sm.* knowledge.
sciccherìa *sf.* smartness.
scientìfico *agg.* scientific.
scienza *sf.* science.
scienziato *sm.* scientist.
scilinguàgnolo *sm.* glib tongue.
scimitarra *sf.* scimitar.
scimmia *sf.* monkey, ape (*anche fig.*).
scimmiesco *agg.* monkeyish.
scimmiottare *vt.* to ape.
scimmiotto *sm.* young monkey.
scimpanzé *sm.* chimpanzee.
scimunito *agg.* silly. ♦ **scimunito** *sm.* blockhead.
scìndere *vt.* to divide: — *le questioni*, to deal (*v. irr.*) with each matter separately.
scintilla *sf.* spark.
scintillamento *sf.* sparkling.
scintillante *agg.* sparkling.
scintillare *vi.* to sparkle.
scintillìo *sm.* sparkling.
scintoismo *sm.* Shintoism.
scintoista *sm.* Shintoist.
scioccamente *avv.* foolishly.
sciocchezza *sf.* **1.** foolishness **2.** foolish thing **3.** trifle.
sciocco *agg.* silly.
sciògliere *vt.* **1.** to melt **2.** (*slegare, disfare*) to untie **3.** (*liberare*) to release **4.** (*risolvere*) to solve. ♦ **sciògliersi** *vr.* to dissolve, to get (*v. irr.*) loose.
scioglilingua *sm.* tongue-twister.
scioglimento *sm.* **1.** dissolution, breaking up **2.** (*epilogo*) unravelling.
sciolina *sf.* ski wax.
scioltezza *sf.* **1.** agility **2.** (*spigliatezza*) ease **3.** (*nel parlare*) fluency.
sciolto *agg.* **1.** melted **2.** (*slegato*) untied **3.** (*agile*) agile **4.** (*disinvolto*) easy || *capelli sciolti*, loose hair; *avere la lingua sciolta*, to have a ready tongue; — *da obblighi*, free from obligations.
scioperante *sm.* striker.
scioperare *vi.* to strike (*v. irr.*).
scioperatàggine *sf.* laziness.
scioperato *agg.* lazy. ♦ **scioperato** *sm.* lazy fellow.
sciòpero *sm.* strike.
sciorinare *vt.* to air, to display (*anche fig.*).
sciovìa *sf.* ski-lift.

sciovinìsmo *sm.* chauvinism.
sciovinista *sm.* chauvinist.
scipitàggine *sf.* insipidity (*anche fig.*).
scipito *agg.* insipid.
scirocco *sm.* sirocco.
sciroppare *vt.* to syrup.
sciroppato *agg.* in syrup.
sciropposo *agg.* syrupy.
scisma *sm.* schism.
scismàtico *agg. e sm.* schismatic.
scissione *sf.* **1.** scission, split (*anche fig.*) **2.** (*fis.; biol.*) fission.
scisso *agg.* divided.
scissura *sf.* **1.** cleft, split **2.** (*fig.*) dissension.
sciupare *vt.* **1.** to spoil (*v. irr.*), to damage **2.** (*sprecare*) to waste.
sciupato *agg.* **1.** spoilt **2.** (*sprecato*) wasted.
sciupìo *sm.* waste.
sciupone *agg.* wasteful. ♦ **sciupone** *sm.* waster.
scivolamento *sm.* sliding.
scivolare *vi.* **1.** to slide (*v. irr.*) **2.** (*involontariamente*) to slip.
scivolata *sf.* **1.** slide **2.** (*involontaria*) slip.
scìvolo *sm.* **1.** (*aer.; mar.*) slipway **2.** skid.
scivolone *sm.* slip.
scivoloso *agg.* slippery.
sclerosi *sf.* sclerosis.
scleròtica *sf.* sclerotic.
scleròtico *agg.* sclerotic.
scoccare *vt. e vi.* **1.** to shoot (*v. irr.*) **2.** (*l'ora*) to strike (*v. irr.*).
scocciare *vt.* to bother.
scocciatore *sm.* bore.
scocciatura *sf.* bother.
scodella *sf.* bowl.
scodellare *vt.* to dish up.
scodinzolare *vi.* to wag the tail.
scodinzolìo *sm.* tail-wagging.
scogliera *sf.* cliff.
scoglio *sm.* **1.** rock **2.** (*fig.*) difficulty.
scoiare *vt.* V. **scuoiare**.
scoiàttolo *sm.* squirrel.
scolapasta *sm.* colander.
scolara *sf.* pupil, schoolgirl.
scolare *vt.* **1.** to drain **2.** (*in un colabrodo*) to strain.
scolaresca *sf.* student-body.
scolaro *sm.* pupil, schoolboy.
scolàstica *sf.* scholasticism.
scolàstico *agg.* **1.** school (*attr.*) **2.** (*dispregiativo*) bookish.
scolatoio *sm.* drain.

scolatura *sf.* draining.

scoliosi *sf.* scoliosis.

scollacciato *agg.* **1.** (*di abito*) low--necked **2.** (*fig.*) coarse.

scollare[1] *vt.* to cut (*v. irr.*) away the neck of.

scollare[2] *vt.* (*staccare*) to unglue.

scollato[1] *agg.* (*di abito*) low-necked.

scollato[2] *agg.* unglued.

scollatura *sf.* neckline.

scollo *sm.* neck-opening.

scolo *sm.* draining.

scolorare *vt.* to discolour. ♦ **scolorarsi** *vr.* to grow (*v. irr.*) pale.

scolorimento *sm.* discolouration.

scolorire *vt.* to bleach.

scolorito *agg.* faded, pale.

scolpare *vt.* to exculpate.

scolpire *vt.* to sculpture.

scombinare *vt.* to upset (*v. irr.*).

scombinato *agg.* screwy.

scombussolamento *sm.* upsetting.

scombussolare *vt.* to upset (*v. irr.*).

scommessa *sf.* bet.

scomméttere *vt.* to bet (*v. irr.*).

scommettitore *sm.* bettor.

scomodamente *avv.* uncomfortably.

scomodare *vt.* to trouble, to bother.

scomodità *sf.* lack of comfort.

scòmodo *agg.* uncomfortable.

scompaginamento *sm.* upsetting, upset.

scompaginare *vt.* to upset (*v. irr.*).

scompagnare *vt.* to break (*v. irr.*) up (a pair).

scompagnato *agg.* odd.

scomparire *vi.* **1.** to disappear **2.** (*non spiccare*) not to stand (*v. irr.*) out.

scomparsa *sf.* **1.** disappearance **2.** (*morte*) death.

scomparso *agg.* **1.** disappeared **2.** (*morto*) dead.

scompartimento *sm.* **1.** partition **2.** (*ferr.*) compartment.

scompartire *vt.* to divide, to share out.

scomparto *sm.* V. *scompartimento*.

scompenso *sm.* lack of balance: — *cardiaco*, cardiac decompensation.

scompiacenza *sf.* unkindness.

scompigliare *vt.* **1.** to upset (*v. irr.*) **2.** (*arruffare*) to ruffle.

scompigliatamente *avv.* confusedly.

scompiglio *sm.* confusion, disorder.

sccomponìbile *agg.* decomposable.

scomponimento *sm.* decomposition.

scomporre *vt.* **1.** to decompose **2.** (*i lineamenti*) to distort.

scompostamente *avv.* in an unseemly manner.

scompostezza *sf.* unseemliness.

scomposto *agg.* **1.** (*sguaiato*) unseemly **2.** decomposed.

scomùnica *sf.* excommunication.

scomunicare *vt.* to excommunicate.

scomunicato *agg. e sm.* excommunicate.

sconcertante *agg.* disconcerting.

sconcertare *vt.* to disconcert, to baffle.

sconcertato *agg.* disconcerted.

sconcerto *sm.* perturbation.

sconcezza *sf.* indecency.

sconciamente *avv.* indecently.

sconcio *agg.* indecent.

sconclusionatamente *avv.* inconclusively.

sconclusionato *agg.* inconclusive.

scondito *agg.* **1.** unseasoned **2.** (*di insalata*) undressed.

sconfessare *vt.* to disown.

sconfessione *sf.* disowning.

sconfìggere *vt.* to defeat.

sconfinamento *sm.* **1.** (*in paese straniero*) crossing the frontier **2.** (*in proprietà privata*) trespass.

sconfinare *vi.* **1.** (*in paese straniero*) to cross the frontier **2.** (*in proprietà privata*) to trespass.

sconfinato *agg.* boundless.

sconfitta *sf.* defeat.

sconfitto *agg.* defeated.

sconfortante *agg.* discouraging.

sconfortare *vt.* to discourage.

sconfortato *agg.* discouraged.

sconforto *sm.* **1.** discouragement **2.** (*dolore*) sorrow.

scongiurare *vt.* **1.** to beseech (*v. irr.*) **2.** (*evitare*) to avoid.

scongiuro *sm.* exorcism.

sconnessione *sf.* disconnectedness.

sconnesso *agg.* **1.** disconnected **2.** (*fig.*) rambling.

sconnèttere *vt.* to disconnect. ♦ **sconnèttere** *vi.* to wander.

sconoscente *agg.* ungrateful.

sconoscenza *sf.* ingratitude.

sconòscere *vt.* to disown.

sconosciuto *agg.* unknown. ♦ **sconosciuto** *sm.* stranger.

sconquassare *vt.* to shatter.
sconquassato *agg.* ramshackle.
sconquasso *sm.* mess, disorder.
sconsacrare *vt.* to deconsecrate.
sconsideratezza *sf.* rashness.
sconsiderato *agg.* thoughtless.
sconsigliare *vt.* to advise against.
sconsigliato *agg.* rash.
sconsolante *agg.* discouraging.
sconsolare *vt.* to dishearten.
sconsolato *agg.* disconsolate.
scontàbile *agg.* discountable.
scontare *vt.* **1.** (*comm.*) to discount **2.** (*detrarre*) to deduct **3.** (*espiare*) to expiate.
scontato *agg.* (*previsto*) expected.
scontentare *vt.* to displease.
scontentezza *sf.* discontent.
scontento *agg.* displeased.
sconto *sm.* discount.
scontrarsi *vr.* to clash.
scontrino *sm.* ticket, check.
scontro *sm.* **1.** encounter **2.** (*di veicoli*) crash **3.** (*fig.*) clash.
scontrosamente *avv.* peevishly.
scontrosità *sf.* bad temper.
scontroso *agg.* bad-tempered.
sconveniente *agg.* **1.** unprofitable **2.** (*indecente*) unseemly.
sconvenientemente *avv.* unbecomingly.
sconvenienza *sf.* **1.** unprofitableness **2.** (*mancanza di correttezza*) unseemliness.
sconvolgente *agg.* upsetting.
sconvòlgere *vt.* to upset (*v. irr.*).
sconvolgimento *sm.* upsetting, confusion.
sconvolto *agg.* upset.
scopa *sf.* broom.
scopare *vt.* to sweep (*v. irr.*).
scoperchiare *vt.* to take (*v. irr.*) off the lid.
scoperta *sf.* discovery.
scopertamente *avv.* openly.
scoperto *agg.* uncovered || *automobile scoperta*, open car; *a capo —*, bare-headed; *giocare a carte scoperte*, to act openly.
scopino *sm.* street-sweeper.
scopo *sm.* aim, purpose: *senza —*, aimless.
scopolamina *sf.* scopolamine.
scoppiare *vi.* **1.** to burst (*v. irr.*) **2.** (*di guerre, epidemie ecc.*) to break (*v. irr.*) out.
scoppiettante *agg.* crackling.
scoppiettare *vi.* to crackle.
scoppiettìo *sm.* crackling.

scoppio *sm.* **1.** burst, explosion: *motore a —*, piston-engine **2.** (*di guerre, rivoluzioni ecc.*) outbreak.
scoprimento *sm.* **1.** discovering **2.** (*di monumento*) unveiling.
scoprire *vt.* **1.** to discover **2.** (*avvistare*) to sight **3.** (*togliere ciò che copre*) to uncover **4.** (*palesare*) to show (*v. irr.*). ♦ **scoprirsi** *vr.* (*rivelarsi*) to reveal oneself.
scopritore *sm.* discoverer.
scoraggiamento *sm.* discouragement.
scoraggiante *agg.* discouraging.
scoraggiare *vt.* to discourage. ♦ **scoraggiarsi** *vr.* to get (*v. irr.*) discouraged.
scoraggiato *agg.* discouraged.
scoramento *sm.* discouragement.
scorato *agg.* disheartened.
scorbùtico *agg.* **1.** (*med.*) scorbutic **2.** (*fig.*) ill-tempered.
scorbuto *sm.* scurvy.
scorciare *vt.* to shorten.
scorciatoia *sf.* short cut.
scorcio *sm.* **1.** foreshortening **2.** (*spazio di tempo*) end, close.
scordare[1] *vt.* to forget (*v. irr.*).
scordare[2] *vt.* (*mus.*) to untune.
scordato[1] *agg.* forgotten.
scordato[2] *agg.* (*mus.*) untuned.
scòrfano *sm.* **1.** sea-scorpion **2.** (*di persona*) fright: *che —!*, what a fright!
scòrgere *vt.* to perceive, to discern.
scoria *sf.* **1.** (*metal.*) dross **2.** (*fig.*) scum.
scornare *vt.* **1.** to horn **2.** (*fig.*) to humiliate.
scornato *agg.* humiliated.
scorno *sm.* shame.
scorpacciata *sf.* blow out: *fare una — di*, to stuff oneself with.
scorpione *sm.* scorpion.
scorporare *vt.* to disembody.
scòrporo *sm.* breaking up.
scorrazzare *vi.* to run (*v. irr.*) about.
scòrrere *vi.* **1.** to run (*v. irr.*) **2.** (*scivolare*) to glide **3.** (*fluire*) to flow **4.** (*di tempo*) to fly (*v. irr.*).
scorrerìa *sf.* raid.
scorrettezza *sf.* incorrectness.
scorretto *agg.* **1.** incorrect **2.** (*di costumi*) dissolute **3.** (*maleducato*) rude.
scorrévole *agg.* **1.** sliding **2.** (*fig.*) fluent.

scorrevolezza *sf.* fluency.

scorribanda *sf.* incursion, raid.

scorrimento *sm.* sliding.

scorsa *sf.* glance.

scorso *agg.* last, past.

scorsoio *agg.* running.

scorta *sf.* **1.** escort **2.** (*provvista*) supply || *ruota di* —, spare wheel.

scortare *vt.* to escort.

scortecciare *vt.* **1.** to peel **2.** (*un albero*) to bark.

scortese *agg.* rude, impolite.

scortesìa *sf.* rudeness.

scorticare *vt.* to skin.

scorticatura *sf.* scratch.

scortichino *sm.* flaying-knife.

scorza *sf.* **1.** (*corteccia*) bark **2.** (*buccia*) skin, rind.

scoscéndere *vt.* to split (*v. irr.*).

scoscendimento *sm.* **1.** collapse **2.** (*di terreno*) break.

scosceso *agg.* steep, sloping.

scossa *sf.* shock, shake.

scosso *agg.* **1.** shaken **2.** (*fig.*) upset.

scossone *sm.* **1.** shake **2.** (*strattone*) jerk.

scostare *vt.* to shift, to move away. ♦ **scostarsi** *vr.* **1.** to move away **2.** (*staccarsi*) to turn off.

scostumatezza *sf.* dissoluteness.

scostumato *agg.* dissolute. ♦ **scostumato** *sm.* dissolute person.

scotennare *vt.* to scalp.

scottante *agg.* burning.

scottare *vt.* **1.** to burn (*v. irr.*) **2.** (*cuc.*) to half-cook **3.** (*fig.*) to hurt (*v. irr.*).

scottatura *sf.* burn.

scotto[1] *sm.* score: *pagare lo* —, to pay (*v. irr.*) one's piper.

scotto[2] *agg.* overdone.

scovare *vt.* **1.** to put (*v. irr.*) up **2.** (*scoprire*) to discover.

scozzare *vt.* to shuffle.

scozzese *agg.* Scotch, Scottish. ♦ **scozzese** *sm.* Scotchman (*pl.* -men).

scozzonare *vt.* **1.** to break (*v. irr.*) in **2.** (*fig.*) to teach (*v. irr.*) the first elements.

screanzatamente *avv.* rudely.

screanzato *agg.* rude, impolite. ♦ **screanzato** *sm.* rude person.

screditare *vt.* to discredit.

screditato *agg.* discredited.

scrédito *sm.* discredit.

scremare *vt.* to skim.

scremato *agg.* skimmed: *latte* —, skim-milk.

scrematura *sf.* skimming.

screpolare *vi.* **1.** to crack **2.** (*della pelle*) to get (*v. irr.*) chapped.

screpolatura *sf.* **1.** crack **2.** (*della pelle*) chap.

screziare *vt.* to variegate.

screziato *agg.* variegated.

screziatura *sf.* variegation.

screzio *sm.* disagreement.

scribacchiare *vt. e vi.* to scribble.

scribacchino *sm.* scribbler.

scricchiolare *vi.* **1.** to creak **2.** (*di denti*) to grind (*v. irr.*).

scricchiolìo *sm.* **1.** creaking **2.** (*di denti*) grinding.

scrigno *sm.* casket: — *di gioielli*, jewel-case.

scriminatura *sf.* (hair-)parting.

scriteriato *agg.* senseless.

scritta *sf.* **1.** inscription **2.** (*cartello*) notice **3.** (*dicitura*) caption.

scritto *sm.* writing.

scrittoio *sm.* writing-desk.

scrittore *sm.* writer.

scrittrice *sf.* woman writer.

scrittura *sf.* **1.** writing: — *a macchina*, typewriting; — *a mano*, handwriting **2.** (*teat.*) engagement **3.** (*giur.*) deed.

scritturare *vt.* to engage.

scrivanìa *sf.* writing-desk.

scrivano *sm.* clerk, copyist.

scrìvere *vt.* to write (*v. irr.*): — *a mano*, to write by hand; — *a penna, a matita*, to write in pen, in pencil; — *sotto dettatura*, to write from dictation; — *a macchina*, to typewrite (*v. irr.*) **2.** (*registrare*) to enter, to record.

scroccare *vt.* to scrounge.

scrocco *sm. vivere a* —, to sponge one's living.

scroccone *sm.* sponger.

scrofa *sf.* sow.

scrofoloso *agg.* scrofulous.

scrollamento *sm.* **1.** shaking **2.** (*di spalle*) shrugging.

scrollare *vt.* **1.** to shake (*v. irr.*) **2.** (*le spalle*) to shrug.

scrollata *sf.* **1.** (*di testa*) shake **2.** (*di spalle*) shrug.

scrosciante *agg.* (*di risa ecc.*) roaring: *pioggia* —, pelting rain.

scrosciare *vi.* **1.** (*di pioggia*) to pelt down **2.** (*fig.*) to roar.

scroscio *sm.* **1.** (*di cascata, torrente ecc.*) roar **2.** (*fig.*) roar, burst || — *di pioggia*, shower.

scrostamento *sm.* peeling.

scrostare vt. **1.** to take (v. irr.) the crust off, to peel off **2.** (dei muri) to remove the plaster from a wall. ♦ **scrostarsi** vr. to fall (v. irr.) off, to peel off.

scrùpolo sm. scruple.

scrupolosamente avv. scrupulously.

scrupolosità sf. scrupulosity.

scrupoloso agg. scrupulous.

scrutare vt. to search, to scan.

scrutatore agg. searching, inquisitive. ♦ **scrutatore** sm. **1.** searcher **2.** (di elezioni) scrutineer.

scrutinare vt. to scrutinize.

scrutinio sm. **1.** (di elezioni) poll **2.** (scolastico) assignment of a term's marks **3.** (attento esame) scrutiny.

scucire vt. to unsew (v. irr.), to unstitch. ♦ **scucirsi** vr. to rip.

scucito agg. **1.** unsewn **2.** (fig.) incoherent.

scucitura sf. unsewing.

scuderia sf. stable.

scudetto sm. **1.** small shield **2.** (sport) (championship) shield.

scudiero sm. squire.

scudisciare vt. to lash.

scudisciata sf. lash.

scudiscio sm. switch, lash.

scudo sm. shield.

scuffia sf. (sbornia) drunkenness.

sculacciare vt. to spank.

sculacciata sf. spank.

sculettare vi. to waddle.

scultore sm. sculptor.

scultòreo agg. sculptural.

scultura sf. sculpture.

scuoiare vt. to skin.

scuola sf. school: — diurna, day-classes; — elementare, primary school; — media inferiore, superiore, secondary school; — pubblica, State school; maestro di —, schoolmaster.

scuòtere vt. **1.** to shake (v. irr.) (anche fig.) **2.** (agitare) to stir.

scuotimento sm. shaking.

scure sf. axe.

scurire vt. **1.** to darken **2.** (pitt.) to tone down. ♦ **scurirsi** vr. to grow (v. irr.) dark.

scuro agg. dark || faccia scura, grim face.

scurrile agg. scurrilous.

scurrilità sf. scurrility.

scusa sf. **1.** excuse, apology **2.** (pretesto) pretext.

scusàbile agg. excusable.

scusare vt. to excuse, to forgive (v. irr.) || scusi!, scusate!, sorry!, excuse me! ♦ **scusarsi** vr. to apologize.

sdebitarsi vr. **1.** to pay (v. irr.) off one's debts **2.** (disobbligarsi) to return a kindness.

sdegnare vt. **1.** to disdain **2.** (provocare lo sdegno) to enrage.

sdegnato agg. indignant.

sdegno sm. disdain, indignation.

sdegnosamente avv. disdainfully.

sdegnoso agg. **1.** (di atti e parole) disdainful **2.** (di persona) haughty.

sdentare vt. to break (v. irr.) the teeth.

sdentato agg. toothless.

sdilinquimento sm. mawkishness.

sdilinquirsi vr. to melt away.

sdoganamento sm. clearing (through the customs).

sdolcinato agg. sugary, affected.

sdolcinatura sf. mawkishness.

sdoppiamento sm. splitting.

sdoppiare vt. to split.

sdraia sf. deck-chair.

sdraiarsi vr. to lie (v. irr.) down.

sdrucciolare vi. to slip, to slide.

sdrucciolévole agg. slippery.

sdrucciolone sm. slip.

sdrucire vt. to tear (v. irr.).

sdrucito agg. torn.

se cong. **1.** if **2.** (dubitativo) whether || — mai, in case; — non altro, at least; — non che, except that; anche —, even if.

sé pron. pers. **1.** one, him, her, it, them **2.** (riflessivi) oneself, himself, herself, itself, themselves || una donna piena di —, a conceited woman; essere fuori di —, to be beside oneself; tornare in —, to recover consciousness; amore di —, selfishness; padronanza di —, self-control; un uomo sicuro di —, a self-confident man; un uomo che si è fatto da —, a self-made man; rispetto di —, self-respect.

sebàceo agg. sebaceous.

sebbene cong. though, although.

sebo sm. sebum.

secante sf. secant.

secca sf. **1.** shoal **2.** (siccità) drought.

seccamente avv. coldly.

seccante agg. (fig.) annoying, irritating || una cosa, persona —, a nuisance.

seccare vt. 1. to dry up 2. (annoiare) to annoy, to irritate. ♦ **seccarsi** vr. (infastidirsi) to be annoyed (with).

seccatore sm. bother.

seccatura sf. 1. (essicamento) drying 2. (noia) bother, nuisance.

secchia sf. pail, bucket.

secchiello sm. bucket.

secchio sm. V. secchia.

secco agg. 1. dry 2. (appassito) withered 3. (magro) thin 4. (brusco) sharp 5. (freddo) cold.

secentesco agg. of the seventeenth century.

secèrnere vt. to secrete.

secessione sf. secession♦

secessionista agg. e sm. secessionist.

seco pron. with him, with her, with them.

secolare agg. 1. secular 2. (in opposizione a ecclesiastico) lay.

secolarizzare vt. to secularize.

secolarizzazione sf. secularization.

sècolo sm. 1. century 2. (epoca) epoch, age || Padre Carlo, al — John Smith, Father Charles, in the world John Smith.

seconda sf. (auto) second gear || a — di (loc. prep.), according to.

secondare vt. to favour.

secondario agg. secondary.

secondino sm. warder.

secondo[1] agg. 1. second 2. (favorevole) favourable. ♦ **secondo** sm. 1. (minuto) second 2. (ufficiale in seconda) executive officer.

secondo[2] prep. according to. ♦ **secondo** avv. second.

secrezione sf. secretion.

sèdano sm. celery.

sedare vt. to soothe.

sedativo agg. e sm. sedative.

sede sf. 1. seat, centre 2. (residenza) residence 3. (eccl.) see 4. (edificio per pubblici uffici) office.

sedentario agg. sedentary.

sedere[1] vi. 1. (stare seduto) to sit (v. irr.), to be sitting 2. (mettersi a sedere) to sit (down).

sedere[2] sm. bottom.

sedia sf. chair: — a dondolo, rocking-chair.

sedicenne agg. 1. (attr.) sixteen--year-old 2. (pred.) sixteen years old.

sedicente agg. would-be.

sedicèsimo agg. sixteenth.

sédici agg. sixteen.

sedile sm. seat, chair.

sedimentario agg. sedimentary.

sedimentazione sf. sedimentation.

sedimento sm. sediment.

sedizione sf. sedition.

sedizioso agg. seditious.

seducente agg. 1. alluring 2. (affascinante) charming.

sedurre vt. to seduce, to tempt.

seduta sf. sitting, session.

seduttore agg. seducing. ♦ **seduttore** sm. seducer.

seduzione sf. 1. seduction 2. (attrazione) attraction.

sega sf. saw.

ségala sf. rye.

segaligno agg. 1. rye (attr.) 2. (di persona) wiry.

segare vt. to saw (v. irr.).

segatura sf. sawdust.

seggio sm. chair, seat: — elettorale, poll.

sèggiola sf. chair.

seggiovia sf. chair-lift.

segherìa sf. saw-mill.

seghettare vt. to jag.

segmentazione sf. segmentation.

segmento sm. segment.

segnalare vt. 1. to signal 2. (far notare) to point out. ♦ **segnalarsi** vr. to distinguish oneself.

segnalatore sm. 1. signaller 2. (segnalatore di direzione) direction indicator.

segnalazione sf. signal: — stradale, traffic signal.

segnale sm. signal: — di pericolo allarme, danger, alarm signal; — di linea libera, occupata (tel.) ringing, engaged tone; — di passaggio a livello, level-crossing signal.

segnalètica sf. signals (pl.).

segnalètico agg. descriptive.

segnalibro sm. book-mark.

segnare vt. 1. to mark 2. (indicare) to show (v. irr.) 3. (sport) to score. ♦ **segnarsi** vr. to cross oneself.

segnatura sf. 1. marking 2. (sport) scoring.

segno sm. 1. sign, mark: passare i —, to overstep the mark 2. (limite) limit 3. (simbolo) symbol.

sego sm. tallow.

segregare vt. to segregate.

segregazione sf. segregation.

segreta sf. dungeon.

segretamente *avv.* in secret.

segretariato *sm.* secretariate.

segretario *sm.* secretary.

segreteria *sf.* **1.** secretariat **2.** (*di ministero*) secretariat of State.

segretezza *sf.* secrecy.

segreto *agg.* secret. ♦ **segreto** *sm.* **1.** secret: *nel — del cuore*, in the depths of one's heart **2.** (*parte interna, intimità*) secrecy.

seguace *sm.* follower, supporter.

seguente *agg.* following, next.

segugio *sm.* bloodhound.

seguire *vt.* e *vi.* **1.** to follow **2.** (*sorvegliare*) to supervise **3.** (*frequentare regolarmente*) to attend.

séguito *sm.* **1.** (*corteo*) retinue **2.** (*successione, sequela*) series **3.** (*continuazione*) continuation || *il — alla prossima puntata*, to be continued **4.** (*comm.*): *a — di*, following up.

sei *agg.* six.

seicento *agg.* six hundred. ♦ **seicento** *sm.* the seventeenth century.

selce *sf.* flint.

selciare *vt.* to pave.

selciato *sm.* pavement.

selenio *sm.* selenium.

selenite *agg.* lunar. ♦ **selenite** *sf.* selenite.

selettività *sf.* selectivity.

selettivo *agg.* selective.

selettore *sm.* selector.

selezionare *vt.* to select.

selezione *sf.* selection.

sella *sf.* saddle.

sellaio *sm.* saddler.

sellare *vt.* to saddle.

sellino *sm.* saddle.

selva *sf.* **1.** wood **2.** (*fig.*) mass.

selvaggina *sf.* game.

selvaggio *agg.* wild, primitive. ♦ **selvaggio** *sm.* savage.

selvàtico *agg.* **1.** wild **2.** (*non socievole*) unsociable.

selvoso *agg.* woody.

semàforo *sm.* traffic-lights (*pl.*).

semàntica *sf.* semantics.

semàntico *agg.* semantic.

sembianza *sf.* features (*pl.*).

sembrare *vi.* **1.** to seem **2.** (*somigliare*) to look like.

seme *sm.* **1.** seed **2.** (*carte da giuoco*) suit.

sementa *sf.* **1.** seeds (*pl.*) **2.** (*epoca della semina*) seed-time.

semente *sf.* seeds (*pl.*).

semenza *sf.* seeds (*pl.*).

semenzaio *sm.* seed-bed.

semestrale *agg.* six-monthly (*attr.*).

semestralmente *avv.* twice a year.

semestre *sm.* half-year.

semiaperto *agg.* half-open.

semicerchio *sm.* semicircle.

semichiuso *agg.* half-closed.

semicircolare *agg.* semicircular.

semiconduttore *sm.* semiconductor.

semidiàmetro *sm.* semi-diameter.

semidìo *sm.* demigod.

semifinale *sf.* semifinal.

semilavorato *agg.* e *sm.* semi-manufactured.

sémina *sf.* sowing.

seminàbile *agg.* fit to be sown.

seminagione *sf.* sowing.

seminare *vt.* to sow (*v. irr.*).

seminario *sm.* seminary.

seminarista *sm.* seminarist.

seminato *agg.* **1.** sown **2.** (*fig.*) strewn.

seminatore *sm.* sower.

seminfermità *sf.* partial infirmity: *— mentale*, partial insanity.

seminudo *agg.* half-naked.

semiserio *agg.* half-serious.

semisfera *sf.* hemisphere.

semita *s.* Semite.

semìtico *agg.* Semitic.

semitono *sm.* semitone.

semivivo *agg.* half-alive.

sémola *sf.* bran.

semolino *sm.* semolina.

semovente *agg.* self-moving.

sempiterno *agg.* everlasting.

sémplice *agg.* simple.

semplicione *sm.* simpleton.

semplicismo *sm.* superficiality.

semplicìstico *agg.* sùperficial.

semplicità *sf.* simplicity.

semplificare *vt.* to simplify.

semplificazione *sf.* simplification.

sempre *avv.* **1.** always: *— avanti!* always onward!; *— meglio, peggio*, better and better, worse and worse; *per —*, for ever; *una volta per —*, once for all **2.** (*tuttora*) still: *vivi — qui?*, do you still live here?

sempreverde *sm.* evergreen.

sènape *sf.* mustard.

senato *sm.* senate.

senatore *sm.* senator.

senatoriale *agg.* senatorial.

senescenza *sf.* senescence.

senile *agg.* senile.

senilità *sf.* senility.

senno *sm.* sense, wisdom.

seno *sm.* **1.** breast, bosom **2.** (*grembo*) womb.

sensale *sm.* broker.

sensatezza *sf.* good sense.

sensato *agg.* sensible.

sensazionale *agg.* sensational.

sensazione *sf.* sensation, feeling.

sensìbile *agg.* sensitive.

sensibilità *sf.* sensitiveness.

sensibilizzare *vt.* to sensitize.

sensibilmente *avv.* **1.** sensitively **2.** (*notevolmente*) sensibly.

sensitività *sf.* sensitivity.

sensitivo *agg.* **1.** sensory **2.** (*sensibile*) sensitive.

senso *sm.* **1.** sense **2.** (*sensazione*) sensation **3.** (*direzione*) direction, way **4.** (*modo*) way, manner.

sensorio *agg.* sensorial.

sensuale *agg.* sensual.

sensualità *sf.* sensuality.

sensualmente *avv.* sensually.

sentenza *sf.* **1.** sentence **2.** (*massima*) saying.

sentenziare *vi.* to judge, to hold (*v. irr.*).

sentenziosamente *avv.* sententiously.

sentenzioso *agg.* sententious.

sentiero *sm.* path.

sentimentale *agg.* sentimental.

sentimentalismo *sm.* sentimentalism.

sentimentalità *sf.* sentimentality.

sentimento *sm.* **1.** sentiment **2.** (*disposizione spirituale*) feeling.

sentinella *sf.* sentry.

sentire *vt.* **1.** to feel (*v. irr.*) **2.** (*udire*) to hear (*v. irr.*) **3.** (*gustare*) to taste **4.** (*odorare*) to smell (*v. irr.*) **5.** (*ascoltare*) to listen to. ◆ **sentirsi** *vr.* to feel.

sentitamente *avv.* heartily.

sentito *agg.* **1.** heart-felt **2.** (*udito*) heard || *per — dire*, by hearsay.

sentore *sm.* inkling: *aver — di*, to suspect.

senza *prep.* without: *— scarpe*, barefoot; *— fine*, endless; *— confronto*, unrivalled; *— numero*, countless; *— testa*, thoughtless.

senzatetto *s.* homeless person.

separare *vt.* to separate. ◆ **separarsi** *vr.* to separate.

separatamente *avv.* separately.

separatismo *sm.* separatism.

separatista *s.* separatist.

separativo *agg.* separative.

separato *agg.* separated.

separazione *sf.* separation.

sepolcrale *agg.* sepulchral.

sepolcro *sm.* sepulchre, tomb.

sepolto *agg.* buried.

sepoltura *sf.* burial.

seppellimento *sm.* burial.

seppellire *vt.* to bury.

seppia *sf.* cuttle-fish.

seppure *cong.* even if.

sequela *sf.* series (*invariato al pl.*)

sequenza *sf.* **1.** series **2.** (*cine*) sequence.

sequestràbile *agg.* seizable.

sequestrare *vt.* to seize.

sequestro *sm.* **1.** seizure **2.** (*per debiti*) distress.

sequoia *sf.* sequoia.

sera *sf.* evening.

seràfico *agg.* seraphic.

serafino *sm.* seraph.

serale *agg.* evening (*attr.*).

serata *sf.* **1.** evening **2.** (*ricevimento serale*) party.

serbare *vt.* **1.** (*mettere in serbo*) to put (*v. irr.*) aside **2.** (*conservare*) to keep (*v. irr.*) || *— odio, rancore*, to nourish hatred, rancour. ◆ **serbarsi** *vr.* to keep, to remain.

serbatoio *sm.* reservoir, tank.

serbo (*nella loc.*) *tenere in —*, to keep (*v. irr.*) aside.

serenamente *avv.* serenely.

serenata *sf.* serenade.

serenìssimo *agg.* Serene Highness

serenità *sf.* serenity.

sereno *agg.* serene, clear || *giudizio —*, objective judgement.

sergente *sm.* sergeant.

sèrico *agg.* silk (*attr.*), silky.

sericoltore *sm.* silkgrower.

sericoltura *sf.* sericulture.

serie *sf.* **1.** series (*invariato al pl.*): *in —*, mass-produced **2.** (*assieme*) set **3.** (*fila*) row.

serietà *sf.* seriousness.

serio *agg.* serious, earnest.

sermone *sm.* **1.** sermon **2.** (*rimprovero*) lecture.

seròtino *agg.* evening (*attr.*).

serpe *sf.* snake.

serpeggiante *agg.* winding.

serpeggiare *vi.* to wind (*v. irr.*).

serpente *sm.* snake, serpent.

serpentina *sf.* **1.** coil **2.** (*di strada*) winding road.

serpentino *agg.* snakelike. ◆ **serpentino** *sm.* serpentine.

serra *sf.* greenhouse.

serraglio *sm.* **1.** menagerie **2.** (*del sultano*) seraglio.
serramànico (*nella loc. avv.*) *coltello a* —, flick-knife.
serramento *sm.* lock.
serrare *vt.* **1.** to shut (*v. irr.*), to close **2.** (*a chiave*) to lock **3.** (*stringere*) to tighten **4.** (*concludere*) to conclude.
serrata *sf.* (*econ.*) lockout.
serratura *sf.* lock: *buco della* —, keyhole.
serva *sf.* maid-servant.
servìbile *agg.* usable.
servigio *sm.* service, favour.
servile *agg.* servile.
servilismo *sm.* servility.
servire *vt.* **1.** to serve **2.** (*di persona di servizio*) to wait on **3.** (*le carte*) to deal (*v. irr.*). ♦ **servire** *vi.* (*occorrere*) to need: *vi serve qualcosa?*, can I help you? ♦ **servirsi** *vr.* **1.** to use **2.** (*a tavola*) to help oneself (to).
servitore *sm.* servant.
servitù *sf.* **1.** servitude, slavery **2.** (*personale di servizio*) servants (*pl.*).
serviziévole *agg.* obliging.
servizio *sm.* **1.** service **2.** (*lavoro*) work: *fuori* —, off duty **3.** (*favore*) favour.
servo *sm.* **1.** servant **2.** (*schiavo*) slave.
servofreno *sm.* brake booster.
sèsamo *sm.* sesame.
sessanta *agg.* sixty.
sessantenne *agg.* **1.** (*attr.*) sixty-year-old **2.** (*pred.*) sixty years old. ♦ **sessantenne** *s.* sixty-year-old person.
sessantèsimo *agg.* sixtieth.
sessantina *sf.* about sixty: *un uomo sulla* —, a man in his sixties.
sessione *sf.* session.
sesso *sm.* sex.
sessuale *agg.* sexual.
sessualità *sf.* sexuality.
sestante *sm.* sextant.
sesterzio *sm.* sesterce.
sestetto *sm.* sextet.
sesto[1] *agg.* sixth.
sesto[2] *sm.* **1.** order **2.** (*arch.*) curve.
sèstuplo *agg. e sm.* sextuple.
seta *sf.* silk.
setacciare *vt.* to sieve.
setaccio *sm.* sieve.
sete *sf.* thirst: *avere* —, to be thirsty.

seterìa *sf.* **1.** silk factory **2.** (*negozio di seta*) silk shop.
setificio *sm.* silk factory.
sétola *sf.* **1.** bristle **2.** (*crine*) hair.
setta *sf.* sect.
settanta *agg.* seventy.
settantenne *agg.* **1.** (*attr.*) seventy-year-old **2.** (*pred.*) seventy years old. ♦ **settantenne** *s.* seventy-year-old person.
settantèsimo *agg.* seventieth.
settario *agg.* sectarian.
settarismo *sm.* sectarianism.
sette *agg.* seven.
settecentesco *agg.* of eighteenth century.
settecento *agg.* seven hundred. ♦ **settecento** *sm.* the eighteenth century.
settembre *sm.* September.
settentrionale *agg.* northern.
settentrione *sm.* north.
setticemìa *sf.* septicaemia.
sèttico *agg.* septic.
settimana *sf.* week.
settimanale *agg.* weekly. ♦ **settimanale** *sm.* weekly magazine.
settimino *sm.* seven months' child.
setto *sm.* septum (*pl.* -ta).
settore *sm.* **1.** (*geom.*) sector **2.** (*campo*) field.
settoriale *agg.* sectorial.
severità *sf.* severity.
severo *agg.* severe, strict.
sevizia *sf.* torture.
seviziare *vt.* to torture.
sezionamento *sm.* dissection.
sezionare *vt.* (*anat.*) to dissect.
sezione *sf.* **1.** section **2.** (*reparto*) department **3.** (*di scuola*) side.
sfaccendato *agg.* idle. ♦ **sfaccendato** *sm.* idler.
sfaccettare *vt.* to facet.
sfacchinare *vi.* to drudge.
sfacciatàggine *sf.* impudence.
sfacciato *agg.* **1.** impudent, cheeky **2.** (*di colori*) gaudy.
sfacelo *sm.* break-up.
sfaldamento *sm.* flaking.
sfaldarsi *vr.* to flake away.
sfamare *vt.* to appease so.'s hunger.
sfarfallare *vi.* to flutter about.
sfarzo *sm.* pomp.
sfarzoso *agg.* sumptuous.
sfasamento *sm.* **1.** (*mecc.; elettr.*) phase-displacement, phase-difference **2.** (*fig.*) inconsequence.
sfasato *agg.* **1.** out of phase **2.** (*fig.*) inconsequent.

sfasciare[1] vt. (togliere le fasce) to unbandage.

sfasciare[2] vt. to smash. ♦ **sfasciarsi** vr. to collapse.

sfasciato agg. (rotto) in pieces.

sfatare vt. to discredit.

sfaticato agg. lazy. ♦ **sfaticato** sm. lazy-bones.

sfatto agg. undone.

sfavillante agg. shining.

sfavillare vi. to shine (v. irr.), to sparkle.

sfavore sm. disfavour, discredit.

sfavorévole agg. unfavourable.

sfebbrato agg. without a temperature.

sfegatarsi vr. to wear (v. irr.) oneself out.

sfegatato agg. fanatic.

sfenòide sm. sphenoid.

sfera sf. 1. sphere 2. (lancetta) hand 3. (mecc.) ball.

sfericità sf. sphericity.

sfèrico agg. spherical.

sferragliare vi. to clang.

sferrare vt. 1. (un attacco) to launch 2. (un colpo) to land a blow. ♦ **sferrarsi** vr. to hurl oneself (at).

sferruzzare vi. to knit (v. irr.).

sferza sf. whip, lash (anche fig.).

sferzare vt. 1. to whip, to lash 2. (fig.) to reprimand.

sferzata sf. 1. lash 2. (fig.) sharp rebuke.

sfiancare vt. to wear (v. irr.) out.

sfiatare vi. to leak. ♦ **sfiatarsi** vr. to talk oneself hoarse.

sfiatato agg. out of breath.

sfiatatoio sm. vent.

sfibbiare vt. to unbuckle.

sfibramento sm. enfeeblement.

sfibrante agg. exhausting.

sfibrare vt. to weaken, to wear (v. irr.) out.

sfibratura sf. breaking.

sfida sf. challenge: in tono di —, defiantly.

sfidante sm. challenger.

sfidare vt. 1. to challenge 2. (affrontare) to face, to dare: — la morte, to face death.

sfiducia sf. mistrust: avere —, to mistrust.

sfiduciare vt. to discourage. ♦ **sfiduciarsi** vr. to become (v. irr.) discouraged.

sfiduciato agg. discouraged.

sfigurare vt. to spoil (v. irr.). ♦

sfigurare vi. to cut (v. irr.) a poor figure.

sfigurato agg. disfigured.

sfilacciare vt. to fray.

sfilacciato agg. frayed.

sfilare[1] vt. to unthread, to unstring (v. irr.).

sfilare[2] vi. to parade.

sfilata sf. 1. march, parade 2. (fila) line, string.

sfinge sf. sphinx.

sfinimento sm. exhaustion.

sfinire vt. to exhaust.

sfinitezza sf. extreme weakness.

sfinito agg. worn out.

sfintere sm. sphincter.

sfiorare vt. to graze, to touch on.

sfiorire vi. to wither, to fade.

sfiorito agg. faded, withered (anche fig.).

sfittare vt. to vacate.

sfitto agg. vacant.

sfocato agg. out of focus.

sfociare vi. to flow.

sfoderare vt. 1. to unline 2. (sguainare) to unsheathe 3. (ostentare) to display.

sfoderato agg. 1. unlined 2. (sguainato) unsheathed.

sfogare vt. to give (v. irr.) vent to ♦ **sfogarsi** vr. to relieve one's feelings.

sfoggiare vi. to show (v. irr.) off.

sfoggio sm. show, ostentation.

sfoglia sf. 1. (lamina) foil 2. (cuc.) pastry.

sfogliare[1] vt. to pluck the petals off.

sfogliare[2] vt. 1. (voltare le pagine) to turn over the pages 2. (dare un'occhiata) to glance through.

sfogliata sf. 1. (cuc.) puff-pastry 2. (di libro) thumbing.

sfogo sm. vent, outlet.

sfolgoramento sm. blazing.

sfolgorante agg. flaming.

sfolgorare vi. to blaze.

sfolgorìo sm. blaze.

sfollagente sm. truncheon.

sfollamento sm. 1. dispersal 2. (mil.) evacuation.

sfollare vt. e vi. to disperse 2. (mil.) to evacuate.

sfollato agg. 1. evacuated. ♦ **sfollato** sm. evacuee.

sfoltire vt. to thin.

sfondamento sm. breaking.

sfondare vt. 1. (rompere il fondo) to break (v. irr.) the bottom 2.

(*mil.*) to break through. ♦ **sfondare** *vi.* to have success.

sfondato *agg.* **1.** without a bottom || *scarpe sfondate*, worn-out shoes **2.** (*insaziabile*) voracious.

sfondo *sm.* background.

sforbiciare *vt.* to cut (*v. irr.*) with scissors.

sformare *vt.* **1.** to pull out of shape **2.** (*togliere dalla forma*) to remove from the mould. ♦ **sformarsi** *vr.* to get (*v. irr.*) out of shape.

sformato *agg.* shapeless.

sfornare *vt.* **1.** to take (*v. irr.*) out of the oven **2.** (*produrre*) to bring (*v. irr.*) out.

sfornito *agg.* destitute, lacking (in).

sfortuna *sf.* bad luck.

sfortunato *agg.* unlucky.

sforzare *vt.* to strain, to force. ♦ **sforzarsi** *vr.* to try hard.

sforzatamente *avv.* **1.** with much effort **2.** (*in modo forzato*) forcedly.

sforzato *agg.* **1.** forced **2.** (*fig.*) false.

sforzatura *sf.* (*cosa sforzata*) far-fetched thing.

sforzo *sm.* **1.** effort **2.** (*mecc.*) stress.

sfottere *vt.* to pull so.'s legs.

sfracellare *vt.* to smash. ♦ **sfracellarsi** *vr.* to smash.

sfrangiare *vt.* to undo (*v. irr.*), to form a fringe. ♦ **sfrangiarsi** *vr.* to fray.

sfrangiatura *sf.* fraying.

sfrattare *vt.* to evict.

sfratto *sm.* eviction.

sfrecciare *vi.* to dart.

sfregamento *sm.* rubbing.

sfregare *vt.* to rub.

sfregiare *vt.* to disfigure.

sfregiato *agg.* disfigured.

sfregio *sm.* slash, scar.

sfrenare *vt.* to unbridle.

sfrenatezza *sf.* unrestraint.

sfrenato *agg.* wild, unbridled.

sfrigolare *vi.* to sizzle.

sfrigolìo *sm.* sizzle.

sfringuellare *vi.* to twitter.

sfrondare *vt.* **1.** to strip off leaves **2.** (*fig.*) to curtail.

sfrontatezza *sf.* effrontery.

sfrontato *agg.* brazen, impudent. ♦ **sfrontato** *sm.* impudent fellow.

sfrusciare *vi.* to rustle.

sfruscìo *sm.* rustling.

sfruttamento *sm.* exploitation.

sfruttare *vt.* to exploit.

sfruttatore *sm.* profiteer.

sfuggente *agg.* receding: *sguardo —*, elusive look.

sfuggévole *agg.* transitory.

sfuggire *vi.* to escape, to slip. ♦ **sfuggire** *vt.* to avoid.

sfuggita *sf. di —*, quickly: *vedere qu. di —*, to have a glimpse of so.

sfumare *vt.* to shade. ♦ **sfumare** *vi.* **1.** to evaporate **2.** (*fig.*) to come (*v. irr.*) to nothing.

sfumatamente *avv.* softly.

sfumato *agg.* **1.** vanished **2.** (*di colori*) soft.

sfumatura *sf.* **1.** (*lo sfumare*) shading **2.** (*gradazione*) shade.

sfuriata *sf.* outburst.

sgabello *sm.* stool.

sgabuzzino *sm.* closet.

sgambettare *vi.* to kick (one's legs) about.

sgambetto *sm.* trip: *fare lo —*, to trip (so.); (*fig.*) to supplant.

sganasciamento *sm.* dislocation (of so.'s jaw).

sganasciarsi *vr. — dalle risa*, to laugh oneself silly.

sganascione *sm.* slap.

sganciare *vt.* **1.** to unhook **2.** (*ferr.*) to uncouple **3.** (*di bombe*) to release. ♦ **sganciarsi** *vr.* (*liberarsi di qu.*) to get (*v. irr.*) away (so.).

sgangherare *vt.* to unhinge.

sgangherato *agg.* **1.** unhinged **2.** (*sguaiato*) wild.

sgarbatamente *avv.* impolitely.

sgarbato *àgg.* rude, impolite.

sgarberìa *sf.* rudeness.

sgarbo *sm.* offence.

sgargiante *agg.* gaudy.

sgarrare *vi.* **1.** to be wrong **2.** (*di orologio*) (*se è avanti*) to gain; (*se è indietro*) to lose (*v. irr.*).

sgattaiolare *vi.* to slip away.

sgelare *vi.* to thaw. ♦ **sgelarsi** *vr.* to thaw.

sgelo *sm.* thawing.

sghembo *agg.* oblique: *di —*, obliquely.

sgherro *sm.* hired assassin.

sghignazzare *vi.* to guffaw.

sghignazzata *sf.* guffaw.

sghimbescio (*nella loc. avv.*) *di —*, awry.

sghiribizzo *sm.* whim.

sgobbare *vi.* to work hard.

sgobbone *sm.* **1.** hard worker **2.** (*studentesco*) swot.

sgocciolare *vi.* to drip.
sgocciolìo *sm.* dripping.
sgolarsi *vr.* to shout oneself hoarse.
sgombrare *vt.* to clear.
sgombro *agg.* **1.** clear (of) **2.** (*fig.*) free (from).
sgomentare *vt.* to dismay.
sgomento *agg.* dismayed. ♦ **sgomento** *sm.* dismay.
sgominare *vt.* to rout.
sgonfiamento *sm.* deflation.
sgonfiare *vt.* to deflate.
sgonfio *agg.* deflated.
sgorbia *sf.* gouge.
sgorbiare *vt.* to scrawl.
sgorbio *sm.* **1.** scrawl **2.** (*pittura mal fatta*) daub **3.** (*fig.*) deformed man (*pl.* men).
sgorgare *vi.* to gush, to flow.
sgozzare *vt.* to cut (*v. irr.*) so.'s throat.
sgradévole *agg.* unpleasant.
sgradito *agg.* **1.** disagreeable **2.** (*mal accetto*) unwelcome.
sgrammaticato *agg.* ungrammatical.
sgranare *vt.* **1.** to shell: — *gli occhi*, to open one's eyes wide **2.** (*mangiare*) to devour.
sgranatrice *sf.* husker.
sgranchire *vt.* to stretch.
sgranocchiare *vt.* to munch.
sgrassare *vt.* to take (*v. irr.*) the grease off: — *il brodo*, to skim the grease from the broth.
sgravare *vt.* **1.** to lighten **2.** (*fig.*) to relieve.
sgravio *sm.* **1.** lightening **2.** (*fig.*) relief.
sgraziato *agg.* awkward.
sgretolamento *sm.* pounding.
sgretolare *vt.* to pound. ♦ **sgretolarsi** *vr.* to crumble.
sgridare *vt.* to scold.
sgroppare[1] *vt.* (*sciogliere*) to untie.
sgroppare[2] *vi.* (*di cavallo*) to buck.
sgroppata *sf.* bucking.
sgrossamento *sm.* rough-shaping.
sgrossare *vt.* **1.** to rough **2.** (*dirozzare*) to refine.
sgrovigliare *vt.* to unravel.
sguaiato *agg.* **1.** unbecoming **2.** (*volgare*) coarse.
sguainare *vt.* to unsheathe.
sgualcire *vt.* to crease.
sgualdrina *sf.* harlot, whore.
sguardo *sm.* look, glance: *dare uno —*, to have a look.

sguarnire *vt.* **1.** to untrim **2.** (*mil.*) to dismantle.
sguàttero *sm.* scullery-boy.
sguazzare *vi.* to wallow.
sguinzagliare *vt.* to unleash.
sgusciare *vt.* to shell. ♦ **sgusciare** *vi.* to slip away.
si[1] *pron.* **1.** (*riflessivo*) oneself, himself, herself, itself, themselves **2.** (*rec.*) (*fra due*) each other; (*fra molti*) one another **3.** (*pron. indef.*) one, people, we, they: — *dice*, people say.
si[2] *sm.* (*mus.*) si, B.
sì *avv.* yes: *penso di —*, I think so; — *certo*, certainly; *e — che*, yet; *uno —, uno no*, every other one; *forse che —, forse che no*, maybe yes, maybe no.
sia *cong.* **1.** (*o l'uno o l'altro*) whether... or, either... or **2.** (*entrambi*) both... and.
siamese *agg.* e *s.* Siamese.
sibarita *s.* sybarite.
siberiano *agg.* Siberian.
sibilante *agg.* **1.** hissing **2.** (*fonetica*) sibilant.
sibilare *vi.* to whistle, to hiss.
sibilla *sf.* sibyl.
sibillino *agg.* sibylline.
sìbilo *sm.* hiss, whistle.
sicario *sm.* cut-throat.
sicché *cong.* **1.** so... that **2.** (*dunque*) therefore.
siccità *sf.* drought.
siccome *cong.* as, since.
siciliano *agg.* e *sm.* Sicilian.
sicomoro *sm.* sycamore.
sicumera *sf.* presumption.
sicura *sf.* safety belt.
sicurezza *sf.* **1.** (*certezza*) certainty **2.** (*immunità da pericoli*) safety || *dispositivo di —*, safety device; *misura di —*, precautionary measure; *uscita di —*, emergency door; *rasoio, spilla di —*, safety-razor, pin.
sicuro *agg.* **1.** (*certo*) sure: — *di sé*, self-confident **2.** (*immune da pericoli*) safe **3.** (*che non sbaglia*) unfailing **4.** (*calmo, saldo*) calm, steady **5.** (*esperto*) skilful.
siderale *agg.* sidereal.
siderurgìa *sf.* metallurgy of iron.
siderùrgico *agg.* iron (*attr.*): *stabilimento —*, iron-works (*pl.*). ♦ **siderùrgico** *sm.* iron worker.
sidro *sm.* cider.
siepe *sf.* hedge.

siero *sm.* serum.
sieroso *agg.* serous.
sieroterapìa *sf.* serotherapy.
siesta *sf.* nap.
siffatto *agg.* such.
sifìlide *sf.* syphilis.
sifone *sm.* siphon.
sigaraia *sf.* cigar-seller.
sigaretta *sf.* cigarette.
sìgaro *sm.* cigar.
sigillare *vt.* to seal.
sigillatura *sf.* sealing.
sigillo *sm.* seal.
sigla *sf.* monogram.
siglare *vt.* to initial.
significare *vt.* **1.** to mean (*v. irr.*) **2.** (*comunicare*) to signify **3.** (*simboleggiare*) to represent.
significativo *agg.* meaningful.
significato *sm.* **1.** meaning **2.** (*valore*) import.
signora *sf.* **1.** lady, woman (*pl.* women) **2.** (*seguito da cognome*) Mrs: *la — Smith*, Mrs. Smith **3.** (*vocativo*) Madam: *buon giorno —*, good morning Madam **4.** (*padrona*) mistress **5.** (*donna ricca*) rich lady **6.** (*moglie*) wife (*pl.* wives).
signore *sm.* **1.** gentleman, man (*pl.* -men) **2.** (*seguito da cognome*) Mr.: *il — Smith*, Mr. Smith **3.** (*padrone*) master **4.** (*vocativo*) Sir: *sì —! yes, Sir!* **5.** (*uomo ricco*) lord **6.** (*Dio*) God, Lord.
signoreggiare *vt.* to rule.
signorìa *sf.* **1.** (*di uomo*) Lordship; (*di donna*) Ladyship **2.** (*dominio*) dominion.
signorile *agg.* **1.** (*riferito a uomo*) gentlemanlike; (*riferito a donna*) ladylike **2.** (*elegante*) luxury.
signorilità *sf.* distinction, high class.
signorina *sf.* **1.** young lady **2.** (*seguito da cognome*) Miss: *la — Smith*, Miss Smith **3.** (*vocativo*) Madam: *Buon giorno —*, good morning Madam **4.** (*padroncina*) young mistress **5.** (*donna non sposata*) unmarried woman.
signorotto *sm.* squire.
silenziatore *sm.* silencer.
silenzio *sm.* silence.
silenzioso *agg.* silent ‖ *una strada silenziosa*, a noiseless street.
sìlfide *sf.* sylph.
silfo *sm.* sylph.
sìlice *sf.* silica.

silicio *sm.* silicon.
silicone *sm.* silicone.
silicosi *sf.* silicosis.
sìllaba *sf.* syllable.
sillabare *vt.* to syllabize.
sìllabo *sm.* summary.
sillogismo *sm.* syllogism.
sillogìstico *agg.* syllogistic.
silo *sm.* silo (*pl.* silos).
siluramento *sm.* **1.** torpedoing **2.** (*fig.*) firing.
silurante *sf.* torpedo-boat.
silurare *vt.* **1.** to torpedo **2.** (*fig.*) to dismiss.
siluriano *agg.* Silurian.
siluro *sm.* (*mil.; zool.*) torpedo.
silvestre *agg.* sylvan.
silvicoltore *sm.* forester.
silvicoltura *sf.* forestry.
simbiosi *sf.* symbiosis.
simboleggiare *vt.* to symbolize.
simbòlico *agg.* **1.** symbolic **2.** (*nominale*) nominal.
simbolismo *sm.* symbolism.
simbolista *agg. e sm.* symbolist.
sìmbolo *sm.* symbol.
similare *agg.* similar.
sìmile *agg.* **1.** like, similar **2.** (*pred.*) alike **3.** (*tale*) such. ♦ **sìmile** *sm.* fellow-creature.
similitùdine *sf.* **1.** likeness **2.** (*lett.*) simile.
simmetrìa *sf.* symmetry.
simmètrico *agg.* symmetric(al).
simonìa *sf.* simony.
simonìaco *agg. e sm.* simoniac.
simpatìa *sf.* liking.
simpàtico *agg.* nice, pleasant.
simpatizzante *agg.* sympathizing. ♦ **simpatizzante** *s.* sympathizer.
simpatizzare *vi.* **1.** to sympathize **2.** (*rec.*) to take (*v. irr.*) a liking to each other.
simposio *sm.* symposium (*pl.* -ia).
simulacro *sm.* **1.** simulacre **2.** (*finzione*) sham.
simulare *vt.* to feign.
simulato *agg.* simulated.
simulatore *sm.* simulator.
simulazione *sf.* simulation.
simultaneità *sf.* simultaneity.
simultàneo *agg.* simultaneous (with).
sinagoga *sf.* synagogue.
sincerarsi *vr.* to make (*v. irr.*) sure.
sincerità *sf.* sincerity.
sincero *agg.* sincere, true.
sincopare *vt.* to syncopate.

sincopato *agg.* syncopated.
sincope *sf.* 1. (*med.*) syncope 2. (*mus.; gramm.*) syncopation.
sincronismo *sm.* synchronism.
sincronizzare *vt.* to synchronize.
sincronizzazione *sf.* synchronization.
sindacale *agg.* trade-union (*attr.*).
sindacalismo *sm.* trade-unionism.
sindacalista *s.* trade-unionist.
sindacare *vt.* 1. to control 2. (*criticare*) to criticize.
sindacato *sm.* trade-union.
sindaco *sm.* 1. mayor 2. (*di società*) auditor.
sindrome *sf.* syndrome.
sinecura *sf.* sinecure.
sinfonia *sf.* symphony.
sinfonico *agg.* symphonic.
singhiozzare *vi.* to sob.
singhiozzo *sm.* 1. hiccup 2. (*di pianto*) sob.
singolare *agg.* 1. singular 2. (*singolo*) single.
singolarità *sf.* singularity.
singolarmente *avv.* 1. (*ad uno ad uno*) singly 2. (*segnatamente*) particularly.
singolo *agg.* single, individual.
singulto *sm.* 1. hiccup 2. (*di pianto*) sob.
sinistra *sf.* 1. left: alla mia —, on my left 2. (*mano*) left hand 3. (*parte*) left-hand side || uomo di — (*pol.*), left-winger.
sinistramente *avv.* sinisterly.
sinistrato *agg.* 1. (*di edificio*) bomb-damaged 2. (*di persona*) injured. ♦ **sinistrato** *sm.* (damage) sufferer.
sinistro *agg.* 1. left 2. (*truce*) sinister, grim. ♦ **sinistro** *sm.* 1. accident, mishap 2. (*boxe*) left.
sinologo *sm.* Sinologist.
sinonimia *sf.* synonymy.
sinonimo *agg.* synonymous. ♦ **sinonimo** *sm.* synonym.
sinora *avv.* till now, so far.
sinovite *sf.* synovitis.
sintassi *sf.* syntax.
sintattico *agg.* syntactic(al).
sintesi *sf.* synthesis (*pl.* -ses).
sintetico *agg.* synthetic.
sintetizzare *vt.* to synthetize.
sintomatico *agg.* symptomatic.
sintomo *sm.* symptom.
sintonia *sf.* syntony.
sintonizzare *vt.* to tune in.
sinuosità *sf.* winding.

sinuoso *agg.* winding.
sinusite *sf.* sinusitis.
sionismo *sm.* Zionism.
sionista *s.* Zionist.
sipario *sm.* curtain.
sirena *sf.* 1. (*mit.*) siren, mermaid 2. (*acustica*) hooter.
siringa *sf.* syringe.
siringare *vt.* to syringe.
sismico *agg.* seismic.
sismografo *sm.* seismograph.
sismologia *sf.* seismology.
sismologo *sm.* seismologist.
sistema *sm.* system: — di vita, way of life.
sistemare *vt.* 1. (*mettere in ordine*) to arrange 2. (*definire*) to settle.
sistematico *agg.* systematic(al).
sistemazione *sf.* 1. (*ordine*) arrangement 2. (*collocazione di macchinari*) layout 3. (*il sistemarsi*) settling 4. (*lavoro*) job.
sito *sm.* place.
situare *vt.* to place.
situazione *sf.* situation.
slabbrare *vt.* to chip the rim of.
slabbratura *sf.* chipping.
slacciare *vt.* 1. to untie 2. (*sbottonare*) to unbutton.
slanciarsi *vr.* to rush.
slanciato *agg.* slim.
slancio *sm.* 1. rush 2. (*energia*) energy.
slargare *vt.* to widen.
slattamento *sm.* weaning.
slattare *vt.* to wean.
slavato *agg.* pale.
slavina *sf.* landslide; (*di neve*) snowslide.
slavo *agg.* e *sm.* Slav.
sleale *agg.* unfair.
slealtà *sf.* disloyalty.
slegare *vt.* to untie.
slegato *agg.* 1. untied 2. (*di discorso ecc.*) disconnected.
slitta *sf.* sleigh.
slittamento *sm.* skidding.
slittare *vi.* 1. to slide (*v. irr.*) 2. (*di ruote*) to skid.
slogamento *sm.* dislocation.
slogare *vt.* to dislocate.
slogatura *sf.* dislocation.
sloggiare *vi.* to clear out. ♦ **sloggiare** *vt.* to drive (*v. irr.*) out.
smaccato *agg.* sickly-sweet.
smacchiare *vt.* to clean.
smacchiatore *sm.* stain-remover.
smacchiatura *sf.* cleaning.
smacco *sm.* mortification.

smagliante agg. dazzling.
smagliare vt. to unravel. ♦ **smagliarsi** vr. (di calze) to ladder.
smagliato agg. unravelled.
smagliatura sf. 1. (di calze) ladder.
smagnetizzare vt. to demagnetize.
smagnetizzazione sf. demagnetization.
smagrire vt. e vi. to thin.
smagrito agg. thin, grown thin.
smaliziare vt. to smarten up. ♦ **smaliziarsi** vr. to wisen.
smaliziato agg. cunning.
smaltare vt. to enamel: — le unghie, to paint one's nails.
smaltato agg. 1. enamelled 2. (di unghie) painted.
smaltire vt. to digest: — la sbornia, to get (v. irr.) over one's drunkenness.
smalto sm. enamel: — per unghie, nail-polish.
smanceria sf. mawkishness.
smangiare vt. to corrode.
smania sf. 1. great desire 2. (agitazione) frenzy.
smaniare vi. 1. to yearn (for) 2. (essere agitati) to be restless.
smanioso agg. 1. eager 2. (agitato) restless.
smantellamento sm. dismantling.
smantellare vt. to dismantle.
smarcare vt. to unmark.
smargiassata sf. swagger.
smargiasseria sf. bragging.
smargiasso sm. braggart.
smarginare vt. to trim the edge.
smarrimento sm. 1. loss 2. (turbamento) bewilderment.
smarrire vt. to lose (v. irr.). ♦ **smarrirsi** vr. 1. to lose one's way 2. (di lettera, pacco) to miscarry 3. (turbarsi) to be bewildered.
smascellarsi vr. to dislocate one's jaws.
smascherare vt. to unmask.
smembramento sm. dismemberment.
smembrare vt. to dismember.
smemorataggine sf. 1. lack of memory 2. (dimenticanza) lapse of memory.
smemorato agg. absent-minded.
smentire vt. to deny. ♦ **smentirsi** vr. 1. to contradict oneself 2. (venir meno) to be untrue to oneself.
smentita sf. denial.
smeraldo sm. emerald.

smerciare vt. to sell (v. irr.) off.
smercio sm. sale.
smerigliare vt. 1. to polish with emery 2. (di vetri) to frost glass.
smerigliato agg. emery: carta smerigliata, emery paper; vetro —, frosted glass.
smeriglio sm. emery.
smerlo sm. scallop.
smesso agg. cast off.
smettere vt. to stop, to leave (v. irr.) off: — un vestito, to cast (v. irr.) off a dress.
smezzare vt. to halve.
smidollato agg. (di persona) spineless.
smilitarizzare vt. to demilitarize.
smilitarizzazione sf. demilitarization.
smilzo agg. thin.
sminuire vt. to diminish. ♦ **sminuirsi** vr. to belittle oneself.
sminuzzare vt. 1. (tritare) to mince 2. (tagliuzzare) to chop up 3. (sbriciolare) to crumble.
smistamento sm. 1. clearing 2. (ferr.) shunting 3. (di corrispondenza) sorting.
smistare vt. 1. (di corrispondenza) to sort out 2. (ferr.) to shunt.
smisuratamente avv. beyond measure.
smisurato agg. enormous, huge.
smobilitare vt. to demobilize.
smobilitazione sf. demobilization.
smoccolare vt. to snuff.
smoccolatoio sm. snuffers (pl.).
smoccolatura sf. snuffing.
smodato agg. immoderate.
smoderatezza sf. immoderateness.
smoderato agg. immoderate.
smontàbile agg. demountable.
smontaggio sm. disassembling.
smontare vt. 1. (far scendere) (da cavallo) to unhorse; (da un'automobile) to drop 2. (scomporre in parti) to take (v. irr.) to pieces 3. (mecc.) to disassemble 4. (fig.) to dishearten, to cool. ♦ **smontare** vi. 1. (da un treno, tram ecc.) to get (v. irr.) off 2. (da un'automobile) to get (v. irr.) out 3. (da cavallo) to dismount 4. (dal lavoro) to go (v. irr.) off duty 5. (sbiadire) to fade.
smorfia sf. grimace.
smorfioso agg. affected.
smorto agg. pale.
smorzamento sm. 1. (di luci) shad-

ing **2.** (*di colori*) toning down **3.** (*di suoni*) lowering **4.** (*di sete; fig.*) quenching.

smorzare *vt.* **1.** (*di luci*) to shade **2.** (*di colori*) to tone down **3.** (*di suoni*) to lower **4.** (*di sete; fig.*) to quench **5.** (*spegnere*) to put (*v. irr.*) down.

smottamento *sm.* landslip.

smottare *vi.* to slip.

smozzicare *vt.* **1.** to hack to pieces **2.** (*di parole*) to clip.

smunto *agg.* pale.

smuòvere *vt.* **1.** to shift **2.** (*fig.*) to move.

smussare *vt.* **1.** to round off **2.** (*fig.*) to soften.

smussato *agg.* **1.** blunted **2.** (*fig.*) softened.

snaturare *vt.* to pervert.

snaturato *agg.* unnatural.

snazionalizzare *vt.* to denationalize.

snebbiare *vt.* **1.** to dispel the fog **2.** (*fig.*) to clear.

snellezza *sf.* slenderness.

snellire *vt.* **1.** to make (*v. irr.*) slender **2.** (*fig.*) to simplify. ◆ **snellirsi** *vr.* to grow (*v. irr.*) slender.

snello *agg.* slender.

snervante *agg.* enervating.

snervare *vt.* to enervate.

snidare *vt.* **1.** to flush **2.** (*fig.*) to dislodge.

snobbare *vt.* to snob.

snobismo *sm.* snobbery.

snocciolare *vt.* **1.** to stone **2.** (*fig.*) to tell (*v. irr.*).

snodare *vt.* **1.** to untie **2.** (*rendere agile*) to make (*v. irr.*) supple. ◆ **snodarsi** *vr.* (*di strade*) to wind (*v. irr.*).

snodato *agg.* **1.** supple **2.** (*di cosa*) jointed.

snodo *sm.* joint.

soave *agg.* sweet.

soavità *sf.* sweetness.

sobbalzare *vi.* **1.** to jerk **2.** (*trasalire*) to start.

sobbalzo *sm.* **1.** jerk **2.** (*sussulto*) start.

sobbarcarsi *vr.* to take (*v. irr.*) upon oneself.

sobborgo *sm.* suburb.

sobillare *vt.* to stir up.

sobillatore *sm.* instigator.

sobrietà *sf.* sobriety.

sobrio *agg.* sober.

socchiùdere *vt.* **1.** to half-close **2.** (*aprire un po'*) to half-open.

socchiuso *agg.* half-closed, half-open.

sòccida *sf.* agistment.

soccòmbere *vi.* to succumb.

soccòrrere *vt.* to help, to assist.

soccorritore *agg.* helpful. ◆ **soccorritore** *sm.* helper.

soccorso *sm.* help || *pronto* —, first aid.

socialdemocràtico *agg.* socialdemocratic.

socialdemocrazìa *sf.* socialdemocracy.

sociale *agg.* social.

socialismo *sm.* Socialism.

socialista *agg. e sm.* Socialist.

socialità *sf.* sociality.

socializzare *vt.* to socialize.

socializzazione *sf.* socialization.

società *sf.* **1.** society **2.** (*comm.*) company: — *anonima*, joint-stock company; — *a responsabilità limitata*, limited company || *entrare in* —, to enter into partnership.

sociévole *agg.* sociable.

socievolezza *sf.* sociability.

socio *sm.* **1.** member **2.** (*comm.*) partner.

sociologìa *sf.* sociology.

sociològico *agg.* sociological.

sociòlogo *sm.* sociologist.

socràtico *agg.* Socratic.

soda *sf.* soda.

sodalizio *sm.* **1.** society **2.** (*confraternita*) brotherhood.

sodare *vt.* to consolidate.

sodatura *sf.* (*tessile*) fulling.

soddisfacente *agg.* satisfactory.

soddisfare *vt.* **1.** to satisfy **2.** (*adempiere*) to fulfil **3.** (*far fronte a*) to discharge **4.** (*riparare*) to make (*v. irr.*) amends.

soddisfazione *sf.* satisfaction.

sodio *sm.* sodium.

sodo *agg.* solid, firm: *uovo* —, hard-boiled egg; *darle sode a qu.*, to strike (*v. irr.*) so. hard.

sofferente *agg.* **1.** suffering **2.** (*malaticcio*) poorly.

sofferenza *sf.* pain.

soffermare *vt.* to stop. ◆ **soffermarsi** *vr.* to stop.

soffiare *vt. e vi.* to blow (*v. irr.*): *soffiarsi il naso*, to blow one's nose.

soffiata *sf.* puff.

soffiato *agg.* puffed.

soffiatore *sm.* blower.

soffiatura *sf.* blowing.

sòffice *agg.* soft.

soffietto *sm.* **1.** bellows (*pl.*) **2.** (*edit.*) blurb.

soffio *sm.* puff, whiff.

soffione *sm.* **1.** blow-pipe **2.** (*geol.*) fumarole.

soffitta *sf.* garret.

soffitto *sm.* ceiling.

soffocamento *sm.* choking.

soffocante *agg.* choking: *caldo —,* sultry heat.

soffocare *vt.* **1.** to choke **2.** (*reprimere*) to repress.

soffocato *agg.* choked.

sòffoco *sm.* sultriness.

soffóndere *vt.* to suffuse.

soffrìggere *vt.* to fry slightly.

soffrire *vt.* **1.** to suffer **2.** (*sopportare*) to stand (*v. irr.*).

soffuso *agg.* suffused.

sofisma *sm.* sophism.

sofista *sm.* sophist.

sofìstica *sf.* sophistry.

sofisticare *vi.* to quibble. ◆ **sofisticare** *vt.* to adulterate.

sofisticato *agg.* **1.** sophisticated **2.** (*adulterato*) adulterated.

sofisticazione *sf.* adulteration.

sofisticherìa *sf.* quibbling.

sofìstico *agg.* sophistical.

soggettista *sm.* scenario writer.

soggettivismo *sm.* subjectivism.

soggettività *sf.* subjectivity.

soggettivo *agg.* subjective.

soggetto *agg. e sm.* subject.

soggezione *sf.* **1.** subjection **2.** (*timidezza*) shyness.

sogghignare *vi.* to sneer.

sogghigno *sm.* sneer.

soggiacere *vi.* to be subjected

soggiogare *vt.* to subdue.

soggiornare *vi.* to stay.

soggiorno *sm.* stay: *stanza di —,* living-room.

soggiùngere *vt.* to add.

soglia *sf.* threshold.

sògliola *sf.* sole.

sognante *agg.* dreaming: *occhi sognanti,* dreamy eyes.

sognare *vt.* to dream (*v. irr.*): — *ad occhi aperti,* to have daydreams.

sognatore *agg.* dreaming. ◆ **sognatore** *sm.* dreamer.

sogno *sm.* dream.

soia *sf.* soya.

solaio *sm.* attic.

solamente *avv.* only.

solare *agg.* **1.** solar **2.** (*radioso*) radiant.

solatìo *agg.* sunny.

solcare *vt.* **1.** to plough **2.** (*fig.*) to furrow.

solcato *agg.* **1.** ploughed **2.** (*fig.*) furrowed.

solcatura *sf.* ploughing, furrowing.

solco *sm.* **1.** (*agr.*) furrow **2.** (*ruga*) wrinkle **3.** (*mar.*) wake **4.** (*di ruota sul terreno*) track.

solcòmetro *sm.* log.

soldataglia *sf.* soldiery.

soldatesco *agg.* soldierly.

soldato *sm.* soldier.

soldo *sm.* **1.** penny **2.** (*denaro*) money **3.** (*salario*) pay: *essere al — di qu.,* to be in so.'s pay.

sole *sm.* sun: *bagno di —,* sun-bathing; *colpo di —,* sunstroke; *un giorno di —, senza —,* a sunny day, a sunless day; *tramonto del —,* sunset.

soleggiare *vt.* to sun-dry.

soleggiato *agg.* sunny.

solenne *agg.* solemn.

solennità *sf.* **1.** solemnity **2.** (*cerimonia*) ceremony.

solennizzare *vt.* to solemnize.

solenòide *sm.* solenoid.

solere *vi.* to use (*usato solo al passato*).

solerte *agg.* diligent.

solerzia *sf.* diligence.

soletta *sf.* sole.

solfa *sf.* **1.** scale **2.** (*fig.*) old story.

solfara *sf.* sulphur mine.

solfare *vt.* to sulphur.

solfatara *sf.* solfatara.

solfato *sm.* sulphate.

solfeggiare *vt.* to sol-fa.

solfeggio *sm.* solfeggio.

solfito *sm.* sulphite.

solfuro *sm.* sulphide.

solidale *agg.* solid (for).

solidamente *avv.* solidly.

solidarietà *sf.* solidarity.

solidarizzare *vi.* to be solid (for).

solidificare *vt.* to solidify.

solidificazione *sf.* solidification.

solidità *sf.* **1.** solidity **2.** (*di colori*) fastness.

sòlido *agg.* **1.** solid **2.** (*di colori*) fast **3.** (*fig.*) sound. ◆ **sòlido** *sm.* solid.

soliloquio *sm.* soliloquy.

solipsismo *sm.* solipsism.

solista *s.* soloist.

solitamente *avv.* usually.
solitario[1] *agg.* solitary. ♦ **solitario** *sm.* 1. hermit 2. *(brillante)* solitaire.
solitario[2] *sm.* (*a carte*) solitaire.
sòlito *agg.* usual, customary: *essere* —, to be used to (doing); *di* —, usually.
solitùdine *sf.* loneliness.
sollazzare *vt.* to amuse.
sollazzo *sm.* amusement.
sollecitante *agg.* urging.
sollecitare *vt.* 1. (*far premura*) to urge 2. (*brigare*) to solicit 3. (*affrettare*) to hurry up.
sollecitazione *sf.* 1. solicitation 2. (*preghiera*) entreaty.
sollécito *agg.* 1. (*rapido*) prompt 2. (*preoccupato*) solicitous 3. (*premuroso*) obliging.
sollecitùdine *sf.'* 1. (*rapidità*) promptness 2. (*interessamento*) concern 3. (*gentilezza*) kindness.
solleone *sm.* dog-days (*pl.*).
solleticante *agg.* alluring.
solleticare *vt.* to tickle.
sollético *sm.* 1. tickle: *soffrire il* —, to be ticklish 2. (*fig.*) itch.
sollevamento *sm.* lifting.
sollevare *vt.* 1. to lift 2. (*issare*) to hoist 3. (*fig.*) to raise 4. (*dar sollievo*) to relieve. ♦ **sollevarsi** *vr.* 1. to rise (*v. irr.*) 2. (*riaversi*) to recover 3. (*insorgere*) to rebel.
sollevato *agg.* (*rasserenato*) cheered up.
sollevazione *sf.* (*rivolta*) rising.
sollievo *sm.* relief.
sollùchero *sm. andare in* —, to go (*v. irr.*) into raptures.
solo *agg.* 1. alone (*pred.*): *da* —, by oneself 2. (*unico*) only. ♦ **solo** *avv.* only.
solstizio *sm.* solstice.
soltanto *avv.* only.
solùbile *agg.* soluble.
solubilità *sf.* solubility.
soluzione *sf.* solution.
solvente *agg.* e *sm.* solvent.
solvenza *sf.* (*comm.*) solvency.
solvìbile *agg.* solvent.
solvibilità *sf.* solvency.
soma *sf.* load, burden.
somaràggine *sf.* stupidity.
somaro *sm.* ass.
somàtico *agg.* somatic.
somigliante *agg.* alike, similar.
somiglianza *sf.* likeness.
somigliare *vi.* to look like.

somma *sf.* 1. (*mat.*) addition 2. (*di denaro*) sum.
sommamente *avv.* extremely.
sommare *vt.* to add.
sommariamente *avv.* summarily.
sommario *agg.* e *sm.* summary.
sommèrgere *vt.* to submerge.
sommergìbile *agg.* submersible. ♦ **sommergìbile** *sm.* submarine.
sommergibilista *sm.* submariner.
sommersione *sf.* submersion.
sommerso *agg.* submerged.
sommessamente *avv.* 1. submissively 2. (*a bassa voce*) in a low voice.
sommesso *agg.* 1. submissive 2. (*di voce*) low.
somministrare *vt.* to administer.
somministratore *sm.* giver.
somministrazione *sf.* giving.
sommissione *sf.* V. *sottomissione.*
sommità *sf.* summit, top.
sommo[1] *agg.* 1. highest 2. (*fig.*) supreme.
sommo[2] *sm.* summit, top.
sommossa *sf.* rising.
sommovimento *sm.* movement, agitation.
sommozzatore *sm.* frogman (*pl.* -men).
sommuòvere *vt.* to stir up.
sonagliera *sf.* collar with bells.
sonaglio *sm.* 1. harness-bell 2. (*giocattolo*) rattle || *serpente a sonagli,* rattlesnake.
sonante *agg.* resounding || *denaro* —, ready money.
sonare *vt.* 1. to sound 2. (*musica*) to play 3. (*di orologio*) to strike (*v. irr.*). ♦ **sonare** *vi.* (*di campanello*) to ring (*v. irr.*).
sonata *sf.* (*mus.*) sonata.
sonatore *sm.* player.
sonda *sf.* 1. (*mar.*) sounding line 2. (*med.*) probe 3. (*min.*) drill.
sondaggio *sm.* 1. sounding 2. (*med.*) probing 3. (*min.*) drilling.
sondare *vt.* 1. to sound 2. (*fig.*) to throw (*v. irr.*) out.
sonerìa *sf.* 1. (*di orologio*) striking--mechanism 2. alarm.
sonetto *sm.* sonnet.
sonnacchiosamente *avv.* drowsily.
sonnacchioso *agg.* 1. sleepy 2. (*fig.*) torpid.
sonnambulismo *sm.* sleep-walking.
sonnàmbulo *sm.* sleep-walker.
sonnecchiare *vi.* to doze.
sonnellino *sm.* nap.

sonnìfero *sm.* sleeping pills (*pl.*).
sonno *sm.* sleep: — *profondo*, sound sleep.
sonnolento *agg.* drowsy.
sonnolenza *sf.* drowsiness.
sonoramente *avv.* sonorously.
sonorità *sf.* sonority.
sonorizzare *vt.* to post-score.
sonorizzazione *sf.* post-scoring.
sonoro *agg.* **1.** sonorous **2.** (*rumoroso*) loud **3.** (*cine*) sound.
sontuosamente *avv.* sumptuously.
sontuosità *sf.* sumptuousness.
sontuoso *agg.* sumptuous.
soperchierìa *sf.* V. *soverchierìa*.
sopire *vt.* **1.** to make (*v. irr.*) drowsy **2.** (*calmare*) to soothe.
sopore *sm.* doze.
soporìfero *agg.* soporific.
sopperire *vi.* **1.** to provide (for) **2.** (*supplire*) to make (*v. irr.*) up (for).
soppesare *vt.* **1.** to weigh in one's hand **2.** (*considerare*) to weigh.
soppiantare *vt.* to supplant.
soppiatto (*nella loc. avv.*) *di* —, stealthily.
sopportàbile *agg.* bearable.
sopportabilità *sf.* bearableness.
sopportabilmente *avv.* bearably.
sopportare *vt.* to bear (*v. irr.*).
sopportazione *sf.* endurance.
soppressare *vt.* to press.
soppressione *sf.* **1.** suppression **2.** (*abolizione*) abolition.
soppresso *agg.* **1.** suppressed **2.** (*abolito*) abolished.
sopprìmere *vt.* **1.** to suppress **2.** (*abolire*) to abolish.
sopra *prep.* **1.** (*con contatto*) on, upon **2.** (*senza contatto*) over **3.** (*al di sopra*) above. ◆ **sopra** *avv.* **1.** above **2.** (*al piano superiore*) upstairs.
soprabbondanza *sf.* V. *sovrabbondanza*.
soprabbondare *vi.* V. *sovrabbondare*.
sopràbito *sm.* overcoat.
sopraccaricare *vt.* V. *sovraccaricare*.
sopraccàrico *sm.* V. *sovraccàrico*.
sopraccennato *agg.* above-mentioned.
sopracciglio *sm.* eyebrow.
sopraccitato *agg.* V. *sopraddetto*.
sopraccoperta *sf.* **1.** (*di libro*) jacket **2.** (*di letto*) counterpane. ◆ **sopraccoperta** *avv.* (*mar.*) on deck.

sopraddetto *agg.* above-mentioned.
sopraelevare *vt.* **1.** (*edil.*) to increase the height of **2.** (*di strade, rotaie ecc.*) to bank.
sopraelevazione *sf.* **1.** (*edil.*) heightening **2.** (*di strade, rotaie ecc.*) superelevation.
sopraffare *vt.* to overwhelm.
sopraffazione *sf.* **1.** overwhelming **2.** (*abuso*) abuse.
sopraffino *agg.* first-rate.
sopràggiùngere *vi.* **1.** to arrive **2.** (*accadere*) to happen.
sopraggiunta *sf.* addition.
sopraindicato *agg.* V. *sopraddetto*.
sopralluogo *sm.* investigation on the spot.
soprammercato (*nella loc. avv.*) *per* —, moreover.
soprammèttere *vt.* to place on.
soprammòbile *sm.* knick-knack.
soprannaturale *agg.* supernatural.
soprannome *sm.* nickname.
soprannominare *vt.* to nickname.
soprannùmero *sm.* excess.
soprano *sm.* soprano.
soprappassaggio *sm.* overbridge.
soprappensiero *avv.* lost in thought.
soprappiù *sm.* extra, addition.
soprapprezzo *sm.* extra charge.
soprascarpa *sf.* galosh.
soprascritta *sf.* inscription.
soprascritto *agg.* above-written.
soprasensìbile *agg.* supersensible.
soprassalto *sm.* jerk: *di* —, all of a sudden.
soprassedere *vi.* **1.** to wait **2.** (*rimandare*) to postpone.
soprassoldo *sm.* extra pay.
soprastruttura *sf.* superstructure.
soprattassa *sf.* extra tax.
soprattutto *avv.* above all.
sopravanzare *vt.* **1.** (*superare*) to surpass **2.** (*avanzare*) to be left over.
sopravanzo *sm.* surplus.
sopravvalutare *vt.* to overrate.
sopravvenire *vi.* **1.** (*di persone*) to turn up **2.** (*di cose*) to come (*v. irr.*) about.
sopravvento *sm.* **1.** (*mar.*) windward **2.** (*fig.*) upper hand: *prendere il* —, to get (*v. irr.*) the upper hand.
sopravvissuto *agg. e sm.* surviving. ◆ **sopravvissuto** *sm.* survivor.
sopravvivenza *sf.* survival.

sopravvìvere *vi.* to survive.
sopruso *sm.* abuse of power.
soqquadro *sm.* confusion: *a* —, topsy-turvy.
sorbettare *vt.* to freeze (*v. irr.*).
sorbetto *sm.* sherbet.
sorbire *vt.* to sip. ♦ **sorbirsi** *vr.* to put (*v. irr.*) up with.
sorcio *sm.* mouse (*pl.* mice).
sordamente *avv.* dully.
sordidamente *avv.* filthily.
sordidezza *sf.* filthiness.
sòrdido *agg.* filthy.
sordina *sf.* (*mus.*) mute: *in* — (*fig.*), on the sly.
sordità *sf.* deafness.
sordo *agg.* deaf.
sordomuto *sm.* deaf-mute.
sorella *sf.* sister.
sorellastra *sf.* half-sister.
sorgente *sf.* spring, source.
sòrgere *vi.* to rise (*v. irr.*).
sorgiva *sf.* spring-water.
sorgivo *agg.* spring (*attr.*).
soriano *agg.* syrian: *gatto* —, tabby cat.
sormontare *vt.* 1. to surmount 2. (*superare*) to overcome (*v. irr.*).
sornione *agg.* sly. ♦ **sornione** *sm.* sly person.
sorpassare *vt.* 1. to overtake (*v. irr.*) 2. (*sport*) to outrun (*v. irr.*).
sorpassato *agg.* old-fashioned.
sorpasso *sm.* overtaking.
sorprendente *agg.* surprising.
sorprèndere *vt.* 1. (*cogliere inaspettatamente*) to catch (*v. irr.*) 2. (*meravigliare*) to surprise.
sorpresa *sf.* surprise: *di* —, by surprise.
sorrèggere *vt.* to support.
sorridente *agg.* smiling.
sorrìdere *vi.* 1. to smile 2. (*attrarre*) to appeal.
sorriso *sm.* smile.
sorsata *sf.* sip.
sorseggiare *vt.* to sip.
sorso *sm.* gulp, sip.
sorta *sf.* kind, sort.
sorte *sf.* 1. destiny, lot 2. (*avvenire*) future.
sorteggiare *vt.* to draw (*v. irr.*) lots (for).
sorteggio *sm.* draw.
sortilegio *sm.* witchcraft.
sortire[1] *vt.* to get (*v. irr.*).
sortire[2] *vi.* to come (*v. irr.*) out.
sortita *sf.* sally.
sorvegliante *sm.* overseer.

sorveglianza *sf.* overseeing.
sorvegliare *vt.* to oversee (*v. irr.*).
sorvolare *vt.* 1. to fly (*v. irr.*) over 2. (*passar sopra*) to pass over.
sorvolo *sm.* flying over.
sosia *sm.* double.
sospèndere *vt.* 1. (*attaccare*) to suspend 2. (*interrompere*) to defer.
sospensione *sf.* 1. (*incertezza; chim.*) suspension 2. (*interruzione*) interruption.
sospensiva *sf.* suspension.
sospensivo *agg.* suspensive.
sospeso *agg.* 1. hanging 2. (*interrotto*) suspended.
sospettàbile *agg.* liable to suspicion.
sospettare *vt.* to suspect.
sospetto *sm.* suspicion.
sospettosamente *avv.* suspiciously.
sospettoso *agg.* suspicious.
sospìngere *vt.* to drive (*v. irr.*) || *ad ogni piè sospinto*, at every moment.
sospirare *vi.* 1. to sigh 2. (*fig.*) to pine. ♦ **sospirare** *vt.* to long (for).
sospirato *agg.* (*desiderato*) longed for.
sospiro *sm.* sigh.
sosta *sf.* 1. (*fermata*) stop 2. (*pausa*) pause.
sostantivamente *avv.* substantively.
sostantivare *vt.* to substantivize.
sostantivo *sm.* substantive, noun.
sostanza *sf.* substance || *in* — (*in breve*), in short.
sostanziale *agg.* substantial.
sostanzialmente *avv.* substantially.
sostanzioso *agg.* substantial.
sostare *vi.* to stop.
sostegno *sm.* support.
sostenere *vt.* 1. to support 2. (*affermare*) to maintain 3. (*tener alto*) to keep (*v. irr.*) up.
sostenìbile *agg.* 1. supportable 2. (*di opinioni*) maintainable.
sostenimento *sm.* 1. support 2. (*sostentamento*) sustenance.
sostenitore *sm.* supporter.
sostentamento *sm.* sustenance.
sostenuto *agg.* 1. stiff, distant 2. (*comm.*) steady.
sostituìbile *agg.* replaceable.
sostituire *vt.* to replace.
sostituto *sm.* substitute.
sostituzione *sf.* replacement.
sostrato *sm.* substratum (*pl.* -ta).

sottacere *vt.* to keep (*v. irr.*) (sthg.) from.

sottaceti *sm. pl.* pickles.

sottana *sf.* 1. skirt 2. (*di prete*) cassock.

sottecchi (*nella loc. avv.*) *di* —, stealthily.

sotterfugio *sm.* subterfuge.

sotterramento *sm.* burial.

sotterrànea *sf.* underground.

sotterràneo *agg.* underground. ♦ **sotterràneo** *sm.* 1. (*di basilica*) vault 2. (*di castello*) dungeon.

sotterrare *vt.* to bury.

sottigliezza *sf.* 1. thinness 2. (*acutezza*) subtlety.

sottile *agg.* 1. thin 2. (*fig.*) subtle.

sottilizzare *vi.* to split (*v. irr.*) hairs.

sottilmente *avv.* 1. finely 2. (*con acutezza*) subtly.

sottintèndere *vt.* to imply.

sottinteso *agg.* implied. ♦ **sottinteso** *sm.* allusion.

sotto *prep.* 1. under 2. (*al di sotto, più in basso*) below, beneath 3. (*in espressioni di tempo*) — *Natale*, at Christmas; *essere* — *gli esami*, to be close to the exams. ♦ **sotto** *avv.* 1. underneath, below 2. (*al piano di sotto*) downstairs.

sottobanco *loc. avv.* underthecounter.

sottobosco *sm.* underbrush.

sottocchio *avv.* in front of: *tenere qc.* —, to keep (*v. irr.*) an eye on sthg.

sottochiave *avv.* under lock and key.

sottocoperta *sf.* (*mar.*) below deck.

sottocoppa *sf.* saucer.

sottocutàneo *agg.* subcutaneous.

sottofondo *sm.* 1. (*edil.*) foundation 2. (*sfondo*) background.

sottogamba (*nella loc. avv.*) *prendere qc.* —, to make (*v. irr.*) light of sthg.

sottolineare *vt.* 1. to underline 2. (*fig.*) to lay (*v. irr.*) stress (on).

sottolineatura *sf.* underlining.

sottomano *avv.* 1. (*di nascosto*) underhand 2. (*a portata di mano*) at hand.

sottomarino *agg. e sm.* submarine.

sottomesso *agg.* 1. subdued 2. (*obbediente*) submissive.

sottométtere *vt.* to subject. ♦ **sottométtersi** *vr.* to submit (oneself).

sottomissione *sf.* 1. subdual 2. (*obbedienza*) submission.

sottopassaggio *sm.* subway.

sottoporre *vt.* 1. (*al giudizio di qu.*) to submit 2. (*subire, far subire*) to subject 3. (*esporre*) to expose.

sottoposto *sm.* subordinate.

sottoprodotto *sm.* by-product.

sottoscritto *agg.* subscribed. ♦ **sottoscritto** *sm.* undersigned.

sottoscrìvere *vt.* 1. to sign 2. (*comm.*) to underwrite. ♦ **sottoscrivere** *vi.* to subscribe.

sottoscrizione *sf.* subscription.

sottosegretario *sm.* under-secretary.

sottosopra *avv.* 1. upside down 2. (*in disordine*) topsy-turvy.

sottospecie *sf.* subspecies (*invariato al pl.*).

sottostante *agg.* below.

sottostare *vi.* 1. (*essere sotto*) to be below 2. (*essere soggetto*) to be subjected 3. (*sottomettersi*) to submit.

sottosuolo *sm.* subsoil.

sottotenente *sm.* second lieutenant.

sottotìtolo *sm.* subtitle.

sottovalutare *vt.* to undervalue.

sottovento *avv.* (*mar.*) leeward.

sottoveste *sf.* petticoat.

sottovoce *avv.* in a low voice.

sottrarre *vt.* 1. (*mat.*) to subtract 2. (*portar via*) to take (*v. irr.*) away 3. (*rubare*) to steal (*v. irr.*) 4. (*salvare da*) to deliver. ♦ **sottrarsi** *vr.* to avoid (sthg.).

sottrazione *sf.* subtraction.

sottufficiale *sm.* non-commissioned officer.

sovente *avv.* often, frequently.

soverchiare *vi.* to overcome (*v. irr.*).

soverchierìa *sf.* oppression.

soviètico *agg. e sm.* Soviet.

sovrabbondante *agg.* superabundant.

sovrabbondanza *sf.* superabundance.

sovrabbondare *vi.* to superabound.

sovraccaricare *vt.* to overload.

sovraccàrico *sm.* overload.

sovraccoperta *sf. e avv.* V. *sopraccoperta.*

sovranità *sf.* 1. sovereignty 2. (*supremazia*) supremacy.

sovrannaturale *agg.* V. *soprannaturale.*

sovrano *agg.* sovereign.

sovrappopolare *vt.* to overpopulate.

sovrappopolato *agg.* overpopulated.

sovrappopolazione *sf.* overpopulation.

sovrapporre *vt.* to superimpose.

sovrapposizione *sf.* superimposition.

sovrastampa *sf.* overprint.

sovrastante *agg.* impending, overhanging.

sovrastare *vi.* **1.** to overhang (*v. irr.*) over **2.** (*fig.*) to impend **3.** (*essere superiore*) to be superior.

sovreccedente *agg.* superabundant.

sovreccedenza *sf.* surplus.

sovreccitàbile *agg.* overexcitable.

sovreccitabilità *sf.* overexcitability.

sovreccitare *vt.* to overexcite.

sovreccitazione *sf.* overexcitement.

sovrimposta *sf.* additional tax.

sovrimpressione *sf.* (*foto; cine*) superimposure.

sovrintendente *sm.* superintendent.

sovrintendenza *sf.* superintendence.

sovrumano *agg.* superhuman.

sovvenzionare *vt.* to subsidize.

sovvenzione *sf.* subsidy.

sovversione *sf.* overthrow.

sovversivo *agg.* subversive. ♦ **sovversivo** *sm.* subverter.

sovvertimento *sm.* subversion.

sovvertire *vt.* to overthrow (*v. irr.*).

sozzo *agg.* filthy.

sozzume *sm.* filth.

spaccalegna *sm.* wood-cutter.

spaccamontagne *sm.* braggart.

spaccapietre *sm.* stone-breaker.

spaccare *vt.* **1.** to split (*v. irr.*) **2.** (*rompere*) to break (*v. irr.*) || *il mio orologio spacca il minuto*, my watch is dead right; *il sole spacca le pietre*, the sun is blazing down.

spaccatura *sf.* split, cleft.

spacchettare *vt.* to unpack.

spacciare *vt.* **1.** (*vendere*) to sell (*v. irr.*) **2.** (*mettere in circolazione*) to circulate **3.** (*far credere*) to make (*v. irr.*) (so.) believe **4.** (*uccidere*) to kill. ♦ **spacciarsi** *vr.* to pretend to be || *lo danno per spacciato* (*di malato*), they give him up.

spacciato *agg.* done for.

spacciatore *sm.* **1.** seller **2.** (*di monete false*) forger.

spaccio *sm.* **1.** shop **2.** (*vendita*) sale.

spacco *sm.* **1.** split **2.** (*di abiti*) vent.

spacconata *sf.* bluff.

spaccone *sm.* boaster.

spada *sf.* sword.

spadaccino *sm.* fencer.

spadino *sm.* court-sword.

spadroneggiare *vi.* to lord it.

spaesato *agg.* (*fig.*) lost.

spaghetto *sm.* **1.** (*piccolo spago*) string **2.** (*fam.*) (*paura*) fright.

spagliare *vt.* to take (*v. irr.*) the straw off.

spagnoletta *sf.* **1.** (*di filo*) spool **2.** (*arachide*) peanut.

spagnolismo *sm.* Hispanicism.

spagnolo *agg.* Spanish. ♦ **spagnolo** *sm.* Spaniard.

spago *sm.* string.

spaiare *vt.* to uncouple.

spaiato *agg.* odd.

spalancare *vt.* to open wide.

spalancato *agg.* wide open.

spalare *vt.* to shovel away.

spalatore *sm.* shoveller.

spalatura *sf.* shovelling.

spalla *sf.* **1.** shoulder **2.** (*pl.*) back (*sing.*) **3.** (*teat.*) stooge man || *alle spalle*, behind; *vivere alle spalle di qu.*, to live on so.

spallata *sf.* **1.** push with the shoulders **2.** (*alzata di spalle*) shrug.

spalleggiare *vt.* to back.

spalletta *sf.* parapet.

spalliera *sf.* **1.** back **2.** (*di piante*) espalier.

spallina *sf.* **1.** shoulder-strap **2.** (*mil.*) epaulette.

spalluccia *sf.* *far spallucce*, to shrug one's shoulders.

spalmare *vt.* to smear.

spalto *sm.* glacis.

spampanare *vt.* to strip a vine of its leaves.

spàndere *vt.* **1.** to spread (*v. irr.*) **2.** (*versare*) to shed (*v. irr.*) **3.** (*scialacquare*) to squander.

spanna *sf.* span.

spannare *vt.* to skim.

spannocchiare *vt.* to husk.

spappolare *vt.* to pulp. ♦ **spappolarsi** *vr.* to become (*v. irr.*) mushy.

sparare[1] *vt.* to shoot (*v. irr.*), to fire.

sparare² *vt.* (*squartare*) to split (*v. irr.*).

sparata *sf.* **1.** discharge **2.** (*spacconata*) brag.

sparato *sm.* (*di camicia*) shirt-front.

sparatore *sm.* shooter.

sparatoria *sf.* shooting.

sparecchiare *vt.* to clear.

spareggio *sm.* **1.** disparity **2.** (*sport*) deciding game.

spàrgere *vt.* **1.** to scatter **2.** (*divulgare*) to spread (*v. irr.*) **3.** (*versare; di luce*) to shed (*v. irr.*).

spargimento *sm.* **1.** spreading **2.** (*versamento*) shedding || — *di sangue*, bloodshed.

sparigliare *vt.* to unmatch.

sparire *vi.* to disappear.

sparizione *sf.* disappearance.

sparlare *vi.* to speak (*v. irr.*) badly.

sparo *sm.* shot.

sparpagliare *vt.* to scatter. ♦ **sparpagliarsi** *vr.* to scatter.

sparso *agg.* **1.** (*versato*) shed **2.** (*sciolto*) loose.

spartano *agg.* Spartan.

spartiacque *sm.* watershed.

spartineve *sm.* snow-plough.

spartire *vt.* to share out.

spartito *sm.* score.

spartizione *sf.* sharing.

sparuto *agg.* lean, spare.

spàrviero *sm.* sparrow-hawk.

spasimante *sm.* wooer.

spasimare *vi.* **1.** to suffer agonies **2.** (*fig.*) to yearn.

spàsimo *sm.* pang.

spasmo *sm.* spasm.

spasmodicamente *avv.* spasmodically.

spasmòdico *agg.* spasmodic.

spassare *vt.* to amuse || *spassarsela*, to have a very good time.

spassionato *agg.* impartial.

spasso *sm.* **1.** amusement: *che* —!, what fun! **2.** (*passeggiata*) *andare a* —, to go (*v. irr.*) for a walk; *essere a* —, to be out of work.

spassoso *agg.* funny, amusing.

spàstico *agg.* spastic.

spato *sm.* spar.

spàtola *sf.* broad knife.

spatriare *vt.* V. *espatriare*.

spauracchio *sm.* **1.** scarecrow **2.** (*fig.*) bugbear.

spaurire *vt.* to frighten. ♦ **spaurirsi** *vr.* to get (*v. irr.*) frightened.

spaurito *agg.* frightened.

spavalderìa *sf.* boldness.

spavaldo *agg.* bold, arrogant.

spaventapàsseri *sm.* scarecrow.

spaventare *vt.* to frighten, to scare. ♦ **spaventarsi** *vr.* to be frightened.

spaventato *agg.* frightened, scared.

spavento *sm.* fright.

spaventoso *agg.* dreadful, frightful.

spaziale *agg.* space (*attr.*).

spaziare *vt.* to space. ♦ **spaziare** *vi.* to range.

spaziatura *sf.* spacing.

spazieggiare *vt.* to space.

spazientirsi *vr.* to lose (*v. irr.*) one's patience.

spazio *sm.* **1.** space **2.** (*posto*) room.

spazioso *agg.* wide.

spazzacamino *sm.* chimney-sweep.

spazzamine *sm.* mine-sweeper.

spazzaneve *sm.* snow-plough.

spazzare *vt.* to sweep (*v. irr.*).

spazzata *sf.* sweep.

spazzatura *sf.* (*rifiuti*) sweepings (*pl.*): *bidone della* —, dust-bin; *carro della* —, dust-cart.

spazzino *sm.* **1.** road-sweeper **2.** (*spazzaturaio*) dustman (*pl.* -men).

spàzzola *sf.* brush || *capelli a* —, crew-cut.

spazzolare *vt.* to brush.

spazzolata *sf.* brush.

spazzolino *sm.* (small) brush: — *da denti*, tooth-brush.

spazzolone *sm.* scrubbing-brush.

specchiarsi *vr.* **1.** to look at oneself in a mirror **2.** (*riflettersi*) to be mirrored.

specchiera *sf.* looking-glass.

specchietto *sm.* **1.** hand-mirror **2.** (*tabella*) table || — *retrovisore*, driving-mirror.

specchio *sm.* **1.** mirror **2.** (*prospetto*) register **3.** (*modello*) model || — *d'acqua*, sheet of water.

speciale *agg.* special.

specialista *s.* specialist.

specialità *sf.* speciality.

specializzare *vt.* to specialize. ♦ **specializzarsi** *vr.* to specialize.

specializzazione *sf.* specialization.

specie *sf.* **1.** kind **2.** (*scientifico; teol.*) species (*pl. invariato*) || *far* —, to surprise.

specificamente *avv.* specifically.

specificare *vt.* to specify.

specificazione *sf.* specification.

specifico *agg. e sm.* specific.

specioso *agg.* specious.

speculare[1] *vi.* to speculate (on): — *al rialzo, al ribasso,* to speculate for the advance, for the fall.

speculare[2] *agg.* mirror-like.

speculativo *agg.* speculative.

speculatore *agg.* speculative. ♦ **speculatore** *sm.* speculator.

speculazione *sf.* speculation.

spedire *vt.* 1. to send (*v. irr.*) 2. (*via mare*) to ship 3. (*via terra*) to forward.

speditamente *avv.* 1. quickly 2. (*correntemente*) fluently.

speditezza *sf.* 1. quickness 2. (*nel parlare*) fluency.

spedito *agg.* 1. (*svelto*) quick 2. (*nel parlare*) fluent.

speditore *sm.* sender.

spedizione *sf.* 1. forwarding 2. (*per mare*) shipment 3. (*di lettere, pacchi*) dispatch 4. (*scientifico; mil.*) expedition || — *per via aerea,* air-freight.

spedizioniere *sm.* forwarding agent.

spègnere *vt.* 1. (*un fuoco*) to put (*v. irr.*) out 2. (*gas, luce ecc.*) to turn off 3. (*fig.*) to stifle || — *la sete,* to quench one's thirst. ♦ **spègnersi** *vr.* 1. to go (*v. irr.*) out 2. (*fig.*) to fade 3. (*morire*) to pass away.

spegnimento *sm.* extinction.

spegnitoio *sm.* snuffer.

spelacchiare *vt.* to tear (*v. irr.*) out the hair of. ♦ **spelacchiarsi** *vr.* to lose (*v. irr.*) one's hair.

spelacchiato *agg.* 1. scanty-haired 2. (*di stoffe, pellicce*) worn-out.

spelare *vt.* to balden. ♦ **spelarsi** *vr.* V. spelacchiarsi.

spelato *agg.* 1. hairless 2. (*di indumento*) worn.

spelatura *sf.* 1. hairless patch 2. (*di indumento*) worn patch.

speleologìa *sf.* speleology.

speleològico *agg.* speleological.

speleòlogo *sm.* speleologist.

spellare *vt.* to skin. ♦ **spellarsi** *vr.* to peel.

spellatura *sf.* 1. skinning 2. (*parte spellata*) graze.

spelonca *sf.* den.

spendaccione *sm.* spendthrift.

spèndere *vt.* to spend (*v. irr.*) (*anche fig.*).

spennacchiare *vt.* to pluck. ♦ **spennacchiarsi** *vr.* to lose (*v. irr.*) one's feathers.

spennare *vt.* to pluck.

spennellare *vt.* 1. to brush 2. (*med.*) to paint.

spennellata *sf.* touch of the brush.

spennellatura *sf.* (*med.*) painting.

spensieratamente *avv.* thoughtlessly.

spensieratezza *sf.* thoughtlessness.

spensierato *agg.* thoughtless.

spento *agg.* 1. extinguished, out (*pred.*) 2. (*estinto*) extinct 3. (*smorto*) dull.

speràbile *agg.* to be hoped (for).

speranza *sf.* hope.

speranzoso *agg.* hopeful.

sperare *vt.* e *vi.* to hope (for sthg., in so.).

spèrdersi *vr.* 1. to get (*v. irr.*) lost 2. (*dileguare*) to vanish.

sperduto *agg.* 1. scattered 2. (*isolato*) secluded 3. (*smarrito*) lost.

sperequazione *sf.* inequality.

spergiurare *vi.* to swear (*v. irr.*) falsely: *giurare e —,* to swear again and again.

spergiuro *sm.* 1. perjury 2. (*di persona*) perjurer.

spericolato *agg.* reckless. ♦ **spericolato** *sm.* daredevil.

sperimentale *agg.* experimental.

sperimentalismo *sm.* experimentalism.

sperimentalmente *avv.* experimentally.

sperimentare *vt.* 1. to experiment (with) 2. (*mettere alla prova*) to test.

sperimentato *agg.* 1. (*provato*) tried 2. (*esperto*) experienced.

sperimentatore *sm.* experimenter.

sperimentazione *sf.* experimentation.

sperma *sm.* sperm.

spermatozoo *sm.* spermatozoon (*pl.* -zoa).

speronare *vt.* 1. (*mar.*) to ram 2. (*un cavallo*) to spur.

speronata *sf.* 1. (*mar.*) ramming 2. (*colpo di sperone*) spur.

sperone *sm.* V. sprone.

sperperamento *sm.* squandering.

sperperare *vt.* to squander.

sperperatore *sm.* squanderer.

spèrpero *sm.* dissipation.

sperticato *agg.* excessive.

spesa *sf.* 1. expense: *far fronte a una —,* to meet (*v. irr.*) an expense 2. (*compera*) shopping: *andare a far spese,* to go (*v. irr.*) shopping.

spesare vt. to maintain.
spesato agg. essere —, to have all expenses paid.
spessire vt. to thicken. ♦ **spessirsi** vr. to thicken.
spesso[1] agg. 1. thick 2. (frequente) frequent.
spesso[2] avv. often.
spessore sm. thickness.
spettàbile agg. respectable.
spettàcolo sm. 1. spectacle 2. (teat.) performance.
spettacoloso agg. spectacular.
spettante agg. due.
spettanze sf. pl. dues.
spettare vi. 1. to be (for so.) 2. (essere dovuto) to be due.
spettatore sm. 1. spectator 2. (testimone) witness || gli spettatori, the audience.
spettegolare vi. to gossip.
spettinare vt. to ruffle so.'s hair. ♦ **spettinarsi** vr. to ruffle one's hair.
spettinato agg. uncombed.
spettrale agg. spectral.
spettro sm. 1. ghost 2. (fis.) spectrum (pl. -ra).
spettroscopìa sf. spectroscopy.
spettroscòpico agg. spectroscopic(al).
spettroscopio sm. spectroscope.
speziale sm. (farmacista) chemist.
spezie sf. pl. spices.
spezzàbile agg. breakable.
spezzare vt. to break (v. irr.). ♦ **spezzarsi** vr. to break.
spezzatino sm. stew.
spezzato agg. broken.
spezzettamento sm. chopping.
spezzettare vt. to chop.
spezzone sm. 1. (mil.) incendiary bomb 2. (metal.) cut-down size.
spia sf. 1. spy 2. (indizio) evidence 3. (di porta) peep-hole || — luminosa, warning light; fare la —, to play the spy.
spiaccicare vt. to squash. ♦ **spiaccicarsi** vr. to get (v. irr.) squashed.
spiacente agg. sorry.
spiacere vi. V. dispiacere.
spiacévole agg. unpleasant.
spiacevolmente avv. unpleasantly.
spiaggia sf. 1. beach 2. (riva) (sea)shore.
spianamento sm. 1. levelling 2. (il radere al suolo) razing.
spianare vt. 1. to level 2. (radere al suolo) to raze 3. (appianare, lisciare) to smooth. ♦ **spianarsi** vr. to become (v. irr.) smooth.
spianata sf. 1. levelling 2. (luogo spianato) open space 3. (arch.) esplanade 4. (in un bosco) clearing.
spianato agg. 1. levelled 2. (liscio) smooth.
spiano (nella loc. avv.) a tutto —, profusely; (sodo) hard.
spiantare vt. 1. to pull out 2. (rovinare) to ruin. ♦ **spiantarsi** vr. (rovinarsi) to go (v. irr.) to ruin.
spiantato agg. (fig.) penniless. ♦ **spiantato** sm. (fig.) pauper.
spiare vt. 1. to spy (upon) 2. (aspettare) to watch (for).
spiattellare vt. to blab (out).
spiazzo sm. 1. open space 2. (nel bosco) clearing.
spiccare vt. 1. to pick 2. (tagliare) to cut (v. irr.) off 3. (pronunciare) to enunciate distinctly 4. (emettere) to issue || — un salto, to take (v. irr.) a leap; — il volo, to fly (v. irr.) up; — una tratta, to draw (v. irr.) a bill. ♦ **spiccare** vi. to stand (v. irr.) out.
spiccatamente avv. distinctly.
spiccato agg. 1. (marcato) marked 2. (nitido) clear.
spicchio sm. 1. slice 2. (di agrumi) segment 3. (di aglio) clove 4. (geom.) sector || a spicchi, sliced.
spicciare vt. to dispatch. ♦ **spicciarsi** vr. to hurry up.
spicciativo agg. V. spiccio.
spiccicare vt. 1. to detach 2. (pronunciare) to utter.
spiccio agg. 1. quick 2. (franco) straightforward || andar per le spicce, to go (v. irr.) straight to the point; moneta spiccia, small change.
spicciolata (nella loc. avv.) alla —, few at a time.
spìccioli sm. pl. change (solo sing.).
spicco sm. far —, to stand (v. irr.) out.
spidocchiare vt. to delouse.
spiedo sm. spit.
spiegàbile agg. explainable.
spiegamento sm. 1. spreading out 2. (mil.) deployment.
spiegare vt. 1. to explain 2. (stendere) to spread (v. irr.) out 3. (di vele) to unfurl 4. (mil.) to deploy. ♦ **spiegarsi** vr. 1. (farsi

capire) to make (*v. irr.*) oneself understood **2.** (*stendersi*) to spread out.

spiegazione *sf.* explanation.

spiegazzare *vt.* to crumple.

spietatamente *avv.* ruthlessly.

spietatezza *sf.* ruthlessness.

spietato *agg.* ruthless.

spifferare *vt.* to blurt out.

spiffero *sm.* draught.

spiga *sf.* **1.** spike **2.** (*di cereali*) ear.

spigare *vi.* to ear.

spighetta *sf.* braid.

spigliatamente *avv.* easily.

spigliatezza *sf.* ease.

spigliato *agg.* easy.

spigo *sm.* lavender.

spigolare *vt.* to glean (*anche fig.*).

spigolatore *sm.* gleaner.

spigolatrice *sf.* gleaner.

spigolatura *sf.* gleaning.

spìgolo *sm.* edge.

spigoloso *agg.* edgy.

spilla *sf.* **1.** pin **2.** (*gioiello*) brooch.

spillare *vt.* **1.** to draw (*v. irr.*) **2.** (*fig.*) to worm.

spillo *sm.* pin: — *da balia,* safety-pin.

spillone *sm.* (*per cappello*) hat-pin.

spilorcerìa *sf.* stinginess.

spilorcio *agg.* stingy. ♦ **spilorcio** *sm.* miser.

spilungona *sf.* lanky woman.

spilungone *sm.* lanky man.

spina *sf.* **1.** thorn **2.** (*lisca*) fishbone **3.** (*elettr.*) plug **4.** (*mecc.*) pin **5.** (*di botte*) bung **6.** (*fig.*) sorrow, grief || — *dorsale,* backbone; *a — di pesce,* herring-bone.

spinacio *sm.* spinach (*solo sing.*).

spinale *agg.* spinal.

spinare *vt.* (*pesce*) to bone.

spinato *agg.* (*a spina di pesce*) herring-bone || *filo —,* barbed wire.

spinetta *sf.* spinet.

spìngere *vt.* **1.** to push **2.** (*condurre*) to drive (*v. irr.*) **3.** (*stimolare*) to urge **4.** (*portare*) to carry. ♦ **spìngersi** *vr.* to push.

spino *sm.* thorn.

spinone *sm.* (*cane*) griffon.

spinosità *sf.* thorniness.

spinoso *agg.* thorny.

spinta *sf.* **1.** push **2.** (*stimolo*) incentive **3.** (*mecc.; edil.*) thrust.

spinterògeno *sm.* (battery) coil ignition.

spinto *agg.* **1.** (*eccessivo*) excessive **2.** (*audace*) risky.

spintone *sm.* shove || *farsi avanti a spintoni,* to elbow one's way forward.

spiombare *vt.* to unseal.

spionaggio *sm.* espionage.

spioncino *sm.* peep-hole.

spione *sm.* spy.

spiovente *agg.* **1.** drooping **2.** (*inclinato*) sloping. ♦ **spiovente** *sm.* **1.** slope **2.** (*sport*) high kick.

spiòvere *vi.* **1.** to stop raining **2.** (*ricadere*) to come (*v. irr.*) down.

spira *sf.* coil.

spiraglio *sm.* **1.** small hole **2.** (*barlume*) gleam.

spirale *sf.* **1.** spiral **2.** (*molla*) spring.

spirante *agg.* **1.** (*soffiante*) blowing **2.** (*morente*) passing away **3.** (*esalante*) exhaling.

spirare *vi.* **1.** (*soffiare*) to blow (*v. irr.*) **2.** (*morire*) to pass away **3.** (*scadere*) to expire **4.** (*emanare*) to emanate. ♦ **spirare** *vt.* to exhale.

spiritato *agg.* **1.** possessed **2.** (*spaventato*) frightened.

spirìtico *agg.* spiritualistic.

spiritismo *sm.* spiritualism.

spiritista *s.* spiritualist.

spiritìstico *agg.* V. *spiritico.*

spìrito *sm.* **1.** spirit **2.** (*fantasma*) ghost **3.** (*arguzia*) wit **4.** (*alcool*) alcohol || *far dello —,* to be witty.

spiritosàggine *sf.* witticism.

spiritosamente *avv.* wittily.

spiritoso *agg.* **1.** witty **2.** (*alcoolico*) alcoholic.

spirituale *agg.* spiritual.

spiritualismo *sm.* spiritualism.

spiritualista *agg.* spiritualistic. ♦ **spiritualista** *s.* spiritualist.

spiritualità *sf.* spirituality.

spiritualizzare *vt.* to spiritualize.

spiritualmente *avv.* spiritually.

spizzicare *vt.* to nibble.

spìzzico (*nella loc. avv.*) *a —,* little by little.

splendente *agg.* bright.

splèndere *vi.* to shine (*v. irr.*).

splèndido *agg.* splendid.

splendore *sm.* splendour.

spocchia *sf.* haughtiness.

spocchioso *agg.* haughty.

spodestamento *sm.* **1.** dispossession **2.** (*da posizione autorevole*) dethronement.

spodestare *vt.* **1.** to dispossess **2.** (*detronizzare*) to dethrone.

spoetizzare *vt.* to disenchant.

spoglia *sf.* **1.** (*di animale*) skin **2.** (*veste*) dress **3.** (*bottino*) spoils (*pl.*) || *spoglie mortali*, mortal remains.

spogliare *vt.* **1.** to strip **2.** (*derubare*) to rob **3.** (*saccheggiare*) to plunder. ♦ **spogliarsi** *vr.* **1.** to strip **2.** (*di alberi*) to shed (*v. irr.*) **3.** (*privarsi*) to strip oneself (of).

spogliarello *sm.* strip-tease.

spogliatoio *sm.* **1.** dressing-room **2.** (*teat. ecc.*) cloak-room.

spoglio *agg.* bare. ♦ **spoglio** *sm.* **1.** (*computo*) counting **2.** (*esame*) examination **3.** (*vestito smesso*) cast-off || *fare lo —*, to go (*v. irr.*) through.

spola *sf.* shuttle.

spoletta *sf.* **1.** spool **2.** (*di arma*) fuse.

spoliazione *sf.* spoliation.

spolmonarsi *vr.* to talk oneself hoarse.

spolpare *vt.* **1.** to take (*v. irr.*) the flesh off **2.** (*fig.*) to skin.

spolpato *agg.* **1.** stripped of the flesh **2.** (*fig.*) skinned.

spolverare *vt.* to dust.

spolveratura *sf.* **1.** dusting **2.** (*fig.*) smattering.

spolverino *sm.* dust-coat.

spolverizzare *vt.* to dust.

spòlvero *sm.* **1.** dusting **2.** (*disegno*) perforated pattern.

sponda *sf.* **1.** edge **2.** (*di fiume*) bank **3.** (*di mare*) shore **4.** (*parapetto*) parapet.

sponsali *sm. pl.* nuptials.

spontaneamente *avv.* spontaneously.

spontaneità *sf.* spontaneity.

spontàneo *agg.* spontaneous.

spopolamento *sm.* depopulation.

spopolare *vt.* to depopulate. ♦ **spopolarsi** *vr.* to become (*v. irr.*) depopulated.

spopolato *agg.* (*deserto*) deserted.

spora *sf.* spore.

sporàdico *agg.* sporadic.

sporcaccione *sm.* dirty man

sporcare *vt.* to dirty.

sporcizia *sf.* dirt.

sporco *agg.* dirty.

sporgente *agg.* protruding.

sporgenza *sf.* protrusion.

spòrgere *vi.* to put (*v. irr.*) out. ♦ **spòrgere** *vt.* to put (*v. irr.*) out. ♦ **spòrgersi** *vr.* to lean (*v. irr.*) out.

sport *sm.* sport.

sporta *sf.* basket.

sportello *sm.* **1.** door **2.** (*di biglietteria*) ticket-window **3.** (*di ufficio postale ecc.*) counter.

sportivamente *avv.* sportingly.

sportivo *agg.* sporting. ♦ **sportivo** *sm.* sportsman (*pl.* -men).

sporto *agg.* **1.** leaning out **2.** (*proteso*) outstretched.

sposa *sf.* bride.

sposalizio *sm.* wedding.

sposare *vt.* to marry. ♦ **sposarsi** *vr.* to get (*v. irr.*) married.

sposo *sm.* bridegroom.

spossamento *sm.* exhaustion.

spossante *agg.* exhausting.

spossare *vt.* to exhaust.

spossatezza *sf.* V. *spossamento*.

spossato *agg.* weary.

spossessare *vt.* to dispossess.

spostàbile *agg.* shiftable.

spostamento *sm.* **1.** shifting **2.** (*cambiamento*) change.

spostare *vt.* **1.** to shift, to move **2.** (*cambiare*) to change. ♦ **spostarsi** *vr.* to shift.

spostato *agg.* out of one's place (*pred.*). ♦ **spostato** *sm.* misfit.

spranga *sf.* bar.

sprangare *vt.* to bar.

sprazzo *sm.* flash: *— d'ingegno*, brain-wave.

sprecare *vt.* to waste.

spreco *sm.* waste.

sprecone *sm.* waster.

spregévole *agg.* despicable.

spregiare *vt.* to scorn.

spregiativo *agg.* **1.** scornful **2.** (*gramm.*) pejorative. ♦ **spregiativo** *sm.* (*gramm.*) pejorative.

spregio *sm.* contempt.

spregiudicatamente *avv.* open-mindedly.

spregiudicatezza *sf.* open-mindedness.

spregiudicato *agg.* open-minded.

sprèmere *vt.* **1.** to squeeze **2.** (*torcere*) to wring (*v. irr.*) out. ♦ **spremersi** *vr.* to rack oneself.

spremilimoni *sm.* lemon-squeezer.

spremitura *sf.* **1.** squeezing **2.** (*di panni bagnati*) wringing.

spremuta *sf.* squash.

spremuto *agg.* **1.** squeezed **2.** (*di panni*) wrung.

spretare *vt.* to unfrock. ♦ **spretarsi** *vr.* to renounce one's priesthood.

spretato *agg.* unfrocked. ♦ **spretato** *sm.* unfrocked priest.
sprezzante *agg.* scornful.
sprezzare *vt.* V. *disprezzare.*
sprezzo *sm.* scorn.
sprigionamento *sm.* **1.** exhalation **2.** (*violento*) bursting out.
sprigionare *vt.* to emit. ♦ **sprigionarsi** *vr.* **1.** to be emitted **2.** (*con violenza*) to burst (*v. irr.*) out.
sprimacciare *vt.* to shake (*v. irr.*) up.
sprizzare *vt. e vi.* to spurt: — *scintille,* to spit (*v. irr.*) sparks; — *gioia,* to burst (*v. irr.*) with joy.
sprizzo *sm.* spurt.
sprofondamento *sm.* **1.** sinking **2.** (*crollo*) collapse.
sprofondare *vt.* (*far cadere*) to cause to collapse. ♦ **sprofondare** *vi.* **1.** to sink (*v. irr.*) **2.** (*crollare*) to collapse **3.** (*fig.*) to be absorbed. ♦ **sprofondarsi** *vr.* **1.** to sink **2.** (*crollare*) to collapse **3.** (*fig.*) to be absorbed.
sproloquio *sm.* long rigmarole.
spronare *vt.* to spur.
spronata *sf.* spurring.
sprone *sm.* **1.** spur **2.** (*mar.*) ram ‖ *a spron battuto,* at full speed.
sproporzionato *agg.* disproportionate, out of proportion (*pred.*).
sproporzione *sf.* disproportion.
spropositato *agg.* **1.** full of blunders **2.** (*fig.*) enormous.
spropòsito *sm.* **1.** blunder **2.** (*eccesso*) excess ‖ *a —,* off the point.
sprovveduto *agg.* **1.** (*incauto*) unwary **2.** (*sprovvisto*) devoid **3.** (*impreparato*) unprepared.
sprovvisto *agg.* devoid ‖ *alla sprovvista,* unawares.
spruzzare *vt.* **1.** to spray **2.** (*inzaccherare*) to splash.
spruzzata *sf.* spray.
spruzzatore *sm.* sprayer.
spruzzatura *sf.* spraying.
spruzzo *sm.* **1.** spray **2.** (*di liquido sporco*) splash.
spudoratezza *sf.* shamelessness.
spudorato *agg.* shameless.
spugna *sf.* **1.** sponge **2.** (*tessuto*) sponge-cloth ‖ *cancellare con la —,* to sponge; *bere come una —,* to drink (*v. irr.*) like a fish.
spugnatura *sf.* sponge down.
spugnosità *sf.* sponginess.

spugnoso *agg.* spongy.
spulciare *vt.* **1.** to look for fleas (on) **2.** (*esaminare; fig.*) to peruse **3.** (*raccogliere; fig.*) to gather here and there.
spuma *sf.* foam.
spumante *agg.* foaming. ♦ **spumante** *sm.* sparkling wine.
spumare *vi.* to foam.
spumeggiante *agg.* foaming.
spumeggiare *vi.* to foam.
spumoso *agg.* foamy.
spuntare[1] *vt.* **1.** (*smussare*) to blunt **2.** (*tagliare*) to trim **3.** (*staccare*) to unpin ‖ *spuntarla,* to succeed. ♦ **spuntarsi** *vr.* **1.** (*smussarsi*) to get (*v. irr.*) blunt **2.** (*staccarsi*) to become (*v. irr.*) unpinned.
spuntare[2] *vi.* **1.** (*sorgere*) to rise (*v. irr.*) **2.** (*germogliare*) to sprout **3.** (*di capelli*) to begin (*v. irr.*) to grow **4.** (*apparire*) to appear.
spuntato *agg.* pointless.
spuntatura *sf.* **1.** (*lo smussare*) blunting **2.** (*il tagliare*) trimming.
spuntino *sm.* snack.
spunto *sm.* **1.** cue **2.** (*punto di partenza*) starting point.
spuntone *sm.* spike.
spurgare *vt.* **1.** to clean **2.** (*med.*) to discharge. ♦ **spurgarsi** *vr.* (*espettorare*) to expectorate.
spurgo *sm.* **1.** (*lo spurgare*) discharging **2.** (*l'espettorare*) expectorating **3.** (*ciò che viene espulso*) discharge.
spurio *agg.* spurious.
sputacchiare *vi.* V. *sputare.*
sputacchiera *sf.* spittoon.
sputacchio *sm.* spittle.
sputare *vt.* to spit (*v. irr.*).
sputasentenze *sm.* wiseacre.
sputo *sm.* spit.
squadra *sf.* **1.** (*da disegno*) square **2.** (*gruppo; sport*) team **3.** (*di operai*) gang **4.** (*mil.*) squad **5.** (*mar.*) squadron ‖ — *mobile,* flying squad.
squadrare *vt.* **1.** to square **2.** (*guardare*) to look (so.) up and down.
squadratura *sf.* squaring.
squadriglia *sf.* squadron.
squadro *sm.* squaring.
squadrone *sm.* squadron.
squagliamento *sm.* melting.
squagliare *vt.* to melt. ♦ **squagliarsi** *vr.* **1.** to melt **2.** (*andar via*) to steal (*v. irr.*) away.
squalìfica *sf.* disqualification.

squalificare vt. to disqualify.

squàllido agg. dreary.

squallore sm. dreariness.

squalo sm. shark.

squama sf. scale.

squamare vt. to scale. ♦ **squamarsi** vr. to scale.

squamoso agg. scaly.

squarciagola (nella loc. avv.) a —, at the top of one's voice.

squarciamento sm. tearing.

squarciare vt. 1. to tear (v. irr.) 2. (fig.) to dispel. ♦ **squarciarsi** vr. to be torn.

squarcio sm. gash.

squartare vt. to mangle.

squartatore sm. mangler.

squassare vt. to jolt.

squasso sm. jolt.

squattrinato agg. penniless.

squilibrare vt. to unbalance. ♦ **squilibrarsi** vr. to lose (v. irr.) one's balance.

squilibrato agg. unbalanced. ♦ **squilibrato** sm. lunatic.

squilibrio sm. 1. lack of balance 2. (mentale) derangement.

squillante agg. 1. shrill 2. (di trombe) blaring 3. (di campane) pealing.

squillare vi. 1. to ring (v. irr.) 2. (di trombe) to blare.

squillo sm. 1. ring 2. (di tromba) blare.

squinternare vt. 1. to ruin 2. (fig.) to upset (v. irr.).

squisitezza sf. exquisiteness.

squisito agg. exquisite.

squittìo sm. squeak.

squittire vi. to squeak.

sradicare vt. to uproot.

sragionare vi. to talk nonsense.

sregolatezza sf. disorderliness.

sregolato agg. disorderly.

stabbio sm. 1. sty 2. (letame) manure.

stàbile , sm. building. ♦ **stàbile** agg. 1. stable 2. (permanente) permanent: in pianta —, on the permanent staff.

stabilimento sm. 1. (fabbrica) factory 2. (edificio, lo stabilire) establishment.

stabilire vt. 1. to establish 2. (decidere) to decide. ♦ **stabilirsi** vr. to settle.

stabilità sf. stability.

stabilizzare vt. to stabilize.

stabilizzatore sm. stabilizer.

stabilizzazione sf. stabilization.

stabilmente avv. firmly.

stacanovismo sm. Stakhanovism.

staccàbile agg. detachable.

staccare vt. 1. to take (v. irr.) off 2. (tagliare) to cut (v. irr.) off 3. (separare) to separate 4. (slegare) to unfasten || — un assegno, to issue a cheque. ♦ **staccarsi** vr. 1. to come (v. irr.) off 2. (sciogliersi) to break (v. irr.) loose 3. (scostarsi) to move away 4. (separarsi) to part 5. (distaccarsi) to pull ahead (of) 6. (esser diverso) to differ.

stacciare vt. to sieve.

staccio sm. sieve.

staccionata sf. fence.

stacco sm. detachment.

stadera sf. steelyard.

stadio sm. 1. stadium (pl. -ia), sports ground 2. (fase) stage.

staffa sf. stirrup || perder le staffe (fig.), to lose (v. irr.) one's self--control.

staffetta sf. 1. courier 2. (sport) relay race.

staffilare vt. to lash.

staffilata sf. lash.

staffile sm. whip.

stafilococco sm. staphylococcus (pl. -ci).

staggio sm. 1. (di scala) shaft 2. (di sedia) back leg.

stagionale agg. seasonal.

stagionare vt. to season.

stagionato agg. 1. seasoned 2. (fig.) oldish.

stagionatura sf. seasoning.

stagione sf. season.

stagnaio sm. tinsmith.

stagnante agg. stagnant.

stagnare[1] vi. to stagnate.

stagnare[2] vt. 1. to tin 2. (saldare) to solder 3. (impermeabilizzare) to waterproof 4. (fermare) to staunch.

stagnatura sf. tinning.

stagnino sm. tinker.

stagno[1] sm. tin.

stagno[2] sm. (bacino d'acqua) pond.

stagno[3] agg. water-tight.

stagnola sf. tin-foil.

staio sm. bushel.

stalagmite sf. stalagmite.

stalattite sf. stalactite.

stalla sf. stable.

stalliere sm. stable-boy.

stallo sm. stall.

stallone sm. stallion.

stamattina *avv.* this morning.

stambecco *sm.* ibex.

stamberga *sf.* hovel.

stambugio *sm.* hole.

stame *sm.* (*bot.*) stamen.

stamigna *sf.* bunting.

stampa *sf.* **1.** print **2.** (*atto di stampare*) printing **3.** (*periodici, giornali*) press **4.** (*genere*) stamp || *agenzia di* —, news-agency; *errore di* —, misprint.

stampare *vt.* **1.** to print **2.** (*mecc.*) to press **3.** (*coniare*) to coin. ♦ **stamparsi** *vr.* — *in mente*, to impress (sthg.) firmly on one's mind.

stampatello *sm.* block letters (*pl.*).

stampato *sm.* **1.** printed matter **2.** (*modulo*) form.

stampatore *sm.* printer.

stampatrice *sf.* printing-press.

stampella *sf.* crutch.

stamperìa *sf.* printing-office.

stampigliare *vt.* to stamp.

stampo *sm.* **1.** die, mould **2.** (*genere*) stamp.

stanare *vt.* to drive (*v. irr.*) out.

stancare *vt.* **1.** to tire **2.** (*infastidire*) to annoy. ♦ **stancarsi** *vr.* **1.** to get (*v. irr.*) tired **2.** (*annoiarsi*) to get bored.

stanchezza *sf.* tiredness.

stanco *agg.* tired.

standardizzare *vt.* to standardize.

stanga *sf.* **1.** bar **2.** (*di carro*) shaft **3.** (*di passaggio a livello*) barrier.

stangare *vt.* **1.** to bar **2.** (*percuotere*) to thrash.

stanghetta *sf.* **1.** (*degli occhiali*) bar **2.** (*di serratura*) bolt.

stanotte *avv.* tonight.

stantìo *agg.* stale.

stantuffo *sm.* **1.** piston **2.** (*di pompa ecc.*) plunger.

stanza *sf.* **1.** room **2.** (*strofa*) stanza || *prendere, avere* —, to settle.

stanziamento *sm.* appropriation.

stanziare *vt.* to appropriate. ♦ **stanziarsi** *vr.* to settle.

stappare *vt.* to uncork.

stare *vi.* **1.** to stay **2.** (*abitare*) to live **3.** (*di salute, essere*) to be **4.** (*in piedi*) to stand (*v. irr.*) **5.** (*dipendere*) to depend (on) **6.** (*spettare*) to be up **7.** (*andare*) to go (*v. irr.*) **8.** (*di abito*) to suit || — *per*, to be going (to); *lasciar* —, to leave (*v. irr.*) alone; *sta' a sentire!*, listen!; *ben ti sta!*, it

serves you right!

starnazzare *vi.* to flutter.

starnutire *vi.* to sneeze.

starnuto *sm.* sneeze.

stasare *vt.* to unclog.

stasera *avv.* this evening.

stasi *sf.* **1.** standstill **2.** (*med.*) stasis (*pl.* -ses).

statale *agg.* State (*attr.*), of the State. ♦ **statale** *s.* State employee.

stàtica *sf.* statics.

stàtico *agg.* static.

statista *sm.* statesman (*pl.* -men).

statistica *sf.* statistics.

statizzare *vt.* to nationalize.

statizzazione *sf.* nationalization.

stato *sm.* **1.** state, condition (*anche posizione sociale*) **2.** (*giur.*) status **3.** (*pol.*) State || *ufficio di* — *civile*, registry office; *ufficiale di* — *civile*, registrar.

statua *sf.* statue.

statuaria *sf.* statuary.

statuario *agg.* statuesque.

statuire *vt.* to decree.

statunitense *agg.* United States (*attr.*). ♦ **statunitense** *sm.* United States citizen.

statura *sf.* stature.

statuto *sm.* statute.

stazionamento *sm.* standing.

stazionare *vi.* **1.** to stay **2.** (*di vetture*) to be parked.

stazionario *agg.* stationary.

stazione *sf.* station.

stazza *sf.* tonnage.

stazzare *vt.* to have the tonnage of.

stecca *sf.* **1.** (*di ombrello, ventaglio*) rib **2.** (*da biliardo*) cue **3.** (*di persiana*) slat **4.** (*di busto*) whalebone **5.** (*stonatura*) false note.

steccare *vt.* **1.** (*chiudere con steccato*) to fence in **2.** (*mus.*) to fluff. ♦ **steccare** *vi.* **1.** (*cantando*) to sing (*v. irr.*) a false note **2.** (*suonando*) to play a false note.

steccato *sm.* fence.

stecchito *agg.* **1.** (*secco*) dried up **2.** (*magro*) skinny **3.** (*morto*) stone dead.

stecco *sm.* **1.** stick **2.** (*persona magra*) bag of bones.

stecconata *sf.* paling.

stele *sf.* stele (*pl.* -lae).

stella *sf.* star: — *marina*, starfish; *a forma di* —, starlike.

stellare *agg.* **1.** stellar **2.** (*a forma di stella*) star-shaped.

stellato *agg.* starry.

stelletta *sf.* **1.** (*tip.*) asterisk **2.** (*mil.*) star.

stelloncino *sm.* short paragraph.

stelo *sm.* stem.

stemma *sm.* coat-of-arms.

stemperare *vt.* **1.** to mix **2.** (*diluire*) to spin out. ♦ **stemperarsi** *vr.* to dissolve.

stempiarsi *vr.* to go (*v. irr.*) bald.

stendardo *sm.* standard.

stèndere *vt.* **1.** to spread (*v. irr.*) **2.** (*allungare*) to stretch **3.** (*scrivere*) to draw (*v. irr.*) up **4.** (*rilassare*) to relax || — *il bucato*, to hang (*v. irr.*) out the washing. ♦ **stèndersi** *vr.* **1.** to stretch **2.** (*adagiarsi*) to lie (*v. irr.*) down.

stenodattilografìa *sf.* shorthand and typewriting.

stenografare *vt.* to write (*v. irr.*) down in shorthand.

stenografìa *sf.* shorthand.

stenògrafo *sm.* shorthand-writer.

stentare *vi.* **1.** to have difficulty (in) **2.** (*mancare del necessario*) to be in need.

stentato *agg.* **1.** hard **2.** (*cresciuto a stento*) stunted.

stento *sm.* privation: *a* —, hardly, with difficulty.

stentòreo *agg.* stentorian.

steppa *sf.* steppe.

sterco *sm.* dung.

stereofonìa *sf.* stereophony.

stereofònico *agg.* stereophonic.

stereografìa *sf.* stereography.

stereogràfico *agg.* stereographic(al).

stereoscopìa *sf.* stereoscopy.

stereoscopio *sm.* stereoscope.

stereotipato *agg.* stereotyped.

stereotipìa *sf.* stereotyping.

stèrile *agg.* barren.

sterilità *sf.* barrenness.

sterilizzare *vt.* to sterilize.

sterilizzatore *agg.* sterilizing. ♦ **sterilizzatore** *sm.* sterilizer.

sterilizzazione *sf.* sterilization.

sterlina *sf.* pound.

sterminare *vt.* to exterminate.

sterminatezza *sf.* immensity.

sterminato *agg.* (*smisurato*) immense.

sterminatore *sm.* exterminator.

sterminio *sm.* extermination.

sterno *sm.* breast-bone.

sterpaglia *sf.* brushwood.

sterpo *sm.* dry twig.

sterrare *vt.* to dig (*v. irr.*) up.

sterratore *sm.* navvy.

sterzare *vt.* to steer.

sterzata *sf.* sudden turn.

sterzo *sm.* (*auto*) steering-gear.

stesso *agg.* **1.** (*medesimo*) same **2.** (*intensivo*) *se* —, oneself; *io, me* —, myself; *tu, te* —, yourself; *egli, lui* —, himself; *ella, lei stessa*, herself; *esso* —, itself; *noi stessi*, ourselves; *voi stessi*, yourselves; *loro stessi*, themselves **3.** (*proprio*) very. ♦ **stesso** *sm.* same. ♦ **stesso** *avv.* all the same

stesura *sf.* **1.** (*redazione*) draft **2.** (*di contratto*) drawing up.

stetoscopio *sm.* stethoscope.

stìgmate *sf.* *pl.* **1.** stigmata (*pl.*) **2.** (*marchio*) brand (*sing.*).

stigmatizzare *vt.* to stigmatize.

stilare *vt.* to draw (*v. irr.*) up.

stile *sm.* style: *aver* —, to be stylish; *con* —, stylishly.

stilettata *sf.* stab.

stilista *s.* stylist.

stilìstica *sf.* stylistics.

stilizzare *vt.* to stylize.

stilizzazione *sf.* stylization.

stilla *sf.* drop.

stillare *vi.* e *vt.* to ooze. ♦ **stillarsi** *vr.* — *il cervello*, to rack one's brain.

stiliicidio *sm.* dripping.

stilo *sm.* stylus.

stilogràfica *sf.* fountainpen.

stilogràfico *agg.* stylographic(al).

stima *sf.* **1.** (*valutazione*) estimate **2.** (*buona opinione*) esteem.

stimàbile *agg.* estimable.

stimare *vt.* **1.** (*valutare*) to estimate **2.** (*tenere in considerazione*) to esteem **3.** (*ritenere*) to consider.

stimatore *sm.* estimator.

stimolante *agg.* stimulating. ♦ **stimolante** *sm.* stimulant.

stimolare *vt.* to stimulate.

stìmolo *sm.* **1.** stimulus (*pl.* -li) **2.** (*pungolo*) goad.

stinco *sm.* shin.

stingere *vt.* to fade. ♦ **stingersi** *vr.* to fade.

stinto *agg.* faded.

stipare *vt.* to cram.

stipato *agg.* crammed (with).

stipendiare *vt.* to pay (*v. irr.*) a salary (to so.).

stipendio *sm.* salary.

stìpite *sm.* jamb.

stipulante *agg.* stipulating. ♦ **stipulante** *s.* stipulator.

stipulare *vt.* to stipulate.

stipulazione *sf.* stipulation.

stiracchiare *vt.* 1. to stretch 2. (*distorcere*) to twist.

stiracchiato *agg.* (*fig.*) forced.

stiramento *sm.* 1. stretching 2. (*muscolare*) strain.

stirare *vt.* 1. to stretch 2. (*col ferro da stiro*) to iron.

stiratura *sf.* ironing.

stirerìa *sf.* (*e tintoria*) laundry shop.

stirpe *sf.* 1. stock 2. (*progenie*) issue.

stitichezza *sf.* constipation.

stìtico *agg.* constipated.

stiva *sf.* hold.

stivale *sm.* boot.

stivaletto *sm.* ankle-boot.

stizza *sf.* anger.

stizzire *vt.* to vex. ♦ **stizzirsi** *vr.* to get (*v. irr.*) cross.

stizzito *agg.* cross.

stizzoso *agg.* peevish.

stoccata *sf.* thrust: *lanciare una —* (*fig.*), to gibe (at).

stoffa *sf.* 1. cloth 2. (*fig.*) stuff.

stoicismo *sm.* stoicism.

stòico *agg. e sm.* stoic.

stoino *sm.* door-mat.

stola *sf.* stole.

stolidità *sf.* stolidity.

stòlido *agg.* stolid.

stoltezza *sf.* foolishness.

stolto *agg.* foolish. ♦ **stolto** *sm.* fool.

stomacare *vt.* to sicken. ♦ **stomacarsi** *vr.* to sicken.

stomachévole *agg.* sickening.

stòmaco *sm.* stomach: *dare di —*, to vomit; *restare sullo —*, to lie (*v. irr.*) on one's stomach.

stomatite *sf.* stomatitis.

stomatologìa *sf.* stomatology.

stonare *vi.* 1. to be out of tune 2. (*fig.*) to be out of place 3. (*di colori*) to clash. ♦ **stonare** *vt.* to upset (*v. irr.*).

stonato *agg.* 1. out of tune 2. (*fig.*) out of place 3. (*turbato*) upset 4. (*di nota*) false.

stonatura *sf.* false note.

stoppa *sf.* tow.

stoppaccio *sm.* wad.

stoppare *vt.* 1. to plug 2. (*sport*) to stop.

stoppia *sf.* stubble.

stoppino *sm.* wick.

stopposo *agg.* 1. towy 2. (*di carne*) stringy.

stòrcere *vt.* 1. to twist 2. (*un'articolazione*) to sprain || *— gli occhi*, to roll one's eyes. ♦ **stòrcersi** *vr.* 1. to twist 2. (*lussarsi, slogarsi*) to wrench.

stordimento *sm.* 1. dizziness 2. (*meraviglia*) bewilderment.

stordire *vt.* 1. to stun 2. (*di alcoolici*) to dull 3. (*assordare*) to deafen 4. (*innervosire*) to drive (*v. irr.*) crazy. ♦ **stordirsi** *vr.* to dull one's senses.

stordito *agg.* 1. (*sbalordito*) bewildered 2. (*sbadato*) heedless 3. (*sciocco*) foolish.

storia *sf.* 1. history 2. (*racconto*) story.

storicismo *sm.* historical method.

storicità *sf.* historicity.

stòrico *agg.* historical. ♦ **stòrico** *sm.* historian.

storiografìa *sf.* historiography.

storiògrafo *sm.* historiographer.

stormire *vi.* to rustle.

stormo *sm.* 1. flight 2. (*folla*) crowd || *suonare a —*, to ring (*v. irr.*) the tocsin.

stornare *vt.* to divert.

stornello[1] *sm.* ditty.

stornello[2] *sm.* (*zool.*) starling.

storno[1] *agg.* dapple-grey.

storno[2] *sm.* (*zool.*) starling.

storno[3] *sm.* (*comm.*) transfer.

storpiare *vt.* 1. to cripple 2. (*rovinare*) to mangle.

storpiatura *sf.* 1. crippling 2. (*fig.*) mangling 3. (*cosa malfatta*) botch.

storpio *sm.* cripple.

storta *sf.* 1. twist 2. (*in una articolazione*) sprain 3. (*chim.*) retort.

storto *agg.* 1. twisted 2. (*piegato*) crooked 3. (*di occhi*) squinting 4. (*sbagliato*) wrong.

stortura *sf.* 1. deformity 2. (*errore*) mistake.

stoviglie *sf. pl.* kitchenware (*sing.*).

stràbico *agg.* squinting. ♦ **stràbico** *sm.* squinter.

strabiliante *agg.* amazing.

strabiliare *vt.* to amaze (*anche far strabiliare*). ♦ **strabiliare** *vi.* to be amazed. ♦ **strabiliarsi** *vr.* to be amazed.

strabismo *sm.* squint.

straboccare *vi.* 1. to overflow 2. (*fig.*) to abound (in).

strabocchévole *agg.* overflowing.

strabuzzare *vt.* *— gli occhi*, to roll one's eyes.

stracàrico agg. overloaded (with).

stracciare vt. to tear (v. irr.). ♦ **stracciarsi** vr. to tear.

stracciato agg. 1. torn 2. (di persona) in rags.

straccio agg. torn, in rags || carta straccia, waste paper. ♦ **straccio** sm. rag: — per la polvere, duster.

straccione sm. ragamuffin.

straccivéndolo sm. rag-and-bone-man (pl. -men).

stracotto agg. overdone. ♦ **stracotto** sm. stew.

strada sf. 1. road 2. (di città) street 3. (percorso; fig.) way || — a senso unico, one-way street; — ferrata, railway; — maestra, main road.

stradale agg. road (attr.), of the road: fondo —, road-bed.

stradino sm. roadman (pl. -men).

strafalcione sm. blunder.

strafare vi. to overdo (v. irr.).

strafottente agg. 1. (noncurante) unconcerned 2. (arrogante) arrogant.

strage sf. 1. slaughter 2. (distruzione) destruction || fare una —, to slaughter.

stragrande agg. enormous.

stralciare vt. 1. (comm.) to remove 2. (fig.) to take (v. irr.) off.

stralcio sm. 1. removal 2. (estratto) extract.

strale sm. dart.

stralunare vt. — gli occhi, to roll one's eyes, to open one's eyes wide.

stralunato agg. 1. (di occhi) rolling, wild-eyed 2. (di persona) upset.

stramazzare vi. to fall (v. irr.) heavily.

stramberìa sf. oddity.

strambo agg. odd.

strame sm. litter.

strampalato agg. queer.

stranezza sf. oddity.

strangolamento sm. strangling.

strangolare vt. to strangle.

strangolatore sm. strangler.

straniero agg. foreign. ♦ **straniero** sm. foreigner.

strano agg. strange.

straordinario agg. extraordinary.

strapazzare vt. 1. to ill-use 2. (sgridare) to scold 3. (far lavorare troppo) to overwork 4. (di uova) to scramble. ♦ **strapazzarsi** vr. to overwork oneself.

strapazzata sf. 1. scolding 2. (fatica) overwork.

strapazzo sm. overwork: abiti da —, working-clothes; scrittore da —, hack.

strapieno agg. full up.

strapiombare vi. 1. to lean (v. irr.) 2. (scendere a precipizio) to fall (v. irr.) perpendicularly.

strapiombo sm. precipice: a —, sheer.

strapotente agg. very powerful.

strappare vt. 1. (lacerare) to tear (v. irr.) 2. (togliere) to snatch 3. (estirpare) to pull up 4. (un dente) to pull out 5. (estorcere) to wring (v. irr.). ♦ **strapparsi** vr. (lacerarsi) to tear.

strappo sm. 1. tear 2. (strappata) pull 3. (infrazione) breach || — muscolare, sprain.

strapuntino sm. folding seat.

straricco agg. immensely rich.

straripamento sm. overflowing.

straripare vi. to overflow.

strascicare vt. 1. to drag 2. (i piedi) to shuffle 3. (le parole) to drawl.

stràscico sm. 1. train 2. (residuo) after-effect 3. (rete) trawl.

strascinare vt. V. trascinare.

stratagemma sm. stratagem.

stratega sm. strategist.

strategìa sf. strategy.

stratègico agg. strategic(al).

stratificare vt. to stratify.

stratificazione sf. stratification.

strato sm. 1. layer 2. (di rivestimento) coat 3. (della società) class.

stratosfera sf. stratosphere.

stratosfèrico agg. stratospheric(al).

strattone sm. 1. pull 2. (sobbalzo) jerk || a strattoni, jerkily; (a intervalli) by fits and starts.

stravagante agg. odd, queer.

stravaganza sf. oddity.

stravecchio agg. very old.

stravedere vi. to see (v. irr.) badly: — per qu., to be crazy about so.

stravincere vt. to crush. ♦ **stravincere** vi. to win (v. irr.) all along the line.

stravizio sm. excess.

stravòlgere vt. 1. to twist 2. (gli occhi) to roll.

stravolto agg. 1. (turbato) upset 2. (di occhi) rolling.

straziante agg. tormenting, heart-rending (solo fig.).

straziare *vt.* to tear (*v. irr.*).

strazio *sm.* torment: *far — di*, to play havoc with.

strega *sf.* witch.

stregare *vt.* to bewitch.

stregone *sm.* wizard.

stregoneria *sf.* witchcraft.

stremare *vt.* to exhaust.

stremo *sm.* extreme.

strenna *sf.* gift.

strenuo *agg.* brave.

strepitare *vi.* to shout.

strèpito *sm.* din, uproar.

strepitoso *agg.* uproarious: *successo —*, striking success.

streptococco *sm.* streptococcus (*pl. -ci*).

streptomicina *sf.* streptomycin.

stretta *sf.* 1. grasp 2. (*calca*) press 3. (*gola*) gorge || *— di mano*, handshake; *essere alle strette*, to be in dire straits; *mettere alle strette qu.*, to put (*v. irr.*) so. with his back against the wall.

strettezza *sf.* 1. narrowness 2. (*povertà*) financial difficulty.

stretto *agg.* 1. narrow 2. (*serrato, piccolo*) tight 3. (*rigoroso*) strict 4. (*pigiato*) packed. ♦ **stretto** *sm.* strait.

strettoia *sf.* narrow passage.

stria *sf.* streak.

striare *vt.* to streak.

stricnina *sf.* strychnine.

stridente *agg.* 1. shrill 2. (*discordante*) jarring.

stridere *vi.* 1. to creak 2. (*di insetti*) to chirp 3. (*contrastare*) to jar.

stridio *sm.* 1. creaking 2. (*di insetti*) chirping.

strido *sm.* 1. scream 2. (*di animale*) screech.

stridulo *agg.* shrill.

striglia *sf.* curry-comb.

strigliare *vt.* 1. to curry 2. (*fig.*) to rebuke.

strillare *vi.* to scream.

strillo *sm.* scream.

strillone *sm.* newsboy.

striminzito *agg.* 1. stunted 2. (*di persona*) thin.

strimpellare *vt.* 1. (*di violino*) to scrape 2. (*di pianoforte*) to strum.

strinare *vt.* to singe.

stringa *sf.* lace.

stringare *vt.* 1. to lace tightly 2. (*fig.*) to condense.

stringato *agg.* 1. laced 2. (*fig.*) concise.

stringente *agg.* 1. (*urgente*) urgent 2. (*convincente*) persuasive.

stringere *vt.* 1. to press 2. (*restringere, avvitare*) to tighten 3. (*abbracciare*) to clasp 4. (*impugnare*) to grasp 5. (*fare*) to make (*v. irr.*) || *— la mano a*, to shake (*v. irr.*) hands with; *— i pugni*, to clench one's fists; *stringi stringi*, in conclusion. ♦ **stringere** *vi.* to be tight. ♦ **stringersi** *vr.* 1. to press (against) 2. (*far spazio*) to squeeze up || *— nelle spalle*, to shrug one's shoulders.

stringimento *sm.* 1. pressing 2. (*restringimento, legamento, avvitamento*) tightening 3. (*l'impugnare*) clasp 4. (*fitta*) pang.

striscia *sf.* 1. strip 2. (*riga*) stripe 3. (*scia*) trail || *a strisce*, striped.

strisciante *agg.* 1. creeping 2. (*servile*) fawning.

strisciare *vi.* 1. to creep (*v. irr.*) 2. (*fig.*) to grovel. ♦ **strisciare** *vt.* 1. to drag 2. (*i piedi*) to shuffle 3. (*radere*) to graze 4. (*fig.*) to fawn (on).

stritolamento *sm.* crushing.

stritolare *vt.* to crush.

strizzare *vt.* 1. to squeeze 2. (*torcere*) to wring (*v. irr.*) || *— l'occhio*, to wink (at so.).

strizzata *sf.* 1. squeeze 2. (*il torcere*) wring.

strofa *sf.* stanza.

strofinaccio *sm.* 1. duster 2. (*per asciugare*) towel.

strofinamento *sm.* rubbing.

strofinare *vt.* to rub.

strombatura *sf.* splay.

strombazzare *vt.* e *vi.* to trumpet.

strombettare *vi.* 1. to blow (*v. irr.*) a trumpet 2. (*auto*) to honk.

stroncare *vt.* 1. to break (*v. irr.*) off 2. (*fig.*) to demolish.

stroncatura *sf.* harsh criticism.

stronzio *sm.* strontium.

stropicciare *vt.* 1. to rub 2. (*i piedi*) to shuffle 3. (*sgualcire*) to crease. ♦ **stropicciarsi** *vr.* 1. (*gli occhi*) to rub oneself 2. (*sgualcirsi*) to crease.

stropiccio *sm.* *— di piedi*, shuffling.

strozzare *vt.* 1. to strangle 2. (*ostruire*) to obstruct 3. (*fig.*) to choke.

strozzato *agg.* 1. strangled 2. (*soffocato*) choked 3. (*con strozzature*) with narrow passages 4. (*med.*)

strangulated **5.** (*ostruito*) obstructed.

strozzatura *sf.* **1.** strangling **2.** (*il soffocare*) choking **3.** (*ostruzione*) obstruction **4.** (*restringimento*) narrow passage **5.** (*med.*) strangulation.

strozzinaggio *sm.* usury.

strozzino *sm.* usurer.

struggente *agg.* pining.

strùggere *vt.* **1.** to melt **2.** (*fig.*) to wear (*v. irr.*) out. ◆ **strùggersi** *vr.* **1.** to melt **2.** (*affliggersi*) to be distressed **3.** (*languire*) to be consumed (with), to pine (for).

struggimento *sm.* longing.

strumentale *agg.* instrumental.

strumentalismo *sm.* instrumentalism.

strumentare *vt.* to instrument.

strumentazione *sf.* instrumentation.

strumento *sm.* instrument.

strusciare *vt.* **1.** to rub **2.** (*adulare*) to fawn (on). ◆ **strusciarsi** *vr.* to rub (oneself).

strutto *sm.* lard.

struttura *sf.* structure.

strutturale *agg.* structural.

strutturare *vt.* to structure.

strutturazione *sf.* structure.

struzzo *sm.* ostrich.

stuccare[1] *vt.* **1.** to stucco **2.** (*turare*) to fill.

stuccare[2] *vt.* **1.** (*nauseare*) to sicken **2.** (*annoiare*) to bore. ◆ **stuccarsi** *vr.* **1.** to get (*v. irr.*) sick **2.** (*annoiarsi*) to get bored.

stuccatura *sf.* **1.** plastering **2.** (*di dente*) filling.

stucchévole *agg.* **1.** filling **2.** (*nauseante*) sickening **3.** (*noioso*) boring.

stucco *sm.* **1.** stucco **2.** (*per vetri*) putty || *restare di* —, to be nonplussed.

studente *sm.* student.

studentesco *agg.* student (*attr.*).

studiacchiare *vt.* to study fitfully.

studiare *vt.* to study. ◆ **studiarsi** *vr.* to try.

studiato *agg.* (*affettato*) affected.

studio *sm.* **1.** study **2.** (*progetto*) plan **3.** (*cine*) studio || *programma di studi*, curriculum; *essere allo* —, to be under consideration.

studioso *agg.* studious. ◆ **studioso** *sm.* scholar.

stufa *sf.* stove.

stufare *vt.* **1.** to stew **2.** (*fig.*) to bore. ◆ **stufarsi** *vr.* to get (*v. irr.*) bored.

stufato *sm.* stew.

stufo *agg.* fed up (with).

stuoia *sf.* mat.

stuolo *sm.* crowd.

stupefacente *agg.* stupefying. ◆ **stupefacente** *sm.* drug.

stupefare *vt.* to stupefy. ◆ **stupefarsi** *vr.* to be stupefied.

stupefazione *sf.* stupefaction.

stupendamente *avv.* wonderfully.

stupendo *agg.* wonderful.

stupidàggine *sf.* stupidity.

stupidità *sf.* stupidity.

stùpido *agg. e sm.* stupid.

stupire *vt.* to astonish. ◆ **stupirsi** *vr.* to be astonished.

stupito *agg.* astonished.

stupore *sm.* astonishment.

stupro *sm.* rape.

sturare *vt.* **1.** to uncork **2.** (*botti*) to unbung.

stuzzicadenti *sm.* tooth-pick.

stuzzicare *vt.* **1.** to prod **2.** (*frugare*) to pick **3.** (*molestare*) to tease **4.** (*stimolare*) to whet.

su *prep.* **1.** on **2.** (*senza contatto; rivestimento*) over **3.** (*al di sopra di*) above **4.** (*circa*) about || *nove volte* — *dieci*, nine times out of ten. ◆ **su** *avv.* **1.** up **2.** (*al piano superiore*) upstairs **3.** (*indosso*) on || — *per giù*, more or less; *in* — (*in avanti*), onwards; *più* —, further up; —, *andiamo!*, come on!

sua *agg. e pron.* V. *suo.*

suadente *agg.* persuasive.

subàcqueo *agg.* underwater (*attr.*). ◆ **subàcqueo** *sm.* frogman (*pl.* -men).

subaffittare *vt.* to sublease.

subaffitto *sm.* sublease.

subalpino *agg.* subalpine.

subalterno *agg. e sm.* subaltern.

subbuglio *sm.* **1.** turmoil **2.** (*disordine*) mess.

subconscio *sm.* subconscious.

subcosciente *agg. e sm.* subconscious.

subdolamente *avv.* underhand.

sùbdolo *agg.* sly.

subentrare *vi.* to take (*v. irr.*) the place (of).

subire *vt.* to undergo (*v. irr.*).

subissare *vt.* **1.** (*sprofondare*) to sink (*v. irr.*) **2.** (*fig.*) to overwhelm.

subisso *sm.* (*gran quantità*) shower.
subitaneità *sf.* suddenness.
subitàneo *agg.* sudden.
sùbito *avv.* **1.** at once **2.** (*presto*) soon || — *prima*, just before; — *dopo*, just after.
sublimare *vt.* to sublimate.
sublimato *sm.* sublimate.
sublimazione *sf.* sublimation.
sublime *agg. e sm.* sublime.
sublimità *sf.* sublimity.
sublocazione *sf.* subletting.
sublunare *agg.* sublunar.
subodorare *vt.* to suspect.
subordinare *vt.* to subordinate.
subordinata *sf.* subordinate clause.
subordinato *agg. e sm.* subordinate.
subordinazione *sf.* subordination.
subornare *vt.* to suborn.
subornazione *sf.* subornation.
substrato *sm.* substratum (*pl.* -ta).
suburbano *agg.* suburban.
suburbio *sm.* suburb.
succèdere *vi.* **1.** to succeed **2.** (*capitare*) to happen. ♦ **succèdersi** *vr.* to follow one another.
successione *sf.* succession.
successivamente *avv.* afterwards.
successo *sm.* **1.** success **2.** (*esito*) outcome || *aver* —, to be successful.
successore *sm.* successor.
succhiare *vt.* to suck.
succhiata *sf.* suck.
succhiello *sm.* gimlet.
succinto *agg.* **1.** (*di abiti*) scanty **2.** (*conciso*) concise.
succo *sm.* **1.** juice **2.** (*fig.*) pith.
succosità *sf.* **1.** juiciness **2.** (*fig.*) pithiness.
succoso *agg.* **1.** juicy **2.** (*fig.*) pithy.
sùccubo *agg.* entirely dominated (by).
succulento *agg.* **1.** juicy **2.** (*gustoso*) rich.
succursale *sf.* branch.
sud *sm.* south: *del* —, southern, south (*attr.*); *verso* —, southwards.
sudare *vi.* to sweat: — *sette camicie*, to toil hard; — *freddo*, to be in a cold sweat.
sudario *sm.* shroud.
sudata *sf.* sweat.
sudaticcio *agg.* clammy.
sudato *agg.* **1.** sweaty **2.** (*fig.*) hard-earned.
suddetto *agg.* above-mentioned.

suddiàcono *sm.* subdeacon.
sudditanza *sf.* subjection.
sùddito *sm.* subject.
suddivìdere *vt.* to subdivide.
suddivisione *sf.* subdivision.
sùdicio *agg.* dirty.
sudicione *sm.* dirty fellow.
sudiciume *sm.* dirt.
sudore *sm.* **1.** sweat **2.** (*fig.*) toil.
sudorìfero *agg.* **1.** (*che secerne sudore*) sudoriferous **2.** (*che produce sudore*) sudorific.
sue *agg. e pron.* V. *suo*.
sufficiente *agg.* **1.** sufficient **2.** (*altezzoso*) conceited **2.** (*voto sufficiente*) pass mark.
sufficienza *sf.* **1.** sufficiency **2.** (*alterigia*) conceit **3.** (*voto sufficiente*) pass mark || *aria di* —, superior air; *a* —, enough.
suffisso *sm.* suffix.
suffragare *vt.* **1.** to support **2.** (*eccl.*) to pray for.
suffragio *sm.* **1.** suffrage **2.** (*approvazione*) approval.
suggellare *vt.* to seal.
suggello *sm.* seal.
suggerimento *sm.* **1.** suggestion **2.** (*teat.*) prompting.
suggerire *vt.* **1.** to suggest **2.** (*dar l'imbeccata; teat.*) to prompt.
suggeritore *sm.* prompter.
suggestionàbile *agg.* impressionable.
suggestionabilità *sf.* impressionability.
suggestionare *vt.* to influence. ♦ **suggestionarsi** *vr.* to will oneself (to do sthg.), to be influenced.
suggestione *sf.* suggestion.
suggestività *sf.* suggestiveness.
suggestivamente *avv.* evocatively.
suggestivo *agg.* evocative.
sùghero *sm.* **1.** cork **2.** (*albero*) cork-tree.
sugna *sf.* pork fat.
sugo *sm.* **1.** juice **2.** (*di carne*) gravy **3.** (*di pomodoro*) sauce **4.** (*fig.*) gist.
sugosità *sf.* V. *succosità*.
sugoso *agg.* V. *succoso*.
suicida *agg.* suicidal. ♦ **suicida** *s.* suicide.
suicidarsi *vr.* to commit suicide.
suicidio *sm.* suicide.
suino *agg.* swine (*attr.*) || *carne suina*, pork. ♦ **suino** *sm.* swine (*pl. invariato*).
sulfamìdico *sm.* sulphonamide.

sulfùreo *agg.* sulphureous.
sultanato *sm.* sultanate.
sultanina *sf.* sultana.
sultano *sm.* sultan.
summenzionato *agg.* aforesaid.
sunto *sm.* summary.
suo *agg.* 1. (*di lui*) his 2. (*di lei*) her 3. (*di esso*) its 4. (*formula di cortesia*) your. ◆ suo *pron.* 1. (*di lui*) his 2. (*di lei*) hers 3. (*di esso*) its 4. (*formula di cortesia*) yours || i suoi (*famigliari*), his, her family.
suòcera *sf.* mother-in-law.
suòcero *sm.* father-in-law.
suoi *agg.* e' *pron.* V. suo.
suola *sf.* sole.
suolo *sm.* soil, ground.
suonare *vt.* V. sonare.
suono *sm.* sound.
suora *sf.* nun, sister.
superàbile *agg.* surmountable.
superaffollato *agg.* overcrowded.
superalimentare *vt.* 1. to overrish 2. (*mecc.*) to overcharge.
superalimentazione *sf.* 1. overfeeding 2. (*mecc.*) overcharging.
superamento *sm.* 1. overcoming 2. (*auto*) overtaking.
superare *vt.* 1. (*oltrepassare*) to exceed 2. (*auto*) to overtake (*v. irr.*) 3. (*attraversare*) to cross 4. (*vincere*) to overcome (*v. irr.*) 5. (*una persona*) to surpass 6. (*un esame, una prova*) to pass.
superbia *sf.* pride.
superbo *agg.* 1. proud 2. (*magnifico*) superb.
superdotato *agg.* highly gifted.
superficiale *agg.* superficial.
superficialità *sf.* superficiality.
superficie *sf.* 1. surface 2. (*area*) area.
superfluo *agg.* superfluous. ◆ superfluo *sm.* surplus.
superiora *sf.* Mother Superior.
superiore *agg.* 1. superior 2. (*sovrastante*) upper 3. (*più avanzato*) advanced. ◆ superiore *sm.* superior.
superiorità *sf.* superiority.
superlativo *agg.* e *sm.* superlative.
supermercato *sm.* supermarket.
supernutrizione *sf.* overfeeding.
supersònico *agg.* supersonic.
supèrstite *agg.* surviving. ◆ supèrstite *s.* survivor.
superstizione *sf.* superstition.
superstizioso *agg.* superstitious.

superuomo *sm.* superman (*pl.* -men).
supervisione *sf.* supervision.
supervisore *sm.* supervisor.
supinamente *avv.* supinely.
supino *agg.* supine.
suppellèttile *sf.* furnishings (*pl.*).
supplementare *agg.* supplementary.
supplemento *sm.* 1. supplement 2. (*spesa supplementare*) additional charge 3. (*di biglietto ferroviario*) excess fare.
supplente *agg.* temporary. ◆ supplente *s.* temporary teacher.
supplenza *sf.* temporary post.
suppletivo *agg.* supplementary.
sùpplica *sf.* 1. entreaty 2. (*petizione*) petition.
supplicante *agg.* e *s.* suppliant.
supplicare *vt.* to entreat.
supplichévole *agg.* entreating.
supplire *vi.* 1. (*compensare*) to make (*v. irr.*) up (for) 2. (*sostituire*) to substitute (for). ◆ supplire *vt.* to take (*v. irr.*) the place of.
supplizio *sm.* torment: andare al —, to go (*v. irr.*) to the scaffold.
supporre *vt.* to suppose.
supporto *sm.* support.
supposizione *sf.* supposition.
supposta *sf.* suppository.
supposto che *cong.* suppose (that).
suppurare *vi.* to suppurate.
suppurazione *sf.* suppuration.
supremazìa *sf.* supremacy.
supremo *agg.* supreme: Comando — (*mil.*), headquarters (*pl.*).
surclassare *vt.* to outclass.
surgelare *vt.* to deep-freeze (*v. irr.*).
surrealismo *sm.* surrealism.
surrealista *agg.* e *s.* surrealist.
surrealìstico *agg.* surrealistic.
surrenale *agg.* suprarenal.
surrettizio *agg.* surreptitious.
surriscaldamento *sm.* overheating.
surriscaldare *vt.* to overheat. ◆ surriscaldarsi *vr.* to get (*v. irr.*) overheated.
surrogàbile *agg.* replaceable.
surrogare *vt.* to replace.
surrogato *sm.* substitute.
surrogazione *sf.* (*giur.*) surrogation.
suscettìbile *agg.* 1. susceptible 2. (*permaloso*) touchy.
suscettibilità *sf.* 1. susceptibility 2. (*permalosità*) touchiness || urtare la — di qu., to hurt (*v. irr.*) so.'s feelings.

suscitare vt. 1. to provoke 2. (eccitare) to stir up.
suscitatore sm. provoker.
susina sf. plum.
susino sm. plum-tree.
susseguente agg. following.
susseguire vi. to follow.
sussidiare vt. 1. to support 2. (di governo) to subsidize.
sussidiario agg. subsidiary.
sussidio sm. subsidy.
sussiego sm. haughtiness.
sussistenza sf. 1. existence 2. (sostentamento) subsistence 3. (mil.) Catering Corps.
sussistere vi. 1. to subsist 2. (reggere) to hold (v. irr.) water.
sussultare vi. 1. to start 2. (di cose) to shake (v. irr.).
sussulto sm. start.
sussurrare vt. e vi. 1. to whisper 2. (criticare) to murmur.
sussurro sm. whisper.
sutura sf. suture.
suturare vt. to suture.
svagare vt. 1. to divert 2. (divertire) to amuse. ♦ **svagarsi** vr. 1. to divert one's mind 2. (divertirsi) to amuse oneself.
svagatezza sf. absent-mindedness.
svagato agg. absent-minded.
svago sm. amusement.
svaligiamento sm. 1. robbery 2. (di una casa) burglary.
svaligiare vt. 1. to rob 2. (una casa) to burgle.
svaligiatore sm. 1. robber 2. (di case) burglar.
svalutare vt. 1. to devaluate 2. (sottovalutare) to undervalue.
svalutazione sf. devaluation.
svanire vi. 1. to disappear 2. (dileguarsi, di luce ecc.) to fade.
svanito agg. 1. (dileguato) vanished 2. (di mente) feeble-minded.
svantaggio sm. disadvantage.
svantaggioso agg. disadvantageous.
svaporamento sm. evaporation.
svaporare vi. to evaporate.
svariare vt. to vary.
svariato agg. various.
svarione sm. blunder.
svasare vt. (mecc.) to flare.
svasato agg. (di abito) bell-shaped.
svasatura sf. 1. (di abito) bell-shaping 2. (mecc.; lo svasare) flaring 3. (apertura) countersink.
svàstica sf. swastika.
svecchiamento sm. renewal.

svecchiare vt. to renew.
svedese agg. Swedish. ♦ **svedese** sm. Swede.
sveglia sf. 1. early call 2. (orologio) alarm clock 3. (mil.) reveille.
svegliare vt. to wake (v. irr.) (up). ♦ **svegliarsi** vr. to wake (up).
sveglio agg. 1. awake (pred.) 2. (fig.) quick-witted.
svelare vt. 1. to reveal, to disclose 2. (togliere il velo) to unveil.
svelenire vt. (fig.) to remove the sting from.
svèllere vt. to extirpate.
sveltezza sf. quickness.
sveltire vt. 1. to quicken 2. (scaltrire) to wake (v. irr.) up || — la figura, to slim. ♦ **sveltirsi** vr. 1. to become (v. irr.) quick(er) 2. (scaltrirsi) to wake up.
svelto agg. 1. quick 2. (slanciato) slender 3. (intelligente) smart. ♦ **svelto** avv. fast || —!, hurry up!
svenare vt. to open so.'s veins. ♦ **svenarsi** vr. to cut (v. irr.) one's veins.
svéndere vt. to undersell (v. irr.).
svéndita sf. (clearance) sale.
svenévole agg. maudlin.
svenimento sm. faint.
svenire vi. to faint.
sventagliare vt. to fan.
sventare vt. to baffle.
sventatezza sf. 1. thoughtlessness 2. (atto sventato) thoughtless action.
sventato agg. (sbadato) thoughtless. ♦ **sventato** sm. scatter-brain.
sventola sf. (schiaffo) slap.
sventolare vt. e vi. to wave. ♦ **sventolarsi** vr. to fan oneself.
sventolìo sm. waving.
sventramento sm. 1. disembowelment 2. (demolizione) demolition.
sventrare vt. 1. to disembowel 2. (demolire) to demolish.
sventura sf. misfortune: per —, unluckily; per colmo di —, to crown it all.
sventuratamente avv. unfortunately.
sventurato agg. unfortunate.
svenuto agg. unconscious.
svergognare vt. to shame.
svergognatamente avv. shamelessly.
svergognato agg. shameless.
svernamento sm. wintering.
svernare vi. to winter.

svestire vt. to undress. ♦ **svestirsi** vr. to undress.

svettare vt. to lop. ♦ **svettare** vi. to stand (v. irr.) out.

svezzamento sm. weaning.

svezzare vt. to wean.

sviamento sm. 1. diversion 2. (il traviare) leading astray 3. (il traviarsi) going astray.

sviare vt. 1. to divert 2. (traviare) to lead (v. irr.) astray. ♦ **sviarsi** vr. 1. to be diverted 2. (traviarsi) to go (v. irr.) astray.

sviato agg. led astray (pred.).

svignàrsela vr. to slink (v. irr.) away.

svigorire vt. to weaken. ♦ **svigorirsi** vr. to grow (v. irr.) weak.

svilimento sm. depreciation.

svilire vt. to depreciate.

sviluppare vt. 1. to develop 2. (sciogliere) to loosen 3. (sprigionare) to generate. ♦ **svilupparsi** vr. to develop.

sviluppatore sm. (foto) developer.

sviluppo sm. 1. development 2. (sprigionamento) generation.

svincolamento sm. 1. release 2. (doganale) clearance 3. (riscatto) redemption.

svincolare vt. 1. to release 2. (sdoganare) to clear 3. (riscattare) to redeem. ♦ **svincolarsi** vr. to get (v. irr.) free.

svisare vt. (travisare) to twist.

sviscerare vt. 1. to disembowel 2. (fig.) to dissect.

sviscerato agg. passionate.

svista sf. oversight.

svitare vt. to unscrew.

svìzzero agg. e sm. Swiss.

svogliatezza sf. 1. unwillingness 2. (pigrizia) laziness.

svogliato agg. 1. unwilling 2. (pigro) lazy. ♦ **svogliato** sm. lazy-bones.

svolazzare vi. to flutter.

svolazzo sm. 1. fluttering 2. (tratto di penna) flourish.

svòlgere vt. 1. to unwind (v. irr.) 2. (trattare) to develop 3. (mettere in opera) to carry out. ♦ **svòlgersi** vr. 1. to unwind 2. (svilupparsi) to develop 3. (accadere) to take (v. irr.) place.

svolgimento sm. 1. unwinding 2. (trattazione) treatment 3. (corso) course 4. (sviluppo) development.

svolta sf. 1. turn 2. (fig.) turning

point ‖ fare una —, to turn.

svoltare vi. to turn.

svuotamento sm. emptying.

svuotare vt. 1. to empty 2. (fig.) to deprive.

T

tabaccàio sm. tobacconist.

tabaccare vt. to snuff.

tabaccherìa sf. tobacconist's.

tabacchiera sf. snuff-box.

tabacco sm. tobacco.

tabella sf. 1. (lista) list 2. (quadro) board.

tabellone sm. notice board.

tabernàcolo sm. tabernacle.

tabù sm. taboo.

tabulatore sm. tabulator.

tacca sf. 1. notch 2. (fig.) condition.

taccagnerìa sf. stinginess.

taccagno agg. stingy. ♦ **taccagno** sm. miser.

tacchino sm. turkey.

taccia sf. 1. reputation 2. (accusa) charge.

tacciare vt. to charge (with).

tacco sm. heel.

taccuino sm. note-book.

tacere vi. to be silent: far —, to silence.

tachicardìa sf. tachycardia.

tachìmetro sm. tachometer.

tacitare vt. 1. to hush up 2. (un creditore) to pay (v. irr.) off.

tàcito agg. 1. silent 2. (non espresso) tacit.

taciturno agg. silent.

tafano sm. gad-fly.

tafferuglio sm. brawl.

taglia sf. 1. (riscatto) ransom 2. (ricompensa) reward 3. (misura) size.

tagliacarte sm. paper-knife (pl. -knives).

taglialegna sm. wood-cutter.

tagliando sm. coupon.

tagliapietre sm. stone-cutter.

tagliare vt. 1. to cut (v. irr.) 2. (attraversare) to cut across: — via, to cut off ‖ — a pezzi, to cut into pieces; — la corda (fig.), to run (v. irr.) away; — la strada a qu., to bar so.'s way. ♦ **tagliarsi** vr. to cut.

tagliatelle *sf. pl.* noodles.
tagliato *agg.* **1.** cut **2.** (*inclinato, disposto*) cut out, fit: *essere — fuori*, to be cut off.
tagliatore *sm.* cutter.
taglieggiare *vt.* to ransom.
tagliente *agg.* sharp.
tagliere *sm.* trencher.
taglio *sm.* **1.** cut **2.** (*il tagliare*) cutting **3.** (*parte tagliente, orlo*) edge **4.** (*dimensione*) size **5.** (*raccolto*) harvest.
tagliola *sf.* snare.
taglione *sm.* retaliation.
tagliuzzare *vt.* to mince.
talare *agg.* talaric: *veste —*, cassock.
talco *sm.* talc: *— borato*, talcum powder.
tale *agg.* **1.** such **2.** (*per tralasciare i dati determinati*) such and such: *il — giorno*, on such and such day **3.** (*suddetto*) above-mentioned || *— e quale*, exactly like, exactly as. ♦ **tale** *pron. indef.* someone.
talea *sf.* scion.
talento *sm.* talent.
talismano *sm.* talisman.
tallonare *vi.* to follow.
talloncino *sm.* slip.
tallone *sm.* heel.
talora *avv.* sometimes.
talpa *sf.* mole.
taluno *agg.* some. ♦ **taluno** *pron.* someone (*pl.* some people).
talvolta *avv.* V. *talora.*
tamarindo *sm.* tamarind.
tambureggiare *vi.* to drum.
tamburellare *vi.* to drum one's fingers on.
tamburino *sm.* drummer.
tamburo *sm.* **1.** drum **2.** (*mecc.*) cylinder.
tamponamento *sm.* **1.** plugging **2.** (*med.*) tamponage **3.** (*auto*) bumping.
tamponare *vt.* **1.** to plug **2.** (*med.*) to tampon **3.** (*auto*) to bump (against).
tampone *sm.* **1.** plug **2.** (*med.*) tampon **3.** (*di carta asciugante*) blotter.
tana *sf.* den.
tanfo *sm.* stench.
tangente *agg. e sf.* tangent.
tangenza *sf.* tangency: *punto di —*, tangential point.
tangenziale *agg.* tangential.
tànghero *sm.* boor.
tangìbile *agg.* tangible.
tangibilità *sf.* tangibility.

tànnico *agg.* (*chim.*) tannic.
tannino *sm.* tannin.
tanto *avv.* **1.** so **2.** (*coi verbi*) so much **3.** (*di tempo*) so long **4.** (*ad ogni modo*) anyhow || *— quanto*, as much as; *— ... quanto*, as... a (*sia... sia*) both ... and; *— meglio* so much the better; *— per cam biare*, just for a change. ♦ **tanto** *agg.* so much (*pl.* so many): *— ... quanto*, as much... as (*pl.* a many... as). ♦ **tanto che** *cong* so (that).
tapiro *sm.* tapir.
tappa *sf.* **1.** (*luogo*) halting-place **2.** (*parte di viaggio*) stage **3** (*sport*) lap.
tappare *vt.* **1.** to stop **2.** (*con tappo* to cork.
tapparella *sf.* rolling shutter.
tappeto *sm.* carpet.
tappezzare *vt.* **1.** (*con carta*) to pa per **2.** (*coprire*) to cover **3.** (*fode rare*) to upholster.
tappezzerìa *sf.* **1.** (*di carta*) paper **2.** (*di stoffa*) tapestry.
tappezziere *sm.* **1.** (*per pareti*) pa per hanger **2.** (*per divani ecc.* upholsterer.
tappo *sm.* **1.** plug **2.** (*per bottiglia* cap.
tara *sf.* **1.** tare **2.** (*med.; difetto* taint.
taràntola *sf.* tarantula.
tarare *vt.* **1.** (*mecc.*) to set (*v. irr.* **2.** (*calibrare*) to calibrate **3** (*comm.*) to tare.
tarato *agg.* **1.** (*comm.*) tared **2** (*mecc.*) set **3.** (*med.*) with a tain **4.** (*fig.*) corrupted.
tarchiato *agg.* sturdy.
tardare *vi.* to be late. ♦ **tardare** *vt.* to delay.
tardi *avv.* late: *far —*, to be late.
tardivo *agg.* **1.** (*arretrato*) backward **2.** (*che viene tardi*) tardy.
tardo *agg.* **1.** tardy **2.** (*ottuso*) du **3.** (*di tempo*) late || *a tarda notte* late in the night; *tarda età*, ol age.
targa *sf.* **1.** (*di metallo*) plate **2.** (*d* (*marmo*) slab **3.** (*auto*) number plate.
targare *vt.* (*auto*) to give (*v. irr.*) number-plate (to a car).
tariffa *sf.* tariff.
tarlarsi *vr.* to get (*v. irr.*) worm -eaten.
tarlatura *sf.* worm-hole.

tarlo *sm.* **1.** woodworm **2.** (*fig.*) gnawings (*pl.*).

tarma *sf.* moth.

tarmarsi *vr.* to get (*v. irr.*) moth--eaten.

tarpare *vt.* to clip.

tartagliare *vi.* to stammer.

tartàrico *agg.* tartaric.

tàrtaro *sm.* tartar.

tartaruga *sf.* tortoise.

tartassare *vt.* to harass.

tartina *sf.* canapé.

tartufo *sm.* truffle.

tasca *sf.* pocket.

tascàbile *agg.* pocket (*attributivo*).

tassa *sf.* **1.** tax **2.** (*d'iscrizione*) fee.

tassàbile *agg.* taxable.

tassàmetro *sm.* taximeter: — *di parcheggio*, parking meter.

tassare *vt.* to tax.

tassativo *agg.* peremptory.

tassazione *sf.* taxation.

tassello *sm.* dowel.

tassì *sm.* taxi.

tassista *sm.* taxi-driver.

tasso[1] *sm.* (*comm.*) rate.

tasso[2] *sm.* (*bot.*) yew.

tasso[3] *sm.* (*zool.*) badger.

tastare *vt.* to feel (*v. irr.*): — *il terreno* (*fig.*), to feel one's way.

tastiera *sf.* keyboard.

tasto *sm.* **1.** key **2.** (*tatto*) feel **3.** (*argomento*) subject.

tastoni *avv.* a —, gropingly; *andare a* —, to grope.

tàttica *sf.* tactics.

tàttico *agg.* tactical. ♦ **tàttico** *sm.* tactician.

tàttile *agg.* tactile.

tatto *sm.* **1.** touch **2.** (*fig.*) tact || *con* —, tactfully.

tatuaggio *sm.* tattoo.

tatuare *vt.* to tattoo.

taumatùrgico *agg.* thaumaturgic(al).

taumaturgo *sm.* thaumaturge.

taurino *agg.* bull-like (*attr.*): *dal collo* —, bull-necked.

tauromachìa *sf.* bullfight.

tautologìa *sf.* tautology.

taverna *sf.* tavern.

taverniere *sm.* tavern-keeper.

tàvola *sf.* **1.** table **2.** (*asse*) board **3.** (*di marmo*) slab **4.** (*illustrazione*) plate.

tavolaccio *sm.* plank-bed.

tavolata *sf.* table.

tavolato *sm.* **1.** (*di pavimento*) plank floor **2.** (*mar.*) planking **3.**

(*geogr.*) plateau.

tavolozza *sf.* palette.

tazza *sf.* cup: — *da tè*, tea-cup.

te *pron.* you.

tè *sm.* tea.

teatrale *agg.* theatrical.

teatro *sm.* theatre: — *di posa*, studio.

tècnica *sf.* technique.

tecnicismo *sm.* technicality.

tècnico *agg.* technical. ♦ **tècnico** *sm.* technician.

tecnologìa *sf.* technology.

tecnològico *agg.* technological.

tedesco *agg.* e *sm.* German.

tediare *vt.* to bore.

tedio *sm.* boredom.

tedioso *agg.* boring.

tegame *sm.* saucepan.

teglia *sf.* bakepan.

tégola *sf.* tile: *coprire di tegole*, to tile.

teiera *sf.* tea-pot.

teismo *sm.* theism.

tela *sf.* **1.** cloth **2.** (*teat.*) curtain **3.** (*dipinto*) painting **4.** (*per dipingere*) canvas || — *cerata*, oilcloth; — *di sacco*, sackcloth; — *di lino*, linen; — *di ragno*, cobweb.

telaio *sm.* **1.** loom **2.** (*ossatura, cornice*) frame.

telecàmera *sf.* camera.

telecomandare *vt.* to radiocontrol.

telecomunicazione *sf.* telecommunication.

telefèrica *sf.* cableway.

telefonare *vt.* to (tele)phone.

telefonata *sf.* (telephone) call.

telefonìa *sf.* telephony.

telefònico *agg.* telephone (*attr.*): *cabina telefonica*, telephone booth.

telefonista *sm.* (telephone) operator. ♦ **telefonista** *sf.* switchboard girl.

telèfono *sm.* (tele)phone: *dare un colpo di* —, to ring (*v. irr.*) up.

telefoto *sf.* telephotograph.

telegiornale *sm.* (television) news (-reel).

telegrafare *vt.* to telegraph.

telegrafìa *sf.* telegraphy.

telegràfico *agg.* telegraphic(al).

telegrafista *sm.* telegraphist.

telègrafo *sm.* **1.** telegraph **2.** (*ufficio*) telegraph-office.

telegramma *sm.* telegram, wire: *fare un* — *a qu.*, to wire so.

telèmetro *sm.* **1.** telemeter **2.** (*in arma da fuoco; foto*) rangefinder.

teleobbiettivo *sm.* telephoto lens.
teleologìa *sf.* teleology.
telepatìa *sf.* telepathy.
telerìe *sf. pl.* linen (*sing.*): *commerciante in* —, linen-draper.
teleschermo *sm.* television screen.
telescopio *sm.* telescope.
telescrivente *sf.* teletypewriter.
teleselezione *sf.* long distance dialing.
telespettatore *sm.* televiewer.
teletipìa *sf.* teletype.
teletrasméttere *vt.* to telecast (*v. irr.*).
televisione *sf.* television: *guardare la* —, to watch television; *alla* —, on television; *trasmettere per* —, to telecast.
televisivo *agg.* televisional, television (*attr.*): *trasmissione televisiva*, telecast.
televisore *sm.* television set.
tellùrico *agg.* telluric.
telo *sm.* sheet.
telone *sm.* **1.** (*teat.*) curtain **2.** (*cine*) screen.
tema[1] *sf.* (*paura*) fear: *per* — *che*, lest.
tema[2] *sm.* **1.** theme **2.** (*scolastico*) composition.
temàtica *sf.* themes (*pl.*).
temàtico *agg.* thematic(al).
temerarietà *sf.* rashness.
temerario *agg.* rash.
temere *vt. e vi.* **1.** to fear **2.** (*patire*) not to stand (*v. irr.*) || · *temo di sì*, I fear so; *temo di no*, I fear not.
temìbile *agg.* dreadful.
tèmpera *sf.* **1.** (*metal.*) hardening **2.** (*pitt.*) distemper || *dipingere a* —, to distemper.
temperamatite *sm.·* pencil-sharpener.
temperamento *sm.* **1.** temperament **2.** (*alleviamento*) mitigation.
temperante *agg.* temperate.
temperanza *sf.* temperance.
temperare *vt.* **1.** to temper **2.** (*matite*) to sharpen.
temperato *agg.* **1.** temperate **2.** (*di matita*) sharpened.
temperatura *sf.* temperature.
temperino *sm.* penknife (*pl.* -knives).
tempesta *sf.* tempest, storm.
tempestare *vt.* **1.** (*assalire*) to assail **2.** (*importunare*) to harass **3.** (*cospargere*) to strew (*v. irr.*) (sthg.

with). ◆ **tempestare** *vi.* **1.** to storm **2.** (*grandinare*) to hail.
tempestività *sf.* timeliness.
tempestivo *agg.* timely.
tempestoso *agg.* stormy.
tempia *sf.* temple.
tempio *sm.* temple.
tempo *sm.* **1.** time **2.** (*atmosferico*) weather **3.** (*gramm.*) tense **4.** (*fase*) stage **5.** (*cine*) part || *un* —, once; *col passare del* —, in the long run; *molto* — *prima, dopo*, long before, after; *a* — *perso*, in one's spare time; *per* —, early.
temporale[1] *agg.* temporal.
temporale[2] *agg.* (*anat.*) temporal.
temporale[3] *sm.* storm.
temporalesco *agg.* stormy.
temporaneità *sf.* temporariness.
temporàneo *agg.* temporary.
temporeggiare *vi.* to temporize.
tempra *sf.* **1.** temper **2.** (*metal.*) hardening **3.** (*fig.*) character.
temprare *vt.* **1.** to temper **2.** (*fig.*) to strengthen **3.** (*plasmare*) to form.
temprato *agg.* (*abituato*) inured.
tenace *agg.* tenacious.
tenacia *sf.* tenacity.
tenaglia *sf.* pincers (*pl.*).
tenda *sf.* **1.** curtain **2.** (*da campo*) tent.
tendaggio *sm.* curtain.
tendente *agg.* tending.
tendenza *sf.* **1.** tendency **2.** inclination.
tendenziale *agg.* tendential.
tendenziosità *sf.·* tendentiousness.
tendenzioso *agg.* tendentious.
tèndere *vt.* **1.** (*protendere*) to stretch (out) **2.** (*mettere in tensione*) to tighten. ◆ **tèndere** *vi.* **1.** to tend **2.** (*mirare*) to aim (at).
tendina *sf.* curtain.
tèndine *sm.* tendon.
tenditore *sm.* turnbuckle.
tènebra *sf.* darkness.
tenebroso *agg.* **1.** dark **2.** (*sinistro*) sinister.
tenente *sm.* lieutenant.
tenere *vt.* **1.** to keep (*v. irr.*) **2.** (*sostenere, considerare, contenere*) to hold (*v. irr.*) || — *una lezione*, to give (*v. irr.*) a lesson. ◆ **tenersi** *vr.* (*seguire*) to follow: — *al corrente*, to keep tabs on.
tenerezza *sf.* tenderness.
tènero *agg.* tender. ◆ **tènero** *sm.* **1.** (*parte tenera*) tender part **2.** (*affetto*) sympathy.

tenia *sf.* tapeworm.

tennis *sm.* tennis.

tennista *s.* tennis-player.

tenore *sm.* tenor.

tenorile *agg.* tenor (*attr.*).

tensione *sf.* tension.

tentacolare *agg.* tentacular.

tentàcolo *sm.* tentacle.

tentare *vt.* **1.** to tempt **2.** (*provare*) to try.

tentativo *sm.* attempt.

tentatore *agg.* tempting. ♦ **tentatore** *sm.* tempter.

tentazione *sf.* temptation.

tentennamento *sm.* **1.** shaking **2.** (*traballamento*) tottering **3.** (*esitazione*) hesitation.

tentennare *vt.* to shake (*v. irr.*). ♦ **tentennare** *vi.* **1.** to totter **2.** (*esitare*) to waver.

tentoni *agg.* gropingly.

tenue *agg.* **1.** small **2.** (*leggero*) soft.

tenuità *sf.* **1.** smallness **2.** (*levità*) slightness.

tenuta *sf.* **1.** (*proprietà*) estate **2.** (*capacità*) capacity **3.** (*abiti*) clothes (*pl.*) **4.** (*tec.*) seal || — *di strada*, roadability; *a — d'acqua*, watertight.

teocràtico *agg.* theocratic(al).

teocrazìa *sf.* theocracy.

teologale *agg.* theological.

teologìa *sf.* theology.

teològico *agg.* theologic(al).

teòlogo *sm.* theologian.

teorema *sm.* theorem.

teorìa *sf.* **1.** theory **2.** (*fila*) string.

teòrico *agg.* theoretic(al).

teorizzare *vi.* to theorize.

tepore *sm.* lukewarmness.

teppa *sf.* rabble.

teppista *sm.* teddy-boy.

terapèutico *agg.* therapeutic(al).

terapìa *sf.* therapy.

terebinto *sm.* terebinth.

tèrgere *vt.* to wipe (off).

tergicristallo *sm.* windscreen wiper.

tergiversare *vi.* to hesitate.

tergiversazione *sf.* hesitation.

tergo *sm.* back: *segue a* —, please turn over.

termale *agg.* thermal: *stazione* —, spa.

terme *sf. pl.* thermal springs.

tèrmico *agg.* thermic.

terminale *agg.* terminal.

terminare *vt. e vi.* to end.

tèrmine *sm.* **1.** term **2.** (*limite*) limit **3.** (*fine*) end || *contratto a* —, time-contract; *portare a* —, to carry out.

terminologìa *sf.* terminology.

tèrmite *sf.* termite.

termocoperta *sf.* thermal blanket.

termodinàmica *sf.* thermodynamics.

termoelèttrico *agg.* thermoelectric(al).

termòforo *sm.* warming pad.

termògeno *agg.* thermogenetic.

termoiònico *agg.* thermionic.

termòmetro *sm.* thermometer: *il* — *segna...*, the thermometer stands at...

termonucleare *agg.* thermonuclear.

termos *sm.* vacuum bottle.

termosifone *sm.* (*radiatore*) radiator.

termòstato *sm.* thermostat.

ternario *agg.* ternary.

terno *sm.* tern. ♦ **terno** *agg.* triple.

terra *sf.* **1.** (*globo terracqueo*) earth **2.** (*paese; l'opposto del mare*) land **3.** (*terreno*) ground || — —, earthbound; *raso* —, to the ground.

terracotta *sf.* terracotta: *vasellame di* —, earthenware.

terraferma *sf.* dry land.

terraglia *sf.* pottery.

terranova *sm.* (*cane*) Newfoundland dog.

terrapieno *sm.* **1.** bank **2.** (*di fiume*) embankment. ·

terràqueo *agg.* terraqueous.

terrazza *sf.* **1.** terrace **2.** (*balcone*) balcony.

terrazziere *sm.* digger.

terrazzo *sm.* V. *terrazza*.

terremoto *sm.* earthquake.

terreno[1] *agg.* earthly.

terreno[2] *sm.* ground.

tèrreo *agg.* **1.** earthy **2.** (*di colorito*) wan, sallow.

terrestre *agg.* terrestrial, earthly.

terrìbile *agg.* terrible.

terriccio *sm.* mould.

terriero *agg.* land (*attr.*).

terrificante *agg.* terrifying.

terrificare *vt.* to terrify.

terrina *sf.* tureen.

territoriale *agg.* territorial.

territorio *sm.* territory.

terrore *sm.* terror: *incutere* — *a qu.*, to strike (*v. irr.*) so. with terror.

terrorismo *sm.* terrorism.

terrorista *s.* terrorist.
terroristico *agg.* terroristic.
terrorizzare *vt.* to terrorize.
terroso *agg.* earthy.
terso *agg.* clear.
terza *sf.* **1.** (*di scuola, treno*) third class **2.** (*di auto*) third gear.
terzetto *sm.* trio.
terziario *agg.* e *sm.* tertiary.
terzina *sf.* tercet.
terzino *sm.* (*sport*) full back.
terzo *agg.* third. ♦ **terzo** *sm.* **1.** third **2.** (*terza persona*) third person || *terzi,* third party.
terzùltimo *agg.* e *sm.* last but two.
tesa *sf.* brim.
tesaurizzare *vt.* to treasure.
teschio *sm.* skull.
tesi *sf.* thesis (*pl.* -ses).
teso *agg.* taut.
tesoreria *sf.* treasury.
tesoriere *sm.* treasurer.
tesoro *sm.* **1.** treasure **2.** (*pol.*) treasury.
tèssera *sf.* **1.** card **2.** (*di mosaico*) tessera (*pl.* -rae).
tesseramento *sm.* **1.** rationing **2.** (*reclutamento*) enrolment.
tesserare *vt.* **1.** to ration **2.** (*arruolare*) to enrol.
tèssere *vt.* to weave (*v. irr.*).
tèssile *agg.* textile. ♦ **tèssile** *sm.* weaver.
tessitore *sm.* weaver.
tessitura *sf.* **1.** weaving **2.** (*disposizione dei fili*) texture.
tessuto *sm.* **1.** fabric **2.** (*med.; fig.*) tissue || *negozio di tessuti,* draper's shop.
testa *sf.* head: *colpo di —,* rash act; *essere in — a tutti,* to be ahead of everybody.
testamentario *agg.* testamentary.
testamento *sm.* will.
testardàggine *sf.* stubbornness.
testardo *agg.* stubborn.
testata *sf.* **1.** head **2.** (*colpo*) butt **3.** (*di giornale*) heading.
teste *s.* witness: *— d'accusa, di difesa,* witness for the prosecution, the defence.
testìcolo *sm.* testicle.
testimonianza *sf.* **1.** witness **2.** (*prova*) evidence || *far —,* to bear (*v. irr.*) witness.
testimoniare *vt.* e *vi.* **1.** to witness **2.** (*attestare*) to testify.
testimonio *sm.* witness.
testo *sm.* text.

testuale *agg.* **1.** textual **2.** (*esatto*) exact.
tetànico *agg.* tetanic.
tètano *sm.* tetanus.
tetraedro *sm.* tetrahedron.
tetràggine *sf.* gloom.
tetràgono *agg.* (*fig.*) steadfast.
tetralogìa *sf.* tetralogy.
tetro *agg.* gloomy.
tettarella *sf.* dummy.
tetto *sm.* roof: *— a capanna,* saddle roof.
tettoia *sf.* shed.
tettònica *sf.* tectonics.
teutònico *agg.* Teutonic. ♦ **teutònico** *sm.* Teuton.
ti *pron.* **1.** you, to you **2.** (*r.*) yourself.
tiara *sf.* tiara.
tibia *sf.* tibia.
tic *sm.* tic.
ticchettare *vi.* to tick.
ticchettio *sm.* ticking.
ticchio *sm.* fancy.
tièpido *agg.* tepid.
tifo *sm.* **1.** typhus **2.** (*fig.*) fanaticism.
tifone *sm.* typhoon.
tifoso *sm.* **1.** typhus patient **2.** (*fig.*) fan.
tiglio *sm.* lime.
tigna *sf.* ringworm.
tignola *sf.* moth.
tigrato *agg.* striped.
tigre *sf.* tiger.
timbrare *vt.* **1.** to stamp **2.** (*lettere*) to postmark || *— a secco,* to emboss.
timbratura *sf.* **1.** stamping **2.** (*postale*) postmarking.
timbro *sm.* **1.** stamp **2.** (*di suono*) timbre **3.** (*postale*) postmark || *— a secco,* embossed stamp.
timidezza *sf.* shyness.
tìmido *agg.* shy.
timo *sm.* thyme.
timone *sm.* helm.
timoniere *sm.* helmsman (*pl.* -men).
timorato *agg.* **1.** respectful **2.** (*scrupoloso*) scrupulous.
timore *sm.* fear: *aver —,* to fear, to be afraid.
timoroso *agg.* fearful.
tìmpano *sm.* **1.** eardrum **2.** (*mus.*) kettle-drum **3.** (*arch.*) gable.
tinca *sf.* tench.
tinello *sm.* living-room.
tìngere *vt.* to dye (*v. irr.*). ♦ **tìngersi** *vr.* to dye oneself.

tino *sm.* vat.

tinozza *sf.* tub.

tinta *sf.* **1.** (*colore*) hue **2.** (*materia colorante*) dye **3.** (*tingitura*) dyeing.

tinteggiare *vt.* to paint.

tintinnare *vi.* to tinkle.

tintinnìo *sm.* tinkling.

tintore *sm.* **1.** dyer **2.** (*anche per lavature a secco*) cleaner.

tintoria *sf.* **1.** dyeworks (*pl.*) **2.** (*negozio anche per lavature a secco*) dry cleaners' shop.

tintura *sf.* V. tinta.

tìpico *agg.* typical.

tipo *sm.* **1.** type **2.** (*modello*) pattern **3.** (*individuo*) fellow.

tipografìa *sf.* **1.** typography **2.** (*mecc.*) letterpress printing.

tipogràfico *agg.* typographic(al).

tipògrafo *sm.* typographer.

tiraggio *sm.* draught.

tiralìnee *sm.* drawing-pen.

tiranneggiare *vt.* to tyrannize.

tirannìa *sf.* tyranny.

tirànnico *agg.* tyrannical.

tirànnide *sf.* tyranny.

tiranno *sm.* tyrant.

tirante *sm.* **1.** (*mecc.*) connecting rod **2.** (*arch.*) tie-beam.

tirapiedi *sm.* drudge.

tirare *vt.* **1.** to draw (*v. irr.*), to pull **2.** (*scagliare*) to throw (*v. irr.*). ♦ **tirare** *vi.* **1.** (*sparare*) to shoot (*v. irr.*) **2.** (*di tiraggio*) to draw **3.** (*di vestito*) to be tight. ♦ **tirarsi** *vr.* to draw.

tirata *sf.* **1.** pull **2.** (*invettiva*) tirade.

tiratore *sm.* shooter.

tiratura *sf.* **1.** (*tip.*) printing **2.** (*numero di copie stampate*) circulation.

tirchierìa *sf.* niggardliness.

tirchio *agg.* niggardly.

tiritera *sf.* rigmarole.

tiro *sm.* **1.** (*trazione*) draught **2.** (*lancio*) throw **3.** (*sparo*) shot **4.** (*scherzo*) trick.

tirocinio *sm.* apprenticeship.

tiròide *sf.* thyroid.

tisana *sf.* ptisan.

tisi *sf.* consumption.

tìsico *agg. e sm.* consumptive.

tisiologìa *sf.* phthisiology.

tisiòlogo *sm.* phthisiologist.

titànico *agg.* titanic.

titillare *vt.* to tickle.

titolare *agg.* **1.** regular **2.** (*nominale*) titular. ♦ **titolare** *s.* **1.** regular holder **2.** (*proprietario*) owner **3.** (*capo*) principal.

titolato *agg.* titled.

tìtolo *sm.* **1.** title **2.** (*qualifica*) qualification **3.** (*documento*) document **4.** (*comm.*) security.

titubante *agg.* hesitating.

titubanza *sf.* hesitation.

titubare *vi.* to hesitate.

tizianesco *agg.* **1.** Titianesque **2.** (*di capelli*) titian.

tizio *sm.* fellow.

tizzone *sm.* brand.

toccare *vt.* to touch || — *un porto*, to call at. ♦ **toccare** *vi.* **1.** (*capitare*) to happen **2.** (*spettare*) to fall (*v. irr.*).

toccasana *sm.* cure-all.

tocco¹ *agg.* (*pazzoide*) touched.

tocco² *sm.* **1.** touch **2.** (*battito*) knock **3.** (*rintocco*) toll || *al* —, at one o'clock.

tocco³ *sm.* (*berretto*) toque.

toga *sf.* gown.

togato *agg.* gowned.

tògliere *vt.* **1.** to take (*v. irr.*) **2.** (*liberare*) to relieve. ♦ **tògliersi** *vr.* **1.** to get (*v. irr.*) off **2.** (*un indumento*) to take off || — *la vita*, to commit suicide.

toletta *sf.* toilet.

tolleràbile *agg.* tolerable.

tollerante *agg.* tolerant.

tolleranza *sf.* tolerance.

tollerare *vt.* **1.** to tolerate **2.** (*sopportare*) to bear (*v. irr.*).

tomaia *sf.* vamp.

tomba *sf.* grave.

tombale *agg.* grave (*attr.*).

tombino *sm.* manhole.

tòmbola *sf.* **1.** (*gioco*) "tombola" **2.** (*caduta*) tumble.

tombolare *vi.* to tumble down.

tomismo *sm.* Thomism.

tomista *agg. e sm.* Thomist.

tomo *sm.* **1.** tome **2.** (*persona*) chap.

tònaca *sf.* frock: *gettare la* —, to give (*v. irr.*) up the frock.

tonalità *sf.* tonality.

tonante *agg.* thundering.

tondeggiante *agg.* roundish.

tondeggiare *vi.* to be roundish.

tondello *sm.* round.

tondo *agg. e sm.* round || *chiaro e* —, clearly.

tonfo *sm.* splash.

tònico *agg. e sm.* tonic.

tonificare *vt.* to brace.

tonnellaggio *sm.* tonnage.

tonnellata *sf.* ton.

tonno *sm.* tunny.

tono *sm.* **1.** tone **2.** (*accordo*) tune **3.** (*mus.*) strain.

tonsilla *sf.* tonsil.

tonsillectomìa *sf.* tonsillectomy.

tonsillite *sf.* tonsillitis.

tonsura *sf.* tonsure.

tonsurare *vt.* to tonsure.

tonto *agg.* dull. ♦ **tonto** *sm.* dunce.

topaia *sf.* (*fig.*) hovel.

topazio *sm.* topaz.

tòpica *sf.* **1.** topic **2.** (*errore*) blunder.

tòpico *agg.* topical.

topo *sm.* mouse (*pl.* mice), rat || — *di biblioteca* (*fig.*), bookworm; — *di albergo* (*fig.*), hotel thief.

topografìa *sf.* topography.

topogràfico *agg.* topographic(al).

topologìa *sf.* topology.

toponomàstica *sf.* toponymy.

toppa *sf.* **1.** (*pezza*) patch **2.** (*di serratura*) keyhole || *mettere una* —, to patch up.

torace *sm.* thorax, chest.

torba *sf.* peat.

torbidezza *sf.* **1.** turbidity **2.** (*esser fosco*) gloominess.

tòrbido *agg.* **1.** turbid **2.** (*fosco*) gloomy **3.** (*inquieto*) troubled. ♦ **tòrbido** *sm.* (*disordine*) disorder: *pescare nel* —, to fish in troubled water.

torbiera *sf.* peat-bog.

tòrcere *vt.* **1.** to wring (*v. irr.*) **2.** (*attorcigliare*) to twist || *dare del filo da* —, to give (*v. irr.*) a lot of trouble; — *il naso* (*fig.*), to turn up one's nose (at). ♦ **tòrcersi** *vr.* to twist.

torchiare *vt.* to press.

torchiatura *sf.* pressing.

torchio *sm.* press.

torcia *sf.* torch.

torcicollo *sm.* stiff-neck.

torcitore *sm.* twister.

torcitura *sf.* twist.

tordo *sm.* thrush.

torero *sm.* bullfighter.

torma *sf.* swarm.

tormalina *sf.* tourmaline.

tormenta *sf.* blizzard.

tormentare *vt.* to torment. ♦ **tormentarsi** *vr.* to worry.

tormentato *agg.* (*inquieto*) restless.

tormento *sm.* torment.

tormentoso *agg.* tormenting.

tornaconto *sm.* profit.

tornado *sm.* tornado.

tornante *sm.* bend.

tornare *vi.* **1.** to return **2.** (*di conti*) to be correct.

tornasole *sm.* litmus.

torneo *sm.* tournament.

tornio *sm.* lathe.

tornire *vt.* **1.** (*mecc.*) to turn **2.** (*fig.*) to polish.

tornito *agg.* **1.** (*rotondo*) round **2.** (*ben fatto*) well-shaped.

tornitore *sm.* turner.

toro *sm.* bull.

torpediniera *sf.* torpedo-boat.

torpedo *sf.* torpedo.

torpedone *sm.* (motor-)coach.

tòrpido *agg.* torpid.

torpore *sm.* torpor.

torre *sf.* tower.

torrefare *vt.* **1.** to torrefy **2.** (*caffè*) to roast.

torrefazione *sf.* **1.** torrefaction **2.** (*di caffè*) roasting **3.** (*negozio*) coffee store.

torreggiare *vi.* to tower.

torrente *sm.* torrent.

torrentizio *agg.* torrent-like.

torrenziale *agg.* torrential.

torretta *sf.* (*mil.; mar.*) turret.

tòrrido *agg.* torrid.

torrione *sm.* donjon.

torrone *sm.* nougat.

torsione *sf.* torsion.

torso *sm.* **1.** trunk **2.** (*di statua*) torso.

tòrsolo *sm.* **1.** (*di verdura*) stump **2.** (*di frutta*) core.

torta *sf.* cake.

tortiera *sf.* bakepan.

torto *agg.* **1.** (*piegato*) bent **2.** (*contorto*) twisted.

torto *sm.* **1.** wrong **2.** (*colpa*) fault || *aver* —, to be wrong; *far* — *a qu.*, to wrong so.; *a* —, wrongly.

tòrtora *sf.* turtle-dove.

tortuosità *sf.* tortuosity.

tortuoso *agg.* tortuous.

tortura *sf.* torture.

torturare *vt.* to torture. ♦ **torturarsi** *vr.* to worry.

torvo *agg.* grim.

tosare *vt.* to shear (*v. irr.*).

tosatrice *sf.* clippers (*pl.*).

tosatura *sf.* shearing.

toscano *agg.* e *sm.* Tuscan.

tosse *sf.* cough.

tossicchiare *vi.* to keep (*v. irr.*) on coughing.

tossicità *sf.* toxicity.

tòssico *agg.* toxic. ♦ **tòssico** *sm.* toxicant.

tossicologìa *sf.* toxicology.

tossicòlogo *sm.* toxicologist.

tossicomanìa *sf.* toxicomania.

tossina *sf.* toxin.

tossire *vi.* to cough.

tostapane *sm.* toaster.

tostare *vt.* 1. to toast 2. (*caffè*) to roast.

tosto[1] *avv.* at once.

tosto[2] *agg.* hard || *faccia tosta*, cheek.

tosto[3] *sm.* toast.

totale *agg. e sm.* total: *in —*, in all.

totalità *sf.* 1. totality 2. (*numero complessivo*) mass.

totalitario *agg.* totalitarian.

totalitarismo *sm.* totalitarianism.

totalizzare *vt.* 1. to totalize 2. (*sport*) to score.

totalizzatore *sm.* totalizer.

tovaglia *sf.* (table-)cloth.

tovagliolo *sm.* napkin.

tozzo[1] *agg.* squat, stocky.

tozzo[2] *sm.* piece: *un — di pane*, a crust of bread.

tra *prep.* 1. (*fra due persone, cose, gruppi*) between 2. (*fra più di due*) among 3. (*nel mezzo di*) amid 4. (*di tempo*) (with)in.

traballare *vi.* 1. to stagger 2. (*di vettura*) to jolt || *entrare, uscire traballando*, to stagger in, out.

trabeazione *sf.* trabeation.

trabìccolo *sm.* ramshackle vehicle.

traboccare *vi.* to overflow.

trabocchetto *sm.* trap.

tracagnotto *agg.* squat.

tracannare *vt.* to gulp down.

traccia *sf.* 1. trace 2. (*segno*) mark 3. (*orme*) footsteps (*pl.*) 4. (*schema*) outline.

tracciare *vt.* to trace (out): *— a grandi linee*, to outline.

tracciato *sm.* layout.

tracciatore *sm.* tracer.

trachea *sf.* windpipe.

tracheale *agg.* tracheal.

tracheite *sf.* tracheitis.

tracolla *sf.* baldric: *portare qc. a —*, to carry sthg. across one's back.

tracollare *vi.* 1. to lose (*v. irr.*) one's balance 2. (*cadere*) to collapse.

tracollo *sm.* collapse: *portare al —*, to bring (*v. irr.*) to ruin.

tracoma *sm.* trachoma.

tracotante *agg.* haughty.

tracotanza *sf.* haughtiness.

tradimento *sm.* 1. treason 2. (*infedeltà*) betrayal || *a —* (*agg.*), treacherous, (*avv.*) treacherously.

tradire *vt.* 1. to betray 2. (*di coniuge*) to be unfaithful (to).

traditore *agg.* treacherous. ♦ **traditore** *sm.* traitor.

tradizionale *agg.* traditional.

tradizionalismo *sm.* traditionalism.

tradizionalista *s.* traditionalist.

tradizione *sf.* tradition: *per —*, traditionally.

tradotta *sf.* troop-train.

traducìbile *agg.* translatable.

tradurre *vt.* to translate: *— in atto*, to carry out; *— in carcere*, to take (*v. irr.*) to prison.

traduttore *sm.* translator.

traduzione *sf.* translation.

traente *s.* (*comm.*) drawer.

trafelato *agg.* breathless.

trafficante *sm.* dealer.

trafficare *vi.* 1. to deal (*v. irr.*) 2. (*affaccendarsi*) to bustle about.

tràffico *sm.* 1. traffic 2. (*comm.*) trade.

trafìggere *vt.* to pierce (through).

trafila *sf.* 1. procedure 2. (*mecc.*) draw-plate.

trafilare *vt.* to draw (*v. irr.*).

trafiletto *sm.* paragraph.

traforare *vt.* 1. to perforate 2. (*ricamare*) to embroider with open-work.

traforato *agg.* 1. perforated 2. (*ricamato a traforo*) open-work (*attr.*).

traforatrice *sf.* fret-sawing machine.

traforo *sm.* 1. perforation 2. (*galleria*) tunnel 3. (*falegnameria*) fretwork 4. (*ricamo*) open-work.

trafugamento *sm.* stealing.

trafugare *vt.* to steal (*v. irr.*).

tragedia *sf.* tragedy.

tragediògrafo *sm.* tragedian.

traghettare *vt.* to ferry.

traghetto *sm.* ferry-boat.

tragicità *sf.* tragicalness.

tràgico *agg.* tragical. ♦ **tràgico** *sm.* tragedian.

tragicòmico *agg.* tragicomic(al).

tragicommedia *sf.* tragicomedy.

tragitto *sm.* 1. way 2. (*viaggio*) journey.

traguardo *sm.* goal.

traiettoria *sf.* trajectory.

trainare *vt.* to haul.

tràino *sm.* 1. haulage 2. (*carro*) truck.

tralasciare vt. to leave (v. irr.) out, to omit.

tralcio sm. shoot.

traliccio sm. 1. (tela) ticking 2. (per costruzioni) trellis || — di ferro, iron framework.

tralice (nella loc. avv.) in —, askance.

tralignamento sm. degeneration.

tralignare vi. to degenerate.

tralùcere vi. to shine (v. irr.) (through).

tram sm. tramcar.

trama sf. 1. weft 2. (fig.) plot.

tramaglio sm. trammel.

tramandare vt. to hand down.

tramare vt. 1. to weave (v. irr.) 2. (fig.) to plot.

trambusto sm. bustle.

tramenare vt. e vi. to move about.

tramenìo sm. bustle.

tramestare vt. to rummage.

tramestìo sm. 1. rummaging 2. (trepestio) stamping.

tramezzare vt. to partition.

tramezzino sm. sandwich.

tramezzo sm. partition.

tràmite sm. path: — qu., through so.

tramoggia sf. hopper.

tramontana sf. 1. north 2. (vento) north wind || perder la —, to lose (v. irr.) one's head.

tramontare vi. 1. to set (v. irr.) 2. (svanire) to fade.

tramonto sm. 1. setting 2. (del sole) sunset 3. (declino) decline.

tramortimento sm. swoon.

tramortire vt. to stun.

trampoliere sm. wader.

trampolino sm. spring-board.

tràmpolo sm. stilt.

tramutare vt. to change. ♦ tramutarsi vr. to change.

trancia sf. 1. shears (pl.) 2. (fetta) slice.

tranciare vt. to shear.

tranello sm. snare.

trangugiare vt. to swallow.

tranne prep. but.

tranquillante agg. tranquillizing. ♦ tranquillante sm. tranquillizer.

tranquillità sf. calmness.

tranquillizzare vt. 1. to calm 2. (rassicurare) to reassure.

tranquillo agg. calm: star —, to keep (v. irr.) quiet; sta' —!, do not worry!

transalpino agg. transalpine.

transatlàntico agg. transatlantic. ♦ transatlàntico sm. liner.

transazione sf. 1. transaction 2. (accomodamento) arrangement 3. (compromesso) compromise.

transcontinentale agg. transcontinental.

transetto sm. transept.

trànsfuga s. runaway.

transìgere vt. e vi. to compromise.

transistore sm. transistor.

transitàbile agg. practicable.

transitabilità sf. practicability.

transitare vi. to pass through.

transitivo agg. e sm. transitive.

trànsito sm. transit.

transitorio agg. transitory.

transizione sf. transition.

transoceànico agg. transoceanic.

transustanziazione sf. transubstantiation.

tranvìa sf. tramway.

tranviario agg. tramcar (attr.).

tranviere sm. 1. tram-driver 2. (bigliettario) tram-conductor.

trapanare vt. 1. to drill 2. (med.) to trepan.

trapanazione sf. 1. drilling 2. (med.) trepanation.

tràpano sm. 1. drill 2. (med.) trepan.

trapassare vt. to pierce through. ♦ trapassare vi. (morire) to die.

trapasso sm. 1. (morte) death 2. (giur.; comm.) transfer.

trapelare vi. to leak out.

trapezio sm. 1. trapezium 2. (da ginnastica) trapeze.

trapiantare vt. to transplant. ♦ trapiantarsi vr. (stabilirsi) to settle.

trapianto sm. 1. transplantation 2. (tessuto trapiantato) graft.

trappista sm. Trappist.

tràppola sf. trap: prendere in —, to trap.

trapunta sf. quilt.

trapuntare vt. 1. to quilt 2. (ricamare) to embroider.

trapunto agg. 1. quilted 2. (ricamato) embroidered || — di stelle, starry.

trarre vt. 1. to draw (v. irr.) 2. (ottenere) to get (v. irr.). ♦ trarsi vr. to draw.

trasalire vi. to startle: far —, to startle.

trasandato agg. shabby.

trasbordare *vt.* 1. to transfer 2. (*traghettare*) to ferry.

trasbordo *sm.* 1. transfer 2. (*traghetto*) ferrying across.

trascendentale *agg.* transcendental.

trascendentalismo *sm.* transcendentalism.

trascendente *agg.* transcendent.

trascendenza *sf.* transcendence.

trascéndere *vt.* to transcend. ♦ trascéndere *vi.* to let (*v. irr.*) oneself go.

trascinare *vt.* 1. to drag 2. (*affascinare*) to fascinate.

trascòrrere *vt.* (*il tempo*) to spend (*v. irr.*). ♦ trascòrrere *vi.* 1. (*di tempo*) to pass 2. (*lasciar correre*) to pass over.

trascorso *agg.* past. ♦ trascorso *sm.* (*errore*) slip.

trascrittore *sm.* transcriber.

trascrìvere *vt.* 1. to transcribe 2. (*giur.*) to register.

trascrizione *sf.* 1. transcription 2. (*giur.*) registration 3. (*trapasso*) transfer.

trascuràbile *agg.* negligible.

trascurare *vt.* to neglect. ♦ trascurarsi *vr.* not to care of oneself.

trascuratezza *sf.* 1. negligence 2. (*sciatteria*) slovenliness.

trascurato *agg.* 1. (*negligente*) careless 2. (*sciatto*) sloven.

trasecolare *vi.* to be amazed.

trasecolato *agg.* amazed.

trasferìbile *agg.* transferable.

trasferimento *sm.* transfer.

trasferire *vt.* to transfer. ♦ trasferirsi *vr.* to (re)move.

trasferta *sf.* 1. transfer 2. (*indennità*) travelling allowance || *in* —, on transfer; *partita in* — (*sport*), out match.

trasfigurare *vt.* to transfigure. ♦ trasfigurarsi *vr.* to become (*v. irr.*) transfigured.

trasfigurazione *sf.* transfiguration.

trasfóndere *vt.* 1. to transfuse 2. (*fig.*) to instil.

trasformàbile *agg.* convertible.

trasformare *vt.* to change, to turn. ♦ trasformarsi *vr.* to change.

trasformatore *sm.* transformer.

trasformazione *sf.* transformation.

trasformismo *sm.* transformism.

trasfusione *sf.* transfusion.

trasgredire *vt.* e *vi.* to infringe.

trasgressione *sf.* infringement.

trasgressore *sm.* infringer.

traslazione *sf.* 1. transfer 2. (*fis.; eccl.*) translation.

traslocare *vt.* e *vi.* to move.

trasloco *sm.* removal.

traslùcido *agg.* translucent.

trasméttere *vt.* to transmit.

trasmettitore *sm.* transmitter.

trasmigrare *vi.* to transmigrate.

trasmigrazione *sf.* transmigration.

trasmissìbile *agg.* transmissible.

trasmissione *sf.* 1. transmission 2. (*giur.*) transfer 3. (*mecc.*) drive || — *radio*, broadcast; — *televisiva*, telecast.

trasmittente *agg.* transmitting.

trasognato *agg.* dreamy.

trasparente *agg.* transparent.

trasparenza *sf.* transparence.

trasparire *vi.* 1. to shine (*v. irr.*) through 2. (*esser trasparente*) to be transparent || *lasciar* —, to betray.

traspirare *vi.* to transpire.

traspirazione *sf.* transpiration.

trasporre *vt.* to transpose.

trasportàbile *agg.* transportable.

trasportare *vt.* 1. to carry 2. (*fig.*) to carry away. ♦ trasportarsi *vr.* to go (*v. irr.*).

trasportatore *sm.* conveyer: — *a nastro*, belt-conveyer.

trasporto *sm.* transport: *nave da* —, cargo; *spese di* —, carriage.

trasposizione *sf.* transposition.

trastullare *vt.* to amuse. ♦ trastullarsi *vr.* 1. (*giocare*) to play 2. (*scherzare*) to trifle.

trastullo *sm.* 1. plaything 2. (*divertimento*) amusement.

trasudamento *sm.* sweating.

trasudare *vt.* e *vi.* to sweat.

trasversale *agg.* transversal, cross (*attr.*). ♦ trasversale *sf.* 1. transversal 2. (*strada*) cross-road.

trasvolare *vt.* to fly (*v. irr.*) across.

trasvolata *sf.* flight (across).

tratta *sf.* 1. (*traffico*) trade 2. (*comm.*) draft || — *a vista*, sight draft; *spiccare una* — *su qu.*, to draw (*v. irr.*) upon so.

trattàbile *agg.* 1. tractable 2. (*di argomento*) that can be dealt with.

trattabilità *sf.* tractability.

trattamento *sm.* 1. treatment 2. (*paga*) salary.

trattare *vt.* 1. to treat 2. (*maneggiare*) to handle 3. (*commerciare*) to deal (*v. irr.*) (in) 4. (*negoziare*) to negotiate 5. (*un argomento*) to deal (with). ♦ trattarsi *v. imp.* to be a question of, to be involved.

trattativa *sf.* negotiation.

trattato *sm.* **1.** (*patto*) treaty **2.** (*libro*) treatise.

trattazione *sf.* treatment.

tratteggiare *vt.* **1.** to outline **2.** (*ombreggiare*) to hatch.

trattéggio *sm.* **1.** (*abbozzo*) outline **2.** (*ombreggiatura*) hatching.

trattenere *vt.* **1.** to keep (*v. irr.*) **2.** (*dedurre*) to deduct **3.** (*frenare*) to refrain || — *il respiro,* to hold (*v. irr.*) one's breath. ♦ **trattenersi** *vr.* (*fermarsi*) to stay || *non posso trattenermi dal fare,* I cannot help doing.

trattenimento *sm.* (*festa*) party.

trattenuta *sf.* deduction.

trattino *sm.* **1.** dash **2.** (*di unione*) hyphen.

tratto *sm.* **1.** (*tirata*) pull **2.** (*colpo*) stroke **3.** (*linea*) line **4.** (*brano*) passage **5.** (*estensione di spazio*) way **6.** (*lineamento*) feature **7.** (*comportamento*) manners (*pl.*) || *d'un —,* suddenly; *di — in —,* now and then.

trattore[1] *sm.* (*mecc.*) tractor.

trattore[2] *sm.* (*oste*) inn-keeper.

trattorìa *sf.* inn.

tratturo *sm.* cattle-track.

tràuma *sm.* trauma.

traumàtico *agg.* traumatic.

traumatologìa *sf.* traumatology.

travagliare *vt.* V. *tormentare.*

travaglio *sm.* **1.** (*fatica*) labour **2.** (*cruccio*) trouble.

travasare *vt.* to pour off.

travaso *sm.* **1.** pouring off **2.** (*med.*) effusion.

travatura *sf.* truss.

trave *sf.* beam.

travéggole *sf. pl. avere le —,* to mistake (*v. irr.*) one thing for another.

traversa *sf.* **1.** (*sbarra*) cross-bar **2.** (*via*) side-road.

traversata *sf.* crossing.

traversìa *sf.* misfortune. ♦

traversina *sf.* sleeper.

traverso *agg.* **1.** transverse, cross (*attr.*) **2.** (*obliquo*) slanting || *di —,* askance; *andare per — (fig.),* to go (*v. irr.*) wrong with.

travestimento *sm.* disguise.

travestire *vt.* to disguise (as).

traviamento *sm.* corruption.

traviare *vt.* to mislead (*v. irr.*). ♦
traviarsi *vr.* to go (*v. irr.*) astray.

travisamento *sm.* alteration.

travisare *vt.* to alter.

travolgente *agg.* sweeping.

travòlgere *vt.* **1.** to sweep (*v. irr.*) away **2.** (*investire*) to run (*v. irr.*) over.

trazione *sf.* traction.

tre *agg.* three.

trebbiare *vt.* to thrash.

trebbiatrice *sf.* thrasher.

trebbiatura *sf.* thrashing.

treccia *sf.* plait: *farsi le trecce,* to plait one's hair.

trecento *agg.* three hundred || *il — (secolo),* the fourteenth century.

tredicenne *agg.* thirteen years old, thirteen-year-old (*attr.*).

tredicèsimo *agg.* thirteenth.

trédici *agg.* thirteen.

tregua *sf.* **1.** truce **2.** (*riposo*) rest.

tremante *agg.* **1.** trembling **2.** (*di freddo*) shivering.

tremare *vi.* **1.** to tremble **2.** (*di freddo*) to shiver.

tremendo *agg.* awful.

trementina *sf.* turpentine.

tremila *agg.* three thousand.

trèmito *sm.* **1.** tremble **2.** (*di freddo*) shiver.

tremolante *agg.* **1.** trembling **2.** (*di luce*) flickering **3.** (*di stelle*) twinkling.

tremolare *vi.* **1.** to tremble **2.** (*di luce*) to flicker **3.** (*di stelle*) to twinkle.

tremolìo *sm.* **1.** tremble **2.** (*di luce*) flickering **3.** (*di stelle*) twinkle.

tremore *sm.* V. *trèmito.*

treno *sm.* **1.** train: — *accelerato,* slow train; — *direttissimo,* fast train; — *rapido,* express train **2.** (*tenore*) way of living, routine.

trenta *agg.* thirty.

trentenne *agg.* thirty years old, thirty-year-old (*attr.*).

trentennio *sm.* period of thirty years.

trentèsimo *agg.* thirtieth.

trentina *sf.* about thirty.

trepestìo *sm.* stamping.

trepidante *agg.* anxious.

trepidare *vi.* to be anxious.

trepidazione *sf.* anxiety.

treppiede *sm.* tripod.

tresca *sf.* intrigue.

tréspolo *sm.* trestle.

trìade *sf.* triad.

triangolare *agg.* triangular.

triangolazione *sf.* triangulation.

triàngolo sm. triangle.
tribale agg. tribal.
tribolare vi. **1.** to toil **2.** (soffrire) to suffer. ♦ **tribolare** vt. to vex.
tribolazione sf. suffering.
tribordo sm. starboard.
tribù sf. tribe.
tribuna sf. **1.** (per oratori) platform **2.** (sport) stand.
tribunale sm. court.
tribuno sm. tribune.
tributare vt. to bestow.
tributario agg. **1.** tributary **2.** (fiscale) fiscal. ♦ **tributario** sm. tributary.
tributo sm. tribute.
tricheco sm. walrus.
triciclo sm. tricycle.
triclinio sm. triclinium (pl. -nia).
tricolore agg. e sm. tricolour.
tricorno sm. tricorn.
tricromìa sf. **1.** trichromatism **2.** (pezzo singolo) trichromatic print.
tridente sm. **1.** trident **2.** (per fieno) hayfork.
tridimensionale agg. tridimensional.
triedro sm. trihedron.
triennale agg. e sm. triennial.
triennio sm. period of three years.
trifase agg. three-phase (attr.).
trifoglio sm. clover.
trigèmino agg. e sm. trigeminal: parto —, birth of triplets.
trigèsimo agg. thirtieth: nel — della sua morte, on the thirtieth day after his death.
trigonometrìa sf. trigonometry.
trilione sm. **1.** (in sistema italiano, francese e americano = 1000⁴) billion; (amer.) trillion **2.** (in sistema inglese e tedesco = 1000⁶) trillion; (amer.) quintillion.
trillare vi. **1.** to trill **2.** (squillare) to ring (v. irr.).
trillo sm. **1.** trill **2.** (di sveglia, telefono) ring.
trilogìa sf. trilogy.
trimestrale agg. quarterly.
trimestre sm. **1.** quarter **2.** (scol.) term **3.** (paga trimestrale) quarterage.
trimotore agg. three-engined aeroplane.
trina sf. lace.
trincare vt. to gulp. ♦ **trincare** vi. to drink (v. irr.).
trincea sf. trench.
trincerare vt. to entrench.

trincetto sm. shoemaker's knife (pl. knives).
trinchetto sm. albero di —, foremast; vela di —, foresail.
trinciante agg. sharp. ♦ **trinciante** sm. carver.
trinciare vt. **1.** to cut (v. irr.) (up) **2.** (carne) to carve || — giudizi, to judge rashly.
trinciato sm. cut-tobacco.
trinità sf. trinity.
trinomio sm. trinomial.
trionfante agg. triumphant.
trionfare vt. to triumph.
trionfatore sm. triumpher.
trionfo sm. triumph.
tripartito agg. tripartite.
tripartizione sf. tripartition.
triplicare vt. to treble.
triplo agg. triple. ♦ **triplo** sm. **1.** triple **2.** (tre volte tanto) three times as much.
trippa sf. (cuc.) tripe.
tripudiare vi. to exult.
tripudio sm. exultation.
trisàvolo sm. great-great-grand-father.
trisìllabo agg. trisyllabic. ♦ **trisìllabo** sm. trisyllable.
triste agg. sad.
tristezza sf. **1.** sadness **2.** (dolore) grief.
tristo agg. wicked.
tritacarne sm. mincer.
tritare vt. to mince.
tritatutto sm. mincer.
trito agg. (fig.) trite.
tritolo sm. trinitrotoluene.
trìttico sm. triptych.
trittongo sm. triphthong.
tritume sm. crumbs (pl.).
triturare vt. to triturate.
triumvirato sm. triumvirate.
triùmviro sm. triumvir.
trivalente agg. trivalent.
trivella sf. **1.** (min.) drill **2.** (falegnameria) auger.
trivellare vt. to drill.
trivellazione sf. drilling: torre di —, derrick.
triviale agg. coarse.
trivialità sf. **1.** coarseness **2.** (detto triviale) coarse expression.
trofeo sm. trophy.
troglodita sf. troglodyte.
troglodìtico agg. troglodytic(al).
trògolo sm. trough.
troia sf. (zool.) sow.
tromba sf. **1.** trumpet **2.** (di scale)

well || — d'aria, tornado; — d'acqua, water-spout.

trombettiere sm. trumpeter.

trombone sm. 1. (mus.) trombone 2. (schioppo) blunderbuss || suonatore di —, trombonist.

trombosi sf. thrombosis.

troncare vt. 1. to cut (v. irr.) off 2. (fig.) to break (v. irr.) off.

tronco¹ agg. 1. cut off 2. (fig.) broken.

tronco² sm. 1. trunk 2. (d'albero abbattuto) log 3. (geom.) frustum || — ferroviario, railway section; licenziare in —, to sack on the spot.

troncone sm. stump.

troneggiare vi. to dominate (sthg.).

tronfio agg. 1. conceited 2. (di stile) bombastic.

trono sm. throne.

tropicale agg. tropical.

tròpico sm. tropic.

tropismo sm. tropism.

troposfera sf. troposphere.

troppo avv. 1. (con agg. e avv.) too 2. (con v.) too much 3. (di tempo) too long. ♦ **troppo** agg. e pron. too much (pl. too many): anche —, only too; essere di —, to be unwelcome.

trota sf. trout (pl. invariato).

trottare vi. to trot: far — qu. (fig.) to make (v. irr.) so. run.

trottata sf. trot.

trottatore sm. trotter.

trotterellare vi. 1. to trot along 2. (di bambini) to toddle.

trotto sm. trot: mettere un cavallo al —, to trot a horse.

tròttola sf. top.

trovare vt. 1. to find (v. irr.) 2. (far visita) to see (v. irr.) 3. (pensare) to think (v. irr.). ♦ **trovarsi** vr. 1. (essere) to be 2. (sentirsi) to feel (v. irr.).

trovata sf. trick.

trovatello sm. foundling.

trovatore sm. troubadour.

truccare vi. 1. to make (v. irr.) up 2. (sport) to fix.

truccatore sm. maker-up.

truccatura sf. make-up.

trucco sm. 1. trick 2. (cosmetici) make-up 3. (inganno) deceit.

truce agg. grim.

trucidare vt. to slay (v. irr.).

tràciolo sm. shaving.

truculento agg. truculent.

truffa sf. cheat.

truffaldino agg. cheating.

truffare vt. to cheat.

truffatore sm. cheat.

truismo sm. truism.

truppa sf. troop.

tu pron. you.

tua agg. e pron. V. tuo.

tuba sf. 1. tuba 2. (cappello) top-hat.

tubare vi. to coo.

tubatura sf. piping.

tubercolare agg. tubercular.

tubercolina sf. tuberculin.

tubercolosario sm. sanatorium.

tubercolosi sf. tuberculosis: — polmonare, consumption.

tubercoloso agg. tuberculous. ♦ **tubercoloso** sm. consumptive.

tùbero sm. tuber.

tuberosa sf. tuberose.

tubino sm. bowler-hat.

tubo sm. 1. tube 2. (di conduttura) pipe 3. (anat.) canal.

tubolare agg. tubular.

tue agg. e pron. V. tuo.

tuffare vt. to plunge, to dip. ♦ **tuffarsi** vr. to plunge, to dive.

tuffatore sm. diver.

tuffo sm. plunge, dive.

tufo sm. tuff.

tugurio sm. hovel.

tulipano sm. tulip.

tumefare vt. to swell (v. irr.). ♦ **tumefarsi** vr. to swell.

tumefatto agg. swollen.

tumefazione sf. swelling.

tùmido agg. tumid: labbra tumide, thick lips.

tumore sm. tumour.

tumulare vt. to bury.

tumulazione sf. burial.

tùmulo sm. 1. tumulus (pl. -li) 2. (tomba) grave.

tumulto sm. tumult.

tumultuante agg. riotous.

tumultuare vi. to riot.

tumultuoso agg. tumultuous.

tundra sf. tundra.

tungsteno sm. tungsten.

tùnica sf. tunic.

tunnel sm. tunnel.

tuo agg. your. ♦ **tuo** pron. yours.

tuoi agg. e pron. V. tuo || i —, your family.

tuonare vi. to thunder.

tuono sm. thunder.

tuorlo sm. yolk.

turàcciolo sm. 1. stopper 2. (di su-

ghero) cork || *mettere il — a una bottiglia,* to cork a bottle.

turare *vt.* to stop, to fill up. ♦ **turarsi** *vr.* **1.** to stop **2.** (*chiudersi*) to shut oneself up.

turba[1] *sf.* crowd.

turba[2] *sf.* (*med.*) trouble.

turbamento *sm.* **1.** perturbation **2.** (*eccitazione*) excitement **3.** (*sconvolgimento*) upsetting.

turbante *sm.* turban.

turbare *vt.* **1.** to upset (*v. irr.*) **2.** (*agitare intorbidando*) to muddy. ♦ **turbarsi** *vr.* to get (*v. irr.*) upset.

turbina *sf.* turbine.

turbinare *vi.* to whirl.

tùrbine *sm.* **1.** whirl **2.** (*uragano*) hurricane.

turbinìo *sm.* whirling.

turbinoso *agg.* **1.** whirling **2.** (*tumultuoso*) tumultuous.

turbolento *agg.* boisterous.

turbolenza *sf.* boisterousness.

turbomotore *sm.* turbojet engine.

turbonave *sf.* turboship.

turboreattore *sm.* (*aer.*) turbojet.

turcasso *sm.* quiver.

turchese *sm.* turquoise.

turchino *agg.* deep blue.

turco *agg.* Turkish. ♦ **turco** *sm.* Turk.

turgidezza *sf.* turgidity.

tùrgido *agg.* turgid.

turìbolo *sm.* censer.

turismo *sm.* tourism.

turista *s.* tourist.

turìstico *agg.* tourist (*attr.*).

turlupinare *vt.* to swindle.

turlupinatura *sf.* swindle.

turno *sm.* **1.** turn **2.** (*servizio*) duty || *di —,* on duty; *a —,* on turn.

turpe *agg.* filthy.

turpiloquio *sm.* coarse language.

turpitùdine *sf.* baseness.

turrito *agg.* turreted.

tuta *sf.* overalls (*pl.*): *— spaziale,* spacesuit.

tutela *sf.* **1.** guardianship **2.** (*protezione*) protection.

tutelare *vt.* to guard.

tutelare *agg.* tutelary.

tutore *sm.* guardian.

tuttavìa *cong.* yet.

tutto *agg.* all, whole (*pl.* all); (*ogni*) every || *tutt'e due,* both; *tutt'al più,* at the most; *tutt'altro che,* anything but; *tutt'altro!,* on the contrary! ♦ **tutto** *pron.* all,

everything (*pl.* all); (*ognuno*) everybody. ♦ **tutto** *s.x.* whole: *del —,* quite.

tuttofare *agg. cameriera —,* maid-of-all-work.

tuttora *avv.* still.

U

ubbìa *sf.* whim.

ubbidiente *agg.* obedient.

ubbidienza *sf.* obedience.

ubbidire *vi.* to obey (so., sthg.).

ubicare *vt.* to locate.

ubicato *agg.* situated.

ubicazione *sf.* location.

ubiquità *sf.* ubiquity.

ubriacare *vt.* to make (*v. irr.*) drunk. ♦ **ubriacarsi** *vr.* to get (*v. irr.*) drunk.

ubriacatura *sf.* intoxication.

ubriachezza *sf.* drunkenness.

ubriaco *agg.* drunk. ♦ **ubriaco** *sm.* drunken man (*pl.* men).

ubriacone *sm.* drunkard.

uccellagione *sf.* feathered game.

uccellare *vi.* to fowl.

uccelliera *sf.* aviary.

uccello *sm.* bird.

uccìdere *vt.* **1.** to kill **2.** (*assassinare*) to murder **3.** (*con pugnale*) to stab to death **4.** (*con arma da fuoco*) to shoot (*v. irr.*). ♦ **uccìdersi** *vr.* **1.** to get (*v. irr.*) killed **2.** (*suicidarsi*) to commit suicide, to kill oneself.

uccisione *sf.* killing.

uccisore *sm.* killer.

udìbile *agg.* audible.

udienza *sf.* hearing.

udire *vt.* to hear (*v. irr.*).

uditivo *agg.* auditory.

udito *sm.* hearing.

uditore *sm.* **1.** listener **2.** (*nella scuola*) auditor.

uditorio *sm.* audience.

ufficiale *agg.* official. ♦ **ufficiale** *sm.* **1.** officer **2.** (*governativo, postale*) official.

ufficialità *sf.* official character.

ufficialmente *avv.* officially.

ufficiare *vi.* to officiate.

ufficio *sm.* office: *capo —,* head clerk; *d'—,* officially; *— informazioni,* information bureau.

ufficiosamente *avv.* unofficially.

ufficioso *agg.* unofficial.

ufo (*nella loc. avv.*) **a —**, without paying.

ugello *sm.* nozzle.

uggia *sf.* boredom: *questo libro mi è venuto in —*, I have grown tired of this book.

uggiolare *vi.* to whine.

uggioso *agg.* dull.

ùgola *sf.* 1. uvula 2. (*voce*) voice.

uguaglianza *sf.* equality.

uguagliare *vt.* 1. to be equal (to) 2. (*rendere uguale*) to make (*v. irr.*) equal.

uguale *agg.* 1. equal 2. (*simile*) like, alike (*pred.*) 3. (*stesso*) same.

ugualitario *agg.* equalitarian.

ugualmente *avv.* 1. equally 2. (*lo stesso*) all the same.

ùlcera *sf.* ulcer.

ulcerare *vt.* to ulcerate. ♦ **ulcerarsi** *vr.* to ulcerate.

ulcerato *agg.* ulcerated.

ulcerazione *sf.* ulceration.

ulceroso *agg.* ulcerous.

ulteriore *agg.* further.

ulteriormente *avv.* further on.

ultimamente *avv.* 1. recently 2. (*da ultimo*) finally.

ultimare *vt.* to finish.

ultimazione *sf.* conclusion.

ùltimo *agg.* 1. last 2. (*il più recente*) latest 3. (*estremo*) utmost.

ultramicroscòpico *agg.* ultramicroscopic(al).

ultramoderno *agg.* ultramodern.

ultrasensìbile *agg.* ultrasensitive.

ultrasònico *agg.* ultrasonic.

ultrasuono *sm.* ultrasound.

ultraterreno *agg.* supernatural.

ultravioletto *agg.* ultraviolet.

ululare *vi.* 1. to howl 2. (*di sirena*) to hoot.

ululato *sm.* 1. howl 2. (*di sirena*) hoot.

umanésimo *sm.* Humanism.

umanista *sm.* humanist.

umanìstico *agg.* humanistic.

umanità *sf.* humanity.

umanitario *agg.* humanitarian.

umanitarismo *sm.* humanitarianism.

umanizzare *vt.* to humanize.

umano *agg.* 1. human 2. (*comprensivo*) humane.

umerale *agg.* humeral.

umettare *vt.* to moisten.

umidità *sf.* humidity, dampness.

ùmido *agg.* damp.

ùmile *agg.* humble.

umiliante *agg.* humiliating.

umiliare *vt.* to humble.

umiliazione *sf.* humiliation.

umiltà *sf.* 1. humbleness 2. (*virtù dell'umile*) humility.

umore *sm.* humour: *essere di buon —*, to be in a good humour.

umorismo *sm.* humour.

umorista *s.* humorist.

umorìstico *agg.* humorous.

una *art. e agg.* V. **uno.**

unànime *agg.* unanimous.

unanimità *sf.* unanimity: *all'—*, unanimously.

uncinare *vt.* to hook.

uncinato *agg.* hooked ‖ *croce uncinata*, swastika.

uncinetto *sm.* crochet-hook: *lavorare all'—*, to crochet.

uncino *sm.* hook.

undicèsimo *agg.* eleventh.

ùndici *agg.* eleven.

ùngere *vt.* to grease.

unghia *sf.* 1. nail 2. (*di equino*) hoof 3. (*fig.*) clutch.

unghiata *sf.* scratch: *dare un'—*, to scratch.

unguento *sm.* ointment.

ungulato *agg.* hoofed.

unicamente *avv.* only.

unicellulare *agg.* unicellular.

unicità *sf.* uniqueness.

ùnico *agg.* 1. only 2. (*senza uguale*) unique.

unificare *vt.* 1. to unify 2. (*uniformare*) to standardize.

unificatore *agg.* unifying. ♦ **unificatore** *sm.* unifier.

unificazione *sf.* 1. unification 2. (*uniformazione*) standardization.

uniformare *vt.* 1. to conform 2. (*rendere conforme*) to standardize. ♦ **uniformarsi** *vr.* to conform (to).

uniforme[1] *agg.* uniform.

uniforme[2] *sf.* uniform.

uniformemente *avv.* uniformly.

uniformità *sf.* uniformity.

unigènito *agg.* only child.

unilaterale *agg.* unilateral.

unilateralmente *avv.* unilaterally.

uninominale *agg.* uninominal.

unione *sf.* union.

unionista *sm.* unionist.

unipolare *agg.* unipolar.

unire *vt.* to unite, to join. ♦ **unirsi** *vr.* to unite, to join.

unìsono *sm.* unison.

unità *sf.* **1.** unity **2.** (*fis.; mat.; mil.*) unit.

unitamente *avv.* unitedly: — *a*, together with.

unitario *agg.* unitary.

unito *agg.* **1.** united **2.** (*accluso*) enclosed.

universale *agg.* universal.

universalità *sf.* universality.

universalizzare *vt.* to universalize.

università *sf.* university.

universitario *agg.* university (*attr.*). ♦ **universitario** *sm.* university student.

universo *agg.* whole. ♦ **universo** *sm.* universe.

unìvoco *agg.* univocal.

uno, un, una *art.* a, an (*davanti a vocale e h muta*). ♦ **uno, un, una** *agg.* one. ♦ **uno, una** *pron.* **1.** one **2.** (*un tale*) a man; (*una tale*) a woman || — *a* —, one by one; *l'* — *e l'altro*, both; *l'* — *o l'altro*, either; *né l'* — *né l'altro*, neither; *l'* — *l'altro*, each other; *un po' per* —, a part each; *costano 5 sterline l'*—, they cost 5 pounds each.

unto *agg.* greasy.

untume *sm.* grease.

untuosamente *avv.* (*fig.*) unctuously.

untuosità *sf.* **1.** greasiness **2.** (*fig.*) unctuousness.

untuoso *agg.* **1.** greasy **2.** (*fig.*) unctuous.

unzione *sf.* unction.

uomo *sm.* man (*pl.* men): *un* — *da nulla*, a nobody.

uopo *sm.* esser d'—, to be necessary; *all'*—, if necessary.

uovo *sm.* egg: *rosso d'*—, yolk; *cercare il pelo nell'*—, to split (*v. irr.*) hairs.

uragano *sm.* hurricane.

uranìfero *agg.* uranic.

uranio *sm.* uranium.

uranite *sf.* uranite.

uranografìa *sf.* uranography.

urbanésimo *sm.* urbanization.

urbanista *s.* town planner.

urbanìstica *sf.* town-planning.

urbanìstico *agg.* town-planning.

urbanità *sf.* urbanity.

urbanizzare *vt.* to urbanize.

urbanizzazione *sf.* urbanization.

urbano *agg.* **1.** urban **2.** (*cortese*) urbane.

ùrea *sf.* urea.

uremìa *sf.* uraemia.

urèmico *agg.* uraemic.

uretra *sf.* urethra.

urgente *agg.* urgent.

urgentemente *avv.* urgently.

urgenza *sf.* urgency.

ùrgere *vt.* to urge. ♦ **ùrgere** *vi.* to be urgent.

uricemìa *sf.* uricaemia.

ùrico *agg.* uric.

urina *sf.* V. *orina*.

urinare *vi.* V. *orinare*.

urlare *vt.* e *vi.* **1.** to shout, to scream **2.** (*di vento, animale; per il dolore*) to howl.

urlatore *agg.* shouting. ♦ **urlatore** *sm.* shouter.

urlo *sm.* **1.** shout **2.** (*di vento, animale; per il dolore*) howl.

urna *sf.* **1.** urn **2.** (*per i voti*) ballot-box || *andare alle urne*, to go (*v. irr.*) to the polls.

urogallo *sm.* grouse.

urologìa *sf.* urology.

uròlogo *sm.* urologist.

urtante *agg.* irritating.

urtare *vt.* **1.** to knock **2.** (*infastidire*) to irritate **3.** (*offendere*) to hurt (*v. irr.*). ♦ **urtarsi** *vr.* to get (*v. irr.*) cross. ♦ **urtarsi** *vr. rec.* to collide.

urticante *agg.* urticating.

urticaria *sf.* nettle rash.

urto *sm.* **1.** push **2.** (*scontro, contrasto*) collision || *essere in* —, to be at variance.

urtone *sm.* shove.

usanza *sf.* **1.** custom **2.** (*abitudine personale*) habit.

usare *vt.* to use: — *una cortesia*, to do (*v. irr.*) a favour. ♦ **usare** *vi.* **1.** to be accustomed; (*solo al passato*) to use **2.** (*essere di moda*) to be fashionable.

usato *agg.* **1.** used **2.** (*in uso*) in use **3.** (*abituale*) usual **4.** (*non nuovo*) second-hand.

uscente *agg.* **1.** retiring **2.** (*con espressioni di tempo*) closing.

usciere *sm.* **1.** usher **2.** (*ufficiale giudiziario*) bailiff.

uscio *sm.* door: *abitare* — *a* — (*con*), to live next door (to).

uscire *vi.* **1.** to go (*v. irr.*) out, to come (*v. irr.*) out **2.** (*sboccare*) to lead (*v. irr.*) **3.** (*uscire di strada*) to go off || *uscirne bene, male*, to come off well, badly.

uscita sf. 1. way out 2. (atto di uscire) going out, coming out 3. (spese) expense || strada senza —, blind-alley.

usignolo sm. nightingale.

uso¹ agg. accustomed.

uso² sm. use: d'—, usual; all'— di, after the fashion of.

ùssaro sm. hussar.

ustionare vt. to scald.

ustionato agg. scalded.

ustione sf. scald.

usuale agg. usual.

usufruire vi. to benefit (by).

usufrutto sm. usufruct.

usufruttuario agg. e sm. usufructuary.

usura sf. 1. usury 2. (logorio) wear and tear.

usuraio sm. usurer.

usurpare vt. to usurp.

usurpatore agg. usurping. ♦ **usurpatore** sm. usurper.

usurpazione sf. usurpation.

utènsile sm. utensil.

utente s. user.

uterino agg. uterine.

ùtero sm. uterus (pl. -ri).

ùtile agg. useful. ♦ **ùtile** sm. profit.

utilità sf. 1. usefulness 2. (vantaggio) profit || non ne vedo l'—, I do not see the use of it.

utilitaria sf. (auto) utility car.

utilitario agg. e sm. utilitarian.

utilitarismo sm. utilitarianism.

utilitarìstico agg. V. utilitario.

utilizzàbile agg. utilizable.

utilizzare vt. to utilize.

utilizzatore agg. utilizing. ♦ **utilizzatore** sm. utilizer.

utilizzazione sf. utilization.

utopìa sf. utopia.

utopista s. utopian.

utopìstico agg. utopian.

uva sf. grapes (pl.): — passa, raisin.

uxoricida sm. uxoricide.

uxoricidio sm. uxoricide.

V

vacante agg. vacant.

vacanza sf. 1. holiday 2. (posto vacante) vacancy.

vacca sf. cow.

vaccaro sm. cowherd.

vaccherìa sf. cowhouse.

vacchetta sf. cowhide.

vaccinàbile agg. that can be vaccinated.

vaccinare vt. to vaccinate.

vaccinazione sf. vaccination.

vaccino sm. vaccine.

vaccinògeno agg. vaccinogenous.

vaccinoterapìa sf. vaccinotherapy.

vacillamento sm. 1. unsteadiness 2. (di luce) flickering 3. (fig.) wavering.

vacillante agg. 1. unsteady 2. (di luce) flickering 3. (fig.) uncertain.

vacillare vi. 1. to be unsteady 2. (di luce) to flicker 3. (fig.) to waver.

vacuità sf. vacuity.

vacuo agg. vacuous.

vademecum sm. vade-mecum.

vagabondaggio sm. vagrancy.

vagabondare vi. to wander.

vagabondo agg. vagabond. ♦ **vagabondo** sm. vagrant.

vagamente avv. vaguely.

vagante agg. wandering.

vagare vi. to wander.

vagheggiamento sm. longing (for).

vagheggiare vt. to long (for).

vagheggino sm. gallant.

vaghezza sf. 1. charm 2. (indeterminatezza) vagueness.

vagina sf. vagina (pl. -nae).

vagire vi. to wail.

vagito sm. wail.

vaglia¹ sf. (valore) worth.

vaglia² sm. money order: — postale, postal order.

vagliare vt. to sieve 2. (fig.) to weigh.

vagliatura sf. screening.

vaglio sm. 1. sieve 2. (fig.) sifting.

vago agg. 1. vague 2. (leggiadro) pretty.

vagoncino sm. wag(g)on.

vagolare vi. to rove.

vagone sm. carriage, coach.

vaio¹ agg. dark grey.

vaio² sm. vair.

vaiolo sm. smallpox.

valanga sf. avalanche.

valchiria sf. Walkyrie.

valente agg. 1. skilful 2. (valoroso) brave.

valentemente avv. 1. skilfully 2. (valorosamente) bravely.

valentìa sf. 1. skill 2. (valore) worth.

valentuomo *sm.* worthy man.

valenza *sf.* valence.

valere *vi.* **1.** to be worth: — *la pena*, to be worth while; *far —: i propri diritti*, to assert one's rights; *farsi —*, to make (*v. irr.*) oneself appreciated **2.** (*contare*) to count **3.** (*servire*) to be of use **4.** (*essere valido*) to be valid. ♦ **valersi** *vr.* to avail oneself (of).

valeriana *sf.* valerian.

valévole *agg.* valid.

valicàbile *agg.* that can be crossed.

valicare *vt.* to cross.

vàlico *sm.* pass.

validamente *avv.* validly.

validità *sf.* validity.

vàlido *agg.* **1.** valid **2.** (*fondato*) well-grounded **3.** (*forte*) strong.

valigerìa *sf.* leatherware shop.

valigia *sf.* suit-case; *fare le valigie*, to pack up.

vallata *sf.* valley.

valle *sf.* valley.

valletto *sm.* valet.

vallo *sm.* rampart.

vallone *agg. e sm.* Walloon.

valore *sm.* **1.** value **2.** (*coraggio*) bravery.

valorizzare *vt.* **1.** to turn to account **2.** (*accentuare*) to emphasize.

valorizzazione *sf.* **1.** turning to account **2.** (*comm.*) valorization.

valorosamente *avv.* bravely.

valoroso *agg.* brave.

valsente *sm.* commercial value.

valuta *sf.* **1.** value **2.** (*moneta*) currency: — *estera*, foreign currency.

valutàbile *agg.* valuable.

valutare *vt.* **1.** to value **2.** (*considerare*) to consider.

valutazione *sf.* **1.** evaluation **2.** (*considerazione*) careful consideration.

valva *sf.* valve.

vàlvola *sf.* **1.** valve **2.** (*elettr.*) fuse **3.** (*radio*) valve, tube.

valvolare *agg.* valvular.

valzer *sm.* waltz: *ballare il —*, to waltz.

vampa *sf.* **1.** blaze **2.** (*al viso*) flush.

vampata *sf.* **1.** blaze **2.** (*folata*) blast **3.** (*al viso*) flush.

vampeggiante *agg.* blazing.

vampeggiare *vi.* to blaze.

vampiro *sm.* vampire.

vanagloria *sf.* vainglory.

vanagloriarsi *vr.* to boast.

vanaglorioso *agg.* boastful.

vanamente *avv.* vainly.

vandàlico *agg.* vandalic.

vandalismo *sm.* vandalism.

vàndalo *agg. e sm.* vandal.

vaneggiamento *sm.* raving.

vaneggiare *vi.* to rave.

vanesio *agg.* foppish. ♦ **vanesio** *sm.* fop.

vanga *sf.* spade.

vangare *vt.* to spade.

vangata *sf.* blow with a spade.

vangatore *sm.* spademan.

vangatura *sf.* spading.

vangelo *sm.* Gospel.

vaniglia *sf.* vanilla.

vanigliato *agg.* vanilla-flavoured.

vaniloquio *sm.* empty talk.

vanità *sf.* vanity.

vanitoso *agg.* conceited.

vano¹ *agg.* vain.

vano² *sm.* space, room.

vantaggio *sm.* **1.** advantage **2.** (*sport*) lead.

vantaggiosamente *avv.* advantageously.

vantaggioso *agg.* advantageous.

vantare *vt.* **1.** to boast (of) **2.** (*lodare*) to praise **3.** (*millantare*) to brag. ♦ **vantarsi** *vr.* to boast (of).

vanterìa *sf.* boast.

vanto *sm.* boast.

vànvera (*nella loc. avv.*) *a —*, at random.

vapore *sm.* **1.** steam **2.** (*mar.*) steamer.

vaporetto *sm.* steamboat.

vaporiera *sf.* steam-engine.

vaporizzare *vt.* to vaporize.

vaporizzatore *sm.* vaporizer.

vaporizzazione *sf.* vaporization.

vaporosità *sf.* **1.** haziness **2.** (*di abito*) gauziness.

vaporoso *agg.* **1.** hazy **2.** (*di abito*) gauzy.

varare *vt.* to launch (*anche fig.*).

varcare *vt.* to cross, to pass.

varco *sm.* passage, opening: *aprirsi un — fra la folla*, to force one's way through the crowd.

variàbile *agg.* variable, unsteady.

variabilità *sf.* variability, unsteadiness.

variante *sf.* variant.

variare *vt.* **1.** to vary **2.** (*di mercato*) to fluctuate.

variato *agg.* V. *vario*.

variazione *sf.* variation, change.

varice *sf.* varix (*pl.* varices).

varicella *sf.* chicken-pox.

varicoso *agg.* varicose.

variegato *agg.* variegated.

varietà *sf.* variety.

vario *agg.* **1.** varied **2.** (*differente*) various **3.** (*parecchi*) several.

variopinto *agg.* many-coloured.

varo *sm.* launch.

vasaio *sm.* potter.

vasca *sf.* basin: — *da bagno*, bath (tub).

vascello *sm.* vessel.

vascolare *agg.* vascular.

vaselina *sf.* vaseline.

vasellame *sm.* **1.** (*di terracotta*) earthenware **2.** (*di porcellana*) china **3.** (*d'argento, d'oro*) silver, gold plate.

vaso *sm.* **1.** vase **2.** (*rotondo*) pot **3.** (*recipiente; anat.*) vessel.

vasocostrittore *agg. e sm.* vasoconstrictor.

vasodilatatore *agg. e sm.* vasodilator.

vasomotore *agg.* vasomotor.

vasomotorio *agg.* vasomotor.

vassallaggio *sm.* **1.** (*stor.*) vassalage **2.** subjection.

vassallo *agg. e sm.* **1.** (*stor.*) vassal **2.** subject.

vassoio *sm.* tray.

vastità *sf.* **1.** vastness **2.** (*estensione*) expanse.

vasto *agg.* wide, large.

vate *sm.* **1.** prophet **2.** (*poeta*) poet.

Vaticano *agg.* Vatican.

vaticinare *vt.* to prophesy.

vaticinio *sm.* prophecy.

vattelappesca *inter.* who knows!

ve *pron:* you: — *lo scrissi*, I wrote it to you. ♦ **ve** *avv.* there: — *ne sono due*, there are two.

ve' *inter.* look, see.

vecchiaia *sf.* old age.

vecchiezza *sf.* great age.

vecchio *agg.* **1.** old **2.** (*antico*) ancient **3.** (*stantio*) stale. ♦ **vecchio** *sm.* old man.

veccia *sf.* vetch.

vece *sf.* stead, place.

vedere *vt.* to see (*v. irr.*): — *la luce* (*nascere*), to be born; *far* —, to show (*v. irr.*); *farsi* —, to show oneself; *non* — *l'ora di*, to look forward to (*con gerundio*). ♦ **vedersi** *vr.* ` **1.** to see oneself **2.** (*vedersela*) to deal (*v. irr.*) with.

vedetta *sf.* **1.** (*sentinella*) watchman (*pl.* -men) **2.** (*posto di osservazione*) look-out.

védova *sf.* widow.

vedovanza *sf.* widowhood.

vedovile *agg.* **1.** (*di vedova*) of a widow **2.** (*di vedovo*) of a widower.

védovo *sm.* widower.

vedretta *sf.* small steep glacier.

veduta *sf.* **1.** sight, view **2.** (*opinione*) view, idea.

veemente *agg.* vehement.

veemenza *sf.* vehemence.

vegetale *agg. e sm.* vegetable.

vegetare *vi.* to vegetate.

vegetariano *agg. e sm.* vegetarian.

vegetativo *agg.* vegetative.

vegetazione *sf.* vegetation.

vègeto *agg.* **1.** (*di pianta*) thriving **2.** (*di persona*) vigorous, strong ‖ *vivo e* —, hale and hearty

veggente *sm.* seer.

veglia *sf.* **1.** waking **2.** (*il vegliare*) watch.

vegliardo *sm.* old man.

vegliare *vi.* **1.** to be awake **2.** (*far la veglia*) to watch.

veglione *sm.* masked ball.

veìcolo *sm.* vehicle.

vela *sf.* sail.

velame *sm.* **1.** veil **2.** (*mar.*) sails (*pl.*).

velare *vt.* to veil.

velario *sm.* curtain.

velatura *sf.* sails (*pl.*).

veleggiare *vi.* to sail.

veleno *sm.* poison.

velenoso *agg.* poisonous, venomous.

veletta *sf.* **1.** (*mar.*) topsail **2.** (*di cappello*) veil.

veliero *sm.* sailing-ship.

velina *sf.* tissue-paper.

velismo *sm.* sailing.

velìvolo *sm.* aeroplane.

velleità *sf.* foolish ambition, fancy.

vellicare *vt.* to tickle.

vello *sm.* fleece.

vellutato *agg.* velvety: *pelle vellutata*, downy skin.

velluto *sm.* velvet.

velo *sm.* veil.

veloce *agg.* fast, quick, swift.

velocìpede *sm.* velocipede.

velocità *sf.* speed, velocity: *a tutta* —, at full speed; *limite di* —, speed limit; *cambio di* — (*auto*), gearbox; *indicatore di* —, speedometer.

velòdromo *sm.* cycle-racing track.

veltro *sm.* greyhound.
vena *sf.* vein.
venale *agg.* venal.
venalità *sf.* venality.
venare *vt.* 1. to vein 2. (*di legno*) to grain.
venato *agg.* 1. veined 2. (*di legno*) grained.
venatorio *agg.* venatorial.
venatura *sf.* 1. vein 2. (*di legno*) grain.
vendemmia *sf.* vintage.
vendemmiare *vi.* to gather grapes.
vendemmiatore *sm.* vintager.
véndere *vt.* to sell (*v. irr.*): — *a buon mercato*, to sell cheaply; — *a credito*, to sell on credit; — *all'ingrosso, al minuto*, to sell wholesale, by retail; — *a rate*, to sell by instalments.
vendetta *sf.* revenge.
vendìbile *agg.* salable.
vendicare *vt.* to revenge.
vendicativo *agg.* revengeful.
vendicatore *sm.* revenger.
véndita *sf.* sale: — *all'asta*, auction.
venditore *sm.* seller.
venduto *agg.* 1. sold 2. (*fig.*) corrupted.
veneficio *sm.* poisoning.
venèfico *agg.* poisonous.
veneràbile *agg.* venerable.
venerando *agg.* venerable.
venerare *vt.* to worship.
venerazione *sf.* worship.
venerdì *sm.* Friday: — *Santo*, Good Friday.
vènere *sf.* 1. Venus 2. (*fig.*) beauty.
venèreo *agg.* venereal.
veneziana *sf.* Venetian-blind.
veniale *agg.* venial.
venire *vi.* 1. to come (*v. irr.*): — *al sodo*, to come to the point; — *in mente*, to come into one's head; — *meno*, to faint; — *alla luce*, to come to light 2. (*riuscire*) to turn out 3. (*derivare*) to derive.
venoso *agg.* venous.
ventaglio *sm.* fan.
ventata *sf.* gust of wind.
ventèsimo *agg.* twentieth.
venti *agg.* twenty.
ventilare *vt.* to ventilate.
ventilato *agg.* airy, windy.
ventilatore *sm.* fan.
ventilazione *sf.* ventilation.
ventina *sf.* score: *essere sulla* — (*di anni*), to be about twenty.

vento *sm.* wind.
ventosa *sf.* sucker.
ventosità *sf.* flatulence.
ventoso *agg.* windy.
ventrale *agg.* ventral.
ventre *sm.* 1. abdomen 2. (*fam.*) tummy.
ventrìcolo *sm.* ventricle.
ventriera *sf.* body-belt.
ventriglio *sm.* gizzard.
ventriloquio *sm.* ventriloquism.
ventrìloquo *sm.* ventriloquist.
ventura *sf.* chance, fortune.
venturo *agg.* next, coming.
venustà *sf.* beauty.
venusto *agg.* beautiful.
venuta *sf.* coming, arrival.
vera *sf.* wedding-ring.
verace *agg.* true.
veracità *sf.* veracity, truth.
veramente *avv.* really, truly, indeed.
veranda *sf.* verandah.
verbale *agg.* verbal. ♦ **verbale** *sm.* minutes (*pl.*).
verbalizzare *vt.* to record.
verbo *sm.* 1. verb 2. (*parola*) word.
verbosità *sf.* verbosity.
verboso *agg.* verbose.
verdastro *agg.* greenish.
verde *agg.* green.
verdeggiante *agg.* verdant.
verdeggiare *vi.* to be verdant.
verdemare *sm.* sea-green.
verderame *sm.* verdigris.
verdetto *sm.* verdict.
verdògnolo *agg.* greenish.
verdura *sf.* vegetables (*pl.*).
verecondia *sf.* modesty.
verecondo *agg.* modest.
verga *sf.* 1. twig 2. (*bacchetta*) rod.
vergare *vt.* (*scrivere*) to write (*v. irr.*).
vergata *sf.* blow with a rod.
vergato *agg.* 1. striped 2. (*scritto*) written || *carta vergata*, laid paper.
verginale *agg.* virginal.
vérgine *agg. e sf.* virgin.
vergìneo *agg.* virginal.
verginità *sf.* virginity.
vergogna *sf.* shame: *aver* —, to be ashamed.
vergognarsi *vr.* to be, to feel (*v. irr.*) shamed.
vergognosamente *avv.* shamefully.
vergognoso *agg.* 1. shameful 2. (*timido*) shy.
veridicamente *avv.* veraciously.
veridicità *sf.* veracity.

verìdico *agg.* veracious.
verìfica *sf.* verification.
verificàbile *agg.* verifiable.
verificare *vt.* to verify, to check.
verificatore *sm.* verifier.
verificazione *sf.* V. *verifica.*
verismo *sm.* realism.
verista *sm.* realist.
verìstico *agg.* realistic.
verità *sf.* truth: *dire la* —, to tell (*v. irr.*) the truth.
veritiero *agg.* truthful.
verme *sm.* worm.
vermìfugo *agg. e sm.* vermifuge.
vermiglio *agg.* bright red.
verminoso *agg.* verminous.
vernàcolo *agg.* vernacular.
vernice *sf.* **1.** paint **2.** (*apparenza*) varnish.
verniciare *vt.* to paint, to varnish.
verniciatura *sf.* painting, varnishing.
vero *agg.* true, real.
verosimigliante *agg.* likely.
verosimiglianza *sf.* likelihood.
verosìmile *agg.* likely, probable.
verricello *sm.* windlass.
verro *sm.* boar.
verruca *sf.* wart.
versamento *sm.* **1.** pouring **2.** (*comm.*) payment, deposit.
versante *sm.* side, slope.
versare *vt.* **1.** to pour **2.** (*rovesciare*) to spill (*v. irr.*) **3.** (*comm.*) to pay (*v. irr.*).
versàtile *agg.* versatile.
versatilità *sf.* versatility.
versato *agg.* **1.** poured out **2.** (*esperto*) versed.
verseggiare *vt.* to versify.
verseggiatore *sm.* versifier.
versetto *sm.* **1.** short line **2.** (*della Bibbia*) verse.
versificare *vt.* to versify.
versificatore *sm.* versifier.
versificazione *sf.* versification.
versione *sf.* version, translation.
verso[1] *sm.* **1.** verse, line **2.** (*suono*) sound **3.** (*direzione*) way.
verso[2] *prep.* **1.** towards, to **2.** (*contro*) against **3.** (*circa*) about.
vèrtebra *sf.* vertebra (*pl.* -rae).
vertebrale *agg.* vertebral.
vertebrato *agg. e sm.* vertebrate.
vertenza *sf.* **1.** dispute **2.** (*giur.*) litigation.
vèrtere *vi.* to be about, to concern.
verticale *agg.* vertical.
verticalità *sf.* verticality.

vèrtice *sm.* **1.** vertex (*pl.* vertices) **2.** (*fig.*) height, top.
vertìgine *sf.* dizziness (*solo sing.*).
vertiginoso *agg.* dizzy.
verza *sf.* cabbage.
vescica *sf.* bladder.
vescovado *sm.* bishop's residence.
vescovile *agg.* episcopal.
véscovo *sm.* bishop.
vespa *sf.* wasp.
vespaio *sm.* **1.** wasps' nest **2.** (*fig.*) hornets' nest.
vespro *sm.* **1.** evening **2.** (*relig.*) evensong.
vessare *vt.* to vex.
vessatorio *agg.* vexatious.
vessazione *sf.* vexation.
vessillo *sm.* flag.
vestaglia *sf.* dressing-gown.
vestale *sf.* vestal.
veste *sf.* **1.** dress **2.** (*eccl.*) vestment **3.** (*qualità*) capacity.
vestiario *sm.* clothes (*pl.*).
vestìbolo *sm.* hall.
vestigio *sm.* vestige.
vestimento *sm.* V. *veste.*
vestire *vt.* **1.** to dress **2.** (*fig.*) to clothe **3.** (*indossare*) to wear (*v. irr.*). ♦ **vestirsi** *vr.* to dress oneself.
vestito *sm.* **1.** (*da uomo*) suit **2.** (*da donna*) frock, dress.
vestizione *sf.* (*eccl.*) ceremony of taking the habit **2.** (*di monaca*) ceremony of taking the veil.
veterano *sm.* veteran.
veterinaria *sf.* veterinary science.
veterinario *sm.* veterinary.
veto *sm.* veto.
vetraio *sm.* glazier.
vetrame *sm.* glassware.
vetrata *sf.* glass partition: — *a colori,* stained glass window.
vetrato *agg.* glazed: *carta vetrata,* glass-paper.
vetrerìa *sf.* glass-work.
vetrificàbile *agg.* vitrifiable.
vetrificare *vt.* to vitrify.
vetrificazione *sf.* vitrification.
vetrina *sf.* shop-window.
vetrioleggiare *vt.* to vitriolize.
vetriolo *sm.* vitriol.
vetro *sm.* **1.** glass **2.** (*di finestra*) window-pane.
vetrocromìa *sf.* glass-painting.
vetroso *agg.* glassy.
vetta *sf.* top, summit.
vettore *sm.* vector.
vettoriale *agg.* vectorial.

vettovagliamento *sm.* provisi-n-ing.

vettovagliare *vt.* to provision.

vettura *sf.* 1. coach 2. (*automobile*) car || — *di piazza*, taxi-cab.

vetturino *sm.* cabman (*pl.* -men).

vetustà *sf.* antiquity.

vetusto *agg.* ancient.

vezzeggiare *vt.* to fondle.

vezzeggiativo *sm.* petname.

vezzo *sm.* 1. habit 2. (*collana*) necklace.

vezzosamente *avv.* charmingly.

vezzoso *agg.* charming.

vi[1] *pron.* you, to you.

vi[2] *avv.* 1. (*qui*) here 2. (*là*) there.

via[1] *sf.* 1. street 2. (*strada di comunicazione*) road 3. (*cammino*) way (*anche fig.*) 4. (*linea di condotta*) course. ◆ *via*, come: *dare il* —, to give (*v. irr.*) the starting.

via[2] *avv.* away: *andar* —, to go (*v. irr.*) away.

viabilità *sf.* state of a road.

viadotto *sm.* viaduct.

viaggiante *agg.* travelling.

viaggiare *vi.* to travel: — *in treno, automobile, aereo*, to travel by train, by car, by air.

viaggiatore *sm.* traveller: — *di commercio*, commercial traveller.

viaggio *sm.* 1. journey, trip 2. (*per mare*) voyage 3. (*in aereo*) flight.

viale *sm.* avenue; (*di giardino*) alley.

viandante *sm.* wayfarer.

viàtico *sm.* viaticum (*pl.* -ca).

viavai *sm.* coming-and-going.

vibrante *agg.* vibrating (with).

vibrare *vi.* 1. to vibrate 2. (*colpi*) to strike (*v. irr.*).

vibràtile *agg.* vibratile.

vibrato *agg.* energetic.

vibratore *sm.* vibrator.

vibrazione *sf.* vibration.

vicariato *sm.* vicariate.

vicario *sm.* vicar.

viceconsole *sm.* vice-consul.

vicedirettore *sm.* assistant-director.

vicegovernatore *sm.* vice-governor.

vicenda *sf.* vicissitude 2. (*evento*) event 3. (*successione*) succession.

vicendévole *agg.* mutual.

vicendevolmente *avv.* mutually.

vicepresidente *sm.* vice-president.

viceré *sm.* viceroy.

vicesegretario *sm.* vice-secretary.

viceversa *avv.* vice versa. ◆ *vice-versa cong.* whereas.

vicinale *sf.* local road.

vicinanza *sf.* 1. vicinity: *in* — *di*, close to 2. (*adiacenze*) neighbourhood: *nelle vicinanze*, in the neighbourhood.

vicinato *sm.* 1. neighbourhood 2. (*i vicini*) neighbours (*pl.*).

vicino[1] *agg.* near, close. ◆ *vicino sm.* neighbour.

vicino[2] *avv.* near, near by. ◆ *vicino prep.* near, close to.

vicissitùdine *sf.* vicissitude.

vìcolo *sm.* lane, alley.

vìdeo *sm.* video.

vidimare *vt.* 1. (*firmare*) to sign 2. (*autenticare*) to authenticate.

vidimazione *sf.* 1. (*firma*) signature 2. (*autenticazione*) authentication.

vietare *vt.* to forbid (*v. irr.*).

vietato *agg.* forbidden: — *fumare*, no smoking; — *entrare*, no admittance.

vieto *agg.* antiquated.

vigente *agg.* in force.

vìgere *vi.* to be in force.

vigilante *agg.* watchful.

vigilanza *sf.* watch.

vigilare *vt.* to watch over.

vigilato *agg.* watched.

vigile *agg.* watchful. ◆ *vìgile sm.* policeman (*pl.* -men).

vigilia *sf.* 1. eve 2. (*relig.*) fast.

vigliaccamente *avv.* in a cowardly way.

vigliaccherìa *sf.* 1. cowardice 2. (*azione vigliacca*) cowardly action.

vigliacco *agg.* cowardly.

vigna *sf.* vineyard.

vigneto *sm.* vineyard.

vignetta *sf.* cartoon.

vigore *sm.* vigour: *in* —, in force.

vigoroso *agg.* vigorous.

vile *agg.* 1. cowardly 2. (*meschino*) mean 3. (*basso*) low.

vilipèndere *vt.* to despise.

vilipendio *sm.* contempt.

villa *sf.* villa.

villaggio *sm.* village.

villanìa *sf.* 1. rudeness 2. (*azione villana*) rude action.

villano *agg.* rude. ◆ *villano sm.* peasant, countryman (*pl.* -men).

villeggiante *s.* holiday-maker.

villeggiatura *sf.* holiday: *luogo di* —, (holiday) resort.

villino *sm.* cottage.

villoso *agg.* hairy.

viltà *sf.* 1. cowardice 2. (*azione vile*) cowardly action.

vilucchio *sm.* bearbind.

viluppo *sm.* tangle.

vìmine *sm.* withe: *paniere di vimini,* wicker basket.

vinaccia *sf.* dregs of pressed grapes (*pl.*).

vinaio *sm.* wine-merchant.

vinario *agg.* wine (*attr.*).

vincente *agg.* winning. ♦ **vincente** *sm.* winner.

vìncere *vt.* **1.** to win (*v. irr.*) **2.** (*battere*) to beat (*v. irr.*) **3.** (*sopraffare*) to overcome (*v. irr.*) **4.** (*superare*) to outdo (*v. irr.*).

vincìbile *agg.* conquerable.

vìncita *sf.* **1.** win **2.** (*denaro vinto*) winnings (*pl.*).

vincitore *agg.* winning. ♦ **vincitore** *sm.* winner.

vinco *sm.* withe.

vincolare *vt.* **1.** to bind (*v. irr.*) **2.** (*comm.*) to lock up.

vincolato *agg.* **1.** bound **2.** (*comm.*) locked up.

vìncolo *sm.* tie, bond.

vinello *sm.* light wine.

vinìcolo *agg.* wine (*attr.*).

vinificazione *sf.* wine-making.

vino *sm.* wine.

vinto *agg.* **1.** that has been won **2.** (*sconfitto*) beaten **3.** (*sopraffatto*) overcome ‖ *darsi —,* to give (*v. irr.*) in. ♦ **vinto** *sm.* **1.** (*al giuoco o in qualsiasi contesa*) loser **2.** (*in battaglia*) vanquished man.

viola[1] *sf.* **1.** violet: *— del pensiero,* pansy. ♦ **viola** *agg.* e *sm.* violet.

viola[2] *sf.* (*mus.*) viola.

violàcee *sf. pl.* violaceae.

violàceo *agg.* violet.

violare *vt.* to violate.

violatore *sm.* violator.

violazione *sf.* violation: *— di domicilio,* house-breaking.

violentare *vt.* **1.** to violate, to rape **2.** (*fig.*) to do (*v. irr.*) violence to.

violento *agg.* violent.

violenza *sf.* violence, rape.

violetto *agg.* violet.

violinista *s.* violin-player.

violino *sm.* violin.

violoncellista *s.* violoncellist.

violoncello *sm.* violoncello.

viòttola *sf.* path, lane.

viòttolo *sm.* path, lane.

vìpera *sf.* **1.** adder **2.** (*fig.*) viper.

viperino *agg.* viperous.

viraggio *sm.* (*foto*) toning.

virago *sf.* virago.

virare *vt.* e *vi.* **1.** to veer: *— di bordo,* to veer round **2.** (*fig.*) to turn about.

virata *sf.* veer.

virginale *agg.* virginal.

virginia *sm.* Virginia.

vìrgola *sf.* **1.** (*gramm.*) comma **2.** (*mat.*) point.

virgolette *sf. pl.* inverted commas: *tra —,* in inverted commas.

virgulto *sm.* shoot.

virile *agg.* manly.

virilità *sf.* **1.** manliness **2.** (*età virile*) manhood.

virilmente *avv.* manfully.

virologìa *sf.* virology.

virosi *sf.* virosis (*pl.* -ses).

virtù *sf.* virtue.

virtuale *agg.* virtual.

virtualità *sf.* virtuality.

virtuosismo *sm.* virtuosity.

virtuoso *agg.* virtuous.

virulento *agg.* virulent.

virulenza *sf.* virulence.

virus *sm.* virus.

viscerale *agg.* visceral.

vìscere *sm.* **1.** vital organ **2.** (*f. pl.*) *le viscere,* viscera.

vischio *sm.* **1.** mistletoe **2.** (*pania*) bird-lime.

vischiosità *sf.* stickiness.

vischioso *agg.* sticky.

viscidità *sf.* viscidity.

vìscido *agg.* **1.** sticky **2.** (*scivoloso*) slippery.

vìsciola *sf.* wild cherry.

visconte *sm.* viscount.

viscontessa *sf.* viscountess.

viscosità *sf.* viscosity.

viscoso *agg.* viscous.

visìbile *agg.* visible, clear.

visibilio *sm.* great number: *andare in —,* to go (*v. irr.*) into raptures.

visibilità *sf.* visibility.

visiera *sf.* **1.** (*di elmo*) visor **2.** (*di berretto*) peak.

visionario *agg.* e *sm.* visionary.

visione *sf.* vision: *prendere — di,* to look over; *prima — (cine),* first screening.

vìsita *sf.* **1.** visit, call: *fare una —,* to pay (*v. irr.*) a visit **2.** (*persona che visita*) visitor **3.** (*med.*) examination.

vìsitare *vt.* to visit.

visitatore *sm.* visitor.

visivo *agg.* visual.

viso *sm.* face: *— a —,* face to face.

visone *sm.* mink.

vispo *agg.* lively, brisk.

vista *sf.* **1.** sight **2.** (*occhi*) eyes (*pl.*).

vistare *vt.* to visa.

visto[1] *sm.* visa.

visto[2] *agg.* seen || — *che*, since as.

vistoso *agg.* **1.** showy **2.** (*fig.*) considerable.

visuale *agg.* visual. ◆ **visuale** *sf.* sight.

vita[1] *sf.* **1.** life (*pl.* lives): *a* —, for life; *in* —, during one's life **2.** (*necessario per vivere*) living: *costo della* —, cost of living.

vita[2] *sf.* (*anat.*) waist.

vitaiolo *sm.* bon viveur.

vitalba *sf.* clematis.

vitale *agg.* vital.

vitalità *sf.* vitality.

vitalizio *agg.* for life. ◆ **vitalizio** *sm.* annuity.

vitamina *sf.* vitamin.

vitamìnico *agg.* vitaminic.

vite[1] *sf.* vine.

vite[2] *sf.* (*mecc.*) screw.

vitello *sm.* calf (*pl.* calves).

viticcio *sm.* vine-tendril.

vitìcolo *agg.* viticultural.

viticoltore *sm.* viticulturist.

viticoltura *sf.* grape-growing.

vìtreo *agg.* vitreous.

vìttima *sf.* victim.

vittimismo *sm.* victimization.

vitto *sm.* **1.** food **2.** (*pasti in pensione o albergo*) board: — *e alloggio*, board and lodging.

vittoria *sf.* victory.

vittorioso *agg.* victorious.

vituperare *vt.* to vituperate.

vituperio *sm.* insult.

viuzza *sf.* lane.

viva *inter.* hurrah!

vivacchiare *vi.* to live poorly.

vivace *agg.* **1.** lively, sprightly **2.** (*pronto, sveglio*) quick **3.** (*di colori*) bright.

vivacemente *avv.* **1.** lively **2.** (*prontamente*) quickly **3.** (*vivamente*) brightly.

vivacità *sf.* **1.** liveliness **2.** (*di colori*) brightness.

vivaio *sm.* **1.** (*di pesci*) fish-pond **2.** (*di piante*) nursery.

vivamente *avv.* deeply, keenly.

vivanda *sf.* food.

vivandiere *sm.* sutler.

vivente *agg.* alive (*pred.*), living. ◆ **vivente** *sm.* living being.

vìvere *vt. e vi.* to live: *cessare di*

—, to die; *insegnare a* — *a qu.*, to teach (*v. irr.*) so. good manners; — *alle spalle di qu.*, to sponge on so.

vìveri *sm. pl.* victuals.

vìvido *agg.* vivid.

vivificare *vt.* to enliven.

vivificatore *agg.* vivifying. ◆ **vivificatore** *sm.* vivifier.

vivìparo *agg. e sm.* viviparous.

vivisezione *sf.* vivisection.

vivo *agg.* **1.** living, alive (*pred.*) || *a viva forza*, by main force; *argento* —, quicksilver; *calce viva*, quicklime; *farsi* —, to turn up **2.** (*vivace*) lively **3.** (*profondo, acuto*) deep, sharp **4.** (*vivido*) vivid **5.** (*di colori*) bright.

viziare *vt.* **1.** to spoil (*v. irr.*) **2.** (*guastare*) to vitiate.

viziato *agg.* **1.** spoilt **2.** (*guasto*) vitiated.

vizio *sm.* **1.** vice **2.** (*cattiva abitudine*) bad habit.

vizioso *agg.* vicious. ◆ **vizioso** *sm.* vicious man.

vocabolario *sm.* **1.** vocabulary **2.** (*dizionario*) dictionary.

vocàbolo *sm.* word.

vocale[1] *agg.* vocal.

vocale[2] *sf.* vowel.

vocalizzare *vt. e vi.* to vocalize.

vocalizzo *sm.* vocalization.

vocativo *agg. e sm.* vocative.

vocazione *sf.* vocation, bent.

voce *sf.* **1.** voice: *a* — *alta, bassa*, in a loud, low voice; *parlare sotto* —, to whisper **2.** (*diceria*) rumour **3.** (*articolo di elenco*) item.

vociare *vi.* to shout.

vociferare *vi.* **1.** to shout **2.** (*spargere una voce*) to rumour.

vocìo *sm.* shouting.

voga[1] *sf.* (*mar.*) rowing.

voga[2] *sf.* **1.** (*moda*) fashion **2.** (*energia*) energy.

vogare *vi.* (*mar.*) to row.

vogata *sf.* row.

vogatore *sm.* rower.

voglia *sf.* **1.** wish: *aver* —, to feel (*v. irr.*) like **2.** (*volontà*) will.

voglioso *agg.* desirous, willing.

voi *pron.* you: — *stessi*, you yourselves.

volano *sm.* battledore and shuttlecock.

volante[1] *agg.* flying: *cervo* —, kite; *foglio* —, loose sheet. ◆ **volante** *sf.* (*di polizia*) flying squad.

volante² *sm.* steering-wheel.

volantino *sm.* leaflet.

volare *vi.* to fly (*v. irr.*): *far* —, to blow (*v. irr.*).

volata *sf.* **1.** flight **2.** (*corsa*) rush **3.** (*sport*) final sprint.

volàtile¹ *agg.* (*chim.*) volatile.

volàtile² *sm.* bird.

volatilizzare *vt.* to volatilize. ♦ **volatilizzarsi** *vr.* to volatilize.

volente *agg.* — *o nolente*, willy-nilly.

volenterosamente *avv.* willingly.

volenteroso *agg.* V. *volonteroso*.

volentieri *avv.* willingly.

volere¹ *vt.* **1.** (*forte volontà*) (*pres. indicativo e congiuntivo*) will; (*passato indicativo e congiuntivo, condizionale*) would **2.** (*desiderio*) to want, to wish: *voglio che egli venga*, I want him to come **3.** (*gradire*) to like (*costr. pers.*): *vorrei, avrei voluto*, I should like, I should have liked **4.** (*desiderio intenso*) to wish: *vorrei essere ricco!*, I wish I were rich! **5.** (*aver bisogno di*) to need, to require **6.** (*con espressioni di tempo*) to take (*v. irr.*): *ci vogliono due ore per andare alla stazione*, it takes two hours to go to the station **7.** (*cercare*) to ask for: *c'è qualcuno che ti cerca*, there is somebody asking for you **8.** (*essere disposti*) to be willing || *che tu voglia o no*, whether you like it or not; *vuoi ... vuoi (sia ... sia)*, both ... and; *Dio lo voglia, Dio non voglia!*, God grant it, God forbid!

volere² *sm.* will, wish.

volgare *agg.* vulgar, common.

volgarità *sf.* vulgarity.

volgarizzare *vt.* to divulge.

volgarizzatore *sm.* popularizer.

volgarizzazione *sf.* popularization.

volgarmente *avv.* vulgarly, commonly.

vòlgere *vt.* to turn.

vòlgere *sm.* course.

volgo *sm.* common people.

voliera *sf.* aviary.

volitivo *agg.* **1.** strong-willed **2.** (*gramm.*) volitive.

volo *sm.* flight: *prendere il* —, to run (*v. irr.*) away; *capire qc. al* —, to grasp sthg. immediately.

volontà *sf.* will: *di sua spontanea* —, of his own free-will.

volontariamente *avv.* voluntarily.

volontario *agg.* voluntary. ♦ **volontario** *sm.* volunteer.

volontarismo *sm.* voluntarism.

volonteroso *agg.* willing.

volpe *sf.* fox.

volpino *agg.* foxy: *cane* —, Pomeranian.

volpone *sm.* old fox.

volta¹ *sf.* **1.** time: *una* —, once; *due, tre volte*, twice, three times; *ancora una* —, once again; *una* — *e mezzo*, half as much; *una* — *o l'altra*, sooner or later; *rare volte*, seldom; *una* — *tanto*, once in a while; *c'era una* —, once upon a time there was **2.** (*turno*) turn: *a mia* —, in my turn.

volta² *sf.* **1.** (*curva*) bend **2.** (*arch.*) vault.

voltafaccia *sm.* volte-face.

voltaggio *sm.* voltage.

voltàmetro *sm.* voltameter.

voltare *vt.* to turn.

voltastòmaco *sm.* sickness.

voltata *sf.* bend, turning, curve.

volteggiare *vi.* **1.** to whirl **2.** (*svolazzare*) to fly (*v. irr.*) about.

volteggio *sm.* vaulting.

volto¹ *sm.* **1.** face **2.** (*aspetto*) aspect.

volto² *agg.* **1.** turned **2.** (*rivolto*) directed.

volùbile *agg.* changeable.

volubilità *sf.* inconstancy.

volume *sm.* volume.

volumètrico *agg.* volumetric.

voluminoso *agg.* voluminous, bulky.

voluta *sf.* volute.

volutamente *avv.* intentionally.

voluttà *sf.* **1.** delight **2.** (*dei sensi*) voluptuousness.

voluttuario *agg.* voluptuary.

voluttuosamente *avv.* voluptuously.

voluttuoso *agg.* voluptuous.

vòmere *sm.* **1.** ploughshare **2.** (*anat.*) vomer.

vomitare *vt.* to vomit, to be sick.

vòmito *sm.* vomiting: *conato di* —, retch.

vòngola *sf.* mussel.

vorace *agg.* voracious, greedy.

voracità *sf.* voracity, greed.

voràgine *sf.* chasm.

vorticare *vi.* to whirl.

vòrtice *sm.* whirl: — *di vento*, whirlwind.

vorticosamente *avv.* in whirls.
vorticoso *agg.* whirling.
vostro *agg. poss.* your || *in vece vostra*, instead of you. ♦ **vostro** *pron. poss.* yours || *rispondiamo alla vostra del 3 giugno* (*comm.*), in reply to your letter of June 3rd; *sono dalla vostra*, I am on your side.
votante *agg.* voting. ♦ **votante** *sm.* voter.
votare *vt.* to vote. ♦ **votarsi** *vr.* to devote oneself.
votato *agg.* 1. passed 2. (*dedicato*) devoted.
votazione *sf.* voting.
votivo *agg.* votive.
voto *sm.* 1. (*promessa solenne*) vow 2. (*augurio*) wish 3. (*per elezioni*) vote 4. (*scolastico*) mark: *prendere un bel, brutto —*, to get (*v. irr.*) a good, bad mark.
vulcànico *agg.* volcanic.
vulcanismo *sm.* vulcanism.
vulcanizzare *vt.* to vulcanize.
vulcanizzato *agg.* vulcanized.
vulcanizzazione *sf.* vulcanization.
vulcano *sm.* volcano.
vulneràbile *agg.* vulnerable.
vulnerabilità *sf.* vulnerability.
vuotare *vt.* to empty: *— il sacco*, to speak (*v. irr.*) out one's mind.
vuoto *agg.* 1. empty 2. (*sprovvisto*) devoid. ♦ **vuoto** *sm.* 1. empty space 2. (*recipiente vuoto*) empty 3. (*vacuità*) emptiness.

X

xenofobìa *sf.* xenophobia.
xenòfobo *sm.* xenophobe.
xilòfono *sm.* xylophone.
xilografìa *sf.* 1. (*incisione*) xylograph 2. (*arte*) xylography.

Z

zaffata *sf.* whiff.
zafferano *sm.* saffron.
zaffiro *sm.* sapphire.
zàino *sm.* knapsack.
zampa *sf.* 1. paw 2. (*con zoccolo*) hoof 3. (*di uccello*) claw 4. (*di insetto*) leg || *zampe di gallina* (*scrittura*), scrawl; (*rughe*) crow's feet.
zampata *sf.* blow with a paw.
zampettare *vt.* to toddle.
zampillante *agg.* gushing.
zampillare *vi.* to gush.
zampillo *sm.* gush.
zampino *sm.* little paw || *mettere lo — in una faccenda*, to have a hand in the matter.
zampogna *sf.* 1. reed-pipe 2. (*cornamusa*) bag-pipe.
zampognaro *sm.* piper.
zanna *sf.* 1. fang 2. (*di elefante*) tusk.
zanzara *sf.* mosquito.
zanzariera *sf.* mosquito-net.
zappa *sf.* hoe.
zappare *vt.* to hoe.
zappata *sf.* blow with a hoe.
zappatore *sm.* 1. hoer 2. (*mil.*) pioneer.
zappatura *sf.* hoeing.
zar *sm.* czar.
zarina *sf.* czarina.
zarista *s.* czarist.
zàttera *sf.* raft.
zavorra *sf.* 1. ballast 2. (*fig.*) rubbish.
zavorrare *vt.* to ballast.
zàzzera *sf.* mane.
zazzeruto *agg.* shockheaded.
zebra *sf.* zebra.
zebrato *agg.* striped.
zebratura *sf.* stripes (*pl.*).
zebù *sm.* zebu.
zecca[1] *sf.* mint: *nuovo di —*, brand-new.
zecca[2] *sf.* (*zool.*) tick.
zecchino *sm.* sequin: *oro —*, first-quality-gold.
zèfiro *sm.* zephyr.
zelante *agg.* zealous.
zelantemente *avv.* zealously.
zelo *sm.* zeal.
zenit *sm.* zenith.
zénzero *sm.* ginger.
zeppo *agg.* crammed (with).
zerbino *sm.* door-mat.
zerbinotto *sm.* dandy.
zero *sm.* 1. nought 2. (*in gradazioni*) zero 3. (*tel.*) 0 || *ridursi a —*, to come (*v. irr.*) to nought.
zia *sf.* aunt.
zibaldone *sm.* miscellany.
zibellino *sm.* sable.
zigano *agg. e sm.* tzigane.
zìgomo *sm.* cheek-bone.

zigrinare *vt.* to knurl.
zigrinato *agg.* knurled.
zig-zag (*nella loc. avv.*) a —, zigzag.
zigzagare *vi.* to zigzag.
zimbello *sm.* **1.** decoy **2.** (*fig.*) laughing-stock.
zincare *vt.* to zinc.
zincatura *sf.* zinc-plating.
zinco *sm.* zinc.
zincografìa *sf.* zincography.
zingaresco *agg.* gipsy (*attr.*).
zìngaro *sm.* gipsy.
zio *sm.* uncle.
zircone *sm.* zircon.
zirconio *sm.* zirconium.
zitella *sf.* spinster.
zittire *vt.* to hiss.
zitto *agg.* silent: *star* —, to be silent.
zizzania *sf.* **1.** darnel **2.** (*fig.*) discord.
zoccolaio *sm.* clog-maker.
zoccolare *vi.* to clatter about with one's clogs.
zòccolo *sm.* **1.** clog **2.** (*di animale*) hoof **3.** (*piedistallo*) base.
zodiacale *agg.* zodiacal.
zodìaco *sm.* zodiac.
zolfanello *sm.* match.
zolfatara *sf.* V. *solfatara.*
zolfatura *sf.* sulfurization.
zolfo *sm.* sulphur
zolla *sf.* clod.
zolletta *sf.* lump.
zona *sf.* zone, area.
zonzo (*nella loc. avv.*) *andare a* —, to loaf.
zoo *sm.* zoo.
zoofilìa *sf.* zoophilia.
zoòfilo *agg.* zoophilous. ◆ **zoòfilo** *sm.* animal-lover.

zoofobìa *sf.* zoophobia.
zoologìa *sf.* zoology.
zoològico *agg.* zoological.
zoòlogo *sm.* zoologist.
zootecnìa *sf.* zootechny.
zootècnico *agg.* zootechnic: *patrimonio* —, live-stock. ◆ **zootècnico** *sm.* animal expert.
zoppicamento *sm.* limping.
zoppicante *agg.* lame.
zoppicare *vi.* **1.** to limp **2.** (*di mobile*) to be shaky.
zoppo *agg.* **1.** lame **2.** (*di mobile*) shaky. ◆ **zoppo** *sm.* lame person.
zoticàggine *sf.* boorishness.
zòtico *agg.* boorish. ◆ **zòtico** *sm.* boor.
zuavo *sm.* zouave || *calzoni alla zuava*, knickerbockers.
zucca *sf.* **1.** pumpkin **2.** (*testa*) pate.
zuccherare *vt.* to sugar.
zuccherato *agg.* sugared.
zuccheriera *sf.* sugar-basin.
zuccherificio *sm.* sugar-refinery.
zuccherino *sm.* **1.** sweet **2.** (*fig.*) sugar-plum.
zùcchero *sm.* sugar.
zucchina *sf.* vegetable marrow.
zucconàggine *sf.* **1.** (*ottusità*) dullness **2.** (*ostinatezza*) stubbornness.
zuccone *sm.* **1.** (*ottuso*) blockhead **2.** (*testardo*) donkey.
zuffa *sf.* brawl.
zufolare *vt.* e *vi.* to whistle.
zufolìo *sm.* whistle.
zùfolo *sm.* **1.** whistle **2.** (*mus.*) pipe.
zuppa *sf.* soup.
zuppiera *sf.* tureen.
zuppo *agg.* soaked.
zuzzurellone *sm.* skittish boy.

NOMI PROPRI, STORICI E GEOGRAFICI

Abele Abel.
Abissinia Abyssinia.
Abramo Abraham.
Achille Achilles.
Ada Ada.
Adamo Adam.
Adolfo Adolph.
Adone Adonis.
Adriano Hadrian.
Adriatico (Mar) Adriatic Sea.
Afganistan Afghanistan.
Africa Africa.
Afrodite Aphrodite.
Agamennone Agamemnon
Agata Agatha.
Agnese Agnes.
Agostino Augustin.
Aia (L') The Hague.
Aiace Ajax.
Albania Albania.
Alberto Albert.
Aldo Aldous.
Alessandra Alexandra.
Alessandro Alexander.
Alessio Alexis.
Alfredo Alfred.
Algeri Algiers.
Algeria Algeria.
Alice Alice.
Alpi Alps *pl.*
Alsazia Alsace.
Amazzoni (Rio delle) Amazon.
Ambrogio Ambrose.
Amburgo Hamburg.
Amelia Amelia.
America America.
Amleto Hamlet.
Andalusia Andalusia.
Ande Andes *pl.*
Andrea Andrew.
Angelo Angel.
Anna Ann(e).
Annibale Hannibal.
Antartide Antarctica.
Antonino Antoninus.
Antonio Ant(h)ony.
Apollo Apollo.
Appennini Apennines *pl.*
Arabia Arabia.
Aragona Aragon.
Arcadia Arcadia.
Archimede Archimedes.

Argentina Argentina.
Arianna Ariadne.
Aristofane Aristophanes.
Aristotele Aristotle.
Armando Armand.
Arnaldo Arnold.
Aroldo Harold.
Arrigo Henry.
Arturo Arthur.
Asia Asia.
Atene Athens.
Atlantico Atlantic.
Augusta Augusta.
Augusto Augustus.
Australia Australia.
Austria Austria.
Azzorre Azores *pl.*

Babele Babel.
Babilonia Babylon.
Bacco Bacchus.
Balcani Balkans *pl.*
Baldassarre Balthazar.
Baleari Balearic Islands *pl.*
Baltico (Mar) Baltic Sea.
Baltimora Baltimore.
Barbara Barbara.
Barcellona Barcelona.
Barnaba Barnaby, Barnabas.
Bartolomeo Bartholomew.
Basilea Basel.
Basilio Basil.
Battista Baptist.
Beatrice Beatrix.
Belgio Belgium.
Belgrado Belgrade.
Benedetto Benedict.
Bengala Bengal.
Beniamino Benjamin.
Berenice Berenice.
Berlino Berlin.
Bermude Bermudas *pl.*
Bernardo Bernard.
Berta Bertha.
Betlemme Bethlehem.
Bianca Blanche.
Birmania Burma.
Boemia Bohemia.
Bolivia Bolivia.
Bonifacio Boniface.
Bosforo Bosporus.

Brandeburgo Brandenburg.
Brasile Brazil.
Bretagna Brittany.
Bruto Brutus.
Bulgaria Bulgaria.

Cadice Cadiz.
Caino Cain.
Caio Caius.
Cairo Cairo.
California California.
Calvino Calvin.
Cambogia Cambodia.
Campidoglio Capitol.
Canadà Canada.
Caraibi (Mar dei) Caribbean Sea.
Carlo Charles.
Carlomagno Charlemagne.
Carlotta Charlotte.
Carolina Caroline.
Carpazi Carpathian Mountains *pl*.
Cartagine Carthage.
Cascemir Cashmere, Kashmir.
Caspio (Mar) Caspian Sea.
Cassio Cassius.
Cassiopea Cassiopeia.
Castiglia Castile.
Caterina Catherine.
Catone Cato.
Caucaso Caucasus.
Cecilia Cecily.
Cecilio Cecil.
Cecoslovacchia Czechoslovakia.
Cenerentola Cinderella.
Cesare Caesar.
Chiara Clara.
Cicerone Cicero.
Cile Chile.
Cina China.
Cinzia Cynthia.
Cipro Cyprus.
Cirillo Cyril.
Ciro Cyrus.
Clara Clara.
Claudio Claudius, Claude.
Clemente Clement.
Clementina Clementine.
Cleopatra Cleopatra.
Clitennestra Clytemnestra.
Colombia Colombia.
Colonia Cologne.
Congo Congo.
Corea Korea.
Corfù Corfu.
Corinto Corinth.
Cornelio Cornelius.
Cornovaglia Cornwall.
Corrado Conrad.

Corsica Corsica.
Costantino Constantine.
Costantinopoli Constantinople.
Costanza Constance.
Creta Crete.
Crimea Crimea.
Cristina Christine.
Cristo Christ.
Cristoforo Christopher.
Cuba Cuba.

Dafne Daphne.
Damasco Damascus.
Damocle Damocles.
Daniele Daniel.
Danimarca Denmark.
Danubio Danube.
Danzica Danzig.
Dardanelli Dardanelles *pl*.
Dario Darius.
Davide David.
Debora Deborah.
Delfo Delphi.
Democrito Democritus.
Demostene Demosthenes.
Desdemona Desdemona.
Diana Diana.
Didone Dido.
Diocleziano Diocletian.
Diogene Diogenes.
Dionigi, Dionisio Dionysius.
Domenico Dominic.
Domiziano Domitian.
Dorotea Dorothy.
Dublino Dublin.

Ebridi Hebrides *pl*.
Edgardo Edgar.
Edimburgo Edinburgh.
Edipo Oedipus.
Edmondo Edmund.
Edoardo Edward.
Egeo (Mar) Aegean Sea.
Egitto Egypt.
Elena Helen.
Eleonora Eleanor.
Elettra Electra.
Elia Elias, Elijah.
Elisa Eliza.
Elisabetta Elizabeth.
Ellade Hellas.
Emanuele Emanuel.
Emilia Emily.
Enea Aeneas.
Enrichetta Henrietta, Harriet.
Enrico Henry, Harry.
Epaminonda Epaminondas.

Epicuro Epicurus.
Eraclito Heraclitus.
Erasmo Erasmus.
Erberto Herbert.
Ercole Hercules.
Eritrea Eritrea.
Ermete Hermes.
Ernesto Ernest.
Erode Herod.
Erodoto Herodotus.
Esaù Esau.
Eschilo Aeschylus.
Esiodo Hesiod.
Esopo Aesop.
Ester Esther.
Etiopia Ethiopia.
Ettore Hector.
Euclide Euclid.
Eufrate Euphrates.
Eugenio Eugene.
Euripide Euripides.
Europa Europe.
Eva Eve.
Evelina Evelyn.
Ezechiele Ezekiel.

Farsalo Pharsalus.
Fausto Faust(us).
Federico Frederic.
Fedra Phaedra.
Felice Felix.
Ferdinando Ferdinand.
Filadelfia Philadelphia.
Filippi Philippi.
Filippine Philippines *pl.*
Filippo Philip.
Finlandia Finland.
Firenze Florence.
Formosa Formosa.
Francesca Frances.
Francesco Francis.
Francia France.
Franco Frank.
Francoforte Frankfurt.

Gabriele Gabriel.
Galilea Galilee.
Galles Wales.
Gallia Gaule.
Genova Genoa.
Geova Jehovah.
Gerardo Gerard.
Geremia Jeremiah.
Gerico Jericho.
Germania Germany.
Gerolamo Jerome.
Gerusalemme Jerusalem.

Gesù Jesus.
Giacobbe Jacob.
Giacomo James.
Giamaica Jamaica.
Giappone Japan.
Giasone Jason.
Giava Java.
Gibilterra Gibraltar.
Gilberto Gilbert.
Ginevra Geneva.
Giobbe Job.
Giona Jonah, Jonas.
Gionata Jonathan.
Giordano Jordan.
Giorgio George.
Giosuè Joshua.
Giovanna Jane, Jean, Joan.
Giovanni John.
Giove Jove, Jupiter.
Giovenale Juvenal.
Giuda Judas, Jude.
Giudea Judea.
Giuditta Judith.
Giulia Julia, Julie.
Giuliana Juliana.
Giuliano Julian.
Giulietta Juliet.
Giulio Julius.
Giunone Juno.
Giuseppe Joseph.
Giuseppina Josephine.
Goffredo Geoffrey, Jeffrey.
Golgota Golgotha.
Golia Goliath.
Gran Bretagna Great Britain.
Grazia Grace.
Grecia Greece.
Gregorio Gregory.
Groenlandia Greenland.
Guaiana Guiana.
Gualtiero Walter.
Guascogna Gascony.
Guglielmo William.
Guido Guy.
Guinea Guinea.
Gustavo Gustavus.

Iacopo James.
Iberia Iberia.
Icaro Icarus.
Ignazio Ignatius.
Ilario Hilary.
Imalaia Himalaya.
India India.
Indostan Hindustan.
Inghilterra England.
Innocenzo Innocent.
Ionio (Mar) Ionian Sea.

Ippolito Hippolytus.
Irene Irene.
Iride Iris.
Irlanda Ireland.
Irlanda (Stato Libero di) Eire.
Isabella Isabel.
Isacco Isaac.
Isaia Isaiah.
Iside Isis.
Islanda Iceland.
Ismaele Ishmael.
Israele Israel.
Italia Italy.
Iugoslavia Yugoslavia.

Lamberto Lambert.
Lancillotto Launcelot.
Laocoonte Laocoon.
Lapponia Lapland.
Laura Laura.
Lazio Latium.
Lazzaro Lazarus.
Leandro Leander.
Leonardo Leonard.
Leone Leo(n).
Leonida Leonidas.
Leopoldo Leopold.
Lete Lethe.
Letizia Letitia.
Libano Lebanon.
Libia Libya.
Licurgo Lycurgus
Lidia Lydia.
Liegi Liege.
Lione Lyons.
Lisbona Lisbon.
Livio Livy.
Livorno Leghorn.
Lodovico Ludwig.
Lombardia Lombardy.
Londra London.
Lorena Lorraine.
Lorenzo Lawrence.
Losanna Lausanne.
Lotario Lothar.
Lovanio Louvain.
Luca Luke.
Lucerna Lucerne.
Lucia Lucy.
Luciano Lucian.
Lucifero Lucifer.
Lucio Lucius.
Lucrezio Lucretius.
Luigi Louis, Lewis.
Luigia, Luisa Louise.
Lussemburgo Luxemburg.
Lutero Luther.

Maddalena Magdalene.
Maiorca Majorca.
Malesia Malaya.
Malta Malta.
Manciuria Manchuria.
Manfredi Manfred.
Manica (La) The Channel.
Mantova Mantua.
Maometto Mohammed.
Maratona Marathon.
Marcello Marcellus.
Marco Mark.
Margherita Margaret.
Maria Mary.
Marianna Marianne.
Mario Marius.
Marocco Morocco.
Marta Martha.
Marte Mars.
Martino Martin.
Marziale Martial.
Massimiliano Maximilian.
Matilde Matilda.
Matteo Matthew.
Matusalemme Methuselah.
Maurizio Maurice.
Mecca, La Mecca.
Mecenate Maecenas.
Mediterraneo Mediterranean.
Medusa Medusa.
Mefistofele Mephistopheles.
Melanesia Melanesia.
Menelao Menelaus.
Mercurio Mercury.
Merlino Merlin.
Mesopotamia Mesopotamia.
Messalina Messalina.
Messico Mexico.
Micene Mycenae.
Michele Michael.
Mida Midas.
Milano Milan.
Minerva Minerva.
Minosse Minos.
Minotauro Minotaur.
Mitridate Mithridates.
Molucche Moluccas *pl.*
Monaco (Principato di) Monaco.
Monaco di Baviera Munich.
Mongolia Mongolia.
Mosa Meuse.
Mosca Moscow.
Mosè Moses.
Mozambico Mozambique.

Napoleone Napoleon.
Napoli Naples.
Narciso Narcissus.

Nerone Nero.
Nettuno Neptune.
Nicola, Niccolò Nicholas.
Nilo Nile.
Nizza Nice.
Noè Noah.
Normandia Normandy.
Norvegia Norway.
Nuova Zelanda New Zealand.

Oceania Oceania.
Ofelia Ophelia.
Olanda Holland.
Olimpo Olympus.
Oliviero Oliver.
Omero Homer.
Orazio Horace, Horatio.
Orcadi Orkneys *pl.*
Oreste Orestes.
Orfeo Orpheus.
Orione Orion.
Orlando Roland.
Orsola Ursula.
Osiride Osiris.
Osvaldo Oswald.
Otello Othello.
Ovidio Ovid.

Pacifico Pacific.
Padova Padua.
Paesi Bassi Netherlands *p.*.
Palestina Palestine.
Pancrazio Pancras.
Paola Paula.
Paolina Pauline.
Paolo Paul.
Papuasia Papua.
Paride Paris.
Parigi Paris.
Parnaso Parnassus.
Partenone Parthenon.
Patagonia Patagonia.
Patrizia Patricia.
Patrizio Patrick.
Pechino Peking.
Peloponneso Peloponnesus.
Penelope Penelope.
Pensilvania Pennsylvania.
Pericle Pericles.
Perseo Perseus.
Persia Persia.
Perù Peru.
Piemonte Piedmont.
Pietro, Piero Peter.
Pigmalione Pigmalion.
Pindaro Pindar.
Pio Pius.

Pirenei Pyrenees *pl.*
Pireo Piraeus.
Pitagora Pythagoras.
Platone Plato.
Plinio Pliny.
Plutarco Plutarch.
Polinesia Polynesia.
Polonia Poland.
Pompeo Pompey.
Portogallo Portugal.
Praga Prague.
Prometeo Prometheus.
Prussia Prussia.
Puglia Apulia.

Quintino Quentin.

Rachele Rachel.
Raffaele, Raffaello Raphael.
Raimondo Raymond.
Ramsete Ramses.
Rebecca Rebecca.
Remo Remus.
Reno Rhine.
Riccardo Richard.
Roberto Robert.
Rodano Rhone.
Rodi Rhodes.
Rodolfo Rudolph.
Rodrigo Roderick.
Rolando Roland.
Roma Rome.
Romania Ro(u)mania.
Romeo Romeo.
Romolo Romulus.
Rosa Rose.
Rosalia Rosalie.
Rosalinda Rosalind.
Rossana Roxana.
Rubicone Rubicon.
Ruggero Roger.
Russia Russia.

Saffo Sappho.
Salomone Solomon.
Samuele Samuel.
Sansone Samson.
Sara Sarah.
Sardegna Sardinia.
Sassonia Saxony.
Satana Satan.
Saturno Saturn.
Saul Saul.
Savoia Savoy.
Scandinavia Scandinavia.
Scipione Scipion.

Scozia Scotland.
Sebastiano Sebastian.
Sempione Simplon.
Serse Xerxes.
Siam Siam.
Siberia Siberia.
Sibilla Sibyl.
Sicilia Sicily.
Silla Sulla.
Silvestro Silvester.
Silvia Sylvia.
Simeone Simeon.
Simone Simon.
Siracusa Syracuse.
Siria Syria.
Smirne Smyrna.
Socrate Socrates.
Sodoma Sodom.
Sofia Sophia.
Sofocle Sophocles.
Somalia Somaliland.
Spagna Spain.
Sparta Sparta.
Stati Uniti United States (of America - U.S.A.).
Stefano Stephen.
Stoccolma Stockholm.
Strasburgo Strasbourg.
Sudan S(o)udan.
Susanna Susan(nah).
Svezia Sweden.
Svizzera Switzerland.

Tacito Tacitus.
Tailandia Thailand.
Tamigi Thames.
Tangeri Tangier(s).
Tasmania Tasmania.
Tebe Thebes.
Telemaco Telemachus.
Temistocle Themistocles.
Teodorico Theodoric.
Terenzio Terence.
Teresa Theresa.
Termopili Thermopylae pl.
Terranova Newfoundland.
Teseo Theseus.
Tevere Tiber.
Tiberio Tiberius.
Tirolo Tirol, Tyrol.

Tirreno (Mar) Tyrrhenian Sea.
Tito Titus.
Tiziano Titian.
Tobia Tobias.
Tolomeo Ptolemy.
Tommaso Thomas.
Tonchino Tonkin, Tongking.
Torino Turin.
Toscana Tuscany.
Traiano Trajan.
Tristano Tristan, Tristram.
Troia Troy.
Tullio Tully.
Tunisi Tunis.
Tunisia Tunisia.
Turchia Turkey.

Uberto Hubert.
Ucraina Ukraine.
Ugo Hugh.
Ulisse Ulysses.
Umberto Humbert.
Ungheria Hungary.
Urbano Urban.
URSS USSR (Union of Socialist Soviet Republics).

Valentino Valentine.
Valeria Valeria.
Valerio Valerius.
Varsavia Warsaw.
Vaticano Vatican.
Venere Venus.
Veneto Venetia.
Venezia Venice.
Vesuvio Vesuvius.
Vienna Vienna.
Vincenzo Vincent.
Virgilio Virgil.
Virginia Virginia.
Vittoria Victoria.
Vittorio Victor.
Viviana, Viviano Vivian.
Vulcano Vulcan.

Zaccaria Zachary.
Zurigo Zurich.

SIGLE E ABBREVIAZIONI USATE IN ITALIA

A., *alto*: H., high.
A.C., *Automobile Club*: A.A., Automobile Association.
a.C., *avanti Cristo*: B.C. Before Christ.
A.D., *Anno Domini, nell'anno del Signore*: A.D., Anno Domini, (After Christ).
ago., *Agosto*: Aug., August.
A.M., *Aeronautica Militare*: A.F., Air Force.
am., amer., *americano*: Am., American.
anon., *anonimo*: anon., anonymous.
app., *appendice*: app., appendix.
appross., *approssimativo*: approx., approximate.
apr., *aprile*: Apr., April.
A.R., *altezza reale*: R.H., Royal Highness.
ar., *arrivo*: arr., arrival.
ass., *associazione*: ass., association.

b.f., *bassa frequenza*: L.F., low frequency.
boll., *bollettino*: bull., bulletin.
brev., *brevetto*: pat., patent.

C., *centigradi*: cent., centigrade.
c., 1. *conto*: acc., account **2.** *cubico*: cu., cubic.
ca., 1. *circa*: a., about **2.** *corrente alternata*: a.c., alternating current.
cad., *cadauno*: ea., each.
Cap., *capitano*: Capt., captain.
cap., *capitolo*: c., chapter.
capit., *capitolo*: c., chapter.
Capp., *capitoli*: cc., chapters.
Card., *Cardinale*: Card., cardinal.
C/c, *conto corrente*: c/a, current account.
cc., *corrente continua*: dc., direct current.
C.D., *Corpo Diplomatico*: C.D., Corps Diplomatique.
C.E.E.A., *Comunità europea per l'energia atomica*: A.E.C., Atomic Energy Commission.
cent., centg., *centigrado*: cent., centigrade.
Cf., *confronta*: cp., compare.

cm., *centimetro*: cent., centimetre.
c.m., *corrente mese*: inst., instant.
cm.c., *centimetro cubo*: c.c., cubic centimetre.
Col., *colonnello*: col., colonel.
coll., *collegio*: coll., college.
coop., *cooperativa*: coop., co-operative.
C.P., *Casella Postale*: P.O.B., Post Office Box.
C.S., *Corte Suprema*: Sup. Ct., Supreme Court.

D., *dottore*: dr., doctor.
d.C., *dopo Cristo*: A.D., Anno Domini.
dic., *dicembre*: Dec., December.
Dirett., *direttore*: dir., director.
dom., *domenica*: Sun., Sunday.
dott., *dottore*: dr., doctor.
dozz., *dozzina*: doz., dozen.

E, *est*: E, East.
ecc., *eccetera*: etc., and so on.
ed., 1. *edito*: ed., edited **2.** *edizione*: ed., edition.
Egr., *egregio*: Esq., Esquire.
es., *esempio*: ex., example.

feb., *febbraio*: Feb., February.
fed., *federazione*: fed., federation.
F.lli, *fratelli*: br., bros., brothers.

g., *grammo*: g., gram.
Gen., *generale*: Gen., General.
gen., 1. *generale*: gen., general **2.** *gennaio*: Jan., January.
giov., *giovedì*: Thur., Thursday.

h., *ora*: h., hour.
H.P., *cavallo vapore*: H.P., horse power.

ibid., *ibidem, nello stesso luogo*: ibid., in the same place.
id., *idem, come sopra*: id., the same.
iun., *iunior, giovane*: jr., junior.

kg., *chilogrammo*: kg., kilogram.
km., *chilometro*: km., kilometre.
kw., *chilowatt*: kw., kilowatt.

l., 1. *latino*: Lat., Latin **2.** *litro*: l., litre.
lat., *latitudine*: lat., latitude.
lib., *libro*: b., book.
long., *longitudine*: long., longitude.
L.st., *Lira sterlina*: L., pound.
lun., *lunedì*: Mon., Monday.

M., *monte*: Mt., mount.
m., 1. *morto*: d., dead **2.** *mese*: m., month **3.** *metro*: m., metre **4.** *minuto*: m., minute.
M.AA.EE., *Ministero degli Affari Esteri*: F.O., Foreign Office.
Magg., *Maggiore*: Maj., Major.
mar., *marzo*: Mar., March.
mart., *martedì*: Tues., Tuesday.
mass., *massimo*: max., maximum.
m.c.d., *minimo comun denominatore*: L.C.D., Lowest Common Denominator.
m.c.m., *minimo comune multiplo*: L.C.M., Least Common Multiple.
M.E.C., *Mercato Comune Europeo*: E.C.M., European Common Market.
mer(c)., *mercoledì*: Wed., Wednesday.
mg., *milligrammo*: mg., milligram.
mm., *millimetro*: mm., millimetre.
M/n., *motonave*: Ms., motorship.
ms., *manoscritto*: ms., manuscript.
mss., *manoscritti*: mss., manuscripts.
Mus., *museo*: mus., museum.

N., 1. *nato*: b., born **2.** *Nord*: N., North **3.** *numero*: N., Number.
nov., *novembre*: Nov., November.
N.U., *Nazioni Unite*: U.N., United Nations.

O., *ovest*: W., West.
on., *onorevole*: hon., honourable.
O.N.U., *Organizzazione Nazioni Unite*: U.N.O., United Nations Organization.
ott., *ottobre*: Oct., October.

P., *padre*: fr., father.
p., *pagina*: p., page.
P.A., *Patto Atlantico*: N.A.T.O.,

North Atlantic Treaty Organization.
paragr., *paragrafo*: par., paragraph.
p.at., *peso atomico*: a.w., atomic weight.
P.C., *Partito Comunista*: C.P., Communist Party.
p.e., *per esempio*: e.g., for example (exempli gratia).
pres., *presidente*: pres., president.
proc., *procuratore*: att., attorney.
prof., *professore*: prof., professor.
P.S., *poscritto*: P.S., postscript.
p.za, *piazza*: sq., square.

Q.G., *Quartier Generale*: G.H., General Headquarters.

ref., *referenze*: ref., reference.
reg., *registro*: reg., register.
Rev., *Reverendo*: rev., Reverend.
R.M., *ricchezza mobile*: PAYE, Pay As You Earn.
R.U., *Regno Unito*: U.K., United Kingdom.

S., 1. *Santo*: St., Saint **2.** *secolo*: cen., century **3.** *società*: co., Company **4.** *Sud*: S., South.
sab., *sabato*: Sat., Saturday.
S.A.R., *Sua Altezza Reale*: H.R.H., His (Her) Royal Highness.
Sc., *scuola*: sch., school.
S.E., *Sua Eccellenza*: H.E., His Excellency.
segg., *seguenti*: fol., following.
segr., *segretario*: sec., secretary.
serg., *sergente*: sergt., sergeant.
sett., *settembre*: Sept., September.
sig., *signore*: Mr., Mister.
sig.na, *signorina*: Miss.
sig.ra, *signora*: Mrs., Mistress.
S.M.B., *Sua Maestà Britannica*: H.B.M., His (Her) Britannic Majesty.
S.O., *Sud Ovest*: S.W., South West.
s.p.a., *società per azioni*: inc., incorporated.
spec., 1. *speciale*: spec., special **2.** *specialmente*: spec., specially.
s.r.l., *società a responsabilità limitata*: ltd., limited (in inglese); corp., corporation (in americano).
S.S., *Sua Santità*: H.H., His Holiness.
S.U., *Stati Uniti*: U.S., United States.

S.U.A., *Stati Uniti d'America*: U.S.A., United States of America.

T., *tonnellata*: t., ton.
T.B.C., *tubercolosi*: T.B., Tuberculosis.
tel., *telefono*: tel. telephone.

U., *unione*: U., Union.
U.P., *Unione postale*: P.U., Postal Union.
U.R.S.S., *Unione Repubbliche So-* cialiste Sovietiche: U.S.S.R., Union of Socialist Soviet Republics.

V., 1. *vaglia*: P.O., Postal Order
 2. *volume*: vol., volume.
v., *verso*: v., verse.
Ven., *Venerabile*: Ven., Venerable.
ven., *venerdì*: Fr., Friday.
vesc., *vescovo*: Bp., Bishop.
v.le, *viale*: Ave., Avenue.
vol., *volume*: vol., volume.
voll., *volumi*: voll., volumes.
vv., *versi*: vv., verses.